# BANK MANAGEMENT:
## Text and Cases

**FOURTH EDITION**

# BANK MANAGEMENT:
## Text and Cases

**GEORGE H. HEMPEL**
*Southern Methodist University*

**DONALD G. SIMONSON**
*University of New Mexico*

**ALAN B. COLEMAN**
*Southern Methodist University*

**JOHN WILEY & SONS, INC.**
New York • Chichester • Brisbane • Toronto • Singapore

ACQUISITIONS EDITOR   Whitney Blake
MARKETING MANAGER   Debra Riegert
SENIOR PRODUCTION EDITOR   Jennifer Knapp
DESIGNER   EriBen Graphics/Dorothy Bungert
MANUFACTURING MANAGER   Inez Pettis
ILLUSTRATION   Jaime Perea

This book was set in Bodoni Book by Achorn Graphic Services and
printed and bound by Malloy Lithographing. The cover was printed by Lehigh Press.

*Library of Congress Cataloging in Publication Data:*
Hempel, George H.
    Bank management : text and cases / George H. Hempel, Donald G.
Simonson, Alan B. Coleman. — 4th ed.
        p.    cm.
    Includes indexes.
    ISBN 0-471-55256-9
    1. Bank management.  2. Bank management—Case studies.
I. Simonson, Donald G.   II. Coleman, Alan B.   III. Title.
HG1615.H45    1994
332.1'068—dc20                                                93-24354
                                                                CIP

Printed in the United States of America

10 9 8 7 6 5

# About the Authors

**Dr. George H. Hempel** is Corrigan Professor of Finance and President and CEO of the Southwestern Graduate School of Banking Foundation at Southern Methodist University. He has written 15 other books and numerous articles on various topics in banking and finance. Dr. Hempel has served on banking boards, as a consultant to banks, and in numerous banking professional educational programs. He is past president of the Financial Management Association, a professional association whose over 10,000 members include approximately 70 percent of all U.S. finance professors.

**Dr. Donald G. Simonson** is New Mexico Bankers Professor of Finance and Director of the Western States Banking School at the University of New Mexico. Prior to his academic career, he was employed at Martin Marietta and Mobil Oil. Dr. Simonson has published extensive research in banking and finance journals and has served on the faculties of a number of regional and national schools of banking. He has directed numerous educational programs for officers and directors of banks and is Senior Contributing Editor of *United States Banker* magazine.

**Dr. Alan B. Coleman** is a retired Caruth Professor of Finance from Southern Methodist University. He had previously served as president of two corporations, Dean of Southern Methodist's School of Business, and President of the Southwestern Graduate School of Banking Foundation. Dr. Coleman is the author of three other casebooks and has written numerous cases in banking and finance. He serves on the boards of and as consultant to several banks and businesses.

# Preface

Managing a commercial bank in the mid-1990s promises to be a challenging task. A difficult economic environment, a changing regulatory environment, a rapid rate of technological development, an increasingly intense level of competition, and some worrisome trends in the banking industry have combined to create a demand for strong bank management. The purpose of this book is to present the management concepts and techniques that will help current and potential managers succeed in this challenging period. We have included 27 up-to-date cases in which bankers and students can test their ability to solve problems in modern banking situations. Instructions for a microcomputer simulation that uses any of several of the case banks as a starting point is included in an ending appendix.

This book is divided into four parts. Each part has four or more cases in which readers apply the concepts and techniques discussed in the part. Part I is an introduction to bank management. In Chapter 1 we review the dynamic nature of bank management and the banking structures. In Chapter 2 we move to an examination of the meanings of the typical items on bank financial statements. Chapter 3 introduces a basic model for measuring bank returns and risk. Chapter 4 discusses the overall measurement of bank performance and includes more sophisticated return and risk measures and a discussion of how to use the recently revised Uniform Bank Performance Reports.

In Part II we examine basic asset, liability, and capital management decisions. Chapter 5 demonstrates how bank reserve requirements are measured and met. We present methods for measuring short-term, seasonal, and long-term liquidity needs and then discuss methods for meeting such needs. Chapter 6 evaluates the ways that the securities portfolio affects a bank's profitability and risk. We discuss several techniques for increasing returns without significantly increasing risks. In Chapter 7, the methods of acquiring deposits and short-term liabilities are evaluated, as well as the cost of these funds. We also examine the potential profit on the various types of deposits and short-term liabilities. Chapter 8 covers how a bank determines and obtains the appropriate amount and mix of capital funds. The implications of newly passed capital standards are examined. Chapter 9 emphasizes capital acquisition and management. Methods of evaluating the choice between senior equity and external equity, and a discussion of the newer forms of senior capital, are among the topics covered.

Part III (Chapters 10–14) covers the lending function of commercial banks. The primary types of bank loans are described, and the ways a bank may organize to compete successfully in lending are discussed. In this part we present details on such topics as credit analysis, loan pricing, and structuring a loan for the primary types of bank loans.

Part IV emphasizes integrative management techniques. In Chapter 15 we introduce techniques for managing a bank's overall interest sensitivity position and for increasing the interest margin. Chapter 16 discusses advanced alternatives for measuring and managing interest rate risk. Duration and hedging techniques are included in this chapter. In Chapter 17 we describe the use of new financial products and methods of pricing in bank management. Chapter 18 is a new chapter on bank mergers and acquisitions. Reasons for the trend toward more mergers and acquisitions and a discussion of valuation techniques, are included in this chapter. Chapter 19 includes some important concepts of international finance and suggests how banks should be managed in a changing international environment. Chapter 20 includes a method for determining actual and potential risk–return trade-offs and a system for long-range planning.

A separate Instructors Manual, which includes a summary, teaching objectives, and suggested questions for each case, is available for professors and bank training directors. Cases appropriate for each chapter are outlined. Coupons that adopting instructors can use to obtain a disk with microcomputer programs accompanying cases (free) and the microcomputer simulation (at a nominal charge) that may be used with this book are also included in the Instructors Manual.

We are indebted to several professors and bankers. William S. Townsend of Rauscher, Pierce, Refsnes helped with the initial formulation of the book and with ideas on how to incorporate cases with the text material. Harry Blythe of Ohio State University provided assistance and helpful comments throughout the preparation of the earlier editions. In addition, we wish to thank Tim Sidley of Mellon Bank, Dwight Crane of Harvard University, Dick Roberts and Bud Baker of Wachovia Corporation, Bill Alberts of the University of Washington, Don Wright of First Interstate Lakewood Bank, George Parker of Stanford University, Don Tuttle of Indiana University, James McNulty of Florida International University and Frank Shackelford of Indiana National Bank for their helpful comments on this or earlier editions.

Case materials were obtained from George Parker of Stanford University,

Harry Blythe and David Cole of Ohio State University, Oliver Hickle and John Falkenberg of United Bank of Denver, Keith B. Johnson and Gerson M. Goldberg of the University of Connecticut, Dick Snelsire of First Wachovia, Phillip White of the University of Colorado, Brian Garrison of Central Bank & Trust, and Bradford M. Johnson of Sterne, Agee & Leach, Inc. Valuable research assistance was supplied by Sumon Mazumdar, a Southern Methodist University graduate student. Primary secretarial assistance was provided by Kay McKee.

Helpful suggestions were also generated from those using earlier editions of this book at Wharton, Southern Methodist University, Texas Tech University, University of Illinois, University of Missouri, Southwestern Graduate School of Banking, University of Hawaii, Stanford University, Western States School of Banking, University of New Mexico, Washington University, Indiana University, Ohio State University, University of Oklahoma, and the Graduate School of Banking at Colorado University. In spite of the help received, deficiencies undoubtedly remain. For these we take full responsibility and urge readers to call them to our attention.

*George H. Hempel*
*Donald G. Simonson*
*Alan B. Coleman*

# Contents

**PART TWO    BASIC ASSET, LIABILITY, AND CAPITAL DECISIONS 143**

**PART THREE  MANAGING THE LOAN PORTFOLIO 367**

# PART I

# INTRODUCTION TO BANK MANAGEMENT

# The Changing Nature of Bank Management

The management of a commercial bank has become increasingly challenging. Concepts and techniques gainfully used only a few years ago now seem outdated. The markets that banks use to finance themselves have changed dramatically in the last few years. Protection from regulation and from geographic and product constraints appears to have almost disappeared. To some bank managements, the increasing complexity of banking decisions is worrisome; to many others, however, it presents an opportunity to reward good management. The purpose of this book is to present up-to-date concepts and techniques that can help bank managers in this challenging period.

This introductory chapter briefly discusses the economic role of commercial banks and the current structure of banking and its regulation. It then examines the dynamic and increasingly challenging nature of the bank funding environment and of the financial markets affecting banking and concludes with an outline of the primary topics covered in this book.

## ROLE OF COMMERCIAL BANKING IN THE U.S. ECONOMY[1]

The primary role of commercial banks can be understood by looking at the financial flows in our economy over a specified time period. Figure 1-1 illus-

[1]The economic role of financial intermediaries is discussed in greater depth in *Two Faces of Debt* (Federal Reserve Bank of Chicago, 1985) and George H. Hempel and Jess B. Yawitz, *Financial Management of Financial Institutions* (Englewood Cliffs, N.J.: Prentice-Hall, 1977).

**FIGURE 1-1    Simplified Graph of Financial Flows in the U.S. Economy**

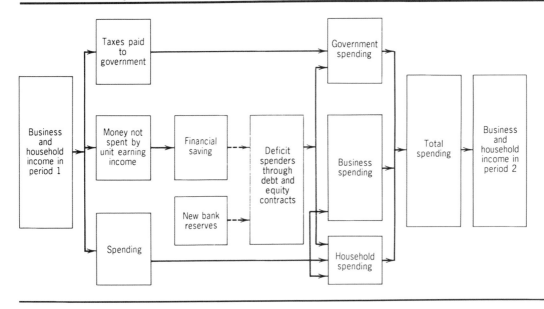

trates the three ways in which the business and household income for a period can be used. First, part of this income is taxed by government units. The remaining "disposable" amount is either spent or not spent by the unit earning the income. What happens to each of these three uses of income? Taxes paid to governments are typically spent by these units and constitute a part of total spending and a part of business and household income in the next period. Funds spent by the unit earning them find their way into the spending stream and provide household and business income for the following period. Money not spent by the unit earning the income, plus any new reserves provided from the Federal Reserve, are transferred for varying periods of time to units that want to spend more than they earned in that particular period. These "borrowed" funds are rapidly returned to the spending stream by deficit-spending governments, businesses, and households.

Although some of the transfers of funds from surplus units to deficit units are made directly through borrowing or equity contracts, the different desires of surplus and deficit units create the need for financial intermediaries. Such differing desires might include size, maturity, legal character, marketability, liquidity, divisibility, redeemability, and risk. For example, many surplus units have relatively small amounts of funds and want to be able to convert to cash easily and to have relatively short maturities. On the other hand, deficit units often want large amounts of funds for long periods of time, with the assurance that they will be forced to pay only when payments are scheduled. The institutions that try to meet the diverse desires of the surplus and deficit units are

**FIGURE 1-2    Financial Intermediaries in the Flow Between Surplus and Deficit Units**

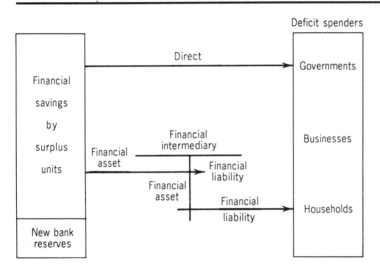

called financial intermediaries.[2] In facilitating the flow of funds between surplus and deficit units (see Figure 1-2), financial intermediaries create two separate markets. They purchase primary securities from deficit units and sell secondary, indirect liabilities to surplus units. In this way, a financial intermediary is able to tailor its asset and liability structure to satisfy the desires of both the ultimate borrowers and ultimate lenders in the economy. Financial intermediaries simply substitute their own more desirable (to the surplus units) financial liabilities for the financial liabilities of the deficit unit. By holding a diversified portfolio of assets, many intermediaries can reduce risk beyond the reduction available to individual units. They also assist deficit units in finding funds in the desirable amount and form.

In the fully developed U.S. financial system, surplus units are able to choose from a wide variety of alternative financial assets, including primary securities of deficit units and the numerous secondary liabilities offered by financial intermediaries. Deficit units can usually acquire purchasing power in a desirable form, either directly from surplus units or, more commonly, from a financial intermediary. Liquidity and marketability of the securities created in the direct or indirect flows between surplus and deficit units are vastly improved by the existence of a secondary market (the New York Stock Exchange is an example) in which securities may be traded. Such a setting en-

---

[2]Brokers or agents are also institutions that serve as go-betweens and receive commissions for their services. Typically, they do not hold financial assets for a long period themselves, and their services help match surplus and deficit units but do not overcome the differences that may exist between surplus and deficit units.

courages economic efficiency, since the allocation of financing is based on a unit's profitability and ability to pay rather than on the form of financing. This greater efficiency should stimulate both capital accumulation and economic growth.

Commercial banks are financial intermediaries that supply financial services to surplus and deficit units in the U.S. economy. Most bank assets are financial in nature, consisting primarily of money owed by such nonfinancial economic units as households, businesses, and governments. Commercial banks issue contractual obligations, primarily in deposit or borrowing form, to obtain the funds to purchase these financial assets. A bank's capital results from the sale of stock or the accumulation of retained earnings and generally represents a relatively minor source of funds.

The role of commercial banking can, therefore, be stated very simply: to fill the diverse desires of both the ultimate borrowers and lenders in our economy. A commercial bank must obviously compete with other banks, with other financial intermediaries, with direct market transactions, and with any other organization that wishes to perform the task of filling the diverse desires of surplus and deficit units. A bank will be successful only if it performs its economic role as well as or better than its competition.

The difficulty of performing this role successfully can be understood by considering the problems banks have in balancing the diverse desires of the four groups affected by their actions: surplus units, deficit units, bank owners, and bank regulators. Banks not only must issue liabilities in a form acceptable to surplus units, but also must pay a high enough return to outbid competitors. Virtually every surplus unit (whether a household, business, or government) will choose the highest return available in an acceptable form. A higher return to the surplus unit, of course, means a higher cost to the bank acquiring that unit's funds. Deficit units, on the other hand, want the bank to lend them money at the lowest cost available for the desirable form. What borrower would pay 15 percent for a loan when the same loan is available at 14 percent? Corporate and government treasurers tend to be even more sensitive to differences in interest costs. The problem is that the lower the cost to the borrower, the lower the return to the bank.

In addition to pleasing the surplus and deficit units, bank management must be concerned about a third group, the bank's owners. There must be an adequate difference between what the bank earns from the deficit units and what it pays surplus units for the funds (plus personnel and overhead costs) if it is to make an acceptable profit. The owners would prefer to earn more for themselves by paying less to surplus units and charging more to deficit units, but competition limits both of these actions.

As if keeping surplus units, deficit units, and owners satisfied is not enough, bank management must also be concerned with a fourth group, bank regulators. In general terms, regulators are interested in limiting the risks a bank takes in obtaining and employing funds. Limiting risks, however, tends to limit the ability to pay a high return to surplus units, to lend to deficit units at low costs, and to earn an adequate spread between these costs (revenues for the bank) and returns (expenses for the bank) for the shareholders. In a competitive environment, a bank management that can keep these four economic groups satisfied has done a remarkable job.

## CURRENT BANKING STRUCTURE AND REGULATION

The current banking structure and regulation of commercial banks in the United States defies logical explanation and is primarily the result of our historical development.[3] The purpose here is to describe briefly the current (as of 1993) banking structure and regulation. Nearly all commercial banks in the United States are privately owned. Most banks can choose if they wish to be unit banks or part of a branch system, to be members of a holding company, and to seek correspondent relationships with other commercial banks. Available data on the number of banks in the United States in selected years from 1811 to 1992 and on the banking structure are summarized in Tables 1-1 and 1-2, respectively.

Since the passage of the National Banking Act in 1863, a bank has been able to choose between seeking a national charter from the Comptroller of the Currency or a state charter under the supervision of its state's banking regulatory body. Since the formation of the Federal Reserve in 1913, national banks have had to become members of the Federal Reserve, but state banks can choose whether to become members. Figure 1-3 shows that the number of commercial banks has dropped over the last decade because new charters have been less than mergers and failures.

### Unit versus Branch Banking

Most banks in the United States have traditionally been unit banks—single-office institutions primarily serving their local communities. At the end of 1992 there were 11,465 insured commercial banks in the United States. Of these, 4,646 were unit banks, down from 9,375 at the end of 1971. Although still over 40 percent of all commercial banks, the unit bank might well be placed on the endangered species list. The tide toward multiple-office banking is running strong. The number of branch banking offices increased from 4,613 in 1948 to 10,605 in 1960, 23,362 at the end of 1971, and 52,438 at the end of 1992.[4] This increase has resulted from both the establishment of new branches in growing communities and the absorption of previously independent banks through mergers. The pros and cons of multiple-office banking and bank mergers are still in the forefront of bank policy considerations today.

---

[3] The historical development of banks and bank regulation is covered in D. R. Dewey, *Financial History of the United States* (New York: Longman, 1934); Raymond W. Goldsmith, *Financial Intermediaries in the American Economy Since 1900* (Princeton, N.J.: Princeton University Press, 1958); Paul B. Trescott, *Financing American Enterprise* (New York: Harper & Row, 1963); and H. R. Kroos and M. R. Blyn, *A History of Financial Institutions* (New York: Random House, 1971).

[4] Data from Federal Deposit Insurance Corporation, 1993.

**TABLE 1-1 Number and Total Assets of Commercial Banks**

| Year | Number of Banks | Total Assets (dollars in millions) |
|------|-----------------|------------------------------------|
| 1811 | 88 | $ 42 |
| 1820 | 307 | 103 |
| 1830 | 329 | 110 |
| 1866 | 1,391 | 1,673 |
| 1880 | 3,355 | 3,399 |
| 1900 | 13,053 | 11,388 |
| 1920 | 30,909 | 53,094 |
| 1930 | 24,273 | 74,290 |
| 1940 | 15,076 | 79,729 |
| 1950 | 14,676 | 179,165 |
| 1960 | 13,999 | 230,046 |
| 1970 | 14,199 | 518,220 |
| 1980 | 15,120 | 1,704,000 |
| 1981 | 15,213 | 1,781,700 |
| 1982 | 15,329 | 1,972,100 |
| 1983 | 15,380 | 2,113,100 |
| 1984 | 15,023 | 2,348,900 |
| 1985 | 14,797 | 2,581,600 |
| 1986 | 14,559 | 2,763,400 |
| 1987 | 13,987 | 2,998,300 |
| 1988 | 13,398 | 3,101,200 |
| 1989 | 12,916 | 3,283,900 |
| 1990 | 12,568 | 3,367,800 |
| 1991 | 12,123 | 3,411,000 |
| 1992 | 11,659 | 3,652,700 |

SOURCES: *The Statistical History of the United States from Colonial Times to the Present* (Stamford, Conn.: Fairfield Publishers, 1974); *Statistical Abstract of the United States;* Board of Governors of the Federal Reserve System, Federal Reserve Bulletin.

Branch banking has been a controversial subject since the earliest days of the United States. As early as 1790, Secretary of the Treasury Alexander Hamilton had grave doubts about it.[5] Nevertheless, both the First and Second Banks of the United States were branch banking institutions.[6] In many instances the early state banks also had branches. The 406 state banks existing in 1834 operated 100 branches. On the eve of the Civil War, there were 170 state bank branches in 11 states. However, the existence of over 1,500 banks by that time indicated a clear trend toward unit banking.

Opposition to branch banking arose from two directions. First, the remoteness of some branches (as well as of some unit banks) tended to facilitate

[5] "Report on a National Bank" (December 13, 1970), in *Papers on Public Credit, Commerce and Finance,* ed. Samuel McKee, Jr. (New York: Columbia University Press, 1934).

[6] The Second Bank, organized in 1816, had established 19 offices in 14 states by October 1817.

## TABLE 1-2 Data on Banking Structure, December 31, 1992[a]

| Structure | Number of Banks |
|---|---|
| National banks (examined by Comptroller of the Currency) | 3,599 |
| Federal Reserve member banks—national banks plus (examined by Federal Reserve) | 956 |
| Bank covered by FDIC—all Federal Reserve members plus (examined by state and FDIC) | 6,910 |
| State non-FDIC banks (examined by state banking authority) | 194 |
| Total banks | 11,659 |
| Branch offices (of 6819 banks) | 52,438 |
| Total banking offices | 64,097 |

| | Number[b] | Banks Controlled | Assets (dollars in billions) |
|---|---|---|---|
| One-bank holding companies | 4,898 | 4,894[c] | |
| Multibank holding companies | 851 | 3,284 | |
| Total holding company banks | 5,749 | 8,178 | $3,087 (84.5% of $3,653 Total Assets) |

[a] Fifty states and the District of Columbia.

[b] After eliminating tiered one- and multibank holding companies.

[c] A few banks are partially owned by two one-bank holding companies.

Source: Federal Reserve System and Federal Deposit Insurance Corporation, 1993.

## FIGURE 1-3 Structural Changes Among FDIC-Insured Commercial Banks 1980–1992

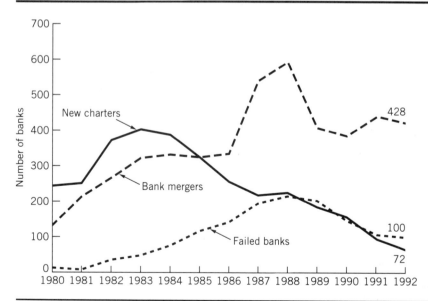

Source: *Quarterly Banking Profile*, FDIC, Washington, D.C. 1993.

9

some of the worst abuses of the note-issue privilege in the days of wildcat banking, so that banking reform and early attempts at bank supervision often led to the abolition of the branch banking privilege.[7] Second, the Jacksonian campaign against the Second Bank of the United States and the subsequent Populist campaigns for cheap money were in a real sense directed against the concentration of monetary power in large eastern banks, some of which were branch institutions. The resultant political furor helped to establish the emotional tone that is still evident in much of the popular and political opposition to branch banking.[8]

When the National Banking Act was passed in 1863, the question of branches was not even discussed. The Federal Reserve Act of 1913 extended the privilege of membership to state banks without prohibiting them from operating existing branches but did not accord the right to establish new branches to national banks, for which membership was compulsory. Limited branch powers were gradually granted to national banks and subsequently extended until 1952, when all national banks were empowered to establish branches as freely as banks chartered by the respective states.

The history of banking in the United States, therefore, starts with branch banking, veers in the direction of unit banking, and is now quite rapidly swinging back again. Opposition to branch banking is still strong in some areas, however, and state laws concerning the establishment of branches vary from one part of the country to another. Statewide branching is permitted in 29 states; branching is permitted in an extensively limited manner in 4 states; while the remaining 17 states allow limited branching.[9]

Against this background of diversity in law and tradition, those who are responsible for managing banks must attempt a logical assessment of the virtues and deficiencies of unit banking. The issues are obviously not clear-cut, or they would have been resolved long ago. Nor is the available evidence entirely conclusive, even when weighted objectively. It is, nevertheless, incumbent on bank management and legislative bodies regulating bankers to evaluate the banking structure, actual and prospective, in the light of economic reality and the expanding needs of a complex and dynamic economy.

## The Bank Holding Company

Bank holding companies are also an integral part of our current banking structure. There are two general types of bank holding companies, one-bank and

---

[7] By the early 1840s, Massachusetts, New York, and Rhode Island had passed legislation providing that no one should conduct the business of banking except at his or her place of residence.

[8] In *Old Kent Bank and Trust Company* v. *William McC. Martin et al.*, Judge Washington, dissenting, said, "There has long been public hostility to the extension, by means of branches, of a bank's geographic area of operation. At one time branch banking was almost uniformly forbidden in the U.S. Many persons feared, and still fear that, among other things, unrestrained bank operations would enable a few wealthy urban banks to extend their operations to a point where the independence and prosperity of the poorer banks . . . would be seriously jeopardized."

[9] *Profile of State-Chartered Banking*, Conference of State Bank Supervisors, 1992.

multibank. Prior to the 1970 amendments, one-bank holding companies did not fall within the definition of the Bank Holding Company Act of 1956 and were, therefore, not subject to the specific control of the Board of Governors of the Federal Reserve System. Under our current laws, a one-bank holding company is created when an existing bank organizes a holding company of which the bank becomes a subsidiary. Multibank holding companies own a controlling interest in the stock of two or more banks. Many smaller banks (with assets under $200 million) have formed one-bank holding companies to gain tax or capital advantages, or both, from that form of organization. The holding company form of organization appeals to larger banks for two additional reasons. Multibank holding companies can be used to acquire additional banks (particularly important in states limiting branching), and either type can be used to form or acquire additional subsidiaries in financially related activities.

The Board of Governors, under the authority of the 1970 amendments, has established a "laundry list" of such permissible activities. Table 1-3 lists activities found permissible by regulation or order and activities that have been specifically denied. Numerous other financial activities have been neither approved nor denied.[10]

At the end of 1992, bank holding companies controlled 8,178 banks, and approximately 4,000 subsidiaries engaged in, or were authorized to engage in, various other activities. Not all of these subsidiaries are currently active. At that time, there were 5,749 holding company groups in the United States controlling 84.5 percent of the assets of all commercial banks. Of these, 4,898 were one-bank holding companies.[11]

Under the current legislative structure, multibank holding companies have usually been pushed into one of two different patterns of organization and decision making. First, some holding companies operate very much like a branching system. Although each bank has a separate board of directors, the subsidiary board tends to have little power. All banks have the same name and same functions (e.g., investment loan rates and deposit rates are done entirely at the holding company level).

The second pattern emphasizes that the distinctive feature of any form of bank holding company lies in its ability to realize many of the benefits and render most of the services of widespread branch banking organizations while retaining the decentralization of management that can preserve the "local touch." Each banking unit of this form of holding company system typically is managed by a board of directors composed of local citizens who retain a substantial measure of autonomy in forming lending policies and dealing with local management problems. Without a substantial grant of local autonomy, the outstanding citizens and business leaders of the various communities could hardly be induced to serve as directors, because in most cases they hold only a nominal stock interest in the bank or the holding company. Given enough local authority, they regard their directorships as a form of community service.

[10] The American Bankers Association provided this list.
[11] Board of Governors of the Federal Reserve System.

---

**TABLE 1-3  Permissible and Denied Nonbanking Activities by Bank Holding Companies**

| Permitted by Regulation | Permitted by Order | Denied by Federal Reserve |
|---|---|---|
| 1. Extensions of credit[a] <br> Mortgage banking <br>    Finance companies— <br>    consumer, sales and <br>    commercial <br> Credit cards <br> Factoring <br> 2. Industrial bank, Morris Plan bank, industrial loan company <br> 3. Servicing loans and other extensions of credit[a] <br> 4. Trust company[a] <br> 5. Investment or financial advising[a] <br> 6. Full-payout leasing of personal or real property[a] <br> 7. Investments in community welfare projects[a] <br> 8. Providing bookkeeping or data-processing services[a] <br> 9. Acting as insurance agent or broker primarily in connection with credit extensions[a] <br> 10. Underwriting credit life, accident, and health insurance <br> 11. Providing courier services[a] <br> 12. Management consulting for unaffiliated banks[a,b] <br> 13. Sale at retail of money orders with a face value of not more than $1,000, travelers checks, and savings bonds[a,b] <br> 14. Performing appraisals of real estate[b] <br> 15. Audit services for unaffiliated banks <br> 16. Issuance and sale of travelers checks <br> 17. Management consulting to nonbank depository institutions | 1. Issuance and sale of travelers checks[a,c] <br> 2. Buying and selling gold and silver bullion and silver coin[a] <br> 3. Issuing money orders and general-purpose, variable denominated payment instruments[a,b,c] <br> 4. Futures commission merchant to cover gold and silver bullion and coins[a,b] <br> 5. Underwriting certain federal, state, and municipal securities[a,b] <br> 6. Check verification[a,b] <br> 7. Financial advice to consumers[a,b] <br> 8. Issuance of small-denomination debt instruments[b] | 1. Insurance premium funding (combined sales of mutual funds and insurance) <br> 2. Underwriting life insurance not related to credit extension <br> 3. Real estate brokerage[a] <br> 4. Land development <br> 5. Real estate syndication <br> 6. General management consulting <br> 7. Property management <br> 8. Computer output microfilm services <br> 9. Underwriting mortgage guaranty insurance[d] <br> 10. Operating a savings and loan association[b,e] <br> 11. Operating a travel agency[a,b] <br> 12. Underwriting property and casualty insurance[b] <br> 13. Underwriting home loan life mortgage insurance[b] <br> 14. Orbanco: Investment note issue with transactional characteristics |

[a] Activities permissible to national banks.

[b] Added to list since January 1, 1975.

[c] To be decided on a case-by-case basis.

[d] Board orders found these activities closely related to banking but denied proposed acquisitions as part of its "go slow" policy.

[e] Operating a thrift institution has been permitted by order in Rhode Island and New Hampshire only.

The relationship of the holding company to its subsidiary banks in this holding company pattern is largely that of an informed and helpful stockholder. This role combines many of the functions often rendered to country banks by their city correspondents, with provision for effective group action in such fields as accounting, loan participation, purchasing, or investment analysis. This form of holding company has, in short, covered many staff functions for its constituent banks. This holding company form of organization also tends to encourage a certain amount of healthy rivalry among its units. Such competition provides stimulus for experimentation and can lead to a diversity of approaches that is less likely to be found in a branch organization, where final management authority stems from one top-management team and a single board of directors.

## Correspondent Banking in the United States

The correspondent banking system is an entirely informal arrangement whereby a smaller bank maintains deposit balances with larger banks in nearby cities and looks to them for a wide variety of services and assistance. The city banks, in turn, keep correspondent balances with still larger banks in the principal money centers. Before the establishment of the Federal Reserve System, checks were collected entirely through this network of correspondent banks (often by roundabout routing). Most important, the correspondent system served as a means of mobilizing the supply of credit and channeling it to areas where and when it was needed. Thus, correspondent banks provided liquidity and credit fluidity to a diverse economy. Country banks could deposit their idle funds with their correspondents, who invested them in money market loans (theoretically, at least). Then, at times of peak demand for seasonal agricultural credit, the country banks not only could draw down their balances but also could borrow from their correspondents. The inadequacies of these arrangements, which did not include a central bank, were evident in recurring panics and finally led to the establishment of the Federal Reserve System. Nevertheless, without correspondent relationships, the early credit needs of the country could hardly have been met at all.

The correspondent banks are still active in the collection of checks and still supply credit to the smaller banks for the balances that the latter maintain. In addition, correspondent banks perform many services that would otherwise be unobtainable for smaller banks and their customers. They give investment advice, provide safekeeping for customers' securities, arrange for the purchase and sale of securities, arrange international financial transactions, trade in federal funds, participate in loans too large for the small banks, sell participation in large loans to small banks with surplus funds, and provide a wide range of other services.

The larger correspondent banks, nearly all of which are members of the Federal Reserve System, indirectly channel the benefits of that system to those banks that are not members and at the same time provide some services even to member banks (such as giving investment advice) that would be inappropriate for the central bank to perform.[12] The correspondent banking system tends to extend economies of scale to smaller banks. Smaller banks experience infrequent demands for some services, such as international financial transactions, but must generally be prepared to offer such services to customers. Returns would rarely compensate the initial investment required for small-scale production of these services. Larger banks, however, encounter sufficient demand from the public and from other commercial banks to provide these services profitably and at a lower unit cost to their customers. Aside from direct expenses incurred in providing these services or the fees required for data processing, correspondents rarely charge customer banks. The deposit balances that a bank holds with its correspondent are expected to compensate for the services.[13]

The volume of interbank demand deposits provides some indication of the usage of correspondent services. In 1896, correspondent balances represented 10 percent of total demand deposits in commercial banks. These balances climbed to 13 percent in 1913, just before the organization of the Federal Reserve System, and then fell gradually to 7 percent in 1928. They reached roughly 12 percent of total demand deposits in the late 1940s, declined to 9 percent by the early 1960s, and then rose back to approximately 11 percent by early 1976. The rather sharp increase in the late 1960s and 1970s appears to have been caused by the increasing need for correspondent services and the substantial increase in loan participation among correspondent banks. By 1993 this percentage had dropped back to below 8 percent. This drop-off probably resulted from the higher interest rates in much of the 1980s, which have encouraged banks to minimize idle balances, and from the Depository Institution Deregulation and Monetary Control Act of 1980, which encourages nonmember banks to hold reserves at the Federal Reserve.[14]

## The Regulatory Structure

Regulation of banking is currently divided among 3 federal agencies and 50 state agencies. Areas of responsibility overlap, yet the duties of the diverse regulatory agencies are generally carried out smoothly and efficiently. Indeed, the pluralism of bank regulatory authority in the United States may have led to a regulatory environment superior to one charted by a single authority.

---

[12] One of the primary advantages Federal Reserve membership gave larger banks was the ability to pass on many benefits of system membership to their smaller correspondents. The Depository Institution Regulation and Monetary Control Act of 1980, which requires the Federal Reserve to price its services to members, to allow nonmembers to receive some "Fed" services, and increasingly to encourage nonmember banks to hold reserves at the Fed, is changing this aspect of correspondent relationships.

[13] By far the largest share of these compensating correspondent balances is held as demand deposits. A recent survey found that fewer than 6 percent of the banks favored a fee arrangement. This general preference for demand deposits as compensation for correspondent services may exist partly because nonmember banks can normally count correspondent balances toward reserve requirements. Many banks, however, charge fees for computer services.

[14] *All Bank Statistics*, 1896–1955 (Washington, D.C.: U.S. Board of Governors of the Federal Reserve System, 1959); Federal Reserve Bulletins, 1956–1993.

Bank regulation encompasses a wide variety of technical functions relating to the operation of banks. These concern the following:

1. The issuance and enforcement of regulations.
2. The chartering of banks.
3. The periodic examination of banks and the requirement that bank management take steps to correct unsatisfactory or unsound conditions found through such examinations.
4. The review and analysis of periodic reports of conditions, earnings, and expenses.
5. The rendering of counsel and advice, when requested, on bank operating problems, particularly in the case of smaller banks.
6. The approval of proposed changes in the scope of corporate functions exercised by individual banks and of proposed changes in their capital structures.
7. Authorization for the establishment of branches and for the exercise of trust powers.
8. The approval of bank mergers and consolidations.
9. The organization and regulation of bank holding companies.
10. The regulation of bank service corporations.
11. The liquidation of banks.

All of these functions are not performed by each of the four types of supervisory agencies, but they are all the responsibility of at least one of the agencies. The purpose of this section is to summarize the broad aspects of the regulatory environment in which commercial banks must operate.[15]

The diffusion of bank regulatory authority does not mean that banks are not closely regulated. Banking is more closely regulated in the United States than in any other developed country in the world. At the same time, no other country has as many banks relative to its population. These facts are not unrelated. On the contrary, the degree and character of bank regulation in the United States spring directly from the nature of our banking structure.

As noted in the preceding paragraphs, the diversity of U.S. banking structures developed in response to the often conflicting desires of different segments of the public. Despite the recent trend toward consolidation, there are still thousands of banks chartered by both state and federal governments that for the most part are locally owned and operated. Left to their own and often inadequate devices in the past, hundreds of banks failed. Americans apparently wanted to preserve this diverse structure without sacrificing banking safety. The American system of bank regulation, therefore, has developed over the years in response to the desire for a banking system that is both sound and responsive to the credit needs of a dynamic economy. One of the basic responsibilities of bank regulatory authorities should be to ensure the continuance of a responsible bank regulatory system.

---

[15]More complete descriptions of the regulatory structure for banks are contained in Part 10 of the *Bankers Handbook*, ed. William H. Baughn and Charles E. Walker (Homewood, Ill.: Dow-Jones–Irwin, 1989), and in *Bank Supervision* (St. Louis: Federal Reserve Bank), 1988.

The limitation of banking activities through detailed provisions of regulation and law is a distinctive feature of banking in the United States. All banks derive their powers from the banking laws, which are, in this sense, permissive. On the other hand, banking laws specifically limit the powers granted and are thus essentially restrictive. The restrictions are designed to prevent, if possible, U.S. banks from making the mistakes that caused widespread bank failures in the past.

Both state and federal regulatory authorities are concerned with regulation and supervision. They administer the banking laws, promulgate and interpret regulations issued thereunder, and exercise impersonal and objective judgments regarding bank policies to further the public interest. They use the examination process to review both the legality and the soundness of an individual bank's operations.

As noted earlier, the historical development of the American banking structure has given rise to a multiplicity of regulatory agencies at both the state and federal levels. Under our concept of dual banking, national banks are chartered and supervised by the Office of the Comptroller of the Currency, whereas state banks are chartered and supervised primarily by the banking authorities of the respective states. Most state-chartered banks, however, have come under one form or another of federal supervision and regulation. With the establishment of the Federal Reserve System, those state-chartered banks that became members submitted voluntarily to many of the legal restrictions imposed on national banks and to examination and supervision by the Board of Governors of the Federal Reserve System.

With the advent of federal deposit insurance, nearly all the remaining state banks accepted supervision by the Federal Deposit Insurance Corporation (FDIC) as a condition of insurance. There are now roughly 200 nonmember, noninsured commercial banks that are subject to no direct federal supervision.

Moreover, the jurisdictions of these three federal regulatory agencies overlap, and individual banks are subject to the rules of more than one agency. National banks, for example, while chartered and supervised solely by the Comptroller of the Currency, are required to be members of the Federal Reserve System, and their deposits are insured by the FDIC. Both of these latter agencies have the power to examine national banks (a power seldom exercised), but both review reports of examinations made by national bank examiners. National banks are also subject to some state laws, such as those governing branching authority and legal holidays.

The crisscrossing of regulatory responsibility is further illustrated by the rules regarding changes in banking structure. All holding company transactions, including those involving nonmember banks, are subject to the jurisdiction of the Board of Governors of the Federal Reserve System. The establishment of *de novo* branches requires the approval of the chartering authority, state or national, and, for state banks, the additional approval of either the Board of Governors or the FDIC, depending on member or nonmember insured status. Merger applications follow the same course, except that each of the three federal agencies must seek the advice of the other two and of the Department of Justice regarding the competitive factors involved.

The three federal regulatory agencies and the state agencies are responsible for bank examination, the foundation of bank regulation. American banking is highly competitive because of the large number of banks in the country. In most communities there are two or more sources of banking services. Bank examinations in the United States are primarily designed to protect depositors from unsound banking practices rather than to provide a substitute for competition. Bank examinations, completed by any of the four major types of regulatory agencies, emphasize review and appraisal of earning ability, asset quality, capital adequacy, liquidity, and management ability.

Two factors that give rise to the need for examination are inherent in banking. The first involves the bank's loans and investments, which lead to the creation of demand deposits. Since these demand deposits make up the major portion of the nation's money supply, the quality of bank credit underlies the value of money. The second factor is the nature of the financial intermediary role that banks fulfill in the economy. Banks receive savings and demand deposits that are highly liquid. The banks invest these deposits in other, less liquid assets. To prevent a liquidity crisis, banks must hold some liquid assets, have adequate capital, and maintain professional management.

Two major concerns about the diversity and practices of our regulatory system deserve special mention. First, rivalry and feuding among the chief bank regulatory agencies have made bankers uncertain about how to handle many important banking functions. Areas of regulatory disagreement include interstate acquisitions, limited-service banks, loans to other countries, disclosure of financial condition, entry into insurance and investment banking, capital requirements, and brokered deposits. Overlapping responsibilities, bureaucratic power plays, and different opinions would seem to make rational decisions much harder. Some bankers, however, prefer this diversity, because they say that they can always find one regulatory official who agrees with them on most issues.

The second major area of concern is the premiums for FDIC deposit insurance and the excessive risk that such insurance encourages. The level premium for any risk bank would be the same as that of life insurance firms selling equal-cost life insurance to a 30- and a 70-year-old person. Furthermore, since the risk of failure is passed on with explicit insurance up to $100,000, and sometimes higher, implicit insurance or guarantees (e.g., the Continental Illinois Bank bailout), banks may take higher risks without incurring higher costs in the quest for high returns. For the last decade, academics have generally criticized such subsidies and the possible excessive risks to which they may lead. Recently, many bankers and legislators have joined the ranks of the concerned. The Federal Deposit Insurance Corporation Improvement Act (FDICIA), passed in December 1991, represents an initial attempt to address this concern. This act is evaluated later in this chapter.

Joint consideration of some problems by the various regulatory bodies has been a positive trend. For example, representatives from each of the major bank regulatory groups have met to consider bank capital requirements. Additionally, the Federal Financial Institutions Examination Council has been given a broader role in coordinating regulatory initiatives. This council includes representatives from the Federal Reserve, FDIC, Comptroller, Office of Thrift Supervision, and National Credit Union Administration. In our opinion, more consistent and uniform bank regulation should lead to better bank management.

### Banking Problems

The risks in banking have been particularly visible in the 1980s and early 1990s. Large companies, such as Braniff and International Harvester, have failed or been unable to pay their debts. Foreign countries, such as Poland, Brazil, and Mexico, have delayed payments on their obligations to banks. The banking community was shocked in May 1982, when Drysdale Government Securities, Inc., a small, aggressive New York securities dealer, defaulted on $160 million owed to other government securities dealers. Chase Manhattan Bank and Manufacturers Hanover Trust, which acted as Drysdale's agent in the securities market, covered Drysdale's debts at an after-tax cost of $117 and $9 million, respectively. In July 1982, federal regulators closed Penn Square Bank in Oklahoma. Much of that bank's $250 million in uninsured deposits has not been recovered. In addition, Penn Square had packaged about $2 billion worth of poor-quality loan participations for other banks, including Continental Illinois Bank, Seattle First National Bank, and Chase Manhattan Bank. In August another small securities market fund, Lombard-Wall, was forced into bankruptcy. Again several banks were its primary creditors.

In 1983 the forced merger of SeaFirst Corporation into Bank of America and of First National Bank of Midland into Republic Bancorporation of Dallas showed that even banks with billions of dollars in assets could have severe problems. A further shock occurred in 1984, when federal regulators guaranteed all deposits, without maximum, of Continental National Bank and Trust Company and were still forced to nationalize the bank. Numerous other well-regarded banks reported losses (e.g., InterFirst Corporation, First City Bancorporation, Crocker National, and First Chicago Corporation) or suffered higher borrowing costs because of higher perceived risk (e.g., Manufacturers Hanover in 1983 and 1984). Stress on financial institutions was accentuated by the failure of several government securities dealers (e.g., E.S.M. Securities and Bevill Bresler) and failures and forced takeovers of state-insured savings and loan associations (S&Ls) in Ohio and Maryland in the mid-1980s. Problems in energy, agriculture, and real estate put additional pressures on commercial banks in geographic regions heavily dependent on these economic sectors from the mid-1980s through the early 1990s. The northeastern U.S. real estate problems led to problems in northeastern commercial banks in the early 1990s.

Table 1-4 shows the number of bank suspensions from 1890 to 1933. Table 1-5 shows the number of bank failures and forced mergers in the United States since the FDIC began keeping records. After 1943, fewer than 10 banks

**TABLE 1-4    Bank Suspensions, 1890–1933**

| Year | Total Bank Suspensions |
|---|---|
| 1890–1899 | 1,294 |
| 1900–1909 | 797 |
| 1910–1919 | 849 |
| 1920 | 168 |
| 1921 | 505 |
| 1922 | 367 |
| 1923 | 646 |
| 1924 | 775 |
| 1925 | 618 |
| 1926 | 976 |
| 1927 | 669 |
| 1928 | 499 |
| 1929 | 659 |
| 1930 | 1,352 |
| 1931 | 2,294 |
| 1932 | 1,456 |
| 1933 | 4,004 |

SOURCES: *The Statistical History of the United States from Colonial Times to the Present* (Stamford, Conn.: Fairfield Publishers, 1974); *Statistical Abstract of the United States.*

closed each year until 1975, when the toll rose to 14. It dropped to 10 or fewer until 1982, when failures suddenly jumped to 42. That number rose to 48 in 1983, 80 in 1984, 120 in 1985, 145 in 1986, and 203 in 1987, peaking at 221 in 1988. The number of failures fell slowly after 1988, but the dollar amount increased from 1989 to 1992. To be sure, failures in the last decade are still less than half of the 4,000 or so bank failures in 1933, when there was no insurance system in place to cushion the blow. Nevertheless, the rash of failures reflects the existence of trouble spots in the economy (e.g., agriculture, defense, energy, real estate), as well as the uneven management capabilities of bankers.

## A CHALLENGING AND CHANGING ENVIRONMENT IN THE MID- AND LATE 1990s

Anticipating the environment in which commercial banks will make their management decisions during the next several years is clearly important. It is, of course, impossible to predict accurately all aspects of the future environment for bank management decisions. Some reasonable inferences, however, can be made about the future environment by studying economic trends, recent legislation, and developments in the banking industry. The following discussion of the future environment is divided into three parts: the regulatory environment, the trends in the banking industry, and the changing nature of the

**TABLE 1-5  FDIC-Insured Banks Closed as a Result of Financial Difficulties (dollars in thousands)**

| Year of Deposit Payoff or Deposit Assumption | No. of Banks | Disbursements | Recoveries to Dec. 31, 1991 | Estimated Additional Recoveries | Losses[a] |
|---|---|---|---|---|---|
| 1934 | 9 | 941 | 734 | — | 207 |
| 1935 | 25 | 9,108 | 6,423 | — | 2,685 |
| 1936 | 69 | 15,206 | 12,873 | — | 2,333 |
| 1937 | 75 | 20,204 | 16,532 | — | 3,672 |
| 1938 | 74 | 34,394 | 31,969 | — | 2,425 |
| 1939 | 60 | 81,828 | 74,676 | — | 7,152 |
| 1940 | 43 | 87,899 | 84,103 | — | 3,796 |
| 1941 | 15 | 25,061 | 24,470 | — | 591 |
| 1942 | 20 | 11,684 | 10,996 | — | 688 |
| 1943 | 5 | 7,230 | 7,107 | — | 123 |
| 1944 | 2 | 1,532 | 1,492 | — | 40 |
| 1945 | 1 | 1,845 | 1,845 | — | — |
| 1946 | 1 | 274 | 274 | — | — |
| 1947 | 5 | 2,038 | 1,979 | — | 59 |
| 1948 | 3 | 3,150 | 2,509 | — | 641 |
| 1949 | 4 | 2,685 | 2,316 | — | 369 |
| 1950 | 4 | 4,404 | 3,019 | — | 1,385 |
| 1951 | 2 | 1,986 | 1,986 | — | — |
| 1952 | 3 | 1,525 | 733 | — | 792 |
| 1953 | 2 | 5,359 | 5,359 | — | — |
| 1954 | 2 | 1,029 | 771 | — | 258 |
| 1955 | 5 | 7,315 | 7,085 | — | 230 |
| 1956 | 2 | 3,499 | 3,286 | — | 213 |
| 1957 | 1 | 1,031 | 1,031 | — | — |
| 1958 | 4 | 3,051 | 3,023 | — | 28 |
| 1959 | 3 | 1,835 | 1,738 | — | 97 |
| 1960 | 1 | 4,765 | 4,765 | — | — |
| 1961 | 5 | 6,201 | 4,699 | — | 1,502 |
| 1962 | 3 | 1,983 | 1,827 | 0 | — |
| 1963 | 2 | 19,172 | 18,886 | — | 286 |
| 1964 | 7 | 13,712 | 12,171 | 0 | 1,540 |
| 1965 | 5 | 11,479 | 10,816 | 0 | 663 |
| 1966 | 7 | 10,020 | 9,541 | 234 | 245 |
| 1967 | 4 | 8,097 | 7,087 | 0 | 1,010 |
| 1968 | 3 | 6,476 | 6,464 | 0 | 12 |
| 1969 | 9 | 42,072 | 41,910 | 0 | 162 |
| 1970 | 7 | 51,566 | 51,501 | 0 | 272 |
| 1971 | 6 | 171,646 | 171,430 | 23 | 193 |
| 1972 | 1 | 16,189 | 14,501 | (8) | 1,704 |
| 1973 | 6 | 435,238 | 368,852 | (1,101) | 67,487 |
| 1974 | 4 | 2,403,277 | 2,259,633 | 143,604 | 40 |

**TABLE 1-5**   *(continued)*

| Year of Deposit Payoff or Deposit Assumption | No. of Banks | Disbursements | Recoveries to Dec. 31, 1991 | Estimated Additional Recoveries | Losses[a] |
|---|---|---|---|---|---|
| 1975 | 13 | 332,046 | 292,431 | 23,303 | 16,312 |
| 1976 | 16 | 599,337 | 559,430 | 39,720 | 247 |
| 1977 | 6 | 26,650 | 20,654 | 3,903 | 2,093 |
| 1978 | 7 | 548,568 | 510,613 | 28,940 | 9,015 |
| 1979 | 10 | 90,351 | 74,246 | 5,238 | 10,867 |
| 1980 | 10 | 152,355 | 114,764 | 7,010 | 30,585 |
| 1981 | 10 | 998,433 | 366,908 | 43,518 | 588,007 |
| 1982 | 42 | 2,262,079 | 824,149 | 122,674 | 1,315,256 |
| 1983 | 48 | 3,695,633 | 2,050,340 | 275,667 | 1,369,626 |
| 1984 | 80 | 7,863,086 | 5,345,560 | 351,763 | 1,985,763 |
| 1985 | 120 | 2,865,563 | 1,508,850 | 285,330 | 1,071,383 |
| 1986 | 144 | 4,892,583 | 2,770,918 | 274,165 | 1,847,500 |
| 1987 | 201 | 5,025,908 | 2,691,892 | 162,171 | 2,171,845 |
| 1988 | 221 | 13,034,043 | 3,624,988 | 2,249,063 | 7,159,992 |
| 1989 | 206 | 10,562,090 | 4,206,437 | (154,936) | 6,510,589 |
| 1990 | 159 | 10,369,855 | 5,826,682 | 601,990 | 3,941,183 |
| 1991 | 108 | 19,790,422 | 4,068,166 | 8,307,830 | 7,396,426 |
| 1992 | 100 | — | — | — | — |
| Total | 2,007 | 86,465,085 | 38,165,402 | 12,770,101 | 35,529,492 |

[a] Includes estimated losses in active cases. Not adjusted for interest or allowable return, which was collected in some cases in which the disbursement was fully recovered.

Source: Federal Deposit Insurance Corporation, *Annual Report of the FDIC, 1991* (Washington, D.C.: U.S. Government Printing Office, 1992).

money and capital markets. A fourth area, the changing economic environment in the 1990s, should be studied by examining current economic periodicals.

## The Legislative and Regulatory Environment

Table 1-6 summarizes the key provisions of 12 major legislative acts (often with subsequent amendments) that greatly affect banking, and Table 1-7 describes the regulations of the Federal Reserve.

The Depository Institutions Deregulation and Monetary Control Act of 1980 (HR 4986), the Garn–St. Germain Depository Institutions Act of 1982 (HR 6267), the Financial Institutions Reform, Recovery, and Enforcement Act of 1989 (FIRREA), and the Federal Deposit Insurance Corporation Improvement Act of 1991 (FDICIA) have led to greater changes in bank management than any legislation since the 1930s. HR 4986 includes nine titles on such diverse

**TABLE 1-6  Major Provisions of Legislation Affecting Banks**

*National Banking Act* (many amendments)—created the Comptroller of the Currency, which charters, examines, and supervises banks that choose to become national (rather than state) banks.

*Federal Reserve Act* (many amendments)—created a system of 12 Federal Reserve banks to control the supply of money and credit and supervise state chartered banks that are members of the Federal Reserve. Control now centralized in the Board of Governors and the Open Market Committee. Supervises bank holding companies.

*Edge Act*—allows commercial banks to open subsidiary offices in other states to transact international business.

*Bank Holding Company Act* (many amendments)—defines a holding company and states the criteria the Board of Governors of the Federal Reserve System must apply to determine which nonbank activities a holding company may engage in.

*Federal Deposit Insurance Act* (many amendments)—created the FDIC, which insures deposit accounts in member banks up to $100,000 (at present). Examines and supervises state banks.

*Glass–Steagall Act*—requires separation of investment activities and commercial banking.

*McFadden Act*—prohibits interstate banking.

*Douglas Amendment to the Bank Holding Company Act*—prohibits bank holding companies from interstate expansion.

*Depository Institution Deregulation and Monetary Control Act of 1980*—authorized NOW accounts; provided for the phaseout of Regulation Q; increased FDIC insurance to $100,000; altered the competitive relationship between banks and other financial institutions; created the Depository Institutions Deregulation Committee (DIDC).

*Depository Institutions Act of 1982* (Garn–St. Germain)—authorized money market accounts; requires the end of the interest rate differential favoring thrifts; gives broader asset powers to S&Ls and thrift institutions.

*Financial Institutions Reform, Recovery, and Enforcement Act of 1989 (FIRREA)*—reformed the regulatory structure of S&Ls; provided the structure and financing (inadequate) for bailout of the S&L industry; added acceptable levels of penalties for some regulatory standards (particularly capital adequacy); and called for a comprehensive study of deposit insurance.

*Federal Deposit Insurance Corporation Improvement Act of 1991 (FDICIA)*—made a number of reforms addressing the safety and soundness of deposit insurance funds, supervision, accounting, prompt regulatory action, least-cost resolution, and federal insurance for state-chartered depository institutions. The act also expands regulation of foreign banks, implements changes in consumer protection laws, and provides for netting procedures to reduce the systemic risks within the borrowing system.

---

**TABLE 1-7  Summary of Major Federal Reserve Regulations**

---

1. Monetary policy–related regulations
   A     Loans to depositories
   D     Reserve requirements
   U, T  Credit by banks, by brokers and dealers, and by others
   G, X  Rules for margin borrowers
   Q     Interest rate ceilings on various types of deposits
2. Bank safety and soundness regulations
   F     Financial disclosure to stockholders and others
   L     Interlocking directorates in banking
   O     Loans to officers, directors, and stockholders
   P     Security devices and procedures
   R     Interlocking relationships between banks and the securities industry
3. Regulations covering the international activities and holding company activities of banks
   K     International banking
   Y     Bank holding company activities
4. Regulations covering activities of the Federal Reserve Banks
   H     Membership in the Federal Reserve
   I     Stock ownership in Federal Reserve Banks
   J     Federal Reserve check processing rules and procedures
   N     Reserve Banks' relations with foreign banks and governments
   V     Loan guarantees
5. Consumer protection regulations
   AA   Unfair and deceptive practices
   B     Equal credit opportunity
   BB   Community reinvestment
   C     Home mortgage disclosure
   DD   Truth-in-savings
   E     Electronic fund transfers
   M     Consumer leasing
   R     Flood insurance
   S     Financial privacy
   Z     Truth-in-lending

---

subjects as nationwide authorization of Negotiable Order of Withdrawal (NOW) accounts, expanded asset and liability powers for thrift institutions, fees for services provided by the Federal Reserve, preemption of state usury laws, and simplification of truth-in-lending regulations. Table 1-8 summarizes HR 4986's immediate and probable long-term impact on bank financial management.

The passage of HR 6267 in 1982 probably has had the most far-reaching effect on bank management. Money market accounts and Super NOW accounts were the new depository instruments permitted by this act. Banks were able to compete freely with money market funds for the first time. However, at the same time, the pricing protection of Regulation Q, which set the minimum rates banks could pay on time and savings deposits, tended to disappear.

**TABLE 1-8  Immediate and Longer-Run Effects of HR 4986 on Bank Management Decisions**

| Actions | Impact Effects | Subsequent Effects |
|---|---|---|
| Lower (higher) reserve requirements | Increased (decreased) earning assets and earnings | After transition period, more equitable competitive environment (less of a differential license fee based on size) |
| | | Decreased variation in relative growth rates among various types of deposits |
| | | Reduction in correspondent balances |
| Federal Reserve pricing | Increased explicit costs paid to Federal Reserve | Changes in retail checking services (truncation, pricing) |
| | | Changes in cash management practices and float |
| | | Reduction in correspondent balances |
| | | Greater reliance on explicit pricing (fees, service charges) |
| | | Stimulus to debit cards, electronic fund transfer systems (EFTS), direct deposits, point-of-sale terminals (POS), automated teller machines |
| Nationwide NOW accounts | Higher interest expense of core deposits | Higher average "personal checking" balances |
| | | Reduced not sufficient funds (NFS), overdrafts |
| | | Higher reserve requirements on automated transfer (ATS) balances that are switched to NOW accounts |
| Phaseout of Regulation Q ceilings | Gradual increase in interest costs and pressures on margins | Greater discretion in product design of savings instruments |
| | | Decreased variation in relative size and growth rates of various types of deposits |
| | | Reliance on explicit interest instead of premiums; enhanced value of one-stop banking |
| Higher FDIC insurance level | Higher insurance fees | Potential for marketing distinction vis-à-vis money market funds, Sears, American Express, and Merrill Lynch |
| Expanded powers for thrifts | Costly entry of thrifts into several new markets | Greater competition for obtaining and profitably using bank funds |
| | | Narrowing of spread between attracting and employing funds |
| Relaxation of many state usury laws | Loan rates more consistent with market | Enhancement of ability to hold interest margins stable over credit cycles |
| | | Reduction of artificial barrier on fund allocation |

Banks had to price (some for the first time) such accounts in a very competitive market. Interest margins came under increasing pressure in the mid-1980s as a result of this legislation.

Although changes in banking as a result of HR 4986 and HR 6267 have been significant, the laws have several important deficiencies. For example, there is no provision for removing the remaining constraints on interstate expansion by banks or bank holding companies. Restrictions now imposed under the Glass-Steagall Act, such as those aimed at comingled investment accounts, were not addressed. The long-term implications of those low-yielding, fixed-rate mortgages that will remain a significant part of the portfolios of many thrift institutions and some banks for years to come were not explicitly considered. These and similar issues cannot be ignored. The problem is that banking legislation and regulation tend to be following, not leading, influences on bank management. Legislation and regulation tend to validate or legitimize successful innovation in the banking industry.

While there was no comprehensive banking legislation in the mid-1980s, there have been several regulatory or legislative changes. Bank capital adequacy regulations were tightened and brought closer to uniformity in 1985.

Some states began allowing interstate banking. Many other states passed reciprocal pacts allowing banks in their respective states to cross state lines. On March 31, 1986, all regulated size minimums and interest rate limits were removed. In 1988 the three federal bank regulatory agencies passed new capital guidelines that would use risk weighting of assets as a major determinant of bank capital adequacy. These guidelines became fully effective at the start of 1993.

In addition, the Tax Reform Act of 1986 has had and will have a substantial impact on bank financial management decisions and on bank earnings. Rules limiting the ability to deduct the provision for loan loss expenses for tax purposes and for computing minimum income tax levels will lead to changes in the use of this provision and will probably decrease the reported after-tax earnings of many larger banks. The elimination of the tax-exempt status of income on nearly all larger state and local bond issues will change bank investment decisions appreciably.

The Competitive Equality Banking Act, which passed in the summer of 1987, was primarily defensive and not comprehensive. The main purpose of the legislation was to provide additional funding for the Federal Savings and Loan Insurance Corporation. Much tougher requirements to qualify as a "nonbank" bank, maximum time limits on when deposited funds must be available, and a temporary moratorium on the expansion of most nontraditional banking activities (such as security underwriting) were included in this legislation.

The Financial Institutions Reform, Recovery, and Enforcement Act (FIRREA), which passed in the late summer of 1989, was a comprehensive national legislation affecting banking. FIRREA reformed bank regulation by (1) bringing S&L supervision under the auspices of the Office of Thrift Supervision, a new division of the Comptroller of the Currency; (2) bringing S&L deposit insurance (supposedly in a segregated account) under the control of the FDIC; and (3)

**TABLE 1-9    Principal Provisions of the Federal Deposit Insurance Corporation Improvement Act of 1991**

| Provision | Section | Effective Date |
|---|---|---|
| Improved examinations | Section 111 | December 19, 1992 |
| Independent annual audits | Section 112 | January 1, 1993 |
| Revised accounting principles | Section 121 | December 19, 1992 |
| Small business lending reporting | Section 122 | June 19, 1992 |
| Prompt corrective action | Section 131 | December 19, 1992 |
| Standards for safety and soundness | Section 132 | December 1, 1993 |
| Least-cost resolution | Section 141 | January 1, 1995 |
| Discount window advances | Section 142 | December 19, 1993 |
| Foreign bank supervision | Title II, Subtitle A | December 19, 1993 |
| Study of regulatory burden | Section 221 | December 19, 1992 |
| Amendments to Home Mortgage Disclosure Act | Section 224 | January 1, 1992 |
| Branch closure rules | Section 228 | December 19, 1992 |
| Truth-in-savings | Title II, Subtitle F | September 19, 1992 |
| Limits on brokered deposits | Section 301 | June 19, 1992 |
| Risk-based assessments | Section 302 | January 1, 1994 |
| State bank powers | Section 303 | December 19, 1992 |
| Real estate lending standards | Section 304 | March 19, 1993 |
| Improved capital standards | Section 305 | June 19, 1993 |
| Insider loans | Section 306 | May 18, 1992 |
| Interbank liabilities | Section 308 | December 19, 1992 |
| Pass-through insurance | Section 311 | December 19, 1992 |
| Two-window deposit system | Section 321 | June 19, 1992 |
| Private reinsurance system | Section 322 | June 19, 1993 |
| Purchased mortgage servicing rights | Section 475 | February 19, 1992 |

creating the Resolution Trust Corporation to resolve problems by selling or liquidating financially troubled S&Ls and by liquidating the remaining assets of these associations. Although the long-term effects of this act are unknown, commercial banks have been affected indirectly by fallout, such as higher deposit insurance, higher regulatory costs, public indignation at the high cost of the bailout, and tougher regulatory standards and examinations. Despite its comprehensive nature, FIRREA failed to directly address obvious concerns, such as banking powers, market value accounting, deposit insurance, and interstate banking.

The Federal Deposit Insurance Corporation Improvement Act of 1991 (FDICIA) was enacted on December 19, 1991, as PL 102-242, 105 Stat. 2236. The Bush administration had proposed legislation to reform the financial system that included nationwide branching, expanded powers for banks, and a huge $70 billion loan to shore up the depleted deposit insurance fund. While it got the loan, the primary result was one of the strictest and most sweeping pieces of financial regulation in decades. Table 1-9 lists the provisions in

FDICIA with the effective dates. Seven of these provisions will now be summarized.

Section 131 of FDICIA encourages early and prompt intervention, affecting the timing of failures. Five capital categories were established in the legislation: well capitalized, adequately capitalized, undercapitalized, significantly undercapitalized, and critically undercapitalized. Table 1-10 lists the mandatory supervisory actions applicable to banks in each capital category. (The capital standards for these categories are described in Chapter 8.) FDICIA includes the requirement that an institution must be closed by its primary supervisor if it is critically undercapitalized for a prolonged period. In general, the law defines a critically undercapitalized institution as having tangible capital that is less than 2 percent of total assets. This early intervention requirement became effective on December 19, 1992. Under previous law, an institution was closed only after its capital had been exhausted.

Section 132 of FDICIA requires the appropriate bank regulatory agency to prescribe standards of safety and soundness. These standards include but are not limited to items related to internal control, directors' qualifications, and management compensation. Even a bank's share price will be subject to review by regulators. Many bankers object to the imposition of regulations at the micro level of many of the safety and soundness standards. They claim that government mandates are being imposed as a substitute for private decision making in the business of banking.

Section 141 of FDICIA requires that the resolution transactions chosen for failing banks must be the least costly to the deposit insurance fund of all possible methods of meeting that obligation. Prior law only required that the resolution selected be less costly than a payout of insured deposits and a liquidation of assets.

Title II, Subtitle A, of FDICIA strengthens the authority of the Federal Reserve to supervise foreign banks' entry into and operation in the U.S. banking system. Annual examinations are required for each office of a foreign bank. Offices of foreign banks are subject to individual lending limits similar to those U.S. banks face. Also, any foreign bank operating in the United States that seeks to acquire more than 5 percent of the voting shares of a U.S. bank or bank holding company must obtain prior approval from the Federal Reserve.

Title II, Subtitle F, of FDICIA contains the Truth in Savings Act, which requires depository institutions to provide clear, uniform disclosure of interest rates and fees. The purpose of the Truth in Savings Act is to allow consumers to make more informed comparisons among the various services offered by depository institutions. However, many analysts argue that the requirements imposed on banks and other depository institutions by this section of FDICIA are beyond what is necessary for consumers to make an informed choice.

Section 301 of FDICIA includes a prohibition on the acceptance of brokered deposits by undercapitalized banks.

Section 302 includes a requirement that the FDIC must charge higher deposit insurance premiums to banks that pose greater risks to the insurance fund.

**TABLE 1-10    Mandatory Supervisory Actions Applicable to Institutions in Each Capital Category**

Well Capitalized and Adequately Capitalized

   May not make any capital distribution or pay a management fee to a controlling person that would leave the institution undercapitalized.

Undercapitalized

   Subject to the provisions applicable to well-capitalized and adequately capitalized institutions.

   Subject to increased monitoring.

   Must submit an acceptable capital restoration plan within 45 days and implement that plan.

   Growth of total assets must be restricted.

   Approval from the appropriate banking agency is required prior to acquisitions, branching, and new lines of business.

Significantly Undercapitalized

   Subject to all provisions applicable to undercapitalized institutions.

   Bonuses and raises to senior executive officers must be restricted.

   Subject to discretionary actions such as the following:

      Severe restrictions on asset growth or reduction of total assets may be required.

      May be required to elect a new board of directors.

      Dismissal of any director or senior executive officer and their replacement by new officers, subject to agency approval, may be required.

      May be prohibited from accepting deposits from correspondent institutions.

      Controlling bank holding company may be prohibited from paying dividends without Federal Reserve approval.

Critically Undercapitalized

   Must be placed in receivership within 90 days unless the appropriate agency and the FDIC concur that another action would better achieve the purposes of prompt corrective action.

   Must be placed in receivership if it continues to be critically undercapitalized, unless specific statutory requirements are met.

   After 60 days, must be prohibited from paying principal or interest on subordinated debt without prior approval from the FDIC.

   Activities must be restricted. At a minimum, may not do the following without prior written approval from the FDIC:

      Enter into any material transaction other than in the usual course of business.

      Extend credit for any highly leveraged transaction.

      Make any material change in accounting methods.

      Engage in any "covered transactions," as defined in Section 23A of the Federal Reserve Act, which concerns affiliate transactions.

      Pay excessive compensation or bonuses.

      Pay interest on new or renewed liabilities at a rate that would cause the weighted average cost of funds to exceed significantly the prevailing rate in the institution's market area.

Current trends indicate that some additional legislative or regulatory developments are likely in the near future. One strong possibility is further relaxation of state boundary constraints in providing financial services. These constraints are already partly overcome by the offices opened as a result of the Edge Act, loan production offices, bank holding company subsidiaries, nonbank banks, and eased state banking laws, but using such loophole opportunities is not particularly efficient. Improved electronic technology and the need for domestic rather than international takeovers of weakened depository institutions should provide added incentives for some kind of legislative or regulatory action. It is likely that by the mid-1990s at least regional, and probably nationwide, banking will be legally permitted.

Legislative action in other areas in the near future is difficult to predict. Key areas in which some type of action may be forced on legislative or regulatory bodies include (1) further definitions of the financial services that banks will be allowed to provide (insurance, underwriting of securities, etc.); (2) ground rules for competition between money market funds, brokerage firms, and other nondepository firms with depository institutions; (3) payment of interest on reserves; (4) resolution of the nonbank banks' situation; and (5) further limits on clearing times. Regulators and accountants seem likely to force banks to move toward market values for bank assets, liabilities, and resulting equity (see the Appendix to Chapter 6 for details). It is uncertain at this time whether many of these items will be covered in a comprehensive financial institutions act or whether legislation will follow the market in a piecemeal fashion.

## Trends in the Banking Industry

A complete examination of the future environment for bank financial management decisions must include a review of the current status of the banking industry itself. How much flexibility will the industry have to face the challenging economic and regulatory environment? Will future technology help or hurt the industry? Will competitive pressure be intraindustry or interindustry?

In 1950, as a result of the Depression and World War II, commercial banks held over 60 percent of their total assets in their cash and due from bank accounts or in Treasury securities (see Table 1-11). At the same time, funds were acquired primarily through checking accounts. Non-interest-bearing (demand) deposits made up over 70 percent of the total liabilities and capital in 1950. The low average return of banking assets, caused by the banks' asset mix and low interest rates, meant that banks paid relatively low returns on time and savings deposits and were often not aggressive in trying to obtain funds from such accounts.

The primary emphasis in bank management during the 1950s and early 1960s was on shifting from Treasury securities and cash and due from bank accounts to riskier assets with higher returns. Emphasis on time and savings deposits as sources of funds increased somewhat, but non-interest-bearing (demand) deposits still contributed well over one-half of the total sources of funds for most banks. Furthermore, the total deposits and assets of all commer-

**Table 1-11    Percentage Distribution of Assets and Liabilities of Commercial Banks**

|  | 1950 | 1964 | 1978 | 1992 |
|---|---|---|---|---|
| **Assets** | | | | |
| Cash and due from banks | 24 | 18 | 14 | 11 |
| Treasury and agency securities | 37 | 21 | 8 | 13 |
| Other securities | 7 | 10 | 13 | 16 |
| Loans | 31 | 49 | 60 | 54 |
| Other assets | 1 | 2 | 5 | 6 |
| Total assets | 100 | 100 | 100 | 100 |
| **Liabilities and Capital** | | | | |
| Non-interest-bearing deposits | 70 | 55 | 28 | 14 |
| Interest-bearing deposits | 22 | 34 | 52 | 64 |
| Borrowings | 0 | 1 | 9 | 12 |
| Other liabilities | 1 | 2 | 4 | 3 |
| Capital accounts | 7 | 8 | 7 | 7 |
| Total liabilities and capital | 100 | 100 | 100 | 100 |

SOURCES: Selected *Federal Reserve Bulletins*, *FDIC Annual Reports*, and *Quarterly Banking Profiles*, 1950–1993.

cial banks grew at an annual rate of less than 5 percent from 1950 to 1964. During this period, the combined assets of nonbank depository intermediaries grew at an annual rate of roughly 12 percent. The reasons for this low growth in banks vis-à-vis other financial institutions included (1) slow demand deposit growth as corporate treasurers began to utilize efficient cash management techniques; (2) significantly lower average rates paid on time and savings deposits compared to those paid by many other intermediaries; and (3) generally conservative attitudes toward attracting funds by bank managers.

The prevailing philosophy of bank financial managers appeared to emphasize the profitable lending of attracted funds at the cost of the increased risk of shifting from Treasury securities to loans. The excess liquidity and low portfolio credit risk of banks during the immediate postwar period were substantially reduced. As Table 1-11 illustrates, from 1950 to 1964, cash and due from bank accounts and Treasury securities fell from 61 to 39 percent of bank assets, while loans rose from 31 to 49 percent.

By the mid-1960s, banks were responding to their relatively slow growth during the preceding 15 years by (1) requiring loan customers to keep larger demand deposit balances; (2) paying competitive rates on time and savings accounts within the confines of Regulation Q; and (3) aggressively offering certificates of deposit, savings certificates, and other new liability instruments. Management's emphasis changed from asset selection to the acquisition of funds—that is, to liability management. The more aggressive acquisition of funds was part of a shift in bank strategy away from the high margins and slow growth of the 1950s toward lower margins and more rapid growth in the mid-1960s. This shift was encouraged by the gradual relaxation of Regulation

Q and by allowing banks to use certificates of deposit and other liability forms to compete more effectively for funds. The strong demand for credit from the mid-1960s throughout most of the 1970s allowed banks to employ the substantially larger amounts of funds they were able to attract.

The surge in asset and loan growth was pronounced—the rate of asset growth doubled—averaging nearly 10 percent annually from 1964 to 1978. By comparison, in this same period, the assets of nonbank depository intermediaries grew at an average annual rate of slightly less than 7 percent. It is noteworthy that this rapid growth slowed in the late 1970s because of intensified competition with money market funds, brokerage houses, and other institutions offering banklike financial instruments or services. The liability innovations created to compete with these institutions, such as insured money market accounts, long-term savings certificates, and Super NOW accounts, are proving costly and may lead to complex liability management problems.

The change in the composition and financing of the rapid growth from 1964 to 1978 and the less rapid growth through 1992 has many implications for the future. Non-interest-bearing deposits declined from 55 percent of total liabilities and capital in the mid-1960s to 28 percent in 1978 and 14 percent in 1992. Time and savings deposits increased from 34 percent of total liabilities and capital in 1964, to 52 percent by 1978, to 64 percent in 1992. Borrowing and other liabilities increased from a relatively small source of funds in the 1960s to roughly 15 percent of total liabilities and capital by 1992. On the asset side, cash and due from bank accounts and Treasury securities declined absolutely as well as relatively, while loans continued their rapid growth, increasing from 49 to 60 percent of the total assets from 1964 to 1978. The path from 1978 to 1992 contained two movements. Loans grew from 60 to 64 percent of total assets from 1978 to 1987, then fell rapidly to 54 percent of total assets by 1992. The declining loan demand in the late 1980s and early 1990s led to proportionate increases in Treasury securities and other securities. Nearly all of the other securities were state and local issues until passage of the Tax Reform Act of 1986, which removed most of the tax advantage of state and local securities. Mortgage-backed securities were the fastest growing segment of other securities in the late 1980s and early 1990s.

These broad trends indicate that banks will probably be exposed to substantial risks in the 1990s. Options, such as conversion from low-cost core demand and savings deposits to interest-sensitive deposits and shifts from high-quality securities to higher-earning, higher-risk securities, have already been partially utilized. Therefore, management flexibility is limited in the challenging economic and regulatory environment predicted for the 1990s.

Technological changes in the 1990s promise to complicate further efforts to predict how banks will fare. The pace of technological change for banks in the last few years has been slower than many predicted. On average, the industry is still dominated by a paper-based, brick-and-mortar, customer—bank-employee interaction delivery system. Recent developments, however, indicate that banks are moving away from this system. The technology exists to alter banks' delivery systems rapidly. This technology consists of advances in computer capabilities, which permit easy and inexpensive gathering, storing, analyzing, and retrieving of customer data. Also, advances in communication hardware and software permit convenient access to customer records at great distances. This revolution in delivery system capabilities has significant implications for bank management decisions.

Automatic teller machines (ATMs) have become widely accepted in most areas of the country. By the mid-1990s, the vast majority of bank transactions probably will be by electronic impulse made away from the banks' physical location by means of automated clearinghouses, direct payroll crediting, direct bill paying, widespread use of debit cards, and point-of-sale (POS) terminals. Furthermore, some individuals can now sit at home and pay bills, make deposits, shift among types of deposits, shift from deposits to other financial assets, and so forth, all by electronic impulse. By the late 1990s, such home banking may be commonplace. Commercial banks are finding that to compete effectively on a cost basis, they must use these and other methods to reduce significantly the costs of the most common transactions; that is, it is more cost-effective to keep most customers away from the bank except for unusual transactions.

In the long run, such technology will increase productivity and reduce costs in banking; however, the transition period will be difficult. This difficulty is compounded by the trying economic and regulatory environment predicted. Some banks will be willing and able to take the high costs and risks involved. Those who drag their feet may find themselves rapidly becoming noncompetitive.

The status of banking is also affected by the competitive environment. Competition with other banks will probably intensify for several reasons: (1) the lack of product differentiation for some banking services; (2) the disappearance of Regulation Q, which had prohibited rate competition for some categories of deposits; (3) the continuing decline in geographic constraints restricting banking competition; and (4) the greater use of advanced technology, which may increase the ability of banks to compete with each other.

Competition with other depository institutions is also likely to increase. The prediction by bank management that other depository institutions will be unable to compete because of their inferior asset positions and lack of experience in many banking areas seems overoptimistic. The opposite will probably occur. Some of the remaining or financially aided thrifts will be very competitive in both attracting and employing funds. Even though 70 percent of their assets must be related to residential mortgages, thrifts have acquired permission to become involved in most traditional areas of commercial banking. Thrifts are also able to provide some financial services that are still prohibited for banks. After some failures, restructuring, and tremendous cost to the taxpaying public, the surviving, aggressive thrifts may reappear as even more formidable competition than they were in the past.

Nondepository financial organizations appear likely to use their substantial competitive edge—fewer restrictions, no reserves, no capital requirements, less regulation—to offer more and more banklike financial services. Some of the nondepository organizations providing banklike services are known. For example, much has been written about money market funds and brokerage firms, such as Merrill Lynch, that offer cash management accounts. If Merrill Lynch or G. E. Capital was classified as a bank, it would rank in the top 10 in size among the roughly 13,000 U.S. banks. The combination of financial giants, such as Bache with Prudential and American Express with Shearson, may be indicative of very competitive financial supermarkets in the near future. In addition, other nondepository financial organizations, such as life insurance companies and private pension funds, are looking carefully at segments of banking services they believe would be profitable.

More and more companies whose primary business activities are non-financial appear to be interested in starting to offer financial assets, liabilities, and services that will compete with many banking products and services. For example, Sears has opened financial centers at many of its stores—centers that offer consumer savings certificates, insurance, real estate, and money market mutual funds. J. C. Penney is reportedly offering market rates of inter-est to savers who prepay their charge accounts. More and more nonfinancial companies are likely to provide formidable competition for banks in the coming years.

Finally, changing the public perception is a problem for the banking industry. In the protective legislative and regulatory environment during the three decades following World War II, the power and prestige of bankers remained as secure as their vaults. Now, at the start of the 1990s, bankers appear to have fallen from the ranks of the esteemed. The public, who in the past accorded bankers blind trust, seem to be rebelling against skyrocketing fees, poor-quality loans, poor services, impersonal treatment, and the inability of bank managers to measure and manage risks. The clearest evidence of the public's concern is the thousands of bank customers who have been attracted to nonbank institutions because of the financial products and services they offer.

One of the causes of this change in perception has been the growing number of bank failures and forced mergers. Names of failed banks or those that were involuntarily merged or nationalized, such as Penn Square, SeaFirst, Bank of New England, First National Bank of Midland, First Republic, MCorp, and Continental Illinois Bank, are well known by the public. In addition, the fact that roughly 800 of the nearly 12,000 banks were still on regulators' "prob-lem list" at the end of 1992 (up from under 300 in 1980 and 1981) is well publicized.

## Effect of the Changing Money and Capital Markets

Another development that has affected bank financial management is the con-tinuing change in the money and capital markets. These changes include (1) the globalization of money and capital markets; (2) the evolution of numerous new securities in these markets; and (3) the development of new secondary markets for many financial assets. The last two changes have led to the ability to securitize many financial assets.

The pace of globalization of the money and capital markets seemed to quicken during the very tight monetary situation of the early 1980s. Now many medium-sized and all larger-sized businesses in the United States and other countries can raise funds in financial markets throughout the world. Larger banks can purchase funds and raise capital in nearly all of the financial markets in the world; many bank customers, however, have not attained access to these markets. The ability of larger American corporations to finance themselves in many markets has reduced banks' share in financing such corporations and has reduced the interest spread banks earn on the portion of financing they have retained.

Many new securities have been developed in the last decade or so. Early innovations, such as zero-coupon securities and bonds with put options, have been replaced with increasingly complex issues, such as bonds adjusted for changes in inflation and exchange rates and dutch auction preferred stocks. Banks are affected by the development of new securities in the following ways: (1) banks can issue and have issued such new securities to finance their own needs; (2) banks can acquire these new (and often complex) securities as part of their asset portfolios; and (3) corporate customers of banks have the additional option of using these new securities instead of bank financing.

The development of new secondary markets for many financial assets has had a profound effect on bank funding and financial management. Banks can now sell financial assets they have originated, such as mortgages, installment loans, and credit card loans. If sold without recourse, these assets are no longer on the selling bank's balance sheet and currently are not included in capital adequacy calculations. In addition, some embryonic market in nonperforming loans and loans to less developed countries may offer greater flexibility in managing problem loans.

Securitization of financial assets—that is, the issuance of a security instrument backed by financial assets—is an outgrowth of the development of new securities and new secondary markets. The previous holder of the financial assets receives the proceeds from the sale of the securities less any commissions, credit enhancement fees, and so forth. Some banks have already securitized mortgages, installment loans, and credit card loans they held as assets. Nonperforming loans and loans to less developed countries are proposed for securitization. If securitization is without recourse, the securitized assets are no longer on the bank's balance sheet and currently are not included in capital adequacy calculations.

## An Approach to Bank Management in This Challenging Environment

Where does the combination of a difficult economic environment, a changing regulatory environment, increasingly sharp competition, a virtual technological revolution, concerns about recent trends in banking, and continuing changes in the money and capital markets leave the banking industry? The environment for bank management decisions will clearly be a challenging one in the coming years. Some banks and other depository institutions will fail. There will be numerous acquisitions and mergers in the banking and depository industries. The number of banks will probably decline by 30 to 40 percent over the next decade, and the decline in other depository institutions may be even greater. Well-managed banks can and will be very successful during such times. The purpose of this book is to present the concepts and techniques that will help bank managers be successful in this challenging period.

This book is divided into four parts. In the first part (Chapters 1 through 4) we deal with basic materials on measuring bank performance. Chapter 1 contains an introduction to the changing nature of bank management. Chapter 2 covers the basic items on a bank's balance sheet and income statement. Topics such as loan loss accounting, sources and uses of funding, repricing schedules, off–balance sheet items, risks banks take, and risk–return trade-offs are discussed in Chapter 3. Chapter 4 includes an evaluation of the finance performance of an actual bank and enhances the risk and return measures discussed in the preceding chapters. Uniform bank performance reports are also presented and evaluated.

Part Two (Chapters 5 to 9) covers many of the key elements of bank asset, liability, and capital management. Chapter 5 discusses how reserve requirements are calculated, how many corporate cash management principles apply to banks, and how to evaluate correspondent relationships, as well as how a bank measures and fills its liquidity needs. Chapter 6 covers such topics as how a bank should inventory its investment needs, formulate investment policies, and develop investment strategies.

Chapter 7 discusses such topics as how a bank should inventory its funding needs, risks associated with funding decisions, contingency funding, and strategies for attracting funds. It also includes an extensive section on measuring and using the cost of funds. Chapter 8 covers the purposes of bank capital, methods of appraising capital adequacy, steps in financial planning, determination of total capital needs, and the new risk-based capital requirements. Chapter 9 includes an evaluation of the use of capital notes, debentures, preferred stock, and common stock; a discussion of new forms of capital, such as perpetual debt, floating-rate preferred, and dutch auction preferred; and an introduction to management techniques such as allocating capital to lines of business and dividend policy.

Part Three (Chapters 10 through 14) discusses the lending function of commercial banks in considerable detail. How a bank should organize to compete successfully in lending and lending policy are discussed in Chapter 10. Credit analysis is emphasized in Chapter 11. In Chapter 12 the primary types of bank commercial loans are described. This chapter presents details on credit analysis, loan pricing, and so on, for these types of loans. Consumer lending is covered in Chapter 13, and Chapter 14 discusses selected specialized areas of bank lending.

Part Four (Chapters 15 to 20) covers integrative bank management decisions and new products and techniques. Chapter 15 covers the need for interest-sensitivity analysis, the strengths and weaknesses of gap analysis, methods for correcting some of the gapping, and simulation techniques. Duration analysis and strategies for hedging interest-rate risk are covered in Chapter 16.

Chapter 17 examines new investment and funding alternatives, such as mortgage-backed securities, collateralized mortgage obligations, floating rate notes, Euro Securities, zero coupon securities, and deposits tied to stock indices. It also introduces new methods for pricing off–balance sheet items and contingency claim products. The processes for acquiring new or failing banks are emphasized in Chapter 18. Chapter 19 discusses the increasing importance of global banking for banks and for the world economy, and covers international banking activities in foreign exchange, interbank deposits, swaps, and other markets.

The book concludes with Chapter 20, which covers techniques for tying together asset and liability management. Included in this chapter are a method for determining risk–return trade-offs, a system for bank long-range planning, and a discussion of potential successful strategies a bank might apply in these challenging times.

The 27 selected cases and the bank microcomputer simulation that appear in the book illustrate most of the key ideas and techniques.

Just reading about the concepts and techniques espoused in this book is not enough. Bank managers and students of banking should reinforce their learning by applying the concepts and techniques to the case situations and simulations covered in these chapters. This will not only reinforce the learning process but will indicate the applicability of the concepts and techniques to real-life situations as well.

## Discussion Questions

1. Define surplus unit, deficit unit, and financial intermediary. What are the primary functions of financial intermediaries?
2. Describe what surplus units, deficit units, bank owners, and bank regulators desire from bank management. Are these desires complementary or in conflict?
3. Name the two principal chartering bodies for U.S. commercial banks. If a bank wanted to form a holding company, what regulatory body would it apply to?
4. Describe the principal services performed by correspondent banks in the United States. Will correspondent banking grow or decline in coming years?
5. Discuss the current impact of the following legislation:
   a. National Banking Act
   b. Federal Reserve Act
   c. Glass-Steagall Act
   d. Depository Institutions Act of 1982
   e. Financial Institutions Reform, Recovery, and Enforcement Act
   f. Federal Deposit Insurance Corporation Improvement Act

6. Discuss the principal immediate and long-run effects of the Federal Deposit Insurance Corporation Improvement Act of 1991.
7. List the principal provisions of any major banking legislation that has passed since 1993.
8. Describe the principal trends in the primary categories of bank assets and liabilities from 1950 to 1992.
9. Discuss the competition that banks face from nondepository financial organizations at the present time. Do you believe this type of competition will intensify in future years?
10. Has the number of newly chartered banks been greater than the number of banks that have been closed? Why?

# CHAPTER 2

# Understanding a Bank's Financial Statements

This chapter introduces and briefly explains the primary data used in evaluating a bank. To facilitate this effort, the balance sheet and income statement of an example bank—Community National Bank—are detailed, and supplementary financial information and qualitative factors that may affect a bank's performance are discussed. Additionally, financial reporting areas that can often be confusing, such as loan loss accounting, repricing schedules, and off–balance sheet items, are described and clarified. Finally, sources of banking information are listed. Readers who are familiar with this introductory material may want to proceed to Chapter 3.

## UNDERSTANDING A BANK'S BALANCE SHEET

Balance sheets for Community National Bank for 1990, 1991, and 1992 appear in Table 2-1 and reflect average daily balances rather than end-of-the-year figures. End-of-the-year figures are useful in a few situations; average balances, however, should usually be used for measuring a bank's performance because distortions may occur if balances on only one day are considered.

In broad terms, Community National Bank's assets represent the uses of funds it has been able to attract. The bank's liabilities and net worth record the specific sources of funds. Liabilities are nonowner claims on the bank's assets. The net worth is the value of the bank's assets minus the value of its liabilities. Since most bank assets and liabilities are valued at cost or adjusted (toward their maturity value) cost rather than by their market values, many analysts worry about the usefulness of the resulting net worth.

## TABLE 2-1  Community National Bank Average Balance Sheets (dollars in thousands)

| | 1990 $ | 1990 % | 1991 $ | 1991 % | 1992 $ | 1992 % |
|---|---|---|---|---|---|---|
| **Assets** | | | | | | |
| Cash and due from banks | $ 10,217 | 8.8% | $11,698 | 8.9% | $ 13,205 | 9.0% |
| Short-term instruments | | | | | | |
|   Fed funds sold | 2,723 | 2.3% | 2,200 | 1.7% | 1,504 | 1.0% |
|   Other short-term investments | -0- | -0- | -0- | -0- | -0- | -0- |
| Investment securities | | | | | | |
|   Taxable securities | 16,697 | 14.4% | 18,625 | 13.8% | 26,925 | 18.4% |
|   Tax-exempt securities | 17,012 | 14.7% | 16,330 | 12.3% | 15,176 | 10.4% |
| Trading account securities | -0- | -0- | -0- | -0- | -0- | -0- |
| Loans | | | | | | |
|   Commercial loans | 29,659 | 25.6% | 31,561 | 23.7% | 32,817 | 22.4% |
|   Consumer loans | 19,679 | 17.0% | 26,938 | 20.2% | 28,141 | 19.3% |
|   Real estate loans | 16,054 | 13.9% | 20,869 | 15.7% | 22,154 | 15.2% |
|   Other loans | 123 | .1% | 262 | .2% | 341 | .2% |
|   Total loans | $ 65,515 | 56.5% | $ 79,630 | 59.8% | $ 83,453 | 57.1% |
|   Less: Reserve for loan loss | 480 | .4% | 686 | .5% | 777 | .5% |
| Net loans | $ 65,035 | 56.1% | $ 78,944 | 59.3% | $ 82,676 | 56.6% |
| Direct lease financing | -0- | -0- | -0- | -0- | -0- | -0- |
| Bank premises and equipment | 3,260 | 2.8% | 3,503 | 2.6% | 3,781 | 2.6% |
| Other real estate owned | -0- | -0- | 240 | .2% | 240 | .2% |
| Other assets | 1,006 | .9% | 1,615 | 1.2% | 2,651 | 1.8% |
|   Total assets | $115,950 | 100.0% | $133,155 | 100.0% | $146,158 | 100.0% |
| **Liabilities and Net Worth** | | | | | | |
| Demand deposits | $ 18,986 | 16.4% | $ 19,125 | 14.4% | $ 21,632 | 14.8% |
| NOW and Super NOW | 15,689 | 13.5% | 16,983 | 12.7% | 19,107 | 13.1% |
|   Total demand deposits | $ 34,675 | 29.9% | $ 36,108 | 27.1% | $ 40,739 | 27.9% |
| Passbook savings | 9,162 | 7.9% | 7,185 | 5.4% | 6,843 | 4.7% |
| Money market accounts | 10,725 | 9.2% | 16,710 | 12.5% | 20,012 | 13.7% |
| Savings certificates | 18,401 | 15.9% | 20,425 | 15.3% | 19,338 | 13.2% |
| CDs, $100,000 and over | 20,159 | 17.4% | 27,165 | 20.4% | 32,078 | 21.9% |
| Public and other time deposits | 10,163 | 8.8% | 10,403 | 7.8% | 11,664 | 8.7% |
|   Total savings and time | $ 68,610 | 59.2% | $ 81,888 | 61.4% | $ 89,935 | 61.5% |
|   Total deposits | $103,285 | 89.1% | $117,996 | 88.5% | $130,674 | 89.4% |
| Short-term borrowing | | | | | | |
|   Fed funds purchased | 1,715 | 1.5% | 2,463 | 2.0% | 2,175 | 1.5% |
|   Other short-term borrowing | 1,405 | 1.2% | 1,654 | 1.2% | 1,384 | .9% |
| Other liabilities | 790 | .7% | 950 | .7% | 1,091 | .7% |
| Long-term debt | -0- | -0- | -0- | -0- | -0- | -0- |
| Shareholders' equity | | | | | | |
|   Common stock (par $1) | $ 963 | .8% | $ 1,013 | .8% | $ 1,103 | .7% |
|   Surplus | 1,348 | 1.2% | 1,798 | 1.3% | 1,795 | 1.2% |
|   Undivided profits | 6,444 | 5.6% | 7,281 | 5.5% | 8,023 | 5.5% |
|   Equity reserves | -0- | -0- | -0- | -0- | -0- | -0- |
|   Total equity | $ 8,755 | 7.6% | $ 10,092 | 7.6% | $ 10,834 | 7.4% |
| Total liabilities and net worth | $115,950 | 100.0% | $133,155 | 100.0% | $146,158 | 100.0% |

The following paragraphs provide a brief description of the principal bank asset accounts.

*Cash and due from banks* generally includes four categories of cash assets:

1. Currency and coin held in the bank's vault.
2. Deposits with the Federal Reserve Bank, which are used to meet legal reserve requirements and may also serve as a balancing account for checking clearance, transactions in Treasury securities, wire transfers, and so on.
3. Deposits with correspondent banks, which Fed nonmember banks can use to help meet legal requirements and all banks can use to compensate their correspondents for services performed.
4. Cash items in the process of collection, that is, items deposited in the Federal Reserve or correspondent banks for which credit has not been received. Since a bank does not earn interest on any of these four categories of cash assets, they are labeled nonearning assets and banks generally exert considerable effort to minimize their cash assets.

*Short-term instruments* include interest-bearing short-term assets such as Fed funds sold (excess reserves that one bank lends to another), securities purchased under agreement to resell, and other bank certificates of deposit. Such short-term instruments have obvious appeal to banks with extra funds for a short period; however, some banks use these short-term assets continuously as a way of employing attracted funds.

*Investment securities* are interest-bearing debt securities that a bank owns. These securities may be of any maturity and are valued at market value (for securities held for possible sale) or at what the bank paid for them plus or minus an amortized adjustment toward the maturity value of the principal. The income on taxable securities is subject to federal income tax. The largest amount of taxable securities held by most banks is securities of the U.S. government—Treasury bills, notes, and bonds. Many banks do have sizable holdings of securities of U.S. government agencies, such as the Federal Home Loan Bank. Some banks also hold either corporate debt or debts of foreign governments or businesses. Tax-exempt securities held by banks are general obligation or revenue bonds issued by states or their political subdivisions. The interest on such bonds may be partially exempt from federal income taxes; however, the 1986 Tax Reform Act eliminated most of the tax exemption on most state and local issues purchased after August 1986. Realized appreciation or depreciation on these bonds' principal value, however, is subject to such taxes. Banks are not permitted to buy corporate stocks.

*Trading account securities* are any of the preceding debt securities (usually Treasury securities), which are held primarily for resale within relatively short periods. These securities must be valued at market rather than at book value, and appreciation or depreciation in value must be reported as an ordinary gain or loss on the income statement.

*Loans* are the primary earning assets of most banks in the United States. The bank lends funds to a customer and in return gets a promissory note from the customer promising to pay interest, at either a fixed or a variable rate, and to repay the principal balance of the loan. Loans are usually categorized by type of user and by use of the funds. The following are the three major categories for most banks:

1. Commercial loans, which are short- or intermediate-term loans to businesses typically for seasonal buildup of accounts receivable or inventory or for permanent working capital or plant and equipment.
2. Consumer loans, which include automobile loans, other consumer durable loans, home improvement loans, credit card loans, and other installment and single-payment loans to finance personal expenditures.
3. Real estate loans, which include temporary construction financing as well as long-term loans to finance residences, office buildings, retail outlets, and factories. Most long-term loans made prior to the early 1980s were amortizing and fixed-rate; however, some recent real estate loans have been variable-rate or renegotiable on rate every few years.

Other types of loans include agricultural loans, loans to banks and other financial institutions, loans to brokers and dealers, and any other loans that do not fit into the preceding loan categories.

*The reserve for loan losses* represents the balance in the valuation portion of a bank's bad debt reserve. A bank builds up this reserve to absorb future loan losses. Contributions to the reserve are made according to strict Internal Revenue Service tax rules. This reserve is increased by tax-deductible charges to income and decreased by charged-off loan losses. The valuation reserve is subtracted from total loans to arrive at a bank's net loans.

*Net loans* are total loans less any unearned income and the reserve for loan losses. Since 1976, only net loans have been reported as bank assets.

*Direct lease financing* consists of the outstanding balances on all types of leases on property acquired by a bank for the purpose of lease financing.

*Bank premises and equipment* includes all the bank's premises, facilities, equipment, furniture, fixtures, and leasehold improvements. These items are on the books at their depreciated book value and are classified as nonearning assets because they usually do not directly create an income stream.

*Other real estate owned* refers to all real estate actually owned by the bank, excluding bank premises and equipment. A major item included under this category is real estate acquired through foreclosure.

*Other assets* is a catchall category of other assets not large enough to warrant a separate account, such as customer liability to the bank on acceptances, prepaid expenses, and balances with savings and loan associations. If the items become significant, they will appear as a separate balance sheet item.

The liabilities and net worth side of a bank's balance sheet separates all the bank's sources of funds into appropriate categories. The categories can be based on the form of the organization supplying the funds, such as individual, partnership, and corporate deposits versus public deposits, or on the form of the contract, such as passbook savings versus money market deposits. The following paragraphs emphasize the form of the contract, but they include some of the principal forms of the organization using each contract.

*Demand deposits* are non-interest-bearing checking accounts of individuals, partnerships, corporations, and governmental units. The majority of these accounts generally come from businesses (partnerships or corporations) because (1) businesses are usually forced to leave compensating demand deposit balances with the bank in order to get loans, (2) individuals are usually eligible for interest-bearing checking accounts, and (3) governmental units keep most of their deposits in interest-bearing accounts.

*NOW and Super NOW accounts* are checking accounts of individuals and partnerships that receive interest as long as they meet the specifications set by the bank. The proper legal title for these accounts is Negotiable Order of Withdrawal accounts, and prior to March 31, 1986, they were subject to Regulation Q limits set by the Depository Institutions Deregulation Committee.

*Passbook (or statement) savings* are savings deposits that have no specified maturity. These deposits were subject to Regulation Q rate maximums set by the Depository Institutions Deregulation Committee until March 31, 1986. They do not have contractual provisions requiring the depositor to give written notice of an intention to withdraw funds. Businesses are usually not permitted to hold this type of deposit.

*Money market accounts* are savings deposits of individuals and partnerships. This type of deposit was created in December 1982 to provide banks with an instrument that could compete effectively with money market mutual funds. There are no rate maximums, and regulatory limits on minimum size and maximum free withdrawals were removed on December 31, 1985. Most banks pay rates that vary according to an average rate on a short-term money market instrument and will probably continue to use minimum sizes and maximum free withdrawals to market this account.

*Savings certificates* are time deposits evidenced by nonnegotiable instruments that specify the interest rate and the maturity date, which must be seven days or longer. These certificates are no longer subject to Regulation Q rate ceilings, and there are usually interest penalties if the deposits are withdrawn prior to maturity. These certificates can be held by businesses, and some have floating rates—often tied to those of similar-maturity Treasury securities.

*Certificates of deposit (CD's) $100,000 and over* are larger than savings certificates and often negotiable, with maturities of 14 days or greater. They are not subject to rate ceilings, and they can be either fixed or variable obligations. The negotiable CDs are denominated in amounts ranging from $100,000 to $100 million, with $1 million being the standard trading unit and six months to one year the most popular maturity range. Principal purchasers are treasurers of large businesses; however, state and local governments and wealthy individuals also have purchased significant amounts.

*Public and other time deposits* is a catchall category of time and savings deposit accounts. The primary category of public deposits is usually time deposits of state and local governments. In many states, securities must be pledged as collateral for such deposits. Other time deposits include time deposits of commercial banks, other financial intermediaries, and foreign governments and financial institutions.

*Short-term borrowing* of a commercial bank may consist of Federal funds purchased and other forms of short-term borrowing. Federal funds purchased are excess reserves of one bank that are purchased by another bank or possibly another institution. These purchases are often made on a daily basis but generally cannot be easily renewed. For the banking system, Federal funds purchased are roughly equal to Federal funds sold, and the rate on Federal funds is determined by the amount of excess reserves available versus the demand for this form of funding. Securities sold under an agreement to repurchase are a form of short-term borrowing that represent a bank's obligation to buy back securities it has temporarily sold. Because the purchaser owns the securities during this period, these "repos" constitute, in effect, secured borrowing. Other short-term borrowing forms include discount borrowings from the Federal Reserve, Eurodollars, and commercial paper (issued by bank holding companies).

*Other liabilities* is a catchall category for remaining liabilities. Items usually found in this category include accrued taxes and expenses, dividends payable, liabilities on acceptances, trade payables, and other miscellaneous liabilities.

*Long-term debt* includes bank capital notes and debentures with maturities exceeding one year. These notes or debentures are not insured and may be either straight (nonconvertible) or convertible into the bank's common stock. Long-term debt is a source of funds and may also be treated as part of capital by some regulatory bodies (the Comptroller and the Federal Reserve at the present time) if the debt meets certain requirements. The requirements usually include subordination to deposits and other liabilities, minimum average maturity when issued (usually 8 to 10 years), and minimum remaining maturity (usually 2 years).

*Stockholder's equity* represents the difference between the book value of a bank's assets and its liabilities. It includes up to five possible items— preferred stock, common stock, surplus, undivided profits, and equity reserves. Preferred stock pays a fixed or variable dividend that is not a tax-deductible expense; therefore, banks do not often use preferred stock. The common stock account is the total par or stated value of all the bank's outstanding shares. The surplus account can be increased by the sale of common stock at a premium above its par value and by transfers from the undivided profits account. The undivided profits account is similar to the retained earnings account for most nonfinancial businesses. After-tax net income increases undivided profits, and cash or stock dividends and capital transfers reduce undivided profits. Equity reserves include contingency reserves (the emphasis generally on reserves that are not a tax-deductible expense), such as reserves for security gains or losses and the contingency portion of provisions for possible loan losses. The book value of a bank's common stock is the summation of the common stock, surplus, undivided profits, and equity reserve accounts.

**TABLE 2-2   Community National Bank Income Statements for Specified Years Ended December 31 (dollars in thousands)**

|  | 1990 | 1991 | 1992 |
|---|---|---|---|
| **Interest Income:** | | | |
| Short-term instruments | $ 279 | $ 159 | $ 153 |
| Taxable securities | 1,792 | 1,850 | 1,920 |
| Tax-exempt securities | 1,098 | 1,068 | 1,025 |
| Commercial loans | 4,109 | 3,665 | 3,533 |
| Consumer loans | 2,898 | 3,229 | 3,408 |
| Real estate loans | 1,936 | 2,923 | 2,224 |
| Other loans | 16 | 29 | 32 |
| Total interest income | $12,128 | $12,023 | $12,295 |
| **Noninterest Income:** | | | |
| Service charges and fees | 657 | 947 | 1,061 |
| Other noninterest income | 309 | 349 | 486 |
| Total operating income | $13,094 | $13,519 | $13,842 |
| **Interest Expense:** | | | |
| NOW and Super NOW accounts | $ 535 | $ 547 | $ 593 |
| Passbook savings | 482 | 345 | 296 |
| Money market accounts | 885 | 1,321 | 1,155 |
| Savings certificates | 1,626 | 1,637 | 1,494 |
| CD's $100,000 and over | 2,434 | 2,266 | 2,603 |
| Other time deposits | 1,091 | 865 | 939 |
| Short-term borrowing | 346 | 409 | 198 |
| Other liabilities | 62 | 89 | 85 |
| Long-term debt | 0 | 0 | 0 |
| Total interest expense | $ 7,461 | $ 7,479 | $ 7,363 |
| **Noninterest Expense:** | | | |
| Provision for loan losses | $ 297 | $ 403 | $ 517 |
| Salaries and benefits | 2,505 | 2,721 | 3,002 |
| Occupancy expense | 806 | 883 | 969 |
| Other expenses | 571 | 628 | 687 |
| Total expense | $11,640 | $12,114 | $12,538 |
| Net income before taxes | $ 1,454 | $ 1,205 | $ 1,304 |
| Income taxes | 139 | 38 | 102 |
| Net income | $ 1,315 | $ 1,167 | $ 1,202 |
| Cash dividends paid | $ 481 | $ 506 | $ 507 |

# UNDERSTANDING A BANK'S INCOME STATEMENT

Table 2-2 contains the 1990, 1991, and 1992 income statements for Community National Bank. Interest income on a bank's earning assets is the primary source of bank income, whereas the interest expense required to obtain the funds employed by the bank is usually the bank's primary cost category. Other income items, such as service charges, fees, and net trust income, are important sources of revenues for most banks. Other expenses, most notably the costs associated with the bank's employees and its premises and equipment, are usually significant expenditures for a bank.

A description of the income statement items listed in Table 2-2 follows.

*Interest income* on short-term instruments, taxable securities, tax-exempt securities, commercial loans, real estate loans, and other loans is the interest the bank receives on each of these specific asset categories. All interest income, less associated expenses, is taxable, with the exception of some of the interest income on tax-exempt securities. A method of calculating the tax-equivalent interest income on such securities is discussed in the following section.

*Service charges and fees* include income from maintenance fees and various activity fees that most banks charge on their demand deposit accounts under a certain size. Businesses usually receive a credit against these charges based on their average balances, whereas fees on individual deposits are often waived if a minimum balance requirement is met. Fees for originating loans or guaranteed lines of credit are often included in this category.

*Other noninterest income* includes the net income from the bank's trust department (if it has one), commissions on insurance premiums, income from direct lease financing, trading account income, safe deposit rental fees, and miscellaneous noninterest income sources.

*Interest expense* on NOW and Super NOW accounts, passbook savings, savings certificates, money market accounts, CDs of $100,000 and over, other time deposits, short-term borrowing, other liabilities, and long-term debt includes the interest expense on each of these specific deposit or liability categories. Every category of interest expense is a deductible expense for determining a bank's income taxes.

*Provision for loan losses* is the amount charged against earnings to establish a reserve sufficient to absorb expected loan losses. Internal Revenue Service rules set the maximum amount that can be a tax-deductible expense and that can be included in the valuation reserve account on the balance sheet. Management, based on its knowledge of the quality of the loan portfolio and the opinions of the regulatory authorities, may charge more or less than the maximum tax-deductible amount if it believes this amount is more appropriate for possible loan losses.

*Salaries and benefits* represent the total compensation paid to all officers and employees of the bank. This compensation includes not only salaries and wages but also unemployment and social security taxes paid, contributions to retirement or pension plans, cost of medical or health services, and other fringe benefits provided officers and employees.

*Occupancy expense* consists of depreciation on premises and equipment, the rental or leasing cost of offices or machines, and taxes on premises and equipment.

*Other expenses* is a general category for a bank's remaining operating expenses. This account usually includes such expenses as advertising, premiums on deposit insurance and fidelity insurance, directors' fees, supplies and postage, and costs associated with temporary employees. This category now includes security gains or losses from the sale, exchange, redemption, or retirement of investment securities above or below the value at which these securities are carried on the bank's books.

*Net income before taxes* is the difference between total operating income and total expenses. Although banks pay the existing corporate income tax rates, net operating income is usually adjusted to determine taxable income. The primary adjustment is usually to subtract the interest on tax-exempt securities from net operating income before taxes; however, other adjustments may be needed if the bank uses other tax avoidance techniques.

*Net income* is income before taxes less the estimated federal, state, and local income taxes payable for that year. Some bank regulators and analysts favor using net operating income after taxes as the primary dollar measure of a bank's income. This is computed by eliminating nonoperating events, such as significant gains or losses on the sale of securities or extraordinary items.

## SUPPLEMENTARY INFORMATION

Items from a bank's balance sheet and income statement are generally accompanied by other information that is useful in evaluating bank performance. Table 2-3 is an example of useful supplementary data that are usually available in a bank's annual report or its 10-K report. Following is a brief description of the supplementary items:

*Earning assets* refers to all assets earning an explicit interest return. Cash and due from banks and bank premises and equipment are the two major asset categories that are not earning assets.

*Risk assets* are earning assets subject to either credit risk or interest rate risk. Some banks still calculate risk assets as earning assets less all government securities; however, Community National Bank uses a more appropriate designation of earning assets less all short-term instruments and investment securities maturing within one year.

*Maturity of investment securities* classifies the book value of a bank's investment securities into selected maturity categories. This information is helpful in understanding the interest sensitivity of the securities portfolio and the potential appreciation or depreciation of this portfolio if interest rates change.

*Market to book value of securities* shows the percentage of book value of

**TABLE 2-3   Community National Bank Supplementary Information (dollars in thousands)**

|                                                          | 1990      | 1991      | 1992      |
|----------------------------------------------------------|-----------|-----------|-----------|
| Earning assets                                           | $101,467  | $115,899  | $126,281  |
| Risk assets                                              | $ 92,700  | $108,241  | $119,046  |
| Maturities of investment securities:                     |           |           |           |
|   Under one year                               | $  6,044  | $  5,458  | $  5,731  |
|   One to five years                            | 11,421    | 14,218    | 15,372    |
|   Five to ten years                            | 9,653     | 9,824     | 15,808    |
|   Over ten years                               | 6,591     | 5,255     | 5,190     |
| Market to book value of securities:                      |           |           |           |
|   Taxable securities                           | 96.81%    | 98.17%    | 108.91%   |
|   Tax-exempt securities                        | 90.04%    | 96.01%    | 103.18%   |
| Loan losses less recoveries                              | $    287  | $    320  | $    424  |
| Past-due loans:                                          |           |           |           |
|   Commercial                                   | $    552  | $    681  | $    845  |
|   Consumer                                     | 964       | 1,433     | 1,688     |
|   Real estate                                  | 251       | 388       | 436       |
|   Other                                        | 1         | 3         | 3         |
| Interest rate sensitivity (one year):                    |           |           |           |
|   Interest-sensitive assets                    | $ 50,664  | $ 59,766  | $ 70,352  |
|   Interest-sensitive liabilities               | 46,741    | 66,182    | 81,749    |
| Number of employees                                      | 126       | 132       | 136       |
| Average market price per share (est.)                    | 13        | 12        | 10        |
| Tax-equivalent interest income on tax-exempt securities  | 1,633     | 1,577     | 1,498     |
| Total tax-equivalent interest income                     | 12,663    | 12,532    | 12,768    |
| Total tax-equivalent revenues                            | 13,629    | 13,828    | 14,315    |

a bank's securities that is represented by the market value of those securities. The difference between the market value (calculated by multiplying the book value by the market-to-book-value percentage) and the book value of securities represents the unrealized appreciation or depreciation in the securities portfolio.

*Loan losses less recoveries* represent the actual loan losses the bank has recognized during the year less any recoveries of previous loan losses.

*Past-due loans* are loans on which interest or principal payments or both have not been paid at the contracted time. Usually a bank allows a short grace period (e.g., 30 or 60 days) before it classifies a loan as past due. Past-due loans differ from classified loans, provisions for possible loan losses, and loan losses, although all these categories give some idea of the credit quality of a bank's loan portfolio. Many banks also report nonperforming loans or renegotiated loans.

*Interest rate sensitivity* refers to a comparison of the sensitivity of cash flows on assets and liabilities to changes in interest rates. Interest-sensitive assets (liabilities) are any category of assets (liabilities) on which interest income (expense) will change in the specified time period in response to interest rate changes. The time period of such sensitivity should be identified. Many banks measure rate sensitivity for several time periods (e.g., 30 days, 90 days, six months, and one year) because of sizable time differences in sensitivity between assets and liabilities. A dollar gap (difference between sensitive assets and sensitive liabilities), as well as the ratio of sensitive assets to sensitive liabilities, is often calculated.

*The number of employees* should be the number of full-time officers and employees plus the full-time equivalent of a bank's part-time employees. Temporary employees generally are not included.

*Average market price per share* is available for larger banks whose shares are actively traded. Problems may arise if a bank is the nondominant member of a bank holding company or if the bank is small and does not have an active market for its shares.

*Tax-equivalent interest income on tax-exempt securities* is a hypothetical figure that makes the income on tax-exempt securities comparable with the taxable income on most other bank earning assets. The formula for determining the tax-equivalent income on tax-exempt securities is the Tax Equity and Fiscal Responsibility Act (TEFRA) adjusted tax-exempt interest income divided by 1 minus the bank's marginal tax rate. There was no TEFRA adjustment before 1983. In 1983 and 1984 tax-exempt income was adjusted downward by 15 percent times the estimated cost of funds. From the start of 1985 to August 1986, tax-exempt income was adjusted downward by 20 percent times the cost of funds, and in August 1986, tax-exempt income was adjusted downward by 100 percent times the estimated cost of funds for larger municipal issues.

*Total tax-equivalent interest income* is the total interest income (from the income statement) less the interest income on tax-exempt securities (also from the income statement) plus the tax-equivalent interest income on tax-exempt securities. The current corporate federal income tax rate is 35 percent, and many securities are exempt from state or local income taxes. Tax-exempt interest income is declining for most banks due to TEFRA and the Tax Reform Act of 1986.

*Total tax-equivalent revenues* is total tax-equivalent interest income plus all noninterest income and minus all noninterest expenses.

## AN INTRODUCTION TO LOAN LOSS ACCOUNTING

While a thorough analysis of loan loss accounting is a legal and accounting nightmare, the basics can be clarified by a simple example. The reconciliation of the loan loss reserve accounts for Community National Bank in 1992 appears in Table 2-4. The reserves for loan loss balances are year-end balance sheet figures rather than the average balances found in Table 2-1. The provision for loan losses figure can be found in the income statement in Table 2-2. The figure for actual loan losses less recoveries is part of the supplementary information in Table 2-3.

Community National Bank had a Reserve for Loan Losses of $731,300 as

**TABLE 2-4   Community National Bank Reconciliation of Reserve for Loan Loss Accounts, 1992**

| | |
|---|---:|
| Reserve for loan losses, Dec. 31, 1991 | $   731,300 |
| Loan losses during 1992 less any recoveries from previous loan losses | − 423,820 |
| Provisions for loan loss, 1992 | + 517,220 |
| Reserve for loan losses, Dec. 31, 1992 | $824,700 |

of December 31, 1991. During the year this reserve would be decreased by the actual loan losses Community National charged off and increased by any recoveries of loans previously charged off. Toward the end of the accounting period (here we assume it is an annual period, but for most banks it is quarterly), Community National makes an additional provision for loan losses to bring the period-ending reserve to the desired level. This provision is an expense item on the income statement and is usually deductible as an expense establishing taxable income.[1]

The desired level of the ending reserve for loan losses should be based primarily on management's knowledge of the current loan portfolio. Specifically, management must continually review problem loans and overall portfolio quality, current and expected economic and financial conditions, loss experience relative to outstanding loans, and examinations by internal and outside auditors and the regulatory authorities to determine the adequacy of this reserve.

## OFF–BALANCE SHEET INFORMATION

During the 1980s, banks developed new means of doing business that did not appear on their balance sheets as assets and liabilities. Later we will see that these off–balance sheet items may have a significant impact on bank returns and risk. At this point, some of the more common off–balance sheet activities are introduced and possible sources of information are disclosed.

There are two broad categories of off–balance sheet information. The first consists of activities that generate income and/or expenses without the creation or holding of an underlying asset or liability. A simple example would

[1]The relative simplicity of loan loss reserve accounting often breaks down because of varying tax and regulatory rules (differences may be caused by regulatory jurisdiction and even size of bank—the Tax Reform Act of 1986 made different rules for very large banks). The reserve for loan losses can have up to three parts: (1) a valuation portion that results from tax-deductible provisions for loan losses, (2) a contingency portion that is a nondeductible transfer and is shown as a contra asset or an offset to equity capital as a "reserve for contingencies and other capital reserves," and (3) a deferred tax portion that represents the tax effect on the difference between the deduction allowed for income tax purposes and that claimed for financial reporting purposes and that is included under "other liabilities." Fortunately, all of Community National Bank's reserve is contained in the valuation portion.

---

**TABLE 2-5    Primary Types of Off–Balance Sheet Commitments and Contingent Claims**

---

1. Financial guarantees
   a. Standby letter of credit
   b. Lines of credit
   c. Revolving loan commitments
   d. Note issuance facilities
   e. Securitization with recourse
2. Trade finance
   a. Commercial letters of credit
   b. Acceptance participations
3. Investment activities
   a. Forward commitments
   b. Financial futures
   c. Interest rate swaps
   d. Options
   e. Currency swaps

---

be cases in which the bank acted as a broker (taking a fee for arranging for funds to be provided to borrowers without making loans or raising deposits) rather than as a dealer (making and holding loans and the funding source). Other banking services, such as cash management, that generate fee income without requiring assets or liabilities also fit in the category.

The second category of off–balance sheet activities involves the bank's commitments and contingent claims. A commitment means that the bank commits to some future action and receives a fee for making such a commitment. A contingent claim is an obligation by a bank to take action (e.g., to lend funds or buy securities) if a contingency is realized. The claim does not appear on the balance sheet until it is exercised (e.g., the loan is made or the security is purchased). The bank, however, has usually underwritten an obligation of a third party and has increased income and taken risk.

Table 2-5 shows some more common commitments and contingent claims grouped into three subcategories: (1) financial guarantees, (2) trade finance, and (3) investment activities. A financial guarantee is an undertaking by a bank (the guarantor) to stand behind the obligation of a third party and to carry out that obligation if the third party fails to do so. For example, in standby letters of credit, the bank must pay the beneficiary if the third party defaults on a financial obligation of the performance contract. A line of credit is a nonfee, informal agreement between a bank and a customer that the bank will typically make a loan up to the maximum agreed amount to that customer unless conditions have changed materially. In contrast, a revolving loan agreement is a formal agreement between the bank and a customer that obligates the bank to lend funds according to the terms of the contract. Note issuance facilities—Euronotes, revolving underwriting facilities (RUFs), and standby note issuance facilities (SNIFs)—and securitization of assets with resource are other examples of financial guarantees.

Trade finance includes commercial letters of credit and acceptance participations, both of which are used to finance international trade. A letter of credit involves a bank's guarantee that its customer will pay a contractual debt to a third party. An acceptance participation is all or part of a banker's acceptance (a time draft the originating bank has agreed to pay at maturity) that has been purchased and for which the purchasing bank has a contingent liability.

Investment activities that do not appear on a bank's balance sheet include forward commitments, financial futures, interest rate swaps, options (puts, calls, collars), and currency swaps. These activities have the same characteristics as the other off–balance sheet commitments and contingent claims. A bank usually receives a fee or changes a risk position immediately for an activity that does not appear on the balance sheet now but for which the bank may have to take future actions. Off–balance sheet investment activities are described in detail in Chapters 6 and 15.

Table 2-6 is a copy of the Federal Financial Institutions Examining Committee Schedule RC-L on which banks report non–balance sheet commitments and contingencies. These commitments and contingencies may have a significant effect on the return and capital adequacy measures discussed in the following chapter. One of the most important aspects of the recently adopted risk-backed capital rules is the requirement that capital be held for most non–balance sheet items.

## NONFINANCIAL INFORMATION

Nonfinancial information also affects a bank's overall financial condition. A checklist of such information was developed by Michael Knapp and is summarized in Table 2-7. Many of the items are self-explanatory; however, a few deserve further explanation. For example, recent dismissal of an audit firm or significant management turnover may indicate internal conflict regarding the quality of financial or operating policies. Outside directors who lack experience, expertise, or interest may encourage dominant management personalities who may dictate weak lending, investment, or funding policies. Poor loan documentation and overvalued or nonexistent collateral are frequent shortcomings at poorly managed banks. The key point is that information such as that listed in Table 2-7 is an important supplement to a bank's financial information.

## SOURCES AND QUALITY OF INFORMATION

The sources of banking information range from the bank's annual financial reports to the detailed financial analysis available in the Uniform Bank Performance Reports. Consulting firms, industry associations, and computer-based services also provide important information for evaluating a bank's performance.

**TABLE 2-6   Schedule RC-L—Commitments and Contingencies**
**Please read carefully the instructions for the preparation of Schedule RC-L**

| Dollar Amounts in Thousands | C360 Bil | Mil Thou | |
|---|---|---|---|
| 1. Commitments to make or purchase loans or to extend credit in the form of lease financing arrangements (report only the unused portions of commitments that are fee paid or otherwise legally binding)............... | | | 1. |
| 2. Futures and forward contracts (exclude contracts involving foreign exchange): | | | |
| a. Commitments to purchase ....................................................... | | | 2.a. |
| b. Commitments to sell.................................................................. | | | 2.b. |
| 3. When-issued securities: | | | |
| a. Gross commitments to purchase ............................................. | | | 3.a. |
| b. Gross commitments to sell...................................................... | | | 3.b. |
| 4. Standby contracts and other option arrangements: | | | |
| a. Obligations to purchase under option contracts......................... | | | 4.a. |
| b. Obligations to sell under option contracts................................ | | | 4.b. |
| 5. Commitments to purchase foreign currencies and U.S. dollar exchange (spot and forward) | | | 5. |
| 6. Standby letters of credit: | | | |
| a. Standby letters of credit: | | | |
|   (1) To U.S. addressees (domicile) .............................................. | | | 6.a.(1) |
|   (2) To non-U.S. addressees (domicile)...................................... | | | 6.a.(2) |
| b. Amount of standby letters of credit in Items 6.a.(1) and 6.a.(2) conveyed to others through participations............................................ | | | 6.b. |
| 7. Commercial and similar letters of credit............................................ | | | 7. |
| 8. Participations in acceptances (as described in the instructions) conveyed to others by the reporting bank ......................................... | | | 8. |
| 9. Participations in acceptances (as described in the instructions) acquired by the reporting (nonaccepting) bank .............................................. | | | 9. |
| 10. Securities borrowed ...................................................................... | | | 10. |
| 11. Securities lent ............................................................................. | | | 11. |
| 12. Other significant commitments and contingencies (list below each component of this item over 25% of Schedule RC, Item 28, "Total equity capital")........................................................................................ | | | 12. |
| | | | |
| | | | |
| | | | |

**Memoranda**

| | Bil | Mil Thou | |
|---|---|---|---|
| 1. Loans originated by the reporting bank that have been sold or participated to others during the calendar quarter ending with the report date (exclude the portions of such loans retained by the reporting bank; see instructions for other exclusions)................................................... | | | M.1. |
| 2. Notional value of all outstanding interest rate swaps ......................... | | | M.2. |

SOURCE: Adapted from Schedule RC-L by the Federal Financial Institutions Examination Commission.

---

**TABLE 2-7    Checklist of Nonfinancial Information Affecting a Bank's Financial Condition**

---

1. Is the bank insured by the FDIC?
2. Is the bank audited by a CPA firm?
3. Has the bank recently changed independent auditors?
4. Have there been significant management changes in recent years?
5. How much banking experience and general business experience do the outside directors possess?
6. Do the outside directors appear to have significant influence on the bank's operations?
7. Does the bank have a loan review committee?
8. What is the general quality and financial strength of correspondent banks?
9. Does the bank use a conservative method of defining nonperforming loans?
10. Does the bank offer substantial interest rate premiums to depositors?
11. Have bank regulators recently required the bank to sign administrative agreements or cease-and-desist orders?

---

SOURCE: Michael C. Knapp, "Avoiding Problem Banks," *Journal of Accountancy* (May, 1985), p. 103.

Much more detailed information and quantitative analytical analysis of a bank are available for all insured commercial banks in the Uniform Bank Performance Reports. These reports provide a detailed five-year financial profile for the requested bank and a similar profile for a "peer" group and are prepared from quarterly call report data by the Federal Financial Institutions Examination Council. The contents of a typical Uniform Bank Performance Report are explored in Chapter 4. There are also a number of consulting firms that specialize in bank analysis. Most of the data used by consulting firms come from computer tapes of quarterly call report data.

The bottom portion of Table 2-8 lists some of the more widely used sources of general banking information. The American Bankers Association is the largest industry trade group and has periodicals and studies on various aspects of banking. The FDIC Information Service provides the public with current information on the banking industry and the availability of banking data. The Bank Administration Institute is a nonprofit organization that funds and publishes research of interest to bankers and their customers. INNERLINE and the Money Market Monitor are two computer-based services that track the financial health of banks and market interest rates. The only daily banking paper published in the United States is the *American Banker*. It reports on innovative banking services and provides constant surveillance of legislative and judicial actions that significantly influence the industry.

The quality of information, particularly financial information, on a bank also deserves mention at this point. Three areas of concern are briefly discussed: (1) the use of point-of-time data, (2) the use of book value data, and (3) the discretion allowed in determining some key data. Most of the annual and quarterly report data by banks are given at a particular point of time.

**TABLE 2-8  Primary Sources of Banking Information**

| Source | Information Provided | Availability |
|---|---|---|
| **Financial Information** | | |
| Annual financial report | Basic financial statements and supplemental disclosures | By request from bank |
| Quarterly call report | Reports of condition and income—contain essentially the same information supplied in a bank balance sheet and income statement | By request from Data Base; Federal Deposit Insurance Corporation; 550 17th Street N.W.; Washington, D.C. 20429 (small fee for copying and postage) |
| Annual Form 10-K (bank holding companies) | Securities and Exchange Commission—required financial statements and other extensive financial disclosures, including nature and extent of foreign loans and related-party transactions | By request from the bank holding company. Included in annual report. |
| **Financial Analysis** | | |
| Uniform Bank Performance Report | Detailed 15- to 20-page comparative analytical report | By request from Federal Financial Institutions Examination Council; 1776 G Street N.W., Suite 701; Washington, D.C. 20006 ($25 per report) |
| Bank analysts | In-depth information and reports on specific banks | Keefe, Bruyette & Woods; 2 World Trade Center, 85th Floor; New York, N.Y. 10048 |
| | | Sheshunoff & Company; P.O. Box 13203; Capitol Station; Austin, Tex. 78711 |
| | | Financial Institutions Analysts and Consultants, Inc.; 3 Embarcadero Center, Suite 1830; San Francisco, Calif. 94111 |
| **General Information** | | |
| American Bankers Association | Information and studies on banking industry | ABA Public Information Office; 1120 Connecticut Avenue N.W.; Washington, D.C. 20036 |
| FDIC Information Service | General information on the banking industry and current status of the availability of information on specific banks | FDIC; Corporate Communications Office; 550 17th Street N.W.; Washington, D.C. 20429 |
| Bank Administration Institute | Various research studies in the banking field | 60 Gould Center; Rolling Meadows, Ill. 60008 (varying fees) |
| INNERLINE | On-line access to call report data base | American Banker; State Street Plaza; New York, N.Y. 10004 (fee schedule available on request; |

**TABLE 2-8**   *(continued)*

| Source | Information Provided | Availability |
|---|---|---|
| | | least expensive rate is $30 per month) |
| Money Market Monitor | On-line access to data base containing current interest rates on money market certificates and jumbo CD's by over 200 U.S. banks | American Banker ($7.50 per use accessed via INNERLINE) |
| *American Banker* | Overview of current banking events and financial market data | Daily financial newspaper ($675 annually) |

Source: Michael C. Knapp, "Avoiding Problem Banks," *Journal of Accountancy* (May, 1985), p. 101. Costs updated to 1992.

Because many financial assets and liabilities are short term or can be bought, sold, or repaid in a short period, some point-of-time data may be misleading. Most bank analysts prefer daily averages of balances in assets and liabilities for many measures of banking performance.

Second, banking financial information is generally stated in book value rather than market value terms. This is particularly surprising because most banking assets and liabilities are financial ones that are generally more amenable to valuation (market values exist or can be estimated from very similar instruments) than the nonfinancial assets and liabilities of other businesses. About the only balance sheet item most banks provide market value information on (in footnotes to financial statements) is their security holdings. Other key assets, such as loans, and liabilities, such as long-term borrowings, are expressed in book value terms, with no hints about market values. Since the book value of common equity is the difference between the book value of assets and the book value of liabilities, one has to wonder what book value of common equity measures.

Finally, numerous types of bank financial information are affected by accounting rules, tax rules, and management decisions. For example, the provision for loan losses and the resulting reserve for loan losses, described earlier in this chapter, is probably affected more by accounting rules, tax rules, and management decisions than by economic realities. One has to wonder why some banks have reserves against 60 percent of their nonperforming loans (another rather arbitrary number), while other banks have reserves against only 20 percent of their nonperforming loans. Also, why, in the spring of 1987, did most large banks suddenly deem necessary a significant increase in reserves against losses on loans to less developed countries? Changes in the rules or management interpretation of such rules may make some aggregative information questionable and comparison between banks highly suspect.

## Discussion Questions

1. Briefly describe the following balance sheet accounts:
   a. Cash and due from banks
   b. Consumer loans
   c. Other real estate owned
   d. Demand deposits
   e. Money market accounts
   f. Federal Funds purchased
2. What are the principal noninterest expenses of a commercial bank? Should provision for loan losses be an interest expense or a noninterest expense? What are the principal sources of noninterest income of a commercial bank?
3. Define the following terms:
   a. Earning assets
   b. Risk assets
   c. Interest rate sensitivity
   d. Tax-equivalent interest income
4. List and briefly describe the off–balance sheet activities that involve the bank's commitments and contingent claims.
5. What types of nonfinancial information would you want on a bank if you were considering investing in its stock? Making a large deposit? Accepting a management position at the bank?
6. Some accountants and regulators are advocating market value accounting for commercial banks. Would you be in favor of such a proposal? Explain the arguments for and against market value accounting.

# CHAPTER 3

# A Model for Measuring Returns and Risks in Banking

Many banks will have to take and manage higher risks in the 1990s in order to make acceptable returns. It will be increasingly important for a bank to be able to measure the risks taken to produce acceptable returns during the coming period of challenging external factors and deregulation. A bank's performance will affect its valuation in the market, its ability to acquire other banks or to be acquired at a good price, and its ability to be funded in the deposit and financial markets. Although a bank cannot change its past performance, thorough evaluation of this performance is the necessary first step in planning for an acceptable future performance.

## USING BASIC IDEAS FROM BUSINESS FINANCE

All too often bankers seem to conclude that commercial banks are so different from nonfinancial businesses that most of the concepts developed in analyzing such businesses are not appropriate for commercial banks. Such a conclusion is unwarranted. Although banks are unique in certain ways, most of the primary concepts developed for profit-oriented, private corporations are generally appropriate for analyzing commercial banks.

### Attaining the Primary Objective

The activities of a business can be described either in operating terms or in financial terms. In operating terms, a business firm buys raw materials and combines them with capital and labor to produce goods or services. These goods or services are then sold to others at prices high enough to yield returns above the cost of the raw materials, capital, and labor. In financial terms, the business obtains funds through creditor and ownership sources; spends funds for raw materials, labor, and capital; and recovers funds (hopefully in excess of the amount spent).

According to current financial theory, business management's basic objective should be to maximize the value of the owners' investment in the business. For larger, publicly held businesses operating in efficient capital markets, this objective is obtained by maximizing the market price per share. Efficient capital markets help management in seeking the highest returns for the appropriate risk level. The task is more difficult for smaller firms, some of which do not have actively traded shares. Nevertheless, the firm's management (which for smaller firms is also often its owners) tries to maximize the value of the owners' investment by seeking to achieve the highest returns for the risk level deemed appropriate by the owners. Unfortunately, the manager cannot rely on an efficient market mechanism to assist in making decisions on trade-offs between returns and risks.

### Beginning Return Measures for a Company

In order to determine whether a company's management has been successful in achieving its objectives, interested parties analyze the company's return and risk measures. Table 3-1 presents a simplified balance sheet, an income statement, and an introductory profitability analysis for the fictional ABC Manufacturing Company.

These introductory profitability analyses include the beginning items in a typical return-on-equity model, as illustrated in Table 3-2. The return-on-equity model, first developed by the DuPont Corporation, disaggregates return on equity into its basic components, which can be analyzed to identify areas in which a business may want to improve.

### Additional Information Needed

Additional information is needed to analyze ABC's performance. A more in-depth profitability analysis is needed to evaluate the firm's returns. Risk measures, such as variability of sales, nature of costs, coverage of fixed operating and financial costs, and variability of the firm's returns versus returns on a diversified portfolio, need to be calculated. The firm's return and risk measures are often compared with those of similar businesses. Generally, higher returns are available if higher risks are taken. Finally, the firm's management tries to balance the trade-offs between returns and risks by maximizing the value of the owners' investment in the firm.

### Parallels with Banking

Like a nonfinancial business, a commercial bank obtains funds from creditor and ownership sources; spends funds for its raw materials, labor, and capital;

**TABLE 3-1    ABC Manufacturing Company**

### Average Balance Sheet for 1993

| Assets | | Liabilities and Net Worth | |
|---|---|---|---|
| Cash | $ 500,000 | Current liabilities | $ 3,000,000 |
| Accounts receivable | 3,000,000 | Long-term debt | 2,000,000 |
| Inventory | 2,000,000 | Common stock | 1,000,000 |
| Plant and equipment | 4,500,000 | Retained earnings | 4,000,000 |
| | $10,000,000 | | $10,000,000 |

### Income Statement for Year 1993

| | |
|---|---|
| Revenue (or sales) | $20,000,000 |
| Cost of goods sold | 15,000,000 |
| Gross operating income | 5,000,000 |
| Selling and administrative expenses | 3,000,000 |
| Net operating income | 2,000,000 |
| Interest | 400,000 |
| Taxable income | 1,600,000 |
| Taxes (34%) | 544,000 |
| Net income | $ 1,056,000 |

### Profitability Analysis

| | | |
|---|---|---|
| Gross margin | $\dfrac{\text{Gross operating income}}{\text{Revenue}} =$ | $\dfrac{5,000,000}{20,000,000} = 25\%$ |
| Net margin (before interest and taxes) | $\dfrac{\text{Net operating income}}{\text{Revenue}} =$ | $\dfrac{2,000,000}{20,000,000} = 10\%$ |
| Net margin (after interest and taxes) | $\dfrac{\text{Net income}}{\text{Revenue}} =$ | $\dfrac{1,056,000}{20,000,000} = 5.28\%$ |
| Asset utilization (assets turnover) | $\dfrac{\text{Revenues}}{\text{Assets}} =$ | $\dfrac{20,000,000}{10,000,000} = 2\times$ |
| Return on assets | $\dfrac{\text{Net income}}{\text{Assets}} =$ | $\dfrac{1,056,000}{10,000,000} = 10.56\%$ |
| Leverage multiplier | $\dfrac{\text{Assets}}{\text{Equity}} =$ | $\dfrac{10,000,000}{5,000,000} = 2\times$ |
| Return on equity | $\dfrac{\text{Net income}}{\text{Equity}} =$ | $\dfrac{1,056,000}{5,000,000} = 21.12\%$ |

**TABLE 3-2    Return-on-Equity Model**

Return on equity

$\dfrac{\text{Net income}}{\text{Equity}}$ = Leverage multiplier $\dfrac{\text{Assets}}{\text{Equity}}$ × Return on assets $\dfrac{\text{Net income}}{\text{Assets}}$

Return on assets = Net margin $\dfrac{\text{Net income}}{\text{Revenues}}$ × Asset utilization $\dfrac{\text{Revenues}}{\text{Assets}}$

Net margin $\dfrac{\text{Net income}}{\text{Revenues}}$ = Gross margin $\dfrac{\text{Gross operating income}}{\text{Revenues}}$ − Required expense Coverage $\dfrac{\text{Expenses}}{\text{Revenues}}$

Asset utilization $\dfrac{\text{Revenues}}{\text{Assets}}$ — Receivables turnover — Inventory turnover — Fixed-asset turnover

and hopes to recover funds in excess of the amount spent. The raw material purchased is funds, rather than iron, cloth, or food, and the product sold is funds packaged in a usable form, instead of steel, clothing, or groceries. As in a nonfinancial business, bank management's basic objective should be to maximize the value of the owners' investment in the bank. Useful information on the appropriate trade-offs between returns and risk is obtained from relatively efficient markets for most publicly held banks. The management of smaller banks seeks to achieve the highest returns for the risk level deemed appropriate by the owners and top management.

### A Simplified Bank Example

The simplified financial information on XYZ Commercial Bank in Table 3-3 illustrates some of these similarities. Note that, like ABC Manufacturing, XYZ Bank has short- and long-term assets and that funds were obtained from current liabilities, long-term liabilities, and either issued or retained common equity. The proportions of assets and liabilities are often different for banks compared with nonfinancial businesses, since banks tend to have limited amounts in fixed assets (such as premises) and equity capital, and substantially larger amounts in short-term financial assets and liabilities. XYZ Bank's income statement includes revenue and expense items similar to those of ABC

**TABLE 3-3   XYZ Commercial Bank**

### *Average Balance Sheet for 1993*

| *Assets* | | *Liabilities and Net Worth* | |
|---|---|---|---|
| Cash and due from banks | $   8,000,000 | Current liabilities | $ 70,000,000 |
| Short-term loans and securities | 60,000,000 | Long-term liabilities | 23,000,000 |
| Long-term loans and securities | 30,000,000 | Common stock | 1,000,000 |
| Premises and equipment | 2,000,000 | Undivided profits | 6,000,000 |
| | $100,000,000 | | $100,000,000 |

### *Income Statement for Year 1993*

| | |
|---|---|
| Revenues—interest | $9,000,000 |
| Interest expenses | 4,000,000 |
| Net interest income | 5,000,000 |
| Overhead—people and premises | 3,000,000 |
| Net operating income | 2,000,000 |
| Taxes (34%) | 680,000 |
| Net income | $1,320,000 |

### *Profitability Analysis*

| Interest margin | $\dfrac{\text{Net interest income}}{\text{Earning assets}} = \dfrac{5{,}000{,}000}{90{,}000{,}000} = 5.6\%$ |
|---|---|
| Net margin (after tax) | $\dfrac{\text{Net income}}{\text{Revenues}} = \dfrac{1{,}320{,}000}{9{,}000{,}000} = 14.7\%$ |
| Asset utilization | $\dfrac{\text{Revenues}}{\text{Assets}} = \dfrac{9{,}000{,}000}{100{,}000{,}000} = 9.0\%$ |
| Return on assets | $\dfrac{\text{Net income}}{\text{Assets}} = \dfrac{1{,}320{,}000}{100{,}000{,}000} = 1.32\%$ |
| Leverage multiplier | $\dfrac{\text{Assets}}{\text{Equity}} = \dfrac{100{,}000{,}000}{7{,}000{,}000} = 14.3\times$ |
| Return on equity | $\dfrac{\text{Net income}}{\text{Equity}} = \dfrac{1{,}320{,}000}{7{,}000{,}000} = 18.86\%$ |

Manufacturing. The same basic profitability analysis (see Table 3-3) can be applied to the XYZ Bank example.

The meaning of each of the return measurements in Table 3-3 is reviewed; then the results are compared with the similar results for ABC Manufacturing Company. Probably the most important measure is the return on equity in which income after all expenses and taxes is divided by common equity capital (par value, paid in surplus, undivided profits, and capital reserves). Return on equity tells bank management the amount that has been earned on the book value of common shareholders' investment in the bank. This measure also reflects revenue generation, operational efficiency, financial leverage, and tax planning as well as possible in a single figure.

A bank's return on equity is derived from its return on assets and its leverage multiplier. Return on assets is net income divided by the total assets, and should reflect bank management's ability to utilize the bank's financial and real resources to generate net income. Many regulators believe return on assets is the best measure of bank efficiency. Since return on assets is lower for financial intermediaries such as commercial banks than for most nonfinancial businesses, most intermediaries must utilize financial leverage (fixed- or limited-cost funding) heavily to increase return on equity to a competitive level. The leverage multiplier to be applied to return on assets is calculated by dividing assets by assets minus all liabilities, borrowing, and preferred stock.

Return on assets is itself a derivative of the net (or profit) margin times the asset utilization (or yield). Asset utilization is revenues divided by assets and reflects how many assets are employed as earning assets and the yields earned on these earning assets. Net margin is net income divided by revenues. Net margin is affected by the interest margin—interest yields on assets and interest cost of funds—and by the burden (or overhead). The burden reflects the difference between noninterest expense and interest income.

The overall results in Table 3-3 indicate that the XYZ Bank had asset utilization and return on assets but that the higher leverage multiplier tended to make the resulting return on equity competitive with that of ABC Manufacturing. This would, of course, have to be true if the two types of businesses are to compete in the markets for new equity capital.

Just as additional information is needed to analyze ABC's performance, more in-depth profitability analysis is necessary to evaluate the bank's returns. Risk measures, similar to such measures for nonfinancial businesses and some specific to banks and similar financial institutions, should be calculated. The bank's return and risk measures should then be compared with those of similar banks. As with nonfinancial firms, generally higher returns are available if the bank takes higher risks. The bank's management tries to maximize the owners' investment in the bank by balancing the trade-offs between the risks and returns. Bank management should keep such parallel concepts in mind when analyzing the key measures of returns made and risks taken by commercial banks.

## KEY RETURN AND RISK MEASURES
## FOR A SAMPLE BANK

Smithville Bank, an example of a commercial bank in a hypothetical environment, will be used to illustrate further how to measure bank returns and risks and how to evaluate their interrelationships.

To keep this example basic, it is assumed that the bank can obtain funds in only five ways: (1) transaction deposits consisting of demand deposit (checking) and NOW accounts; (2) short-term time and savings deposits consisting of passbook savings, money market deposit accounts, and time deposits maturing within 180 days; (3) long-term time deposits, which mature in over 180 days; (4) money borrowed from other sources; and (5) equity capital representing the owners' investment and earnings retained in the bank. Similarly, it is assumed that, after meeting its cash and premises requirements, the bank can employ the funds it has obtained in only five ways: (1) short-term high-quality debt securities maturing within 180 days, (2) long-term high-quality debt securities maturing in over 180 days, (3) good-quality loans whose rate varies with changes in interest rates, (4) medium-quality loans whose rate varies with changes in interest rates, and (5) good-quality fixed-rate loans.

Table 3-4 presents the basic conditions in the hypothetical environment in which Smithville Bank must operate. Although this environment is not

**TABLE 3-4   Hypothesized Environment**

|  | Rates |
|---|---|
| **Reserve and cash requirements:** | |
| Transaction deposits | 15% |
| Time deposits | 4% |
| **Potential earnings available:** | |
| Short-term securities | 5% |
| Long-term securities (currently) | 7% |
| Long-term securities (held) | 8% |
| High-quality, variable-rate loans | 7% |
| Medium-quality, variable-rate loans | 9% |
| Fixed-rate loans (currently) | 8% |
| Fixed-rate loans (held) | 9% |
| **Expenses in environment:** | |
| Transaction deposits | 3% |
| Short-term time deposits | 4% |
| Long-term time deposits | 5% |
| Borrowings | 4% |
| Other expenses (net of other income) | $2 million |
| Income tax rate | 34% |

meant to be representative of any particular time period, the reserves, revenues, and expenses are not far from those that existed in the early 1990s.
Furthermore, the relationships between rates are reasonably representative of
many periods of time. Short-term securities yield 5 percent versus 7 percent
on long-term securities because of the greater price fluctuations (interest rate
risk) on the long-term securities. Loans tend to yield more than securities
because of their greater credit risk. Also, higher-quality loans yield less than
medium-quality loans, and variable-rate loans yield less than fixed-rate loans.
On the cost side, transaction deposits cost less than time deposits but have
higher required reserves and may cause more liquidity pressures on assets.
Long-term time deposits cost more than short-term ones because of interest
rate risk.

### The Bank's Financial Statements

The balance sheet and income statements for Smithville Bank are summarized
in Table 3-5. It is assumed that Smithville Bank has obtained $30 million in
transaction deposits (demand deposits and NOW accounts), $30 million in
short-term time and savings deposits, and $30 million in longer-term time
deposits. Furthermore, the bank has borrowed an additional $3 million and

**TABLE 3-5    Smithville Bank**

*Balance Sheet (dollars in thousands)*

| Assets | | Liabilities and Net Worth | |
|---|---|---|---|
| Cash and due from banks | $   6,900 | Transaction deposits | $ 30,000 |
| Short-term securities | 15,000 | Short-term time deposits | 30,000 |
| Long-term securities | 15,000 | Long-term time deposits | 30,000 |
| High variable loans | 20,000 | | 3,000 |
| Medium variable loans | 20,000 | Borrowings | 7,000 |
| Fixed-rate loans | 20,000 | Equity capital | |
| Premises and other assets | 3,100 | | $100,000 |
| | $100,000 | | |

*Income Statement (dollars in thousands)*

| | |
|---|---|
| Revenues | $6,950 |
| Interest expenses | − 3,720 |
| Other expenses (net) | − 2,000 |
| Operating income | $1,230 |
| Taxes | −   418 |
| Net income | $   812 |

has equity capital totaling $7 million. In employing these funds, the bank held $6.9 million in reserves and other cash accounts—15 percent of $30 million in transaction deposits and 4 percent of $60 million in time deposits—and had premises and other assets worth $3.1 million. The bank's management invested $15 million in liquid short-term securities and lent $20 million, respectively, in high-quality variable-rate loans, low-quality variable-rate loans, and fixed-rate loans. The remaining $15 million was invested in long-term securities. Fortunately, the $15 million of long-term securities and $20 million of fixed-rate loans had been invested in higher rate environments and had average yields of 8 and 9 percent, respectively.

The income statement for Smithville Bank is calculated from the account balances and rates available in the environment. For example, revenues are calculated as follows:

| Category | Balance | × | Yield | = | Revenue |
|---|---|---|---|---|---|
| Cash and due from banks | $ 6,900 | | 0% | | $ 0 |
| Short-term securities | 15,000 | | 5% | | 750 |
| Long-term securities | 15,000 | | 8% | | 1,200 |
| High variable loans | 20,000 | | 7% | | 1,400 |
| Medium variable loans | 20,000 | | 9% | | 1,800 |
| Fixed-rate loans | 20,000 | | 9% | | 1,800 |
| Premises | 3,100 | | 0% | | 0 |
| Total revenues | | | | | $6,950 |

Note that although returns on long-term securities and fixed-rate loans average 8 and 9 percent, respectively, increases in these accounts would earn 7 and 8 percent, respectively. Interest expenses are similarly calculated:

| Category | Balance | × | Cost | = | Expenses |
|---|---|---|---|---|---|
| Transaction deposits | $30,000 | | 3% | | $ 900 |
| Short-term deposits | 30,000 | | 4% | | 1,200 |
| Long-term deposits | 30,000 | | 5% | | 1,500 |
| Borrowing | 3,000 | | 4% | | 120 |
| Total interest expenses | | | | | $3,720 |

The operating income is the total revenues less the total interest expenses and other expenses. The net income is the operating income less income taxes, assumed in this example to be 34 percent.

**TABLE 3-6   Introductory Return and Risk Measurements (Smithville Bank Figures)**

| Category | Equation | | Calculations | | Results |
|---|---|---|---|---|---|
| Interest margin | $\dfrac{\text{Int. inc.} - \text{int. ex.}}{\text{Earning assets}}$ | $=$ | $\dfrac{6{,}950 - 3{,}720}{90{,}000}$ | $=$ | $3.59\%$ |
| Net margin | $\dfrac{\text{Net income}}{\text{Revenues}}$ | $=$ | $\dfrac{812}{6{,}950}$ | $=$ | $11.68\%$ $\times$ |
| Asset utilization | $\dfrac{\text{Revenues}}{\text{Assets}}$ | $=$ | $\dfrac{6{,}950}{100{,}000}$ | $=$ | $6.95\%$ $=$ |
| Return on assets | $\dfrac{\text{Net income}}{\text{Assets}}$ | $=$ | $\dfrac{812}{100{,}000}$ | $=$ | $0.81\%$ $\times$ |
| Leverage multiplier | $\dfrac{\text{Assets}}{\text{Equity}}$ | $=$ | $\dfrac{100{,}000}{7{,}000}$ | $=$ | $14.29\times$ $=$ |
| Return on capital | $\dfrac{\text{Net income}}{\text{Equity}}$ | $=$ | $\dfrac{812}{7{,}000}$ | $=$ | $11.60\%$ |
| **Risk Measures** | | | | | |
| Liquidity risk | $\dfrac{\text{Short-term securities}}{\text{Deposits}}$ | $=$ | $\dfrac{15{,}000}{90{,}000}$ | $=$ | $16.67\%$ |
| Interest rate risk[a] | $\dfrac{\text{I.s. assets}}{\text{I.s. liabilities}}$ | $=$ | $\dfrac{55{,}000}{63{,}000}$ | $=$ | $0.87$ |
| Credit risk | $\dfrac{\text{Medium loans}}{\text{Assets}}$ | $=$ | $\dfrac{20{,}000}{100{,}000}$ | $=$ | $20.00\%$ |
| Capital risk | $\dfrac{\text{Capital}}{\text{Risk assets}}$ | $=$ | $\dfrac{7{,}000}{75{,}000}$ | $=$ | $9.33\%$ |

[a]Short-term securities and all variable-rate loans are interest-sensitive assets, whereas transaction deposits, short-term time and savings deposits, and borrowings are treated as interest-sensitive liabilities. Transaction deposits are treated as interest sensitive because more and more of such deposits are interest-bearing deposits, all of which are not covered by Regulation Q.

### Measuring Returns

How well has this bank performed? Has it earned acceptable returns? What risks has it taken to achieve these returns? Table 3-6 shows how to calculate 10 introductory return and risk measurements for Smithville Bank. The return measurements and their relationships are similar to those appearing in Table 3-2. The first return measurement is the interest margin in percentage terms, which is interest income minus interest expense divided by earning assets (all securities and loans). Interest income less both interest expense and other expenses divided by revenues is labeled the net margin. This net margin times asset utilization (revenues divided by assets) equals the return on assets. It is important to note that this asset utilization is strongly affected by how much a bank has invested in earning assets. When the return on assets is multiplied by the leverage multiplier (assets divided by equity), the result is the return on equity. This return on equity (net income divided by equity capital) is the most important measurement of banking returns because it is influenced by how well the bank has performed on all other return categories and indicates whether a bank can compete for private sources of capital in the economy.

### Measuring Risks

Risk measures are related to the return measurements because a bank must take risks to earn adequate returns. Four basic categories of risk measurements are described in this section, and introductory measurements for Smithville Bank are calculated in Table 3-6.

**Liquidity Risk**  A bank's liquidity risk refers to a comparison of its liquidity needs for deposit outflows and loan increases with its actual or potential sources of liquidity from either selling an asset it holds or acquiring an additional liability. For the sample bank, this risk is approximated by comparing a proxy of the bank's liquidity needs, its deposits, with a proxy for the bank's liquidity sources and its short-term securities. Although both variables are only rough approximations (funding loans may be a major liquidity need, and purchasing liabilities may be an important source of liquidity), this relationship is a beginning indicator of most banks' liquidity risk. The trade-offs that generally exist between returns and risks are demonstrated by observing that a shift from short-term securities to long-term securities or loans raises a bank's returns but also increases its liquidity risk. The inverse would be true if short-term securities were increased. Thus, a higher liquidity ratio for the sample bank would indicate a less risky and less profitable bank.

**Interest Rate Risk**  The bank's interest rate risk is related to the changes in asset and liability returns and values caused by movements in interest rates. A beginning measurement of this risk is the ratio of interest-sensitive assets to interest-sensitive liabilities. Particularly in periods of wide interest rate movements, this ratio reflects the risk the bank is willing to take that it can predict the future direction of interest rates. If a bank has a ratio above 1.0, the bank's returns will be lower if interest rates decline and higher if they increase. Given the difficulty of predicting interest rates, at least some banks have concluded that the way to minimize interest rate risk is to have an interest sensitivity ratio close to 1.0. Such a ratio may be hard for some banks to achieve and often may be reached only at the cost of lower returns on assets, such as short-term securities or variable-rate loans.

**Credit Risk**  The credit risk of a bank is defined as the risk that the interest or principal, or both, on securities and loans will not be paid as promised. In the Smithville Bank example, the credit risk is estimated by observing the proportion of assets that are medium-quality loans. The relative amount of past-due loans or loan losses would be a better measure, but such data are not available in this example. The credit risk is higher if the bank has more medium-quality loans, but returns are usually higher too. Returns tend to be lower if the bank chooses to lower its credit risk by having a smaller portion of its assets in medium-quality loans.

**Capital Risk**    The capital risk of a bank indicates how much asset values may decline before the position of its depositors and other creditors is jeopardized. Thus, a bank with a 10 percent capital-to-assets ratio could withstand greater declines in asset values than a bank with a 5 percent capital-to-assets ratio. The capital risk of Smithville Bank is measured by examining the percentage of the bank's risk assets that are covered by its capital. The capital risk is inversely related to the leverage multiplier and, therefore, to the return on equity. When a bank chooses (assuming this is allowed by its regulators) to take more capital risk, its leverage multiplier and return on equity, *ceteris paribus*, are higher. If the bank chooses (or is forced to choose) to lower its capital risk, its leverage multiplier and return on equity are lower.

## Setting Objectives for Returns and Risks

Clearly, returns are increased by increasing one or more of the four primary risks a bank may take. Obviously, bank management would prefer the highest returns for a given level of risks and the lowest risks for a given level of returns. Two questions remain for the bank manager: What degree of total risk should a bank take to increase returns? How much of which type of risk should a bank take?

The answers to these questions are difficult and not exact. For assistance a bank can look at its past performance and determine its satisfaction with the returns obtained and risks taken. The bank can find return and risk measurements for similar individual banks or peer groups of banks and compare these with its own similar measures. If the bank's stock is actively traded, the bank can take actions that will maximize its market price. Exact answers are hard to come by. Constraints, such as the nature of a bank's market, the level of competition it faces, the areas in which it has special management expertise, and the stance of its regulators means that each bank has individual characteristics that affect its desired return–risk trade-offs.

The following three steps should prove helpful. The first step for bank management is to assess how other similar individual banks and groups of banks have made their risk–return decisions. Any bank can obtain information on other individual banks or peer groupings from the FDIC, Federal Reserve, Comptroller's Office, or numerous private bank service companies. Many banks' regulatory reports include a comparison with peer group banks. The second step is to compare a bank's performance (return and risk) measurements with those of selected similar banks. Significant variances in these measurements should be justified. There are many reasons for differences, such as different markets or different management philosophies; however, many banks may find one or several areas for improvement. The final step is to set reasonable (challenging but attainable) objectives, given a bank's past performance, the performance of its peers, and its environment.

**TABLE 3-7   Performance Objectives for Smithville Bank**

| Return Measures | Objective | Actual |
|---|---|---|
| Interest margin | 4.00% | 3.59% |
| Net margin | 11.00% | 11.68% |
| Asset utilization | 9.00% | 6.95% |
| Return on assets | 1.00% | 0.81% |
| Leverage multiplier | 14.00× | 14.29× |
| Return on equity | 14.00% | 11.60% |
| **Risk Measures** | | |
| Liquidity risk | 23.00% | 16.67% |
| Interest rate risk | 1.00 | 0.87 |
| Credit risk | 20.00% | 20.00% |
| Capital risk | 10.00% | 9.33% |

### Comparison with Objectives

Assume that after careful study of its past performance and that of its peers, Smithville Bank decided on the performance objectives in the first column in Table 3-7. These objectives should be compared with the bank's actual performance for the period being examined (see Table 3-6). Smithville Bank's return on equity was somewhat below its objective, and the return composition for achieving this target was slightly different from those objectives. The bank's interest margin and resulting return on assets were below the objectives, but an above-target leverage multiplier brought the return on equity closer to, though still below, its objective.

Analysis of the risk measures showed that the bank's liquidity and interest rate risks were substantially different from its objectives. Smithville Bank was able to get close to its return-on-equity objective only by taking higher risks than desired in these areas, as well as taking a greater capital risk to provide a higher leverage multiplier. The bank appears to be vulnerable to substantial increases in either interest rates or loan demand. Based on the preceding analysis, Smithville Bank might set future goals such as increasing its net interest margin, increasing liquid assets, and balancing its interest rate sensitivity position. Such action would be expected to increase the value of the shareholders' investment in the bank.

## RETURN–RISK TRADE-OFFS

Two additional Smithville Bank examples illustrate the difficulty in obtaining conflicting goals and the trade-offs between returns and risks taken by nearly every commercial bank. It is assumed that in the year following the initial example (see Table 3-5), Smithville's deposits grew by $10 million and its

**TABLE 3-8    Emphasis on Liquidity and Balanced Interest Sensitivity (for Smithville Bank)**

### Balance Sheet (dollars in thousands)

| Assets | | Liabilities | |
|---|---|---|---|
| Cash and due from banks | $ 7,300 | Transaction deposits | $ 30,000 |
| Short-term securities | 25,600 | Short-term time deposits | 35,000 |
| Long-term securities | 15,000 | Long-term time deposits | 35,000 |
| High variable loans | 20,000 | Borrowings | 3,000 |
| Medium variable loans | 20,000 | Equity capital | 8,000 |
| Fixed-rate loans | 20,000 | | |
| Premises | 3,100 | | |
| | $111,000 | | $111,000 |

### Income Statement (dollars in thousands)

| | |
|---|---|
| Revenues | $7,480 |
| Interest expenses | −4,170 |
| Other expenses | −2,000 |
| Operating income | 1,310 |
| Taxes (34%) | −  445 |
| Net income | $  865 |

### Introductory Return and Risk Measures

| Return Measures | Objective | Previous | Emphasizing Liquidity |
|---|---|---|---|
| Interest margin | 4.00% | 3.59% | 3.29% |
| Net margin | 11.00% | 11.68% | 11.56% |
| Asset utilization | 9.00% | 6.95% | 6.74% |
| Return on assets | 1.00% | 0.81% | 0.78% |
| Leverage multiplier | 14.00× | 14.29× | 13.88× |
| Return on equity | 14.00% | 11.60% | 10.81% |
| **Risk Measures** | | | |
| Liquidity risk | 23.00% | 16.67% | 25.60% |
| Interest rate risk | 1.00 | 0.87 | 0.96 |
| Credit risk | 20.00% | 20.00% | 18.02% |
| Capital risk | 10.00% | 9.33% | 10.67% |

capital grew by $1 million. Available returns and expenses remained the same (see Table 3-4). The bank's management set its highest priorities on increasing the bank's liquidity position and on making the bank less vulnerable to interest rate fluctuations. To achieve these objectives, the bank chose to place all the newly attracted funds, less those required as reserves and cash, into short-term securities. The resulting balance sheet, income statement, and return–risk measures are shown in Table 3-8.

## Results of Lower Risk

Smithville Bank's management decisions improved its risk position measurably. The bank's liquidity risk, credit risk, and capital risk were all better than the targeted objectives. Its interest sensitivity position moved from 0.87 to 0.96—toward its targeted goal of 1.00. However, the other side of the bank's performance, its returns, had deteriorated. Both the interest margin and the net margin declined appreciably because the bank's use of the funds obtained emphasized the more liquid, variable-return securities that had lower yields than other alternatives. The resulting return on assets and on capital fell to 0.78 percent and 10.81 percent, respectively, even further below the bank's goals of 1.00 and 14.00 percent. Thus, Smithville Bank was unable to obtain its risk objectives without hurting its return performance significantly. The bank's owners would probably be unhappy with such management decisions.

## Results of Improving Returns

Using the same figures (Smithville's deposits grew by $10 million and its capital grew by $1 million, with returns and expenses the same as those in Table 3-4), the second example assumes that the bank's management decided to emphasize increasing returns. The bank chose to invest the newly attracted funds, less those required as reserves, to the two asset categories that produced the highest returns. The resulting balance sheet, income statement, and return–risk measures are shown in Table 3-9.

## Management, Owner, and Regulatory Perspectives

The new management decisions improved Smithville Bank's returns appreciably. The interest margin improved slightly, and the net margin and asset utilization rate improved significantly. The resulting return on assets and return on capital increased to 1.00 and 13.88 percent, respectively, very close to the bank's objectives of 1.00 and 14.00 percent. The costs to obtain these increased returns were taking risks considerably higher than those in the previous year and higher than the bank's objectives. Smithville's liquidity deteriorated further; its earnings were even more sensitive to interest rate movements; and it had taken slightly above-average credit risk. The bank's capital risk improved slightly from the previous year; however, it was still significantly below the bank's objective. The bank's owners might be happy with the higher returns, but other parties, such as large depositors and regulators, might become concerned about the risks the bank had taken to obtain these returns.

## Additional Return–Risk Trade-off Situations

With the aid of a microcomputer, management can try many variations of the Smithville Bank example—changing the bank's liability structure, increasing or decreasing its capital position, varying the external environment so that

**TABLE 3-9   Emphasis on Profitability (for Smithville Bank)**

### Balance Sheet (dollars in thousands)

| Assets | | Liabilities | |
|---|---|---|---|
| Cash and due from banks | $ 7,300 | Transaction deposits | $ 30,000 |
| Short-term securities | 15,000 | Short-term time deposits | 35,000 |
| Long-term securities | 15,000 | Long-term time deposits | 35,000 |
| High variable loans | 20,000 | Borrowings | 3,000 |
| Medium variable loans | 25,500 | Equity capital | 8,000 |
| Fixed-rate loans | 25,100 | | |
| Premises | 3,100 | | |
| | $111,000 | | $111,000 |

### Income Statement (dollars in thousands)

| | |
|---|---|
| Revenues | $7,853 |
| Interest expenses | −4,170 |
| Other expenses | −2,000 |
| Operating income | 1,683 |
| Taxes (34%) | − 572 |
| | $1,111 |

### Introductory Return and Risk Measures

| Return Measures | Objective | Previous | Emphasizing Returns |
|---|---|---|---|
| Interest margin | 4.00% | 3.59% | 3.66% |
| Net margin | 11.00% | 11.68% | 14.14% |
| Asset utilization | 9.00% | 6.95% | 7.07% |
| Return on assets | 1.00% | 0.81% | 1.00% |
| Leverage multiplier | 14.00× | 14.29× | 13.88× |
| Return on equity | 14.00% | 11.60% | 13.88% |
| *Risk Measures* | | | |
| Liquidity risk | 23.00% | 16.67% | 15.00% |
| Interest-rate risk | 1.00 | 0.87 | 0.86 |
| Credit risk | 20.00% | 20.00% | 22.97% |
| Capital risk | 10.00% | 9.33% | 9.35% |

rates are higher or lower, and so forth. Four such situations are summarized in Table 3-10. The results are always similar. To increase its returns, the bank must take additional risk. Conversely, lower risk means lower returns.

**Liquid, Low-Capital Situation**   The first situation summarized in Table 3-10 is based on the assumption that regulatory authorities allow the liquid version of Smithville bank (see Table 3-8) to have a lower capital position and, therefore, a higher leverage multiplier. It is assumed that the liquid Smithville

**TABLE 3-10    Additional Risk Return Situations for Smithville Bank**

| | Objective | (1) Liquid Low-Capital Bank | (2) Profitable High-Capital Bank | (3) Shifting Fund Sources Bank | (4) Rapid Purchased-Growth Bank |
|---|---|---|---|---|---|
| *Return Measures* | | | | | |
| Interest margin | 4.00% | 3.21% | 3.74% | 3.42% | 3.50% |
| Net margin | 11.00% | 10.85% | 14.82% | 12.52% | 15.79% |
| Asset utilization | 9.00% | 6.74% | 7.07% | 7.03% | 6.98% |
| Return on assets | 1.00% | 0.73% | 1.05% | 0.88% | 1.10% |
| Leverage multiplier | 14.00× | 18.50× | 11.10× | 13.88× | 13.00× |
| Return on equity | 14.00% | 13.53% | 11.64% | 12.20% | 14.32% |
| *Risk Measures* | | | | | |
| Liquidity | 23.00% | 25.60% | 15.00% | 17.00% | 18.36% |
| Interest rate risk | 1.00 | 0.94 | 0.92 | 0.98 | .90 |
| Credit risk | 20.00% | 18.02% | 22.97% | 19.82% | 20.00% |
| Capital risk | 10.00% | 8.00% | 11.68% | 9.45% | 10.10% |

Bank is required to hold $2 million less capital and obtains this $2 million through borrowing. Although return on assets is lower because of the cost of borrowing the additional $1 million, return on equity is significantly higher than that for the liquid situation in Table 3-8 because of the higher leverage multiplier. Risks are the same, except that capital risk is considerably higher than the 10 percent objective.

**Profitable, High-Capital Situation**    The second situation summarized in Table 3-10 assumes that the regulatory authorities require $2 million of additional capital for the higher-profit, high-risk version of Smithville Bank. (The original data for this revision appears in Table 3-9.) The asset structure is left unchanged from Table 3-9, but borrowing falls to $1 million and capital is raised by $2 million. With the lower leverage multiplier, the return on capital falls from 13.88 to 11.64 percent and, except for capital risks, the risk measures all remain high. Raising capital lowered profitability and did not improve the bank's liquidity, interest sensitivity, or credit risk situation.

**Shifting Fund Sources Situation**    In the third situation, it is assumed that Smithville Bank's sources of funds changed appreciably. Transaction deposits fell to $20 million, and the bank was able to remain the same size by attracting $5 million more in short-term and savings deposits and $5 million more in long-term time deposits. The funds attracted were invested approximately equally in five categories of earning assets. The results in this situation are worrisome (particularly because they may be close to what happened in the late 1980s). Profits are below average (the return on equity is 12.20 percent) and liquidity risk, interest rate risk, and capital risk are all lower risk than the target objectives.

**Rapid Purchased-Growth Situation**   The fourth and final situation depicts the case in which Smithville Bank decides to grow rapidly, from $111 million to $130 million in the following year. Funds are attracted by aggressive bidding to obtain $5 million in new short-term time and savings deposits, $5 million in new long-term time deposits, and $7 million in new borrowings. For this situation, capital is increased to $10 million, and approximately equal amounts are invested in each of the five categories of earning assets. The results, as summarized in Table 3-10, indicate that Smithville Bank exceeded targeted profits, liquidity, and interest rate risk. A bank having above-average growth clearly needs to consider the effects on its return–risk position of how the growth is financed and how the funds obtained are employed.

## Discussion Questions

1. According to current financial theory, what should be the objectives of the management of a nonfinancial firm? What differences, if any, should there be in the management's objectives for a commercial bank?
2. What are the five primary components of the return-on-equity model? Write the formulas for each of these components, and show how the components are interrelated.
3. Describe the four basic categories of financial risk that banks take. List several ratios for measuring risk in each of these categories.
4. How should a bank establish its objective for selected risk and return measures?
5. Give two examples of how a bank can increase its return on assets and return on equity by taking greater risks.
6. Give a brief example illustrating the effect on returns and risk when a bank takes additional credit risks.
7. What are the effects on the return and risk measures of a bank repurchasing some of its common stock in the market?
8. Give several examples of how a bank might take additional liquidity risk. Describe the effects of these measures on the bank's return measures.

CHAPTER **4**

# Evaluation of
# a Bank's Performance

This chapter brings together and enhances the information generally available for a bank (discussed in Chapter 2) and the model for measuring returns and risks (discussed in Chapter 3). The chapter opens with an evaluation of the 10 key return and risk measures for Community National Bank. These are compared with similar measures for a peer group, and selected supplemental ratios are presented. The chapter continues with a discussion of techniques for increasing the sophistication of return and risk measures. It then turns to a discussion of value maximization as a way to target the appropriate risk–return trade-offs. The chapter closes with a discussion of Uniform Bank Performance Reports and possible indicators of poor performance.

## AN EXAMPLE OF EVALUATING A BANK'S PERFORMANCE

The key risk–return measures from Chapter 3 are computed and analyzed for Community National Bank (from information in Chapter 2) in this section. Table 4-1 illustrates the calculation of the key ratios measuring the bank's returns and risks it has taken to obtain these returns. Two risk measures are modified because more information is available than was available for the sample bank. Liquidity risk is now measured by comparing the difference between liquid assets (short-term instruments and securities maturing within a year) and short-term borrowing (a proxy for how much of the bank's borrowing capacity is used) to total deposits. Credit risk is now measured by dividing past-due loans by net loans.

**TABLE 4-1  Community National Bank Return–Risk Ratios**

| | | 1990 | | 1991 | | 1992 | |
|---|---|---|---|---|---|---|---|
| Interest margin (te)[a] | $\dfrac{\text{Interest income (te)}^{[a]} - \text{Int. expense}}{\text{Earning assets}}$ | $\dfrac{12{,}663 - 7{,}461}{101{,}467}$ | = 5.13% | $\dfrac{12{,}532 - 7{,}479}{115{,}899}$ | = 4.36% | $\dfrac{12{,}768 - 7{,}363}{126{,}281}$ | = 4.28% |
| Net margin (te)[a] | $\dfrac{\text{Net income (at)}^{[b]}}{\text{Revenues (te)}^{[a]}}$ | $\dfrac{1{,}315}{13{,}629}$ | = 9.65% | $\dfrac{1{,}167}{13{,}828}$ | = 8.44% | $\dfrac{1{,}202}{14{,}315}$ | = 8.40% |
| Asset utilization (te)[a] | $\dfrac{\text{Revenues (te)}^{[a]}}{\text{Assets}}$ | $\dfrac{13{,}629}{115{,}950}$ | = 11.75% | $\dfrac{13{,}828}{133{,}155}$ | = 10.38% | $\dfrac{14{,}315}{146{,}158}$ | = 9.79% |
| Return on assets | $\dfrac{\text{Net income (at)}^{[b]}}{\text{Assets}}$ | $\dfrac{1{,}315}{115{,}950}$ | = 1.13% | $\dfrac{1{,}167}{133{,}155}$ | = 0.88% | $\dfrac{1{,}202}{146{,}158}$ | = 0.82% |
| Leverage multiplier | $\dfrac{\text{Assets}}{\text{Equity}}$ | $\dfrac{115{,}950}{8{,}755}$ | = 13.24 × | $\dfrac{133{,}155}{10{,}092}$ | = 13.19 × | $\dfrac{146{,}158}{10{,}824}$ | = 13.50 × |
| Return on equity | $\dfrac{\text{Net income (at)}^{[b]}}{\text{Equity}}$ | $\dfrac{1{,}315}{8{,}755}$ | = 15.02% | $\dfrac{1{,}167}{10{,}092}$ | = 11.56% | $\dfrac{1{,}202}{10{,}824}$ | = 11.10% |
| Liquidity risk | $\dfrac{\text{Liquid assets} - \text{short-term borrowing}}{\text{Total deposits}}$ | $\dfrac{8{,}767 - 3{,}120}{103{,}285}$ | = 5.46% | $\dfrac{7{,}658 - 4{,}117}{117{,}996}$ | = 3.00% | $\dfrac{7{,}235 - 3{,}559}{130{,}674}$ | = 2.81% |
| Interest rate risk | $\dfrac{\text{Interest-sensitive assets}}{\text{Interest-sensitive liabilities}}$ | $\dfrac{50{,}664}{46{,}741}$ | = 1.08 | $\dfrac{59{,}766}{66{,}182}$ | = 0.90 | $\dfrac{70{,}352}{81{,}749}$ | = 0.86 |
| Credit risk | $\dfrac{\text{Past-due loans}}{\text{Net loans}}$ | $\dfrac{1{,}768}{65{,}035}$ | = 2.72% | $\dfrac{2{,}505}{82{,}944}$ | = 3.02% | $\dfrac{2{,}972}{92{,}676}$ | = 3.20% |
| Capital risk | $\dfrac{\text{Equity}}{\text{Risk assets}}$ | $\dfrac{8{,}755}{92{,}700}$ | = 9.44% | $\dfrac{10{,}092}{108{,}241}$ | = 9.32% | $\dfrac{10{,}824}{119{,}046}$ | = 9.09% |

[a] Tax equivalent.
[b] After taxes.

### Analysis of Key Return–Risk Ratios

Once such calculations are completed, the next concern is the interpretation of the resulting return–risk ratios. Several sources may serve as a beginning basis for comparison. First, trends in a bank's own return–risk measures over time often provide useful insights. Second, comparison of a bank's return–risk measures with the same measures for reasonably similar banks is helpful in identifying areas of strength and weakness. Reasonably similar banks could include individual banks of like size and in comparable markets or a grouping of peer banks of similar size and in comparable markets. Averages and often various percentile groupings of return–risk measures for peer groupings are available from the three national regulatory agencies and numerous service companies. Finally, a bank can compare its return–risk measures with its own planned targets or objectives for such measures. Interpreting comparisons with any of these sources should be done carefully. Even favorable trends in a bank's own return–risk ratios may still be at an undesirable level. Totally identical individual banks or groupings of banks are difficult, if not impossible, to identify. A bank's planned objectives are typically based on its own and its peer group's performance in recent years, which may still be at an unacceptable level. In addition, the directors and top management of a bank may choose different strategies and trade-offs between return and risk from peer banks to achieve an acceptable level of performance. Clearly, comparative ratios are only the first step in analyzing a bank's key return–risk ratios.

The skill and complexities in analyzing a bank's key return–risk ratios can be illustrated by trying to interpret the trends in Table 4-1 and by comparing Community National Bank's key ratios with the average ratios for peer banks of similar size and in regions and markets similar to those of Community Bank, which appear in Table 4-2. In the case of its interest margin, Community

**TABLE 4-2    Key Return–Risk Ratios for Peer Banks of Community National Bank[a]**

|  | 1990 | 1991 | 1992 |
|---|---|---|---|
| Interest margin (te) | 5.09% | 5.08% | 5.11% |
| Net margin (te) | 9.65% | 8.83% | 8.77% |
| Asset utilization (te) | 11.30% | 10.25% | 9.67% |
| Return on assets | 1.09% | .91% | .85% |
| Leverage multiplier | 13.92× | 14.06× | 14.08× |
| Return on equity | 15.17% | 12.80% | 11.97% |
| Liquidity risk | 10.32% | 9.98% | 10.07% |
| Interest rate risk | 1.06 | 1.04 | 1.01 |
| Credit risk | 2.01% | 2.37% | 3.12% |
| Capital risk | 9.45% | 9.36% | 9.24% |

[a]Based on banks with assets of from $100 million to $500 million in regions and markets similar to those of Community National Bank.

National would probably be somewhat concerned with the decline in its interest margin from above average to below average from 1990 to 1992. The below-average interest margin in 1992 might not be of much concern if the bank's other costs, such as salaries and occupancy costs, were below average. Often more retail-oriented (consumer-oriented) banks have high interest margins and high other costs. Wholesale (large business customer) banks often tend to have relatively lower margins but considerably lower other costs.

Community National Bank's net margin, which reflects both its interest margin and its ability to cover all other costs, including taxes, is clearly cause for considerable concern. The bank's net margin (using approximated tax-equivalent income) declined markedly from 1990 to 1992 and was over 1 percent below the average net margin of peer banks in 1992. Clearly, other costs in addition to interest expense had risen rapidly and were above average. Techniques for investigating this problem will be discussed later.

Community National's asset utilization was slightly above average and was rising by a magnitude similar to that of its peer banks. This tends to verify that Community's problem was expense control rather than failure to earn an adequate gross yield on assets. The return on assets that resulted from the low net margin and the average asset utilization fell from slightly above average in 1990 to below that of peer banks in 1991 and 1992. A below-peer-average leverage multiplier further hurt Community National's return on equity because of the low return on assets in 1991 and 1992. The bank's return on equity was nearly equal to that of its peer banks in those years.

Examination of the risk position of Community National Bank produced some surprising results. Because of its lower than average returns, it seems logical to expect the bank to be taking lower risks. The opposite proved true for the four primary risk categories. Community National Bank appeared to be taking a substantial liquidity risk. Its liquid assets seemed low and its short-term borrowings appeared high relative to its deposits and the liquidity ratio, recognizing these variables for its peer banks. Community National experienced a rapid growth in interest-sensitive liabilities in 1991 and 1992. By 1992 the bank's interest rate risk (interest-sensitive assets divided by interest-sensitive liabilities) had fallen to 0.86. This strong net liability sensitivity indicates that the bank is gambling on a decline in the level of interest rates. Community National's credit risk (measured by past-due loans) is also above the similar measurement for its peers. Finally, in spite of a small common stock issue in 1991, its capital risk is slightly higher; that is, the bank's equity capital is a smaller proportion of risk assets than it is for its peer banks.

In summary, analysis of the key risk–return ratios for Community National Bank indicates that the bank's low return on equity is primarily caused by higher than average expenses. Better control of these expenses should be a top priority in coming years. Of equal concern is the conclusion that the bank is taking above-average risk in each of the four primary risk categories. Community National appears to be gambling that interest rates will fall and that the liquidity needs of the bank will be relatively small. The bank has no area of significant strength to give it flexibility if bad times come. Using the preceding analysis as a starting base, supplemental ratios can be developed to enable Community National to understand its performance in greater depth and to serve as a guide to specific future actions.

## Supplemental Measures of Bank Performance

Once the key return–risk ratios have been used to spot the areas of greatest concern, supplemental measures of bank performance can be used to identify specific strengths and weaknesses. Table 4-3 contains an example of such supplemental ratios for Community National Bank. The emphasis at this time is on the types of supplemental measures a bank may use. Trends, targets, and peer group figures are helpful as a basis for evaluating such supplemental ratios, but these are not presented here.

The first four categories of supplemental measures are particularly useful for detailed understanding of the factors underlying a bank's net margin and return on assets. The first category measures the yields on each type of earning asset. A bank like Community National is able to see the trends in yields on various earning assets, to examine how its gross returns compare with those of its peers on specific assets, and to identify assets on which yields might be improved. The second category looks at noninterest sources of income to examine a bank's performance in earning income from sources other than interest on its earning assets. Although noninterest income is relatively small for most banks, adequate returns can be the margin of success for a bank. Furthermore, many bank analysts feel that noninterest income will be a growing contributor to bank returns in future years. The other two categories emphasize the interest costs of a bank's various sources of funds and its cost efficiency in other overhead areas, such as salaries and occupancy expenses. Rising or above-average costs can be indicative of potential problem areas.

The bank's asset and liability composition often provides useful supplemental information to its key return–risk ratios. The current environment and a bank's specific market will obviously affect its mixture of assets and liabilities; however, bank management decisions also have an impact in this important area. Analysis of these compositions in conjunction with yields on assets and cost of fund sources often proves helpful. As an example, specific costs of fund sources for Community National Bank are generally at acceptable levels. It is the change in the composition of liabilities from low-cost sources, such as demand deposits and passbook savings, to high-cost sources, such as money market accounts and large CDs, that has caused the bank's interest margin to deteriorate. Continued increases in many noninterest expenses have led to even greater deterioration in the bank's net margin.

Examining the annual growth rates of selected items, the next category of supplemental measures provides helpful insights on both returns and risks. For example, rapid loan growth tends to lead to higher returns and higher risk.

**TABLE 4-3   Community National Bank Supplemental Measures**

|  | 1990 | 1991 | 1992 |
|---|---|---|---|
| **Yield on Earning Assets** | | | |
| Short-term instruments | 10.25% | 7.22% | 3.52% |
| Taxable securities | 10.73 | 10.04 | 7.50 |
| Tax-exempt securities | 6.45 | 6.54 | 6.75 |
| Tax-exempt securities (te)[a] | 9.60 | 9.66 | 9.87 |
| All investment securities (te)[a] | 10.16 | 9.86 | 8.38 |
| Commercial loans | 13.85 | 11.61 | 10.77 |
| Consumer loans | 14.72 | 11.99 | 12.11 |
| Real estate loans | 12.06 | 9.69 | 10.04 |
| Other loans | 13.01 | 11.07 | 9.38 |
| All loans (net) | 13.77 | 11.33 | 11.12 |
| All earning assets (te)[a] | 12.87 | 10.81 | 10.11 |
| **Noninterest Income** | | | |
| Service charges and fees/revenues | 5.02% | 7.00% | 7.66% |
| Other noninterest income/revenues | 2.36 | 2.58 | 3.51 |
| Total noninterest income/earning assets | 0.95 | 1.12 | 1.23 |
| **Cost of Fund Sources** | | | |
| NOW and Super NOW | 3.41% | 3.22% | 3.10% |
| Passbook savings | 5.26 | 4.80 | 4.31 |
| Money market accounts | 8.25 | 7.90 | 5.77 |
| Savings certificates | 8.83 | 8.01 | 7.73 |
| CDs of $100,000 and over | 12.07 | 8.34 | 8.11 |
| Other time deposits | 10.74 | 8.31 | 8.05 |
| All interest-bearing deposits | 8.37 | 7.06 | 6.49 |
| Short-term borrowing | 11.09 | 9.93 | 5.56 |
| Other liabilities | 7.85 | 9.37 | 7.79 |
| All interest-bearing funds | 8.53 | 7.26 | 6.54 |
| Interest expense/earning assets | 7.35 | 6.45 | 5.83 |
| **Cost Efficiency** | | | |
| Provision for loan losses/revenues | 2.27% | 2.98% | 3.73% |
| Salaries and benefits/revenues | 19.13 | 20.13 | 21.69 |
| Salaries and benefits/employees | $19,881.00 | $20,613.00 | $22,074.00 |
| Total assets ($ thousand)/employee | $920.00 | $1,008.00 | $1,074.00 |
| Occupancy expenses/revenues | 6.16 | 6.53 | 7.00 |
| Occupancy expenses/total assets | 0.70 | 0.66 | 0.66 |
| Other expenses/revenues | 4.36 | 4.65 | 4.96 |
| Taxes/net income before taxes | 9.56 | 3.15 | 7.82 |
| Taxes (net income (bt)[b] − tax-exempt income) | 39.04 | 37.73 | 36.56 |
| Noninterest expenses/earning assets | 3.83 | 3.65 | 3.69 |
| Total expenses/earning assets | 11.47 | 12.61 | 11.91 |
| **Composition of Assets** | | | |
| Earning assets/total assets | 87.52% | 87.04% | 86.40% |
| Details appear on balance sheet | | (See Table 2-1) | |

**TABLE 4-3**   *(continued)*

| | | | |
|---|---|---|---|
| **Composition of Liabilities** | | | |
| Details appear on balance sheet | | (See Table 2-1) | |
| **Annual Growth Rates** | | | |
| Assets | | 14.84% | 9.77% |
| Loans (net) | | 27.54 | 11.73 |
| Deposits | | 14.24 | 10.74 |
| Capital | | 15.27 | 7.25 |
| **Supplemental Liquidity Ratios** | | | |
| Liquid assets/total assets | 7.56% | 5.75% | 4.95% |
| Total borrowing/stockholder equity | 35.63 | 40.79 | 32.88 |
| Volatile deposits/total deposits | 34.20 | 28.21 | 33.47 |
| **Supplemental Interest-Sensitivity Ratios** | | | |
| Interest-sensitive assets/assets | 43.69% | 44.88% | 48.12% |
| Interest-sensitive liabilities/assets | 40.31 | 49.70 | 55.93 |
| Net sensitive assets/assets | 3.38 | −4.82 | −7.80 |
| **Supplement Credit Risk Measures** | | | |
| Risk assets/total assets | 79.95% | 81.29% | 81.45% |
| Provisions for loan losses/net loans | 0.45 | 0.49 | 0.56 |
| Valuation reserves/net loans | 0.74 | 0.83 | 0.84 |
| **Supplemental Capital Ratios** | | | |
| Debt capital/total capital | 0.00% | 0.00% | 0.00% |
| Capital/assets | 7.55 | 7.58 | 7.40 |
| Capital/loans | 13.46 | 12.17 | 11.68 |

[a] Tax equivalent.

[b] Before taxes.

More rapid growth in assets than in deposits is indicative of a bank using borrowed sources of funds extensively. The growth rate of capital in relation to the growth rate of assets and loans often dictates the bank's future capital position. (This is discussed in detail in the chapters on bank capital.)

Finally, the four categories of supplemental risk ratios add greater depth in understanding the risks a bank takes when trying to obtain higher returns. For example, in the liquidity risk category, the sources of liquidity are estimated by looking at liquid assets in relation to total assets and at total borrowings as a percentage of stockholders' equity. Volatile deposits (large CDs and public time deposits) as a percentage of total deposits and the rate of growth in loans (from the preceding ratio category) serve as beginning approximations of liquidity needs.

## INCREASING THE SOPHISTICATION OF RETURN AND RISK MANAGEMENT

The methodology applied so far to Community National Bank is widely adopted by bankers, analysts, and regulators. Methods for increasing the sophistication of this traditional approach to return and risk measures are discussed in the next two sections.

### An Alternative Breakdown of Return on Equity[1]

The traditional way of looking at the return on equity (ROE) is to express it as the product of the return on assets (ROA) and the leverage multiplier (M). The ROA term, however, reflects the bank's asset utilization, its debt–equity mix, the percentage cost of its debt funds, and the ratio of noninterest expenses to assets. Thus, the term confounds the impact on the ROE of the way two distinct sets of management decisions are carried out: those focusing on investment strategy (identifying and exploiting asset purchase decisions) and those focusing on financial strategy (determining the best mix of equity and various kinds of debt). As a consequence, the equation does not tell management as much as it really needs to know about the underlying causes of its performance.

The purpose of this section is to present and describe an alternative method of breaking down ROE that is free of this confounding problem and that, therefore, can help management probe more deeply into these underlying causes. This method expresses the bank's ROE as the *sum* of two components. The first is the operating, or pre-interest expense, rate of return that the bank earns on the funds it has invested in loans, securities, cash, and other assets; more briefly, it is the bank's return on invested funds (ROIF). It reflects both the productivity and the efficiency of the bank's asset purchase operations. The second component is the bank's return on financial leverage (ROFL). It reflects both the degree to which the bank trades on its equity and the terms of that trading. In summary:

$$ROE = ROIF + ROFL$$

The following paragraphs explain this alternative ROE approach and then use it to analyze the changes in Community National Bank's ROE over the years 1990, 1991, and 1992.

Like most businesses, a commercial bank assembles a pool of debt and equity funds and then invests this pool in financial and nonfinancial assets at some rate identified here as the ROIF. This return can be defined both as a simple ratio and as the difference between two ratios.

---

[1]The approach was developed and enthusiastically supported by Dr. William W. Alberts of the University of Washington and Marakon Associates. A more detailed description appears in William W. Alberts, "Explaining a Bank's ROE: An Alternative Approach," *The Bankers Magazine*, March–April, 1989.

$$ROIF = \frac{Operating\ income}{Assets}$$

where operating income is given by the equation

Operating income = revenues − operating expenses − unadjusted taxes

Revenues are defined as the sum of interest income on loans and securities, service charges and fees, and other noninterest income. Operating expenses are defined as the sum of the loan loss provision, personnel expenses, and other noninterest expenses. Unadjusted taxes are defined as the product of the tax rate, $t$, and taxable income, calculated before deduction of the bank's interest expense.

For the second definition, the yield or asset utilization is made comparable by "netting down" (at $t$) the taxable revenues to their after-tax equivalent:

$$Yield = \frac{Tax\text{-}exempt\ revenues + (1 - t) \times Taxable\ revenues}{Assets}$$

For example, for Community National Bank in 1990 with taxable revenues of $11,996, tax-exempt revenues of $1,098, and $t$ equal to 39 percent:

$$Yield = \frac{1,098 + (0.61 \times 11,996)}{115,950} = \frac{8,416}{115,950} = 7.26\%$$

Since the operating expenses (noninterest expenses) are tax deductible, they must also be adjusted (at $t$) when calculating the operating expense ratio:

$$Operating\ expense\ ratio = \frac{(1 - t)(Noninterest\ expense)}{Assets}$$

The bank's operating expense ratio for 1990 was

$$\frac{(.61)297}{115,950} + \frac{(.61)2,505}{115,950} + \frac{(.61)1,377}{115,950} = 0.15\% + 1.32\% + 0.72\% = 2.20\%$$

The ROIF, then, is given by

$$ROIF = 7.26\% - 2.20\% = 5.06\%$$

The second component of the alternative ROE breakdown, ROFL, measures the impact on the ROE of the fact that the bank is raising debt funds at some particular cost and then investing these funds in assets that generate some particular ROIF. More specifically, given the magnitude of the bank's assets and given that

$$\text{Assets} = \text{Invested funds} = \text{Debt} + \text{Equity}$$

the bank's ROFL is the *product* of (1) the difference, or spread, between the ROIF and the *after-tax* cost of the debt funds, $K_d(1 - t)$ and (2) the debt–equity ratio, $L$. Expressed as an equation:

$$\text{ROFL} = [\text{ROIF} - K_d(1 - t)][L]$$

where

$$K_d(1 - t) = \frac{\text{Interest expense} \times (1 - t)}{\text{Debt}}$$

Again, using Community National Bank in 1990 as the example, the debt–equity ratio and after-tax cost of debt were

$$L = \frac{\text{Debt}}{\text{Equity}} = \frac{107,195}{8,755} = 12.24\times$$

$$K_d(1 - t) = \frac{7,461}{107,195}(1 - .39) = 4.25\%$$

Community National's leverage spread, ROIF minus the after-tax cost of debt, was $5.06\% - 4.25\% = 0.81\%$. Thus, the bank was able to invest \$107 million in debt funds costing 4.25 percent after taxes at an ROIF of 5.06 percent. The bank's ROFL for 1990 was

$$\text{ROFL} = [5.06\% - 4.25\%][12.24] = 9.92\%$$

and the alternative ROE equation for 1990 was

$$\text{ROE} = \text{ROIF} + \text{ROFL}$$

$$= 5.06\% + 9.92\%$$

$$= 14.98\%$$

which is similar to the 15.02 percent given for the bank. The slight difference is caused primarily by using a rounded tax figure.

The magnitude of the ROFL for any bank is sensitive both to the magnitude of the leverage spread and to the magnitude of the leverage ratio. Specifically, here is the way the ROFL varies with the leverage spread, given a leverage ratio equal to Community National's ratio for 1990:

| Debt/ Equity | Debt/ Assets | Leverage Spread | ROFL |
|---|---|---|---|
| 12.24× | 92.4% | .25% | 3.06% |
| 12.24× | 92.4% | .50% | 6.12% |
| 12.24× | 92.4% | .75% | 9.18% |
| 12.24× | 92.4% | 1.00% | 12.24% |

and here is the way the ROFL varies with the leverage ratio, given a leverage spread equal to Community National's spread for 1990:

| Debt/ Equity | Debt/ Assets | Leverage Spread | ROFL |
|---|---|---|---|
| 8.09× | 89.0% | .81% | 6.55% |
| 10.11× | 91.0% | .81% | 8.19% |
| 13.29× | 93.0% | .81% | 10.76% |
| 19.00× | 95.0% | .81% | 15.39% |

In short, for a debt–equity ratio in the region of 12× (and therefore a debt–assets ratio in the region of 92 percent), each 0.25 percentage point increase in the spread adds about three percentage points to the ROFL. Turning the coin, for a leverage spread in the region of 0.81 percent, increasing the debt–assets ratio by increments of two percentage points increases the debt–equity ratio, and thus the leverage spread, by progressively larger increments. Note in particular that increasing the debt–assets ratio from 93 to 95 percent adds almost five percentage points to the ROFL.

But this "magnification effect" of leverage has a dark side, of course. If the ROIF is *less* than the after-tax cost of debt, the ROE will be less than the ROIF and could easily be negative. For example, suppose that

$$\text{ROIF} = 4.75\%$$

$$K_d(1 - t) = 5.25\%$$

$$L = 13.00\times$$

then

$$\text{ROE} = 4.75\% + [-.50\%][13.00] = 4.75\% - 6.50\% = -1.75\%$$

Further, with a negative spread, the ROE *decreases* as the leverage ratio increases.

**FIGURE 4-1    The Alternative ROE Equation**

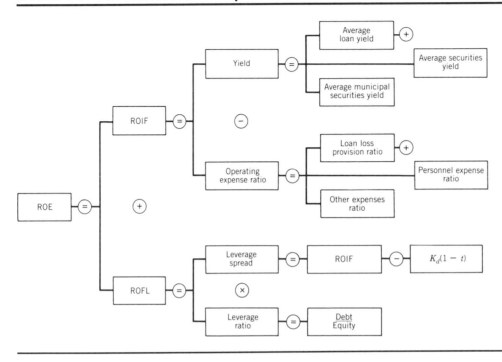

Figure 4-1 summarizes in graphic form this alternative method for breaking down ROE. Applied to Community National's ROE in 1990, 1991, and 1992, the alternative method shows:

|  | 1990 | 1991 | 1992 |
|---|---|---|---|
| Yield | 7.26% | 6.60% | 6.22% |
| Operating expense ratio | 2.20% | 2.12% | 2.23% |
| ROIF | 5.06% | 4.38% | 3.99% |
| ROIF | 5.06% | 4.38% | 3.99% |
| $K_d(1 - t)$ | 4.25% | 3.77% | 3.43% |
| Leverage spread | .81% | .61% | .56% |
| Leverage ratio | 12.24× | 12.19× | 12.50× |
| ROFL | 9.92% | 7.44% | 7.00% |
| ROIF + ROFL = ROE | 14.98%[a] | 11.72%[a] | 10.99%[a] |

[a]Slight difference with actual figures caused by rounding the tax figure to the nearest percent.

What does this alternative method tell management about the causes of the decrease in the ROE to 11.72 percent in 1991? First, since the ROIF decreased and the leverage ratio did not change materially, it was the decrease of 0.20 percent in the leverage spread that drove the ROE down. Second, the leverage spread decreased because the after-tax cost of debt decreased proportionately less than the ROIF. Third, the ROIF decreased more than the cost of debt, not because the bank's cost management deteriorated, but because the bank had deterioration in yields on its earning assets.

Why did the ROE decrease further in 1992? On the one hand, the ROIF decreased 0.39 percent (partly because of the increase in the tax rate and partly because of a decrease in yields on most loans and securities). On the other hand, the ROFL decreased 0.44 percent. Since the decrease in the ROIF was smaller than the decrease in the ROFL, the ROE decreased from 11.72 percent to approximately 10.99 percent.

It is worth noting that for 1992 a combination of the same 0.56 percent leverage spread and a debt–assets ratio of, say, 94.4 percent would have resulted in an ROE of 14.27 percent, calculated as follows:

$$\text{ROE} = 3.99\% + [.61\%][16.86] = 3.99\% + 10.28\% = 14.27\%$$

Summing up, the alternative ROE equation makes it clear that Community National's management allowed a dramatic deterioration to take place in 1991 in the relationship between its interest revenues and its interest expenses. Specifically, the spread between its overall yield and its overall after-tax cost of debt was cut almost in half. As a consequence, its ROFL also was cut sharply. Since in 1990 Community National's ROFL was nearly twice the size of its ROIF (a relationship that is typical for the banking business), this drop in the ROFL in 1991 and 1992 caused a sharp drop in the ROE.

## Improving Risk Measurement

In the very challenging environment of the early 1990s, banks must take considerable risks to earn a reasonable return. The measurement and management of such risks is one of the most important aspects of bank financial management. Beginning measures of risk were discussed in the preceding chapter and at the beginning of this chapter. This section elaborates on the types of risks a bank must take to be profitable and on the measurement of such risks. Many of the subsequent chapters in this book emphasize the management of the various risks in banking.

Figure 4-2 shows one way of classifying the risks a bank must take to achieve acceptable returns. There are four broad classes of risk: (1) environmental risks, which the bank must take as a regulated firm that is a key part of the payments system in the United States; (2) management risks, which are caused by the people managing a bank; (3) delivery risks, which are taken as the bank delivers financial services; and (4) financial risks, which are taken in managing the balance sheet.

Environmental risk is a catchall category that refers to risks the bank must guard against but over which it has, at best, limited control. Legislative

## FIGURE 4-2    Classification of Banking Risks

| Banking Characteristics | Risk Class | Risk Category |
|---|---|---|
| Environment | Environmental risks | Legislative risk |
| | | Economic risk |
| | | Competitive risk |
| | | Regulatory risk |
| Human resources | Management risks | Defalcation risk |
| | | Organizational risk |
| | | Ability risk |
| | | Compensation risk |
| Financial services | Delivery risks | Operational risk |
| | | Technological risk |
| | | New-product risk |
| | | Strategic risk |
| Balance sheet | Financial risks | Credit risk |
| | | Liquidity risk |
| | | Interest rate risk |
| | | Leverage risk |

risk refers to changing the laws that affect commercial banks. Economic risks are associated with national and regional economic factors that can affect bank performance materially. Competitive risks arise because most bank products and services can be offered by more and more financial and nonfinancial firms. Finally, regulatory risk involves living with some rules that place a bank at a competitive disadvantage and the ever-present danger that legislators or regulators will change the rules in a manner unfavorable to the bank.

Management risks include the risk of dishonesty by an officer or employee; the risk that the bank will not have an effective organization; the risk that management lacks the ability to make good decisions consistently; and the risk that the bank's compensation plans do not provide appropriate management incentive.

There are four major risks associated with the delivery of financial services. Operational risk, sometimes called burden risk, is the ability of the bank to deliver its financial services in a profitable manner. Both the ability to deliver services and the ability to control the overhead associated with such delivery are important elements. Technological risk refers to the risk of current delivery systems becoming inefficient because of the development of new delivery systems. New-product risk is the danger associated with introducing new products and services. Lower than anticipated demand, higher than anticipated cost, and lack of managerial talent in new markets can lead to severe problems with new products. Strategic risk refers to the ability of the bank to select geographic and product areas that will be profitable for the bank in a complex future environment.

**FIGURE 4-3   Measuring and Managing Financial Risks**

| Financial Risk | Traditional Measures | Lead Measures | Management Techniques |
|---|---|---|---|
| 1. Credit risk | Loans/assets<br>Nonperforming loans/loans<br>Loan losses/loans<br>Reserves for losses/loans | Loan concentration<br>Loan growth<br>High lending rates<br>Reserves to nonper-<br>forming loans | Credit analysis<br>Credit documentation<br>Credit controls<br>Special risk assessment |
| 2. Liquidity risk | Loans/deposits<br>Liquid assets/deposits | Purchased funds<br>Borrowing cost<br>Liquid assets<br>Borrowings/deposits | Liquidity plan<br>Contingency plan<br>Cost/pricing models<br>Development of funding sources |
| 3. Interest rate risk | Interest-sensitive assets/<br>interest-sensitive<br>liabilities<br>Gap | Gap buckets<br>Duration<br>Dynamic gaps | Dynamic gap management<br>Duration analysis |
| 4. Leverage risk | Equity/deposits<br>Equity/assets<br>Capital/assets | Risk-adjusted assets/equity<br>Growth in assets vs.<br>growth in equity | Capital planning<br>Sustainable growth analysis<br>Dividend policy<br>Risk-adjusted capital adequacy |

There are also four primary categories of financial risks. Credit risk, also called default or asset quality risk, is the probability of receiving cash flows from assets when promised. Liquidity risk, or funding risk, indicates the potential ability of a bank to fund its financial needs. Interest rate risk refers to the potential negative effect on the net cash flows and values of assets and liabilities resulting from interest rate changes. Leverage risk, also called capital risk, is a function of the capital cushion a bank has to protect its depositors and borrowers from declines in asset value. The interaction between these risks should be apparent. For example, a bank that has little risk of declines in net asset values and that has low credit and interest rate risks can afford to take more leverage risk.

Figure 4-3 contains traditional and possible lead measures of the four categories of financial risk. The traditional measures were discussed in the preceding chapter and the first part of this chapter. The lead measures are discussed later. Management techniques used to control for these financial risks are listed in Figure 4-3 and discussed in numerous other chapters in this book.

Credit risk is taken, at least to some degree, by nearly all banks and may lead to serious problems or failure if excessive. Traditional measures, such as loans to assets, nonperforming loans to loans, loan losses to loans, and reserves for losses to loans, were previously discussed. These measures tend to suffer because they lag behind the returns gained by taking higher credit risk. Potential lead indicators for credit risk include loan concentration in geographic or industry areas, rapid loan growth, high yields on categories of loans, and the ratio of loan loss reserves to nonperforming loans. Although none of these measures is a perfect predictor, weaknesses in one, and particularly more than one, of the indicators are often a sign of future credit problems. Such management techniques as credit analysis, credit documentation, and credit controls and assessment of such special risks as foreign or fraud risks are discussed in Chapters 9 through 13 of this book.

Traditional measures of liquidity risk, such as the loan-to-deposit ratio or the proportion of liquid assets to deposits, generally tend to focus on the liquidity of assets on the balance sheet. More progressive or lead measures should focus more on actual or potential cash flows to meet cash needs. For example, how much a bank has in purchased or volatile funds may be indicative of the bank's need for liquidity and of how much of its potential borrowing reserve the bank has used. The same may be true for a bank that has to pay higher than average borrowing costs. The difference between liquid assets (a positive for liquidity sources) and borrowings (a use of a bank's borrowing potential) related to some proxy for potential liquidity needs (e.g., volatile funds) may be a good lead indicator of liquidity risk. Management techniques for controlling liquidity risk include a liquidity plan, a contingency plan, a good cost-pricing model, and the continuous development of funding sources. These and other liquidity and funding management techniques are discussed in Chapters 5 and 7.

Interest rate risk has traditionally been measured by the ratio of interest-sensitive assets to interest-sensitive liabilities or the gap or difference between interest-sensitive assets and interest-sensitive liabilities. Problems with these traditional measures include difficulty in selecting the maturity to use as the criterion for sensitivity, concern that reinvestment and changing rates may affect interest sensitivity quickly and measurably, and failure to consider value sensitivity to rate changes. More progressive or lead measures of interest rate risk include gap measures at several different maturity times, or "buckets"; dynamic gap measures based on selected reinvestment and rate assumptions; and duration measures for the bank's assets, liabilities, and non–balance sheet items. Management techniques for controlling and managing interest rate risk are discussed in Chapter 14.

Traditional measures of leverage risk or capital adequacy usually emphasize equity capital as a percentage of assets and may also include equity-to-deposits or capital-to-assets ratios. Weaknesses of these measures include emphasis on static balance sheet values, no recognition of differences in risk among various assets, no recognition of off–balance sheet items, and the use of book rather than market values for both assets and equity. Improved and lead measures of capital risk might include comparisons of risk-adjusted or risk-weighted assets with equity or total capital, measures recognizing off–balance sheet items as part of capital adequacy, and measures comparing the growth in assets or risk-adjusted assets to the growth in equity capital. Measurement and management of leverage risk start with capital planning and include such techniques as sustainable growth analyses, dividend policy effects, and recognition of risk-adjustment capital adequacy. These and similar techniques for controlling and managing leverage risk are discussed in Chapter 8.

## The Appropriate Trade-off between Risks and Returns

The trade-offs between risk and return have already been discussed and were illustrated in the Smithville Bank example in Chapter 3. There is no question that some risks have to be taken to get adequate returns. The big question is how many.

Figure 4-4 gives one approach to answering this trade-off question. The basic emphasis is that bank management should be trying to maximize the value of the owners' investment in the bank. This value maximization involves both returns and risks and the balance between the two. Return variables

**FIGURE 4-4    Elements of Goal of Maximizing Value to Owners**

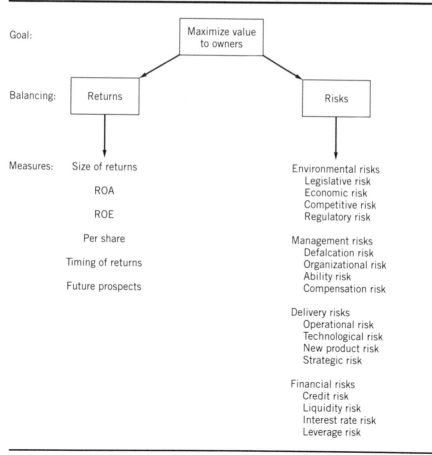

include not only the return measures covered, such as ROA and ROE, but also the timing of returns and future return prospects. The quality or riskiness of returns is related to the size, timing, and future prospects of returns. Returns can be increased and made faster by taking more financial and operating risks. Timing of returns and future prospects are affected by the operating risk and, to a lesser degree, the financial risks. The environmental risks typically do not increase returns but serve as constraints on return and risk decisions.

Management of larger banks or holding companies whose stock trades in an active market should use the market price of its bank's common shares as a guide to balancing risk–return trade-offs. A bank's market price should represent its returns times some multiple that the market places on these returns. The multiple probably depends primarily on the risks the bank has undertaken to obtain its returns and the future prospects of the bank. The bank should take on additional risks if the market price increases, because the increase in returns more than offsets the lower return multiple resulting from the higher risks the bank has taken. If the market price declines, the previous lower returns but lower risk and higher multiple is the preferable alternative.

For banks whose stock is not actively traded, the following equations might provide some guidance. Maximization of value to owners is estimated by discounting net cash benefits to shareholders. This condition can be expressed algebraically as

$$W = \frac{B_1}{(1 + r)^1} + \frac{B_2}{(1 + r)^2} + \frac{B_3}{(1 + r)^3} + \cdots + \frac{B_n}{(1 + r)^n} \tag{4.1}$$

where $W$ is the wealth position of its shareholders; $B$ denotes the net cash benefits to the shareholders in periods 1, 2, 3, . . . , and $n$; and $r$ is the appropriate rate of discount that reflects both the timing and the risk associated with the net cash receipts.

The key variables constituting $B$ and $r$ are shown in the following equations:

$$B = R - (C + O + T) \tag{4.2}$$

$$r = i + p \tag{4.3}$$

In Equation 4.2, $R$ denotes the gross receipts from the financial institution's assets, $C$ represents the costs of its financial liabilities, $O$ is the overhead costs associated with $R$ and $C$, and $T$ is the taxes the bank must pay. Depreciation and other noncash costs are generally a relatively small percentage of $O$, so net cash benefits and net income are reasonably similar for most financial institutions. In Equation 4.3, $i$ is an estimated riskless interest rate that reflects the time value of money, and $p$ is the appropriate risk premium associated with the assets and liabilities of the bank. By substituting Equations 4.2 and 4.3 into Equation 4.1, the following is obtained:

$$W = \frac{R_1 - (C_1 + O_1 + T_1)}{1 + (i + p)^1} + \frac{R_2 - (C_2 + O_2 + T_2)}{1 + (i + p)^2}$$
$$+ \cdots + \frac{R_n - (C_n + O_n + T_n)}{1 + (i + p)^n} \tag{4.4}$$

The interdependent nature of these variables should be evident. $R$ represents the flow of benefits from the stock of assets and $C$ represents the flow of negative benefits (costs from the stock of liabilities) that the bank has created to obtain funds. $O$, which has both fixed and variable components, will depend at least partially on the nature of the asset and liability positions. For taxable institutions, $T$ can be taken as a variable cost that is a function of $R - (C + O)$. While the riskless rate ($i$) is beyond the bank's control, it will tend to be strongly correlated with both $R$ and $C$. Finally, $p$ is a function of the interaction of the risks associated with the assets and liabilities portfolios. Conceptually, it is useful to think of the required return ($i + p$) determined by the market's perception of the riskiness of the bank's asset, liability, and capital composition.

To make prudent financial management decisions, bank managers must consider the combined impact of all relevant variables. For example, if management considers purchasing liabilities of 8 percent and investing the proceeds in assets earning 10 percent, they must take account of changes in $O$, $T$, and $p$ from the transaction. It may well be that, in spite of the positive spread between $R$ and $C$, the total effect, including increases in overhead, taxes, or risks, may actually reduce the wealth of the bank's shareholders.

## Uniform Bank Performance Reports

The uniform bank performance report (UBPR) is probably the most comprehensive information source for analyzing commercial banks. A UBPR is prepared annually for each insured commercial bank by the Federal Financial Institutions Examinations Council (FFIEC). The UBPR provides a detailed five-year financial report on a bank and a similar profile for a peer group of banks that can be used for comparative purposes. The FFIEC prepares these reports from a data base of financial information from filed quarterly reports.

The three major sections and the principal subsections of each are listed in Table 4-4. Six sample pages from a demonstration UBPR appear as Table 4-5. The summary ratios section, page 1 of the UBPR, is used as an example. Notice that the summary ratios are grouped into five categories, with three measures reported for each ratio:

1. The selected bank's ratio.
2. Mean ratios for the peer group.
3. Percentile ranking of the requested bank's ratio within the peer group.

The most efficient use of a UBPR probably comes from studying this summary ratio section, identifying potential strengths and weaknesses, and

---

**TABLE 4-4  Typical UBPR's Table of Contents**

---

**TABLE 4-5**

---

```
CERT # 99999  DSB # 99999999      XXXXXXXXXXXXXXXXXXXXXXXXX(BANK NAME)XXXXXXXXXXXXXXXXXXXXXX  XXXXXXXXXXXXXX(CITYST)XXXXXXXXXXX
CHARTER # 99999                                        SUMMARY RATIOS                                          PAGE 01

                                  MM/DD/YY              MM/DD/YY              MM/DD/YY              MM/DD/YY          MM/DD/YY
                              ----------------      ----------------      ----------------      --------------    --------------
AVERAGE ASSETS ($000)             $999999999            $999999999            $999999999            $999999999       $999999999
NET INCOME ($000)                 $999999999            $999999999            $999999999            $999999999       $999999999
NUMBER OF BANKS IN PEER GROUP     $999999999            $999999999            $999999999            $999999999       $999999999

EARNINGS AND PROFITABILITY    BANK  PEER 99 PCT    BANK  PEER 99 PCT    BANK  PEER 99 PCT    BANK  PEER 99     BANK  PEER 99
--------------------------    ------- ------- ---  ------- ------- ---  ------- ------- ---  ------- -------   ------- -------
PERCENT OF AVERAGE ASSETS:
  INTEREST INCOME (TE)        $999.99 $999.99  99  $999.99 $999.99  99  $999.99 $999.99  99  $999.99 $999.99   $999.99 $999.99
  - INTEREST EXPENSE          $999.99 $999.99  99  $999.99 $999.99  99  $999.99 $999.99  99  $999.99 $999.99   $999.99 $999.99
  NET INTEREST INCOME (TE)    $999.99 $999.99  99  $999.99 $999.99  99  $999.99 $999.99  99  $999.99 $999.99   $999.99 $999.99
  + NON-INTEREST INCOME       $999.99 $999.99  99  $999.99 $999.99  99  $999.99 $999.99  99  $999.99 $999.99   $999.99 $999.99
  - OVERHEAD EXPENSE          $999.99 $999.99  99  $999.99 $999.99  99  $999.99 $999.99  99  $999.99 $999.99   $999.99 $999.99
  - PROVISION: LOAN&LEASE LOSSES $999.99 $999.99 99 $999.99 $999.99 99  $999.99 $999.99  99  $999.99 $999.99   $999.99 $999.99
  = PRETAX OPERATING INCOME (TE) $999.99 $999.99 99 $999.99 $999.99 99  $999.99 $999.99  99  $999.99 $999.99   $999.99 $999.99
  + SECURITIES GAINS (LOSSES) $999.99 $999.99  99  $999.99 $999.99  99  $999.99 $999.99  99  $999.99 $999.99   $999.99 $999.99
  = PRETAX NET OPERATING INC(TE) $999.99 $999.99 99 $999.99 $999.99 99  $999.99 $999.99  99  $999.99 $999.99   $999.99 $999.99
  NET OPERATING INCOME        $999.99 $999.99  99  $999.99 $999.99  99  $999.99 $999.99  99  $999.99 $999.99   $999.99 $999.99
  ADJUSTED NET OPERATING INCOME $999.99 $999.99 99 $999.99 $999.99  99  $999.99 $999.99  99  $999.99 $999.99   $999.99 $999.99
  ADJUSTED NET INCOME         $999.99 $999.99  99  $999.99 $999.99  99  $999.99 $999.99  99  $999.99 $999.99   $999.99 $999.99
  NET INCOME                  $999.99 $999.99  99  $999.99 $999.99  99  $999.99 $999.99  99  $999.99 $999.99   $999.99 $999.99

MARGIN ANALYSIS:
AVG EARNING ASSETS TO AVG ASSTS $999.99 $999.99 99 $999.99 $999.99 99  $999.99 $999.99  99  $999.99 $999.99   $999.99 $999.99
AVG INT-BEARING FUNDS TO AV AST $999.99 $999.99 99 $999.99 $999.99 99  $999.99 $999.99  99  $999.99 $999.99   $999.99 $999.99
INT INC (TE) TO AVG EARN ASSETS $999.99 $999.99 99 $999.99 $999.99 99  $999.99 $999.99  99  $999.99 $999.99   $999.99 $999.99
INT EXPENSE TO AVG EARN ASSETS $999.99 $999.99 99 $999.99 $999.99 99  $999.99 $999.99  99  $999.99 $999.99   $999.99 $999.99
NET INT INC-TE TO AVG EARN ASST $999.99 $999.99 99 $999.99 $999.99 99  $999.99 $999.99  99  $999.99 $999.99   $999.99 $999.99

LOAN & LEASE ANALYSIS
---------------------
NET LOSS TO AVERAGE TOTAL LN&LS $999.99 $999.99 99 $999.99 $999.99 99  $999.99 $999.99  99  $999.99 $999.99   $999.99 $999.99
EARNINGS COVERAGE OF NET LOSS(X) $999.99 $999.99 99 $999.99 $999.99 99 $999.99 $999.99  99  $999.99 $999.99   $999.99 $999.99
LOSS RESERVE TO NET LOSSES (X)  $999.99 $999.99 99 $999.99 $999.99 99  $999.99 $999.99  99  $999.99 $999.99   $999.99 $999.99
LOSS RESERVE TO TOTAL LN&LS     $999.99 $999.99 99 $999.99 $999.99 99  $999.99 $999.99  99  $999.99 $999.99   $999.99 $999.99
% NONCURRENT LOANS & LEASES     $999.99 $999.99 99 $999.99 $999.99 99  $999.99 $999.99  99  $999.99 $999.99   $999.99 $999.99
```

**TABLE 4-5**   (continued)

```
LIQUIDITY
--------
VOLATILE LIABILITY DEPENDENCE  $999.99 $999.99  99    $999.99 $999.99  99    $999.99 $999.99  99    $999.99 $999.99    $999.99 $999.99
NET LOANS & LEASES TO ASSETS   $999.99 $999.99  99    $999.99 $999.99  99    $999.99 $999.99  99    $999.99 $999.99    $999.99 $999.99

CAPITALIZATION
--------------
PRIMARY CAP TO ADJ AVG ASSETS  $999.99 $999.99  99    $999.99 $999.99  99    $999.99 $999.99  99    $999.99 $999.99    $999.99 $999.99
CASH DIVIDENDS TO NET INCOME   $999.99 $999.99  99    $999.99 $999.99  99    $999.99 $999.99  99    $999.99 $999.99    $999.99 $999.99
RETAIN EARNS TO AVG TOTAL EQUITY $999.99 $999.99 99   $999.99 $999.99  99    $999.99 $999.99  99    $999.99 $999.99    $999.99 $999.99

GROWTH RATES
------------
ASSETS                         $999.99 $999.99  99    $999.99 $999.99  99    $999.99 $999.99  99    $999.99 $999.99    $999.99 $999.99
PRIMARY CAPITAL                $999.99 $999.99  99    $999.99 $999.99  99    $999.99 $999.99  99    $999.99 $999.99    $999.99 $999.99
NET LOANS & LEASES             $999.99 $999.99  99    $999.99 $999.99  99    $999.99 $999.99  99    $999.99 $999.99    $999.99 $999.99
VOLATILE LIABILITIES           $999.99 $999.99  99    $999.99 $999.99  99    $999.99 $999.99  99    $999.99 $999.99    $999.99 $999.99
```

```
note:  this UBPR page layout is for the FFIEC 031 call reporter
CERT # 99999  DSB # 99999999      XXXXXXXXXXXXXXXXXXXXXXXXXX(BANK NAME)XXXXXXXXXXXXXXXXXXXXXXXX XXXXXXXXXXXXX(CITYST)XXXXXXXXXXXXXX
CHARTER # 99999                   INCOME STATEMENT - REVENUES AND EXPENSES ($000)                            PAGE 02
```

|                              | MM/DD/YY   | MM/DD/YY   | MM/DD/YY   | MM/DD/YY   | MM/DD/YY   | PERCENT CHANGE<br>--------------<br>1 YEAR |
|------------------------------|-----------|-----------|-----------|-----------|-----------|--------|
| INTEREST AND FEES ON LOANS   | $999999999 | $999999999 | $999999999 | $999999999 | $999999999 | $999.99 |
| INCOME FROM LEASE FINANCING  | $999999999 | $999999999 | $999999999 | $999999999 | $999999999 | $999.99 |
| FULLY TAXABLE                | $999999999 | $999999999 | $999999999 | $999999999 | $999999999 | $999.99 |
| TAX-EXEMPT                   | $999999999 | $999999999 | $999999999 | $999999999 | $999999999 | $999.99 |
| ESTIMATED TAX BENEFIT        | $999999999 | $999999999 | $999999999 | $999999999 | $999999999 |         |
| INCOME ON LOANS & LEASES (TE)| $999999999 | $999999999 | $999999999 | $999999999 | $999999999 | $999.99 |
| U.S. TREAS & AGENCY SECURITIES | $999999999 | $999999999 | $999999999 | $999999999 | $999999999 | $999.99 |
| TAX-EXEMPT SECURITIES INCOME | $999999999 | $999999999 | $999999999 | $999999999 | $999999999 | $999.99 |
| ESTIMATED TAX BENEFIT        | $999999999 | $999999999 | $999999999 | $999999999 | $999999999 |         |
| OTHER SECURITIES INCOME      | $999999999 | $999999999 | $999999999 | $999999999 | $999999999 | $999.99 |
| INVESTMT INTEREST INCOME (TE)| $999999999 | $999999999 | $999999999 | $999999999 | $999999999 | $999.99 |
| INTEREST ON DUE FROM BANKS   | $999999999 | $999999999 | $999999999 | $999999999 | $999999999 | $999.99 |
| INT ON FED FUNDS SOLD & RESALES | $999999999 | $999999999 | $999999999 | $999999999 | $999999999 | $999.99 |
| TRADING ACCOUNT INCOME       | $999999999 | $999999999 | $999999999 | $999999999 | $999999999 | $999.99 |
| TOTAL INTEREST INCOME (TE)   | $999999999 | $999999999 | $999999999 | $999999999 | $999999999 | $999.99 |
| INT ON DEPOSITS IN FOREIGN OFF | $999999999 | $999999999 | $999999999 | $999999999 | $999999999 | $999.99 |
| INTEREST ON CD'S OVER $100M  | $999999999 | $999999999 | $999999999 | $999999999 | $999999999 | $999.99 |
| INTEREST ON ALL OTHER DEPOSITS | $999999999 | $999999999 | $999999999 | $999999999 | $999999999 | $999.99 |
| INT ON FED FUNDS PURCH & REPOS | $999999999 | $999999999 | $999999999 | $999999999 | $999999999 | $999.99 |
| INT BORROWED MONEY (+NOTE OPT) | $999999999 | $999999999 | $999999999 | $999999999 | $999999999 | $999.99 |
| INT ON MORTGAGES & LEASES    | $999999999 | $999999999 | $999999999 | $999999999 | $999999999 | $999.99 |
| INT ON SUB NOTES & DEBENTURES | $999999999 | $999999999 | $999999999 | $999999999 | $999999999 | $999.99 |
| TOTAL INTEREST EXPENSE       | $999999999 | $999999999 | $999999999 | $999999999 | $999999999 | $999.99 |
| NET INTEREST INCOME (TE)     | $999999999 | $999999999 | $999999999 | $999999999 | $999999999 | $999.99 |
| NON-INTEREST INCOME          | $999999999 | $999999999 | $999999999 | $999999999 | $999999999 | $999.99 |
| ADJUSTED OPERATING INC (TE)  | $999999999 | $999999999 | $999999999 | $999999999 | $999999999 | $999.99 |
| OVERHEAD EXPENSE             | $999999999 | $999999999 | $999999999 | $999999999 | $999999999 | $999.99 |
| PROVISION FOR LOAN&LEASE LOSSES | $999999999 | $999999999 | $999999999 | $999999999 | $999999999 | $999.99 |
| PROV: ALLOCATED TRANSFER RISK | $999999999 | $999999999 | $999999999 | $999999999 | $999999999 |         |
| PRETAX OPERATING INCOME (TE) | $999999999 | $999999999 | $999999999 | $999999999 | $999999999 | $999.99 |
| SECURITIES GAINS (LOSSES)    | $999999999 | $999999999 | $999999999 | $999999999 | $999999999 | $999.99 |
| PRETAX NET OPERATING INC (TE)| $999999999 | $999999999 | $999999999 | $999999999 | $999999999 | $999.99 |
| APPLICABLE INCOME TAXES      | $999999999 | $999999999 | $999999999 | $999999999 | $999999999 |         |
| CURRENT TAX EQUIV ADJUSTMENT | $999999999 | $999999999 | $999999999 | $999999999 | $999999999 |         |
| OTHER TAX EQUIV ADJUSTMENTS  | $999999999 | $999999999 | $999999999 | $999999999 | $999999999 |         |
| APPLICABLE INCOME TAXES (TE) | $999999999 | $999999999 | $999999999 | $999999999 | $999999999 |         |
| NET OPERATING INCOME         | $999999999 | $999999999 | $999999999 | $999999999 | $999999999 | $999.99 |
| NET EXTRAORDINARY ITEMS      | $999999999 | $999999999 | $999999999 | $999999999 | $999999999 |         |
| NET INCOME                   | $999999999 | $999999999 | $999999999 | $999999999 | $999999999 | $999.99 |
| CASH DIVIDENDS DECLARED      | $999999999 | $999999999 | $999999999 | $999999999 | $999999999 | $999.99 |
| RETAINED EARNINGS            | $999999999 | $999999999 | $999999999 | $999999999 | $999999999 | $999.99 |
| MEMO: NET INTERNATIONAL INCOME | $999999999 | $999999999 | $999999999 | $999999999 | $999999999 | $999.99 |

**TABLE 4-5**    *(continued)*

```
note:  this UBPR page layout is for the FFIEC 031 call reporter
CERT # 99999  DSB # 99999999    XXXXXXXXXXXXXXXXXXXXXXXX(BANK NAME)XXXXXXXXXXXXXXXXXXXXXX XXXXXXXXXXXX(CITYST)XXXXXXXXXXXXXX
CHARTER # 99999                 NON-INTEREST INCOME AND EXPENSES ($000) AND YIELDS                      PAGE 03
```

| NON-INTEREST INCOME & EXPENSES | MM/DD/YY | MM/DD/YY | MM/DD/YY | MM/DD/YY | MM/DD/YY |
|---|---|---|---|---|---|
| FIDUCIARY ACTIVITIES | $999999999 | $999999999 | $999999999 | $999999999 | $999999999 |
| DEPOSIT SERVICE CHARGES | $999999999 | $999999999 | $999999999 | $999999999 | $999999999 |
| TRADING COMMISSIONS & FEES | $999999999 | $999999999 | $999999999 | $999999999 | $999999999 |
| FOREIGN EXCHANGE TRADING | $999999999 | $999999999 | $999999999 | $999999999 | $999999999 |
| OTHER FOREIGN TRANSACTIONS | $999999999 | $999999999 | $999999999 | $999999999 | $999999999 |
| OTHER NONINTEREST INCOME | $999999999 | $999999999 | $999999999 | $999999999 | $999999999 |
| NONINTEREST INCOME | $999999999 | $999999999 | $999999999 | $999999999 | $999999999 |
| PERSONNEL EXPENSE | $999999999 | $999999999 | $999999999 | $999999999 | $999999999 |
| OCCUPANCY EXPENSE | $999999999 | $999999999 | $999999999 | $999999999 | $999999999 |
| OTHER OPER EXP(INCL INTANGIBLES) | $999999999 | $999999999 | $999999999 | $999999999 | $999999999 |
| TOTAL OVERHEAD EXPENSE | $999999999 | $999999999 | $999999999 | $999999999 | $999999999 |
| :INCLUDING INT ON MORTG & LEASE | $999999999 | $999999999 | $999999999 | $999999999 | $999999999 |
| DOMESTIC BANKING OFFICES (#) | $999999999 | $999999999 | $999999999 | $999999999 | $999999999 |
| FOREIGN BRANCHES (#) | $999999999 | $999999999 | $999999999 | $999999999 | $999999999 |
| AVG ASSETS PER DOMESTIC OFFICE | $999999999 | $999999999 | $999999999 | $999999999 | $999999999 |
| NUMBER OF EQUIV EMPLOYEES | $999999999 | $999999999 | $999999999 | $999999999 | $999999999 |

| PERCENT OF AVERAGE ASSETS | BANK | PEER 99 | PCT | BANK | PEER 99 | PCT | BANK | PEER 99 | PCT | BANK | PEER 99 | BANK | PEER 99 |
|---|---|---|---|---|---|---|---|---|---|---|---|---|---|
| PERSONNEL EXPENSE | $999.99 | $999.99 | 99 | $999.99 | $999.99 | 99 | $999.99 | $999.99 | 99 | $999.99 | $999.99 | $999.99 | $999.99 |
| OCCUPANCY EXPENSE | $999.99 | $999.99 | 99 | $999.99 | $999.99 | 99 | $999.99 | $999.99 | 99 | $999.99 | $999.99 | $999.99 | $999.99 |
| OTHER OPER EXP(INCL INTANGIBLES) | $999.99 | $999.99 | 99 | $999.99 | $999.99 | 99 | $999.99 | $999.99 | 99 | $999.99 | $999.99 | $999.99 | $999.99 |
| TOTAL OVERHEAD EXPENSE | $999.99 | $999.99 | 99 | $999.99 | $999.99 | 99 | $999.99 | $999.99 | 99 | $999.99 | $999.99 | $999.99 | $999.99 |
| :INCLUDING INT ON MORTG & LEASES | $999.99 | $999.99 | 99 | $999.99 | $999.99 | 99 | $999.99 | $999.99 | 99 | $999.99 | $999.99 | $999.99 | $999.99 |
| OVERHEAD LESS NON-INT INCOME | $999.99 | $999.99 | 99 | $999.99 | $999.99 | 99 | $999.99 | $999.99 | 99 | $999.99 | $999.99 | $999.99 | $999.99 |
| OTHER INCOME & EXPENSE RATIOS: | | | | | | | | | | | | | |
| AVG PERSONNEL EXP PER EMPL($000) | $999.99 | $999.99 | 99 | $999.99 | $999.99 | 99 | $999.99 | $999.99 | 99 | $999.99 | $999.99 | $999.99 | $999.99 |
| AVG ASSETS PER EMPL ($MILLION) | $999.99 | $999.99 | 99 | $999.99 | $999.99 | 99 | $999.99 | $999.99 | 99 | $999.99 | $999.99 | $999.99 | $999.99 |
| MARGINAL TAX RATE | $999.99 | $999.99 | 99 | $999.99 | $999.99 | 99 | $999.99 | $999.99 | 99 | $999.99 | $999.99 | $999.99 | $999.99 |

| YIELD ON OR COST OF: | BANK | PEER 99 | PCT | BANK | PEER 99 | PCT | BANK | PEER 99 | PCT | BANK | PEER 99 | BANK | PEER 99 |
|---|---|---|---|---|---|---|---|---|---|---|---|---|---|
| TOTAL LOANS & LEASES (TE) | $999.99 | $999.99 | 99 | $999.99 | $999.99 | 99 | $999.99 | $999.99 | 99 | $999.99 | $999.99 | $999.99 | $999.99 |
| LOANS IN DOMESTIC OFFICES | $999.99 | $999.99 | 99 | $999.99 | $999.99 | 99 | $999.99 | $999.99 | 99 | $999.99 | $999.99 | $999.99 | $999.99 |
| REAL ESTATE | $999.99 | $999.99 | 99 | $999.99 | $999.99 | 99 | $999.99 | $999.99 | 99 | $999.99 | $999.99 | $999.99 | $999.99 |
| COMMERCIAL & INDUSTRIAL | $999.99 | $999.99 | 99 | $999.99 | $999.99 | 99 | $999.99 | $999.99 | 99 | $999.99 | $999.99 | $999.99 | $999.99 |
| INDIVIDUAL | $999.99 | $999.99 | 99 | $999.99 | $999.99 | 99 | $999.99 | $999.99 | 99 | $999.99 | $999.99 | $999.99 | $999.99 |
| AGRICULTURAL | $999.99 | $999.99 | 99 | $999.99 | $999.99 | 99 | $999.99 | $999.99 | 99 | $999.99 | $999.99 | $999.99 | $999.99 |
| LOANS IN FOREIGN OFFICES | $999.99 | $999.99 | 99 | $999.99 | $999.99 | 99 | $999.99 | $999.99 | 99 | $999.99 | $999.99 | $999.99 | $999.99 |
| TOTAL INVESTMENT SECURITIES (TE) | $999.99 | $999.99 | 99 | $999.99 | $999.99 | 99 | $999.99 | $999.99 | 99 | $999.99 | $999.99 | $999.99 | $999.99 |
| U.S. TREASURIES & AGENCIES | $999.99 | $999.99 | 99 | $999.99 | $999.99 | 99 | $999.99 | $999.99 | 99 | $999.99 | $999.99 | $999.99 | $999.99 |
| TAX-EXEMPT MUNICIPALS (BOOK) | $999.99 | $999.99 | 99 | $999.99 | $999.99 | 99 | $999.99 | $999.99 | 99 | $999.99 | $999.99 | $999.99 | $999.99 |
| TAX-EXEMPT MUNICIPALS (TE) | $999.99 | $999.99 | 99 | $999.99 | $999.99 | 99 | $999.99 | $999.99 | 99 | $999.99 | $999.99 | $999.99 | $999.99 |
| OTHER SECURITIES | $999.99 | $999.99 | 99 | $999.99 | $999.99 | 99 | $999.99 | $999.99 | 99 | $999.99 | $999.99 | $999.99 | $999.99 |
| INTEREST-BEARING BANK BALANCES | $999.99 | $999.99 | 99 | $999.99 | $999.99 | 99 | $999.99 | $999.99 | 99 | $999.99 | $999.99 | $999.99 | $999.99 |
| FEDERAL FUNDS SOLD & RESALES | $999.99 | $999.99 | 99 | $999.99 | $999.99 | 99 | $999.99 | $999.99 | 99 | $999.99 | $999.99 | $999.99 | $999.99 |
| TOTAL INT-BEARING DEPOSITS | $999.99 | $999.99 | 99 | $999.99 | $999.99 | 99 | $999.99 | $999.99 | 99 | $999.99 | $999.99 | $999.99 | $999.99 |
| TRANSACTION ACCOUNTS | $999.99 | $999.99 | 99 | $999.99 | $999.99 | 99 | $999.99 | $999.99 | 99 | $999.99 | $999.99 | $999.99 | $999.99 |
| MONEY MARKET DEPOSIT ACCOUNTS | $999.99 | $999.99 | 99 | $999.99 | $999.99 | 99 | $999.99 | $999.99 | 99 | $999.99 | $999.99 | $999.99 | $999.99 |
| OTHER SAVINGS DEPOSITS | $999.99 | $999.99 | 99 | $999.99 | $999.99 | 99 | $999.99 | $999.99 | 99 | $999.99 | $999.99 | $999.99 | $999.99 |
| LARGE CERTIFICATES OF DEPOSIT | $999.99 | $999.99 | 99 | $999.99 | $999.99 | 99 | $999.99 | $999.99 | 99 | $999.99 | $999.99 | $999.99 | $999.99 |
| ALL OTHER TIME DEPOSITS | $999.99 | $999.99 | 99 | $999.99 | $999.99 | 99 | $999.99 | $999.99 | 99 | $999.99 | $999.99 | $999.99 | $999.99 |
| FOREIGN OFFICE DEPOSITS | $999.99 | $999.99 | 99 | $999.99 | $999.99 | 99 | $999.99 | $999.99 | 99 | $999.99 | $999.99 | $999.99 | $999.99 |
| FEDERAL FUNDS PURCHASED & REPOS | $999.99 | $999.99 | 99 | $999.99 | $999.99 | 99 | $999.99 | $999.99 | 99 | $999.99 | $999.99 | $999.99 | $999.99 |
| OTHER BORROWED MONEY | $999.99 | $999.99 | 99 | $999.99 | $999.99 | 99 | $999.99 | $999.99 | 99 | $999.99 | $999.99 | $999.99 | $999.99 |
| SUBORDINATED NOTES & DEBENTURES | $999.99 | $999.99 | 99 | $999.99 | $999.99 | 99 | $999.99 | $999.99 | 99 | $999.99 | $999.99 | $999.99 | $999.99 |
| ALL INTEREST-BEARING FUNDS | $999.99 | $999.99 | 99 | $999.99 | $999.99 | 99 | $999.99 | $999.99 | 99 | $999.99 | $999.99 | $999.99 | $999.99 |

```
CERT # 99999  DSB # 99999999    XXXXXXXXXXXXXXXXXXXXXXXX(BANK NAME)XXXXXXXXXXXXXXXXXXXXXX XXXXXXXXXXXX(CITYST)XXXXXXXXXXXXXX
CHARTER # 99999                 BALANCE SHEET - PERCENTAGE COMPOSITION OF ASSETS AND LIABILITIES         PAGE 06
```

| | MM/DD/YY | | | MM/DD/YY | | | MM/DD/YY | | | MM/DD/YY | | MM/DD/YY | |
|---|---|---|---|---|---|---|---|---|---|---|---|---|---|
| ASSETS, PERCENT OF AVG ASSETS | BANK | PEER 99 | PCT | BANK | PEER 99 | PCT | BANK | PEER 99 | PCT | BANK | PEER 99 | BANK | PEER 99 |
| TOTAL LOANS | $999.99 | $999.99 | 99 | $999.99 | $999.99 | 99 | $999.99 | $999.99 | 99 | $999.99 | $999.99 | $999.99 | $999.99 |
| LEASE FINANCING RECEIVABLES | $999.99 | $999.99 | 99 | $999.99 | $999.99 | 99 | $999.99 | $999.99 | 99 | $999.99 | $999.99 | $999.99 | $999.99 |
| LESS:  RESERVES | $999.99 | $999.99 | 99 | $999.99 | $999.99 | 99 | $999.99 | $999.99 | 99 | $999.99 | $999.99 | $999.99 | $999.99 |
| NET LOANS & LEASES | $999.99 | $999.99 | 99 | $999.99 | $999.99 | 99 | $999.99 | $999.99 | 99 | $999.99 | $999.99 | $999.99 | $999.99 |
| SECURITIES OVER 1 YEAR | $999.99 | $999.99 | 99 | $999.99 | $999.99 | 99 | $999.99 | $999.99 | 99 | $999.99 | $999.99 | $999.99 | $999.99 |
| SUBTOTAL | $999.99 | $999.99 | 99 | $999.99 | $999.99 | 99 | $999.99 | $999.99 | 99 | $999.99 | $999.99 | $999.99 | $999.99 |
| INTEREST-BEARING BANK BALANCES | $999.99 | $999.99 | 99 | $999.99 | $999.99 | 99 | $999.99 | $999.99 | 99 | $999.99 | $999.99 | $999.99 | $999.99 |
| FEDERAL FUNDS SOLD & RESALES | $999.99 | $999.99 | 99 | $999.99 | $999.99 | 99 | $999.99 | $999.99 | 99 | $999.99 | $999.99 | $999.99 | $999.99 |
| TRADING ACCOUNT ASSETS | $999.99 | $999.99 | 99 | $999.99 | $999.99 | 99 | $999.99 | $999.99 | 99 | $999.99 | $999.99 | $999.99 | $999.99 |

## TABLE 4-5    *(continued)*

| | | | | | | | | | | | | | | | | | | |
|---|---|---|---|---|---|---|---|---|---|---|---|---|---|---|---|---|---|---|
| DEBT SECURITIES 1 YEAR & LESS | $999.99 | $999.99 | 99 | | $999.99 | $999.99 | 99 | | $999.99 | $999.99 | 99 | | $999.99 | $999.99 | | $999.99 | $999.99 |
| TEMPORARY INVESTMENTS | $999.99 | $999.99 | 99 | | $999.99 | $999.99 | 99 | | $999.99 | $999.99 | 99 | | $999.99 | $999.99 | | $999.99 | $999.99 |
| TOTAL EARNING ASSETS | $999.99 | $999.99 | 99 | | $999.99 | $999.99 | 99 | | $999.99 | $999.99 | 99 | | $999.99 | $999.99 | | $999.99 | $999.99 |
| NON-INT CASH & DUE FROM BANKS | $999.99 | $999.99 | 99 | | $999.99 | $999.99 | 99 | | $999.99 | $999.99 | 99 | | $999.99 | $999.99 | | $999.99 | $999.99 |
| PREMISES, FIX ASSTS & CAP LEASES | $999.99 | $999.99 | 99 | | $999.99 | $999.99 | 99 | | $999.99 | $999.99 | 99 | | $999.99 | $999.99 | | $999.99 | $999.99 |
| OTHER REAL ESTATE OWNED | $999.99 | $999.99 | 99 | | $999.99 | $999.99 | 99 | | $999.99 | $999.99 | 99 | | $999.99 | $999.99 | | $999.99 | $999.99 |
| ACCEPTANCES & OTHER ASSETS | $999.99 | $999.99 | 99 | | $999.99 | $999.99 | 99 | | $999.99 | $999.99 | 99 | | $999.99 | $999.99 | | $999.99 | $999.99 |
| SUBTOTAL | $999.99 | $999.99 | 99 | | $999.99 | $999.99 | 99 | | $999.99 | $999.99 | 99 | | $999.99 | $999.99 | | $999.99 | $999.99 |
| TOTAL ASSETS | $999.99 | $999.99 | 99 | | $999.99 | $999.99 | 99 | | $999.99 | $999.99 | 99 | | $999.99 | $999.99 | | $999.99 | $999.99 |
| STANDBY LETTERS OF CREDIT | $999.99 | $999.99 | 99 | | $999.99 | $999.99 | 99 | | $999.99 | $999.99 | 99 | | $999.99 | $999.99 | | $999.99 | $999.99 |

LIABILITIES, PERCENT OF AVG ASST

| | | | | | | | | | | | | | | | | | | |
|---|---|---|---|---|---|---|---|---|---|---|---|---|---|---|---|---|---|---|
| DEMAND DEPOSITS | $999.99 | $999.99 | 99 | | $999.99 | $999.99 | 99 | | $999.99 | $999.99 | 99 | | $999.99 | $999.99 | | $999.99 | $999.99 |
| ALL NOW & ATS ACCOUNTS | $999.99 | $999.99 | 99 | | $999.99 | $999.99 | 99 | | $999.99 | $999.99 | 99 | | $999.99 | $999.99 | | $999.99 | $999.99 |
| MMDA SAVINGS | $999.99 | $999.99 | 99 | | $999.99 | $999.99 | 99 | | $999.99 | $999.99 | 99 | | $999.99 | $999.99 | | $999.99 | $999.99 |
| OTHER SAVINGS DEPOSITS | $999.99 | $999.99 | 99 | | $999.99 | $999.99 | 99 | | $999.99 | $999.99 | 99 | | $999.99 | $999.99 | | $999.99 | $999.99 |
| TIME DEPOSITS UNDER $100M | $999.99 | $999.99 | 99 | | $999.99 | $999.99 | 99 | | $999.99 | $999.99 | 99 | | $999.99 | $999.99 | | $999.99 | $999.99 |
| CORE DEPOSITS | $999.99 | $999.99 | 99 | | $999.99 | $999.99 | 99 | | $999.99 | $999.99 | 99 | | $999.99 | $999.99 | | $999.99 | $999.99 |
| TIME DEPOSITS OVER $100M | $999.99 | $999.99 | 99 | | $999.99 | $999.99 | 99 | | $999.99 | $999.99 | 99 | | $999.99 | $999.99 | | $999.99 | $999.99 |
| DEPOSITS IN FOREIGN OFFICES | $999.99 | $999.99 | 99 | | $999.99 | $999.99 | 99 | | $999.99 | $999.99 | 99 | | $999.99 | $999.99 | | $999.99 | $999.99 |
| FEDERAL FUNDS PURCH & REPOS | $999.99 | $999.99 | 99 | | $999.99 | $999.99 | 99 | | $999.99 | $999.99 | 99 | | $999.99 | $999.99 | | $999.99 | $999.99 |
| OTHER BORROWINGS (+NOTE OPT) | $999.99 | $999.99 | 99 | | $999.99 | $999.99 | 99 | | $999.99 | $999.99 | 99 | | $999.99 | $999.99 | | $999.99 | $999.99 |
| VOLATILE LIABILITIES | $999.99 | $999.99 | 99 | | $999.99 | $999.99 | 99 | | $999.99 | $999.99 | 99 | | $999.99 | $999.99 | | $999.99 | $999.99 |
| ACCEPTANCES & OTHER LIABILITIES | $999.99 | $999.99 | 99 | | $999.99 | $999.99 | 99 | | $999.99 | $999.99 | 99 | | $999.99 | $999.99 | | $999.99 | $999.99 |
| TOTAL LIABILITIES(INCL MORTG) | $999.99 | $999.99 | 99 | | $999.99 | $999.99 | 99 | | $999.99 | $999.99 | 99 | | $999.99 | $999.99 | | $999.99 | $999.99 |
| SUBORDINATED NOTES & DEBENTURES | $999.99 | $999.99 | 99 | | $999.99 | $999.99 | 99 | | $999.99 | $999.99 | 99 | | $999.99 | $999.99 | | $999.99 | $999.99 |
| ALL COMMON & PREFERRED CAPITAL | $999.99 | $999.99 | 99 | | $999.99 | $999.99 | 99 | | $999.99 | $999.99 | 99 | | $999.99 | $999.99 | | $999.99 | $999.99 |
| TOTAL LIABILITIES & CAPITAL | $999.99 | $999.99 | 99 | | $999.99 | $999.99 | 99 | | $999.99 | $999.99 | 99 | | $999.99 | $999.99 | | $999.99 | $999.99 |
| TOTAL BROKERED DEPOSITS | $999.99 | $999.99 | 99 | | $999.99 | $999.99 | 99 | | $999.99 | $999.99 | 99 | | $999.99 | $999.99 | | $999.99 | $999.99 |

CERT # 99999   DSB # 99999999
CHARTER # 99999

XXXXXXXXXXXXXXXXXXXXXXXXXX(BANK NAME)XXXXXXXXXXXXXXXXXXXXXXXXXX XXXXXXXXXXXXXX(CITYST)XXXXXXXXXXXXXX
ANALYSIS OF LOAN & LEASE LOSS RESERVE AND LOAN MIX
PAGE 07

| CHANGE: LOAN&LEASE RESERVE($000) | MM/DD/YY | MM/DD/YY | MM/DD/YY | MM/DD/YY | MM/DD/YY |
|---|---|---|---|---|---|
| BEGINNING BALANCE | $999999999 | $999999999 | $999999999 | $999999999 | $999999999 |
| GROSS LOAN & LEASE LOSSES | $999999999 | $999999999 | $999999999 | $999999999 | $999999999 |
| RECOVERIES | $999999999 | $999999999 | $999999999 | $999999999 | $999999999 |
| NET LOAN & LEASE LOSSES | $999999999 | $999999999 | $999999999 | $999999999 | $999999999 |
| PROVISION FOR LOAN & LEASE LOSS | $999999999 | $999999999 | $999999999 | $999999999 | $999999999 |
| OTHER ADJUSTMENTS | $999999999 | $999999999 | $999999999 | $999999999 | $999999999 |
| ENDING BALANCE | $999999999 | $999999999 | $999999999 | $999999999 | $999999999 |
| NET ATRR CHARGE-OFFS | $999999999 | $999999999 | $999999999 | $999999999 | $999999999 |
| OTHER ATRR CHARGES (NET) | $999999999 | $999999999 | $999999999 | $999999999 | $999999999 |
| AVERAGE TOTAL LOANS & LEASES | $999999999 | $999999999 | $999999999 | $999999999 | $999999999 |

| ANALYSIS RATIOS | BANK | PEER 99 | PCT | BANK | PEER 99 | PCT | BANK | PEER 99 | PCT | BANK | PEER 99 | BANK | PEER 99 |
|---|---|---|---|---|---|---|---|---|---|---|---|---|---|
| LOSS PROVISION TO AVERAGE ASSETS | $999.99 | $999.99 | | $999.99 | $999.99 | | $999.99 | $999.99 | | $999.99 | $999.99 | $999.99 | $999.99 |
| LOSS PROVISION TO AVG TOT LN&LS | $999.99 | $999.99 | 99 | $999.99 | $999.99 | 99 | $999.99 | $999.99 | 99 | $999.99 | $999.99 | $999.99 | $999.99 |
| NET LOSS TO AVERAGE TOTAL LN&LS | $999.99 | $999.99 | 99 | $999.99 | $999.99 | 99 | $999.99 | $999.99 | 99 | $999.99 | $999.99 | $999.99 | $999.99 |
| GROSS LOSS TO AVERAGE TOT LN&LS | $999.99 | $999.99 | 99 | $999.99 | $999.99 | 99 | $999.99 | $999.99 | 99 | $999.99 | $999.99 | $999.99 | $999.99 |
| RECOVERIES TO AVERAGE TOT LN&LS | $999.99 | $999.99 | 99 | $999.99 | $999.99 | 99 | $999.99 | $999.99 | 99 | $999.99 | $999.99 | $999.99 | $999.99 |
| RECOVERIES TO PRIOR PERIOD LOSS | $999.99 | $999.99 | 99 | $999.99 | $999.99 | 99 | $999.99 | $999.99 | 99 | $999.99 | $999.99 | $999.99 | $999.99 |
| LOSS RESERVE TO TOTAL LN&LS | $999.99 | $999.99 | 99 | $999.99 | $999.99 | 99 | $999.99 | $999.99 | 99 | $999.99 | $999.99 | $999.99 | $999.99 |
| LOSS RESERVE TO NET LOSSES (X) | $999.99 | $999.99 | 99 | $999.99 | $999.99 | 99 | $999.99 | $999.99 | 99 | $999.99 | $999.99 | $999.99 | $999.99 |
| LOSS RESV TO NONACCRUAL LN&LS(X) | $999.99 | $999.99 | | $999.99 | $999.99 | | $999.99 | $999.99 | | $999.99 | $999.99 | $999.99 | $999.99 |
| EARN COVERAGE OF NET LOSSES (X) | $999.99 | $999.99 | 99 | $999.99 | $999.99 | 99 | $999.99 | $999.99 | 99 | $999.99 | $999.99 | $999.99 | $999.99 |

LOAN MIX, % AVERAGE GROSS LN&LS

| | BANK | PEER 99 | PCT | BANK | PEER 99 | PCT | BANK | PEER 99 | PCT | BANK | PEER 99 | BANK | PEER 99 |
|---|---|---|---|---|---|---|---|---|---|---|---|---|---|
| CONSTRUCTION & DEVELOPMENT | $999.99 | $999.99 | 99 | $999.99 | $999.99 | 99 | $999.99 | $999.99 | 99 | $999.99 | $999.99 | $999.99 | $999.99 |
| 1 - 4 FAMILY RESIDENTIAL | $999.99 | $999.99 | 99 | $999.99 | $999.99 | 99 | $999.99 | $999.99 | 99 | $999.99 | $999.99 | $999.99 | $999.99 |
| HOME EQUITY LOANS | $999.99 | $999.99 | 99 | $999.99 | $999.99 | 99 | $999.99 | $999.99 | 99 | $999.99 | $999.99 | $999.99 | $999.99 |
| OTHER REAL ESTATE LOANS | $999.99 | $999.99 | 99 | $999.99 | $999.99 | 99 | $999.99 | $999.99 | 99 | $999.99 | $999.99 | $999.99 | $999.99 |
| TOTAL REAL ESTATE | $999.99 | $999.99 | 99 | $999.99 | $999.99 | 99 | $999.99 | $999.99 | 99 | $999.99 | $999.99 | $999.99 | $999.99 |

## TABLE 4-5    *(continued)*

| | | | | | | | | | | | | | | | |
|---|---|---|---|---|---|---|---|---|---|---|---|---|---|---|---|
| FINANCIAL INSTITUTION LOANS | $999.99 | $999.99 | 99 | $999.99 | $999.99 | 99 | $999.99 | $999.99 | 99 | $999.99 | $999.99 | | $999.99 | $999.99 | |
| AGRICULTURAL LOANS | $999.99 | $999.99 | 99 | $999.99 | $999.99 | 99 | $999.99 | $999.99 | 99 | $999.99 | $999.99 | | $999.99 | $999.99 | |
| COMMERCIAL & INDUSTRIAL LOANS | $999.99 | $999.99 | 99 | $999.99 | $999.99 | 99 | $999.99 | $999.99 | 99 | $999.99 | $999.99 | | $999.99 | $999.99 | |
| LOANS TO INDIVIDUALS | $999.99 | $999.99 | 99 | $999.99 | $999.99 | 99 | $999.99 | $999.99 | 99 | $999.99 | $999.99 | | $999.99 | $999.99 | |
| MUNICIPAL LOANS | $999.99 | $999.99 | 99 | $999.99 | $999.99 | 99 | $999.99 | $999.99 | 99 | $999.99 | $999.99 | | $999.99 | $999.99 | |
| ACCEPTANCES OF OTHER BANKS | $999.99 | $999.99 | 99 | $999.99 | $999.99 | 99 | $999.99 | $999.99 | 99 | $999.99 | $999.99 | | $999.99 | $999.99 | |
| FOREIGN OFFICE LOANS & LEASES | $999.99 | $999.99 | 99 | $999.99 | $999.99 | 99 | $999.99 | $999.99 | 99 | $999.99 | $999.99 | | $999.99 | $999.99 | |
| ALL OTHER LOANS | $999.99 | $999.99 | 99 | $999.99 | $999.99 | 99 | $999.99 | $999.99 | 99 | $999.99 | $999.99 | | $999.99 | $999.99 | |
| LEASE FINANCING RECEIVABLES | $999.99 | $999.99 | 99 | $999.99 | $999.99 | 99 | $999.99 | $999.99 | 99 | $999.99 | $999.99 | | $999.99 | $999.99 | |

MEMORANDUM (% OF AVG TOT LOANS):

| | | | | | | | | | | | | | | | |
|---|---|---|---|---|---|---|---|---|---|---|---|---|---|---|---|
| COMMERCIAL PAPER IN LOANS | $999.99 | $999.99 | 99 | $999.99 | $999.99 | 99 | $999.99 | $999.99 | 99 | $999.99 | $999.99 | | $999.99 | $999.99 | |
| LOAN & LEASE COMMITMENTS | $999.99 | $999.99 | 99 | $999.99 | $999.99 | 99 | $999.99 | $999.99 | 99 | $999.99 | $999.99 | | $999.99 | $999.99 | |
| LOANS SOLD DURING THE QUARTER | $999.99 | $999.99 | 99 | $999.99 | $999.99 | 99 | $999.99 | $999.99 | 99 | $999.99 | $999.99 | | $999.99 | $999.99 | |
| OFFICER, SHAREHOLDER LOANS | $999.99 | $999.99 | 99 | $999.99 | $999.99 | 99 | $999.99 | $999.99 | 99 | $999.99 | $999.99 | | $999.99 | $999.99 | |
| OFFICER, SHAREHOLDER LNS TO ASST | $999.99 | $999.99 | 99 | $999.99 | $999.99 | 99 | $999.99 | $999.99 | 99 | $999.99 | $999.99 | | $999.99 | $999.99 | |

NET LOSSES BY TYPE OF LN&LS

-------------------------------

| | | | | | | | | | | | | | | | |
|---|---|---|---|---|---|---|---|---|---|---|---|---|---|---|---|
| REAL ESTATE LOANS | $999.99 | $999.99 | 99 | $999.99 | $999.99 | 99 | $999.99 | $999.99 | 99 | $999.99 | $999.99 | | $999.99 | $999.99 | |
| COMMERCIAL AND INDUSTRIAL LOANS | $999.99 | $999.99 | 99 | $999.99 | $999.99 | 99 | $999.99 | $999.99 | 99 | $999.99 | $999.99 | | $999.99 | $999.99 | |
| LOANS TO INDIVIDUALS | $999.99 | $999.99 | 99 | $999.99 | $999.99 | 99 | $999.99 | $999.99 | 99 | $999.99 | $999.99 | | $999.99 | $999.99 | |
| ALL OTHER LOANS & LEASES | $999.99 | $999.99 | 99 | $999.99 | $999.99 | 99 | $999.99 | $999.99 | 99 | $999.99 | $999.99 | | $999.99 | $999.99 | |

CERT # 99999  DSB # 99999999    XXXXXXXXXXXXXXXXXXXXXXXXX(BANK NAME)XXXXXXXXXXXXXXXXXXXXXXXX XXXXXXXXXXXXX(CITYST)XXXXXXXXXXXXX
CHARTER # 99999                 MATURITY AND REPRICING DISTRIBUTION AS OF MM/DD/YY                                PAGE 09

CUMULATIVE PERCENT OF ITEM

| | ITEM TOTAL AS A PERCENT OF ASSETS | | | PERCENT REPRICED WITHIN 3 MONTHS | | | PERCENT REPRICED WITHIN 12 MONTHS | | | PERCENT REPRICED WITHIN 5 YEARS | | |
|---|---|---|---|---|---|---|---|---|---|---|---|---|
| **ASSETS** | BANK | PEER | 99 PCT | BANK | PEER | 99 PCT | BANK | PEER | 99 PCT | BANK | PEER | 99 PCT |
| LOANS AND LEASES (EXCL NONACC) | $999.99 | $999.99 | 99 | $999.99 | $999.99 | 99 | $999.99 | $999.99 | 99 | $999.99 | $999.99 | 99 |
| FIXED RATE BY MATURITY | $999.99 | $999.99 | 99 | $999.99 | $999.99 | 99 | $999.99 | $999.99 | 99 | $999.99 | $999.99 | 99 |
| FLOATING RATE BY REP INTERVAL | $999.99 | $999.99 | 99 | $999.99 | $999.99 | 99 | $999.99 | $999.99 | 99 | $999.99 | $999.99 | 99 |
| DEBT SECURITIES | $999.99 | $999.99 | 99 | $999.99 | $999.99 | 99 | $999.99 | $999.99 | 99 | $999.99 | $999.99 | 99 |
| FIXED RATE BY MATURITY | $999.99 | $999.99 | 99 | $999.99 | $999.99 | 99 | $999.99 | $999.99 | 99 | $999.99 | $999.99 | 99 |
| FLOATING RATE BY REP INTERVAL | $999.99 | $999.99 | 99 | $999.99 | $999.99 | 99 | $999.99 | $999.99 | 99 | $999.99 | $999.99 | 99 |
| FEDERAL FUNDS SOLD (OVERNIGHT) | $999.99 | $999.99 | 99 | 100.00 | 100.00 | | | | | | | |
| SECURITIES PURCHASED UNDER AGREEMENT TO RESELL* | $999.99 | $999.99 | 99 | | | | | | | | | |
| INTEREST-BEARING BANK BALANCES* | $999.99 | $999.99 | 99 | | | | | | | | | |
| TRADING ACCOUNT ASSETS | $999.99 | $999.99 | 99 | 100.00 | 100.00 | | | | | | | |
| TOTAL INTEREST-BEARING ASSETS | $999.99 | $999.99 | 99 | | | | | | | | | |

**LIABILITIES**

| | | | | | | | | | | | | |
|---|---|---|---|---|---|---|---|---|---|---|---|---|
| DEPOSITS IN FOREIGN OFFICES* | $999.99 | $999.99 | 99 | | | | | | | | | |
| CD'S OF $100,000 OR MORE | $999.99 | $999.99 | 99 | $999.99 | $999.99 | 99 | $999.99 | $999.99 | 99 | $999.99 | $999.99 | 99 |
| FIXED RATE BY MATURITY | $999.99 | $999.99 | 99 | $999.99 | $999.99 | 99 | $999.99 | $999.99 | 99 | $999.99 | $999.99 | 99 |
| FLOATING RATE BY REP INTERVAL | $999.99 | $999.99 | 99 | $999.99 | $999.99 | 99 | $999.99 | $999.99 | 99 | $999.99 | $999.99 | 99 |
| OTHER TIME DEPOSITS* | $999.99 | $999.99 | 99 | $999.99 | $999.99 | 99 | | | | | | |
| MONEY MARKET DEPOSIT ACCOUNTS | $999.99 | $999.99 | 99 | 100.00 | 100.00 | | | | | | | |
| OTHER SAVINGS DEP (EXCL MMDA)* | $999.99 | $999.99 | 99 | | | | | | | | | |
| NOW ACCOUNTS | $999.99 | $999.99 | 99 | 100.00 | 100.00 | | | | | | | |
| FEDERAL FUNDS PURCH (OVERNIGHT) | $999.99 | $999.99 | 99 | 100.00 | 100.00 | | | | | | | |
| SECURITIES SOLD UNDER AGREEMENT TO REPURCHASE* | $999.99 | $999.99 | 99 | | | | | | | | | |
| OTHER BORROWED MONEY* | $999.99 | $999.99 | 99 | | | | | | | | | |
| SUBORDINATED NOTES & DEBENTURES* | $999.99 | $999.99 | 99 | | | | | | | | | |
| TREASURY NOTES | $999.99 | $999.99 | 99 | 100.00 | 100.00 | | | | | | | |
| TOTAL INTEREST-BEARING LIABS | $999.99 | $999.99 | 99 | | | | | | | | | |

*INDICATED ITEMS ARE NOT REPORTED BY MATURITY/REPRICING INTERVAL AS OF MARCH 31, 1988.
OTHER TIME DEPOSITS ARE NOT BROKEN DOWN BEYOND THREE MONTHS.

then following up on specific items contained in the detailed analysis in the three remaining sections. Analysts who wish to interpret the detailed UBPR measures will be helped considerably by the *UBPR User's Guide* (revised 1988), which is available from the FFIEC.

UBPR users should also be aware of at least three weaknesses of these reports. First, the reports are prepared from a regulatory point of view. Any available market price, per share data, or return-on-equity measures that are important from the shareholder's perspective are ignored. Second, the data are accounting data, which are generally based on historical costs and ignore values that are generally more important to decision makers. Third, the data are usually quarterly averages, which are neither daily averages nor year-end data that appear in many other banking reports. Often bank analysts end up with three sets of measures—one based on daily averages, one based on quarterly averages, and one based on year-end figures. In spite of such weaknesses, UBPRs remain one of the key sources for evaluating bank performance.

### Indicators of Failure

Banks that fail usually do not measure up in managing credit risk, the skill that commercial banks are supposed to perform best. Banks that lack credit risk management skills and that are located in geographic markets under economic stress are especially prone to fail. Undoubtedly, energy-related economic stress contributes to the high rate of bank failure in the nation's energy belt. (Out of the 96 bank failures in the first six months of 1987, 51 occurred in Louisiana, Oklahoma, and Texas.)

In addition to the abnormally poor performance of energy credits, the credit risks taken by banks in the energy belt historically have been greater than the risks accepted by most banks in other parts of the country. First, the regional economy is thinner and rather highly concentrated. Often loan applicants have short credit histories or lack credit standing in other ways. But for many of the banks in the region, such deals were the only ones around. In addition, Louisiana, Oklahoma, and Texas long have been the site of an especially robust entrepreneurial spirit, perhaps fueled by the go-for-broke nature of energy exploration and development. Many past nonenergy loan deals made in the area probably would not have been bankable in other parts of the nation.

Regardless of the region, however, certain indicators of poor financial performance bestow a sort of economic mark of Cain on banks that are prone to fail. Certainly, poor loan performance (poor credit risk management) is one prominent such indicator. But there are others.

Several recent research projects by academicians and regulatory economists have identified certain bank financial ratios as leading indicators of failure. The researchers looked at failed banks' ratios for a year or more before actual failure to see if they could anticipate the actual failures. In essence, they tried to discover *failure proneness*. Some important leading indicators of failure appear to include the following:

| Ratio | Effect |
| --- | --- |
| Return on assets | $(-)$ |
| Loans to assets | $(+)$ |
| Capital to assets | $(-)$ |
| Purchased funds to assets | $(+)$ |
| Net charge-offs to loans | $(+)$ |
| Commercial and industrial loans to assets | $(+)$ |

The plus or minus sign in the "Effect" column gives the relationship of the ratio to bank failure. For example, return on assets is negatively related to failure; higher returns on assets indicate less likelihood of failure. All research shows that the larger a bank's allocation to loans, the more failure-prone the bank. Also, a low capital ratio increases the chances of failure. Similarly, banks with large purchased funds positions are more likely to fail. Some researchers have concluded that a large net ratio of charge-offs to loans suggests pending failure. Interestingly, other researchers found little statistical evidence of this relationship. Finally, at least one major research project singled out the ratio of commercial and industrial loans to total assets as an apparent precursor to failure.

In actuality, of course, banks that fail tend to exhibit all these ratios at unfavorable levels. It is the combination of the ratios, not any one ratio alone, that is important. And when the combined ratios are sufficiently out of bounds, the results can be lethal.

One way to understand the severity or out-of-bounds nature of a bank's financial ratios is to look at the ratios recently displayed by banks before failure. Table 4-6 shows a set of such ratios for 48 smaller banks that failed in 1985. In addition, it shows average ratios for small banks with $0–25 million in assets with a return-on-equity ranking in the lowest 20 percent and an identical set of ratios for small banks that ranked in the top 20 percent in terms of return on equity. The point of this is to determine how closely the bottom 20 percent return on equity banks resemble banks that later failed or, alternatively, to see if they are more like the top 20 percent banks. The result is that banks that find themselves in the bottom 20 percent return on equity group can gauge the severity of their relatively poor performance.

Thus, for example, the table indicates that the average net interest margin as a percentage of average assets for return on equity banks in the bottom 20 percent is 91 basis points below that of the banks in the top 20 percent (3.69 percent minus 4.60 percent) and 98 basis points above that of soon-to-fail banks. The banks in the bottom 20 percent, in other words, are positioned about halfway between the top performers and the soon-to-fail banks. (Interest income and interest expense percentages of average assets differ partly because of differences in time periods; the data for the banks in the top and bottom 20 percent are from 1986, whereas the data for the failed banks are from 1985.) Similarly, provision for loan losses for the bottom 20 percent of

**TABLE 4-6  Performance Profile of U.S. Banks with Assets of $0–25 Million**

|  | 829 Banks, Top 20% ROE | 871 Banks, Bottom 20% ROE | 48 Failed Banks, 1985 |
|---|---|---|---|
| Average assets, mean (dollars in thousands) | $14,960 | $14,370 | $18,703 |
| 1. Total interest income | 9.83% | 9.05% | 9.66% |
| Total interest expense | 5.23 | 5.36 | 6.95 |
| Net interest margin (NIM) | 4.60 | 3.69 | 2.71 |
| Provision for loan losses (PLL) | 0.36 | 3.05 | 6.95 |
| NIM net of PLL | 4.24 | 0.64 | (3.63) |
| Total noninterest income | 1.54 | 1.20 | 1.04 |
| Total noninterest expense | 3.62 | 4.73 | 10.56 |
| Income taxes, extraordinary items | 0.52 | (0.38) | (0.01) |
| Net income | 1.63% | −2.51% | −13.14% |
| 2. Return on average equity | 18.11% | −34.28% | −249.68% |
| Equity + LL reserves to assets | 9.71 | 7.93 | 5.19 |
| Equity formation rate | 10.84% | −24.26% | −98.24% |
| 3. Earning assets to total assets | 83.07% | 84.03% | 85.63% |
| Net overhead to earning assets | 2.83 | 8.04 | 11.19 |
| Growth rate of total assets | 8.50 | −2.88 | −10.20 |
| 4. Nonperforming loans to capital | 11.93% | 64.75% | 235.89% |
| Net charge-offs to loans | 0.67 | 5.11 | 9.09 |
| Recoveries to charge-offs | 32.05 | 9.40 | — |
| 5. Net loans to total assets | 47.40% | 53.79% | 64.30% |
| Real estate loans to loans | 41.02 | 31.83 | 30.78 |
| Agricultural loans to loans | 14.11 | 18.20 | 17.02 |
| Commercial and industrial loans to loans | 18.44 | 26.32 | 35.75 |
| Credit card and personal loans to loans | 25.23 | 22.08 | 21.40 |
| 6. Brokered deposits to total deposits | 0.09 | 0.35 | 1.94% |

banks falls well within the range between the top 20 percent and failing banks, although it is materially closer to the top 20 percent of banks. Individual banks in the bottom 20 percent that have provisions approaching 7 percent of assets, however, look a lot like failing banks.

Noninterest income and expense as a percentage of average assets for failing banks is partly inflated by an often severe shrinkage in assets. Average banks in the bottom 20 percent, although severely disadvantaged in noninterest expense compared with high-performing banks, do not resemble failing banks. As shown in the table, the latter produced a 10.56 percent noninterest expense ratio compared with 4.73 percent for banks in the bottom 20 percent.

Return on assets (net income as a percentage of average assets) and return on average equity were extremely poor in 1986 for the banks in the bottom 20 percent. Again, fortunately, these banks' return on assets and return on equity do not, on average, approach the catastrophic depths of failing banks' return on assets and return on equity.

Equity formation (depletion) rates for the banks in the bottom 20 percent is dangerously negative at −24.26 percent. Failing banks, of course, bleed equity through loan writeoffs at rates that eventually prove fatal. (Equity formation rates do not include "additions" to capital via increases in loan loss reserves.)

The shrinkage of assets by the banks in the bottom 20 percent at a 2.88 percent annual rate is indicative of the same involuntary downsizing found in failing banks. The latter show about a 10 percent average shrinkage rate, portending their imminent collapse.

Nonperforming loans for banks with a return on equity in the bottom 20 percent represent about 65 percent of capital, indicating a very severe threat to capital. Failing banks, on the other hand, strongly signal their pending insolvency, with average levels of nonperforming loans that drown capital by 236 percent. Net charge-offs by banks in the bottom 20 percent, at over 5 percent of loans, similarly appear to threaten solvency. Charge-offs at a 9 percent rate are more severe for failing banks and, at that, are probably unrealistically small, because managements of failing banks resist recognizing that loan book values are untenable.

The pattern of net loans to total assets is quite revealing. As formal research has concluded, the large allocations of assets to loans appears to be a characteristic of failure-prone banks. Banks in the bottom 20 percent in terms of return on equity exhibit a tendency toward large allocations that might be a tipoff to trouble. Part of this relationship between increasing loan ratios and poor performance, however, might be artificial. As noted, poorly performing banks tend to be in a shrinkage mode. In addition, they may not be able to collect on outstanding loans but they are reluctant to charge them off even when there is clearly little value in them. The combination of shrinking assets and carrying bad loans inflates the loan allocation ratios.

The loan mix ratios reported in Table 4-6 reveal some fascinating information. Clearly, the banks in the top 20 percent in return on equity book an abnormal share of real estate and personal (including credit card) loans. Poorly performing banks—those in the bottom 20 percent in terms of return on equity and the soon-to-fail banks—carry significantly higher proportions of agricultural and commercial and industrial loans. Previously, the loan mix of the banks in the bottom 20 percent resembled the failing banks' loan mix far more than it resembled that of the top-performing banks.

Finally, failing banks tend to be distinguishable by their aggressive position in brokered deposits. Presumably, these banks are forced to replace losses in core deposits with purchased money. The average 1.94 percent of deposits that failing banks take through brokers is not a major funding source. But, given the virtual absence of such funds among top-performing banks, the presence of brokered deposits seems clearly associated with troubled banks.

To be sure, the resemblance of the financial ratio profile of banks in the bottom 20 percent in terms of return on equity to that of failing banks does not suggest imminent failure, but banks in this group appear to be leaning in that direction. If the prediction that the present wave of failures will continue is accurate, the early victims logically will be those banks in the bottom 20 percent in return on equity with a financial profile like that of the soon-to-fail banks reported in Table 4-6.

## Discussion Questions

1. Competition has forced the net interest margins of most banks to narrow significantly. What measures will show how a bank is responding to this competitive challenge?
2. Explain how you would interpret a bank's asset utilitization figures. Why are these figures low compared with those of most other industries?
3. What supplementary ratios might a bank use to evaluate its cost efficiency and its liquidity position?
4. What are the primary differences between the return on equity model discussed in Chapter 3 and the alternative method (developed and enthusiastically supported by Dr. William W. Alberts) proposed in this chapter? Which of these methods would you use? Why?
5. Describe the following four classes of banking risks:
   a. Environmental risks
   b. Delivery risks
   c. Management risks
   d. Financial risks
6. What are the meanings of the following categories of risk?
   a. Defalcation risk
   b. Technological risk
   c. Leverage risk
   d. Regulatory risk
7. How would you suggest a bank should attempt to reach the appropriate trade-off between returns and risks? Would your answer be different for a bank with $100 million in assets that is closely held (by a limited number of large equity holders) and a $20 billion bank whose stock is actively traded?
8. What measures of credit risk are included in a bank's UBPR? Explain how you would interpret the information.
9. Discuss which financial ratios you would look at to determine the failure proneness of a bank.

# FIRST NATIONAL BANK OF PARK CITIES

## INTRODUCTION

Mr. Tom Turner had long held the ambition of organizing and directing a new community-oriented commercial bank. He had never seriously explored the possibility of such an entrepreneurial experience, however, since nearly all his banking affiliations had carried him toward large, well-established bank holding companies.

Nonetheless, from time to time, Turner had mentioned his interests to business associates and friends in his residential community, an independent incorporated town entirely surrounded by the City of Dallas. He continued to receive enough encouragement and enthusiasm from his friends to believe that his goal of directing a new independent bank might indeed be feasible and that possibly significant financial support might be available to him.

By mid-1983, Turner began spending part of his time studying and researching the possibility of a new bank in the Park Cities area within Dallas, and exploring specific investment interest among his friends and business colleagues.

By the end of 1983, Turner had developed a preliminary strategy for a new community bank, and he had identified a group of some 15 to 20 organizers and investors who had expressed serious interest in the project.

In the early stages of his explorations of this venture, Turner had identified several key questions and judgmental issues that would have to be resolved if this effort was to move forward. Some of the principal early considerations were as follows:

1. Was there a real need and a profitable opportunity for another new bank in the Dallas–Park Cities area, given the many new financial institutions that had already been opened in recent years?

2. How much capital would be required for such a venture, and how difficult would it be to earn a competitive rate of return on that necessary capital base?

3. How difficult might the competitive environ-

ment prove to be, and how could Turner make his projected bank a uniquely different institution, meeting customers' needs in ways that would justify the opening of still another community bank in Dallas?

4. What kind of strategic plan and marketing effort would be required to "sell" the projected new bank to its community?

5. What would be the management requirements of such a venture, including the formation of a board of directors, and the operating challenges and problems that such a new enterprise might encounter?

6. Should the proposed new bank seek a national or a state (Texas) bank charter?

Some of the answers to these questions gradually became clearer as Turner continued to study the possibilities and as interested potential investors began to express their ideas and suggestions. The following data summarize some of the preliminary planning and analytical data that Turner assembled as he became increasingly serious about the formation of a new bank.

## THE PROPOSED BANK'S GEOGRAPHIC LOCATION

The proposed Park Cities Bank would be located on the southwest corner of the intersection of Hillcrest Avenue and University Boulevard in Dallas, Texas. The market area encompasses the two cities of Highland Park and University Park (the Park Cities) and a portion of the City of Dallas. The area extends approximately 1.6 miles north, 1.9 miles south, 0.7 mile east, and 1.8 miles to the west from the proposed location.

This site would be especially attractive since it represents a combination of two towns that form an inner-city community within Dallas and because three of the boundaries (north, east, and west) are major traffic arteries in Dallas and form natural barriers for the marketplace. The southerly boundary has been chosen because residents of the Park Cities tend to identify and conduct their retail and banking business within their community.

The primary market area for the deposits and loans is outlined in Exhibit 1, which shows the bank's potential market area in relation to the Dallas/Fort Worth metroplex and the central portion of the City of Dallas.

The proposed bank would be well located in its market area, providing convenient access for the entire community through two major north–south thoroughfares. Moreover, there would be numerous retail establishments surrounding the proposed bank's site. Customers who patronized those stores would be able to complete their shopping and banking at one convenient location. Finally, the new bank would be located across the street from the Southern Methodist University campus, one of the market area's largest employers. The organizers believed the bank could attract the university's administration, faculty, staff, and students as customers.

## THE MARKET ECONOMY

### Population, Housing, and Income Characteristics

The market area for the projected new institution would span two of Texas's most vibrant cities, Highland Park and University Park. Known as the Park Cities, they cover approximately 6 square miles and are completely surrounded by the City of Dallas. They are among the most affluent communities in the state. In 1980, for example, median family income in Highland Park was $52,742, and in University Park it was $33,763. In contrast, median family income in the State of Texas as a whole for that year was $19,619 and for the United States it was $19,928. Thus, median family income was 168.8 percent higher in Highland Park and 72.1 percent higher in University Park than in Texas as a whole. The area's residents are, generally speaking, very successful and affluent.

Population figures for the Park Cities indicate a stable population base. The cities of Highland Park and University Park have been completely developed for many years and, consequently, are not expected to experience sharp increases in population growth. Community stability coupled with considerable residential redevelopment and renovation of existing homes has created one of the most desirable residential areas in the Dallas metroplex.

Exhibit 2 provides income and housing data for the Park Cities, and it summarizes current population estimates for Highland Park and University Park. A solid indicator of the area's general affluence is its housing values. In 1982, the State Property Tax Board confirmed the average value of a single-family residence in the Highland Park Independent School District (whose boundaries closely parallel those of the proposed bank's market area) to be $226,000.

### Employment and Commercial Activity

Although the (new) projected bank's market area economy would be anchored in its own retail and commercial activity, the location under study would be convenient to all primary employment centers in Dallas. To the east, the Central Expressway corridor contains approximately 4.9 million square feet of office space; to the south, the Dallas Central Business District has over 16 million square feet; the Turtle Creek Corridor, which passes through the center of the proposed market area, contains 1.5 million square feet of office space; on the west, the Stemmons Freeway area has over 6 million square feet of office space; north of the market area, the LBJ/Far North Dallas area comprises over 7 million square feet of office space.

### Retail Sales

Retail sales for the cities of Highland Park and University Park in 1982 were estimated to be $62,017,135 and $107,723,720, respectively. (See Exhibit 3.) These figures reflect a 97 percent increase over 1978 sales in Highland Park and a 64 percent increase in University Park. The yearly increase in estimated retail sales figures summarized in Exhibit 3 demonstrates an outstanding retail growth trend for the Park Cities. There are nine retail shopping centers located within the proposed bank's market area.

At the northern boundary market area is one of Dallas's largest regional shopping malls—NorthPark Shopping Center. Built in 1973, NorthPark has over 1 million square feet. The mall caters to Dallas's more affluent consumers, anchor tenants being Neiman-Marcus, Woolf Brothers, and Lord & Taylor.

## THE COMPETITIVE ENVIRONMENT

A major area of concern to Tom Turner, however, was the intense competition coming from both new and established banks. The market area was currently served by 10 banks, 3 of which were organized in 1982 and opened in early 1983. An 11th bank had recently received charter approval and was currently in organization. There was also a new charter application currently pending in the Comptroller of the Currency's office.

All of these market-area banks provide a reasonably full range of services to area residents. Each of them would, of course, compete with the proposed bank. Additionally, many other financial institutions in Dallas County would offer some competition for the projected institution because of previously established banking connections, long term in many cases, by Park Cities residents.

At year's end 1982, deposits in these directly competing banks totaled $1,083,516,000; total loans were $806,212,000. These figures represent a 144.6 percent increase in deposits and a 177.5 percent increase in loans since 1977. (See Exhibit 4.) The organizing group for the Park Cities Bank fully realized that competition for such an affluent customer base would be intense. Accordingly, they could not just offer "me too" banking services and expect to attract customers without somehow differentiating the new bank from all the others. The real challenge, therefore, would be to design a marketing and customer services program that would clearly make the new bank stand apart.

### Deregulation of Financial Institutions

The Garn–St. Germain Depository Institutions Act of 1982 was signed into law on October 15, 1982, and it brought about significant changes in the competitive environment for financial institutions. Mr. Turner realized that provisions of the legislation would affect the marketplace for *de novo* banks, as well as for all banks. New provisions of the law dealing with chartering of thrift institutions, liberalizing investment opportunities, raising lending limits to individual customers, and expanding insurance activities of bank holding companies all would have effects on bank competition. Moreover, the establishment of new deposit accounts, the ability of thrift institutions to make commercial loans, and the phasing out of interest rate ceilings on time and savings deposits under Regulation Q signaled major changes that would directly affect newly established banks.

In any event, Turner and the other organizers recognized that competition from existing and new banks in the market area, and from new competitors to banks generally, would present perhaps the greatest challenge to any new bank's profit potential.

Of the 11 banks in the market area, 4 were newly chartered and therefore likely to offer substantial competition for the proposed bank. Of these, Central National Bank is located on the east side of North Central Expressway, with only difficult access to the proposed market. Grand Bank–Central, Oak Lawn Bank, and Sherry Lane National Bank, however, are located on the west side of North Central Expressway and would be expected to provide vigorous competition in the southern and western portions of the proposed bank's market.

The organizers were confident that the convenience of the Park Cities bank location to all parts of its market area would reduce the competitive impact from Grand Bank–Central and Oak Lawn Bank. Nonetheless, they realized that they would have to implement an aggressive marketing strategy for the proposed bank that would include extensive outreach throughout the market area, highlighting the new bank's competitive rates and its full line of services.

Nearly all of the probable organizers had long-standing ties to the Park Cities. It was their intention, therefore, to make use of their substantial professional and social contacts to attract loan and deposit business. Moreover, it was anticipated that the sale of the new bank's common stock to residents and enterprises throughout the Park Cities would serve to strengthen further the bank's relationship to its market area and, thereby, its competitive effectiveness.

In addition to the 11 banks in the immediate area, there are 12 S&L offices, 1 credit union, and 3 mortgage and/or insurance companies. In short, competition would be intense.

## PLANS AND STRATEGIES FOR OPERATION

The organizers' goal was to create a profitable and growing bank to service the needs of the residents, employees, and businesses in the market area. To achieve this result, a strong deposit base would have to be secured, a sound investment and lending strategy developed, and a stable asset–liability mix created. To achieve these pre-opening goals, the organizers discussed designating preliminary committees with differing responsibilities. These committee members were considered as likely members of a future board of directors.

A building committee would oversee the planning and construction of the bank facility and would supervise the purchase of office furniture and equipment. A personnel committee would assist in the selection of a vice-president, cashier, and other staff personnel. An operations committee would examine operating systems and consider the various security measures needed to protect the bank's assets. A loan committee would establish the bank's lending policy. Once the bank opened, this group would serve as the standing loan committee. An investment committee would determine the bank's investment strategy. These groups would have responsibility for managing the bank's portfolio prior to opening (after raising the initial capital) and continuing with this responsibility once the bank began operating. An asset–liability committee would provide oversight supervision for the bank's assets and liabilities.

Finally, a marketing committee would study how common stock could be sold, how a public relations campaign plan might be organized, how to maximize value from the bank's opening ceremonies, and how to market the new bank continually to its publics.

### Sources of Deposits

The prime sources of deposits for the bank would be the residents, employees, and businesses in the bank's market area. The probable organizers and board of directors together with the bank's marketing strategies would, it was hoped, ensure access to these target markets.

The organizers had diverse business and financial interests that represented a majority of the important aspects in the market area's economy. Consequently, they would be in a position to contact individuals and companies, and encourage such potential customers to become depositors and to move some or all of their banking relations to the new institution. Mr. Turner proposed that each organizer-director be responsible for gener-

ating $1 million in deposits during the first operating year.

Marketing campaigns would be directed to the area's business and professional community. The organizers also intended to use advertising and public programs to communicate the proposed bank's services. They believed that recent legislation creating new deposit accounts would enable the Park Cities bank to compete effectively with money market funds for deposits.

### Lending and Investment Strategies

The loan policy would need to meet all of the communities' needs. To begin operations, however, the founders expected to receive some assistance from correspondent banking relationships in obtaining the initial loans. It was anticipated that most of the loan portfolio would soon be originated by the bank itself. Mr. Turner planned to solicit and originate loans through the directors, the customer base, advertising, and direct contact with the local community through an officer call program.

In outlining a loan policy, Mr. Turner considered the following loans to be possibilities:

1. Interim construction loans.
2. Loans secured by marketable bonds, generally not to exceed 95 percent of the market value of U.S. government and federal agencies, 85 percent of state and political subdivisions, and 80 percent of the market value of corporate obligations.
3. Loans secured by marketable securities listed on a recognized stock exchange, not to exceed 75 percent of the market value.
4. Loans secured by over-the-counter stocks with adequate margins.
5. Loans secured by time or savings deposits with interest rates charged not less than 1 percent more than those earned on the deposits where such deposits are with the bank.
6. Loans to professional men and women (i.e., doctors, lawyers, dentists, and CPAs).
7. Participation loans.
8. Floor-plan loans which a significant banking relationship could develop.
9. Loans to business concerns secured by equipment, generally for 36 to 60 months, not to exceed the equipment's estimated useful life.
10. Aircraft loans at 75 percent of cost or appraised value, whichever is less.
11. Loans to companies secured by inventory

with a margin of at least 50 percent. The inventory value and marketability must be determined and monitored.

12. Loans to companies secured by assignment of acceptable accounts receivable with a 30 percent margin. Accounts receivable would be from companies whose financial strength and payment record are known to be favorable.

13. Unsecured loans to businesses that exhibit a satisfactory balance sheet and earnings statement. These loans would largely be short-term and self-liquidating.

14. Unsecured loans to individuals who are commercial customers.

A proposed investment policy had been developed along the following lines:

1. U.S. Treasury securities and U.S. government agency obligations would be the principal taxable portfolio component, as distinct from corporate bonds.

2. Maturities of taxable securities generally would be no longer than 7 years, and the average life of such securities would be 4.5 years or less.

3. U.S. government-guaranteed securities (taxable or tax-exempt) would be included within the guidelines that apply to taxable securities.

4. The quality of all tax-exempt securities would be no lower than "A" as established by major rating services or, in the absence of ratings, in the opinion of recognized bond dealers.

5. Investments would also consist of local and state obligations with maturities not to exceed 10 years.

6. Intermediate- and long-term bonds would be acquired so long as the average maturity of the tax-exempt portfolio did not exceed 10 years and the intermediate maturity did not exceed 7 years.

7. Tax-exempt securities of Texas issuers would be emphasized as far as practical.

8. Attention would be focused at all times on diversification in the investment portfolio. Diversification should include geographical and industrial categories.

### Asset–Liability Mix

The asset–liability mix proposed by the bank organizers would, it was hoped, minimize risk due to interest rate fluctuations. Mr. Turner planned to maintain a rate-sensitive asset (RSA) to rate-sensitive liability (RSL) ratio of between 0.8 and 1.2. This policy was intended to stabilize the bank's long-run earning power. When a board-designated committee believed interest rates would rise, it could take actions to increase the RSA/RSL ratio toward 1.2. On the other hand, the committee could decide to decrease the RSA/RSL ratio toward 0.8 when it concluded that rates might decline.

### Physical Facilities

The organizers were considering permanent facilities that would be located on approximately 23,000 square feet at the southwest corner intersection of Hillcrest Avenue and University Boulevard. The bank would lease space in a projected 30,000-square-foot, two-story building. Mr. Turner anticipated that the opening needs would total 7,500 square feet with an option to expand, eventually occupying the entire building. The bank would initially be operating four teller stations, reserving space to add two additional future teller positions.

### Assumptions Used to Determine Pro Forma Balance Sheets and Income Statements

The pro forma balance sheets and income statements developed by Mr. Turner were derived by forecasting total deposit levels for the first three years and then constructing income statements based on assumptions about cost and operating ratios. Deposits were projected based upon average market-area income, the growth and development of area residential and commercial markets, and the other banks' experience in Dallas County. (See Exhibits 5 to 7.)

The key assumptions were as follows:

1. Deposits and expenses would be accrued uniformly throughout the year. This permitted averages to be used in determining the profit-loss statement. Since the bank would have its initial capital invested in government securities at opening, it was assumed that investment securities would average $5.18 million for the first year.

2. Loans and discounts were estimated to yield 13.5 percent throughout the three-year period. Investment securities would yield an estimated 11 percent for the three years. The average cost of time deposits was assumed at 8.5 percent for the period. NOW accounts were estimated to cost 5.25 percent, and Super NOW accounts would average 8.5 percent. These rates were estimated from recent interest levels and average rates forecast during the three-year period.

3. Employee wages and benefits were increased from the initial base at 10 percent annually. The level of wages and the annual increases were determined from discussions by the organizers about appropriate levels necessary to attract competent employees in the Dallas County market.

4. The demand-deposit/time-deposit ratio was 20 to 80 percent. This assumption was based upon area bank experience and the anticipation that time deposits would continue to constitute a larger fraction of total deposits.

5. The loan-to-deposit ratio was forecast at 60, 65, and 70 percent, respectively, for the first three years. These ratios reflected the experience of newly chartered urban banks in Texas.

6. The first-year $20 million deposit forecast was large for suburban banks. The organizers believed, however, that this level of deposits was realistic because (a) the market was the most affluent in Dallas; (b) the bank's marketing plan assigned an "obligation" level of $1 million in deposits that each organizer would, it was hoped, be able to attract during the first year; and (c) Mr. Turner had served as the principal banker for business firms and individuals that he believed would shift deposits to the new institution.

7. Although Mr. Turner expected to attract public funds, the amount and timing of these deposits would be highly variable. Accordingly, no such funds were incorporated in the pro forma forecasts.

A short biographical comment on each of the bank's probable organizers follows.

**Tom E. Turner**   Mr. Turner was currently serving full-time coordinating the bank's organizing effort. He graduated from the University of Texas (BBA–General Business) and the Southwestern Graduate School of Banking at Southern Methodist University. He was previously employed by Inter-First Bank Dallas, entering the executive training program in 1963 and becoming a vice-president in the Correspondent–Southwest Division of that bank in 1965.

In 1973, Mr. Turner joined BancTexas, Dallas. At the time of his resignation in May 1983, Mr. Turner was a senior vice-president, serving as the group head of the bank's Correspondent Division/National and as a member of the Senior Credit Policy Committee and the Senior Loan Committee. In these positions, he was responsible for loan and deposit

portfolios in excess of $100 million and he supervised a 15-person staff.

A resident of the Park Cities, Mr. Turner brought over 21 years of banking experience in Dallas to the investing group. As an executive officer of important Dallas banks, he had been actively involved in the formation of lending policies and in the careful scrutiny of credit applications. Furthermore, he had experience in serving the needs of individuals and businesses located within the proposed bank's market area.

In his prior position, Mr. Turner was responsible for managing the accounts of several bank directors and the personal accounts of major business customers. Turner believed that serving the financial needs of executives would prove very helpful in developing the proposed bank's services.

**Webber W. Beall, Jr.**   Mr. Beall was a partner in the law firm of Touchstone, Bernays, Johnston, Beall & Smith. He graduated from Southern Methodist University (BBA–Accounting) in 1954 and Southern Methodist University School of Law (LLB) in 1959. Mr. Beall's knowledge of the market-area residents, both socially and professionally, would enable him to contribute to business development and the profit potential of the proposed bank.

**William P. Carr, Jr.**   Mr. Carr was an owner of Carr Petroleum Corporation, Inc., a family-owned oil and gas business operating properties in Texas, New Mexico, and Kansas and drilling on properties located in these states, as well as in Colorado and Nebraska. Mr. Carr graduated from the University of Texas in 1963 (BS–Economics). Prior to his current position, he was an investment banker with First Southwest Company. He served on numerous boards of business, educational, and charitable institutions.

**Edward F. Doran**   Mr. Doran is the co-owner and co-manager of Doran Chevrolet–Peugeot, Inc. He is a graduate of Southern Methodist University (BBA–General Business). He was very knowledgeable about the market area's business and residents and was in a good position to attract customers to the proposed bank.

**R. William Gribble, Jr.**   Mr. Gribble was the owner of Gribble Oil Corporation, an independent oil and gas production company. He is a graduate of the University of Texas (BS–Geology) and the University of Oklahoma (BS–Geological Engineering). Mr. Gribble intended to support the new bank with his business and personal accounts while assisting in bringing new customers to the institution.

**Harrell S. "Buddy" Hayden**   Mr. Hayden was the managing partner of Hayden & Smith Co., a commercial real estate sales and leasing company. He is a graduate of the University of Texas (BBA–Marketing). He was a past president of the Greater Dallas Board of Realtors and had served on the Texas Association of Realtors' board of directors. Mr. Hayden had actively participated in the bank's site selection. He was a lifelong resident of the Park Cities.

**James E. Herring**   Mr. Herring was president and chairman of the board of Marcom International, Inc., a commodity trading and commodity futures brokerage. Mr. Herring attended the University of Houston and is a graduate of the University of Texas (BBA–Finance) and Harvard Graduate School of Business. Mr. Herring served as a director of Tascosa National Bank of Amarillo from 1970 to 1979.

**Henry D. Lindsley III**   Mr. Lindsley was the chairman of the board of Higginbotham-Bartlett Company of New Mexico, a retail lumber and hardware concern. He is a graduate of the University of Texas (BBA). Mr. Lindsley had served as a director of First National Bank of Brownsville (Texas). He and his family were lifelong residents of Dallas.

**Edwin J. Luedtke, Jr.**   Mr. Luedtke was a partner in the firm of Luedtke, Aldridge, Pendleton, Inc., a commercial real estate development and brokerage company. He is a graduate of Rice University (BA and BS) and the University of Virginia (MBA).

**Michael A. McBee**   Mr. McBee was a partner in an oil and gas exploration and production company. He is a graduate of the New Mexico Military Institute. Mr. McBee and his family were lifelong residents of Dallas.

**Donald J. Malouf**   Mr. Malouf was an attorney serving as president of the law firm Malouf, Lynch & Jackson, a professional corporation. He is a graduate of the University of Texas (BA and MBA) and Southern Methodist University School of Law (LLB). Mr. Malouf had prior experience as a director of other financial institutions.

**Robert A. Massad**   Mr. Massad was the president of MAS/TER Realty, Inc., a full-service real estate company engaged in the brokerage, development, management, and acquisition of real estate in the Dallas area. He is a graduate of Southern Methodist University (BBA–Banking and Finance). Mr. Massad had a great deal of experience in analyzing and financing the acquisition of real estate in the Dallas area.

**Matthew C. Roberts III**   Mr. Roberts was a self-employed investor. He is a graduate of Southern Methodist University (BS–Geology). Mr. Roberts had been active in the Dallas–Park Cities area all of his life. Moreover, he had served as a director of Terrell State Bank (now InterFirst Bank–Terrell) for over 14 years.

**Wade C. Smith**   Mr. Smith was an attorney and is the managing partner of the firm Touchstone, Bernays, Johnston, Beall & Smith. He is a graduate of the University of Texas and the University of Texas School of Law and has been consistently active in community activities in both Dallas and the Park Cities.

**Tom J. Stollenwerck**   Mr. Stollenwerck was an attorney and partner in the firm Touchstone, Bernays, Johnston, Beall & Smith. He is a graduate of Southern Methodist University and Southern Methodist University School of Law.

**John C. Vogt**   Mr. Vogt was the president of International Supply Co., Inc., a wholesale distributor of plumbing, utility, and industrial supplies. He is a graduate of the University of Texas. He was a resident of the Park Cities and was a member of numerous civic and charitable area organizations.

The organizing group, under Tom Turner's leadership, was greatly encouraged by the prospects for a new bank in the Park Cities area. The members believed that as much as $5 million in common stock could be raised from the organizers and some area residents to launch this new venture. They realized, however, that there were some real risks attached to this undertaking. In particular, they were concerned with the level of competition, which was currently strong and growing; the challenges in marketing and selling a new bank to the Park Cities community, given the presence of several other well-sponsored new banking organizations; and finally, the attractiveness of the return on investment for this new institution. Although they had gathered the necessary data and had completed a preliminary charter application, the group was still uncertain whether the final decision should be made to invest this large amount of capital and to proceed with the venture.

**EXHIBIT 1    First National Bank of Park Cities—Map Showing Bank Competitors**

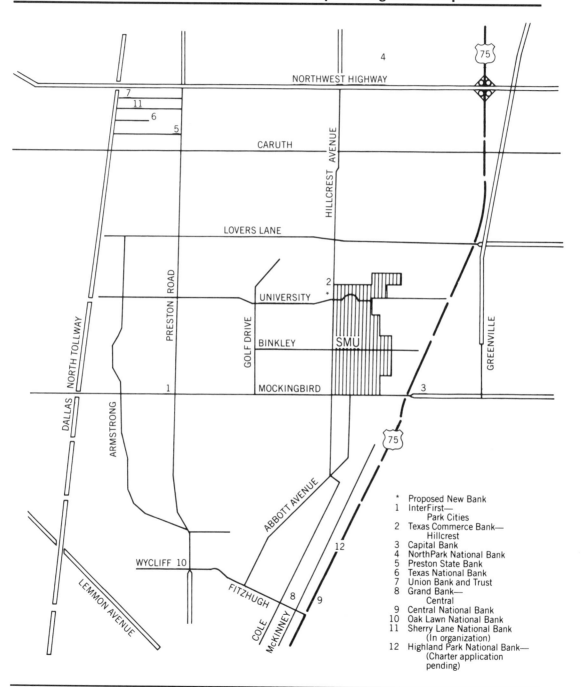

SOURCE: Southwestern Graduate School of Banking.

**EXHIBIT 2    First National Bank of Park Cities—Economic Data for the Park Cities**

|  | City of Highland Park | City of University Park |
|---|---|---|
| **Demographics** | | |
| Total population, 1980 final census | 8,909 | 22,254 |
| Estimated population, Jan. 1, 1983 | 8,950 | 23,300 |
| Households, 1980 | 3,702 | 8,597 |
| Average household size, 1980 | 2.41 | 2.24 |
| **Income** | | |
| Median family income, 1980 | $52,742 | $33,763 |
| **Housing** | | |
| Total housing units, 1980 | 3,950 | 9,040 |
| Vacant units, 1980 | 248 | 443 |
| Occupancy rate (percent), 1980 | 93.7 | 95.1 |
| Single-family units, 1980 | 3,132 | 7,458 |
| Multifamily units, 1980 | 818 | 1,578 |
| Median housing value, 1980 | $200,100 | $126,900 |

SOURCE: U.S. Bureau of the Census, 1980, and North Central Texas Council of Governments.

**EXHIBIT 3    Estimated Retail Sales for the Cities of Highland Park and University Park**

| Year | University Park | Percent Change | Highland Park | Percent Change |
|---|---|---|---|---|
| 1982 | $107,723,720 | + 7.45 | $62,017,135 | +22.94 |
| 1981 | 100,251,400 | + 4.41 | 50,443,090 | + 6.50 |
| 1980 | 96,019,811 | +23.69 | 47,364,877 | +18.93 |
| 1979 | 77,626,933 | +18.27 | 39,825,047 | +26.80 |
| 1978 | 65,632,793 | — | 31,406,769 | — |

SOURCE: Texas Comptroller of Public Accounts, Sales Tax Office.

# EXHIBIT 4
## SELECTED MARKET-AREA BANKS, LOAN AND DEPOSIT SUMMARY 1977-1982

| | 1982 | | 1981 | | 1980 | | 1979 | | 1978 | | 1977 | |
|---|---|---|---|---|---|---|---|---|---|---|---|---|
| | Deposits | Loans | Deposits | Loans | Deposits | Loans | Deposits | Loans | Deposits | Loans | Deposits | Loans |
| InterFirst Bank-Park Cities | $214,320,000 | $160,635,000 | $173,333,000 | $119,762,000 | $137,809,000 | $93,819,000 | $97,232,764 | $73,234,716 | $81,569,070 | $62,993,882 | $70,034,774 | $46,363,461 |
| Texas Commerce Bank-Hillcrest | 80,485,000 | 53,646,000 | 65,079,000 | 24,735,000 | 57,967,955 | 31,310,212 | 55,139,881 | 29,000,460 | 52,020,788 | 22,772,425 | 52,466,301 | 28,689,923 |
| Capital Bank | 83,125,000 | 50,794,000 | 68,888,526 | 45,017,412 | 55,658,207 | 32,012,366 | 48,417,032 | 29,980,232 | 31,381,372 | 22,890,986 | 23,885,127 | 16,150,610 |
| NorthPark National Bank | 262,233,600 | 175,878,600 | 225,921,000 | 154,200,000 | 188,671,254 | 104,854,507 | 143,249,554 | 82,278,323 | 103,998,109 | 65,985,780 | 81,134,537 | 46,334,174 |
| Grand Bank-Central | In organization | | | | | | | | | | | |
| Preston State Bank | 391,260,818 | 330,594,007 | 372,024,313 | 273,547,621 | 344,662,965 | 228,574,392 | 294,920,225 | 214,707,936 | 237,812,309 | 178,236,720 | 205,081,288 | 143,460,301 |
| Texas National Bank | 14,630,173 | 9,440,030 | In organization | | | | | | | | | |
| Union Bank and Trust | In organization | | | | | | | | | | | |
| Central National Bank | 37,461,347 | 25,224,417 | 29,335,600 | 12,812,637 | 22,609,540 | 9,988,313 | 20,850,157 | 16,952,675 | 13,845,990 | 11,016,694 | 10,379,483 | 9,586,010 |
| Oak Lawn Bank | In organization | | | | | | | | | | | |
| Sherry Lane National Bank | In organization | | | | | | | | | | | |
| Highland Park National Bank | Charter pending | | | | | | | | | | | |
| Total Market-Area Banks | $1,083,516,000 | $806,212,000 | $934,582,000 | $630,075,000 | $807,380,000 | $500,558,000 | $659,810,000 | $446,155,000 | $520,627,000 | $363,896,000 | $442,981,000 | $290,584,000 |

SOURCE: *Texas Banking Red Book*, 1978-1983, Banker's Digest, Inc.; FDIC Call Reports.

**EXHIBIT 5  First National Bank of Park Cities—Pro Forma Balance Sheet (dollars in thousands)**

| | Year-end Balance | | | | | | Average Balance for Income Generation | | |
| --- | --- | --- | --- | --- | --- | --- | --- | --- | --- |
| | First Year | Percentage | Second Year | Percentage | Third Year | Percentage | First Year | Second Year | Third Year |
| Cash and due from banks | $ 2,175 | (9) | $ 3,562 | (10) | $ 4,637 | (10) | 5,180 | 9,264 | 10,250 |
| Investment securities | 8,633 | (36) | 9,894 | (29) | 10,605 | (24) | 6,000 | 15,750 | 23,750 |
| Loans | 12,000 | (50) | 19,500 | (56) | 28,000 | (62) | | | |
| Fixed assets | 679 | (3) | 598 | (2) | 517 | (1) | | | |
| Other assets | 716 | (3) | 1,020 | (3) | 1,332 | (3) | | | |
| Total assets | $24,203 | (100) | $34,574 | (100) | $45,090 | (100) | | | |
| Demand deposits | $ 4,000 | (17) | $ 6,000 | (17) | $ 8,000 | (18) | 2,000 | 5,000 | 7,000 |
| Time and savings deposits | 16,000 | (66) | 24,000 | (69) | 32,000 | (71) | 8,000 | 20,000 | 28,000 |
| Total deposits | $20,000 | (83) | $30,000 | (87) | $40,000 | (89) | 10,000 | 25,000 | 35,000 |
| Other liabilities | 475 | (2) | 678 | (2) | 884 | (2) | | | |
| Common stock | 2,000 | (8) | 2,000 | (6) | 2,000 | (4) | | | |
| Surplus | 2,000 | (8) | 2,000 | (6) | 2,000 | (4) | | | |
| Undivided profits | (272) | (−1.1) | (104) | (−0.3) | 206 | (0.5) | | | |
| Total capital funds | $ 3,728 | (15) | $ 3,896 | (11) | $ 4,206 | (9) | | | |
| Total liabilities and capital | $24,203 | (100) | $34,574 | (100) | $45,090 | (100) | | | |

*Note:* Because of rounding, percentages do not always equal 100%.

**EXHIBIT 6    First National Bank of Park Cities—Operating Income and Expense (dollars in thousands)**

| | First Year | Second Year | Third Year |
|---|---|---|---|
| **Operating Income** | | | |
| Interest and fees on loans | $ 810 | $2,126 | $3,206 |
| Interest on investment securities | 570 | 1,019 | 1,125 |
| Other operating income[a] | 160 | 230 | 310 |
| Total operating income | $1,540 | $3,375 | $4,641 |
| **Operating Expense** | | | |
| Officer salaries and benefits | $ 235 | $ 289 | $ 358 |
| Employee salaries and benefits | 195 | 320 | 487 |
| Interest on deposits | 680 | 1,700 | 2,300 |
| Net occupancy expense[b] | 276 | 276 | 276 |
| Provision for loan losses | 60 | 158 | 238 |
| Other expenses[c] | 247 | 464 | 594 |
| Total operating expense | $1,693 | $3,207 | $4,253 |
| Subtotal: Income minus expense | $ (153) | $ 168 | $ 388 |
| Income taxes | — | — | 78 |
| Net operating income (loss) | (153) | 168 | 310 |
| Beginning capital funds | $4,000 | $3,728 | $3,896 |
| Less organization expense[d] | (119) | — | — |
| Add/subtract net operating income/loss | (153) | 168 | 310 |
| Ending capital funds | $3,728 | $3,896 | $4,206 |
| Number of officers | 4 | 5 | 6 |
| Number of other employees | 13 | 20 | 29 |

[a] Includes service charges, insufficient check fees, exchange fees, and so on.

[b] Includes rental of building, amortization of leasehold improvements, and furniture and equipment expense.

[c] Includes stationery, printing, postage, data processing, accounting, examination fees, advertising, telephone, and so on.

[d] Includes Mr. Turner's salary, in addition to the Comptroller's filing fee, and the attorney's and economist's fees.

**EXHIBIT 7   First National Bank of Park Cities—Information on Loans and Deposits**
**(dollars in thousands)**

| | First Year | (%) | Second Year | (%) | Third Year | (%) |
|---|---|---|---|---|---|---|
| | | | *Year-end* | | | |
| **Loan Detail** | | | | | | |
| Real estate loans | $ 2,400 | (20) | $ 3,900 | (20) | $ 5,600 | (20) |
| Commercial loans | 4,800 | (40) | 7,800 | (40) | 11,200 | (40) |
| Installment loans | 4,200 | (35) | 6,825 | (35) | 9,800 | (35) |
| Other loans | 600 | (5) | 975 | (5) | 1,400 | (5) |
| Total | $12,000 | | $19,500 | | $28,000 | |
| **Demand Deposit Detail** | | | | | | |
| NOW accounts | $ 200 | (5) | $ 300 | (5) | $ 400 | (5) |
| Regular checking | 1,800 | (45) | 2,700 | (45) | 3,600 | (45) |
| Corporate and business checking | 2,000 | (50) | 3,000 | (50) | 4,000 | (50) |
| Public funds | — | (0) | — | (0) | — | (0) |
| Total | $ 4,000 | | $ 6,000 | | $ 8,000 | |
| **Time and Savings Deposits Detail** | | | | | | |
| Automatic transfers | — | (0) | — | (0) | — | (0) |
| Regular passbook savings | $ 800 | (5) | $ 1,200 | (5) | $ 2,000 | (6) |
| Money market deposits and Super NOW accounts | 10,400 | (65) | 15,600 | (65) | 18,000 | (56) |
| Money market CDs less than $10,000 | 800 | (5) | 1,200 | (5) | 2,000 | (6) |
| CDs over $10,000 | 800 | (5) | 1,200 | (5) | 2,000 | (6) |
| CDs over $100,000 | 3,200 | (20) | 4,800 | (20) | 8,000 | (25) |
| Public funds | — | (0) | — | (0) | — | (0) |
| Total | $16,000 | | $24,000 | | $32,000 | |

**EXHIBIT 8    First National Bank of Park Cities—National Bank Charters Compared to State Bank Charters**

## 1. STATUTORY REQUIREMENTS

### National Bank

The Comptroller of the Currency ("Comptroller") charters national banks pursuant to the standards set forth in the National Bank Act of 1864, the Federal Deposit Insurance Act of 1935, and the Community Reinvestment Act. The Comptroller's decision is based upon objective facts and subjective judgment. The National Bank Act sets forth the procedure necessary to obtain a charter.

The broad statutory factors considered by the Comptroller in deciding whether to approve or disapprove applications to organize new banks are derived from the Federal Deposit Insurance Act and include: (12 C.F.R. #5.20(b))

1. The bank's future earnings prospects.
2. The general character of its management.
3. The adequacy of its capital structure.
4. The convenience and needs of the community to be served by the bank.
5. The financial history and condition of the bank.
6. The compliance with the National Bank Act.
7. Whether the corporate powers are consistent with the Federal Deposit Insurance Act.

Although a literal reading of the National Bank Act requires the Comptroller to grant a charter if the statutory standards are met, the Comptroller's discretion to deny a charter is unquestioned.

The Act provides that a national bank may be organized by five or more natural persons who enter into articles of association specifying the objectives for which the association is formed. The organizers also prepare an organization certificate stating the name of the association, which must include the word "national," the place of operation, the amount of capital stock, the number of shares, the names and addresses of shareholders, the number of shares held by each shareholder, and the fact that the certificate is made to enable the persons to organize a bank under the national banking laws. (12 C.F.R. #27,28)

The initial capital of a national bank is the amount of its unimpaired common stock plus the amount of preferred stock outstanding and unimpaired. The statutory minimum capital of a national bank depends upon the population of the city where the bank is located. (12 U.S.C. #51)

| Population of City | Capital Requirement for National Bank |
|---|---|
| 1. 6,000 or fewer inhabitants | Not less than $50,000 |
| 2. 6001–50,000 inhabitants | Not less than $100,000 |
| 3. More than 50,000 | Not less than $200,000 |

However, this statutory minimum is deemed inadequate by the Comptroller; generally at least $1 million in capital is required before authorization to commence business. (12 C.F.R. #5.20(c)(3)(iii))

**EXHIBIT 8**   (continued)

## State Bank (Texas Civil Statutes)

### Art. 342-300. *Application for and Granting of Charters*

*Approval*

A. Applications for a State bank charter shall be granted only upon good and sufficient proof that all of the following conditions presently exist:

1. A public necessity exists for the proposed bank.
2. The proposed capital structure is adequate.
3. The volume of business in the community where such proposed bank is to be established is such as to indicate profitable operation of the proposed bank.
4. The proposed officers and directors have sufficient banking experience, ability, and standing to render success of the proposed bank probable.
5. The applicants are acting in good faith.

The burden to establish said conditions shall be upon the applicants.

B. Applicants desiring to incorporate a State bank shall file with the Banking Commissioner an application for charter upon official forms prepared and prescribed by the Commissioner. All persons subscribing to the capital stock of the proposed bank shall sign and verify under oath a statement of such stock subscribed, and which statement shall truly report the number of shares and the amount to be paid in consideration; the names, identity, title and address of any other persons who will be beneficial owners of such stock or otherwise share an interest or ownership in said stock, or who will pay any portion of the consideration; whether said stock is to be pledged as security for any loan; whether a loan has been committed or is intended for the subscription and purchase of said stock, and if so, the name and address of such person or corporation which is intended to loan funds for said purchase; the names of any cosigners, guarantors, partners or other persons liable for the repayment of any loan financing the purchase of such stock. Provided, however, that the verified statement of subscribers to stock shall be confidential and privileged from public disclosure prior to the final determination by the Board of the application for a charter, unless the Board shall find that public disclosure prior to public hearing and final determination of the charter application is necessary to a full development of the factual record.

C. The Commissioner shall require deposit of such charter fees as are required by law and shall proceed to conduct a thorough investigation of the application, the applicants and their personnel, and the charter conditions alleged. The actual expense of such investigation and report shall be paid by the applicants, and the Commissioner may require a deposit in an estimated amount, the balance to be paid in full prior to hearing of the application. A written report of the investigation shall be furnished to the State Banking Board and shall be made available to all interested parties at their request.

D. Upon filing of the application, the Commissioner shall promptly set the time and place for public hearing of the application for charter, giving the applicants reasonable notice thereof. Before the 10th day preceding the day on which the hearing is held, the Commissioner shall publish notice of the hearing in a newspaper of general circulation in the county where the proposed bank is to be located. After full and public hearing the Board shall vote and determine whether the necessary conditions set out in Section A above have been established. Should the Board, or a majority of the Board, determine all of the said conditions affirmatively, then the application shall be approved; if not, then the application shall be denied. If approved, and when the Commissioner receives satisfactory evidence that the capital has been paid in full in cash, the Commissioner shall deliver to the incorporators a certified copy of the Articles of Association, and the bank shall come into corporate existence. Provided however, that the State Banking Board may make its approval of any application conditional, and in such event shall set out such condition in the resolution granting the charter, and the Commissioner shall not deliver the certified copy of the Articles of Association until such condition has been met, after which the Commissioner shall in writing inform the State Banking Board as to compliance with such condition and delivery of the Articles of Association.

### Article 342-301. *Powers*

Subject to the provisions of this Code, five (5) or more persons, a majority of whom are residents of this state, may incorporate a state bank, with any one or more of all the following powers:

(a) To receive time and demand deposits at interest or without interest; to lend money with or without security at interest; and to buy, sell and discount bonds, negotiable instruments and other evidences of indebtedness.

(b) To act as fiscal agent or transfer agent and in such capacity to receive and disburse money and to transfer registered and countersigned certificates of stock, bonds or other evidences of indebtedness.

(c) To act as trustee under any mortgage or bond issue and to accept and execute any trust not inconsistent with the laws of this state.

(d) To act under the order or appointment of any court of record, without giving bond, as guardian, receiver, trustee, executor, administrator and, although without general depository powers, as depository for any moneys paid into court.

(e) To purchase, invest in, and sell bills of exchange, bonds, mortgages and other evidences of indebtedness, and to lend money and to charge and collect interest thereon in advance or otherwise.

(f) To receive savings deposits with or without the payment of interest.

(g) To receive time deposits with or without the payment of interest.

(h) To issue, sell and negotiate notes, bonds and other evidences of indebtedness, and, in addition, to issue and sell, for cash or on an installment basis, investment certificates, creating no relation of debtor and creditor between the bank and the holder, to be retired solely out of specified surplus, reserves, or special retirement account, and containing such provisions relative to yield, retirement, penalties, withdrawal values, and obligations of the issuing bank as may be approved by the Commissioner.

A state bank shall have all incidental powers necessary to exercise its specific powers.

### Article 342-303. *Capital, Surplus and Reserve Requirements*

Repealed by Acts 1981, 67th Leg., eff. May 20, 1981.

---

**EXHIBIT 8**   *(continued)*

---

*Art. 342-304. Articles of Association*
The articles of association of a state bank shall be signed and acknowledged by each incorporator and shall contain:

1. The name of the corporation.
2. The city or town and the county of its domicile.
3. Such of the powers listed in Article 1 of this Chapter as it shall choose to exercise.
4. The capital and the denomination and number of shares.
5. The number of directors.
6. The period of duration, which may be perpetual.

## 2.  NATIONAL OR STATE CHARTERS

### National Bank

| Advantages | Disadvantages |
|---|---|
| Free use of check-clearing facilities | Must hold stock in the Federal Reserve System equal to 3% of its capital and surplus, and such amount must be kept in non-income-producing status |
| Use of the Federal Reserve discount window | |
| Automatically become members of FDIC | |
| | Not permitted to lend on unimproved real estate |
| | Can make loans to a single customer up to only 15% of capital and surplus if it is unsecured; 25% if it is secured |

### State Bank

| Advantages | Disadvantages |
|---|---|
| May count correspondent balances as a part of its reserve requirement and still produce income from those reserves | Must elect membership and be approved by FDIC |
| Is permitted to lend on unimproved real estate | |
| Can make loans to a single customer up to a level equal to 20% of capital and surplus | |

# CASE 2

## IMPERIAL NATIONAL BANK

Mr. Geoffrey Mellors, recently appointed president of Imperial National Bank of Alpine, Texas, decided in early 1988 to invite an experienced independent consultant to review the overall organization and strategic policies of his bank. This comprehensive review was prompted by the concern expressed by two members of the board of directors about the new directions taken by the bank during the past year. The sudden accidental death of the late chairman of the board and president had caused the Imperial National Bank to acquire an immediate change of leadership. That new leadership, in the person of Geoffrey Mellors, had also rather quickly brought substantial change in the bank's approach to business development and its traditional pattern of operations. Accordingly, at a recent board meeting, two of the older and more experienced board members politely but firmly suggested that it might prove advisable for an independent consultant to evaluate the bank's total situation. The board and the new president then could jointly consider the new activities undertaken by the bank, as well as its problems and opportunities, based on an objective assessment. The material that follows summarizes the preliminary information gathered by a consultant, selected by Mellors, regarding the organization, liquidity, investments, loan activities, and personnel of Imperial National Bank.

There were five commercial banks in Alpine with total deposits on December 31, 1987, of about $240 million. Three of these banks had been operating for 20 to 40 years. The other two had been organized for less than 10 years, one having been incorporated only 4 years ago. The largest bank in Alpine had deposits of about $112 million, the second largest had deposits of about $60 million, and the third largest was the Imperial National Bank, with deposits at year-end 1987 of $46 million. The deposits of the remaining two banks totaled approximately $12 million each.

Imperial National Bank's stock was held by about 125 stockholders, with one, a director but not an officer, owning 25 percent of the outstanding stock. Cash dividends ranging between 10 and 15 percent of par value had been paid in recent years, as well as several stock dividends. Imperial's board of directors was composed of 15 members, all of whom had business interests in Alpine, although 2 lived in Brownwood. Their investments in Imperial National Bank were not an important part of their financial holdings. The president and executive vice-president were the only two bank officers on the board. About two-thirds of the directors were 55 to 65 years old.

Imperial National was located in a three-story building about 20 years old, part of which was rented as office space. The structure had been partly remodeled about six years ago, and three drive-in windows had been added. The bank's equipment was fairly efficient, but no effort has been made to acquire the most modern facilities.

Twenty years ago, an important part of the bank's business was agricultural, but by 1987 only a modest part of the bank's volume involved agriculture. In fact, Alpine's growth had resulted primarily from the fact that its business was fairly well distributed among personal, retail, and commercial banking business. Local building and construction activity had also produced a considerable volume of construction loans on which the bank's past record had proven good.

Recently, Imperial National Bank had not found it necessary to buy Federal funds or to borrow to any great extent. In the past, however, borrowing had been necessary on a few occasions. Imperial National Bank had been a modest net seller of Federal funds during the past few months. The bank had an arrangement with City National Bank, its principal correspondent, to borrow Federal funds of up to $900,000 if needed. In this connection, City National Bank stipulated, as a condition of this line, that total borrowings and Federal funds purchases from all sources would not at any time exceed $900,000.

## BANK OFFICERS AND ORGANIZATION

Mr. Mellors lived in Alpine and had served on the bank's board for several years. He owned about 5 percent of the bank's stock, which he inherited from his father. Mellors was a 40-year-old lawyer, having obtained a law degree at Southern Methodist University. He did not practice law, however, but occupied himself with looking after his personal wealth, which was substantial, and that of his wife, who had inherited a large amount of local urban property. During the last 10 years, Mellors had also been heavily engaged in real estate development and construction. He had long believed that frequent use of substantial credit constituted one of the best ways to make money. He felt that Imperial National Bank had not been as aggressive as it should have been in its loan policies and that over the years the bank had not taken advantage of many opportunities for business that would have proven quite profitable. Although he had mentioned this from time to time as a board member, Mellors had never pressed the matter with the bank's former management. He had made it clear to certain people, however, that he would be available to serve as the bank's chief executive should the necessity arise. Moreover, Mellors had increased his stock ownership by purchasing the holdings of the two former chief executives. He financed these stock purchases through a loan with the same correspondent, City National Bank, that handled his real estate financing.

Since becoming president of Imperial National Bank, Mellors had devoted some of his time to reconsidering several loan proposals declined by the prior management. A number of these transactions were subsequently approved, several from geographic regions outside the bank's normal service area. Mellors felt that his more aggressive approach to bank management would materially increase Imperial's profit performance.

Following is a summary of the other members of management:

The executive vice-president, George Parrott, was 35 years of age. He grew up in Alpine, was single, graduated from the local high school, and had attended college for a year and a half. At that time he joined the bank, and during these years he had gained experience in most phases of bank operations except commercial loan and investment activities. During the past five years, Parrott had served primarily in the bank's consumer loan division.

Stephen Beard, vice-president, was 38 years old, was married, and had two children. He earned a BA degree from the University of New Mexico, majoring in social sciences. Beard was a relative newcomer to Imperial National Bank, having held his present position since December 1986, when he was recommended to the board by Mellors. Previously, Beard had been employed for 13 years in various capacities by City National Bank. Beard had worked in various divisions at City National Bank, including the credit department, but for the last eight years he had served in the correspondent bank division. One of his duties was to act as City National's contact officer for Imperial National Bank.

The bank employed two assistant vice-presidents, one of whom aided the executive vice-president in the consumer credit division while the other worked with the new vice-president, Steve Beard, in handling smaller personal and commercial loans. Each of these men was about 31 years old, and neither of them held a college degree. The cashier at Imperial National, Henry Murar, had been employed since graduating from high school. He was 35 years of age, and for the past 5 years he had been in charge of paying and receiving tellers and the bookkeeping, proof, and transit departments. There was an assistant cashier who assisted Murar in handling the teller's responsibilities and who served as head teller. Finally, another assistant cashier had charge of bookkeeping, proof, and transit activities. In total, the bank had 47 employees, 9 of whom were officers.

Imperial National had no formal training program. The bank made relatively little use of committees. The only active committee was the loan committee, composed of three board members who were not officers, plus the president, executive vice-president, and vice-president. The committee met weekly and reviewed all loans above $1,000. It was charged with responsibility for decisions on all major loans or lines of credit, although there had not been a clear definition of these latter two terms since Mellors assumed office.

**EXHIBIT I    Imperial National Bank of Alpine—Population and Bank Data on Alpine**

| Year | Population | No. Banks |
|---|---|---|
| 1965 | 20,800 | 2 |
| 1970 | 26,800 | 3 |
| 1975 | 32,400 | 3 |
| 1980 | 38,600 | 4 |
| Mid-1980s | 49,900 | 5 |

**Total Bank Deposits—Alpine (dollars in thousands)**

| | 1983 | 1984 | 1985 | 1986 | 1987 |
|---|---|---|---|---|---|
| Bank A | $ 79,856 | $ 91,818 | $ 94,420 | $105,874 | $111,684 |
| Imperial National Bank | 31,774 | 32,842 | 38,484 | 42,318 | 45,876 |
| Bank B | 47,710 | 50,442 | 67,216 | 56,332 | 59,746 |
| Bank C | 3,208 | 4,246 | 6,050 | 9,170 | 12,014 |
| Bank D | 3,016 | 4,466 | 7,912 | 9,874 | 12,298 |
| Total deposits | $165,564 | $183,814 | $214,082 | $223,568 | $241,618 |

**EXHIBIT 2**    Imperial National Bank of Alpine—Assets, Liabilities, Reserves, and Capital (dollars in thousands)

| | 12/31/85 | 6/30/86 | 12/31/86 | 6/30/87 | 12/31/87 |
|---|---|---|---|---|---|
| **Assets** | | | | | |
| Cash and balances | $ 5,148 | $ 4,908 | $ 5,602 | $ 6,190 | $ 5,736 |
| Federal funds sold | 0 | 0 | 0 | 0 | 250 |
| U.S. Treasury securities | 2,234 | 2,900 | 3,764 | 2,646 | 2,310 |
| Securities U.S. govt. agencies | 3,556 | 3,174 | 3,374 | 3,956 | 4,068 |
| Obligations of state and political subdivisions | 6,878 | 7,186 | 7,430 | 8,398 | 7,792 |
| Other securities | 314 | 50 | 56 | 56 | 56 |
| Trading account securities | 0 | 0 | 0 | 0 | 0 |
| Loans & discounts—net | 22,752 | 24,636 | 25,182 | 26,932 | 29,434 |
| Fixed assets[a] | 650 | 618 | 580 | 590 | 626 |
| Other assets | 86 | 216 | 218 | 310 | 334 |
| Total assets | $41,618 | $43,688 | $46,206 | $49,078 | $50,606 |
| **Liabilities** | | | | | |
| Transaction deposits | $13,382 | $14,180 | $14,958 | $15,954 | $16,244 |
| Time & savings deposits | 19,586 | 20,706 | 21,836 | 22,962 | 23,754 |
| Deposits of U.S. govt. | 324 | 280 | 568 | 670 | 478 |
| Deposits of state and political subdivisions | 4,528 | 4,126 | 4,086 | 4,238 | 4,730 |
| Deposits of commercial banks | 438 | 382 | 574 | 492 | 406 |
| Other deposits | 196 | 180 | 296 | 306 | 264 |
| Total deposits | $38,454 | $39,854 | $42,318 | $44,622 | $45,876 |
| Federal funds purchased and other liabilities for borrowed money | 0 | 0 | 0 | 0 | 0 |
| Mortgage indebtedness | 6 | 6 | 6 | 6 | 6 |
| Other liabilities | 512 | 828 | 782 | 856 | 1,068 |
| Total liabilities | $38,972 | $40,688 | $43,106 | $45,484 | $46,950 |
| **Capital Accounts** | | | | | |
| Capital | 570 | 650 | 650 | 658 | 658 |
| Surplus[b] | 856 | 1,064 | 1,233 | 1,238 | 1,504 |
| Undivided profits[c] | 1,184 | 1,296 | 1,210 | 1,698 | 1,446 |
| Reserves | 36 | 0 | 7 | 0 | 48 |
| Total capital accounts | $ 2,646 | $ 3,010 | $ 3,100 | $ 3,594 | $ 3,656 |
| Total liabilities, reserves, and capital accounts | $41,618 | $43,698 | $46,206 | $49,078 | $50,606 |

[a] Includes bank premises owned, real estate owned other than bank premises, and investments and other assets that directly represent bank premises or other real estate.

[b] Stock dividends declared in 1986 and 1987. Changes among capital accounts are not material in this case.

[c] Ibid.

## EXHIBIT 3  Imperial National Bank of Alpine—Operating Income and Expense
### (dollars in thousands)

|  | 12/31/85 | 12/31/86 | 12/31/87 |
|---|---|---|---|
| **Operating Income** | | | |
| Income from loans (including income from sale of Federal funds) | $2,070 | $2,458 | $3,139 |
| Interest and dividends on investments | 592 | 692 | 896 |
| Noninterest income | 198 | 234 | 241 |
| Total operating income | $2,860 | $3,384 | $4,276 |
| **Operating Expense** | | | |
| Interest on deposits | 1,388 | 1,392 | 1,703 |
| Employee compensation and benefits | 562 | 694 | 775 |
| Net operating expense of bank premises plus furniture, equipment, depreciation, and rent | 101 | 103 | 124 |
| Provision for loan loss | 108 | 127 | 205 |
| Other operating expense | 312 | 544 | 677 |
| Total operating expense | $2,471 | $2,860 | $3,484 |
| Income before income tax and security gains or losses | 389 | 524 | 792 |
| Applicable income tax | 41 | 66 | 142 |
| Income after tax and before security gain or loss | $ 348 | $ 458 | $ 650 |
| Net security gain or loss | 6 | 10 | 16 |
| Net income | $ 354 | $ 468 | $ 666 |
| Cash dividend declared on common stock | $ 58 | $ 100 | $ 74 |

## EXHIBIT 4  Imperial National Bank of Alpine—Loans and Discounts
### (dollars in thousands)

|  | 12/31/85 | 12/31/86 | 12/31/87 |
|---|---|---|---|
| Real estate loans | $ 6,136 | $ 7,566 | $ 9,338 |
| Loans to financial institutions | 1,111 | 914 | 1,107 |
| Loans for purchasing or carrying securities | 68 | 73 | 137 |
| Loans to farmers | 1,915 | 2,008 | 2,344 |
| Commercial and industrial loans | 5,768 | 6,487 | 7,685 |
| Loans to individuals | 7,486 | 7,847 | 8,450 |
| All other loans | 350 | 461 | 627 |
| Total loans, gross | $22,834 | $25,356 | $29,688 |
| Less reserve for loan loss | 82 | 174 | 254 |
| Total loans, net | $22,752 | $25,182 | $29,434 |

## EXHIBIT 5  Imperial National Bank of Alpine—Security Portfolio (dollars in thousands)

| Type | Book Value | Market Value | Maturity—Book | | |
|------|-----------|-------------|---------------|---|---|
| | | | Within 1 Yr. | 1–5 Yrs. | Over 5 Yrs. |
| U.S. Treasury securities | $ 2,310 | $ 2,146 | $ 400 | $ 910 | $1,000 |
| Agency securities | 4,068 | 3,789 | 800 | 800 | 2,468 |
| State & local securities | 7,792 | 7,215 | 950 | 3,432 | 3,410 |
| Total | $14,170 | $13,150 | $2,150 | $5,142 | $6,878 |

## EXHIBIT 6  Imperial National Bank of Alpine—Static Repricing Gap (dollars in thousands)

| | Within 30 Days | 30 Days–6 Mos. | 6 Mos.–1 Yr. |
|---|---|---|---|
| Repricing assets | $ 6,387 | $ 2,079 | $ 1,981 |
| Repricing liabilities | 4,821 | 5,788 | 4,722 |
| Gap | $ 1,566 | $ –3,709 | $ –2,741 |
| Cumulative gap | 1,566 | –2,143 | –4,884 |

## EXHIBIT 7  Imperial National Bank of Alpine—Ratios for Imperial and Peer Banks

| | Imperial Bank | | Peer Banks[a] | |
|---|---|---|---|---|
| | 1987 | 1986 | 1987 | 1986 |
| **Profitability** | | | | |
| 1. Return on assets | 1.3 | 1.0 | 1.12 | 1.04 |
| 2. Return on equity (including reserves) | 18.2 | 15.1 | 14.51 | 13.66 |
| 3. Cash dividends paid as percent of net income | 11.1 | 21.4 | 26.13 | 27.08 |
| **Sources and Disposition of Income** | | | | |
| *Percentage of Total Assets:* | | | | |
| 4. Total operating income | 8.4 | 7.3 | 7.67 | 7.54 |
| 5. Salaries, wages, and fringe benefits | 1.2 | 1.3 | 1.45 | 1.44 |
| 6. Interest on deposits | 4.1 | 3.6 | 3.10 | 3.05 |
| 7. Interest on borrowed money | 0.0 | 0.1 | .04 | .05 |
| 8. Net occupancy expense of bank premises | 0.7 | 0.7 | .28 | .29 |
| 9. All other operating expense | 0.6 | 0.4 | 1.47 | 1.57 |
| 10. Total operating expense | 6.9 | 6.2 | 6.34 | 6.40 |
| 11. Income after tax, before security gain or loss | 1.3 | 1.0 | 1.09 | .99 |
| 12. Net income | 1.3 | 1.0 | 1.12 | 1.04 |

**EXHIBIT 7**   (continued)

| | Imperial Bank | | Peer Banks[a] | |
|---|---|---|---|---|
| | **1987** | **1986** | **1987** | **1986** |
| *Percentage of Total Operating Income:* | | | | |
| 13. Interest on U.S. Treasury securities | 4.1 | 6.0 | 7.67 | 7.30 |
| 14. Interest on U.S. govt. agency securities | 7.0 | 5.3 | 5.04 | 4.97 |
| 15. Interest on obligations of state & local govts. | 9.8 | 9.0 | 9.45 | 10.70 |
| 16. Interest and dividends on all other securities | 0.1 | 0.1 | .40 | .43 |
| 17. Interest and fees on loans | 72.2 | 70.5 | 63.97 | 62.86 |
| 18. Interest on Fed. funds sold and repos | 1.2 | 2.1 | 3.79 | 3.49 |
| 19. All other operating income | 5.6 | 6.9 | 9.68 | 10.25 |
| 20. Total operating income | 100.0 | 100.0 | 100.00 | 100.00 |
| 21. Trust dept. income (included in item 19) | 0.0 | 0.0 | .61 | .67 |
| 22. Salaries and employee benefits | 18.1 | 20.5 | 18.89 | 19.03 |
| 23. Interest on deposits | 39.8 | 40.8 | 40.68 | 40.78 |
| 24. Interest on borrowed money | 0.0 | 0.0 | .37 | .48 |
| 25. Interest on subordinated debt and debentures | 0.0 | 0.0 | .21 | .21 |
| 26. Net occupancy expense of bank premises | 2.9 | 3.0 | 3.74 | 3.49 |
| 27. Provision for loan loss | 4.8 | 3.8 | 3.46 | 4.51 |
| 28. All other operating expense | 15.8 | 16.1 | 15.63 | 15.98 |
| 29. Total operating expense | 81.5 | 84.5 | 82.98 | 84.92 |
| 30. Income before tax & securities gain or loss | 18.5 | 15.5 | 17.02 | 15.08 |
| 31. Income after tax & before securities gain/loss | 15.2 | 13.5 | 14.32 | 12.78 |
| 32. Net securities gain (+), loss (−), after tax effect | 0.3 | 0.3 | .38 | .60 |
| 33. Net income | 15.5 | 13.8 | 14.70 | 13.38 |

**Rates of Return on Securities and Loans**
*Return on Securities:*

| | | | | |
|---|---|---|---|---|
| 34. Interest on U.S. Treasury securities | 6.0 | 6.4 | 6.85 | 6.86 |
| 35. Interest on securities of U.S. govt. agencies | 6.9 | 6.3 | 7.28 | 7.53 |
| 36. Interest on obligations of state & local govts. | 5.1 | 5.0 | 4.92 | 5.04 |
| 37. Interest & dividends on all other securities | 2.9 | 2.9 | 6.07 | 6.51 |

*Return on Loans:*

| | | | | |
|---|---|---|---|---|
| 38. Interest and fees on loans | 10.6 | 9.7 | 9.68 | 9.62 |
| 39. Net losses (−) or recoveries (+) on loans | −0.4 | −0.4 | −.38 | −.60 |

**Distribution of Total Assets/
Percentage of Total Assets
(Average Balances):**

| | | | | |
|---|---|---|---|---|
| 40. Cash assets | 12.0 | 11.9 | 11.72 | 12.49 |
| 41. U.S. Treasury securities | 5.9 | 6.8 | 8.67 | 8.15 |
| 42. Securities of other U.S. govt. agencies | 7.9 | 7.6 | 5.24 | 5.05 |
| 43. Obligations of state and local govts. | 16.2 | 16.3 | 14.60 | 16.12 |
| 44. All other securities | 0.1 | 0.3 | .48 | .46 |
| 45. Loans | 56.1 | 55.2 | 53.36 | 53.67 |
| 46. Real estate | 1.2 | 1.4 | 2.27 | 2.30 |
| 47. All other assets | 0.6 | 0.4 | 1.66 | 1.76 |

**EXHIBIT 7**  *(continued)*

| | *Imperial Bank* | | *Peer Banks*[a] | |
|---|---|---|---|---|
| | **1987** | **1986** | **1987** | **1986** |
| **Distribution of Loans/** | | | | |
| **Percent of Gross Loans (Year End):** | | | | |
| 48.  Real estate loans | 31.5 | 30.0 | 21.14 | 19.87 |
| 49.  Loans to farmers | 7.9 | 8.0 | 8.60 | 8.20 |
| 50.  Commercial and industrial loans | 25.9 | 25.8 | 26.52 | 28.50 |
| 51.  Consumer loans to individuals | 28.5 | 31.2 | 31.87 | 30.79 |
| 52.  Fed. funds sold with agreements to repurchase | 0.8 | 0.0 | 8.08 | 8.44 |
| 53.  All other loans | 5.4 | 5.1 | 3.79 | 4.26 |
| **Other Ratios** | | | | |
| 54.  Total capital accounts and reserves to total assets | 7.2 | 6.7 | 7.99 | 8.01 |
| 55.  Time and savings deposits to total deposits | 57.9 | 58.0 | 59.41 | 58.12 |
| 56.  Interest on time & savings deposits | 5.9 | 5.7 | 5.76 | 5.81 |
| 57.  Interest on large CDs | n/a | n/a | 6.42 | 6.35 |
| 58.  Income tax to net income plus income tax | 17.9 | 12.6 | 14.74 | 14.30 |
| 59.  Interest and fees on loans | 10.5 | 9.6 | 9.60 | 9.60 |

[a]Commercial banks in Eleventh Federal Reserve District with total deposits from $25,000,000 to $50,000,000.

## CASE 3    KEYSTONE NATIONAL BANK

At the end of 1990, Keystone National Bank had total resources of $410 million. It served its market area with 16 offices and a staff of 295 full-time equivalent officers and employees.

Early in 1991, Mr. Matthew Killian, executive vice-president of Keystone Bank, was reviewing the financial data he had assembled for the asset and liability management committee (ALCO). Mr. Killian had joined the bank the previous November, along with Mr. Bryce Wilson, who was named chairman of the board and chief executive officer. Shortly after the two men had assumed their new positions, Mr. Wilson instructed Mr. Killian to respond to the report of national bank examiners, dated October 17, 1990, which was highly critical of the bank's policies and procedures for monitoring and controlling its risk position. Mr. Killian was asked to review the bank's performance and, as soon as he completed his evaluation, to present his recommendations for corrective measures to the ALCO.

The examiners had found much to criticize. They specifically made note of three areas of concern. First, the bank's exposure to credit, interest-rate, and liquidity risks was judged excessive in relation to its capital strength and earnings performance. Second, the bank funded approximately 25 percent of its assets through large CDs, more than twice the peer bank average of about 12 percent. Finally, the bank's financial reports and written policy statements regarding interest-rate and liquidity risk management did not provide the data and specific guidelines needed to make well-reasoned asset and liability management decisions.

During the past few weeks, Mr. Killian had worked on evaluating Keystone's recent operating performance and its financial condition. He was also occupied with designing an information system of financial reports that would be useful in managing the bank's resources and that would meet the examiners' criticism.

For his analysis of Keystone's performance, Mr. Killian put together the financial data of eight banks for the last two years, 1989 and 1990. While none of the eight banks competed with Keystone National, each was about the same size, with total assets that ranged from about $300 million to just under $600 million. Also, the banks selected to form a suitable peer group were located in areas with economic and demographic characteristics similar to those of Keystone's market. The balance sheet and income statement data for Keystone and the peer group banks are shown in Exhibits 1 and 2. Exhibit 3 contains key financial ratios for Keystone and its peers.

The two primary financial reports designed by Mr. Killian for management's use in making asset and liability management decisions were an interest-rate sensitivity report (Exhibit 4) and a liquidity report (Exhibit 5). Mr. Killian felt that the reports would improve management's ability to monitor and understand Keystone's risk position.

In preparing for the ALCO meeting at which he would discuss his findings and present his recommendations, Mr. Killian talked to each member of the committee and obtained their views on the outlook for the local and national economies in 1991. The consensus estimate of the ALCO members was that interest rates would bottom out by the end of the second quarter and would increase during the last half of the year. Mr. Killian's summary of this forecast appears in Exhibit 6.

## EXHIBIT I    KEYSTONE NATIONAL BANK Average Balance Sheet (dollars in thousands)

| | 1990 | | | 1989 | | |
|---|---|---|---|---|---|---|
| | Keystone | | Peers | Keystone | | Peers |
| | $ | % | % | $ | % | % |
| Cash and due from banks | 27,424 | 7.03 | 6.87 | 25,869 | 7.16 | 6.97 |
| Interest-bearing bank balances | 8,348 | 2.14 | 3.10 | 7,299 | 2.02 | 2.98 |
| Federal funds sold and resales | 10,884 | 2.79 | 5.24 | 9,683 | 2.68 | 4.95 |
| **Investment securities:** | | | | | | |
| U.S. Treasuries & Federal agencies | 35,226 | 9.03 | 12.17 | 35,913 | 9.94 | 12.96 |
| State and local government securities | 24,654 | 6.32 | 7.93 | 26,628 | 7.37 | 9.04 |
| Other securities | 5,930 | 1.52 | 1.75 | 4,805 | 1.33 | 1.21 |
| Total investment securities | 65,810 | 16.87 | 21.85 | 67,346 | 18.64 | 23.21 |
| **Loans and leases:** | | | | | | |
| Commercial | 96,589 | 24.76 | 17.06 | 90,867 | 25.15 | 17.03 |
| Real estate | 69,516 | 17.82 | 23.51 | 56,218 | 15.56 | 21.59 |
| Consumer | 82,935 | 21.26 | 14.87 | 74,247 | 20.55 | 14.89 |
| Other loans | 16,306 | 4.18 | 4.29 | 17,776 | 4.92 | 4.82 |
| Lease financing | 1,053 | .27 | .35 | 831 | .23 | .31 |
| Total loans and leases | 266,399 | 68.29 | 60.08 | 239,939 | 66.41 | 58.64 |
| Less reserve for losses | 3,199 | .82 | .73 | 2,746 | .76 | .66 |
| Net loans and leases | 263,200 | 67.47 | 59.35 | 237,193 | 65.65 | 57.98 |
| Bank premises and equipment, net | 7,295 | 1.87 | 1.69 | 7,045 | 1.95 | 1.84 |
| Other assets | 7,139 | 1.83 | 1.90 | 6,865 | 1.90 | 2.07 |
| Total assets | 390,100 | 100.00 | 100.00 | 361,300 | 100.00 | 100.00 |
| Total earning assets | 351,441 | 90.09 | 90.27 | 324,267 | 89.75 | 89.78 |
| Noninterest-bearing demand deposits | 67,058 | 17.19 | 17.14 | 63,264 | 17.51 | 17.32 |
| Interest-bearing demand deposits | 29,375 | 7.53 | 8.24 | 29,012 | 8.03 | 8.80 |
| Regular savings | 21,104 | 5.41 | 7.89 | 18,860 | 5.22 | 8.07 |
| Money market deposit accounts | 44,159 | 11.32 | 18.39 | 38,876 | 10.76 | 15.96 |
| Time deposits under $100,000 | 82,857 | 21.24 | 23.86 | 77,788 | 21.53 | 24.57 |
| Time deposits $100,000 and over | 98,032 | 25.13 | 11.49 | 88,048 | 24.37 | 11.68 |
| Total deposits | 342,585 | 87.82 | 87.01 | 315,848 | 87.42 | 86.40 |
| Federal funds purchased | 14,551 | 3.73 | 4.77 | 15,211 | 4.21 | 5.15 |
| Other liabilities | 7,295 | 1.87 | 1.24 | 6,937 | 1.92 | 1.37 |
| Total liabilities | 364,431 | 93.42 | 93.02 | 337,996 | 93.55 | 92.92 |
| Shareholders' equity | 25,669 | 6.58 | 6.98 | 23,304 | 6.45 | 7.08 |
| Total liabilities and equity capital | 390,100 | 100.00 | 100.00 | 361,300 | 100.00 | 100.00 |

**EXHIBIT 2    KEYSTONE NATIONAL BANK Income Statement—Taxable-Equivalent Basis— Percentage of Average Total Assets (dollars in thousands)**

| | 1990 Keystone $ | 1990 Keystone % | 1990 Peers % | 1989 Keystone $ | 1989 Keystone % | 1989 Peers % |
|---|---|---|---|---|---|---|
| **Interest income:** | | | | | | |
| Loans and leases | 30,467 | 7.81 | 6.80 | 30,156 | 8.35 | 7.27 |
| Investment securities | 7,001 | 1.79 | 2.33 | 7,677 | 2.12 | 2.64 |
| Interest-bearing bank balances | 689 | .18 | .27 | 718 | .20 | .29 |
| Federal funds sold | 775 | .20 | .38 | 794 | .22 | .42 |
| Total interest income | 38,932 | 9.98 | 9.78 | 39,345 | 10.89 | 10.62 |
| **Interest expense:** | | | | | | |
| Interest on deposits | 18,828 | 4.83 | 4.70 | 19,835 | 5.49 | 5.40 |
| Interest on short-term borrowings | 989 | .25 | .34 | 1,156 | .32 | .39 |
| Total interest expense | 19,817 | 5.08 | 5.04 | 20,991 | 5.81 | 5.79 |
| Net interest margin | 19,115 | 4.90 | 4.74 | 18,354 | 5.08 | 4.83 |
| Provision for loan losses | 2,146 | .55 | .43 | 1,770 | .49 | .41 |
| Adjusted net interest margin | 16,969 | 4.35 | 4.31 | 16,584 | 4.59 | 4.42 |
| Noninterest income | 3,511 | .90 | .94 | 3,324 | .92 | .97 |
| **Noninterest expense:** | | | | | | |
| Personnel | 6,671 | 1.71 | 1.61 | 6,540 | 1.81 | 1.70 |
| Occupancy and equipment | 2,302 | .59 | .52 | 2,276 | .63 | .57 |
| Other noninterest expense | 5,110 | 1.31 | 1.24 | 4,914 | 1.36 | 1.28 |
| | 14,083 | 3.61 | 3.37 | 13,730 | 3.80 | 3.55 |
| Net overhead | 10,572 | 2.71 | 2.43 | 10,404 | 2.88 | 2.58 |
| Income before income taxes | 6,397 | 1.64 | 1.88 | 6,178 | 1.71 | 1.84 |
| Applicable income taxes | 2,849 | .73 | .84 | 2,746 | .76 | .82 |
| Net income | 3,548 | .91 | 1.04 | 3,432 | .95 | 1.02 |

**EXHIBIT 3 KEYSTONE NATIONAL BANK Key Financial Ratios—Average Balances and Taxable-Equivalent Income**

| | 1990 | | 1989 | |
|---|---|---|---|---|
| | Keystone National | Peer Group | Keystone National | Peer Group |
| **Profitability measures:** | | | | |
| 1. Return on assets | .91% | 1.04% | .95% | 1.02% |
| 2. Net profit margin | 8.36 | 9.70 | 8.04 | 8.80 |
| 3. Asset yield or utilization | 10.88 | 10.72 | 11.81 | 11.59 |
| 4. Return on equity capital | 13.82 | 14.90 | 14.73 | 14.41 |
| 5. Leverage or equity multiplier | 15.20× | 14.33× | 15.50× | 14.12× |
| **Spread management (% of earning assets):** | | | | |
| 6. Net interest margin | 5.44% | 5.25% | 5.66% | 5.38% |
| 7. Adjusted net interest margin | 4.83 | 4.77 | 5.11 | 4.92 |
| 8. Net overhead burden | 3.01 | 2.69 | 3.21 | 2.87 |
| **Asset management (% of assets):** | | | | |
| 9. Fed. funds sold & int.-bearing bk. balances | 4.93% | 8.34% | 4.70% | 7.93% |
| 10. U.S. Treasuries & Federal agencies | 9.03 | 12.17 | 9.94 | 12.96 |
| 11. State and local government securities | 6.32 | 7.93 | 7.37 | 9.04 |
| 12. Net loans and lease financing | 67.47 | 59.35 | 65.65 | 57.98 |
| 13. Bank premises and equipment | 1.87 | 1.69 | 1.95 | 1.84 |
| **Liability management (% of assets):** | | | | |
| 14. Noninterest demand deposits | 17.19% | 17.14% | 17.51% | 17.32% |
| 15. Interest-bearing demand deposits | 7.53 | 8.24 | 8.03 | 8.80 |
| 16. Regular and money market savings | 16.73 | 26.28 | 15.98 | 24.03 |
| 17. Time deposits under $100,000 | 21.24 | 23.86 | 21.53 | 24.57 |
| 18. Time deposits $100,000 and over | 25.13 | 11.49 | 24.37 | 11.68 |
| 19. Short-term borrowings | 3.73 | 4.77 | 4.21 | 5.15 |
| **Expense control:** | | | | |
| 20. Interest expense/assets | 5.08% | 5.04% | 5.81% | 5.79% |
| 21. Interest expense/int. paying liabilities | 6.83 | 6.75 | 7.84 | 7.80 |
| 22. Assets per FTE employee (thousands $) | $1,322 | $1,485 | $1,216 | $1,352 |
| 23. Personnel expense/assets | 1.71% | 1.61% | 1.81% | 1.70% |
| 24. Other operating expenses/assets | 1.90 | 1.76 | 1.99 | 1.85 |
| 25. Provision for loan losses/assets | .55 | .43 | .49 | .41 |
| **Asset yield enhancement:** | | | | |
| 26. Interest income/assets | 9.98% | 9.78% | 10.89% | 10.62% |
| 27. Interest income/earning assets | 11.08 | 10.83 | 12.13 | 11.83 |
| 28. Noninterest income/assets | .90 | .94 | .92 | .97 |
| 29. Loan income/loans and leases | 11.44 | 11.32 | 12.57 | 12.40 |
| 30. Yield on investment securities | 10.64 | 10.66 | 11.40 | 11.37 |
| **Credit quality (% of loans and leases):** | | | | |
| 31. Net charge-offs | .64% | .52% | .60% | .47% |
| 32. Past-due & nonaccrual loans & leases | 1.93 | 1.58 | 1.89 | 1.71 |

**EXHIBIT 3**    (continued)

|  | *1990* | | *1989* | |
| --- | :---: | :---: | :---: | :---: |
|  | **Keystone National** | **Peer Group** | **Keystone National** | **Peer Group** |
| **Liquidity measures:** | | | | |
| 33. Temporary investments/assets | 10.64% | 15.07% | 11.02% | 16.15% |
| 34. Volatile liabilities/assets | 28.86 | 16.26 | 28.58 | 16.83 |
| 35. Net loans & leases/core deposits | 107.62 | 78.59 | 104.12 | 77.60 |
| **Interest sensitivity measures (% of assets):** | | | | |
| 36. Assets repricing in one year | 51.92% | 51.95% | 53.06% | 52.24% |
| 37. Liabilities repricing in one year | 60.37 | 57.83 | 59.84 | 55.04 |
| 38. One-year GAP | (8.45) | (5.88) | (6.78) | (2.80) |
| **Capital adequacy and loan loss coverage:** | | | | |
| 39. Equity capital/assets | 6.58% | 6.98% | 6.45% | 7.08% |
| 40. Net loans & leases/equity capital | 10.25× | 8.50× | 10.18× | 8.19× |
| 41. Loan loss reserve/loans and leases | 1.20% | 1.22% | 1.14% | 1.13% |
| 42. Cash dividends/net income | 33.34 | 38.64 | 33.90 | 34.67 |
| 43. Internal capital generation rate | 9.21 | 9.14 | 9.74 | 9.41 |

## GLOSSARY OF SELECTED TERMS

**Adjusted net interest margin.** The yield realized on earning assets less total interest expense and the provision for loan losses divided by average earning assets.

**Asset yield or utilization.** Total operating income (interest income on a taxable-equivalent basis plus noninterest income) divided by average total assets.

**Core deposits.** Interest-bearing and noninterest-bearing demand deposits, regular savings, money market savings, and CDs under $100,000.

**Earning assets.** Interest-bearing assets including total loans and leases, investment securities, Federal funds sold, interest-bearing deposits with other banks, and other money market instruments.

**FTE employees.** Full-time equivalent employees.

**Gap.** The difference between rate-sensitive assets and rate-sensitive liabilities over a specified time period.

**Internal capital generation rate.** The annual rate of increase in common stockholders' equity that results from retained earnings. The rate is computed by multiplying the return on average common stockholders' equity by the earnings retention rate (the percentage of earnings retained).

**Leverage or equity multiplier.** Average total assets divided by average common stockholders' equity.

**Net charge-offs.** The difference between gross loan charge-offs and recoveries on loans.

**Net interest margin.** The difference between the yield realized on earning assets (on a taxable equivalent basis) and total interest expense divided by average earning assets.

**Net loans and leases.** Gross loans less unearned income and the loan loss reserve.

**Net overhead.** The difference between noninterest income and noninterest expense divided by average earning assets.

**EXHIBIT 3** *(continued)*

**Net profit margin.** Net income after taxes divided by total operating income (on a taxable equivalent basis).

**Nonaccrual loans and leases.** Loans and leases on which interest accruals have been discontinued, usually due to the borrower's financial difficulties.

**Noninterest expense.** All operating expenses other than interest expense and the provision for loan losses, including salaries, fringe benefits, occupancy costs, etc.

**Noninterest income.** All income other than interest and fees on earning assets, including trust department income, deposit service charge income, other service charges, etc.

**Personnel expense.** Salaries, wages, and officers' and employees' benefits.

**Return on assets.** Net income after taxes divided by average total assets.

**Return on equity capital.** Net income after taxes divided by average common stockholders' equity.

**Taxable equivalent.** Income, chiefly on state and local government securities, that is exempt from Federal income tax, is restated to a taxable equivalent basis by dividing such income by $(1 - t)$, where $t$ is the full statutory tax rate. All yield calculations reflect this adjustment.

**Temporary investments.** Interest-bearing deposits with banks, Federal funds sold, trading account securities, and investment securities with remaining maturities of one year or less.

**Volatile liabilities.** Large CDs and other time accounts in amounts of $100,000 and more, Federal funds purchased, repurchase agreements, foreign office deposits, interest-bearing demand notes issued to the U.S. Treasury, and other liabilities for short-term borrowed funds.

## EXHIBIT 4   KEYSTONE NATIONAL BANK—Interest Rate Sensitivity Report, December 31, 1990 (dollars in thousands)

| | 1–7 Days | 8–30 Days | 31–60 Days | 61–90 Days | 91–120 Days | 121–150 Days | 151–180 Days | 181–365 Days | Over 365 days | Total |
|---|---|---|---|---|---|---|---|---|---|---|
| Cash and due from banks | | | | | | | | | $ 28,795 | $ 28,795 |
| Interest-bearing bank balances | | $ 1,557 | $ 832 | $ 3,929 | $ 1,662 | $ 785 | | | | 8,765 |
| Investment securities | $ 2,625 | 505 | 2,148 | 3,074 | | 7,586 | | $ 7,467 | 45,696 | 69,101 |
| Federal funds sold and resales | 11,428 | | | | | | | | | 11,428 |
| Commercial loans | 59,187 | 4,180 | 3,762 | 4,026 | 3,226 | 2,262 | $ 1,978 | 8,762 | 13,635 | 101,418 |
| Real estate loans | 10,532 | 1,284 | 1,052 | 1,708 | 1,131 | 1,137 | 1,125 | 6,766 | 48,257 | 72,992 |
| Consumer loans | 296 | 3,527 | 4,104 | 7,208 | 4,710 | 4,692 | 4,753 | 17,536 | 40,256 | 87,032 |
| Other loans and lease financing | 696 | 536 | 880 | 1,048 | 1,413 | 1,218 | 2,094 | 3,600 | 6,742 | 18,227 |
| Other assets | | | | | | | | | 15,156 | 15,156 |
| **Total assets** | **$85,064** | **$ 11,689** | **$ 12,778** | **$ 20,993** | **$ 12,142** | **$ 17,680** | **$ 9,950** | **$ 44,131** | **$198,537** | **$412,964** |
| Noninterest-bearing demand deposits | | | | | | | | | 70,411 | 70,411 |
| Interest-bearing demand deposits | | 18,506 | | | | | | | 12,338 | 30,844 |
| Regular savings | | 234 | 415 | 508 | 465 | 509 | 281 | 3,766 | 15,981 | 22,159 |
| Money market deposit accounts | | 46,367 | | | | | | | | 46,367 |
| Time deposits under $100,000 | 714 | 2,558 | 22,575 | 4,602 | 2,445 | 6,795 | 2,661 | 19,626 | 25,024 | 87,000 |
| Time deposits $100,000 and over | 1,565 | 14,267 | 10,046 | 21,842 | 18,024 | 11,734 | 6,587 | 16,943 | 1,925 | 102,933 |
| Federal funds purchased | 15,279 | | | | | | | | | 15,279 |
| Other liabilities | | | | | | | | | 7,660 | 7,660 |
| Shareholders' equity | | | | | | | | | 26,952 | 26,952 |
| Loan loss reserve | | | | | | | | | 3,359 | 3,359 |
| **Total liabilities and equity capital** | **$17,558** | **$ 81,932** | **$ 33,036** | **$ 26,952** | **$ 20,934** | **$ 19,038** | **$ 9,529** | **$ 40,335** | **$163,650** | **$412,964** |
| Periodic GAP | $67,506 | $(70,243) | $(20,258) | $ (5,959) | $ (8,792) | $ (1,358) | $ 421 | $ 3,796 | $ 34,887 | 0 |
| Cumulative GAP | $67,506 | $ (2,737) | $(22,995) | $(28,954) | $(37,746) | $(39,104) | $(38,683) | $(34,887) | | |
| Cumulative GAP as percent of assets | 16.35% | (.66%) | (5.57%) | (7.01%) | (9.14%) | (9.47%) | (9.37%) | (8.45%) | | |
| Cumulative GAP as percent of equity capital | 250.47% | (10.16%) | (85.32%) | (107.43%) | (140.05%) | (145.09%) | (143.53%) | (129.44%) | | |

135

**EXHIBIT 5    KEYSTONE NATIONAL BANK** Liquidity Report for Maturing and Volatile Funds—First Quarter, 1991 (dollars in thousands)

| | Maturing Funds | Volatile Funds | Loan Demand/ Deposit Growth |
|---|---|---|---|
| **Assets:** | | | |
| Interest-bearing bank balances | $ 6,318 | | |
| Investment securities | 8,352 | | |
| Federal funds sold | 11,428 | | |
| Principal payments: | | | |
| Commercial loans | 15,172 | | |
| Real estate loans | 6,606 | | |
| Consumer loans | 15,135 | | |
| Other loans and lease financing | 2,658 | | |
| Total | $65,669 | | |
| **Liabilities:**[a] | | | |
| Non-interest-bearing demand deposits | | $ 8,300 | |
| Interest-bearing demand deposits | | 2,100 | |
| Regular savings | 1,157 | | |
| Money market deposit accounts | | 3,500 | |
| Time deposits under $100,000 | 22,837 | | |
| Time deposits $100,000 and over | 47,720 | | |
| Federal funds purchased | 15,279 | | |
| Total | $86,993 | $13,900 | |
| Estimated new loan demand | | | $35,000 |
| Estimated new core deposits[a] (excluding large CDs) | | | $21,000 |

[a] All deposit amounts are adjusted for required cash reserves.

**EXHIBIT 6    Keystone National Bank—Asset and Liability Management Committee Consensus View of Local and National Economic Conditions**

## LOAN DEMAND

Loan demand in 1991, especially in real estate and consumer credit card activity, will pick up in our market area in response to increased population as three major national firms— an electronics company, an automotive parts and accessories manufacturer, and a building materials supplier—will open new facilities and hire about 2,700 employees during the year. Nationally we see a recession in the first two quarters, followed by reasonable recovery in the latter half of 1991.

## INTEREST RATES

In spite of an economic slowdown in the United States, business activity is stronger than anticipated in our region. Easy monetary policy suggests that the Fed will attempt to increase money growth during the year to stem the recession. Short-term interest rates will fall about 200 basis points, then rise from 50 to 100 basis points above those levels. New York prime should average from 8.50 to 9.00 percent, while 3-month Treasury bill and CD rates should move up to 6.50 to 7.00 percent. All rate bets are off if there is a continuing recession into 1992. If the recession continues or the recovery is weak, all interest rates will continue to fall.

Keystone National Bank will pay competitive deposit rates at the high end to enlarge its base of core deposits. It will not match rates offered by some of the thrifts in our market area but will pay rates above those of our bank competitors.

## CASE 4

# UNITED NATIONAL BANK OF DENVER

In early 1988 Mr. Martin Klop was offered the position of Senior Vice-President–Funds and Financial Management at United National Bank of Denver. Klop had been serving in a similar position for a much smaller bank in western Colorado. The new position represented a potentially attractive career opportunity with a larger bank and at a higher salary. Klop was quite comfortable, however, in his current position, and the president of his bank had urged him to stay. Klop was concerned that the new position might represent some higher risks to him personally. Accordingly, he decided to do a thorough financial analysis of the United National Bank of Denver before accepting the offered position.

The United National Bank of Denver was a wholly owned subsidiary of United Banks of Colorado, a holding company that also had whole or majority interests in approximately 45 other Colorado banks and bank-related entities. The assets of United National Bank represented approximately 60 percent of the holding company's total assets. Klop's major responsibility would be for funds and financial management at United National Bank of Denver. In his interviews, Klop learned that decisions for this bank could be made somewhat independently of the holding company and the other holding company banks.

The United National Bank of Denver was the largest bank in Denver. Because branching was not allowed in Colorado, there were bank holding companies, franchised banks, loan production offices (LPOs), and Edge Act Offices in the state. In 1988, 52 Colorado-chartered banks, 5 foreign banks, 3 franchised banks, several Edge Act corporations, non-bank banks, and LPOs operated offices in the Denver SMSA. There were four banks in Denver (and Colorado) with assets of over $1 billion in early 1988—United National Bank, with assets of $2.9 billion; First Interstate Bank, $2.2 billion; Colorado National Bank, $1.3 billion; and Central Bank, N.A., $1.3 billion. Interstate banking and regional compacts were still prohibited in Colorado. Most Colorado bankers, however, believed that legislation enabling regional banking and complete interstate banking might pass the Colorado legislature by the late 1980s and early 1990s, respectively. First Interstate Bank was part of a California-based holding company that had acquired troubled American National Bank in the early 1980s and that was grandfathered before interstate banking was prohibited.

A booming economy had produced rapid growth in Colorado and the Denver area during the late 1970s and early 1980s. By the mid-1980s, however, falling energy, agriculture, and real estate prices had resulted in a significant slowing of the Denver and Colorado economies. Klop had been told that United National Bank's most recent profit plan assumed a bottoming of the energy recession by late 1987 but a deteriorating commercial real estate market in 1987 and 1988. Clearly, such plans would affect the bank's funds and financial management decisions for the next couple of years. Although Klop believed the long-term outlook for Denver and Colorado was good, he was concerned that it might be at least 1989 before economic growth would return to satisfactory levels.

To help reach his career decision, Klop obtained financial information from the bank and from a UBPR comparing United National Bank with Peer Group 3 (all banks in the United States with assets from $1 to $5 billion). This information can be found as follows: Exhibits 1 and 2 follow case 4; the UBPRs are at the end of this book, beginning on page 844.

Although Klop realized there could be comparability problems between a peer group of U.S. banks, many of which are in branching states, and a nonbranching Colorado bank that was part of a holding company, he assumed the comparisons would still prove helpful in evaluating the performance of United National Bank. He also hoped that his analysis would allow him to identify many of the bank's principal strengths and weaknesses.

**EXHIBIT I    United National Bank of Denver**

*Consolidated Statements of Income*

| (dollars in thousands) | For Three Months Ended March 31, 1988 | 1987 |
|---|---:|---:|
| **Interest Income** | | |
| Deposits with banks | $ 4,371 | $ 2,583 |
| Interest and fees on loans | 32,422 | 30,679 |
| Interest securities: | | |
| U.S. Treasury | 4,758 | 4,320 |
| U.S. government agencies | 287 | 21 |
| States and political subdivisions | 3,605 | 3,960 |
| Other investment securities | 125 | 163 |
| Trading account securities | 93 | 395 |
| Federal funds sold and securities purchased under agreements to resell | 928 | 2,306 |
| Lease financing | 426 | 401 |
| **Total Interest Income** | $47,015 | $44,828 |
| Interest expense | | |
| Deposits | 18,880 | 17,572 |
| Federal funds purchased and securities sold under repurchase agreements | 7,356 | 7,344 |
| Borrowed money | 1,324 | 1,589 |
| Less capitalized interest | — | (24) |
| Total interest expense | $27,560 | $26,481 |
| **Net Interest Margin** | 19,455 | 18,347 |
| Provision for losses | 2,343 | 3,750 |
| Net interest margin after provision for losses | $17,112 | $14,597 |
| **Noninterest Income** | | |
| Trust | 5,650 | 4,714 |
| Service charges on deposits | 3,605 | 3,365 |
| Other service charges, commissions and fees | 4,584 | 3,866 |
| Securities gains | — | 277 |
| Other income | 3,176 | 2,608 |
| Total noninterest income | $17,015 | $14,830 |
| **Noninterest Expense** | | |
| Salaries | 9,457 | 9,389 |
| Pension and employee benefits | 1,540 | 1,353 |
| Net occupancy | 3,154 | 2,776 |
| Furniture and equipment | 1,808 | 1,816 |
| Marketing and community relations | 562 | 675 |
| Data processing services purchased | 5,523 | 5,201 |
| Other expense | 5,513 | 4,741 |
| Total noninterest expense | $27,557 | $25,951 |
| Income before income taxes | 6,570 | 3,476 |
| Income tax (provision) benefit | (951) | 237 |
| **Net Income** | $ 5,619 | $ 3,713 |

**EXHIBIT I**   *(continued)*

*Consolidated Statements of Condition*

| (dollars in thousands) | As of March 31, 1988 | 1987 |
|---|---:|---:|
| **Assets** | | |
| Cash and due from banks | $ 334,321 | $ 456,008 |
| Interest-bearing deposits with banks | 238,211 | 187,641 |
| Investment securities: | | |
| U.S. Treasuries | 281,669 | 274,831 |
| U.S. government agencies | 26,623 | 1,381 |
| States and political subdivisions | 184,828 | 199,082 |
| Other investment securities | 13,288 | 9,289 |
| Total investment securities | $ 506,408 | $ 484,583 |
| Trading account securities | 4,269 | 26,733 |
| Federal funds sold and securities purchased under agreements to resell | 54,240 | 164,245 |
| Loans | 1,308,406 | 1,302,104 |
| Lease financing | 31,961 | 33,840 |
| Less allowance for losses | (35,733) | (26,606) |
| Net loans and lease financing | $1,304,634 | $1,309,338 |
| Real estate acquired through foreclosure | 14,303 | 11,107 |
| Premises and equipment | 80,180 | 80,971 |
| Customers' liability on acceptances outstanding | 807 | 762 |
| Other assets | 61,778 | 56,568 |
| Total assets | $2,599,151 | $2,777,956 |
| **Liabilities and Shareholders' Equity** | | |
| Deposits: | | |
| Demand | $ 615,800 | $ 762,795 |
| Interest with checking | 121,326 | 111,048 |
| Regular savings | 45,633 | 41,986 |
| Money market | 297,664 | 321,016 |
| CDs over $100,000 | 557,053 | 477,147 |
| Other time deposits | 121,423 | 105,799 |
| Foreign time deposits | 74,287 | 106,802 |
| Total deposits | $1,633,186 | $1,926,593 |
| Federal funds purchased and securities sold under repurchase agreements | 491,894 | 580,029 |
| Liabilities for borrowed money | 64,750 | 49,237 |
| Accrued income taxes payable | 16,176 | 19,025 |
| Acceptances outstanding | 807 | 762 |
| Other liabilities | 20,346 | 29,845 |
| Total liabilities | $2,427,159 | $2,605,491 |
| Subordinated notes | 7,000 | 7,000 |
| Shareholders' equity: | | |
| Common stock, $10 par value, 1,325,000 shares authorized and 1,156,000 shares issued | 11,560 | 11,560 |
| Surplus | 34,468 | 34,468 |
| Undivided profits | 119,843 | 119,437 |
| Less Treasury stock at cost: 4,133 shares | (879) | |
| Total shareholders' equity | $ 164,992 | $ 165,465 |
| Total liabilities and shareholders' equity | $2,599,151 | $2,777,956 |

**EXHIBIT 2  United National Bank of Denver Financial Highlights (dollars in thousands)**

| For the Year | 1987 | 1986 | 1985 | 1984 | 1983 | 1982 |
|---|---|---|---|---|---|---|
| Net income | $ 8,645 | $ 22,356 | $ 24,851 | $ 17,773 | $ 13,373 | $ 12,779 |
| Dividends paid | 10,155 | 10,172 | 8,740 | 7,615 | 7,623 | 6,572 |
| Average assets | 2,593,409 | 2,646,613 | 2,560,679 | 2,371,409 | 2,234,158 | 2,127,226 |
| Average loans/leases | 1,309,231 | 1,365,557 | 1,446,125 | 1,401,078 | 1,373,121 | 1,354,383 |
| Average deposits | 1,657,026 | 1,915,397 | 1,864,487 | 1,685,460 | 1,598,003 | 1,407,203 |
| Average shareholders' equity | 160,301 | 157,500 | 143,225 | 130,588 | 121,627 | 109,777 |
| Significant operating ratios: | | | | | | |
| Return on average assets | .33% | .84% | .97% | .75% | .60% | .60% |
| Return on average equity | 5.39 | 14.19 | 17.35 | 13.61 | 11.00 | 11.64 |
| Net charge-offs to average total loans/leases | 1.47 | 1.55 | .87 | .43 | 1.06 | .52 |
| Allowance for losses to total loans/leases (as of December 31) | 2.73 | 2.05 | 1.38 | 1.24 | 1.26 | 1.34 |
| Net interest margin before provision to earning assets[a] | 4.38 | 5.00 | 5.20 | 4.99 | 4.90 | 5.57 |
| Net noninterest expense to earning assets | 2.20 | 1.46 | 2.16 | 2.74 | 2.82 | 3.14 |
| Per share | | | | | | |
| Net income[b] | $7.49 | $19.34 | $21.50 | $15.37 | $11.81 | $12.06 |
| Dividends paid | 8.80 | 8.80 | 7.56 | 6.76 | 6.73 | 6.20 |

[a] Net interest margin calculated on tax-equivalent earnings.

[b] Based on daily weighted average shares of 1,154,302 in 1987; 1,156,000 in 1984 through 1986; 1,132,592 in 1983; and 1,060,000 in 1982.

NOTE: The UBPR's for United National Bank of Denver are found at the end of this book, beginning on page 844.

# BASIC ASSET, LIABILITY, AND CAPITAL DECISIONS

# CHAPTER 5

# Measuring and Providing Reserves and Liquidity

Part II of this book, consisting of Chapters 5 through 8, discusses the basic methods for obtaining and using funds. This chapter covers decisions involving the bank's reserve (or money) position and its liquidity position. Chapter 6 covers management of the bank's security portfolio. Chapters 7 and 8 examine obtaining funds and adequate capital to support asset–liability decisions.

Management's discretion regarding the employment of funds varies considerably. The minimum amount of cash and deposits with Federal Reserve Banks is set by regulatory decision, but the amount to be held in liquid securities is a matter of management choice. This chapter considers how a bank measures its reserve needs and what assets the bank can use to meet these needs. It then measures the various types of liquidity needs and evaluates the methods of meeting them.

## DETERMINING A BANK'S RESERVE NEEDS

A bank's reserve needs are generally set by regulatory requirements and the types of funds attracted by the bank. National banks, which must be members of the Federal Reserve, and state banks that have chosen to be members must meet reserve requirements. Reserve requirements are percentages of the types of funds attracted times the amount of funds attracted in the particular category as set forth in Regulation D of the Federal Reserve. The reserve requirements for state banks that are not members of the Federal Reserve (nonmember banks) were formerly set by the regulatory authority in each state. The Depository Institution Deregulation and Monetary Control Act of 1980 included provisions for equalization of reserve requirements for nonmember banks and for other depository institutions by September 1988.[1] The level of reserves required for all banks, as of January 1, 1993, is shown in Table 5-1.[2]

Table 5-2 shows Form 2900, which member banks use to inform the Federal Reserve Bank of their transaction accounts, other deposits, and vault cash for a week from a Tuesday through the following Monday. Deposits are recorded as of the end of each business day. Therefore, a bank that is open Monday through Friday will record the same amount for its deposits on Friday, Saturday, and Sunday of a statement week. If a bank is also open on Saturday, its Saturday and Sunday deposit totals will be the same. Deposits and vault cash are recorded on a seven-day basis, with the total for the week appearing in column 8 regardless of the days the bank conducts business. The figures contained in Form 2900 are founded for a sample moderate-sized bank not located in a financial center.

Table 5-3 illustrates the calculation of the member bank's reserve needs for two weeks starting the Thursday (two days) after the first Tuesday covered by the bank's transaction deposits but lagged 17 days for nontransaction deposits, emergency liabilities, and vault cash reported on Form 2900. Thus, most banks (those with total deposits of $44 million or more) report their deposits and vault cash on a weekly basis. Reserve needs are figured for a two-week period, which is nearly contemporaneous for transaction deposits and has a 17-day lag for other deposits and vault cash. Demand balances due from depository institutions in the United States and cash items in the process of collection are subtracted from total transaction deposits to find the transaction amounts subject to reserves. In the example, the first $42.4 million of transaction accounts subject to reserves are multiplied by the 3 percent requirement, with the remaining transaction accounts subject to 10 percent reserves. The amount of reserves on transaction accounts is added to reserves based on lagged savings and time deposits and other obligations subject to reserves (at a 0 percent rate in 1993). Vault cash (also lagged) is subtracted from this total amount of reserves to determine the reserves to be maintained at the Federal Reserve directly or on a pass-through basis during the reserve week ending two weeks later.

Figure 5-1 illustrates the timing for the sample bank when the reserves for the October 15 to 28 period are based on the transaction deposits from October 13 to 26 and other deposits from September 15 to 28. The reserves for the following two weeks (October 29 to November 11) would be based on the October 27 to November 9 transaction deposits and on September 29 to

---

[1] For most nonmember banks, reserve requirements were phased in over an eight-year period, beginning with one-eighth in November 1980 and increasing by one-eighth in September of each year after 1980. At the end of 1988, the reserves required for all nonmember banks were to equal or exceed reserve requirements in all states and govern all banks.

[2] Regulation D itself, with detailed descriptions and answers to typical questions, appears in *Federal Reserve Requirements* (Washington, D.C.: Federal Reserve Board of Governors, 1988). *Amendments to Regulation Reserve Requirements* (Washington, D.C.: Federal Reserve Board of Governors) were published in 1992.

**TABLE 5-1    Reserve Requirements for Commercial Banks,
December 14, 1992[a]**

| Type of Deposit and Deposit Intervals[b] | Percent of Deposits | Effective Date |
|---|---|---|
| Net transaction accounts[c,d] | | |
| $0–$42.4 million | 3 | 12/14/91 |
| Over $42.4 million | 10 | 12/14/91 |
| Nonpersonal time and savings deposits[e] | 0 | 12/23/90 |
| Eurocurrency liabilities[f] | 0 | 12/27/90 |
| Ineligible acceptances and obligations by affiliates | | |
| Maturity less than 7 days | 3–10[g] | 12/13/90 |
| Nonpersonal, 7 or more days | 3 | 12/13/90 |

[a]Reserve requirements in effect on December 31, 1992. Required reserves must be held in the form of deposits with Federal Reserve Banks or vault cash. Nonmembers may maintain reserve balances with a Federal Reserve Bank indirectly on a pass-through basis with certain approved institutions.

[b]The Garn–St. Germain Depository Institutions Act of 1982 (Public Law 97-320) requires that $2 million of reservable liabilities (transaction accounts, nonpersonal time deposits, and Eurocurrency liabilities) of each depository institution be subject to a zero percent reserve requirement. The board is to adjust the amount of reservable liabilities subject to this zero percent reserve requirement each year for the succeeding calendar year by 80 percent of the percentage increase in the total reservable liabilities of all depository institutions, measured on an annual basis as of June 30. No corresponding adjustment is to be made in the event of a decrease. On December 30, 1991, the exemption was raised $1.3 million. In determining the reserve requirements of depository institutions, the exemption shall apply in the following order: (1) net NOW accounts (NOW accounts less allowable deductions), (2) net other transaction accounts, and (3) nonpersonal time deposits or Eurocurrency liabilities starting with those with the highest reserve ratio. With respect to NOW accounts and other transaction accounts, the exemption applies only to such accounts that would be subject to a 3 percent reserve requirement.

[c]Transaction accounts include all deposits on which the account holder is permitted to make withdrawals by negotiable or transferable instruments, payment orders of withdrawal, and telephone and preauthorized transfers in excess of three per month for the purpose of making payments to third persons or others. However, money market deposit accounts and similar accounts subject to the rules that permit no more than six preauthorized, automatic, or other transfers per month, of which no more than three can be checks, are not transaction accounts (such accounts are savings deposits subject to time deposit reserve requirements).

[d]The Monetary Control Act of 1980 requires that the amount of transaction accounts against which the 3 percent reserve requirement applies be modified annually by 80 percent of the percentage increase in transaction accounts held by all depository institutions, determined as of June 30 each year. Effective December 15, 1992, the amount was increased from $42.4 million to $46.8 million.

[e]In general, nonpersonal time deposits are time deposits, including savings deposits, that are not transaction accounts and in which a beneficial interest is held by a depositor that is not a natural person. Also included are certain transferable time deposits held by natural persons and certain obligations issued to depository institution offices located outside the United States. For details, see section 204.2 of Regulation D.

[f]Net borrowings from related foreign offices, gross borrowings from unrelated foreign depository institutions, loans to U.S. residents made by overseas branches of domestic depository institutions, and sales of assets by U.S. depositor institutions to their overseas office.

[g]Treated as an addition to net transaction accounts.

**TABLE 5-2**

148

# Report of Transaction Accounts, Other Deposits and Vault Cash

For the week ended Monday, _____ 19___

FR 2900
OMB No. 7100-0087
Hours per response: 1.0 to 12.0
Approval expires August 1994

You must file a *Report of Certain Eurocurrency Transactions* if your institution had any foreign borrowings during the reporting period.

This report is required by law [12 U.S.C. §§248(a), 461, 603, and 615].

The Federal Reserve System regards the information provided by each respondent as confidential. If it should be determined subsequently that any information collected on this form must be released, respondents will be notified.

PLEASE READ INSTRUCTIONS PRIOR TO COMPLETION OF THIS REPORT.

Report all balances as of the close of business each day to the nearest thousand dollars.

| ITEMS | For FRB Use Only | Column 1 Tuesday Mil | Thou | Column 2 Wednesday Mil | Thou | Column 3 Thursday Mil | Thou | Column 4 Friday Mil | Thou | Column 5 Saturday Mil | Thou | Column 6 Sunday Mil | Thou | Column 7 Monday Mil | Thou | Column 8 Total Mil | Thou | |
|---|---|---|---|---|---|---|---|---|---|---|---|---|---|---|---|---|---|---|
| **A. TRANSACTION ACCOUNTS** | | | | | | | | | | | | | | | | | | |
| 1. Demand deposits: | | | | | | | | | | | | | | | | | | |
| a. Due to depository institutions | 2698 | 12 | 221 | 12 | 166 | 12 | 147 | 12 | 144 | 12 | 144 | 12 | 144 | 12 | 162 | 85 | 128 | A.1.a |
| b. Of U.S. Government | 2280 | 8 | 150 | 8 | 162 | 8 | 164 | 8 | 150 | 8 | 150 | 8 | 150 | 8 | 164 | 57 | 090 | A.1.b |
| c. Other demand | 2340 | 28 | 205 | 28 | 214 | 28 | 241 | 28 | 205 | 28 | 205 | 28 | 205 | 28 | 241 | 197 | 516 | A.1.c |
| 2. ATS accounts and NOW accounts/share drafts, and telephone and preauthorized transfers | 6917 | 30 | 010 | 30 | 242 | 30 | 240 | 30 | 210 | 30 | 210 | 30 | 210 | 30 | 241 | 211 | 363 | A.2 |
| 3. Total transaction accounts (must equal sum of Items A.1 through A.2 above) | 2215 | 78 | 586 | 78 | 784 | 78 | 792 | 78 | 709 | 78 | 709 | 78 | 709 | 78 | 808 | 551 | 097 | A.3 |
| **B. DEDUCTIONS FROM TRANSACTION ACCOUNTS** | | | | | | | | | | | | | | | | | | |
| 1. Demand balances due from depository institutions in the U.S. | 0063 | 2 | 190 | 2 | 194 | 2 | 191 | 2 | 192 | 2 | 192 | 2 | 192 | 2 | 191 | 15 | 342 | B.1 |
| 2. Cash items in process of collection | 0020 | 4 | 231 | 4 | 230 | 4 | 230 | 4 | 235 | 4 | 235 | 4 | 235 | 4 | 230 | 29 | 626 | B.2 |
| C. 1. TOTAL SAVINGS DEPOSITS (including MMDAs) | 2389 | 48 | 214 | 48 | 038 | 48 | 165 | 48 | 215 | 48 | 215 | 48 | 215 | 48 | 355 | 337 | 417 | C.1 |
| D. 1. TOTAL TIME DEPOSITS | 2514 | 42 | 565 | 42 | 531 | 42 | 531 | 42 | 506 | 42 | 506 | 42 | 506 | 42 | 526 | 297 | 671 | D.1 |
| E. 1. VAULT CASH | 0080 | | 506 | | 512 | | 498 | | 492 | | 492 | | 492 | | 493 | 3 | 475 | E.1 |
| **F. MEMORANDUM SECTION** | | | | | | | | | | | | | | | | | | |
| 1. All time deposits with balances of $100,000 or more (included in Item D.1 above) | 2604 | 8 | 614 | 8 | 314 | 8 | 414 | 8 | 714 | 8 | 714 | 8 | 714 | 8 | 823 | 60 | 307 | F.1 |
| 2. Total nonpersonal savings and time deposits (included in Items C.1 and D.1 above) | 6918 | 24 | 872 | 24 | 961 | 24 | 821 | 24 | 857 | 24 | 857 | 24 | 857 | 24 | 901 | 174 | 126 | F.2 |

If your institution had no funds obtained through use of ineligible acceptances or through issuance of obligations by affiliates, please check this box and do not complete Schedule AA. ☑

**SCHEDULE AA: OTHER RESERVABLE OBLIGATIONS BY REMAINING MATURITY**

Ineligible Acceptances and Obligations Issued by Affiliates:

| | | | | | | | | | | | | | | | | | | |
|---|---|---|---|---|---|---|---|---|---|---|---|---|---|---|---|---|---|---|
| 1. Maturing in less than 7 days | 2245 | | 0 | | 0 | | 0 | | 0 | | 0 | | 0 | | 0 | | 0 | A.A.1 |
| 2. Maturing in 7 days or more (**Nonpersonal Only**) | 6919 | | 0 | | 0 | | 0 | | 0 | | 0 | | 0 | | 0 | | 0 | A.A.2 |

**TABLE 5-3   Calculation of Required Reserves (for October 15–28, 1992)[a]**

|  | Amount (dollars in thousands) | Required Reserves (%) | Reserve (dollars in thousands) |
|---|---|---|---|
| **Transaction Accounts (Oct. 13–26)** | | | |
| Total transaction accounts | $78,728 | | |
| Less deductions | 6,424 | | |
| Subject to reserves | $72,304 | | |
| Initial amount | 42,400 | 3 | $1,272 |
| Remaining amount | 29,904 | 10 | 2,990 |
| Other reservable transaction obligations | 0 | 10 | — |
| Total transaction reserves | | | $4,262 |
| **Savings and Time Deposits (Sept. 15–28)** | | | |
| Nonpersonal savings and time deposits | $24,875 | 0 | — |
| Eurocurrency transactions | 0 | 0 | — |
| Other reservable obligations | 0 | 3 | — |
| Total other accounts and obligations | | | $ 0 |
| Total reservable deposits and obligations | | | $4,262 |
| Vault cash (Sept. 15–28) | | | 608 |
| Daily average balance, to be maintained at Federal Reserve directly or on pass-through basis (before consideration of carryover) | | | $3,654 |

[a]Based on data in Tables 5-1 and 5-2.

October 12 for other deposits, and so on. In addition, the Federal Reserve allows member banks to carry a reserve excess or deficiency into the following two-week reserve period. Thus, a bank can miss its reserve requirements by up to 2 percent on either side and be allowed to carry this position to meet or increase its new reserve requirement in the next two-week period. An excess or deficiency cannot be carried over to the second two-week period following the week in which the excess or deficiency occurs.

The process of measuring reserve requirements for state nonmember banks varies widely among the regulatory authorities in different states. Reserve requirement percentages, reserve period length, reserve period timing, and carryover provisions differ from state to state. Nevertheless, the basic idea—multiplying deposits in a previous period by reserve requirements to determine reserve needs for a period—holds in most states. Furthermore, the Depository Institution Deregulatory and Monetary Control Act of 1980 standardized the determination of reserves for member and nonmember banks.

**FIGURE 5-1** **Timing Sequence of Measuring and Filling Reserve Needs**

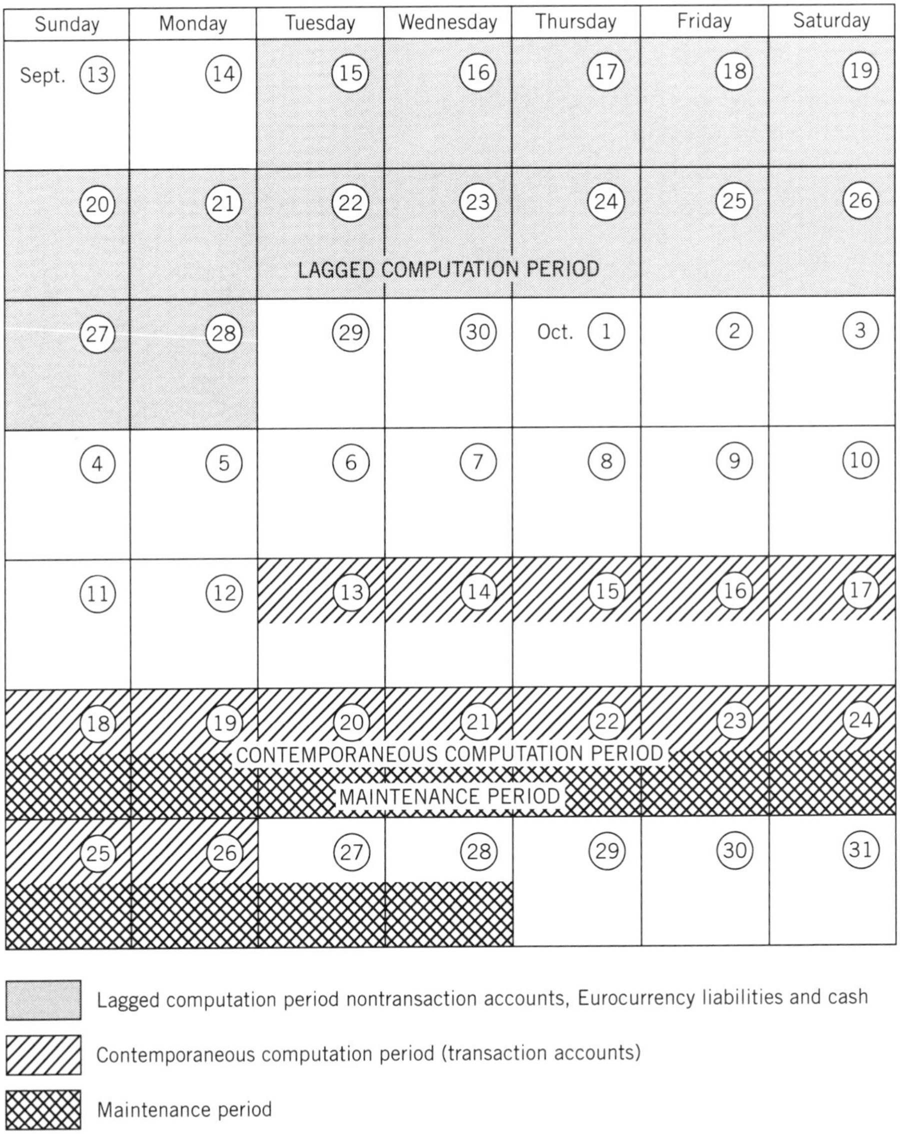

| Sunday | Monday | Tuesday | Wednesday | Thursday | Friday | Saturday |
|--------|--------|---------|-----------|----------|--------|----------|
| Sept. (13) | (14) | (15) | (16) | (17) | (18) | (19) |
| (20) | (21) | (22) | (23) | (24) | (25) | (26) |
| | | LAGGED COMPUTATION PERIOD | | | | |
| (27) | (28) | (29) | (30) | Oct. (1) | (2) | (3) |
| (4) | (5) | (6) | (7) | (8) | (9) | (10) |
| (11) | (12) | (13) | (14) | (15) | (16) | (17) |
| (18) | (19) | (20) | (21) | (22) | (23) | (24) |
| | | CONTEMPORANEOUS COMPUTATION PERIOD | | | | |
| | | MAINTENANCE PERIOD | | | | |
| (25) | (26) | (27) | (28) | (29) | (30) | (31) |

[shaded] Lagged computation period nontransaction accounts, Eurocurrency liabilities and cash

[diagonal lines] Contemporaneous computation period (transaction accounts)

[crosshatch] Maintenance period

## MEETING REQUIRED RESERVES AND MANAGING THE MONEY POSITION

There are four basic asset accounts in what most banks label as their "money" position. Each of these accounts is briefly described.

1. *Currency and coin* (or vault cash) consists of money that the bank holds to meet its daily transaction needs. When a bank has more vault cash than it needs, it deposits the excess in the Federal Reserve or a correspondent bank; the reverse (getting cash from the Fed or a correspondent) is true when the bank has less vault cash than it needs.

2. *Due from the Federal Reserve* represents the deposits of the bank with its Federal Reserve District Bank. This account is the basic reserve account of banks that are members of the Federal Reserve. The net of most checks and electronic funds transfers is ultimately taken from or added to this account. Other ways to increase this account include the purchase of Fed funds, the borrowing of funds from the Federal Reserve, depository currency and coins, and the redemption of maturing Treasury securities. Methods for decreasing Federal Reserve accounts include letting purchased Fed funds mature, selling Fed funds, repaying borrowing from the Federal Reserve, withdrawing coin and currency, and directly purchasing Treasury securities.

3. *Due from other commercial banks* consists of all deposits the bank has in other commercial banks. In most states, nonmember banks are currently permitted to count balances due from other banks to meet required reserves. These nonmember banks use their correspondent banks to clear checks (often through their Federal Reserve account), to conduct Federal funds transactions, and to provide other services as compensation for such balances. Legislation passed in 1980 forced nonmember banks in step-by-step fashion over the following eight years to hold reserves directly (or indirectly through pass-through accounts) in the Federal Reserve. Member banks also hold balances with other banks, but these reserves do not qualify to meet reserve requirements. Services such as loan participations, international transactions, and investment advice are required to compensate banks for balances left in correspondent banks.

4. *Cash items in process of collection* represent checks deposited in Federal Reserve Banks or correspondent banks for which credit has not yet been received. The size of these cash items depends on the volume of checks and the time it takes to clear the checks.

As discussed earlier, the primary objective for a bank should be to maximize the value of the owners' investment in the bank. Since the assets represented by the bank's money position are generally nonearning assets, management's objective should be to minimize the amount invested in such assets without taking excessive risk. The means of achieving this objective can be divided into three groups: cash items in the process of collection, nonreserve correspondent balances, and required reserves.

In managing cash items in the process of collection, banks should generally strive to process and collect cash items as rapidly as possible. This may involve working evenings to process checks earlier, using electronic funds transfer effectively, and flying checks by courier to key collection cities. The primary analytical technique is to ascertain that the marginal benefits—return on assets changed from nonearning to earning assets—exceed the marginal costs of speeding up the collection process.

Demand deposit balances of correspondent banks that cannot be used to meet reserve requirements should be justified by careful evaluation of the service–cost relationship. Larger correspondent banks are usually active in the collection of checks for their "downstream"correspondent banks. In return for deposit balances, many correspondent banks perform services such as giving investment advice, holding securities in safekeeping, arranging for the purchase and sale of securities, trading Federal funds, arranging international financial transactions, participating in loans too large for smaller banks, and selling participations in loans to banks with surplus funds. The services should be provided at a lower cost than that of the recipient bank, yet contribute to the profits of the correspondent bank. The cost of the correspondent balances should be the forgone returns since such balances are nonearning assets. Such costs should not exceed the benefits from the services received.

The final category, required reserves, should be regarded as the dues (explicit cost) of the business of banking. These dues are required to conduct business, but dues above the required amount earn either no return or a return significantly below what the bank can earn on other earning assets. The philosophy in managing the required reserve portion of a bank's money position is usually to meet just the bank's required reserves with acceptable assets—vault cash and deposits at the Federal Reserve and pass-through accounts to the Federal Reserve.

It is important to remember that required reserves are the dues required to be a bank and are used by the Federal Reserve to control the money supply through monetary policy. Required reserves are *not* liquid assets, which can be used to meet loan demands or deposit outflows. Indeed, vault cash and deposits at the Federal Reserve that are required as reserves would seem to be about as nonliquid as bank premises. The interaction between reserves and liquidity is strong. The reserve position of a bank serves as the clearing account for liquidity needs, such as new loans and deposit outflows, and the liquidity position is a buffer for its money position. However, both needs must be met separately.

In managing its money position, a bank must meet its reserve requirements within the time constraints discussed in the preceding section. Random demands for loans and fluctuations in supplies of funds may force it either to buy funds at a higher than optimal price because it needs funds quickly or to employ funds at a lower than optimal return because it has excess reserves to invest immediately. The leeway provided by knowing reserve requirements in advance does not greatly simplify the problem because the balances themselves are subject to change each day. Having determined the bank's requirement at opening time, it is the money-position manager's task to keep track of all important transactions that affect the reserve balance during the day and to take steps to counteract any adverse effects.

The principles of managing the money position are virtually the same in large and small banks. It is the number rather than the nature of the transactions that greatly complicates the task for larger banks in money centers. For the latter, especially for banks serving the New York City money and securities markets, the management of reserve positions is virtually a continuous task. The rapidity with which funds flow through the money market banks reflects the payment for most of the nation's security transactions, as well as the financing of brokers and dealers. This rapidity results from the high degree to which national corporations have consolidated their balances in the money centers, as well as how fully they keep them invested. Finally, the balancing adjustments of all the country banks and the settlement of the Federal funds markets are made on the books of banks in the money centers.

The basic problems involved in managing a money position can be more readily seen in the analysis of procedures that are adequate for the moderate-sized bank not located in a financial center used in Tables 5-1, 5-2, and 5-3. Table 5-4 presents a sample worksheet that such a bank might use to manage its money position. The bank starts by adding its *estimated* contemporaneous reserves for transaction deposits for the October 13 to 26 period to known reserves (based on September 15 to 28 figures) for other deposits and idle cash. The potential excess or deficiency (column 3) can be changed by Federal funds transactions, borrowing from the Federal Reserve, and direct transactions on Treasury securities, with the resulting estimated actual excess or deficiency appearing in column 8 and cumulated in column 9. The estimated contemporaneous reserves will be revised when transaction deposits for October 13 to 19 are reported, and they will be finalized when transaction deposits for October 20 to 26 are calculated. It is the bank's (not the Federal Reserve's) responsibility to make these transaction deposit estimates and to make sure the final required balance is consistent with the contemporaneous transaction deposit reserves. Banks have generally done a good job since contemporaneous reserves were implemented starting February 2, 1984.

Any surplus or deficit position up to 4 percent of daily average reserve requirements from the previous two-week period is placed at the head of columns 3, 8, and 9 on the worksheet in Table 5-4. These amounts are included only in the excess or deficiency figures because they do not, of course, affect the actual amounts of deposits on record. Without the carryover provision, reserve surpluses would be wasted, since reserves earn no interest. Similarly, shortfalls in reserve holdings can also be carried into the next period. Negative carryovers are not permitted for two or more consecutive periods.

A glance at the final column of the worksheet will tell the bank's money manager just where the bank stands at the opening of business each day.[3]

---

[3] Since the Federal Reserve is open only five days a week, no transactions are recorded over the weekend; hence the reserve balance that the bank achieves Friday afternoon will also be its deposit balance for Saturday and Sunday. When holidays occur on Mondays or Fridays, the position is carried a day longer. For example, if a holiday falls on a Monday, the Federal Reserve being closed, the bank's reserve position as of Friday will apply not only to Saturday and Sunday but also to Monday. Hence, locking into a surplus reserve position over a holiday weekend is one method of helping meet reserve requirements for a period.

**TABLE 5-4  Worksheet for Computing Reserve Position**

| Reserve Balances For: | | Required Balances with Federal Reserve Banks[a] | Potential Balances with Federal Reserve Bank | Potential Excess or Deficiency | Federal Funds Actions | | Other Adjustments Affecting Reserve Position[b] | Closing Balances with Federal Reserve Bank | Actual Excess or Deficiency | Accumulated Excess or Deficiency +30 |
| | | | | | Federal Funds Purchased | Federal Funds Sold | | | | |
| Day | Date | (1) | (2) | (3) | (4) | (5) | (6) | (7) | (8) | (9)[c] |
| Thurs. | Oct. 15 | 3,654 | 3,807 | +153 | | | | 3,807 | +153 | +183 |
| Fri. | Oct. 16 | 3,654 | 3,713 | + 59 | | 200 | | 3,513 | −141 | + 42 |
| Sat. | Oct. 17 | 3,654 | 3,713 | + 59 | | 200 | | 3,513 | −141 | − 99 |
| Sun. | Oct. 18 | 3,654 | 3,713 | + 59 | | 200 | | 3,513 | −141 | −240 |
| Mon. | Oct. 19 | 3,654 | 3,452 | −202 | | | | 3,452 | −202 | −442 |
| Tues. | Oct. 20 | 3,654 | 3,209 | −445 | | | | 3,209 | −445 | −887 |
| Wed. | Oct. 21 | 3,654 | 3,461 | −193 | 379 | | | 3,840 | +186 | −701 |
| Thurs. | Oct. 22 | 3,654 | 3,579 | − 75 | 300 | | | 3,879 | +225 | −476 |
| Fri. | Oct. 23 | 3,654 | 3,588 | − 66 | 200 | | | 3,788 | +134 | −342 |
| Sat. | Oct. 24 | 3,654 | 3,588 | − 66 | 200 | | | 3,788 | +134 | −208 |
| Sun. | Oct. 25 | 3,654 | 3,588 | − 66 | 200 | | | 3,788 | +134 | − 74 |
| Mon. | Oct. 26 | 3,654 | 3,720 | + 66 | | | | 3,720 | + 60 | − 8 |
| Tues. | Oct. 27 | 3,654 | 3,681 | + 27 | | | | 3,681 | + 27 | + 19 |
| Wed. | Oct. 28 | 3,654 | 3,740 | + 86 | | 200 | | 3,540 | − 114 | − 95[d] |

[a] Usually estimated on October 15 and October 20 (October 13 to 19 figures available) and finalized on October 27 (October 20 to 26 figures available).
[b] Such as borrowing from the Federal Reserve and payments for and receipts from direct transaction on Treasury securities.
[c] Allowable excess or deficiency in reserve balances brought forward.
[d] Allowable excess or deficiency in reserve balances to be carried forward.

This person then needs to calculate the effects of the debits and credits that he or she believes will be posted to the reserve account during each day. He or she is then in a position to project the current and cumulative average balances as of the close of business the same day. On the basis of this projection, a decision can be made regarding what actions, if any, will be necessary to keep this position in reasonable balance. Table 5-5 provides a suggested form for making these calculations. For small banks with only moderate deposit fluctuations, not much more is needed. For larger banks seeking to keep excess reserves to the barest minimum, a closer scrutiny of daily transactions is necessary.

The bulk of the credits and debits affecting the reserve bank's accounts not located in the money centers is usually evident in the clearing figures each morning (checks presented to it and checks forwarded by it for collection) or is the result of transactions, such as securities purchases and sales, that the bank has originated. In sharp contrast is the situation of banks that operate in the money centers or that carry substantial amounts of due-to-bank balances. During the course of each day, these banks are subject to immediate and unpredictable demands in the form of interbank transfers and other payments arranged in Federal funds by their depositors.

Nevertheless, even for a small community bank, the unpredictable can loom large in the management of its reserve position. The volatility of large deposit accounts can cause money position management to go awry as the result of unexpectedly large withdrawals or even large deposits that cannot be used. Alert money managers will therefore attempt to keep a close watch over the larger depositors and will take notice of the transactions that may affect the reserve position not only on a particular day but later in the reserve-computation period as well. Large deposits and withdrawals can be scanned daily for clues to future deposit swings, and an attempt can be made to get advance notice of future transactions from the financial officers of important corporate customers. At the same time, a calendar of maturing CDs and securities and large loan repayments should be maintained and taken into consideration in the daily adjustments of the reserve position. The money-position manager should also receive a brief daily memorandum of the sources of funds available and a list of correspondent balances and liquidity instruments. Most large banks require that branch managers and department heads report large transactions to the "money desk" as soon as these transactions become known.

In addition to gathering data, the money market manager seeks to match reserve requirements with actual reserve positions. At the start of the statement period, a bank should make a rough forecast of its expected reserve position for each day in the coming period. The manager of the reserve position must then plan out the bank's activity during the period on the basis of the mean forecast of reserve positions and the possible deviations from the mean forecast that might be experienced.

If the projected deposit balances at the Federal Reserve are as shown in Table 5-4, the bank will probably need to buy Federal funds (or borrow from the Federal Reserve) sometime during the period to meet its reserve requirements.

**TABLE 5-5  Estimated Money Position Calculations, Thursday, October 22 (dollars in thousands)**

|  | Previous | Current | Cumulative |
|---|---|---|---|
| Accumulated actual excess or deficiency |  |  | (−)701 |
| Required reserves tonight |  | 3,654 |  |
| Reserve position last night | 3,461 |  |  |
| Transactions affecting reserves today: |  |  |  |
| Net check clearings: (+) net credit or (−) net debit |  | (−) 424 |  |
| Other credits: |  |  |  |
|   Yesterday's immediate cash letter |  | 2,181 |  |
|   Deferred items available today |  | 885 |  |
|   Security sales available today |  | 737 |  |
|   Currency and coin in transit |  | 100 |  |
|   Credit in local clearings |  | — |  |
|   Other |  | — |  |
|     Total other credits |  | (+)3,903 |  |
| Other debits: |  |  |  |
|   Remittances charged today |  | 3,206 |  |
|   Securities purchased charged today |  | — |  |
|   Notes due today |  | — |  |
|   Tax and loan call |  | 100 |  |
|   Currency and coin orders |  | — |  |
|   Debits in local clearings |  | 55 |  |
|   Other |  | — |  |
| Total other debits |  | (−)3,361 |  |
| Net credits minus debits |  | (+) 118 |  |
| Potential balances tonight |  | 3,579 |  |
| Potential excess or deficit tonight |  | (−) 75 | (−)776 |
| Adjusted today: |  |  |  |
|   Credits: |  |  |  |
|     Transfers from bank account |  | — |  |
|     Borrowing from Federal Reserve |  | — |  |
|     Federal funds bought |  | 300 |  |
|     Securities sold for "cash" |  | — |  |
|   Total credits |  | 300 |  |
|   Debits: |  |  |  |
|     Transfers from reserve account |  | — |  |
|     Federal funds sold |  | — |  |
|   Total debits |  | — |  |
| Net adjustments |  | (+) 300 |  |
| Adjusted excess or deficiency |  | (+) 225 | (−)476 |

However, if the possible deviations from these expected levels are small, the reserve manager may want to wait until close to the end of the period and then (since the reserve deficiency is not expected to be large) enter the market and buy funds if necessary. Since the distribution of possible outcomes is small and the expected deficit is also small, the manager can wait until more information is available before acting.

On the other hand, if there is a great deal of uncertainty about the upcoming week, the reserve manager may want to borrow Federal funds early in the period and establish a cushion of reserves so as to avoid borrowing a sizable amount at the last minute. In this case, the bank will sell Federal funds toward the end of the period if reserve positions have worked out to be much closer than forecasted. The bank will act defensively in this time period, sacrificing returns to be able to satisfy legal reserve requirements.

## MEASURING AND FILLING A BANK'S LIQUIDITY NEEDS

A bank's liquidity needs consist of immediate obligations, such as deposit withdrawals or legitimate loan demands, that the bank must meet to be recognized as an ongoing financial intermediary. A bank's liquidity needs and its ability to meet such needs are difficult to measure because the perception and confidence of actual and potential depositors and the money market are all-important but very difficult to quantify.

The traditional way to measure a bank's liquidity position was to look at static liquidity ratios, trying to increase liquidity needs and liquidity sources. For example, a bank would separate its assets into liquid (easily convertible into cash without appreciable loss) and nonliquid components. The bank's liabilities and net worth would be separated into volatile (vulnerable to withdrawal) and reliable (stable) components. Bank managers and regulators would decide the acceptable level for ratios such as temporary assets to total assets or temporary assets to volatile liabilities. The most famous of these ratios is the volatile liability dependency ratio:

$$\frac{\text{Volatile liabilities} - \text{Liquid assets}}{\text{Earning assets}}$$

All of these ratios suffer because they measure liquidity statically (at a point in time) and ignore the dynamic nature of liquidity needs and sources. In the following paragraphs the dynamic nature of liquidity is stressed. A bank's liquidity needs are measured over time; then liquidity sources are matched with these changing needs.

Table 5-6 illustrates the changing liquidity needs for a sample bank with monetary position (reserves, float, and correspondent balances) requirements of 12 percent on transaction accounts and 3 percent on time and savings deposits. During a period of low liquidity need (see section 2 in Table 5-6), the bank's

**TABLE 5-6   Illustration of Liquidity Needs for Sample Bank (dollars in thousands)**

### 1. Starting Position

| Assets | | Liabilities and Capital | |
|---|---|---|---|
| Reserves | 17,100 | Transaction accounts | 100,000 |
| Securities | 75,000 | Savings and time deposits | 170,000 |
| Loans | 200,000 | Borrowings | 10,000 |
| Other assets | 7,900 | Capital | 20,000 |
| | 300,000 | | 300,000 |

### 2. Period of Low Liquidity Need

| Assets | | Liabilities and Capital | |
|---|---|---|---|
| Reserves | 18,000 | Transaction accounts | 105,000 |
| Securities | 84,100 | Savings and time deposits | 180,000 |
| Loans | 200,000 | Borrowings | 5,000 |
| Other assets | 7,900 | Capital | 20,000 |
| | 310,000 | | 310,000 |

### 3. Period of High Liquidity Need

| Assets | | Liabilities and Capital | |
|---|---|---|---|
| Reserves[a] | 15,600 | Transaction accounts | 90,000 |
| Securities[a] | 46,500 | Savings and time deposits | 160,000 |
| Loans | 220,000 | Borrowings[a] | 20,000 |
| Other assets | 7,900 | Capital | 20,000 |
| | 290,000 | | 290,000 |

[a] $20,000 decline in deposits and $20,000 increase in loans financed by additional borrowings of $10,000, lower monetary position of $1,500, and sale of $28,500 of securities.

deposits would be likely to grow while its loan demand might decline or at least grow less rapidly than the increase in deposits. On the other hand, rapid loan growth accompanied by slow growth or declines in deposits leads to a period of high liquidity needs, as illustrated in section 3 of Table 5-6. In this example, a small amount of the $40,000 liquidity needed was provided by the lower required monetary position of $1,500. The majority was supplied by increasing borrowings by $10,000 and selling $28,500 of securities.

One of bank management's more important tasks is measuring and meeting a bank's liquidity needs. A bank's liquidity needs should be measured dynamically. Long-run profitability may be hurt if a bank has too much in low-earning liquidity sources in relation to its needs for such liquidity. On the other hand, too little liquidity may lead to severe financial problems and even a bank failure.

## Measuring Liquidity Needs Dynamically

Daily liquidity needs (hourly in the case of money center banks) are usually met by appropriate management of the money position. There remain, however, short-term, cyclical, and trend needs for liquidity, which the well-managed bank will try to estimate as accurately as possible. The best guides available to most banks are their past experience and knowledge of events likely to affect liquidity needs. After discussing how to measure these liquidity needs dynamically, the appropriate sources for filling these liquidity needs are investigated.

*Short-term liquidity needs* of a bank may arise from several sources. For example, seasonal factors often affect deposit flows and loan demand. Since loans are generally to deposit customers, seasonal increases in loans tend to occur when deposits are at seasonal lows, and vice versa. For example, a bank in a farming community might find high liquidity needs from its loan demand rising and deposits falling in spring, when the need to plant and fertilize crops is high. After the crops are sold in the fall, loans would tend to fall and deposits to increase. Banks that are heavily dependent on one or a few types of customers may find seasonal liquidity needs particularly important. Most seasonal fluctuations can be predicted reasonably accurately on the basis of past experience.

The holders of sizable deposit balances and the customers who borrow in substantial amounts also may influence the short-term liquidity needs of an individual bank to a degree that is directly related to the bank's size. The short-term funding needs of important customers strongly affect the bank's short-term liquidity needs. Some customers' needs are highly predictable, such as the school district that has $5 million in CDs that will be used to pay for a new school building as the certificates mature. The short-term needs of other customers may be very difficult to predict, such as the loan needs of a volatile business that may use its $10 million line of credit (borrowing authority) to finance inventory. Much of the estimation of this type of short-term liquidity need will revolve around a knowledge of the needs and intentions of large customers.

As an example, Fifth National Bank is used in Tables 5-7 and 5-8 to show how a bank may measure its short-term liquidity needs. The balance sheet for Fifth Bank for the end of 1993 appears at the top of Table 5-7. Assume that Fifth National has (1) classified loans as volatile (large customers subject to rapid loan increases or decreases) and other loans (primarily subject to seasonal fluctuations); (2) classified savings and time deposits as vulnerable (subject to large withdrawals or increases) and other deposits (estimated to grow $1 million each month in 1994); and (3) a required monetary position of 12 percent on all transaction accounts and 3 percent on all time and savings deposits. Bank management has estimated monthly patterns for volatile loans and vulnerable deposits. The seasonal indices for transaction accounts and other loans that appear in Table 5-8 were estimated from Fifth Bank's seasonal deposit fluctuations over the past several years.

**TABLE 5-7** **Measuring Liquidity Needs of Fifth National Bank**

*Balance Sheet at End of Year*
*December 31, 1993 (dollars in thousands)*

| Assets | | Liabilities and Capital | |
|---|---|---|---|
| Reserves | $ 17,100 | Transaction accounts | $100,000 |
| Securities | 75,000 | Vulnerable time deposits | 20,000 |
| Loans (volatile) | 20,000 | Other savings and time deposits | 150,000 |
| Loans (other) | 180,000 | Borrowings | 10,000 |
| Other assets | 7,900 | Capital | 20,000 |
| | $300,000 | | $300,000 |

*Monthly Loan and Deposit Fluctuations*

| End of Month | Total Loans | Total Deposits | Estimated Liquidity Needs[a] |
|---|---|---|---|
| January | $192,800 | $273,000 | $ + 10,200 |
| February | 193,200 | 278,000 | + 14,800 |
| March | 205,000 | 269,000 | − 6,000 |
| April | 223,000 | 263,000 | − 30,000 |
| May | 212,200 | 262,000 | − 20,000 |
| June | 198,400 | 264,000 | − 4,400 |
| July | 191,200 | 271,000 | + 9,800 |
| August | 199,800 | 273,000 | + 3,200 |
| September | 210,600 | 273,000 | − 7,600 |
| October | 214,200 | 273,000 | − 11,200 |
| November | 210,600 | 272,000 | − 8,600 |
| December | 210,000 | 277,000 | − 3,000 |

*Balance Sheet, Time of Highest Liquidity Need*
*April 30, 1994 (dollars in thousands)*

| Assets | | Liabilities and Capital | |
|---|---|---|---|
| Reserves | $ 16,350 | Transaction accounts | $ 94,000 |
| Securities | 45,750 | Vulnerable time deposits | 15,000 |
| Loans (volatile) | 25,000 | Other savings and time deposits | 154,000 |
| Loans (other) | 198,000 | Borrowings | 10,000 |
| Other assets | 7,900 | Capital | 20,000 |
| | $293,000 | | $293,000 |

[a]Total loans and deposits for the month minus total at the start of the year without adjustment for required reserves. Minus (−) means that liquidity is needed and plus (+) means added liquidity from the end of the year.

**TABLE 5-8** Seasonal Indexes and Calculation of Monthly Loans and Deposits for Fifth National Bank (dollars in thousands)

| End of Month | Loans (Volatile) | Loans (Other) | | Transaction Accounts | | Vulnerable Time Deposits | Other Time and Savings Deposits |
|---|---|---|---|---|---|---|---|
| | | Index | Amounts | Index | Amounts | | |
| January | $20,000 | 96 | $172,800 | 102 | $102,000 | $20,000 | $151,000 |
| February | 25,000 | 94 | 169,200 | 106 | 106,000 | 20,000 | 152,000 |
| March | 25,000 | 100 | 180,000 | 101 | 101,000 | 15,000 | 153,000 |
| April | 25,000 | 110 | 198,000 | 94 | 94,000 | 15,000 | 154,000 |
| May | 25,000 | 104 | 187,200 | 92 | 92,000 | 15,000 | 155,000 |
| June | 22,000 | 98 | 176,400 | 98 | 98,000 | 10,000 | 156,000 |
| July | 22,000 | 94 | 169,200 | 104 | 104,000 | 10,000 | 157,000 |
| August | 27,000 | 96 | 172,800 | 105 | 105,000 | 10,000 | 158,000 |
| September | 27,000 | 102 | 183,600 | 104 | 104,000 | 10,000 | 159,000 |
| October | 27,000 | 104 | 187,200 | 98 | 98,000 | 15,000 | 160,000 |
| November | 27,000 | 102 | 183,600 | 96 | 96,000 | 15,000 | 161,000 |
| December | 30,000 | 100 | 180,000 | 100 | 100,000 | 15,000 | 162,000 |

The appropriate seasonal index (index for month/index for December) was multiplied by the December transaction accounts and other loans to estimate the dollar amounts in these categories. The various categories of loans and deposits in Table 5-8 are added and used in Table 5-7 to project the bank's estimated liquidity needs from December 31, 1993, to the end of each month in 1994. An estimated balance sheet for the month of highest liquidity needs appears at the bottom of Table 5-7. It is assumed that the liquidity needs from the $23 million increase in loans and $7 million decrease in deposits were financed by a $750,000 drop in required reserves and the sale of $29.250 million of securities. (The methods of filling liquidity needs are discussed in detail in a following section.)

Although the example in Tables 5-7 and 5-8 is a simplified situation, the sample bank serves to illustrate the basic methods for estimating the bank's short-term liquidity needs. Loans and deposits need to be categorized according to their seasonal or other short-term potential fluctuations. There may be as many as 20 to 30 categories of loans and deposits, and many banks use weekly rather than monthly data. Prepared computer programs to estimate short-term liquidity needs are available for both mainframes and microcomputers, and many banks have found their own microcomputer programs are helpful in estimating liquidity needs.

*Cyclical liquidity needs* of a bank are much more difficult to estimate. Such cyclical needs often are out of the control of any individual bank. Economic recession or boom and interest rate movements, particularly when banks may be constrained from changing their own rates because of political pressure or regulation, can cause significant liquidity pressures. Furthermore, the timing of such cyclical pressures can be very difficult to predict. A bank that provides for all potential cyclical liquidity needs would probably end up holding primarily low-earning liquid assets at the cost of significantly lower profitability. The lower risk of this high liquidity position would probably not offset the negative impact of these lower returns.

The impact of cyclical liquidity needs can be illustrated by looking back at Fifth National Bank in Table 5-7. For example, if it is assumed that a cylical boom leads to a 25 percent or $50 million increase in loans, Fifth National will have to sell most of its securities and borrow heavily when interest rates are high and security prices are low. Similar liquidity pressures might occur because of deposit outflows or the market's lack of confidence in a bank's ability to repay debt obligations. Deposit outflows and lack of confidence often stem from operating losses experienced by a bank either from large loan losses or unsuccessful interest rate or foreign exchange gambles. It is doubtful that Fifth National Bank would survive deposit outflows and lender loss of confidence of a magnitude similar to that experienced by Continental Illinois Bank in 1984.

As mentioned earlier, cyclical liquidity pressures are usually difficult to predict. The following methods may give some helpful indications about the magnitude of cyclical liquidity needs. First, cyclical vulnerability to loans may be partially estimated for many banks by looking at the proportion of lines of credit currently used versus the highest use of lines in a previous cyclical boom. For example, if 40 percent of a bank's lines of credit is currently used and if 62 percent was the highest past usage of such lines, the bank might estimate an increase of 22 percent of its total lines as the cyclical liquidity needs from such lines.

Second, correlation patterns between deposit flows and selected indicators, such as the level of rates, changes in rates, and rate ceilings, may provide guidelines for deposit inflows and outflows. Third, a bank's vulnerability to deposit outflows and lack of confidence by lenders should be realistically evaluated. For example, Continental Illinois had over two-thirds of its deposits and borrowings from such nonpersonal sources as large corporate CDs and foreign sources. Large deposits and borrowings from foreign sources were clearly vulnerable to cyclical (or any other) confidence-shattering news. A bank should carefully evaluate its funding diversification, the probable loyalty of its major funding sources, and risks the bank is taking in areas such as credit risk, interest rate risk, and capital risk, which might blemish the bank's name.

Finally, there are statistical programs (in computer software packages) that can remove seasonal and trend effects from a time series of loan and deposit accounts. The residuals should give a rough estimation of the type of cyclical liquidity pressures these accounts were subject to in the past. Thus, if large CDs had fallen 10 to 15 percent in past cyclical periods or confidence crises, the bank might try to make sure it had the ability to meet liquidity needs for 15 percent of its current large CDs.

*Trend liquidity needs* are required by banks for liquidity demands that can be predicted over a longer time span. These longer-term liquidity needs are generally related to the secular trends of the community or markets that a bank serves. In rapidly expanding areas, loans often grow faster than deposits. A bank in such a situation needs sources of liquidity to provide funds for loan expansion.

In stable communities, on the other hand, deposits may show a steady rise while loans remain virtually unchanged. In such cases, the longer view of liquidity requirements may enable the bank to keep more fully invested than it otherwise would. In either case, to gauge the bank's needs for longer-term liquidity, a bank's management must attempt long-range economic forecasting as the basis on which it can reasonably estimate loan and deposit levels for the next year and perhaps five years ahead.

Figure 5-2 illustrates a methodology a bank might use to plan its trend to longer-term liquidity needs. The bank starts by classifying every account on its balance sheet as liquid (convertible into usable funds within less than 90 days with little, if any, loss if the asset is sold) or nonliquid. The accounts listed to the left of the liquidity and nonliquidity columns in Figure 5-2 are representative of the asset types that would fall into each category. Next, the sources of funds, liabilities, and capital, are divided into two categories—volatile (subject to withdrawal because of seasonal, rate, or other pressures) and stable. The accounts listed to the right of the volatile and stable columns are representative of the types of liabilities and capital that would fall into each category. The difference between liquid assets and volatile sources is

**FIGURE 5-2   Illustration of Trend Liquidity Planning for a Bank**

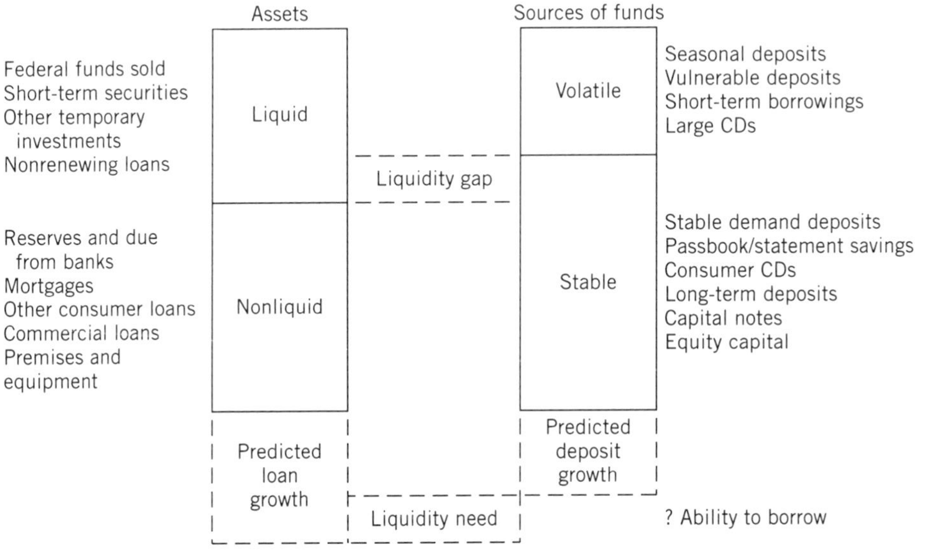

termed the liquidity gap. The gap is positive if liquid assets exceed volatile sources and negative if the reverse is the case.

The broken lines in Figure 5-2 represent expected fund flows during the next period that are added to the balance sheet totals. The primary increase in assets usually comes from loan growth, whereas deposit growth represents the primary source of funds for the bank depicted in Figure 5-2. If predicted loan growth exceeds predicted deposit growth, the bank has a liquidity need that may be covered by reducing a positive liquidity gap or by purchasing funds (methods for meeting liquidity needs are discussed in a following section). On the other hand, if predicted deposit growth exceeds predicted loan growth, the bank can improve its liquidity position or seek to employ the excess liquidity in higher-return assets.

Figure 5-3 illustrates a method for combining short-term and trend liquidity pressures into a unified model for measuring liquidity needs. Again Fifth National Bank is used as the example, but the bank's growth in 1993 and its predicted growth as well as its past and predicted seasonal pattern are the basis for charting liquidity needs. Although the charts in Figure 5-3 are simplified to serve as illustrations, a computer can be used for more elaborate calculations as well as for tracing more detailed charts.

The volatility of Fifth National Bank's deposits is shown in the chart for month-end deposits at the top of Figure 5-3. (For most banks with over $100 million in assets, this chart should be the summation of several charts for specific categories of deposits and should cover successive reserve-computa-

**FIGURE 5-3   Charting Liquidity Needs**

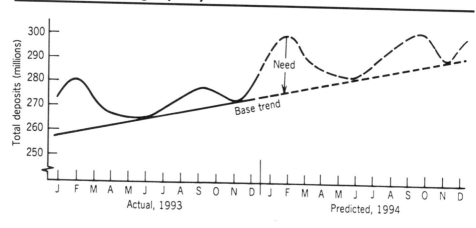

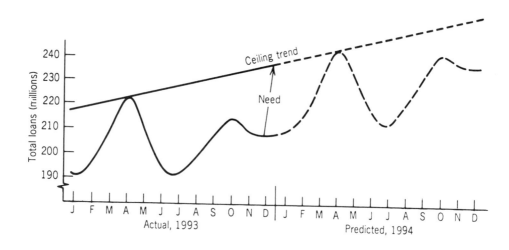

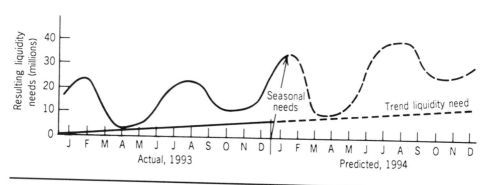

tion periods.) A trend line drawn through or near the low points should indicate the trend of stable deposits. The amount of deposits above this baseline represents the bank's seasonal liquidity needs caused by deposits subject to withdrawal. More complex charts or calculations would recognize liquidity needs for volatile deposits and would be the total of such deposits less the percentage of required reserves held against them. As deposits decline, the release of reserves provides a small part of the requisite liquidity.

The middle chart in Figure 5-3 depicts the liquidity needs from rising and fluctuating loan demands. Part of this demand may be seasonal and can be depicted in a chart of month-end totals. (As with deposits, larger banks will have charts or calculations for several types of loans and will use successive reserve computation periods.) A trend line, drawn through or near the high points, represents the ceiling trend to which loans may be expected to rise periodically or seasonally. The amount by which loans are below the ceiling at any given time represents the bank's potential liquidity needs to meet seasonal loan demands.

The lowest chart in Figure 5-3 traces the combined seasonal and trend liquidity needs for Fifth National Bank. Trend liquidity is calculated by subtracting the changes in the deposit trend line from the changes in the loan trend. If loan growth exceeds deposit growth, there will be a liquidity need; if the reverse is true, there will be a liquidity excess. For example, if the trend line of deposits rose from $250 million to $270 million and the loan trend line rose from $220 million to $250 million in the same period, there would be a trend liquidity need of $10 million. Total seasonal liquidity needs would be the total of deposit deviations from the base trend and loan deviations from the ceiling trend. These seasonal liquidity needs would be added to the trend liquidity previously calculated to trace the bank's total need for liquidity.

Although this method is relatively straightforward, there are numerous practical problems. First, isolating which part of past fluctuations in loans and deposits are seasonal, cyclical, and trend is difficult. Second, forecasting future seasonal patterns and trends based on the past is hazardous at best. Seasonal patterns may change. The trend in deposits may change because of regulatory or competitive actions the bank cannot control. Trends in loans may change because of such actions, economic conditions, or changes in bank lending policies. Third, the method ignores cyclical liquidity needs or liquidity crises due to a lack of confidence, which are often the least predictable and can be the most harmful if not at least partially recognized. Most banks, using methods similar to those illustrated in the charts in Figure 5-3, add some additional liquidity needs for forecasting error and unpredictable cyclical needs. The question is, how much? In spite of such problems, the method seems to offer a bank significant information on its liquidity needs.

*Contingent liquidity needs* are caused by unusual events that are difficult if not impossible to predict. Examples include an unexpected outflow of deposits caused by a rumor about the bank, an unusual increase in loan demand, or the closing of an extensively used funding source. By their very nature, contingency liquidity needs are impossible to forecast accurately. At the same time, every bank should have a plan (and most regulators require a plan) to remain liquid in case some contingency does occur.

Rules of thumb for assessing contingency liquidity needs vary greatly. For example, a retail community bank might believe it should have the ability to cover a contingent deposit outflow of 20 percent. An urban wholesale bank might believe it should have the ability to meet 70 percent of its lines of credit (even though 40 percent is the norm). A larger bank holding company, which uses nondeposit sources extensively, might believe it should be able to cover the disappearance of one of its primary borrowing sources. A bank's primary regulatory body is often a good source for establishing contingency liquidity needs.

## Filling a Bank's Liquidity Needs

Providing for a bank's liquidity needs is often as complex as estimating those needs. Many banks have some estimates of the bank's liquidity needs but do not have adequate policies and procedures for meeting these needs. Various sources that can be used to fill a bank's liquidity needs are described; then methods for matching liquidity needs and sources are discussed.

**Traditional Sources of Liquidity**   The primary traditional sources of liquidity fall into two basic categories. The first category consists of assets in which funds are temporarily invested with the assurance that they either will mature and be paid when liquidity is needed or will be readily salable, without material loss, in advance of maturity. The second category includes the various methods by which banks can borrow or otherwise obtain funds. Large CDs are an example of a classification conflict between deposits, which presumably are used to measure liquidity needs, and funds borrowed to provide liquidity. A general rule of thumb for smaller and medium-sized banks in such conflicts could be to classify deposits that can be readily purchased or sold in an ongoing market as sources of liquidity and to include all other deposits in measuring liquidity needs. Such a rule of thumb for some very large banks might be misleading because a significant proportion of their deposits comes from such marketable sources. These sources are permanent as long as the bank can maintain the confidence of the lender and afford to pay the going market rate.

Most of the primary sources of liquidity are briefly described in Table 5-9. The rule of thumb is that assets must be of high credit quality and either of short maturity or very marketable with little chance of loss. The amount of liquid assets may be limited by the willingness of the bank to hold such assets, which generally earn less than loans or less liquid securities. The use of borrowings or other increases in liabilities to fund liquidity needs is typically limited in one or more ways. Large money center banks and bank holding companies that use purchased liabilities extensively as a source of funds are primarily limited by how much the money market and its participants think such banks can use. Confidence of the money markets is the key variable. Regional banks may have limited access to some markets and will probably

**TABLE 5-9  Potential Traditional Sources of Bank Liquidity**

**Asset Stores of Liquidity**

| | |
|---|---|
| Cash and due from | A bank's money position is a source of liquidity only if (1) there are excess revenues, (2) there are extra balances in correspondent accounts or checks not credited, or (3) deposits drop, freeing decline times 1 − reserve requirement. |
| Federal funds sold | Excess reserves of a bank usually sold to another bank to provide earning asset to selling bank. Most mature daily but can be easily renewed; "term funds" are also short-maturity funds with good market. Unsecured. |
| Short-term U.S. government securities | Treasury bills and notes or bonds close to maturity are widely used sources of liquidity because they are short-term and tend to be bought and sold in active markets. Thought to have no risk of nonpayment. |
| Commercial paper, bankers' acceptances, and negotiable CDs | Obligations of private borrowers that are bought and sold through money market dealers. Generally traded on a discounted basis, and most issues have a fairly active secondary market. Still high quality (i.e., risk of nonpayment very low). |
| Other marketable securities | Short-term government agency and state and local obligations having slightly higher yields than government securities, and yield and secondary markets similar to those for commercial paper, CDs, etc. Must be high quality (range available) if used for liquidity. |
| Securities purchased under agreement to resell (repos) | Temporary purchase of government or other securities in which seller has agreed to repurchase securities at fixed price and set time in the future. Difference between sale and purchase prices is return received by holder. |
| Other liquid assets | Other creditworthy securities, loans, or assets if their maturity conforms with the bank's liquidity needs and if the bank will have no compunction about reducing the size of such assets if necessary. |

**Purchased Forms of Liquidity**

| | |
|---|---|
| Borrowing from Federal Reserve (discounts or advances) | Credit extended on a short-term basis by a Federal Reserve Bank to a bank or other depository institution. Rate, set by Fed, is called discount rate, with penalty rates for frequent or unusually heavy users. Security (securities or acceptable loans) required for either discounts or advances. |
| Federal funds purchased | Purchase of another bank's excess reserves on daily or short-term basis. Other side of Federal funds sold. Purchased through correspondent or informal phone market at existing Federal funds rate. Banks that are continual users often subject to informal limit by sellers. Unsecured; therefore, funds seller checks credit of borrowing bank. |
| Securities sold under agreement to repurchase | Temporary sale of government or other securities in which bank has received funds from purchaser and agreed to rebuy securities at predetermined price. In effect, short-term (often daily) secured borrowing from purchaser. |

**TABLE 5-9**    *(continued)*

| | |
|---|---|
| Large CDs | CDs in minimum amounts of $100,000 that can be issued to corporate treasurers with excess cash. Larger issues may be marketable. Bank must bid at least going market rate. Since unsecured and since insurance limited to $100,000, corporate treasurers check soundness of bank. |
| Public deposits | Treasury tax loan accounts may be retained if bank is willing to pay market rate and has pledgeable securities. Many state and local time deposits go to the bank bidding the highest rate. Often limited by amount of securities available for pledging against public deposits. |
| Eurodollar and other foreign sources | Eurodollars are deposits in U.S. banks held outside the United States with maturities ranging from overnight to a year. Active secondary market with overseas branch essential to continual involvement. Rates set in international market. Other foreign sources also used by very large banks. Bank must not engage in activities or assume risks that could potentially blemish its name. |
| Other liability forms | Other liability sources of liquidity include capital notes, ineligible acceptances, commercial paper sold through holding companies, etc. Key element is that bank can raise funds through such forms if bank pays going market rate and lender has confidence in bank. |

have lower limits on their total usage of purchased liabilities. Once again, lender confidence is an essential ingredient. Smaller banks' access to some markets is closed, and they may find that their usage of borrowed funds is limited to how much their correspondent banks and the Federal Reserve are willing to lend them. These types of limits indicate that banks of any size should have considerable unused borrowing capacity if they plan to borrow to fund liquidity needs.

**Emerging Sources of Liquidity** In addition to these traditional sources, there are several additional methods that banks are using to meet liquidity needs. One method is to purchase long-term securities that have the option of being sold at a set price in the future, which effectively removes the price risk and makes the long-term securities liquid. Another method is to make loans and mortgages in a standardized form so that they can be sold if liquidity is needed. A related method is to securitize (sell as part of collateralized capital market obligations) consumer loans and mortgages. Still another method is for the bank to use capital market obligations (such as commercial paper or notes) to finance its liquidity needs. Clearly, bank financial managers must become more and more innovative in providing sources of liquidity.

## MATCHING LIQUIDITY SOURCES TO LIQUIDITY NEEDS

Banks must choose among various assets, liabilities, and the new emerging sources of liquidity to fill their liquidity needs. The wide variety of potential and actual choices used in providing for liquidity is often a bewildering menu of solutions. The choice among the variety of sources of liquidity should depend on several factors that are discussed in the following paragraphs: (1) purpose of liquidity needed, (2) access to liability markets, (3) management philosophy, (4) costs and characteristics of the various liquidity sources, and (5) interest rate forecasts.

**Purpose of the Liquidity Needed** The reason that liquidity is needed can affect the source of liquidity used to fill that need. Seasonal liquidity needs tend to be reasonably repetitive in extent, duration, and timing. Forecasts of seasonal needs can usually be based on past experience, and most banks should be reasonably confident in making such forecasts. There would, therefore, seem to be only moderate risk associated with the use of purchased forms of liquidity to cover seasonal liquidity needs. There should be a high probability that subsequent cash inflows will provide the funds to repay these purchased forms. The Federal Reserve seems to recognize this in its lending policies by having less stringent requirements for discounts and advances that are clearly for seasonal purposes. The potential gain from using purchased forms to meet seasonal liquidity needs is that the loan and investment portfolios can be structured on the basis of fund availability at seasonal highs. Since loans and investments usually earn higher returns than liquid assets, earnings should be higher from using purchased funds than from building up liquid assets during periods of low seasonal needs.

On the other hand, the use of purchased funds to meet cyclical needs seems less appropriate. Cyclical needs are much more difficult to predict, and when and whether borrowings can be repaid may be a serious concern. The contribution of purchased forms in providing liquidity needs during a cyclical boom may be limited and is likely to be very costly. Loan demands tend to run high in such periods, and liability sources (1) tend to become expensive, (2) may be limited by the market's lack of confidence in a bank's ability to repay its obligations, and (3) may be restricted to only larger and better-known banks. For all but very large banks with good access to broad money market sources, holding liquid assets in slow periods to meet rising loan demand in boom times seems preferable to the use of purchased funds. By holding an adequate amount of liquid assets—an approach that may involve some loss of current income during the early stage of a cyclical expansion—most banks will avoid higher costs and possibly far greater capital losses (from the sale of depreciated bonds) during the later stages of expansion. Put in more precise terms, the essence of liquidity management is to equate the probable earlier loss of income with the subsequent higher fund cost and possible capital losses. Even large banks with many sources of borrowing should not overemphasize purchased funds for cyclical needs. The reputation of such banks is critical in determining access to the money markets, and overemphasis on purchased funds can hurt that reputation.

Meeting longer-term liquidity needs can be more complex. Loan growth exceeds deposit growth for most banks with longer-term liquidity needs. Such net growth can be financed by selling liquid assets or purchasing funds. The problem is that the supply of salable liquid assets and the amount of borrowing permissible are limited in size. Thus, a bank that sells all its liquid assets cannot use this source to finance a continuing excess of loans relative to deposits. A bank that aims for rapid growth is likely to have some limit on how much of its funding sources can be purchased funds. This limit will vary widely, depending on bank size and entry into various financial markets, but there is some limit. The message would seem to be that a bank must finally limit its longer-term liquidity needs. Either more permanent deposit sources must be found or bank loans must be limited in some meaningful way.

A final point related to longer-term liquidity is that any bank should limit its use of purchased forms of liquidity enough to have a borrowing reserve if future unpredicted liquidity needs occur. This may mean that a smaller bank will seldom use purchased funds, keeping its limited ability to borrow as a liquidity or borrowing reserve. A large bank that believes it can purchase additional funds of up to 100 percent of its core deposits may restrict this source to 75 percent in order to have a borrowing reserve for future unpredicted liquidity needs.

**Access to Liability Markets**    The preceding paragraphs on the purposes of needed liquidity have alluded to differences in access to liability markets. This factor is the second primary determinant of the sources of liquidity that banks use to fill their liquidity needs. Many small banks are limited to borrowing from the Federal Reserve or purchasing Federal funds through a larger correspondent. Most members of this group of banks want to avoid borrowing from the Federal Reserve unless the borrowing is classified as seasonal. Furthermore, the use of Federal funds is often limited to between 50 to 100 percent of the borrowing bank's capital base. The result of such limited access to sources of purchased liquidity forms is that most banks in this category use the sale of assets as their primary source of liquidity. The small borrowing reserve that exists is not used but is left available for unpredicted liquidity needs.

The opposite extreme is large banks and bank holding companies located in money center cities. Assuming that they are reasonably managed, such banks and holding companies usually have access to a variety of purchased forms in both domestic and international financial markets. Large bank holding companies have access to a few liability forms (e.g., commercial paper) not available to banks. Furthermore, the total combined size of all purchased forms available to such banks and holding companies tends to be much larger in relation to total assets and capital than that for smaller banks. Large banks and holding companies, therefore, usually have the ability to choose between liquid assets that may be sold and purchased forms of liquidity. The other determinants of filling liquidity should have a strong impact on this choice.

Diversification of funding sources is essential to these large banks and holding companies. Some lenders are more sensitive than others with respect to which banks they will lend money. The most sensitive lenders will cease lending at the first sign of a problem, whereas others tend to be more forgiving. The same attribute applies to markets (e.g., the domestic money market tends to be more sensitive than the Euromarket). By diversifying its funding sources, a bank can take advantage of differences in sensitivity to credit quality across lenders and markets. Two examples of developing diversified funding sources are included in the appendix to this chapter.

Many banks fall between the two size extremes. Purchased sources include not only funds borrowed from the Federal Reserve and Federal funds but also such forms as large CDs (not subject to rate limits) and public funds put up for bid. Such medium-sized banks generally lack access to the commercial paper market and most international markets and have relative borrowing limits between those of the small and large banks. Although there is considerable variation in the sources used to provide for liquidity needs, a typical pattern seems to be to use purchased forms for seasonal needs and liquid asset sales to meet other liquidity needs.

**Managerial Philosophy**   A bank's management philosophy is the third primary determinant of the sources of liquidity banks use to fill their liquidity needs. This philosophy consists of a set of implicit or explicit liquidity guidelines established by top management. The primary liquidity guideline is the extent to which the bank is willing to rely on sources of funds that might disappear in difficult times. A bank that makes little or no use of purchased funding sources for liquidity needs (i.e., one that relies exclusively on its liquid assets) reflects a conservative management philosophy.

At the other end of the spectrum is the bank that seeks out purchased funds from any available source, as long as the total cost of such funds is less than the net rate of return the bank is earning by investing them. Such a bank generally relies heavily on outside sources of funds and reflects an aggressive management philosophy. At the same time, aggressive management must realize that the bank's reputation is critical in determining its access to money market sources. Managements with aggressive liquidity philosophies must neither engage in activity nor assume risks that could potentially blemish the institution's name in the money markets. Most banks in the United States fall somewhere between these two extremes; however, management philosophy has a profound effect on the methods individual banks use to provide for their liquidity needs.

**Cost and Characteristics of Various Liquidity Sources**   The fourth primary determinant of the liquidity sources a bank should use is the cost and characteristics of the various liquidity sources. Usually the source of liquidity chosen by a bank will be the lowest-cost source that achieves the given liquidity need. This lowest-cost principle is subject to the overall constraints imposed by access to financial markets and by the bank's management philosophy. In the case of assets the bank is considering selling to provide for liquidity needs, the "cost" is the income given up during the life of the assets adjusted for any gain or loss, tax effects, and brokerage fees. When considering purchased forms, the cost includes not only interest cost but also reserve requirements, processing costs, insurance fees, and other factors.

In addition to directly comparing costs, banks should also look at differences in costs for different time periods. For example, a bank facing a seasonal increase in loans may finance these loans with either large CDs or repurchase agreements. One fundamental difference between the two instruments is that repurchase agreements are commonly renewed on a daily basis with different customers. Moreover, because they involve the literal sale and repurchase of securities, repos require a great deal of paperwork. Thus, the total costs of repurchase agreements are largely variable, rising steadily as a function of the length of time for which the funds are needed. Issuing CDs, in contrast, involves the bank with high fixed costs (including insurance premiums and non-earning reserves) but no variable costs; once the CDs are issued, no further expenses are incurred. Thus, other considerations aside, the bank should tend to finance a loan expansion of a few days' duration with repurchase agreements and a loan expansion of several weeks' duration with CDs.

**Interest Rate Forecast**   The bank's opinions on the future course of interest rates also affect the choice among alternatives for meeting liquidity needs. Using the previous CDs versus repos example, if interest rates were expected to rise in the future, the cost of CDs would become lower than that of repos at a shorter maturity. Because the repos would have to be rolled over at higher and higher rates, total costs would rise at an increasing rate. Under such circumstances, the bank would prefer to lock in the current low CD rate for all but its most temporary needs. That is, only if the bank needed the funds for a very short time period would it prefer to use repurchase agreements. Alternatively, if interest rates were expected to fall in the future, the total costs of bank borrowing through repurchase agreements would rise at a decreasing rate. In this case, the bank would prefer to avoid a comparatively long-term commitment at the currently high CD rate and instead would prefer to stay in repos to take advantage of the expected lower rates in the future. Thus, in periods when the bank expects interest rates to rise, the tendency is to raise funds through longer-term adjustment instruments. In periods when rates are expected to fall, the tendency is to utilize very short-term sources of funds, such as Federal funds and repurchase agreements.

The shape of the yield curve (maturities versus yields for securities with similar credit risks) for both liquid assets and potential borrowed sources may also affect the choice among the various sources of liquidity. For example, if the yield curve for Treasury bills has a positive slope (which is the normal situation), the yield of a longer-term bill for the period held (remember that one year is the maximum maturity) is usually higher than the yield for a bill with a maturity that matches the holding period. On the funding side, longer-maturity funds usually cost more than shorter-maturity funds. However, in periods of crises, it is reassuring to management to know that the longer-maturity funds will remain with the bank. A liquidity premium may exist on both the asset and funding side.

## MEETING CONTINGENCY AND FUTURE LIQUIDITY NEEDS

### Meeting Contingency Liquidity Needs

Every bank should have a contingency liquidity plan that should enable the bank to meet its contingency needs (discussed earlier). As in meeting other liquidity needs, the primary sources are selling an asset or increasing a liability to provide the needed liquidity. Meeting contingency liquidity needs is particularly difficult because the size of such needs is difficult to predict and because contingency liquidity needs typically arise at the worst possible time for the bank.

A bank needs to keep two facts in mind when looking at potential asset sources to meet contingency needs. First, many bank assets can be sold when the need for funds is truly extreme. The bank's building, branch offices, subsidiaries, and some loans and mortgages are assets most banks would not ordinarily sell to meet seasonal or cyclical liquidity needs, but they may be considered in developing plans to meet contingent liquidity needs. The amount of loss and/or the potential taxation of gains on the sale of such assets must be considered. Second, the sale of such assets is often a one-time event, and it may take many years to build up new assets of the type sold. For example, the sale of a consumer credit card subsidiary can be done once. The beneficial cash flows will no longer accrue to the selling bank, and it would probably take many years to rebuild such an asset to its original earning capacity.

These factors have encouraged many banks (particularly larger ones) to emphasize the development of liability sources to meet contingency liquidity needs. It is generally suggested that a bank should work hard in developing several potential liability sources to meet contingency liquidity needs. For example, a smaller bank might develop Fed funds lines of credit with several of its upstream correspondent banks. In addition, such a bank should have pledgeable collateral at its Federal Reserve Bank so that the commercial bank can borrow there if contingency liquidity needs arise. A larger bank, which usually has access to a much broader group of sources, should have several liability sources open for its use at all times. Correspondent bank and Federal Reserve sources should be available. Large corporate and public sector accounts should be courted—both for current business and as an emergency source of funds. Open market sources, such as commercial paper, notes, and securitized assets, should be developed as potential sources for such larger banks. In addition, Eurodollar and other foreign deposits might be courted as potential sources of liquidity. The main message is that banks of all sizes should spend considerable time and effort in developing potential liability sources to meet the contingency liquidity needs.

Liquidity crisis management requires a careful, professionally prepared plan. The liquidity crisis plan has three fundamental elements. The first is a program for promoting good communications from the bank's lenders to the funding manager and from the funding manager to the bank's institutional investors and rating agencies. The second element consists of fire drill–type exercises for testing and establishing the marketability of bank assets. Of special interest to large wholesale banks is the possibility for liquidity enhancement available in an ongoing and comprehensive program of loan securitization or liquification by direct negotiation with a network of investors cultivated over time. The final element consists of steps to broaden, deepen, and stabilize markets for the bank's liabilities.

The emphasis on each of these elements is the prevention of a liquidity crisis and not damage control. Preparedness is the sole weapon available for preventing crises. In the event that a liquidity crisis does befall the bank, however, a liquidity crisis plan centered on good communications and positioning in both asset and liability markets provides the best chance for survival.

## Meeting Future Liquidity Needs

It is easy to become negative about the liquidity situation of banks. Aggregated figures show that liquid assets have decreased and purchased deposits plus borrowed funds have increased markedly for commercial banks in the last couple of decades. Furthermore, the probability of liquidity problems arising as a result of lender and markets' lack of confidence in a bank's ability to repay debt obligations appears to have risen markedly in the late 1980s. There are, however, three positive aspects about bank liquidity that have emerged in recent years—more realistic regulatory liquidity assessment, the decline in rate ceilings on funding sources, and the development of interest rate hedging instruments, which allow banks to separate liquidity risk from interest rate risk.

As late as the 1980s, the primary regulatory authorities tended to look at static balance sheet measures of liquidity. Typically, the amount of unpledged, short-term securities was compared with some proxy for liquidity needs, such as total deposits. If this ratio met a preestablished target, the bank was deemed to be liquid. The static and arbitrary nature of this type of liquidity measure coupled with the rapidly changing nature of banking weakened the usefulness of regulatory liquidity evaluations.

The emerging approach used by the three federal regulatory authorities seems much more reasonable. The examiner asks bank management for the bank's information on its liquidity needs and its ability to meet those needs. If the examiner believes the bank's system for assessing liquidity provides appropriate information and the bank's liquidity is adequate, the bank meets the regulatory requirements. If the bank's method for measuring liquidity is weak, the examiner compares his or her calculation of the bank's short-term liquidity needs with the bank's ability to meet such needs. Liquidity needs include estimated credit demands, probable deposit volatility, and borrowed funds that must be repaid. Sources of meeting these needs include securities maturing in less than a year, other securities with market values exceeding book value, and other assets that appear to be readily sellable with little loss. The examiner is satisfied if sources exceed needs. If needs exceed sources, the examiner will consider the bank's ability to sell securities under agreement to repurchase (repos) and the bank's ability to borrow (e.g., Federal funds) before making the final regulatory liquidity decision.

The decline in rate ceilings on funding sources was documented in the section on bank sources of funds. Over 90 percent of bank interest-bearing funds were subject to rate ceilings in the late 1970s, but virtually none have been subject to any rate ceilings since March 31, 1986. There will no longer be liquidity crunches, or deposit outflows, created when rates on open market instruments exceed Regulation Q rate limits on bank deposits. Banks with reasonable credit reputations and an ability to pay the going market rate should be able to purchase liquidity.

Finally, new risk management tools—financial futures, options, caps, floors, and interest rate swaps—share the common feature of allowing for the differentiation of liquidity risk and interest rate risk. Using these tools enables banks to manipulate the effective interest rate maturity of embedded assets and liabilities without altering the balance sheet. Liquidity can be managed separately and does not need to be sacrificed for the sake of managing interest rate risk.

## Discussion Questions

1. What basic factors determine the reserve needs of a bank?
2. Which types of deposits have contemporaneous reserves and which types have a lagged computation period?
3. Describe each of the four basic accounts in what most banks label as their money position.
4. Discuss some of the techniques that commercial banks use to manage their reserve balances.
5. What are the two primary liquidity needs of most banks? What two broad sources can be used to meet these needs?
6. Discuss how a bank can measure its seasonal, cyclical, and trend liquidity needs.
7. What purchased forms of liquidity are typically available to a smaller bank? To a larger bank? When may a larger bank be unable to obtain purchased funds?
8. Discuss the factors that affect the liquidity forms a bank should use in providing for its liquidity needs.
9. Should the shape of the yield curve affect short-term asset maturity decisions? Short-term liability maturity decisions?
10. Discuss the changing liquidity needs of banks in the early 1990s. How has regulatory evaluation of a bank's liquidity position changed in response to any changes you list?

# CHAPTER 6

# Managing the Security Portfolio

A bank's security portfolio consists primarily of impersonal financial assets that pay the bank a limited (usually fixed) return until the assets (usually a debt instrument) mature. The traditional pattern that many banks still follow consists of four sequential steps to employ the funds they are able to attract. First, they meet the legal reserve requirement. Second, adequate provisions are made for the bank's liquidity needs. Some of this liquidity need may be met through borrowing, but the majority of the liquidity needs of most banks (including money center and large regional banks) are met through having cash flows or liquid assets available to meet such needs. Third, the bank meets the loan demands in its market area, which may range from a small community to the world. Loans, which generally tend to be made on a personal contact basis, usually have higher yields than securities and are an important aid in attracting deposits. Fourth and finally, any remaining funds are invested in the bank's security portfolio.

This traditional pattern of treating securities as the residual use of funds inevitably leads to timing problems in their purchase and sale. In recessions and periods of slow economic growth, when loan demands and interest rates tend to be lower, banks usually have relatively large amounts of funds to invest in securities. In the ensuing boom period, when loan demands and interest rates tend to be high, banks are usually unable to purchase securities and may be forced to sell previously purchased securities at losses in order to finance loan growth. Strategies for mitigating the problems resulting from investing funds in securities at the wrong times are examined in this chapter.

The economic conditions in the late 1970s and early 1980s—inflation, high loan demands, relatively high and fluctuating interest rates—led to a different kind of concern about the management of a bank's security portfolio. Most bank managers concentrated their efforts on making loans and then acquiring funds to finance these loans. Good management of the security portfolio came to mean purchasing only very short-term securities. Many high-earning-performance banks in the late 1970s and early 1980s had large loan portfolios and small security portfolios. This led at least some banks to downplay the importance of managing the security portfolio.

As interest rates fell in the middle and later 1980s and the early 1990s, banks began to use the portfolio in a different way. Gains were taken by selling many securities. The profits on security sales made a bank's net income higher for the year in which gains were taken. The security sales, however, necessitated either accepting lower income in future years for similar-quality securities or taking more risk (credit liquidity, rate risk, or some combination thereof) to try to maintain the income on the securities. Again, management of the security portfolio appeared to take a back seat to other pressures in the bank.

Many of the actions when rates rose or fell seem questionable if one looks at the functions of a bank's security portfolio in both the current and future environments. First, a bank's security portfolio often remains a primary source of liquidity. Even large banks with access to many markets for purchased funds still look at the security portfolio as a source of liquidity. For many small banks, the security portfolio is the primary source of the liquidity. Thus, the security portfolio is important in reducing liquidity risk (a function of the interrelationship between liquidity needs and liquidity sources). Second, and equally important, a bank's security portfolio is an important contributor to bank earnings. In 1992, for example, 29.7 percent of the total revenue of all banks in the United States came from banks' securities portfolios.[1] Because of the much lower cost of acquiring and managing securities compared with loans,[2] it appears that the security portfolio's proportionate contribution to banks' net income is even higher than its contribution to total revenues. Other important contributions of the security portfolio include providing acceptable collateral for public deposits; allowing borrowing from the Federal Reserve; providing a vehicle for repurchase agreements; dressing up the balance sheet for customers and regulators; and allowing impersonal flexibility that can be used in managing a bank's overall maturity and interest-sensitivity position. Such essential functions indicate that managing the security portfolio still deserves considerable attention.

This chapter is divided into two sections. The first section covers the types of securities banks usually purchase and the method of measuring returns and risks on such securities. The second section covers the five steps a bank's management should follow in actively managing its security portfolio.

---

[1] *FDIC Quarterly Banking Profile* (Washington, D.C.: FDIC, 1993).

[2] See *Functional Cost Analysis: National Average Reports*, various years. Published annually by the Federal Reserve Board of Governors.

# DISTINGUISHING CHARACTERISTICS OF DEBT SECURITIES

Because current U.S. law prohibits commercial banks from owning common stock in other corporations, we will limit our discussion here to debt securities that banks are eligible to purchase.

*Maturity* is one of the differentiating characteristics among debt instruments. Banks can choose from among the numerous money market instruments with maturities ranging from one day to one year discussed in this chapter. In addition, longer-term securities nearing maturity should be treated as short-term instruments. Banks can also choose from among numerous intermediate and long-term securities. (A discussion of the manner in which maturity affects returns is included in the following material on risks.)

The *taxation* of income and security gains and losses is a second characteristic that affects the investment instruments banks typically select. In general, security gains increase taxable income, and losses decrease taxable income and are, therefore, taxed at the bank's ordinary income tax rate. Most interest income is taxable to banks; however, income on Treasury and many U.S. agency issues and on in-state state and local issues is not subject to state and local income taxes. Also, interest income on all state and local bond issues prior to August 1986 and on smaller general obligations after that date is, after deducting 20 percent of the average financing cost, exempt from a bank's federal income tax.

There are *four potential sources of risk* in the purchase of debt securities. First, the bank may be forced to sell prior to maturity a particular security that does not have broad marketability. Price concessions required to sell the security may decrease the security's return appreciably. This risk is called *marketability risk*.

A second source of risk, known as *interest rate risk*, derives from changes in the general level of interest rates. Changes in the market value of outstanding securities are inversely related to changes in interest rates. For most bonds, the magnitude of such changes will be greater with instruments of longer maturity. This rate of increase declines as the maturity of the security decreases. The magnitude of changes in market value for a given change in rate also depends on the proportion of the return that is coupon versus principal; generally, the lower the coupon, the greater the price volatility of the bond. Preference should be given to the duration of a bond rather than to its maturity in evaluating interest rate risk. Interest rate risk also includes reinvestment risks, that is, the rate at which cash flows from the bond can be reinvested and the time when some uncertain cash flows due to repayment before maturity or call will occur.

A third risk is the possibility of nonpayment of interest or principal, or both. The possibility of nonpayment, often labeled the *credit risk* (or default risk), is a relevant consideration for most debt securities, except those that are obligations of the federal government.

Finally, there is a *purchasing power risk* associated with all debt instruments. If dollars received as interest or principal payments purchase less than the dollars used to purchase the debt instruments, the investor suffers a loss of purchasing power. The investor attempts to overcome this risk by requiring a higher return or by having dollar liabilities that are paid in lower-purchasing-power dollars, or both. To the extent that interest rate and price level changes are positively correlated, it is difficult to separate interest rate and purchasing power risk. That is, nominal (market) interest rates normally adjust to changes in the expected rate of inflation.

The formula for converting nominal rates of return $(R_n)$ to real rates $(R_r)$ is

$$R_r = \frac{1 + R_n}{1 + q} - 1$$

where $q$ denotes the actual rate of change in the general price level over the holding period. This equation is commonly expressed as

$$R_r = R_n - q$$

*Specific terms of an instrument* are the final distinguishing characteristic. Issues that are callable or that have specific or implicit buy-back or put options are clearly different from the same basic types of issues that do not have these options or specific terms. More and more debt instruments have specific terms that distinguish them from generic securities.

## SHORT-TERM INSTRUMENTS

Banks are often significant investors in various types of short-term instruments. These instruments generally mature in less than a year, so the risk of fluctuations in the price of the instruments is relatively low; however, reinvestment risk is relatively high. There are many short-term instruments that banks may use. Descriptions of the most commonly used instruments and their primary characteristics follow and are summarized in Table 6-1.

*Federal funds sold* are short-term loans to other banks through the Federal Reserve System. They are used to meet the borrowing bank's reserve requirements at the Federal Reserve. Federal funds sold represent the excess reserves that are offered in the market at competitively determined interest rates to banks needing funds to meet reserve requirements. The market for Federal funds is predominantly short term, as over 80 percent of total Federal fund transactions are done overnight. Banks generally lend their Federal funds on an unsecured basis, although collateral can be required to secure a borrowing position. The credit risk assumed by a bank will depend upon the financial condition of the borrowing bank. The Federal funds market is important because it is the core of the overnight credit market in the United States, and many other money market rates are fundamentally tied to the current and expected Federal funds rates.

**TABLE 6-1    Short-Term Instruments Purchased by Commercial Banks**

| Security | Issuer | Brief Description |
|---|---|---|
| Federal funds sold | Other commercial banks | Excess reserves of a bank usually sold to another bank to provide earning assets to selling bank; most mature daily but can be easily renewed; "term funds" are also short-maturity funds with a good market; unsecured |
| Treasury bills | Federal government | Highly marketable debt with no credit risk; sold on discount basis |
| Agency notes | Government agencies | Obligations of federal agencies; very high quality and nearly as marketable as federal debt |
| State and local notes | State and local governments | Short-term tax or bond anticipation obligations of state and local governments; interest is generally tax exempt for banks but not for most other investors |
| Commercial paper | Business or finance companies | High-quality business promissory notes; sold on discount basis |
| Negotiable CDs | Commercial banks and other financial institutions | Large interest-bearing deposits that can be traded before maturity |
| Bankers' acceptances | Businesses backed by commercial bank | Paper used to finance international trade, backed by commercial bank to improve credit quality |
| Securities purchased under agreement to resell (repos) | Commercial banks or businesses | Temporary purchase of government or other securities in which seller has agreed to repurchase securities at fixed price and set time in the future; difference between sale and purchase prices is return received by holder |
| Broker call loans | Securities brokers | Loans created when securities dealers borrow from bank to finance securities position of their clients |

*Treasury bills* are short-term obligations of the U.S. government. These securities are sold weekly on a discount auction basis in maturities of three and six months, and monthly offerings are made for one-year maturities. The discount prices of Treasury bills are determined by sealed auction bids and are sold in minimum amounts of $10,000 and in additional $5,000 increments. These securities are free from default risk, since they are the direct obligation of the U.S. government. The secondary market for Treasury bills is very active, and the resulting marketability risk associated with ownership is nonexistent. Interest income is subject to federal income tax but is exempt from state and local taxes.

*Repurchase agreements* involve the acquisition of funds by the sale of securities with the agreement to repurchase the securities at a given time, within one year, at a specified price. The securities underlying this transaction are typically Treasury and agency obligations. The repo transaction is short term, with maturities ranging from overnight to six months. Interest paid on repos is fully taxable, and the rate paid on repos is determined by the initial selling price plus a negotiated rate of interest. Repos are a close substitute for Federal funds from an investment perspective but pay a somewhat lower rate because of the securities that collateralize the underlying transaction. The credit risk of this transaction is virtually eliminated, as is interest rate risk, as the borrower must provide additional collateral if interest rates move in an unfavorable manner, causing a decrease in the value of the collateral.

*Agency notes* are the credit obligations of federally sponsored agencies that obtain their funding requirements by selling either debt or pass-through securities in the money and capital markets. These agencies are wholly owned by the private sector and hence do not have the credit guarantee of the federal government. Federally sponsored credit agencies finance their loan programs and secondary market purchases through the issuance of notes and pass-through securities. Interest on these securities is usually exempt from state and local taxes, and discount notes are by far the most popular form of issuance. The maturities of discount notes range from overnight to 360 days, but the maturity of a particular note depends upon which agency has issued the debt. The sponsored agencies typically pay lower returns than other private borrowers as a result of the unique features of the agencies and their generally low level of credit risk. There is an active secondary market for agency notes, similar to that for Treasury securities, so that the marketability risk of these securities is minimal.

*State and local notes* are short-term municipal securities and are obligations of state and local governments, and of the districts and authorities they create, to be repaid by the issuer's ability to tax or borrow or from the cash flow generated from a specific project. State and local notes with original maturities of less than one year are classified as short-term obligations. The interest on these obligations is exempt from federal tax and can be exempted from state and local taxes in the state of issue for individuals and most other potential purchasers except those using borrowed money to purchase the obligations. The actual yield to an investor will depend upon the investor's marginal tax rate; however, banks are subject to nondeductibility of 100 percent of the average cost of funds to finance these notes. The tax-exempt status of the interest payments to investors other than banks means that the notes carry an initial coupon rate below that of other obligations. This low interest rate tends to make these notes less appealing to banks than to most other investors. The credit risk of these securities is determined by the financial condition of the issuer and is borne by the investor. The secondary market is often thin and is made by dealers who underwrote the original issue. Thus, marketability risk is a concern, since the secondary market for municipal obligations is not as liquid as that for other investment alternatives.

*Commercial paper* is the short-term, unsecured borrowing of both financial and nonfinancial corporations used to meet short-term working capital needs. Commercial paper is issued in bearer form and is issued in maturities tailored to meet the needs of the issuing corporation. Maturities typically range from 1 to 270 days. Commercial paper is generally issued on a discount basis, with interest fully taxable. The yield on commercial paper is typically close to that of large negotiable CDs and bankers' acceptances. Since these obligations are generally short term, and most paper is issued with 5- to 45-day maturities, interest rate risk is not pervasive. However, there is not an active secondary market, and liquidity risk can be a problem. Commercial paper also has the credit risk of the underlying issuer of the obligation. Rating agencies such as Standard and Poors and Moody's provide credit ratings that help determine the premium an investor will require for the credit risk.

*Negotiable CDs* are CDs issued by banks that have a defined face amount, interest rate, and maturity but have a feature that allows them to be traded in a secondary market. Most negotiable CDs are issued in negotiable form to provide easy marketability. They have maturities that range from a minimum of seven days to 12 months. The most popular maturities are one, two, three, and six months. Rates on negotiable CDs are quoted on an interest-bearing basis, and interest is subject to full taxation. Yields are typically found to be at a premium to Treasury bills of similar maturities. This is due to the underlying credit risk of those CDs that exceed the $100,000 FDIC insurance limit and the fact that Treasury bills are exempt from state and local taxes. Although there is an active secondary market for negotiable CDs, it does not have the depth or breadth of the Treasury market.

*Bankers' acceptances (BAs)* are highly marketable short-term money market instruments that are used primarily to finance international trade. The BA represents a commercial bank's unconditional guarantee to pay a specified amount at a specified time. BAs are issued in maturities that range from 30 to 270 days and generally are structured to match the flow of goods and services that are being financed by the underlying transaction. These securities are issued at a discount, and the interest earned is subject to full taxation. Yields on BAs are generally similar to those on large negotiable CDs. The credit risk of a BA is minimized, since it has the unconditional guarantee of the accepting bank and is the secondary liability of the drawer or initiator of the transaction for the full face amount. BAs are traded in a highly active secondary market; thus, the marketability risk and interest rate risk of this type of security are minimized.

*Broker call loans*, although technically loans, amount to money market securities. They are created when securities brokers borrow from banks to finance the securities positions of their clients for short intervals, collateralizing the loans with securities salable on stock exchanges. They provide attractive yields, often in excess of one percentage point over interest rates on commercial paper or BAs. Call loans are so called because they can be called by investors on 24-hour notice.

# LONG-TERM DEBT SECURITIES

Banks invest in long-term debt securities primarily to obtain higher interest income. Currently (late 1993) they carry (on their books) the value of the

**TABLE 6-2   Longer-Term Securities Purchased by Banks**

| Security | Issuer | Brief Description |
|---|---|---|
| Treasury notes and bonds | Federal government | Longer-term interest-bearing notes and bonds that are obligations of the federal government |
| Agency bonds | Government agencies | Longer-term interest-bearing bonds of federal agencies |
| General obligations | State and local governments | Bonds backed by full faith, credit, and taxing power of issuing unit; interest may be partially tax exempt (subject to TEFRA and tax reform limits) |
| Revenue bonds | State and local governments | Bonds backed by revenues from specific projects or tax source; interest on new issues is subject to 100% TEFRA. |
| Corporate bonds | Business | Interest-bearing long-term business debt with varying degrees of quality and marketability |
| Mortgage-backed bonds | Consumers (packaged) | Interest-bearing long-term debt backed by grouping of mortgages and guarantee of government agency |

securities they own at cost (plus or minus any accretion of discount or amortization of premium) rather than at market value. If interest rates fall and prices rise, banks obtain gains, taxed as ordinary income, only when they sell securities. If rates rise and prices fall, banks may sell securities to obtain losses against ordinary income. This system of valuing securities at cost unless the securities are sold is being changed in 1994 (see the later discussion). A description of the primary characteristics of long-term securities follows and Table 6-2 gives a summary.

### Treasury Notes and Bonds

The lack of credit risk on U.S. Treasury securities and the highly efficient market for such securities explain the importance of Treasury securities to the commercial banking system. Income from all Treasury securities is subject to federal income taxes but is exempt from state and local income taxes. Marketable Treasury securities may be used as security for deposits of public monies and for loans from Federal Reserve Banks.

There are three basic types of marketable Treasury securities—bills, notes, and bonds. The characteristics of Treasury bills were discussed in the section on short-term securities. The primary difference between notes and bonds is their maturity. Treasury notes are issued with a maturity of not less than 1 year and not more than 10 years. These notes are available in minimum denominations of $10,000 in either registered or bearer form. Interest is paid on the registered bearer notes semiannually when the appropriate coupon is surrendered. Treasury bonds mature more than 10 years after the date of issuance. Bonds are available in either registered or bearer form and pay interest semiannually. Treasury bonds cover a wide range of maturities; maturity selections by buyers are based on portfolio requirements and on the willingness to assume interest rate risk. Nearly all Treasury issues are non-callable.

## Agency Obligations

The amount of outstanding securities that is not a direct obligation of the Treasury but that, in one way or another, involves federal sponsorship or guarantee has increased rapidly in recent years. Yields on securities of federal agencies are generally somewhat higher than yields on Treasury securities of similar maturity. Although agency securities are not the direct obligations of the federal government, they are regarded in the investment community as being of a credit quality nearly equal to that of Treasury securities. It is generally felt that the U.S. government would not allow a default on any of these bonds. Agency issues are, therefore, treated as non–credit risk assets and usually may be carried separately from risk assets in a bank's statement of condition. Although all agency securities are subject to federal income taxes, most of them are exempt from state and local income taxes. In addition, agency securities may be used as collateral to secure the fiduciary, trust, and public funds of the U.S. government and of many state and local governments. Some agency issues have slight marketability risk. The interest rate risk on agency securities is similar to that on Treasury securities; however, some agency securities are callable.

## State and Local Government Bonds

The increasing demand of state and local governments for funds has resulted in a rapidly growing market for state and local securities. The interest payments on this type of indebtedness used to be exempt from federal income taxes and are usually still exempt from income taxes imposed within the state of issue. Commercial banks used to be the dominant purchaser of state and local bonds; however, reduced taxable earnings primarily from increased loan losses at some banks, other methods of reducing taxes, and reduction of tax exemption on state and local securities to banks have caused banks' dominance to decline.[3]

Intermediate and longer-term state and local bonds can be divided into

---

[3] Commercial bank holdings of state and local securities fell from about 50 percent of all state and local securities outstanding in the early 1970s to about 14 percent at the end of 1992. The drop in banks' share of state and local securities—particularly among larger banks—reflects expansion into leasing, lending subject to foreign tax credits, and other activities that reduce the availability of taxable income that could be sheltered by state and local securities. Loan losses by some banks in 1982–1987 also made tax-exempt income less desirable. Passage of TEFRA and tax reform legislation in 1986 has kept banks from gaining exemption to federal income taxes on larger state and local issues purchased after August 1986.

three broad categories. Housing authority bonds are issued by local housing agencies to build and administer low-rent housing projects. Although the bonds are issued under the auspices of local housing agencies, the Housing Act of 1949 provided that the full faith and credit of the United States is pledged to the payment of all amounts agreed to be paid by the local agencies.

A bond is considered a general obligation if all the property in a community can be assessed and taxed at a level that will produce the revenues necessary to pay the debt. The primary tangible tax base is real estate on which the taxing authorities possess a lien equivalent to a first mortgage. Sales taxes, income taxes, and governmental subsidies are also important state or local revenue sources. The pledge of full faith and credit by a state or local unit usually includes a promise to levy taxes at whatever level debt service payments require.

Revenue bonds are payable solely from the earnings of a designated public project or undertaking. This type of bond includes all obligations not payable from or guaranteed by the general taxing power of the state or local government. The revenue supporting these bonds may come from (1) specifically dedicated taxes, such as those on cigarettes, gasoline, and beer; (2) tolls for roads, bridges, airports, or marine port facilities; (3) revenues from publicly owned utilities; and (4) rent payments on buildings or office space. Some banks have become heavy purchasers of industrial revenue bonds or pollution-control bonds, which are secured by revenues promised to the issuing unit by large corporations. Banks have also purchased recently popular issues, such as single-family mortgage revenue bonds and revenue bonds issued by nonprofit organizations—primarily hospitals.

The housing authority bonds, which are guaranteed by the federal government, are virtually free of credit risk. The credit risks inherent in other types of state and local debt are related to the ability and willingness of the governmental unit either to pay its obligations or to revise its capitalization. With general obligation bonds, the ability to pay is mainly contingent on the economic background of a community, the diversity of industry, the stability of employment, and so on. The ability to pay revenue bonds can generally be ascertained by comparing operating income with debt service requirements. This ability to pay could be changed by recapitalization, the issuance of additional debt with a credit position and a claim on taxing power or earnings equal to or superior to those of the existing bonds. Issues of revenue bonds usually specify the extent to which additional debt may be undertaken. There is usually no such protection for general obligation bonds.

Marketability risk varies widely among state and local issues and may be quite high for smaller issues. Interest rate risk is primarily a function of maturity, as is true of Treasury and agency securities. Two other characteristics of state and local debt are particularly pertinent for commercial banks. First, nearly all general obligations have serial maturities. A bank could, therefore, buy one issue with maturities in several years. Second, the 1982 TEFRA allowed deductions for only 85 percent of the interest cost on funds used to buy state and local securities. The Deficit Reduction Act of 1984 further reduced that share to 80 percent. The Tax Reform Act of 1986 prohibited banks from deducting interest costs or carrying larger issues of state and local securities purchased after August 1986. The bonds of issuers of general-purpose obligations totaling less than $10 million annually are still subject to the 80 percent TEFRA.

### Corporate Bonds

A corporate bond is an obligation (usually long term) of a private corporation. Although a governmental body may generally be assumed to have a continuing existence, a private corporation is subject to the vicissitudes of a market economy. The credit risk assumed by purchasers of corporate bonds is, therefore, a serious consideration; the failure of the enterprise may result in permanent and total loss. Marketability risk and interest rate risk are similar to those of state and local issues. Most corporate bonds are callable.

Banks have not purchased corporate bonds much in the past because there have been only brief interludes in recent history when the tax-equivalent yield on state and local bonds did not exceed the yields on corporate bonds of equal quality. The market for corporate bonds was primarily composed of institutions subject to minimal or no federal income taxation. In the early 1980s, however, there were enough banks with no taxable income so that the banking industry had become a factor in the corporate bond market. The worry in the early 1990s is that banks may purchase junk bonds (below investment grade) or bonds subject to event risk, such as leveraged buy-outs. Bank regulators are developing rules to eliminate or severely limit such security holdings.

## NEW BANK PORTFOLIO INSTRUMENTS

The later 1980s and early 1990s have seen less traditional bank portfolio instruments replace state and local securities as commercial banks' primary new investment purchases. There has been tremendous growth in commercial bank holdings of mortgage-backed securities and, to a lesser extent, other asset-backed securities. In addition to lowered or no tax exemption for state and local securities, a combination of attractive yield spreads, low credit risk, fairly stable prepayment rates, and favorable risk-based capital requirements have made mortgage-backed securities the most popular new portfolio instrument for many commercial banks. At the end of 1992, commercial banks held slightly over $250 billion of mortgage-backed securities, nearly 20 percent of that market. Banks must realize that these and other new instruments have complicated risks that should be carefully analyzed. Mortgage-backed securities and some of the other new bank portfolio instruments are described in the following paragraphs.

Two mortgage-backed instruments that made their initial appearance in the late 1970s are Government National Mortgage Association (GNMA) fully modified *mortgage-backed pass-through securities* and the Federal Home Loan

Mortgage Corporation (FHLMC) *mortgage participation certificates*. The cash flow to pay debt service on both securities comes from the selected groups of mortgages backing the security. The GNMA pass-throughs represent a share in a pool of Federal Housing Administration (FHA) or Veterans Administration (VA) mortgages. GNMA guarantees the timely payment of principal and interest on these securities, and this guarantee is backed by the full faith and credit of the U.S. government. The participation certificates represent undivided interests in specified residential conventional mortgages underwritten and owned or partly owned by the FHLMC. These securities are not guaranteed by the U.S. government, but the FHLMC itself does guarantee debt service payments. Early prepayment by mortgagers has typically caused the average maturity of these instruments to be less than the 12-year basis used for determining initial yield quotations.

In addition to the government-sponsored agencies, private institutions have issued mortgage pass-through certificates. These are participants in a pool of trusteed mortgages that may be either conventional, FHA, or VA; they are not guaranteed by the issuing institution. Banks also may buy securities backed by the cash flows from credit cards or installment loans. Typically, mortgages and other asset-backed securities are issued through major underwriters for public distribution and many have active secondary markets.

Another potential security is the *mortgage guaranteed or insured by the federal government*. FHA-issued and VA-guaranteed mortgages may be purchased by commercial banks from several federal agencies, as well as from other banks or nonbank financial intermediaries. The government-sponsored Federal National Mortgage Association and GNMA have contributed to the development of a national secondary mortgage market, purchasing and making purchase commitments where and when investment funds are in short supply and selling when and where investment funds are available. Even with the efforts of these agencies, however, the liquidity of guaranteed or insured mortgages may be limited in periods of restrictive monetary conditions.

There are several *derivative securities* from mortgage-backed and other securities. The derivative securities redistribute the cash flows from the backing securities into different tranches. One form, called *collateralized mortgage obligations (CMOs)*, consists of maturity tranches in which investors could buy the short-, intermediate-, or longer-term cash flows from the backing security. Short average-life CMO tranches have been particularly popular for banks, as they seem to provide a better match against the short maturity of interest-bearing liabilities. Among these, sequential pay and planned amortization classes (PACs) were perceived as the closest alternative to commercial banks' traditional holdings in Treasury and agency notes. Another form (called STRIPS, for Separate Trading of Registered Interest and Principal Securities) divides the cash flows into income stream (called IOs) and principal stream tranches (called POs).

*Floating-rate notes* are also a relatively new security. Although variable-rate securities have been around for nearly a decade, the exchangeable variable-rate note made its debut in 1984. The interest rate on such notes typically floats (is reset each quarter) for five years, then becomes fixed for five years. The governmental or corporate borrower can exchange the variable-rate notes for those with a fixed rate of interest based on Treasury rates.

*Adjustable-rate preferred stocks* are a relatively new vehicle that has proved to be a good investment for some banks. These stocks are usually repriced annually at a preselected basis point spread below one or several predetermined interest rate indices. Some stocks are repriced every seven weeks through a dutch auction mechanism in which the highest bidder (lowest dividend) gets the stock. The major appeal of these and similar stocks is that 80 percent of the dividend is exempt from corporate income taxes. A simplified example of an adjustable-rate preferred stock with a yield 100 basis points below the intermediate-term Treasury yield illustrates this appeal. If the Treasury yield is 9 percent, the preferred yield is 8 percent, and the bank has a 34 percent marginal income rate tax, the after-tax yield of the Treasury is $9 \times (1 - 0.34)$, or 5.94 percent, and that of the preferred is $8 - 8(.2)(.34)$, or 7.46 percent. Banks that are prohibited from holding preferred stocks invest in these and other preferred stocks through their holding companies.

In addition, numerous combinations and permutations of the preceding instruments have become available for banks and others to buy in the early 1990s. For example, banks can buy *zero coupon* state and local bonds or corporate bonds, which do not pay coupon interest but have predetermined appreciation to maturity. There is no reinvestment risk on these bonds, so the yield is certain if the bond is held to maturity. State and local bonds and corporate *bonds with put options*, which let the bank sell them back to the government or company for the full face value after a set period of time (usually two to five years), appeared in the early 1980s.

Off–balance sheet financial instruments—financial futures, options, and interest rate swaps—are discussed in Chapter 16.

## STEPS IN MANAGING THE SECURITY PORTFOLIO

Management of the security portfolio will differ among commercial banks because of differences in size, location, condition, loan demand, and managerial capabilities. There are, however, five basic steps that should lead to sound and flexible bank security portfolio management. The process should start with establishing general criteria and objectives. Next, broad predictions should be made about the economy and interest rates. The security portfolio needs of the bank are inventoried in the third step. In the fourth step, basic policies and strategies for managing the security portfolio are discussed. Fifth, and finally, the delegation of portfolio authority while maintaining control is discussed.

### Establishing General Criteria and Objectives

Policies for managing the security portfolio (often called the *investment portfolio*) generally should be in writing. Written policy statements are highly desirable if for no other reason than that memories may be short. Written policies provide continuity of approach over time, as well as concrete bases for appraising investment portfolio performance. It cannot be emphasized enough that portfolio policies become clear only when the people concerned in their formulation and execution have agreed on their exact wording. All policies, of course, should be reviewed periodically to consider changing circumstances.

The first section of the written portfolio policy should be a clear statement of the objectives of the securities. In the broadest sense, these are the same for all banks: to assist in providing liquidity, to obtain income, to maintain high quality in the portfolio, to keep the bank's funds fully employed, and to provide an adequate supply of liquidity for pledging. Some adaptation to individual circumstances may be necessary, and it is generally useful to state the bank's portfolio objectives carefully to provide continuing and mutual understanding of these objectives. Objectives should be challenging but achievable, understandable, and measurable.

## Coordinating Portfolios with Expected External Environment

It is obviously difficult to forecast key elements of the external environment, such as growth of the economy, interest rates, inflation, and unemployment. Weaknesses in many past forecasts indicate that forecasting is still more of an art than a science. Nevertheless, forecasting of at least general trends in key economic indicators is an important step in the management of the security portfolio. In nearly every security decision there is an implicit forecast of the external environment. For example, the decision between buying long-term versus short-term bonds generally contains an implicit forecast for interest rates and the future inflation rate. It is preferable to make security management decisions consistent with an explicit forecast, rather than to make security decisions that contain an implicit forecast that may or may not be consistent with what the security portfolio manager believes will happen.

Most bank managers have some predictions for the future external environment. Whether these predictions are correct or not is not the major concern; the point is that a bank's security management decisions at that time should be consistent with these predictions. Furthermore, because of the uncertainty of any economic predictions, decisions should be made with adequate safeguards to protect the bank in the case of incorrect predictions. The key point in this second step is that the bank should make its best forecast of the external environment.

## Inventorying Security Management Needs of Bank

After the broad objectives have been established and the external environment forecast, bank management must formulate specific portfolio policies suited to the characteristics and conditions of its bank. There are at least six areas that management should investigate to take an appropriate inventory of the security management of the bank.

**Coordinating Investment and Liquidity Planning**    The first area in inventorying portfolio needs is to decide how the bank's investment strategy should be coordinated with its liquidity position. Some banks, in effect, plan to provide funds to the investment portfolio in exchange for high-quality securities close enough to maturity to qualify as liquidity assets. This strategy is followed principally by banks that establish a policy of structured maturities. Other banks never plan for the liquidity portfolio to draw from the investment portfolios. A discussion on measuring a bank's liquidity needs is included in Chapter 5.

**Evaluating Pledging Requirements**    The second area to evaluate is the pledging requirements necessitated by the bank's public deposits. Some banks have only limited amounts of public deposits, whereas others aggressively seek them. The types of securities acceptable for pledging vary greatly with the type of public deposits. For example, Treasury securities are the only collateral acceptable for securing some public deposits. Other public deposits can be secured by Treasury securities, agency securities, or state and local securities of the same state or municipality depositing the funds. Clearly, bank management must know the bank's specific pledging requirements in inventorying its portfolio needs.

**Assessing the Risk Position**    The third area in inventorying a bank's security management needs is to determine the appropriate proportion of a bank's risk to be taken in the security portfolio. This decision will depend primarily on three considerations. The first is the amount of risk the bank has already assumed in its loan portfolio and other assets. If a bank has aggressively filled loan demands and is in an area where the loan demand is reasonably strong, it may be wise to limit risk exposure in the investment portfolio. The extent of this limitation depends on the second and third considerations.

The second consideration is the bank's capital position relative to the assets it already holds. Bank management should determine whether it has capital in excess of the amount it should hold against its present and anticipated loans and other risk assets. If an excess exists, portfolio policy should encourage increasing the proportion of securities to improve the bank's net income after taxes. If capital funds are inadequate to support additional risks, two alternatives exist. If management believes that the cost of raising new capital exceeds the benefits from a higher-risk portfolio, the bank should take little risk in its investment portfolio. If management believes that the after-tax benefits from a higher-risk portfolio exceed the cost of raising new capital, serious thought should be given to raising additional capital.

The third consideration is a realistic evaluation of the amount of expertise available and the effort applied to the investment portfolio area. Many small and medium-sized banks either do not have the necessary managerial investment expertise or apply what expertise they do have to banking functions other than investments. Some lack of managerial expertise and effort may be overcome through the use of large correspondents or consultants; however, it is generally advisable for a bank in this position to limit the risks it takes with its security portfolio. If such a bank does not take much risk with its other assets and has excess capital, it should compare the costs of providing the necessary expertise with the additional after-tax returns that competently administered policies could generate. The bank will be better off providing the necessary expertise if the incremental returns exceed the additional costs.

**Determining the Tax Position** The fourth logical area in inventorying portfolio needs is to estimate as nearly as possible the bank's net taxable income and to calculate the amount of additional tax-exempt income, if any, that the bank could profitably use. Since tax-exempt income is usually obtained at some sacrifice of gross revenue, it is obviously poor planning to have tax-exempt income exceed current operating earnings. In fact, even if a bank had complete flexibility (i.e., a portfolio large enough to provide all the tax-exempt income it could use), it should not ordinarily plan to eliminate all taxable income. An adequate margin of taxable income should be left to provide for maximum legal tax-free transfers to the reserve for loan losses and to absorb actual losses, should they develop. With regard to the latter, it is important to consider the losses that the bank may wish to take in shifting maturities within the portfolio, a process that will be discussed in greater detail later.

The tax considerations for small banks with incomes of less than $100,000 will usually be different from those affecting large banks because of the disparity in their effective tax rates. Factors other than taxes often determine the investment policies of small banks. For the large banks, tax considerations may weigh heavily in the determination of portfolio policy. Larger banks have many ways of legally reducing or avoiding taxes available to them, such as leasing, lending subject to foreign tax credits, timing of loan or security losses, and accelerated depreciation. Shielding income with tax-exempt securities should be compared with such alternatives. Recently passed tax legislation has limited the securities with tax-exempt income to smaller municipal issues (general-purpose obligations with issues limited to $10 million a year) and to municipal issues acquired before August 1986. (Tax exemption of security income is discussed in Chapter 7.) The new minimum corporate income tax may further mitigate the usefulness of tax-exempt income. Management's objective is still to reduce taxes as much as the existing laws permit without compromising the bank's obligation to make sound loans in its marketplace and to support risk assets with adequate capital funds.

**Estimating the Need for Diversification** The fifth area in the inventorying sequence is an estimation of the need for diversification. The bank should determine the industrial and geographical distributions of its loans and its state and local securities acquired for collateral or community relations. Investment additions in areas of heavy concentration might be limited. Advantages gained by diversification should be weighed against the possible loss of evaluation expertise that bank management may have in areas of concentration.

**Estimating Interest Sensitivity Needs**    The sixth area in inventorying a bank's portfolio needs is to evaluate the interest sensitivity of the bank's other assets and liabilities. A bank is often unable to control completely the interest rate risk associated with the types of loans it may have to make to service community needs or with the type of funds it can attract. An accurate measurement of the interest sensitivity and duration (discussed later in this chapter) of all the bank's nonportfolio assets and liabilities is needed. The portfolio manager will then know the interest sensitivity and duration needed from the investment portfolio to achieve the desired overall position for the bank. Off–balance sheet forms such as financial futures, options, or interest rate swaps may also be used to help achieve the desired overall position.

## Formulating Policies and Strategies for Managing the Security Portfolio

Next, the bank should formulate policies and strategies for managing the security portfolio that are consistent with the bank's written objectives, its economic forecast, and its inventoried needs. Constructive policies and strategies will vary greatly among banks, and each bank should be sure to allow adequate flexibility for management discretion as conditions change. Specific policies and strategies for several key areas of security management are discussed, and then the idea of integrating security portfolio management with total asset and liability management is introduced.

**Size of the Security Portfolio**    The size of the portfolio will be determined by (1) the amount of available funds not required for liquidity purposes and to meet the legitimate loan demands of the community, (2) the amount of securities required for pledging, and (3) the relative profitability of investment in securities. The first is the residual of the bank's liquidity calculations (discussed in Chapter 5), the bank's demand for loanable funds, and the bank's lending policies. The second will vary with the laws of the state in which the bank is located and with the aggressiveness with which the bank seeks public deposits. The third will depend on the profitability of securities in comparison with other competing forms of employing bank funds.

The concept of identifying part of the portfolio as a *core portfolio* is a useful strategy. After providing for all the liquidity needs from the portfolio, a bank may want to identify some or all of the remaining portfolio as a core that management will not use to meet liquidity needs. The bank can be more aggressive with regard to type of security, maturity, and other strategies, knowing it will not be forced to sell the portfolio at an inopportune time.

**Investment Media and Quality Levels**    The essence of establishing flexible portfolio policies and strategies pertaining to security media and quality levels is matching the type and quality of security portfolio instruments with the portfolio needs of the bank. Both the needs and the related policies should be reviewed periodically.

The first portfolio need affecting investment media is the level and acceptable form of the bank's pledging requirements. The bank must have an adequate amount of acceptable securities—Treasury, U.S. agency, or state and local securities—to meet the requirements for public deposits in its political jurisdiction. In cases in which more than one type of security can be used to meet the pledging requirements, the choice will depend on the bank's risk and tax positions. In practically all banks, policymakers should insist that the pledged securities be those eligible securities that the bank is least likely to want to sell. Substitution for pledged securities, though possible, may be a costly and time-consuming process.

Risk position will have a strong impact on the policies affecting the investment media and quality level of the bank. Banks taking considerable lending risk (in relation to their capital position) and banks lacking managerial expertise or effort should limit their purchases to Treasury securities, agency obligations, AAA- or AA-rated state and local securities or AAA- or AA-rated corporate bonds, and federally insured or guaranteed mortgages. Such a policy (in conjunction with reasonable maturity policies) should restrict the risk in the investment portfolio and can be implemented with limited managerial expertise and effort. Many small banks, in particular, should adopt this policy because of their limited senior managerial resources.

On the other hand, banks that have the necessary managerial talent and time and are in a position to take additional risks in their investment portfolio should be less restrictive in their quality limits. Such banks should be able to purchase lower-quality bonds, which usually have higher yields. Before prudent policy allows the purchase of state and local securities or corporate bonds rated below AA, the board of directors and senior management should make sure that talent and time are available for the required credit analysis by the bank staff.

The bank's tax position is an element in determining whether bank policy should encourage the continued holding of state and local securities (acquired before the August 1986 tax reform) with tax-exempt interest payments or of other investment instruments that pay taxable interest. If the yields on tax-exempt state and local obligations continue to range from 10 to 20 percent lower than the yields on other obligations of comparable quality, bank policy may want to emphasize holding state and local obligations as long as the bank's marginal income is taxed at the 34 percent rate. Some smaller state and local issues are still exempt from income taxes; however, care should be taken so that marketability of the portfolio is not unduly limited. When bank income is not taxed or is taxed at a marginal rate below 20 percent, bank policy should usually emphasize switching to taxable securities (including taxable municipals) if they have an adequate yield advantage.

Any desired coordination with the liquidity position will also have an effect on policies determining the investment media and quality levels. If the bank expects to receive periodically a certain volume of securities close enough to maturity to qualify as liquidity assets, bank policy should require that sufficient high-quality, marketable securities will be available to meet such needs.

Finally, if the bank feels that the gains from diversification outweigh the loss of expertise or evaluation that bank management has in areas of concentration, policies should be formulated indicating the portfolio requirements for industrial or geographic diversification.

**Maturity Policies and Strategies** Maturities may present two types of policy problems: the establishment of a maximum maturity limit, if considered sound policy, and the scheduling of maturities within the portfolio. The latter is closely related to the bank's appraisal of the economic climate. Arranging and rearranging portfolio maturities also forces the portfolio manager to make decisions regarding taking profits and losses, with their own special tax considerations. These aspects of the maturity problem are all interrelated but can perhaps be understood more readily if they are examined separately.

There are two risk-related reasons that some banks limit the maximum acceptable maturities in their portfolio. First, the quality of state or local securities and corporate bonds may vary over time. A bank that lacks sufficient managerial expertise or time to evaluate the probability of deterioration in the quality of some securities in its portfolio can reduce its exposure to this risk by setting some fairly short-term limits on the maturities of such securities. The second reason pertains to interest rate movements. If interest rates rise, the prices of long-term bonds deteriorate much more than the prices of short-term bonds. Instead of being able to purchase bonds at higher yields or meet expanding loan demands at profitable rates, the holders of long-term bonds have securities with large, unrealized capital losses.

Commercial bank experience with longer-term bonds generally was unfavorable in the 1970s and early 1980s because of the rising trend of interest rates. Prices of previously purchased bonds deteriorated, and higher yields than those on held securities seemed to be continually available. The reverse was true from mid-1982 through 1992, when interest rates generally trended down and prices of longer-term bonds rose substantially. Still, if a bank is purchasing longer-term securities with the expectation of holding them to maturity, one could readily counsel, "Never buy a yield that you are not willing to live with." In light of the uncertainties of a rapidly changing world, such advice might well limit portfolio commitments to no longer than three years. Even that is a long time to look ahead.

On the other hand, one should not lose sight of the full sweep of history and the long periods in the past during which the secular trend of interest rates was down. Should policymakers be convinced that this particular phase of history was in the process of repeating itself, there would be ample justification for extending maturities beyond 10 or 15 years. And to a certain extent, current tax laws soften the effect of realized losses on investments.

Clearly, one should not be doctrinaire. If the bank lacks managerial expertise or effort in the investment portfolio area or if management expects interest rates to rise and loan demand to be as strong as it was in the late 1970s and early 1980s, it probably should set a fairly short maximum maturity (between three and seven years) for the bulk of its portfolio investments. On the other hand, if the bank has the managerial competence *and* is willing to accept some security losses and to recognize the higher risks and returns generally associated with longer-term bonds, no maximum maturity limit seems necessary. Over the long run, the higher risks associated with these bonds should result in larger profits.

Scheduling maturities within the investment portfolio is undoubtedly the most difficult and exacting task of portfolio management. Other policies can be established, periodically reviewed, and occasionally adapted to new circumstances. Maturity policy, in contrast, requires constant review and decision making as funds become available for investment or as opportunities to improve the income position occur. Probably the most important determinants of maturities are the interest sensitivity and duration of the bank's nonportfolio assets and liabilities. The scheduling of maturities within the investment portfolio should help the bank achieve its desired overall interest sensitivity and duration positions. Portfolio maturities should not be dominated solely by such considerations, however, because maturities of other assets and liabilities can be partially managed and because off–balance sheet hedging instruments, such as financial futures, options, and interest rate swaps, are available. Within established interest sensitivity and duration constraints, there are three major philosophies for scheduling maturities: cyclical maturity determination, spaced or staggered maturities, and a "barbell"maturity structure.

From the previous discussion, it would appear that the ideal course of action in portfolio management would be to hold short-term securities when interest rates are likely to rise and to lengthen maturities when rates are expected to decline. This strategy is tantamount to shortening maturities when business conditions (and the demand for credit) are expected to improve and lengthening maturities when the first signs of a recession appear. There are several problems in the application of this theoretical ideal. First, even in cyclical periods such as the 1960s, bank portfolio managers found themselves under heavy pressure to produce profits (and thereby encouraged to buy longer-term securities) when interest rates were low. When interest rates were high (and expected to decline), banks tended to have only limited amounts to invest in any maturity. Second, business cycles do not always act as the textbooks say they should. For example, the 1970s might be described as 10 years of stagflation and fluctuating, rising interest rates, with only limited vestiges of traditional cyclical movements. As of 1993 there have been three aborted recoveries from a recession that started in 1990. Third, portfolio management can be seen to be closely integrated with economic forecasting, which is considered by some to be a dubious art at best.

Because of the many uncertainties involved in such an ideal approach, banks have frequently been counseled to solve the problem of maturity distribution by spacing maturities more or less evenly within the maximum range. In this way, the bank will assure itself of at least average yields, or a little better. It will not be gambling on changes in the level of rates or the state of the economy. As long as the yield curve is rising, the reinvestment of maturing assets at the longest end of the maturity schedule will assure the bank of

**FIGURE 6-1    Ten-Year Staggered-Maturity Portfolio Distribution of Bonds by Maturity**

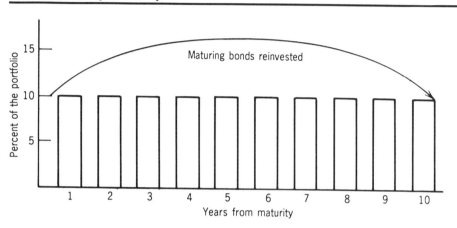

maximum income on a portfolio of which the average maturity will be relatively short. Figure 6-1 illustrates a staggered portfolio in which maturing bonds are invested in bonds that mature in 10 years.

Banks using the barbell maturity structure tend to strengthen their liquidity position by investing a part of their investment portfolio in short-term liquid securities. The remainder of the typical barbell portfolio usually consists of high-yield, very-long-term bonds. Figure 6-2 illustrates a barbell portfolio. Ad-

**FIGURE 6-2    A 30 Percent Short-Term Barbell Portfolio Distribution of Bonds by Maturity**

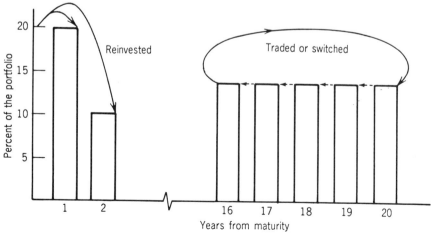

vocates of this maturity philosophy reason that the greater liquidity and higher returns more than compensate for any additional risks. Barbell portfolios tend to be trading portfolios, and it is typical for the long-term proportion of the portfolio to be largest when interest rates are high and for the short-term portion of the portfolio to grow when rates are low. Managerial expertise is clearly a prerequisite for the barbell maturity structure.

For bank management that lacks managerial competence in the investment area or that does not wish to take the trouble to frame a more flexible portfolio policy, average results obtained through regularly spaced (staggered or laddered) maturities are undoubtedly better than what might result from a purely haphazard or intuitive approach to the problem. Spaced maturities are probably an acceptable solution for the small bank. The barbell structure or other flexible approaches are generally preferable for bank managements that have the necessary competence and are willing to exercise judgment. It certainly does not make sense for such managements to invest the proceeds of maturity securities in the longest-term bonds permitted by the bank's policy at a time when the economy is obviously in a slack condition, when banks hold excess reserves, and when money rates are abnormally low.

Not even the most competent investment managers, of course, will be able to call every turn, nor do they need to do so. Alert and informed managers can take advantage of events that have already occurred. They do not need to gamble on the future.

**Trading and Switching Policies and Strategies**   Many banks buy securities and hold them in the bank's portfolio until they mature. This is not the way to maximize returns consistent with reasonable levels of risk. There are times to buy and times to sell (and buy something else), and both large and small banks can take advantage of the broad movements in the securities markets.

A valid distinction can be made between trading and switching. *Trading* is a day-to-day operation that requires easy access to the markets and an expertise not available to many banks. *Switching* involves the mobility of a portfolio in relation to changes in economic conditions and related changes in rate levels. A bank that is alert to switching activities will be in the market far less than a bank that has the capacity to trade actively, but its purchases and sales can, nonetheless, add appreciably to its income over time.

Current (1993) accounting rules applicable to banks do not make a distinction between trading profits and losses and portfolio profits and losses, but value securities for the two purposes differently. A bank may establish a trading account of securities it intends to sell, and the profits and losses resulting from its trades will be shown as a part of its operating earnings. To operate a trading account, a bank must take price appreciation and deterioration as well as actual earnings into its operating results. It must "mark to market," that is, treat price deterioration as an actual loss with respect to those securities that it has designated as its trading account. Since 1983, gains and losses on portfolio transactions are also included as operating earnings; however, securities in the bank investment portfolio are not marked to market but are left valued at their original cost plus any adjustment needed to move this cost toward the securities maturity value. Thus, the value of a bank's investment portfolio on its balance sheets might be misleading.

There is a recent change in accounting rules that forces banks to value much or all of their security portfolios at market value. Standard No. 115 of the Financial Accounting Standards Board (approved in 1993, effective 1994) requires banks to have three categories of securities:

1. Trading accounts of securities the bank intends to sell;
2. Value accounts of securities that the bank may sell (partly based on past activity) with changes in value recognized in an equity reserve, designated "available for sale;" and
3. Investment accounts of securities that the bank will hold to maturity except in emergency situations, designated "hold to maturity."

The first and second accounts would be marked to market, and the third valued at historic cost. Possible distortions in earnings and equity from valuing only certain assets and no liabilities at market values have led to even more comprehensive proposals on valuing both assets and liabilities. The authors' opinions on valuing assets and liabilities and potential effects of such changes are summarized in Appendix 1 at the end of this chapter.

Many securities clearly held for liquidity should probably be treated for accounting purposes as a trading account, whether they are actively traded or not. For the most part, they will be of short maturity and their value as liquidity instruments will be their market value. Those banks that are able to trade their liquidity portfolios because of their own knowledge or because of access to expert advice will probably add appreciably to their income over a period of time.

Intelligent security policies should provide the opportunity to use switching strategies that lead to increased returns. These increases are often beneficial to the bank's stockholders because they involve little, if any, additional risk. Switching maturities and taking profits and losses to the best advantage are technical aspects of security management; however, the general principle discussed here can serve as a beginning guide for establishing rational policies and strategies.

## STRATEGIES DURING TIMES OF MARKET DEPRECIATION

In cyclical periods of high loan demand, high interest rates, and monetary restraint or in trend periods of high inflation and rising interest rates, most bonds in a bank's security portfolio will show market depreciation. This will be the time to take tax losses and possibly to extend maturities in anticipation of lower interest rates and higher security prices. The amount and extent of maturity extensions depend on management's confidence that the cyclical boom or inflationary interest rate spiral is ending. As the manager becomes confident in such periods, security portfolio policy should flexibly encourage three actions: investing any funds available to the investment portfolio at the longer end of the portfolio; "refunding in advance" by selling short-term issues and reinvesting the proceeds of such sales in longer-term bonds; and switching from a security of a given maturity into one of comparable maturity to improve yield and long-term profit potential.

The first and second actions achieve the major portfolio objective of lengthening maturities when losses are taken so that the portfolio can benefit from the expected easing of rates in a later period. The advantages of higher income and greater potential for gain in market price are evident. The third action is more limited in objective but may contribute considerably to the long-run profitability of banks using a barbell type of portfolio policy. For example, assume that a bank owns some 10-year bonds that it bought at par a few years earlier that are currently selling at 80 (remember, bonds are priced in tens of dollars, so that a price of 80 means $800). If the bank sells $1 million par of the bonds for $800,000, the $200,000 loss after taxes costs $132,000 (assuming a marginal tax rate of 34 percent). By reinvesting the $800,000 in similar bonds, the bank will have a built-in future appreciation of $200,000, which after taxes will net it roughly $132,000 at maturity. This is not a break-even proposition, however, because the bank also has $68,000 more in cash (because of the lower taxes) than it would have had if it had not taken the loss. This $68,000 is invested now at the new higher yields and provides higher returns over the remaining life of the bonds, as well as the possibility of appreciation.

One may wonder why all the banks do not sell most of their holdings at a loss in periods of high interest rates. The foremost consideration is how much reduction in reported net income the owners of the bank are willing to accept. Explaining to shareholders that reductions in current profits are advantageous over the long run is not easy. Secondly, banks may be concerned that sale of one security will force other similar securities to be classified as held for sale and valued at market. Also, there is the limitation of taxable income. Losses are valuable only to the extent that they reduce taxes at a high marginal tax rate, such as 35 percent. Finally, since losses reduce income, they also reduce (or lower the increase in) bank capital, thereby encouraging supervisory authorities to ask for more capital.

## STRATEGIES DURING TIMES OF MARKET APPRECIATION

When the economy is clearly in a recession and interest rates are relatively low, at least some bonds will be selling at above-average prices. Portfolio holdings, if acquired at comparatively low prices during a previous period of high interest rates, will show market appreciation. This is the time when banks generally should keep their new investments short. While banks can largely offset the sacrificed income by taking profits in the longer bonds, the strategy of taking profits should be carefully scrutinized.

Taking profits always seems more desirable than absorbing losses, but it can be dangerous merely to take profits and reinvest in comparable (or longer) maturities. To do so is to leave the bank even more vulnerable than before to declines in prices that are bound to come, since these declines will affect booked profits rather than unbooked appreciation. For example, assume that a bank owns some 10-year bonds that it bought at par a few years earlier that are selling for 120. If the bank sells $1 million par value of them for $1.2 million, the $200,000 before-tax gain will be recorded as a $132,000 after-tax gain (assuming a marginal tax rate of 34 percent). The bank will have only $1.132 million to reinvest in the lower rate environment because it has to pay the taxes immediately; therefore, future income flows will usually be lowered. The general rule, therefore, should be: "Do not take profits without shortening maturities." The conviction that the economy is close to the bottom of a recessionary period, which should lead a bank to take profits, should also convince it to shorten maturities in anticipation of a later rise in rates.

Particularly when taking account of changes in the accounting treatment of securities, profits (after taxes), taken in times of low interest rates, should not be looked on as permanent additions to the bank's capital funds. They should be carried as reserves against future security losses, where they will be available to absorb the losses when the next turn in interest rate levels provides new profit possibilities.

Tax considerations should not be overlooked. The distinction between short- and long-term capital gains is not relevant for banks, since all capital gains are taxed as ordinary income and all capital losses are used to reduce ordinary income. Most banks are willing to take losses (reducing taxable income) on any type of security; however, they often prefer to avoid taking gains on state and local securities. The reason is that such gains are subject to federal income taxes, whereas the interest on such bonds acquired before August 1986 is exempt from most or all federal income taxes. Once such bonds are sold, the tax exemption is lost. The interest on state and local bonds acquired before 1983 is completely exempt from federal income taxes. Interest on such securities acquired in 1983 and 1984 is subject to 15 percent disallowance of the allocated funding cost. Interest on such securities acquired from the end of 1984 through August 1986 and selected smaller issues since that date is subject to 20 percent disallowance of the allocated funding cost. New purchases of larger state and local issues should not be evaluated as tax-exempt securities.

## EXAMPLES OF SWITCHING STRATEGIES

Table 6-3 illustrates the basic effects of two security switches. In Example 1, $100,000 of 8 percent federal agency bonds with 14 years remaining to maturity are sold for $90,000, which is approximately a 10 percent yield to maturity. Similar federal agency bonds yielding 10 percent with a similar 14-year maturity are purchased at par. A hypothetical investment of the proceeds from the agency bond sale, $90,000 plus the estimated lower taxes of $3,400 (the bank's

---

**TABLE 6-3    Measuring the Effect of Security Switches**

| Sell | Book Value | Sale Price | Coupon Income | Yield to Maturity (%) |
|---|---|---|---|---|
| **Example 1: Agency Bond Switch at Loss** | | | | |
| $100,000 14-year agency bond | $100,000 | 90,000 | $8,000 | 10 |
| *Purchase* | | | | |
| $100,000 14-year agency bond | $100,000 | | $10,000 | 10 |
| Hypothetical[a] | 93,400[a] | | 9,340[a] | 10 |

Earning effect: Bank will take a $6,600 after-tax loss (10,000 times 1 minus the marginal tax rate of 34%) now, for a $1,340 increase in taxable income each year for 14 years plus a higher value at maturity.

**Example 2: Treasury Bond Switch at Gain**

| Sell | Book Value | Sale Price | Coupon Income | Yield to Maturity (%) |
|---|---|---|---|---|
| $1 million 12-year Treasury bonds | $1,000,000 | $1,100,000 | $80,000 | 6 |
| *Purchase* | | | | |
| $1 million 12-year Treasury bonds | $1,000,000 | | $60,000 | 6 |
| Hypothetical[a] | $1,066,000[a] | | $63,960[a] | 6 |

Earning effect: Bank will take a $66,000 after-tax gain this year ($100,000 times 1 minus the marginal tax rate of 34%) but will have a $16,040 lower taxable income each year for the next 12 years.

[a]Hypothetical amount so that purchase equals proceeds of sale plus lowered taxes or minus higher taxes.

---

34 percent marginal tax rate times the $10,000 of lower income), is made in a similar agency issue. The earnings effect is that the bank takes a $6,600 after-tax loss in the current year and will gain higher income of $1,340 each year for the next 14 years. The $6,600 loss is recovered in roughly 4 years 11 months; moreover, the bonds might have a higher value at maturity. Whether the bank would make such a switch depends on the bank's condition (strong or weak capital, acceptable to have earnings lowered by the loss) and rules of thumb the bank may have developed, such as recovery of loss within half of the remaining life of the bond.

In the second example, $1 million of 8 percent Treasury bonds with 12 years to maturity are sold on a 6 percent yield basis for a gain of $100,000, and the after-tax proceeds are invested in similar-maturity Treasury notes. Assuming that the bank is in a 34 percent marginal income tax bracket, the bank will have only $1,066 million of the $1.1 million proceeds to reinvest in lower-yielding bonds. The results are a $66,000 after-tax profit this year but

$16,040 in lower taxable income each year for the next 12 years. In nearly every switch in which banks realize a gain, this gain is at the cost of lower income in future years. Taking gains makes sense in a few situations, such as when the bank wants to smooth income or increase capital; however, the usual rule is not to take gains unless the proceeds are used to shorten maturities.

Such a rule opens Pandora's box. Portfolio switches that involve changing credit quality or changing the maturity of the security portfolio need to be evaluated under broader criteria than those discussed here. Even the basic analysis without quality or maturity changes is more complex because potential taxable gains or losses at maturity also have to be considered. Nevertheless, the measures presented in Table 6-3 present the basic elements for an analysis of switching opportunities. Many banks now have computer programs to evaluate a large number of potential switches.

**Evaluating Securities with Uncertain Cash Flows**  As pointed out earlier, the interest rate when cash flows are received has a strong impact on the realized yield when a security matures or is sold. The problem becomes more complex if the time when the cash flows will be received is uncertain. Examples are corporate or agency bonds that are callable at the issuer's option or mortgage-backed derivative securities on which the mortgages backing the securities may be refinanced at the borrower's option.

For callable securities, most holders such as banks calculate the yield to call for bonds that sell at a premium above their call price. The appropriate technique for mortgage-backed derivative products is less certain. It becomes more attractive to refinance when mortgage rates fall; however, the decision is made by numerous individual borrowers. Investment bankers and others who sell mortgage-backed securities estimate what will happen to principal and interest cash flows under various scenarios of interest rate changes. These estimations can be used to predict what realized yields will be under various rate scenarios. Generally banks that purchase mortgage-backed securities are better off if yields remain fairly stable. Chapter 17 contains additional discussion on these and similar banking assets with implicit options.

**Securities as an Asset–Liability Balancing Factor**  The preceding discussion of policies and strategies affecting the security portfolio management has ignored one of the most important functions of the portfolio—to serve as a balancing factor for a bank's overall asset–liability structure. The maturity structure, interest sensitivity, overall credit risk, and liquidity needs that result from the type of funds attracted and type of loans made can be at least partially balanced by a bank's security portfolio. Funds attracted and loans made are strongly affected by factors beyond a bank's control, such as competitors' actions and the bank's location. Securities represent nonpersonal assets that, when flexibly managed, can be used to assist the bank in achieving such objectives as a balanced asset–liability maturity structure, the desired interest sensitivity position, an overall credit risk target, and liquidity sources matching liquidity needs. Thus, managing the security portfolio should be evaluated in the context of overall asset–liability management rather than as a separate function.

Two useful measures are duration and immunization. The duration of debt securities explicitly considers the timing of the return of principal and interest payments. The present value of cash flows related to price is weighted by the length of time until they are received. Table 6-4 illustrates how the duration of a seven-year, 12 percent coupon bond is calculated. It is assumed that interest is paid annually and that at the end of the seventh year this bond will pay off $1,120. Notice that the 5.11 years' duration of this bond is less than its term to maturity of 7 years. Other things being equal, the duration of a bond is lower for high-coupon bonds because more money is available for reinvestment earlier. For example, in a 12 percent market, the duration of a 16 percent coupon bond is 4.87 years and the duration of an 8 percent coupon bond is 5.46 years. The duration of a bond can never exceed its term to maturity and will be less than the terms to maturity except for zero coupon bonds. (The duration of a seven-year zero coupon bond is exactly seven years.) Numerous computer software programs are available to calculate duration.

Although some of the claims about the usefulness of duration appear to be overstated, duration would seem to improve management's knowledge about the bank's security portfolio and, more important, its overall asset–liability portfolio. Duration is a better indicator of the interest sensitivity of an asset or liability than the asset's or liability's maturity alone. Duration indicates reinvestment rate risk and relative price volatility better than maturity alone. Some argue that duration is a more appropriate horizontal axis for constructing a yield curve than maturity. Finally, duration figures for various types of assets, or liabilities, are additive in a more meaningful way than maturities. One can question the meaning of the average maturity of a security portfolio.

Immunization recognizes two basic parts of the interest risk of an individual security or security portfolio. One part is the risk of decline in market value if rates rise. Of course, the market value increases if rates fall. The second part is the risk that cash flows will be reinvested at lower rates if interest rates fall; however, cash flows will be reinvested at higher rates if rates rise. Therefore, a rise in rates hurts a security's market value but allows reinvestment at higher rates, whereas a fall in rates hurts because reinvestment is at a lower rate, although the market value of a security rises. Immunization results from the offsetting nature of these two risks when rates move in either direction. A security portfolio would be completely immunized from interest rate movements if reinvestment exactly offsets the market value risk.

The concepts of duration and immunization also can be applied to bank assets other than securities, such as loans and bank liabilities. It is more useful to match the duration of most bank assets with that of most bank liabilities than to measure the duration of a single security or even a portfolio of securities. Likewise, immunization of the bank's total portfolio of assets and liabilities from interest rate movements seems to deserve more attention than immunization of the security portfolio alone. These concepts are, therefore, discussed in detail in Chapter 14.

**TABLE 6-4  Duration Calculation for Bonds with Different Coupons Priced to Yield 12 Percent**

| (1) Year | (2) Cash Flow | (3) Present Value of $1 at 12% | (4) Present Value of Flow | (5) Present Value of Price | (6) Duration (1) × (5) |
|---|---|---|---|---|---|
| **A. Duration of a 12 Percent Coupon Seven-Year Bond Priced to Yield 12 Percent** | | | | | |
| 1 | $ 120 | 0.8929 | $ 107.15 | 0.1071 | .1071 |
| 2 | 120 | 0.7972 | 95.66 | 0.0957 | .1914 |
| 3 | 120 | 0.7118 | 85.42 | 0.0854 | .2562 |
| 4 | 120 | 0.6355 | 76.26 | 0.0763 | .3052 |
| 5 | 120 | 0.5674 | 68.09 | 0.0681 | .3405 |
| 6 | 120 | 0.5066 | 60.79 | 0.0608 | .3648 |
| 7 | 1,120 | 0.4523 | 506.58 | 0.5066 | 3.5462 |
| Sum | | | 1,000.00 | 1.0000 | 5.1114 |
| Price | | | $1,000.00 | | |
| Duration | | | | | 5.11 years |
| **B. Duration of a 16 Percent Coupon Seven-Year Bond Priced to Yield 12 Percent** | | | | | |
| 1 | $ 160 | 0.8929 | $ 142.864 | 0.1208 | 0.1208 |
| 2 | 160 | 0.7972 | 127.552 | 0.1079 | 0.2158 |
| 3 | 160 | 0.7118 | 113.888 | 0.0963 | 0.2889 |
| 4 | 160 | 0.6355 | 101.680 | 0.0860 | 0.3440 |
| 5 | 160 | 0.5674 | 90.784 | 0.0768 | 0.3839 |
| 6 | 160 | 0.5066 | 80.960 | 0.0685 | 0.4108 |
| 7 | 1,160 | 0.4523 | 524.668 | 0.4437 | 3.1061 |
| Sum | | | 1,182.396 | 1.0000 | 4.8703 |
| Price | | | $1,182.40 | | |
| Duration | | | | | 4.87 years |
| **C. Duration of an 8 Percent Coupon Seven-Year Bond Priced to Yield 12 Percent** | | | | | |
| 1 | $ 80 | 0.8929 | $ 71.432 | 0.0873 | 0.0873 |
| 2 | 80 | 0.7972 | 63.776 | 0.0779 | 0.1559 |
| 3 | 80 | 0.7118 | 56.944 | 0.0696 | 0.2087 |
| 4 | 80 | 0.6355 | 50.840 | 0.0621 | 0.2485 |
| 5 | 80 | 0.5674 | 45.392 | 0.0555 | 0.2773 |
| 6 | 80 | 0.5066 | 40.528 | 0.0495 | 0.2971 |
| 7 | 1,080 | 0.4523 | 489.456 | 0.5981 | 4.1866 |
| Sum | | | 818.368 | 1.0000 | 5.4614 |
| Price | | | $818.37 | | |
| Duration | | | | | 5.46 years |

## Implementing Investment Policies and Strategies

There are five key elements in implementing investment policies and strategies successfully. Two of these elements—determining investment objectives and putting portfolio objectives in writing—have been discussed. The other three elements—identifying the purpose and makeup of the portfolio, complying with regulatory rules, and delegating investment authority with adequate controls—are discussed here.

**Identifying the Portfolio**   The *investment account* usually refers to all security holdings of a bank. It is common practice for bank management to provide directors and owners with only a list of the bank's security holdings, showing book values, market prices, and range of maturities. The list is generally subdivided into U.S. government securities, state and municipal securities, and other securities. Few attempts are made, however, to distinguish the liquidity position from the investment portfolio, that is, to identify those securities held specifically for the purpose of liquidity and those held for long-term investment.

Length of maturity alone will not be the distinguishing feature, because under certain circumstances (in anticipation of rising rates, for example), a portion of the investment portfolio could well be held temporarily in short-term issues. The real distinction is the purpose for which the securities are held. Liquidity assets are used to meet estimates of potential deposit withdrawals and increased loan demands. The investment portfolio, by contrast, represents the investment of surplus funds for income. The distinction between securities held for resale or held to maturity may also be useful in this context.

**Complying with Regulatory Rules**   The increase in the relative importance of securities in most banks' asset structures has increased regulatory interest in securities activities by commercial banks. Most of the regulatory bodies seemed particularly concerned about policies and practices involving new derivative products, such as mortgage- or other asset-backed derivative securities. Regulatory treatment has varied among the various regulatory bodies. Finally, in 1991 the Federal Financial Institutions Examination Council adopted a supervisory policy statement on securities activities that should make supervision similar among the various regulatory bodies. The main components of this policy statement are summarized in Appendix 2 at the end of this chapter.

**Delegating Authority but Maintaining Control**   The delegation of authority and retention of control are essential parts of security portfolio policy. In this area the board of directors has the ultimate responsibility, and it should share responsibilities for policy determination with members of senior management. The portfolio manager should be in charge of day-to-day management and may recommend major courses of action or policy changes to the board and senior management.

A bank's investment policy should delegate specific authority to designated officers to purchase or sell securities up to certain amounts, just as a bank's loan policy should permit the bank's lending officer to commit the bank for stated amounts. Opportunities for profitable switching or trading that might be evident to the investment officer, or that might be called to his or her attention by a correspondent bank, a dealer, or an investment advisory service, do not last long in the market. If decisions must be referred to an investment committee, or even to a chief executive officer who may be away from the bank at the moment, portfolio opportunities will be irretrievably lost. A sound policy, therefore, will set trading limits, based on the size of the bank and the investment officer's knowledge and experience, within which he or she should have full discretion. It is relatively simple to compare the results of trading, say every six months, with what would have resulted had no purchases or sales been made. Such a comparison should be a clear indication of the investment officer's acumen.

Compensation plans in the investment area should also recognize good performance. It is important to remember that performance includes assessment of both returns and risks taken.

## SUMMARY

Security portfolio management should recognize differences in size, location, condition, and managerial capabilities among banks. There are, however, five basic steps that should lead to sound, flexible security policies and strategies. Security portfolio policies should be in writing and should start with a statement of the objectives of the security portfolio. After the objectives have been established, the bank should make its forecast for the economy and interest rates. Next, the bank should inventory its own investment needs by identifying the portfolio, estimating pledging requirements, assessing the risk position, determining the tax position, coordinating with the bank's interest-sensitivity position, and estimating the need for diversification. After inventorying its needs, the bank should establish policies and strategies affecting the size, risk, maturity, and marketability of the investment portfolio that are consistent with these needs. Finally, bank policies should delegate authority for action commensurate with responsibility and should reward outstanding performance. All these steps should be coordinated with overall asset–liability management. One of the most important contributions of the security portfolio is that it permits impersonal flexibility in balancing a bank's overall liquidity and interest-sensitivity position.

## Discussion Questions

1. What are the primary functions of a bank's security portfolio in current and future environments?
2. How is the current yield on a bond calculated? How is the yield to maturity

on a bond calculated? Describe situations in which each of these measures is appropriate.

3. What are the four potential sources of risk for debt securities?

4. Name several types of securities banks may use in addition to traditional types—Treasury, agency, state, and local. Describe situations in which banks might seek to use such securities.

5. List and briefly describe the five basic steps that should lead to sound, flexible management of a bank's security portfolio.

6. What are some of the key factors management should look for in inventorying the security management needs of the bank?

7. Discuss the considerations that should affect how much risk a bank should take in its security portfolio.

8. Contrast the advantages and disadvantages of the two major maturity strategies that banks may employ.

9. Give a numerical example of the earnings effect of a Treasury note switch at a loss and a municipal bond switch at a gain.

10. What are the advantages and disadvantages of using the security portfolio as the primary asset–liability balancing mechanism?

11. What is duration? How is it measured? What is the connection between duration and immunization?

# Meaningful Banking Reform Impossible without Changes in Financial Reporting

*by George H. Hempel and Donald G. Simonson*

The 1980s and early 1990s produced many severe problems that threaten the very existence of a system of privately managed depository institutions (commercial banks and thrifts—savings banks, S&Ls, and credit unions). What began as a ripple of challenges in the late 1970s became a virtual tidal wave in the 1980s. High, volatile interest rates gripped the economy in the early 1980s. Extensive experimentation with deregulation occurred, with depository institutions experiencing a breakdown of previous price, product, and geographic barriers. Both intra- and interindustry competition intensified. Depository institutions increasingly were forced to keep up with the accelerating pace and cost of technology in order to deliver financial services efficiently and competitively. Trying to earn an adequate return, many depository institutions responded by acquiring higher-yielding but lower-quality assets. Regulatory and legislative responses (and nonresponses) to many trying situations appear to have exacerbated the overall problem.

The results were particularly disastrous for the S&L industry. In the last decade 847 S&Ls failed, industry dollar size declined over 25 percent, the industry's insurance fund was declared insolvent, and a government (taxpayer) financial rescue is estimated eventually to cost more than $500 billion. Among credit unions, while there have been fewer failures, the number of institutions has declined to approximately half of the number that operated a decade or so ago. The commercial banking industry also suffered during the last decade; there were 1,227 failures from 1982 to 1992, and the number of banks declined from nearly 15,000 to slightly below 12,000. The future for depository institutions remains cause for concern. Predictions that the S&L industry will disappear; that the banking industry's FDIC fund, unless rescued, will be insolvent within a few months; that many large banks will be effectively nationalized; and that the number of banks will decline 50 percent are common.

Because reasonably efficient depository institutions remain vital in financing the U.S. economy, there are numerous ongoing initiatives to try to improve the position and per-

**209**

formance of depository institutions. These proposals come from organizations such as the American Institute of Certified Public Accountants (AICPA), the Financial Accounting Standards Board (FASB), the Securities and Exchange Commission (SEC), and various depository institution regulatory agencies. We believe these initiatives can be grouped into five major categories:

1. *Structural reforms*, for example, relaxing product and geographic restrictions.
2. *Capital reforms*, for example, risk-based capital standards plus overall leverage ratios allowable and early intervention.
3. *Deposit insurance reforms*, for example, numerous proposals to reduce coverage, build fire walls, and so on.
4. *Regulatory reforms*, for example, combining depository insurance funds, proposals to centralize regulation.
5. *Reporting reforms*, for example, proposals to value some or all assets and liabilities (and resulting equity) differently.

Regulators, managers, liquidators, and scholars have actively debated these reforms. Our purpose here is to illustrate that meaningful reforms in the first four categories are impossible without meaningful reform in financial reporting by depository institutions.

We will summarize what we consider to be the basic misconceptions about reporting for depository institutions, present a timeline of the historical cost–market value controversy, discuss the advantages and disadvantages of market value accounting, present other pertinent considerations, and then evaluate all of these variables to reach our conclusions.

## BASIC MISCONCEPTIONS ABOUT REPORTING FOR DEPOSITORY INSTITUTIONS

There are three basic misconceptions about historical cost reporting for depository insti-

tutions. They are:

1. Historical valuation of assets and liabilities is consistent with generally accepted accounting principles (GAAP).
2. Historical cost is used for most other financial institutions in addition to depository institutions.
3. Historical cost has always been used in reporting for depository institutions, practically without challenge.

To illustrate the fallacies of the first misconception, one has to look no further than GAAP rules for valuing assets at the lower of cost or market. The 1938 Supervisory Agreement (Table 6A-1) gave banks permission to leave securities or loans that are deemed to be ultimately collectable at their historical cost, whether value is higher or lower.

The reverse is true for the second misconception. Most nondepository financial institutions (which compete with depository institutions)—such as mutual funds and investment banks—have to account for all or most of their assets and liabilities at market values.

## SUMMARY TIMELINE OF THE HISTORICAL COST–MARKET VALUE CONTROVERSY

Table 6A-1, which summarizes developments in the historical cost–market value controversy over the last seven decades, demonstrates the misconceptions in the third statement. Depository institutions generally used market values prior to the 1938 Supervisory Agreement. Historical cost (the doctrine of ultimate collect ability) enacted in 1938 dominated until the early 1970s. Several proposed changes toward market value accounting were defeated in the 1970s and 1980s. Currently, there are proposals to move toward market value reporting from organizations such as the AICPA, the FASB, the

**TABLE 6A-1    Market Value Accounting—Historical Highlights**

| Time | Event |
|------|-------|
| pre-1930s | Banking school theory of bank supervision—market values used to determine safety and solvency. |
| 1930–1937 | Depression, slow recovery, bank supervision criticized for discouraging new loans. |
| 1938 | Bank supervisory agencies research regulatory agreement:<br>    Investment-grade securities valued at historical cost<br>    Loan at original value if prospects of repayment existed<br>    Named *doctrine of ultimate collectibility*, ignored interest rates and credit risk |
| 1973 | Accountants accept "conceptual framework" with emphasis on economic value; no specific actions taken. |
| 1976 | Proposals (SEC and AICPA) to enforce market values for real estate investment trust debt<br>    Vigorously opposed by bankers and bank regulators<br>    FASB 15 "Accounting by Debtors and Creditors for Restructured Debt" had little real effect |
| Early 1980s | Federal Home Loan Bank Board (FHLBB) proposal to enforce market valuation for securities, including mortgage-backed securities, is soundly rejected by industry panel; instead, regulator accounting is misused to add to historical cost values. |
| 1986 | FASB embarks on project to study improved disclosure about financial instruments and off–balance sheet items; SEC pressures for "investment versus trading" standard. |
| 1987 | FASB exposure draft proposes a comprehensive set of disclosures about the credit risk, liquidity risk, interest rate risk, and market values of all financial instruments. Bankers object vigorously. FASB decides to address project in two phases:<br>1. Off–balance sheet risk<br>2. Market value disclosure |
| 1988 | Accounting Standard Executive Committee (AcSEC) of AICPA agrees to study investment versus trading rules. |
| 1989 | U.S. Treasury issues a notice requesting public comment on the use of market value accounting (required by Financial Institution Reform, Recovery, and Enforcement Act). Office of Thrift Supervision (OTS) issues Thrift Bulletin 13 (TB-13), which requires S&Ls to set limits on, and to calculate the changes in, the mark to market value of their net worth (called *portfolio equity*), assuming parallel shifts in the yield curve of plus or minus 1, 2, 3, and 4 percent. |
| March 1990 | FASB 105: "Disclosure of Information about Financial Instruments with Off Balance Sheet Risk and Financial Instruments with Concentrations of Credit Risk" published: "building block" standard; addresses esoteric instruments (options, futures, swaps, etc.). |
| April 1990 | Office of the Comptroller of the Currency examination guidelines distinguish between a traditional *accounting perspective* that focuses on near-term earnings exposure to interest rate risk and an *economic perspective* that focuses on the interest rate exposure of capital arising from banks' long-term fixed rate positions. |
| Sept. 1990 | SEC Chairman Richard Breeden blasts FASB for failing to provide a standard for market valuing underwater securities, saying that "banks can cook the books" under the current system. |
| Oct. 1990 | AICPA abandons investment versus trading rules study. |

**TABLE 6A-1**   (continued)

| Time | Event |
|------|-------|
| Dec. 1990 | OTS proposes a rule for calculating the capital required to support interest rate risk based on market value equity. <br> FASB issues "Disclosures about Market Values of Financial Instruments," which would require financial and nonfinancial firms to disclose information about market value for all financial instruments. |
| May 1991 | Major issues emerging from FASB disclosure hearings: field testing, definitions, scope, implementation timing, format for disclosure, inclusion of any value changes in income. |
| June 1991 | FASB agrees to consider rules forcing holders of debt securities for investment or trading purposes to book them at current, rather than historical, value. |
| Dec. 1991 | FASB adopts Statement of Financial Standards No. 107, "Disclosures About Fair Value of Financial Instruments." Statement fails to address key issues. <br> Congress passes FDIC Improvement Act of 1991, which requires a task force to solve disclosure issues within one year. |
| May 1992 | FASB does not get sufficient majority to implement Financial Standards No. 107. Reason given: it could not be determined how to mark liabilities to market. <br> FDIC task force does not recommend change to market value accounting. |
| Sept. 1992 | FASB releases (for comment) proposal to value most investment securities at their market value. |
| April 1993 | FASB approves (5 to 2) requirement to value securities held for potential sale at market. Losses or gains in market value (before actual sale) are recognized in an equity reserve. Other proposal on market value accounting to be studied further. |

SEC, the U.S. Congress (hearings on FDIC Improvement Act proposal), and depository institutions regulatory agencies.

With this time line in mind, let's look at the two sides of the issue. Table 6A-2 lists the primary cited disadvantages and advantages of changing to market value accounting.

## THE CONS OF MARKET VALUE ACCOUNTING

1. *There is a lack of sufficient data and valuation models.* Because many bank assets and liabilities are not traded in broad markets in which information is readily available, the validity of data from thinly traded markets is dubious. What is more, a lack of consistent and understandable

valuation models would inevitably lead to wide differences in market value and estimation.

2. *Implementation would exact a high price on an already cost-burdened industry.* Developing sufficient data would be expensive in terms of both time and money; in addition are the costs required to modify existing accounting systems to make current valuations, with respect to loans as well as to other earning assets and interest-bearing liabilities.

3. *A market value perspective can be misleading.* First, market value information will be misused; second, market value reporting will not suit the needs of all users.

4. *Classifying and comparing market values is subject to interpretation.* Determining

**TABLE 6A-2    Disadvantages and Advantages of Changing to Market Value Reporting by Depository Institutions**

**Primary Disadvantages Cited**[a]

1. Lack of data and valuation models.
2. High cost of implementation.
3. Misuse of information.
4. Classification, inclusion, and comparability concerns.
5. Legal concerns.
6. Increased volatility of financial statements.
7. Destroying viability of financial instruments.

**Primary Advantages Cited**[b]

1. Market values available for many assets and liabilities of depository institutions.
2. Relatively inexpensive and relevant valuation models available.
3. Relevant information to depositors, other creditors, investors, and management.
4. Consistency among financial service companies and products.
5. Reporting of values and income consistent with economic principles.
6. Essential to meaningful banking reform.

[a]Described in detail in "Market Value Accounting" (Washington, D.C.: American Bankers Association, 1990).

[b]Described in detail in George H. Hempel, Donald Simonson, Marvin Carlson, Marsha Simonson, and Marcia Cornett, *Market Value Accounting for Financial Services Companies* (Berkeley, Calif.: National Center on Financial Services, 1990).

---

which market value changes should be reflected periodically and which assets and liabilities should be valued is today a matter of controversy. What is more, there is no consistency in interpretation; reporting variations for illiquid assets and liabilities may cause wide disparity in the amounts recorded by different banks.

5. *The issue of market valuation raises some significant legal concerns.* There are three areas of potential legal concern. First, the change could result in future litigation involving securities transactions where nondisclosure is the issue. Second, the change could affect a depository institution's ability to declare and pay dividends. Third, the change could influence relationships between a depository institution and other parties in existing contracts.

6. *The change will encourage the increasing volatility of financial statements.* Partial and comprehensive market value report-

ing will likely increase the volatility of reported assets, liabilities, and income.

7. *The change will destroy the viability of financial instruments.* Shifting away from historical cost accounting will likely destroy the markets for long-term government securities, fixed-rate mortgages, and fixed-rate installment loans.

## THE PROS OF MARKET VALUE ACCOUNTING

1. *Market values are readily available for many bank assets.* The rise of securitization and new secondary markets for loans have produced more objective valuation standards and thus more accurate results. Furthermore, many bank assets and liabilities have market values or analogs, and proxies for smaller denomination deposits may be available from mergers.

2. *Relatively inexpensive and relevant valua-*

*tion guidelines and models are available.* Guidelines and models (e.g., option pricing models) have been developed for estimating market values of remaining assets, liabilities, and off–balance sheet items.

3. *Market valuation is more relevant to depositors, other creditors, investors, and management than are other methods.* Some opponents claim that market value accounting is misleading and produces information that cannot be compared. In reality, market valuations reveal more about the prospects for future earning and viability than do historical costs and are easier to compare.

4. *Conversion to market valuation would create consistency among financial services companies and products.* Nonbank financial services companies, which provide the same financial services as banks, generally use market value reporting. Banks may lose business if they do not conform. As holding companies purchase different types of financial services companies, they may choose where to place their assets and liabilities on the basis of differences in accounting rules applied to their subsidiaries.

5. *Reporting of values and income is consistent with economic principles.* In times of industry stress, politicians, regulators, and bank managers used to disguise troubled institutions' true condition in order to maintain the public's confidence. The foremost means of disguise was to suppress market values and to account for the values of troubled assets in terms of recovery potential. But such an approach violates the economic principles of opportunity cost and time value of money. It also creates an utterly unrealistic view of the institution's position.

6. *Market valuation standards are critical to the industry's safety and soundness.* The absence of objective valuation information in a market-driven economy is costly. Without a reliable information system,

regulators lack a clear view of a bank's returns and risks. Market values provide more meaningful capital measures, better measures of asset quality and interest rate risk, and an early warning indicator of potentially troubled institutions.

## OTHER IMPORTANT CONCERNS IN THE CURRENT CONTROVERSY

There are at least three other important concerns that go beyond the traditional advantages and disadvantages in the market value reporting controversy. The first relates to income statement and residual equity considerations that were not faced in the FASB Financial Standards No. 107. The second deals with the missing question—who should control valuation? The third asks if many of the advantages can be obtained and disadvantages overcome without a complete shift to market value reporting; that is, why not adopt a hybrid solution?

### FASB Omits Income Statement and Residual Equity Questions

There are three unresolved concerns in FASB's Financial Standards No. 107. First, which changes in assets or liability values should flow through the income statement (and change retained earnings)? At present, changes in the value of some financial assets, that is, trading account securities in depository institutions and equities, often flow through the income statement, while changes in the value of most financial assets and nearly all financial liabilities are ignored in the income statement. In our opinion, one of the flagrant omissions in FASB's 107 is ignoring any recognition of changes in value in the income statement.

Second, the special importance and problems of regulated depository institutions are largely ignored in FASB 107. While reasonable resolution of valuation and measurement problems in this area of the economy is extremely important, bank regulatory bodies have to accept some of the responsibility in these areas (the problem is that it is often in their self-interest not to do so).

Third, FASB does not take a stand on how the market value information required by the proposed statement should be displayed in financial statements. We sincerely hope that FASB will take a definitive position. Not to do so will render market value disclosure practically meaningless (a few values will appear in parentheses, others hidden in obscure footnotes, etc.). We would like to see FASB or another appropriate body require a complete supplemental market value balance sheet, including a residual equity and an annual statement of changes in value of the residual equity (earnings and changes in the value of assets or liabilities, etc.)

## The Missing Question—Who Should Control Valuation?

An important issue that seems not to be faced in the testimony, articles, and information we have studied is the question of control. What seems basically at stake in the controversy is who should control the valuation of assets and liabilities and resulting income.

Managers of depositories obviously want to retain as much control as possible. The historical cost system is much more controllable by these managers than (1) GAAP, which generally values assets at the lower of cost or market and flows declines in the value through the income statement, used by the majority of businesses in the United States, or (2) market value reporting, which is used by most financial services companies other than depository institutions. Managers have control mechanisms, such as identifying whether assets are held for trading (marked to market) versus investment purposes; deciding whether and when to sell and take gains or losses or to hold and not

recognize gains or losses; and determining loan loss reserves in as favorable a tax and reporting manner as possible. Under historical cost conditions, managers of depository institutions have strong controls over the timing of income and, for at least a period of time, can control the level of income. The inability to control income, and therefore capital, over longer periods of time was forcefully demonstrated in the 1980s. In the long run, we have seen economic reality dominate, but often at a much higher cost to the public.

Many regulatory agencies would like to assert some or much control over the valuation of assets and liabilities. The degree of control desired has varied over time and among different regulatory agencies. It took the rash of banking failures and problem banks and a rapidly declining deposit insurance fund in the 1980s to reinvolve regulatory agencies strongly in the valuation process. Bank regulatory agencies now appear to be trying to develop a role in the identification of traded versus investment assets and to dominate the identification of loans to be put in reserves (charged to income and changing asset and equity values). Bankers have responded by saying that regulatory control over loan valuation is leading to a credit crunch during the economic recession that started in 1990.

Proponents of market value reporting argue that the financial markets should control valuation of assets, liabilities, and income. If the financial markets are effectively in control, direct valuation of assets, liabilities, and income will be much less under the control of managers and regulators. Markets would directly value actively traded assets and liabilities of depository institutions. Other assets and liabilities of depository institutions would be valued using similar traded securities as proxies. Most of the remaining assets and liabilities will be valued by models dependent on financial market data, such as interest rates. No wonder managers and regulators are concerned. Markets over which they can exert very limited control will effectively determine depository institutions' performance.

In our opinion, many of the claims about inefficient financial markets and the inability of managers of depository institutions to adapt their decisions to valuation by such markets border on the ridiculous. Nevertheless, the main point here, we believe, is who—managers, regulators, or financial markets—should control the valuation of assets and liabilities.

## Gaining Advantages and Overcoming Disadvantages Without Market Value Reporting

Some of the more intriguing opponents of market value reporting argue that some of the advantages of market value reporting can be attained, or the disadvantages of historical cost reporting overcome, without shifting completely to market value reporting. For example, regulators could be supplied with market value information essential to improve regulation, but this information would not be shared with depositors, other creditors, security analysts, or investors. Another method would separate the insured part of a depository institution, which would use historical cost reporting, from the uninsured part, which would use market value reporting, by some type of fire wall.

Interestingly enough, one area in which proponents and opponents of market value reporting often agree is a concern about a partial change to market value reporting. The American Bankers Association study, an opposition view, states that if a partial or piecemeal approach is adopted, there is an even greater possibility that more misleading financial statements will be created.

Proponents share this concern about a partial change to market value reporting. The AcSEC of the AICPA and the FASB

proposal in September 1992 basically recommend classifying more securities as trading account securities, marked to market, versus "permanent" investment accounts securities that are still valued at historical cost. Other assets and all liabilities would still be valued at historical cost. This recommendation is designed to reduce the practice of classifying most securities with losses in the investment account. Proponents of market value reporting point out that changes in the values of expanded trading account securities that were hedged with liabilities or off–balance sheet instruments would show up on the balance sheet and income statement. Offsetting changes in the liabilities or off–balance sheet instruments would not be reported on the balance sheet or income statement. Market value proponents state that this inconsistency means that reported income continues to differ from economic income, and that there are further disincentives to maximizing value.

We strongly believe that partial changes are inappropriate and that there should be a comprehensive change to market value reporting. If a comprehensive change is not accepted, it seems preferable to leave financial statements on a completely historical cost basis, which at least everyone knows is inconsistent with economic values. In our opinion, FASB's December 31, 1990, exposure draft on "Disclosure about Market Value of Financial Instruments" contained a reasoned and comprehensive change in using market values for valuing depository institutions' assets and liabilities.

## OPINIONS ABOUT ADVANTAGES, DISADVANTAGES, AND OTHER CONCLUSIONS

In our opinion, the stated advantages of market valuation outweigh the disadvantages. For one thing, historical cost reporting is less comparable and more subject to misinterpretation than is market value reporting. Legal concerns surrounding market valuation can be overcome. Concern over increased volatility is overstated. Further, it is ludicrous to assume that the change in valuation will destroy markets for financial instruments.

Still, some concerns about market value reporting are legitimate—in part because better data and valuation techniques are needed to control the costs of operating market valuation systems. Nevertheless, we believe the change is essential to the future viability of banks.

The result of the change will be better-managed commercial banks and better-equipped regulators who can make better decisions about an institution. The regulators will also have less excuse for not solving problems at institutions rapidly.

Market value reporting is also essential to improved regulation. Truly meaningful reforms—whether related to structure, capital, deposit insurance, or regulation—will never occur without a change in valuation methods.

In the past, the banking industry has used historical cost to mask and postpone facing depository institution problems. We can no longer afford that luxury because the country cannot afford to bail out the banking industry as it has the S&Ls.

## ACTION BY BANK MANAGERS

Many bankers will no doubt disagree with our opinions. Yet, bank managers would be well advised to prepare for some movement toward market value accounting. First, they should begin developing valuation models, information systems, and accounting systems that will recognize market values as well as historical costs. Second, they should start planning for any changes in their banks' asset and liability composition that the movement toward market value may encourage.

As the 1990s progress, banking will surely and decisively change. Proper reactions to changes, such as the probable movement toward market value accounting, will be essential to successful bank management.

# FFIEC Supervisory Policy Statement on Securities Activities

Effective February 10, 1992, depository institutions are required to comply with the revised policy statement adopted by the Federal Financial Institutions Examination Council (FFIEC). The revised policy describes requirements institutions must meet with respect to: (1) Selection of Securities Dealers; (2) Securities Portfolio Policy, Strategies, and Unsuitable Investment Practices; and (3) Mortgage Derivative Products, other Asset-Backed Products, and Zero-Coupon Bonds.

The following is a summary of the requirements established for each of the areas.

1. Selection of Securities Dealers:
   Depository institutions must know the securities firms and personnel with whom they do business.
   a. Financial Strength:
      Institutions should not execute "transactions with any firm unwilling to provide complete and timely disclosure of its financial condition. Management should review securities firm's financial statements and evaluate the firm's ability to honor its commitments before entering into transactions with the firm and perform periodic reviews thereafter." At a minimum, this ability should be "evidenced by capital strength, liquidity, and operating results gathered from current financial data, annual reports, credit reports, and other sources of financial information."
   b. General Reputation:
      An inquiry into the securities dealer's reputation for financial stability and fair and honest dealings with customers is necessary. "Other depository institutions that have been or are currently customers of the dealer should be contacted. Information from State or Federal securities regulators and securities industry self-regulatory organizations (i.e. NASD) concerning any formal enforcement actions against the dealer, its affiliates or associated personnel should also be investigated." In addition, when the advice of a dealer's sales representative

SOURCE: FFIEC Policy Statement, 1991.

is relied upon, "the background of the sales representative will be checked to determine his or her experience and expertise."

c. Board Review:

"The board of directors or appropriate committee of the board should periodically review and approve:

- a list of securities firms with whom management is authorized to do business,
- limits on the amounts and types of transactions to be executed with each authorized securities firm,
- limits on dollar amounts of unsettled trades,
- safekeeping arrangements,
- repurchase transactions,
- securities lending and borrowing,
- other transactions with credit risk,
- total credit risk with an individual dealer . . ."

"An appropriate committee of the board is one whose membership includes outside directors or whose actions are subject to review and ratification by the board of directors."

d. Possession and Control of Securities:

The board must ensure that "management has established appropriate procedures to obtain and maintain possession and control of securities purchased. Purchased securities and repurchase agreement collateral should only be left in safekeeping with selling dealers when:

- the board or appropriate committee is completely satisfied as to the creditworthiness of the securities dealer,
- the aggregate market value of securities held in safekeeping is within credit limitations approved by the board (or committee) for unsecured transactions."

Federal credit unions are not allowed to keep repo collateral with the broker/dealer.

e. Conflict of Interest:

The board may adopt a policy concerning conflicts of interest with respect to:

- "employees who purchase and sell securities for the depository institution and engage in personal securities transactions with the same securities firms,
- receipt of gifts, gratuities, or travel expenses from approved securities dealer firms or their personnel."

2. Securities Portfolio Policy, Strategies, and Unsuitable Investment Practices:

a. Portfolio Policy:

"A written description of authorized securities investment, trading, and held for sale activities, including the goals and objectives the institution expects to achieve through such activities."

b. Strategies:

"Written descriptions of the way management intends to achieve policy goals and objectives addressing management's plans for each type of security that will be used to carry out the portfolio policy (ex. U.S. Treasuries, mortgage-backed securities, etc.)."

c. Coordination of Policy and Strategies:

"Portfolio policy and strategies should be consistent with the institution's overall business plan which may involve trading, held for sale, and investment activities." Development of policy and strategies should take into account such factors as:

- asset/liability position,
- asset concentrations,
- interest rate risk,

- market volatility,
- management capability,
- desired rate of return.

Securities activities must be conducted in a safe and sound manner. "Policies and strategies must describe anticipated investment activities and either identify anticipated trading and held for sale activities, or state that the institution will not enter into any trading or held for sale activities. Securities trading activity should only be conducted in a closely supervised trading account by institutions with strong capital and earnings and adequate liquidity."

d. Board Review:
"The board of directors should review and approve the overall portfolio policy and management's documented strategies annually, or more frequently if appropriate. Approvals must be adequately documented. The board (or appropriate committee) should review the institution's securities activities and holdings no less than quarterly and oversee the establishment of appropriate systems and internal controls to ensure that policy and strategies are adhered to. Failure to adopt a policy by the board or failure to adhere to the policy approved by the board may result in some or all securities being classified by examiners as held for sale or trading. Held for sale securities must be reported at the lower of cost or market, and trading activities must be reported at market value."

e. Reporting of Securities Activities:
"Securities must be reported in accordance with generally accepted accounting principles (GAAP) consistent with the institutions intent to trade, hold for sale, or hold for investment.

Securities purchased may be reported at their amortized cost only when the depository institution has both the intent and ability to hold the assets for long-term investment purposes. Transactions entered into in anticipation of taking gains on short-term price movements are not suitable portfolio practices and should only be conducted in a closely supervised trading account by institutions that have strong capital, earnings, and adequate liquidity.

"It is an unsafe and unsound practice to report securities holdings that result from trading transactions using reporting standards that are intended for securities held for investment purposes. Securities held for trading must be reported at market value, with unrealized gains and losses recognized in current income. Prices used in periodic revaluations should be obtained from sources independent of the securities dealer doing business with the institution. Prices determined internally by the portfolio manager should be reviewed by persons independent of the portfolio management function.

"It is also an unsafe and unsound practice to report securities held for sale using reporting standards that are intended for securities held for investment purposes. Securities held for sale must be reported at the lower of cost or market value with unrealized losses (and recoveries of unrealized losses) being recognized in current income.

"Infrequent investment portfolio restructuring activities that are carried out in conjunction with a prudent overall business plan and do not result in a pattern of gains being realized with losses being deferred will generally be viewed as an acceptable investment practice. Examiners will particularly scrutinize the patterns or practice of reporting significant amounts of realized gains on sales from investment portfolios that have significant amounts of unrecognized losses. If an examiner determines such a practice has occurred, some or all of the securities reported as held for investment will be designated as held for sale or trading."

Factors relating to investment portfolio securities reporting include:

- the dollar amount of gains realized from sales in relation to the dollar amount of losses realized from sales and in relation to unrealized losses for other investment portfolio securities,
- the dollar amount of gains and losses realized from sales in relation to net income and capital,
- the number of sales transactions resulting in gains and the number resulting in losses,
- the gross dollar volume of securities purchases and sales,
- the rapidity of turnover, including consideration of the length of time securities are owned prior to sale, the length of time securities are held after an unrealized gain is evident, the remaining life of the security at the time of sale,
- the reason for the depository institution's engaging in specific transactions, and whether these reasons are consistent with the portfolio policy and strategies.

Additional considerations relating to an institution's ability to continue to hold investment portfolio securities include:

- the sources and availability of funding,

- the ability to meet margin calls and over-collateralization requirements related to leveraged holdings,
- limitations such as capital requirements, the legality of certain securities holdings, liquidity requirements, legal lending limits, and prudent concentration limits,
- the ability to continue as a going-concern and to liquidate assets in the normal course of business.

f.  Reporting of Loans Held for Sale or Trading:
    "Loans are required to be reported at the lower of cost or market when the institution does not have both the intent and the ability to hold these loans for long-term investment purposes."

g.  Unsuitable Investment Practices:
    The following practices are considered unsuitable with respect to a depository institution's portfolio:

    1.  Gains Trading—The purchase of a security as an investment portfolio asset and the subsequent sale of that same security at a profit after a short-term holding period.
    2.  "When-Issued" Securities Trading—The buying and selling of securities in the period between the announcement of an offering and the issuance and payment date of the securities.
    3.  "Pair-Offs"—A security purchase transaction that is closed-out or sold, at or prior to settlement date or expiration date. "Pair-offs" may also include off–balance sheet contracts (ex. swaps, options on swaps, forward commitments and options on forward commitments).
    4.  Corporate or Extended Settlements—The use of a settlement period in excess of the regular-way settlement period appropriate for

the instrument involved to facilitate speculation is considered a trading activity.

5. Repositioning Repurchase Agreements—A dealer agrees to fund the purchase of a security by buying it back from the purchaser under a resale agreement. The buyer purchasing the security pays the dealer a small "margin" that approximates the actual loss in the security.

6. Short Sales—The sale of a security that is not owned.

7. Delegation of Discretionary Investment Authority—Delegation of purchase and sale authority over the portfolio to a non-affiliated firm or individual relinquishes control over the securities and must be reported as held for sale.

8. Covered Call Writing—Call writing transfers the institution's ability to control the security to an outside party. Securities on which calls have been written should be redesignated as held for sale and reported at the lower of cost or market. If an option contract requires the writer to settle in cash, rather than delivering an investment portfolio security, the institution writing the option maintains the ability to hold the security, thus the security may be reported as an investment. The option must still be reported at the lower of cost or market. Institutions should only initiate a covered call program for securities when the board of directors (or appropriate committee) has specifically approved a policy permitting this activity.

9. "Adjusted Trading"—The sale of a security to a broker or dealer at a price above the prevailing market value and the simultaneous purchase and booking of a different security, frequently a lower grade issue or one with a longer maturity, at a price greater than its market value.

3. Mortgage Derivative Products, Other Asset Backed Products, and Zero-Coupon Bonds:
Mortgage derivative products include CMOs, REMICs, and Stripped MBS. "Mortgage derivative products possessing average life or price volatility in excess of a benchmark fixed rate 30-year mortgage-backed pass-through security are 'high-risk mortgage securities' and are not suitable investments. All high-risk mortgage securities must be carried in the depository institution's trading account or as assets held for sale. Securities that do not meet the definition of a high-risk mortgage security at the time of purchase should be classified as either investments, held-for-sale assets, or trading assets as appropriate. Institutions must determine at least annually that such securities do not fall into the high-risk category. Securities and other products, whether carried on or off the balance sheet (such as CMO swaps, but excluding servicing assets), having high risk characteristics similar to high-risk mortgage securities will be subject to the same supervisory treatment as high-risk mortgage securities."

a. Definition of "High-Risk Mortgage Securities":
A mortgage derivative product that at time of purchase, or a subsequent testing date, meets any of the following tests is a "high-risk mortgage security":

1. The Average Life Test—The security has an expected average life greater than 10.0 years.

2. The Average Life Sensitivity Test—The expected weighted average life of the security:

a. extends by more than 4.0 years, assuming an immediate and sustained parallel shift in the yield curve of plus 300 basis points,

or

b. shortens by more than 6.0 years, assuming an immediate and sustained parallel shift in the yield curve of minus 300 basis points.

3. The Price Sensitivity Test—The estimated change in price of the security is more than 17 percent, due to an immediate and sustained parallel shift in the yield curve of plus or minus 300 basis points.

The same prepayment assumptions and cash flows used to estimate average life sensitivity must be used to estimate price sensitivity. The discount rate used for calculating prices resulting from Treasury curve shifts will be determined using a constant spread to the Treasury curve. The offer side of the market will be used as the base price from which the 17 percent price sensitivity test will be measured.

"In applying the high-risk tests, the assumptions must be reasonable for the underlying collateral. All of the assumptions underlying the analysis must be available for examiner review. Should prepayment assumptions utilized differ significantly from median prepayment assumptions of several major dealers, examiners may use median prepayment assumptions to determine if a particular security is high risk.

In general, floating-rate CMOs will not be subject to the average life, and average life sensitivity tests if it bears a rate that, at the time of purchase or at a subsequent testing date, is below the contractual cap on the instrument. For purposes of the policy, a floating-rate CMO adjusts at least annually on a one-for-one basis with

the corresponding index. The index must be a conventional, widely-used market interest rate index such as the London Interbank Offered Rate (LIBOR). Inverse floating rate CMOs are not included as floating-rate CMOs."

b. Supervisory policy for Mortgage Derivative Products:

"Prior to purchase, a depository institution must determine whether a mortgage security is high risk. A prospectus supplement or other supporting analysis that fully details the cash flows covering each of the securities held by the institution should be obtained and analyzed prior to purchase and retained for examiner review. A prospectus supplement should be obtained as soon as it becomes available."

c. Non-high-risk Mortgage Securities:

"Institutions must ascertain and document prior to purchase, and at least annually that non-high-risk securities held for investment remain non-high-risk. If this assessment is unable to be made through internal analysis, then standard industry calculators available in the mortgage-backed securities marketplace are acceptable and considered independent sources. The assumptions used must be reasonable and are subject to examiner review.

A non-high-risk security may subsequently become a high-risk security, which then must be redesignated as held for sale or trading. The security may be redesignated as non-high-risk only if, at the end of two consecutive quarters, it does not meet the definition of a high-risk security. Once redesignated as a non-high-risk security, it does not need to be tested for another year."

d. High-risk Mortgage Securities:

"An institution may only acquire a high-risk mortgage derivative product to reduce its overall interest rate risk in accordance with safe and sound practices. The policy is not meant to preclude institutions with strong capital, earnings, and adequate liquidity with a closely supervised trading account from acquiring high-risk mortgage securities for trading purposes. Trading must operate in conformance with well developed policies, procedures, internal controls including detailed plans prescribing specific position limits and control arrangements for enforcing these limits. High-risk securities must be reported as trading assets at market value or as held-for-sale assets at the lower of cost or market value.

To acquire high-risk mortgage securities, an institution must have a monitoring and reporting system in place to evaluate the expected and actual performance of such securities. Prior to purchase, an analysis must be conducted that shows that the proposed acquisition of high-risk securities will reduce the institution's overall interest rate risk. Subsequent to purchase, the institution must evaluate at least quarterly whether the high-risk mortgage security has actually reduced interest rate risk. These analyses must be fully documented and will be subject to examiner review. Analyses performed and records constructed to justify purchases on a post-acquisition basis are unacceptable. Reliance on external analysis and documentation from securities dealers without internal analysis by the institution is unacceptable.

Management should also maintain documentation demonstrating that it took reasonable steps to assure that the prices paid for high-risk mortgage securities represented fair market value. Price quotes should be obtained from at least two brokers prior to executing a trade. If quotes cannot be obtained from more than one broker, management should document the reasons for not obtaining such quotes."

Institutions that own high-risk mortgage securities must demonstrate that they have established the following:

1. A board-approved portfolio policy which addresses the goals and objectives the institution expects to achieve through its securities activities, including interest rate risk reduction objectives with respect to high-risk mortgage securities,
2. Limits on the amounts of funds that may be committed to high-risk mortgage securities,
3. Specific financial officer responsibility for and authority over securities activities involving high-risk mortgage securities,
4. Adequate information systems,
5. Procedures for periodic evaluation of high-risk mortgage securities and their actual performance in reducing interest rate risk,
6. Appropriate internal controls.

"The board of directors (or appropriate committee) and the institution's senior management should meet at least quarterly to review all high-risk mortgage securities to determine whether these instruments are adequately satisfying the interest rate risk reduction objectives set forth in the portfolio policy. The depository institution's senior management should be fully knowledgeable about the risks associated with prepayments and their subsequent impact on its high-risk mortgage securities.

Failure to comply with this policy

will be viewed as an unsafe and unsound practice.

Purchases of high-risk mortgage securities prior to date of adoption of this policy generally will be reviewed in accordance with previously-existing supervisory policies.

e. Other Securities:

Securities and other products, whether carried on or off the balance sheet, having characteristics similar to those of high-risk mortgage securities will be subject to the same supervisory treatment as high-risk mortgage securities. Disproportionately large, long-maturity holdings of zero-coupon, stripped, and original issue discount (OID) securities in relation to the total investment portfolio, or total capital of the depository institution, are considered an imprudent investment practice."

# CHAPTER 7

# Trends in the
# Acquisition and Cost
# of Bank Funds

The ability to attract funds at a reasonable cost has become one of the key ingredients of commercial bank management in recent years. For many years after the Depression of the 1930s, banking could be labeled as an industry that emphasized the use of funds. Bank management focused on how to lend and invest the surplus funds that banks were easily able to attract. Although the use of attracted funds is still obviously important, changing conditions, such as the shortage of savings, increased competition for these scarce savings, and increasing loan demands, force banks to place increased emphasis on attracting funds. This shift is demonstrated by the more creative and intensive use of existing sources of funds and in the aggressive development of new sources of funds during the 1970s and early 1980s. Furthermore, while declining loan demand and pressures to increase capital positions have lowered funding needs in the early 1990s, it appears likely that pressures on banks to be able to attract adequate amounts of funds at a reasonable cost will intensify again by the mid-1990s.

The four sections in this chapter address this challenging situation. First, trends in the primary types of funds that banks attract are examined. Second, techniques for measuring the cost of and resulting potential profit from these funding sources are discussed. Third, an assessment is made of the risks associated with acquiring the various types of bank funds. Finally, strategies for acquiring funds that banks use are investigated.

## TYPES AND CHANGING COMPOSITION OF DEPOSITS

The changing trends in total bank funds may provide future challenges to bank management; however, it is the marked and continuing changes in the

**TABLE 7-1   Primary Sources of Funds for Commercial Banks (at the end of 1992)**

| Principal Sources of Bank Funds | Primary Ownership | | | | Maturity | |
| | Individuals | Business | Government | Interbank | None Fixed | Typical Range |
|---|---|---|---|---|---|---|
| Demand deposits | x | x | x | x | x | |
| NOW accounts | x | | x | | x | |
| Super NOW accounts | x | | | | x | |
| Passbook or statement savings deposits | x | | | | x | |
| Money market deposits | x | | x | | x | |
| Time deposits under $100,000 | x | | | | | Seven days to one year |
| Savings certificates | x | | | | | 14 days to eight years |
| Individual retirement and Keogh time deposits | x | | | | x | |
| CDs | x | x | x | | | 14 days to one year |
| Federal funds | | | | x | | Day or term |
| Repurchase agreements | x | x | x | x | | Day to 1 year |
| Other borrowings (Eurodollars, bankers' acceptances, etc.) | x | x | | x | | Day to 270 days |
| Capital notes | x | x | | x | | Over five years |

composition of bank funds sources that have caused drastic changes in bank management in the 1980s. Table 7-1 categorizes and describes the principal types of nonequity sources of funds for commercial banks according to primary ownership, nature of interest paid, and maturity. Table 7-2 shows the amount of funds in these categories of sources of funds as of January 1, 1986, the last time such deposit detail was available. Table 7-3 and Figure 7-1 indicate the net amount of funds in the major categories of funds in selected years from 1950 to 1991. Interbank sources of funds—deposits of other banks, deposits in the process of collection, and Federal funds transactions between affiliates—are eliminated from the figures in Table 7-3 and Figure 7-1. Each of the sources of bank funds is briefly described; then the overall pattern of bank funding and its implications for bank returns and risks are discussed.

**TABLE 7-2** Major Noncapital Sources of Funds for Insured Commercial Banks on January 1, 1986

|  | Billions of Dollars | Percentage of Total |
|---|---|---|
| Demand deposits | $  450.9[a] | 17.7% |
| NOW accounts | 132.2 | 5.2 |
| Super NOW accounts | 47.1 | 1.9 |
| Money market deposits | 335.1 | 13.2 |
| Other savings deposits | 206.9 | 8.1 |
| IRA and Keogh deposits | 61.0 | 2.4 |
| Time deposits under $100,000 | 545.7 | 21.4 |
| Deposit of $100,000 and over | 313.5 | 12.3 |
| Brokered deposits | 25.4 | 1.0 |
| Federal funds purchased and repos | 222.0[b] | 8.7 |
| Demand notes to Treasury | 22.0 | .9 |
| Other borrowed money | 73.4 | 2.9 |
| Mortgage indebtedness | 3.0 | .1 |
| Liabilities on acceptances outstanding | 50.8 | 2.0 |
| All other liabilities | 57.7 | 2.3 |
|  | $2,546.7 | 100.0% |

[a] Includes interbank balances and items in the process of collection.

[b] Fed funds sold to banks and repos with banks totaled $112.3 billion.

SOURCE: Federal Deposit Insurance Corporation, Washington, D.C.

## Demand Deposits

Demand deposits are non-interest-bearing transaction deposits that have no maturity and must be paid by banks when a negotiable instrument, generally in the form of a check or an electronic impulse, is presented. Since demand deposits have no explicit interest cost, they are generally a bank's lowest-cost source of funding; however, increasing costs of processing demand deposit transactions have raised the effective overall cost of demand deposits to close to, if not higher than, the cost of passbook savings. Table 7-2 illustrates that total demand deposits were less than one-fifth of bank noncapital sources of funds by 1986. Table 7-3 and Figure 7-1 further illustrate that the demand deposits fell from 63.3 percent of all commercial bank net sources of funds in 1950 to under one-sixth of these sources by 1991. The reasons for the declining importance of demand deposits in the last three decades include more efficient cash management by individuals, businesses, and governmental units; significantly higher interest rates; and the appearance of competitive instruments, such as NOW accounts and money market instruments at banks and other financial institutions, money market funds, and cash management accounts. A final characteristic of demand deposits is that in recent years they have been a relatively more important source of funds for smaller banks than for

**TABLE 7-3 Noncapital Domestic Net Sources of Funds for All Insured Commercial Banks, Excluding Interbank Deposits**

| End of Year | (Dollars in Billions) | | | | (As a Percentage of Total Deposits and Liabilities) | | | |
|---|---|---|---|---|---|---|---|---|
| | Demand Deposits[a] | Savings Deposits[b] | Time and Other Deposits[b] | Nondeposit Liabilities[c] | Demand Deposits[a] | Savings Deposits[b] | Time and Other Deposits[b] | Nondeposit Liabilities[c] |
| 1947 | 61.8 | | 34.7 | .5 | 63.7 | | 35.8 | .5 |
| 1960 | 94.6 | | 53.5 | 1.4 | 63.3 | | 35.8 | .9 |
| 1962 | 101.5 | | 79.7 | 3.6 | 54.9 | | 43.1 | 2.0 |
| 1964 | 108.3 | | 103.6 | 2.5 | 50.5 | | 48.3 | 1.2 |
| 1966 | 112.9 | | 139.8 | 4.6 | 43.9 | | 54.3 | 1.8 |
| 1968 | 131.5 | | 175.3 | 8.5 | 41.7 | | 55.6 | 2.7 |
| 1970 | 135.2 | 97.2 | 133.8 | 18.6 | 35.1 | 25.2 | 34.8 | 4.8 |
| 1972 | 158.4 | 129.2 | 196.3 | 36.4 | 30.5 | 24.8 | 37.7 | 7.0 |
| 1974 | 185.9 | 146.1 | 255.8 | 52.8 | 28.5 | 22.5 | 40.8 | 8.1 |
| 1976 | 225.8 | 190.3 | 293.1 | 67.0 | 29.1 | 24.5 | 37.8 | 8.6 |
| 1978 | 252.3 | 220.9 | 395.2 | 114.7 | 25.7 | 22.5 | 40.2 | 11.7 |
| 1980 | 302.1 | 201.2 | 558.7 | 161.5 | 24.7 | 16.4 | 45.7 | 13.2 |
| 1981 | 348.2 | 223.7 | 662.5 | 231.0 | 23.7 | 15.3 | 45.2 | 15.8 |
| 1982 | 370.9 | 304.7 | 723.7 | 255.3 | 22.4 | 18.4 | 43.7 | 15.4 |
| 1983 | 389.5 | 462.6 | 682.0 | 265.7 | 21.6 | 25.7 | 37.9 | 14.8 |
| 1984 | 414.3 | 503.5 | 727.4 | 281.0 | 21.5 | 26.1 | 37.8 | 14.6 |
| 1985 | 450.9 | 589.1 | 755.9 | 310.4 | 21.4 | 28.0 | 35.9 | 14.7 |
| 1986 | 472.3 | 1,751.1 | | 359.0 | 18.3 | 67.8 | | 13.9 |
| 1987 | 479.1 | 1,853.6 | | 361.4 | 17.8 | 68.8 | | 13.4 |
| 1988 | 479.4 | 1,952.2 | | 380.9 | 17.0 | 69.4 | | 13.5 |
| 1989 | 483.4 | 2,065.1 | | 418.7 | 16.3 | 69.6 | | 14.1 |
| 1990 | 488.9 | 2,161.0 | | 384.7 | 16.1 | 71.2 | | 12.7 |
| 1991 | 480.2 | 2,207.2 | | 379.1 | 15.7 | 72.0 | | 12.3 |

[a] Net demand deposits were total domestic demand deposits other than domestic commercial interbank and U.S. government less cash items in the process of collection through 1980. After 1980, figures are total demand deposits because adjustments are not available.

[b] Interbank deposits are excluded from both savings and time deposits. NOW, Super NOW, and money market accounts are classified as savings deposits.

[c] Net nondeposit liabilities are all nondeposit liabilities less Federal funds sold and repos of commercial banks.

SOURCES: *Federal Reserve Bulletins*, selected issues; *Statistics on Banking* (Washington, D.C.: FDIC, selected years).

**FIGURE 7-1   Net Sources of Bank Noncapital Funds, 1960–1991**

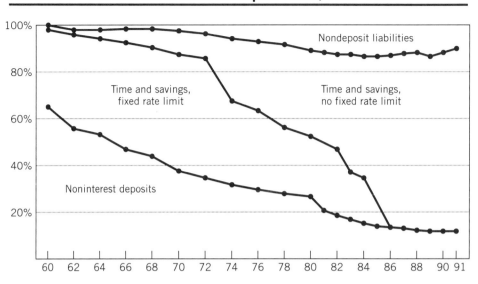

very large banks. This may change as the impact of deregulation is felt further in smaller banks.

### NOW and Super NOW Accounts

NOW accounts are interest-bearing checking accounts, on which Regulation Q rate maximums were dropped on March 31, 1986, which have no maturity and which must be paid by banks upon demand. Although limited amounts of NOW accounts were outstanding in the New England states in the late 1970s, they were not legalized throughout the United States until January 1, 1981. Super NOW accounts, with no rate limits, became available to individuals on January 5, 1983. The typical difference between NOW and Super NOW accounts at banks is that Super NOW accounts pay higher rates but have higher minimum balances and restrictions on activity. There are no legal requirements for rates, minimum balances, or activity. NOW accounts are included with transaction deposits and Super NOW accounts are included with savings deposits in current federal statistics.

### Savings Deposits

Savings deposits are interest-bearing deposits without specific maturity. A check or other order of withdrawal cannot be written directly on a savings account, but withdrawals can be made whenever the depositor desires, and it is easy to shift funds to a demand account on which checks may be written.

These accounts have no fixed maturity, and individuals keep track of their balances through passbooks or periodic bank statements. Passbook savings deposits may be the lowest overall cost source of funds currently available to commercial banks; however, the low rate maximum prior to March 31, 1986, severely restricted the growth of these deposits.

Table 7-3 shows that total savings deposits fell from roughly 25 percent of the net total funds as late as 1976 to slightly above 16 percent at the end of 1980. By the mid-1980s several savings deposit forms—most notably money market accounts—were no longer subject to Regulation Q. Since March 31, 1986, savings deposits have not been subject to Regulation Q or any size or activity limits, and deposits have grown as a share of total noncapital funds.

## Money Market Accounts

Money market deposit accounts are savings deposits of individuals and partnerships. This type of deposit was created in December 1982 to provide banks with an instrument that could compete effectively with money market mutual funds. There are no rate maximums, and regulatory limits on minimum size and maximum free withdrawal were removed on December 31, 1985. Most banks pay rates that vary according to an average rate on a short-term market instrument, and will probably continue to use minimum sizes and maximum free withdrawals to market this account. Money market accounts have grown more rapidly than Super NOW accounts and totaled $335.1 billion, or 21.4 percent of bank noncapital funds in 1986. Lower relative rates slowed the growth of money market deposit accounts in the early 1990s.

## Time Deposits

Time deposits differ from savings deposits primarily because they have a predetermined maturity date, and withdrawals prior to that date are often subject to interest penalties. In the early 1980s total time deposits were consistently above 40 percent of the total noncapital sources of funds (see Tables 7-2 and 7-3). In contrast, time and savings deposits combined were only 36 percent of all net deposits as late as 1960.

There are several categories of time deposits. The first category, CDs of $100,000 or more, is primarily large negotiable CDs of corporations and was $313.5 billion, or 12.3 percent of bank sources of funds, in 1986. The majority of these are fixed rate, with no rate limit, although some variable-rate CDs are included in the total. They have a fixed maturity that usually ranges between 14 and 270 days at the time of issue. A second category, other time deposits of $100,000 or more, is not subject to rate limits; these deposits are nonnegotiable, can have fixed or flexible maturities, and are deposited by individuals, partnerships, corporations, and municipalities. The third major category, time deposits under $100,000, is a catchall category that totaled $545.7 billion, or 21.4 percent of bank noncapital sources of funds, in 1986. This category includes savings certificates with many varying terms, individual retirement and

Keogh time deposits, several types of public time deposits, and miscellaneous and other time deposits. These deposits have no rate limits and no regulatory size minimum.

### Brokered Deposits

Brokered deposits are small and large time deposits obtained by banks from intermediaries seeking insured-deposit accounts on behalf of their customers. Deposit brokers appeared in the early 1980s, when depositors began to face increased risk of loss because of bank failure. An often cited example of this risk was the failure of Penn Square Bank in July 1982. For the first time since the Great Depression, federal regulators liquidated a large bank, as opposed to allowing it to be merged or acquired by a solvent bank with no loss to depositors. Depositors that were not insured (FDIC insurance covers each depositor up to $100,000) suffered large losses, as evidenced by the fact that less than 60 percent of uninsured claims were ever recovered.

Brokers entered deposit markets to bring together depositors (sellers) seeking insured accounts with banks and other depository institutions (buyers) demanding lower-cost, insured-deposit funds. Electronic funds transfer technology enabled brokers cost-effectively to "split" $1 million, for example, into 10 fully insured $100,000 deposit accounts at 10 different depository institutions. Alternatively, brokers could offer smaller depositors better yields than otherwise could be obtained by pooling their deposits and selling "shares" in "participating" large CDs offering higher yields than smaller CDs.

Bank regulators generally have opposed the use of brokered deposits. Regulators seem to believe that since insured depositors are less likely to discipline bank management by withdrawing their funds or charging higher rates on deposits, bank safety and soundness might be compromised to the extent that banks used nationally brokered deposits to grow excessively or to take excessive loan risks. At the present time (early 1993), banks with fully insured brokered deposits in excess of either their total capital (including reserves) or 5 percent of their total deposits must provide monthly reports of the volume, interest rates paid, and usage of such deposits to the FDIC.

### Public Deposits

Public deposits are demand, savings, or time deposits of governmental units. Treasury tax and loan accounts are interest-bearing, demand-type accounts of the U.S. government. Most other governmental units, such as agencies and state and local units, have both non-interest-bearing demand deposits and savings or time deposits. Competition is often intense for such deposits, and many public bodies require a bidding process to make sure their governmental unit gets the highest rate. The federal government and many state and local units still require qualified securities to collateralize the uninsured part of their deposits.

### Correspondent Deposits

Deposits of other banks are a significant source of funds for some upstream correspondent banks. Most correspondent deposits are demand deposits that are left by one bank in another because the latter offers services such as check clearance, international transactions, investment advice, and loan participations. Money earned on such deposits pays the upstream bank for the services. Less than 10 percent of correspondent deposits are savings or time deposits because interest payments would pay for the deposits rather than the upstream bank's services.

## TYPES AND CHANGING COMPOSITION OF SHORT-TERM NONDEPOSIT SOURCES OF FUNDS

Table 7-3 and Figure 7-1 show that less than 1 percent of total net sources of commercial bank funds consisted of net nondeposits as late as 1960. By 1992 nondeposit sources constituted over 12 percent of the total noncapital bank sources of funds. Table 7-4 contains brief descriptions of the major nondeposit sources of bank funds.

The largest nondeposit sources of funds for commercial banks are Federal funds purchased and securities sold under agreement to repurchase (repos). These two accounts, which are combined for reporting purposes, totaled $220.0 billion in 1986, or 51.7 percent of nondeposit bank sources of funds and 8.7 percent of the total sources of bank funds (see Table 7-2). Most Federal funds are one-day purchases of another bank's excess reserves. Security dealers, large businesses, and the Federal Reserve are also able to supply these one-day reserves, so that for commercial banks, total Federal funds purchased usually exceeds the amount of Federal funds sold. There is also a limited amount of Federal funds purchased and sold between banks maturing in periods longer than one day.

Repos provide funds to banks during the period when securities are temporarily sold to another bank, a business, an individual, or other potential temporary purchaser. The temporary selling period typically ranges between 1 and 89 days, and the purchaser has title to the securities unit until the repo is repurchased. Repos usually have a rate slightly below the existing Federal funds rate because they are effectively collateralized by the security sold, whereas Federal funds are usually unsecured. In the early 1980s some banks used small-denomination, "retail" repos, paying rates above Regulation Q ceiling rates on deposits, in order to obtain funds. The total dollar amounts obtained through these retail repos were relatively small.

Commercial banks also use a variety of other borrowing forms, such as discounts and advances from the Federal Reserve, bankers' acceptances, and Eurodollars, as sources of funds. Many of these sources are primarily available to larger banks with international offices. At the present time, commercial banks are prohibited from issuing commercial paper (large, short-term, unse-

---

**TABLE 7-4   Brief Descriptions of Nondeposit Short-term Funding Forms**

| Funding Form | Characteristics |
|---|---|
| Borrowing from Federal Reserve (discounts or advances) | Credit extended on a short-term basis by a Federal Reserve Bank to a bank or other depository institution. Rate is set by the Fed and called the *discount rate*, with penalty rates for frequent or unusually heavy users. Security (securities or acceptable loans) required for either discounts or advances. |
| Federal funds purchased | Purchase of another bank's excess reserves on daily or short-term basis. Other side of Federal funds sold. Purchased through correspondent or informal phone market at existing Federal funds rate. Banks that are continual users often subject to informal limit by sellers. Unsecured; therefore, funds seller checks credit of borrowing bank. |
| Securities sold under agreement to repurchase (repos) | Temporary sale of government or other securities in which bank has received funds from purchase and agreed to rebuy securities at predetermined price. In effect, short-term (often daily) secured borrowing from purchaser. |
| Eurodollar and other foreign sources | Eurodollars are deposits in U.S. banks held outside the United States with maturities ranging from overnight to a year. Active secondary market with overseas branch essential to continual involvement. Rates set in international market. Other foreign sources also used by very large banks. Bank must not engage in activities or assume risks that could potentially blemish its name. |
| Bankers' acceptances | A time draft drawn on a bank by either an exporter or an importer to finance international business transactions. The bank may discount the acceptance in the money market to (in effect) finance the transaction. |
| Other liability forms | Include ineligible acceptances, commercial paper sold through holding companies, and so on. Key element is that bank can raise funds through form if bank pays going market rate and lender has confidence in bank. |

---

cured promissory notes); however, bank holding companies can issue such paper and pass the funds through to banks they own.

## MEASURING AND USING THE COST OF FUNDS

Why should a bank be interested in measuring its cost of funds? Three reasons stand out. First, a bank will generally seek the lowest-cost combination of funds sources available in its market. Other things being equal, a bank will have higher returns when its cost of funds is lower without taking significantly higher risks. Second, a reasonably accurate cost of funds measure is an essential ingredient in determining the returns a bank must obtain on its earning assets. Third, the types of sources of funds a bank obtains and the employment of these sources have a significant impact on the bank's liquidity risk, interest rate risk, and capital risk.

There are several methods of measuring the cost of funds for a bank. Examples and an evaluation of the three most widely used methods—historical average cost, marginal cost of specific sources of funding, and a weighted average expected cost of all sources as a proxy for marginal cost—are presented for Community National Bank. Tables 7-5, 7-6, and 7-7 contain balance sheets, income statements, and supplementary information for Community National through 1992. Table 7-8 contains projections for the bank's fund resources, amount of these attracted funds the bank can employ for 1993 and expected future costs of specific funds sources.

**TABLE 7-5  Community National Bank—Average Balance Sheet (dollars in thousands)**

| | 1990 $ | 1990 % | 1991 $ | 1991 % | 1992 $ | 1992 % |
|---|---|---|---|---|---|---|
| **Assets** | | | | | | |
| Cash and due from banks | $ 10,217 | 8.8% | $ 11,898 | 8.9% | $ 13,205 | 9.0% |
| Short-term instruments | | | | | | |
|   Federal funds sold | 2,723 | 2.3% | 2,200 | 1.7% | 1,504 | 1.0% |
|   Other short-term investments | -0- | -0- | -0- | -0- | -0- | -0- |
| Investment securities | | | | | | |
|   Taxable securities | 16,697 | 14.4% | 18,425 | 13.6% | 16,925 | 18.4% |
|   Tax-exempt securities | 17,012 | 14.7% | 16,330 | 12.3% | 15,176 | 10.4% |
| Trading account securities | -0- | -0- | -0- | -0- | -0- | -0- |
| Loans | | | | | | |
|   Commercial loans | 29,659 | 25.6% | 31,561 | 23.7% | 35,817 | 22.4% |
|   Consumer loans | 19,679 | 17.0% | 26,938 | 20.2% | 28,141 | 19.3% |
|   Real estate loans | 16,054 | 13.9% | 20,869 | 15.7% | 22,154 | 15.2% |
|   Other loans | 123 | .1% | 262 | .2% | 341 | .2% |
|   Total loans | $ 65,515 | 56.5% | $ 79,630 | 59.8% | $ 83,453 | 57.1% |
|   Less valuation reserve | 480 | .4% | 686 | .5% | 777 | .5% |
|   Net loans | $ 65,035 | 56.1% | $ 78,944 | 59.3% | $ 22,676 | 56.6% |
| Direct lease financing | -0- | -0- | -0- | -0- | -0- | -0- |
| Bank premises and equipment | 3,260 | 2.8% | 3,503 | 2.6% | 3,781 | 2.6% |
| Other real estate owned | -0- | -0- | 240 | .2% | 240 | .2% |
| Other assets | 1,006 | .9% | 1,615 | 1.2% | 2,651 | 1.6% |
|   Total assets | $115,950 | 100.0% | $133,155 | 100.0% | $146,158 | 100.0% |
| **Liabilities and Net Worth** | | | | | | |
| Demand deposits | $ 18,986 | 16.4% | $ 19,125 | 14.4% | $ 21,632 | 14.8% |
| NOW and Super NOW | 15,689 | 13.5% | 16,983 | 12.7% | 19,107 | 13.1% |
| Total transaction deposits | $ 34,676 | 29.9% | $ 36,108 | 27.1% | $ 40,739 | 27.9% |

**TABLE 7-5**   *(continued)*

|  | 1990 | | 1991 | | 1992 | |
|---|---|---|---|---|---|---|
|  | $ | % | $ | % | $ | % |
| Passbook savings | 9,162 | 7.9% | 7,185 | 5.4% | 6,863 | 4.7% |
| Money market accounts | 10,725 | 9.2% | 16,710 | 12.5% | 20,012 | 13.7% |
| Savings certificates | 18,401 | 15.9% | 20,425 | 15.3% | 19,338 | 13.2% |
| CDs, $100,000 and over | 20,159 | 17.4% | 27,165 | 20.4% | 32,078 | 21.9% |
| Public and other time deposits | 10,163 | 8.8% | 10,403 | 7.8% | 11,664 | 8.7% |
| Total savings and time | $ 68,609 | 59.2% | $ 81,888 | 61.4% | $ 89,935 | 61.5% |
| Total deposits | $103,285 | 89.1% | $117,996 | 88.5% | $130,674 | 89.4% |
| Short-term borrowing |  |  |  |  |  |  |
| Federal funds purchased | 1,715 | 1.5% | 2,463 | 2.0% | 2,175 | 1.5% |
| Other short-term borrowing | 1,405 | 1.2% | 1,654 | 1.2% | 1,384 | .9% |
| Other liabilities | 790 | .7% | 950 | .7% | 1,091 | .7% |
| Long-term debt | -0- | -0- | -0- | -0- | -0- | -0- |
| Shareholders' equity |  |  |  |  |  |  |
| Common stock (per $1) | $ 963 | .8% | $ 1,013 | .8% | $ 1,013 | .7% |
| Surplus | 1,348 | 1.2% | 1,798 | 1.3% | 1,798 | 1.2% |
| Undivided profits | 6,444 | 5.6% | 7,281 | 5.5% | 8,023 | 5.5% |
| Equity reserves | -0- | -0- | -0- | -0- | -0- | -0- |
| Total equity | $ 8,755 | 7.6% | $ 10,092 | 7.6% | $ 10,834 | 7.4% |
| Total liabilities and net worth | $115,950 | 100.0% | $133,155 | 100.0% | $146,158 | 100.0% |

### Historical Average Cost

The first method of measuring the bank's cost of funds, historical average cost, is probably still the most common. The weighted average cost of funds for Community National Bank is calculated in Table 7-9. The interest cost in dollars ($7.363 million for Community National Bank) is either available or can be calculated by multiplying the average amount in each type of funding account by the average cost of the funds during the period (the year 1992 in this example). The weighted average interest cost, 5.44 percent, is calculated by dividing the dollar interest cost by the total noncapital funds, $135.324 million. The weighted average interest cost for interest-bearing funds (7.10 percent in this example) is calculated by including only interest-bearing funds in the denominator.

Such weighted average cost of funds measures may be helpful in evaluating past funds acquisition performance, but they suffer from four shortcomings. First, some bank funds have to be invested in assets that do not earn returns, such as required reserves, correspondent balances, and fixed assets (e.g., premises). Since the proportion not earning returns varies with different forms of funding, adjustments need to be made both in costs and in the re-

**TABLE 7-6** **Community National Bank—Income Statement for Specified Years Ended December 31 (dollars in thousands)**

|  | 1990 | 1991 | 1992 |
|---|---|---|---|
| Interest income on: |  |  |  |
| Short-term instruments | $ 279 | $ 159 | $ 53 |
| Taxable securities | 1,792 | 1,850 | 2,020 |
| Tax-exempt securities | 1,098 | 1,068 | 1,025 |
| Commercial loans | 4,109 | 3,665 | 3,533 |
| Consumer loans | 2,898 | 3,229 | 3,408 |
| Real estate loans | 1,936 | 2,023 | 2,224 |
| Other loans | 16 | 29 | 32 |
| Total interest income | $12,128 | $12,023 | $12,295 |
| Service charges and fees | 657 | 947 | 1,061 |
| Other noninterest income | 309 | 349 | 486 |
| Total operating income | $13,094 | $13,319 | $13,842 |
| Interest expense on: |  |  |  |
| NOW and Super NOW accounts | $ 535 | $ 547 | $ 593 |
| Passbook savings | 482 | 345 | 296 |
| Money market accounts | 885 | 1,321 | 1,155 |
| Savings certificates | 1,626 | 1,637 | 1,494 |
| CDs, $100,000 and over | 2,434 | 2,266 | 2,603 |
| Other time deposits | 1,091 | 865 | 939 |
| Short-term borrowing | 346 | 409 | 198 |
| Other liabilities | 62 | 89 | 85 |
| Long-term debt | 0 | 0 | 0 |
| Total interest expense | $ 7,461 | $ 7,479 | $ 7,363 |
| Provision for loan losses | $ 297 | $ 403 | $ 517 |
| Salaries and benefits | 2,505 | 2,721 | 3,002 |
| Occupancy expense | 806 | 883 | 969 |
| Other expenses | 571 | 628 | 687 |
| Total expense | $11,640 | $12,114 | $12,538 |
| Net income before tax | $ 1,454 | $ 1,205 | $ 1,304 |
| Income taxes | 139 | 38 | 102 |
| Net income | $ 1,315 | $ 1,167 | $ 1,202 |
| Cash dividends paid | $ 481 | $ 506 | $ 507 |

sulting returns that need to be made to cover the interest costs. Second, the cost of funds should include other expenses associated with attracting funds, such as operating and advertising expenses. Third, there are numerous questions about whether the cost of equity funds should be included in this cost of funds measure and, if so, how. Finally, historical costs can be extremely unreliable as a guide in choosing funds to attract or as an asset pricing guide if interest rates are changing markedly over time, as they did in the 1980s.

**TABLE 7-7   Community National Bank—Supplementary Information (dollars in thousands)**

|  | 1990 | 1991 | 1992 |
|---|---|---|---|
| Earning assets | $101,467 | $115,899 | $126,281 |
| Risk assets | $ 92,700 | $108,241 | $119,046 |
| Maturities of investment securities: |  |  |  |
| Under one year | $  6,044 | $  5,458 | $  5,731 |
| One to five years | 11,421 | 14,218 | 15,372 |
| Five to 10 years | 9,653 | 9,824 | 15,808 |
| Over 10 years | 6,591 | 5,255 | 5,190 |
| Market to book value of securities (%): |  |  |  |
| Taxable securities | 96.81% | 98.17% | 108.91% |
| Tax-exempt securities | 90.04% | 96.01% | 103.18% |
| Past-due loans: |  |  |  |
| Commercial | $    552 | $    681 | $    845 |
| Consumer | 964 | 1,433 | 1,688 |
| Real estate | 251 | 388 | 436 |
| Other | 1 | 3 | 3 |
| Interest rate sensitivity (one year): |  |  |  |
| Interest-sensitive assets | $ 50,664 | $ 59,766 | $ 70,352 |
| Interest-sensitive liabilities | 46,741 | 66,182 | 81,749 |
| Number of employees | 126 | 132 | 136 |
| Average market price per share (est.) | 13 | 12 | 10 |
| Tax equivalent interest income on tax-exempt securities | 1,633 | 1,577 | 1,498 |
| Total tax-equivalent interest income | 12,663 | 12,532 | 12,768 |
| Total tax-equivalent revenues | 13,629 | 13,828 | 14,315 |

**TABLE 7-8   Information for Estimating Required Yields on Sensitive Assets for Community National Bank (dollars in millions)**

1. The bank's holdings of vault cash, deposits with the Federal Reserve and other banks, and other cash items in 1993 are expected to be:
   22 percent of non-interest-bearing demand deposits
   20 percent of interest-bearing demand deposits
    3 percent of all time and savings deposits
2. The bank's investment in premises and equipment and other nonearning assets is expected to be 4 percent in 1993.
3. During 1993, the bank expects its net resources will average $160 million. The average amount and investable amount of the various fund sources are projected as follows (amounts in millions of dollars):

**TABLE 7-8**   *(continued)*

| | Average Amount | Percentage Usable | Amount Investable |
|---|---|---|---|
| Demand deposits, noninterest | $ 24 | 74% | $ 17.76 |
| Demand deposits, interest-bearing | 20 | 76% | 15.20 |
| Passbook savings | 6 | 93% | 5.58 |
| Money market accounts | 25 | 93% | 23.25 |
| Savings certificates | 20 | 93% | 18.60 |
| CDs, $100,000 and over | 34 | 93% | 31.62 |
| Public and other time deposits | 12 | 93% | 11.16 |
| Short-term borrowing | 6 | 96% | 5.76 |
| Other liabilities | 1 | 96% | .96 |
| Stockholders' equity | 12 | 96% | 1.52 |
| Total sources of funds | $160 | | $131.41 |

4. The bank's target rate of return on equity is 14 percent after taxes. Its marginal income tax rate is 34 percent; therefore, the pretax return is $14/(1-.34)$ or 21.2 percent.

5. Costs of each type of funding (percentage):

| | Interest Cost 1992 | Est. Int. Cost 1993 | Net Processing Cost 1993 |
|---|---|---|---|
| Demand deposits, noninterest | 0.0% | 0.0% | 4.6% |
| Demand deposits, interest-bearing | 3.1 | 3.0 | 2.5 |
| Passbook savings | 4.3 | 4.0 | 1.0 |
| Money market deposits | 5.8 | 5.0 | 0.6 |
| Savings certificates | 7.7 | 6.0 | 0.2 |
| CDs, $100,000 and over | 8.1 | 7.0 | 0.1 |
| Public and other time deposits | 8.0 | 7.0 | 0.2 |
| Short-term borrowing | 5.6 | 6.0 | 0.1 |
| Other liabilities | 7.8 | 7.0 | 0.1 |
| Stockholders' equity | 21.2 | 21.2 | 0.0 |

6. Expenses other than interest for 1993 are estimated to be $2.2 million in net processing costs and $1.8 million in net other costs (other expenses of $3.8 million less other income of $2.0 million) for total net noninterest expenses of $4.0 million.

7. Forecast average assets for 1993 (in millions of dollars):

| | Interest Sensitive | Non-sensitive | Total |
|---|---|---|---|
| Cash and due from banks | | 12.1 | 12.1 |
| Short-term securities and instruments | 8.5 | | 8.5 |
| Long-term securities | | 26.0 | 26.0 |
| Loans | 70.0 | 37.0 | 107.0 |
| Bank premises and equipment | | 3.9 | 3.9 |
| Other assets (nonearning) | | 2.5 | 2.5 |
| Total | | | 160.0 |

8. Projected returns on short-term securities purchased in 1993 is 5.0 percent and projected returns on loans is 10 percent.

**TABLE 7-9  Historical Weighted Average Cost Measures (dollars in thousands)**

| Type of Funds | Aver. Amt. | Int. Cost | Interest |
|---|---|---|---|
| 1. Weighted average interest cost of funds: | | | |
| Demand deposits, non-interest-bearing | $ 21,632 | 0% | $    0 |
| Demand deposits, interest-bearing | 19,107 | 3.1% | 593 |
| Passbook savings | 6,843 | 4.3% | 296 |
| Money market accounts | 20,012 | 5.8% | 1,155 |
| Savings certificates | 19,338 | 7.8% | 1,494 |
| CDs, $100,000 and over | 32,087 | 8.1% | 2,603 |
| Public and other time deposits | 11,664 | 8.1% | 939 |
| Short-term borrowing | 3,559 | 5.6% | 198 |
| Other liabilities | 1,091 | 7.8% | 85 |
| | $135,333 | | $7,363 |

Weighted avg. interest cost: $\dfrac{\text{Interest cost \$7,363}}{\text{Total noncapital funds \$135,333}} = 5.44\%$

Weighted avg. interest cost, interest-bearing funds: $\dfrac{\text{Interest cost \$7,363}}{\text{Interest-bearing funds \$103,692}} = 7.10\%$

2. Earning requirements based on weighted average cost of funds:
   a. To cover interest expense:

$$\frac{\text{Interest cost}}{\text{Earning assets}} = \frac{\$7,363}{\$126,281} = 5.83\%$$

   b. To break even:

$$\frac{\text{Interest + All other costs}}{\text{Earning assets}} = \frac{\$7,363 + \$3,628}{\$126,281} = 8.70\%$$

   c. To earn 14% return on capital:

$$\text{Earnings to cover ROE only} = \%\,R \text{ on } E_{bt} \times \frac{\text{Equity}}{\text{Earning assets}}$$

$$= \frac{.14}{1 - 0.34} \times \frac{\$10,824}{\$126,281} = 1.82\%$$

Required to cover costs and ROE = 8.70% + 1.82% = 10.52%

SOURCES: Tables 7-5, 7-6, and 7-7.

**Improvements in Historical Average Cost Measures**  Adjustments are made in the lower part of Table 7-9 to overcome the first three of these shortcomings. In Section 2a, interest cost divided by earning assets adjusts for funds that have to be employed in nonearning assets and shows the return, 5.83 percent, the bank must earn on its earning assets to cover its interest expenses. The so-called break-even yield is calculated in 2b, the total interest expense and net other expenses (noninterest expense less noninterest income) divided by earning assets. This calculation shows how much the bank must earn, 8.70 percent, to cover all its expenses. Finally, one way to recognize the cost of stockholder equity is presented in Section 2c. The before-tax ROE is multiplied by equity divided by earning assets. This earning requirement (1.82 percent) is added to the return required to cover all expenses to indicate the return required on earning assets, 10.52 percent, for the bank to earn 14 percent on its equity capital. The same results could have been obtained by the following computation (amounts in thousands):

| | | |
|---|---|---|
| Interest expenses | $  7,363 | |
| plus | | |
| All other expenses (net) | $  3,628 | |
| plus | | |
| Equity return $10,824 × .2121 | $  2,296 | |
| Total | $ 13,287 | |
| divided by: | | |
| Earning assets | $126,281 | |
| Required to earn 14% ROE | | 10.52% |

In spite of these adaptations, the historical average cost measures seem useful primarily in assessing a bank's past performance. For example, to help explain a bank's earning performance, a bank's actual returns on earning assets can be compared with its break-even yield and the yield required to earn a specified return on capital. If a bank wants guidance about which type of funds to attract, whether or not to take on new assets, or pricing its loans, historical average costs may be very misleading. For example, when rates are rising, the historical average cost of funds is less than the cost of replacing these funds, and the bank might be led into making new loans at unprofitable yields. The reverse could be true when rates fall. If predictions about fluctuating rates in the 1990s are at all accurate, it would seem that a better measure of the cost of bank funds would be essential for a bank to attain reasonable profitability.

## Marginal Cost of Funds

The second measure of the bank's cost of funds, the marginal cost of funds, is a direct result of the deficiencies in using the historical average cost cited earlier. The basic idea is that the bank would use its marginal cost, the cost paid to produce one additional unit of usable funds, to determine the acceptable return on the additional assets purchased with such funds. Also, the bank would seek to attract the lowest-cost source of funds. At first glance these concepts seem easy to implement, but figuring the full cost of a new dollar of funds is difficult, especially if it is necessary to estimate the impact of one source of funds on the cost of other sources.

The simplest approach is to determine a single source of funds a bank wants to use, compute its marginal cost, and use that cost as a basis for pricing new assets. Presumably, the single source selected would be the cheapest one available to the bank. For example, let us assume that Community National Bank hopes to use NOW and Super NOW accounts to finance its asset expansion. The interest cost of these funds is projected to be 3.0 percent, 22 percent of the attracted funds will be employed in nonearning assets, and the cost of acquiring and servicing such accounts is 2.5 percent. Usually the cost of a single marginal source is calculated as follows:

$$\text{Marginal return on funds from single source} = \frac{\text{Interest costs} + \text{Other costs}}{1 - \% \text{ in nonearning assets}}$$

$$= \frac{3.0 + 2.5}{1 - 0.22}$$

$$= 7.05\%$$

Two problems limit the usefulness of this measure. First, the cost of a single source may need to be adjusted to compensate suppliers of other sources of funds for the added risk created by using the single source. For example, if Community National's ratio of debt to equity rose because of the added NOW and Super NOW accounts, uninsured depositors and other creditors and shareholders might demand a higher return. Community National's cost of attracting and holding NOW accounts might be 8.55 percent, the 7.05 percent computed cost plus a 1.5 percent premium because of the higher cost of other sources. A reasonably precise measurement for such a premium seems impossible.

Second, few banks use a single source of funds over a very long period of time. Often several sources provide significant amounts of new funding. One alternative promoted by some banks to overcome this weakness is to use the cost of the most expensive marginal source of funds as the bank's marginal cost of funds.

### Pooled Marginal Cost of Funds

A second alternative is to use an average marginal cost calculation similar to that summarized in Table 7-10 for Community National Bank. In Table 7-10 it is assumed that Community National is expected to grow by $14 million in 1993, primarily through five sources of financing. The interest costs, all other costs, and percentage in nonearning assets expected in 1993 came from Table

**TABLE 7-10    Pooled Marginal Costs of Funding (dollars in millions)**

| Type of Funds | (1) Amount of Increase | (2) Percentage Investable Assets | (3) Investable Amount | (4) Interest & All Other Costs | (5) Total $ Cost (1) × (4) |
|---|---|---|---|---|---|
| Demand deposits, non-interest-bearing | $ 2 | 74% | $ 1.48 | 4.6% | $0.098 |
| Demand deposits, interest-bearing | 1 | 76% | .76 | 5.5% | 0.055 |
| Money market deposits | 5 | 93% | 4.65 | 5.6% | 0.280 |
| CDs, $100,000 and over | 2 | 93% | 1.86 | 7.1% | 0.142 |
| Other time deposits | 3 | 93% | 2.79 | 7.2% | 0.216 |
| Supporting equity | 1 | 96% | .96 | 21.2% | 0.212 |
| Total | $14 | | $12.50 | | $1.003 |

$$\text{Marginal cost} = \frac{\text{Total \$ cost}}{\text{Total amount}} = \frac{1.003}{14.0} = 7.16\%$$

$$\text{Required return on earning assets} = \frac{\text{Total \$ cost}}{\text{Investable funds}} = \frac{1.003}{12.50} = 8.02\%$$

SOURCES: Tables 7-5, 7-6, 7-7, and 7-8.

7-8. The return required on earning assets to cover this "pooled" cost of funds, 8.06 percent in Table 7-10, was found by dividing the total dollar cost of the funds attracted by the amount of funds that could be invested in earning assets. Although the accuracy of this measure might be improved by using the amount each category of funds was expected to rise or fall in 1993, the pooled marginal cost of financing is very sensitive to estimations (or misestimations) of sources of funding in the future.

## Weighted Average Projected Cost

A final way to estimate the cost of funds is to use the weighted average projected cost of all fund sources as an estimation of the marginal cost. Financial theory suggests that if it is assumed that a bank has been financed with the lowest overall cost of funds, its marginal cost of funds should be equal to its weighted average projected cost of funds. It is important to note that the resulting number is *not* a weighted average cost of funds figure, but rather an estimation for the bank's marginal cost of funds if the bank is efficiently financed. Table 7-11 illustrates the calculation of the required overall returns

**TABLE 7-11 Weighted Average Projected Cost of Funds as Estimation of Marginal Cost of Funds (dollars in millions)**

| Types of Funds | (1) Average Amount | (2) Interest and Net Processing Costs | (3) Total $ Cost |
|---|---|---|---|
| Demand deposits, non-interest-bearing | $ 24 | 4.6% | $ 1.104 |
| Demand deposits, interest-bearing | 20 | 5.5 | 1.100 |
| Passbook savings | 6 | 5.0 | 0.300 |
| Money market | 25 | 5.6 | 1.400 |
| Savings certificates | 20 | 6.1 | 1.220 |
| CDs, $100,000 and over | 34 | 7.1 | 2.414 |
| Public and other time deposits | 12 | 7.2 | 0.864 |
| Short-term borrowing | 6 | 6.1 | 0.366 |
| Other liabilities | 1 | 7.1 | 0.071 |
| Stockholders' equity | 12 | 21.2 | 2.545 |
| Totals | $160 | | $11.384 |

$$\text{Weighted average projected cost of funds} = \frac{11.384}{160.0} = 7.12\%$$

$$\text{Required return on noncash assets to cover cost of funds} = \frac{11.384}{141.4} = 8.05\%$$

$$\text{Required return on noncash assets to cover cost of funds plus noninterest items} = \frac{13.184}{141.4} = 9.32\%$$

Sources: Tables 7-5, 7-6, 7-7, and 7-8.

on earning assets based on the projected average cost of funds for 1993. The overall cost of acquiring funds can be estimated by dividing the summation of total dollar acquisition costs, $11.384 million (in column 3) in this example, by the average assets, $160 million (in column 1). The return required on earning assets to cover the cost of funds is calculated by dividing the dollar acquisition cost, $11.384 million, by the earning assets, $141.4 million.

### Which Cost Measure Is Most Appropriate?

Which cost of funds measurement should a bank use? Any of the four measures discussed is appropriate, depending on the purpose of the cost-of-funds figure. The historical average cost of funds is useful in assessing past performance. Marginal cost of specific funds may be helpful in deciding which form of funds the bank should try to attract. It is also important to measure all marginal costs. For example, a bank may believe demand deposits are the cheapest source because they have no explicit interest cost. However, if the acquisition of $1 million in demand deposits costs $200,000 in advertising, personnel calling, and operational costs, demand deposits may be a high-cost source of funds. Furthermore, cost adjustments for changing risks due to a change in funding sources are very difficult to measure. Finally, either the marginal cost of pooled funding or the weighted average projected cost of funds as an estimation of the marginal cost of funding may be acceptable as asset-pricing guides. The weighted average projected cost of funds is used in the example that follows.

## USING COST-OF-FUNDS MEASURES

### Average Return Required on Earning Assets

It is assumed that the objective of Community National Bank is to obtain an interest margin sufficient to cover other costs and to earn an adequate return on the owner's investment. However, costs other than those required to attract funds and income other than interest income have been ignored in the calculations. These cost and income figures can be incorporated by adding in all costs other than the acquisition costs already incorporated, net of all noninterest income items ($3.8 million less $2.0 million) divided by earning assets ($141.4 million), which is 1.27 percent, to the previously calculated required return (8.05 percent).

This resulting required return to cover total net costs of 8.18 percent includes an after-tax return to equity holders of 14 percent. This return, adjusted to a before-tax rate by dividing by 1 minus the marginal bank income tax rate, was treated as a cost of funds similar to other sources. If the forecasted interest rates were approximately correct and the bank earned above 9.32 percent on its assets, the residual after-tax return on equity would be above 14 percent, and vice versa. The concern is how to employ earning assets, which are a mixture of sensitive and nonsensitive assets, so that they will yield an average of 9.32 percent or above.

### Effects of Rate Sensitivity of Assets

Community National Bank is used in Table 7-12 to demonstrate a simplified worksheet that can be used to calculate the yields required on newly priced interest-sensitive assets. The key principle of the worksheet is that to obtain the targeted return on equity, the bank must earn 9.32 percent on its earning assets of $141.4 million, or $13.184 million. The yields on nonsensitive loans and long-term securities are known, and the dollar returns of $3.0 million and $2.64 million, respectively, should be reasonable estimates. Estimated dollar returns on rate-sensitive loans and short-term securities are more complex. In the case of short-term securities, Community National felt that its securities, which were yielding 6 percent at the start of the year, would mature about evenly during the year and that the average yield on newly purchased securities would be 5 percent. The average yield on the $8.5 million of short-term securities would then be 5.5 percent, or $935,000.

**TABLE 7-12  Worksheet for Calculation of the Yield Required on Newly Priced Sensitive Loans** (dollars in thousands)

| Asset Category | Forecasted Average for 1988 | Yield on Nonsensitive Assets | Yield on Sensitive Assets (Old) | Yield on Sensitive Assets (New) | Average Yield | Returns (Dollars) |
|---|---|---|---|---|---|---|
| Short-term securities | $  8,500 | | 6.0% | 5.0% | 5.5% | $   468 |
| Long-term securities | 33,000 | 8.0% | | | 8.0 | 2,640 |
| Loans (nonsensitive) | 30,000 | 10.0% | | | 10.0 | 3,000 |
| Loans (sensitive) | 70,000 | | 10.0% | (3)[a] | (2)[a] | (1)[a] |
| Total earning assets | $141,500 | | | | 9.32% | $13,184 |
| Nonearning assets | 18,500 | | | | 0 | 0 |
| Total assets | $160,000 | | | | 9.32% | $13,184 |

[a]Number in parentheses indicates calculation of the answer in Table 7-13.

**TABLE 7-13    Calculation of the Yield Required on Newly Priced Sensitive Loans (dollars in thousands)**

| | | |
|---|---:|---:|
| 1. Total dollar return on all assets | | $13,184 |
| Dollar returns on: | | |
| Short-term securities | $  468 | |
| Long-term securities | 2,640 | |
| Nonsensitive loans | 3,000 | |
| Cash, premises, etc. | 0 | 6,108 |
| Required dollar return on sensitive loans | | $ 7,076 |

2. Required average yield on all sensitive loans:

$$\frac{7,076}{70,000} = 10.11\%$$

3. Required yield on newly priced sensitive loans:

$$\frac{7,076 - 3,500}{70,000 - 35,000} = \frac{3,576}{35,000} = 10.22\%$$

A calculation similar to that performed on short-term securities could be performed for rate-sensitive loans if the rates on currently outstanding loans are known; if there are reasonable estimates of the repricing, renewal, and maturity profiles of these loans; and if the average rate on newly priced loans can be forecast. A slightly different approach is taken: the current rate and repricing profile are estimated, and the required yield on newly priced sensitive loans to earn 14 percent on equity is calculated. Table 7-13 shows that the calculations can be made by first finding the required dollar yield on sensitive loans by subtracting the returns on short-term and long-term securities and nonsensitive loans from the total return required on all assets. The required average yield on sensitive loans then can be calculated by dividing the required dollar yields on sensitive loans by the average amount of sensitive loans. Finally, if sensitive loans will be repriced about evenly during the year, the required yield on newly priced sensitive loans can be calculated by subtracting the dollar yield at the old sensitive rate and the average amount at the old rate from the numerator and denominator, respectively. The resulting dollar amount divided by the average amount repriced during the year is the average required percentage yield on newly priced sensitive loans (10.22 percent for Community National).

Two final comments about using this type of model seem appropriate. First, the real world is more complex than this simplified model. For example, the growth rates of different types of loans vary, and loan prepayments and extensions occur. This type of model, however, may be made considerably more complex than this simplified example. The authors have worked with banks that have considerably more complex models (generally on microcomputers), which are based on the same basic ideas. Second, even the simplified model presented in this section can be flexibly used. For example, a bank can forecast all rates for the coming year and project the resulting rate of return on equity. Or a bank can leave the new rate on sensitive short-term securities as an unknown to see if the rate calculated by dividing the dollar return on all sensitive loans less the dollar yield on sensitive loans at the previous yield by the average newly priced sensitive loans that are attainable in the market.

The required yield on newly priced sensitive loans can then be compared with the bank's estimates of competitive market rates for the coming year. If market rates are expected to be lower than the required yield, as was the case for the Community National example, the bank will probably earn less than the targeted 14 percent on equity, unless the asset–liability structure is changed or more risk is taken to get increased returns. The bank is likely to earn above 14 percent on equity if expected market rates exceed the required yield on newly priced sensitive loans.

## RISKS ASSOCIATED WITH RAISING FUNDS

Different sources of funds may affect the risks of a bank in different ways. With a goal of achieving the highest value for the stockholders' investment, bank management must consider the risks as well as the costs of the various types of bank sources of funds. This section examines how bank sources of funds affect the primary risks of banking—liquidity risk, interest rate risk, credit risk, and capital risk.

### Liquidity Risk

The liquidity risk associated with bank sources of funds is primarily the probability that depositors or lenders will want to withdraw their funds from the bank. The risk of outflow of such funds differs markedly, depending on the type of deposit, and seems to have changed as economic conditions have changed. The conventional banking wisdom of the 1940s and 1950s generally regarded demand deposits as the most vulnerable source of outflows at most banks. Savings and time deposits, dominated by passbook savings, were thought to be very stable sources of funds. Nondeposit liabilities were an insignificant source of funds for most banks. The primary liquidity pressures on a bank, therefore, came from fluctuations in demand deposits.

By the mid-1960s, the situation had changed appreciably. As interest rates rose, many bank customers managed their demand deposit balances tightly so that transaction need and compensating balances for loans were the major reasons for such deposits. The probability of large declines for all demand deposits in a bank seemed to subside. Savings and time deposits grew rapidly and became more vulnerable to deposit outflows because Regulation Q put most deposits at a competitive disadvantage with open-market instruments when interest rates rose. Therefore the disintermediation of these deposits caused a liquidity problem for banks during credit tightness in 1966, 1969, and 1974. By the early 1970s, banks were willing to buy relatively more expensive deposit or nondeposit liabilities in order to escape the high liquidity risk associated with deposits that were subject to Regulation Q rate limits.

The gradual lifting of Regulation Q and the creation of new deposit and liability forms in the late 1970s and 1980s again changed the liquidity risks associated with a bank's sources of funds. Corporate demand deposits remained at transaction and compensating balance levels and tended to be subject to limited liquidity risk. Consumer demand deposits, which faced the competition from money market funds and interest-bearing NOW and Super NOW accounts of other banks and thrift institutions and which could be competitively priced by balances, increased the liquidity risk. Passbook or statement savings declined steadily in the last few years because of competition from mutual funds, NOW and Super NOW accounts, and money market accounts, and from Regulation Q limits that are considerably below open-market rates.

All bank savings and time deposits were no longer subject to Regulation Q ceilings after March 31, 1986. Thus, banks are now able to compete with other financial institutions and open-market instruments. Since these savings and time deposits have been an increasingly important source of bank funds, commercial banks have probably lowered the liquidity risks associated with *their source of funds*. In the 1970s bank management was more concerned with managing quantity than price, which was often fixed by regulation. In the 1990s banks may be able to get and keep the quantities of funds they desire if they are willing and able to pay the price.

In spite of the increased flexibility in buying deposits and other funds, some banks have faced liquidity problems because of this deposit attraction. Two potential sources of deposit-induced liquidity problems are reviewed here. First, a bank may overemphasize the use of impersonal purchased deposits or funds and cause confidence concerns among actual and potential depositors. Why should an impersonal depositor with deposits exceeding the FDIC insurance limit of $100,000 leave money in a risky bank, even if the depositor receives an above-average rate? The Continental Illinois Bank crisis in 1984 illustrates this point. It is estimated that roughly three-fourths of Continental's funds were from large, uninsured, generally impersonal depositors or lenders. It should not be surprising that many of these depositors and lenders chose to withdraw their funds when the quality of the bank's loan portfolio was perceived to have deteriorated.

Second, brokered deposits, packaged deposits of $100,000 each from any clients of brokerage firms, may represent a unique type of liquidity risk. Since these deposits are insured by the FDIC, they go to the highest rate payer. Brokered deposits may be a temporary source of funds for fast-growing or high-risk commercial banks that temporarily hide the bank's more basic problems. Since these deposits may exacerbate future liquidity pressures, there is regulatory and legislative pressure to limit their use.

In summary, two factors stand out as determining causes of the liquidity risks associated with the withdrawal of funds. First, does the bank have the earnings ability to pay competitive rates? Second, does the bank have the recognized quality that will enable it to use the needed amounts of impersonal, purchased deposits or funds?

## Interest Rate Risk Associated with Funding

The interest rate risk associated with bank sources of funds depends heavily on the interest sensitivity of the assets financed by these funds. For example, if savings certificates, which are repriced every six months, are used to purchase either Federal funds (which are repriced daily) or five-year government bonds, the bank is taking an interest rate risk. The appropriate management technique is to compare the interest sensitivity over time of all sources of funds with the interest sensitivity over time of the assets financed by these funds. It should be emphasized that liquidity risk and interest rate risk may be different for different sources of funds and that there are broad ranges of interest sensitivities among sources of funds.

Variable-rate CDs are an example of a source of funds on which interest rates may vary with changes in market rates but which may pose little liquidity risk over the life of the CD. The same is true for most other non-limit-rate time deposits, as long as the bank is willing to pay the going market rate. The menu of interest sensitivity forms available among bank sources of funds is broad. Federal funds purchased are rate sensitive on a daily basis; repos and large CDs are sensitive to rate changes in a few days to a few months; money market accounts are generally sensitive to rate changes each week; longer-term CDs may not be rate sensitive for several years; and capital notes may not be rate sensitive for 20 to 25 years. If the needed sources of funding for the desired interest sensitivity position are not available at reasonable costs, a bank should consider the use of artificial hedging instruments, such as financial futures, interest rate swaps, and financial options.

In summary, a bank's choice among the fund sources available would seem to depend on the interest cost of the source, other acquisition cost of the source, and its contribution to the liquidity and interest sensitivity balance of the bank.

## Interactions with Credit Risk

A bank's sources of funds do not have a direct effect on its credit risk because depositors or lenders of funds are taking the risk of the bank's not paying them. Two indirect effects, however, are possible. A higher cost of funds may be a side effect of depositors or lenders of funds becoming worried about a bank's ability to pay its claims on time. For example, the problems of Seafirst, Continental Illinois Bank, and InterFirst in 1983 and 1984 raised their cost of funds appreciably. Because of credit concerns about energy and real estate loans, the so-called Texas premium raised the cost of funds for banks in that state nearly 1 percent in 1987. Second, if a bank has a high cost of funds, it may be encouraged to take higher credit risks in its struggle to maintain its profit margin. Deposit insurance partially mitigates the impact of these two indirect effects.

### Interactions with Capital Risk

Finally, a bank's sources of funds have a direct impact on the capital risk and leverage of a bank. A bank's equity costs much more than its deposits and borrowings because of the greater uncertainty associated with the return on equity and because the returns on equity, whether earnings or cash dividends, are not a tax-deductible expense. Thus, a bank may lower its cost of funds by increasing its leverage. As capital risk becomes more pronounced, however, these gains may be illusory. The cost of other sources of funds may rise as capital risk becomes appreciable. In addition, other bank activities, such as new branches and acquisitions, may be curtailed if regulatory authorities feel the bank's capital risk is too high.

## INTRODUCTION TO BASIC FUNDING STRATEGIES

A bank must develop strategies for acquiring funds after it has decided the effects of the various types of funds on its cost of funds and risks. In a broad sense, this means using the marketing concept to determine consumer needs and then communicating to the consumer how the bank will serve these needs. In the following sections several particularly important strategies in acquiring funds are examined—product development, market segmentation, product differentiation, and product attraction.

### Product Development

The first step in product development is to identify bank customers' wants and needs. Once these are identified, a bank should develop and manage its products to fulfill these desires. Although there are some limitations on the product line of every bank—imposed by size, location, regulations, and managerial capabilities—a major shortcoming of most banks is their narrow conception of bank products. Many banks have said in effect that their "products" are making loans and accepting deposits. Banking products should include rendering (at a profit to the bank) all the financial services the customer can use. The willingness (accompanied by regulatory and legislative approval) to develop and market new financial products is one of the keys to banking success in the 1990s.

Product development strategies may be divided into two groups. First, there are those that relate to each individual product—its means of identification, product quality and features, and price. Second, for its whole line of products, the bank must form strategies covering the product assortment, the essential supporting services, hours of business, and bank location and layout.

Some of the basic policy aspects of bank product development for both groups are described briefly in the following paragraphs.

## Market Segmentation

Strategies that have proved useful for nonbanking firms include market segmentation, product differentiation, and image. Market segmentation is the isolation of certain sectors of the total market and the creation of new products so uniquely designed for this sector that no immediate competition exists. This strategy may prove profitable for all banks competing with other financial institutions. One problem with such a strategy for an individual bank is the speed at which other banks can copy most new banking products. This condition leads to the need for product differentiation. Often the purpose is to appeal to different segments of the market with an essentially standardized product. Such product differentiation is a difficult task, and effectively establishing a sense of difference often requires heavier than usual advertising and promotional expenditures.

Many banks have adopted a combination of these strategies for product development. They strive to develop new products to fill customers' wants in some market segments, to match their competition's new product when it appears desirable to do so, and to differentiate their products in the eyes of their customers.

Commercial banks must also develop new financial services to compete successfully with other financial institutions and other institutions offering financial services. Ideas for new banking products may just happen, but they will happen more often if customers' desires are studied and if sensitivity to their potential needs is cultivated among bank employees. Product ideas can come from customers, directors, employees, competing banks, other financial institutions, or trade magazines. Once the ideas are obtained, the development and selection process must start. As many as 50 to 100 new product ideas may yield only one banking product that will ultimately be marketed successfully.

## Product Differentiation and Image

Even if a bank is able to bring new banking products into the market or successfully copy the products of a competitor, it will be likely to face competition from similar products within a relatively short time. Creative pressures will force a need for product identification that often requires at least some differentiation. The brand name, trademark, trade character, slogan, and other identification devices common to manufactured goods all have potential application to bank marketing. They may be employed for individual products or for the entire bank.

The bank's image is related to these identification devices. A bank's image is a complex collection of attitudes and awarenesses on the part of customers and potential customers. All trademarks, brand names, and contacts with bank facilities and bank personnel must combine to create a favorable image in the customer's mind. When a large part of the product is an intangible feeling of confidence, security, and trust, as it is with many bank services, a favorable image is essential. The question of how an individual bank may raise specific types of funds is now addressed.

## Product Attraction

Although individual banks do not have absolute control over the level of their deposits, they can nevertheless influence the amount that they hold. Because deposits and other fund sources are so important to the profitable operation of a bank, most banks tend to compete aggressively for them. Some of the factors determining the level of deposits in a bank cannot be affected significantly by the bank. For example, monetary and fiscal policy, Regulation DD, and the level of general economic activity are exogenous factors that an individual bank must recognize but cannot control. The individual bank can control in varying degrees an intermediate group of factors (e.g., the size and physical location or locations of the bank). Finally, the individual bank determines such factors as its physical features and personnel, its marketing effort, the interest rates it pays on savings and time accounts, the type of loans it is willing to make, and the level of services it offers its depositors. The major factors contributing to the attraction of principal types of deposits are discussed next.

**Corporate Demand Deposits**  At this time, banks are not permitted to pay interest on corporate demand deposits; therefore, each bank must compete primarily on the basis of services rendered the depositor. It has long been held that the failure to charge for a service is not a payment of interest, and this concept has led to the theory of supporting or compensating balances.

As corporate depositors, particularly the larger ones, have become more sophisticated, and as alternative uses of money have become more profitable, corporate treasurers have learned to seek a specific quid pro quo in terms of services for every dollar of their corporation's demand deposits.

The most essential service compensated for by demand deposits is the collection and payment service in all its various forms. Every business that draws checks needs a bank account; those who receive checks need a bank to provide the collection function. The best service is rendered by the bank that can collect checks most quickly, thereby making funds available to the depositor earlier. Out of this need for faster collection has sprung a whole art of *funds mobilization,* in which the Federal Reserve System has cooperated fully. These facilities include arrangements for sending large cash letters directly by wire or air mail to Federal Reserve Banks in other districts (postage paid by the Federal Reserve) or to correspondent banks in major cities, bypassing the Reserve System entirely. Special carrier services have been established to bring checks into major cities more quickly than they can be delivered by mail. Lock-box arrangements have proliferated. Some large banks have special departments whose function is to advise the corporate treasurer on the most effective way to mobilize cash for short-term investment.

Ideally, banks should carefully calculate the costs of these services and make sure that the value of the related deposits compensates them for these costs plus an adequate profit margin. This is usually done by calculating a service charge representing the actual cost plus profit margin and offsetting this charge, in whole or in part, by an earnings credit for balances maintained at the bank. This credit is related to some money market rate representing the value of the funds in the bank. Both the service charges and the earnings credits are competitive rates.

The bank's true net cost of the services it renders to depositors represents its cost of money for those deposits. Faced with higher costs in other markets for funds, most banks are willing to compensate the demand depositor by providing services at a charge somewhat less than the net cost. Some banks waive service charges entirely, figuring that the cost of servicing those accounts is less than the interest they would have to pay on savings or time deposits.

It is very easy, however, to become trapped by this philosophy, and a bank can easily find itself rendering a number of services while double-counting the value of the same demand deposit account. The aggregate cost of these services may well exceed the value of the deposit. It becomes increasingly important, therefore, to look at each account relationship as a whole, and in recent years computer programs have been developed to enable banks to measure the relative total profitability of an account relationship. This involves coordinating in one computer printout all the services performed and their cost, the average collected balances maintained by a given customer (including other related accounts he or she may control) and their value, and credit usage, if any. Small banks can use a microcomputer to look at smaller numbers of large deposit accounts in this fashion.

The bank's willingness to lend money is of almost equal importance in attracting demand deposits, particularly business accounts. Credit availability is an essential need for most businesses at one time or another and is a constant need for some. When funds are in short supply (as they are predicted to be in the foreseeable future), banks will give preference to those customers who maintain demand deposit accounts with them. The offer of credit accommodation is a primary factor in deposit solicitation. For this reason, banks frequently offer "solicitation" lines of credit to businesses with no present need to borrow, and by the same token, businesses maintain deposit balances in anticipation of their possible future borrowing needs. One outstanding example of this relationship is the so-called back-up line of credit supporting a corporation's sale of commercial paper. A company actively using commercial paper to finance its current needs will obtain and advertise the availability of its unused bank lines of credit. The unused lines are typically supported by demand deposit balances of at least 10 percent of the credit available.

The willingness to lend, in short, is another vital service that banks perform for corporations or individuals who maintain or control demand deposit balances. At times when money is extremely scarce, this relationship between deposit balances and credit availability seeps down even to the consumer lending field. For example, nondepositors may seek home mortgage loans in vain.

**Transaction Deposits of Individuals**   Individuals' transaction deposits offer a broad spectrum of opportunities. Individuals can choose to receive interest on their transaction deposits through NOW and Super NOW accounts. NOW and Super NOW accounts usually have a minimum size and a limit on checking activity. Non-interest-bearing demand deposits usually have lower or no balance requirements and often offer more services to the depositors. Service for individuals with non-interest-bearing demand deposits have proliferated in recent years. Many banks have been establishing automated tellers, with which a customer with a "money card" and a secret account number can make deposits or withdraw small amounts of cash 24 hours a day, seven days a week, at scattered and convenient locations. Some banks have instituted systems to allow their customers to pay their bills by telephone. The customer states his or her account number and a personal identification number and then instructs the bank to pay designated amounts to specific payees. The customer can also designate the date on which he or she wishes the payments to be made.

The basic relationship between demand deposits and services rendered is essentially the same whether the depositor is an individual, a business corporation, or a municipality. The most successful bank will be the low-cost producer that can market its services at the lowest price and still maintain an adequate profit margin.

**NOW and Super NOW Accounts**   NOW and Super NOW accounts are available only to individuals. These accounts used to have either rate limitation, activity limitation, or size minimums, but these regulations were removed on March 31, 1986. In such a deregulated environment, banks have to pay rates and offer services that are reasonably competitive with those for similar accounts at thrift institutions and at money market funds. At the same time, a bank should carefully price the complete NOW or Super NOW package to include interest rates, number of transactions permitted without charge, service fees, and minimum size so that the effective cost of the attracted funds is not too high to earn an adequate return.

Advertising and promotional expenditures, as well as a competitive rate package, will continue to be important in attracting NOW and Super NOW accounts. Slight differences in rates are not generally perceived as an overriding concern by most individuals, and once accounts are opened, individuals appear to be hesitant to change to another bank or institution. By the mid-1990s, the authors predict that there will be no distinction between NOW and Super NOW accounts; indeed, many individuals may have a single account that pays an interest rate dependent on the average size and activity in the account.

**Passbook Savings Deposits**   The passbook or statement savings market has been primarily a market of convenience. The primary emphasis of commercial bank advertising in this field has been on "one-stop" or "full-service" banking. The fact that commercial banks, even when they are in close competition with strong thrift institutions, still have large amounts of savings deposits is evidence of the effectiveness of this marketing technique. It has become less effective in recent years, since thrift institutions and banks have been permitted to have NOW and Super NOW accounts. Furthermore, the rapid growth of money market mutual funds has cut heavily into bank passbook and statement savings deposits.

As of March 21, 1986, rate limits on passbook savings were removed. To compete effectively in the passbook savings market (with or without an actual passbook), banks will have to go beyond mere convenience and offer competitive rates and additional services. A bank might offer lower or no charges on checking account facilities to savings deposit customers in some relation to the size of their savings accounts. It might offer a vacation club or special-purpose accounts. Some people save for various reasons; the interest earned is not the only reason for saving. The reason may be general or specific, but the process should be made easy, attractive, and convenient. In spite of all efforts, the passbook or statement savings of individuals in most banks will probably continue declining and be replaced by NOW and Super NOW type accounts in future years.

**Money Market Deposits**   Money market deposits are a special category of savings deposits that have grown rapidly since they were first permitted in late 1982. Most banks place some minimum size on these accounts, and the rate paid may vary with the size. Rates are usually changed weekly in line with some money market index. While rate is the dominant factor in attracting these types of funds, promotion of deposit insurance, convenience, and transferability with other bank accounts have also assisted banks in competing for such deposits. This form of deposit may also be combined with NOW and Super NOW deposits into single account deposits by the early 1990s.

**Time Deposits**   There are several categories of time deposits. The first category, *negotiable CDs of $100,000 or more*, has attracted the largest amounts of funds of any deposit category. These are primarily for corporations and are not subject to interest rate limits. These certificates represent a fruitful source of funds, especially for large banks that lack a large retail deposit base. To be effective in the impersonal CD market, a bank must be large enough and sufficiently well known for its certificates to be traded at reasonable rates in the secondary market.

Although most corporate treasurers will, in theory, buy the certificates of any recognized bank at the highest rate obtainable, if rates are comparable, they are more likely to acquire the certificates issued by one of their banks of account. In times of tight money, banks may put considerable pressure on treasurers with whom they have established contact. By the same token, the treasurer with funds to invest will call a number of banks and "shop and market." Actual rates are often negotiated slightly off the posted rates for large blocks of funds of especially desirable maturities. From the deposit attraction standpoint, it is important that the banker get to know as many treasurers and other shoppers for such funds as possible. Although rate is always the primary factor, personal acquaintance is definitely a plus if several competitive rates are equal.

A second category, *other time deposits of $100,000 or more*, is not subject to rate limits, is not negotiable, can have fixed or flexible maturities, and is purchased by individuals, partnerships, corporations, and municipalities. The majority of these larger time deposits are issued by small or moderate-sized banks to their customers who from time to time have excess cash to invest. Customer-related time deposits of $100,000 and over must be at competitive rates but are kept at the bank primarily by the other relationships the customer has with the bank. Although excessive brokered deposits may lead to liquidity problems (see the previous section) and regulation limits the acceptable amount of brokered deposits, this deposit source should not be completely ignored. Brokered deposits *in moderate amounts* may make sense, and in spite of rates slightly above those of competitors may be less expensive than some other deposit forms. There is little if any acquisition cost, and maturities and terms may be structured to a bank's specific needs.

*Time deposits under $100,000* is a catchall category for remaining time deposits. Many of these deposits are called *savings certificates*. These certificates are issued in a variety of forms to suit the needs and tastes of various classes of customers. They are usually sold in minimum denominations of $1,000. Interest may be paid by check on a monthly or quarterly basis or, in some cases, accumulated to maturity. For customers who cling to the passbook concept, such certificates may be issued in the form of a special passbook. Some certificates are issued with rates tied to Treasury securities with various maturities. Although the interest cost on these certificates will vary over time, the money raised through such deposits will be more permanent because these certificates will always be competitive with market securities. Advertising has been essential in informing the public of the forms of savings certificates a bank is emphasizing.

A majority of *individual retirement and Keogh accounts* fall into this category of time deposits. Such accounts offer banks a relatively new (expanded in 1982 but limited again by the 1986 tax legislation) means for attracting funds. Low- and middle-income individuals, as well as high-income individuals not covered by another retirement plan, can deduct an IRA contribution of up to $2,000 to establish their taxable income. All individuals, including high-income individuals with another retirement plan, benefit from tax-sheltered income on eligible IRA investments. If attractively priced, IRAs should represent a relatively permanent source of funds. IRAs give banks the opportunity to innovate new competitive products with little regulatory constraint. Early ideas regarding interest rates have included rates fluctuating slightly above various-maturity Treasury bill rates or rates set for up to one year. Advertising expenditures to try to attract these deposits have been relatively large for the more aggressive banks.

**Public Deposits**    There are several types of public deposits. Treasury tax and loan accounts are interest-bearing, demand-type accounts of the U.S.

government. It is relatively easy for a bank to become a qualified depository. To keep its prorated share of these deposits for over a day or so, the bank must formally agree to pay a rate based on the market repurchase agreement rate. Qualified securities must be pledged for the uninsured part of these deposits. To attract state or municipal demand deposits, the financial services provided for the state or municipal unit is an important consideration. Attracting state and municipal time deposits depends on factors similar to those affecting large-denomination CDs. In some states, such deposits must go to the institution that bids the highest rate. Competition for state and municipal time deposits can be intense, and banks should be careful that, in the rates they bid, they recognize reserve and pledging requirements and an adequate return on capital. Repurchase agreements in which the bank agrees to rebuy securities it has sold to the political unit are an alternative way of attracting funds from these units. Many states still require pledging of securities against demand and time deposits of the state and its municipalities.

**Correspondent Deposits**  Deposits of other banks are a significant source of funds for some upstream, correspondent banks (over half of a few banks' demand deposits are from other banks). Demand balances are left by one bank in another bank because the latter offers services such as check clearance, international entry, investment advice, and loan participation. The services offered should be significant enough to attract other banks; however, the depository bank should be sure it is making a profit on the funds attracted.

### Nondeposit Sources

Banks should also have fund attraction strategies for nondeposit sources of funds. Some forms, such as Federal funds and commercial paper for bank holding companies, clearly depend on a willingness to pay the going rate. Nonprice strategies are also important. Repurchase agreements depend on the bank having acceptable securities or other assets that can be sold subject to repurchase. A bank may be able to borrow more Federal funds if it has good correspondent relations and a strong capital position. Eurodollar and other foreign sources may be encouraged by foreign offices and connections with foreign banks and businesses.

### Future Possibilities

It appears that one-account banking may gain popularity in the mid-to-late 1990s. One version of such an account would be a flexible format where each customer would have deposits over a certain amount automatically transferred to a variable-rate account. A more complex version would let the customer specify time horizons over which funds would be left with the bank. The customer would receive rates based on the specified maturities, with large penalties for maturity violations. Banks should begin developing this deposit product and plans to promote it as soon as possible.

The age of electronic banking is clearly well under way. Most banks aggressively use automatic teller machines (ATMs) at the present time as a method of attracting funds. A growing number of banks are beginning to use point-of-sale (POS) terminals as part of their strategy for attracting funds. Questions still remain about the cost-effectiveness of some ATM and POS terminals and about sharing and switching systems for such electronic terminals. Home banking is an even newer electronic method for attracting funds. Some proponents believe that over half of all banking transactions will be done at home by the year 2000. Attractive and cost-effective systems are in the developmental stages.

## Discussion Questions

1. Describe the principal actions banks have taken in the last two decades in an attempt to overcome their declining share of the financial intermediation market. Have these actions been successful?
2. Describe the principal types of savings deposits in commercial banks. What are the major differences between these savings deposits and bank time deposits?
3. Briefly describe securities sold under agreement to repurchase (repos). What are the advantages and disadvantages of using repos to fund a bank?
4. Discuss the final steps in the phasing out of Regulation Q. Do you believe that banks now have to manage price rather than quantity?
5. Why should a bank be interested in measuring its cost of funds? Describe the principal methods of measuring the cost of funds for a bank.
6. Define the break-even yield for a bank. How is it calculated?
7. List the three primary ways a bank can estimate its marginal cost of funds. Briefly describe the calculations for each method.
8. How might the types of funds a bank attracts affect the liquidity risk of a bank?
9. Should the interest sensitivity position of a bank affect the types of funds a bank attempts to attract? Briefly describe how a bank might try to change its funding mix.
10. Develop a marketing plan that a bank might use to raise additional demand deposits and additional Super NOW accounts.

# CHAPTER 8

# Capital Planning, Adequacy, and Generation

Capital is a fundamental and vital part of the commercial banking industry. Bank capital enables the establishment of a banking entity by supplying the funds necessary to acquire the physical and human resources that compose it. It is also critical to the perpetuation of that banking entity in its capacity as an ongoing concern. Thus, capital plays an all-important role at the inception of a bank and throughout its life. The subject of capital has become a focal point in the banking industry. Capital adequacy and capital acquisition have become major concerns and topics of discussion, study, and controversy among bank directors, managers, customers, and regulatory authorities. The new risk-based capital rules, plus other capital requirements mandated by the Federal Deposit Insurance Improvement Act of 1991 and implementation of rate risk in capital requirements, have changed many facets of bank management. This chapter and the following one describe how managements can determine and fill the capital needs of their banks.

This chapter starts by investigating capital planning as a part of overall financial planning. The difficult question of how much capital is enough, or capital adequacy, is treated from both a bank management and a regulatory perspective. The chapter ends with an examination of the factors determining a bank's internal or sustainable growth. In Chapter 9 we evaluate the various forms, old and new, of capital that can be raised externally by a commercial bank and introduce capital management techniques to utilize capital more effectively.

# CAPITAL PLANNING IN THE OVERALL FINANCIAL PLAN

The first step in financing a bank's capital needs is the development of an overall financial plan. The amount of capital needed is clearly affected by the bank's financial plan, and the plan is constrained by the amount of capital the bank has raised. The financial planning process starts with a careful analysis of the bank's present position and performance. Next, the bank should predict several key variables, use these variables to develop overall financial projections, and see if the financial results of these projections are consistent with the bank's plans and policies. The sensitivity of these overall results to changes in key variables should also be carefully examined. The bank should then analyze these results, with emphasis on the question of how much capital will be necessary to produce the desired results.

## Analyzing a Bank's Performance

A bank should know where it has been—its accomplishments and failures, strengths and weaknesses—before it projects its future course. The bank must analyze all of the primary aspects of its performance, even when the principal objective is to measure the bank's capital needs. The methods used for analyzing a bank's past performance were discussed in detail in Chapters 3 and 4. The key risk–return measurements for a bank should be compared with those for peer banks in this first step of capital planning.

## Predicting Selected Key Variables in the Future

After a complete analysis of the bank's past performance has been made, the next step is to select a few key variables for the bank and to predict the levels of these variables for targeted future periods. It is important that the predictions for these variables be more than mere extrapolations of past data. They should represent plans that include reasonable policy goals and objectives, as well as observation of trends from past periods.

Selecting a limited number of key variables can be a difficult task. One variable that is usually emphasized is the predicted level of deposits. When predicting the amount of deposits, a bank should consider factors affecting deposit growth that can be controlled (such as promotional efforts, services offered, and rates paid on savings) and factors that cannot be controlled (such as population growth, competition, and economic conditions). Deposits often must be separated by the form of deposit (demand, saving, and time) and by the type of depositor (business, individual, and public) in order to pick up the differences in factors affecting their growth. Furthermore, some banks have the ability to control their level of time deposits and other purchased obligations by changing their rates in the marketplace. Such banks may want to predict demand and passbook deposits and then treat the level of their time deposits as a residual based primarily on their projections of profitable loan and investment opportunities (assuming that they can always purchase the funds required).

Another commonly used key variable is the predicted level of the bank's loans. Both controllable variables (such as the rates charged on various types of loans) and noncontrollable variables (such as local economic conditions and the national business cycle) can affect how much a bank has in its loan portfolio. Often a bank will predict loans equal to a target percentage of deposits; however, this prediction assumes that a bank can cut off loans to customers when demand is strong or can find new loan customers when demand is weak. Both of these predictions seem highly suspect, and it is preferable to predict a range of loan-to-deposit relationships, depending on the national and local economic conditions during the period for which loans are predicted.

Generally, the other key variable or variables should be any other factors that set limits on the progress of the bank during the prediction period. The limiting variable may be the adequacy of trained personnel, target for the spread to be earned on employed assets, rate of opening new branches, or some other factor. The important criterion is that the variables will allow the bank to perform some basic activity, such as increasing deposit or loan growth in a different way than would be possible without that variable.

Once the key variables have been selected, the bank must estimate what will happen to them during the prediction period. Selection of the prediction period is itself a difficult task. Very short-term predictions, such as a month, may be subject to random fluctuations and are usually too short-term and small to have a large impact on capital needs. Longer-term predictions, such as 10 years, are subject to so many changes in noncontrollable factors that to take current actions is unrealistic. The most meaningful time period for predicting the key variables is probably annually for the next three to five years. As an overall projection is developed, it may be necessary to change the predictions for one or more of the key variables or even to change a key variable itself. It is important to note that the availability of capital, which seems like a key variable for at least some banks, is not included as a key variable for the initial overall projection. Instead, the need for capital is established by the overall projection; then the question of the availability of capital is carefully examined.

## Developing an Overall Projection from the Key Variables

The next step, once predictions have been made for the key variables, is to develop pro forma balance sheets and projected income statements for the prediction period. Because these statements are interrelated, they must be developed jointly. (When available, a personal computer should be used to make these predicted statements.) The relationships calculated in analyzing the bank's past performance can be very useful during this step. Prior experience serves as a useful guide to necessary relationships in developing an overall projection and as a check on the reasonableness of assumptions. The management of a bank should have good reasons for projecting figures that depart significantly from prior experience. Generally, the overall balance capital planning the number of categories should be kept as low as possible without materially harming the accuracy of the projection.

The first step in constructing the pro forma balance sheet should be to estimate the bank's major sources of funds. The deposit accounts can be predicted from forecasted growth rates for demand, time, and savings deposits and from the predicted dollar amount of public deposits. The other liabilities account is often a key variable in larger banks in which various forms of liabilities (such as Federal funds or Eurodollars) are purchased. For smaller banks, unless specific information exists, the other liabilities account is often small and may be estimated to remain constant or to grow at about the same rate as deposits and capital.

In predicting the capital accounts, the planner must remember that assets will increase because of additional capital (usually from retained earnings), as well as from new deposits or increases in other liabilities. The amount of retained earnings for a period depends on the level of a bank's earnings in that period, which is partially a function of the amount of earning assets and the bank's cash dividend payout. The uncertainties and interdependencies associated with these variables usually do not materially weaken the financial plan because the amount of retained earnings is only a small proportion of the total additional funds in most time periods. Banks can, therefore, safely use either of two methods initially to predict the capital accounts: (1) leave total capital at the preceding year's-end level (less any scheduled debt repayments) or (2) allow total capital to increase by the increase in earnings estimated from the predicted income statement less any planned cash dividends. No changes should be made on the initial projection except for scheduled debt repayments and possibly for an estimation of retained earnings. (In a later step, specific financing to meet additional capital needs will be reflected in the balance sheet.)

The next step in constructing the pro forma balance sheet is to estimate the uses of the funds from the various sources. The amount in cash and due from banks is estimated by multiplying the various categories of deposits by the reserve requirements for these categories and adding that amount to the minimum correspondent balances and float.

The loan category is often the most difficult to predict. A bank may have a target amount of loans or a desired loan-to-deposit ratio; however, factors such as national, regional, and local economic conditions may make the target difficult to attain. Fortunately, flexibility in security holdings can cushion the lower income if loan demand is low and can provide some extra funds if loan demand is higher than predicted.

The category of fixed assets changes by additions to fixed assets less depreciation on existing equipment. If the amount in this category does not change much, it can be assumed that capital expenditures are roughly equivalent to depreciation. Because noncash expenses (such as depreciation) charged against revenues are usually relatively small for a bank, changes in this category are usually significant only if the bank plans major physical expansion.

The other assets account is a catchall category that usually can be predicted from prior experience, and the investments account is generally used as a balancing residual—that is, it is the difference between total (deposit and other) sources of funds and the previously discussed asset categories (cash and due from banks, loans, fixed assets, and other assets).

All of the predictions for balance sheet accounts are rough estimates, but if the predictions for the key variables are reasonable, the overall forecast will be accurate enough for thoughtful capital planning. Care must be taken at every step to keep the balance sheet in balance. The pro forma balance sheet for the first year provides the base for building the following year's projections; this process continues until each year's projection has been completed.

In situations in which average or year-end balances are readily obtainable, average balances are usually preferable. If an attempt is made to calculate precise earnings on assets and interest on deposits, average figures will have to be considered. One simple alternative is to use an average of beginning and year-end figures for this purpose. A bank with significant seasonal variations, however, will have to use daily, weekly, or monthly average figures.

## Sensitivity Analysis and a Range for the Projections

As the bank continues to make projections year after year, it will probably acquire increasing confidence in those projections. Still, many factors outside a bank's control affect its projections. In preparing to react to an array of possible developments, bank management must envision how sensitive its key variables are to changes beyond the bank's control and the effect of changes in these key variables on the overall forecast. For example, what would happen if a bank's deposits grew at a 20 percent compound rate annually instead of a predicted 10 percent rate? What would be the impact of a substantial drop in loan demand? Bank managers should test only those key variables that they are uncertain about and that might have a significant impact. For example, substantial changes in deposit growth may be important for a bank, but changes in equipment prices may have only a modest effect. One useful technique is to test the key variables by changing them by the greatest amount management thinks is possible and then following the consequences through the projection. If the projected statements are done on a personal computer, changing key variables or the environment by using a group of what-if situations is relatively easy.

If management believes there is a reasonable probability that some key variables may be off by a wide margin and that future events might call for different plans and decisions, two more overall projections should be prepared to bracket the range of possibilities. One projection should be pessimistic, assuming that the identified key variables are at the lower end of reasonable expectations. Capital and other plans and strategies may be appreciably different under this pessimistic outlook. The other projection should be optimistic, assuming that the identified key variables are at the upper end of reasonable expectations. It is interesting to note that this projection is likely to place greater pressure on the bank's ability to raise external capital. In fact, capital requirements could become so great that the availability of capital becomes an important limiting variable in the overall projection.

### Determining Capital Needs from Projections

The final step in the financial planning process is to determine the capital needs based on the bank's projections. The preferred method is to determine what capital management believes is adequate to support the bank's projected assets, deposits, and other liabilities. This amount can then be compared with the bank's actual capital at the start of the year (less any capital repayments) and with its earnings (less anticipated cash dividends). If the amount of capital deemed adequate exceeds the available capital, then management should consider lowering cash dividends and/or raising capital from external sources. If the available capital exceeds the adequate level of capital, the bank might consider raising its cash dividends or buying back some of its stock.

## DETERMINING CAPITAL ADEQUACY

It is also important to determine how much capital is appropriate for an individual bank's financial structure. There are three primary factors affecting the appropriate amount of capital for an individual bank: (1) the purposes of bank capital, (2) the advantages of leverage to owners, and (3) capital adequacy as measured by regulators.

### Purposes of Bank Capital

The first factor, and one of the most difficult to quantify, is the amount of capital needed to meet the purposes of bank capital. Presumably bank capital serves useful purposes, and the level of a bank's capital is inadequate to the extent that it does not serve these purposes. The primary difficulty is that it is impossible to define the purposes of bank capital in a manner that is meaningful and that can be used to measure quantitatively the amount of capital a bank needs. Deciding the purposes of bank capital can be approached by examining similarities between the purposes of capital for a bank and the purposes of capital for a nonfinancial corporation. As Table 8-1 illustrates, the hypothetical ABC Manufacturing Company has financed roughly one-half of its assets in the form of debt and one-half in equity capital. Equity capital assisted ABC Manufacturing in several ways: by providing a substantial proportion of the funds used to finance ABC's assets; by serving as a cushion (loss absorber), which encouraged creditors to lend to the company to help finance ABC's assets; and by improving confidence among creditors, lenders, and customers of the company. The balance sheet of a hypothetical bank, XYZ Commercial Bank (see Table 8-1) shows more short-term assets; therefore, the bank is able to attract considerably more capital from short-term creditors

**TABLE 8-1 Illustration of the Functions of Capital**

### ABC Manufacturing Company

| Assets | | Liabilities | |
|---|---|---|---|
| Cash | $ 50 | Current liabilities | $ 300 |
| Accounts receivable | 300 | Long-term debts | 200 |
| Inventory | 200 | | |
| Plant and equipment | 450 | Equity capital | 500 |
| | $1,000 | | $1,000 |

### XYZ Commercial Bank

| Assets | | Liabilities | |
|---|---|---|---|
| Cash | $ 100 | Current liabilities | $ 700 |
| Short-term loans & investments | 600 | Long-term liabilities | 230 |
| Long-term loans & investments | 260 | | |
| Facilities & equipment | 40 | Equity capital | 70 |
| | $1,000 | | $1,000 |

(depositors and lenders). The relative amount of capital for XYZ Bank is considerably lower than that for ABC Manufacturing; however, the primary purposes—to encourage depositors, improve confidence, and finance badly needed assets—are roughly the same.

Brenton C. Leavitt, of the staff of the board of governors, has stressed four functions of bank capital:

1. To protect the uninsured depositor in the event of insolvency and liquidation.
2. To absorb unanticipated losses with enough margin to inspire continuing confidence to enable the bank, when under stress, to continue as a going concern.
3. To acquire the physical plant and basic necessities needed to render banking services.
4. To serve as a regulatory restraint on unjustified asset expansion.[1]

A brief evaluation of each of Leavitt's four functions of bank capital is an excellent method for determining the basic functions or purposes of bank capital.

The idea that bank capital protects uninsured depositors in the event of insolvency and liquidation carries an element of truth but appears to overstate the case. Many weak-looking bank assets can be phased out with relatively little loss if given sufficient time, competent management, reasonable earnings, adequate liquidity, and the working of the business cycle. Even the staggering

[1]Brenton C. Leavitt, speeches before numerous meetings of bankers and regulators.

losses of the 1930s were ultimately absorbed out of earnings when banks were not forced into liquidation. This is not to say that losses were not charged to capital funds; in the short run, they were. And if too many losses are charged to capital, the bank's doors will inevitably close. Arguments that "enough" bank capital will prevent failures and, even if there is a failure, will protect uninsured depositors are not substantiated. Often the uninsured depositor was the one who, because of fear about poor management, fraud, or lack of liquidity, withdrew his or her funds and caused the bank to fail. The remaining uninsured depositors probably did benefit if the bank had more assets financed by capital; however, it often was several years before such depositors were paid in such situations.

The question of the connection between banking problems and bank capital became even more intense after the widely publicized bank failures and reorganizations in the 1980s. While some of the troubled or failing banks had below-average amounts of capital, it was poor management, large loan losses, and poor liquidity that seemed to be the primary causes of these problems. It is highly questionable whether more capital alone would have kept banks such as Penn Square, Continental Illinois, First Republic, or MCorp open in their existing forms. As George Vojta states:

> The consensus of scholarly research is that the level of bank capital has not been causally related to the incidence of bank failure. Historically, banking crises occurred in periods of prolonged cyclical instability. Failures resulted from a loss of public confidence in the banking system.[2]

The second function cited by Leavitt is conceptually sound and seems to draw more widespread support. A past chairman of the FDIC has stated, "In my view, adequate capital is the least amount necessary for others to have confidence in your bank and its operations."[3] Vojta also stated that bank capital should "provide protection against unanticipated adversity leading to loss in excess of normal expectations. The capital provision against excessive loss permits the bank to continue operations in periods of difficulty until a normal level of earnings is restored."[4]

Maintaining confidence is probably the primary function of bank capital. Uninsured depositors must be confident that their money is safe, and borrowers must be confident that the bank will be in a position to give genuine consideration to their credit needs in bad times as well as good. Furthermore, under the closely supervised, private banking system of the United States, the confidence of the bank supervisor is essential to a bank's continued existence. Confidence is also important to the bank's stockholders. It helps to protect them from failure, which generally results in complete loss of their investment

---

[2]George J. Vojta, *Bank Capital Adequacy*, New York: Citicorp.

[3]Frank Wille, speech before ABA's Correspondent Banking Conference.

[4]Vojta, *Bank Capital Adequacy*.

and deterioration in the bank's market price and, therefore, its ability to raise additional equity capital.

The concern about confidence as the primary function of bank capital is not conceptual but rather one of measurement. Any measure of how much capital is necessary for depositors, borrowers, regulators, shareholders, and other interested parties to remain confident is imprecise at best and may vary widely with economic and regulatory conditions. The bank manager who seeks to maintain capital adequate to serve this function is clearly not dealing with a precise, quantifiable measure.

Bank capital has other important, but probably secondary, functions. As in any business, part of the capital is needed to supply the working tools of the enterprise. This function is immediately evident in the organization of a new bank; the first expenditure of funds supplied by the stockholders is for the banking premises and the equipment needed to begin operations. The provision of such working assets is a continuing function of bank capital. One cannot expect the depositor to supply the funds for new branch buildings or drive-in facilities. One problem in measuring the adequacy of bank capital is determining the extent to which capital may be available to serve other purposes and functions of capital funds, even though it is invested in premises and equipment.

The idea that another secondary function of capital is to restrain unjustified expansion of bank assets is more reasonable than it may at first appear. Regulatory capital requirements may prevent a bank from growing beyond the ability of management to manage, may improve the quality of bank assets, may control the ability of a bank to leverage its growth, and may lead to higher bank earnings on assets. Indeed, capital requirements have been used to prevent unjustified expansion in several recent bank holding company decisions. One warning is that to rely solely, or even primarily, on bank capital requirements to achieve all of these tasks is obviously unsound.

## The Need for Leverage to Improve the Returns to Owners

The second of the three primary factors affecting the appropriate amount of capital for an individual bank is the need for financial leverage to increase returns for the bank's owners. Tables 8-1 and 8-2 illustrate the importance of financial leverage. The ABC Manufacturing Company was 50 percent equity financed, which meant that the firm had a leverage multiplier of 2 times. A 7 percent after-tax return on assets by ABC (approximately the average return on assets for manufacturing companies in 1991) leads to a 14 percent return on equity for ABC Manufacturing.

How can XYZ Commercial Bank, which earns only 0.7 percent on its assets (about average for banks in 1991) satisfy its owners and still have the ability to attract additional equity? XYZ Bank must have significantly more leverage, which means fewer assets financed by equity and a higher leverage multiplier, in order to compete in the equity market with ABC Manufacturing. In Table 8-2 it is assumed that 6 percent of XYZ Bank's assets are financed

**TABLE 8-2  Effects of Financial Leverage on Returns on Equity**

|  | ABC Manufacturing Company[a] | XYZ Commercial Bank[a] | Typical Small Bank[b] | Typical Large Bank[b] |
|---|---|---|---|---|
| Assets | $1,000 | $1,000 | — | — |
| Equity | 500 | 70 | — | — |
| Net earnings | 70 | 9 | — | — |
| Equity-to-assets ratio | 50.0% | 6.0% | 9.4% | 6.1% |
| Return on assets | 7.0% | 0.7% | 1.1% | 0.8% |
| Leverage multiplier | 2.0× | 16.6× | 10.7× | 16.5× |
| Return on equity | 14.0% | 11.6% | 11.3% | 13.8% |

[a]From Table 8-1.

[b]Estimated from the *Quarterly Banking Profile* (Washington, D.C.: FDIC, 1993).

by equity (about average for banks in 1991). The resulting leverage multiplier of 16.67 times leads to a nearly competitive return on equity of 11.6 percent.

This example indicates that in order to attract and keep owners, commercial banks must, and in the real world do, have the financial leverage resulting from low levels of equity in relation to assets. Thus, particularly from the owners' point of view, the appropriate amount of equity capital is little enough to produce at least an adequate return on capital without taking too much capital risk. Three factors tend to keep bank owners from using excessive financial leverage to increase their bank's return on capital.

First, market constraints should keep deficit units from lending excessive amounts to banks in relation to the money provided by bank owners. Some "market" advocates have gone as far as stating that the ability to attract both capital and noncapital funds should be the primary determinant of a bank's capital position. This position seems extreme because it ignores factors such as the existence of deposit insurance and possible market imperfection, which may particularly affect the ability of smaller banks to attract funds. Nevertheless, the market does limit the amounts of capital and noncapital funds available to most banks, and it may do so reasonably efficiently for the larger ones.

Second, banks using the suggested objective of maximizing the market price of their stock will find that overuse of financial leverage will reduce their bank's market price per share. For example, if a bank earning $2.00 per share could increase earnings per share to $2.10 by using additional leverage, the bank should increase leverage only if the market price per share increases. If, for example, the price-earnings multiple fell from 10 to 9 because of the greater risk, the bank would be wise to avoid the additional leverage because its stock price would fall from $20 to $18.90 per share.

Third, regulatory authorities force banks to keep amounts of capital that these authorities deem adequate to protect depositors and the banking system. At the present time, regulatory constraints are the most common factors limiting the use of financial leverage by commercial banks. Such regulatory constraints often conflict with owners' desires for more leverage and higher returns. Regulators usually want more equity capital, whereas owners usually favor less equity capital.

The special characteristics of senior capital, debt, and preferred stock are also important. If a debt or preferred stock issue is acceptable as capital by the appropriate regulatory authority, the issue increases the bank's capital position; however, the same debt or preferred issue also increases financial leverage and the resulting leverage multiplier of the bank. This dual advantage—increased safety *and* increased earnings to owners—encouraged the use of senior capital by banks in the 1960s and 1970s. Factors such as high interest rates, repayment and refinancing difficulties, and regulatory concerns weakened this dual advantage substantially in the 1980s; however, the 1990s may again be favorable to senior capital.

The effect of bank size on the acceptable and permissible levels of financial leverage is also a concern. Table 8-2 shows the effect of financial leverage on a typical small bank and a typical large bank. The typical small bank usually has a higher return on assets and a higher percentage of equity to assets. More equity capital means a lower than average leverage multiplier, which lowers the higher return on assets to nearly an average return on equity. The typical large bank usually has a lower than average return on assets and a lower than average percentage of equity to assets, which produces a higher leverage multiplier, and a close to average return on equity because of the greater leverage.

Several factors can be cited as causes for differences in equity-to-assets ratios and leverage due to bank size. Most large banks have greater management depth, for example. Also, the higher return on assets of many small banks means that they have more risk and should be required to have a higher percentage of equity to assets than large banks. Some regulators have stated that small banks have less diversified asset portfolios than large banks and, therefore, need a relatively larger capital base. This larger capital base is not a major problem as long as small banks are able to earn an above-average return on assets. In the 1980s, small banks' returns on assets declined (the brunt of deregulation hit smaller banks in the mid-1980s), while the average return on assets for large banks improved slightly.

The FDIC figures for U.S. commercial banks with assets under $100 million are as follows:

|  | 1960 | 1970 | 1980 | 1992 |
|---|---|---|---|---|
| Return on assets | .70% | .89% | 1.15% | 1.06% |
| Leverage multiplier (assets ÷ equity) | 13.3× | 13.5× | 12.7× | 10.7× |
| Return on equity | 9.3% | 12.0% | 14.6% | 11.3% |

The capital for large banks, with over $10 billion in assets, varied greatly. As late as 1960, large banks had more capital in relation to assets than average banks. The FDIC figures are as follows:

|  | **1960** | **1970** | **1980** | **1992** |
|---|---|---|---|---|
| Return on assets | 0.95% | 0.69% | 0.52% | .84% |
| Leverage multiplier | | | | |
| (assets ÷ equity) | 11.2× | 18.2× | 27.8× | 16.5× |
| Return on equity | 10.7% | 12.6% | 14.6% | 13.8% |

The reciprocal of the leverage ratio, the ratio of equity capital to assets, had fallen from 9.0 percent in 1960 to 3.6 percent in 1980 but had climbed back to 6.1 percent in 1992. It would seem that the leverage multiplier may decline again if bankers and their regulators become concerned with rising capital costs, off–balance sheet assets, and risk-based capital adequacy requirements.

One feasible explanation of the low equity-to-assets ratios of large banks in the 1980s and early 1990s is that these banks use arbitrage more extensively than most small banks. An extreme example would be a large bank that purchases and sells large amounts of Federal funds daily, often with correspondent banks, at a very low spread between the bid and asked prices. Or a large bank could purchase some type of deposits that it covers with similar maturity assets as a small margin. Small margins on arbitrages are usually justifiable only if little or no additional capital is needed. Such arbitrage transactions tend to build up a large bank's asset size, reduce its return on assets, and reduce its ratio of equity capital to assets. As regulators increased the capital requirements on large banks in the 1980s, these banks responded by reducing low-margin arbitrages, using securitization, and taking as many transactions as possible off the balance sheet. Return on assets and the ratio of equity to assets improved, but return on equity deteriorated.

## Regulatory Capital Adequacy Criteria and Concerns

The third factor affecting the appropriate amount of capital for an individual bank is the amount of capital a bank's regulators believe is adequate. Bank regulators have the responsibility of protecting depositors' funds and the safety of the banking system. Although other factors such as liquidity and interest sensitivity are as important, if not more important, in achieving such objectives, capital adequacy has been a primary concern of regulators for many years.

Federal and state laws prescribe the minimum amount of capital required for the organization of a new bank. The minimum is usually related to the population of the bank's locality. In recent years, as a matter of practical policy, supervisory authorities have usually required new banks to start with more than the legal minimum amount of capital.

Both federal and state laws also have minimum capital requirements for the establishment of branches (where permitted). These legal requirements have little real significance for banking today. They were enacted at a time when banks generally were much smaller. They have not been revised upward, largely because the determination of capital adequacy has become a matter of administrative judgment rather than of definitive law.

With respect to member banks of the Federal Reserve System, the basis for determining capital adequacy is detailed in Section 9 of the Federal Reserve Act and in Regulation H of the Board of Governors of the Federal Reserve. The regulation requires that the net capital and surplus of a member bank shall be adequate in relation to the character and condition of its assets and to its deposit liabilities and other corporate responsibilities. The exact nature of the relationship between capital adequacy and the character and condition of the bank is left to the judgment of the responsible regulatory authority.

The ratio of capital to deposits was widely used as a measure of capital adequacy from the early 1900s until World War II. In the early 1990s, a rule of thumb developed that a bank should have capital funds equal to at least 10 percent of its deposit liabilities. This rule was enacted in some states and received official sanction in 1914 when the Comptroller of the Currency suggested it as the minimum ratio for national banks. During World War II, bank deposits expanded rapidly as the result of bank purchases of U.S. government securities. To have maintained the 10 percent capital-to-deposit ratio in the face of ballooning deposits that were largely created by U.S. government security purchases would have seriously impeded the financing of the war.

The ratio of capital to total assets was used by the FDIC and the Federal Reserve System in the 1940s and early 1950s. No generally accepted standard for adequately capitalized banks was developed for this ratio, although Federal Reserve System authorities suggested that an adequately capitalized bank would have capital equal to at least 8 percent of total assets, and the FDIC used the national average of the ratio for all banks as the standard.

The ratio of capital to total assets, like the ratio of capital to deposits, is unaffected by differences in risks associated with banks' differing asset structures. For example, two banks of equal asset size would require an identical amount of capital, even though one of them might have all of its assets in cash and short-term U.S. government securities and the other might have 85 percent of its assets in loans. Since both ratios have the virtue of simplicity, they are still frequently used as a first quick test of capital adequacy.

In the early postwar years, the Comptroller's Office attempted to overcome the inability of simple ratios to recognize differences in risk on different assets by introducing a capital-to-risk-assets measure. Risk assets, in the broadest sense, were defined as total assets less holdings of cash and U.S. government securities. The theory behind the capital-to-risk-assets measure is that a major function of capital is to protect depositors from risk. Because holding cash carries no risk of loss, and because U.S. government securities carry no credit risk, these assets do not expose depositors to risk and, thus, should be excluded from assets when measuring risk.

The basic capital-to-risk-assets measure recognized one area of risk differential; however, it obviously ignored varying degrees of risk in a bank's remaining assets. This led to the development of a capital-to-adjusted-risk-assets ratio. In addition to relating capital to risk assets, this calculation includes a secondary calculation in which assets that are almost as riskless as cash and U.S. government securities are also deducted from total assets in determining risk assets.

The Federal Reserve responded to the weaknesses in the beginning ratios by developing more comprehensive measures of capital adequacy. In 1952, the Federal Reserve of New York developed a method of measuring the minimum amount of capital an individual bank would need, given its particular asset structure. Assets were divided into six asset categories according to risk. Capital requirements of 0, 5, 12, 20, 50, and 100 percent were assigned to these categories. The sum of the capital requirements of all the categories represented the minimum capital required to be held by a bank.

In 1956, a more complex version of this formula was developed by a staff group at the Board of Governors. Labeled "A Form for Analyzing Bank Capital," it was frequently referred to as the "ABC Formula." It combined a capital adequacy test, similar to the "New York Formula," with a liquidity test, requiring more capital for less liquid banks. The results of this analysis were frequently capital requirements beyond reason, especially for money market banks that practiced arbitrage. The other supervisory authorities never agreed that it was a reasonable approach, and the formula has now been abandoned.

In the late 1960s and early 1970s, national bank examiners moved away from any formula type of analysis. The Comptroller's Office stated:

> formulae, although of some value in assessing capital adequacy, do not take into account other factors of equal or greater importance. The capital position of the bank was, therefore, analyzed and appraised in relation to the character of its management and its asset and deposit position as a going institution under normal conditions, with due allowance for a reasonable margin of safety, and with due regard to the bank's capacity to furnish the broadest service to the public.[5]

In the late 1970s, the Comptroller's Office, the FDIC, and the Federal Reserve agreed to use trends and peer group comparisons of selected ratios to determine capital adequacy. The ratios to be considered included the following:

Equity capital/total assets
Total capital/total assets
Loans/total capital

[5]Part 14a issued under R.S. 324 et seq., as amended; 12 U.S.C. et seq., 1968.

> Classified assets/total capital
> Fixed assets/total capital
> Net rate-sensitive assets/total assets
> Reserve for charge-offs/net charge-offs
> Net charge-offs/loans
> Asset growth rate/capital growth rate

Such comparisons have been combined with other ratios into an overall performance rating scheme called CAMEL (Capital Asset Management Earnings Liquidity) by the regulatory bodies.

In late 1981, the three federal regulatory bodies announced new measures for evaluating capital adequacy. The FDIC stated that equity capital of 6.0 percent or more of total assets is acceptable for FDIC member banks of all sizes. Banks in a strong financial position might fall between 6.0 and 5.0 percent of equity to total assets, whereas any bank below 5.0 percent would be considered undercapitalized. Equity capital consisted of the total of all common stock accounts, 100 percent of equity reserves, a reserve for loan losses, noncallable preferred stock, and debt that must be converted into common stock less 100 percent of doubtful loans and 50 percent of classified loans.

The Comptroller and the Federal Reserve jointly announced a slightly different new method for measuring capital adequacy, stating that most banks' total capital must exceed their total assets by a specified percentage (generally between 6 and 7 percent), depending on the bank's size and financial strength. Total capital consisted of primary capital plus secondary capital. Primary capital was the same as the FDIC's equity capital. Secondary capital included callable preferred, convertible (nonmandatory) debt, and subordinated debt. Debt was reduced 20 percent in value for each year between five years from maturity and its maturity date. Total secondary debt could not be more than 50 percent of primary debt.

In 1985, the three bank regulatory agencies finally agreed to similar capital adequacy guidelines. Banks and bank holding companies of all sizes were supposed to have primary capital of at least 5.5 percent of adjusted total assets and primary and secondary capital of at least 6 percent of total assets. Although a few minor differences still existed, this was the first time banks and holding companies had achieved a reasonable understanding of all regulators' definitions of adequate capital.

This agreement on uniform capital adequacy standards did not mean that those standards were accomplishing the desired objectives. Starting in the mid-1980s, bank regulators became concerned with at least three conditions. First, the capital-to-assets ratios used did not penalize banks for having high-risk assets. In theory, the capital adequacy standards encouraged banks to take higher risks because capital requirements were the same for Treasury bills and high-risk consumer loans. Second, some banks began to use off–balance sheet items extensively because they improved both return on assets and capital-to-assets ratios. Any risk in off–balance sheet assets was ignored in capital adequacy standards. Third, U.S. banks appeared to be at a competitive disadvantage to foreign banks because of the higher capital requirements imposed on most U.S. banks.

In January 1987, these and similar concerns caused the three U.S. federal regulatory agencies, in conjunction with the Bank of England, to release for public comment a proposed risk-based capital adequacy framework. In 1988, bank regulators in these two countries and bank regulatory agencies in 10 other developed, free-world countries adopted reasonably similar risk-based capital adequacy frameworks.

Under the basic framework approved in the United States, a weighted average measure of total assets would be calculated, with the weights corresponding to four different categories of assets grouped according to their risk. The key measure of capital adequacy would be a risk-asset ratio that would be calculated as follows:

$$\text{Risk-asset ratio} = \frac{\text{Designated capital}}{\text{Weighted-risk-asset base}}$$

where the weighted-risk-asset base is the sum of four categories of on–balance sheet risk assets, as shown in Table 8-3, weighted by the appropriate percentage (0, 20, 50, or 100 percent) plus the off–balance sheet items weighted by the appropriate percentage (0, 20, 50, or 100 percent). Table 8-4 describes eligible capital and lists the minimum guidelines effective at the start of 1993.

Table 8-5 presents a simple example comparing conventional versus risk-adjusted capital ratios. Simulations have shown that risk-adjusted capital ratios will exceed current capital requirements for most banks, especially for smaller institutions. The slightly less than 10 percent of banks whose capital requirement will increase tend to have proportionately large amounts in off–balance sheet items. It is hoped that individual banks' requirements set by the different regulators would be affected by on-site examinations of banks' quality and diversity of assets, liquidity, earnings level and stability, management control of risk, and other factors. Thus, the risk-based approach to capital adequacy attempts to link capitalization to bank exposure to risk, with emphasis on loan risk in particular and probability of default in general.

There are several concerns about risk-weighted capital requirements. First is the general concern that minimum required capital will drop for slightly over 90 percent of commercial banks. Second is the total emphasis on credit risk; interest rate risk and liquidity risk are basically ignored. For example, the same capital is required for the 20-year obligation of a borrowing as for the 20-day obligation of the same borrower. Third, banks have found strategies—for example, selling mortgages and buying mortgage-backed securities—that reduce risk-weighted capital requirements without a seemingly significant reduction in overall risk. Finally, a few observers have noted that a bank with only long-term GNMA securities would have no risk-weighted capital requirements.

Reactions to these concerns have come on three fronts. First, regulatory bodies have mandated a required leverage ratio in addition to the risk-weighted

**TABLE 8-3   Summary of Risk Weights and Major Risk Categories for Proposed Risk-Adjusted Capital Requirements**

| Risk Category | Weight | General Description |
|---|---|---|
| On–balance sheet items | | |
| No risk | 0% | Vault cash and balances held with the central bank, domestic national government-guaranteed export loans, gold, and direct claims on the U.S. Treasury and U.S. government agencies. |
| Low risk | 20% | Cash items in the process of collection, short-term claims on U.S. depository institutions and foreign banks, general obligation municipal bonds or claims so guaranteed by U.S. government-sponsored agencies, all claims (including repurchase agreements) fully collateralized by 0% and 20% risk assets, and other low-credit-risk claims. |
| Moderate risk | 50% | One- to four-family residential mortgages, credit equivalents of foreign exchange and interest rate contracts, municipal revenue securities, and other securities in which the government is a shareholder or contributing member. |
| Standard risk | 100% | Long-term claims on U.S. depository institutions and foreign banks, securities issues by foreign governments, fixed assets and all other assets, such as assets typically found in bank loan portfolios. |
| Off–balance sheet items | | |
| | 0% | Unused portion of loan commitments with less than 1 year original maturity and any unconditionally cancellable loan for which a separate credit decision is made with each draw. |
| | 20% | Commercial letters of credit and other self-liquidating, trade-related contingencies. |
| | 50% | Transaction-related contingencies such as a letter of credit backing nonfinancial performance, unused loan commitments with greater than 1 year original maturity, and revolving underwriting facilities, note issuance facilities, etc. |
| | 100% | Direct credit substitutes, standby letters of credit, and assets sold with recourse. |

SOURCE: Summarized from regulators' requirements.

capital requirements. There is slight variation among regulatory bodies, but requirements seem to run from about 4 to 4.5 percent minimum tangible equity (equity minus intangible assets) or Tier I capital to total tangible assets. Second, as of mid-1983, banks with significant interest rate risk were forced to have capital above the minimum risk-weighted requirements. The Office of Thrift Supervision started experimenting with interest-rate-risk-related capital requirements in 1990, and commercial bank regulators followed suit. Third, in late 1991, Congress passed the Federal Deposit Insurance Corporation Improvement Act, which called for rigid regulatory capital requirements for banks starting in late 1992. Basically, commercial banks with (1) over 10 percent Tier

---

### TABLE 8-4    Risk-Based Capital—Types, Ratios, and Minimum Guidelines

---

A. **Eligible Capital**
 1. Core (Tier I)
   a. Common tangible equity
   b. Perpetual preferred stock and qualified, mandatory convertible debt up to 25%
   c. Minority interest in equity of consolidated subsidiaries
 2. Total (Tier II—limited to 100% of Tier I)
   a. Nonspecific loan loss reserve up to 1.25% of risk-adjusted assets (RAA)
   b. Perpetual preferred stock not included in Tier I
   c. Mandatory convertible debt not included in Tier I
   d. Long-term subordinated debt—limited to 50% of Tier I and a phased-out, straight-line basis in the last five years of life
   e. Limited-life preferred stock—included with and treated like long-term subordinated debt

B. **Risk-Based Capital Ratios**

$$\text{Tier I ratio} = \frac{\text{Core capital}}{\text{Risk-adjusted assets}}$$

$$\text{Tier II ratio} = \frac{\text{Total capital}}{\text{Risk-adjusted assets}}$$

C. **Minimum Guidelines Effective 12/31/92**

**Minimum Ratios**

| | |
|---|---|
| Tier I | 4.0% |
| Tier II | 8.0 |
| Shareholders' equity/RAA | 4.0 |

---

### TABLE 8-5    Comparison of Conventional versus Risk-Adjusted Capital Ratios

| Asset Category | Amount | Weight | Risk-weighted Amount |
|---|---|---|---|
| No risk | $ 10,000,000 | 0% | $          0 |
| Low risk | 30,000,000 | 20% | 6,000,000 |
| Moderate risk | 30,000,000 | 50% | 15,000,000 |
| Standard risk | 60,000,000 | 100% | 60,000,000 |
| Off–balance sheet items[a] | 20,000,000 | 100%[a] | 20,000,000 |
| Total assets[a] | $150,000,000 | | |
| Risk-weighted assets | | | $101,000,000 |

Assuming bank had $8,000,000 in primary capital:
   Primary capital to total assets: 8,000,000/150,000,000 = 5.33%
   Primary capital to risk-adjusted assets: 8,000,000/101,000,000 = 7.92%

[a] Off–balance sheet items are not part of the bank's total assets in the traditional capital-to-asset ratio calculation. It is assumed that the off–balance sheet items of this bank were in the 100% weighting category.

I and Tier II capital to risk-weighted assets, (2) over 6 percent Tier I capital to risk-weighted assets, and (3) over 5 percent equity capital to total assets would be classified as well capitalized and would need little if any regulatory permission for activities such as acquisitions, opening new branches, and so on. Banks with (1) under 4 percent Tier I and Tier II capital to risk-weighted assets, (2) under 2 percent Tier I capital to risk-weighted assets, or (3) under 2 percent equity capital to total assets would be classified as critically under-capitalized and would have 90 days to remedy their capital deficiency. If the capital deficiency is not remedied, according to law the bank must be closed. Banks falling between these two extremes will be subject to greater and greater regulatory scrutiny when these three capital ratios are lower. Table 8-6 illustrates the requirements for all five categories.

While the arbitrariness of these capital ratios worries some observers, it seems useful to point out that fewer than 100 banks were in the lowest capital category when the act was first applied in December 1992. Furthermore, Figure

**TABLE 8-6   Bank Classifications According to Capital Ratios under Prompt Corrective Action (FDIC Improvement Act of 1991)**

| Category | Risk-Based Tiers I and II | Capital Tier I | Leverage Tier I/ Assets |
|---|---|---|---|
| 1. Well capitalized: Significantly exceeds required capital standards. *Restrictions:* None. | >10% | >6% | >5% |
| 2. Adequately capitalized: Meets minimum standards. *Restrictions:* Cannot underwrite insurance where state law permits. Requires approval of FDIC to accept brokered funds. | >8% | >4% | >4% |
| 3. Undercapitalized: Fails to meet minimum standards. *Restrictions:* As in 2 above and close monitoring by regulatory agency; capital restoration plan; asset growth restricted; needs approval for acquisitions, branching, new activities. | <8% | <4% | <4% |
| 4. Significantly undercapitalized: Significantly below required minimum standard. *Restrictions:* As in 3 above and must sell new stock to recapitalize; restrictions on transactions with affiliates, as well as on interest paid on deposits and management compensation; must divest troubled affiliates. | <6% | <3% | <3% |
| 5. Critically undercapitalized: Less than 2% leverage capital ratio. *Restrictions:* As in 4 above and prohibition of interest payments on subordinated debt. Placed in receivership or conservatorship within 90 days. | | | <2% |

**FIGURE 8-1   Aggregate Capitalization Increases**

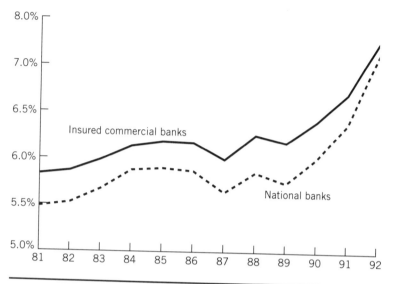

(From *Call Reports.*)

8-1 shows that equity capital has risen relative to total assets throughout the 1980s and early 1990s. Slower asset growth relative to retained earnings has been a major cause of this trend.

## SUSTAINABLE INTERNAL GROWTH

If retained earnings (assuming a reasonable dividend payout, discussed in the next chapter) are sufficient to fill the bank's needs, they are usually the best form of bank equity capital to use. A general rule is that if a bank can finance all of its capital needs internally without hurting its owners or its stock price, it should do so. Retained earnings are not a free source of capital (the cost of retained earnings includes the higher value of cash dividends received today versus those received in future years and possibly a lower stock price because of lower cash dividends); however, they are generally less costly than selling new issues of common equity stock and are subject to direct management control.

The three variables that combine to determine how much of a bank's growth can be sustained through the retention of earnings are (1) the amount of capital the bank and its regulators determine to be adequate, (2) the earnings the bank is able to generate, and (3) the proportion of these earnings that is retained in the bank.

**TABLE 8-7    The Effects of Required Capital Levels of Internally Financed Growth
(dollars in millions)**

| | | | |
|---|---|---|---|
| *Example 1* | | | |
| Start of year for bank with 7% capital-to-assets requirement: | | | |
| Assets    100 | Deposits and borrowings | | 93 |
| | Capital (7%) | | 7 |
| End of year, same capital requirement, $1 retained earnings: | | | |
| Assets    114.3 | Deposits and borrowings | | 106.3 |
| | Capital (7%) | | 8 |
| *Example 2* | | | |
| Start of year for bank with 6% capital-to-assets requirement: | | | |
| Assets    100 | Deposits and borrowings | | 94 |
| | Capital (6%) | | 6 |
| End of year, same capital requirement, $1 retained earnings: | | | |
| Assets    116.7 | Deposits and borrowings | | 109.7 |
| | Capital (6%) | | 7 |
| *Example 3* | | | |
| Start of year for bank with 7% capital-to-assets requirement: | | | |
| Assets    100 | Deposits and borrowings | | 93 |
| | Capital (7%) | | 7 |
| End of year, required capital falls to 6%, $1 retained earnings: | | | |
| Assets    133.3 | Deposits and borrowings | | 125.3 |
| | Capital (6%) | | 8 |

The relationship between the proportion of capital that is deemed to be adequate and how much growth can be financed internally is illustrated in Table 8-7. Retained earnings of $1 million would finance asset growth of $14.3 million if the bank determined that its present 7 percent capital-to-assets requirement was appropriate (see Example I in Table 8-7). The same $1 million would support $16.7 million in asset growth if its capital-to-assets requirement was maintained at 6 percent (Example 2). The lower the capital requirement, the larger the amount of growth a given amount of retained earnings would finance. If the capital-to-asset requirement fell from 7 to 6 percent during the year, $1 million of retained earnings would still finance $16.7 million of asset growth, but an additional $16.7 million of asset growth would be supported by the decline in the capital requirement (Example 3). An increase in the capital required would, of course, reduce the total internally financed asset growth.

The second variable, the earnings a bank is able to generate, should have a direct effect on how much growth the bank is able to finance internally. If the bank used in Example 1 of Table 8-7 was able to earn enough to retain $1.1 million instead of $1 million during the year, the growth financed internally would be proportionately 10 percent, or $1.43 million, greater.

The third variable, the proportion of a bank's earnings that is retained, has a similar direct effect on how much growth the bank is able to finance internally. Assume that the bank in Table 8-7 had earned $1.5 million and paid cash dividends of $0.5 million. Reducing the dividend payout so that cash dividends would fall to $0.4 million would increase retained earnings to $1.1 million, and the growth financed internally would be proportionately greater.

Table 8-8 applies the formulas for calculating sustainable growth to an example bank situation. Equation (c) is the most common formula for calculat-

---

**TABLE 8-8   Calculating a Bank's Capacity for Asset Growth**

**Bank Situation**

| | |
|---|---|
| Average total assets | $500,000,000 |
| Average equity capital | 34,000,000 |
| Expected net profit margin | 8.50% |
| Expected yield on average total assets | 12.00% |
| Expected return on average total assets | 1.02% |
| Leverage multiplier | 14.71× |
| Expected return on average equity capital | 15.00% |
| Cash dividend payout percentage | 40.00% |

1. *The annual growth rate in assets that can be supported by internally generated equity capital* is called the sustainable growth rate. This rate can be determined by any one of the following four equations:

(a)   $$SG = \frac{(PM)(AY)(1 - D)}{EC/TA - (PM)(AY)(1 - D)}$$

(b)   $$SG = \frac{(PM)(AY)(LM)(1 - D)}{1 - (PM)(AY)(LM)(1 - D)}$$

(c)   $$SG = \frac{(ROA)(1 - D)}{EC/TA - (ROA)(1 - D)}$$

(d)   $$SG = \frac{(ROE)(1 - D)}{1 - (ROE)(1 - D)}$$

where

$SG$ = sustainable growth rate, or the annual rate of increase in average total assets that can be supported by internally generated equity capital

$PM$ = profit margin, or net income after taxes divided by total operating income

$AY$ = asset yield, or total operating income divided by average total assets

$D$ = percentage of after-tax net income paid in cash dividends

$EC$ = average equity capital

$TA$ = average total assets

$LM$ = leverage multiplier, or average total assets divided by average equity capital

**TABLE 8-8**    *(continued)*

ROA = return on average total assets, or net income after taxes divided by average total assets
ROE = return on average equity capital, or net income after taxes divided by average equity
   capital

Solving Equation (c):

$$SG = \frac{(.0102)(1 - .40)}{.068 - (.0102)(1 - .40)}$$

   = 9.89 percent

**Proof (dollars in thousands)**

| | |
|---|---:|
| Average total assets, next year | $500,000 |
| | × 1.0989 |
| | $549,450 |
| Required average equity capital | $549,450 |
| | × .068 |
| | $ 37,363 |
| Required increase in average equity capital | $37,363 − $ 34,000 |
| | = $  3,363 |
| Projected net income after taxes | $549,450 |
| | × .0102 |
| | $   5,604 |
| Retained earnings | $   5,604 |
| | × .60 |
| | $   3,363 |

2. *The ROA should support the expected annual growth rate of average total assets.* If the expected annual growth rate of average total assets is 12 percent for this bank, the ROA required to support that growth is

$$ROA = \frac{(EC/TA)(SG)}{(1 + SG)(1 - D)}$$

$$= \frac{(.068)(.12)}{(1.12)(1 - .40)}$$

   = 1.21 percent

3. *The cash dividend payout percentage should support the expected annual growth rate of average total assets.* For this bank, with a desired ratio of equity capital to total assets of 6.8 percent, an expected ROA of 1.02 percent, and a 12 percent expected annual growth rate of average total assets, the cash dividend payout percentage is

$$D = 1 - \left[ \frac{(EC/TA)(SG)}{(ROA)(1 + SG)} \right]$$

**TABLE 8-8**  *(continued)*

$$= 1 - \left[ \frac{(.068)(.12)}{(.0102)(1.12)} \right]$$

$$= 28.57 \text{ percent}$$

4. *The equity capital ratio (EC/TA) should sustain the expected annual growth rate of average total assets.* To sustain an annual growth rate of 12 percent in average total assets, with an ROA of 1.02 percent and a cash dividend payout of 40 percent, the bank's equity capital ratio will decline to

$$\text{EC/TA} = \frac{(\text{ROA})(1 - D)}{\text{SG}} + (\text{ROA})(1 - D)$$

$$= \frac{(.0102)(1 - .40)}{.12} + (.0102)(1 - .40)$$

$$= 5.71 \text{ percent}$$

ing sustainable growth. For the example bank, Equation (c) shows that its assets could grow 9.89 percent before its capital-to-assets ratio of 6.8 percent (a leverage multiplier of 14.71 times) would decline. The formulas can also be applied to solve for the required ROA to support a target annual asset growth rate or to calculate the cash dividend payout that will support a target annual asset growth. The example bank in Table 8-8 needed an ROA of 1.21 percent to support asset growth of 12 percent with a 6.8 percent equity capital ratio (equity capital to total assets) and a 40 percent payout. With an ROA of 1 percent and a 12 percent target asset growth rate, the example bank could pay out 28.57 percent of earnings without hurting its 6.8 percent equity capital ratio.

Finally, Equation (c) can be solved for the equity capital ratio that will result from a capital asset growth rate, an expected ROA, and a planned dividend payout ratio. In Table 8-8 the example bank's equity capital ratio would decline to 5.71 percent if the bank had an annual asset growth rate of 12 percent, an ROA of 1.02 percent, and a cash dividend payout of 40 percent.

A bank's target or planned growth can be compared with its internally supported growth resulting from its earnings, dividend payout, and capital requirements. Returns required for sustainable growth were generated for 7 and 6 percent capital-to-asset ratios in Table 8-9. For target capital to assets of 7 percent, if a bank earned 0.83 on its assets and paid out 60 percent of these earnings as dividends, it could sustain asset growth of 5 percent internally. Earnings of 0.85 percent on assets and a 25 percent payout would sustain growth of 10 percent. For a capital target of 6 percent, earnings of 0.84 on assets and a dividend payout of 35 percent would sustain growth of 10 percent.

**TABLE 8-9** **Return on Assets Required for Sustainable Growth Rates without External Financing**

| *Example 1: Target Leverage (Growth %) of 14.28 × or 7.00%* | | | | | | |
|---|---|---|---|---|---|---|
| **Dividend Payout %** | **5.00** | **7.50** | **10.00** | **12.50** | **15.00** | **17.50** | **20.00** |
| 5.00 | 0.35 | 0.51 | 0.67 | 0.82 | 0.96 | 1.10 | 1.23 |
| 10.00 | 0.37 | 0.54 | 0.71 | 0.86 | 1.01 | 1.16 | 1.30 |
| 15.00 | 0.39 | 0.57 | 0.75 | 0.92 | 1.07 | 1.23 | 1.37 |
| 20.00 | 0.42 | 0.61 | 0.80 | 0.97 | 1.14 | 1.30 | 1.46 |
| 25.00 | 0.44 | 0.65 | 0.85 | 1.04 | 1.22 | 1.39 | 1.56 |
| 30.00 | 0.48 | 0.70 | 0.91 | 1.11 | 1.30 | 1.49 | 1.67 |
| 35.00 | 0.51 | 0.75 | 0.98 | 1.20 | 1.41 | 1.60 | 1.79 |
| 40.00 | 0.56 | 0.81 | 1.06 | 1.30 | 1.52 | 1.74 | 1.94 |
| 45.00 | 0.61 | 0.89 | 1.16 | 1.41 | 1.66 | 1.90 | 2.12 |
| 50.00 | 0.67 | 0.98 | 1.27 | 1.56 | 1.83 | 2.09 | 2.33 |
| 55.00 | 0.74 | 1.09 | 1.41 | 1.73 | 2.03 | 2.32 | 2.59 |
| 60.00 | 0.83 | 1.22 | 1.59 | 1.95 | 2.28 | 2.61 | 2.92 |
| 65.00 | 0.95 | 1.40 | 1.82 | 2.22 | 2.61 | 2.98 | 3.33 |
| 70.00 | 1.11 | 1.63 | 2.12 | 2.59 | 3.04 | 3.48 | 3.89 |
| 75.00 | 1.33 | 1.95 | 2.55 | 3.11 | 3.65 | 4.17 | 4.67 |
| 80.00 | 1.67 | 2.44 | 3.18 | 3.89 | 4.57 | 5.21 | 5.83 |
| 85.00 | 2.22 | 3.26 | 4.24 | 5.19 | 6.09 | 6.95 | 7.78 |
| 90.00 | 3.33 | 4.89 | 6.37 | 7.78 | 9.13 | 10.43 | 11.67 |
| 95.00 | 6.67 | 9.77 | 12.73 | 15.56 | 18.27 | 20.86 | 23.33 |

| *Example 2: Target Leverage (Growth %) of 16.67 × or 6.00%* | | | | | | |
|---|---|---|---|---|---|---|
| **Dividend Payout %** | **5.00** | **7.50** | **10.00** | **12.50** | **15.00** | **17.50** | **20.00** |
| 5.00 | 0.30 | 0.44 | 0.57 | 0.70 | 0.82 | 0.94 | 1.05 |
| 10.00 | 0.32 | 0.47 | 0.61 | 0.74 | 0.87 | 0.99 | 1.11 |
| 15.00 | 0.34 | 0.49 | 0.64 | 0.78 | 0.92 | 1.05 | 1.18 |
| 20.00 | 0.36 | 0.52 | 0.68 | 0.83 | 0.98 | 1.12 | 1.25 |
| 25.00 | 0.38 | 0.56 | 0.73 | 0.89 | 1.14 | 1.19 | 1.33 |
| 30.00 | 0.41 | 0.60 | 0.78 | 0.95 | 1.12 | 1.28 | 1.43 |
| 35.00 | 0.44 | 0.64 | 0.84 | 1.03 | 1.20 | 1.37 | 1.54 |
| 40.00 | 0.48 | 0.70 | 0.91 | 1.11 | 1.30 | 1.49 | 1.67 |
| 45.00 | 0.52 | 0.76 | 0.99 | 1.21 | 1.42 | 1.62 | 1.82 |
| 50.00 | 0.57 | 0.84 | 1.09 | 1.33 | 1.56 | 1.79 | 2.00 |
| 55.00 | 0.63 | 0.93 | 1.21 | 1.48 | 1.74 | 1.99 | 2.22 |
| 60.00 | 0.71 | 1.05 | 1.36 | 1.67 | 1.96 | 2.23 | 2.50 |
| 65.00 | 0.82 | 1.20 | 1.56 | 1.90 | 2.24 | 2.55 | 2.86 |
| 70.00 | 0.95 | 1.40 | 1.82 | 2.22 | 2.61 | 2.98 | 3.33 |
| 75.00 | 1.14 | 1.67 | 2.18 | 2.67 | 3.13 | 3.57 | 4.00 |
| 80.00 | 1.43 | 2.09 | 2.73 | 3.33 | 3.91 | 4.47 | 5.00 |
| 85.00 | 1.90 | 2.79 | 3.64 | 4.44 | 5.22 | 5.96 | 6.67 |
| 90.00 | 2.86 | 4.19 | 5.45 | 6.67 | 7.82 | 8.93 | 10.00 |
| 95.00 | 5.71 | 8.37 | 10.91 | 13.33 | 15.65 | 17.87 | 20.00 |

**TABLE 8-10  Average Sustainable Growth Rate for All Insured U.S. Commercial Banks**

| Ratios | 1980 | 1981 | 1982 | 1983 | 1984 | 1985 | 1986 | 1987 | 1988 | 1989 | 1990 | 1991 | 1992 |
|---|---|---|---|---|---|---|---|---|---|---|---|---|---|
| Leverage ratio[a] | 17.11× | 17.02× | 16.97× | 16.76× | 16.28× | 16.12× | 16.15× | 16.56× | 15.93× | 16.10× | 15.48× | 14.77× | 13.91× |
| Return on assets | 0.80% | 0.77% | 0.71% | 0.67% | 0.64% | 0.70% | 0.61% | 0.12% | 0.82% | 0.49% | 0.49% | 0.56% | .96% |
| Earnings retention rate | 64% | 61% | 56% | 51% | 52% | 53% | 57% | neg.[b] | 60% | 16% | 14% | 23% | .63% |
| Sustainable growth rate | 8.76% | 7.99% | 6.75% | 5.73% | 5.33% | 5.72% | 5.60% | n.a.[b] | 6.32% | 1.28% | 1.07% | 1.94% | 8.80% |

[a] Asset divided by equity capital.

[b] Banks were required to make massive changes to earnings for reserves for loan losses on loans to less-developed countries in 1987. Most banks maintained their dividends, so the dividend payout was over 100% in 1987.

SOURCE: Authors' calculation based on data from *Statistics on Banking* and *Quarterly Banking Profile* (Washington, D.C.: FDIC, various years 1979–1993).

Rapidly growing commercial banks with capital needs clearly exceeding the amount of earnings that can be retained face a complex policy decision. If the bank's management believes that dividends will not significantly affect the market price of the bank's stock, the preferable policy is to pay a modest cash dividend and use typically low-cost retained earnings to finance as much of the expansion as possible. On the other hand, if management believes that dividends will have an *appreciably* positive effect on the bank's stock price, the bank may gain from paying higher dividends and raising more of its needed equity capital by selling higher-priced common stock.

Table 8-10 shows the sustainable growth rate in assets for all insured commercial banks from 1978 to 1992. The leverage ratio, which is the inverse of the capital ratio, remained stable throughout the period. The return on assets exhibited a downward trend through the early and mid-1980s, while the earnings retention rate (1 minus the dividend payout rate) declined continuously from 1978 through 1983 and then began to increase slowly. The overall result of the three preceding variables was a general downward trend in the sustainable growth rate from above 9 percent in 1979 to under 6 percent through the mid-1980s. After even lower sustainable growth rates in the later 1980s, and through 1991, the sustainable growth rate climbed to 8.80 percent in 1992.

## Discussion Questions

1. What are the key ingredients a bank might use in deciding how much capital it needs?
2. Describe how a bank would determine its capital needs from its overall financial plan.
3. What are the purposes of capital for a bank? Are these purposes different from the purposes of equity capital for a nonfinancial corporation?
4. What factors led U.S. regulators to propose and adopt risk-weighted asset capital requirements?
5. Describe the risk-weighted asset capital requirements currently in effect in the United States.
6. What are the additional capital requirements for commercial banks in the United States? Why were these requirements added?
7. What are the current capital adequacy standards for the Comptroller, Federal Reserve, and FDIC?
8. What are the three variables that determine the growth a bank can sustain internally? Show how these variables interrelate to establish a bank's sustainable growth.

# 9

# Capital Acquisition and Management

The preceding chapter discussed the capital planning process, the determination of capital adequacy, and the factors affecting the internal generation of capital. This chapter examines the potential external forms of raising capital and some techniques for choosing among these forms. The chapter closes with an examination of three methods for improving the utilization of capital—allocating capital by lines of business, calculating return on allocated capital, and determining the appropriate dividend policy.

## CHOOSING BETWEEN EXTERNAL EQUITY AND SENIOR CAPITAL

When a bank finds that it may need additional external capital, it must decide whether all of its capital should be common equity capital or whether senior securities (subordinated debt or preferred stock) should be used to fill some of its capital needs. Table 9-1 describes the principal forms for raising capital needs externally, and Figure 9-1 illustrates the amounts raised in the 1980s.

The Comptroller and the Federal Reserve appear to have conceded that, in spite of their objections to capital notes and long-term debentures, the availability of these forms adds needed flexibility to bank management. And although these regulators do not encourage the use of notes and debentures, they do accept such issues. First, such debt instruments add to the basic regulatory purpose of bank capital by providing additional protection for bank depositors and others who would be adversely affected by bank failure. Second, there are some market situations in which a bank cannot sell new common

**TABLE 9-1  Types of Capital That Banks May Issue**

| Type | Description |
|------|-------------|
| Capital notes | Usually smaller-denomination subordinated debt at fixed rate(s) with original maturities of 7 to 15 years. Can be sold to bank customers (retail capital notes). |
| Capital debentures | Generally larger (in denomination and total size) subordinated debt at fixed rates and with original maturity of over 15 years. A few issues have no interest payment and are sold at a deep discount. |
| Convertible debt | Subordinated debt that is usually convertible at the option of the debt holder into common stock of the bank at a predetermined price. Interest is usually 10 to 20% below the rate on straight debt; conversion price is 15 to 25% above stock market prices. A few convertible issues have mandatory conversion. |
| Variable-rate debt | Subordinated debt on which the interest rate varies with some interest-rate index. |
| Option-rate debt | Subordinated debt initially issued as variable-rate debt but convertible into fixed-rate debt at the option of the debt holder during at least some period of the life of the debt. |
| Leasing arrangements | Financial lease, sale, leasebacks, etc., most of which are capitalized and some of which qualify as capital in a manner similar to debt capital. |
| Preferred stock | Stock paying a fixed-rate (nondeductible for corporate income tax) dividend, with a claim on income and assets ahead of common stock. |
| Adjustable-rate preferred stock | Similar to preferred stock, but dividends have no fixed rate. Instead, dividends are adjusted according to some agreed-upon indicator. Includes preferreds with dividends repriced at some percent or basis difference from other yield indices, repriced every seven weeks through a dutch auction mechanism, or repriced based on some measure or facet of bank performance. |
| Convertible preferred stock | Preferred stock that is convertible at the option of the holder into common stock of the bank at a predetermined price. Issued at a lower rate and a higher conversion price than straight issues. Used for some acquisitions and mergers. |
| Common stock | Residual but unlimited claim on income and assets of bank; voting shares that elect board of directors who appoint management. Common stock may be issued; however, some new shares are sold through dividend reinvestment plans, employee stock option plans (ESOPs), and employee stock option trusts (ESOTs). |

**FIGURE 9-1    Capital Issuance by Security Type—Overview: Total Volume Issued from 1980 to 1990, Banks and Bank Holding Companies**

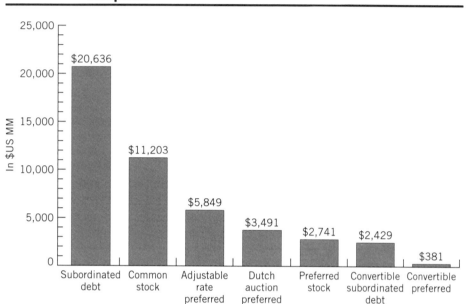

equity because there are no potential buyers or situations in which existing bank stockholders would be severely penalized (generally because the common stock price is significantly below the book value) if regulators were to insist on an injection of new common equity funds.

Noncallable preferred stock and mandatory convertible debt are now accepted as Tier I capital by three federal regulatory authorities under the new risk-weighted capital rules. (The other forms of senior capital in Table 9-1 and Figure 9-1 are Tier II capital.) The restraints against using preferred stock generally come from bank management, which notes that dividends on preferred stock are not tax deductible, as is interest on indebtedness. As a result, financial leverage is usually more favorable for debt issues than for preferred stock issues. Nevertheless, preferred stock should be considered if (1) the bank does not pay income taxes; (2) the bank cannot sell either debt or common stock at anything close to what it believes are reasonable prices; and (3) preferred stock rates, which can be fixed or variable, are now low because of the 70 percent corporate tax exclusion on dividends.

A bank should evaluate three factors when deciding whether all capital should be equity capital: (1) the availability of the various forms of external capital, (2) the need for flexibility in issuing capital in future years, and (3) the financial effects of the various forms of capital, such as leverage, immediate dilution, and earnings per share over longer periods.

The first two factors are dependent upon the size of the bank. Most community banks will find that long-term debentures and preferred stock are not available to them because such securities are attractive only to institutional investors, which would not purchase these types of securities from banks that have less than $100 million in total assets. A market for some forms of senior capital—small-denomination capital notes, convertible debentures, and debt placed directly with a correspondent bank—is available to many community banks, however.

Some community banks have been successful in selling a moderate amount of capital notes in denominations as low as $500 to depositors or friends of the bank at a rate of interest somewhat higher than they pay on long-term savings certificates but below the general market rate for other debt securities. This approach can be an attractive method of raising some additional capital. Although the buyer's investment is difficult to justify in economic terms (except perhaps that earnings are more than those on savings certificates), experience has shown that buyers can sometimes be found. Even so, it is unlikely that the typical community bank can rely on its ability to sell notes whenever it chooses, and meeting maturities on notes already sold could increase the bank's need for common equity at some future date.

The option to sell convertible debentures is also available to some community banks. These debentures are typically sold locally in small denominations to the bank's friends, customers, and stockholders—the same group that would also buy additional common stock in the bank. In addition, direct placement of senior debt with a correspondent bank appears to be an effective and relatively reliable channel for community banks. Bank regulatory authorities have criticized this source, however, because it simply circulates funds within the banking system and fails to add capital strength to the system.

As a bank becomes larger, a separate market develops for its senior securities. There are institutional investors who would not buy common stock from banks but who would consider the bank's capital notes or debentures as an investment. A market for the preferred stock of large banks has also developed among certain corporate institutional investors because of the 70 percent corporate tax exclusion. Senior securities of banks compete in the marketplace with similar securities of other companies. Through security analysis, these securities are appraised as to quality and value. Since the market associates size with marketability, and possibly with quality, the larger the bank, the better the market for its senior securities. A larger bank, therefore, generally has the option of issuing senior securities. Any bank considering this option should evaluate the financial effects of the various forms of capital. Even if senior capital is financially favorable, it is generally not wise to borrow up to the regulatory limit in order to preserve financial flexibility in the future.

The availability of new common equity capital at anything like a reasonable price varies widely among banks. Sufficient amounts of reasonably priced common stock are available to most community banks located in small and medium-sized cities and towns. In such situations, ownership of shares in a local bank is often a source of pride and marks a contribution to the local community. Problems such as maintaining control, ensuring widespread ownership, and moderating of the desire to be on the bank's board of directors seem more common than finding willing buyers for new stock issues.

Large money market centers and regional banks face different problems. They must compete in an impersonal national market for common equities. A bank may find its common stock selling at a low price, either because the entire stock market is depressed or because the market is pessimistic about banks in general.

The availability of new common equity capital may be most limited for small and medium-sized banks in larger cities. These banks do not have the national markets of the larger banks or the community interest and prestige of banks located in smaller communities. Even in the best of times, such banks must work to develop a market for their stock, and there are times when such banks cannot sell common stock.

The need for flexibility in issuing capital in future years may further restrict the use of available senior capital. New equity capital may not be available at a reasonable price, or senior capital may produce more favorable financial results for a bank, or both. While most bank capital should be common equity, external capital does not have to be restricted to equity capital.

## FINANCIAL EFFECTS OF SENIOR CAPITAL

There are two potential financial advantages of senior capital over common stock as a source of capital. First, the issuance of senior capital results in lower immediate dilution of earnings per common share, unless the financing cost exceeds the amount the bank is earning on shareholders' equity. Second, in the long run, senior capital usually increases the earnings per share on common stock because it usually introduces favorable financial leverage, which means that the returns earned on these funds exceed their fixed costs.

For example, assume that the bank in Table 9-2 earns 1.0 percent before taxes on total assets and has a tax rate of 34 percent. Having grown rapidly, the bank now has $500 million in assets but only $30 million in capital funds. The bank examiners suggest that the bank is at the regulatory minimum and that it should raise $5 million in additional capital. The present capitalization consists of 1 million shares of $10 par-value stock and $20 million in surplus, undivided profits, and reserves. Assume further that the bank has three alternative methods of raising the additional capital: (1) selling 166,667 shares of common stock at $30 a share (approximately nine times earnings); (2) selling $5 million of preferred stock with an 8 percent dividend rate; and (3) selling $5 million of subordinated debentures with a 10 percent coupon. Immediately after any of the financing alternatives, the bank will have assets of $505 million and capital of $35 million.

The first section of Table 9-2 illustrates the immediate dilution of earnings per share under the three alternatives. Debt and preferred stock cause less dilution than common stock, and the dilution of earnings per share is higher

**TABLE 9-2   Earnings Results for Alternative Methods of Raising Capital**

| | Present Capital | Additional Capital Financed with Common Stock (at $30 per Share) | Additional Capital Financed with 8% Preferred Stock | Additional Capital Financed with 10% Subordinated Debentures |
|---|---|---|---|---|
| **Earnings on Existing Assets** | | | | |
| Earnings on assets (1.0%) | $5,000,000 | $5,050,000 | $5,050,000 | $5,050,000 |
| Less: Interest | 0 | 0 | 0 | 500,000 |
| Net income before tax | $5,000,000 | $5,050,000 | $5,050,000 | $4,550,000 |
| Less: Taxes (at 34% rate) | 1,700,000 | 1,717,000 | 1,717,000 | 1,547,000 |
| Net income after tax | $3,300,000 | $3,333,000 | $3,333,000 | $3,003,000 |
| Less: Preferred dividends | 0 | 0 | 400,000 | 0 |
| Net for common stock | $3,300,000 | $3,333,000 | $2,933,000 | $3,003,000 |
| Divided by: Number of shares | 1,000,000 | 1,166,667 | 1,000,000 | 1,000,000 |
| Earnings per share | $3.30 | $2.86 | $2.93 | $3.00 |
| **Earnings on Increased Assets** | | | | |
| Earnings on assets (1.0%) | $5,750,000 | $5,800,000 | $5,800,000 | $5,800,000 |
| Less: Interest | 0 | 0 | 0 | 500,000 |
| Net income before tax | $5,750,000 | $5,800,000 | $5,800,000 | $5,300,000 |
| Less: Taxes (at 34% rate) | 1,955,000 | 1,972,000 | 1,972,000 | 1,802,000 |
| Net income after tax | $3,795,000 | $3,828,000 | $3,828,000 | $3,498,000 |
| Less: Preferred dividends | 0 | 0 | 400,000 | 0 |
| Net for common stock | $3,795,000 | $3,828,000 | $3,428,000 | $3,498,000 |
| Divided by: Number of shares | 1,000,000 | 1,166,667 | 1,000,000 | 1,000,000 |
| Earnings per share | $3.80 | $3.28 | $3.43 | $3.50 |

for preferred stock than for debt because the 8 percent preferred dividend is not a tax-deductible expense. There is favorable financial leverage from using both the preferred stock and the debt, but the financial leverage is more favorable with the tax-deductible interest.

The second section of Table 9-2 illustrates what would happen if the bank's assets increased by an additional $75 million over time. Note that the new capital has assisted in financing new assets that contribute to higher earnings. For example, earnings per common share would be $3.28 if the additional capital had been raised by the issuance of common stock and $3.50 and $3.43 if the additional capital had been raised by the issuance of 10 percent debentures or 8 percent preferred stock, respectively. This example portrays favorable financial leverage. The highest earnings per share, of course, would

**TABLE 9-3    Effect of Changing an Important Variable of Earnings per Common Share**

| Variable Changes from Table 9-2[a] | Additional Capital Financed with Common Stock | Additional Capital Financed with Preferred Stock | Additional Capital Financed with Subordinated Debentures |
|---|---|---|---|
| 1. No change | $3.28 | $3.43 | $3.50 |
| 2. Earnings on assets rise to 1.5% before taxes | $4.92 | $5.34 | $5.41 |
| 3. Earnings on assets fall to 0.5% before taxes | $1.64 | $1.51 | $1.58 |
| 4. Cost of debt falls to 6%; preferred to 4% | $3.28 | $3.63 | $3.63 |
| 5. Cost of debt rises to 14%; preferred to 12% | $3.28 | $3.23 | $3.37 |
| 6. Tax rate is 50% | $2.49 | $2.50 | $2.65 |
| 7. Tax rate is 0% | $4.97 | $5.40 | $5.30 |
| 8. Senior capital (when used) was $10 million rather than $5 million[b] | $3.28 | $3.79 | $3.96 |

[a]The specific variable mentioned is the only one allowed to change. All other variables were left the same as in Table 9-2 (assuming that additional capital was raised by one of the three methods and that assets have increased an additional $75 million). Taxes were left at an average rate of 34%.

[b]When senior capital was used, the equity account was reduced from $30 million to $25 million (800,000 shares). Regulators probably would not accept this much senior capital, but the relatively large amount illustrates the effects more clearly. All other variables were left the same as in Table 9-2.

result if no additional capital were raised; however, the bank was seeking a more adequate capital position.

The conclusions that can be derived from Table 9-2 rest primarily on four important variables: (1) the amount the bank can earn on its total capital (or assets with a given proportion of capital) before income taxes, (2) the fixed cost of the senior capital, (3) the effective income tax rate, and (4) the proportion of total capital that is senior capital. Table 9-3 shows the effect on the earnings per common share from Table 9-2 when any one of these variables is changed after the additional capital has been raised and assets have increased by an additional $75 million.

Alternative 1 in Table 9-3 shows the earnings per share as they appeared under the assumptions for the second section of Table 9-2. Alternative 2 shows that when earnings on assets rise, the positive effect of financial leverage, given the same fixed cost for the preferred stock or debt, is even greater. On the other hand, when the return on assets falls, the leverage becomes less favorable—that is, earnings per share were higher when common stock was used—as shown in Alternative 3. Taken together, Alternatives 2 and 3 demonstrate the greater variability of earnings per share when more financial leverage is used.

Alternative 4 shows that if the dividend or interest cost for preferred stock or debt is lower, the earnings per common share are greater. In Alternative 5, higher dividends or interest costs for preferred stock or debt results in lower earnings per common share. In Alternative 5, the increase of 4 percent in the preferred dividend and interest cost means that the leverage from using preferred stock was unfavorable, while the leverage from using debt was much less favorable with the higher interest cost.[1]

Alternatives 6 and 7 examine the impact of different income tax rates. The higher income tax rate in Alternative 6 hurts returns no matter what form of capital is used; however, the pain is less for debentures on which interest is a tax-deductible expense. For Alternative 7, in which there was no corporate income tax, the preferred stock provides more favorable leverage because tax deductibility of interest does not help the debentures. Finally, Alternative 8 shows that greater use of senior capital results in higher earnings per share when financial leverage is favorable. Earnings per share is more volatile, and negative financial leverage is always a possibility when more senior capital is used.

Bank debt instruments, even if not currently required for capital, may also have several advantages over long-term deposits as a source of funds. First, if they meet certain requirements, debt instruments are not subject to reserve requirements. Second, because these instruments have fixed maturities, there is less need for liquidity reserves, and most of the proceeds can be invested in longer-term, higher-yielding assets. Third, the handling and placing costs associated with debt instruments may be lower than the cost of acquiring additional time deposits. Finally, the funds acquired through debt instruments are not subject to the deposit insurance costs of the FDIC.

Balancing the advantages and disadvantages to determine the appropriate amount of senior capital is a difficult task. Small to moderate-sized banks need some financial flexibility. They are generally advised to meet all their capital needs with equity and to issue senior capital only when their capital needs exceed expectations or when the market for their stock is unusually poor. The primary sources, when small or medium-sized banks do decide to issue senior capital, will probably be principal correspondent banks or the banks' existing customers.

Most larger banks should seriously consider the use of some senior capital to meet part of their capital needs. In addition to the advantages of favorable financial leverage, senior capital does not reduce ownership control if current shareholders are unwilling or unable to invest in new common stock. Many larger commercial banks and their holding companies are subject to the 34

---

[1]These results make the naive assumption that the price of the common stock remains the same. The market price of common stock would tend to be higher (meaning fewer shares sold to raise the same amount of capital) when interest rates are lower, and the price of common stock would tend to be lower (more shares for the same amount) when interest rates are higher.

percent corporate income tax and should use subordinated debentures as their source of senior capital.[2]

The amount to be used will depend partially on the current and expected cost of such debentures in relation to the bank's pretax return on its entire capital base. In theory, banks should use senior capital up to the point where the market value of the common shareholders' investment is maximized. The advantages, such as higher earnings per common share, will be weighed against the higher risks, greater variability of earnings, and higher probability of bankruptcy. One rule of thumb is that a bank should use debt within reasonable limits as long as its earnings on total senior and equity capital exceed the current cost of debt by approximately 50 percent or more. Bank managers should limit indebtedness to between one-half and three-fourths of the maximum amount acceptable to regulatory authorities in order to assure themselves of some financial flexibility. The limit should be broad and flexible because of the economies of issuing debt in large blocks.

## NEWER FORMS OF SENIOR CAPITAL

In the 1980s and early 1990s, there was tremendous expansion in the forms of securities issued by corporations (e.g., in 1985 alone, there were over 40 new forms of securities issued by corporations). Bank regulators have closely scrutinized many of these newer forms; however, banks and bank holding companies have found some forms that regulators find acceptable as part of bank capital. Convertible securities and some of the newer forms are evaluated here.

Table 9-4 summarizes the characteristics of 84 bank convertible debt issues from 1969 to 1988. Section 1 shows that over one-half of the 84 issues had an original maturity of 25 years, while 13 others had an original maturity of 10 years or less. Section 2 indicates that the estimated premium (the percentage by which the conversion price exceeds the common stock price at the offering time) ranged between 15 and 20 percent. Nearly 90 percent of the issues had premiums between 10 and 25 percent. Section 3 demonstrates that the interest cost to the bank of a convertible issue was lower than the estimated interest cost of a similar but nonconvertible issue. In cost terms, nearly 70 percent of the issues cost between 100 and 200 basis points (a basis point is .01 percent in cost terms) less than the estimated interest cost of a straight

---

[2]Because preferred dividends must be paid from net earnings after taxes, and because interest on debt capital is normally deductible from earnings before taxes, preferred stock will be attractive only to banks that have a low effective income tax rate or that pay no income taxes. The earnings per share figures in Table 9-3 show that preferred stock produces the same after-tax earnings as similar-cost debt in the no-tax situation. Preferred stock might be attractive in such a situation because of its lower priority and generally smaller charges (because repayment or sinking funds are not usually required). In low-tax situations, interest payments on debt capital may not be deductible from earnings before taxes if the Internal Revenue Service can associate tax-exempt income with the proceeds of the debt issue. Also, preferred dividends may be lower than interest on debt issues because corporate owners have to pay taxes on only 20 percent of preferred dividends received.

**TABLE 9-4  Characteristics of Bank Convertible Debt Issues**

### 1. Maturity of Bank Convertible Debt Issues

| Maturity | Number in Category | Proportion |
|---|---|---|
| 7 years[a] | 2 | 2% |
| 10 years | 11 | 13% |
| 15 years[b] | 4 | 5% |
| 20 years | 19 | 23% |
| 25 years | 47 | 56% |
| 30 years | 1 | 1% |

### 2. Conversion Price Compared with Market Price

| Percentage by Which Conversion Price Exceeds Common Stock Price | Number of Issues | Proportion |
|---|---|---|
| Under 10% | 2 | 5% |
| 10–14.9% | 13 | 32% |
| 15–19.9% | 19 | 46% |
| 20–24.9% | 4 | 10% |
| 25–29.9% | 3 | 7% |
| Data not available | 43 | — |

### 3. Lower Interest Cost on Bank Convertible Issues

| | Number of Issues | Proportion |
|---|---|---|
| **Lower Interest Cost in Actual Yield** | | |
| Under .4% | 1 | 1% |
| .5–.9% | 13 | 16% |
| 1.0–1.4% | 36 | 45% |
| 1.5–1.9% | 18 | 23% |
| 2.0–2.4% | 8 | 10% |
| 2.5% and above | 4 | 5% |
| Not available | 4 | — |
| **Lower Interest Cost in Percentage Terms** | | |
| 5–9.9% | 10 | 13% |
| 10–14.9% | 13 | 16% |
| 15–19.9% | 21 | 26% |
| 20–24.9% | 19 | 24% |
| 25–29.9% | 9 | 11% |
| 30–34.9% | 5 | 6% |
| 35% and above | 3 | 4% |
| Data not available | 4 | — |

**TABLE 9-4** *(continued)*

### 4. *Characteristics of Bank Convertible Bond Issues*

| Characteristic | Number of Issues | Proportion |
|---|---|---|
| **Rights Offering** | | |
| Offered to stockholders | 35 | 55% |
| Not offered to stockholders | 29 | 45% |
| Data not available | 20 | — |
| **Sinking Fund** | | |
| Sinking fund | 23 | 43% |
| No sinking fund | 31 | 57% |
| Data not available | 30 | — |
| **Call Provision[c] (years to call)** | | |
| 1 year or less | 20 | 43% |
| 2–4 years | 5 | 11% |
| 5 years | 15 | 32% |
| 6–9 years | 3 | 6% |
| 10 years | 4 | 9% |
| Over 10 years | 0 | 0% |
| Data not available | 37 | — |

[a] Includes one issue with a maturity of seven and one-half years.

[b] Includes one issue with a maturity of 16 years.

[c] Includes four issues on which the conversion price increased in later years, three issues on which the conversion privilege was delayed, and two issues on which the conversion price was set at a later date.

SOURCES: Data on 84 issues were gathered by the authors from Irving Trust's "Reports of Securities Issued by Commercial Banks and Holding Companies," 1969–1980 prospectus of some individual issues, and Moody's *Bank and Finance Manual*, 1970–1989.

debt issue.[3] In percentage terms, roughly two-thirds of the convertible issues' interest cost was between 10 and 25 percent lower than the estimated interest cost on a straight debt issue. Section 4 shows that over one-half of the issues were offered to existing shareholders through a rights offering. Roughly 43 percent of the bank convertible issues had a sinking fund, and most of these sinking funds began 10 years after the bonds were issued. Of those issues for which call data were available, 43 percent were callable within a year of the time of issue and approximately 85 percent were callable within five years.

[3] Some issues for which common stock premiums could not be calculated provided some interesting sidelights. There were four convertible issues on which the common stock's conversion price was increased in later years. This "step-up" in conversion price tends to encourage conversion just before the time the conversion price will increase if the market price exceeds the prevailing conversion price. Conversion to common stock was delayed for a period ranging from one to five years for three other convertible issues, and on two of these delayed issues, the conversion price was set as a percentage of the common stock price (within a predetermined price range) at the date the issue became convertible.

Nearly all of the issues were callable at decreasing prices starting at between 104 and 106 percent of par value and decreasing to par value.

Some of the characteristics and typical market price performance of an example convertible issue are presented as a prelude to examining the pros and cons of a commercial bank's issuing convertible debt. It is assumed that an example bank can sell $5 million of 25-year convertible debt at an interest cost of 8 percent when the cost of a straight debt issue would be 10 percent. Each $1,000 bond is convertible into 25 common shares—that is, at a price of $40.00 a share when the price at which common stock could be sold is $30 a share. The issue is callable after five years and would result in 125,000 additional shares of common stock if all the bonds were converted.

Table 9-5 illustrates the estimated market price performance of this hypothetical issue. At the time of issue (Condition 1 in Table 9-5), each bond is estimated to sell at a premium of $210 to $250 above its value as a bond and its pure conversion value. The estimated market price of the convertible exceeds both values because the holder owns both a bond, with its prior claims over all forms of equity, and the right to change the bond into 25 shares of common stock at the holder's option. If the common stock falls in value, the holder believes he or she has a price floor provided by the interest payments and security of the bond. If the common stock rises in value, the holder stands to gain because the conversion value will increase at the same rate at which the common stock price increases. Clearly, investors should be, and generally are, willing to pay some premium for the extra protection on the downside and the appreciation potential on the upside.

Conditions 2 through 6 in Table 9-5 illustrate what happens to the estimated market price of the convertible bond if either the level of interest rates changes or the price of the bank's common stock changes. Under Condition 2, interest rates rise to 12 percent and the value of the convertible as a straight bond falls to $640. It is estimated that the market price of the convertible bond will fall to $900, or a premium of $150 over the conversion value, because the bond-value price floor offers considerably less protection if the common stock price falls. If interest rates fall, as under Condition 3, the opposite effect would occur—the estimated market of the convertible bond would rise to $1,090, or a premium of only $90 above the value as a straight bond, because the value of the right to convert the bond to 25 shares of common stock would be below the estimated market of the convertible bond.

Under Conditions 4, 5, and 6, it is assumed that the interest rate remains at 10 percent but that the common stock price changes. The bond value does provide a price floor for the convertible bond when the common stock price falls to $20 per share; however, the estimated premium over the bond value falls to $70 because the right to convert is less valuable. On the other hand, when the common stock price rises above the conversion value (as in Conditions 5 and 6), the convertible bond is estimated to sell at only a small premium over its conversion value because the bond-value price floor is far below the estimated market price of the convertible bond. Finally, if the common stock price rises substantially above its conversion value, the convertible bond will

**TABLE 9-5  Estimated Market Price of a Hypothetical Convertible Bond[a]**

| Conditions | Interest Rate if Straight Bond | Value if Straight Bond[b] | Common Stock Price | Pure Conversion Value | Estimated Market Price of Convertible[c] | Premium Over Bond Value | Premium Over Conversion Value |
|---|---|---|---|---|---|---|---|
| 1. Time of issue | 10% | $ 790 | $30 | $ 750 | $1,000 | $ 210 | $250 |
| 2. Rates to go to 12% | 12 | 640 | 40 | 750 | 900 | 260 | 150 |
| 3. Rates to fall to 8% | 8 | 1,000 | 30 | 750 | 1,090 | 90 | 240 |
| 4. Stock price to $20 | 10 | 790 | 20 | 500 | 860 | 70 | 360 |
| 5. Stock price to $45 | 10 | 790 | 45 | 1,125 | 1,180 | 390 | 55 |
| 6. Stock price to $75 | 10 | 790 | 75 | 1,875 | 1,900 | 1,110 | 25 |
| 7. Rates to 12%, stock to $20 | 12 | 640 | 20 | 500 | 750 | 140 | 250 |

[a] Assuming a $1,000 par value, a convertible bond that has an 8% coupon rate and is convertible at the option of the holder into 25 shares of common stock.

[b] Obtained from standard bond tables.

[c] Estimated market price is the authors' opinion based on the average market price performance of 10 convertible issues of large banks.

---

**FIGURE 9-2** **Graphic Depiction of Estimated Market Price of Hypothetical Convertible Bond**

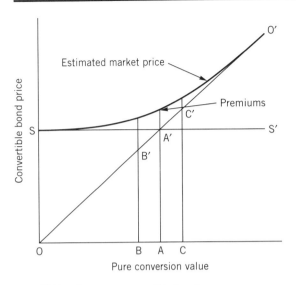

SS′ is value as nonconvertible bond
CC′ is pure conversion value

For situation in Table 9-5:
  SS′ = $790
  OO′ = common stock price x 25
  OA = $750 ($30 per share)
  OB = $500 ($20 per share)
  OC = $1,000 ($ 40 per share)

---

sell at or very slightly above its conversion value. Figure 9-2 illustrates the estimated market price of a convertible bond at a particular level of interest but with varying common stock prices. The premium is furthest above both the bond value (SS′) and the conversion value (OO′) when these two values are close together. If one of these values is dominant, there is little, if any, premium above the estimated market price.

Two final comments on the hypothetical convertible issue seem particularly pertinent. First, conversion occurs at the option of the holder, and there is usually little incentive to convert when the common stock price increases, since the conversion value will increase at roughly the same rate as the common stock price. (The obvious exception occurs when the common stock dividend has been increased until it exceeds the interest return on the convertible issue by a substantial amount.) This lack of incentive is the reason that nearly all convertible issues are callable. When the bank's common stock price increases considerably above its convertible's conversion price, the bank can force conversion of most bonds by calling the issue. Second, the premiums of estimated market price over the bond and conversion values tend to change with stock and bond market conditions. Premiums are generally lower when both bond market and stock market conditions deteriorate (exemplified by Condition 7 in Table 9-5), and they are higher when the bond and stock market conditions are favorable. The typical reason most commercial banks use convertible bonds or convertible preferred stock is the hope of selling common stock at a price considerably above the current price at which common stock could be sold. (Convertible preferred stock is particularly appropriate in unusual situations, such as when the bank has a very low tax rate or when it is financing acquisitions. It has been used more frequently by bank holding companies than by banks.) The earnings per share advantage of selling fewer shares to raise the same amount of capital is obvious. Bank management, however, should be aware that they are counting on the common stock price to rise enough above the conversion price to make the conversion privilege attractive. If the stock price does not rise and conversion does not occur (or cannot be forced to occur by call), then the bank continues with a debt that is at a lower interest or preferred dividend cost than if straight debt had been issued.

Convertible securities nearly always have significantly lower interest or dividend costs than do similar nonconvertible securities. The lower cost of convertibles does not by itself mean that convertibles are "cheaper" than nonconvertibles. A proper appraisal of the cost differences to the issuer of using convertibles or nonconvertibles also must take into account the potential dilution that can result from conversion. (For this reason, a few issuers of convertibles hope that these issues will not be converted.) Whatever the long-term cost differences might be, the lower interest or dividend payments of convertibles may prove advantageous to the issuing bank, particularly in tight money periods.

Convertible securities have several other potential advantages. First, with a call provision, the bank has the flexibility of determining whether an issue selling above the call price will be converted. This flexibility gives the bank a wider range of choices in future financing decisions. Second, in a few situations, the conversion privilege may be necessary as a sweetener to enable a bank to sell a debt or preferred issue. Third, convertible securities may be preferable to common stock in a few situations where the bank is owned by only a few shareholders. Conversion normally does not take place immediately, but rather over time; therefore, convertibles offer the controlling group an opportunity to meet immediate capital needs while obtaining the time to acquire firmer control before conversion takes place. Also, when earnings are decreasing, control may be more of a problem than when the bank is prospering. Conversion normally will not take place unless the bank prospers. Hence, when bank performance is less than satisfactory and the threat of loss of control is greatest, the controlling group is most sheltered from the threat of conversion.

The overall potential advantages of convertibles as a commercial bank's financial strategy are convincing. One can imagine a rapidly growing bank issuing convertibles at a favorable cost, forcing conversion a few years later at a higher price, and then selling a new convertible issue because of the enlarged common equity base. A slower-growing bank, on the other hand, might gain from the lower interest cost, greater flexibility, and better control of the convertible issue over the entire life of the issue.

There is another issue in the question of convertible issues that must be addressed. One might argue that convertible bonds are not advantageous because they are both a senior security and a right to convert to stock. Under the assumption of efficient capital markets, the gains of (in effect) selling common stock above its current price coupled with a lower interest cost would be offset by potential disadvantages to the bank. For example, if bank performance were not satisfactory, the bank would still be forced to make fixed-cost interest payments, which would not be true if the bank had sold common stock. On the other hand, if the bank did very well, it may wish it had waited to sell common stock at an even higher price. The problem with such arguments is that everyone does better with hindsight. Furthermore, the wide fluctuation of premiums on convertible issues under different market conditions and the lower margin requirements on purchases of convertibles raise some questions about the assumption of efficient capital markets. Individual banks may also have special conditions that make convertible issues more favorable to them than to the typical bank in the general market.

There are also two practical considerations that some banks have cited as disadvantages of convertibles. First, earnings per share now must be stated on both a primary basis and a fully diluted basis. The negative connotation of this accounting ruling is that earnings are stated on an as-if-diluted basis even before conversion takes place. If actual and potential shareholders base their investment decision on the fully diluted earnings figure, the hoped-for advantages of favorable leverage may not be fully recognized in the market price of the bank's common stock.

Second, some argue that there is no proper time to issue convertibles. Proponents of this argument hold that common stock should be sold if the bank's common stock is considered to be overvalued. The required equity capital is more likely to be raised on more favorable terms at the present time than in a future period. On the other hand, if the bank believes its common stock is undervalued, the best financial decision is to issue straight debt or preferred stock. Common stock can be sold later when the price of the stock rises to its normal level.

Probably the best way to evaluate the many issues determining whether a bank should use convertible securities is to compare the earnings results if the bank has the alternative of selling convertible debt or preferred stock (see the example in Table 9-2). It is assumed that this example bank can (in addition to the alternative in Table 9-2) raise $5 million of capital by selling 7 percent convertible preferred stock or 8 percent convertible debt. Both issues are convertible at $40 per share or into 125,000 additional shares at the option of the holder. In Table 9-2 the example bank could sell common stock at $30 per

**TABLE 9-6    Earnings Results for Convertible Alternatives**

| | Additional Capital Financed with 7% Convertible Preferred Stock | Additional Capital Financed with 8% Convertible Preferred Debt | After Conversion |
|---|---|---|---|
| **Earnings on Existing Assets** | | | |
| Earnings on assets (1.0%) | $5,050,000 | $5,050,000 | |
| Less: Interest | 0 | 400,000 | |
| Net income before tax | $5,050,000 | $4,650,000 | |
| Less: Taxes (at 34% rate) | 1,717,000 | 1,581,000 | |
| Net income after tax | $3,333,000 | $3,069,000 | |
| Less: Preferred dividends | 350,000 | 0 | |
| Earnings to common stock | $2,983,000 | $3,069,000 | |
| Divided by: Number of shares | 1,000,000 | 1,000,000 | |
| Earnings per share | $2.98 | $3.07 | |
| Fully diluted earnings per share | $2.96 | $2.96 | |
| **Earnings on Increased Assets** | | | |
| Earnings on assets (1.0%) | $5,800,000 | $5,800,000 | $5,800,000 |
| Less: Interest | 0 | 400,000 | 0 |
| Net income before tax | $5,800,000 | $5,400,000 | $5,800,000 |
| Less: Taxes (at 34% rate) | 1,972,000 | 1,836,000 | 1,972,000 |
| Net income after tax | $3,828,000 | $3,564,000 | $3,828,000 |
| Less: Preferred dividends | 350,000 | 0 | 0 |
| Earnings to common stock | $3,478,000 | $3,564,000 | $3,828,000 |
| Divided by: Number of shares | 1,000,000 | 1,000,000 | 1,125,000 |
| Earnings per share | $3.48 | $3.56 | $3.40 |
| Fully diluted earnings per share | $3.40 | $3.40 | $3.40 |

share, preferred stock with an 8 percent dividend, and capital notes with 10 percent interest.

The earnings results with the two convertible alternatives appear in Table 9-6. The first section of this table shows that the immediate dilution per share is lower for the convertible issue than for the straight preferred stock or debt issue (in Table 9-3) because of the lower dividend or interest cost. Furthermore, the fully diluted earnings per share is lower than when common stock was issued at $30 per share because fewer shares of common stock were converted than would be issued if common stock was issued. The second sections of Tables 9-2 and 9-6 illustrate what would happen if the example bank's assets increased by an additional $75 million. Earnings per common share would be $3.28 if the additional capital had been raised by the issuance of common stock; $3.43 and $3.50 if the capital was raised by nonconvertible preferred stock or debentures, respectively; $3.48 and $3.56 if convertible preferred stock or debt, respectively, was used; and $3.40 on a fully diluted basis or after conversion took place.

Before conversion, the convertibles provide more favorable actual earnings per share because of the lower interest or dividend cost of the convertibles. On a fully diluted basis, the convertibles provide more favorable earnings on increased assets than the common stock issue but somewhat less favorable per-share earnings in comparison with the straight debt or preferred issue. Therefore, as long as the common stock price does not rise much above its conversion value, one can argue that the bank gains from the lower interest or dividend cost of the convertible versus the straight security, often at the cost of somewhat lower earnings on a fully diluted basis. Compared with common stock, the financial leverage of the convertible is usually favorable, and the fully diluted earnings per share will always be higher.

Because of these considerations, bank policy should encourage the issuance of convertible debentures, particularly when management believes that the common stock is underpriced and when it wants the additional capital to be permanent rather than temporary.

Mandatory convertible issues, whose conversion is mandatory by the end of a certain period of time, are a variation of regular convertibles. Regulatory authorities prefer this form because the convertibles cannot mature. Regulators classify mandatory convertibles as Tier I capital. Some of these issues have been sold; however, mandatory convertibles have been sold on less favorable terms than regular convertibles, and the bank and security holders lose flexibility with such sales.

Variable-rate debt or option-rate debt are among the other new capital-raising alternatives. Variable-rate debt particularly makes sense in situations in which fixed-rate debt would increase a bank's interest rate risk. Option-rate debt is usually variable-rate debt that can be converted into fixed-rate debt at the option of the debt holder during at least some of the life of the debt. This option increases the price of the debt, which reduces the interest cost to the bank.

The limited number of banks that have no taxable income and have large tax losses to carry forward should consider preferred stock. The 70 percent dividend exclusion for corporate income taxes makes preferred dividend rates lower than yields on bonds. The cost of preferred stock will be less than the cost of debt if the bank has low or no taxes. To escape potential interest-rate risk, preferred stock should either be callable or issued at an adjustable (tied to some interest-rate index) rate. A noncallable, adjustable-rate preferred stock qualifies as primary capital. One interesting form of adjustable-rate preferred stock has its dividend repriced every seven weeks through a dutch auction mechanism.

## EXTERNAL COMMON STOCK ISSUES

Common stock has to be issued when a new bank is formed. Common stock may also be the appropriate form of raising external capital to finance growth.

When a new bank is organized, its capital stock is usually sold to a small group of interested investors. Additional stock may later be offered to this group and their friends; however, if the bank grows rapidly and needs larger amounts of additional common stock, it may have to offer its stock to the public. The pricing of a bank's book value, earning power, and dividends are compared with the prices of actively traded stocks of similar-sized banks for the determination of a reasonable stock price. It is not generally advisable for the issuing bank to try to squeeze the last dollar out of such an offering. The presence of a group of initial shareholders who are satisfied with the appreciation in the market price of their stock will encourage higher common stock prices in future years. The initial public offering should be priced in the popular range for new issues. A stock split may be used to adjust the price of previously issued shares if their value is not between $10 and $30 per share.

Once the stock is reasonably actively traded, the offering price of new issues will be determined primarily by the market price of outstanding shares. In addition to improving its operating efficiency, the bank may take several steps to improve its market price. First, it should foster an effective dividend policy. Second, it should try to publicize the bank and its activities as much as possible (e.g., in the news media and in financial analysts' meetings). It is imperative that the senior management and director always be honest and realistic in presenting information about the bank. The investment community is very slow in forgetting unjustifiably optimistic predictions. The directors and senior management should also use stock splits to keep the market price of the stock in an attractive price range, which is between $20 and $60, according to most financial analysts. (Stock dividends can also be used for this purpose. Stock dividends tend to be smaller than splits, and they force the bank to capitalize a portion of its undivided profits. Smaller stock dividends provide shareholders with a lower-cost opportunity to sell a small portion of their holdings but are more expensive to effect than stock splits.)

Price information is usually available for the issues of larger banks or bank holding companies that are traded on one or more stock exchanges or are traded actively in the over-the-counter market. If a medium-sized bank's stock is not listed on the National Association of Security Dealers Automated Quotation Service (NASDAQ), the bank should try to get enough shareholder base, trading activity, and dealer support (some banks could get on NASDAQ just by getting one or two more dealers to make a market in their stock) to obtain this listing. Advantages of the NASDAQ listing include the widespread publication of stock price quotations and the immediate availability of bid and asked quotations for dealers.

Even the smaller bank, while unable to obtain the NASDAQ listing, should try to make stock price information available. If the bank or a local dealer makes the market, the bank should make sure that the local press gets and publishes the quote on the stock price daily. For infrequently traded stocks of such banks, establishing a reasonable value for the stock is a major problem. Two techniques that a few smaller banks have used successfully to establish a reasonable price are (1) using preemptive rights offerings of new shares to existing shareholders and (2) having periodic stock auctions in which those who wish to buy or sell shares can bid for them or place them in an auctionlike setting.

Other strategies that might improve the bank's market price and its ability to raise equity capital include dividend reinvestment plans (which allow shareholders to reinvest cash dividends automatically in new shares) and purchase by a bank or holding company of some of its own shares. Bank directors and senior management should be flexible in evaluating the probable costs and benefits of these alternative strategies.

Even if a bank's board and its management use the strategies appropriate to their situation and work hard to increase the market's earnings multiple for the bank's stock, the bank's management may believe the market price of the bank's stock to be vastly understated. Often the depressed price may be the result of conditions that a bank's management cannot control. For example, in the late 1980s the multiples for nearly all bank stocks were depressed because of concern about loans to less developed countries, well-publicized banking problems and failures, proposed legislation affecting banks, and other concerns. What should the astute banker do in this hostile environment—particularly if the bank's stock is selling below its book value?

If the bank does not urgently need additional capital, the answer is relatively simple: Do not raise additional equity capital at this time, but do everything possible to strengthen the bank's earnings multiple in future periods in which new capital may be needed. If the bank needs additional capital, it has three options. First, it may decide not to raise additional capital but instead to improve the bank's capital ratios by selling or securitizing assets, slowing asset and deposit growth, or retaining a higher proportion of earnings. Regulatory authorities tend to be relatively lenient in such situations if it is clear that the bank is following such a strategy. A second option is to sell senior capital instead of issuing new shares of common equity. There are limits on the proportion of senior capital a bank may have in its capital structure, and a few banks have used up their ability to exercise this option. The third option is to issue common stock in spite of obviously hostile conditions. In September 1975, for example, the Crocker National Corporation sold 1.5 million shares of its common stock at roughly 75 percent of its book value. This was the first time a major banking institution had offered shares at a price below the book value of its shares. Crocker was forced into this position because $170 million (approximately 30 percent) of its $565 million of capital supporting $6.3 billion in loans was already in debt securities. Crocker's existing shareholders may have been more willing to accept a dilution in their average earnings per share than many bank shareholders because the bank had recently brought in a new top management team, headed by a former Citibank vice-chairman, Thomas B. Wilcox. Since that time, a limited number of other banks have sold new common issues at below book value.

A different version of this third option would be to issue debt or preferred stock that is convertible into common stock. The hoped-for scenario would be that the bank's common stock price would eventually recover, and the bank would have, in effect, sold common stock at 15 to 30 percent above its market price when the capital was raised. Several banks followed this option in the early 1990s.

## CAPITAL MANAGEMENT

Certain management techniques allow banks to utilize their capital effectively and generate higher overall returns on capital. These techniques include allocating capital by lines of business and calculating returns on capital using the new risk-weighted assets-to-capital rules.

The allocation of capital by lines of business is best explained by an example. Table 9-7 presents introductory information on two commercial banks that are similar in size ($100 million in assets) and capital ($6 million), but that emphasize different product lines. Bank A has 50 percent of its assets in national commercial loans and only 10 percent in consumer installment loans. Bank B has 10 percent of its assets in national commercial loans and 50 percent in consumer installment loans. The two banks have agreed, based on past and expected payment records, that national commercial loans require only 50 percent as much capital as average banking lines of business, while consumer installment loans require one and a half times as much capital as average banking lines of business.

If Bank A did not allocate capital, it would effectively allocate $3 million of capital to its national loans and $600,000 to consumer loans. This assumption might lead the bank to erroneous decisions, such as the conclusion that it was just meeting minimum capital adequacy requirements and that it would have to limit growth to retained earnings or its ability to raise external capital. If capital was allocated according to agreed-upon lines of business ($1.5 million to national loans and $900,000 to consumer loans), Bank A would probably find that its capital was more than adequate ($1.2 million above its allocated needs). It could grow without raising capital, and it might even consider larger cash dividends or a stock repurchase plan.

Bank B could come up with equally erroneous decisions if it did not allocate capital by lines of business. The bank would allocate $600,000 of capital to its national business loans and $3 million of capital to its consumer installment loans. It might believe that its capital was adequate (barely) and that it could grow at about the rate of its internal capital generation. If capital was allocated according to the agreed-upon lines of business allocation ($300,000 to national loans and $4.5 million to consumer loans), the bank would be short of capital (needing about $1.2 million more). Bank B might want to raise new capital or reduce assets through sale or securitization. Pricing decisions for Banks A and B would probably be affected by the capital allocation scheme that the banks used.

A related technique would be to calculate the return on capital using the new risk-weighted assets-to-capital rules. Table 9-8 presents an example comparing the returns for securities with those for loans. The cost of funds

**TABLE 9-7 Illustration of Bank Capital Allocation by Lines of Business (dollars in millions)**

### Bank A

**Basic Balance Sheet**

| | | | |
|---|---|---|---|
| National loans | $ 50.0 | Deposits | $ 80.0 |
| Installment loans | 10.0 | Borrowings | 14.0 |
| Other assets | 40.0 | Capital | 6.0 |
| Total assets | $100.0 | Total liabilities & capital | $100.0 |

**Capital Allocated Equally**

| | | | |
|---|---|---|---|
| National loans | $ 50.0 | Allocated capital | $ 3.0 |
| Installment loans | 10.0 | Allocated capital | .6 |
| Other assets | 40.0 | Allocated capital | 2.4 |
| Total assets | $100.0 | Total capital | $ 6.0 |

**Capital Allocated by Management Decision:**

| | | | |
|---|---|---|---|
| National loans | $ 50.0 | Allocated capital | $ 1.5 |
| Installment loans | 10.0 | Allocated capital | .9 |
| Other assets | 40.0 | Allocated capital | 2.4 |
| Total assets | $100.0 | Total capital | $ 4.8[a] |

### Bank B

**Basic Balance Sheet**

| | | | |
|---|---|---|---|
| National loans | $ 10.0 | Deposits | $ 80.0 |
| Installment loans | 50.0 | Borrowings | 14.0 |
| Other assets | 40.0 | Capital | 6.0 |
| Total assets | $100.0 | Total liabilities & capital | $100.0 |

**Capital Allocated Equally**

| | | | |
|---|---|---|---|
| National loans | $ 10.0 | Allocated capital | $ .6 |
| Installment loans | 50.0 | Allocated capital | 3.0 |
| Other assets | 40.0 | Allocated capital | 2.4 |
| Total assets | $100.0 | Total capital | $ 6.0 |

**Capital Allocated by Management Decision:**

| | | | |
|---|---|---|---|
| National loans | $ 10.0 | Allocated capital | $ .3 |
| Installment loans | 50.0 | Allocated capital | 4.5 |
| Other assets | 40.0 | Allocated capital | 2.4 |
| Total assets | $100.0 | Total capital | $ 7.2[b] |

[a]Not all capital allocated.

[b]Exceeds available capital.

**TABLE 9-8    Return on Capital for Security versus Loan under Risk-Weighted Capital Rules (dollars in millions)**

**Assumptions**[a]

| | |
|---|---:|
| Size of investment in securities or loans | $100.0 |
| Capital/risk-weighted asset requirement | 8.0% |
| Securities (guaranteed by U.S. agency, 20% risk weighting) | 9.0% |
| Loans (good quality, 100% risk weighting) | 10.5% |
| Interest cost (deposits and borrowings) | 8.0% |
| Allocated noninterest cost of loans | 2.0% |
| Allocated noninterest cost of securities | .2% |

**Projected Incremental Balance Sheets**

| Securities | $100.00 | Deposits & borrowings | $ 98.40 |
|---|---|---|---|
| | | Required capital | 1.60 |
| | $100.00 | | $100.00 |

| Loans | $100.00 | Deposits & borrowings | $ 92.00 |
|---|---|---|---|
| | | Required capital | 8.00 |
| | $100.00 | | $100.00 |

**Projected Incremental Income Statements**

| | *Securities* | *Loans* |
|---|---|---|
| Interest income | $ 9.00 | $10.50 |
| Interest expense | 7.87 | 7.36 |
| Interest margin | $ 1.13 | $ 3.14 |
| Noninterest cost | .20 | 2.00 |
| Operating income | $  .93 | $ 1.14 |
| Taxes (34%) | .32 | .39 |
| Net income | $  .61 | $  .75 |
| Return on assets | .61% | .75% |
| Return on equity | 38.12% | 9.37% |

[a] Yield on securities and loans and cost of funds are similar to those in the spring of 1990. Functional cost in 1991 is used as the basis for allocated noninterest costs to securities and loans. Risk weighting effective in 1993 used for required capital.

and the gross yields on securities and loans were similar to those existing in the spring of 1990. Noninterest costs were allocated to securities and loans based on a recent functional cost study conducted by the Federal Reserve. It was assumed that the risk-asset weightings were fully effective and that the bank was considering a $100 million investment in either securities or loans.

The results showed that if a bank emphasized the dollar amount of net income or its return on assets, the investment in loans would be more favorable. The net income on loans was approximately $140,000 higher, and the return on assets was 0.14 percent more favorable for loans. Because of the lower risk weighting, however, the return on capital was roughly 38 percent for securities versus approximately 9 percent for loans. If one argues that the loans would attract deposits and cross-sold products, the bank could consider originating the loans and either selling or securitizing them.

The third capital management technique, the dividend policy decision of a bank, should be made to maximize the value of the stockholders' return, which, in turn, should benefit the bank. For the present investor to feel comfortable about his or her investment, a bank's dividend policy should be dependable and there should be assurances that past dividend actions by the bank will be continued in the future. For the potential investor, a consistent dividend policy history is an important factor in evaluating the worth of the bank's stock. Probably the most important element in a bank's dividend policy is establishing a payout (dividends as a percentage of earnings) policy so that dividends will increase as earnings (hopefully) increase. The level and pattern of a bank's dividends are also key elements on which investors rely to help determine the total return that can be expected from their investments and whether or not they will invest at all in a particular bank. Also, if an investor is confident that he or she understands a bank's dividend policy, the investor may place a higher value on that bank's stock.

The level of cash dividends should be set so that the bank can maintain that level over various types of business and economic conditions. Should business or economic conditions be such that earnings and profits are squeezed temporarily, cash dividends should be at a point where the bank is capable of maintaining them for a reasonable period of time until conditions improve. On the other hand, in times of favorable business conditions, dividends should not necessarily be increased immediately. If conditions change and the increased level of dividends cannot be sustained, then a reduction in dividends would be necessary. Cutting dividends is a negative sign to investors and reflects a pessimistic view of the future by management. An increase in dividends is usually viewed as expected prosperity by management; thus investors would anticipate the continuance of the higher dividend level. A good rule to follow, therefore, is that an increase in the dividend level should lag somewhat behind actual increases in earnings in order for management to be sure that it can maintain that level.

With regard to the dividend pattern, consistency is also desirable. Just as with the level of dividends, where fluctuation in the amount of the cash dividend paid is undesirable, the regularity with which this dividend is paid is also important. The income-oriented investor will usually prefer more frequent payments of cash dividends, such as quarterly or semiannually, as opposed to annually. Closer-spaced dividend payments also help increase the investor's confidence because a definite pattern is set up more rapidly by the greater frequency of these payments.

In deciding on the level and pattern of dividends, several factors must be considered by management. These include fulfilling the objectives of the investor, the rate of return a bank can earn on its capital (as opposed to the rate that an individual could earn in an alternative situation), the earnings stability of the bank, and the bank's plans for future growth. Dividend payouts for all insured commercial banks decreased slightly in the 1960s and 1970s, probably because of the large capital needs to finance growth and the relatively poor market for most bank stocks. In the 1980s, this trend was reversed. The increases in dividend payouts appeared to be the result of depressed earnings for many banks; however, some banks believed that higher dividend payouts would lead to higher stock market prices. The dividend increases that accompanied rising earnings for many banks in the early 1990s indicate that at least some bankers conclude that cash dividends paid by publicly held banks tend to have a positive effect on common stock prices.

## Discussion Questions

1. List and describe the basic types of capital that banks may issue.
2. What form has dominated new issues of bank capital over the last decade? Explain the reasons for the dominant form of capital.
3. Evaluate the conditions under which commercial banks should issue convertible subordinated bonds.
4. Explain how a bank should allocate capital among its various lines of business.
5. How do you believe dividends affect a bank's market price? In answering the question, remember that the retention rate is 1 minus the payout rate and that the answer may vary between actively traded banks (or holding companies) and community banks.

## CASE 5

# SHAWNEE NATIONAL BANK*

Shawnee National Bank, a large unit bank located in Kansas City, Missouri, had total resources in early December 1992 of over $1.4 billion (see Exhibit 1). As with other weekly reporting institutions subject to the reserve requirements of the Federal Reserve, the balances that Shawnee National is required to maintain as reserves are based on the average of its daily transaction deposit account balances during a 14-day *computation* period. The reserves required by the Fed must be maintained on an average daily basis during a 14-day *maintenance* period that begins on a Thursday and ends on the second Wednesday thereafter, sometimes called *Settlement Wednesday*. Because the requirement is an average for the period, bank managers are able to exercise judgment concerning the appropriate level of their reserve balances on a day-to-day basis during the maintenance period. At the end of a maintenance period, leeway of up to 4 percent above or below the average total reserve requirement will carry forward into the next maintenance period.

The bank must determine the net daily average reserves that need to be maintained at the Federal Reserve Bank. For a 14-day computation period that ends 3 days before the related maintenance period begins, the bank's average daily cash balance (vault cash) is compiled. This average cash balance is confirmed on the Fed's Daily Position reports, and is carried forward and applied against the gross average reserves required in the corresponding maintenance period.

Since February 1984, the computation period for compiling the transaction account balance ends only 2 days prior to the end of the 14-day maintenance period, giving rise to so-called contemporaneous reserve requirements. At the close of business on Monday of a Settlement Week, Shawnee National has only Tuesday and

Wednesday to bring into line the daily average reserves held at the Fed with the net required reserves for the maintenance period. Even with a good on-line accounting system, this nearly concurrent requirement can present a considerable challenge for the bank's money-desk manager. Numerous noncontrollable transactions (e.g., net checking transactions initiated directly or indirectly by the bank's depositors) and controllable transactions (e.g., Federal funds purchases and sales) affect a bank's balances at its Federal Reserve Bank each day. Shawnee National must keep track of both its transaction deposits and its net reserve balances throughout each business day, reconciling the average daily amounts with the Fed. The Fed's reserve requirements in December 1992 were 10 percent for net transaction balances.[1]

Exhibit 2 contains a summary of Shawnee National's accumulated reserve position for the reserve maintenance period ending Wednesday, December 23, 1992. The associated computation period for transaction accounts ended Monday, December 21, and for vault cash (as a credit) it ended Monday, December 7.

Shawnee National's overall cash position[2] reflected a large number of individual investment, loan, and liquidity decisions made by the bank's officers throughout the year. As a basis for planning, a staff economist forecast the level of depos-

---

*Rewritten by Gerson M. Goldberg and Keith B. Johnson of the University of Connecticut.

[1] The Garn–St. Germain Depository Institution Act of 1982 grants a total exemption to the first $3 million or so of reservable deposits. Also, the next amount of reservable deposits, called a *tranche level*, is subject to only a 3 percent reserve requirement. These adjustments give a relative advantage to a smaller institution. All net transaction amounts above the tranche are reservable at 10 percent. In previous years, other liability accounts have been reservable at various percentages. The level of the exemption and the tranche change annually as follows: For 1993 the exemption increased from $3.6 million to $3.8 million, and the tranche rose from $42.2 million to $46.8 million.

[2] A commercial bank's *cash position* is defined as the sum of cash in the vault, deposits due from correspondent banks and from the Federal Reserve Bank, and items in the process of collection.

its and expected loan demand on a continuous basis for periods of three months, six months, and one year. Once these sources and applications of funds had been estimated and the bank had made its forecast of interest rates for the coming months, the bank could then determine its target asset and liability composition and make asset and/or liability management decisions to move toward that position.

As 1992 began, uncertainty about the outlook for the U.S. economy was unusually great. Had recovery from the recession begun? Was it about to begin? Or might the economy grow at an unacceptably slow rate, leading to fiscal intervention that might rekindle inflationary fears and keep long-term interest rates too high? In this unsettled environment, Shawnee's senior officers decided that the bank would stay well positioned for whatever interest rate changes might develop. A policy of cautious lending limited loan growth, and funds were channeled into short-term securities, even though yields were low and declining. Shawnee's management eschewed higher long-term yields and larger capital gains opportunities that most other banks were vigorously pursuing in 1992.

At mid-year the signals continued to confound forecasters, and concerns mounted that the fledgling recovery was slipping into another dip. Federal Reserve Chairman Alan Greenspan cut short-term rates to their lowest levels in decades, producing an extraordinarily sharply upward-sloping yield curve with a 500 basis point spread between Treasury bills and long Treasury bonds. Finally, convinced that inflation was licked and that long-term rates were unreasonably high, in late summer Shawnee's management belatedly began to shift maturing securities into longer-term government bonds (see Exhibits 3 and 5). This move reduced the bank's liquidity when long-term rates surged in October as it became clear to the markets that the Democrats would win the White House. A moderate but steady climb in "bankable" loan demand during the fall drained Shawnee's liquidity even further.

After the bank's deposit, loan, liability, and investment objectives had been estimated and short-run policies established, Mr. Seth Bradley, a vice-president, managed the daily cash position to adjust for short-run cash fluctuations and to ensure that the bank maintained the required minimum balances with the Federal Reserve Bank. It was Mr. Bradley's objective to minimize the cost of meeting the bank's reserve requirements at the Fed and to invest any temporarily excess funds as profitably as possible.

The month of December was an unusual period for accumulating excess funds. Strong seasonal sales between Thanksgiving and Christmas by several large national mail-order firms located in Shawnee National's market area bolstered local retail activity. The bank's peak period in deposits generally occurred by Christmas, after which it declined rapidly (see Exhibit 4). This rapid decline after Christmas was due to various payments by area agribusinesses for tax management, as many used cash basis accounting.

On Friday, December 18, Mr. Bradley sold $8.0 million in Federal funds, thereby deliberately creating an accumulated reserve deficiency of approximately $35 million (see Exhibit 2) for Monday morning.[3] Mr. Bradley assumed that a $25 million to $30 million reserve buildup would occur on Monday, thereby offsetting the multiple effect of Friday's sale of Federal funds. A large part of this growth in the reserve balance at the Fed was expected to come from immediate credit at the Federal Reserve on one-day items. These items consisted of checks drawn on other banks that Shawnee National forwarded to the Kansas City Clearing House and to its correspondent banks. These checks would increase Shawnee's transaction deposits and, at the margin, its average required reserves for the last day of the contemporaneous computation period. But most important, when these checks were cleared, the full amount of the checks became usable funds on deposit in Shawnee's Federal Reserve account. Mr. Bradley further assumed that the bank would

---

[3] Federal fund sales (loans) on Friday are for three days; thus, the impact on average daily reserves of the net sale of $8.0 million for three days is the equivalent of selling $24.0 million for one day. Federal funds are reserve balances that a commercial bank may either loan to or borrow from other banks to adjust its reserve position. These loans are generally made on an unsecured overnight basis, with repayment expected at the beginning of the next business day. Sales and purchases also can be made for somewhat longer periods. The Federal funds rate is determined by the forces of supply and demand for such funds within the commercial banking system.

experience its typical small reserve drain on Tuesday.[4] Then, with a moderate purchase of Federal funds, the average reserve balances for the maintenance period would closely approximate the legal requirements.

By mid-morning on Monday, December 21, Mr. Bradley realized that his assumptions were not proving correct. The bank opened on Monday with an accumulated reserve deficiency of $35.4 million for the reserve maintenance period that would end on Wednesday, December 23. The large immediate credits to the bank's account at the Federal Reserve had not materialized. A number of factors were responsible:

1. Incoming deposits over the weekend were smaller than expected.

2. A smaller than normal surplus was incurred at the Kansas City Clearing House.

3. A large correspondent bank withdrew funds one day early when in fact the courier plane delivering cash letters to Shawnee had been delayed by blizzard conditions.

4. Several important depositors made larger than normal withdrawals.

5. An adverse arithmetical error of $3 million was made in the general books department.

During Monday the bank experienced slower than usual growth in its reserve balance at the Fed. When combined with Sunday night's unfavorable events, this resulted in only $12.1 million in noncontrollable factors rather than the $30 million Mr. Bradley had expected (see Exhibit 2). Even though the normal noncontrollable factors on Tuesday of −$1 million would most likely change to +$3 million, Mr. Bradley realized that by the close of business on Tuesday, the bank could have an accumulated reserve deficiency of as much as $45.6 million. A deficiency of this size would be difficult to overcome through normal adjustments such as borrowing on its Federal

funds lines or selling short-term Treasury securities.

On Monday afternoon, Mr. Bradley decided that the reserve position at the Fed required immediate attention before the close of business that day. There were several alternatives from which Mr. Bradley could choose in order to adjust the bank's reserve position.

## DISCUSSION OF ALTERNATIVES

### Purchase of Federal Funds

Purchase of Federal funds was the device most commonly used by Shawnee National to adjust its deficit balances at the Federal Reserve Bank. It was Shawnee National's policy, however, to limit net Federal funds purchases to no more than $20 million. The bank did not want to be either an excessive net seller or buyer of Federal funds. Mr. Bradley considered the use of Federal funds as a "fine adjustment" in the bank's reserve position. Since short-term adjustments in reserve balances usually ranged from $5 million to $10 million, Federal funds provided the bank with a convenient means either of profitably employing excess reserves or of offsetting small reserve deficits. The bank's limited use of Federal funds sometimes made it necessary either to extend reserve adjustments over a longer period or to make more permanent adjustments.

### Borrowing from the Federal Reserve

The accumulated reserve deficit could be made up by borrowing from the Federal Reserve Bank. Shawnee National Bank, however, looked upon the use of such borrowing as a privilege. Earlier, on Wednesday, December 9, temporary tightness in the Federal funds market drove the offered rate to 7 percent, more than double the rates prevailing at that time. Mr. Bradley had found it necessary for Shawnee National to borrow at the discount window as Federal funds became unavailable at reasonable rates. Moreover, during the last week of December, the annual additional short-term loan demand by regional agribusinesses for tax management was usually met in part by a seasonal advance at the discount window. Mr. Bradley preferred, therefore, to avoid using the discount window during this week.

---

[4]Shawnee National's proof and transit department worked each Friday and Sunday night to process the heavy volume of banking-by-mail transactions. As a result, incoming items arriving over the weekend were cleared more promptly than by other banks in the area, and Shawnee National generally experienced a peak in usable funds on Monday. This peak typically declined on Tuesday and Wednesday as other banks completed the processing of weekend mail.

## Borrowing by Means of Repurchase Agreements

Shawnee National could sell part of its government or agency portfolio and agree to repurchase it at some future date at a predetermined price or yield. The cost of this form of secured borrowing tended to be lower than that of unsecured forms. There were two potential problems: (1) nearly $74 million of U.S. government and agency securities, as well as $88 million of state and municipal securities, were already pledged to cover government deposits and (2) the maturities of repos were generally overnight, although they could be as long as several months. In Mr. Bradley's opinion, the use of this form might cause the bank to shift permanently to liabilities other than deposits as a source of funds.

## Other Means of Borrowing

Mr. Bradley felt that the bank might obtain the needed funds by offering CDs with rates ranging from 0.25 to 0.50 percent above the existing market rate for comparable CDs. Since Shawnee National was classified as a well-capitalized bank, with its 6.34 percent leverage ratio, he concluded that restrictions on paying higher than prevailing market rates on CDs did not apply. He was concerned, however, about the difficulties some regional banks in the farm belt had experienced in issuing CDs and with the potential maturity of the CDs that Shawnee would offer. Other forms of borrowing, such as the Eurodollar market, ineligible acceptances, and so on, were generally not considered by Mr. Bradley.

## Sale of Short-Term Securities

If the adjustment of the reserve position required funds for more than a few days, short-term securities normally could be sold to provide the necessary funds. However, Mr. Bradley knew that a majority of the short-term securities were pledged as collateral for public deposits. He hoped to be able to retain most of the bank's short-term securities until maturity (see Exhibit 5).

## Brokerage Collateral Loans or Other Loans Callable on Demand

Brokerage collateral loans or other callable loans were usually arranged through Shawnee National's correspondent banks in New York. When the bank negotiated a brokerage collateral loan, it indicated the length of time it wished to employ its funds. Although such loans were callable on demand, the bank would not normally recall the funds until the agreed time had expired.

## Selling a Portion of the Investment Portfolio

On November 30, 1992, Shawnee National's investment portfolio (securities with maturities of over one year) was approximately $270 million (see Exhibit 5). Over half of the securities were pledged as collateral for public deposits, and most of the remaining securities could only be sold at losses. "It may be bad for the bank to take losses at this time," mused Mr. Bradley.

He also realized that he would have to try to make some assessments of Shawnee National's liquidity needs for the remainder of December 1992, especially related to the date in Exhibits 2 and 4. Because of recent discussions among the bank's senior officers, he wondered how the regulatory authorities (the Comptroller of the Currency) would view Shawnee National's liquidity position. The bank's liquidity situation had been a subject of spirited debate among the bank's senior management, with opinions divided as to whether overall liquidity was too high or too low.

Mr. Bradley also was unsure whether he should talk further with senior management regarding the bank's short-term deposit, loan, and investment objectives before he decided on specific actions in managing the reserve position. Bradley was not convinced that he should have sold the $8.0 million of Federal funds on Friday, December 18, thus deliberately creating a reserve deficiency.

By mid-afternoon on Monday, December 21, the accumulated reserve deficiency for the period was approximately $40 million. Mr. Bradley had not decided which of the several alternatives he should choose to reduce or eliminate the deficiency. He knew that he must evaluate the alternatives available, given the preceding considerations, and take action before the close of business on Monday afternoon.

## COST OF ALTERNATIVES

Mr. Bradley wrote down the following cost estimates of the alternatives he believed were available at that time:

| Alternatives | Income Lost | Added Expense |
|---|---|---|
| 1. Purchase of Federal funds | | 2.9–3.2% |
| 2. Borrowing from the Federal Reserve | | 3.0% |
| 3. Borrowing by means of repurchase agreements | | 2.8–3.1% |
| 4. Other means of borrowing (including CDs) | | 3.0–3.3% |
| 5. Sale of short-term securities | 3.0–3.35% | |
| 6. Cancellation of $20 million brokerage participation with New York correspondent | 4.5% | |
| 7. Selling part of the bank's investment portfolio | ? | |

**EXHIBIT I    Shawnee National Bank Statement of Condition, November 30, 1991–1992 (dollars in thousands)**

| Resources | 11/30/91 | 11/30/92 |
|---|---|---|
| Cash and due from banks | $110,358 | $118,835 |
| U.S. government and agency securities | 106,180 | 127,161 |
| State, county, and municipal bonds | 188,428 | 186,945 |
| Federal Reserve Bank stock | 1,070 | 1,560 |
| Loans and discounts, net | 876,437 | 956,324 |
| Accrued interest receivable | 6,724 | 7,427 |
| Customers' liability under letters of credit and acceptances | 11,761 | 12,717 |
| Bank premises, furniture, and fixtures | 26,301 | 29,256 |
| Other resources | 613 | 1,124 |
| Total resources | $1,327,872 | $1,441,349 |
| **Liabilities** | | |
| Transactions deposits | $301,823 | $334,258 |
| Savings deposits | 274,793 | 287,162 |
| Time deposits | 615,534 | 679,121 |
| Other liabilities | 35,424 | 33,234 |
| Capital notes | 16,100 | 15,600 |
| Capital stock | 9,104 | 9,104 |
| Surplus | 28,490 | 30,159 |
| Undivided profits | 46,604 | 52,711 |
| Total liabilities and capital | $1,327,872 | $1,441,349 |

**EXHIBIT 2 Shawnee National Bank Worksheet for Computing Maintenance Period Reserve Position (as of Monday, December 21, 1992, at 2:30 P.M.) (dollars in millions)**

| Required Balances at Fed[a] | (1) Beginning Balance at Fed | (2) Controllable Factors Affecting Reserves | (3) Noncontrollable Factors [Net] Affecting Reserves | (4) Fed Funds Purchased (Sold) [Net] | (5) Other Factors Affecting Reserves[d] | (6) Closing Balances with Fed | (7) Net Reserves Required at Fed[e] | (8) Daily Reserve Excess (Deficiency) | (9) Accumulated Reserve Excess (Deficiency) |
|---|---|---|---|---|---|---|---|---|---|
| WED 12/09 | | | | | | 36.7 | | | (0.4) |
| 1 THU 12/10 | 36.7 | (4.9)[b] | (4.0) | c | | 27.8 | 37.2 | (9.4) | (9.4) |
| 2 FRI 12/11 | 27.8 | | 6.3 | c | | 34.1 | 37.6 | (3.5) | (12.9) |
| 3 SAT 12/12 | 34.1 | | | | | 34.1 | 38.0 | (3.9) | (16.8) |
| 4 SUN 12/13 | 34.1 | | | | | 34.1 | 38.3 | (4.2) | (21.0) |
| 5 MON 12/14 | 34.1 | | 28.4 | c | | 62.5 | 38.4 | 24.1 | 3.1 |
| 6 TUE 12/15 | 62.5 | | (5.9) | (6.8) | | 49.8 | 38.6 | 11.2 | 14.3 |
| 7 WED 12/16 | 49.8 | | 4.7 | (7.4) | | 47.1 | 38.7 | 8.4 | 22.7 |
| 8 THU 12/17 | 47.1 | | (13.5) | c | | 33.6 | 38.9 | (5.3) | 17.4 |
| 9 FRI 12/18 | 33.6 | | (3.7) | (8.0) | | 21.9 | 39.2 | (17.3) | 0.1 |
| 10 SAT 12/19 | 21.9 | | | | | 21.9 | 39.5 | (17.6) | (17.5) |
| 11 SUN 12/20 | 21.9 | | | | | 21.9 | 39.9 | (17.9) | (35.4) |
| 12 MON 12/21 | 21.9 | | 12.1[f] | | | 34.0[f] | 40.1[f] | (6.1)[f] | (41.5)[f] |
| 13 TUE 12/22 | 34.0[f] | | 3.0[f] | | | 37.0[f] | 40.4[f] | (3.4)[f] | (44.9)[f] |
| 14 WED 12/23 | 37.0[f] | | 3.0[f] | | | 40.0[f] | 40.7[f] | (0.7)[f] | (45.6)[f] |

[a]Maintenance period runs from Thursday, December 10, through Wednesday, December 23, 1992, based on a contemporaneous computation period of Tuesday, December 8, through Monday, December 21, 1992.

[b]Purchase of U.S. government securities.

[c]Insignificant net amount.

[d]Borrowing from the Fed window, payments for and receipts from direct Treasury security transactions, etc.

[e]The reserve balance is the average required reserves at the Fed based on cumulative daily deposit data for the computation period plus an additional $0.4 million that was the prior period's deficiency.

[f]Estimated if no adjustments are made.

**EXHIBIT 3   Selected Interest Rates: Averages of Daily Figures**

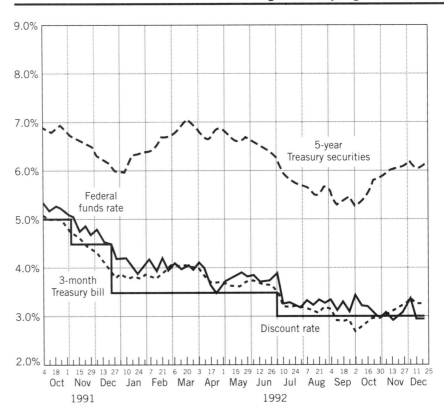

**EXHIBIT 4**    **Shawnee National Bank Reservable Transaction Accounts, December 1989–1991 and December 1–18, 1992 (dollars in millions)**

| Day of Month | 1989 | 1990 | 1991 | 1992 |
|---|---|---|---|---|
| 1 | 252 | — | — | 340 |
| 2 | — | — | 306 | 356 |
| 3 | — | 265 | 310 | 377 |
| 4 | 278 | 269 | 320 | 388 |
| 5 | 288 | 278 | 332 | — |
| 6 | 307 | 291 | 344 | — |
| 7 | 315 | 305 | — | 390 |
| 8 | 341 | — | — | 401 |
| 9 | — | — | 349 | 409 |
| 10 | — | 341 | 366 | 416 |
| 11 | 344 | 350 | 370 | 421 |
| 12 | 363 | 354 | 375 | — |
| 13 | 366 | 364 | 388 | — |
| 14 | 375 | 361 | — | 422 |
| 15 | 380 | — | — | 437 |
| 16 | — | — | 391 | 440 |
| 17 | — | 376 | 393 | 449 |
| 18 | 385 | 372 | 405 | 460 |
| 19 | 387 | 377 | 406 | — |
| 20 | 390 | 381 | 411 | — |
| 21 | 392 | 384 | — | — |
| 22 | 396 | — | — | — |
| 23 | — | — | 422 | — |
| 24 | — | 396 | 424 | — |
| 25 | — | — | — | — |
| 26 | 358 | 375 | 379 | — |
| 27 | 321 | 338 | 345 | — |
| 28 | 291 | 297 | — | — |
| 29 | 253 | — | — | — |
| 30 | — | — | 343 | — |
| 31 | — | 274 | 310 | — |

**EXHIBIT 5**   Shawnee National Bank Maturity Distribution of Securities at Book Value, November 30, 1992 (dollars in thousands)

| Maturity (Years) | U.S. Government Obligations | Federal Agency Obligations | State & Municipal Obligations | Total |
|---|---|---|---|---|
| 1 | 16,038 | 10,690 | 17,932 | 44,660 |
| 2 | 2,101 | 10,921 | 16,529 | 29,551 |
| 3 | 1,566 | 3,172 | 15,072 | 20,350 |
| 4 | 5,031 | 11,613 | 13,572 | 30,216 |
| 5 | 16,401 | 13,854 | 15,070 | 45,325 |
| 6 | 13,095 | 10,746 | 12,145 | 35,986 |
| 7 | 0 | 0 | 9,051 | 9,051 |
| 8 | 0 | 3,219 | 13,138 | 16,357 |
| 9 | 0 | 0 | 12,190 | 12,190 |
| 10 | 0 | 1,974 | 9,144 | 11,118 |
| 11–15 | 0 | 6,200 | 21,245 | 27,445 |
| 15–20 | 0 | 0 | 20,540 | 20,540 |
| Over 20 | 0 | 0 | 11,317 | 11,317 |
| Total | 54,232 | 72,929 | 186,945 | 314,106 |

## CASE 6

# PERALTA NATIONAL BANK

The Asset and Liability Committee (ALCO) of Peralta National Bank gathered promptly in the bank's board room at 8:00 A.M. on October 26, 1992, for its regular monthly meeting. The committee members gradually had become aware that the bank was developing an unusual mix of assets. Loan demand was very weak and, increasingly, the bank was compelled to find appropriate investment instruments in the national money and bond markets for the bank's large supplies of available funds. During 1991 and 1992, the bank experienced substantial increases in its core deposits when it acquired several branches of a failed S&L in the region that was being liquidated by the FDIC. Today's meeting was important because the bank's available funds had continued to grow in the third quarter of 1992, while loans continued to retreat. As a result, the bank's loans-to-deposit ratio stood well below the range that had been targeted by the board of directors.

## ALCO

The members of ALCO included the following:

Chairman of the board, Ed Chalmers

President, Dwight Jamison

Executive vice-president and chief lending officer, George Svoboda

Senior vice-president and chief of operations, including the branches, Lucille Van Order

Senior vice-president and investments officer, Anna Martinez

Senior vice-president and controller, Arnold Weitzman

ALCO (sometimes called the *funds management committee*) had responsibility for the overall financial direction of the bank. ALCO was responsible for controlling the attraction and application of the bank's funds. At its monthly meetings the committee reviewed the status of the bank's liquidity, interest rate sensitivity, investment and loan portfolios, deposit activity and pricing, and capital. ALCO's considered decisions were referred for action to three separate committees for loans, investments, and pricing. ALCO's activities were monitored by the bank's board of directors. All decisions pertaining to the bank's capital position were made by the board.

## ECONOMIC AND INTEREST RATE CONDITIONS

Chairman Ed Chalmers called the meeting to order and asked Arnold Weitzman to distribute the agenda (Exhibit 1). The meeting began with a discussion of national and local economic and interest rate conditions, led by Dwight Jamison. The discussion focused on the continuing steeply positive slope of the yield curve. Jamison directed the committee's attention to the interest rate report shown in Exhibit 2. He noted that short-term interest rates, represented by the three-month Treasury bill, recently had declined to 3 percent, while the yields on long-term Treasury securities, such as the 30-year bond, were 7.5 percent or more. He seemed optimistic that short-term interest rates would remain low. He reminded the committee that the Federal Reserve had lowered the discount rate repeatedly in the past several months and observed that the Fed seemed determined to hold rates down to prevent any interruption of the economic recovery.

However, Jamison cautioned that the presidential election to be held the coming week, on November 3, might change the present outlook. Several prominent economists believed that if the Democratic candidate were elected—and it seemed that he would be—a fiscal stimulus package of increased government spending might ignite inflationary forces and drive interest rates higher. If that happened, he warned, "the stage is set for deposit interest rates to rise rapidly. Banks

that are investing in long-term securities with today's low-cost, short-term deposits could have a lot of difficulty."

Chalmers joined in with the observation that the steep upward yield curve could not continue forever, and he speculated that one of two things would occur: either the low, short-term interest rates would pull down the long-term rates or the high, long-term rates would force the short-term rates to surge. Chalmers commented that financial theory supported the latter result; short-term rates must eventually rise. He said, "It is just a matter of time before short-term rates take off."

## BANK PERFORMANCE

Arnold Weitzman, the bank's controller, distributed the bank's income statements, balance sheets, and ratio analysis (Exhibits 3, 4, and 5, respectively). The committee noted with satisfaction that the bank's profitability remained strong. However, Weitzman explained that although bank profits were up for the first three quarters of 1992, results for the third quarter, as well as for October, were below the bank's profit plan. "The August, September, and October figures show that we are not sustaining the unprecedented net interest margins we made in the first two quarters of this year."

Loan quality was very high, and virtually no losses had been experienced for the past three years. George Svoboda, who had joined the bank several years ago as its chief lending officer, could not avoid gloating over the vast improvement in loan quality. "When I arrived here three and a half years ago, this bank's loan policies were out of control. With the huge losses it had taken, the bank was almost dead in the water. The turnaround in our loan quality is truly remarkable."

President Jamison countered, "George, we may not be taking losses, but it looks to me like we are not taking *loans* either! We seem to have developed a large liquidity position and have no place to invest it. We have finally rebuilt our capital from the disasters in real estate lending this bank experienced in the late 1980s. Is it not time to use our capital for making loans to business? After all, the purpose of our capital is to support that kind of risk taking."

## LOAN ACTIVITY

Since his arrival as head loan officer at Peralta National Bank, George Svoboda had insisted that the bank adopt a comprehensive loan policy and a rigorous structure of loan analysis and approval. The loan policy set strict documentation requirements, and loans were reviewed periodically to ascertain that borrowers were performing as agreed and that loan file data were current. The policy required the board to set the desired mix of commercial, consumer, agricultural, and real estate loans. A new approval process for loan requests consisted of controls at three levels. First, individual loan officers were given approval authority levels that did not require committee action. These ranged from $10,000 for junior officers to $75,000 for President Jamison and Chief Lending Officer Svoboda. Second, the senior loan committee met at least twice weekly to review requests for large loans and lines of credit. This committee also considered any requests that raised the aggregate borrowing of a customer to $100,000 or more. Finally, at the third level of approval, loan requests that raised a single borrower's aggregate borrowings above $500,000 were submitted to a board of directors loan committee.

Recently, real estate loans had constituted about 10 percent of the loan portfolio, which fell far short of the board's desired 25 percent target. Also, the bank's 52 percent loan-to-deposit ratio was well below the board's desired ratio of 65 to 75 percent.

Svoboda reported a continuing shortage of what he considered good-quality loan requests. "In fact," he commented, "since the beginning of this year, we have had quite a few of our strong borrowers reduce or pay off their loans. As you know, we are extremely liquid, but until loan demand becomes more vigorous, I suggest we invest excess funds in short-term, readily marketable securities. The time will come when our borrowers will expect us to have funds immediately available."

Svoboda observed that most economists were predicting slow, if any, loan growth through the first half of 1993. "Our largest borrowers agree," he said. "They are telling us to expect their funding needs to accelerate in the second half of next year. In the meantime, even though the loan portfolio is shrinking, we are still receiving high income because of our new premium pricing policy of charging for loan risk as fully as possible. Concerning the restoration of our capital position, it is true that we have made progress. Our risk-based capital to risk-weighted assets is 11 percent and exceeds the board's minimum 10 percent limit. Also, we have nearly achieved the board's leverage capital limit of 7 percent. However, our capital ratios remain well below those of our peers. I believe we must protect the bank's capital by remaining cautious until highly qualified borrowers return."

## SECURITIES ACTIVITY

Peralta Bank's investment policy required the purchase and sale of investment securities with maturities of greater than one year to be submitted to ALCO for approval. The stated objectives for management of the investment portfolio were as follows:

1. To ensure an adequate degree of safety of invested funds.
2. To provide liquidity.
3. To act as a primary asset pool for the management of interest rate risk.
4. To maximize the return on invested funds.
5. To provide a mix of securities that meets collateral requirements for public deposits.

Anna Martinez, the investment officer, reported that since August, inflows of funds from loan payoffs and a large volume of maturing securities had been reinvested in Treasury bills, interest-bearing interbank deposits, and short-term tranches of mortgage pass-through securities called *planned amortization classes (PACs)*. In addition, the bank had developed a large position in Federal funds sales. Martinez explained that in her opinion, the decline in net interest margin recorded since August was due to the shift from high-yielding loans and securities to low-yielding short-term securities. "However," she explained, "the bank's interest sensitivity position has improved." Martinez distributed the interest sensitivity analyses prepared by her department (Exhibits 6 and 7). Referring to Exhibit 5, she noted, "We are slightly more liability sensitive than our peer banks, but we have twice the volume of assets repriceable in three months as our peers." Regarding the interest sensitivity report shown in Exhibit 6, she commented, "Actually, I am not satisfied that we report the interest sensitivities of our core deposits correctly—especially our demand and NOW deposits. Are some of these truly repriceable in one to three months? Why are they not all shown in the long-term categories?"

Concerning the shape of the yield curve, Martinez argued, "The present yield curve is the steepest that any of us can remember. This is the time to invest in long-term bonds and mortgage-backed securities. The spread between deposit rates at less than 3 percent and 30-year Treasury bond yields at 7.5 percent or—even better—mortgage-backed securities at 8.5 percent is a sure thing. And if interest rates do start to move up, these spreads of $4\frac{1}{2}$ to $5\frac{1}{2}$ percent give us a huge cushion against increases in the cost of our deposits. I believe we could move our whole Federal funds position into long-term securities such as guaranteed mortgage agency securities—Ginnie Maes or Freddie Macs."

## THE DEBATE

Lucille Van Order, the bank's operations officer, had been silent until now. On hearing Martinez's comments, she spoke up concerning the risks of the potential effects of rising interest rates on deposit pricing and long-term securities. "After all, if we are forced to become more competitive on deposit rates and we are locked into long-term securities, our net interest income is going to be damaged." Van Order reminded the committee that the bank's policy for managing interest sensitivity prohibited the bank from taking interest rate positions that could impair the bank's planned net interest income by more than 5 percent if interest rates changed by 1 percent. Referring to Exhibit 7, Van Order noted that a 1 percent rise in interest rates would reduce November's net interest income by 5.4 percent, an amount that exceeded the 5 percent limit on interest rate risk exposure that had been established as policy by the board of directors. She stated that in her opinion, a larger movement in interest rates would do even more serious damage to net interest income.[1]

[1] Investment Department staff members prepared the matrix shown in Exhibit 7 every month, using the bank's computer

At this point, several members of the committee began talking at the same time. Jamison cautioned against extending investment maturities beyond five years, noting that "we may not earn $7\frac{1}{2}$ percent or $8\frac{1}{2}$ percent but 6 percent or 7 percent still would give us an ample spread over 3 percent deposits and we would not be locked in to 30-year securities."

Svoboda countered, observing, "We are going to need those deposits later next year. If interest rates rise, we will have to raise our deposit prices to meet them or we will be left high and dry when our major loan accounts come looking for funds. The best alternative is to invest in short-term securities to just match off the deposits. Besides, this will keep our interest rate sensitivity from getting out of control."

Anna Martinez stated, "Maybe I have some alternatives that can keep everyone satisfied, and serve both our return and risk objectives." She produced an offering statement (Exhibit 8) of mortgage-backed offerings the bank had received yesterday afternoon. Ms. Martinez said, "These issues have no credit risk. The first two issues reprice monthly and the third annually, which would improve our interest rate risk position. And since we have a reputable investment banker making the offerings, we know that the average life calculations are accurate." The looks on the faces around the room hinted to Anna that the real debate was about to start.

simulation model. The matrix quantifies interest rate risk for the current month as well as the coming year. In addition to presenting current net interest income sensitivity, it reveals the bank's future net interest income sensitivity from a static perspective. This static view shows what the interest rate risk will be at future dates if the present balance sheet items are permitted to run off contractually between the present and the future dates shown.

To create the interest rate risk matrix, the bank simulates its expected base net interest income for future dates under a no-rate-change scenario. Then it determines the extent of income variations on the residual assets and liabilities, given certain changes in rates. The bank considers the assumption of immediate rate shocks (shown as positive 1, 2, 3, and 4 percent, as well as negative 1 and 2 percent) to be naive because it involves the instantaneous movement of rates at all maturities. The bank prefers instead the more realistic gradual changes shown. In addition, the bank tests for changes in basis—the risk that the relationship between rates on different financial instruments with equal maturities may vary.

---

**EXHIBIT I    Agenda for Asset and Liability Committee Meeting of October 26, 1992**

---

   I. Outlook for local and national economy and interest rates.
  II. Review of bank's performance:
      a. profitability
      b. loan quality
      c. capital
      d. interest rate sensitivity
      e. liquidity
 III. Loan activity report.
 IV. Securities portfolio status; proposed transactions.
  V. Deposit pricing committee report.
 VI. Proposed action steps.

---

---

**EXHIBIT 2    Yield Curve (as of 10/26/92)**

---

| Maturity | Interest Rate |
|---|---|
| 3 months | 2.971% |
| 6 months | 3.297 |
| 1 year | 3.516 |
| 2 years | 4.340 |
| 3 years | 4.888 |
| 5 years | 5.883 |
| 7 years | 6.428 |
| 10 years | 6.842 |
| 30 years | 7.664 |

---

**EXHIBIT 2**    *(continued)*    **Blue Chip Financial Forecasts**

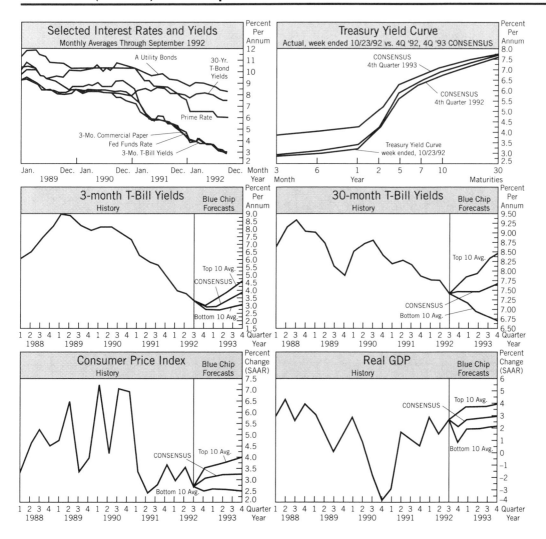

## EXHIBIT 3 Peralta National Bank Balance Sheets (dollars in thousands)

|  | 9/30/92 | 12/31/91 | 12/31/90 | 12/31/89 |
|---|---|---|---|---|
| **Assets** | | | | |
| Cash & due from banks | $ 8,020 | $ 11,510 | $ 12,630 | $ 12,910 |
| Investments | 76,042 | 71,955 | 54,162 | 55,449 |
| Federal funds sold | 41,030 | 200 | 0 | 7,390 |
| Gross: Loans & leases | 137,128 | 163,070 | 150,269 | 127,742 |
| Less: Allowance | 2,360 | 2,300 | 2,270 | 1,900 |
| Net loans & leases | 134,768 | 160,770 | 147,999 | 125,842 |
| Premises, fixed assets | 11,870 | 7,570 | 8,040 | 3,170 |
| Other assets | 13,310 | 13,090 | 12,000 | 2,610 |
| Total assets | $285,040 | $265,095 | $234,831 | $207,371 |
| **Liabilities** | | | | |
| Demand & NOW deposits | $111,910 | $ 92,980 | $ 78,460 | $ 78,040 |
| Money market deposits | 97,520 | 95,960 | 75,630 | 71,390 |
| Savings deposits | 24,580 | 19,520 | 15,410 | 13,690 |
| Time deps. < $100,000 | 22,820 | 25,780 | 23,900 | 14,190 |
| Time deps. > $100,000 | 7,020 | 11,310 | 25,700 | 14,500 |
| Total deposits | 263,850 | 245,550 | 211,660 | 191,810 |
| Other liabilities | 1,030 | 1,650 | 8,470 | 1,790 |
| Equity capital | 20,160 | 17,895 | 14,701 | 13,771 |
| Total liab. & capital | $285,040 | $265,095 | $234,831 | $207,371 |

## EXHIBIT 4 Peralta National Bank Income Statements (dollars in thousands)

|  | Three Quarters Ending 9/30/92 | 12/31/91 | 12/31/90 | 12/31/89 |
|---|---|---|---|---|
| Interest & fees on loans | $12,379 | $17,366 | $17,689 | $15,913 |
| Interest on investments—TE | 5,181 | 6,134 | 5,541 | 4,087 |
| Total interest income—TE | 17,560 | 23,500 | 23,230 | 20,000 |
| Total interest expense | 6,831 | 11,917 | 12,263 | 9,036 |
| Net interest income—TE | 10,729 | 11,583 | 10,967 | 10,964 |
| Noninterest income | 3,840 | 5,540 | 4,410 | 3,470 |
| Adjusted operating inc.—TE | 14,569 | 17,123 | 15,377 | 14,434 |
| Overhead expense | 9,770 | 11,500 | 10,190 | 10,160 |
| Provision: Ln. & ls. losses | 60 | 0 | 400 | 240 |
| Pretax net oper. income | 4,739 | 5,623 | 4,787 | 4,034 |
| Applicable income taxes + tax equivalence adjustment | 1,960 | 2,370 | 2,110 | 1,670 |
| Net income | $ 2,779 | $ 3,253 | $ 2,677 | $ 2,364 |

**EXHIBIT 5  Peralta National Bank Ratio Analysis (all numbers are percents)**

|  | 9/30/92[a] | | 12/31/91 | | 12/31/90 | |
|---|---|---|---|---|---|---|
|  | PNB | Peer | PNB | Peer | PNB | Peer |
| **Income Statement (% of Assets)** | | | | | | |
| Total interest income—TE | 8.45 | 8.17 | 9.26 | 9.07 | 10.25 | 9.52 |
| Total interest expense | 3.28 | 3.77 | 4.70 | 4.93 | 5.41 | 5.42 |
| Net interest income—TE | 5.17 | 4.40 | 4.56 | 4.14 | 4.84 | 4.10 |
| + Noninterest income | 1.85 | 0.53 | 2.18 | 0.53 | 1.95 | 0.56 |
| − Overhead expense | 4.70 | 2.79 | 4.53 | 2.84 | 4.49 | 3.12 |
| − Provision: Ln. & ls. losses | 0.03 | 0.13 | 0.00 | 0.17 | 0.00 | 0.00 |
| Securities gains/losses | 0.00 | 0.02 | 0.00 | 0.01 | 0.00 | 0.00 |
| = Pretax net oper. income | 2.29 | 2.02 | 2.21 | 1.66 | 2.30 | 1.36 |
| Applicable income taxes | | | | | | |
|     + tax equivalent adjustment | 0.94 | 0.68 | 0.94 | 0.58 | 0.93 | 0.43 |
|    Net income | 1.35 | 1.34 | 1.27 | 1.08 | 1.37 | 0.93 |
| **Profitability** | | | | | | |
| Net int. inc./avg. earn. assets | 6.02 | 4.69 | 5.37 | 4.42 | 5.30 | 4.43 |
| Return on avg. assets | 1.35 | 1.34 | 1.27 | 1.08 | 1.37 | 0.93 |
| Return on avg. equity | 19.41 | 13.42 | 19.81 | 10.87 | 22.33 | 9.63 |
| Net overhead | 2.85 | 2.26 | 2.35 | 2.31 | 2.54 | 2.56 |
| Efficiency | 0.67 | 0.57 | 0.67 | 0.61 | 0.66 | 0.67 |
| **Liquidity** | | | | | | |
| Volatile liab. dependence | −16.71 | −5.73 | 1.49 | −13.23 | 12.48 | −18.87 |
| Net ln. & ls. to assets | 47.28 | 54.42 | 61.51 | 55.78 | 63.99 | 56.67 |
| Net ln. & ls. to deposits | 51.97 | 60.23 | 66.41 | 62.95 | 71.00 | 65.48 |
| **Loan Quality** | | | | | | |
| Net loss to avg. ln. & ls. | 0.00 | 0.17 | 0.02 | 0.31 | 0.02 | 0.34 |
| Ln. & ls. allowance to ln. & ls. | 1.56 | 1.76 | 1.30 | 1.75 | 1.40 | 1.82 |
| Noncurrent ln. & ls. to ln. & ls. | 0.32 | 1.13 | 0.90 | 1.28 | 0.20 | 1.35 |
| **Capital** | | | | | | |
| Tier I leverage capital | 6.98 | 9.90 | 6.67 | 9.49 | 6.16 | 9.15 |
| Total RBC to risk-wt. assets | 11.01 | 19.11 | 10.31 | 18.58 | 9.67 | 18.02 |
| Retain. earnings to avg. equity | 11.40 | 8.09 | 13.42 | 5.63 | 6.18 | 5.07 |
| Dividends to net income | 55.60 | 18.77 | 46.04 | 40.42 | 74.95 | 33.18 |
| **Interest Rate Sensitivity (% of Assets)** | | | | | | |
| Assets repriced in 3 months | 42.11 | 23.92 | | | | |
| Liabs. repriced in 3 months | 59.02 | 39.47 | | | | |
|    Net 3-month position | −16.91 | −15.55 | | | | |
| Assets repriced in 6 months | 49.80 | 46.79 | | | | |
| Liabs. repriced in 6 months | 64.11 | 62.47 | | | | |
|    Net 6-month position | −14.31 | −15.68 | | | | |

[a]These data are annualized.

**EXHIBIT 6   Peralta National Bank Interest Sensitivity Analysis (dollars in thousands)**

| | September 30, 1992 | | | | | | |
| | 0–30 | 31–90 | 91–182 | 183–1 yr | 1–2 yrs | >2 yrs | Total |
|---|---|---|---|---|---|---|---|
| **I/S Assets** | | | | | | | |
| FF sold | $ 41,030 | | | | | | $ 41,030 |
| Secs. | 24,221 | $ 8,044 | $10,983 | $ 5,634 | $16,355 | $10,805 | 76,042 |
| Fl. loans | 30,688 | 4,806 | 2,862 | 6,124 | 30 | 88 | 44,598 |
| Fixed: | | | | | | | |
| Comm. lns. | 3,075 | 3,588 | 4,616 | 2,439 | 3,301 | 22,180 | 38,199 |
| Cons. lns. | 510 | 2,617 | 2,478 | 4,128 | 9,023 | 15,044 | 33,800 |
| Cr. cds. | | | | | | 1,829 | 1,829 |
| Agr. lns. | 375 | 868 | 623 | 487 | 1,649 | 1,568 | 5,570 |
| RE lns. | 107 | 178 | 260 | 341 | 1,049 | 11,197 | 13,132 |
| Allow LL | | | | | | (2,360) | (2,360) |
| Total | $100,006 | $20,101 | $21,822 | $19,153 | $31,407 | $60,351 | $251,840 |
| **I/S Liabs.** | | | | | | | |
| FF purch. | | | | | | | |
| Dmd. & NOW | $ 14,439 | $23,879 | $ 9,200 | | $ 3,342 | $61,050 | $111,910 |
| Sav. & MM | 122,100 | | | | | | 122,100 |
| CDs < 100 | 1,986 | 2,142 | 4,876 | $ 4,363 | 3,535 | 5,918 | 22,820 |
| CDs > 100 | 2,050 | 1,584 | 463 | 1,445 | 918 | 560 | 7,020 |
| Oth. liab. | | | | | | | |
| Total | $140,575 | $27,605 | $14,539 | $ 5,808 | $ 7,795 | $67,528 | $263,850 |
| GAP | −40,569 | −7,504 | 7,283 | 13,345 | 23,612 | −7,177 | |
| % GAP | −14.23% | −2.63% | 2.56% | 4.68% | 8.28% | −2.52% | |
| CUM GAP | −40,569 | −48,073 | −40,790 | −27,445 | −3,833 | −11,010 | |
| % C GAP | −14.23% | −16.86% | −14.30% | −9.62% | −1.34% | −3.86% | |

## EXHIBIT 7    Peralta National Bank Rolling 12-Month Interest Rate Risk

**Percent Change in Net Interest Margin Because of:**
**Immediate Rate Shock**

| Occurring on | 11/1/92 | 2/1/93 | 5/1/93 | 8/1/93 | 11/1/93 |
|---|---|---|---|---|---|
| (parallel rate shock) | | | | | |
| 4.00% | −31.6% | | | | |
| 3.00% | −21.1% | | | | |
| 2.00% | −12.0% | | | | |
| 1.00% | −5.4% | −5.3% | −4.7% | −0.5% | +2.3% |
| Base net int. income | $10.2 mm | $10.6 mm | $11.1 mm | $11.3 mm | $11.5 mm |
| Projection (annual) | | | | | |
| −1.00% | 10.8% | | | | |
| −2.00% | 15.6% | | | | |

**Yield Curve Variations**

| | | | | | |
|---|---|---|---|---|---|
| Gradual +2% over 2 yrs. | −3.4% | | | | +1.8% |
| Gradual +4% over 2 yrs. | −7.4% | | | | −0.4% |
| Short rates +2%—2 yrs. | −5.2% | | | | −0.8% |
| Long rates −2%—2 yrs. | −0.3% | | | | −1.7% |

**Basis Risk**

| | | | | | |
|---|---|---|---|---|---|
| Gradual +2% over 2 yrs. | −5.2% | | | | −12.0% |
| Gradual +4% over 2 yrs. | −5.4% | | | | −12.0% |

## EXHIBIT 8    Market Offerings (October 25, 1992)

| | Description | Coupon | Avg. Life (Yrs.) | Price | Yield (%) |
|---|---|---|---|---|---|
| Floating | CMO Floating Rate Class F 1 Mo Libor + 50 − Monthly | 3.75% | 3.5 | 100.00 | 3.75 |
| Floating | CMO Floating Rate Class G 11th District COFI + 100 − Monthly | 5.60% | 2.4 | 100.00 | 5.60 |
| Floating | GNMA ARM 1 Yr CMT + 150 − Annual | 5.50% | 8.5 | 100.00 | 5.50 |
| Fixed | FNMA 7 Yr Balloon | 6.50% | 4.6 | 100.50 | 6.33 |
| Fixed | FNMA 15 Yr | 7.00% | 6.0 | 100.875 | 6.80 |
| Fixed | FNMA 30 Yr | 7.50% | 8.2 | 98.25 | 7.86 |

# CAPITAL SAVINGS BANK, FSB

In spring 1991, Robert Thomas, president and chief executive officer of Capital Savings Bank, FSB, was reviewing detailed financial and operating performance statistics that had recently been assembled by Mrs. Jane Smithson, the savings bank's new executive vice-president for finance. Bob Thomas had requested these summary data to assist him in leading the appraisal of future prospects and operating goals by Capital's board of directors. A two-day board retreat had been scheduled in the next few days for this purpose, and Thomas was preparing a lengthy memorandum and related exhibits as a basis for leading the board discussion concerning Capital's present situation and its likely future opportunities. This searching examination was particularly important to Thomas since his employment could well become affected. There was evidence of growing board dissatisfaction. Moreover, a sizable performance bonus arrangement for key executives could become threatened if financial results did not soon improve. In short, Mr. Thomas was vitally concerned with the future outlook for the bank he directed.

When he had joined Capital Savings and Loan Association in 1979, it had been a rather sleepy $200 million S&L with a home office and two branches in the northern suburbs of a large midwestern city. Capital did what most other S&Ls had done over the last four decades—taking in money through various short-term savings and time deposits and lending money in long-term fixed-rate mortgages at a favorable interest spread.

Then, he thought to himself, all hell broke loose. Inflation increased sharply, forcing interest rates to rise substantially. Paul Volker, chairman of the Federal Reserve Board, declared, on October 6, 1979, that the Federal Reserve would manage reserves and the money supply, thereby permitting market forces to determine interest rates. The prime rate went from 12 to 20 percent, then to 13 percent, and up again to 21.5 percent—all in the next two years. Capital Savings and Loan lost money in 1980, 1981, and 1982; however, the book value of Capital stayed above declining regulatory standards. Thomas vividly recalled that the S&L's market value equity (estimated market value of assets minus estimated market value of liabilities) was negative. He wondered what would have happened if this measure had been applied by the regulatory agencies to Capital Savings and Loan.

Interest rates finally fell in the latter part of 1982 and throughout most of 1983 and 1984. Capital Savings returned to profitability and a positive market value of equity in 1983. The "good old days," however, did not return. Repayment and renegotiation of high-rate mortgages began to reduce the average yield in the association's mortgage portfolio. Intensified competition from investment bankers and government agencies lowered interest spreads on new mortgages. It seemed again that profits were attainable only by taking substantial interest rate risk.

The board of directors and officers of Capital decided that the institution could not be successful in the traditional S&L mode. The federal government encouraged deregulation of the financial service industry with legislation passed in the early 1980s. While S&Ls gained much broader asset and liability powers, they were forced to offer costly and risky new products and services in a highly competitive environment. Interest spread in the traditional mortgage business became too narrow.

Capital's board and officers had reacted aggressively in the middle and later 1980s—opening new branches, bidding for money with new expensive deposits forms, and offering new products and services. This change in operating methods had not gone smoothly, however, particularly in the unusually demanding environment of the middle and later 1980s. Capital changed its name from Capital Savings and Loan to Capital Savings Bank, FSB, but still maintained its mutual charter. In 1986 and 1987, the board and officers became even more aggressive: in acquiring funds, often going to the jumbo deposit market; in growth, purchasing three smaller S&Ls in the metropolitan area; and in asset employment, such as purchasing a mortgage company and making acquisition loans.

While there were some initial successes, the results in 1989 and 1990 were disappointing. Well-publicized problems of thrifts in other parts of the country had kept the cost of funds high. The passage of the Financial Institutions Reform, Recovery, and Enforcement Act (FIRREA) in the summer of 1989 seemed to heighten Capital Savings Bank's problems. A new regulatory agency, the Office of Thrift Supervision, replaced the Federal Home Loan Bank as Capital's primary supervisory regulator. Their deposits were now insured (at higher premiums than banks paid) by the FDIC. Two elements of the FIRREA caused particular concern to Thomas. First, the "Qualified Thrift Lender" (QTL) test was raised from 60 to 70 percent, that is, 70 percent of the savings bank's assets had to be in assets related to residential mortgages. Second, capital standards now had reached the same levels as those for national banks. Changing regulatory rules may cause our downfall yet, thought Thomas during these troubled times.

As he studied the implications of the financial data before him, Thomas wondered if 1990 could possibly prove a typical year in this new financial environment. The stock market crash in October 1987 had brought interest rates and consumer borrowing down somewhat; however, interest rates had risen slightly (on average) in 1988 and 1989, and the profits of Capital Savings Bank had fallen considerably. The recession and the Gulf crisis in 1990 had not helped in this nervous financial and economic environment. The regulators were now criticizing the association for growing too rapidly, for low net worth, for poor liquidity, and for substantial vulnerability to changes in interest rates. Thomas thought, we have been following all the ideas suggested by our consultants—investing in commercial and consumer loans, using competitive salaries to attract more competent employees, and using financial futures and interest-rate swaps to offset our mismatched rate sensitivity position. Unfortunately the use of these "synthetics" in the last three years had reduced Capital's profits significantly in that period.

Currently Capital's board and top officers were considering several conflicting alternative strategies. One was to stay with the basic S&L philosophy—buy funds short-term and lend long-term in the home mortgage market. This might work as long as rates were stable and there was a sharply rising yield curve, but interest rate risk remained high. Futures and swaps instruments might be used to reduce this risk.

A second alternative involved only making variable-rate mortgage loans. Rate risk would be lower, but interest margins would be razor thin under this alternative. A third approach was to sell as much of the current mortgage portfolio as possible and then originate and sell nearly all new mortgages made. Most of the association's assets would then be invested in government-backed, mortgage-backed securities. Repayment risk would be substantial, but this risk might be hedged with futures, swaps, or options.

Finally, one board member had suggested moving into more commercial property mortgages, consumer loans, and even junk bonds. This director acknowledged that credit risk was higher but that yields after provisions for losses were still considerably above yields on high-grade loans and securities. He cited several studies showing that diversified portfolios of lower-quality mortgages, loans, and bonds had substantially higher realized yields over several multiyear time periods. Further, he stated, "Deposit insurance will help us attract funds during brief periods of quality concerns," and asked, "Who cares whether we meet the thrift test or not?" Thomas wondered if the mutual association would have to become a stock association to do this. Moreover, would Capital convert to a bank charter—and, if this were possible, should Capital do so?

As he reflected on all these possibilities, Thomas thumbed through Capital's results for 1986 to 1990, which Mrs. Smithson had provided for the forthcoming board retreat (see Exhibits 1–3). For reference, Mrs. Smithson had put together some similar performance measures for a peer group of 10 relatively similarly sized midwestern S&Ls (see Exhibit 4). Thomas decided to analyze Capital Savings Bank to isolate the association's strengths and weaknesses, in contrast to those of the other associations, before making any proposals or specific suggestions to the board of directors. The principal questions in his mind, however, were: What is the future for our segment of the financial institutions market and Can we become and remain more profitable in this industry? Tough questions indeed!

**EXHIBIT I    Capital Savings Bank, FSB—Average Balance Sheets (dollars in thousands)**

|  | 1986 | 1987 | 1988 | 1989 | 1990 |
|---|---|---|---|---|---|
| **Assets** | | | | | |
| Cash | $ 6,800 | $ 8,000 | $ 10,000 | $ 11,802 | $ 13,259 |
| Government & agency secs. | 13,500 | 15,000 | 18,000 | 17,500 | 28,470 |
| Other investments | 13,850 | 18,000 | 26,750 | 37,502 | 31,233 |
| Accrued interest rec. | 750 | 805 | 1,225 | 1,430 | 1,845 |
| Subtotal | 34,900 | 41,805 | 55,975 | 68,234 | 74,807 |
| FHA/VA mortgages | 28,600 | 30,000 | 33,500 | 38,410 | 43,100 |
| 1–4 dwelling mortgages | 170,000 | 210,000 | 269,000 | 277,405 | 287,312 |
| 5+ dwelling mortgages | 55,600 | 75,000 | 122,500 | 130,103 | 150,034 |
| Other mortgages | 18,500 | 30,000 | 66,000 | 74,210 | 97,007 |
| Mortgage-backed secs. | 78,000 | 95,000 | 101,500 | 98,400 | 116,500 |
| Accrued interest | 4,700 | 5,550 | 7,750 | 8,915 | 10,650 |
| Contras to mortgages | (28,800) | (35,000) | (49,000) | (56,400) | (66,234) |
| Subtotal | 326,600 | 410,550 | 551,250 | 571,043 | 638,369 |
| Commercial mortgages | 3,210 | 5,000 | 7,500 | 21,850 | 58,217 |
| Consumer loans | 8,200 | 12,000 | 14,000 | 25,982 | 37,018 |
| Subtotal | 11,410 | 17,000 | 21,500 | 47,832 | 95,235 |
| Fixed assets | 5,010 | 5,250 | 7,275 | 9,150 | 9,321 |
| Real estate | 6,200 | 9,250 | 18,500 | 21,400 | 28,900 |
| Service Corporation | 8,000 | 10,000 | 14,750 | 18,250 | 23,125 |
| Goodwill | 5,500 | 5,000 | 7,500 | 9,420 | 9,030 |
| Other assets | 9,975 | 12,000 | 18,725 | 19,247 | 28,017 |
| TOTAL ASSETS | $407,595 | $510,855 | $695,475 | $764,576 | $906,804 |
| **Liabilities and Net Worth** | | | | | |
| NOW accounts | $ 31,600 | $ 28,205 | $ 32,860 | $ 38,627 | $ 47,614 |
| Super NOW accounts | 2,800 | 8,400 | 12,850 | 26,581 | 38,928 |
| Passbook savings accts. | 39,675 | 30,205 | 22,855 | 18,423 | 16,847 |
| Money market dep. accts. | 18,400 | 48,900 | 85,706 | 116,927 | 139,129 |
| Time deposits | 253,725 | 316,395 | 417,104 | 447,813 | 498,441 |
| Total deposits | 346,200 | 432,105 | 571,375 | 648,371 | 740,959 |
| Advances—FHLB | 22,000 | 35,000 | 81,000 | 68,400 | 98,000 |
| Borrowed from banks | 8,100 | 10,000 | 2,000 | 4,000 | 8,700 |
| Reverse repos | 4,000 | 2,500 | 5,000 | 4,000 | 12,850 |
| Other borrowings | 3,000 | 4,000 | 5,000 | 5,421 | 7,351 |
| Subtotal | 37,100 | 51,550 | 93,000 | 81,821 | 126,901 |
| Accrued int. payable | 875 | 950 | 1,500 | 1,780 | 2,105 |
| Accounts payable | 220 | 200 | 350 | 420 | 612 |
| Other liabilities | 2,760 | 2,500 | 3,100 | 3,312 | 4,547 |
| Subtotal | 3,855 | 3,650 | 4,950 | 5,512 | 7,264 |
| Reserves | 11,000 | 11,000 | 11,000 | 11,000 | 11,000 |
| Undivided profits | 9,440 | 12,600 | 15,150 | 17,872 | 20,680 |
| Total net worth | 20,440 | 23,600 | 26,150 | 28,872 | 31,680 |
| TOTAL LIAB. & NET WORTH | $407,595 | $510,855 | $695,475 | $764,576 | $906,804 |

**EXHIBIT I** *(continued)*

| | 1986 | 1987 | 1988 | 1989 | 1990 |
|---|---|---|---|---|---|
| **Supplementary Information** | | | | | |
| Interest-earning assets | $366,110 | $461,355 | $618,725 | $688,364 | $801,870 |
| Interest-bearing liabs. | 383,300 | 483,605 | 664,375 | 730,192 | 867,860 |
| Core deposits | 244,878 | 283,102 | 338,401 | 363,447 | 407,222 |
| Nonperforming assets | n/a | 13,324 | 18,267 | 25,894 | 30,174 |
| Loan loss contra | n/a | 4,118 | 5,024 | 8,192 | 9,941 |
| ISA (6 months) | n/a | 104,212 | 138,050 | 172,807 | 230,987 |
| ISL (6 months) | n/a | 320,821 | 431,986 | 492,991 | 576,281 |
| Employees (full equiv.) | 418 | 501 | 620 | 627 | 694 |

**EXHIBIT 2  Capital Savings Bank, FSB—Statements of Consolidated Income**
**(dollars in thousands)**

| | 1986 | 1987 | 1988 | 1989 | 1990 |
|---|---|---|---|---|---|
| **Income** | | | | | |
| Interest income | | | | | |
| Mortgages | $30,650 | $37,195 | $45,800 | $48,578 | $51,503 |
| Mtg.–backed secs. | 9,050 | 11,200 | 11,760 | 9,871 | 10,985 |
| Cons. & com. loans | 1,610 | 2,195 | 2,530 | 5,982 | 10,325 |
| Invest. deps., etc. | 3,180 | 3,675 | 4,925 | 5,815 | 5,771 |
| Total interest inc. | 44,490 | 54,265 | 65,019 | 70,246 | 78,584 |
| Loan fees & svc. chgs. | 4,180 | 5,250 | 7,750 | 8,941 | 11,804 |
| Service corporation | 1,600 | 2,050 | 2,730 | 3,420 | 3,977 |
| Other income | 500 | 700 | 1,050 | 1,207 | 1,301 |
| Total income | $50,770 | $62,265 | $76,545 | $83,814 | $95,666 |
| **Expenses** | | | | | |
| Interest expense | | | | | |
| Deposits | $37,269 | $42,824 | $52,750 | $56,316 | $63,324 |
| FHLB advances | 2,950 | 4,375 | 6,400 | 5,840 | 6,814 |
| Other borrowings | 1,610 | 1,725 | 1,200 | 1,508 | 1,981 |
| Total int. exp. | 41,829 | 48,924 | 60,350 | 63,664 | 72,119 |
| Operating expenses | | | | | |
| Salaries & benefits | $ 3,495 | $ 3,920 | $ 4,725 | $ 4,983 | $ 6,443 |
| Occupancy costs | 1,550 | 1,700 | 2,185 | 2,286 | 2,981 |
| Advertising/other | 1,580 | 1,700 | 2,290 | 2,598 | 2,904 |
| Nonoperating expense | | | | | |
| Loan losses | 880 | 1,000 | 2,545 | 4,700 | 6,108 |
| Other | 6 | 6 | 10 | 12 | 13 |
| Goodwill | 500 | 500 | 595 | 680 | 680 |
| Total expenses | 49,840 | 57,750 | 72,700 | 78,873 | 91,248 |
| Net income bef. taxes | 930 | 4,515 | 3,845 | 4,941 | 4,418 |
| Taxes | 210 | 1,355 | 1,295 | 2,016 | 1,784 |
| Net income | $    720 | $ 3,161 | $ 2,550 | $ 2,935 | $ 2,634 |

**EXHIBIT 3   Capital Savings Bank, FSB—Selected Financial Ratios**

|  | 1986 | 1987 | 1988 | 1989 | 1990 |
|---|---|---|---|---|---|
| 1. Net profit margin | 1.26% | 5.08% | 3.33% | 3.49% | 2.75% |
| 2. Asset utilization | 12.44% | 12.19% | 11.01% | 10.96% | 10.55% |
| 3. Return on assets | .16% | .62% | .37% | .38% | .29% |
| 4. Leverage multiplier | 19.94× | 21.65× | 26.60× | 26.48× | 28.62× |
| 5. Return on equity | 3.13% | 13.39% | 9.75% | 10.13% | 8.31% |
| 6. Growth of assets | 16.35% | 25.33% | 36.14% | 9.94% | 18.60% |
| 7. Growth of deposits | 16.84% | 24.81% | 32.23% | 13.47% | 14.28% |
| 8. Earning assets/assets | 89.82% | 90.31% | 88.96% | 90.03% | 88.43% |
| 9. Interest on earning assets | 12.15% | 11.76% | 10.51% | 10.21% | 9.80% |
| 10. Interest on int.-bear. liab. | 10.91% | 10.12% | 9.08% | 8.72% | 8.31% |
| 11. Net interest spread | 1.24% | 1.64% | 1.43% | 1.49% | 1.49% |
| 12. Net interest margin/EA | .73% | 1.16% | .75% | .96% | .81% |
| 13. Net interest margin/AA | .65% | 1.05% | .67% | .86% | .71% |
| 14. Prov. for loan losses/AA | .22% | .20% | .37% | .61% | .67% |
| 15. Risk-adj: NIM/AA | .43% | .85% | .30% | .25% | .04% |
| 16. Nonint. income/AA | 1.52% | 1.57% | 1.66% | 1.77% | 1.88% |
| 17. Nonint. expense/AA | 1.75% | 1.53% | 1.41% | 1.38% | 1.44% |
| 18. Net burden/AA | .22% | −.05% | −.26% | −.39% | −.45% |
| 19. Income taxes/AA | .05% | .27% | .19% | .26% | .20% |
| 20. Return on assets | .16% | .62% | .37% | .38% | .29% |
| 21. Salary & benefits/AA | .86% | .77% | .68% | .65% | .71% |
| 22. Occupancy costs/AA | .38% | .33% | .31% | .30% | .33% |
| 23. Advertising & OE exp./AA | .39% | .33% | .33% | .34% | .32% |
| 24. Nonoper. expenses/AA | .12% | .10% | .09% | .09% | .08% |
| 25. Liquid assets/AA | 8.56% | 8.18% | 8.05% | 8.92% | 8.25% |
| 26. Borrowed funds/AA | 9.10% | 10.08% | 13.37% | 10.70% | 13.98% |
| 27. Core deposits/AA | 60.08% | 55.42% | 48.66% | 47.54% | 44.91% |
| 28. Real estate/AA | 1.52% | 1.81% | 2.66% | 2.80% | 3.19% |
| 29. Net worth/AA | 5.01% | 4.62% | 3.76% | 3.78% | 3.49% |
| 30. Net worth/EA | 5.58% | 5.12% | 4.23% | 4.19% | 3.95% |
| 31. Net worth/loans | 6.05% | 5.52% | 4.57% | 4.66% | 4.32% |
| 32. ISA/assets | n/a | 19.81% | 19.85% | 22.60% | 25.47% |
| 33. ISL/assets | n/a | 62.80% | 62.11% | 64.48% | 63.55% |
| 34. Gap/assets | n/a | −42.99% | −42.26% | −41.88% | −38.08% |

**EXHIBIT 4    Capital Savings Bank, FSB—Selected Financial Ratios for Peer Institutions**

|  | 1986 | 1987 | 1988 | 1989 | 1990 |
|---|---|---|---|---|---|
| 1. Net profit margin | 5.99% | 6.43% | 6.65% | 6.31% | 6.27% |
| 2. Asset utilization | 12.07% | 11.82% | 12.03% | 11.64% | 11.17% |
| 3. Return on assets | 0.73% | 0.76% | 0.80% | 0.73% | 0.70% |
| 4. Leverage multiplier | 16.10× | 15.80× | 16.01× | 16.62% | 17.13% |
| 5. Return on equity | 11.65% | 12.01% | 12.81% | 12.23% | 12.00% |
| 6. Growth of assets |  | 18.24% | 16.87% | 12.47% | 13.21% |
| 7. Growth of deposits |  | 17.98% | 15.01% | 12.40% | 12.63% |
| 8. Earning assets/assets |  | 89.90% | 88.20% | 88.78% | 89.44% |
| 9. Interest on earning assets |  | 11.41% | 11.44% | 11.06% | 10.71% |
| 10. Interest on int.-bear. liab. |  | 9.43% | 9.50% | 9.18% | 8.82% |
| 11. Net interest spread |  | 1.98% | 1.94% | 1.88% | 1.89% |
| 12. Net interest margin/EA |  | 1.63% | 1.62% | 1.54% | 1.54% |
| 13. Net interest margin/AA |  | 1.46% | 1.43% | 1.37% | 1.37% |
| 14. Prov. for loan losses[a]/AA |  | — | — | — | — |
| 15. Risk-adj: NIM/AA |  | 1.46% | 1.43% | 1.37% | 1.37% |
| 16. Nonint. income/AA |  | 1.21% | 1.40% | 1.49% | 1.51% |
| 17. Nonint. expense[a]/AA |  | 1.68% | 1.73% | 1.85% | 1.89% |
| 18. Net burden/AA |  | .47% | .33% | .36% | .38% |
| 19. Income taxes/AA |  | .23% | .30% | .28% | .29% |
| 20. Return on assets |  | .76% | .80% | .73% | .70% |
| 21. Salary & benefits/AA |  | .76% | .77% | .75% | .74% |
| 22. Occupancy costs/AA |  | .27% | .28% | .28% | .29% |
| 23. Advertising & OE exp./AA |  | .40% | .42% | .40% | .38% |
| 24. Nonoper. expenses/AA |  | .05% | .06% | .05% | .04% |
| 25. Liquid assets/AA |  | 13.80% | 14.50% | 14.87% | 14.39% |
| 26. Borrowed funds/AA |  | 9.94% | 11.50% | 11.36% | 12.01% |
| 27. Core deposits/AA |  | 73.66% | 70.87% | 69.18% | 68.77% |
| 28. Real estate/AA |  | 2.55% | 3.30% | 3.19% | 3.43% |
| 29. Net worth/AA |  | 6.33% | 6.25% | 6.02% | 5.81% |
| 30. Net worth/EA |  | 7.04% | 7.02% | 6.88% | 6.64% |
| 31. Net worth/loans |  | 8.05% | 8.07% | 7.73% | 7.58% |
| 32. ISA/assets |  | 44.28% | 44.07% | 43.98% | 43.70% |
| 33. ISL/assets |  | 61.42% | 60.32% | 61.08% | 59.91% |
| 34. Gap/assets |  | −17.14% | −16.25% | −17.10% | −16.21% |

[a]Included in noninterest expenses.

# MIDLAND FIRST NATIONAL BANK

It was early 1984 and Hugh Leonard, the president and chief executive officer of both the Midland First National Bank and the Midland First Corporation, pondered his first three years on the job. In particular, he was considering three areas: (1) the cause of the bank's roller-coaster performance over the last couple of years; (2) the reasonableness of the bank's $30 million capital offering in 1983; and (3) a strategic plan that would lead to a satisfactory performance in the challenging banking environment over the next few years.

The Midland First National Bank and Trust Co., N.A., was the flagship bank (over 90 percent of total assets) of the Mid-First Corporation, a multibank holding company that owned three bank affiliates. Mid-First also operated six nonbank subsidiaries that were separate entities in the following areas: leasing, consumer finance, mortgage banking, credit life insurance, accident and health insurance, data processing, and discount brokerage. These nonbank subsidiaries were still relatively small, but they had enabled the holding company to expand its financial product line and to grow beyond the geographic borders of the rather slowly developing state in which it was located.

At the end of 1983, Midland First National Bank had resources of just under $6 billion and operated 269 offices throughout the state, which allowed statewide branch banking. Mid-First had been one of the three largest banks in the state for several decades and had become the largest in the state for most of the 1970s. Nonetheless, more aggressive management had allowed two other bank holding companies in the state to grow $1 billion to $2 billion larger in resources than Mid-First Corporation by 1983. The Trust Department at Midland First National was smaller than those at the other large banks in the state, but the bank was planning to emphasize its Trust Department and related services.

In April 1983, Midland and its affiliates had joined a transcontinental ATM system with 33 other large banks. At year end, over 2,500 ATMs were installed across the country, and by 1988 the system called for some 10,000 ATMs in operation nationally. In addition, Midland First National helped organize "Dollar Stations, Inc.," a statewide electronic banking network already serving more than 3 million cardholders. "Our market plans seem good," Leonard concluded, "but why can't we make money?"

In evaluating past performance, Leonard remembered how he had been considered somewhat of a hero when (after arriving in early 1981) the bank's earnings jumped from $0.99 per share for 1980 to $3.41 per share for 1981. Although Mid-First's market price had fluctuated narrowly between $13 and $25 per share (down from $19 to $41 per share in 1978–1979) on the over-the-counter market, Leonard had been widely praised. In 1982, however, some of the praise faded away. Bank earnings fell to $2.76 per share. In spite of this earnings decline, market price had averaged $16 per share, primarily because bank stock prices in general improved as the national outlook brightened. In 1983, earnings fell further to $2.00 per share, but the market price rose to $23 per share in early 1984. Leonard wondered what he had done right in 1981, wrong in 1982 and 1983, and how the bank was positioned to perform in 1984. Exhibits 1 to 5 contain complete financial information for the bank from 1981 to 1983. Exhibits 6 to 8 contain supplemental data on Midland First and its peers from 1981 through 1983.

In evaluating Mid-First Corporation's 1983 capital offering, Leonard thought he should consider the bank's capital adequacy, its dividend policy, the form of capital used, and the bank's potential for future growth. Midland First's ratio of average equity to average total assets had been 6.2 percent for 1979, 5.9 percent for 1980, 6.2 percent for 1981, and 6.1 percent for 1982. In 1981, Leonard had successfully convinced the Comptroller's office that managed asset growth, higher earnings, and lower dividends would return the bank's capital position to an adequate

6 percent level. In fact, however, faster asset growth, lower earnings, and an increase in dividends from $0.20 per quarter in 1981 to $0.25 per quarter in 1982 pushed the Comptroller to strongly encourage the bank to raise additional capital in 1983. It was decided that Mid-First would increase its capital through the issuance of 600,000 fractional shares of adjustable rate cumulative preferred stock (see Exhibit 9). The proceeds would then be used to buy common stock in Mid-First. Accordingly, Mid-First filed a registration statement for $30 million of such shares, which became effective on February 14, 1983. Leonard wondered, however, if the bank had done the right thing. The holding company had sold the preferred issue but still had not bought the common stock of Midland National Bank.

Finally, Leonard's stomach churned when he thought of the future. Midland was in a branch banking state in which reduction in noninterest expense would be difficult to achieve. The very successful new MDAs and Super NOWs had changed the bank's funding mix. This seemed likely to put continuing pressure on the bank's net interest margin. Competition from banks and other institutions within the state would remain high during the foreseeable future. Bank and nonbank financial institutions from other states would become more of a factor in Midland's markets. In 1979 changes in bankruptcy laws also seemed to be encouraging many marginal borrowers not to pay. What strategic plan would work over the next five years? thought Leonard. Here we sit, a $6 billion midwestern bank that urgently must decide what financial products we can profitably sell and whether we should be an "acquirer" or an "acquiree" as geographic boundaries disappear.

Mr. Leonard realized that he and his senior officers must formulate conclusions on several critical questions. Among them were:

1. A thorough analysis and evaluation of the growth and profit performance of Midland First National Bank and Trust Company for 1981 to 1983.

2. A study of the risks Mid-First had taken to achieve its level of profitability.

3. An assessment of the bank's issue of floating-rate preferred stock in 1983. Did the bank need additional capital? If so, would an alternative form of capital be more suitable?

4. A thorough review of Mid-First's strengths and weaknesses.

5. A strategic plan that could lead to at least a satisfactory performance in the challenging period over the next few years.

**EXHIBIT I  Mid-First Corporation—Consolidated Year-end Balance Sheet (dollars in thousands)**

| | December 31 | |
| --- | --- | --- |
| | **1983** | **1982** |
| **Assets** | | |
| Cash and due from banks | $ 480,193 | $ 389,805 |
| Money market instruments | | |
| Interest-bearing deposits with banks | 688,215 | 718,665 |
| Federal Funds sold and securities purchased under resale agreements | 6,322 | 116,850 |
| Other short-term investments | 7,947 | 3,995 |
| Trading account securities | 23,662 | 14,060 |
| Total money market instruments | 726,146 | 853,570 |

**EXHIBIT I**   *(continued)*

|  | December 31 | |
|---|---|---|
|  | **1983** | **1982** |
| Investment securities | 1,089,492 | 937,918 |
| Total loans and leases | 3,477,853 | 3,250,722 |
| Less unearned income | 125,934 | 118,679 |
| Less reserve for losses | 34,201 | 31,170 |
| Net loans and leases | 3,317,718 | 3,100,873 |
| Banking premises and equipment—net | 118,171 | 119,949 |
| Customer liability for acceptances | 197,420 | 302,139 |
| Interest receivable | 73,184 | 68,092 |
| Other assets | 60,111 | 50,009 |
| Total assets | $6,062,435 | $5,822,355 |

**Liabilities**

| Deposits | | |
|---|---|---|
| Demand | $1,140,544 | $1,106,794 |
| Savings and NOW accounts | 936,170 | 1,077,160 |
| Money market accounts | 567,073 | 137,090 |
| Time | 2,363,608 | 2,174,126 |
| Total savings, time, and money market accounts | 3,766,851 | 3,388,376 |
| Total deposits | 4,907,395 | 4,495,170 |
| Short-term borrowings | 492,816 | 587,493 |
| Other liabilities | 83,516 | 96,348 |
| Bank acceptances | 197,420 | 302,139 |
| Long-term debt | 16,718 | 13,679 |
| Total liabilities | 5,697,865 | 5,494,829 |

**Shareholders' Equity**

| Capital shares | | |
|---|---|---|
| Preferred shares—$25.00 par value; authorized 800,000 shares; issued 12,000 adjusted-rate cumulative shares in 1983 | 300 | |
| Common shares—$6.66⅔ par value; authorized 10,000,000 shares; issued 8,049,309 shares in 1983 | 53,662 | 53,639 |
| Capital surplus | 127,260 | 98,430 |
| Retained earnings | 183,687 | 175,614 |
| Less common Treasury shares | 339 | 157 |
| Total shareholders' equity | 364,570 | 327,526 |
| Total liabilities and shareholders' equity | $6,062,435 | $5,822,355 |

**EXHIBIT 2  Midland First National Bank and Trust Company—Average Balance Sheet and Yield Information, 1981–1983 (dollars in millions; tax-equivalent basis)**

| | 1983 | | | 1982 | | | 1981 | | |
| --- | --- | --- | --- | --- | --- | --- | --- | --- | --- |
| | Average Outstanding | Income/ Expense | Yield Rate | Average Outstanding | Income/ Expense | Yield Rate | Average Outstanding | Income/ Expense | Yield Rate |
| **Interest-Earning Assets** | | | | | | | | | |
| Loans and leases[a] | | | | | | | | | |
| Commercial | $1,617 | $191.5 | 11.84% | $1,393 | $210.8 | 15.15% | $1,123 | $211.9 | 18.87% |
| Real estate | 866 | 93.3 | 10.53 | 867 | 93.2 | 10.75 | 896 | 96.9 | 10.81 |
| Consumer—net | 551 | 86.9 | 16.24 | 544 | 86.4 | 16.47 | 624 | 90.5 | 14.89 |
| Leases | 68 | 11.0 | 16.07 | 70 | 12.0 | 17.02 | 61 | 10.2 | 16.51 |
| Foreign | 119 | 12.4 | 10.41 | 100 | 15.2 | 15.24 | 51 | 9.0 | 17.70 |
| Total loans and leases | 3,241 | 395.1 | 12.25 | 2,974 | 417.6 | 14.14 | 2,755 | 418.5 | 15.28 |
| Interest and dividends on investment securities | | | | | | | | | |
| Taxable | 618 | 59.4 | 9.62 | 502 | 48.1 | 9.58 | 617 | 54.5 | 8.83 |
| Tax-exempt | 387 | 35.2 | 9.10 | 462 | 40.3 | 8.71 | 482 | 45.6 | 9.47 |
| Total investment securities | 1,005 | 94.6 | 9.42 | 964 | 88.4 | 9.16 | 1,099 | 100.1 | 9.11 |
| Deposits with banks and other short-term investments | | | | | | | | | |
| Domestic | 54 | 4.6 | 8.52 | 74 | 9.6 | 13.13 | 143 | 23.4 | 16.37 |
| Foreign | 597 | 60.9 | 10.20 | 714 | 104.2 | 14.60 | 272 | 46.1 | 16.92 |
| Trading account securities | 16 | 1.5 | 9.46 | 24 | 2.9 | 12.47 | 4 | 0.6 | 15.49 |
| Total interest-earning assets | 4,913 | 556.7 | 11.37 | 4,750 | 622.7 | 13.16 | 4,273 | 588.7 | 13.83 |
| **Other Assets** | | | | | | | | | |
| Cash and due from banks | 413 | | | 446 | | | 448 | | |
| Banking premises and equipment—net | 119 | | | 119 | | | 107 | | |
| Reserve for loan and lease losses | (32) | | | (29) | | | (26) | | |
| Other assets | 395 | | | 389 | | | 250 | | |
| Total other assets | 895 | | | 925 | | | 779 | | |
| Total assets | $5,808 | $556.7 | 9.59% | $5,675 | $622.7 | 10.97% | $5,052 | $588.7 | 11.65% |

[a]Includes loan fees of $14.8 million in 1983 and $13.5 million in 1982; nonaccrual loans are included in the average outstandings for calculation of yields.

**EXHIBIT 2** (continued)

| | 1983 | | | 1982 | | | 1981 | | |
|---|---|---|---|---|---|---|---|---|---|
| | Average Outstanding | Income/ Expense | Yield Rate | Average Outstanding | Income/ Expense | Yield Rate | Average Outstanding | Income/ Expense | Yield Rate |
| **Interest-Bearing Liabilities** | | | | | | | | | |
| **Deposits** | | | | | | | | | |
| Savings and NOW accounts | $ 959 | $ 49.3 | 5.14% | $1,066 | $ 54.6 | 5.12% | $1,066 | $ 54.7 | 5.13% |
| Money market accounts | 485 | 39.1 | 8.06 | 4 | 0.6 | 15.24 | | | |
| **Time** | | | | | | | | | |
| Six-month money market certificates | 683 | 60.9 | 8.91 | 881 | 112.5 | 12.77 | 823 | 117.0 | 14.22 |
| Other CDs | 624 | 72.5 | 11.62 | 587 | 67.9 | 11.57 | 445 | 37.6 | 8.45 |
| CDs over $100,000 | | | | | | | | | |
| Domestic | 489 | 44.5 | 9.11 | 586 | 73.0 | 12.46 | 516 | 79.5 | 15.41 |
| Foreign | 30 | 2.9 | 9.66 | 62 | 9.0 | 14.53 | 49 | 7.9 | 15.98 |
| Other time CDs | 153 | 18.6 | 12.17 | 82 | 11.4 | 13.89 | 34 | 2.9 | 8.58 |
| Total time CDs | 1,979 | 199.4 | 10.08 | 2,198 | 273.8 | 12.46 | 1,867 | 244.9 | 13.12 |
| Total deposits | 3,423 | 287.8 | 8.41 | 3,268 | 329.0 | 10.07 | 2,933 | 299.6 | 10.22 |
| Short-term borrowings | 613 | 53.9 | 8.79 | 710 | 84.0 | 11.84 | 562 | 86.1 | 15.32 |
| Long-term debt | 17 | 1.5 | 8.81 | 13 | 1.2 | 9.21 | 13 | 1.2 | 8.93 |
| Total interest-bearing liabilities | 4,053 | 343.2 | 8.47 | 3,991 | 414.2 | 10.38 | 3,508 | 386.9 | 11.03 |
| **Other Liabilities** | | | | | | | | | |
| Demand deposits | 1,026 | | | 990 | | | 985 | | |
| Other liabilities | 371 | | | 371 | | | 253 | | |
| Total other liabilities | 1,397 | | | 1,361 | | | 1,238 | | |
| Shareholders' equity | 358 | | | 323 | | | 306 | | |
| Total liabilities and shareholders' equity | $5,808 | $343.2 | 5.91% | $5,675 | $414.2 | 7.30% | $5,052 | $386.9 | 7.66% |
| Net interest income | | $213.5 | 2.90% | | $208.5 | 2.78% | | $201.8 | 2.80% |
| Net yield on interest earnings assets | | | 4.35% | | | 4.39% | | | 4.72% |
| Net yield on total assets | | | 3.68% | | | 3.67% | | | 3.99% |

**EXHIBIT 3   Midland First National Bank and Trust Company—Average Balance Sheet**

| | Percent Distribution | | |
| --- | --- | --- | --- |
| | **1983** | **1982** | **1981** |
| **Interest-Earning Assets** | | | |
| Loans and leases | | | |
| Domestic | 53.8% | 50.6% | 53.3% |
| Foreign | 2.0 | 1.8 | 1.0 |
| Investment securities | | | |
| Taxable | 10.6 | 8.8 | 12.2 |
| Tax-exempt | 6.7 | 8.1 | 9.5 |
| Total investment securities | 17.3 | 16.9 | 21.7 |
| Short-term investments | | | |
| Federal funds sold | 0.7 | 0.8 | 2.5 |
| Repurchase agreements | 0.3 | 0.2 | 0.1 |
| Total short-term investments | 1.0 | 1.0 | 2.6 |
| Deposits with banks | | | |
| Domestic | | 0.3 | 0.2 |
| Foreign | 10.3 | 12.6 | 5.4 |
| Trading account securities | 0.3 | 0.4 | 0.1 |
| Total interest-earning assets | 84.7 | 83.6 | 84.3 |
| Other assets | | | |
| Cash and due from banks | 7.1 | 7.9 | 8.9 |
| Banking premises and equipment—net | 2.0 | 2.1 | 2.1 |
| Reserve for loan and lease losses | (0.6) | (0.5) | (0.5) |
| Other assets | 6.8 | 6.9 | 5.2 |
| Total other assets | 15.3 | 16.4 | 15.7 |
| Total assets | 100.0% | 100.0% | 100.0% |
| **Interest-Bearing Liabilities** | | | |
| Deposits | | | |
| Savings and NOW accounts | 16.5% | 18.8% | 21.1% |
| Money market accounts | 8.4 | 0.1 | |
| Time | | | |
| Six-month money market certificates | 11.8 | 15.5 | 16.3 |
| Other CDs | 10.7 | 10.4 | 8.6 |
| CDs, over $100,000 | | | |
| Domestic | 8.4 | 10.3 | 10.4 |
| Foreign | 0.5 | 1.1 | 0.9 |
| Other time certificates | 2.6 | 1.4 | 0.7 |
| Total time certificates | 34.0 | 38.7 | 36.9 |
| Total deposits | 58.9 | 57.6 | 58.0 |
| Short-term borrowings | 10.6 | 12.5 | 11.1 |
| Long-term debt | 0.3 | 0.3 | 0.3 |
| Total interest-bearing liabilities | 69.8 | 70.4 | 69.4 |
| Other liabilities | | | |
| Demand deposits | 17.6 | 17.4 | 19.5 |
| Other liabilities | 6.4 | 6.5 | 5.0 |
| Total other liabilities | 24.0 | 23.9 | 24.5 |
| Shareholders' equity | 6.2 | 5.7 | 6.1 |
| Total liabilities and shareholders' equity | 100.0% | 100.0% | 100.0% |

**EXHIBIT 4  Midland First National Bank and Trust Company—Percentage of Average Assets for Peer Group Banks with Assets from $3 Billion to $10 Billion**

|  | 1983 | 1982 | 1981 |
|---|---|---|---|
| Cash and due from banks | 8.25% | 8.96% | 10.81% |
| Investment securities |  |  |  |
| U.S. Treasuries and federal agencies | 6.99 | 6.04 | 6.15 |
| State and local governments | 7.63 | 8.17 | 9.18 |
| Other | 0.47 | 0.49 | 0.56 |
| Total investment securities | 15.09 | 14.70 | 15.89 |
| Interest-bearing deposits in banks | 10.75 | 10.75 | 9.36 |
| Trading account securities | 0.46 | 0.43 | 0.44 |
| Federal funds sold and resales | 3.89 | 4.07 | 3.37 |
| Loans, net of unearned income |  |  |  |
| Commercial, financial, agricultural | 23.98 | 24.03 | 23.66 |
| Real estate—construction | 2.99 | 2.71 | 2.22 |
| Real estate—mortgage | 9.26 | 9.76 | 9.59 |
| Consumer | 8.59 | 8.31 | 8.81 |
| Foreign | 4.82 | 5.20 | 5.50 |
| Other | 2.75 | 2.47 | 2.37 |
| Total loans | 52.39 | 52.48 | 52.15 |
| Less: Reserve for loan losses | 0.75 | 0.63 | 0.61 |
| Net loans | 51.64 | 51.85 | 51.54 |
| Direct-lease financing | 0.88 | 0.89 | 0.91 |
| Premises and equipment, net | 1.57 | 1.46 | 1.43 |
| Other assets | 7.47 | 6.89 | 6.25 |
| Total assets | 100.00 | 100.00 | 100.00 |
| Total earning assets | 84.79 | 83.17 | 82.12 |
| Demand deposits | 18.47 | 19.09 | 21.52 |
| Savings and time deposits |  |  |  |
| Savings deposits | 6.09 | 7.74 | 7.65 |
| NOW accounts | 3.00 | 3.09 | 2.46 |
| Super-NOW accounts and MMDAs | 7.85 | NA | NA |
| Money market certificates | 5.23 | 8.54 | 8.39 |
| Other time deposits under $100,000 | 7.77 | 6.28 | 4.49 |
| Time deposits, $100,000 and over | 14.59 | 16.67 | 16.64 |
| Deposits in foreign offices | 9.96 | 11.11 | 11.33 |
| Total savings and time deposits | 54.49 | 53.43 | 51.06 |
| Total deposits | 72.76 | 72.52 | 72.58 |
| Federal funds purchased and repos | 13.51 | 12.65 | 12.72 |
| Other short-term borrowings | 2.47 | 2.58 | 2.43 |
| Other liabilities | 5.26 | 6.56 | 6.45 |
| Total liabilities | 94.20 | 94.31 | 94.18 |
| Subordinated debt | 0.34 | 0.37 | 0.46 |
| Shareholders' equity | 5.46 | 5.32 | 5.36 |
| Total liabilities and equity capital | 100.00% | 100.00% | 100.00% |

**EXHIBIT 5 Midland First National Bank and Trust Company—Statement of Income**
(dollars in thousands except per-share amounts)

|  | 1983 | 1982 | 1981 |
|---|---:|---:|---:|
| **Income from Earning Assets** | | | |
| Interest and fees on loans and leases | $393,949 | $415,999 | $416,888 |
| Interest and dividends on investments | | | |
|    Taxable | 59,443 | 48,095 | 54,448 |
|    Tax-exempt | 22,977 | 26,577 | 27,647 |
| Other interest income | 65,489 | 113,850 | 69,469 |
| Interest on trading account securities | 1,457 | 2,963 | 575 |
|    Total income from earning assets | 543,315 | 607,484 | 569,027 |
| **Cost of Money** | | | |
| Interest on savings, NOW, and MMDA accts. | 88,431 | 55,183 | 54,755 |
| Interest on time deposits | 199,416 | 273,820 | 244,925 |
| Interest on short-term borrowings | 53,871 | 84,034 | 86,054 |
| Interest on long-term debt | 1,517 | 1,197 | 1,197 |
|    Total cost of money | 343,235 | 414,234 | 386,931 |
|    Net interest income | 200,080 | 193,250 | 182,096 |
|    Provision for loan and lease losses | 38,656 | 22,382 | 22,444 |
| Net interest income after provision for losses | 161,424 | 170,868 | 159,652 |
| **Other Income** | | | |
| Service and return charges on deposits | 19,720 | 17,409 | 15,327 |
| Trust fees | 7,972 | 6,987 | 7,014 |
| Credit card fees | 16,774 | 12,878 | 8,743 |
| Securities gains (losses) | (333) | (4,155) | (5,629) |
| Miscellaneous | 20,296 | 16,304 | 19,015 |
|    Total other income | 64,429 | 49,423 | 44,470 |
| Net interest income (after provision for losses) and other income | 225,853 | 220,291 | 204,122 |
| **Operating Expenses** | | | |
| Personnel | 113,559 | 105,047 | 95,338 |
| Occupancy | 18,350 | 18,165 | 16,977 |
| Equipment | 20,822 | 18,997 | 17,222 |
| Communications | 6,160 | 4,893 | 4,145 |
| Marketing and advertising | 5,156 | 4,166 | 4,977 |
| Taxes other than income taxes | (3,442) | 7,276 | 4,592 |
| Stationery, printing, and supplies | 10,502 | 10,451 | 10,168 |
| Other | 36,176 | 30,109 | 24,428 |
|    Total operating expenses | 207,283 | 199,104 | 177,847 |
| **Earnings** | | | |
| Income before applicable income taxes | 18,570 | 21,187 | 26,275 |
| Applicable income tax benefits | (45) | 1,011 | 1,147 |
|    Net income | $ 18,525 | $ 22,198 | $ 27,422 |
| Average common shares outstanding | 8,030 | 8,044 | 8,046 |
| Net income per common share | $2.00 | $2.76 | $3.41 |

# EXHIBIT 6 Midland First National Bank and Trust Company—Interest Rate Sensitivity Position, December 31, 1983 (dollars in millions)

| | 0–90 Days | 91–180 Days | 181–270 Days | 271–365 Days | Cumulative: 1 Year |
|---|---|---|---|---|---|
| **Use of Funds** | | | | | |
| Loans and leases | | | | | |
|   Variable-rate | $1,401.1 | | | | $1,401.1 |
|   Fixed-rate | 267.2 | $ 93.1 | $ 70.2 | $ 90.0 | 520.5 |
| Investment securities | 33.3 | 72.5 | 40.5 | 54.8 | 201.1 |
| Bank CDs | 654.2 | 27.0 | 0.4 | 6.6 | 688.2 |
| Funds sold and misc.[a] | 57.9 | | | | 57.9 |
|   Total | $2,413.7 | $ 192.6 | $111.1 | $151.4 | $2,868.8 |
| **Source of Funds** | | | | | |
| Money market accounts | $ 567.1 | | | | $ 567.1 |
| Demand, savings, and consumer time | 586.7 | $ 349.7 | $ 32.6 | $ 70.1 | 1,039.0 |
| CDs greater than $100,000 | 636.9 | 86.7 | 8.8 | 9.2 | 741.6 |
| Borrowed funds and misc.[b] | 521.6 | 10.3 | | | 531.9 |
|   Total | $2,312.3 | $ 446.7 | $ 41.4 | $ 79.3 | $2,879.6 |
| Rate sensitivity gap | $ 101.4 | $(254.1) | $ 69.7 | $ 72.1 | $ (10.8) |
| As percentage of total assets | 1.7% | 4.2% | 1.1% | 1.2% | .2% |

[a]Includes contractual floating-rate receipts on $20 million (notational principal amount) of interest rate swaps.

[b]Includes contractual payment on $10 million (notational principal amount) of interest rate swaps and $30 million of variable-rate preferred stock.

# EXHIBIT 7  Midland First National Bank and Trust Company—Information on Investment Securities

| | 1983 Book Amount | 1983 Market Amount | 1982 Book Amount | 1982 Market Amount | *Maturity Distribution as of December 31, 1983* | | | | | | | |
| | | | | | *Within 1 Year* | | *After 1 but within 5 Years* | | *After 5 but within 10 Years* | | *After 10 Years* | |
| | | | | | Amount | Rate[a] | Amount | Rate[a] | Amount | Rate[a] | Amount | Rate |
|---|---|---|---|---|---|---|---|---|---|---|---|---|
| U.S. Treasury | $ 382 | $377 | $ 308 | $308 | $153 | 9.84% | $229 | 10.03% | | | | |
| U.S. government agencies | 301 | 255 | 215 | 194 | 30 | 9.03 | 33 | 9.23 | $ 11 | 7.25% | $227 | 9.46 |
| State and political subdivisions | 384 | 294 | 396 | 310 | 3 | 11.32 | 27 | 10.23 | 202 | 8.68 | 152 | 8.37 |
| Other | 23 | 20 | 19 | 15 | | | 7 | 13.03 | | | 16 | 6.28 |
| Total securities | $1,090 | $946 | $ 938 | $827 | $186 | 9.73% | $296 | 10.03% | $213 | 8.60% | $395 | 9.02% |
| Interest-bearing deposits with banks | 688 | | 719 | | 666 | 10.13% | 22 | 10.97% | | | | |
| Total | $1,778 | | $1,657 | | $852 | 10.04% | $318 | 10.10% | $213 | 8.60% | $395 | 9.02% |

[a]The weighted average rates are based upon book value and effective yields weighted for the scheduled maturity of each security. Tax-exempt maturities have been adjusted to a tax-equivalent basis using a 34% tax rate.

**EXHIBIT 8  Midland First National Bank and Trust Company—Data Comparison (percents, unless marked)**

| | Midland First National Bank and Trust Company—Selected Data | | | Selected Data, Peer Group Banks | | |
|---|---|---|---|---|---|---|
| | 1983 | 1982 | 1981 | 1983 | 1982 | 1981 |
| 1. Year-end maturities of investment securities | | | | | | |
| Under 1 year | 17.08 | 5.22 | 5.31 | 28.63 | 17.41 | 18.94 |
| One to 5 years | 27.15 | 39.66 | 32.86 | 34.37 | 37.03 | 35.15 |
| Five to 10 years | 19.54 | 17.49 | 18.98 | 16.90 | 20.62 | 19.92 |
| Over 10 years | 36.23 | 37.63 | 42.85 | 20.03 | 24.94 | 25.99 |
| | 100.00 | 100.00 | 100.00 | 100.00 | 100.00 | 100.00 |
| 2. Year-end market-to-book value | | | | | | |
| Taxable securities | 92.07 | 95.27 | 85.01 | 97.55 | 99.66 | 91.42 |
| Tax-exempt securities | 77.81 | 78.43 | 63.38 | 90.34 | 90.04 | 81.72 |
| 3. Yield on average investment securities | | | | | | |
| U.S. Treasuries and federal agencies | 9.60 | 9.58 | 8.83 | 10.39 | 10.85 | 10.27 |
| Tax-exempt securities—tax equivalent | 9.11 | 8.72 | 9.46 | 13.28 | 14.05 | 13.61 |
| Total securities—tax equivalent | 9.47 | 9.17 | 9.11 | 12.04 | 12.90 | 12.25 |
| 4. Provision for loan losses | | | | | | |
| Provision/average total assets | 0.64 | 0.39 | 0.44 | 0.40 | 0.35 | 0.29 |
| Provision/average total loans | 1.18 | 0.77 | 0.83 | 0.75 | 0.65 | 0.55 |
| 5. Loan losses | | | | | | |
| Gross loan losses/average total loans | 1.28 | 0.93 | 1.02 | 0.81 | 0.67 | 0.54 |
| Recoveries/average total loans | 0.20 | 0.24 | 0.31 | 0.20 | 0.16 | 0.17 |
| Net loan losses/average total loans | 1.08 | 0.69 | 0.71 | 0.61 | 0.51 | 0.37 |
| 6. Loan loss reserve | | | | | | |
| Ending reserve/total loans | 1.02 | 1.02 | 1.05 | 1.33 | 1.21 | 1.18 |
| Ending reserve/net loan losses | 0.98× | 1.56× | 1.50× | 3.25× | 2.80× | 3.99× |
| Ending reserve/nonaccrual loans | 0.50× | 0.42× | 0.98× | 0.77× | 1.00× | 1.52× |
| 7. Earnings coverage of net loan losses | 1.31× | 2.39× | 2.82× | 6.10× | 5.04× | 6.86× |
| 8. Nonaccrual loans/year-end total loans | 1.94 | 2.38 | 1.02 | 2.13 | 2.19 | 1.20 |
| 9. Renegotiated loans/year-end total loans | 1.57 | 1.52 | 1.31 | 0.93 | 1.52 | 1.87 |
| 10. Loan yields | | | | | | |
| Commercial loans | 11.82 | 15.13 | 18.87 | 11.67 | 15.95 | 18.89 |
| Real estate loans | 10.50 | 10.75 | 10.81 | 11.00 | 11.93 | 12.39 |
| Consumer loans | 13.29 | 15.88 | 14.50 | 13.93 | 14.82 | 14.56 |
| Foreign loans | 11.87 | 15.24 | 17.65 | 12.07 | 15.43 | 17.64 |
| Total loans | 12.05 | 14.05 | 15.25 | 11.91 | 14.30 | 16.10 |

| | | | | | | |
|---|---|---|---|---|---|---|
| 11. Yield on interest-bearing deposits of banks | 9.98 | 14.44 | 16.75 | 10.21 | 14.01 | 16.78 |
| 12. Yield on Federal funds sold and resales | 9.30 | 12.39 | 16.10 | 8.67 | 12.40 | 16.16 |
| 13. Profitability ratios | | | | | | |
|     Profit margin—tax equivalent | 2.98 | 3.30 | 4.33 | 6.41 | 5.51 | 5.32 |
|     Asset yield or utilization—tax equivalent | 10.69 | 11.84 | 12.54 | 11.08 | 12.71 | 13.73 |
|     Return on average total assets | 0.32 | 0.39 | 0.54 | 0.71 | 0.70 | 0.73 |
|     Leverage or equity multiplier | 16.27× | 17.57× | 16.51× | 18.32× | 18.80× | 18.65× |
|     Return on average equity capital | 5.18 | 6.87 | 8.95 | 13.01 | 13.16 | 13.61 |
| 14. Noninterest income/average total assets | 1.10 | 0.87 | 0.88 | 1.15 | 1.04 | 0.99 |
| 15. Personnel expense | | | | | | |
|     Personnel expense per FTE employee | $20,470.00 | $17,820.00 | $15,130.00 | $24,150.00 | $23,000.00 | $20,050.00 |
|     FTE employees per $1 million average assets | 1.08 | 1.09 | 1.24 | 0.69 | 0.67 | 0.70 |
| 16. Funds costs | | | | | | |
|     All interest-paying funds | 8.46 | 10.38 | 11.03 | 8.70 | 11.27 | 13.25 |
|     All interest-paying deposits | 8.44 | 10.07 | 10.22 | 8.59 | 11.15 | 12.71 |
|     Domestic CDs—100,000 or more | 9.13 | 12.46 | 15.41 | 9.22 | 12.56 | 15.65 |
|     Deposits in foreign offices | 10.34 | 14.53 | 15.98 | 10.09 | 13.56 | 16.50 |
|     Federal funds purchased and repos | 8.55 | 11.84 | 15.32 | 8.90 | 11.80 | 15.85 |
| 17. Interest rate sensitivity | | | | | | |
|     Year-end market rate assets/total assets | 49.39 | 42.59 | 38.55 | 54.21 | 52.75 | 49.63 |
|     Year-end market rate funds/total assets | 49.58 | 41.18 | 40.09 | 51.39 | 47.98 | 50.40 |
| 18. Liquidity measures | | | | | | |
|     Net market rate position/total assets | (0.19) | 1.41 | (1.54) | 2.82 | 4.77 | (0.77) |
|     Temporary investments/total assets | 15.31 | 15.50 | 14.32 | 19.74 | 20.10 | 17.37 |
|     Core deposits/total assets | 68.21 | 66.27 | 63.50 | 49.49 | 46.88 | 44.51 |
|     Volatile liabilities/total assets | 21.92 | 23.25 | 24.82 | 39.37 | 42.32 | 43.24 |
|     Volatile liabilities dependence | 22.93 | 17.30 | 15.38 | 28.09 | 33.39 | 40.48 |
|     Federal funds purchased/total capital | 1.52× | 1.63× | 2.20× | 2.51× | 2.34× | 2.35× |
| 19. Capital measures | | | | | | |
|     Primary capital (total assets + loss reserve) | 5.73 | 6.13 | 6.17 | 6.23 | 5.91 | 5.93 |
|     Total capital (total assets + loss reserve) | 5.73 | 6.13 | 6.17 | 6.46 | 6.28 | 6.37 |
|     Primary capital (risk assets + loss reserve) | 8.35 | 8.78 | 8.96 | 9.32 | 8.45 | 8.47 |
|     Total capital (risk assets + loss reserve) | 8.35 | 8.78 | 8.96 | 9.76 | 8.98 | 9.10 |
|     Primary capital/total loans and leases | 11.08 | 11.46 | 11.93 | 11.72 | 11.15 | 11.25 |
|     Total capital/total loans and leases | 11.08 | 11.46 | 11.93 | 12.38 | 11.84 | 12.08 |
| 20. End-of-period growth rates | | | | | | |
|     Total assets | 4.28 | 5.66 | 10.18 | 11.12 | 10.49 | 10.07 |
|     Total loans | 7.39 | 9.52 | 3.43 | 11.63 | 8.68 | 13.97 |
|     Core deposits | 7.39 | 8.94 | 3.52 | 14.28 | 12.80 | 4.43 |
|     Volatile liabilities | 6.87 | (7.02) | 23.80 | 6.06 | 7.44 | 15.68 |
|     Primary capital | 2.94 | 4.47 | 7.18 | 12.33 | 9.44 | 9.98 |
|     Total capital | 2.83 | 4.66 | 7.86 | 10.71 | 9.32 | 9.08 |
| 21. Cash dividends declared/net income | 50.00 | 36.24 | 23.48 | 36.73 | 43.41 | 42.08 |

---

**EXHIBIT 9    Prospectus, Mid-First Corporation—600,000 Fractional Shares of 12,000
Adjustable Rate Cumulative Preferred Shares, 1983 Series ($25 par value)**

---

Each Fractional Share ("Share") representing 1/50th of an Adjustable Rate Cumulative Preferred Share, 1983 Series of Mid-First Corporation (the "Company") entitles the holder to all rights and preferences of such a fraction of an Adjustable Rate Cumulative Preferred Share, 1983 Series. Each Share will have a total liquidation value of $50. See "Description of Fractional Shares of Adjustable Rate Cumulative Preferred Shares, 1983 Series."

The dividend rate on each Share for the initial dividend period ending May 31, 1983, will be $9\frac{1}{2}\%$ per annum and such dividend will be paid June 1, 1983. Thereafter, dividends will be payable at a rate (the "Applicable Rate") which for any quarterly dividend period will be equal to 2.00% less than the highest of the "Treasury Bill Rate," the "Ten Year Constant Maturity Rate" and the "Twenty Year Constant Maturity Rate" determined in advance of such dividend period. However, the Applicable Rate for any dividend period will not be less than 6% per annum nor greater than 13% per annum. Dividends, when and as declared by the Board of Directors of the Company, will be payable quarterly on the first day of March, June, September and December of each year. See "Description of Fractional Shares of Adjustable Rate Cumulative Preferred Shares, 1983 Series—Adjustable Rate Dividends."

The Shares are redeemable, in whole or in part, at the option of the Company on or after March 1, 1988, and prior to March 1, 1993, at a price equivalent to $51.50 per Share and thereafter at a price equivalent to $50.00 per Share plus, in each case, dividends accrued to the redemption date. See "Description of Fractional Shares of Adjustable Rate Cumulative Preferred Shares, 1983 Series."

These securities have not been approved or disapproved by the Securities and Exchange Commission nor has the commission passed upon the accuracy or adequacy of this prospectus. Any representation to the contrary is a criminal offense.

---

|  | Price to Public[a] | Underwriting Discounts and Commissions[b] | Proceeds to Company[c] |
|---|---|---|---|
| Per share | $50.00 | $1.30 | $48.70 |
| Total | $30,000,000 | $780,000 | $29,220,000 |

[a] Plus accrued dividends, if any, from date of original issue.

[b] The Company has agreed to indemnify the Underwriters against certain liabilities, including liabilities under the Securities Act of 1933.

[c] Before deducting expenses estimated at $95,000.

---

The Shares are offered by the several Underwriters when, as and if issued by the Company and accepted by the Underwriters and subject to their right to reject orders in whole or in part. It is expected that the certificates representing the Shares will be ready for delivery on or about February 23, 1983.

---

# WELLS FARGO BANK*

At 3:00 P.M. on August 31, 1981, Frank Newman, executive vice-president and chief financial officer of Wells Fargo & Company, had just received a phone call from Donald Moore of Morgan Stanley & Co. Mr. Moore, a vice-president within the Financial Institutions Business Unit of this investment banking firm, was responsible for keeping Wells Fargo, an important client of the firm, informed of market opportunities, as well as initiating financing ideas and executing any transactions which might develop.

Their telephone conversation centered on an innovative financing idea called a *stock-for-debt* swap. In light of his bank's current financial position, the overall outlook for 1981 earnings, and the market for bank stocks, Mr. Newman wondered how Wells Fargo would benefit from such a transaction. In 1980 Morgan Stanley had completed a somewhat similar transaction for Wells Fargo, a cash repurchase of sinking fund bonds. As a pure cash transaction, the previous exchange was not completely analogous to the stock-for-debt swap being proposed.

## COMPANY DESCRIPTION

Wells Fargo & Company is a bank holding company whose principal asset is Wells Fargo Bank, the 11th largest bank in the U.S. and the 3rd largest west of the Mississippi on the basis of deposits. As of December 31, 1980, the bank had total assets of $21.8 billion and total net loans of $14.9 billion.

Wells Fargo is primarily a domestically oriented bank, with U.S. activities accounting for 85

*This case was written by Donald Moore and Mike Pepe of Morgan Stanley & Company, with assistance from George G. C. Parker, senior lecturer in management at the Stanford Graduate School of Business, and Bowen H. McCoy, managing director for Morgan Stanley & Company. Financial support for this project was provided in part by the Program in Finance of the Graduate School of Business, Stanford University. Copyright © 1981 by the Board of Trustees of the Leland Stanford Junior University. Used by permission.

percent of consolidated earnings. Retail banking activities are conducted through 383 branch offices throughout California and constitute the most significant portion of the company's business, accounting for almost 70 percent of the loan portfolio and 48 percent of consolidated earnings in 1980. Consumer banking services include savings programs, checking accounts, credit card services, home mortgage loans, and installment loans.

## FINANCIAL PERFORMANCE

### 1974–1979

During the period 1974–1979, Wells Fargo was one of the best performing banks in the country. Consistent growth was achieved in both the size of the bank's operations, as measured by its asset base, and in net income from operations (before security transactions). Assets grew by approximately 11 percent per annum, while net income increased at an impressive rate of over 22 percent per annum during the six-year period. The increase in the bank's earnings could be attributed largely to a substantial improvement in profitability, with return on assets increasing from 0.41 percent to 0.64 percent and return on equity increasing from 10.36 percent to 15.62 percent during the six-year period. Exhibit 1 illustrates this performance.

### 1980

Despite a 14.5 percent increase in assets in 1980, the bank's earnings declined to 1.2 percent, as return on assets decreased from 0.68 percent to 0.55 percent and return on equity decreased from 16.48 percent to 13.98 percent.

Earnings suffered in 1980 principally because of a decline in loan volume coupled with a narrower spread between the yield on earning assets and the rates paid on interest-sensitive liabilities. A drop in real estate lending activity resulted in a significant decline in real estate loan origination fees, an important source of income to Wells Fargo. Moreover, the bank's cost of funds increased from 7.35 percent in 1979 to 9.10 percent in 1980 due to a shift in the mix of the bank's liabilities. Relatively low-cost consumer deposits, such as savings, declined as a proportion of total funding sources while more costly deposits and borrowings, such as six-month Treasury certificates, commercial paper, and Federal funds, increased. Since a portion of the bank's consumer installment and single-family mortgage portfolios were funded on a short-term basis with interest-sensitive liabilities, the company's net interest spread—the difference between the average yield on earning assets (on a tax equivalent basis and including loan fees) and the average cost of funding assets—decreased from 4.47 percent in 1979 to 3.89 percent in 1980. Exhibit 2 tracks the increases in Wells Fargo's cost of funds from 1974 to 1980.

## 1981

These trends continued during the first six months of 1981, as average earning assets increased 13 percent, while the interest spread narrowed from 3.92 percent in the first six months of 1980 to 3.81 percent in the first six months of 1981. Contributing to the decline in spread was a continuing shift in the composition of consumer deposits to higher paying, interest-sensitive instruments, which are more expensive than traditional sources of bank funds. The bank's sizable portfolio of residential mortgages also adversely affected the results because it included a number of long-term mortgages with low, fixed rates of interest which were funded with interest-sensitive liabilities.

Income in the first quarter rose $5.6 million or 10 percent over the comparable period in 1980, including an $8.8 million gain on the sale of equity securities from a 49 percent-owned unconsolidated small business investment company.

## Common Stock Performance

In 1976 and 1977, Wells Fargo's common stock was trading at or close to book value. In April 1977, Wells Fargo sold 2 million shares of common stock at $27 1/8 per share when book value per share was $27. The net proceeds of $52 million served to strengthen Wells Fargo's capital base; by the end of 1977, average equity, as a percent of average assets, an important measure of leverage for a bank holding company, had in-

creased to 4.35 percent. However, this ratio declined steadily (see Exhibit 1) to a low of 3.86 percent for the first six months of 1981.

Wells Fargo's leverage had increased, as assets had grown faster than equity. In addition, the company was aware of the regulatory agencies' concern over the banking industry's declining capital ratios. Wells Fargo believed full utilization of its leverage capacity would impair its flexibility, thereby restricting the company's ability to take advantage of business opportunities that were expected with deregulation. In order to remedy this situation, the company had filed for $35 million of preferred stock in April 1981, but the fixed-income market subsequently declined and the cost of borrowing to Wells Fargo became unattractive. The issuance of common shares was also unattractive—with the stock trading at $26 1/4 compared to a book value of over $41 per share. Nevertheless, a common stock offering would augment the company's capital base and strengthen its equity position.

### Environment for Fixed-Income Securities

The U.S. capital markets during 1980 and through the first six months of 1981 were characterized by both absolute increases in interest rates and extreme volatility. During the 12-month period ending June 1981, for example, yields on U.S. Treasury notes with six-year maturities increased from 11.00 percent to 14.25 percent. The deterioration in the corporate bond market was even more pronounced with yields on intermediate term (3–10 years) corporate issues rising to 100 to 150 basis points above Treasury, eliminating the most favorable elective tax options associated with this transaction. The new rule stated that only depreciable assets could be written down, therefore enabling an issuer to defer taxes for only five to seven years. Purchasing discount bonds with cash lost some of its attractiveness in that Wells Fargo could only defer for five to seven years taxes payable on the difference between the face value of the bonds (the original sales price) and the discount repurchase price.

### Stock-for-Debt Swap

During their telephone conversation, Mr. Moore and Mr. Newman discussed the way in which a stock-for-debt recapitalization could be structured. Morgan Stanley could buy Wells Fargo's outstanding debt securities from institutional investors for Morgan Stanley's own account and, if agreement were reached between Wells Fargo and Morgan Stanley, the investment banker could then exchange its holdings of Wells Fargo debt securities for newly issued Wells Fargo stock with an equivalent market value. Morgan Stanley could then resell the shares of Wells Fargo stock to equity investors.

Mr. Newman believed that the exchange would be beneficial to Wells Fargo for several reasons. Wells Fargo would increase its equity base by the sum of the gains achieved on the debt retirement and the value of the shares issued in the exchange. As a result, a stock-for-debt recapitalization could have a favorable impact on Wells Fargo's leverage ratios. It would permit the company to retire discount debt at a time when bond prices were at record lows without incidence of "forgiveness of indebtedness" taxation. As noted above, on a cash purchase of an outstanding debt instrument bought at a discount, there was a tax liability on the gain which could only be deferred five to seven years. In a stock-for-debt recapitalization, however, there was no tax liability. Wells Fargo would record a gain equivalent to the difference between the principal amount of the bonds retired and the value of the bonds tendered in the exchange.

### The Mechanics of the Transaction

Effecting a stock-for-debt exchange was a somewhat complicated transaction which involved a number of areas of expertise within an investment bank. A specialized group of fixed-income salespersons and traders determined the amount of outstanding bonds which could be purchased at various prices and devised a strategy for purchasing the bonds in negotiated transactions with institutional investors. Because tax law required that exchanges could only take place between principals, Morgan Stanley would acquire the bonds for its own account. When Morgan Stanley had acquired sufficient bonds to effect an exchange, and if an agreement could be reached between Morgan Stanley and Wells Fargo on an appropriate exchange ratio, then the contemplated exchange could take place. Wells Fargo would have to file a Registration Statement with the Securities and Exchange Commission cov-

ering the new shares to be issued. Subsequent to the filing, Morgan Stanley would commence its marketing effort to develop interest in the shares which it would receive as principal. Later, the SEC would declare the Registration Statement effective and Morgan Stanley and Wells Fargo would attempt to reach agreement as to an appropriate exchange ratio. For example, if a price of $11.9 million were agreed upon, Morgan Stanley would deliver $17 million principal amount of debt (market value of $11.9 million) in exchange for an equivalent amount of Wells Fargo common stock. The number of shares of common stock would be based upon a negotiated market price including an underwriter's spread of 4 percent. Thereafter, Morgan would attempt to reoffer the stock to institutional investors.

### FRANK NEWMAN'S DECISION

Wells Fargo & Company's second quarter of 1981 earnings were down 11 percent from the second quarter of 1980 principally because interest rates paid for Federal funds and negotiable certificates of deposit during the quarter were the highest in U.S. banking history. To give greater flexibility in a fluctuating interest-rate environment, the bank's long-range plan called for a continued shift in the emphasis of its loan portfolio to interest-sensitive loans in the real estate, commercial, corporate, and international areas.

Without the stock-for-debt swap, the controller's department of the bank estimated operating earnings per share to be $5.30.

It was unclear to Mr. Newman whether earnings per share from the swap would be considered operating or nonoperating earnings on the income statements.

Mr. Newman believed that current market conditions provided an economically attractive opportunity to augment the bank's equity position and liability mix through the stock-for-debt transaction. During their telephone conversation, Mr. Moore told the Wells Fargo executive vice-president that he was confident that Morgan Stanley could purchase up to $17 million aggregate principal amount of the bank's 8.60 percent debentures due in 2002 at an average cost of $640 per $1000 debenture. However, before Mr. Newman recommended the recapitalization to the board of directors, he had to consider the following:

- The economic benefits of the transaction. Estimated cash flows associated with the repurchase of the 8.60 percent sinking fund debentures due 2002 are provided in Exhibit 5.
- The impact on earnings per share this year and in the future.
- The contribution the recapitalization would make to the company's equity position and leverage.
- The perception of the financial community and the impact on Wells Fargo's common stock.
- The reaction of the bank's regulators.

The before-tax cost of new borrowing for Wells Fargo was thought by Newman to be approximately equal to the yield to maturity on a before-tax basis of the existing notes outstanding.

As he thought about these issues, Mr. Newman glanced at a document sent to him by Morgan Stanley that provided a hypothetical analysis of the stock-for-debt transaction (see Appendix). He also knew that several Wall Street firms were estimating earnings of $5.50 per share in 1981 and $6.25 for 1982. Wells Fargo's common stock on the New York Stock Exchange closed at $27.75 per share, down $.125 from the prior day's close.

**EXHIBIT 1   Wells Fargo & Company—Financial Performance, 1974–1981 (June) (dollars in millions)**

| | 1974 | 1975 | 1976 | 1977 | 1978 | 1979 | 1980 | Latest 12 Months Ended 6/30/81 |
|---|---|---|---|---|---|---|---|---|
| Average equity | $ 444.0 | $ 477.0 | $ 517.0 | $ 613.0 | $ 706.0 | $ 790.0 | $ 871.0 | $ 938.0 |
| Average assets | 11,799.0 | 11,740.0 | 12,352.0 | 14,097.0 | 16,650.0 | 19,269.0 | 22,055.0 | 24,274.0 |
| Net income | 46.0 | 55.4 | 62.3 | 85.4 | 110.1 | 123.4 | 121.9 | 127.4 |
| Return on average assets | 0.41% | 0.47% | 0.50% | 0.61% | 0.66% | 0.64% | 0.55% | 0.52% |
| Return on average equity | 10.98 | 11.48 | 12.04 | 14.09 | 16.41 | 16.48 | 13.98 | 13.98 |
| Average equity/average assets | 3.76 | 4.06 | 4.19 | 4.35 | 4.24 | 4.10 | 3.95 | 3.86 |
| Earnings per share | $ 2.46 | $ 2.74 | $ 3.10 | $ 3.99 | $ 5.16 | $ 5.75 | $ 5.32 | $ 5.42 |
| Number of shares outstanding | — | — | — | — | — | — | — | 23,505,535 |

**EXHIBIT 2   Wells Fargo & Company—Cost of Funds, 1974–1981**

| | 1974 | 1975 | 1976 | 1977 | 1978 | 1979 | 1980 | Latest 12 Months Ended 6/30/81 |
|---|---|---|---|---|---|---|---|---|
| Cost of all funds[a] | 6.87% | 5.20% | 4.56% | 4.53% | 5.52% | 7.35% | 9.10% | 9.69% |
| Cost of interest-bearing liabilities[b] | 8.20 | 6.35 | 5.65 | 5.67 | 6.83 | 8.90 | 10.84 | 11.23 |
| Net interest spread[c] | 1.68 | 2.65 | 2.87 | 3.02 | 3.19 | 2.93 | 2.15 | 1.80 |

[a] Defined as interest expense divided by average earning assets.
[b] Defined as interest expense divided by interest-bearing liabilities.
[c] Defined as earning asset yield less cost of interest-bearing funds.

**EXHIBIT 3  Wells Fargo & Company—Market Information**

| | 1974 | 1975 | 1976 | 1977 | 1978 | 1979 | 1980 | 6/30 1981 |
|---|---|---|---|---|---|---|---|---|
| **Common stock prices** | | | | | | | | |
| High | $ 27.125 | $ 20.500 | $ 27.000 | $ 28.875 | $ 33.250 | $ 33.375 | $ 29.000 | $ 36.125 |
| Low | 9.500 | 12.875 | 15.625 | 24.125 | 24.000 | 25.375 | 21.625 | 30.625 |
| Close as of 12/31 | 13.000 | 15.500 | 27.000 | 26.875 | 27.125 | 26.875 | 28.500 | 33.000 |
| Price change in relation to S&P's 400[a] (%) | — | 90.4 | 133.0 | 151.0 | 148.8 | 130.6 | 108.5 | 121.7 |
| Price/earnings ratio | 5.3 | 5.7 | 8.7 | 6.7 | 5.3 | 4.7 | 5.4 | 6.1[b] |
| Market value/book value | 0.57 | 0.63 | 1.01 | 0.91 | 0.82 | 0.73 | 0.71 | 0.80 |
| **Selected Per-Share Statistics** | | | | | | | | |
| Earnings per share | $ 2.46 | $ 2.74 | $ 3.10 | $ 3.99 | $ 5.16 | $ 5.75 | $ 5.32 | $ 5.42[b] |
| Book value per share | 22.95 | 24.74 | 26.79 | 29.46 | 32.94 | 36.58 | 39.93 | 41.46 |
| Dividend per share | 0.96 | 0.96 | 0.99 | 1.12 | 1.40 | 1.72 | 1.92 | 0.96 |
| Dividend yield | 7.40% | 6.20% | 3.70% | 4.20% | 5.20% | 6.40% | 6.70% | 5.8% |

[a] Based on close, 1974 = 100.

[b] Latest 12 months.

**EXHIBIT 4**  Wells Fargo & Company—Analysis of Partial Prepurchase of 8.60 Percent Sinking Fund Debentures Due 4/1/2002 and Cash Flow Analysis for a Prepurchase of $5, 500,000[a]

| Semiannual Period | Old Issue | | | Total Savings | Net Savings |
| --- | --- | --- | --- | --- | --- |
| | Balance Outstanding | After-tax Interest | Sinking Fund Payment | | |
| 0 | $5,500,000 | $      0 | $      0 | $      0 | $(4,070,000) |
| 1 | 5,500,000 | 127,710 | 0 | 127,710 | 127,710 |
| 2 | 5,500,000 | 127,710 | 0 | 127,710 | 127,710 |
| 3 | 5,500,000 | 127,710 | 0 | 127,710 | 127,710 |
| 4 | 5,500,000 | 127,710 | 0 | 127,710 | 127,710 |
| 5 | 5,500,000 | 127,710 | 0 | 127,710 | 127,710 |
| 6 | 5,500,000 | 127,710 | 0 | 127,710 | 127,710 |
| 7 | 5,500,000 | 127,710 | 0 | 127,710 | 127,710 |
| 8 | 5,500,000 | 127,710 | 0 | 127,710 | 127,710 |
| 9 | 5,500,000 | 127,710 | 0 | 127,710 | 127,710 |
| 10 | 5,500,000 | 127,710 | 0 | 127,710 | 127,710 |
| 11 | 5,500,000 | 127,710 | 0 | 127,710 | 127,710 |
| 12 | 5,500,000 | 127,710 | 0 | 127,710 | 127,710 |
| 13 | 5,500,000 | 127,710 | 3,000,000 | 3,127,710 | 3,127,710 |
| 14 | 2,500,000 | 58,050 | 0 | 58,050 | 58,050 |
| 15 | 0 | 58,050 | 2,500,000 | 2,558,050 | 2,558,050 |
| Total | | $1,733,760 | $5,500,000 | $7,233,760 | $ 3,163,760 |

[a]Net present value discounted at 7.56% (after tax) = $575,633. Internal rate of return (after tax) = 10.17%. Sinking fund bonds at a price of 74 or $4,070,000.

**EXHIBIT 5   Wells Fargo & Company—Analysis of Partial Prepurchase of 8.60 Percent Sinking-Fund Debentures Due 4/1/2002 and Cash Flow Analysis for a Prepurchase of $17,000,000**[a]

| Semiannual Period | Old Issue Balance Outstanding | After-tax Interest | Sinking-fund Payment | Total Savings | Net Savings |
|---|---|---|---|---|---|
| 0 | $17,000,000 | $      0 | $ | $       0 | ($10,880,000) |
| 1 | 17,000,000 | 394,740 | 0 | 394,740 | 394,740 |
| 2 | 17,000,000 | 394,740 | 0 | 394,740 | 394,740 |
| 3 | 17,000,000 | 394,740 | 0 | 394,740 | 394,740 |
| 4 | 17,000,000 | 394,740 | 0 | 394,740 | 394,740 |
| 5 | 17,000,000 | 394,740 | 0 | 394,740 | 394,740 |
| 6 | 17,000,000 | 394,740 | 0 | 394,740 | 394,740 |
| 7 | 17,000,000 | 394,740 | 0 | 394,740 | 394,740 |
| 8 | 17,000,000 | 394,740 | 0 | 394,740 | 394,740 |
| 9 | 17,000,000 | 394,740 | 0 | 394,740 | 394,740 |
| 10 | 17,000,000 | 394,740 | 0 | 394,740 | 394,740 |
| 11 | 17,000,000 | 394,740 | 0 | 394,740 | 394,740 |
| 12 | 17,000,000 | 394,740 | 0 | 394,740 | 394,740 |
| 13 | 16,500,000 | 394,740 | 500,000 | 894,740 | 894,740 |
| 14 | 16,500,000 | 383,130 | 0 | 383,130 | 383,130 |
| 15 | 13,500,000 | 383,130 | 3,000,000 | 3,383,130 | 3,383,130 |
| 16 | 13,500,000 | 313,470 | 0 | 313,470 | 313,470 |
| 17 | 10,500,000 | 313,470 | 3,000,000 | 3,313,470 | 3,313,470 |
| 18 | 10,500,000 | 243,810 | 0 | 243,810 | 243,810 |
| 19 | 7,500,000 | 243,810 | 3,000,000 | 3,243,810 | 3,243,810 |
| 20 | 7,500,000 | 174,150 | 0 | 174,150 | 174,150 |
| 21 | 4,500,000 | 174,150 | 3,000,000 | 3,174,150 | 3,174,150 |
| 22 | 4,500,000 | 104,490 | 0 | 104,490 | 104,490 |
| 23 | 1,500,000 | 104,490 | 3,000,000 | 3,104,490 | 3,104,490 |
| 24 | 1,500,000 | 34,830 | 0 | 34,830 | 34,830 |
| 25 | 0 | 34,830 | 1,500,000 | 1,534,830 | 1,534,830 |
| Total | | $7,639,380 | $17,000,000 | $24,639,380 | $13,759,380 |

[a]Sinking-fund bonds at a price of 64 or $10,880,000.

**CASE**

**9**

# APPENDIX: STOCK-FOR-DEBT RECAPITALIZATION—AN ILLUSTRATIVE EXAMPLE

ABC Corporation is considering a stock-for-debt recapitalization. Among its outstanding debt obligations are the following:

1. $75 million 8.40 percent debentures due 1987.
2. $100 million 7⅜ percent debentures due 1992.

Morgan Stanley is aware that an insurance company that owns $20 million of the 8.40 percent debentures needs to take a loss for tax purposes and is willing to sell its debentures for 74¾ (14.84 percent yield), which, with costs and fees, implies a cost to ABC of $75. Further, Morgan Stanley believes it can accumulate $25 million principal amount of the 7⅜ percent debentures at an average cost, including fees, of $67. ABC currently has 16 million shares outstanding on which it currently pays an annual dividend of $1.60. ABC's stock closed yesterday at $40.

## THE EXCHANGE

The total market value of securities that can be accumulated for exchange is $31,750,000.

$$\begin{array}{l} \$20 \text{ million} \times 0.75 = \phantom{0}15.00 \\ \$25 \text{ million} \times 0.67 = \phantom{0}\underline{16.75} \\ \phantom{\$25 \text{ million} \times 0.67 = 0} \$31.75 \end{array}$$

Based on yesterday's closing price and a discount to Morgan Stanley of 5 percent, ABC would issue 835,526 new shares (5.2 percent increase in shares outstanding) in exchange for the debt obligations as follows:

$$\frac{31,750,000}{40 - (0.05 \times 40)} = 835,526$$

## ACCOUNTING EFFECTS

ABC's capitalization prior to the exchange is as follows:

| August 31, 1981 (dollars in thousands) | |
| --- | --: |
| 8.40% debentures due 1987 | $ 75,000 |
| 7⅜% debentures due 1992 | 100,000 |
| Stockholders' equity | 650,061 |
| Total | $825,061 |
| Book value per share | $40.63 |

On the exchange, ABC would report a gain of $13.25 million (principal amount of debt retired less its market value).

In the 12 months ended August 31, ABC had earned $6.02 per share ($96.3 million in aggregate). Pro forma for the exchange, per share earnings rise to $6.62 per share (10 percent increase).

In future years, the exchange will have a dilutive effect on earnings per share, as the increase in shares outstanding will not be fully offset by higher net income (which results from reduced interest expense). Looking at the 12 months ended August 31, on a pro forma basis, but this time excluding the impact of the gain exchange, one would find earnings per share of $5.83, a 3.1 percent decrease.

The exchange does have favorable impacts on ABC's capitalization. Long-term debt is reduced by the principal amount of debt retired, or $45 million. Stockholders' equity is increased by the market value of stock issued ($31.75 million) plus the gain recognized ($13.25 million), or $45 million in total.

# HILLSIDE NATIONAL BANK

Phil Forbes sat comfortably on the leather sofa in Jeff Stevens' office. He fumbled with a notepad and pencil as Jeff plopped down in the chair behind his desk.

It was early in January 1992. Forbes had started with Hillside National Bank five years earlier, and his progression to vice-president for finance fit the career path that Stevens, the bank's president, had mapped out for him. Over the five years, the bank had grown slowly but steadily to just over $80 million in assets. Hillside's population of 18,000 was stable, with little visible prospect for increasing.

The bank had remained rather trouble-free over the years under Jeff's leadership. Jeff was well liked in the community, and he was a detailed-minded executive where credit controls and other internal matters were concerned.

## MARCY STATE BANK

Jeff immediately leveled with Phil Forbes on the business at hand—the opportunity to buy Marcy State Bank in the nearby town of Marcy. "I want you to check their numbers carefully so that I can reassure the board that we'll have no surprise need for capital beyond what we need to complete the cash purchase." Jeff went on to explain that Hillside Bancorp, the legal holding company framework for Hillside National Bank, would be the acquirer, and that the company's regulators would require a capital injection of $1.2 million into the holding company in order to complete the transaction.

"The majority shareholder wants to work with us," Jeff continued. "The firm price is $2.4 million, the current book value of the bank. We know that recent acquisitions of small banks in the state have been priced at 1.2 to 1.8 times book and in a range of 6 to 10 times earnings. Our loan people and I have been looking at their loan portfolio, and there are some problems. But

then we expected problems, considering that they never managed to put together a decent lending group up there. And when you consider the real estate shakeout in Marcy over the past couple of years, that bank certainly could be worse off than it is."

It was clear to Phil that the opportunity to acquire Marcy State might provide a one-time chance for Hillside Bancorp to dramatically improve its prospects for the future (an abbreviated balance sheet for Hillside Bancorp, the holding company parent of Hillside National, is shown in Exhibit 1). The competition in Hillside probably would prohibit much growth for Hillside National, and the bank had done about all it could for now to strengthen itself. By contrast, according to several directors, the community of Marcy had great potential.

Marcy was an attractive community situated on the tree-lined shore of a large recreational lake about 30 miles west of Hillside. The town had a population of 7,000 year-round residents, although a growing segment of the population, including three of Hillside National's directors, consisted of high-season residents who owned second homes in Marcy. The town's growth had been interrupted by the 1980s' bust in the regional oil and gas industry, but recently a gradual resumption of growth indicated that the effects of the bust were moderating and that more rapid growth soon would follow.

There were a total of three banks in Marcy. One was equal in size to Marcy State and was affiliated with a moderate-sized holding company headquartered in the capital. Another was a *de novo* bank, chartered two years ago, that already held $12 million in deposits. But Hillside National Bank's target, Marcy State, a $38 million bank, had a checkered past. It was chartered 15 years ago, and it seemed to hire and fire a president every year or two. Also, the present ownership had felt compelled to provide a modest capital injection in early 1991.

## FINANCIAL BACKGROUND

Exhibits 2A and 2B present two years of balance sheet and income statement data, including the just completed statements for December 31, 1991. Several facts about the bank's financial condition were especially germane to the proposed acquisition:

1. Phil figured that loan writeoffs, on the high side, would be just over $1 million in 1992 and that the bank's lending activity would retrench, resulting in initial overall shrinkage in the loan portfolio during 1992.

2. Phil considered that the application of purchase accounting rules to the acquisition would result in markdowns of Marcy State's loan values and book equity value. He figured the downward adjustment of equity would be fully offset by the creation of approximately $750,000 in goodwill and by the recognition of a core deposit base intangible asset of $250,000.

3. At the proposed acquisition date (January 15, 1992), the bank would have a net operating loss carryover of approximately $900,000, the use of which would be limited by the tax laws to about $225,000 per year.

## PROJECTING THE FUTURE

Phil Forbes knew that the board would want reasonable assurance that no further capital injections would be required in the near term. Hillside National's holding company was adequately capitalized for now, but under the proposed acquisition, it was expected that half of the purchase price would have to be injected into the holding company in the form of fresh (cash) capital. Several members of the board agreed that their pro rata share of the cash injection "would be a stretch."

Exhibit 3 presents Forbes' pro forma balance sheet and income statements for 1992 and 1993. He knew the bank would have to meet the risk-based and leverage capital standards specified under the "prompt corrective action" regulation of the Federal Deposit Insurance Corporation Improvement Act of 1991. Exhibit 4A gives an abbreviated schedule of the risk weight classifications under risk-based capital standards. The minimum ratios under the prompt corrective action rules shown in Exhibit 4B indicate that examiners would expect the bank to maintain at least an 8 percent risk-based capital ratio as well as a 4 percent Tier I leverage capital ratio. The regulators could require even more capital for a bank they considered in trouble. Exhibit 5 can be used to apply the risk-based capital requirements to Phil Forbes' projections.

### EXHIBIT I    Hillside Bancorp—Balance Sheet, December 31, 1991

| Assets | | Liabilities and Equity | |
|---|---|---|---|
| Cash | $ 50,000 | Accounts payable | $ 100,000 |
| Equity invested in subsidiary bank | 6,000,000 | Notes payable | 4,000,000 |
| Other assets | 50,000 | Shareholders' equity | 2,000,000 |
| Total | $6,100,000 | Total | $6,100,000 |

**EXHIBIT 2A  Marcy State Bank—Statement of Condition (dollars in thousands)**

|  | December 31, 1990 | December 31, 1991 |
|---|---|---|
| Cash and due from banks | $ 6,400 | $ 2,600 |
| Investment securities | 8,500 | 6,500 |
| Federal funds sold | 0 | 2,200 |
| Loans | 26,450 | 25,960 |
| Allowance for loan losses | (350) | (960) |
| Premises and equipment | 900 | 900 |
| Other real estate owned | 300 | 400 |
| Other assets | 700 | 500 |
| Total assets | $42,900 | $38,100 |
| Demand deposits | 9,800 | 6,600 |
| Interest-bearing checking accts. | 2,900 | 3,000 |
| Money market deposits | 8,600 | 8,200 |
| Savings accounts | 1,300 | 1,000 |
| CDs < $100M | 5,700 | 7,800 |
| CDs > $100M | 9,800 | 8,300 |
| Total deposits | 38,100 | 34,900 |
| Other liabilities | 1,800 | 800 |
| Shareholders' equity | 3,000 | 2,400 |
| Total liab. and equity | $42,900 | $38,100 |

**EXHIBIT 2B  Income Statement (dollars in thousands)**

|  | Year Ended 12/31/90 | Year Ended 12/31/91 |
|---|---|---|
| Interest income | $ 3,500 | $ 3,500 |
| Interest expense | 1,800 | 1,900 |
| Net interest income | 1,700 | 1,600 |
| Provision for loan losses | 460 | 840 |
| Net int. income after PLL | 1,240 | 760 |
| Noninterest income | 370 | 320 |
| Noninterest expenses: | | |
| Salaries and benefits | 690 | 710 |
| Occupancy and FF & E | 410 | 370 |
| Other | 1,090 | 830 |
| Total nonint. expense | 2,190 | 1,910 |
| Net income (loss) before taxes | (580) | (830) |
| Income taxes (credit) | (40) | (70) |
| Net income (loss) | ($540) | ($760) |

**EXHIBIT 3   Marcy State Bank—Pro Forma Statement of Condition
(dollars in thousands)**

|  | December 31, 1992[a] | December 31, 1993 |
|---|---|---|
| Cash and Federal balances (cat. 1) | $ 1,800 | $ 2,000 |
| Placements with banks (cat. 2) | 600 | 600 |
| Investment securities |  |  |
|   Treasuries (cat. 1) | 1,800 | 2,000 |
|   Govt.-sponsored agencies (cat. 2) | 1,900 | 2,000 |
| Federal funds sold (cat. 2) | 3,000 | 1,000 |
| Loans (also see footnote below) |  |  |
|   Residential mortgages (cat. 3) | 14,000 | 16,000 |
|   Con. and commercial (cat. 4) | 10,000 | 11,600 |
| Allowance for loan losses | (200) | (200) |
| Premises and equip. (cat. 4) | 900 | 900 |
| Other real estate owned (cat. 4) | 500 | 600 |
| Intangible assets | 225 | 200 |
| Goodwill | 725 | 700 |
| Other assets (cat. 4) | 500 | 600 |
|     Total assets | $35,750 | $38,000 |
| Demand deposits | 6,000 | 6,000 |
| Interest-bearing checking accounts | 3,000 | 3,000 |
| Money market deposits | 9,500 | 10,700 |
| Savings accounts | 1,200 | 1,200 |
| CDs < $100M | 7,900 | 8,300 |
| CDs > $100M | 4,810 | 5,120 |
|     Total deposits | $32,410 | $34,320 |
| Other liabilities | 800 | 700 |
| Stockholders' equity | 2,540 | 2,980 |
|     Total liab. and equity | $35,750 | $38,000 |

[a]Loan commitments expected to total $3 million on December 31, 1992, and $4.5 million on December 31, 1993. Original maturities were over 1 year.

## EXHIBIT 4A    Risk Weighting Categories for Risk-Based Capital Standard

Category 1 (0% risk weight)
  Cash
  Federal balances
  Federal Reserve Bank stock
  Treasuries/guaranteed U.S. govt. agency debt
Category 2 (20% risk weight)
  Collateralized loans
  Due from nonofficial banks
  Government-sponsored agency debt
  General obligation bonds
Category 3 (50% risk weight)
  Revenue bonds
  Residential mortgages
Category 4 (100% risk weight)
  Commercial and consumer loans
  Other loans
  Other assets
  Other real estate owned
  Furniture, fixtures, and equipment
Off–balance sheet items
  Loan commitments, maturities > 1 year (50% conversion factor [c.f.])
  Standby letters of credit (100% c.f.)
  Risk participation in bankers' acceptances (100% c.f.)
  Interest rate swaps, options (100% c.f.)

Under the transition rules for risk-based capital requirements, banks must hold total capital of 7.25% of total risk-weighted assets by December 31, 1991. Required capital of up to 1.5% of this requirement can be loan loss reserves. By December 31, 1992, total capital must be 8.00% of risk-weighted assets, and up to 1.25% of this requirement can be loan loss reserve.

It is anticipated that Marcy State Bank will make up its capital requirements exclusively with stockholders' equity and allowable loan loss reserves.

Goodwill and other intangible assets are not admissible as capital.

**EXHIBIT 4B   Bank Classifications According to Capital Ratios under Prompt Corrective Action (FDIC Improvement Act of 1991)**

|  | Risk-Based Capital | | Leverage Tier I/ Assets |
|---|---|---|---|
|  | Tiers I & II | Tier I | |
| 1. Well capitalized: Significantly exceeds required capital standards.<br>*Restrictions:* None. | >10% | >6% | >5% |
| 2. Adequately capitalized: Meets minimum standards.<br>*Restrictions:* Cannot underwrite insurance where state law permits. Requires approval of FDIC to accept brokered funds. | >8% | >4% | >4% |
| 3. Undercapitalized: Fails to meet minimum standards.<br>*Restrictions:* As in 2 above and close monitoring by regulatory agency; capital restoration plan; asset growth restricted; needs approval for acquisitions, branching, new activities. | <8% | <4% | <4% |
| 4. Significantly undercapitalized: Significantly below required minimum standard.<br>*Restrictions:* As in 3 above and must sell new stock to recapitalize; restrictions on transactions with affiliates, as well as on interest paid on deposits and management compensation; must divest troubled affiliates. | <6% | <3% | <3% |
| 5. Critically undercapitalized: Less than 2% leverage capital ratio.<br>*Restrictions:* As in 4 above and prohibition of interest payments on subordinated debt. Placed in receivership or conservatorship within 90 days. | | | <2% |

**EXHIBIT 5 Risk-Based Capital Requirements—Marcy State Bank Pro Forma Statement of Condition (dollars in thousands)**

| | December 31, 1992 | December 31, 1993 | Risk-Based Capital | | |
| --- | --- | --- | --- | --- | --- |
| | | | Weight | 12/31/92 Risk-wtd. | 12/31/93 Risk-wtd. |
| Cash and Federal balances | $ 1,800 | $ 2,000 | 0.00% | | |
| Placements with banks | 600 | 600 | 20.00% | | |
| Investment securities | | | | | |
| Treasuries | 1,800 | 2,000 | 0.00% | | |
| Govt.-sponsored agencies | 1,900 | 2,000 | 20.00% | | |
| Federal funds sold | 3,000 | 1,000 | 20.00% | | |
| Loans | | | | | |
| Residential mortgages | 14,000 | 16,000 | 50.00% | | |
| Cons. and commercial | 10,000 | 11,600 | 100.00% | | |
| Allowance for loan losses | (200) | (200) | — | | |
| Premises and equip. | 900 | 900 | 100.00% | | |
| Other real estate owned | 500 | 600 | 100.00% | | |
| Intangible assets | 225 | 200 | — | | |
| Goodwill | 725 | 700 | — | | |
| Other assets | 500 | 600 | 100.00% | | |
| Total assets | $35,750 | $38,000 | | | |
| Loan commitments at $3 million, $4.5 million on 12/31/92, 12/31/93 | | | 50% | | |
| *Total Risk-Weighted Assets* | | | | | |

| | | |
|---|---|---|
| Demand deposits | $ 6,000 | $ 6,000 |
| Interest-bearing checking accts. | 3,000 | 3,000 |
| Money market deposits | 9,500 | 10,700 |
| Savings accounts | 1,200 | 1,200 |
| CDs < 100M | 7,900 | 8,300 |
| CDs > 100M | 4,810 | 5,120 |
| Total deposits | $32,410 | $34,320 |
| Other liabilities | $ 800 | $ 700 |
| Stockholders' equity | 2,540 | 2,980 |
| Total liab. and equity | $35,750 | $38,000 |

| *Qualifying Capital:* | *12/31/92* | *12/31/93* |
|---|---|---|
| Stockholders' equity | | |
| + Loan loss reserve[a] | | |
| − Intangible assets | | |
| − Goodwill | | |
| Total | | |
| Risk-wtd. capital ratio = (Tiers I & II) | | |
| Leverage ratio[b] = | | |

[a] Maximum allowed is the lesser of
1. 1.25% of risk weighted assets or
2. Allowances for loan losses on the balance sheet.
[b] Leverage ratio = total equity/total assets

# CHAPTER 10

# The Bank Credit Organization

Most bankers believe that the defining business of banking is lending. While the traditional scope of bank lending is changing, this view is confirmed by national data on banking. For example, approximately $2 trillion in bank loans are currently outstanding. Interest and fees on these loans contribute nearly two-thirds of banks' total operating income. By 1993, loans had fallen to slightly less than half of banks' total assets. Also, bankers know that, historically, the main path to professional advancement and high salary as a bank employee has always been through the lending function, although today other major paths to progress increasingly are opening as bank operations, financial management, trust activities, and other activities become more crucial and complex.

In the future, bank lending may not be a perpetually growing business. There are several reasons for bank loans to grow more moderately. For example, under the newly established risk-based capital rules (see Chapter 8), loans to consumers and businesses require the backing of more capital than other types of bank assets. This bias of higher capital standards puts such loans at a cost disadvantage because of the high cost of capital. Also, as we will show in later chapters, loans may decline as a proportion of total bank assets because of the trend toward loan securitization and because of the entry of other, nonbank, institutional providers of loans. In the 1980s, banks began to securitize many types of loans, including home mortgage loans, consumer loans, and even business loans. Through securitization, banks are able to move loans off their balance sheets and relieve themselves of expensive capital requirements for backing the loans.

Bank loans may also decline in the future because certain traditional customers of banks continue to discover more efficient alternative lenders, such as the commercial paper market or business finance companies. Finally, bank lending to consumers and businesses declines cyclically when the economy goes through recessionary periods such as that of the early 1990s. At such times, borrowers operate defensively and attempt to reduce their indebtedness by paying back their loans and avoiding new borrowing.

Bank loans finance diverse groups in the economy. Manufacturers, distributors, service firms, farmers, builders, home buyers, commercial real estate developers, consumers, and others all depend on bank credit. The ways in which banks allocate their loanable funds strongly influence the economic development of the community and the nation. Most bankers believe it is in their own best interests to supply credit within their own communities because credit helps communities to grow. In addition, banking regulators prompt banks to comply with the Community Reinvestment Act, which requires banks to evaluate their communities' credit needs closely and to service and stimulate local economic activities.

Every bank bears a degree of risk when it lends to private borrowers such as businesses and consumers, and, without exception, every bank experiences some loan losses when certain borrowers fail to repay their loans as agreed. Whatever the degree of risk taken, loan losses can be minimized by organizing and managing the lending function in a highly professional manner.

## MANAGING CREDIT RISK

This section reviews the principles of managing the risks of bank lending. The trends in lending show that lending opportunities have declined among low-risk borrowers. As just described, commercial paper, securitization, and nonbank competition have pushed banks to find viable loan business among riskier classes of borrowers. For example, large, stable corporate borrowers that once were the mainstays of banks' loan portfolios have shifted to open market sources like commercial paper and the bond market, which have lower transactions costs.

Recent banking history shows how critical it is for banks to control the risks of lending. Poor loan quality was the main factor in the growing number of U.S. bank failures during the past decade, which culminated in an average of nearly 200 failures per year from 1987 to 1992. In a study of national banks that failed in the mid-1980s, the Comptroller of the Currency found that the consistent element in the failures was the inadequacy of the banks' management systems for controlling loan quality.[1] In reporting its findings, the Comptroller's office listed several basic faults in lending procedures, including the following:

[1]This study was reported by Joseph F. Apadoford, "Credit Quality: CEOs Set the Tone," *Magazine of Bank Administration* (June 1988), pp. 20–22.

1. Inattention to loan policies.
2. Overly generous loan terms and lack of clear standards.
3. Disregard of banks' own policies.
4. Unsafe concentration of credit.
5. Poor control over loan personnel.
6. Loan growth beyond the banks' ability to control quality.
7. Poor systems for detecting loan problems.
8. Lack of understanding of borrowers' cash needs.
9. Out-of-market lending.

## Credit Culture

To overcome their deficiencies in systems and procedures that spawn poor loans, banks must develop a *credit culture* supported by well-conceived *management strategies* for controlling credit risk. The first step is to determine an appropriate credit culture that is consistent with the business values of the management team. For a bank to set a correct credit culture, it must establish its priorities with respect to the marketplace. Priorities may range from emphasizing long-term, consistent performance of the loan portfolio with highly conservative underwriting standards to emphasizing aggressive loan growth and market share with highly flexible standards. The first set of priorities is the lower-risk one and suggests goals of superior loan quality with stable earnings; the second set is the higher-risk one and suggests acceptable loan quality with superior earnings.

## Credit Risk Management Strategy

Once the credit culture and priorities have been set, the bank must design its *credit risk management strategy*. Bank credit risk is divided into two basic parts—*transaction risk* and *portfolio risk*. Although most of our discussion in this part of the book is devoted to transaction risk, we will first define portfolio risk. Portfolio risk can be further divided into *intrinsic risk* and *concentration risk*. Intrinsic risk is the risk that is unique to the specific borrower, such as the borrower's customer base, its geographic market, its leverage, and so forth. Concentration risk stems from the dollar amounts or proportions of banks' loan portfolios that are tied up in certain industries or types of loans (e.g., energy, commercial real estate, less developed countries, highly leveraged transactions), as well as certain geographic areas.

Transaction risk is addressed in terms of three elements: the bank's credit organization, with which it administers the credit function; the bank's credit investigation and analysis systems; and the bank's standards for underwriting loans—for example, the terms written into its loan agreements, the kinds of collateral it accepts, and so forth. In this chapter we review banks' credit organizations. We explain the need for and the formulation of a loan policy to steer banks toward the desired makeup and control of their loan portfolios. We also cover the technical aspects of loan administration, basically

---

**FIGURE 10-1    A Typical Lending Organization in a Medium-Sized Bank**

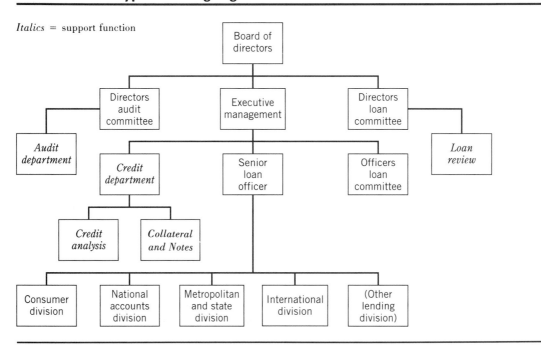

*Italics* = support function

---

the legal and pecuniary protection of the loan portfolio. Finally, we explain the indirect controls on the loan portfolio that result from regulation and the examination of banks by various bank supervisory agencies. In Chapter 11 we review methods of banks' credit investigation and analysis, and in Chapters 12 and 13 we discuss credit underwriting standards for business and consumer loans, respectively.

## THE LENDING ORGANIZATION

The organizational structure of the lending function varies with a bank's size and type of business. An officer of a small bank may perform all of the detailed work associated with making a loan, including credit investigation and analysis, negotiation, customer contact, periodic review of the loan file, and, at times, collection. In larger banks, individual loan officers specialize in consulting and negotiating with customers, and there is greater compartmentalization of support functions such as credit analysis, loan review, and loan collection. The next chapter will explain the main tasks of loan officers.

Figure 10-1 shows a representative loan organization for a medium-sized bank. An important checks-and-balances feature of lending organizations is to have the loan review department and the audit department report directly to the board of directors via appropriate directors' committees. This arrangement preserves the independence of these functions and protects them from the undue influence of the officers who make loans and who may not want to face up to potentially adverse information about their loan customers.

## Loan Divisions

The various loan divisions shown in Figure 10-1 perform the basic functions of generating loan business and supporting customers. In larger banks, the divisions usually are organized along geographic, industry, or product lines. Large banks develop lending expertise in such specialized businesses as energy, mining, public utilities, specialized lines of manufacturing, or commercial real estate. Separate loan divisions are necessary to service the special needs of these industries. At the same time, national and regional loan divisions that cut across different industries are needed to serve geographically dispersed customers.

## Credit Department

The primary mission of the credit department is to evaluate the creditworthiness and debt payment capacity of present loan customers and new loan applicants. This evaluation process is covered in detail in the next chapter. Because of the technical nature of its credit evaluation function, the credit department is an excellent place to train new loan officers. Trainees are exposed to a variety of good and not so good loan cases on which they assist loan officers in making credit decisions.

The credit department may also be responsible for loan review, although in larger banks this function is likely to be handled by a separate department. Credit departments are sometimes responsible for collections of past-due loans. This function is usually handled by specialists within the department.

## Collateral and Note Department

A crucial and complex loan function is the perfection of the bank's security interest in collateral offered in support of a loan. Chapter 12 presents the details and documents that are used to take a security interest in collateral offered by prospective borrowers. The legal complications and paperwork generated in this function often justify its separation from other activities in a unit such as the collateral and note department. This department also performs the discount function: the monitoring and crediting of payments received on outstanding notes.

## Loan Committees

Loan committees are responsible for approving banks' larger loan requests. All banks need effective committees for the review of major loan proposals and loan delinquencies. Usually, two or three committees are needed: a directors' loan committee, an officers' loan committee, and, for banks with an excessive number of troubled loans, a special assets committee. Loans above certain minimum sizes must be submitted to the officers' loan committee, consisting of the bank's most experienced loan officers. The officers' committee meets frequently. In large banks it may meet daily, whereas in small banks it may meet only once a week.

The loan officers' committee serves as a check on, not a substitute for, the individual loan officer's judgment. The committee's duties are as follows:

1. Review major new loans.
2. Review major loan renewals and ascertain the reasons for renewal.
3. Review delinquent loans and determine the cause of delinquency.
4. Ensure compliance with stated bank policy.
5. Ensure full documentation of loans.
6. Ensure consistency in the treatment of loan customers.

Banks differ in how they structure the loan approval process. Some banks give relatively large loan limits to their loan officers, with the ability to combine their limits with other officers to approve most of the acceptable loan applications. Other banks grant smaller loan limits, do not permit combining of loan limits, and rely mostly upon loan committees to approve loans. The first system results in greater flexibility and efficiency; the second system results in greater control and safety.

The directors' loan committee reviews major loans approved by the officers' committee. It is usually composed of the bank's president, the most senior loan officers, and two or more external members of the board of directors. The committee makes a final judgment on the officers' loan committee decisions, giving closer scrutiny to the largest credits. It is especially concerned with conformance to bank loan policy. The directors' loan committee also reviews significant past-due loans and credit problems.

A special assets committee is sometimes created in banks that have experienced a significant increase in regulator-criticized loans. This committee monitors the progress of problem loans and tries to determine how to work out effectively the loans through creative cooperation with distressed borrowers and through persistent collection efforts.

## LOAN POLICY FORMULATION

The composition and quality of a bank's loans should be a reflection of its loan policy. The policy reflects the bank's lending culture, including its priorities, specifying procedures, and means of monitoring lending activity. As such, it provides guidance and focus to the bank's lending activities. To ensure that such direction is unambiguous and is communicated to all concerned, the loan policy must be in written form. Indeed, the Comptroller of the Currency puts great emphasis on a written loan policy being handed down from the board of directors to management. From the Comptroller's viewpoint, a written loan policy should obtain three results:

1. Produce sound and collectible loans.
2. Provide profitable investment of bank funds.
3. Encourage extensions of credit that meet the legitimate needs of the bank's market.

Loan policies may change over time. For example, immediately after World War II, most banks considered consumer loans to be inappropriate.[2] However, as the demand for consumer durable goods and housing increased, the resulting attractive interest rate spreads on consumer and mortgage finance encouraged banks to shift loan funds to these markets. For a decade or so during the late 1970s and early 1980s, many large banks adopted policies to seek loans aggressively in Third World countries. This policy thrust was abruptly interrupted when, starting in 1982, many less developed nations failed to meet loan repayment schedules. Many banks' loan policies moved into another, similarly trendy loan market in commercial real estate in the early and mid-1980s. This market was boosted artificially by new tax incentives for investment in real estate and by regulatory encouragement. A sweeping change in policy was forced upon banks when, beginning in the 1980s, low-cost nonbank lenders acquired an increasing share of the market for top-rated corporate loans. As a result of this nonbank competition, many banks redirected their efforts to smaller and higher-risk middle-market corporate borrowers.

In addition, loan policies vary over the credit cycle. In periods of tight money, banks often have to restrict their loan growth. By contrast, when funds are plentiful and the economy is weak, banks may require their borrowers to show greater balance sheet and earnings strengths than during boom periods. To find solid loans during such periods, some banks may decide to lend outside their normal market areas. Clearly, the loan policy should be adaptable to changes in cyclical and secular circumstances. In fact, it is crucial that loan policies be updated routinely to reflect current circumstances and to maintain their relevance as control tools. A well-managed bank may review its loan policy on an annual basis to ensure that the policy adequately addresses the types of risks the bank is willing to take in its dynamic market area.

## Loan Policy Outline

A representative outline for a written loan policy is shown in Table 10-1. The outline is divided into three parts. The first part contains general policy statements that specify in broad terms the mission of the bank's loan department and the desired qualities of the loan portfolio. The second part describes technical principles and procedures to be followed in structuring and administering

---

[2]The postwar evolution of bank lending policies is reviewed in D. A. Hayes, "Bank Lending Policies: Domestic and International" (Ann Arbor: Division of Research, Graduate School of Business Administration, University of Michigan, 1977).

---

**TABLE 10-1   Outline for a Written Loan Policy**

I. General policy statements
   A. Objectives
   B. Strategies
      1. Loan mix
      2. Liquidity and maturity structure
      3. Size of portfolio
   C. Trade area
   D. Credit standards
      1. Types of loans
      2. Secured vs. unsecured guidelines
      3. Collateral
      4. Terms
   E. Loan authorities and approval
II. Principles and procedures
   A. Insurance protection
   B. Documentation standards and security
     interest
   C. Problem loan collections and charge-offs
   D. Legal constraints and compliance
   E. Loan pricing
   F. Financial information required from
     borrowers
   G. Ethical issues and conflicts of interest
   H. Loan review

III. Parameters and procedures by type of loan
   A. Real estate mortgage loans[a]
      1. Loan description
      2. Purpose of loan proceeds
      3. Preferred maturities
      4. Pricing; rates, fees, balances
      5. Minimum and maximum amounts
      6. Insurance requirements
      7. Perfection of collateral
      8. Channels of approval for policy
   B. Interim construction financing
   C. Accounts receivable loans
   D. Inventory loans
   E. Term loans
   F. Securities purchase loans
   G. Agricultural loans
   H. Small business loans
   I. Consumer loans
   J. Purchased loans

[a] Factors 1–8 in Section A also pertain to each loan category that follows (Sections B to J).

---

the loan portfolio. The third part introduces detailed procedures and parameters that apply to each of the various types of loans made by the bank. In the following sections of this chapter, the general policy statements included in the first part are discussed. Then several of the technical procedures indicated in the second part are considered.

### Loan Objectives and Strategies

The objectives section of the loan policy statement sets forth the bank's external and internal missions. Included are statements about its perceived business role in its trade area, perceived market niche, desired profitability, maintenance of public confidence, and degree of competitiveness and aggressiveness. It might quantify loan growth and earning objectives, including the desired size of the loan portfolio in relation to total deposits or total assets.

    A meaningful loan policy will express risk management strategies in concrete terms. Banks' loans comprise a portfolio of loan types, geographical area, and risk. In the case of portfolio risk, the desired loan mix should be quantified: for example, working capital commercial loans, 40 percent; consumer loans, 30 percent; real estate loans, 15 percent; term commercial loans, 15 percent.

In practice, a desired percentage range of loans by type will prove to be more flexible. Portfolio mix expresses the diversification sought by the bank in its loan placements. Diversification reduces the portfolio concentration risk associated with large concentrations of loans in a single category. Banks in one-industry communities sometimes have few chances to diversify their loans. For them, participation with correspondent banks might be a good way to achieve geographical diversification. This section of the policy statement may also describe the maximum amount the bank is willing to lend to any one customer—called the bank's *in-house limit*. This limit might be set at, say, 60 or 80 percent of the bank's legal lending limit (legal limits are described later in this chapter under "Legal and Regulatory Controls on Lending"). Finally, the types of loans and borrowers that the bank considers to be undesirable should be mentioned.

The bank's liquidity strategy should be indicated because it acts as a constraint on lending activity and because liquidity is partly determined by the maturity structure of the loan portfolio. The desired size of the loan portfolio expresses the bank's intended aggressiveness in expanding its loan portfolio. A highly aggressive loan policy comes with both good news and bad news. The good news is that a large loan portfolio may increase bank earnings. The bad news is that an aggressive policy may lead to lower credit standards, marginal loans, and large loan losses.

## Trade Area

Both a primary and a secondary trade area should be designated to instruct loan officers on the bank's geographic priorities. Banks understand their own trade areas best and are more apt to misjudge the quality of loans originating outside their areas. For example, loan officers will be less alert to the economic deterioration of communities outside their trade areas. Banks should (1) define the area to be serviced routinely by each of their officers, (2) set limits on loan participation with other bank customers outside the area, and (3) process any other loans as an exception to policy.

Trade area definitions must comply with the Community Reinvestment Act. This act is discussed in Chapter 13.

The extent of a trade area obviously depends on the size and special characteristics of banks. The trade area for large money center banks is not limited geographically but is national and international in scope. Also, geographic limits mean less to many regional banks with lending expertise in narrow fields, such as oil and gas, meat packing, electronics, or public utilities, or to regional banks that have major relationships with corporations with national and international locations.

## Credit Standards

The written loan policy states the types of loans the bank considers desirable. Desirable loans routinely include the primary lending function to grant short-term loans to business customers in the trade area to the extent that resources and opportunities permit. For such working capital-type loans, a minimum out-of-the-bank period, say 30 to 60 days each year, should be specified. Non-working capital short-term loans should indicate a specific source of re-payment.

Other, less conventional loans are also normally discussed in the policy statement. Cautions should appear about lending to new businesses that are not well capitalized or backed by a strong private guarantor or a federal guaran-tor such as the Small Business Administration or Farm Home Administration.

The types of loans to be avoided should be mentioned. Loans to acquire a business or to buy out stockholders in the borrower's present business may be prohibited. The funds from such capital loans effectively replace part of a firm's equity with debt. The borrower normally expects to repay the loan from earnings of the business, which may drain the business of needed equity funds. Also, in new-acquisition borrowing, the borrower is usually less familiar with the business than the former owner, so that future profits may slip below their historic level. The policy may limit such loans to cases in which the borrower's other resources are ample or in which former owners guarantee the loan.

So-called bridge loans are often cited as contrary to bank loan policy. Such loans "bridge" a firm's needs until it can raise additional permanent funds. The bank's exposure is especially great when repayment depends on a small firm's ability to sell stock under uncertain future market conditions. Speculative loans also are frequently proscribed by policy unless the borrower can qualify independently on the basis of his or her normal business perfor-mance. If a borrower has depleted working capital funds through speculative activity, loans to replenish the working capital normally would not be per-mitted.

Loan policy should indicate both desirable and unacceptable types of collateral. It should further indicate circumstances in which unsecured lending is prohibited. The quality and liquidity of collateral must be verified, and maximum loan-to-collateral-value ratios should be applied before a secured loan is approved.

Responsibilities and procedures for appraisals should be specified, in-cluding the time intervals between reappraisals. Special attention must be paid to regulations covering appraisals under FIRREA, passed in 1989. This legislation contains specific parameters governing the frequency and quality of appraisals. FIRREA also establishes special requirements on the credentials of independent appraisers.

## Loan Authorities and Approvals

The loan policy should establish lending limits for all loan officers and for combinations of officers and loan committees. Bankers look upon increases in an individual's lending authority as a privilege that must be earned empirically. Limits for individuals will normally be predicated on their experience and length of service as lenders. Secured loans will carry higher limits than unsecured loans for comparable purposes, and seasonal working capital loans may carry higher limits than term loans. Individual officers' lending authorities for any one borrower are determined by totaling all of the borrower's existing loans, credit lines, and credit requests under consideration. Joint authorities might be used to approve larger loans than the officers involved would be permitted to approve individually, although in such cases it should be made clear that each officer is responsible for monitoring the performance of the loan. Division heads (e.g., commercial, real estate, or dealer) or branch heads should be held responsible for loans made by their subordinate officers. Individual officers' limits also depend on the bank's capital base and its ultimate legal, or in-house, loan limit. For example, a vice-president in a bank with $50 million in assets may have a loan limit of $25,000, whereas an officer of identical rank in a $5 billion bank may have a $200,000 limit.

The real value of a well-conceived loan policy—one that is consistent with a bank's credit culture—is its role as a communication tool. In this role, the loan policy establishes the bank's strategy for managing credit risk by specifying the bank's standards and organizational objectives to its loan personnel.

## PRINCIPLES AND PROCEDURES

Part II of the loan policy outline in Table 10-1 deals with several procedural areas. It sets forth policy in relation to the technical requirements of the loan function.

### Insurance Protection

Most borrowers are exposed to risks that threaten their ability to repay their bank loans. Life insurance on key personnel is especially important to protect against loss of death or disability that strikes the borrower or one of the borrower's indispensable employees. A catastrophic fire or flood may interrupt the borrower's business or destroy the loan collateral.

The loan policy should indicate the types of borrowers who must be insured. The policy must designate the bank as loss payee, or, when the cash value of a life insurance policy is offered as protection, this must be properly assigned to the bank in a binder issued by the insurer. An increasingly common form of protection is the credit life policy written by the bank. Credit life is simply term life insurance written on consumer loan customers. It pays off outstanding balances due the bank in the event of the customer's death.

A somewhat different form of protection is obtained through reinsurance. If the borrower defaults, reinsurance pays off and the insurance company pursues collection on its own behalf on the bank's defaulted note. Reinsurance premiums are rather costly, and the bank's policy should indicate what classes of borrowers, if any, should be under reinsurance programs.

## Documentation Standards

Loan policy should prescribe uniform credit files and documentation procedures. Such requirements are routine for most medium-sized and larger banks; however, too often, documentation procedures in many small banks are determined by the preferences of individual loan officers. Customers' credit files should be organized around an effective documentation system that promotes uniformity and almost certainly results in lower loan losses, especially when coupled with a well-designed loan review program (discussed in the next section). The credit files are administered by the credit department.

A uniform loan documentation checklist should be required for each credit file. The listed documents include only those most frequently used in various types of lending transactions:

1. The basic loan agreement.
2. The credit application.
3. The borrower's financial statements.
4. Credit reports.
5. Evidence of perfection of security interest (e.g., UCC-1 financing statement).
6. Assignment of rents or leases on real estate or other productive property.
7. The borrower's life or casualty insurance policies (showing the bank as the loss payee).
8. Corporate borrowing resolution or partnership agreement.
9. Subordination agreement.
10. Continuing guarantee.
11. Financial statements on the guarantor.
12. Correspondence.
13. Copies of existing and paid-off promissory notes.

The basic loan agreement is the pivotal loan document used to set forth the conditions of the loan transaction. The loan agreement ties all the loan documents together. It spells out the ground rules, procedures, and mechanics, including the terms of repayment, as well as loan covenants. Loan covenants are covered in Chapter 12.

Other data and documents pertaining to the credit file should also be included in the loan documentation. Of special concern is item 5—*perfection of security interests*—which pertains to documents that establish the bank's legal claim to collateral in the event of default. This item accounts for much of the attention banks give to its documentation. It is discussed in detail in Chapter 12; the law governing security interests is covered by Article 1 of the Uniform Commercial Code.

Item 8—the *corporate borrowing resolution* or *partnership agreement*—indicates those employees of the borrowing firm who are authorized to commit the borrower to indebtedness. Loan officers must confirm that the name of the person who signs a loan agreement appears on the appropriate borrowing authorization instrument. The loan officer should obtain a certified copy of the instrument for the credit file. Item 9—a *subordination agreement*—is used when it is necessary to subordinate a prior loan and lender to the present loan agreement with the bank. In cases in which a corporate borrower's loan is backed by a guarantor, such as a suretyship, the credit line should contain the signed personal guarantee document, called a *continuing guarantee*. A continuing guarantee is often required of a firm's majority stockholders to ensure that the loan is protected against the possibility of corporate insolvency. Without a guarantee, stockholders might permit their insolvent corporation simply to abandon its debt obligations.

It would be difficult to exaggerate the need for careful loan documentation. It is necessary for protecting the bank in the event of a default and enforcing the bank's secured position against collateral. A crucial dimension of loan documentation is to use the documents to monitor the performance of a loan to ensure that the borrower complies with the loan agreement and that deterioration in the borrower's financial condition does not go unnoticed. The early recognition of a borrower's problem that might create a cash flow interruption and a default may permit the bank to protect its position before a major loan loss occurs.

Increasingly, banks are conducting loan previews before loan funds are disbursed. Loan previews examine all materials pertaining to a pending loan to ensure that documentation is complete; that the loan conforms to policy, laws, and regulations; and that a workable security interest in collateral has been obtained.

## CONTROLLING LOAN LOSSES

### The Loan Review Function

It is said that banks never make bad loans; at least, they are not bad at the time they are made. However, banks find that invariably a small portion of their loans become delinquent and eventually must be written off. This basic risk of the lending function is not entirely bad; banks would be remiss in not bearing such risk in the course of underwriting a variety of business enterprises and consumer needs. When a bank does not experience at least a few loan losses, this is likely to be a sign that the bank is passing up profitable opportunities. Nevertheless, well-managed banks should do all they can to minimize loan losses.

Most banks conduct loan reviews to reduce losses and monitor loan quality. Loan reviews consist of a periodic audit of the ongoing performance of some or all of the active loans in the bank's loan portfolio. Its essence is credit analysis, although, unlike the credit analysis conducted by the credit department as part of the loan approval process (discussed in Chapter 11), credit analysis in loan review occurs after the loan is on the books. To fulfill its basic objective of reducing loan losses, the following points should be emphasized in loan review:

1. To detect actual or potential problem loans as early as possible.
2. To provide an incentive for loan officers to monitor loans and to report deterioration in their own loans.

3. To enforce uniform documentation.
4. To ensure that loan policies, banking laws, and regulations are followed.
5. To inform management and the board about the overall condition of the loan portfolio.
6. To aid in establishing loan loss reserves.

The true purpose of loan review is actually a source of some confusion. Most bankers would cite an "early warning" purpose wherein loan review provides the basic defense against deteriorating credit quality. They would claim that loan review can detect, in timely fashion, the changes in credit quality that can occur quickly in loan agreements. Gregory Udell argues, however, that the infrequency of review and, for some loans, the absence of review (discussed later in this section) inherent in formal loan review systems make it impossible always to catch early deterioration in loans.[3] Udell argues persuasively that the fundamental purpose of loan review is to reinforce a "credit culture" within the lending organization. The credit culture relies on loan officers, not the loan review department, as the basic defense against deteriorating credit quality. Indeed, banking regulators refer to loan officers as the "first line of defense" against credit problems.

The rationale for depending on the credit culture is that loan officers are privy to crucial information about borrowers' financial condition, and they are the first persons in the bank to know about changes in credit quality. Thus, correct loan review procedures attempt to overcome the disincentives for loan officers to monitor their loans. The disincentives include time and energy taken away from other tasks, the fear of discovering quality deterioration that might reflect poorly on loan officers' original credit judgments, and the personal friendships and bonding that often occur between loan officers and their corporate borrowers.

The credit culture must offset such disincentives by establishing a climate in which it is clear that lenders are accountable for devoting appropriate attention to monitoring credit quality. Loan officers are viewed as responsible for communicating changes in the quality of their loans. Loan review reinforces this responsibility by detecting, after the fact, how diligently loan officers actually reported changes in quality. The net result is that loan review has the function of monitoring loan officers (who are responsible for monitoring the loans), not loan performance itself.

## Loan Review Procedures

The procedures for loan review should be formalized in written form in the loan policy. In general, all the materials needed for loan review should be in the credit files set up for each loan made. Historically, the process required the arduous task of manually handling many files. Now, however, many banks have begun to store credit file data on computers.

---

[3]Gregory F. Udell, *Designing the Optimal Loan Review Policy* (Madison, Wis.: Herbert V. Prochnow Educational Foundation, 1987).

The scope of a bank's loan review operation is partly a matter of bank size. Some large banks establish a separate loan review staff directly under executive management to ensure its independence of loan personnel. There is a compelling logic to this approach, because the chief executive officer is ultimately accountable for loan quality and can act directly to remedy deficiencies. Medium-sized banks may make the review operation an additional duty of the credit department or assign it to the audit department. The smallest banks often do not have a loan review program, or they depend on loan officers to conduct the loan review as time permits. Loan officers should, of course, monitor their own loans continuously. In addition, however, it is vital that there be an independent loan review to, in effect, monitor the loan officer. Within the formal loan review system itself, loan officers should not review their own loans; human nature prevents people, including loan officers, from being objective when reviewing their own work.

Whatever means are used to conduct loan review, the following points should be covered:

1. Financial condition and repayment ability of the borrower.
2. Completeness of documentation.
3. Consistency with the loan policy.
4. Perfection of the security interest on collateral.
5. Legal and regulatory compliance.
6. Apparent profitability.

Most banks are unable to review regularly every loan on their books. Some banks review all loans in excess of a certain cutoff value and review only a random sample of loans below the cutoff. The frequency of review of individual loans is determined by the size and quality of the loan; large, poor-quality loans are reviewed most frequently. Many banks have a loan grading system that establishes the quality and, therefore, the frequency of review of each loan. Table 10-2 shows an example of such a system.

As a general rule, each year a bank should review at least as much of its loan portfolio as its regulator would review in an examination. For example, 70 percent of the commercial loan portfolio might be reviewed in a year's time, along with a random sampling of homogeneous loan pools such as consumer and residential loan portfolios.

## Correcting Problem Loans

Figure 10-2 graphs net loan losses as a percentage of loans outstanding for all U.S. banks from 1976 to 1992. In the 1970s there was a clear relationship between loan losses and periods during and following recessions; for example, loan losses declined for several years beginning in 1976 following the recession years of 1974 and 1975. Recession and its attendant poor economic conditions produce declines in firms' sales and profit margins. Falling sales may generate unexpected increases in corporate inventories, and falling profits cause firms to attempt to cut overhead. These changes can be readily observed in a borrower's financial statements and may foretell a coming delinquency.

**TABLE 10-2  A Loan Grading System**

| Loan Rating | Review Schedule | General Description | | Specific Circumstances |
|---|---|---|---|---|
| A | 360 days | Top grade | 1 | Unsecured loans to very substantial companies with unquestionable financial strength |
| | | | 2 | Loans adequately secured by cash surrender value, government bond, CDs, or savings accounts |
| | | | 3 | Loans well secured by listed stock |
| B | 180 days | Good | 1 | Loans where the risk is reasonable but the overall situation is less desirable than grade A |
| | | | 2 | Loans adequately secured by listed stock |
| | | | 3 | Loans generously secured by receivables, inventory, and other readily marketable collateral |
| C | 90 days | Marginal | 1 | Loans that require more than average service and attention to collateral and financial information or counseling |
| | | | 2 | Loans for which collateral values are less than standard |
| | | | 3 | Loans that are not conforming to the repayment schedule but are not seriously past due. Credit-worthiness of collateral values are in evidence |
| D | 30 days (minimum) | Workout doubtful loss | 1 | All loans classified by bank examiners |
| | | | 2 | Unusually high credit risks that require constant supervision |

SOURCE: Margaret A. Hoffman and Gerald C. Fischer, *Credit Department Management* (Philadelphia: Robert E. Morris Associates, 1980).

Beginning about 1983, loan losses for the banking system began a sharp rise that finally flattened out in 1987. This rise in losses was not related to national economic conditions but rather to concentrations of loans in some banks among borrowers in the Third World and in energy, farming, and real estate. These sectors of the economy suffered from a combination of causes, including disinflationary trends that followed the severe inflation of 1979–1982, declines in export markets, and a reaction to earlier profligate international lending by certain aggressive banks. The pattern of the 1980s caused well-managed banks to implement and enforce sounder loan policies and to use their loan review functions to detect inappropriate concentrations of loans that might expose them to pyramiding losses. The rise in loan losses resumed from 1988 to 1990 following overinvestment in real estate and the approaching recession of 1990–1991.

In general, the loan policy should require diligence on the part of all loan personnel to detect and attempt to correct problem loans. Although loan review personnel are important in the early detection of problem loans, individual loan officers frequently have special ongoing knowledge to contribute. Loan officers attempt to maintain good rapport with their borrowers. If the bor-

**FIGURE 10-2   Net Loan Losses as Percent of Loans Outstanding**

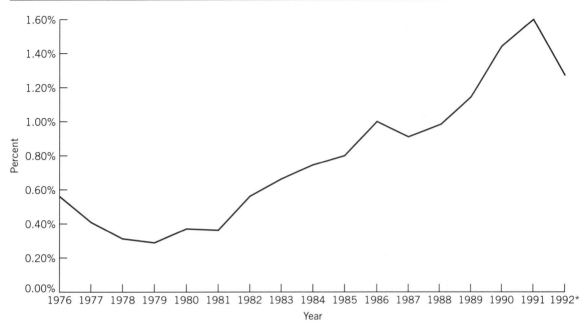

* Annualized thru 9/30/92

rower's business deteriorates, the loan officer frequently will find that this rapport deteriorates as well. Any unexplained change in the borrower's attitude toward the loan officer or the bank may be a clue to the borrower's financial difficulties. Unexpected declines in deposit balances and the occurrence of overdrafts are signs of such difficulties.

Other clues include late payments of principal and interest and abnormal delays by the borrower in submitting periodic financial statements as required in the loan agreement. Delays might indicate a reluctance to submit unfavorable financial results to the bank. In the event of such delays, the loan officer should immediately inquire about the reasons. Payment delinquencies also must be followed up quickly because they frequently indicate that the borrower is undergoing a financial crisis.

Other indicators of trouble include the following:

1. Disturbing trends in financial statements.
2. Management turnover.
3. Cancellation of insurance.
4. Security interest filed against the borrower by other creditors.
5. Notice of a lawsuit, tax liens, or other legal action against the borrower.

6. Deteriorating relations with trade suppliers.
7. Death or illness of principals.
8. Marital difficulties of principals.
9. Loss of key source of revenue.
10. Deterioration of labor relations.
11. Natural disaster.
12. Rapid growth.

When a problem loan is detected, the responsible loan officer should take immediate corrective action to prevent further deterioration and to minimize potential loss. The preferred solution to a problem loan is to negotiate a plan of action with the borrower to try to protect both the bank and the borrower from possible loss. The plan of action is actually a revised loan agreement. It should set forth a new repayment schedule, provide covenants limiting the customer's activities, establish requirements for the customer to report operating and financial activities for the bank to monitor, and specify the extent of the bank's authority to participate in management decisions. Often banks operate a special assets division that takes charge of such problem loans. There are at least two important advantages in operating a special assets division. First, the loan is administered by officers who specialize in situations that involve actual or potential litigation; second, the loan relationship can be managed more objectively. Both of these advantages act to reduce the potential loss to the bank.

Problems with secured loans may arise when the collateral is inadequate. The market value of certain types of collateral, such as securities, may fall below the loan value. Also, the loan may have been inadequately secured at the outset because of either improper documentation or an excessive loan-to-value ratio. An obvious solution would be to obtain additional collateral in the form of marketable securities, cash value of life insurance, receivables, inventory, or even real estate equity.

A problem loan might be remedied through the addition of guarantees or endorsements. Of course, the extent of the improvement in the bank's position is directly related to the financial strength of the guarantors.

Loan officers must be especially alert to detect fraud. Possible types of fraud include false financial statements, false documents, securities, and titles for collateral. In the event of bankruptcy, proof that fraud was used in obtaining a loan may be the basis for gaining legal access to a borrower's resources ahead of other creditors.

In any case, the earlier the bank's officers detect pending loan problems, the more likely they will be able to take action to protect the bank's position by requiring the borrower to provide additional security or, perhaps, by encouraging the borrower to refinance the loan at another institution. Whatever the solution, early detection of problems reduces potential losses to the bank.

### Borrower's Financial Statements

Loans should always be supported by concrete financial data. The data may consist of a small consumer borrower's personal financial statement or a multinational corporate borrower's unqualified audited financial statement studied by professional analysts, CPAs, and attorneys. The loan policy should establish certain guidelines for such data. Normally, common dated balance sheets and income statements for at least the immediate past three years are required of commercial borrowers.

For small banks that deal regularly with small businesses, the professionalism of the borrower's financial statements can be expected to vary a great deal. Small businesses often present statements prepared by an owner who has no formal training in accounting. Statements prepared by professional accountants may be compiled, indicating that they are derived solely from the company's accounts without audit. Even professionally audited statements may contain broad disclaimers as to the integrity of certain information presented. When financial data are insufficient, the loan officer should ask the customer for clarification. For example, it is frequently necessary to clarify how receivables, inventory, or equipment are valued and whether or not they have been pledged for other purposes. Also, the delinquency of trade payables or the maturity of other debt may need clarification. Written clarifications of such issues should be a part of the credit file.

Personal financial statements should be required of all co-makers, guarantors, or endorsers. Details of real estate owned, stocks and bonds, mortgages, loans, and other debt maturities should be included so that the borrower's personal net worth is clearly indicated.

### Interest Rate Policy

Interest rates charged on loans potentially depend on one or more of several considerations, such as the following:

1. The bank's cost of funds (sometimes including the cost of equity funds).
2. The riskiness of the borrower.
3. Compensating balances and fees.
4. Interest rates charged by competitors.
5. Usury ceilings.
6. Other banking relationships with the borrower.

Chapter 12 deals with many of these considerations in its discussion of the pricing and profitability of commercial loans. General guidelines should be included as part of the loan policy's principles and procedures. For example, the bank's own prime loan rate—the interest rate quoted to the bank's most creditworthy borrowers—should be explained. Most small or medium-sized banks' prime rates are based on a national prime rate but are modified according to their customer base and market competitive situation. Legal challenges to the prime rate concept (discussed in Chapter 12) are nullifying its use at many banks. Bank pricing policy for single-pay, balloon maturity loans (*bullet* loans) versus fully amortized loans might be indicated. Also, lawful exceptions to established usury ceilings are sometimes detailed for the benefit of loan officers.

### Unethical Conduct and Conflicts of Interest

The success of any bank depends partly on its customers' confidence that the bank's employees will not exploit their unique positions of trust for unethical gain. Bankers deal more directly and routinely with money than perhaps any other professional group. The exchange of money is the basis, and not just the outcome, of customer interaction. Bankers also deal with highly sensitive and confidential information related to their customers. As a result, the potential for conflicts of interest is unusually serious.

Loan policy statements frequently list improper activities or relationships that loan officers should avoid. Such a list should include acceptance of gifts of value or loans from customers or loan applicants, investment in a customer's business or other uses of privileged information for personal gain, and improper use of credit information on a customer. On the last point, the Robert Morris Associates Code of Ethics for the Exchange of Credit Information is used by many banks to govern the exchange of credit information. The code prescribes controls on the creditors' sharing between themselves of their credit experiences with customers without unduly violating the customers' right to privacy.

Conflicts of interest may also arise between the commercial loan division and the trust department when the loan division has inside information on a firm whose securities are held by the trust department. Policy should prohibit the trust department's access to such files.

### Common Reasons for Loan Losses

Well-managed banks regularly conduct what might be called an "autopsy" on loans that resulted in losses for the bank. This step is the strongest feedback available on the effectiveness of loan policies, documentation, loan officers, and the loan review function. Invariably, losses reflect on parts of the lending function that may require correction or revision. While a thorough review of failed credits is painful, it probably teaches lending personnel about the importance of controls on the lending function better than any hypothetical exercise could possibly do. Table 10-3 lists common causes for loan failures that were uncovered in loan autopsies recently conducted in a sample of 60 small to medium-sized banks.

## LEGAL AND REGULATORY CONTROLS ON LENDING

Historically, commercial banking has been one of the most tightly regulated industries in the United States. There are several reasons. First, banking risks must be minimal because banks are pivotal in our payments system, and because taxpayers ultimately guarantee banks' deposits and must pay for losses from an epidemic of bank failures, just as they did for the massive failures of S&Ls in the late 1980s and early 1990s. In the case of the payments system, the public's confidence in the nation's monetary system and its currency depends on the safety of its banks. Second, commercial banks are instruments

**TABLE 10-3    Twenty Common Reasons for Loan Losses**[a]

1. Collateral overvalued; improperly margined, failure to get appraisal.
2. Dispersal of funds before documentation finished.
3. Officer making "good ole boy" loans, bypassing the loan committee, personal friendship of loan officer with borrower.
4. Loan to a new business with an inexperienced owner-manager.
5. Renewing a loan for increasing amounts, with no additional collateral taken.
6. Repeatedly rewriting loan to cover delinquent interest due.
7. Not analyzing borrower's cash flows and repayment capacity.
8. Failure of officer to review loan's status frequently enough.
9. Funds not applied as represented; diverted to borrower's personal use (no attempt to verify to what purpose money was applied).
10. Funds used out of the bank's market area; poor communications with borrower.
11. Repayment plan not clear or not stated on the face of the note.
12. Failure to receive or infrequent receipt of borrower's financial statements.
13. Failure to realize on collateral because borrower raised nuisance legal defenses.
14. Bank's failure to follow its own written policies and procedures.
15. Bank president too dominant in pushing through loan approvals.
16. Ignoring overdraft situation as a tip-off to borrower's major financial problems.
17. Failure to inspect borrower's business premises.
18. Lending against fictitious book net worth of business, with no audit or verification of borrower's financial statement.
19. Failure to get or ignoring negative credit bureau reports or other credit references.
20. Failure to call loan or to move against collateral quickly when deterioration becomes obviously hopeless.

[a]1990 unpublished survey, Western States School of Banking, Albuquerque, New Mexico.

of national monetary policy. Tight control over banks ensures an elastic currency by enforcing desired and more predictable behavior by banks. Third, memories of past banking panics and failures make special precautions politically appealing. In the case of the taxpayer's guarantee of bank deposits, the taxpayer is protected by the banking industry–supported system of deposit insurance. The taxpayer relies upon regulatory control of bank's loan quality to avoid drains on deposit insurance resources. Finally, incentives and controls are sometimes placed on banks' power to create credit in order to allocate credit to socially desirable ends.

Although not all of these reasons directly address the bank lending function, they do result in prominent regulation of the loan portfolio, from which most of the risk in banking is derived.

### Legal Provisions

Regulatory constraints on lending activity are reflected in enacted legislation and interpretive decisions of supervisory agencies. Regulations that deal with limited types of loans (commercial, consumer, real estate) are discussed in Chapters 12, 13, and 14.

Loans to single affiliated borrowers are limited to prevent the concentration of a bank's assets. In the case of national banks, the 1982 Depository Institutions Act established a complex mechanism for limiting loans to single borrowers or a combination of borrowers who are in a common enterprise or who are otherwise financially interdependent. Generally, the limit is 15 percent of the bank's capital and surplus plus an additional 10 percent for loans fully secured by readily marketable collateral. Still higher limits are possible for loans to a combination of certain organizations and their subsidiaries. For the purpose of defining capital, eligible notes and debentures have been included since the early 1960s. There are several exceptions to these limits, including drafts or bills of exchange used to finance domestic and international trade. Also, goods secured by shipping documents are exempt, and those secured by warehouse receipts are partially exempt.

The Financial Institutions Regulatory Act of 1978 tightly restricted loans to insiders (executive officers, directors, and principal shareholders). In 1983, insider borrowing rules were relaxed somewhat. Executive officers were permitted to borrow 2.5 percent of bank capital and surplus, with a ceiling of $100,000. Under the "insider abuse" clause of the Federal Deposit Insurance Corporation Improvement Act of 1991 (FDICIA), banks may not extend credit to their executive officers, directors, and principal shareholders on preferential terms such as low interest rates and insufficient collateral but must apply the terms offered to outside borrowers. Also, loans to such insiders must not bear more than nominal risk. FDICIA requires that all loans to insiders be approved in advance by the bank's board of directors. This law limits the amount of aggregate credit extended to insiders and their affiliated interests to the amount of the bank's unimpaired capital and surplus. Exceptions may be made for community banks with under $100 million in deposits if the board believes that this provision would impede the flow of credit in the bank's community. In such cases, the aggregate credit to insiders cannot exceed two times the bank's unimpaired capital and surplus. Loans to bank examiners are illegal.

Regulation U sets margin restrictions on credit granted to acquire or carry securities and is intended to prevent speculation in securities markets. The regulation does not apply to loans secured by stocks, assuming that loan proceeds are not to be used to acquire stocks.

National banks are limited in the size of their real estate loan portfolios to the largest of either capital and surplus or 70 percent of time and savings deposits. Loans on real estate are confined to improved farm, business, and residential properties.

Many states have usury laws that establish ceilings on interest rates charged consumers and small businesses by state banks. National banks are permitted to charge up to 1 percentage point above the Federal Reserve discount rate. A federal preemption of state usury ceilings was effective during most of the period from the late 1970s through the mid-1980s, permitting banks to earn market rates of interest on previously restricted loans.

### Supervisory Examination of Loan Quality

In-bank examination by federal or state regulatory authorities has as its primary goals the evaluation of the following:

1. The bank's liquidity and solvency.
2. The bank's compliance with banking laws and regulations.
3. The quality and liquidity of the bank's assets.
4. The sufficiency of internal controls and safeguards.
5. The adequacy of capital.
6. The soundness of managements' policies.

The evaluation of each of these factors directly or indirectly involves the quality of the loan portfolio. Indeed, since it typically contains the majority of bank assets, the loan portfolio probably occupies more examiner time than all the other examination procedures combined. Considering that several thousand person-hours might be spent on a single examination of a $1 billion bank, depending on the extent of the bank's problems, it is clear that the loan portfolio receives considerable examiner attention. The examiner's summary evaluation regarding the condition of the bank and the soundness of its management is influenced heavily by the examiner's assessment of the bank's loans.

Loan examination, in its broadest aspects, requires an evaluation of the bank's lending policy and the administration of the whole loan portfolio. Problems in the loan portfolios of many banks often stem from inexperienced and poorly paid managers at the top. Loan problems also arise because of inadequate internal loan review systems in which loan officers, management, and directors are not alerted to deteriorating loans in need of follow-up and correction. Other problems occur because of failure to ascertain how loan proceeds are to be used, failure to establish clear loan repayment programs, failure to obtain sufficient credit information, and too much dependence on collateral.

Ultimately, however, the examiner's evaluation of the loan portfolio comes down to appraisal of individual loans. Some of the evaluation process is quite mundane and includes detailed steps such as proving each note to the general ledger, verifying the accuracy of collateral described in the note, recording loan details on the examiner's line card, and verifying that loan proceeds have actually been disbursed in the manner intended in the note.

Other aspects of the evaluation process are less mundane and require the examiner to have substantial experience, judgment, perceptiveness, and analytical ability in evaluating the risk of a loan. Primarily, the measurement of loan risk must be based on the willingness and ability of the borrower to perform as agreed in the loan negotiation. Consideration is given to the character, capacity, financial responsibility, and record of the borrower. Tests are made to determine if the borrower's actual and potential earning or liquid assets will cover interest payments and enable the loan principal to be repaid on the agreed schedule.

After a detailed review and discussion of individual loans with bank officers, the examiner will provide the bank with a listing of all loans warranting "criticism." Generally, criticized loans have above-average levels of risk or present risks at the time of the examination that the bank would not ordinarily undertake. Criticized loans are further broken down into the following categories:

1. *Other assets especially mentioned (OAEM)* are assets that are currently protected but *potentially weak*. The risks to these loans may be relatively minor, yet constitute an unwarranted risk in light of the circumstances surrounding them.
2. *Substandard* loans are inadequately protected by the net worth and paying capacity of the borrower or the pledged collateral. The bank will likely sustain some loss if deficiencies are not corrected.
3. *Doubtful* loans have all the weaknesses of substandard loans but have deteriorated such that they have a high probability of substantial loss.
4. *Loss* loans are considered uncollectible and of little or no value as a bank asset.

After deriving a list of criticized loans, the examiner assesses the adequacy of the bank's reserve for loan losses. The examiner's list of criticized loans is used as the basis for determining the adequacy of the reserve. As shown in the following example, the examiner applies an estimated loss percentage to each category of criticized loans. The total of these calculations is the amount of the *required reserve*, according to the examiner. If the total is equal to or less than the bank's actual loan loss reserve, the examiner considers the bank to be *adequately reserved*. If the required reserve is greater than the bank's actual loan loss reserve, the bank is *underreserved*, and the bank will be compelled to debit its current earnings and credit its loan loss reserve in an amount sufficient to raise the loan loss reserve to the required level estimated by the examiner.

| Criticized Loan Category | Estimated Loss Amount | Percentage | Reserve Requirement |
|---|---|---|---|
| OAEM | $1,000,000 | 2 | $ 20,000 |
| Substandard | 3,000,000 | 10 | 300,000 |
| Doubtful | 1,000,000 | 50 | 500,000 |
| Loss | 500,000 | 100 | 500,000 |
| Totals | $5,500,000 | | $1,320,000 |
| Less: Actual loan loss reserve | | | 820,000 |
| Amount underreserved | | | $ 500,000 |

In this example, the bank would be required to charge its earnings with a $500,000 provision for loan losses. Such a charge would come as an unpleasant surprise to the shareholders and directors of the bank. To avoid such a situation, bankers are well advised to criticize their bank's loans realistically. The example also highlights the importance of detecting problem loans as early as possible.

There is good evidence that examiners are rather successful in evaluating and classifying problem loans. Of the loans they examine, they manage to classify most of those that are subsequently charged off (although not all the loans they classify are charged off). In a long-term study of the classification of loans by examiners in a sample of 12 banks, it was found that of the charged-off loans that had been previously examined, 87 percent were adversely classified. Examiners also appear to be successful in assigning loans to the substandard, doubtful, and loss classification categories according to their relative risks of default. In the aforementioned 12-bank sample, higher charge-off rates occurred for the lowest classification categories; 10 percent of substandard, 58 percent of doubtful, and 95 percent of loss classifications were eventually charged off.[4]

## SUMMARY

Effective organization and control of the lending function are vital to the profitability and solvency of every bank. The lending function is perhaps the most diverse and complex activity in banking. Also, for most banks, it is the function involving risk to management, depositors, and stockholders.

The key tool for control and for communicating the bank's lending goals and strategies is the written loan policy. A formal loan policy is handed down from the board of directors to the loan officers for implementation; that is, loan officers' lending authority is derived from the directors. Bank directors are ultimately responsible for the quality and condition of the loan portfolio, and, as in all matters pertaining to the bank, they must answer to stockholders and bank regulatory authorities for deficiencies. Regulators expect the directors to conduct a regular internal examination of the loan portfolio in order to assess the quality and documentation of the loans, to review specific large credits, to ensure that proper loan approval policies and other policies are being followed, and generally to evaluate the performance of loan officers.[5]

Inherent in loan policy is the directors' attitude toward risk taking. Taking risks is a natural part of lending to consumers, businesses, farmers, and others, and inevitably losses will occur. The bank can do much to minimize loan losses in relation to the risks it does take, however, through a loan policy that mandates complete and uniform loan information and documentation; prompt action on delinquencies; secondary protection in the form of insurance on borrowers; and adequate collateral, profitable pricing, and, most important, loan review.

[4]Kenneth Spong and Thomas Hoenig, "Bank Examination Classifications and Loan Risk," *Economic Review*, Federal Reserve Bank of Kansas City (June 1979), pp. 15–25.

[5]Margaret A. Hoffman and Gerald C. Fischer, *Credit Department Management* (Philadelphia: Robert Morris Associates, 1980).

Small banks have had a tendency to rely on the bank examiner to perform their loan review or credit examination. Although examiners appear to be quite proficient in classifying problem loans, regulatory examinations were less frequent in the 1980s in relation to earlier periods. Examination personnel had not increased at the same pace as bank assets or new regulations and compliance requirements. However, a serious spate of troubled banks with problem loans in the mid-1980s added pressure for greater examination capacity. It appears that, in the future, banks of all sizes will need to provide for a professional and uniform internal loan review function. This function should be independent of the loan divisions and the loan approval channels.

In the next chapter we discuss credit analysis, a loan function that is perhaps the most basic of all in minimizing loan losses. Through credit analysis, the bank attempts to determine the ability of a borrower to repay legitimate extensions of credit. By refusing credit to a potential borrower who, on analysis, cannot demonstrate sufficient financial strength, the bank hopes to improve its chances to avoid unnecessary losses in its loan portfolio.

## Discussion Questions

1. Discuss the loan quality checks and balances that are built into the loan organization structure of typical banks. Is there a difference in loan committees fulfilling a review function versus a decision-making function on proposed loans?

2. What is the function of the loan policy? Why do regulators insist that loan policies be written?

3. Loan policies often list types of legal loans that are undesirable, even if made to profitable borrowers. List five types of such loans. What are the common ingredients of these types?

4. In the Penn Square Bank failure of 1982, poor or missing documentation was cited on many of the bank's loans and on many loans the bank sold to other banks. From historical accounts of the failure (see any financial newspaper or magazine account written at the time or since), find several quotations of examiners and correspondent banks regarding the quality of Penn Square's loan documentation.

5. The upsurge of bad loans in the mid-1980s has made loan review crucial, yet some bankers object to the cost of this "nonproductive" function. Discuss the economies of loan review in a small bank that is under pressure to hold down its overhead expenses.

6. Discuss the value of the following as indicators of a bank's loan quality:
   a. Reserve for loan losses (balance sheet).
   b. Provision for loan losses (income statement).
   c. Net loan charge-offs (loans charged off minus recoveries on previously charged-off loans).

7. Should banks require all borrowers to submit financial statements that are audited by CPAs?

8. Banks employ "workout specialists," who excel at collecting bad loans. Compare and contrast the technical and personal characteristics of workout specialists with those of regular loan officers.
9. What factors make it difficult for banks to apply the same credit standard to bank directors and senior managers that they apply to regular borrowers?
10. Examiners sometimes adversely classify loans that a bank's management considers sound and collectible. What circumstances might produce this difference of opinion?
11. What is the effect on bank capital adequacy when examiners adversely classify loans? Should the effect be the same on highly profitable banks as it is on banks with poor profits?

CHAPTER **11**

# Lending Principles and the Business Borrower

In its fullest meaning, credit analysis is the process of assessing the risk of lending to a business or an individual. Credit risk must be evaluated against the benefits the bank expects to derive from making the loan. The direct benefits are simply the interest and fees earned on the loan and, possibly, the deposit balances required as a condition of the loan. Indirect benefits consist of the initiation or maintenance of a relationship with the borrower that may provide the bank with increased deposits and with demand for a variety of bank services. In Chapters 12, 13, and 14 we will discuss the ways in which banks structure the loans they make in order to provide benefits commensurate with loan risks.

Credit risk assessment has both qualitative and quantitative dimensions; the qualitative dimensions of risk are generally more difficult to assess. The steps in qualitative risk assessment consist primarily of gathering information on the borrower's record of financial responsibility, determining his or her true purpose for wanting to borrow funds, identifying the risks confronting the borrower's business under future industry and economic conditions, and estimating the degree of commitment the borrower is expected to have regarding repayment. The quantitative dimension of credit risk assessment consists of the analysis of historical financial data and the projection of future financial results to evaluate the borrower's capacity for timely repayment of the loan and, indeed, the borrower's ability to survive possible industry and economic reverses.

The first section of this chapter introduces the four fundamental lines of inquiry in credit analysis. The second section discusses the resources and procedures used in credit investigation. The remainder of the chapter is devoted to financial statement analysis. The third section deals with the techniques of financial analysis, especially aspects of working capital analysis and financial forecasting. An appendix is included for readers who wish to review the basics of financial ratio analysis.

## FOUR BASIC CREDIT FACTORS

The essence of all credit analysis can be captured in four basic credit factors or lines of inquiry:

1. The borrower's character and soundness.
2. The intended use of loan funds.
3. The primary source of loan repayment.
4. Secondary sources of repayment.

### Character and Soundness

Most bankers agree that the paramount factor in a successful loan is the honesty and goodwill of the borrower. Dishonest borrowers do not feel morally committed to repay their debts. A determined, skilled, and dishonest borrower usually can get a loan through misrepresentation. Because loan officers must spread their time over many loan relationships, they do not have time to uncover elaborate schemes to defraud the bank.

To be sure, it is important to recognize that default does not always occur because of moral failing and willful neglect on the part of the borrower. Perhaps equally important are intelligence, personal discipline, and managerial skills and instincts. These qualities are sometimes easier to evaluate than blatant dishonesty—but not much easier. Loan officers must devote ample time in attempting to determine the competence of borrowers.

Finally, perhaps the subtlest task loan officers face is to discover the true quality of a borrower's business or project. Even competent and essentially honest borrowers are motivated to represent their plans and prospects in the best possible light when they are applying for funding. Without being deceitful, they often will not reveal their innermost fears or doubts. Thus, the loan officer tends to receive only part of the information needed to make a balanced credit decision. More than any other factor, it is this *asymmetry* in credit information volunteered by borrowers that compels loan officers to analyze carefully other, more objective information.

The bank must protect itself from dishonest, incompetent, or overly subjective borrowers by thoroughly investigating the credit background of the borrower. The borrower's previous credit relationships can be evaluated from records of the local credit bureau, suppliers, past banking relationships, and customers. If the borrower has built a record of prompt payment of interest and principal, it is likely that future loans will be similarly serviced. If the borrower has been routinely late in paying past debts, the reasons should be determined. If previous creditors have experienced losses, the loan officer should almost automatically reject the application.

## Use of Loan Funds

At first glance, the borrower's need and proposed use for funds usually seem perfectly clear. In many commercial loans, this is frequently not the case. More often than not, determining the true need and use for funds requires good analytical skills in accounting and business finance. An understanding of the loan's intended use helps the analyst to understand whether the loan request is reasonable and acceptable.

Ostensibly, most business loans are made for working capital purposes—usually additions to current assets. However, the specific purpose for the loan may be substantially different. The loan proceeds may provide emergency funds to meet the firm's payroll; they may be used to pay aggrieved suppliers' overdue accounts; they may be used to replace working capital that was depleted to purchase fixed assets; or they may replace funds depleted through operating losses. A common need for funds arises when collections of receivables slow down. The analyst should also determine whether working capital needs are seasonal or permanent. Frequently, short-term loans are made to finance working capital needs that initially appear seasonal but subsequently prove to be permanent needs arising from general sales growth. As a result, short-term loans often become de facto term loans that support permanent increases in accounts receivable, inventory, and fixed assets.

Assets financed by longer-term term commercial loans should meet the legitimate needs of the borrower's business. An asset purchased in the hope of profiting from its resale is speculative. Banks ordinarily do not lend for such a purchase because it does not contribute to the economic needs of the business.

## Primary Source of Repayment

The analyst's accounting and finance skills are crucial in determining the ability of the borrower to repay a loan from cash flow. For seasonal working capital loans, cash flows are generated by means of the orderly liquidation of the seasonal buildup in inventories and receivables. In term loans, cash flows are generated from earnings and noncash expenses (depreciation, depletion, etc.) charged against earnings. The analyst must ascertain the timing and sufficiency of these cash flows and evaluate the risk of cash flows falling short.

Sources of repayment other than cash flows from operations should be viewed with caution. The borrower may plan on a future injection of investor capital to repay the loan. Unfortunately, if the firm fails to produce attractive profits, outsiders usually withhold future investment in the firm. The customer may be depending on borrowing (*takeout* funds) from another institution to repay the bank. Unless a formal commitment exists from another institution, this source suffers from the same limitation as a planned equity injection. An exception is the interim construction loan in which another, long-term lender has formally committed to provide takeout funds. The future sale of a fixed asset usually is not a reliable source of loan repayment. If the borrower is either unwilling or unable to sell the asset at the time of the loan, a future, possibly forced, sale of the asset to repay the loan is highly speculative.

### Secondary Sources of Repayment

In general, cash flow from business operations is the most dependable source of loan repayment. However, if sufficient cash flows fail to materialize, the bank can prevent a loss if it has secured a secondary source of repayment.

Collateral should always be viewed as a secondary, not a primary, source of repayment. Banks hope to avoid foreclosing on collateral because foreclosure entails much time and expense. Collateral value should cover, in addition to the loan amount and interest due, the legal costs of foreclosure and interest during foreclosure proceedings. Collateral is the preferred secondary source of repayment.

Other secondary sources are guarantors and co-makers. However, collection from guarantors and co-makers often requires expensive litigation and results in considerable ill will between the bank, borrower, and guarantor.

## CREDIT INVESTIGATION

The purpose of credit investigation is to acquire enough information to determine the loan applicant's willingness and capacity to service the proposed loan. The investigation attempts to develop an understanding of the nature of the borrower in terms of the four basic credit factors just discussed: the borrower's character, the true purpose of the loan, the primary source of repayment, and the secondary sources of repayment. There are three fundamental sources of information: customers, internal bank sources, and external sources available through institutions outside the bank.

### Customer Interview

Despite possible lack of objectivity, the loan customer ordinarily will provide the most important information needed in a credit investigation. The prospective borrower should indicate the type and amount of loan requested, designate the proposed source and plan of repayment, identify the collateral or guarantors, name other previous and current creditors, list primary customers and trade suppliers, identify the firm's accountant, indicate the principal officers and shareholders, and give personal and business histories. The borrower also should provide documents needed to establish the lending relationship, including such items as the latest three or more years of business financial statements, personal financial statements, personal income tax returns, borrowing authorities, evidence of insurance, and continuing guarantees.

Lenders can quickly gather a wealth of supporting information using well-planned questions during the interview. What are the characteristics of the borrower's market? How are the products sold and distributed to the market? How important is price, quality, or service in selling the product? What is the production process? Are labor relations a problem? Who are the principal owners and executives, and what are their experience and educational backgrounds? Who would be in charge in the event that the present chief executive officer became unavailable? Does the firm have a strategic planning program? How will future markets of opportunity differ from those of today, and what resources will be needed to serve them? These and related questions serve to build the lender's comprehensive grasp of the strengths and weaknesses of a loan applicant.

### Internal Sources of Information

If the loan customer has existing relationships with the bank, a great deal of information is internally available to the bank about the customer's willingness and capacity to service the proposed loan. The investigator should study credit files on any current or previous borrowings, examine checking account activity, and review other deposits previously or currently held. These sources will indicate the degree of the bank's satisfaction with past payment performance, and they may reveal any tendency to overdraw deposit accounts. These sources will also identify primary customers, suppliers, and other creditors with whom the borrower has had financial transactions.

Values shown on a borrower's personal financial statement usually require validation. For example, bank accounts and CDs can be verified from bank statements. Ownership of stock, bonds, or mutual funds can be verified from stock and bond certificates or brokerage account statements. The value of a home or of other real estate can be verified with qualified appraisals or property tax statements. The validation of personal liability is equally important and usually is done from external sources, as described in the next subsection.

Income tax returns are very useful for validating almost every aspect of a borrower's personal finances, including income sources, assets, and liabilities. Special schedules that form part of income tax returns provide details on expenses claimed as deductions, income from investment and employment, and gains and losses on investment activities. Schedules on income averaging; income from rents, royalties, estates, or trusts; and depreciation expense on property all combine to provide a complete picture of the applicant's income and expense that is difficult to construct from other sources.

### External Sources of Information

Several service agencies provide credit reporting on businesses and business principals.

*Business Information Report*, published by Dun and Bradstreet, summarizes the financial history and current payment status of businesses. This basic credit report provides a composite credit rating, describes the promptness of trade payments by the subject firm, and indicates the highest credit balance carried during the most recent year. Other details include balance sheets, sales and profit records, insurance coverage, lease obligations, biographical information on principals, the firm's history, and its recent business trends.

*The Credit Interchange Service* of the National Association of Credit Management (NACM) is a national subscription service that provides information on a firm's current trade payment habits. The NACM sponsors local associations of trade suppliers and financial institutions, which share their credit listings and records on their payment experiences with businesses in their market areas.

*Credit bureaus* are local, regional, and national organizations that produce payment and employment information on individuals. Although this information source is generally used in connection with a consumer loan request, it may be used to obtain the payment history of principals in a business. Banks and other financial institutions are legitimate credit references and should be consulted. In the exchange of commercial credit information, bank officers are expected to govern themselves according to principles such as those set forth in the Robert Morris Associates Code of Ethics for the Exchange of Credit Information. This code describes ethical standards for confidentiality and accuracy in making and replying to credit inquiries.

A variety of commercial publications provides descriptive written and statistical information. These include *Moody's Industrial Manuals, Polk's City Directories, Standard and Poor's Corporation Records, Thomas' Registers*, and other special-purpose directories. Articles on individual firms or industries are published in many trade publications and may be found through the *Business Periodical Index* at any library. Official public information sources include filings of titles and mortgages, registration of corporation status, and business licenses.

## Spreadsheets and Statement Spreading

Bankers generally use so-called spreadsheets for recording a credit applicant's financial information (Tables 11-1 and 11-2). Spreadsheets permit the analyst to organize financial data in a consistent manner. This frequently requires that certain data submitted by the applicant be reclassified to match the bank's purposes. For example, an item included as a current asset in the applicant's statement might be reclassified as noncurrent on the spreadsheet if the credit analyst has doubts about its liquidity. An example of such an item might be a note due from one of the business's officers or principals.

The spreadsheet is arranged to allow easy comparison of current and historical trends and is readily updated, as the columns are completed from left to right. Spreadsheets typically are structured to permit entry of up to five years of financial statement history.

Columns are provided for common size ratios for each balance sheet and income statement account. Space is provided for several key financial ratios and for analysis of changes in net worth and working capital. Supplementary forms are often used to enter a time series of other key ratios.

## TABLE 11-1 General Spread Form

**GENERAL SPREAD FORM**

| NAME | | | | | | | | | |
|---|---|---|---|---|---|---|---|---|---|
| AUDITED STATEMENT | | | | | | | | | |
| STATEMENT DATE | | | | | | | | | |
| CASH | | | | | | | | | |
| MARKETABLE SECURITIES | | | | | | | | | |
| NOTES RECEIVABLE | | | | | | | | | |
| ACCOUNTS RECEIVABLE | | | | | | | | | |
| INVENTORY | | | | | | | | | |
| | | | | | | | | | |
| | | | | | | | | | |
| ALLOW. FOR DOUBT. ACCT. | | | | | | | | | |
| TOTAL CURRENT ASSETS | | | | | | | | | |
| FIXED ASSETS—NET | | | | | | | | | |
| NON-MARKETABLE SECURITIES | | | | | | | | | |
| NON-CURRENT RECEIVABLES | | | | | | | | | |
| PREPAID AND DEFERRED EXPENSES | | | | | | | | | |
| | | | | | | | | | |
| | | | | | | | | | |
| | | | | | | | | | |
| INTANGIBLES | | | | | | | | | |
| TOTAL NON-CURRENT ASSETS | | | | | | | | | |
| TOTAL ASSETS | | | | | | | | | |
| CURRENT MTY OF TERM DEBT | | | | | | | | | |
| NOTES PAYABLE | | | | | | | | | |
| ACCOUNTS PAYABLE | | | | | | | | | |
| ACCRUED EXPENSE & MISC. | | | | | | | | | |
| | | | | | | | | | |
| | | | | | | | | | |
| INCOME TAX LIABILITY | | | | | | | | | |
| TOTAL CURRENT LIABILITIES | | | | | | | | | |
| | | | | | | | | | |
| SUBORDINATED DEBT | | | | | | | | | |
| TOTAL LIABILITIES | | | | | | | | | |
| MINORITY INTEREST | | | | | | | | | |
| DEFERRED INCOME/RESERVES | | | | | | | | | |
| TREASURY STOCK | | | | | | | | | |
| PREFERRED STOCK OUTSTANDING | | | | | | | | | |
| COMMON STOCK OUTSTANDING | | | | | | | | | |
| CAPITAL SURPLUS | | | | | | | | | |
| RETAINED EARNINGS (DEFICIT) | | | | | | | | | |
| | | | | | | | | | |
| NET WORTH | | | | | | | | | |
| TANGIBLE NET WORTH | | | | | | | | | |
| | | | | | | | | | |
| WORKING CAPITAL | | | | | | | | | |
| EXCESS CUR. ASSETS OVER TOT. LIAB. | | | | | | | | | |
| CURRENT RATIO | | | | | | | | | |
| CASH. MKT. SEC. & A/R TO CURR. LIAB. | | | | | | | | | |
| A/R COLLECTION PERIOD—DAYS | | | | | | | | | |
| NET SALES TO INVENTORY | | | | | | | | | |
| COST OF SALES TO INVENTORY | | | | | | | | | |
| INVENTORY TO WORKING CAPITAL | | | | | | | | | |
| SR DEBT TO (TANG. N.W. & SUB. DEBT) | | | | | | | | | |
| NET PROFIT (LOSS) TO AVG. NET WORTH | | | | | | | | | |

## TABLE 11-2  Income Statement Analysis

**NAME**

| | | | | | | | | |
|---|---|---|---|---|---|---|---|---|
| PERIOD COVERED (MONTHS) | | | | | | | | |
| STATEMENT DATE | | | | | | | | |
| NET SALES | | | | | | | | |
| COST OF SALES | | | | | | | | |
| GROSS PROFIT | | | | | | | | |
| SELLING EXPENSES | | | | | | | | |
| GENERAL & ADMINISTRATIVE EXP. | | | | | | | | |
| TOTAL OPERATING EXPENSES | | | | | | | | |
| OPERATING PROFIT | | | | | | | | |
| OTHER INCOME (EXPENSE)—NET | | | | | | | | |
| NET PROFIT (LOSS) BEFORE TAXES | | | | | | | | |
| INCOME TAXES | | | | | | | | |
| NET PROFIT (LOSS) AFTER TAXES | | | | | | | | |
| ADDITIONAL DATA | | | | | | | | |
| DIVIDENDS—PREFERRED STOCK | | | | | | | | |
| DIVIDENDS—COM. STOCK or WITHDRAW | | | | | | | | |
| OFFICER REMUNERATION | | | | | | | | |
| INTEREST EXPENSE | | | | | | | | |
| OTHER CHANGES IN WORTH | | | | | | | | |
| CONTINGENT LIABILITIES | | | | | | | | |
| LEASE OBLIGATIONS | | | | | | | | |
| ANALYSIS OF CHANGES IN WORTH OR SURPLUS | | | | | | | | |
| AT BEGINNING OF PERIOD | | | | | | | | |
| ADD NET PROFIT | | | | | | | | |
| DEDUCT DIVIDENDS OR WITHDRAW | | | | | | | | |
| | | | | | | | | |
| | | | | | | | | |
| | | | | | | | | |
| | | | | | | | | |
| WORTH OR SURPLUS REPORTED | | | | | | | | |
| ANALYSIS OF WORKING CAPITAL | | | | | | | | |
| AT BEGINNING OF PERIOD | | | | | | | | |
| ADD. NET PROFIT | | | | | | | | |
| NON-CASH CHARGES | | | | | | | | |
| | | | | | | | | |
| | | | | | | | | |
| | | | | | | | | |
| MISCELLANEOUS | | | | | | | | |
| TOTAL ADDITIONS | | | | | | | | |
| DEDUCT: | | | | | | | | |
| DIVIDENDS/WITHDRAWALS | | | | | | | | |
| PLANT EXPENDITURES | | | | | | | | |
| | | | | | | | | |
| | | | | | | | | |
| MISCELLANEOUS | | | | | | | | |
| TOTAL DEDUCTIONS | | | | | | | | |
| NET CHANGE (+ OR −) | | | | | | | | |
| AT END OF PERIOD | | | | | | | | |
| | | | | | | | | |
| W/C AS ABOVE | | | | | | | | |
| INVENTORY | | | | | | | | |
| EXCESS OF W/C OVER INVENTORY | | | | | | | | |
| ANALYST INITIALS | | | | | | | | |

## Credit Analysis Rationale: A Case Example

The calculation of financial ratios provides the basis of most technical, quantitative credit analysis. For the uninitiated reader, the appendix contains a review of some commonly used financial ratios. This section demonstrates, through a simple case example, the kind of analytical reasoning used in credit evaluation. Tables 11-3, 11-4, and 11-5 present, respectively, balance sheets, income statements, and key financial ratios for three years for a small television and appliance retailer. In addition, each table includes the most recent comparable data on a local competitor and on the sample of TV and appliance retailers from Robert Morris Associates' (RMA) *Statement Studies*.

Even a cursory look at the common size balance sheets and income statements reveals a great deal about the character of the loan applicant's business. Table 11-3 shows that the accounts receivable make up only 14 percent of the 1990 assets of the firm, compared with 19 percent for its local competitor and 21 percent for the RMA firms. From these comparative data, the firm appears to have good control of its credit sales. It also appears to be overinvested in inventory, which represents 72 percent of its assets versus 66 percent for the local competitor and 46 percent for RMA firms. This suggests that the firm stocks slow-moving items or has a more complicated product mix, or both. On the other hand, the firm has less invested in fixed assets.

The firm's funds come predominantly from floor plan and long-term debt. Both categories of debt far exceed in importance the same sources for RMA firms, although the local competitor firm relies even more heavily on floor-plan debt. The applicant's accounts payable appear to be relatively small for this line of business and suggest little conflict with trade creditors. The firm's equity base is dramatically smaller than those of other firms, offering much less protection to its creditors.

Table 11-4 shows that the firm's 1990 cost of sales in relation to total income is 81.7 percent, compared with a cost of sales in the 70 percent range for other firms. In this retail business, an unusually high cost of sales suggests the likelihood of underpricing—the use of price cutting as a sales tool. Operating expenses, consisting of the sum of wages and salaries, sales expense, and other operating expense, totaled only 15 percent of income in 1990, compared with 26 percent for the local competitor and 25 percent for RMA firms. This indicates an exceptionally low-cost operation capable of supporting somewhat lower product prices. Unfortunately, all other (nonoperating) expenses nearly wiped out the firm's remaining revenues, so that the net income compared unfavorably with that of other firms.

It is obvious that the common size balance sheet and income statement highlight some key differences among firms in a similar line of business. However, common size ratios occasionally are misleading. If one asset account is grossly large, other asset accounts appear relatively small in ratio terms, even though they are about the amount expected in dollar terms. For example, it is possible for a firm's total assets to be so inflated by gross overinvestment in, say, fixed assets that all other asset proportions, such as the inventory common size ratio, are dwarfed and falsely appear insufficient. Thus, liquidity, lever-

**TABLE 11-3  TV and Appliance Retailer—Comparative Balance Sheet (dollars in thousands)**

| | 12/31/88 | Percentage of Total Assets | 12/31/89 | Percentage of Total Assets | 12/31/90 | Percentage of Total Assets | Local Competitor 1990 | RMA Ratios |
|---|---|---|---|---|---|---|---|---|
| **Assets** | | | | | | | | |
| Cash | $ 11 | 6% | $ 12 | 5% | $ 16 | 6% | 5% | 11% |
| Accounts receivable | 12 | 13 | 48 | 21 | 41 | 14 | 19 | 21 |
| Inventory | 122 | 69 | 147 | 65 | 203 | 72 | 66 | 46 |
| Total current assets | 155 | 88 | 207 | 91 | 260 | 92 | 90 | 78 |
| Net fixed assets | 21 | 12 | 21 | 9 | 24 | 8 | 10 | 22 |
| Total assets | $176 | 100% | $228 | 100% | $284 | 100% | 100% | 100% |
| **Liability and Equity** | | | | | | | | |
| Accounts payable | $ 16 | 9% | $ 10 | 4% | $ 4 | 1% | 2% | 12% |
| Flooring finance | 112 | 64 | 127 | 56 | 149 | 53 | 63 | 34 |
| Total current liabilities | 128 | 73 | 137 | 60 | 153 | 54 | 65 | 46 |
| Long-term debt | 23 | 13 | 57 | 25 | 90 | 33 | 8 | 10 |
| Total equity | 25 | 14 | 34 | 15 | 37 | 13 | 27 | 44 |
| Total liabilities and equity | $176 | 100 | $228 | 100 | $284 | 100 | 100 | 100 |

**TABLE 11-4  TV and Appliance Retailer—Comparative Statement of Income (dollars in thousands)**

| | 1988 | Percentage of Total Income | 1989 | Percentage of Total Income | 1990 | Percentage of Total Income | Local Competitor 1990 | RMA Ratios |
|---|---|---|---|---|---|---|---|---|
| **Income** | $713.4 | 100.0% | $866.2 | 100.0% | $911.7 | 100.0% | 100.0% | 100.0% |
| Less: Cost of sales | 592.2 | 83.0 | 706.2 | 81.5 | 745.1 | 81.7 | 70.5 | 71.3 |
| Gross profit | $121.2 | 17.0 | $160.0 | 18.5 | $166.6 | 18.3 | 29.5 | 28.7 |
| **Operating Expenses** | | | | | | | | |
| Wages and salaries | $ 46.4 | 6.5 | $ 60.1 | 6.9 | $ 54.7 | 6.0 | 17.7 | — |
| Sales expense | 19.6 | 2.7 | 24.3 | 2.8 | 39.7 | 4.4 | 4.2 | 25.2 |
| Other operating expense | 30.0 | 4.2 | 41.6 | 4.8 | 42.1 | 4.6 | 4.1 | — |
| Operating profit | $ 25.2 | 3.5 | $ 34.0 | 3.9 | $ 30.1 | 3.3 | 3.5 | 3.5 |
| **All Other Expenses** | $ 15.9 | 2.2 | $ 21.3 | 2.5 | $ 22.9 | 2.5 | 0.5 | 0.7 |
| Profit before taxes | 9.3 | 1.3 | 12.7 | 1.5 | 7.2 | 0.8 | 3.0 | 2.8 |
| Income taxes | 2.4 | 0.3 | 3.9 | 0.5 | 4.4 | 0.5 | 0.4 | — |
| Net income | $ 6.9 | 1.0 | $ 8.8 | 1.0 | $ 2.8 | 0.3 | 2.6 | 2.8 |

## TABLE 11-5   TV and Appliance Retailer—Financial Ratio Analysis

| | 1988 | 1989 | 1990 | Local Competitor 1990 | RMA Ratios |
|---|---|---|---|---|---|
| **Liquidity** | | | | | |
| Current | 1.2 | 1.5 | 1.7 | 1.4 | 1.7 |
| Quick | 0.3 | 0.4 | 0.4 | 0.4 | 0.7 |
| **Leverage** | | | | | |
| Debt to total assets | 0.86 | 0.85 | 0.87 | 0.72 | 0.54 |
| Interest coverage | 1.7 | 2.0 | 1.2 | 2.6 | 3.5 |
| Fixed charge coverage | 1.4 | 1.5 | 1.1 | 2.3 | N/A |
| **Activity** | | | | | |
| Inventory turnover | 5.4× | 5.2× | 4.3× | 4.9× | 5.7× |
| Average collection period (days) | 14 | 15 | 18 | 20 | 27 |
| Fixed assets turnover | 34× | 41× | 39× | 30× | 13× |
| Cash-to-cash cycle (days) | 87 | 90 | 109 | 101 | 98 |
| **Profitability** | | | | | |
| Profit margin on sales | 1.0% | 1.0% | 0.3% | 2.6% | 2.8% |
| Return on (average) total assets | 4.6% | 4.6% | 1.1% | 7.4% | 6.8% |
| Return on (average) net worth | 32.6% | 29.8% | 7.9% | 26.2% | 17.5% |

age, activity, and profitability ratios are necessary to complete a clear analytical picture.

Table 11-5 shows that the firm's current ratio of 1.7 is in line with that of the RMA firms and exceeds that of the local competitor. However, the firm's quick ratio of 0.4 is well below the RMA quick ratio. Together the current and quick ratios indicate that the firm's balance sheet liquidity depends predominantly on inventory. If inventory is obsolete or otherwise not readily marketable, the firm would have great difficulty meeting its short-term obligations. It should be noted that there is no provision for the current portion of long-term debt, a current liability. If a portion of long-term debt is to be repaid currently, the firm's liquidity would be further squeezed.

The firm's 1990 debt ratio of 0.87 indicates that, in relation to its peers, it offers a very small equity cushion for its creditors. Only 13 percent of its funds come from its owners, whereas 28 percent of its local competitor's funds and 46 percent of RMA firms' funds came from owners. The 1990 interest coverage ratio of 1.2 and the fixed charge ratio of 1.1 are far short of those of the other firms. This indicates insufficient earnings or excessive interest payments, or a combination of the two.

Inventory turnover of 4.3 times in 1990 for the firm compares unfavorably with 4.9 times for the local competitor and 5.7 times for RMA firms, again suggesting excessive investment in inventory. A similarly unfavorable comparison exists for the firm's cash-to-cash cycle of 109 days versus 101 days and 98 days, respectively, for its competitor and the RMA firms. This factor, when considered along with the firm's favorable average collection period of 18 days, is further indicative of an abnormally large inventory; specifically, the short average collection period demonstrates that receivables are not the cause of the long cash-to-cash cycle and implies that the cause is too much inventory. The firm's fixed-asset turnover of 39 times compared with 30 times and 13 times for its peers indicates that relatively little is invested in illiquid buildings and equipment.

Table 11-5 shows that the firm's profitability lags far behind that of its peers. Its return on sales of 1.0, 1.0, and 0.3 percent for the last three years compares poorly with its competitor's 2.6 percent and the RMA firms' 2.8 percent. As determined from its common size income statement, this poor performance is due to the extreme underpricing of its merchandise. A similarly unfavorable return on assets, bottoming out at 1.1 percent in 1990, further reflects poor earnings and may indicate excessive investment in assets, particularly inventory. Despite poor earnings performance, the firm's return on net worth figures for 1988 and 1989 are biased upward, in relation to those of its peers, because of the small amount of equity in the firm (the denominator in the return-on-net-worth ratio). If the firm operates at a loss in the future, its return on net worth would be dramatically biased negatively by the small amount of equity.

Financial analysis alone is not always sufficient to determine the creditworthiness of a firm. As a loan applicant, the firm would have to provide additional information such as the purpose of the loan and how the loan would affect the financial statements and ratios. However, the previous evidence indicates that the historical earnings, liquidity, inventory management, pricing, and equity support of the firm are all deficient. In the case of the TV and appliance retailer, financial analysis creates substantial doubt about the advisability of extending credit to the firm.

## WORKING CAPITAL ANALYSIS AND FINANCIAL PROJECTIONS

### Concept of Net Working Capital

Historically, the major role of banks in commercial lending has been to finance nonpermanent additions to working capital, defined simply as all current assets. Such additions enable a business to increase its cash balances and inventory in anticipation of seasonal bulges in sales and temporarily to extend larger amounts of credit to its customers as an aftereffect of such sales. Working capital loans are said to be self-liquidating because repayment occurs with an orderly reduction in inventories as sales rise, followed by reductions in receivables after collections are made on credit sales. The repayment of these traditional commercial loans is largely independent of long-term profitability and long-term cash flows.

**FIGURE 11-1    Net Working Capital**

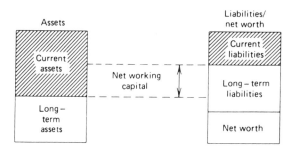

The measure known as *net working capital*, defined as current assets minus current liabilities, indicates the amount of a firm's working capital that is financed by long-term or so-called permanent sources of funds.[1] This relationship is illustrated in Figure 11-1. The assets and the liabilities/net worth sides of the balance sheet are represented by two bars. Each bar is divided into short-term and long-term items. Net working capital is a good indicator of a firm's liquidity because it identifies the part of a firm's most liquid assets that is supported by reliable (long-term) funds; that is, it is the amount of current assets that is not subject to claims by holders of current liabilities. Everything else being equal, a loan officer would have greater confidence in a borrower with a large net working capital position than one with little net working capital.

A corollary measure of liquidity is *net liquid assets*, which is a rough indication of the absolute dollar amount of liquidity in the firm. It is derived by subtracting from current assets the amount invested in inventory and all current liabilities. Inventory is subtracted because its liquidity often is suspect.

## Sources and Uses of Funds Analysis

In evaluating a working capital loan proposal, it is not enough simply to determine a borrower's net working capital position for one historic point in time. The loan officer should attempt to understand the dynamics in the borrower's balance sheet as seasonal activity ebbs and flows. Historical comparisons of the firm's balance sheet in a base period with its balance sheet during peak business activity will demonstrate how working capital is provided and used in operation. Table 11-6 shows comparative January 1990 and June 1990 balance sheets for a wholesaler of garden supplies whose sales and funds requirements usually peak in June. The differences between January 1990 and June 1990 in each account are recorded at the right as either a source or a use

[1]In practice, net working capital is often incorrectly called simply *working capital*.

**TABLE 11-6**    **Comparative Balance Sheets—Sources and Uses of Funds, Garden Wholesalers (dollars in thousands)**

|  | January 1990 | June 1990 | January to June Sources | Uses |
|---|---|---|---|---|
| **Assets** | $ 30 | $   15 | $ 15 | — |
| Cash | 30 | 15 | 15 | — |
| Accounts receivable | 150 | 450 | — | $300 |
| Inventory | 300 | 550 | — | 250 |
| Current assets | 480 | 1,015 | 15 | 550 |
| Net fixed assets | 180 | 175 | 5 | — |
| Total assets | $660 | $1,190 | | |
| **Liabilities and Net Worth** | | | | |
| Accounts payable | $ 60 | $   200 | $140 | — |
| Notes payable | 0 | 385 | 385 | — |
| Current liabilities | 60 | 585 | 525 | 0 |
| Long-term debt | 200 | 190 | — | 10 |
| Common stock | 50 | 50 | — | — |
| Retained earnings | 350 | 365 | 15 | — |
| Total liabilities and net worth | $660 | $1,190 | | |
| Total sources and uses | | | $560 | $560 |

of funds. Decreases in assets and increases in liabilities constitute sources of funds, whereas increases in assets and decreases in liabilities are uses of funds.

In the case of Garden Wholesalers, the net working capital improved hardly at all from January to June 1990. A total of $535,000 was used for a net increase in current assets ($550,000 in uses and $15,000 in sources), of which $525,000, or nearly all of it, was financed by increases in current liabilities. Nearly three-fourths of the increased current liabilities were provided by bank funds in the form of $385,000 in notes payable, and a little over one-fourth was provided by trade credit in the form of $140,000 in new accounts payable to suppliers. Garden Wholesalers' cash flows from depreciation (assumed to be $5,000) and retained earnings were rather insignificant sources of funds for financing additions to working capital.

### Financial Projections

The sources and uses of funds analysis can also be used to make simple financial projections. Suppose that in the following January, Garden Wholesalers' bank attempts to determine the firm's need for funds for the peak of the coming season. The loan officer should review all the factors affecting sales and funds flows, including economic conditions, industry and local market conditions, the impact of potential regulation, and the characteristics of the firm's operation. From these factors it can be determined that by June 1991 receivables will increase by $425,000, inventories by $350,000, and accounts payable by $230,000. Also, a $100,000 addition to fixed assets, $5,000 in depreciation, and $20,000 in retained earnings will occur. Finally, an estimate of change in cash balances and a partial repayment of long-term debt are included. Table 11-7 shows that, starting with the end of the January 1991 balance sheet, the forecasted uses exceed the forecasted sources, indicating a need for new external funds of $675,000 (including refinancing of January's notes payable). The sources of the new funds are assumed to be a $575,000 bank loan and a $100,000 addition to long-term debt; the latter is considered to be the source of financing for the addition to fixed assets. Net working capital will increase nominally from $440,000 to $455,000.

A more detailed projection is probably warranted in the form of a cash budget. Preparation of a cash budget requires projecting specific cash inflows

**TABLE 11-7    Financial Projection, New Funds Requirements for Garden Wholesalers (dollars in thousands)**

| | January 31, 1991 | January to June, 1991 (Projected) Sources | January to June, 1991 (Projected) Uses | June 30, 1991 (Projected) |
|---|---|---|---|---|
| **Assets** | | | | |
| Cash | $ 30 | — | — | $   30 |
| Accounts receivable | 175 | — | 425 | 600 |
| Inventory | 350 | — | 350 | 700 |
| Current assets | 555 | 0 | 775 | 1330 |
| Net fixed assets | 170 | 5 | 100 | 265 |
| Total assets | $725 | | | $1,595 |
| **Liabilities and Net Worth** | | | | |
| Accounts payable | $ 70 | $230 | — | $  300 |
| Notes payable | 45 | ? ← 575 | $ 45 | 575 |
| Current liabilities | 115 | 230    100 | | 875 |
| Long-term debt | 180 | ? ← | 10 | 270 |
| Common stock | 50 | — | — | 50 |
| Retained earnings | 380 | 20 | — | 400 |
| Total liabilities and net worth | $725 | $255 | $930 | $1595 |

930
−255
675

New funds needed
to balance

| **Net Working Capital** | $440 | | | $  455 |

**TABLE 11-8  Cash Budget for Garden Wholesalers, 1991 (dollars in thousands)**

|  | February | March | April | May | June |
|---|---|---|---|---|---|
| **Cash Inflows** | | | | | |
| Collections | $100 | $ 75 | $305 | $369 | $476 |
| Issue bonds | — | 100 | — | — | — |
| **Cash Disbursements** | | | | | |
| Accounts payable | 70 | 110 | 150 | 200 | 220 |
| Operating expenses | 20 | 20 | 20 | 20 | 20 |
| Wages | 100 | 130 | 180 | 250 | 300 |
| Taxes paid | — | — | 23 | — | 22 |
| Repayment on long-term debt | — | — | — | 10 | — |
| Additions to fixed assets | — | 50 | — | — | 50 |
| **Cash and Loan Summary** | | | | | |
| Net inflow (outflow) | (90) | (135) | (58) | (111) | (136) |
| Beginning cash | 30 | 30 | 20 | 22 | 26 |
| Loan increase (repayment) | 90 | 125 | 60 | 115 | 140 |
| Accumulated loan | 135 | 260 | 320 | 435 | 575 |
| Ending cash | $ 30 | $ 20 | $ 22 | $ 26 | $ 30 |

and cash disbursements on a monthly or even more frequent basis. The cash budget more closely identifies the amounts and timing of specific draws against a credit line extended by a bank or, alternatively, it identifies periods of excess cash in which short-term money market investments can be considered.

Table 11-8 shows a monthly cash budget for Garden Wholesalers for the same period covered in the balance sheet projection in Table 11-7. The cash budget is divided into three parts: cash inflows, cash disbursements, and a cash and loan summary. It projects monthly additions to and subtractions from the firm's balances and reflects bank borrowings to replenish cash balances. Note that the June cash balance and bank loan concur with the respective accounts on the pro forma June 1991 balance sheet in Table 11-7. In addition, the cash budget directly reflects transactions indicated in the sources and uses analysis in Table 11-7, such as the long-term debt repayment, issuance of new bonds, and payments on the addition to fixed assets. Still other cash budget entries are more directly related to the pro forma income statement (not shown), and the sum of every month's profit or loss is ultimately reflected in pro forma $20,000 additions to retained earnings shown in Table 11-7.

Although the pro forma income statement is not shown, most of its ingredients are implicit in the sources and uses projections and the monthly cash budget. Sales for January 31 to June 30, 1991, are not shown in the previous example, although they generally lead the cash collections shown in Table 11-8 by a more or less regular time period. The firm's cost of goods sold can be derived from the beginning inventory level plus additions to inventory minus ending inventory. Additions to inventory usually can be derived from purchases plus employee wages. Operating expenses and taxes constitute other expense items. The aggregate of sales, cost of goods sold, and other expense items provide the information needed to develop a pro forma income statement consistent with the pro forma balance sheet and cash budget.

Simply stated, the cash budget or cash flow analysis gives estimates of the borrower's cash inflows and outflows for a short interval of time. The example of Garden Wholesalers indicated the pattern of cash needs and subsequent loan take-downs as the firm approached its seasonal peak of activity. The example can easily be extended further into the future as the firm's activity subsides, generating cash for repayment of the loan. A more complete cash budget then shows when and whether the loan can be repaid.

## Cash Flow from Operations

It should be obvious by now that cash flow does not appear directly on balance sheets or income statements. However, in the final analysis, lenders must rely upon cash flow to repay loans. In the short run, there is often very little similarity between net income and cash flow. Thus, it is perilous to count on net income as a source of repayment. This simple fact—income does not equal cash flow—frequently is puzzling to beginner analysts.

Although it is not revealed directly in balance sheets and income statements, cash flow from a firm's operations can be derived through adjustments to these financial statements. The adjustments unlock the accrual accounting convention that forms the basis of financial statements. Balance sheet noncash assets represent historical cash inflows and potential cash outflows. By unlocking this accrual convention, we reveal the implicit present cash flows. Changes in assets, liabilities, and net worth, along with events that create income and expense, all contain cash flow information.

The rules for converting accrual accounting to cash basis accounting are straightforward. To convert revenues to receipts, one starts with revenues, subtracts increases in related assets, and adds increases in related liabilities. A symmetrical approach is followed to convert expenses (an accrual concept) to actual cash expenditures. In this case one starts with expenses, adds related increases in assets, and subtracts related increases in liabilities. Table 11-9 summarizes these rules.

The example of Textile Distributors, Inc., demonstrates the adjustments needed to unlock cash flow information. Table 11-10 presents balance sheets

## TABLE 11-9  Converting Accrual Income to Cash Flow

| To Get Cash | Related Assets | Related Liabilities |
|---|---|---|
| Receipts | Subtract | Add |
| Expenditures | Add | Subtract |

**TABLE 11-10  Textile Distributors, Inc.—Balance Sheets and Income Statement
(dollars in thousands)**

| | *Balance Sheets* | |
|---|---|---|
| | **December 31, 1989** | **December 31, 1990** |
| **Assets** | | |
| Cash | $   88 | $   72 |
| Accounts receivable | 1,142 | 1,532 |
| Inventory | 212 | 392 |
| Current assets | 1,442 | 1,996 |
| Net fixed assets | 44 | 100 |
| Total assets | 1,486 | 2,096 |
| **Liabilities and Net Worth** | | |
| Accounts payable | $1,008 | $1,332 |
| Notes payable—bank | 200 | 400 |
| Accrued expenses | 24 | 40 |
| Current liabilities | 1,232 | 1,772 |
| Common stock | 170 | 170 |
| Retained earnings | 84 | 154 |
| Total liabilities and net worth | $1,486 | $2,096 |

| *Income Statement* | | |
|---|---|---|
| *1990* | | |
| Net sales | | $   5,483 |
| Cost of goods sold | | − 4,495 |
| Gross profit | | 988 |
| Less: | | |
| Office salaries | $   112 | |
| Depreciation | 23 | |
| General and administrative | 642 | |
| Total operating expense | | − 777 |
| Operating income | | 211 |
| Interest expense | | − 38 |
| Net income before taxes | | 173 |
| Income taxes | | − 70 |
| Net income after taxes | | 103 |
| Less dividends | | − 33 |
| Retained earnings | | $     70 |

**TABLE 11-11    Textile Distributors, Inc.—Cash Provided from Operations, 1990 (dollars in thousands)**

| | | |
|---|---:|---:|
| **Net Cash Received** | | |
| Sales | $ 5,483 | |
| + Beginning accounts receivable | +1,142 | |
| | 6,625 | |
| − Ending accounts receivable | −1,532 | |
| − Net cash received | | $5,093 |
| **Cash Disbursed for Inventory** | | |
| Cost of goods sold | 4,495 | |
| + Ending inventory | + 392 | |
| | 4,887 | |
| − Beginning inventory | − 212 | |
| = Goods available for sale | 4,675 | |
| + Beginning accounts payable | +1,008 | |
| | 5,683 | |
| − Ending accounts payable | −1,332 | |
| = Total cash disbursed for inventory | | 4,351 |
| **Cash Disbursed for Expenses** | | |
| − Total expenses | 885 | |
| − Noncash charges | − 23 | |
| | 862 | |
| + Beginning accrued expenses | + 24 | |
| | 886 | |
| − Ending accrued expenses | − 40 | |
| | 846 | |
| − Beginning prepaid expenses | − 0 | |
| | 846 | |
| + Ending prepaid expenses | + 0 | |
| = Total expenses | | 846 |
| Cash surplus or deficient | | $ (104) |

for years' end 1989 and 1990 and a statement of income for 1990. Table 11-11 gives an analysis of cash provided during 1990 and consists of adjustments that essentially unravel the accruals represented on the balance sheets. A careful study of Table 11-11 will reveal its reasoning to anyone who is well acquainted with the logic of accrual accounting.

Consider Figure 11-2, which diagrams the first part of Table 11-11, "Net Cash Received." Textile Distributors sells everything on credit. Therefore, sales do not fully correspond with cash received; rather, sales initially is added

---

**FIGURE 11-2    Net Cash Received in 1990—Textile Distributors, Inc.**

| | Beginning A/R  $ 1,142,000 | |
|---|---|---|
| | Ending A/R  $ 1,532,000 | |
| Sales | | Net cash recieved |
| $ 5,483,000 | = Deferred collections = $ 390,000 | $ 5,093,000 |

---

to accounts receivable. The accounts receivable account is better thought of as a deferred collections account. If accounts receivable increase during the period, as in Figure 11-2, sales will overstate the net cash received because additional deferred collections are created.

Other adjustments are made in the second section, "Cash Disbursed for Inventory," to account for cash disbursed to produce goods and the accrual effects of changes in inventory and accounts payable. The third section, "Cash Disbursed for Expenses," can be used for similar adjustments to accrued expenses (liabilities), prepaid expenses (assets), accrued taxes, depreciation, interest, and other accrued items.

Note that overall, Textile Distributors' net cash flow during 1990 was a negative $104,000, despite a strong net income of $103,000. Clearly, a lender that depended on net income to reduce Textile's loan would have been greatly disappointed.

## Long-Term Financial Requirements

The principle of sources and uses of funds analysis to obtain balance sheet projections is as valid for long-term as it is for short-term estimates of funds requirements. For long-term purposes, however, the emphasis is on overall financial needs and not simply on the financing of temporary additions to working capital. The approach is to project the balance sheet for some future period—say, three to five years from the present. The differences between the future and present accounts indicate how funds will be used (invested) in the interim and determine how much external financing will be required. The future balance sheet is established using at least two kinds of data. First, discrete planning data are usually given, such as a planned dollar amount to be invested in new equipment or plant expansion. The second kind of data are derived by relating certain balance sheet accounts to key planning variables. For example, receivables and inventories may be a percentage of the sales anticipated in the future period. The ratios used to relate an account to sales may be derived from the firm's experience or may be equal to known norms in the firm's industry, such as those given in the RMA *Statement Studies*.

**TABLE 11-12  Three-year Balance Sheet Projection for a Manufacturing Firm (dollars in thousands)**

|  | June 1990 | June 1993 | Sources | Uses |
|---|---|---|---|---|
| **Assets** | | | | |
| Cash | $   70 | $   50 | $   20 | — |
| Accounts receivable | 700 | 800 | — | $   100 |
| Inventory | 850 | 1,280 | — | 430 |
| Current assets | 1,620 | 2,130 | | |
| Fixed assets | | | | |
| Gross | 1,800 | 2,300 | — | 500 |
| Accumulated depreciation | (300) | (450) | 150 | — |
| Net fixed assets | 1,500 | 1,850 | | |
| Total assets | 3,120 | 3,980 | | |
| **Liabilities and Net Worth** | | | | |
| Accounts payable | 250 | 320 | 70 | — |
| Notes payable | 300 | 610 | 310 | — |
| Current liabilities | 550 | 930 | | |
| Long-term debt (old) | 1,300 | 1,000 | — | 300 |
| Long-term debt (new) | — | 348 | 348 | — |
| Total long-term debt | 1,300 | 1,348 | | |
| Common stock | 200 | 200 | — | — |
| Retained earnings | 1,070 | 1,502 | 432 | — |
| Total liabilities and net worth | $3,120 | $3,980 | | |
| Total sources and uses | | | $1,330 | $1,330 |

To illustrate, in Table 11-12 we have constructed a balance sheet for three years into the future (June 1993) for a manufacturer, taking the actual June 1990 balance sheet as a base. The following guidelines are applied:

1. Sales will be $4.8 million during each of the next three years.
2. Minimum cash should be $50,000.
3. Receivables represent sales for the most recent 60 days (two months).
4. Inventories will turn over three times per year. Inventories are valued at the cost of goods, which will be 80 percent of sales.
5. Additions to fixed assets will total $500,000. Depreciation will be $50,000 per year.
6. Accounts payable will be equal to one-fourth of inventories.
7. Existing long-term debt will be retired at a rate of $100,000 per year.
8. After-tax profits will total 5 percent of sales each year. Forty percent of profits will be paid out in dividends.
9. Net working capital must be at least $1.2 million.

Each June 1993 balance sheet account is derived either explicitly or implicitly from the guidelines. The explicit derivations are as follows:

1. Cash = <u>$50,000</u> as specified.
2. Accounts receivable = 2 months/12 months/year × $4.8 million sales = <u>$800,000</u>.
3. Inventory = 0.80 × $4.8 million sales/3× turnover = <u>$1.28 million</u>.
4. Net fixed assets = $1.5 million (June 1990) + $500,000 additions = $50,000 depreciation × 3 years = <u>$1.85 million</u>.
5. Accounts payable = $1.28 million inventory × 1/4 = <u>$320,000</u>.
6. Notes payable = $2.13 million current assets − $320,000 payables − $1.2 million required net working capital = <u>$610,000</u>.
7. Total long-term debt = plug figure to balance the balance sheet after deducting $100,000 × 3 years of old debt retirement.
8. Retained earnings = $1.07 million (June 1990) + 0.05 aftertax profit × $4.8 million sales × 3 years × 0.6 retention rate = <u>$1.502 million</u>.

The sources and uses data in Table 11-12 reveal a lot about the financial dynamics of the firm over the coming three-year period. One debatable issue is the allocation of new debt between bank loans (notes payable) and new long-term debt. If the additions to working capital are considered permanent, the firm's banker might consider financing part or all of it through term lending in the future, or the banker might urge that other long-term sources, such as the bond market, be tapped.

## SUMMARY

Well-managed banks carefully assess the risk they incur in lending to a business borrower. They investigate the borrower's credit background, ascertain the reason for borrowing, and usually identify a source of repayment that is related to the successful business operations of the borrower.

Credit analysis requires the cooperation of the borrower and of informants both inside and outside the bank. Subjective judgment must be used in evaluating a borrower's trustworthiness and, therefore, his or her moral commitment to repay the loan as agreed.

The borrower's ability to repay is mostly a matter of financial analysis. Historical financial analysis is two-dimensional. Time series analysis is used to spot evolving financial strengths and weaknesses with the perspective of the passage of time. Cross-sectional analysis permits the analyst to determine how effectively the borrower has performed in relation to other firms with like market opportunities and risks.

Funds flow analysis demonstrates the dynamic funds needs of the firm. Its use in financial projections provides a comprehensive view of the future and gives the analyst a reality check against the borrower's request.

Chapter 12 discusses commercial loan negotiation and reviews the considerations that determine the terms and structure of the loan.

# Appendix: Financial Ratio Analysis

The more technical part of credit analysis and its use in making loan decisions has to do with concrete methods of analysis of financial statements. These methods of analysis generally rely on financial ratios calculated from various combinations of balance sheet and income statement accounts. Financial ratios may relate balance sheet accounts to one another, relate income statement accounts to one another, or cross-relate balance sheet and income statement accounts. Financial ratios are usually separated into categories based on the intended purposes or characteristics of the firm. The following are five frequently used classifications:

1. Common size ratios.
2. Profitability ratios.
3. Liquidity (short-term solvency) ratios.
4. Financial leverage (long-term solvency) ratios.
5. Activity or turnover ratios.

Short-term lenders are concerned foremost with liquidity ratios and, to a lesser extent, with activity ratios. Long-term lenders are mainly interested in profitability and financial leverage ratios.

Common size ratios are perhaps the simplest form of financial ratio. They express each balance sheet account as a percentage of total assets and each income statement account as a percentage of total revenue to create common size statements. The purpose of common size statements is to reduce firms of different sizes to a common basis and reveal underlying differences in their allocation of assets, sources of funds, and expenses.

Profitability ratios give the firm's profitability in relation to some investment base or to net sales. They attempt to measure the overall operational efficiency of the firm's management. The following three ratios—return on equity, return on assets, and profit margin—are most commonly used, although many others can be constructed.

Return on equity =

$$\frac{\text{Net income available to common stock}}{\text{Common stock equity}}$$

Return on equity is a summary measure of how effectively common stockholders' funds have been employed, including the effectiveness of the use of financial leverage. The numerator is after-tax income less any preferred dividends. The denominator is the average of balance sheet equity over the period of income and is usually derived by averaging the equity at the beginning and end of the period.

$$\text{Return on assets} = \frac{\text{Net income after tax}}{\text{Average total assets}}$$

Return on assets indicates the efficiency with which management employed the total capital resources available to it. It is a better measure of operating performance than return on equity because the latter is affected by the degree of financial leverage. The denominator can be formed by averaging the beginning and ending values of total assets.

$$\text{Profit margin} = \frac{\text{Net income after tax}}{\text{Net sales}}$$

Profit margin measures the profit per dollar of net sales. Its complement (1 − profit margin) indicates the expense incurred to generate $1 of revenue and reveals the effectiveness of cost controls and pricing policies.

Liquidity ratios indicate the firm's capacity for meeting its short-term liabilities as they become due. Two ratios are usually evaluated, the current ratio and the quick ratio.

$$\text{Current ratio} = \frac{\text{Current assets}}{\text{Current liabilities}}$$

The current ratio indicates the extent to which the claims of short-term creditors are covered by assets that can be readily converted into cash without loss. High current ratios suggest a high margin of safety for short-term creditors. However, the ratio

does not consider differences in the quality of receivables and inventories.

$$\text{Quick (acid-test) ratio} = \frac{\text{Current assets} - \text{Inventories}}{\text{Current liabilities}}$$

Concern over the quality of liquidity of inventories is purged in the quick ratio. Only the "quick" assets of cash, marketable securities, and receivables are included. For many industries in which inventory values may be suspect, the quick ratio is a more reliable measure of liquidity than the current ratio.

Because of their role as short-term lenders, banks have sought more reliable measures of liquidity than the static data reflected in the current and quick ratios. One such measure is the cash flow interval ratio, which relates quick assets to the firm's daily operating expenditures and other known cash disbursements. It indicates the number of days of net funds expenditures covered by quick assets. The cash budget, discussed earlier in this chapter, can be used in daily form to derive daily cash disbursements.

Financial leverage ratios indicate (1) the degree to which creditors, rather than owners, are financing a firm and (2) the firm's ability to meet long-term interest and principal payments on debt. From a lender's viewpoint, the amount of equity represents a cushion against operating losses or against a decline in the value of the firm's assets. As a result, lenders prefer to hold financial leverage within safe limits. On the other hand, the use of debt permits owners to control a firm with less personal investment. Assuming that borrowed funds can be invested to earn a rate of return greater than their cost, owners are motivated to increase financial leverage. Three ratios are commonly used to analyze the degree of financial leverage—debt ratio, interest coverage ratio, and fixed-charge coverage ratio.

$$\text{Debt ratio} = \frac{\text{Total debt}}{\text{Total assets}}$$

The debt ratio represents the portion of assets being financed by creditors. It is a measure of the financial risk of the firm. Generally, the more debt in the firm's financial structure, the more volatile its earnings and the greater the risk to owners and creditors.

Interest coverage ratio =

$$\frac{\text{Pretax income plus interest}}{\text{Interest expenses}}$$

The interest coverage ratio indicates the margin of safety that earnings provide creditors in relation to interest charges. A more liberal measure that is sometimes of value includes depreciation in the numerator to reflect the coverage provided by total cash flow.

Fixed-charge coverage ratio =

$$\frac{\text{Pretax income} + \text{Interest} + \text{Lease payments}}{\text{Interest} + \text{Lease expenses}}$$

The fixed-charge coverage ratio simply extends the interest coverage ratio to account for contractual commitments under leasing agreements. Here again, depreciation may be added to the numerator to obtain the coverage of fixed charges by cash flow and not just income. In both types of coverage ratios, the cyclical volatility of earnings must be analyzed to determine the appropriate coverage multiple.

Activity ratios indicate the intensity with which various assets are used to achieve a given sales level. In effect, they test for the operating efficiency of specific groups of assets. We will next discuss four of the more widely used activity ratios—average collection period, inventory turnover, fixed-asset turnover, and cash-to-cash cycle.

Average collection period =

$$\frac{\text{Accounts receivable}}{\text{Sales per day}}$$

When compared with the credit policy and terms granted by the firm, the average collection period measures the quality of credit extended and the effectiveness of collections. It indicates, on average, the time the firm must wait to collect after making a sale. Another important analysis of accounts receivable is the receivables' aging schedule, which classifies the proportion of receivables according to the period of time they have been outstanding, such as 1 to 30 days, 31 to 60 days, and over 60 days. The average collection period and the aging schedule together indicate the degree of liquidity of receivables. Relatively short collection periods combined with an aging schedule with very few overdue accounts suggest liquid and high-quality receivables.

Inventory turnover ratio =

$$\frac{\text{Cost of sales (annual)}}{\text{Average inventory}}$$

The inventory turnover ratio indicates the effectiveness of management's inventory controls. It measures the number of times per year that the firm rolls over its entire investment in inventory. If the turnover of inventory is too high, it may indicate a less than optimal inventory level, which would result in stockouts and lost sales. A too low turnover may indicate poor purchasing, production, and handling controls or obsolete merchandise. The cost of sales is used in the numerator, since inventory is usually valued at cost.

Fixed-asset turnover =

$$\frac{\text{Net sales}}{\text{Average net fixed assets}}$$

**FIGURE 11A-1   Cash-to-cash Cycle (dollars in thousands)**

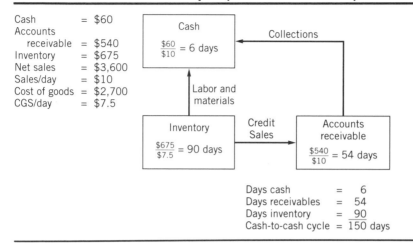

Cash          = $60
Accounts
  receivable  = $540
Inventory     = $675
Net sales     = $3,600
Sales/day     = $10
Cost of goods = $2,700
CGS/day       = $7.5

Days cash          =     6
Days receivables   =    54
Days inventory     =    90
Cash-to-cash cycle = 150 days

Fixed-asset utilization is measured by the rate at which the product value flows through the firm's plant and equipment. Low rates of flow or turnover indicate below-capacity operations; a high rate of flow may reflect inadequate investment in plant and equipment. Differences in depreciation policies distort this ratio so that appropriate adjustments must be considered.

$$\text{Cash-to-cash cycle} = \frac{\text{Average cash}}{\text{Net sales per day}}$$

$$+ \text{ Average collection period}$$

$$+ \frac{\text{Average inventory}}{\text{Cost of sales per day}}$$

The cash-to-cash cycle measures the turnover rate of working capital. As shown in Figure 11A-1, it represents the time required for a single dollar to move through the working capital cycle. Funds are invested first in operating cash balances, then converted to inventories by means of purchases of labor and material, then transformed into receivables as inventory is sold on credit, and finally, returned to cash as receivables are collected.

## SOURCES OF COMPARATIVE FINANCIAL DATA

Unfortunately, financial ratios cannot be analyzed easily in isolation because there are no reliable absolute standards to determine what their values should be. As a result, financial ratios must be analyzed in two basic comparative modes: cross-sectional and time series. Cross-sectional analysis compares the firm's ratios with those of peer firms in its industry for the same period or point in time. This section mainly discusses cross-sectional analysis and the use of comparative financial data of similar firms.

Time series analysis is concerned with the historical trend of the firm's ratios, that is, it measures the firm against itself at different points in time. Time series analysis can detect trends that may indicate potential problems before they occur. For example, the analyst may find that a firm experiencing rapid sales growth has a steadily falling profit margin because of a rising trend in its cost of goods sold. Without a time series perspective, the euphoria of rapid growth might conceal a dangerous deterioration in profit margins.

Several sources of comparative financial ratios are used by analysts in both time series and cross-sectional analysis.

*Statement Studies*, published annually by RMA, is the most familiar such source to bankers. Table 11A-1 shows a standard summary page from this publication consisting of financial ratios for a sample of family clothing retailers. A common size balance sheet and income statement and a series of liquidity, leverage, activity, and profitability ratios are presented for several hundred types of businesses. The ratios are derived from a sample of over 40,000 sets of statements submitted by bank loan officers throughout the nation. The ratios are reported by firm size so that a small firm can be compared with other small firms in its industry and a large firm can be compared with large firms. The most recent three years of time series data are given for the entire sample of firms in each line of business. In addition, three stratified values are reported for each ratio: upper quartile, median, and lower quartile. The distributional data for ratios give the analyst a better sense of the difference between a loan applicant's ratios and those of its peers.

Dun and Bradstreet publishes *Key Business Ratios in 125 Lines of Business*. This publication reports 14 ratios and, like the annual *Statement Studies*, gives the interquartile ranges. It does not, however, provide the ratios by firm size categories, nor does it report recent historical or time series data.

The *Almanac of Business and Industrial Financial Ratios*, published by Prentice-Hall, reports financial ratios for 170 lines of business and industries. The sample of firm data is taken from Internal Revenue Service corporate tax filings and is quite accurate and complete. However, the data are available only with a two- to three-year lag.

## RATIO INTERRELATIONSHIPS: THE DUPONT SYSTEM

Crucial information about the financial condition of a firm is revealed in several financial ratios, not just one. A combination or a system of financial ratios can reveal a great deal about the sources of a firm's profit performance. No single ratio can explain more than one facet of the firm's performance.

The DuPont system of analysis breaks the summary profitability ratio return on equity into its constituent leverage, profit margin, activity, and common size ratios. This system enables the analyst simultaneously to view the key relationships governing a business enterprise. Return on equity (ROE) may be defined as follows:

$$\text{ROE} = \frac{\text{Total assets}}{\text{Equity}}$$
$$\times \frac{\text{Net income after taxes}}{\text{Total assets}}$$

ROE is simply a multiple of total assets/equity—the dollars of assets supported by a single dollar of equity in the firm—and return on assets (ROA). ROA can be defined as follows:

$$\text{ROA} = \frac{\text{Sales}}{\text{Total assets}}$$
$$\times \frac{\text{Net income after taxes}}{\text{Sales}}$$

The term sales/total assets is the activity ratio called *total assets turnover*, and the term net income after taxes/sales is the profitability ratio called *profit margin*.

Total assets can be further broken into the assets' side of the common size balance sheet, and the net income after taxes can be shown as the residual from the common size income statement. Figure 11A-2 graphically presents the complete system.

## TABLE 11A-1  Industry Statistics for Retailers—Family Clothing

| Current Data — 62(6/30-9/30/81) 0-1MM 110 | 1-10MM 57 | Current Data — 114(10/1/81-3/31/82) 10-50MM 6 | 50-100MM 3 | ALL 176 | ASSET SIZE / NUMBER OF STATEMENTS | Comp. Hist. 6/30/77-3/31/78 ALL 164 | 6/30/78-3/31/79 ALL 158 | 6/30/79-3/31/80 ALL 156 | 6/30/80-3/31/81 ALL 185 | 6/30/81-3/31/82 ALL 176 |
|---|---|---|---|---|---|---|---|---|---|---|
| % | % | % | % | % | **ASSETS** | % | % | % | % | % |
| 8.1 | 9.4 | | | 8.4 | Cash & Equivalents | 8.5 | 8.5 | 8.6 | 8.9 | 8.4 |
| 13.2 | 15.6 | | | 14.4 | Accts. & Notes Rec. - Trade(net) | 15.2 | 14.5 | 14.4 | 14.0 | 14.4 |
| 54.8 | 49.4 | | | 52.2 | Inventory | 52.1 | 53.9 | 51.6 | 51.9 | 52.2 |
| 1.5 | 1.3 | | | 1.4 | All Other Current | 1.7 | 1.1 | 1.6 | 1.1 | 1.4 |
| 77.6 | 75.7 | | | 76.4 | Total Current | 77.5 | 78.0 | 76.2 | 75.9 | 76.4 |
| 16.8 | 17.6 | | | 17.6 | Fixed Assets (net) | 17.3 | 17.4 | 18.2 | 17.3 | 17.6 |
| .8 | 1.1 | | | .8 | Intangibles (net) | .4 | .4 | .7 | 1.0 | .8 |
| 4.8 | 5.6 | | | 5.2 | All Other Non-Current | 4.8 | 4.2 | 5.0 | 5.8 | 5.2 |
| 100.0 | 100.0 | | | 100.0 | Total | 100.0 | 100.0 | 100.0 | 100.0 | 100.0 |
| | | | | | **LIABILITIES** | | | | | |
| 10.4 | 11.3 | | | 10.6 | Notes Payable-Short Term | 9.9 | 10.5 | 9.9 | 9.5 | 10.6 |
| 3.9 | 2.4 | | | 3.4 | Cur. Mat.-L/T/D | 2.8 | 3.3 | 4.0 | 3.0 | 3.4 |
| 16.6 | 17.0 | | | 16.6 | Accts. & Notes Payable - Trade | 16.1 | 17.1 | 15.2 | 16.2 | 16.6 |
| 5.2 | 6.2 | | | 5.5 | Accrued Expenses | 4.9 | 5.6 | 5.5 | 6.1 | 5.5 |
| 3.5 | 3.1 | | | 3.4 | All Other Current | 3.0 | 3.7 | 3.6 | 3.4 | 3.4 |
| 39.6 | 40.1 | | | 39.5 | Total Current | 36.8 | 40.3 | 38.1 | 38.4 | 39.5 |
| 14.0 | 12.3 | | | 14.3 | Long Term Debt | 16.4 | 15.4 | 16.7 | 15.2 | 14.3 |
| 2.4 | 2.1 | | | 2.4 | All Other Non-Current | .8 | 2.2 | 1.3 | 2.2 | 2.4 |
| 44.0 | 45.5 | | | 43.8 | Net Worth | 46.1 | 42.1 | 43.9 | 44.2 | 43.8 |
| 100.0 | 100.0 | | | 100.0 | Total Liabilities & Net Worth | 100.0 | 100.0 | 100.0 | 100.0 | 100.0 |
| | | | | | **INCOME DATA** | | | | | |
| 100.0 | 100.0 | | | 100.0 | Net Sales | 100.0 | 100.0 | 100.0 | 100.0 | 100.0 |
| 61.8 | 58.9 | | | 60.7 | Cost Of Sales | 61.3 | 61.2 | 59.7 | 60.7 | 60.7 |
| 38.2 | 41.1 | | | 39.3 | Gross Profit | 38.7 | 38.8 | 40.3 | 39.3 | 39.3 |
| 33.1 | 38.0 | | | 34.7 | Operating Expenses | 34.7 | 35.5 | 37.1 | 35.2 | 34.7 |
| 5.1 | 3.1 | | | 4.6 | Operating Profit | 4.0 | 3.4 | 3.3 | 4.1 | 4.6 |
| 1.8 | .5 | | | 1.4 | All Other Expenses (net) | .5 | -.9 | .3 | .9 | 1.4 |
| 3.3 | 2.6 | | | 3.1 | Profit Before Taxes | 3.4 | 4.3 | 2.9 | 3.2 | 3.1 |
| | | | | | **RATIOS** | | | | | |
| 3.2 / 2.0 / 1.5 | 2.4 / 1.9 / 1.5 | | | 3.0 / 2.0 / 1.5 | Current | 3.3 / 2.2 / 1.6 | 3.0 / 2.0 / 1.5 | 3.0 / 2.1 / 1.5 | 2.9 / 2.0 / 1.5 | 3.0 / 2.0 / 1.5 |
| (109) 1.0 / .4 / .2 | 1.2 / .6 / .2 | | | (175) 1.1 / .5 / .2 | Quick | (163) 1.2 / .6 / .2 | 1.1 / .6 / .2 | 1.1 / .6 / .2 | (184) 1.1 / .6 / .2 | (175) 1.1 / .5 / .2 |
| 1 398.6 / 10 36.2 / 40 9.1 | 1 692.2 / 23 15.7 / 47 7.8 | | | 1 329.9 / 12 29.7 / 45 8.1 | Sales/Receivables | 1 390.7 / 13 27.5 / 48 7.6 | 2 228.1 / 16 23.3 / 46 7.9 | 2 199.3 / 15 24.3 / 43 8.4 | 2 225.4 / 12 30.1 / 42 8.6 | 1 329.9 / 12 29.7 / 45 8.1 |
| 107 3.4 / 146 2.5 / 228 1.6 | 101 3.6 / 135 2.7 / 174 2.1 | | | 107 3.4 / 135 2.7 / 203 1.8 | Cost of Sales/Inventory | 101 3.6 / 140 2.6 / 192 1.9 | 101 3.6 / 140 2.6 / 192 1.9 | 101 3.6 / 135 2.7 / 192 1.9 | 101 3.6 / 130 2.8 / 192 1.9 | 107 3.4 / 135 2.7 / 203 1.8 |
| 3.4 / 5.7 / 10.6 | 4.3 / 5.7 / 9.4 | | | 3.6 / 5.6 / 9.5 | Sales/Working Capital | 3.7 / 4.9 / 9.4 | 3.9 / 5.8 / 10.4 | 3.8 / 5.4 / 9.3 | 4.3 / 6.1 / 10.5 | 3.6 / 5.6 / 9.5 |
| (97) 5.4 / 2.5 / 1.2 | (44) 4.3 / 2.0 / 1.0 | | | (149) 5.2 / 2.4 / 1.2 | EBIT/Interest | (132) 8.3 / 3.5 / 1.7 | (127) 8.7 / 3.7 / 1.4 | (126) 6.5 / 2.7 / 1.3 | (149) 5.8 / 2.5 / 1.2 | (149) 5.2 / 2.4 / 1.2 |
| (40) 3.8 / 1.8 / .8 | (30) 6.3 / 2.0 / .4 | | | (77) 4.7 / 2.0 / .6 | Cash Flow/Cur. Mat. L/T/D | (69) 5.8 / 2.2 / .9 | (66) 8.8 / 3.3 / 1.2 | (72) 3.8 / 1.9 / .8 | (79) 4.3 / 2.1 / .8 | (77) 4.7 / 2.0 / .6 |
| .1 / .3 / .7 | .2 / .4 / .7 | | | .2 / .4 / .7 | Fixed/Worth | .2 / .3 / .6 | .2 / .4 / .6 | .1 / .4 / .6 | .2 / .4 / .8 | .2 / .4 / .7 |
| .6 / 1.3 / 2.7 | .7 / 1.4 / 2.2 | | | .7 / 1.4 / 2.6 | Debt/Worth | .6 / 1.1 / 2.4 | .7 / 1.4 / 2.7 | .6 / 1.2 / 2.4 | .7 / 1.2 / 2.5 | .7 / 1.4 / 2.6 |
| (106) 32.7 / 14.7 / 1.9 | 22.8 / 8.8 / 1.0 | | | (172) 30.3 / 13.7 / 1.9 | % Profit Before Taxes/Tangible Net Worth | (161) 30.4 / 14.2 / 5.6 | (154) 30.7 / 14.8 / 3.8 | (151) 28.9 / 14.0 / 3.7 | (181) 30.2 / 16.0 / 3.2 | (172) 30.3 / 13.7 / 1.9 |
| 13.1 / 5.6 / 1.0 | 9.4 / 4.9 / .3 | | | 12.1 / 5.3 / .9 | % Profit Before Taxes/Total Assets | 13.8 / 6.2 / 1.9 | 13.0 / 6.2 / 1.5 | 13.1 / 6.2 / 1.1 | 13.6 / 6.4 / 1.2 | 12.1 / 5.3 / .9 |
| 46.1 / 19.9 / 11.0 | 27.5 / 15.5 / 8.7 | | | 35.0 / 17.8 / 9.2 | Sales/Net Fixed Assets | 33.7 / 16.6 / 8.7 | 31.1 / 16.6 / 9.1 | 30.3 / 15.7 / 8.4 | 37.6 / 16.4 / 9.6 | 35.0 / 17.8 / 9.2 |
| 2.8 / 2.1 / 1.6 | 2.6 / 2.1 / 1.8 | | | 2.7 / 2.1 / 1.7 | Sales/Total Assets | 2.6 / 2.1 / 1.7 | 2.9 / 2.2 / 1.7 | 2.7 / 2.1 / 1.8 | 2.8 / 2.2 / 1.8 | 2.7 / 2.1 / 1.7 |
| (98) .7 / 1.2 / 1.7 | (52) .8 / 1.4 / 1.7 | | | (159) .8 / 1.3 / 1.8 | % Depr., Dep., Amort./Sales | (148) .7 / 1.1 / 1.8 | (144) .8 / 1.2 / 1.7 | (143) .8 / 1.3 / 1.7 | (169) .8 / 1.2 / 1.8 | (159) .8 / 1.3 / 1.8 |
| (76) 2.2 / 3.9 / 6.5 | (35) 2.6 / 3.8 / 5.4 | | | (115) 2.3 / 3.9 / 6.2 | % Lease & Rental Exp/Sales | (114) 2.4 / 3.8 / 5.2 | (103) 2.3 / 3.3 / 4.7 | (116) 2.3 / 3.4 / 5.5 | (125) 2.1 / 3.1 / 4.8 | (115) 2.3 / 3.9 / 6.2 |
| (59) 3.3 / 7.1 / 11.0 | (21) 1.9 / 3.2 / 6.7 | | | (80) 2.7 / 6.1 / 10.3 | % Officers' Comp/Sales | (75) 2.8 / 4.6 / 7.5 | (81) 2.9 / 4.5 / 6.8 | (76) 3.3 / 5.0 / 7.9 | (83) 2.9 / 5.8 / 9.2 | (80) 2.7 / 6.1 / 10.3 |
| 102364M | 313974M | 201550M | 485254M | 1103142M | Net Sales ($) | 533356M | 688600M | 654166M | 1280864M | 1103142M |
| 45060M | 139757M | 104543M | 252708M | 542068M | Total Assets ($) | 252776M | 333144M | 308714M | 534308M | 542068M |

©Robert Morris Associates 1982          M = $thousand   MM = $million

[1] RMA cautions that the statistics be regarded only as a general guideline and not as an absolute industry norm. This is due to limited samples within categories and different methods of operations by companies within the same industry. RMA recommends that the figures be used only as general guidelines in addition to other methods of financial analysis.

**FIGURE IIA-2    DuPont System of Analysis**

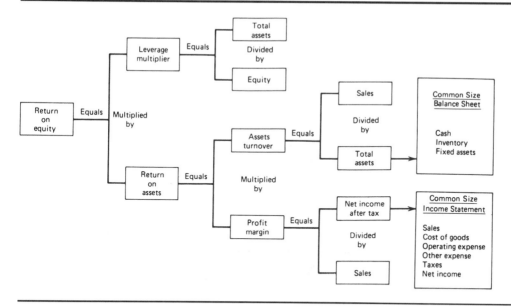

## Discussion Questions

1. Why are banks counseled not to lend money on the strength of collateral alone?

2. Develop a list of questions that a loan officer might present to a prospective borrower to gain a comprehensive understanding of the borrower's business.

3. Why do loan officers usually assign priority to the importance of the four basic credit factors indicated in the text, namely, the borrower's character, use of loan funds, primary source of repayment, and secondary sources of repayment? What arguments can you give for alternatively ranking sources of repayment ahead of the use of funds?

4. How would you evaluate the primary source of repayment on a loan to a business for the purchase of a corporate aircraft?

5. Using data in the annual report for a corporation, fill in the spreadsheets given in Tables 11-1 and 11-2. Complete one year only.

6. List and discuss the services offered by several key credit reporting agencies.

7. From a corporation's annual reports, compute financial ratios for three years, including liquidity, leverage, activity, and profitability ratios. Discuss the trends of the firm's strengths and weaknesses.

8. How does the definition of liquidity differ from the two alternative views of net working capital?

9. Using balance sheet and income statement data from a corporate report, construct a statement of cash provided from operations.

10. In credit analysis, how would the emphasis differ for a seasonal, self-liquidating loan versus a term loan to be repaid over several years?

# CHAPTER 12

# Commercial Lending

Commercial and industrial borrowers are the second largest users of bank loans after real estate borrowers. In mid-1993, these loans accounted for $535 billion out of $2,067 billion in total loans held by banks, or over one quarter.

Banks have developed a wide array of business lending skills and are adept at tailoring loans to businesses under varied conditions for a large number of purposes. Nearly every type of business borrows bank funds at some time. Even large public utilities, with their relatively free access to open-market long-term funds, routinely borrow "bridge" funds from banks to span the periodic issuance of their securities.

The business uses of bank credit include the following:

1. Seasonal working capital.
2. Long-term working capital.
3. New fixed assets.
4. Replacement of fixed assets.
5. Changes in payment patterns.
6. Unexpected one-time expenses.
7. Refinance of old debt.

There are many other purposes for business borrowing. Each purpose creates a need for a more or less unique loan arrangement. This chapter begins with a discussion of bank competitiveness in markets for commercial credit. Then we explain the types of loans banks make and how they structure them. Finally, we discuss collateral considerations, loan pricing, and the types of restrictions and covenants used in loan agreements.

# ARE BANK LOANS COMPETITIVE?

Commercial banks have encountered a great deal of competition in the market for loans to business. The stiffest competition comes from the intermediation of credit directly through the financial markets, such as the commercial paper market. Finance companies also compete aggressively with banks for loans to business. Some observers believe that the commercial banking system is in a "Darwinian struggle" to hold its share of the market for credit.[1]

To these observers, the system of allocating financial resources through commercial banks is less viable than it was 20 years ago. They portray bank lending as archaic because it involves ponderous decision making by committees, administered pricing, subordination to a broader customer relationship, and a high cost of bank funds (especially the cost of bank capital) to carry the loans on the bank's own balance sheet. In this view, bank lending amounts to a clublike activity that imposes unnatural costs on the intermediation of loanable funds.

In contrast to bank lending is a more modern system of loans created through the open markets. The open-market system competes for business credit without the need for bureaucratic organizations. The open markets rely on investment bankers, not commercial bankers, not only to originate but also to trade credit agreements in the markets. In this system, pricing is far more efficient because loanable funds are allocated through impersonal open-market bidding and trading activity.

However, despite the apparent efficiency of the open market, banks offer advantages and strengths as credit intermediaries that the open market does not. Banks have special skills for gathering and processing credit information that enable them to play a unique role in (1) screening undeserving loan applicants, (2) ensuring that credit is made available impartially and objectively, and (3) seeing to it that outstanding credit agreements are monitored and enforced. Banks have other advantages too. Historically, they have been able to fund loans at lower costs than nonbank intermediaries. Part of the lower cost is due to banks' relatively inexpensive sources of funds. First, depositors place a high value on deposit insurance, which allows banks to raise deposit funds at below-market interest rates. Also, banks attract substantial amounts of demand deposits that do not bear interest. In addition, banks have an advantage in monitoring loans because, typically, their borrowers maintain deposit accounts with them. This enables banks to observe the behavior of borrowers' cash flows and their ability to repay loans.[2]

However, banks' information advantage may be decreasing. New technologies for storing and transmitting data have reduced the costs of information and communication by a factor of perhaps 20 in the last 20 years. As a result,

---

[1] Alex Pollack, "Financial Innovations and the Merging of Commercial and Investment Banking Activities," Twenty-third Annual Conference on Bank Structure and Competition, Federal Reserve Bank of Chicago (May 1987).

[2] This point is developed in Eugene F. Fama, "What's Different about Banks?" *Journal of Monetary Economics* (January 1985), pp. 29–39.

information is becoming widely available at very low cost. In addition, large banks in highly competitive deposit markets are finding it too expensive to fund loans on their balance sheets with deposits and equity capital. Nondiscretionary costs of deposit insurance premiums and reserve requirements actually raise deposit costs to somewhat more than their stated rates. Equity cost rates are much higher, of course, and regulatory capital requirements ensure that banks incur a significant cost of equity to carry loans on their balance sheets. Thus, large banks are finding that it is cheaper to fund the loans they originate by quickly selling them to remove them from their balance sheets. Alternatively, banks may use certain qualified loans as collateral for the support of securities they issue in the financial markets. This latter approach is a process known as securitization.

In the final analysis, it seems clear that banks are no longer competitive in the market for large amounts of high-quality credit. In this market, there is far less need for bankers' unique information-gathering advantages for screening borrowers and for structuring and monitoring loan agreements. Large borrowers are attracted to the commercial paper market, which in 1992 accounted for 15 percent of the total business credit. Commercial paper can be issued quickly and in widely varied amounts, beginning at $1 million. Credit rating agencies provide their own valuable monitoring services for commercial paper borrowers. But despite the advantages of open-market borrowing, large borrowers do not find banks irrelevant. Even the strongest borrowers are motivated to seek a credit relationship with banks because such relationships add to the value of the borrowing firms. A banking relationship adds value by signaling to the borrowing firm's investors that the firm has the advantage of being scrutinized and expertly advised by a bank.[3]

The borrowing firms that are most likely to have valuable relationships with banks tend to be smaller firms and firms that produce products and services for less stable or less established markets. The lending bank is required to develop a great deal of information on the creditworthiness of these firms and to be highly flexible about how it structures the loan; how it monitors the loan; and, if things go awry, how it resolves borrowers' distress. Traditionally, banks excel at these functions. However, in recent years, commercial finance companies have taken a share of this business away from banks, accounting in 1992 for nearly 20 percent of business borrowing. Commercial finance companies fund their lending activities in the commercial paper market. They specialize in asset-based loans such as loans secured by accounts receivable, inventory, or equipment. In addition to financing purchases of such assets, companies can pledge existing working capital and equipment to obtain finance company lines of credit. However, many firms are not naturally positioned to borrow from finance companies. For example, service companies do not hold sufficient collateral to obtain asset-based loans.[4]

---

[3] See, for example, Christopher James, "Some Evidence on the Uniqueness of Bank Loans," *Journal of Financial Economics* (December 1987), pp. 217–235.

[4] See the discussion in Sean Becketti and Charles Morris, "Are Bank Loans Still Special?" *Economic Review*, Federal Reserve Bank of Kansas City, Third Quarter, 1992, pp. 71–84.

# TYPES OF LOANS

Although they are highly flexible and diverse, we can classify bank loans according to their maturity, type of collateral, and other special features. This section classifies bank loans into four types: short-term loans, bridge loans, revolving credit loans, and term loans. At any particular time, individual borrowers may have any number of each type of loan. This simple classification permits us to focus on the ways banks structure each type.[5]

## Short-Term Loans

**Source of Repayment**   Well over half of bank commercial loans are made for a short term, that is, for periods of less than a year. Most of these loans are for financing increases in inventory for seasonal borrowers. The loan is repaid when the borrower's inventory is sold and its receivables are collected. Short-term loans also finance borrowers with short-lived and project-oriented needs for funds—for example, service businesses such as accounting or engineering design firms.

**Analysis**   Retailers and manufacturers are regular users of seasonal working capital lines of credit. Through a line of credit, a bank indicates its intention to provide credit up to the amount of the line. The lender analyzes borrower-prepared projected monthly balance sheets and income statements. The projections show the need for funds for financing seasonal bulges in working capital as inventory, sales, and receivables expand in sequence. This sequence is known as the *working capital cycle*. The projections should reveal the expected peak loan need, the timing of takedowns, the link between bank and supplier credit, and the amount and time of the bank's maximum reliance on inventory support of its loan.

**Facility**   A loan facility is defined as the structure and terms established in a loan agreement. In the case of lines of credit, the facility is very flexible and overcomes the need to extend a series of short-term loans. The borrower takes down only part of the line as the need arises. As a result, the borrower is not left to borrow redundant funds. Interest is charged only on the amount actually borrowed, and the loan is repaid as cash flows back into the firm with the usual seasonal decline in sales, inventory, and receivables.

Normally, as a condition of the credit line, the agreement requires that the customer be out of debt to the bank for some period of time during the year. This required *rest period* is usually 30 to 90 consecutive days and is intended to provide confirmation that the customer's need for funds is not continuous and permanent. If the need appears to be continuous and permanent, the bank may seek to increase the collateral and otherwise restructure the loan. Seasonal lines of credit can "revolve" in the sense that amounts

---

[5]Parts of the following discussion of loan types are based on Edgar M. Morsman, Jr., "Commercial Loan Structuring," *The Journal of Commercial Bank Lending* (November 1991), pp. 24–42.

repaid can be reborrowed within the line. However, they generally do not revolve; amounts repaid are seldom reborrowed.

Lines of credit should not be confused with loan commitments. Commitments are enforceable obligations to advance funds under agreed-upon terms. By contrast, lines of credit can be revoked without the consent of borrowers.

A letter of agreement may be used to specify the line amount; define how the proceeds against a line are to be used; restrict the use of funds for other purposes, such as the purchase of fixed assets or the repayment of other debt; and spell out the expiration date. Despite their lack of enforceability, credit lines normally are honored faithfully by banks. Even an infrequent failure to honor its lines would risk a bank's reputation and its standing with present and potential customers. Of course, if the borrower's soundness deteriorates, lines of credit are subject to reduction or even cancellation. On the other hand, formal commitments obligate the bank to advance funds as established in a formal loan agreement, unless the borrower fails to fulfill the terms and conditions set forth.

Normally, the total of banks' open lines exceeds their practical capacity to honor all of them simultaneously. An "oversold" position such as this is a reasonable posture for a bank to take because it is virtually impossible that all line-of-credit customers would try to take down a large part of their lines at the same time. A bank can hedge against such an occurrence and preserve flexibility by structuring forward agreements informally so that they are not legally binding.

**Collateral** Line-of-credit borrowings usually are secured with inventory, accounts receivable, or fixed assets. The use of a formula for advancing funds against a borrowing base (defined later in this chapter) is not normal for seasonal borrowing. Because inventory values often are difficult to determine, the bank is most exposed when the borrower's seasonal inventory reaches its peak. In addition, however, as the inventory is sold, the lender must be concerned with the quality of receivables. This concern requires an understanding of the firm's credit policy, including how the firm checks on the credit of its own customers, how it sets customers' credit limits and denies credit, its collection procedures, and other considerations.

### Bridge Loans

**Source of Repayment** Another type of short-term loan is the bridge loan. Such loans can be thought of as project-type loans that bridge a period of time up to a specific event that generates sufficient funds for repayment of the loan. For example, money center and regional banks lend large sums to investment bankers to bridge their underwriting and placement of securities issues until the issues can be sold to investors. Sales to investors generate the funds needed to pay off the banks. Interim construction and real estate loans are normally short-term loans to builders or land developers for the purpose of acquiring and improving real estate. Such loans are secured by the subject real estate and are conditional on a commitment of long-term takeout funds from a permanent lender. The takeout funds are the source of repayment at the completion of the project for the bank making the bridge loan. Interim construction lending is the norm for the construction of single-family and multi-family housing, office buildings, shopping centers, warehouses, hotels, and restaurants, as well as for land development. Another type of bridge loan is one that spans the period until an issue of long-term debt or equity can be completed. On completion of the issue, the proceeds are used to retire the bridge loan.

**Analysis**    The bridge loan lender must make two kinds of evaluations. First, the lender must determine the probability that the bridge event will occur as projected; for example, the lender should assess the probability that construction takeout funds will, in fact, be forthcoming. Second, the lender must analyze the ability of the borrower to repay the loan if the projected event does not occur—for example, if the construction takeout commitment is not fulfilled.

**Facility**    Bridge loan maturities are tailored to the timing of the payoff event. If repayment is not completed at the time of the event, the lender must conclude that a failure has occurred.

**Collateral**    When a bridge loan finances the acquisition or building of an asset for immediate resale, the collateralization usually is as simple as taking a security interest in the asset itself. If the bridge loan is for financing or bridging a security underwriting, the lender ensures that repayment is made directly from the proceeds of the security offering. However, the lender must determine if the borrower can repay from other sources if the sale or refinancing event does not succeed.

## Revolving Credit Loans

Revolving credit loans finance the expansion of current assets or the retirement of current liabilities. This type of credit often is called *asset-based* lending because the amounts borrowed are tied to a *borrowing base* formula that limits the outstanding amount to a margin percentage on the borrower's receivables, inventory, or, in extractive industries, reserves owned. This credit is the long-term equivalent of short-term line-of-credit loans entailing a commitment to advance funds up to a maximum line for longer terms, that is, for as much as five years. The need for funds arises most often because the borrower cannot fund its increasing sales from internal sources such as retained earnings.

**Source of Repayment**    During the life of the revolving credit loan, repayment is derived from collections from the borrower's customers. With revolving credit, however, further advances are made when the borrowing firm periodically increases its inventories. Thus, repayment is indefinite and often remains so until the loan is converted to a term loan with a definite repayment schedule. Whether conversion to a term loan is appropriate or not depends upon the likelihood that long-term earnings will be adequate to repay the loan. Another source of repayment may be refinancing with an alternative lender or through a securities offering to market investors. The risk of nonrepayment is greater for revolving credit than for other types of loans because of the borrower's unresolved earnings power and the duration of the borrower's need.

**Analysis**   It is imperative to analyze the operating capabilities of revolving credit borrowers because such borrowers maintain a tenuous balancing act that matches the bank's financing to growing inventories, sales, and collections. This requires sharp internal controls and reporting systems. Debt ratios usually are higher than average and must be managed wisely so that financing costs are tolerable. The lender must determine how the borrower can demonstrate long-term earnings power capable of methodically repaying the current loan.

**Facility**   Revolving credit loans are made on a revocable basis. A loan agreement specifies the credit limit available and the conditions under which funds are advanced and repaid. Advances are made against evidence of adequate working collateral, with reports on the status of the collateral submitted frequently.

**Collateral**   Normally, revolving credit advances are made against a borrowing base of eligible receivables and inventories. Advances support the growth of inventories or the decrease in current liabilities, such as the reduction of excessive trade credit outstanding. Experienced lenders determine the quality of inventories and receivables and, therefore, the margins to be applied in a borrowing base advance formula. As a general rule, commodity-like raw materials inventories qualify for a higher advance rate than an end product from the borrower's conversion process. Commodity-like products are more likely to be sold to manufacturers who need similar raw materials. Alternatively, such inventories can usually be returned to the supplier, net of a restocking charge. By contrast, goods-in-process inventories may not be accepted as collateral at all because the bank is likely to find it extremely difficult to supervise the finishing of production in a failed firm. Also, finished goods inventories usually are less valuable than raw material inventories because finished goods inventories, especially specialized goods, often are difficult to liquidate. Lenders must also be wary of any category of inventories subject to obsolescence or spoilage.

Of the two, receivables constitute better collateral, whereas inventories must be viewed on a highly discounted liquidation basis. However, even though receivables generally are better collateral, the lender should margin them conservatively, usually providing an advance rate of 60 to 95 percent, to discount past-due accounts of customers and to deduct profit margins in order to restrict the recognition of value to actual value added to products sold net of the profit margin and of returns and allowances.

## Term Loans

Term loans are loans (other than consumer and real estate loans) with maturities over one year. Often they finance the purchase of fixed assets or the broad expansion of production capacity, but they may also be made to finance a change in company control or an acquisition or to take out a revolving credit loan.

For some highly rated companies with access to the bond market, term loans offer a viable "privately placed" alternative source of long-term funds. Their advantage over bonds is that term loans can be executed *quickly, flexibly*, and with *low issuance costs*. Because term loans are negotiated directly with a bank, an agreement can be reached more quickly and can be tailored to the specific case of the borrower, whereas a public bond issue must go through a lengthy registration process with the SEC. Typically, bonds are burdened with extensive terms or "boiler plate" to conform to the expectations of a broad bondholder public. Also, unlike the 20- to 30-year maturities usually associated with bonds, most term loans have intermediate maturities of less than 10 years.

**Source of Repayment**    The repayment source for term loans must consist of stable, long-term sources of cash. In the long run, sufficient earnings power is imperative, although cash flows arising from depreciation tax shelters may be a significant source for capital-intensive borrowers with high rates of depreciation. For loans made to finance fixed assets, repayment should be scheduled before the end of the useful life of the asset.

**Analysis**    The analysis of term loan borrowers focuses on what might be called the *long-term income statement*. The lender must understand the long-term earnings potential of the company. This implies a broad-based analysis of the firm's products and management, its industry, and its competitive strength within the industry. Long-term earnings projections are required, as well as sensitivity analyses that test the effects of unfavorable developments in sales volumes, profit margins, asset turnover rates, and direct and overhead expense ratios. In lending on specific fixed assets, it should be determined whether the assets will produce sufficient profitability to warrant their purchase.

**Facility**    Term loans typically are outstanding for a specified period of time and are amortized with payments of interest and principal on a quarterly or, ideally, monthly basis. Monthly payments have the advantages of more frequent compounding of the interest rate earned. They also provide the bank with more frequent confirmation that the borrower is remaining current on its debt and that its ability to repay has not deteriorated. A formal loan agreement is prepared, with terms and covenants spelling out the duties of the bank and the borrower, including certain rights that accrue to the bank if the borrower fails to comply with the requirements of the agreement. Loan proceeds are normally disbursed when the loan agreement is closed or shortly thereafter. In reality, term loans provide intermediate term credit; maturities are usually limited to 10 years and are predominantly in the 2- to 5-year range.

**Collateral**    The bank loan is normally secured by the borrower's fixed assets, including a mortgage on land and structures or a perfected security interest on equipment. Working capital is less often used for collateral in term loans but is used to support seasonal or revolving credit loans. The collateral value of secured assets is the assets' liquidation value, usually under assumed distress conditions.

## TAKING A SECURITY INTEREST

When a bank takes a security interest in collateral of the borrower, the bank obtains the right to sell the collateral assets and apply the proceeds to the loan if the borrower cannot repay the loan as agreed. Most bank loans to businesses are made on this basis. Although short-term loans to high-quality borrowers are not secured, most long-term loans are secured. In fact, the loan policies of many small and medium-sized banks generally forbid most unsecured term loans. Large banks, in dealing with large prime borrowers, are more liberal in granting unsecured loans, because such borrowers tend to have stronger equity support in their capital structures, more stable cash flows, and more certain investment opportunities.

Banks follow precise procedures to establish and document their legal claim to the proceeds of collateral assets in the event of default. Different procedures and documents are required for real, as opposed to personal, property. There is also a difference in the procedures for securing personal property, depending on whether the property remains in the possession of the bank or the borrower. These distinctions are illustrated in Figure 12-1, a schematic diagram of the methods and documents for gaining an enforceable security interest.

### Real Property

When real estate (land and improvements, including structures) collateral is offered, the bank must record the associated mortgage with a public agency such as the county clerk. This recording or filing protects the bank against subsequent claims by third parties. A title search is required to establish the existence of defects in the title in the form of other possible claims on the real estate. A major concern is the status of taxes and assessments on the real estate. These items are senior to all other claims; ideally, the borrower should

**FIGURE 12-1    Methods and Documents for Taking Security Interest**

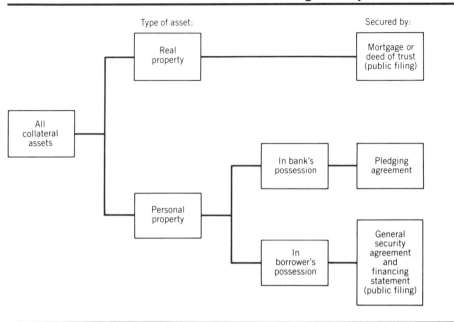

be current on them. Title companies sell title insurance to protect the bank against loss due to defects that were not disclosed by the title search.

In addition to matters of title, there are other routine considerations in real estate–secured lending. A professionally prepared appraisal is necessary to document the real estate's value in the present market or in case of possible liquidation. A certified survey is required to ascertain the secured property's physical location and dimensions and to ensure that improvements are properly located on the borrower's (and not infringing on someone else's) property. Evidence of insurance on the property is needed, including the designation of the bank as payee in the event of loss.

## Personal Property in the Bank's Possession

A security interest in the property of the borrower is perfected when the bank or its agent actually takes physical possession of it. The borrower completes a pledge agreement, which authorizes the bank to hold the collateral and to derive cash from it in the event of default. Because the asset is already in the bank's possession, it is not necessary to file a pledge agreement publicly.

There are several considerations in dealing with the more common types of collateral secured under pledge agreements. When negotiable securities are held as loan collateral, the borrower must execute a stock power assignment. The stock power simply authorizes the bank to sell the stock upon default of the loan. Stock loans are subject to Regulation U, under which the Federal Reserve Board controls the margin financing of stock purchases. The bank must report the purpose of stock loans and observe additional restrictions if the purpose is to purchase stock on margin.

Loans secured by the cash value or face value of a life insurance policy require a special pledge agreement to assign the policy to the bank. To be valid, the bank's security interest in the policy must be formally acknowledged by the issuing insurance company.

Banks commonly take a security interest in a savings account or CD belonging to an owner or stockholder of a borrowing firm. If the borrower's deposit is in another financial institution, that institution must formally acknowledge the assignment. This third-party notice perfects the lending bank's claim. To secure a borrower's deposits within the lending bank, a pledge agreement is important to block the possible withdrawal of the funds by the borrower.

### Personal Property in the Customer's Possession

Under the Uniform Commercial Code, a bank perfects its security interest in collateral property held by the borrower with a public filing of a general security agreement. The general security agreement simply grants the bank a security interest. It is accompanied by a financing statement that describes the collateral and gives the legal names and addresses of the borrower and the bank. The financing statement officially "places the world on notice" of the collateral position granted to and taken by the bank. To survive beyond their normal five-year expiration term, financing statements must be renewed by the filing of a continuation statement.

### Guarantees

As noted in Chapter 10, guarantees of loans to small corporations are often required of major stockholders to prevent firms from avoiding indebtedness under the shield of limited corporate liability. In general, loans should not be made on the strength of a guarantee; they should be based on the business source of repayment. The bank's position may be strengthened somewhat if the proposed guarantor signs as a co-maker instead. This may prevent litigation that could arise in loans with guarantors when the guarantors contest a possible later restructuring of the loan.

### Accounts Receivable Financing

Accounts receivable financing is a form of collateralized lending with a particularly intimate link between the loan and its collateral. The bank lends money against an agreed percentage (50 to 90 percent) of accounts receivable assigned to it. The borrowing firm usually continues its regular credit and collection functions, and its customers are not notified of the assignment of their debt to the bank. Collections are automatically paid down on the loan, and new loan funds are granted as new receivables are generated.

This type of financing has advantages for both the bank and the borrower. It gives the bank access to the readily convertible collateral of weaker borrowers who otherwise might not provide a viable loan market. Credit is well controlled since receivables financing permits borrowing only as the borrower generates sales. It also provides for automatic repayment of the loan as collections come in.

Accounts receivable financing gives relatively weak borrowers access to credit they otherwise might not obtain. The credit is *evergreen* in that no rest period is required. The amount of credit is more or less tailored to the rolling needs of the borrower, particularly because financing reacts to expanding sales, thus supporting the necessary buildup of inventories. However, the cost of accounts receivable financing is higher than the cost paid by a borrower that is qualified for unsecured lending.

Banks proceed cautiously because of the unusual reliance on the collateral in receivables financing. The collateral needs to be examined carefully and continually to ensure performance and to eliminate ineligible receivables from the borrowing base.

## Factoring

Accounts receivable financing is often confused with factoring. In factoring, a bank or a commercial factor actually purchases selected accounts receivable from its customer at a percentage of their face value. In a strict sense, then, factoring is not a form of collateralized lending but rather an outright purchase of the customer's assets. The bank notifies the borrower's debtors to remit all payments directly to the bank and not to the customer. Generally, the customer is required to maintain a cash reserve against losses due to buyers' claims against the customer firm.

Table 12-1 summarizes the differences between accounts receivable financing and factoring.

**TABLE 12-1    Accounts Receivable Financing versus Factoring**

|  | *Accounts Receivable* | |
|---|---|---|
|  | Financing | Factoring |
| Credit function performed by | Borrower | Bank |
| Collection function performed by | Borrower | Bank |
| Proceeds allowed via | Loan | Purchase |
| Cash reserve required | No | Yes |
| Account ownership | Borrower | Bank |
| Debtor notification | No | Yes |
| Cost | Lower | Higher |

### Inventory Financing

For our purposes, inventory financing can be defined as any loan that is secured by inventory and scheduled to be repaid from the sale of that inventory. Like accounts receivable financing, it is a highly specialized lending service to business; it is often combined with accounts receivable financing. Lending against inventory is a high-risk venture because such financing is usually extended to businesses that are financially weak. Also, the lender frequently encounters problems related to the valuation and marketability of inventory, as well as difficulties in physical control of the inventory.

There are several forms of inventory lending. All of the borrower's inventories can be used as security on a loan under a *floating lien*. However, the seller is not constrained from selling inventories, so that the bank cannot control specific inventory items. The floating lien may be used to provide continuing security on receivables created when the inventory is sold.

*Trust receipt financing*, also known as *floor plan finance*, is vitally important in many retail businesses and involves transitory legal ownership of inventory by the bank. Typically, the borrower is provided funds with which to pay for goods received from suppliers. The borrower holds the goods in trust for the bank by issuing the bank a trust receipt. As sales occur, the borrower transmits the proceeds to the bank. Contracts from the borrower's credit sales are also frequently sold to the bank, so that the bank, in effect, provides continuous financing.

Trust receipts can be issued only on specifically identifiable goods. The goods must be easily verified when the bank runs its audit of the customer's inventory. Trust receipts are most convenient when used to finance new- and used-automobile dealers, other durable consumer goods retailers, and machinery dealers.

*Warehousing financing* facilitates inventory lending by providing controls on the disposition of a borrower's inventories. Two different warehousing arrangements are used: the public warehouse and the field warehouse. The *public warehouse* is owned and operated remotely from the borrower's site by an independent third party in the storage business. The *field warehouse* is controlled by an independent third-party operator on the borrower's site and is more suitable when the goods handled are too bulky to relocate or when goods are moved in and out with great frequency.

In both public and field warehouse arrangements, the independent third party receives and stores the inventories and provides the bank with warehouse receipts. The bank then creates a deposit for the borrower at an advance rate, typically in the range of 50 to 80 percent of the value of the receipted goods. As the borrower's customers submit orders for the goods, the bank releases goods to make the sales, and the proceeds of the sales are remitted directly to the bank to repay the loan. The costs of warehouse financing are quite high and become prohibitive for smaller operations. Banks undertake a major risk in warehouse financing because of the difficulty of verifying the quality of goods on which they acquire warehouse receipts. Fraud has also played a prominent part in warehouse finance. The great salad oil scandal of the early

1960s, in which banks advanced millions of dollars against warehouse receipts for which no goods existed, stands as testimony to the inherent risk of this type of loan.

### Participation Agreements

Banks sometimes find it beneficial to sell or *participate* part of a commercial loan to another bank or other lender. Alternatively, banks frequently have opportunities to acquire a participation in loans originated by others. The basis of participation usually is established either as pro rata or lifo. The *pro rata* basis entitles the participant to a set proportion of the loan, without distinction as to subordination. The *lifo* basis, in effect, layers participants for subordination purposes. Each participant is lined up ahead of or behind other participants, based on their order of entry. State and federal laws and regulations often govern the role of participation agents for banks.

In many large participated commercial loans, a *multilender loan agreement* often is used. This agreement sets forth the identities of each participating lender on all loan documents and indicates the proportional interest each has in the agreement, as well as the collateral supporting the loan. This permits each lender to hold its own promissory note. In addition, a formal agreement establishes the lead bank as the *managing agent* and the other participants as *co-agents*, and it clarifies the rights and obligations of the managing bank in administering the loan and the participation agreement.

The net effect of such formalization of participation agreements is that each participant acquires a direct contractual relationship with the borrower that does not depend on the lead bank. This arrangement has the obvious advantage of protecting the participant against the possible failure of the lead bank.

## LOAN COVENANTS

In making any business loan, there is the risk that the loan's purpose will go awry or that the borrower's financial condition will deteriorate to the extent that repayment of the loan is jeopardized. These risks increase with the length of time a loan is outstanding. Loan agreements set up a conflict between borrowers and lenders.[6] Intuitively, it should be clear that borrowing firms or, more precisely, their shareholders have an incentive to take on risky activities in the expectation of a payoff commensurate with the risk. If the activities fail totally, the borrowing firms' shareholders' stake is wiped out and the lending bank is left with a worthless claim. If the activities succeed, however, the shareholders enjoy excess returns and the lenders recover a set amount of interest and principal, without the prospect of excess returns. To protect them-

---

[6] A comprehensive analysis of loan or bond covenants is found in Clifford W. Smith, Jr., and Jerold B. Warner, "On Financial Contracting," *Journal of Financial Economics* (June 1979), pp. 117–161.

selves against such risk, banks write restrictive covenants into loan agreements. Term loans usually are set up with the most extensive loan covenants, although standard boiler-plate covenants are typically a part of all loan agreements.

### Affirmative versus Negative Covenants

There are two types of covenants in most term loan agreements: affirmative and negative. *Affirmative covenants* set out the borrower's obligation to submit financial statements regularly, to maintain adequate insurance, to certify compliance with provisions of the loan agreement periodically, to pay principal and interest as scheduled, and to conform to other requirements for reporting on company activities. *Negative covenants* range from requiring the borrower to maintain reasonable financial health to outright restraints or prohibitions on the borrower's activities. Because negative covenants might restrict or impose costs on the borrower, they are the subject of other intense negotiations.

There may be many negative covenants in a term loan agreement or just a few. The banker must determine, in each case, the types of covenants to include and how they should be quantified.

### Objectives of Covenants

In framing the loan agreement covenants, the banker must first decide what he or she wants to control and achieve. Covenants may be classified by their objectives as follows:

1. Cash flow control.
2. Trigger call or restructuring of the loan.
3. Balance sheet control.

The most common objective is *cash flow control*, that is, assurance that the cash flow from the borrower's operations will be available to service the interest and principal of the loan. For term loans, the most important factor in cash flow is profits. The banker reviews the firm's business plan and the way in which the proceeds of the loan will be used. If the firm's plans are considered too risky, the banker might use loan covenants to force a modification, such as reducing the amount that the firm will invest in a high-risk venture or even prohibiting the firm from entering a new, high-risk market or product line.

However, it is not enough that a borrower's future profits seem assured. The banker may insist on covenants preventing dividend payments, excessive capital investments, or repayment of debts owed to other lenders in order to ensure that future cash flows will repay the bank's loan.

The *trigger* type of loan covenant establishes critical financial thresholds that, when violated, trigger the bank's right to some form of protective recourse. For example, if the borrower fails to maintain minimum profitability or a minimum net working capital level, the bank might gain the right to call the entire loan. This call would protect the bank against deterioration in the value of the firm's working capital: If the firm cannot repay the loan on call, the bank's recourse lies in the firm's assets. Alternatively, a call on the loan opens the way for the bank to increase the loan interest rate, increase the collateral, or write stricter covenants.

*Balance sheet control* covenants are aimed at restricting future actions by the firm that will weaken the balance sheet, often as a reaction to changes in the firm's business situation. Covenants may be used to limit further indebtedness or depletion of current assets in order to maintain an acceptable debt-to-equity ratio, current ratio, or other balance sheet standards.

## PRICING CONCEPTS

The profitability of banks depends on how the prices they charge for loans and myriad services compare with their costs of funds and operations. As the major source of revenue, loan prices, including loan interest rates, fees, and compensating balances, have a crucial role in bank profitability. Indeed, because loans represent the central activity of banking and are the basis of most banks' relationships with their major customers, loan pricing tends to be the focal point of both revenues and costs.

### Price versus Base Rate

The national prime rate is a loan rate administered by the large money market banks. The banks adjust the prime, with considerable public fanfare, to signal the softening or hardening of loan conditions. Their adjustment of the prime often is not closely synchronized with changes in short-term open-market rates, such as the Federal funds rate.

Since the late 1970s, when as much as 90 percent of their loans were linked to the prime rate, money center banks have moved away from the prime rate as a benchmark used in loan pricing. As indicated in Table 12-2, only one-fifth of business loans made by nine of the largest money center banks

**TABLE 12-2    Pricing Business Loan Base Rates at U.S. Banks (percentage of loans)**

| Rate Basis | Nine Money Center Banks | Other Large Banks | Other Banks |
|---|---|---|---|
| Prime rate | 21.1% | 29.0% | 54.0% |
| Federal funds rate | 37.7 | 25.8 | 16.7 |
| Other domestic money market rate | 25.5 | 20.7 | 12.0 |
| Foreign rate | 4.3 | 9.4 | 6.2 |
| Other | 11.4 | 15.1 | 11.0 |

SOURCE: Thomas D. Simpson, "Developments in the United States Financial System since the Mid-1970s," *Federal Reserve Bulletin* (January 1988), pp. 1–13.

were based on the prime rate in a recent year. The remainder of their business loans shifted to one of several open-market reference rates. This was due to new sources of competition for these loans, especially from foreign banks that sought loan business in the United States through their offshore branches and agencies. Thirty-seven percent of large business loans by money center banks were tied to the Federal funds rate, and about one-quarter was tied to other domestic money market rates, such as the CD or Treasury bill rate. Only a small fraction was tied to external interest rates such as the London Interbank Offering Rate (LIBOR).

For other large banks, the prime rate was still somewhat more important as a pricing benchmark rate, although the open market–based rate had increased significantly during the past 20 years. Slightly over half of small bank business loans remained linked to the prime rate, although here too, market-based pricing demonstrated a considerable gain.

The movement from large, prime-based short-term loans to pricing on money market base rates probably will never be reversed. The movement occurred, as noted earlier in the chapter, because of price competition from an expanding commercial paper market and from foreign banks, both of which were historically more open to unrestrained competition. Nevertheless, local banks' prime rates are still the basis of pricing most small loans, and many large revolving credits are frequently based on prime. In addition, the rates on certain consumer loans and many construction loans continue to be based on the prime rate.

Some smaller banks have given up the practice of quoting loan prices based on a prime rate because of publicity from court cases challenging prime rate lending practices during the 1980s. Plaintiffs claimed that banks misled customers by implying that the prime rate was the interest rate charged to their most creditworthy customers when, in fact, they made loans at interest rates below their stated primes. It was alleged that although the term *prime rate* is not clearly defined, it is vaguely represented as the lowest commercial loan rate available. Some of the plaintiffs claimed that the defendant banks violated antitrust laws because they all fixed their prime rates at noncompetitive levels. In any case, the practice by large banks of quoting a national prime rate as an indicator of loan tightness, although not as a specific loan offer rate, seems likely to persist.

### Floating Rates

When money market rates of interest fluctuated dramatically during the early 1980s, banks' loan pricing systems became largely based on floating rates. When market rates rise, the cost of many sources of bank funds rises as well, and if bank loans are all at fixed rates, bank profitability becomes squeezed. Recognizing this effect of rate fluctuations, banks have made a major shift to floating-rate provisions in business loans. This pricing tactic ties the loan rate to a base rate that responds to the movement of market rates in general or to a rate designated as the prime rate.

The first large-scale introduction of floating-rate loans dates from the early 1970s. At that time, large banks offered floating rates that were guaranteed not to exceed an average or absolute *cap*.[7] This ceiling rate policy had the effect of partly protecting the bank against rising market rates and of giving the customer a guarantee against unlimited increases in rate. However, market rates unexpectedly rose to record heights in 1973 and 1974, leaving rates on many outstanding loans at caps well below market and, in some cases, below the banks' changing cost of money. As a result, banks have generally rejected the cap rate tactic during more recent periods of rising rates.[8] By the early 1980s, banks surveyed by the Federal Reserve System were making over half of their loans on an open-ended, floating-rate basis.[9] In recent years, banks have been able to protect their profit margins on such loans using off–balance sheet instruments to hedge these rates, including financial futures and option-based caps.

Beginning in the early 1980s, a period of soaring interest rates, banks aggressively shifted their loan pricing to a floating-rate basis. Key banking legislation during this period removed interest rate restraints on bank deposits. This change forced most bankers to focus on the interest sensitivity of their balance sheets for the first time. Banks with large positions in fixed-rate loans found themselves exposed to considerable interest rate risk when deposit rates rose sharply, and they quickly adopted a floating rate loan pricing strategy. Floating rates based on LIBOR have become highly important. LIBOR is a widely quoted rate on short-term European money market credits. It largely determines the overseas lending rates of large U.S. banks, particularly when the spread between U.S. money market base rates and LIBOR rates favors the latter. Also, U.S. banks' access to overseas sources of funds has recently made LIBOR an increasingly popular base rate among borrowers of regional and even small banks.

## Pricing Classifications

For pricing purposes, we can divide customers into three basic types:

1. Prime customers.
2. Perceived-value customers.
3. Relationship customers.

The various aspects of loan pricing apply differently to each of these customer types.

---

[7] An interesting discussion of these developments appears in Randall C. Merris, "Business Loans at Large Commercial Banks: Policies and Practices," *Economic Perspectives* (Federal Reserve Bank of Chicago) (November-December 1979), pp. 15–23.

[8] An exception occurred in the mid-1980s among several major banks that used financial futures and bond options to hedge the risk of floating-rate loans with cap rates.

[9] Warren T. Trepeta, "Changes in Bank Lending Practices," *Federal Reserve Bulletin* (September 1981), pp. 671–686.

**Prime Customers**    Large banks have customers who are eligible to borrow short-term funds at the banks' lowest or base loan rates, typically just above an open-market rate of interest. Such customers are the banks' largest and most creditworthy borrowers—in essence, prime customers. Loan pricing for prime customers should not be confused with prime rate pricing. Prime customers have alternative sources of funds from the commercial paper market, foreign banks, and nonbank institutions. To get their business, banks must offer competitive lending rates. Banks know they cannot make loans to prime customers if they attempt to charge a rate higher than their lowest rate.

Unlike weaker and more local borrowers, large prime customers tend not to tie their borrowing needs to their needs for other bank services. Rather, they seek only a limited relationship in their banking dealings. As a result, banks are less able to bundle the pricing of loans and services together for prime customers. Instead, banks must price loans to be competitive with market sources of funds. The lack of interplay between lending and other services offered by banks makes loan pricing for prime customers uniquely straightforward.

**Perceived-Value Customers**    Another method for pricing loans or, for that matter, any other bank service is based on the value of the funds or services to the customer. The reasoning is that the bank can probably expect to attract customers if the price of bank loans or services does not exceed their applied value to the customers. This conclusion appears to be based on sound economic reasoning; from the customers' viewpoint, services whose marginal costs are below the marginal (perceived) benefits provided are worth the cost. Thus, according to this approach, the bank's pricing should be derived from knowledge of the value that customers perceive in borrowed funds or services. Obviously, no two customers perceive value exactly alike, and any given price might exceed the value perceived by some customers but not the value perceived by others. In essence, using this approach, the bank's task is to estimate the elasticities of demand for its customers and to price its funds or services to that the price–quality combination maximizes net revenue. Theoretically, in this context, the prime borrowers discussed earlier have infinitely elastic demand for funds because no one will borrow at above-market rates and all will try to borrow at below-market rates. Clearly, because prime borrowers have alternative sources of funds and services, competition for their business is intense.

One of two basic circumstances in which pure perceived value pricing works is when the customer lacks these alternative sources. If, for example, a single bank is the only feasible source of loan funds for a local customer, that customer should be willing to borrow at any rate up to the value it places on the use of the funds (although the bank might refuse such a loan if it considers a high rate to be detrimental to the borrower's financial health). Of course, if the rate exceeds the customer's perceived value, a rational customer will not borrow at all.

The other circumstance in which perceived value pricing works is when customers view a loan or other bank service as part of a total banking relationship. A bank may price a loan or service above the customer's alternative sources of supply (and below the value perceived by the customer) if the customer uses a wide array of bank services. For example, even though a bank may charge the highest price in the market for funds wire transfers, its business customers probably will not switch their wire transfer activity to another institution if they want to continue using the bank's other services. Despite its high price, they probably will continue to use the bank's wire transfer service. In this case, the most important criterion is that the wire transfer cost does not exceed its perceived value.

**Relationship Customers**   Loan pricing for the majority of borrowers, those that can be classified between prime and weak marginal borrowers, is conditioned by a strong customer relationship. A strong relationship exists when the customer uses a broad range of banking services, borrows regularly, and is a good source of future loan demand. To such a borrower, loan rates are usually established nominally at a spread above the base cost of funds. However, the focus of concern is the yield on the total activities, including loans, associated with the relationship.

## LOAN PRICING AND PROFITABILITY MODELS

### Spread Pricing Model

Two basic approaches to loan pricing are distinguished according to the bank's relationship to the borrower. The first approach is *spread pricing* over the bank's cost of funds and is suitable for prime borrowers who, as noted, do not necessarily tie their borrowing needs to their needs for other bank services; that is, they seek a rather limited relationship in most of their dealings with the bank. Banks tend to price such loans to be competitive with other sources of funds available to the borrower.

For purposes of spread pricing, the cost of bank funds is, conceptually, the transfer price charged by the funds-gathering function of the bank. To be most competitive, the bank may fund the loan with *duration-matched* funds and price it at a markup (spread) over the cost of such funds. The typical cost benchmark for these funds might be the interest rate offered on the bank's short-term CD or perhaps a blended cost based on a mix of the CD rate and an overnight rate such as the Federal funds rate or repurchase agreement rate. By duration-matching the loan and its funding source in this way, the bank hopes to eliminate the interest rate risk of holding the loan in its portfolio. Alternatively, the bank may view the transfer price of its funds for financing the loan to be the weighted average of its deposit and other sources of funds. In this case, the funds-gathering function of the bank transfers the *pooled* rate on all funds. Whether it uses a duration-matched or a pooled transfer price, the price should be based on the marginal, not average, cost of funds. Clearly, the interest rate to be charged the borrower on a specific new loan will be

**TABLE 12-3    Spread Loan Pricing Model**

|  | Percent |
|---|---|
| 1. Value of bank funds | 6.00% |
| 2. Servicing fees | 0.10 |
| 3. Commitment fee on average unused portion: | 0.75 |
| 4. Commitment fee income = | |
| unused portion × (3): 1/3 × 0.75% = | 0.25 |
| 5. Collected balances: percent of loan usage: | 11.00 |
| 6. Value of balances = | |
| (5) × usable portion × value of funds: | |
| 11% × 0.85 × 6% | 0.56 |
| 7. Desired spread over value (cost of funds): | 4.00 |
| 8. Loan price = (1) + (7) − (2) − (4) − (6) = | |
| 6.00% + 4.00% − 0.10% − 0.25% − 0.56% = | 9.09% |

at the margin and will be independent of the historic rates on the bank's existing loans. The value of the bank's funds, no less, should be based on marginal costs.

Given the appropriate value or transfer price of funds, the spread is then determined by the bank's target return on the funds used by the bank to finance the loan, plus a premium for the credit risk involved. Table 12-3 presents a model applied to the spread pricing of such a loan. In meeting the bank's spread target, the customer is credited with bank income generated from servicing and commitment fees (lines 2 and 4 in Table 12-3) and with the value of deposit balances held by the borrower in the bank (line 6). The value of bank funds (line 1) may be set equal to the all-in cost of bank liabilities or to the earnings rate on risk-free assets such as Treasury bills. The borrower's deposit balances are adjusted downward to account for the fact that reserve and float requirements reduce the usability of these funds (resulting in usable funds equal to 85 percent of total funds, shown in line 6 of the table). The desired spread of 4 percent over the bank's cost of funds shown in line 6 might be appropriate for a small, somewhat high-risk borrower. Of course, comparable spreads in the case of high-quality, large corporate loans are much smaller than in this example and would produce a lower loan interest rate.

## Customer Profitability Models

For most banks, particularly small banks, loans arise out of a broader relationship with the borrower. With increased competition for good customers and the desire to treat them equitably, banks have developed pricing techniques that recognize in detail the many aspects of a single customer relationship. They now tend to price explicitly computerized payroll, wire funds transfers, lockboxes, and other services provided in addition to interest rate pricing on loans. According to this approach, loans should be priced so that the profitability of a bank's total relationship with a borrower meets its profitability standard. The method used for analyzing loan pricing in this more complete customer relationship is the *loan account profitability model*. This model simply compares the revenues and costs of a customer relationship. To be profitable, the total relationship must show that

$$\text{Revenues} > \text{Costs}$$

These two quantities, total revenues and total costs, must be fully and carefully identified.

## Revenues

Table 12-4 lists the sources of revenue stemming from all aspects of the bank's relationship with the hypothetical ABC Corporation. All explicit service charges, as well as loan interest, are included. The service charges are not incorporated in the loan interest rate but are priced independently on the basis of the customer's actual activity. In this way, the customer does not pay for more or less of the bank's services than it uses, and high-service users are not subsidized by low-service users. ABC Corporation has a $3.5 million line of credit and uses an average of $1.2 million during the year.

## Costs

The costs associated with the ABC Corporation loan are listed in Table 12-5. There are two basic types of costs: the cost of bank funds and the cost of other services provided. The amount of bank funds required to support the loan is divided between the bank's pool of nonequity funds and equity capital.

Most banks recognize that their risky assets, such as the ABC loan, are theoretically supported by bank equity against the risk of a decline in value. If a risky asset declines in value, the bank's capital absorbs or cushions the

---

**TABLE 12-4    Revenue Derived from the ABC Corporation**

| | |
|---|---:|
| Loan interest | |
| Commercial loan, $1,200,000 average at 12% | $144,000 |
| Commitment fee income =<br>    unused line, $2,300,000 at 0.5% | 11,500 |
| Loan service (includes officer's time, legal fees, and other fees) | 2,448 |
| General bank services (includes depository charges, wire<br>    charges, etc.) | 2,960 |
| Total revenue derived | $160,908 |

**TABLE 12-5    Costs Assigned to ABC Corporation**

| | |
|---|---:|
| Cost of funds: | |
| a. Charge for equity capital funds, $120,000 (30.00%)[a] | $36,000 |
| b. Charge for net general funds used (see Table 12-6) $929,000 (9.60%) | 89,184 |
| c. ABC demand deposits, $215,000 (5.00%)[b] | 4,375 |
| d. ABC CD, $50,000 (10.35%)[c] | 5,175 |
| Cost of services (including depository and transfer items, allocated costs of loan dept.) | 10,620 |
| Total net cost | $145,354 |

[a]Return on equity stated on a pretax basis rather than on the more familiar after-tax basis, because all revenues and costs for ABC are likewise stated on a pretax basis.

[b]Cost of servicing.

[c]Interest expense plus cost of servicing.

decline and shields creditors, including uninsured depositors, from the decline. In pricing the ABC loan, the lending bank charges for the equity it allocates for accounting purposes to support the loan. In the ABC example, the basis of equity allocation is the bank's ratio of equity to risk assets, which is 10 percent. On this basis, the bank's return on its total equity must be earned by all of its risky assets. For the bank in question, the expected return on equity is 30 percent, stated on a pretax basis.

As shown in Table 12-5, the amount of equity capital funds to support the average loan ($1.2 million) times the bank's ratio of equity to risk assets (10 percent) is $120,000. The charge for equity capital funds, therefore, is $120,000 times the bank's required pretax return on equity (30 percent), or $36,000.

The remaining funds for supporting the loan ($1,200,000 − $120,000 = $1,080,000) must come from the bank's pooled other sources of funds, which is simply a weighted mix of the various types of deposits and borrowed funds. However, ABC Corporation already provides some of these funds in the form of deposits it maintains with the bank. As shown in the net pooled funds used calculation in Table 12-6, ABC is given credit for its own demand deposit and CD accounts before assessing a charge for pooled funds; in effect, the bank loans ABC its own deposits first. The credits are net of reserve requirements and float in order to recognize that ABC's deposits are not all available to be loaned out; reserves and float force the bank to tie up some funds in cash items that cannot be used for lending. After deducting the net funds provided by ABC and the allocation for equity capital derived earlier, the bank must provide an additional $929,000. The charge for these funds is set forth in Table 12-5 and is based on ABC's weighted marginal cost for pooled funds, equal to 9.60 percent.

The remainder of Table 12-5 is straightforward. The costs associated with

---

### TABLE 12-6   Net Pooled Funds Used by the ABC Corporation

| | | |
|---|---:|---:|
| Total funds required | | $1,200,000 |
| Less: (a) Equity capital funds | | 120,000 |
| (b) ABC demand deposit | $125,000 | |
| Less: reserves and float (18%) | 22,500 | |
| Funds provided | | 102,500 |
| (c) ABC CD | 50,000 | |
| Less reserves 3% | 1,500 | |
| Funds provided | | 48,500 |
| Net pooled funds used | | $ 929,000 |

---

ABC's demand deposit account and CD must be included, because these costs were excluded from the charge for pooled funds used. The loan-handling charge is derived from the bank's cost account system, which allocates total loan department expense to the loans outstanding on the basis of loan amounts. The remaining cost items are self-explanatory.

The total relationship with ABC appears to have excess value to the bank. Revenues exceed costs even when costs include the desired return on equity funds. Comparing the total revenues in Table 12-4 and the total costs in Table 12-5 yields the following:

$$\text{Revenues} - \text{Cost} = \$160,908 - \$145,354 = \$15,554$$

Before declaring the $15,554 excess value, however, the bank must assess the relative riskiness of its loan to ABC. If the loan risk is more than the average risk of the bank's risk assets, the bank must determine whether or not $15,554 is an adequate compensation for this additional risk. If it is not, a higher loan interest rate should be considered.

### Significance of Customer Profitability Models

While the example of ABC Corporation implies that customer profitability models are used for input into the loan-pricing decision, in reality such models probably serve a much broader function. Lending officers must assign priorities to the use of their time wisely in view of the multiple demands on their time. Without a specific guide, officers' time is often spent in reacting to the most vocal customers, cultivating and placating the largest customers, and resolving problem loan situations. A system of customer profitability measurement, on the other hand, assists officers in comparing the profitability of loan accounts under their responsibility, indicating which accounts merit more of their scarce time.

### Cost Accounting Systems

Clearly, customer profitability analysis assumes that the bank has a good understanding of its costs. Actually, many banks are latecomers in developing and accepting cost accounting techniques. Historically, banks have applied a majority of their staffs and their creative efforts to procuring low-cost deposits and servicing depositors without charge. The slow-to-die tradition of not charging to recover the costs of many deposit-related services retarded the development of accounting systems to determine banks' costs for those services.

However, most large banks are developing sophisticated cost accounting systems. Other banks participate in the Federal Reserve System's Functional Cost Analysis program or use the data generated by this program as a reference point for cost-dependent decision making. The functional cost analysis program collects uniform cost and income data from a group of participating Federal Reserve member banks. The data are structured to indicate the profitability and cost characteristics of various functional activities in banks.

### Pricing Loans Using Financial Futures

In the early 1980s, banks moved to floating-rate pricing of loans to protect their profits against the volatility of interest rates. Soaring interest rates drove up the cost of funding loans, and bankers were quick to see that their loan rates floated up with the cost of money. However, floating-rate pricing has deprived many borrowers of an important product. Borrowers often prefer fixed-rate loans; they are more at ease when the future price of their outstanding debt is known. Floating rates present borrowers with uncertainty. Financial futures contracts are one means by which banks can offer borrowers fixed-rate loans while protecting themselves against a rise in the cost of funding such loans. (See Chapter 15 for a more technical analysis of financial futures contracts.)

Perhaps the simplest way to provide a futures hedge is to grant a fixed-rate loan, fund it with short-term money, and simultaneously sell (short) financial futures. Bankers price the loan at a profitable spread over the present cost of short-term funds, and the futures position locks in the present cost of funds. If interest rates rise and drive up the cost of bank funds, the bank is able to take a gain on its futures position. Depending on one's point of view, the gain offsets the rising cost of funds or replaces revenue the bank forfeits by not floating its loan rate. The duration of the futures position must match the maturity of the loan in order to protect the bank throughout the life of the loan.

A slightly more complicated approach is an *anticipatory hedge*. Often a prospective borrower would like to fix the rate on a loan the borrower anticipates needing at a later date. Rate fixing is particularly appealing if the borrower feels that loan rates are favorable in the present but fears that they will rise before the money is needed. For a fee, the borrower's bank will lock in today's loan rate by hedging its own cost of funding the loan at a later date. Table 12-7 gives an example of such an anticipatory hedge. The middle column

**TABLE 12-7  A Bank's Anticipatory Hedge of a Six-Month Fixed-Rate Loan**

|  | **Cash Transactions** | **Futures Transactions** |
|---|---|---|
| January 1, 1994 | Bank commits to fund a $1 million, six-month, fixed-rate loan priced at 7% three months later (April); current CD rate = 5% | Bank sells two June 1994, 91-day Eurodollar futures at a price of 95.62 (4.38%) |
| April 1, 1994 | Bank disburses a $1 million loan funded with six-month CDs; spot CD rate = 6% | Bank offsets its hedge by buying two June 1994 Eurodollar futures contracts at 94.70 (5.30%) |
| Summary | Interest cost due to rate rise in CD market (1%) | Yield gain on futures position due to decline (rise) in futures price (rate)—.92 (0.92%) |
|  | Increased cost:<br>1/2 year × 1% × $1,000,000<br>= $5,000 | Gain:<br>Two contracts × 1/4 year ×<br>0.92% × $1,000,000 = $4,600 |

|  |  |
|---|---|
| Cost | $5,000 |
| Gain | 4,600 |
| Net loss | $  400 |

describes the transactions dealing with the bank's funding of the loan with CDs (the "cash" side of the hedge), and the right-hand column describes the futures transactions. In the case shown, the borrower anticipates a need for a six-month $1 million loan in April, three months in the future. Today's (January's) rate on a six-month loan will be fixed at 7 percent, or two points over the cost of the bank's six-month CD, which is 5 percent. The bank sells two June 91-day Eurodollar futures contracts to hedge against a rise in the cost of CDs. The CDs are the nominal funding source for the fixed-rate loan. The 91-day Eurodollar contracts have a maturity, or face value, of $1 million each. Two such contracts are used to hedge the $1 million of CDs because the dollar interest cost on a six-month CD is expected to change approximately twice as much as the interest yield on a single 91-day Eurodollar futures contract; this is due to the difference in their terms to maturity (one is six months; the other, three months).

The results show that CD rates did in fact rise by 1 percent from the time the loan commitment was made in January until the loan was actually funded in April. However, the futures hedge largely protected the bank against the $5,000 increase in the cost of funding the loan. The hedge was not perfect because of basis risk; the price (yield) on the Eurodollar futures did not change fully with the change in the CD rate.

There are many other ways that banks can use the futures markets to offer fixed-rate loans. In addition, banks can advise borrowers on booking futures positions for their own accounts to hedge against rate increases on floating-rate loans. To date, only a small number of banks are active users of the futures markets. It is likely that an increasing number of banks will become informed on futures hedging techniques as the competition for business loans continues to intensify.

# NONINTEREST ASPECTS OF LOAN PRICING

## Direct Factors

In our previous discussion, we neglected loan pricing aspects other than the explicit interest rate charged. However, there are important considerations in pricing loans other than direct interest charges. Foremost among the noninterest factors of loan pricing are compensating balance requirements and commitment fees. Both of these factors directly affect banks' yield on loans.

**Compensating Balances**    Compensating balance requirements obligate the borrower to hold demand deposits or low-interest time deposits as part of a loan agreement. Balance requirements are also sometimes set on loan commitments. The balance requirement on loans usually requires that balances average an agreed-on percentage of the loan amount. An alternative way of setting the balance requirements is with reference to a percentage of a minimum, not an average, balance. The predominant use of an average requirement allows the borrower to draw balances down to well below the average requirement when loan funds are applied to their intended purpose and then to raise the average balance as funds accumulate to well above the average requirement, pending repayment of the loan.

Average balance requirements range from 10 to 20 percent, with 15 percent perhaps being most common. At times, balance requirements are applied to both the loan and the total commitment; for example, "10 and 10" indicates balances of 10 percent on the loan and 10 percent on the total commitment. This actually results in a 20 percent requirement on the loan and 10 percent on the unused commitment.

One rationale for compensating balance requirements is that they ensure that borrowers will remain as customers on both sides of the balance sheet, that is, as both borrowers and providers of funds. Banks obviously do not want their borrowers to redeposit loan proceeds at another institution. Another rationale is that compensating balances permit banks to pay implicit interest that they are prohibited from paying explicitly under Regulation Q. The implicit interest arises from the fact that banks can charge lower loan rates because borrowers' balances have considerable value to them. It is also argued that the compensating balance requirement simply adds discipline to the borrower's management of working balances, much of which the borrower would maintain on deposit in any case. Finally, compensating balances reflect a traditional belief among some that the central function of banks is to take deposits. At the extreme, this belief states that loans are made to ensure the availability of deposits in the present and the future.

The cost to the borrower of compensating balance requirements can be directly reflected in the cost of a loan. If a borrower needs $80,000 but must retain an average compensating balance of 20 percent, the borrower must obtain a $100,000 loan. If the loan rate is 16 percent, or a cost to the borrower of $16,000 in interest charges annually, the effective rate on the $80,000 portion of the loan usable by the borrower is then 20 percent ($16,000 divided by $80,000). Of course, these factors apply only if the borrower would otherwise maintain a zero deposit balance—a most unlikely event. The actual amount of redundant borrowing is the amount by which the required average balance exceeds the amount that the borrower would otherwise maintain.

Compensating balances are criticized as being an inefficient pricing mechanism because, although they raise the effective borrowing costs, banks must hold idle reserves against the additional deposits and therefore cannot fully invest them in earning assets. This rationale strikes some borrowers and bankers as questionable. In some instances, among banks that have moved toward unbundled and explicit pricing, balance requirements have been replaced by fees or higher loan rates. Banks that substitute fees or higher rates for balances reflect their belief in lending, rather than deposit taking, as the bank's central function; they do not hold the traditional belief that lending is primarily a tool for obtaining deposits. Their concerns are, first, to generate good loans and, second, as skillful liabilities managers, to obtain deposits or purchased sources of money to fund the loans.

Nevertheless, in periods of tight money and high interest rates, compensating balances tend to become more attractive to banks than fees. During such times, the balances ought to provide the banks with higher yields, because interest rates increase on banks' earning assets, where the cost to banks for handling compensating balances is relatively unaffected. However, borrowers attempt to economize on demand deposits as interest rates rise, and they are inclined to resist restrictive balance requirements.

**Commitment Fees**   Formal loan commitments arise mostly for revolving credits and, to a lesser extent, for term loans and short-term credits. They set forth a bank's firm obligation to provide a specified amount of credit in the future at a specified price or pricing formula. Unlike the informal loan commitment on seasonal short-term credit, the formal commitment also frequently sets forth the fee to the borrower for making future credit available. In essence, the commitment fee is the price for a call on future credit.

Commitment fees on revolving credits are more prevalent because of the delay and relative unpredictability of the takedown by the customer. For the usual commitment period of two to five years, fees on the unused portion average about 0.5 percent. They may increase to as much as 0.75 percent during periods of tight money and may fall below 0.5 percent in periods of slack loan demand.

In theory, commitment fees are related to the bank's cost of preparing to meet borrowers' future calls for credit, either by maintaining liquidity on its balance sheet or, alternatively, by preserving its own capacity to borrow funds. There are logical explanations for both kinds of costs. The bank may feel compelled to hold assets in short-term government securities to ensure that it has liquidity for backing up commitments to meet borrowers' future calls for loan funds. By maintaining liquidity in this way, the bank forgoes returns on higher-yielding assets and, instead, holds low-yielding liquid assets. Alternatively, the bank may maintain its own borrowing capacity in the money markets to meet future calls on credit. In this case, the bank forgoes borrowing in the money markets and investing in earning assets currently in order to ensure its ability to borrow in the future when loan commitments are called.

### Indirect Factors

In addition, there are several indirect noninterest factors involved in loan pricing. These include collateral requirements, loan maturity limits, and loan covenants. In our discussion of loan pricing so far, we have ignored the effect of these factors or have assumed that they remain constant for every loan. In fact, these indirect factors are important variables in any loan negotiation. If the terms involving collateral, maturity, and loan covenants become more restrictive, the risk to the bank is reduced and the effective cost to the customer increases. Highly restrictive terms ought to ease other, more direct, pricing elements. Specifically, shortened loan maturities, increased collateral, and more restrictive loan covenants should result in a lowering of some or all of the direct pricing elements of loan rates, commitment fees, and compensating balance requirements.

In addition, the indirect noninterest pricing factors are frequently used as a means of rationing loan funds, particularly during periods of tight money when banks struggle to find sufficient funds. To qualify for a larger loan at the going rate of interest, certain borrowers are required to put up more collateral and accept shorter loan maturities and stricter covenants. Borrowers subject to these forms of credit rationing are generally those with few, if any, alternative sources of funds. (Earlier, these borrowers were characterized as perceived-value customers.) If indirect or direct pricing factors are too restrictive, that is, too costly, perceived-value customers became rationed out of the loan market altogether.

## SUMMARY

Most banks actively seek to make business loans. In the past, banks offered only short-term, self-liquidating credit. Such loans were usually for temporary additions to working capital that would soon be sold off to generate cash for repayment of the loans. This type of loan included a requirement that borrowers pay off their loans sometime during the year. Borrowers often refinanced their loans at other banks to meet this *clean-up* rule and then later returned to the bank of origin to renew the loan. Bankers call such loans *evergreen loans*.

Evergreen loans engaged banks in term lending despite their intentions to grant short-term loans. From such beginnings, many banks have shifted aggressively to longer-term credits to finance plant and equipment. This shift has produced dramatic changes in bank lending principles by tieing loans to borrowers' long-term profitability as a primary source of repayment and by routinely tying loans to collateral as a secondary source of repayment. Large banks in particular provide revolving credits, revolving credit commitments, and term loans structured to meet intermediate-term financing needs of business.

A crucial dimension of term credits is the negotiation of covenants. Restrictive or negative covenants can be classified into three categories according to their objectives. Cash flow covenants have as their objective the protection of cash flows for loan repayment. They can be used to restrict the borrower's actions that introduce unacceptable risks to earnings or to restrict uses of cash flow other than for loan repayment. Trigger covenants protect the bank from the borrower's financial deterioration by establishing minimum financial standards that, when violated, authorize the bank to call or restructure the loan. Balance sheet covenants protect the loan by restraining the borrower from taking actions that would unduly weaken the balance sheet and jeopardize the value of collateral assets.

For most borrowers, loan interest rates are typically set on a prime-plus basis to account for the risk associated with the credit. However, banks are increasingly pricing loans in the context of a total customer relationship. Customer profitability analysis explicitly prices and tracks the costs of individual (unbundled) services rendered, in addition to the usual loan and deposit aspect of the relationship.

Compensating balances and commitment fees directly affect loan yield and the cost to the customer of borrowing. Some argue that compensating balance requirements are an anachronism left over from an era when the main focus of banking was taking deposits. Although balance requirements are being replaced by fees in some banks, they will undoubtedly persist in some banks into the future.

## Discussion Questions

1. Distinguish between open lines of credit and commitments that are usually associated with revolving credit agreements.
2. Discuss the pros and cons of a business making term loans from a bank as opposed to issuing its bonds in the open capital markets.
3. What are the key documents used by banks to take a security interest in collateral under the Uniform Commercial Code? Review the purposes of these documents.
4. What are the features that distinguish accounts receivable financing and factoring?
5. Trace the cash flows that occur when a bank provides floor plan financing for a dealer in new automobiles.

6. What are the characteristics that distinguish public warehousing finance from field warehousing finance?

7. Describe and give examples of negative loan covenants for the purpose of
   a. Cash flow control.
   b. Calling of a loan for noncompliance.
   c. Balance sheet control.

8. How does the prime rate differ from the base rate? What caused many banks to abandon the use of prime rate loans?

9. Discuss the "net yield on the net funds used" measure applied in loan pricing. From this measure, how does one determine if a loan is correctly priced?

10. How should bank shareholders' return on equity be incorporated into loan pricing formulas?

11. Determine the true cost of funds to a borrower on a loan that has
    a. A 10 percent interest rate on borrowed funds.
    b. An 8 percent compensating balance on borrowed funds and a 4 percent balance on the unborrowed portion of the commitment.
    c. A 0.5 percent commitment fee on unborrowed funds.
    d. An average of 50 percent of the unused commitment.

12. All else equal, will borrowers prefer to leave compensating balances or to pay commitment fees when interest rates are abnormally high? Why?

# CHAPTER 13

# Consumer Lending

The individual consumer has always been an important player in the business of banking. Consumers' deposits are the largest source of commercial banks' funds, totaling roughly two-thirds of bank funds in 1992. By contrast, consumers have borrowed from banks on a large scale for a much shorter period of time.

The predominant type of borrowing used by consumers is installment credit loans that the consumer repays on an amortizing basis, typically over several years. This type of credit did not come into its own until after World War II. Earlier, society tended to frown upon the use of installment credit, believing that it violated norms of moral and prudent behavior because it allowed the borrowers to use money they had not yet earned. Following World War II, installment lending was quickly legitimized by millions of consumers who were eager to obtain new automobiles, household appliances, and other durable goods that had not been available during the war. As a result, the level of total consumer lending in the United States quickly rose in the postwar era from a modest $2.5 billion in 1945 to $29 billion by 1955. By mid-1993, outstanding consumer credit from all categories of lenders stood at over $800 billion, $390 billion of which was held by commercial banks.

The growth over nearly 50 years in consumer lending reflects the steady rise of income and employment and the increased job security of millions of middle-class families. Growing and secure future personal income is a crucial criterion for extending credit to consumers because it allows them to acquire goods or services today based on tomorrow's income. In this regard, recessionary and slow economic conditions such as those in 1990–1993 create uncertainty about many consumers' future incomes and cause consumer borrowing to decline.

In part, the longer-term growth of consumer lending reflects aggressive marketing by banks and other financial institutions in competing for the consumer loan market. Newer forms of credit such as credit cards, overdraft facilities, home equity credit, and longer maturities have made credit more attractive and more available to consumers. The percentage of households with installment debt increased steadily until the recession of the early 1990s. This occurred in all age categories, not just among younger families, although the latter were likely to be most heavily in debt.

Since the mid-1970s, consumer debt has grown more rapidly than personal income, indicating a sharp rise in the ratio of consumer credit to disposable income. This has caused some observers to conclude that U.S. households risk exceeding their debt capacity. This ratio stood at about 5 percent in the mid-1970s and reached a peak of 19 percent in the late 1980s. Then the ratio declined to below 18 percent during the 1990–1992 recession. Some observers deny that consumers are close to exceeding their ability to pay and cite households' consistently high levels of liquidity. Data show that the ratio of consumer installment credit outstanding to the amount of consumer-held liquid assets (meaning assets that are readily convertible into cash) has remained at around 20 percent for the past 25 years or so. This ratio falls moderately during recessions and rises slightly during economic expansions.

One researcher has concluded that, because of the existence of credit cards and below-market interest rate financing from manufacturers, lenders have become less able to ration credit during periods of credit restraint. Consumer credit has also become more affordable because of below-market prices on manufacturers' credit and ongoing shifts of market share from finance companies and retailers to commercial banks. Consumers, meanwhile, have expanded the purposes for borrowing to include more purchases of luxury goods and services such as recreational possessions and activities. Concurrent with these developments is the rise in consumer debt delinquencies and personal bankruptcies. These changes do not necessarily portend major future losses for banks. They do, however, call for banks to maintain good controls on their consumer lending underwriting standards.[1]

## COMMERCIAL BANK CONSUMER CREDIT

As noted in Table 13-1, by mid-1992 nonmortgage consumer debt held by U.S. commercial banks totaled $360 billion, or about 18 percent of the $2,090 billion in total loans banks held. Banks held $326 billion out of the $718 billion (45 percent) in consumer installment debt held by all major holders, including finance companies, credit unions, retailers, savings institutions, and gasoline

[1]Charlene Sullivan, "Consumer Credit: Are There Limits?" *Journal of Retail Banking* (Winter 1986–1987), pp. 5–18.

**TABLE 13-1 Consumer Debt Held by Commercial Banks, 1971 and 1992 (dollars in billions)**

|                | 1971   | 1992    |
|----------------|--------|---------|
| Installment    | $51.2  | $326.3  |
| Automobile     | 20.8   | 109.0   |
| Revolving      | 7.4    | 128.5   |
| Mobile home    | 4.4    | 9.3     |
| Other          | 18.6   | 88.8    |
| Noninstallment | 14.0   | 33.4    |
| Total          | $65.2  | $359.7  |

companies. Table 13-1 gives a breakdown by type of consumer loan held by banks in 1971 and 1992.

Banks are the most frequently used suppliers of credit services to households. Table 13-2 shows that banks lead other depository institutions and nondepository sources in the percentage of household users as a source for credit, including bank credit cards, mortgages, motor vehicle loans, home equity or other credit lines, and all other types of credit. However, about 40 percent of households now have at least one kind of credit relationship with nondepository institutions. This nondepository percentage appears to be growing as numerous large and highly diversified companies such as AT&T, General Electric, General Motors, the Fidelity Group of mutual funds, and insurance companies like Equitable, Prudential, and John Hancock have entered the credit card business and, to some extent, the mortgage business.[2]

## Automobile Lending

*Direct* automobile loans are simply loans made to consumers for the purchase of automobiles, where the automobiles secure the loans through chattel mortgages. *Indirect* automobile loans are loans acquired from automobile dealers. In the latter arrangement, the consumer applies for a loan to the dealer, who conveys essential information regarding the consumer's creditworthiness to the bank. Typically, banks attempt to aid auto dealers in executing their transactions by indicating acceptance or rejection of such credit requests as quickly as possible. Banks acquire indirect loans from automobile dealers in "packages." In the dealer relations of many banks, it is understood that the individual loans in a package will vary in quality; that is, dealers are normally permitted some borrowers of marginal creditworthiness for the size of the loan or collateral value involved. As a result, delinquencies and losses on indirect

[2]David Lawrence, "Consumer Banking: Still the Bank's Profit Center," *The Bankers Magazine* (March-April 1992), pp. 18–22.

**TABLE 13-2  Percentage of Households Using Credit Services by Type of Credit and Source**

| Type of Account | Any Source | Financial Institution | | | | | | | | | | Non-financial Source |
|---|---|---|---|---|---|---|---|---|---|---|---|---|
| | | All | Depository | | | | Nondepository | | | | | |
| | | | All | Commercial Bank | Savings | Credit Union | All | Finance Company | Brokerage | Other | | |
| All consumer credit | 80.0 | 74.9 | 68.0 | 56.6 | 20.9 | 13.7 | 32.8 | 21.1 | 1.1 | 14.8 | | 25.0 |
| Bank credit card | 56.5 | 55.8 | 54.0 | 45.5 | 5.9 | 6.3 | 7.9 | .2 | .8 | 7.1 | | 1.5 |
| Mortgage | 40.8 | 37.2 | 26.3 | 14.1 | 12.8 | 1.1 | 13.3 | 5.3 | .1 | 8.2 | | 5.8 |
| Motor vehicle | 34.9 | 33.8 | 21.8 | 13.7 | 3.1 | 6.0 | 13.7 | 13.5 | * | .1 | | 1.3 |
| Home equity or other credit line | 10.8 | 10.6 | 8.8 | 5.6 | 1.5 | 1.9 | 2.1 | 1.8 | .3 | 0 | | .3 |
| Other | 28.2 | 13.8 | 10.4 | 6.2 | 2.2 | 2.6 | 4.1 | 4.0 | * | 1 | | 18.6 |

SOURCE: Gregory E. Elliehausen and John D. Wolken, "Banking Markets and the Use of Financial Services by Households," *Federal Reserve Bulletin* (March 1992), p. 178.

automobile loans run as high as twice those on direct loans. In addition, banks pay automobile dealers a rebate on loans provided by the dealers. Finally, in the interest of maintaining and promoting their dealer relations, banks frequently offer *floor-plan financing* to dealers at favorable rates, as well as financing support for dealers' automobile leasing programs. However, the attractiveness of the relationship changes over the business cycle; during periods of high loan demand, many banks play down these support factors.

After several decades of generally rapid growth, automobile debt is now declining periodically at commercial banks because of aggressive, below-market financing by automobile manufacturers. Both direct and indirect lending on new automobiles are affected by such developments. For both types of loans, maturities have consistently increased, as auto finance companies now routinely offer 60-month loans on new cars. In mid-1992, maturities averaged 54 months for new cars and 48 months for used cars. Interest rates on new-car loans range between 2 and 2.5 percent over the banks' prime rates, and used-car loans run as much as 6 percent over prime.

## Revolving Credit

Credit and debit card overdraft loans (included as revolving installment credit in Table 13-1) account for one of the highest rates of consumer debt growth. Credit card and debit card lending is based on preauthorized lines of credit that can be taken down as the consumer takes cash advances or makes purchases from any of the more than 1.5 million merchants who accept such cards. This easy access to credit through plastic cards has been helped dramatically by the rapid deployment of electronic banking devices. These devices include automated teller machines (ATMs), at which bank customers conduct direct deposit and cash withdrawal transactions, and point-of-sale (POS) machines at merchants' locations, which credit the merchants' accounts and either debit the cardholders' checking accounts or trigger an overline debit in payment for goods and services. As indicated in a later section of this chapter, card-type lending was hampered at times during the 1980s by state usury laws, which restrict the interest rates charged for this high-risk credit, and by laws that prohibit bank card issuers from charging the consumer an annual fee for card services. While these usury restraints were modified and liberalized in many states during the 1980s, there are recurring calls by consumer rights advocates to institute a federal ceiling on credit card fees and interest rates.

## Home Equity Credit

Personal revolving lines of credit can be extended either secured or unsecured. They may total as little as $1,000 but often amount to tens of thousands of dollars. When the loans are unsecured, the borrower must demonstrate considerable financial strength. A popular secured version of this type of credit is the line of credit secured by equity in the borrower's home. The home equity line of credit was widely offered by banks beginning in the mid-1980s, and its popularity was boosted sharply as a result of the Tax Reform Act of 1986. This law curtailed the deductions of interest expense on more traditional consumer loans, including auto, credit card, and other nonmortgage loans. The deductibility of interest on mortgage loans, however, continued to be available up to the purchase price of the home (plus improvements). In effect, then, the after-tax cost of home equity credit fell relative to the after-tax costs of other types of consumer credit. From bankers' points of view, home equity credit was a fortuitous replacement in their loan portfolios for automobile loans that, at times, declined dramatically.

In addition to their cost competitiveness, home equity loans have other positive qualities. The use of a home as collateral usually provides the bank with collateral that has the potential for appreciation. With automobile loans, on the other hand, rapid depreciation must be expected. Moreover, home equity lines are frequently drawn upon for home improvement, thereby further increasing the value of the collateral on which the loan is based.

A survey in the late 1980s determined that the appraised value of the average house supporting a home equity loan was $101,000 and the average outstanding balance on the first mortgage was $39,000, leaving available equity of $62,000. In addition, the loan-to-appraised-value limit applied by the average bank surveyed was 77 percent, indicating that, on average, about $39,000 could be borrowed ($101,000 $\times$ 77 percent $-$ $39,000). Thus, there appears to be very good potential growth for home equity credit.

Most banks that provide home equity credit offer it on an open-ended (revolving), variable-rate basis. About one-half of issuing banks also offer a closed-end version of the product. Home equity credit usually is priced on a variable-rate basis, with the rate set at about 2 percent over the national or local prime rate. Compared with other sources of credit, home equity lines of credit appear to be a relative bargain for consumers.

## Mobile Home Financing

Mobile home financing is not unlike the financing of automobiles. Most mobile home financing is indirect, that is, arranged through dealers. Bank relationships with mobile home dealers often include financing of their inventory.

Mobile home financing grew rapidly in the 1960s and 1970s with the explosive growth of the industry. The continuing high cost of conventional housing indicates that mobile home sales and mobile home financing will probably continue to grow, although the relatively poor credit quality of this market has resulted in a slight reduction of mobile home lending by commercial banks. Many mobile home borrowers do not have solid credit histories, and default and delinquency rates on these loans are relatively high. Compared with conventional home mortgages, mobile home loans have shorter maturities, normally 10 to 12 years, and interest rates 4 to 5 percent higher than those of home first mortgages. Table 13-3 lists the prevailing national interest rates for the predominant types of consumer credit in November, 1992.

**TABLE 13-3   Interest Rates for Several Types of Consumer Loans, November 1992**

| Type of Loan | Rate |
| --- | --- |
| Home equity line of credit | 9.50% |
| Credit card | 17.97 |
| New car loan | 10.67 |
| Personal loan | 14.28 |
| Mobile home | 12.83 |

SOURCE: *Federal Reserve Bulletin*, November 1992, p. 82.

## SECURITIZATION OF CONSUMER LOANS

A breakthrough in bank loan portfolio management occurred in 1985 with the first securitization of consumer loans on bank balance sheets. *Securitization* is a method in which banks sell part of their loan portfolios to investors in the form of securities. Although the market for securitized mortgages (called *mortgage-backed securities*) dominates the field, there have been significant conversions of automobile loans and credit card loans into securities. In 1992, securitized automobile loans and credit card loans totaled $109 billion, up from only $15 billion just five years earlier. Chapter 16 discusses securitization in greater detail.

## INTEREST CHARGE CONSIDERATIONS

### Add-On Rates

For automobile loans and most other types of consumer installment loans, interest charges are quoted in terms of an *add-on* rate. The add-on rate is applied to the original loan principal and is charged over the life of the loan despite the amortization of principal by means of installment payments. For example, suppose that an add-on rate of 8 percent is charged on a $1,200, one-year loan to be repaid in monthly installments. The interest amount of $96 (8 percent of $1,200) is added up front on the amount borrowed, and monthly payments are determined by dividing principal plus interest, or $1,296, by 12 (the number of payments). Although interest in the amount of $96 is charged, the average outstanding loan balance during the year will be only $600. The resulting effective annual rate will be nearly 16 percent, or double the add-on rate quoted.

When more than one payment is made over the life of the loan, the add-on rate will always result in an effective rate that exceeds the nominal rate. This is because the borrower does not have the full use of the amount borrowed for the whole time period. Also, the more frequent the installment payments, the higher the effective rate. Installment loan rates must also be quoted in annual percentage rates (APRs), and the total dollar finance charge must be disclosed in accordance with truth-in-lending legislation and Regulation Z, discussed later in this chapter.

### Bank Discount Rate

Another method for calculating loan interest is based simply on the amount to be repaid. The amount loaned is equal to the amount to be repaid minus the interest amount. Suppose that $1,200 is borrowed at 15 percent and repaid after one year. The interest amount will be 15 percent of $1,200, or $180. In the simple interest method, the $180 interest amount would be for the use of $1,200 over the entire year. In the bank discount method, however, the $180 would be deducted from $1,200, leaving $1,020 to be used for the year. The effective interest rate in this case would be 17.647 percent ($180 divided by $1,020), or considerably more than 15 percent. The bank discount method is sometimes used for single-payment consumer loans and for small business loans. Once again, Regulation Z requires the bank to disclose the true annual percentage rate.

### State Usury Ceilings

As with credit card and other revolving loans, installment loan interest rates are subject to usury limits in many states. The usury ceilings usually specify limits on add-on, as well as true annual percentage rates; lenders obviously cannot avoid legal interest limits by quoting on an add-on basis with the appearance of bargain rates. In the middle and late-1980s, a temporary federal preemption of state usury laws at times went into effect. With implementation of this legislation, lenders were able to make consumer loans competitive with the then prevailing competitive high market interest rates. However, this legislation permitted individual states to override the federal preemption by reestablishing their own structures of usury ceilings.

### Variable-Rate Consumer Loans

In the early 1980s, banks began to employ variable-rate pricing for installment loans in response to the soaring cost of bank funds in an era of high and volatile market rates of interest. At the time, variable rates were already well accepted by corporate borrowers, but their acceptance by consumers was uncertain. A prolonged period of generally falling interest rates beginning in early 1984, however, quickly won over consumers to variable rates. As a result, for many banks in the 1990s, variable-rate installment lending dominates fixed-rate lending by a considerable margin. If interest rates should begin a prolonged rise, on the other hand, it remains to be seen whether consumers will continue to accept installment loans priced on a variable-rate basis.

## Prepayment Penalties

The assessment of charges on consumer loans that are paid off early is an important aspect of consumer loan charges. A method must be used to refund unearned income to the consumer when a loan is prepaid. However, the bank is entitled to collect more than the interest that would be prorated to the length of time the loan is outstanding because of the high average loan balance during the early part of the loan period and because the bank incurs origination costs that it initially expects to recover over the full life of the loan.

The usual approach to determining the customer's rebate is the *Rule of 78s* method. The method varies the rebate amount according to the time at which prepayment occurs and is based on the sum of the installment period numbers. The finance charge in any one month that a prepayment occurs is a proportion of the sum-of-the-months' digits over the maturity of the loan. For a 12-month loan, the sum of the digits is

$$1 + 2 + 3 + \ldots + 12 = 78$$

thus the name *Rule of 78s*. In this case, the bank's total charge in the first month will be 12 times the amount charged in the 12th month: 12/78ths of the total finance charge is earned in the first month, 11/78ths in the second month, and so forth, to 1/78th in the 12th month. For example, if the customer repays the loan in the second month, the bank will keep 23/78ths [(12 + 11) / 78)] of the total finance charge. The method is appealing to bankers because it is relatively simple to compute.

The Rule of 78s is sometimes criticized as being arbitrary and unfair to the borrower. The mathematically accurate method of computing loan prepayment charges is called the *actuarial method*. This method calculates the earned finance charge on the actual (declining) balance before prepayment occurred. Historically, bankers found the actuarial method to be too complicated and time-consuming, although hand-held financial calculators and simple computer software now facilitate its use. In most cases, the Rule of 78s method does approximate the actuarial method reasonably well. However, the Rule of 78s is not a good approximating tool if the annual percentage rate is very high or the loan maturity is unusually long, or both.

# CREDIT ANALYSIS IN CONSUMER LENDING

Banks' consumer lending activities involve handling a large number of customers. Each borrower represents a relatively small amount of loan business, and banks need to process a great many of these loans to generate a substantial dollar volume of nonmortgage consumer loan business. With such large numbers of borrowers, it is vital for bank management to exercise effective control over the consumer credit-granting process.

Most banks with large numbers of consumer credit applications supplement their analyses with statistical credit scoring. This automated analysis

**TABLE 13-4  Steps in Consumer Credit Analysis**

1. Determine loan purpose and amount
2. Obtain information
    a. Consumer credit
    b. Personal financial statement
    c. Income tax returns
    d. Business financial statements
3. Investigate and verify information
4. Analysis
    a. Financial statements
    b. Cash flow
5. Evaluate collateral, if required
6. Price and structure the credit
7. Negotiate with applicant

system is a means of evaluating applications using a form of score card that lists application characteristics such as income level, job tenure, residence ownership, established credit with retailers or other lenders, and so forth. The application is awarded point values for each characteristic, and the total number of points indicates whether or not the applicant qualifies for a loan. Acceptability is predicated on the bank's data base of past applicants with similar creditworthiness profiles and the historical incidence of these applicants' success or failure in paying off loans from the bank. Statistical credit scoring models are described more fully in the next section.

Credit scoring is seldom used as the sole criterion for granting consumer credit. Other factors, such as debt payment capacity, present economic conditions, and collateral requirements, must meet the bank's underwriting standards. Subjective information—such as personality and the apparent character of the borrower, the potential for a profitable relationship in the future, and other extenuating and nonquantifiable factors—causes credit analysis to be a highly judgmental process. *Credit analysis* is the process by which both quantifiable and subjective factors are evaluated simultaneously and judged. The objective of this process is to minimize loan losses and nonperforming loans. The steps in consumer credit analysis are outlined in Table 13-4.

### Loan Types

Nonmortgage consumer credit products are differentiated according to the purpose, amount, source of repayment, and term of the loan. The type of loan product suitable for a qualified applicant must be determined in the interview process. The following types of credit products are typically offered by an aggressive retail loan department:

1. Checking revolving overdraft line of credit.
2. Large personal revolving line of credit, including home equity credit.
3. Installment loan.
    a. Short term.
    b. Long term.
4. Single-payment loan.

**Checking Overdraft Line**    The checking revolving loan is usually restricted to small loan amounts, seldom over several thousand dollars, and offers protection against overdrafts. The borrower simply triggers the line by writing checks in excess of his or her account balance, usually with notice to the bank. The account bears a high rate of interest and is normally unsecured. A solid record of disciplined credit activity is required. Many banks consider the checking overdraft line of credit too aggressive and too risky.

**Other Installment Loans**    Installment loans are made for a fixed amount and may be either unsecured or secured. By definition, installment loans are repayable in two or more installments. Repayment schedules are set up to amortize the principal fully, usually on a monthly basis, over the life of the loan. Maturities typically are 4 to 5 years, although long-term installment credit may extend as far as 20 years. Although loans may be unsecured or secured, unsecured loans usually do not exceed three years or so in maturity.

Installment loans are often made to buy automobiles, which constitute the collateral. As noted earlier, at times automobile lending by banks declined drastically in the 1980s. The decline occurred because of the aggressive financing programs launched by automobile manufacturers in which below-market financing rates, occasionally even including zero rates, were offered as a sales tool. As described earlier, home equity is also used as collateral for installment loans. The purpose of such loans appears to be mostly home improvement and debt consolidation.

**Single-Payment Loans**    The support for a single-payment loan usually is a single source of repayment available at the time of maturity. Repayment typically does not come from regular income sources, but from sources such as maturing securities, including certificates of deposits or bonds, or from the planned sale of common stock or real estate. This type of loan depends a great deal on the validity of the source of repayment, so the lender must be meticulous in verifying and validating the source.

## Obtaining Information

As in commercial lending, the most valuable credit information available in consumer lending is supplied by the loan applicant. A bank asks nonmortgage consumer borrowers to provide this information on the bank's own standardized credit application forms. The form generally requires data on employment, income, living arrangements, marital status, assets owned, and outstanding debt.

On unsecured loans and secured loans over, say, $5,000, banks should require a current personal financial statement. They should also require income tax returns and business financial statements on self-employed applicants. Internal Revenue Service Form 1040 income tax returns should be accompanied by supporting schedules that detail deductions and income from investments, dividends, businesses owned, rents, royalties, and other sources.

An important secondary source of credit information is credit reporting agencies. These agencies gather extensive data on consumers' credit histories, including a listing of outstanding debts, legal actions, and promptness of payment. Credit agencies compile these data from information supplied by creditors. Regulation B governs the way in which creditors maintain their customers' credit records and how they report the records to credit agencies or other inquirers. Originally one intent of the regulation was to enable married women to build a credit record when credit is extended jointly to married couples. This Regulation B provision corrected a previously common practice of creditors that omit a spouse (usually the wife) from the credit history on accounts for which the spouse was jointly liable. On the other hand, Regulation B prohibits creditors from associating a person with a spouse's bad credit history if he or she was not responsible for the debts of the spouse.

**Investigation and Verification** Before banks can depend fully on primary financial documents submitted by the borrower, the information they contain must be verified. Personal financial statements are usually self-prepared, and they should be tested for accuracy and realism. Direct verification can be made by contacting present creditors about indebtedness reported by potential borrowers, employers, and other organizations with official knowledge of the borrower's income. On assets offered as collateral, legal searches should be conducted to determine if there are previous claimants who have filed under the Uniform Commercial Code. Appraisals on both real and personal property may be required to establish an estimate of collateral values.

**Information and Equal Credit Opportunity** Under the Equal Credit Opportunity Act (ECOA) and Regulation B, under which the ECOA is implemented, borrowers have the right to withhold information that is irrelevant to the loan transaction. Because of the complexities of Regulation B, it is not always clear to bankers what information they are not permitted to require of consumer borrowers. To avoid requesting proscribed information, most banks model their loan application forms on a standard form published by the Federal Reserve Board that conforms with Regulation B.

In general, the information that is not required is that which might be used to discriminate against the applicant. Information concerning the borrower's marital status generally must not be required if the borrower applies for individual credit as opposed to joint credit. An exception is permitted for secured loans, because, in the event of default, the bank's access to the collateral might be affected by the borrower's marital status. This is particularly important in community property states, where assets owned by a married person may also be owned by the person's spouse. In cases in which the bank can legally inquire about marital status, it cannot inquire whether the applicant is divorced. Such information might be used unfairly in judging the applicant's general stability.

The bank cannot require an applicant (often a separated or divorced person) to provide information on alimony, child support, or separate maintenance income unless the applicant wishes to offer the information in support of her (or his) creditworthiness. The bank may, however, require disclosure of the liability to pay alimony, child support, and separate maintenance, since such payments clearly could impair the applicant's ability to repay the loan.

A bank cannot discriminate against female loan applicants because of their potential to bear children. A bank can, however, inquire about present dependents, including their ages and expenses. Regulation B prohibits inquiries about an applicant's race, color, religion, or national origin. The bank may not refuse credit to aliens because they are not citizens, although it may inquire about their immigration status to determine creditworthiness.

It might seem that Regulation B interferes with a bank's natural desire to know as much as it can about a loan applicant in order to be comfortable about its evaluation of creditworthiness. However, Regulation B probably does not prevent inquiries that are clearly germane to the evaluation. It does attempt to block the use of extraneous information that might reinforce unreasoned and often subconscious biases that lenders sometimes develop. On the other hand, some bankers believe that they should avoid requiring too much information so that loan applicants will not feel that their privacy is being invaded. In this regard, requiring too much information may inhibit the bank's efforts to market its consumer lending service.

## Cash Flow and Statement Analysis

As in commercial lending, the primary criteria for consumer credit are the financial standing and debt service capacity of the borrower. Collateral pledged as a secondary source of repayment is used to reduce the risk and to help define the amount and maturity of the loan, but it is not a basis per se for making the loan.

Assets should be reviewed to determine how much liquidity they afford. On credit line loans, underwriting standards sometimes require liquid assets to equal or exceed the amount of the line. Diversification of assets is important to provide more stable values. The borrower's tangible net worth must be calculated, and intangible assets should be ruled out. Credit line borrowing might require that tangible net worth be three or more times the amount of the credit line. The borrower's total income should be from stable sources that are dependable. Secondary or collateral sources should be determined. A thorough understanding of the borrower's financial status is important in structuring the loan to fit the borrower's repayment capability and needs. When collateral is called for, the loan should be structured with an appropriate collateral value margin.

Ultimately, the primary concern in consumer loan analysis is to identify a specific source of repayment. The usual source is income from wages. This requires an evaluation of employment stability and of other claims on income, such as debt payment obligations and a reasonable level of subsistence. The process of determining if adequate resources are available to repay a loan is referred to as *cash flow analysis*.

The monthly debt-to-income ratio is used to determine the amount of income needed to meet the borrower's total monthly debt obligations:

$$\text{Debt-to-income ratio} = \frac{\text{Total monthly payments}}{\text{Gross monthly income}}$$

The debt-to-income ratio compares the regular sources of income, exclusive of contingent or unverifiable income, to fixed monthly obligations. The latter includes items such as mortgage payments, installment and charge card payments, and monthly support and child care payments, in addition to the payment requirements of the proposed bank loan. The fixed obligations do not include normal daily living expenses. The underwriting standards of many banks require that the debt-to-income ratio not exceed 40 percent. On large credit line borrowings, gross income should be two or more times the amount of the credit line.

### Balancing Loan Losses and Opportunities

Two basic types of errors can be made in evaluating loan applications, and they should be balanced to minimize overall losses. The first type of error is the obvious one of granting a loan to a borrower who ultimately does not pay satisfactorily. The bank risks the direct loss of income and, potentially, the loss of its funds when it lends to such customers. To prevent these losses, the bank can tighten its lending standards, but it does so at the risk of disqualifying good borrowers. The elimination of good borrowers is the second type of error in evaluating applications: Tightening credit standards may lead the bank to deny loans to applicants who would have paid exactly as agreed. Of course, this type of error can be offset by liberalizing the granting of credit, which increases the probability of including unsatisfactory borrowers. In the simplest terms, the bank's loan application evaluation system should achieve an acceptable trade-off of losses due to default and opportunity losses due to the rejection of borrowers who would have paid satisfactorily.

## CREDIT EVALUATION SYSTEMS

We have discussed in depth what might be called *judgmental credit analysis*. Here we summarize that system and describe in detail the alternative credit scoring system mentioned earlier and known as *statistical* or *empirical credit analysis*. The two systems are compared and contrasted at the end of the section.

### Judgmental Credit Analysis

The judgmental system of consumer credit analysis relies on the consumer loan officer's experience and insight when appraising a borrower's ability and willingness to repay. This evaluation is similar to the evaluation of a business loan at perhaps a lower level of sophistication. As in commercial lending, the consumer loan officer also must assess the applicant's character, use of funds, primary source of repayment, and any secondary or collateral sources of repayment.

In the judgmental method of credit analysis, character can be evaluated from the applicant's credit history and from the degree of dependability demonstrated through length and consistency of employment, length and type of residence, apparent sincerity, and other factors. The loan officer must be as objective as possible and, under the ECOA, must not apply subjective values or personal biases. In using judgmental systems, the ECOA prohibits taking into direct account the applicant's age, although the lender may consider age as a factor in the applicant's future income because age usually is a determinant of time to retirement and life expectancy. Prospective retirement and life expectancy are germane when setting loan maturity.

The applicant's income is almost always the primary source of the repayment of consumer loans. Income, as noted earlier, must be adequate in relation to the borrower's debts and other financial obligations. The loan officer must also evaluate secondary sources of repayment and establish the present and probable future value of collateral offered.

## Empirical Credit Analysis

Empirical consumer credit analysis, referred to earlier as *credit scoring*, assigns point values to various applicant characteristics. The points are added up to award the applicant a numerical score, which is then compared with a predetermined accept-reject score, and credit is denied to those whose scores are below this level. An example of one bank's credit scoring system is given in Table 13-5. Note that each applicant characteristic used in a scoring system is weighted to have greater or less effect than other characteristics. For example, "Time with present employer" may have more influence than "Own or rent principal residence." Under the ECOA, such systems cannot use race, color, religion, national origin, or immigration status.

Unlike judgmental systems, empirical systems of analysis can consider age, but only as a positive factor. In congressional testimony on the ECOA, it was determined that most creditors find that creditworthiness increases with age, and to prohibit the use of age in credit scoring systems would reduce the points usually awarded to older applicants. However, for credit scoring systems using age, the ECOA requires "a demonstrably and statistically sound empirically derived credit system." There should be no age penalty for elderly applicants. When using age as an attribute of the applicant, Regulation B requires that credit scoring systems do the following:

1. Be based on data from an appropriate sample of creditors' applicants.
2. Separate creditworthy from noncreditworthy applicants "at a statistically significant rate."
3. Be periodically reevaluated as to their ability to predict good versus bad loans.

**TABLE 13-5    Sample Credit Scoring System Characteristics and Weights**

| | Points | | Points |
|---|---|---|---|
| 1. Own or rent principal residence | | e. Loan only | 10 |
| a. Owns/buying | 40 | f. None given | 10 |
| b. Rents | 8 | g. No answer | 10 |
| c. No answer | 8 | 6. Major credit card/dept. store | |
| d. Other | 25 | a. Major CC(s) and | |
| 2. Time at present address | | department store(s) | 40 |
| a. Under 6 months | 12 | b. Major CC(s) only | 40 |
| b. 6 months–2 years | 15 | c. Department store(s) only | 30 |
| c. 2 years–6½ years | 22 | d. None | 10 |
| d. Over 6½ years | 35 | 7. Finance company reference | |
| e. No answer | 12 | a. One | 15 |
| 3. Time with present employer | | b. Two or more | 10 |
| a. Under 1½ years | 12 | c. None | 5 |
| b. 1½–3 years | 15 | d. No answer | 10 |
| c. 3 years–5½ years | 25 | 8. Income | |
| d. Over 5½ years | 48 | a. $0–15,000 | 5 |
| e. Retired | 48 | b. $15,000–25,000 | 15 |
| f. Unemployed with | | c. $25,000–40,000 | 30 |
| alimony/child support/public | | d. Over $40,000 | 50 |
| assistance | 25 | 9. Monthly payments | |
| g. Homemaker | 25 | a. $10–200 | 35 |
| h. Unemployed–no public | | b. $200–500 | 25 |
| assistance | 12 | c. Over $500 | 10 |
| i. No answer | 12 | d. No payments | 45 |
| 4. Applicant's age | | e. No answer | 10 |
| a. Under 45 years | 4 | 10. Derogatory ratings | |
| b. 45 years or older | 20 | a. No investigation | 0 |
| c. No answer | 4 | b. No record | 0 |
| 5. Banking reference | | c. Two or more derogatory | −20 |
| a. Checking and savings | 60 | d. One derogatory | 0 |
| b. Checking | 40 | e. All positive ratings | 15 |
| c. Savings | 40 | | |
| d. Loan and checking and/or savings | 30 | | |

The appeal of a credit scoring system is that its allegedly pure objectivity clearly precludes discriminatory evaluation of credit applications. However, this system requires highly sophisticated statistical tools, which make it expensive to derive and to revalidate periodically. The derivation is based on multivariate statistical methods of either multiple regression or a technique known as *multiple discriminant analysis (MDA)*. The latter technique is an especially good solution to the credit scoring problem, and its conceptual base is explained in the following discussion.

**FIGURE 13-1    Illustration of a Credit Scoring System**

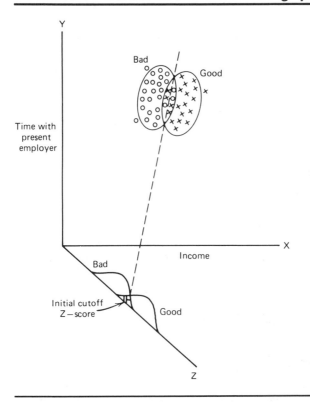

(SOURCE: Adapted from Paul E. Green and Donald S. Tull, *Research for Marketing Decisions*. Englewood Cliffs, N.J.: Prentice-Hall, 1970.)

The objective of credit scoring is to predict from applicant characteristics whether a borrower is a good (creditworthy) or bad (not creditworthy) risk. MDA determines the statistical importance of each characteristic and how the characteristics can be combined to distinguish bad from good.

The statistical concept of MDA can be illustrated in a diagram. Figure 13-1 shows a three-dimensional diagram of a simple credit scoring system with only two applicant characteristics—time with present employer on the Y axis and income on the X axis. In reality, credit scoring systems use as many as 10 to 15 characteristics, but they cannot be plotted like the system in Figure 13-1 because each characteristic requires its own dimension; that is, 10 characteristics would require 10 dimensions to plot! The profiles of both bad and good past borrowers are plotted in two dimensions in Figure 13-1, with circles designating bad and Xs designating good. The boundaries of each group are drawn to enclose a specified proportion of related points, such as 98 percent. Notice that the boundary enclosing 98 percent of one group also encloses a small proportion of the other group. Now we draw a straight line through the points at which the group boundaries intersect and project the line to the Z axis. This is the line, condensed into a *Z score*, which best separates the bad group points from the good ones. Also, the bad and good group points themselves are projected onto the Z axis, where they form frequency distributions of their Z scores. These distributions overlap, indicating the existence of a few bad borrowers in the good borrowers' group (Type 1 error) and a few good borrowers among the bad borrowers' group (Type 2 error). The cutoff Z score can be adjusted toward the origin in Figure 13-1 to liberalize credit granting. This adjustment would reduce the elimination of good borrowers but would also increase the acceptance of bad borrowers. Adjusting further away from the origin would reduce the acceptance of bad borrowers but would also eliminate more good borrowers.

The credit scoring system illustrated in Figure 13-1 combines the two characteristic profiles of good and bad borrowers into simple numbers. The line projected to the Z axis that best discriminates between good and bad borrowers implicitly assigns unique weights to each of the two characteristics.

Statistically derived credit scoring systems have two technical flaws that are commonly cited. First, the borrower data used are historical and might be obsolete in detecting current predictors of creditworthiness. Second, the data consist of only those loan applications that have been accepted and omit applications that have been rejected. There can never be an actual record of the creditworthiness of rejected applications.

## Judgmental versus Empirical Systems

In comparing the effectiveness of judgmental and credit scoring empirical systems for evaluating consumer loan applications, it is important to consider their ability to predict the creditworthiness of an applicant.[3] If creditworthiness can usually be predicted, the bank is protected against abnormal losses on its loans and is assured of a dependable flow of payments of interest and principal. However, there are other factors to consider in this comparison. Perhaps equally important is management's control over the process of granting credit. Control factors such as consistency and objectivity are important to the bank's reputation and to its obligation to comply with laws and regulations.

Both systems are capable of using the same applicant characteristics. However, credit scoring assigns weights to each characteristic and reflects a hierarchy of their significance. In other words, credit scoring consistently weighs each characteristic according to its statistical importance in relation to other characteristics. Judgmental systems are subject to variation of the hierarchy of significance and, in addition, may consider certain intangible factors that cannot be quantified. Credit scoring considers only characteristics that

---

[3]A good reference on this topic is Gary G. Chandler and John Y. Coffman, "A Comparative Analysis of Empirical versus Judgmental Credit Evaluation," *Journal of Retail Banking* (September 1979), pp. 15–26.

historically have been associated with creditworthiness, whereas judgmental systems may use other factors, some of which may be contrary to regulations.

A feature of credit scoring systems is that these systems consider the multitude of creditworthiness characteristics simultaneously. Judgmental systems cannot do this because of the processing limitations of the human mind. Loan officers probably weight the information they do use differently from one applicant to the next.

The volume of credit granted and the amount of loan losses are difficult to control under judgmental credit evaluation. Control requires an explicit consumer loan policy that describes credit standards. Policy statements that refer to the many possible relevant characteristics of consumers are difficult to convey and difficult to monitor. As a result, policy tends to be carried out inconsistently across loan analysts. Credit scoring, on the other hand, removes all issues of policy interpretation.

Judgmental methods of evaluation are better able to take into account present and future changes in economic conditions. An experienced analyst should be able to incorporate significant changes in the environment quickly in predicting a loan applicant's future creditworthiness. Credit scoring systems usually are less effective when major environmental changes are occurring. At such times, they suffer from the fact that they are based on customer data from an unrepresentative period in the past.

In practice, many banks use a combination of judgmental and credit scoring systems. Credit scoring readily isolates clearly noncreditworthy and clearly creditworthy applicants. The applicants that fall between these groups are then subjected to further information inquiries and to judgmental evaluation. For example, all applicants scoring below X are rejected, all scoring Y (higher than X) and above are granted credit, and all scoring between X and Y are evaluated further.

## REPORTING THE CREDIT DECISION

The final step in the consumer lending process is notifying the borrower of the decision. Of course, an affirmative decision by the bank is simply conveyed along with actual credit to the customer's deposit account or other means granting the customer access to funds.

If the loan application is unsuccessful, the bank is required under the Fair Credit Reporting Act of 1971 to report the denial of credit to the applicant. The bank either must provide the applicant with the reasons for the denial or advise the applicant of his or her right to a statement of the principal reason or reasons. If the denial is based wholly or partly on information from a credit bureau, the bank must provide the name and address of the bureau. The bank does not have to reveal anything the credit bureau's report contains.

The purpose of the Fair Credit Reporting Act is to enable consumers to trace the reasons for the denial of credit so that they can refute or challenge the accuracy of unfavorable information. The consumer is given the right to full disclosure of the contents of his or her credit bureau file.

## BANKS AND CREDIT CARD FINANCE

### Growth of Bank Credit Cards

In recent years, lending associated with bank credit cards has been the fastest growth area in consumer lending. Bank credit cards first became popular nearly 30 years ago. At that time, individual banks issued the cards to their existing customers and recruited local merchants who agreed to accept them from the customers. Participating merchants daily presented the bank with sales vouchers signed by their card-using customers. The merchants' bank accounts then received immediate credit, less the bank's discount. The arrangement provided benefits to all three parties. The bank collected fees derived from discounting merchants' sales vouchers and charged interest on cardholder balances that were carried beyond the grace, or free, period of 25 days or so. Cardholders enjoyed unquestioned credit from participating merchants, avoided the burden of carrying cash for large purchases, and did not have the hassle of uncertain acceptance of written checks. Merchants expanded their sales appeal to a growing pool of cardholders.

However, the local bank credit card plan had serious drawbacks. The card's usefulness was restricted to a circle of participating merchants in the card banks' market areas. Also, bank card plans proliferated among competing banks, forcing merchants either to choose one plan to the exclusion of others or to operate with perhaps several parallel systems. These drawbacks were overcome in the late 1960s when two national credit card plans emerged to replace the local bank cards. These two plans—VISA and MasterCard—distribute their cards through a network of regional issuing banks, which, in turn, enlist smaller agent banks that further distribute the cards. Issuing banks retain control of the approval of new card applicants, including establishment of the credit limit assigned to each applicant. The issuing banks (not their agent banks) extend revolving credit to cardholders who do not wish to pay their monthly statements in full within the due date. In addition, issuing banks collect merchants' fees and incur the costs associated with operating the card system.

An important and complex feature of the national bank card systems is the worldwide communications credit record maintained on card users. Merchants call into their card-issuing bank on their automatic dial-up stations for credit authorizations on card users if transactions exceed the merchant's *floor limit*. The issuing bank accesses the card user's file through telecommunications lines to determine whether the proposed purchase would put the card user over his or her credit limit and whether the card has been canceled or reported lost or stolen. The worldwide character of this credit interchange system permits authorization within seconds on card users from distant issuing banks.

**TABLE 13-6   Largest Ten Credit Card Issuers (December 1990)**

|  | Credit (in $ billions) | Outstanding Percentage of Issuers | Number of Accounts (in millions) | Percentage of Issuers |
|---|---|---|---|---|
| Citicorp | $31.5 | 12.7% | 20.4 | 3.3% |
| Sears Roebuck and Co. | 17.5 | 7.1 | 45.3 | 7.4 |
| GECC Retailer Financial Serv. | 8.6 | 3.5 | 31.0 | 5.1 |
| Chase Manhattan Bank USA | 8.5 | 3.4 | 9.0 | 1.0 |
| Central Atlantic Bank | 6.9 | 2.8 | 4.8 | 0.8 |
| Amer. Exps. Cent. Bk. (Optima) | 6.8 | 2.8 | 2.2 | 0.4 |
| First Chicago Corp. | 6.5 | 2.6 | 6.6 | 1.1 |
| Greenwood Trust Co. (Discover) | 6.4 | 2.6 | 21.6 | 3.5 |
| Bank of America | 5.9 | 2.4 | 4.7 | 0.8 |
| J.C. Penney Co. | 4.6 | 1.9 | 28.0 | 4.6 |
| American Express | 4.6 | 1.9 | 18.0 | 2.9 |

In 1991, there existed over 6,000 credit card issuers in the United States and more than 600 million active accounts based on 1 billion cards outstanding. However, banks represent only about two-thirds of the credit card credit outstanding. Various nonbank cards exist and, in addition, pursuant to the Competitive Equality Banking Act of 1987, *credit card banks* were authorized permitting nonbanks to issue VISA or MasterCard credit cards. Recent card issuers include huge corporations such as AT&T, Ford Motor Company, Sears, Prudential Insurance, General Electric, Amoco, and others. The top 10 credit card issuers at the end of 1990 are listed in Table 13-6.

The appeal of VISA and MasterCard to consumers is their worldwide acceptance. Cardholders can purchase an almost unlimited array of goods and services from merchants throughout the United States and in many foreign countries. Increasingly, large retail chains with their own credit card systems are accepting the two major bank cards in order to remain competitive. The VISA and MasterCard cards are not only a convenient form of consumer credit, they are also a convenient form of payment. In this regard, national bank cards are as acceptable and effective as currency.

### Issues in Credit Card Pricing

The pricing and other features of the two bank credit card programs are similar. Merchant discount fees generally range from 1 to 6 percent, with high-volume merchants paying lower percentages. It is doubtful, however, that banks' revenue from merchant discounts exceeds the cost of providing immediate cash against merchant sales, absorbing credit risk, and performing monthly billing services.

In the past, the usury laws of many states governed what banks could charge consumers for the use of credit cards. Until recently, these laws prohibited banks from charging consumers annual fees for the use of their cards. In most states, banks were prohibited from levying a finance charge on card users who made full payment on their card purchases within a *grace period*, usually 25 days after billing.[4] Finally, usury statutes limited interest charges on revolving or unpaid balances.

As a practical matter, these price regulations were eliminated by the U.S. Supreme Court's *Marquette National Bank* v. *First of Omaha Service Corporation* (439 U.S. 99) decision in 1978. In this seminal case, the Court held that bank interest rates were restricted by the state in which the bank is located, not the state in which the customer is located. As a result, banks set up the card operations in states without interest rate ceilings.

The absence of an interest rate ceiling in South Dakota attracted the largest bank credit operation in the world when Citibank located its credit card operation there in 1980. By operating from a state that has no usury ceiling, Citicorp is free to set its own rate for its card users everywhere. A similar move to Delaware was made by Chase Manhattan Bank when, in 1981, that state removed pricing statutes affecting credit cards.

Periodically, bank credit card pricing comes under fire because of what some observers perceive to be unfair pricing practices. This criticism often stems from the observation that interest rates on credit card outstanding balances do not decline when general market rates of interest decline. The most recent threat of an interest rate ceiling occurred in late 1991 when President George Bush suggested that such a ceiling would make credit available more widely. In reality, bank credit card operations do appear to be highly profitable. Figure 13-2 depicts credit card profitability for VISA U.S.A. during the period 1978–1991. Net income on VISA outstandings was established to be 3.5 percent in early 1991, or about 2.2 percent after taxes. By comparison, banks as a group do well if they can earn 1.0 percent on total assets after taxes.

Highly educated and high-income consumers are most likely not to have revolving credit card balances, thus avoiding payment of finance charges. They use their bank card for its payment convenience, not as a means of gaining access to credit. As a result, banks must rely on income from their revolving credit card users to subsidize the free services given to nonrevolving users.

In sum, banks in many states are forced to give away credit card services to consumers who are most able to pay for them. In the future, in the interest of more equitable pricing, it is likely that all banks will be permitted to charge annual user fees or per-transaction fees. Another possibility is that banks will levy finance charges from the date of purchase. The effect of these changes is not clear. In general, such changes would probably reduce credit card use by consumers who do not presently pay for card services.

---

[4]The grace period gives card users who make purchases early in the monthly cycle the use of the bank's funds for almost two months. This free period does not apply to card users who make partial payments on their outstanding balances; in cases of partial payment, retrospective finance charges are applied to the whole balance.

**FIGURE 13-2    VISA U.S.A. Card Profitability Trends (Return on Average Outstandings)**

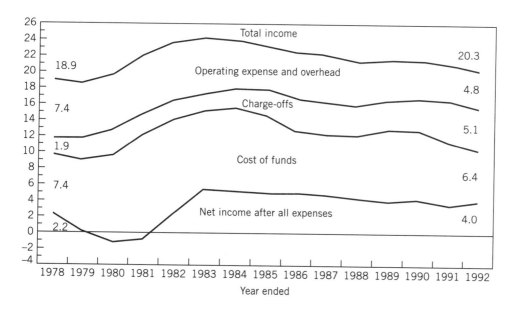

## Debit Cards

Nonpaying consumers might switch to the use of debit cards, which electronically debit the consumer's deposit account at the time of purchase and credit the merchant's account. Both types of cards—the credit card and the debit card—serve as a means of payment as readily as cash. However, debit cards have several efficiencies that credit cards do not possess. With debit cards, card users forgo check writing, card-issuing banks need not prepare monthly billings, and, in the simplest debit card system, credit risk is eliminated. If enough consumers substitute debit cards for credit cards, ultimately banks' credit card lending might be reduced. It is likely, however, that banks will offer to tie debit cards to personal lines of credit in the form of overdraft protection. With this arrangement, if the consumer's debit card–based purchases exceed the funds in the consumer's bank account, a prearranged line of credit will be triggered. The size of the credit line for overdraft protection for a given consumer presumably will be identical to the credit limit on a credit card issued to that consumer. In either case, the bank will be exposed to the same risk of default. The total effect on the volume of consumer credit extended by banks remains to be seen.

It is also uncertain whether the two national credit card associations will

**TABLE 13-7  Delinquency Rates at Large Commercial Banks**

| Type of Loan | Delinquency Rate |
|---|---|
| Real estate loans | 5.26% |
| Commercial and industrial loans | 6.39 |
| Consumer loans | 3.36 |
| Other loans | 7.00 |
| All loans | 5.45 |

SOURCE: "Developments in the U.S. Financial System Since the Mid-1970s," *Federal Reserve Bulletin*, January 1988, pp. 1–13.

dominate future debit card plans. Despite their success in gaining the world-wide acceptance of merchants, these associations are accepted reluctantly by their issuing banks. These banks would prefer to preserve more of their own identity instead of subordinating it to the MasterCard or VISA names. They also are reluctant to share with their local bank competitors the electronic transaction networks that will undoubtedly be the heart of future debit card plans.

## CONSUMER LOAN LOSSES AND THE BANKRUPTCY CODE

Historically, consumer loans have experienced the highest loss rates of all types of loans. However, the recent data in Table 13-7 show that, for large banks, delinquency rates on consumer loans were well below those on most other loans. Nevertheless, banks must make a determined effort to try to recover principal and interest from seriously delinquent borrowers. And most consumers conscientiously work to stay current in repaying their loans. However, consumers who are under severe financial pressure can deter the collection effort of banks and other creditors by filing for bankruptcy under the Federal Bankruptcy Code. The code permits consumers to eliminate part of their indebtedness without being rendered destitute; that is, consumers are permitted to retain certain assets that will help them achieve financial rehabilitation.

### Bankruptcy Reform

For most of the twentieth century, bankruptcy procedures in the United States were governed by bankruptcy laws written in 1898. In 1978, Congress passed the Bankruptcy Reform Act, which modernized and consolidated into one consistent code the many amendments and court rulings since 1898. In part, the 1978 law attempted to remove the stigma of bankruptcy by identifying persons filing for bankruptcy as *debtors* instead of *bankrupts*. A stated objective of the Bankruptcy Reform Act was to "better protect the American consumer and the unfortunate debtor." This objective was provided for in the new code by setting forth a generous list of debtor assets that are exempt from the claims of creditors when the debtor files for bankruptcy. This provision is intended to make it more feasible for financially distressed debtors to repay their debts voluntarily over time.

Two parts of the Bankruptcy Code provide relief for debtors while protecting certain of their assets. The first part, under Chapter 8 of the code, provides for liquidation of the debtor's assets to service debts. The second part, providing debtor relief, under Chapter 13, sets forth procedures for repayment planning based on the debtor's future earnings (the *wage earner plan*).

**Chapter 8**    Chapter 8 provides for conversion of the debtor's assets to cash and the pro rata distribution of the cash proceeds to creditors. The cash distribution results in a formal discharge of the debts. Certain debts, including taxes, alimony, child support, funds received through embezzlement, or debts incurred through misrepresentation, cannot be discharged. In relation to the previous outdated code, the new code significantly liberalizes the list of protected debtor's assets that are exempted from liquidation. These exempted, subsistence-related assets include a portion of home equity, a motor vehicle, and a limited amount of jewelry, household goods, funds in a retirement account, and tools of trade. Moreover, debtors may choose between federal and state exemption provisions, selecting the more favorable option. The liberal exemption of household goods in California, for example, is quite favorable to debtors in comparison with the federal provisions. However, most states have opted out of the federal statute by setting their own—typically lower—exemption levels.

**Chapter 13**    Chapter 13 provides for debtors to retain all of their assets while repaying their debts out of future earnings on the basis of a schedule approved by the court. Initially, the repayment schedule is distributed to all creditors who file a proof of claim with the courts. Secured creditors vote on the debtor's repayment plan. Unsecured creditors may not vote, but the value they receive under Chapter 13 must not be less than what they would receive under Chapter 8 liquidation, as estimated by the court. Unfortunately, the liberal asset exemptions of Chapter 8 usually result in no distribution at all to unsecured creditors. As a result, the repayment plans submitted to the creditors and the court under Chapter 13 often provide little or no payment to unsecured creditors. This loophole is highly controversial and appears to deny these creditors a fair remedy.

Once the debtor has paid off the creditors according to the plan, the court formally grants a discharge. The new code liberalizes the old code's wage earner plan concept by extending it to self-employed persons and by permitting unrestricted joint filings of married couples. Under another section of the code, Chapter 12, many of the concepts discussed earlier that protect consumers are extended to businesses. In order to file for Chapter 13 bankruptcy reorganization, a debtor must meet a ceiling amount of $350,000.

Creditors are prohibited or *stayed* from taking direct action against a debtor who has filed for bankruptcy or against his or her property. For example, if a borrower has filed for bankruptcy, a bank cannot use a setoff against its borrower's account, nor can the bank foreclose on a mortgage or repossess an automobile it financed for the debtor.

## Criticism and Reform of the 1978 Bankruptcy Code

Bankers contend that the 1978 Bankruptcy Code so liberalized bankruptcy procedures that it actually encouraged debtors to use the bankruptcy court to abandon their debts. In the opinion of one banker, "Congress may have inadvertently created a law by which most people in the United States could lawfully walk out on their debts while keeping all of their property."[5] In fact, the rise of personal bankruptcy filings nationally following the effective date of the new code on October 1, 1979, seems to support this contention. The revised code, combined with the 1981–1982 recession, appeared to drive bankruptcy filings to a peak of 316,000 in 1981. By 1984, as the economy strengthened, bankruptcies fell to 284,000. However, they have grown sharply since then, to a record 944,000 filings in 1991.

Statistical studies have demonstrated that of consumers who filed for a Chapter 8 set-aside of their debts, about 20 percent had the financial ability to repay their debts over several years.[6] In fairness, these consumers were candidates for servicing their debts under a court-approved Chapter 13 repayment schedule. Such abuses led to further reform of the code in 1984. One of the 1984 reforms—the "substantial abuse" test—allows the bankruptcy court to dismiss its earlier granting of Chapter 8 relief when it finds that a debtor's current income and expenses do permit the debtor to service his or her debts. However, the court cannot consider projections of the debtor's future income. Another reform simply lowers the amounts of property the debtor can exempt under Chapter 8.

The banking industry contends that bankruptcy proceedings are overdue for additional reform to provide better statistical information, simplify procedures for creditors, and eliminate growing abuses by debtors. One study concluded that about one-third of bankruptcy petitions in a large western city had a possibly fraudulent basis. Reform proposals emphasize the need to provide creditors with more timely and complete notice and expedited procedures and to encourage greater use of Chapter 13 reorganizations in place of Chapter 8 liquidations.[7]

Bankers point out that the costs of writing off bad consumer debts must

[5]Frank Sennott, "Bankruptcy Abuse Jeopardizes Consumer Credit Privileges," *American Banker* (March 24, 1981), pp. 13, 14, 17.

[6]Credit Research Center, "Consumer's Right to Bankruptcy: Origins and Effect," and "Costs and Benefits of Personal Bankruptcy" (West Lafayette, Ind.: Credit Research Center), 1981.

[7]George Cleland, "ABA Attacks a Growth Industry—Bankruptcy," *ABA Banking Journal*, Vol. 84 (May 1992), p. 14.

be passed along to other consumers. Otherwise, it is argued, banks could not afford to continue with their consumer lending programs. However, another lesson is also implied in the profusion of bankruptcies. That lesson is that bankers must realistically evaluate a consumer's ability to pay, and they must avoid making easy credit available to marginal borrowers.

## CONSUMER REGULATION AND COMPLIANCE

During the decade beginning in the late 1960s, Congress passed a comprehensive regulatory legislation package to protect consumers in their dealings with financial institutions. Table 13-8 lists and describes the most significant regulations and laws included in this package. As described previously in this chapter, Regulation B (Equal Credit Opportunity) and the Fair Credit Reporting Act are vital considerations in the process of credit investigation and analysis. Regulation Z (Truth in Lending) has had such a significant impact on bank compliance efforts that it warrants separate discussion in a later section. Several regulations deal primarily with housing and mortgage matters and are relevant to the discussion of real estate lending in Chapter 12.

Banks have developed intricate systems of internal controls to be sure that they comply with these regulations. These controls ensure that documentation required by the new regulations is produced, and they set up mechanisms to monitor functional compliance.

Most banks employ a compliance officer, who is responsible to senior management, to ensure that the bank's compliance program is effective. Large banks may have several compliance officers. Small banks usually assign the compliance function to an officer who carries conventional banking responsibilities as well. Compliance programs create a lot of expense for banks. However, noncompliance is potentially much more expensive, because it can lead to severe pecuniary penalties and even prison sentences for managers who knowingly fail to observe consumer regulations.

A bank's policies and procedures in relation to regulatory compliance are generally set forth in a compliance manual. This manual contains the bank's policy statement on compliance; detailed procedures, including instructions to employees on completing loan and consumer disclosure forms; and instructions on the filing and retention of documents proving compliance. The compliance manual serves two basic purposes. First, its existence satisfies examiners who wish to see the bank's policies and procedures made explicit. Second, and probably more important, it serves as a control tool to instruct and inform bank personnel uniformly.

### Truth in Lending

Originally passed by Congress in 1968, the Truth in Lending Act and the associated Regulation Z, enforced by the Federal Reserve System, represent a major compliance burden on banks. The Truth in Lending Act, like much

---

**TABLE 13-8   Regulations and Laws Pertaining to Consumer Lending**

Regulation AA (Consumer Inquiries and Complaints)
Sets forth procedures for investigating and processing complaints by a consumer in relation to the denial of credit. (Applies to state member banks.)

Regulation B (Equal Credit Opportunity)
Prohibits discrimination against a credit applicant on the basis of race, sex, color, marital status, religion, age, receipt of public assistance, and national origin in any credit transaction.

Regulation BB (Community Reinvestment)
Forbids the arbitrary consideration of geographic factors or redlining in granting credit within the financial institution's local community. Redlining consists of blanket refusal to grant credit within circumscribed (redlined) neighborhoods deemed by the bank to be in physical and economic decline.

Regulation C (Home Mortgage Disclosure)
Details reporting requirements of geographical data on mortgages to enable regulators to detect redlining practices. The 1989 amendments to the Home Mortgage Disclosure Act expand disclosure requirements on the disposition of loan applications and on the race or national origin, gender, and annual income of loan applicants and borrowers.

1989 Amendments to Home Mortgage Disclosure Act
Expand disclosure on the disposition of loan applications and on the race or origin, gender, and annual income of loan applicants and borrowers.

Regulation E (Electronic Funds Transfer)
Limits consumer liability for unauthorized use of lost credit or debit cards. Controls issuance of cards and specifies information to be supplied consumer in using electronic transfer devices.

Regulation Z (Truth in Lending)
Requires that consumers be given meaningful and consistent information on the cost of credit. Certain nonprice information must also be disclosed.

Fair Housing Act
Prohibits discrimination in housing and housing credit on the basis of race, color, religion, national origin, or sex. This act preceded passage of the Equal Credit Opportunity Act, which defined several additional bases of discrimination. The Fair Housing Act prohibits redlining housing credit.

Fair Credit Reporting Act
Grants consumers access to their credit bureau records, and entitles them to check the source of information and its accuracy. Denials of credit by banks on the basis of credit bureau information must be reported to consumers.

Real Estate Settlement Procedures Act
Requires detailed statement of settlement costs on real estate transactions and reporting of borrowers' rights in the granting of mortgage credit.

---

consumer protection legislation, was prompted by what Congress considered to be abuses by creditors. Congress believed that banks and other lenders were not giving consumers enough information about credit. It thought that the terminology used by lenders varied too widely, causing confusion and poor borrowing decisions by consumers. The Truth in Lending Act was designed to standardize the methods of disclosing loan terms to creditors, so that consumers could effectively shop for the best deal on a loan among alternative lenders. The act emphasized disclosure of key credit information in straightforward terms by focusing on the *finance charge* and the *annual percentage rate (APR)*.

The finance charge simply expresses the total dollar amount of the cost of credit. This total includes not only interest costs but also ancillary charges, such as points[8] or credit insurance premiums. In addition to the finance charge, the lender must disclose prepayment penalties, charges in the event that the borrower defaults, and any security interest taken on collateral.

The second crucial provision of the Truth in Lending Act specifies standard rules for determining the APR. The APR is the simple annual rate computed by the actuarial method. For example, the lender cannot represent the add-on rate used in installment contracts as the APR. Unlike the add-on rate, the APR must be computed in such a way that any declining loan balance outstanding is recognized. In the case of credit card or other revolving-type credit, the APR is the monthly percentage finance charge multiplied by 12. For example, if an open-ended credit plan charges 1.75 percent per month on the unpaid balance, the APR would be 21 percent.

In general, lenders must "clearly and conspicuously" disclose all material terms of the loan and must do so before the credit is extended. The Truth in Lending Act further regulates credit advertising. Most important, the lender cannot advertise one feature of its credit offer without stating other details, such as the means of determining the finance charge and the actual APR.

The Truth in Lending Act contains provisions for certain civil penalties to force compliance. Initially, an automatic $100 minimum civil penalty was imposed for violations.

As passed in 1968, the Truth in Lending Act was so exacting in its requirements that consumers were confused about the technical details of statements of disclosure regarding loan terms. Many frustrated consumers failed to read the disclosure statements, making the technical details self-defeating. Furthermore, compliance by lenders was difficult under the disclosure requirements and ambiguities of the act, coupled with the Federal Reserve System's literal interpretations. Compliance was made even more difficult by the highly technical finding in over 15,000 civil lawsuits filed in federal courts under the Truth in Lending Act through 1980.

Finally, in 1980, Congress passed the Truth in Lending Simplification and Reform Act, which reduced some of the original disclosure requirements, exempted agricultural credit from the provisions of the act, and provided standard disclosure forms that ensured compliance if used by lenders.

## SUMMARY

The granting of all types of credit to consumers by banks has grown dramatically in the past 30 or more years. This type of credit now makes up over

---

[8] One point represents 1 percent of the total loan amount charged "on the front end" as a loan origination fee. For example, three points on a $10,000 loan equals $300.

one-third of the average bank's loan portfolio. Installment credit is mostly used for the purchase of household durables and automobiles. Revolving credit, especially that associated with credit or debit cards, is increasingly used to purchase a wide variety of personal goods and services. Card-type transactions are valued by consumers for their convenience as a virtual cash substitute as well as a source of credit.

The mix of consumer credit appears to be changing rapidly. Credit extended by means of credit cards and, increasingly, debit cards is expanding rapidly. The future growth of this form of consumer debt seems assured as electronic devices that utilize them proliferate. On the other hand, automobile loan lending as a proportion of total bank consumer lending probably has shrunk permanently as auto manufacturers have usurped the market for this type of loan.

Installment lending is characterized by low amounts per loan and large numbers of loans. Banks have to organize efficiently to receive, analyze, and evaluate loan applications and to advise consumers of their decisions. Formal credit scoring systems are an appropriate approach to efficient processing at banks with particularly high rates of installment loan applications. For large banks, the benefits of a credit scoring system probably outweigh the costs of maintaining and updating the system using the sophisticated statistical techniques on which such systems are based. However, no credit scoring system can be entirely devoid of judgment; applications that fall in the gray area need further individual attention. Small banks probably cannot justify a statistically verified scoring system tailored to their clientele. These banks will probably always need to depend primarily on judgment.

Consumer lending is further complicated by a host of federal consumer protection regulations that require careful compliance. Part of any major consumer lending program in a bank must be a system for monitoring and documenting the bank's adherence to consumer regulations. Regulation B (Equal Credit Opportunity Act) and Regulation Z (Truth in Lending Act), in particular, demand the bank's comprehension and careful implementation. Recognition of the complexity of such regulations is growing, and as a result, Congress is regularly promoting legislation to simplify them.

## Discussion Questions

1. Distinguish between direct and indirect automobile loans. Why should banks seek both types of this loan business, instead of just one or the other?
2. Determine the effective annual rate on a two-year loan of $1,200 with an 8 percent add-on rate, paid in monthly installments.
3. How does conversion to floating-rate consumer loans affect the interest sensitivity of bank balance sheets?
4. What is the purpose or rationale for the Rule of 78s?
5. Cite the purpose and some basic provisions of the Equal Credit Opportunity Act and its operational equivalent, Regulation B.

6. Summarize the pros and cons of judgmental and empirically based credit evaluation systems.
7. Why has the credit card system evolved from a system whereby many banks issued their own cards to one dominated by VISA and MasterCard?
8. What are the advantages of the proposed debit card over the present credit card? Why have debit cards been accepted so slowly?
9. Some observers claim that the 1978 Bankruptcy Reform Act encourages debtors to abandon their debts with the help of the bankruptcy courts. What provisions of the act might lend credence to this statement?
10. What are the main provisions of the Truth in Lending Act?

# Special Markets for Bank Loans

Chapters 11 and 12 covered in a general way the major facets of making commercial loans. Chapter 11 presented the principles of credit investigation and the analysis of business borrowers. Four factors are basic in evaluating the likelihood that a loan will be repaid promptly and in full. First, the lender must determine the borrower's character and credit history. Second, the lender must ascertain the specific use of the loan funds and the appropriateness of such use. Third, the lender must evaluate the source of repayment normally related to the borrower's primary operating activity. Finally, the lender needs to identify a secondary (collateral) source of repayment. Chapter 12 discussed the general considerations involved in structuring a loan. These considerations included term to maturity, the process of securing collateral and extracting cash from it, pricing, commitments, and covenants.

Though covered in general terms, most of these facets of evaluating and structuring loans also apply to a cross section of loans made to special customer groups or made routinely for specialized purposes.

This chapter reviews selected special-purpose types of loans in light of the principles and considerations covered in Chapters 11 and 12. The types of loans we will review include the following:

1. International.
2. Agricultural.
3. Real estate.
4. Government guaranteed.
5. Lease financing.

# INTERNATIONAL LOANS[1]

Commercial banks are at the heart of the international financial system. They facilitate world trade and support the international expansion of multinational corporations by financing an array of international transactions. Their major role in short-term finance is to guarantee customers' international trade obligations, discount international paper, and facilitate international payments. Many larger U.S. banks, those with several billion dollars or more in total assets, engage directly in these aspects of international banking. Smaller banks can offer international loan-related services through correspondent relationships with larger banks.

U.S. banks' role as creditors in international finance consists of direct lending to U.S. customers overseas and to foreign entities, including banks and nonbanks. All U.S. money center banks, as well as many large regional banks, do a significant amount of this type of lending.

## Short-Term Finance

International trade credit and the documents associated with it are more complicated than their domestic equivalents. This is because international trade cuts across two bodies of laws and regulations, and because the buyers and sellers (importers and exporters) are less familiar with and less accessible to one another than buyers and sellers in the same country. These complications often require the help of banks to intermediate import-export transactions.

**Simple Trade Account**    In the simplest form of international trade, the *open-account* basis, banks have only a simple transactions role. In open-account trade, the importer and exporter are well known to each other and probably have established a successful working relationship. The importer orders goods and promptly pays for them when the goods and title thereto are received.

Almost as simple is the *foreign collection* basis, in which a bank is used to transmit collected funds. Before the goods it has bought can be shipped, the importer must place funds with its bank so that the exporter is assured that payment will be made with collected funds. In this instance, the bank is merely an agent and not a lender.

**Bank Drafts**    Financial instruments, such as bank drafts and letters of credit, reduce some of the uncertainties of international transactions. A *sight draft* is usually prepared by the exporter and addressed to the importer, ordering the importer to pay on receipt of the goods and the draft. When the draft is signed and "accepted" by the importer and formally acknowledged by the importer's bank, the exporter can use the draft as collateral to borrow funds

---

[1] See Chapter 19 for a discussion of recent international lending activity by U.S. banks.

from his or her own bank, creating, in effect, an international form of accounts receivable financing. A sight draft generally implies only the promise of the importer to pay. However, acceptance by the importer's bank makes the draft an irrevocable instrument of payment.

An alternative form of draft is the *time draft*, which allows a specified period of time after the goods are delivered and the draft is presented before payment is due. For example, payment terms might be 30, 60, or 90 days' sight. A time draft that has been accepted by the importer's bank is called a *banker's acceptance*. When the bank accepts the draft, the bank guarantees that it will pay the draft on maturity; that is, it effectively replaces the importer's credit with its own credit. As a rule, the exporter, as well as the investment markets, put greater stock in the bank's creditworthiness than in the importer's creditworthiness.

The exporter may attempt to sell the banker's acceptance to an investor at a discount that is consistent with the market rate on banker's acceptances at the time. Alternatively, the bank may effectively extend credit by buying the acceptance from the exporter at the appropriate discount. The bank typically sells it in the banker's acceptance market and later, at maturity, pays off the investor at par as the payment from the importer comes due.

**Commercial Letters of Credit**   The sight or time draft transactions just described usually involve commercial or documentary letters of credit. The letter of credit (L/C) typically is issued by the importer's bank, that is, the issuing bank. The issuing bank's L/C signifies that the bank agrees to pay the importer's obligation to an exporter resulting from a sales agreement, contingent on receiving documentation proving that shipment was made. In return for the L/C, the importer warrants that he or she will pay the bank the sales amount and any fees.

The L/C is crucial to exporters if a foreign customer is not well known or if the customer's credit is suspect for any reason. The L/C substitutes the issuing bank's credit and reputation for those of the importer.

The issuing bank sends the L/C covering the amount of the sale to the exporter's bank (called the *paying bank*) in the exporter's country. The paying bank, in turn, sends the L/C to the exporter. When shipment is made, the exporter presents its sight or time draft along with proof-of-shipment documents to its (paying) bank. The exporter's bank then pays the seller, debits the account of the importer's bank, and sends the shipping documents and the draft on to the importer's bank. Upon receipt of the documents and draft, the importer's bank debits the importer's account (in the case of a sight draft; alternatively, with a time draft, the importer's account is debited on maturity) and conveys the documents, representing title to the goods, to the importer.

Figure 14-1, based on an agreement by an American computer manufacturer (exporter) to sell computer equipment to a Singaporan buyer (importer), illustrates the transactions just described. In Step 1, the buyer's bank in Singapore issues its L/C to the computer manufacturer's bank in Wisconsin, which

## FIGURE 14-1    Typical Path of Letter of Credit

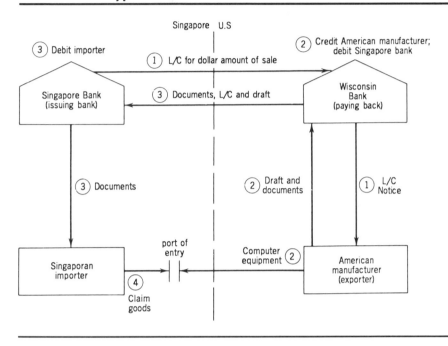

sends it to the manufacturer. In Step 2, the manufacturer in Wisconsin ships the computer equipment to Singapore and presents the sight draft and shipping documents to its bank. The bank in Wisconsin credits the manufacturer's account for the amount of the sale, debits the Singaporan issuing bank's account, and sends the documents to the issuing bank. In Step 3, the Singaporan bank receives the documents, debits the dollar equivalent amount from the buyer's account, and presents the documents to the buyer. Finally, in Step 4, with the shipping documents and effective title in hand, the buyer claims the computer equipment.

L/Cs may be confirmed or unconfirmed and revocable or irrevocable. Confirmed irrevocable L/Cs bear the guarantee of payment by both the issuing and confirming (paying) banks. An unconfirmed irrevocable L/C bears the guarantee of the issuing bank only, and a revocable L/C carries only the importer's promise to pay and does not carry either bank's guarantee.

## Insuring against Foreign Exchange Risk[2]

An ever-present dimension of international trade, particularly with credit sales, is the risk of changing currency values. International transactions are invari-

[2]See Chapter 19 on international banking for a more complete discussion of the use of the foreign exchange market, including hedging, speculation, and swaps.

ably denominated in the currency of either (1) the exporter's nation, (2) the importer's nation, or (3) a third nation. In the case of the computer sale, if payment terms are 90 days and the sale is in terms of U.S. dollars, the Singaporan importer faces foreign exchange risk, because the value of the dollar may increase in relation to the Singaporan dollar during the credit period. Then, when payment comes due, the importer may be forced to pay out more Singaporan dollars for any fixed U.S. dollar amount. If the sale is denominated in Singaporan dollars, then the U.S. manufacturer is exposed to changing currency values and the risk that the Singaporan dollar may appreciate relative to the U.S. dollar. This foreign exchange risk compounds the credit risk that might already be borne by the manufacturer when it extends 90-day credit to the importer unless it requires an irrevocable confirmed L/C. Finally, transactions denominated in a third nation's currency potentially expose both exporter and importer to foreign exchange risk.

Banks assist traders in covering or insuring against exchange risks by putting them in the forward market. The *forward market* offers contracts to sell or buy a foreign currency at some future date at a guaranteed rate of exchange. In the case just described, the Singaporan importer could cover the dollar transaction 90 days hence by contracting in the 90-day forward market to buy or sell U.S. dollars. For example, suppose that the current (spot) exchange rate for U.S. dollars to Singaporan dollars is $1.65 U.S. and the 90-day forward rate is $1.60 U.S.; that is, the Singaporan dollar is at a forward discount. This relationship may indicate that the Singaporan dollar is expected to fall in value in relation to the U.S. dollar, which would result in an increase in the Singaporan dollar price of the computer equipment. As protection against further increases in price, the importer would sell Singaporan dollars against U.S. dollars for delivery in 90 days. The amount of forward Singaporan dollars sold would be the approximate amount of the computer equipment sales agreement.

Hedging permits a firm to lock in against the fluctuations in currency values at an amount equal to the forward discount. In this case, regardless of whether the Singaporan dollar appreciates or even depreciates more than implied by the forward rate, the net cost of foreign exchange exposure will correspond to the discount on the forward Singaporan dollar in relation to the present or spot rate.

### Direct Loans

Direct international loans take several forms. Private-sector firms in industrial nations borrow long term under guarantees by their respective governments. Governments and private borrowers in less-developed countries (LDCs) borrow large blocks of funds from syndicates of international banks. Many of the latter types of loans are not guaranteed and may represent unusual risks to banks.

Banks with large international credits limit their concentrations of loans in any one country according to the perceived country risk. *Country risk* generally refers to the economic and political conditions of a country. In any case, a loan to the foreign nation's government or its agencies is generally safer than a loan to a private-sector borrower. Even loans to governments may be unsafe, however, because of what is called *sovereign risk*. When foreign governments experience economic or political pressures, there is a risk that they will divert resources to the correction of their domestic problems at the expense of servicing their debts to external lenders. In the 1980s, several LDCs requested the rescheduling of bank loans at considerable sacrifice in interest income to the banks involved.[3] At the extreme, governments may simply repudiate their debts; that is, they may no longer recognize their obligations to external creditors.

Clearly, the credit analysis process for international lending is a big, sometimes global, task. Banks with major foreign loans must understand the foreign country's history, forecast its future economic performance, and monitor its internal political and structural changes. In addition, because of nations' economic interdependence, banks must be cognizant of how their client nations are affected by changes in the world economy.

Country risk can be evaluated the same way as domestic credit risk to distinguish between acceptable and unacceptable borrowers.[4] The analysis should break down the country's request for credit into four questions that are analogous to those raised with any borrower: Is the borrower willing to repay? What is the use of funds? What is the primary source of repayment? What is the secondary source of repayment?

A debtor country's willingness to repay has a lot to do with its ability to accept economic discipline in managing its growth. Repayment of external debt may require a nation to slow its growth. If the country uses external debt to fuel its growth at a rate that its citizens demand, it may be unwilling to accept the political risk of an abrupt slowdown. In these circumstances, the debtor nation may prefer to default on its debts. It may find that negotiating to obtain concessions from its creditors to reschedule its debt payments is more palatable than dealing with the political instability that might be associated with retarded growth in the domestic economy.

Banks should analyze a country's use of borrowed funds and the primary repayment source in a straightforward manner. What assets does the country intend to purchase with the funds? Do these assets (such as new industry, education, or public works) promise to produce a rate of return in excess of the interest cost of the subject debt, and will the assets generate increased export earnings? Export earnings, in this sense, are analogous to the net income of a corporation. The ability of the debtor nation to earn hard currency, such as the U.S. dollar or the Japanese yen, is crucial in this phase of the analysis. For a U.S. bank lender, the issue is the availability of dollars earned by the country for repayment. Alternatively, other lenders, such as the International Monetary Fund, might be available to take out the bank.

---

[3] The recent experience of U.S. bank loans to LDCs is reviewed in more depth in Chapter 19.

[4] A thoughtful discussion on this topic can be found in Daniel R. Denison, "A Pragmatic Model for Country Risk Analysis," *Journal of Commercial Bank Lending* (March 1984), pp. 29–37.

Secondary sources of repayment are significantly different when loaning to foreign nations than when loaning to domestic corporate borrowers. The secondary source is the nation's ability to reduce its imports in relation to its exports. In a debt crisis, the nation must be able to divert to debt repayment the hard currency used to finance imports. Once again, the key is often the willingness to slow down growth and to let export earnings catch up with or exceed outlays for imports.

## Loan Syndications and Security Underwriting

A vigorous international market for large loans has existed only since the early 1970s. Since then, wholesale loans to sovereign (government) and corporate borrowers in large denominations up to billions of dollars have involved international banks in several ways. A group of banks may form a cooperative lending syndicate. Alternatively, individual banks may underwrite securities for international borrowers through their overseas merchant banking subsidiaries, or they may securitize loans for placement directly with investors.

Loan syndication generally has played the greatest role, although this role was diminished for a while in the mid-1980s. In the 1990s, the syndicated loans market has been dominated by the largest international banks. This domination marks a dramatic change from a market that was previously open to the participation of small institutions.

In the syndicated loans market, a group of cooperating banks joins with one or more lead banks for each new loan transaction. The lead bank receives a *mandate* from the borrower to form a *lead management group*. This group is responsible for carefully documenting the loan (called a *facility*) and for taking significant responsibility for its financing. Frequently the "loan" is in actuality a standby facility that may be only partially drawn upon. In any case, the lead group further selects several *co-manager* banks that agree to provide smaller portions of the financing and to assist in bid preparation and syndicate management. Traditionally, a *general syndication* is rounded out with the selection of more numerous *participant* banks, which take smaller parts of the total financing. In the late 1980s, however, returns on syndicated credit facilities became so thin that small participant banks were priced out of syndication because they could not *make the rate* (could not provide funds at a positive spread).

By the early 1990s, the focus of the syndicated loans market had shifted from sovereign to corporate financing. This occurred, in part, because of the general halt of lending to LDCs following banks' write-offs of massive amounts of loans made to these nations in the 1980s. The shift also occurred because corporations rushed in for syndicated loans when prices on syndications were forced down by competition among international banks that had become extremely liquid.

Although they are now smaller than the largest foreign banks, large U.S. banks lead in arranging syndicated loans. For example, Table 14-1 shows that U.S. banks made the list of the top 10 international loan arrangement managers

**TABLE 14-1    Syndicated Loan Volume January 1 to March 31, 1988, by Type of Currency**

| Currency | Volume (dollars in millions) |
|---|---|
| U.S. dollar | $63,095 |
| Pound sterling | 20,129 |
| French franc | 2,479 |
| Yen | 2,114 |
| ECU (European Currency Units) | 1,998 |
| Australian dollar | 1,899 |
| Others | 2,973 |
| Total | $94,687 |

in a recent period. Syndicated loans are made in any of several lending currencies, of which the U.S. dollar is by far the most common.

The banks do not fund the loan from their balance sheets but instead have to raise the money, usually from the London Interbank Eurodollar market, to loan to the borrower. The loan is priced at the banks' own cost of borrowing (LIBOR) plus a spread to cover credit risk and other costs of making the loan and, to be sure, a margin of profit. The syndicated loan agreement usually stipulates that the funding for the loan will be rolled over every three to six months, with the price being adjusted as refundings occur at new market rates of interest. The costs covered by the all-in price on the loan include front-end or underwriting fees and commitment fees keyed to the unused portion of the loan. With banks' high liquidity, the market in the early 1990s became so competitive that some loan facilities were priced as low as five basis points over LIBOR.

Eurobonds and other types of international bonds have become increasingly important competition for syndicated loans.[5] In the 1980s a number of banks opened merchant banking subsidiaries in London, broadening their wholesale activities to include underwriting a variety of financial instruments, especially Eurobonds. These underwritings would not be permitted in a foreign branch under the Glass-Stegall Act, which prohibits investment banking activities by U.S. banks. Banks and their merchant banking subsidiaries are now very active in underwriting Eurobonds; as a result, they compete against their own syndication efforts. In 1983, Eurobond issues exceeded syndicated loan volume for the first time. By 1986, however, the syndicated loans market again dominated the Eurobond market, and this dominance increased through the end of the 1980s.

Several reasons are cited for the dominance of syndicated lending. The

[5] See Katherine Campbell, "Euromarkets: The Age of Hybrid," *The Banker* (September 1984), pp. 21–42.

reasons focus on the flexibility it provides borrowers. Primarily the banking market is a superior source of funding, compared with the Eurobond market, because of the speed with which very large amounts of funds can be made available. For example, large, high-quality corporate borrowers have raised several billion dollars in a matter of days. Moreover, credit facilities are flexibly administered and permit variable amounts of funds to be taken down as needed, with no more than 48 hours' advance notice to the lead management group.

Other types of financing in the wholesale capital market are provided by merchant banking firms. These firms underwrite innovative instruments such as commercial paper, interest rate swaps, and revolving credit facilities. These forms of financing basically involve channeling investors' funds directly to borrowers; they do not entail funding by the banks. The use of international bonds and these latter types of financing have been referred to as the *securitization* of Euromarkets, that is, the substitution of transferable financial securities for syndicated loan agreements. For now, syndicated loans dominate Euro-capital markets, but bonds and related types of financing, most of which are forms of financing created by American bank subsidiaries, define alternative strategies for competition in international financial markets.

## AGRICULTURAL LOANS

For about 28 percent of all commercial banks, farm loans are significant, exceeding 25 percent of their loan portfolios. These rural-area banks hold more than half of all commercial bank farm loans. However, farm-related lending comprises only about 5 percent of the loans made by the banking industry as a whole.

Although farm loans are not a major factor in the banking industry, banks are a major part of the market for farm credit. In 1987, bank loans to farmers and to financial agricultural production totaled $49 billion, which constituted 25 percent of the market for farm credit. Of this debt, $40 billion, or four-fifths, was non–real estate debt; banks' market share of farm real estate debt was comparatively minor. Non–real estate farm debt is dominated by production loans that finance the crop cycle; funds needed for the planting season are not repaid until the crop is harvested and marketed. Farmers sometimes delay the sale of crops by storing them in the hope of getting a better price later on. This frequently results in further demand for loan funds to carry the unsold crops and to finance ongoing operations. Farm capital equipment is another source of loan demand. Increasingly, sophisticated and expensive farm mechanization has added considerably to farm term loans.

### Farm Credit Evaluation

Loan officers in agricultural-area banks must have experience with farm problems and must develop the ability to judge the risks of adverse commodity prices, crop failure, and poor financial planning by the farmer.

In judging the farmer's ability to service bank debt, it is important to consider the farmer's financial leverage. One measure of financial leverage is the *debt–assets ratio*, which shows what proportion of the farm's assets are subject to the claims of debt holders rather than the claims of the owners.

In the early 1980s this ratio deteriorated dangerously. The stage was set for this deterioration by a tremendous growth in both farm debt and equity values beginning in the mid-1960s.[6] The parallel rise in both debt and equity values resulted in a steady debt–assets ratio until 1980 and concealed farmers' and lenders' exposure to declining farm income in the 1980s.

Overall, total farm debt from all lenders grew from $54.4 billion in 1970 to a peak of $204.8 billion in 1985. Agriculture experienced an extraordinary boom in the inflationary environment of the 1970s. Farm exports and domestic demand flourished, and both farmers and lenders were euphoric over the apparently endless rise in crop prices, farm income, and land values. With record returns on farm assets in the mid-1970s, farmers and investors began to bid aggressively on farmland, driving the average price for an acre of farmland from $189 in 1970 to $628 by 1979. During the same period, farm equity rose from $262 billion in 1970 to $849 billion in 1979. As noted, the rise in equity supported more and more debt, and farmers borrowed heavily to invest in equipment, buildings, and especially land.

In the early 1980s, export markets for agriculture dried up and poor crop production in several years severely strained farmers. Interest rates soared and put further pressure on farmers' debt service capability. Prices for farm acreage fell, reducing farm equity from a high of $1,065 billion in 1979 to $530 billion in 1986.[7] With decreasing asset values, debt–asset ratios escalated to a record 24 percent by 1985 from an average of 16 percent during the 1970s and rendered many farmers technically insolvent. According to the Department of Agriculture, in 1985 one-third of all farmers were in serious financial trouble. These farmers accounted for nearly two-thirds of all farm debt, putting farm lenders at serious risk. It was estimated that 12 percent of all farmers failed in 1985.

Although an apparently strong debt–assets ratio suggests that a farm is solvent, as it did for many farmers in the 1970s, it does not reveal the cash flow problems that a farmer often faces. A second and more meaningful measure of financial leverage in the short run is the ratio of interest to return on assets. This measure, the *reciprocal coverage ratio*, gives a more dynamic view of the farmer's cash flow and ability to service debt from current income. For the farm industry, this ratio rose dramatically throughout the 1970s and was especially high in the early 1980s, when interest rates were high. This trend signifies the increased share of the return on farm assets going to creditors for interest payments. Unfortunately, the interest–return ratio is unstable because the farmer's return on assets is relatively volatile, due to the uncertainties of

---

[6] See "Federal Credit Agencies: Misdirected Policies Disrupt Markets," *Savings Institutions* (September 1986), pp. 78–83, for a good overview.

[7] Emanuel Melichor, "Turning the Corner on Troubled Farm Debt," *Federal Reserve Bulletin* (July 1987), pp. 523–536.

weather and crop prices. As the ratio increases generally, the lender's cushion against such uncertainties is seriously eroded. The ratio of interest to return on assets rose from 8 percent in 1970 to about triple that level in the 1980s.

Not surprisingly, then, the farm crisis was transmitted to agricultural banks and other farm lenders. Charge-offs of non–real estate farm loans peaked at 3.4 percent of outstanding farm loans at banks. Over 200 agriculture-dependent banks failed due to farm loan problems in the 1980s. Meanwhile, farmland values, which were the basis of many ill-advised bank credit extensions, fell back toward the preinflationary levels of the mid-1970s.

### Farm Loan Competition

Table 14-2 shows the amount and share of farm debt held by various lenders, including commercial banks. The major nonbank financial institutional lenders are described in this section. Individuals and others are nonfinancial institutional lenders whose extensions of farm credit stem from their primary, nonfinancial business. Much of farms' non–real estate credit arises from trade receivables.

**Table 14-2    Farm Debt Outstanding, Recent Year**

|  | Amount (dollars in billions) | Percent |
|---|---|---|
| **Total Debt** | | |
| Banks | 41.3 | 26.2 |
| FCS | 45.5 | 28.9 |
| Life insurance companies | 10.2 | 6.5 |
| FmHA | 23.9 | 15.2 |
| Individuals and others | 36.3 | 23.1 |
| Total | 157.3 | 100.0 |
| **Real Estate Debt** | | |
| Banks | 11.7 | 13.1 |
| Federal land banks | 35.0 | 39.1 |
| Life insurance companies | 10.2 | 11.4 |
| FmHA | 9.5 | 10.6 |
| Individuals and others | 23.1 | 25.8 |
| Total | 89.4 | 100.0 |
| **Non–Real Estate Debt** | | |
| Banks | 29.6 | 43.7 |
| PCAs | 10.6 | 15.6 |
| FmHA | 14.4 | 21.2 |
| Individuals and others | 13.2 | 19.5 |
| Total | 67.8 | 100.0 |

The *production credit associations* (PCAs) are a major part of the federally supervised cooperative Farm Credit System (FCS). This system is regulated by the Farm Credit Administration through 12 regional Farm Credit Districts. The system consists of three cooperative lending groups:[8]

1. Twelve federal land banks and 388 local federal land bank associations that finance farm real estate.
2. Thirteen banks for cooperatives, which lend to farmers' supporting operations, such as marketing, supply, and business service cooperatives.
3. Thirty-seven federal intermediate credit banks (FICBs) and 315 local PCAs.

The FCS's role in non–real estate farm lending is performed by the 315 PCAs. The PCAs are borrower-owned cooperatives that lend short- and intermediate-term funds to farmers for crop and livestock operations. The PCAs are funded by the FICBs, which, in turn raise their funds through bond issues in the national financial markets.

The Farmers Home Administration (FmHA) is a federal government agency that engages in direct lending to farmers and guarantees farm loans originated by commercial banks. The FmHA was authorized under the Emergency Agricultural Credit Act of 1979 (amended in 1980) to lend funds to farmers who are temporarily unable to acquire funds from their normal lenders at reasonable rates. Like the FICBs, the FmHA raises its funds in the national capital markets.

The Commodity Credit Corporation (CCC) is a federal government agency that is involved in a unique aspect of farm lending. The CCC is an instrument of the government's price support and farm income policies, and provides price support and crop storage loans. Lending by the CCC fluctuates erratically, depending on commodity prices. If market prices fall below the amount per bushel that the CCC is willing to provide, farmers rush into the CCC program. This happened during the 1982–1986 period of depressed crop prices.

Since 1975, and as indicated in Table 14-2, the FCS has been the largest lender to agriculture, a position it wrested away from commercial banks. Along with banks, the FCS experienced a serious crisis in the mid-1980s. By 1986, 14.4 percent of its outstanding loans and 42.9 percent of the FmHA's loans were delinquent. The federal land banks alone lost $2.1 billion in 1985.

The net effect on banks of the government-supported credit agencies is indirect. Before the aggressive lending via federal agencies in the 1970s, commercial banks tended to supply a rather steady stream of credit to the farm sector. This supply of credit was restricted by the limited investment opportunities available. With rising commodity prices and a boom in exports, however, the federal agencies fueled an explosive growth in farm debt. As a result, farm investment in modern equipment, irrigation systems, and land exceeded the value of the resulting gains in productivity. In the 1980s, when the farm economy deteriorated due to high interest rates, declining food and

---

[8]Data apply to the beginning of 1986: *Annual Report of Farm Credit Administration and Cooperative Farm Credit System* (Washington, D.C.: Farm Credit Administration, 1987).

commodity prices, inflation, and the collapse of export markets, farmers could not support the huge debt overload taken on during the boom. All lenders suffered enormous losses. It is possible, however, that the crisis experienced in commercial banks would have been avoided had not government-supported credit lured farmers into assuming unprecedented burdens of debt.

Beginning in 1985, farm debt began to decline as farmers sought a way out of their excessively leveraged position. Between 1985 and 1992, farm credit market debt decreased by over $12 billion.

## REAL ESTATE LOANS

Except for savings institutions of all kinds, commercial banks lend more funds for the purchase, development, and construction of real estate properties than any other type of lender.

Table 14-3 lists the estimated value of residential mortgage debt outstanding, by types of holder, in March 1992. In early 1992, banks held $530 billion in residential mortgages outstanding, exclusive of mortgages held by bank trust departments. The bank holdings of mortgage debt represented 17 percent of the $3,105 billion in total residential mortgage debt outstanding held by all types of lenders.

**Table 14-3   Residential Mortgage Debt Outstanding, by Holder, March 1992 (dollars in billions)**

| Holder | One- to Four-Family | Multifamily | Total |
|---|---|---|---|
| Commercial banks | 492.8 | 37.7 | 530.5 |
| Savings institutions | 525.6 | 77.6 | 603.2 |
| Life insurance companies | 11.5 | 30.4 | 41.9 |
| Federal agencies | | | |
|   FmHA | 18.5 | 10.3 | 28.7 |
|   FHA/VA | 4.1 | 7.3 | 11.4 |
|   FNMA | 124.1 | 12.4 | 136.5 |
|   FHLMC | 26.2 | 2.7 | 28.9 |
|   Federal land banks | 2.3 | — | 2.3 |
| Mortgage pools and trusts | | | |
|   GNMA | 409.3 | 13.4 | 422.7 |
|   FHLMC | 360.9 | 7.0 | 367.9 |
|   FNMA | 380.6 | 9.3 | 389.9 |
| Individuals and others | 457.1 | 83.7 | 540.8 |
|    Total | 2,813.0 | 291.8 | 3,104.8 |

SOURCE: *Federal Reserve Bulletin* (November 1992).

Abbreviations: FmHA, Farmers Home Administration; FHA, Federal Housing Administration; VA, Veterans Administration; FNMA, Federal National Mortgage Association; FHLMC, Federal Home Loan Mortgage Association; GNMA, Government National Mortgage Association.

The $530 billion in mortgage debt held by banks in 1992 accounted for 31 percent of total bank loans outstanding of $1.9 trillion. However, the significance of mortgages in bank loan portfolios differed with the size of the bank. For large banks with assets of over $750 million, mortgages represented nearly 30 percent of loans, whereas they represented almost one-third of small banks' loans. For some small banks, particularly those located in developing suburban locations, mortgages often constituted well over half of their loan portfolios.

Residential mortgage loan originations fluctuate with the volume of new home construction and especially with the level of mortgage interest rates. Table 14-4 demonstrates that originations flourished in 1992 and 1993, when rates declined. As discussed subsequently, many mortgage loans are not held permanently by their originators. For example, mortgage bankers operate on turnover and quickly sell the mortgages they originate in the secondary market. At times, such as the 1992–1993 period, mortgage originations include a large number of refinancings as mortgagors pay off their old mortgages and simultaneously refinance their homes at lower interest rates. As shown in Table 14-4, refinancings surged during the low-rate period of 1991–1993.

The fraction of mortgages originated on an adjustable rate basis reflects mortgagors' interest rate expectations. As shown in Table 14-4, when mortgagors perceive that interest rates are relatively high, they prefer adjustable rate mortgages. At perceived low interest rates, they prefer fixed-rate mortgages.

## Legal Restrictions

National banks must conform to the requirements of 12 U.S. Code 371 governing real estate loans. This section of the code considers a loan to be a real estate loan if it is secured either by a lien (mortgage, deed of trust, or other) or

---

**Table 14-4  One- to Four-Family Mortgage Origination Activity, 1989–1994**

|  | 1989 | 1990 | 1991 | 1992 | *Forecast* 1993 | 1994 |
|---|---|---|---|---|---|---|
| One- to four-family mortgage originations (dollars in billions) | 483 | 453 | 540 | 825 | 800 | 710 |
| Mortgage interest rates (%) |  |  |  |  |  |  |
| Fixed | 10.12 | 10.13 | 9.24 | 8.36 | 7.97 | 7.31 |
| Adjustable | 8.80 | 8.36 | 7.10 | 5.48 | 5.16 | 5.43 |
| Refinancings (percent of total) | 19 | 16 | 30 | 38 | 38 | 20 |
| Adjustable rate (percent of loans closed) | 39 | 28 | 23 | 23 | 17 | 14 |

SOURCE: David Lereah, "Cautiously Optimistic," *Mortgage Banking* (January 1993), pp. 14–19.

by a leasehold agreement on the subject real estate and if its original maturity is at least 60 months. The code requires the following:

1. A loan on unimproved real estate must not exceed 66.67 percent of the property's appraised value.
2. A loan on real estate improved by a building must not exceed 90 percent of the property's appraised value.
3. Real estate loans generally should be fully amortized within 30 years.
4. Total real estate loans must not exceed the bank's capital plus unimpaired surplus or the bank's time and savings deposits, whichever is greater.
5. Total second mortgages plus the amount unpaid on all prior liens must not exceed 20 percent of the bank's capital plus unimpaired surplus.

The loan-to-value restrictions set forth in the code do not apply to government-insured or government-guaranteed mortgages or to privately insured mortgages.

### Residential Mortgages

As shown in Table 14-5, mortgages are classified by type of property. One- to four-family residential properties account for over one-half of bank mortgage loans. Mortgages on single-family residences make up most of these loans. Many banks appear to avoid permanent mortgage lending on large apartments and condominiums, preferring to leave such loans to life insurance companies or pension funds. Banks view apartments and condominiums as high risk and as requiring an imprudently large concentration of funds. To the extent that banks make such mortgages, they tend to be of relatively short maturity and at low loan–value ratios.

### Government-Backed Mortgages

Many residential mortgages held by banks are *conventional* loans, meaning that they are not insured or guaranteed by a government agency. However, a growing proportion are not conventional and are supported by government agencies. The Federal Housing Administration (FHA) insures and the Veterans

**Table 14-5   Commercial Bank Real Estate Debt Outstanding, 1992**

| Type of Property | Amount (dollars in billions) | Percent |
|---|---|---|
| One- to four-family residential | 492.8 | 56 |
| Multifamily residential | 37.7 | 4 |
| Commercial, construction, land development | 330.9 | 38 |
| Farm | 18.9 | 2 |
| Total | 880.3 | 100 |

Administration (VA) guarantees payment of principal and interest on certain qualifying residential mortgages originated by banks and other private lenders. FHA or VA backing is available for loans that meet certain standards, set periodically by the agencies involved, including the following:

1. Maximum loan–value ratio.
2. Interest rate restriction.
3. Maximum loan size.
4. Minimum down payment.

Residences that are subject to FHA- and VA-backed mortgages must also meet certain construction and design standards. These features reduce the risk of the subject mortgages, make them more attractive to lending institutions, and thereby increase the flow of mortgage funds. These same features also make it possible for lenders to accumulate a bundle of guaranteed or insured, standardized mortgages for sale either to larger institutional investors, the Federal National Mortgage Association (FNMA, or "Fannie Mae"), or the public by means of the Government National Mortgage Association (GNMA, or "Ginnie Mae"). The ability to package standardized loans helps banks to overcome the lack of marketability of small-denomination, single loans whose characteristics would otherwise be highly dissimilar.

**Secondary Markets**  The ability to sell their mortgages helps banks and S&Ls to avoid the problem of illiquidity associated with borrowing from short-term depositors and lending long term. Fannie Mae, a privately financed and managed association, developed the first resale market for mortgages. Although Fannie Mae was initially authorized to purchase and sell only FHA mortgages, it has become active in purchasing VA and, beginning in the 1970s, conventional loans. Actually, Fannie Mae does not create a pure secondary market, because it deals only in mortgages on which forward purchase commitments have been made. Banks and other institutions bid for Fannie Mae purchase commitments of a certain amount, and the commitment price is established at auction. Successful bidders acquire a commitment from Fannie Mae that assures them of a resale market for a bundle of loans to be made anytime up to the expiration date of the commitment.

Ginnie Mae is a government agency established in 1968 under the Department of Housing and Urban Development. Ginnie Mae shares with Fannie Mae the objective of making mortgages more liquid. Ginnie Mae developed the mortgage-backed *pass-through* security on which it guarantees the payment of principal and interest. To create a pass-through security issue, Ginnie Mae acquires pools of FHA and VA mortgages from banks and other lenders and uses the pools to back its securities. Payments to Ginnie Mae securities holders are passed through from payments made on the underlying pool of mortgages. Ginnie Mae's guarantee makes its securities attractive to investors who would not otherwise invest in the mortgage market. All of this activity increases the flow of money ultimately available to mortgage lenders.

The Federal Home Loan Mortgage Corporation (FHLMC, or "Freddie

Mac"), created in 1970, accomplishes for conventional mortgages what Ginnie Mae accomplished for FHA and VA mortgages. Like Ginnie Mae, Freddie Mac sells participations in mortgage pools and guarantees payment of interest and principal. But unlike Ginnie Mae, Freddie Mac deals in conventional mortgages and has truly advanced the marketability of these non-government-supported loans. Freddie Mac does, however, require private insurance on most mortgages in which it deals.

Among them, the three federal credit agencies—FNMA, GNMA, and FHLMC—are the biggest buyers of mortgages. These agencies buy mortgages and pool them either to sell shares in the pool or to issue securities that are backed by the pool as collateral.

In addition to the three mortgage associations, there exists a substantial interinstitutional market. Banks, S&Ls, and mutual savings banks are able to sell bundles of mortgages to larger banks, insurance companies, and other institutional investors.

During the 1980s, a huge secondary market developed based on mortgage-backed securities and derivatives of these securities. The basic mortgage-backed market consisted of over $1.2 trillion in marketable securities by 1993 and was continuing to grow. In Chapter 17 we discuss this market and the investment properties of the market's mortgage-derivative securities. We confine the discussion here to the basic mortgage instrument and the credit or underwriting standards observed by mortgage lenders.

**Credit Standards** Much of the impetus for the development of the huge mortgage-backed securities market was the 1980s environment of turbulent interest rates and soaring costs of interest-sensitive bank funds. In this threatening environment, banks continued to originate mortgages but deemphasized the holding of mortgages, selling them whenever they could. In essence, the secondary mortgage market produced a separation of mortgage origination, which is a regional activity, from mortgage funding, which has become national. As a result, the marketability of mortgages has become so important to banks that their mortgage loan standards increasingly call for conformance to the standards of the secondary market. The standards of the national mortgage associations and of institutional investors, described earlier, profoundly influence the approach banks take to mortgage lending.

Table 14-6 lists the primary credit underwriting standards observed by Freddie Mac, Fannie Mae, and the private mortgage insurance companies in 1993. The standards listed in Table 14-6 should not be viewed in absolute terms; a particularly favorable ratio may offset an unfavorable ratio. For example, lenders might accept a ratio of housing expense to owner's income that significantly exceeds 25 percent if the loan–value ratio is well below the maximum listed. This specific relationship is common in areas such as California, where housing values rose much faster than home buyers' incomes. If a home buyer's previous home has appreciated dramatically in price, he or she will probably be able to produce considerable equity for the purchase of the next home. In this case, a favorable loan–value ratio of 70 or 60 percent would

**Table 14-6    Credit Underwriting Standards for Mortgage Resale Organizations: One- to Four-Family Residential Properties (in effect March 1993)**

| Standard | FHLMC | FNMA | Private Mortgage Insurance Co. |
|---|---|---|---|
| Maximum loan amount[a] | 1 unit  $203,150<br>2 units $259,850<br>3 units $314,100<br>4 units $390,400 | 1 unit  $203,150<br>2 units $259,850<br>3 units $314,100<br>4 units $390,400 | No maximum |
| Loan–value ratio | | | |
| 1. Primary res. fixed | 95% | 95% | 95% |
|    ARM | 90% | 95% | 95% |
|    Refinance | 90% | | |
| 2. Secondary res. | 80% | | |
|    Refinance | 70% | | |
| 3. Non-owner occupied | Not accepted | 70% | 90% |
| Down payment minimum | 5% | 5% | 5% cash<br>or land equity |
| ARM | Accepted with (1) Annual rate cap (1% or 2%) or (2) life rate cap (normal, 6%)[b] | Accepts full range of ARMs. Standard is 2% annual and 6% life rate cap | Acceptability based on adjusted rate index, frequency of adjustment, and payment increase |
| Maximum ratio of housing expense to gross income[c] | 25–28% | 28% | 25–30% |
| Maximum monthly ratio of debt payment to income | 33–36% | 33–36% | 33–38% |

[a] Limits for FHLMC mortgages are 50% higher in Alaska, Guam, Hawaii, and the Virgin Islands.

[b] If the loan–value ratio is greater than 75%, the borrower must qualify for the maximum rate in year 2.

[c] Expense includes principal, interest, taxes, and homeowners association dues.

SOURCE: FHLMC, FNMA, Bank Administration Institute.

offset an abnormally large housing-expense–income ratio of 40 percent or more.

**Adjustable-Rate Mortgages**[9]    The standards listed in Table 14-6 are generally tied to traditional fixed-interest-rate and fixed-monthly-payment mortgages. Beginning in April 1981, however, legislators and federal regulators authorized wide use of the adjustable rate mortgage (ARM). Since then, during

[9] A good overview of ARM features and pricing is found in Frank E. Nothoft, Frank Veterans, and Michael K. Stamper, "Designing ARMs," *Secondary Mortgage Markets* (Winter 1987–1988), pp. 2–7.

periods when market interest rates have been abnormally high, as in the early 1980s, ARMs have tended to dominate mortgage financing. During low-rate periods, such as the one beginning in 1986, the ARM has all but disappeared as mortgagors have sought to lock in low fixed rates. When interest rates rise, as from the 1986 low, however, and the difference between adjustable and fixed rates widens, as it did in 1987 and 1988, borrowers shift quickly to ARMs with the expectation that interest rates will eventually fall again. In the late 1980s, a period of gently rising interest rates, banks and other lenders introduced attractive adjustable-rate pricing features to lure still more borrowers to ARMs.

By the end of the 1980s, borrowers were more knowledgeable about ARMs than they had been earlier in the decade. They needed to be more knowledgeable because lenders began to offer pricing structures with a dizzying menu of features, such as teaser rates, several adjustment period options, different margins, a variety of lifetime and periodic adjustment caps, and possible convertibility. *Teasers* are initial discounts that reduce monthly payments substantially, typically for the initial year. The rate adjustment period for ARMs is normally one year. Some lenders, however, offer three-year ARMs for which the rate is reset every third year. In a way, the three-year ARM is a compromise between the fixed-rate mortgage and the standard one-year ARM because its rate holds constant for a full three years.

Lenders may also vary the *margin*, defined as the amount added to the adjustment index (usually the one-year Treasury bill rate). A higher margin is sometimes used to offset the cost to the lender of a teaser rate. Lenders may also vary the adjustment caps offered on an ARM. A 2 percent cap (the one most often used) restricts the annual rate adjustment to 200 basis points. One percent caps are less frequently offered but are still common.

Lifetime rate caps restrict the amount that the interest rate can increase during the life of the loan. A lifetime cap of 6 percent is perhaps the most common. Lifetime interest rate ceilings will be used on all ARMs in the future in conformance with the Competitive Equality Banking Act of 1987.

An innovation introduced in 1987 was the convertible ARM. This type of ARM permits the borrower to convert an ARM to a fixed rate during a window in the life of the loan (e.g., between the second and fifth years). The major attraction of convertibility is the low cost of effectively refinancing, thereby avoiding the expense of actually paying the origination costs on a new mortgage after prepaying an old one.

The advantage of a wide variety of pricing features on ARMs is the flexibility it gives lenders and borrowers in tailoring the loan to the borrower's needs. For example, an initial discount (teaser) might be combined with a high margin to accommodate a young, low-income borrower who expects a rapid increase in earning power. On the other hand, this flexibility runs counter to the needs of the secondary market, which thrives on standardization. The federal agencies are particularly focused on creating a standardized ARM product that will develop market liquidity and be understood readily by the investor.

By the end of the 1980s, however, numerous pools of ARMs had been securitized and a deepening of the secondary market for ARMs seemed assured.

## Nonresidential Mortgages

Bank mortgages are made on commercial properties, consisting primarily of shopping centers, business and professional (e.g., medical or dental) office buildings, warehouses, hotels and motels, restaurants, and other commercial structures. Many such mortgages are direct extensions of banks' regular relationships with commercial customers (e.g., mortgage financing of a warehouse for a manufacturer who is a regular working capital loan customer).

In comparison with residential lending, most commercial mortgage financing by banks has shorter maturities (10 to 15 years) and smaller loan–value ratios (60 to 70 percent). Unlike residential mortgages, commercial mortgages have been based on variable interest rates for several years; typical rates float above the bank's prime rate.

## Construction Loans

Many commercial properties are permanently financed by nonbank lenders, especially life insurance companies and, to a lesser extent, private pension funds. Nevertheless, banks do a substantial volume of interim lending to finance the construction of these properties, as well as residential projects. Construction financing is a relatively high-risk activity. It often involves a large loan commitment over a period of time long enough to cover the planning, building, and final acceptance by owners or permanent lenders. Construction time is subject to many contingencies, including poor weather, materials shortages, and labor stoppages; on large projects, the construction time may be several years. In addition, faulty construction and underestimation of costs are common. Finally, building contractors tend to be very modestly capitalized in relation to the value of their construction projects and are, therefore, less cushioned against insolvency.

Construction lending can be classified into two types: loans for which a permanent takeout commitment exists and loans without a takeout. In situations with a takeout commitment, a long-term lender such as a life insurance company agrees to advance permanent funding on completion and acceptance of the construction. Interim construction loans usually require regular supervision, including site inspections, commitment takedowns against construction progress, and assurance that subcontractor and other claimants are satisfied. Long-term takeout lenders usually are not equipped to offer these services.

Banks must treat a construction loan that is not backed by a takeout commitment as they would treat a high-risk working capital loan. In a sense, the process of converting construction materials into a finished product is similar to a typical manufacturing process. However, a collateral position is frequently awkward. Contractors must usually post a performance bond, and the project collateral is normally subject to the claim of the bond's underwriter.

Because of their risks, construction loans are priced above most bank commercial loans. Commitment fees are 1 to 1.5 percent (instead of the 0.5 percent typical on commercial loans), and loan interest rates float at 2 percent or more over the prime rate.

# GUARANTEED SMALL BUSINESS LOANS

Small businesses represent enormous potential for bank lending, particularly for small banks. There are an estimated 14 million small business firms operating in the United States, and most of these firms must shop for borrowed funds at some time. In total, 99 percent of all firms in the United States are small, but they employ 57 percent of the private work force and account for 50 percent of domestic private production.

Unfortunately, because small firms are riskier borrowers than large, well-established firms, they have few alternative sources of credit. Historically, banks have loaned predominantly to the low-risk minority of small business firms. Business finance companies traditionally have loaned to select higher-risk firms at substantially higher interest rates than those on bank loans. However, with the establishment of the Small Business Administration (SBA) in 1953, another credit alternative became available in the form of guaranteed loans.

## SBA Loan Guarantee Program

The SBA offers a loan guarantee program in which a participating bank can obtain a guarantee up to 90 percent of the principal of a qualified small business loan. Currently, the SBA extends its 90 percent guarantee to a principal value of up to $500,000. In 1991 more than 19,000 SBA-guaranteed loans were made, for a total of $4.6 billion. The total dollar volume was projected at $6.0 billion for 1992.[10] However, until recently, many banks believed that participation in the SBA loan guarantee program was too inefficient to make it worth their effort. SBA guarantees were restricted to a narrow range of loan purposes. In addition, the SBA tied the interest rates on guaranteed loans closely to a base rate it determined in relation to its own borrowing rate and other factors. SBA application procedures and lengthy loan approval times further deterred bank participation.

Recently, however, SBA pricing and procedure rules have been greatly loosened and simplified. Interest rates on floating-rate loans can now be set up to 2.25 to 2.75 percent (depending on the maturity) over the prime rate. Loan types now vary from long-term, fixed-asset financing (504 programs) to

---

[10]Patricia Saiki, "The Advantages of Making Loans with the SBA," *Journal of Commercial Lending* (November 1992), pp. 18–22.

a pilot program line of credit with guarantees for up to five years (known as the *Green Line* program). Moreover, the approval process has been speeded up, partly through simplification and partly because the SBA now certifies participating banks to conduct the SBA's credit evaluation. This latter step eliminates the delays of sending the application forms to the SBA, waiting for the SBA to conduct its own evaluation, and waiting for the SBA to advise the bank of its approval or denial. These factors, and the increased liquidity due to the development of a secondary market, make SBA-guaranteed loans increasingly viable and profitable.

The present application procedure for SBA-guaranteed loans requires the borrower to complete several forms, including a detailed cash flow analysis. Although they appear quite technical, the requirements are no more stringent than those required by a conscientious bank loan officer from a borrower in applying for a conventional loan. The SBA typically responds with its decision in 7–10 days.

## Secondary Market

The SBA-guaranteed portions of loans are readily marketable. Qualified institutional investors are often eager to bid on the guaranteed portions at prices that provide them yields close to those of government-issued securities. Banks retain the nonguaranteed portions of the loans and continue to service them for an attractive fee. The economics of this transaction often are quite favorable to the originating bank.

To illustrate this process, suppose that the bank makes a $500,000 SBA 90 percent guaranteed loan and sells the guaranteed portion of $450,000. Furthermore, suppose that the loan is priced at a fixed rate of 2 percent over a prime rate of 6 percent at a time when short-term U.S. Treasury bills are yielding 4.5 percent. Investors might thereby bid for the 90 percent guaranteed portion at a price that yields 5 percent. At that yield to investors, the bank will collect a guaranteed spread of 3 percent (8 − 5 percent) on the entire guaranteed portion of the loan just for servicing the loan. In addition, of course, the bank will continue to earn 8 percent on the nonguaranteed 10 percent of the loan that it still owns. As shown in Table 14-7, this arrangement yields a 35 percent overall return on bank funds invested in the loan.

Although the loan terms appear extremely favorable to the bank, the rates and servicing spreads shown are achievable. In addition, compensating balances requirements might be included in the final loan agreement. The inclusion of compensating balances as an offset to the net amount of bank funds invested would increase the yield to the bank even more.

The extraordinary yields possible with making and selling SBA guarantees readily illustrate the distortion that results from market intervention. In the present case, public policy implemented through the SBA calls for diverting funds to high-risk, small firms from other uses of funds. The high yields indicated provide a powerful incentive for banks to allocate funds to SBA-guaranteed loans to small business.

**Table 14-7    Yield on a $500,000 SBA-Guaranteed Loan Sold in the Secondary Market**

| | | |
|---|---|---|
| Income | | |
| $450,000 at 3% | = | $13,500 |
| 50,000 at 8% | = | 4,000 |
| Total | | $17,500 |
| Bank funds invested | = | 50,000 |
| Gross yield to bank | = | $\dfrac{17,500}{50,000} = 35\%$ |

The marketability of SBA-guaranteed loans received a boost when the SBA began to securitize these loans. As with securitization in the mortgage and consumer markets, the SBA pools loans and sells pay-through-type securities that are supported and serviced by the underlying loan pool. Chapter 17 reviews loan securitizations in greater depth, including their prepayment and pricing characteristics.

The ability to sell SBA loans provides banks with immediate liquidity and frees up bank funds to make additional loans. The guaranteed portions of SBA loans are government obligations and can be eliminated from the bank's loan portfolio for the purpose of determining legal capital requirements. Also, the guaranteed portions do not have to be counted against regulatory loan limits. Thus, regulators permit loans to be made that are larger than legal lending limits because the government guarantees amounts in excess of the limits.

## LEASE FINANCING

Lease financing by banks is a unique means of funding a firm's need for capital equipment without actually lending to the firm. Like term loans, leases typically give the lessee firm the use of an asset over most of the asset's life and, in addition, include the right to purchase the asset at the expiration of the lease term. The distinction between a term loan to purchase equipment and a lease covering the same equipment is formalized in the Federal Reserve's Regulation Y, which restricts leasing by bank holding companies to situations in which the lease is the "functional equivalent to an extension of credit." Types of assets that are commonly leased include the following:

- Computers.
- Production machinery.
- Transportation equipment.
- Pollution control equipment.
- Medical equipment.
- Material-handling machinery.
- Oil drilling equipment.

## Financial versus Operating Leases

The principle of leasing recognizes that it is the use of an asset that gives it value, and not ownership of the asset. In a lease agreement, the lessor owns equipment that it makes available for the lessee's use in return for rental fees and possibly other benefits. There are two basic types of leases—financial and operating; however, banks can offer only financial leases.

In a *financial lease*, the lessor expects to recover the entire acquisition cost of the leased asset plus a profit. The lessor's proceeds include the rental fees, salvage value, and, either directly or indirectly, tax benefits due to investment tax credits and tax deferrals from accelerated depreciation. Financial leases are not cancelable by either party, and they are usually *net* leases, which means that the lessee is responsible for maintenance, insurance, and applicable taxes. To qualify as a financial lease (and not a sale) under the rules of the Internal Revenue Service (IRS), the lease should include (1) an option for the lessee to buy the asset, usually at fair market value, (2) a lease term not exceeding 30 years, and (3) rental payments that provide a reasonable rate of return to the lessor. Qualification as a financial lease and not a sale, according to the IRS, is necessary to enable the lessee to deduct as expense the full amount of rental payments.

*Operating leases*, on the other hand, are cancelable and do not bind the lessee for a long period. Their term is significantly shorter than the asset's economic life. Also, unlike the arrangement with the financial lease, the lessor is responsible for maintenance, insurance, and applicable taxes.

For many years, banks could not hold an equity position in real earning property. Finally, in 1963, the Comptroller of the Currency authorized national banks to own and lease real property; subsequently, the Federal Reserve extended the same privilege to bank holding companies. Bank acquisitions of real earning assets can occur only in response to a customer's request to enter into a financial lease agreement. Banks are specifically forbidden to acquire real assets in anticipation of unidentified customers' leasing needs.

## Forms of Bank Participation in Lease Financing

The value of direct-lease financing by banks in 1992 totaled $39 billion. This activity took place in two basic forms: straight leases and leveraged leases.

**Straight Leasing**   The most straightforward form of leasing is the direct lease, in which the bank provides 100 percent financing. The customer firm develops specifications for an asset needed in its operations. The customer then determines the manufacturer or dealer that is best able to supply the asset and makes arrangements for a purchase. Then the bank acquires the asset, which is delivered to the customer; simultaneously, the bank completes an agreement to lease the asset to the customer.

Most often, this type of leasing negotiation evolves out of a total banking relationship with an established customer. However, some leasing deals are developed by brokers who bring together a client needing to lease equipment and a bank willing to participate. A broker relationship might be especially good for a bank that does not have loan officers experienced with leasing.

Banks also get involved in a modified form of lease financing through leasing companies. In this approach, the bank does not take an ownership position in the asset. The leasing company acquires the asset, using bank loan funds, and then leases the asset to a client. The lessor pledges the asset against its loan through a security agreement and also pledges the lease revenues.

**Leveraged Leasing**  A somewhat more sophisticated form of leasing in which banks may engage is leveraged leasing. Typically, a bank holding company affiliate acts as the lessor and sets up an ownership trust, which acquires an asset to be leased. The holding company provides only a small part of the funds for purchase of the asset, and the trust borrows the remaining funds from an institutional lender such as an insurance company. The holding company funds represent the equity investment and must be at least 20 percent of the cost of the asset. In other words, the purchase is leveraged with up to 80 percent borrowed funds.

The institutions providing the debt funds to the trust do not have recourse to the holding company bank (lessor). They look to the ability of the lessee to make rental payments and to the collateral value of the asset. To the bank holding company, the profitability of leveraged leasing is heavily affected by the tax benefits of owning the asset. The principal tax benefits are the investment tax credit and the tax deductibility of accelerated depreciation and interest on borrowed funds. In relation to the amount of equity invested, these benefits are multiplied by leveraging with debt. Generally, the tax benefits of ownership are more significant to the bank holding company than to the lessee, and the benefits are passed through to the lessee in the form of lower lease rental payments. For example, a public hospital (nontaxable) lessee would benefit from leveraged leased medical equipment because of tax advantages that accrue to the lessor and are passed on through reduced costs of leasing. On the other hand, if the lessee is able to take full advantage of the tax benefits, there may be little financial advantage in leveraged leasing.

## SUMMARY

Our discussion of several special- or narrow-purpose loan markets centered on the uniqueness of each. For example, international L/C services involve a unique type of commitment financing conditioned on individual trade transactions. Moreover, when a time L/C is used, the bank's commitment may be made negotiable and sold as a banker's acceptance. Real estate loans, SBA-guaranteed loans, and agricultural loans are all strongly influenced by the unique role played by government or quasi-government agencies in markets for these loans. Direct-lease financing actually does not entail a loan per se but creates a rental agreement.

However, most of the general loan principles and considerations presented in Chapters 11 and 12 are readily applicable to each of these loan markets. First, the borrower's character and ability to pay are always a central issue. In each lending category we have discussed, an unscrupulous and determined borrower can defraud the bank of loan funds.

Second, the primary source of repayment must be carefully evaluated, as it is the basis of any loan. For example, a mortgagee must demonstrate that his or her monthly income is an adequate multiple of the proposed monthly mortgage payment. Also, an importer using international time L/C services must be able to resell imported goods promptly to cover any credit received. SBA-guaranteed borrowers must offer a source of loan repayment derived from business operations. Farm borrowers must be expected to generate funds for loan repayment out of crop or livestock production.

Finally, secondary sources of repayment in the form of collateral are important in almost all loan markets. For example, the appraised value of a home is the secondary source of repayment in the event of default on a home mortgage. In lease agreements, the equipment being leased is already the bank's asset and can be liquidated for value should the lessee fail to meet rental payments. Farmers put up their equipment or real estate as secondary sources of loan recovery should they fail to produce saleable agricultural commodities.

It is clear that different markets for bank loans have unique and sometimes technical factors that differentiate them and require loan officers with narrow expertise. However, general lending factors such as those discussed in this chapter are common to all loan situations and are the basis for most loan decisions.

## Discussion Questions

1. What is the significance of revocability versus irrevocability and confirmed versus unconfirmed designations for international L/Cs?
2. Describe the steps that lead to the creation of a banker's acceptance.
3. Describe the transactions in the forward foreign exchange market through which an American exporter can hedge the value of export sales to a foreign buyer when the sale is denominated in the buyer's currency.
4. Explain how the credit evaluation of a foreign borrower is analogous to evaluating the basic credit factors for a business borrower.
5. It has been said that agricultural loans must be supported by the farmer's income statement and not the farmer's balance sheet, as was the case in the past. Explain.
6. Distinguish among the roles played in the mortgage market by the FHA, VA, GNMA, FNMA, and FHLMC.
7. "Alternative mortgage instruments might simply substitute credit risk for interest rate risk in the bank." Explain.
8. In lending on major commercial properties, why don't permanent lenders,

such as life insurance companies and pension funds, also provide the interim funds used during the construction stage?

9. What are a bank's risk–reward trade-offs of lending to small business under the SBA-guaranteed loan program? How do these trade-offs compare with conventional working capital line-of-credit lending?

10. Distinguish between financial and operating leases.

11. Why might leveraged leasing be more attractive to bankers than straight leasing?

## CASE 11 ATHLETEQUIP COMPANY, INC.

### BACKGROUND

Athletequip Company was founded in Toledo, Ohio, in 1964 as a partnership by Mr. Charles O. Ball and Mr. Clark L. Alexander. Mr. Alexander died in 1969, leaving his share of the partnership to his wife, Sharon, who sold it back to Charles Ball. Mr. Ball continued the business with the assistance of his wife, Elizabeth, and his two sons, Gregory and Phillip, who were then students of business administration at the local state university. The company was incorporated in 1974, with Charles Ball as president and Gregory and Phillip, who had at that time completed their degrees, as vice-president and treasurer, respectively. In 1979 the Balls moved the business to Alhambra, California, its present site. The elder Ball died in 1980, leaving the bulk of his estate—and controlling interest in the company—to his wife and sons.

Athletequip, Inc., was engaged in the manufacture of athletic garments, specializing in uniforms and jackets. About half of the inventory on hand usually consisted of football practice pants, with the balance consisting of yardage goods and goods-in-process on firm purchase orders. Because of the nature of these products, a substantial portion of sales was made on a specific order basis, with orders taken throughout the year as institutions were able to anticipate their needs. This enabled the company to maintain a fairly level production cycle.

Goods were distributed throughout the United States. Sales were made to sporting goods stores and directly to high schools and colleges. Although the market was highly competitive, Athletequip had been quite successful, particularly in the area of football uniforms. Of the 1,330 U.S. colleges that play football, Athletequip outfitted 330 teams. In fact, the company estimated that it manufactured at least 25 percent of all football game pants used in the country last year.

Selling terms extended by Athletequip were 3/10–net 30 to stores, and extended terms were given to high schools and colleges, with those invoices being payable in October of each year.

The company employed 89 persons and had 6 salesmen on commission and salary.

### MANAGEMENT

Gregory S. Ball assumed the presidency of the company upon the death of his father in 1980. At that time he was 31 years old and had been involved in the company for 11 years. In spite of his youth, he had shown great skill in his trade, and under his direction, Athletequip had grown in the past 12 years from a company with total assets of $238,000 and net sales of $756,000 to one with $698,000 in total assets and $1,727,000 in net sales.

Phillip M. Ball had served as vice-president and chief financial officer since 1980. Currently 39, he was highly regarded in the industry for his integrity and entrepreneurship.

John T. Ryan, age 36, joined the company in 1985 as sales manager. He held a BBA in marketing from California State University and, upon coming to Athletequip, had 12 years' sales experience with a nationally known firm.

The company was well thought of in the community, and the Ball brothers were actively involved in both civic and business organizations.

### BANK RELATIONSHIPS

Athletequip, Inc., had been a customer of the Third First State Bank in Alhambra since the company's arrival in 1979. However, ownership of that bank changed hands about six months ago, accompanied by a change in management personnel. Therefore, those familiar with the principals of Athletequip, Inc., were no longer with the bank.

There was also some question regarding the Third First Bank's ability to meet the increasing credit requirements of the company, as these would likely exceed the bank's legal lending limit.

Athletequip had inquired at various times regarding services such as payroll and account reconciliation; however, the bank's response had been largely unsatisfactory.

Athletequip, Inc., had been a long-time prospect of the Commerce National Bank in Alhambra and had now requested that Commerce establish a $550,000 line of credit to be used in expanding its operations. The company rented office and plant facilities of approximately 45,000 square feet from a partnership owned by the Balls; however, operating capacity in the present location had been reached, and Athletequip needed to move in the near future. The cost of a new plant and equipment would approximate $400,000, and plans for financing would be considered at a future time.

## FINANCIAL INFORMATION

Financial statements of Athletequip, Inc., for the past three calendar years are presented in Exhibits 1–4. Changes in the equity section reflect the purchase by the company from Elizabeth Ball of 700 shares of $10 par value stock for $50 per share. For inheritance tax purposes, Mrs. Ball is contemplating disposal of all of her stock within the next few years. The credit report on the company and its principals appears in Exhibit 5, and industry comparisons are shown in Exhibit 6.

## QUESTIONS

1. Consider the loan as requested. Include in the presentation the use of ratios, a source and application of funds statement, reconcilement of net worth, and a basic trend and comparative analysis.

2. Upon conclusion of the analysis, the bank will meet with the principals of Athletequip, Inc., at which time additional information may be obtained. Consider the types of questions to be asked and additional information to be requested, as well as the bank's position in regard to the loan request.

## EXHIBIT 1    Athletequip Company, Inc.—Balance Sheet (Prepared without Audit)

| | *End of Year* | | |
| | 1992 | 1991 | 1990 |
| --- | --- | --- | --- |
| **Assets** | | | |
| Current Assets | | | |
| Cash | $ 55,251 | $ 67,261 | $ 97,397 |
| Accounts receivable—less allowance for bad debts | 169,734 | 139,442 | 107,553 |
| Inventory | 301,184 | 295,498 | 242,674 |
| Prepaid expenses | 5,272 | 4,012 | 2,120 |
| | $531,441 | $506,213 | $449,744 |

**EXHIBIT I**  *(continued)*

| | End of Year | | |
| --- | --- | --- | --- |
| | **1992** | **1991** | **1990** |
| Fixed Assets | | | |
| Machinery and equipment | $189,412 | $162,937 | $140,739 |
| Automobiles and trucks | 14,303 | 14,545 | 14,545 |
| Office furniture and equipment | 42,228 | 27,042 | 23,474 |
| Leasehold improvements | 73,688 | 74,413 | 73,025 |
| | $319,631 | $278,937 | $251,783 |
| Less allowance for depreciation and amortization | 164,686 | 137,954 | 103,939 |
| | $154,945 | $140,983 | $147,844 |
| Other Assets | 11,436 | 13,336 | 9,474 |
| Total Assets | $697,822 | $660,532 | $607,062 |
| **Liabilities and Stockholders' Equity** | | | |
| Current Liabilities | | | |
| Accounts payable | $ 88,110 | $ 79,621 | $ 80,027 |
| Notes payable—secured—Alhambra State Bank— portion due within one year | 2,125 | 8,500 | 8,500 |
| Contracts payable—autos—portion due within one year | 2,846 | 1,217 | 4,287 |
| Accrued taxes | 14,210 | 18,000 | 17,458 |
| Accrued expenses | 54,464 | 11,003 | 29,997 |
| Deferred income | | 450 | 450 |
| Federal taxes on income payable | 10,075 | 45,498 | 27,969 |
| | $171,830 | $164,289 | $168,688 |
| Other Liabilities | | | |
| Contracts payable—auto—portion due after one year | 949 | | 1,217 |
| Notes payable—Elizabeth Ball | 35,000 | | |
| Notes payable—secured—Alhambra State Bank— portion due after one year | | 3,125 | 10,625 |
| | $ 35,949 | $ 3,125 | $ 11,842 |
| Total Liabilities | 144,789 | $167,414 | $180,530 |
| Stockholders' Equity | | | |
| Capital stock—common—authorized 20,000 shares of $10.00 par value per share | $ 93,000 | $100,000 | $100,000 |
| Paid-in surplus | | 586 | 586 |
| Retained earnings | 397,043 | 392,532 | 325,946 |
| | 490,043 | $493,118 | $426,532 |
| Total Liabilities and Stockholders' Equity | $697,822 | $660,532 | $607,062 |

**EXHIBIT 2  Athletequip Company, Inc.—Statement of Earnings (Prepared without Audit)**

Year Ending

| | 1992 | | 1991 | | | 1990 | | |
|---|---|---|---|---|---|---|---|---|
| | Dollars | % of Sales | Dollars | % of Sales | Increase or Decrease | Dollars | % of Sales | Increase or Decrease |
| Sales | $1,726,769 | 100.00 | $1,739,224 | 100.00 | $(12,455) | $1,607,121 | 100.00 | $132,103 |
| Cost of Sales | 1,093,130 | 63.30 | 1,081,909 | 62.21 | 11,221 | 1,036,048 | 64.47 | 45,861 |
| Gross Profit on Sales | 633,639 | 36.70 | 657,315 | 37.79 | (23,676) | 571,073 | 35.53 | 86,242 |
| Operating Expenses | | | | | | | | |
| Advertising | 37,793 | 2.19 | 26,154 | 1.50 | 11,639 | 29,081 | 1.81 | (2,927) |
| Depreciation and amortization | 33,001 | 1.91 | 34,015 | 1.96 | (1,014) | 27,585 | 1.72 | 6,430 |
| Discounts on sales | 36,743 | 2.13 | 36,460 | 2.10 | 283 | 31,739 | 1.98 | 4,721 |
| Employees' profit-sharing plan | 28,000 | 1.62 | 25,966 | 1.49 | 2,034 | 20,000 | 1.24 | 5,966 |
| Factory supplies and expense | 11,123 | .64 | 17,477 | 1.01 | (6,354) | 21,682 | 1.35 | (4,205) |
| Insurance | 21,150 | 1.22 | 20,478 | 1.18 | 672 | 16,275 | 1.01 | 4,203 |
| Outside sales commissions | 65,636 | 3.80 | 62,518 | 3.59 | 3,118 | 62,827 | 3.91 | (309) |
| Rent—net | 60,425 | 3.50 | 59,586 | 3.43 | 839 | 48,524 | 3.02 | 11,062 |
| Salaries | 145,778 | 8.44 | 132,069 | 7.59 | 13,709 | 116,080 | 7.22 | 15,989 |
| Taxes | 44,587 | 2.58 | 37,661 | 2.17 | 6,926 | 36,316 | 2.26 | 1,345 |
| Travel and entertainment | 38,607 | 2.24 | 29,721 | 1.71 | 8,886 | 22,278 | 1.39 | 7,443 |
| Other | 76,193 | 4.41 | 69,834 | 4.02 | 6,359 | 68,772 | 4.28 | 1,062 |
| | 599,036 | 34.68 | 551,938 | 31.73 | 47,098 | 501,159 | 31.18 | 50,779 |
| Net Earnings from Operations | $ 34,603 | 2.00 | $ 105,377 | 31.73 | $(70,774) | $ 69,914 | 4.35 | $ 35,463 |
| Other Income | $ 5,983 | .35 | $ 6,707 | .38 | $ (724) | $ 6,687 | .42 | 20 |
| Net Earnings before Provision for Federal Taxes on Income | $ 40,586 | 2.35 | $ 112,084 | 6.44 | $(71,498) | $ 76,601 | 4.77 | $ 35,483 |
| Provision for Federal Taxes on Income | 10,075 | .58 | 45,498 | 2.61 | (35,423) | 27,969 | 1.74 | 17,529 |
| Net Earnings | $ 30,511 | 1.77 | $ 66,586 | 3.83 | $(36,075) | $ 48,632 | 3.03 | $ 17,954 |

**EXHIBIT 3   Athletequip Company, Inc.—Statement of Cost of Sales (Prepared without Audit)**

| | 1992 | | 1991 | | | 1990 | | |
| --- | --- | --- | --- | --- | --- | --- | --- | --- |
| | Dollars | % of Sales | Dollars | % of Sales | Increase or Decrease | Dollars | % of Sales | Increase or Decrease |
| Opening inventory | $ 295,498 | 17.1 | $ 242,674 | 14.0 | $ 52,824 | $ 221,284 | 13.8 | $21,390 |
| Purchases | 528,647 | 30.6 | 539,426 | 31.0 | (10,779) | 518,331 | 32.3 | 21,095 |
| Supplies | 71,141 | 4.1 | 88,992 | 5.1 | (17,851) | 75,994 | 4.7 | 12,998 |
| Labor—plant | 427,983 | 24.8 | 435,010 | 25.0 | (7,027) | 397,517 | 24.7 | 37,493 |
| Outside work | 71,044 | 4.1 | 71,306 | 4.1 | (262) | 65,595 | 4.1 | 5,711 |
| | $1,394,313 | 80.7 | $1,377,408 | 79.2 | $ 16,905 | $1,278,721 | 79.6 | $98,687 |
| Closing inventory | 301,184 | 17.4 | 295,498 | 17.0 | 5,686 | 242,674 | 15.1 | 52,824 |
| Cost of sales | $1,093,129 | 63.3 | $1,081,910 | 62.2 | $11,219 | $1,036,047 | 64.5 | $45,863 |

## EXHIBIT 4A  General Spread Form—Athletequip Company, Inc. (in thousands of dollars)

| NAME | ATHLETEQUIP COMPANY, INC. | | | |
|------|-----------|----------|----------|----------|
| 1 AUDITED STATEMENT | | No | No | No |
| 2 STATEMENT DATE | | 12-31-90 | 12-31-91 | 12-31-92 |
| 3 CASH | | 97 | 67 | 55 |
| 4 MARKETABLE SECURITIES | | | | |
| 5 NOTES RECEIVABLE | | | | |
| 6 ACCOUNTS RECEIVABLE | | 108 | 139 | 170 |
| 7 INVENTORY | | 243 | 295 | 301 |
| 8 | | | | |
| 9 | | | | |
| 10 | | | | |
| 11 ALLOW. FOR DOUBT. ACCT. | | | | |
| 12 TOTAL CURRENT ASSETS | | 448 | 501 | 526 |
| 13 FIXED ASSETS—NET | | 148 | 141 | 155 |
| 14 NON-MARKETABLE SECURITIES | | | | |
| 15 NONCURRENT RECEIVABLES | | | | |
| 16 PREPAID AND DEFERRED EXPENSES | | 2 | 4 | 6 |
| 17 OTHER ASSETS | | 9 | 14 | 11 |
| 18 | | | | |
| 19 | | | | |
| 20 | | | | |
| 21 INTANGIBLES | | | | |
| 22 TOTAL NONCURRENT ASSETS | | 159 | 159 | 172 |
| 23 TOTAL ASSETS (12 + 22) | | 607 | 660 | 698 |
| 24 CURRENT MTY. OF TERM DEBT | | 13 | 10 | 5 |
| 25 NOTES PAYABLE | | | | |
| 26 ACCOUNTS PAYABLE | | 80 | 80 | 88 |
| 27 ACCRUED EXPENSE & MISC. | | 47 | 29 | 69 |
| 28 NOTE PAYABLE—ELIZ. BALL | | | | 35 |

| # | Item | | | |
|---|------|---|---|---|
| 29 | | | | |
| 30 | | | | |
| 31 | INCOME TAX LIABILITY | 28 | 45 | 10 |
| 32 | TOTAL CURRENT LIABILITIES | 168 | 164 | 207 |
| 33 | TERM DEBT | 12 | 2 | 1 |
| 34 | | | | |
| 35 | SUBORDINATED DEBT | | | |
| 36 | TOTAL LIABILITIES (32 + 33 + 34 + 35) | 181 | 166 | 208 |
| 37 | MINORITY INTEREST | | | |
| 38 | DEFERRED INCOME/RESERVES | | | |
| 39 | TREASURY STOCK | | | |
| 40 | PREFERRED STOCK OUTSTANDING | | | |
| 41 | COMMON STOCK OUTSTANDING | 100 | 100 | 93 |
| 42 | CAPITAL SURPLUS | 1 | 1 | — |
| 43 | RETAINED EARNINGS (DEFICIT) | 326 | 393 | 397 |
| 44 | | | | |
| 45 | | | | |
| 46 | NET WORTH (39 thru 45) | 427 | 494 | 490 |
| 47 | TANGIBLE NET WORTH (46 − 21) | 427 | 494 | 490 |
| 48 | WORKING CAPITAL (12–32) | 280 | 337 | 319 |
| 49 | CUR. ASSETS LESS TOT. LIAB. | 267 | 335 | 318 |
| 50 | CURRENT RATIO (12–32) | 2.7 | 3.1 | 2.5 |
| 51 | CASH, MKT. SEC. & A/R TO CUR. LIAB. | 1.2 | 1.3 | 1.1 |
| 52 | A/R COLLECTION PERIOD—DAYS | 24 | 29 | 35 |
| 53 | NET SALES TO INVENTORY | 6.6 | 5.9 | 5.7 |
| 54 | COST OF SALES TO INVENTORY | 4.3 | 3.7 | 3.6 |
| 55 | INVENTORY TO WORKING CAPITAL | .87 | .88 | .94 |
| 56 | SR. DEBT ÷ (TANG. N.W. & SUB. DEBT) | .42 | .34 | .42 |
| 57 | NET PROFIT (LOSS) TO AVG. NET WORTH | .11 | .15 | .06 |

# EXHIBIT 4A   (continued)

NAME   ATHLETEQUIP COMPANY, INC.

| | 12 mos | % | 12 mos | % | 12 mos | % |
|---|---|---|---|---|---|---|
| 58 PERIOD COVERED (MONTHS) | | | | | | |
| STATEMENT DATE | 12-31-90 | % | 12-31-91 | % | 12-31-92 | % |
| 59 NET SALES | 1,607 | | 1,739 | | 1, | |
| 60 COST OF SALES | 1,036 | 65 | 1,082 | 62 | 1,093 | 63 |
| 61 GROSS PROFIT | 571 | 36 | 657 | 38 | 634 | 37 |
| 62 SELLING EXPENSES | 146 | | 155 | | 169 | |
| 63 GENERAL & ADMINISTRATIVE EXP. | 355 | | 397 | | 430 | |
| 64 TOTAL OPERATING EXPENSES (62 + 63) | 501 | | 552 | 32 | 599 | 35 |
| 65 OPERATING PROFIT (61 – 64) | 70 | | 105 | 6 | 35 | 2 |
| 66 OTHER INCOME (EXPENSE)—NET | 7 | | 7 | | 6 | |
| 67 NET PROFIT (LOSS) BEFORE TAXES | 77 | | 112 | 6 | 41 | 2 |
| 68 INCOME TAXES | 28 | | 45 | 3 | 10 | |
| 69 NET PROFIT (LOSS) AFTER TAXES | 49 | | 67 | 4 | 31 | 2 |
| ADDITIONAL DATA | | | | | | |
| 70 DIVIDENDS—PREFERRED STOCK | | | | | | |
| 71 DIVIDENDS—COM. STOCK OR WITHDRAW | | | | | | |
| 72 OFFICER REMUNERATION | | | | | | |
| 73 INTEREST EXPENSE | | | | | | |
| 74 OTHER CHANGES IN WORTH (80 thru 83) | | | | | | |
| 75 CONTINGENT LIABILITIES | | | | | | |
| 76 LEASE OBLIGATIONS | | | | | | |
| ANALYSIS OF CHANGES IN WORTH OR SURPLUS | | | | | | |
| 77 AT BEGINNING OF PERIOD | | | 427 | | 494 | |
| 78 ADD NET PROFIT | | | 67 | | 31 | |
| 79 DEDUCT DIVIDENDS OR WITHDRAW. | | | | | | |
| 80 TREAS. STK.—PURCH. & CANCEL'D | | | | | (35) | |

| Line | Description | | | |
|---|---|---|---|---|
| 81 | | | | |
| 82 | | | | |
| 83 | | | | |
| 84 | WORTH OR SURPLUS REPORTED (46) | | 494 | 490 |
| | **ANALYSIS OF WORKING CAPITAL** | | | |
| 85 | AT BEGINNING OF PERIOD | | 280 | 337 |
| 86 | ADD: NET PROFIT | 49 | 67 | 31 |
| 87 | NON-CASH CHARGES | 28 | 34 | 33 |
| 88 | DECR. OTHER DEF'D ASSETS | | | 1 |
| 89 | | | | |
| 90 | | | | |
| 91 | MISCELLANEOUS | | | |
| 92 | TOTAL ADDITIONS (86 thru 91) | 77 | 101 | 65 |
| 93 | DEDUCT: | | | |
| 94 | DIVIDENDS/WITHDRAWALS | | | |
| 95 | PLANT EXPENDITURES | | 27 | 47 |
| 96 | CANCEL TREAS. STK | | | 35 |
| 97 | INCR. OTHER DEF'D ASSETS | | 7 | |
| 98 | DECR. DEF'D LIABILITIES | | 10 | 1 |
| 99 | MISCELLANEOUS | | | |
| 100 | TOTAL DEDUCTIONS (93 thru 99) | | 44 | 83 |
| 101 | NET CHANGE (+ OR −) (92 − 100) | | +57 | (18) |
| 102 | AT END OF PERIOD (85 + 101) | 280 | 337 | 319 |
| 103 | | | | |
| 104 | W/C AS ABOVE (102 same as 48) | 280 | 337 | 319 |
| 105 | INVENTORY | 243 | 295 | 301 |
| 106 | W/C LESS INVENTORY (104 − 105) | 37 | 42 | 18 |
| | ANALYST INITIALS | JEB | JEB | JEB |

**EXHIBIT 4B    General Spread Form**

NAME    ATHLETEQUIP COMPANY, INC. (in thousands of dollars)

| | 12-31-91 | 3-31-92 | 6-30-92 | 9-30-92 | 12-31-92 |
|---|---|---|---|---|---|
| 1 AUDITED STATEMENT | No | No | No | No | No |
| 2 STATEMENT DATE | 12-31-91 | 3-31-92 | 6-30-92 | 9-30-92 | 12-31-92 |
| 3 CASH | 67 | 1 | 4 | 1 | 55 |
| 4 MARKETABLE SECURITIES | | | | | |
| 5 NOTES RECEIVABLE | | | | | |
| 6 ACCOUNTS RECEIVABLE | 139 | 443 | 567 | 844 | 170 |
| 7 INVENTORY | 295 | 217 | 257 | 219 | 301 |
| 8 | | | | | |
| 9 | | | | | |
| 10 | | | | | |
| 11 ALLOW. FOR DOUBT. ACCT. | | | | | |
| 12 TOTAL CURRENT ASSETS | 501 | 661 | 828 | 1,064 | 526 |
| 13 FIXED ASSETS—NET | 141 | 140 | 139 | 145 | 155 |
| 14 NON-MARKETABLE SECURITIES | | | | | |
| 15 NONCURRENT RECEIVABLES | | | | | |
| 16 PREPAID AND DEFERRED EXPENSES | 4 | 9 | 16 | 8 | 5 |
| 17 OTHER ASSETS | 14 | 11 | 11 | 11 | 11 |
| 18 | | | | | |
| 19 | | | | | |
| 20 | | | | | |
| 21 INTANGIBLES | | 1 | 1 | 1 | |
| 22 TOTAL NONCURRENT ASSETS | 159 | 161 | 167 | 165 | 171 |
| 23 TOTAL ASSETS (12 + 22) | 660 | 822 | 995 | 1,229 | 697 |
| 24 CURRENT MTY. OF TERM DEBT | 10 | | | | 5 |
| 25 NOTES PAYABLE | | 145 | 279 | 443 | |
| 26 ACCOUNTS PAYABLE | 80 | 64 | 96 | 125 | 88 |
| 27 ACCRUED EXPENSE & MISC. | 29 | 11 | 5 | 19 | 69 |
| 28 NOTE PAYABLE—ELIZ. BALL | | | | | 35 |

| # | | Col 1 | Col 2 | Col 3 | Col 4 | Col 5 |
|---|---|---|---|---|---|---|
| 29 | | | | | | |
| 30 | | | | | | |
| 31 | INCOME TAX LIABILITY | 45 | 64 | 59 | 70 | 10 |
| 32 | TOTAL CURRENT LIABILITIES | 164 | 284 | 439 | 657 | 207 |
| 33 | TERM DEBT | 2 | 5 | 2 | 2 | 1 |
| 34 | | | | | | |
| 35 | SUBORDINATED DEBT | | | | | |
| 36 | TOTAL LIABILITIES (32 + 33 + 34 + 35) | 166 | 289 | 441 | 659 | 208 |
| 37 | MINORITY INTEREST | | | | | |
| 38 | DEFERRED INCOME/RESERVES | | | | | |
| 39 | TREASURY STOCK | | | | | |
| 40 | PREFERRED STOCK OUTSTANDING | | | | | |
| 41 | COMMON STOCK OUTSTANDING | 100 | 100 | 100 | 100 | 93 |
| 42 | CAPITAL SURPLUS | 1 | 1 | 1 | 1 | |
| 43 | RETAINED EARNINGS (DEFICIT) | 393 | 432 | 453 | 469 | 397 |
| 44 | | | | | | |
| 45 | | | | | | |
| 46 | NET WORTH (39 thru 45) | 494 | 533 | 554 | 570 | 490 |
| 47 | TANGIBLE NET WORTH (46 – 21) | 494 | 532 | 553 | 569 | 490 |
| 48 | WORKING CAPITAL (12–32) | 337 | 377 | 389 | 407 | 319 |
| 49 | CUR. ASSETS LESS TOT. LIAB. | 335 | 372 | 387 | 405 | 318 |
| 50 | CURRENT RATIO (12–32) | 3.1 | 2.33 | 1.89 | 1.62 | 2.5 |
| 51 | CASH, MKT. SEC. & A/R TO CUR. LIAB. | 1.3 | 1.56 | 1.30 | 1.29 | 1.1 |
| 52 | A/R COLLECTION PERIOD—DAYS[a] | 29 | 78 | 110 | 162 | 35 |
| 53 | NET SALES TO INVENTORY[a] | 5.9 | 9.4 | 7.2 | 8.6 | 5.7 |
| 54 | COST OF SALES TO INVENTORY | 3.7 | | | | 3.6 |
| 55 | INVENTORY TO WORKING CAPITAL | .88 | .58 | .66 | .54 | .94 |
| 56 | SR. DEBT ÷ (TANG. N.W. & SUB. DEBT) | .34 | .54 | .80 | 1.16 | .42 |
| 57 | NET PROFIT (LOSS) TO AVG. NET WORTH[a] | .15 | .03 | .23 | .19 | .06 |

[a] Annualized.

525

**EXHIBIT 5A    Athletequip Company, Inc.—Credit Report**

| | Date of Report April 3, 1993 | Started | Rating |
|---|---|---|---|
| ATHLETEQUIP COMPANY, INC., MFG ATHLETIC GARMENTS ALHAMBRA, CALIF 91103 | | 1964 SUMMARY PAYMENTS SALES WORTH EMPLOYS CONDITION TREND | A+1 DISC PPT $1,700,000+ $488,650 95 SOUND UP |

GENE BALL, PRES., TREAS., & CHIEF EXECUTIVE
PHIL BALL, VICE-PRESIDENT
ELIZABETH BALL, SECRETARY

| PAYMENTS | HC | OWE | P DUE TERMS | | March 11, | SOLD |
|---|---|---|---|---|---|---|
| | 27500 | 11000 | 1 30 | | Disc | Over 3 years |
| | 20000 | 400 | | 30 | Ppt | Over 3 years to 6-B |
| | 4000 | 500 | | 30 | Ppt | Over 3 years |

| HIGHLIGHTS | | *Dec. 31, 1992* | *Dec. 31, 1991* |
|---|---|---|---|
| | Net Working Capital | $  359,611 | $   341,924 |
| | Net Worth | 490,043 | 493,118 |
| | Net Sales | 1,726,769 | 1,739,224 |

This old, established business has all along maintained a sound financial condition. Net worth has shown increases over the past several years as a result of retention of earnings, but it declined slightly this year. Volume continues to show moderate increases each year.

Current financial statement shows a satisfactory working capital condition despite the slight reduction in sales and net worth.

**CURRENT**   On March 3, Mrs. Emma Little, bookkeeper, submitted financial statement of Dec. 31, 1992, as the latest available for publication.

While complete operating figures are not submitted for publication, sales for the year ending Dec. 31, 1992, were $1,727,000 compared to $1,739,000 for the previous year.

Mrs. Little stated that sales for the first three months of this year are in excess of $470,000 and that sales for the fiscal year will probably approach $2,000,000.

*Banking*

Relations are maintained with one local bank, where balances average in high five to low six figures. Loans granted to low five figures secured by accounts receivable, with high four figures currently outstanding. The account is well regarded.

**EXHIBIT 5B   Athletequip, Inc.—Financial Statement of Principals[a]**

| | Elizabeth Ball | Phillip Ball | Gregory Ball | Combined |
|---|---|---|---|---|
| | | *Names* | | |
| **Assets** | | | | |
| Cash | $ 18,000 | $  9,434 | $  6,298 | $   33,732 |
| Listed securities | 30,000 | 30,809 | 27,059 | 87,868 |
| Unlisted securities | 92,232 | 180,804 | 180,804 | 453,840 |
| Co. profit sharing | 5,650 | 12,500 | 12,500 | 30,650 |
| Real estate | 235,639 | 281,643 | 275,100 | 792,382 |
| Vans Inv. | 3,800 | 3,800 | 3,800 | 11,400 |
| C.V.L.I. | | 2,430 | 4,529 | 6,959 |
| Receivables | 65,521 | | | 65,521 |
| Auto | 6,000 | 3,100 | 1,500 | 10,600 |
| Other | | 2,000 | | 2,000 |
| Total | $456,842 | $526,520 | $511,590 | $1,494,952 |
| **Liabilities** | | | | |
| Real estate | $ 28,940 | $ 88,945 | $ 90,430 | $  208,315 |
| Contracts | 2,376 | | | 2,376 |
| Taxes | 1,967 | 3,023 | 5,150 | 10,140 |
| Total | $ 33,283 | $ 91,968 | $ 95,580 | $  220,831 |
| Net Worth | 423,559 | 434,552 | 416,010 | 1,274,121 |
| Total | $456,842 | $526,520 | $511,590 | $1,494,952 |
| N.W. w/o Athletequip | $331,327 | $253,748 | $235,306 | $  820,381 |

[a] All statements dated April 1, 1993.

**EXHIBIT 6   Industry Ratios—Manufacturing—Sporting and Athletic Goods**

| | Low 10% | Average | High 10% |
|---|---|---|---|
| Current ratio | 1.2× | 1.8× | 2.7× |
| Quick ratio | .5× | .8× | 1.2× |
| Days sales in receivables | 72d | 54d | 36d |
| Days COGS inventory | 166d | 111d | 72d |
| Sales/working capital | 3.6× | 7.2× | 12.4× |
| Sales/net fixed assets | 6.5× | 10.9× | 20.9× |
| Sales/total assets | 1.5× | 1.7× | 2.4× |
| EBIT/interest | .7× | 2.1× | 4.2× |
| Cash flow/current maturity debt | .3 | 2.4 | 7.1 |
| Total debt/equity | 351% | 168% | 94% |
| Return on assets | .4% | 5.0% | 15.6% |
| Return on equity | 1.6% | 16.4% | 37.4% |

# FLAIR DRESS MANUFACTURING COMPANY, INC.

## BACKGROUND

The Flair Dress Manufacturing Company was organized as a partnership in 1978 by James S. McDonald and Raymond J. Thompson. The business was incorporated in 1983, and George A. Lawson purchased a 50 percent interest. McDonald, Flair's president, died in 1989, and upon his death the company repurchased his stock from his widow and canceled it. At this time, George Lawson assumed the presidency of the company.

The company manufactured a popular line of dresses, skirts, blouses, and slacks, which were sold to department stores, chain stores, and specialty shops throughout the United States. Allied Stores, Sears Roebuck and Company, and J. C. Penney Company accounted for 45 percent of sales from the 7,500 accounts on the company's mailing list. Peak sales occurred in February and August. Forty percent of sales were confirmed orders, and 60 percent were from stock. About 55 percent of billings were on the 8 percent-10EOM (end-of-month) discount terms.

The company employed 563 people and had 19 salesmen on commission and salary. All buildings and equipment are owned by Flair.

## MANAGEMENT

George Lawson, age 54, had been president of Flair, Inc., since 1989. He came to the company in 1985 from Atlas Garment Company, where he was employed for 10 years, the last 4 as a partner. He is believed by those in the industry to be capable and progressive.

Raymond J. Thompson, co-founder of Flair, Inc., was 62 years of age and had been vice-president and manager of the sales division since the company's incorporation in 1983. He was well regarded in the industry.

John T. (Jack) Mitchell, 40, joined the company in 1987 as assistant sales manager. He received his BA from Columbia University in 1977. After graduation he accepted a position with Allied Stores and was a buyer for Allied for three years

prior to coming to Flair. He has worked closely with Thompson and would likely assume direction of the sales division upon Thompson's departure.

L. J. Peters, 52, graduated from Vanderbilt University in 1961 with a BS degree in industrial engineering. He worked with Bobbie Brooks in various areas of production for several years before coming to Flair in 1981. Peters was operations manager and worked closely with Lawson in design supervision.

Thomas C. Kindel, 29, graduated from Rice University in 1986 with a BBA degree in accounting. He came to Flair in 1988 and has headed the accounting department for the past two years.

## CURRENT SITUATION

George Lawson and Raymond Thompson have disagreed in recent months over issues of management policy, and Lawson had acquired the option to purchase Thompson's one-third ownership. If he should exercise the option, Lawson would become the sole stockholder. Lawson would, however, then sell 10 percent of the outstanding stock to Mitchell and 10 percent to Peters.

As a result of these transactions, Flair, Inc., would have new officers as follows:

George A. Lawson, president
John T. Mitchell, vice-president—sales
L. J. Peters, vice-president—operations
Thomas Kindel, secretary–treasurer

Lawson felt that Thompson's withdrawal from the firm would not adversely affect either sales or operations. It is not known what Thompson planned to do if his interest was purchased.

Thompson's interest can be purchased for $350,000 as follows:

| | |
|---|---|
| $100,000 | Cash |
| 250,000 | Note from the company payable to Thompson, $50,000 a year for five years plus 9% interest |
| Total | $350,000 |

## BANK RELATIONSHIP

Flair, Inc., had been a customer of the First State Bank for the past 15 years. The bank's experience with the company had been good; open lines of credit of $500,000 had been approved each year. The credit record for this and the preceding three years has been as follows:

|      | High     | Low          |
|------|----------|--------------|
| 1987 | $500,000 | $175,000     |
| 1986 | 450,000  | 50,000       |
| 1985 | 400,000  | –0– no debt  |
| 1984 | 500,000  | 125,000      |

Collected balances average in the low six figures.

George Lawson was now requesting a loan for the company of $100,000 for five years, with repayment to be made from earnings. The proceeds of this loan would be paid to Thompson as the cash portion of his settlement.

Lawson was also requesting a one-year reaffirmation of the company's $500,000 open line of credit. This line would be used in the company's normal operations and would be repaid for 45 to 60 days during the late spring.

## FINANCIAL INFORMATION

The company's balance sheets and profit and loss statements for the past four years are given in Exhibits 1 and 2. The statements were prepared by a CPA but were rendered without an opinion. All statements are dated May 31, which is the company's fiscal year end.

Inventory was valued at the lower cost of market.

|                          | Current   | Percent |
|--------------------------|-----------|---------|
| Raw material and supplies | $375,000  | 41.5    |
| Work in progress         | 217,000   | 24.1    |
| Finished goods           | 310,000   | 34.4    |
| Totals                   | $902,000  | 100.0   |

Receivables were aged as follows:

|                  | Prior     | Percent |
|------------------|-----------|---------|
| Current          | $461,000  | 85.3    |
| 30–60 days       | 32,000    | 5.9     |
| 60–90 days       | 16,000    | 3.0     |
| 90 days and over | 31,000    | 5.8     |
| Totals           | $540,000  | 100.0   |

Bad debt expense averaged $8,300 a year for the past four years. The reserve for bad debts was $9,200 at May 31, 1993.

Lawson had been receiving an annual salary of $50,000 and Thompson one of $45,000.

Dun and Bradstreet rated the firm A + 1 and reported that supplier relations were uniformly favorable, with discounts being taken for prompt payments.

## QUESTIONS

1. Review the financial data and indicate trends in the firm's liquidity and leverage positions. Are they in line with industry standards? Consider the impact of the additional debt.

2. Analyze trends in sales, profit margins, and cash flow. Would the firm be able to generate sufficient cash flow to service the additional debt?

3. What are the implications of the concentration of receivables for the firm's liquidity and future sales prospects? Would future sales be affected by Thompson's departure?

4. Assume that you will make both loans. Structure the conditions for each loan, indicating repayment provisions and the content of the loan agreement.

**EXHIBIT 1    Flair Dress Manufacturing Company—Balance Sheet (Prepared without Audit) As of December 31, 1990–1993**

|  | 1993 | 1992 | 1991 | 1990 |
|---|---|---|---|---|
| **Assets** | | | | |
| Cash | $ 273,000 | $ 70,000 | $ 32,000 | $ 25,000 |
| Prepaid and deferred expenses | 27,000 | 10,000 | 9,000 | 49,000 |
| Fixed assets—net of depreciation | 243,000 | 228,000 | 372,000 | 413,000 |
| Accounts receivable—net | 540,000 | 615,000 | 380,000 | 461,000 |
| Other receivables | 0 | 0 | 0 | 75,000 |
| Inventory | 902,000 | 918,000 | 1,138,000 | 935,000 |
| Total assets | $1,985,000 | $1,841,000 | $1,931,000 | $1,958,000 |
| **Liabilities** | | | | |
| Notes payable | $ 450,000 | $ 400,000 | $ 320,000 | $ 365,000 |
| Current maturities of term debt | 0 | 0 | 31,000 | 31,000 |
| Long-term debt | 0 | 0 | 143,000 | 285,000 |
| Accrued expenses | 141,000 | 94,000 | 190,000 | 112,000 |
| Accounts payable | 562,000 | 614,000 | 583,000 | 552,000 |
| Capital stock | 400,000 | 400,000 | 400,000 | 400,000 |
| Retained earnings | 432,000 | 333,000 | 264,000 | 213,000 |
| Total liabilities | $1,985,000 | $1,841,000 | $1,931,000 | $1,958,000 |

**EXHIBIT 2    Flair Dress Manufacturing Company—Statement of Earnings (Prepared without Audit) For the Year Ending December 31, 1990–1993**

|  | 1993 | 1992 | 1991 | 1990 |
|---|---|---|---|---|
| Net sales | $7,206,000 | $7,114,000 | $6,781,000 | $6,120,000 |
| Cost of sales | 5,856,000 | 5,868,000 | 5,601,000 | 4,978,000 |
| Gross profit | 1,350,000 | 1,246,000 | 1,180,000 | 1,142,000 |
| Total operating expenses | 1,064,000 | 1,015,000 | 975,000 | 887,000 |
| Operating profit | 286,000 | 231,000 | 205,000 | 255,000 |
| Income taxes | 137,000 | 112,000 | 104,000 | 123,000 |
| Net profit | $ 149,000 | $ 119,000 | $ 101,000 | $ 132,000 |
| Depreciation | $44,000 | $46,000 | $47,000 | $53,000 |
| Dividends paid | $50,000 | $50,000 | $50,000 | –0– |

# CENTURY CABLE COMPANY, INC.

## BACKGROUND

Century Cable Company, Inc., a manufacturer of battery cables, was founded in 1982 in Denver, Colorado, as a partnership by John H. Loren and Alexander M. Parsons. Loren and Parsons each made an initial investment of $30,000, and they shared equally in the company's management. The company was incorporated in 1990. At this time, Loren assumed the presidency and Parsons became vice-president. This title designation was, however, more a matter of formal necessity than a definition of rank in the organization. Loren became primarily involved in sales, while Parsons took charge of production.

Century Cable, Inc., sold its battery cables and related products throughout much of the United States. Over 90 percent of sales were made through distributors. The production process involved some fabrication as well as assembly. The company employed 23 persons.

During the first three years, Century sustained operating losses, but beginning in the late 1980s the company became profitable and its performance showed modest but steady improvement into the beginning of the 1990s. This was especially true since the two principal officers received reasonably generous salaries and perquisites, totaling nearly $130,000 per year for each of them.

Late in 1991, Alex Parsons was compelled to move to California for family reasons, and he offered to sell his company interest to Loren for $110,000. A short-term bank loan was negotiated for that purpose, and in December 1991 Century, Inc., acquired all of Parsons' stock, treating the transaction as a treasury stock acquisition. At about the same time, John Loren hired a new production manager, Jane R. Scott.

## MANAGEMENT

John H. Loren, age 43, held a master's degree in electrical engineering from the University of Colorado and was employed by a large national battery manufacturing corporation before founding Century, Inc., in 1982. He had proved to be a capable manager.

Jane R. Scott, age 32, became the company's production manager in late 1991. She had received a BBA degree from Colorado State University in 1981 and was assistant manager for production in a large manufacturing firm in Boulder, Colorado, before coming to Century. John Loren was satisfied that Scott could fill the management gap created by Parsons' departure.

## BANK RELATIONSHIP

Since its founding 10 years ago, Century Cable, Inc., had been a customer of the First Colorado State Bank in Denver. In 1991, the company had negotiated a $160,000 line of credit with First Colorado State, which was fully utilized by the end of the year. The firm had been gradually increasing its bank borrowing for the past several years. The credit was secured by accounts receivable and inventory under a loan agreement. The most recent loan agreement was intended to restrain operations and expansion so that the company could devote its efforts to strengthening its financial position, which was not viewed by Henry Brookings, the loan officer, as being sufficiently strong. Borrowings were limited to $160,000, or 80 percent of acceptable receivables and inventory, whichever was lower. Although Brookings increased the credit line from $100,000 in 1991 to help finance the company's purchase of Parsons' stock, he had some misgivings about this action.

Century, Inc., had made steady progress during recent years, but the bank had become somewhat concerned about recent information that accounts receivable collections had slowed. Delinquency percentages, which for some time had been quite modest, were beginning to increase. Credit reports and credit inquiries directed to the bank also began to suggest that the company had begun "stretching" its accounts payable.

Accordingly, Brookings decided to call on Loren to review the company's current situation. During the visit it quickly became apparent that Century was experiencing serious cash flow problems. Nonetheless, Loren thought these problems could be resolved because the difficulties resulted primarily from some slowness in collecting accounts receivable. Loren did not seem unduly concerned.

About three weeks after Brookings' visit, Loren came to the bank with news that a large number of battery cables that had been recently produced were defective. After several months of use, the plastic cable head was cracking and coming loose from the battery terminal. Distributors were, of course, reluctant to pay for inventory purchases until this situation had been corrected. Loren estimated that it would require at least $50,000 to replace defective goods and to correct the production problem. He indicated to Brookings that the product failure was the direct result of a defect in material supplied by a major chemical company. The chemical company had solicited Century's business for some time before obtaining a contract to sell this product to Century, beginning in 1991. The contract appeared to contain a warranty covering quality and production specifications that Loren believed would apply to the cracking problem Century had en-

countered. He planned to pursue the matter, taking whatever legal steps might be necessary to recover losses from the supplier.

During the meeting with Brookings, Loren also reported that demand for the company's products remained good and that the firm had a backlog of orders totaling nearly $250,000, a record high. The company, however, had utilized all of its $160,000 line of credit as of April 1992, and cash flow pressures continued. Though he remained optimistic that these current operating problems could be resolved promptly, Loren pressed Brookings to consider an increase in the firm's secured line of credit up to perhaps $200,000 to $225,000. Loren said that, as of March 31, 1992, inventory and accounts receivable had totaled nearly $300,000. Hence, on an 80 percent advance basis, Loren felt that the higher credit level could be properly secured.

Brookings promised Loren to review Century's total situation and to respond to Loren within the next few days. After Loren left the bank, Brookings summarized the recent data and noted several questions that required resolution, including how much and what kind of money Century needed, what options were open to the bank, and his own assessment of Century's management.

**EXHIBIT I   General Spread Form—Century Cable Company, Inc. (dollars in thousands)**

NAME   Century Cable Company, Inc.

| AUDITED STATEMENT | Audit | Audit | Audit | Audit | Audit |
|---|---|---|---|---|---|
| STATEMENT DATE | 12-31-87 | 12-31-88 | 12-31-89 | 12-31-90 | 12-31-91 |
| CASH | 6 | 8 | 16 | 18 | 20 |
| MARKETABLE SECURITIES | | | | | |
| NOTES RECEIVABLE | | | | | |
| ACCOUNTS RECEIVABLE | 90 | 96 | 94 | 98 | 132 |
| INVENTORY | 90 | 100 | 114 | 110 | 136 |
| | | | | | |
| ALLOW. FOR DOUBT. ACCT. | | | | | |
| TOTAL CURRENT ASSETS | 188 | 204 | 224 | 226 | 288 |
| FIXED ASSETS—NET | 60 | 74 | 70 | 84 | 86 |
| NONMARKETABLE SECURITIES | | | | | |
| NONCURRENT RECEIVABLES | | | | | |
| PREPAID AND DEFERRED EXPENSES | 4 | 4 | 4 | 4 | 4 |
| | | | | | |
| INTANGIBLES | | | | | |
| TOTAL NONCURRENT ASSETS | 64 | 78 | 74 | 88 | 90 |
| TOTAL ASSETS | 252 | 282 | 298 | 314 | 378 |
| CURRENT MTY. OF TERM DEBT | 2 | 8 | 8 | 8 | 8 |
| NOTES PAYABLE | 66 | 66 | 60 | 26 | 100 |
| ACCOUNTS PAYABLE | 66 | 68 | 68 | 70 | 98 |
| ACCRUED EXPENSE & MISC. | 18 | 20 | 22 | 24 | 28 |

**EXHIBIT 1** (continued)

| NAME | Century Cable Company, Inc. | | (dollars in thousands) | | |
|---|---|---|---|---|---|
| INCOME TAX LIABILITY | | | | | |
| TOTAL CURRENT LIABILITIES | 234 | 128 | 158 | 162 | 152 |
| TERM DEBT | 14 | 8 | 16 | 24 | 16 |
| SUBORDINATED DEBT | | | | | |
| TOTAL LIABILITIES | 248 | 136 | 174 | 186 | 168 |
| MINORITY INTEREST | | | | | |
| DEFERRED INCOME/RESERVES | | | | | |
| TREASURY STOCK | (110) | | | | |
| PREFERRED STOCK OUTSTANDING | | | | | |
| COMMON STOCK OUTSTANDING | 60 | 60 | 60 | 60 | 60 |
| CAPITAL SURPLUS | | | | | |
| RETAINED EARNINGS (DEFICIT) | 180 | 118 | 64 | 36 | 24 |
| NET WORTH | 130 | 178 | 124 | 96 | 84 |
| TANGIBLE NET WORTH | | | | | |
| WORKING CAPITAL | 54 | 98 | 66 | 42 | 36 |
| EXCESS CUR. ASSETS OVER TOT. LIAB. | 20 | 45 | 25 | 9 | 10 |
| CURRENT RATIO | 1.23 | 1.77 | 1.42 | 1.26 | 1.24 |
| CASH, MKT. SEC. & A/R TO CURR. LIAB. | .65 | .91 | .70 | .64 | .63 |
| A/R COLLECTION PERIOD—DAYS | 41 days | 35 days | 38 days | 41 days | 40 days |
| NET SALES TO INVENTORY | 8.5 | 9.2 | 7.8 | 8.5 | 8.8 |
| COST OF SALES TO INVENTORY | | | | | |
| INVENTORY TO WORKING CAPITAL | 2.5 | 1.1 | 1.7 | 2.4 | 2.6 |
| SR. DEBT TO (TANG. N.W. & SUB. DEBT) | 1.91 | .76 | 1.40 | 1.93 | 2.00 |
| NET PROFIT (LOSS) TO AVG. NET WORTH | .40 | .36 | .25 | .13 | .26 |

| PERIOD COVERED (MONTHS) STATEMENT DATE | 12 mos. 12-31-87 | % | 12 mos. 12-31-88 | % | 12 mos. 12-31-89 | % | 12 mos. 12-31-90 | % | 12 mos. 12-31-91 | % |
|---|---|---|---|---|---|---|---|---|---|---|
| NET SALES | 812 | | 856 | | 884 | | 1016 | | 1160 | |
| COST OF SALES | | | | | | | 814 | | 954 | |
| GROSS PROFIT | 136 | 17 | 138 | 16 | 168 | 19 | 202 | 20 | 206 | 18 |
| SELLING EXPENSES | | | | | | | | | | |
| GENERAL & ADMINISTRATIVE EXP. | | | | | | | | | | |
| TOTAL OPERATING EXPENSES | | | | | | | | | | |
| OPERATING PROFIT | | | | | | | | | | |
| OTHER INCOME (EXPENSE)—NET | | | | | | | | | | |
| NET PROFIT (LOSS) BEFORE TAXES | | | | | | | | | | |
| INCOME TAXES | | | | | | | | | | |
| NET PROFIT (LOSS) AFTER TAXES | 20 | 2.5 | 12 | 1.5 | 28 | 3.2 | 54 | 5.3 | 62 | 5.3 |
| ADDITIONAL DATA | | | | | | | | | | |
| DIVIDENDS—PREFERRED STOCK | | | | | | | | | | |
| DIVIDENDS—COM. STOCK OR WITHDRAW | | | | | | | | | | |
| OFFICER REMUNERATION | | | | | | | | | | |
| INTEREST EXPENSE | | | | | | | | | | |
| OTHER CHANGES IN WORTH | | | | | | | | | | |
| CONTINGENT LIABILITIES | | | | | | | | | | |
| LEASE OBLIGATIONS | | | | | | | | | | |
| ANALYSIS OF CHANGES IN WORTH OR SURPLUS | | | | | | | | | | |
| AT BEGINNING OF PERIOD | | | 84 | | 96 | | 124 | | 178 | |
| ADD NET PROFIT | 20 | | 12 | | 28 | | 54 | | 62 | |
| DEDUCT DIVIDENDS OR WITHDRAW | | | | | | | | | | |
| PURCHASE TREAS. STOCK | | | | | | | | | (110) | |
| WORTH OR SURPLUS REPORTED | 84 | | 96 | | 124 | | 178 | | 130 | |

**EXHIBIT I** (continued)

NAME    Century Cable Company, Inc.

### ANALYSIS OF WORKING CAPITAL

|  | | | | | |
|---|---|---|---|---|---|
| AT BEGINNING OF PERIOD | | 36 | 42 | 66 | 98 |
| ADD: NET PROFIT | 20 | 12 | 28 | 54 | 62 |
| NON-CASH CHARGES | 8 | 12 | 12 | 14 | 14 |
| INCR.—TERM DEBT | | 8 | | | 6 |
| MISCELLANEOUS | | | | | |
| TOTAL ADDITIONS | | 32 | 40 | 68 | 82 |
| DEDUCT: | | | | | |
| DIVIDENDS/WITHDRAWALS | | | | | |
| PLANT EXPENDITURES | | 26 | 8 | 28 | 16 |
| PURCHASE TREAS. STOCK | | | | | 110 |
| DECR. TERM DEBT | | | 8 | 8 | |
| MISCELLANEOUS | | | | | |
| TOTAL DEDUCTIONS | | 26 | 16 | 36 | 126 |
| NET CHANGE (+ OR −) | | +6 | +24 | +32 | −44 |
| AT END OF PERIOD | 36 | 42 | 66 | 98 | 54 |
| W/C AS ABOVE | 36 | 42 | 66 | 98 | 54 |
| INVENTORY | 92 | 100 | 114 | 110 | 136 |
| EXCESS OF W/C OVER INVENTORY | (56) | (58) | (48) | (12) | (82) |
| ANALYST INITIAL | JEB | JEB | JEB | JEB | JEB |

## CASE 14    BOSTWICK STORES

Mr. Henry Hardwick, senior vice-president of Bay State National Bank in Framingham, Massachusetts, was preparing for a meeting with one of Bay State's branch managers and a possible new customer, Mr. Carl Bostwick. He had approached the manager of Bay State's branch in nearby Marlboro to ask whether the bank might be interested in establishing a credit relationship with Bostwick Stores.

The company had for some years divided its business among three small, independent banks in its market area. Bostwick had become gradually convinced, however, that it would be more efficient, perhaps less costly, and more reliable for the company to deal with a single larger bank that would be able to handle all of Bostwick's growing credit requirements. Accordingly, Carl Bostwick had contacted the Marlboro branch of Bay State National Bank to explore possible mutual interests. Since the company's combined credit needs would far exceed the branch office lending authority, a meeting was arranged with Mr. Hardwick, a senior and experienced lending officer, to discuss the matter in greater detail.

The branch manager told Hardwick that Bostwick wanted to consolidate all company borrowing with a single lender, and a figure of $450,000 was mentioned, suggesting the size of the credit facility that Bostwick had in mind. It also became clear in the preliminary discussions that most, or all, of this amount would be needed on an intermediate-term basis, perhaps in the range of five to seven years. In any case, Mr. Bostwick expressed his own opinion that the company would prefer financing of that kind and size.

To assist Mr. Hardwick in preparing for his meeting with Bostwick, the branch manager obtained a credit report on Bostwick Stores (see Exhibit 1). He also obtained from the company summary financial statements for the most recent five years, plus an interim report for the first four months of 1988.

These materials, gathered just two days before the planned meeting of the three men, were forwarded to Mr. Hardwick for his review and as preparation to explore Bostwick's interests.

The local manager had visited the Bostwick Department Store and examined the facility to gain some firsthand familiarity with the company's operations. He reported to Hardwick that the department store was attractive, the merchandise looked fresh and effectively displayed, and the sales staff was courteous and attentive. He saw nothing in his cursory visit to the Bostwick Department Store to suggest any obvious problem from a visitor's or casual customer's point of view.

Hardwick began to study the financial data and the credit report summarized below as a basis for his meeting with Bostwick. Although he was not sure of the specific credit request that might emerge from the meeting, the branch manager made two suggestions:

1. Consider what Bay State Bank's reaction would be to a $450,000 five- to seven-year term loan request; or,

2. If that credit commitment presented a problem, be prepared to offer a counterproposal sufficient to finance the company's operating needs at an appropriate level.

The branch manager was quite interested in acquiring Bostwick as a new customer, and Bay State was also anxious to add new, good-quality customers. Credit demand had been somewhat slower than desired in recent months; thus, both bankers were anxious to book new business.

Nonetheless, Mr. Hardwick wanted to study the limited available data before his initial meeting with Bostwick to ascertain answers to at least three important questions:

1. How financially successful had this organization been?

2. How much and what type of financing did Bostwick really need?

3. What would be the likely sources of repayment for the amount of credit required?

Hardwick wanted to use his meeting with Bostwick to demonstrate the bank's interest in attracting new customers while being somewhat cautious that any credit arrangements made good business sense for *both* the borrower and the lender.

### Credit Report: Bostwick Stores

Carl Bostwick, general partner, age 54
Harry Bostwick, general partner, age 45
Thomas Bostwick, general partner, age 49
Marie Dalton, general partner, age 52
Stuart Bostwick, general partner, age 51

The company was founded in 1947 by Claude Bostwick. He died in 1953, leaving as heirs his widow, Rita, and seven children, five of whom continued their association and involvement with this business. All five of the general partners are married.

The department store formerly owned the real estate used in the operation of this business. In 1981, however, the articles of co-partnership were revised to eliminate the real estate as a partnership asset, transferring it to the five individual members of the firm as tenants in common. The new real estate entity was styled "Bostwick Realty Company" and was owned equally by the five family members. The relationship between the department store and the real estate company was as tenant and landlord, since the store used all the real estate owned by the separate entity. Tax and accounting advantages motivated this arrangement. (See Exhibits 6 and 7 for summary financial information on the realty company.)

Two mortgages were outstanding on the real property. This property had an original book value of $250,000, but its current market value is probably about double that amount. There are two mortgages on the property: The first, arranged in 1973, totaling $400,000, is funded by the Metropolitan Life Insurance Company, carrying interest at 9.25 percent, with a balance as of September 30, 1987, of $298,000. There had been a small second mortgage with County National Bank, but that debt had been repaid in full by 1987.

The Bostwick Department Store operates as a general merchandise establishment, with 18 departments, comprising primarily wearing apparel, shoes, dry goods, cosmetics, household furnishings, and appliances. Customers for the store's single location come primarily from the Marlboro area or from transients. The town has a population of about 30,000, and its local economy is primarily related to trade, services, and a moderate amount of agriculture. There are two other general merchandise department stores in Marlboro, of which Bostwick is the smallest. It has, however, been able to compete effectively against the other stores and is attractively profitable on a pretax basis.

Customer sales are about two-thirds for cash and about one-third on 30-day charge accounts and on installment terms. Bostwick maintains about 6,500 accounts eligible for 30-day terms and several hundred additional accounts that qualify for installment credit extending up to 18 months.

Bostwick experiences the typical seasonality of department stores, with November and December representing by far the heaviest sales months of the year. The company employs 65 regular full-time employees and 35 more on a part-time basis.

Bostwick conducts its merchandising activities in three adjoining three-story buildings of moderate size, comprising a total of some 60,000 square feet. In addition, there are two warehouse locations for storage, inventory, and maintenance purposes. A nearby, conveniently located parking lot is available for store patrons. All properties are in good condition and well maintained. The main retail store facilities have been extensively renovated in recent years, and are attractive and pleasant. As noted earlier, all the real estate is owned separately by the partners.

This comprised the principal information available to Mr. Hardwick as he prepared for his meeting with Carl Bostwick the following day.

# EXHIBIT I Retailers—Department Stores SIC #5311 [a]

Current Data periods: 31 statements (6/30–8/30/83); 135 statements (10/1/83–3/31/84).

| ASSET SIZE | Current Data: 0-1MM | 1-10MM | 10-50MM | 50-100MM | ALL | Hist. 6/30/79-3/31/80 ALL | 6/30/80-3/31/81 ALL | 6/30/81-3/31/82 ALL | 6/30/82-3/31/83 ALL | 6/30/83-3/31/84 ALL |
|---|---|---|---|---|---|---|---|---|---|---|
| **NUMBER OF STATEMENTS** | 32 | 70 | 45 | 19 | 166 | 180 | 199 | 211 | 236 | 166 |
| **ASSETS** | % | % | % | % | % | % | % | % | % | % |
| Cash & Equivalents | 8.5 | 5.8 | 7.7 | 4.5 | 6.7 | 6.8 | 7.4 | 7.2 | 7.0 | 8.7 |
| Accts. & Notes Rec.—Trade(net) | 19.1 | 26.3 | 21.4 | 13.8 | 22.2 | 18.9 | 19.2 | 18.8 | 19.9 | 22.2 |
| Inventory | 51.5 | 45.0 | 36.8 | 41.0 | 43.6 | 47.2 | 43.7 | 43.2 | 42.4 | 43.6 |
| All Other Current | 1.6 | 1.7 | 1.8 | 1.8 | 1.7 | 1.5 | 1.8 | 1.8 | 1.2 | 1.7 |
| Total Current | 80.6 | 78.9 | 67.7 | 61.1 | 74.2 | 74.4 | 72.1 | 70.8 | 70.4 | 74.2 |
| Fixed Assets (net) | 15.0 | 16.5 | 25.6 | 29.4 | 20.1 | 20.0 | 21.3 | 20.3 | 21.4 | 20.1 |
| Intangibles (net) | .7 | .6 | .5 | .8 | .6 | .6 | .4 | .6 | .3 | .6 |
| All Other Non-Current | 3.7 | 4.1 | 6.3 | 8.6 | 5.1 | 5.0 | 6.2 | 8.3 | 7.9 | 5.1 |
| Total | 100.0 | 100.0 | 100.0 | 100.0 | 100.0 | 100.0 | 100.0 | 100.0 | 100.0 | 100.0 |
| **LIABILITIES** | | | | | | | | | | |
| Notes Payable—Short Term | 12.0 | 12.7 | 3.5 | 4.7 | 9.2 | 8.9 | 7.8 | 7.5 | 8.5 | 9.2 |
| Cur. Mat.—L/T/D | 1.9 | 2.4 | 2.9 | 3.2 | 2.5 | 2.2 | 1.9 | 1.9 | 2.1 | 2.5 |
| Accts. & Notes Payable—Trade | 12.7 | 14.2 | 15.2 | 14.5 | 14.2 | 13.8 | 14.4 | 14.0 | 13.9 | 14.2 |
| Accrued Expenses | 4.0 | 5.2 | 7.0 | 9.1 | 5.9 | 5.2 | 5.3 | 5.6 | 5.5 | 5.9 |
| All Other Current | 7.4 | 3.5 | 4.0 | 2.3 | 4.3 | 5.5 | 4.0 | 3.5 | 2.8 | 4.3 |
| Total Current | 38.0 | 38.0 | 32.5 | 33.8 | 36.0 | 35.6 | 33.6 | 32.5 | 32.8 | 36.0 |
| Long Term Debt | 13.3 | 13.5 | 17.9 | 26.7 | 16.2 | 16.5 | 17.7 | 14.6 | 16.2 | 16.2 |
| All Other Non-Current | 1.2 | 1.7 | 4.4 | 6.1 | 2.8 | 2.5 | 3.3 | 3.8 | 4.6 | 2.8 |
| Net Worth | 47.5 | 46.7 | 45.2 | 33.4 | 44.9 | 45.4 | 45.4 | 49.1 | 46.3 | 44.9 |
| Total Liabilities & Net Worth | 100.0 | 100.0 | 100.0 | 100.0 | 100.0 | 100.0 | 100.0 | 100.0 | 100.0 | 100.0 |
| **INCOME DATA** | | | | | | | | | | |
| Net Sales | 100.0 | 100.0 | 100.0 | 100.0 | 100.0 | 100.0 | 100.0 | 100.0 | 100.0 | 100.0 |
| Cost Of Sales | 64.4 | 64.1 | 65.5 | 64.2 | 64.5 | 65.9 | 65.4 | 64.2 | 64.4 | 64.5 |
| Gross Profit | 35.6 | 35.9 | 34.5 | 35.8 | 35.5 | 34.1 | 34.6 | 35.8 | 35.6 | 35.6 |
| Operating Expenses | 34.2 | 35.1 | 30.9 | 30.8 | 33.3 | 31.1 | 31.6 | 32.4 | 32.3 | 33.3 |
| Operating Profit | 1.5 | .8 | 3.6 | 5.0 | 2.2 | 2.9 | 3.1 | 3.4 | 3.4 | 2.2 |
| All Other Expenses (net) | -.5 | -.2 | -.4 | 1.9 | -.1 | .4 | .8 | .3 | .7 | -.1 |
| Profit Before Taxes | 1.9 | 1.0 | 4.0 | 3.1 | 2.2 | 2.6 | 2.2 | 3.1 | 2.7 | 2.2 |
| **RATIOS** | | | | | | | | | | |
| Current | 4.8 / 2.2 / 1.4 | 3.1 / 2.2 / 1.6 | 2.8 / 2.2 / 1.6 | 2.3 / 1.9 / 1.4 | 2.9 / 2.1 / 1.5 | 3.1 / 2.3 / 1.7 | 2.9 / 2.2 / 1.6 | 3.1 / 2.3 / 1.7 | 3.4 / 2.3 / 1.6 | 2.9 / 2.1 / 1.5 |
| Quick | 1.8 / .5 / .3 | 1.4 / .9 / .5 | 1.5 / .9 / .5 | .9 / .7 / .2 | 1.4 / .8 / .4 | 1.4 / .8 / .2 | 1.4 / .9 / .3 | 1.5 / .8 / .3 | 1.7 / 1.0 / .4 (236) | 1.4 / .8 / .4 |
| Sales/Receivables | 4 93.7 / 15 23.6 / 41 8.8 | 21 17.6 / 48 7.4 / 64 5.7 | 5 72.7 / 37 9.9 / 69 5.3 | 2 181.7 / 11 32.1 / 63 5.8 | 5 70.3 / 37 9.8 / 63 5.8 | 4 100.3 / 29 12.4 / 59 6.2 | 4 101.8 / 38 12.2 / 61 6.0 | 3 133.0 / 38 9.5 / 60 6.1 | 4 102.0 / 42 8.7 / 62 5.9 | 5 70.3 / 37 9.8 / 63 5.8 |
| Cost of Sales/Inventory | 78 4.7 / 122 3.0 / 152 2.4 | 91 4.0 / 104 3.5 / 135 2.7 | 74 4.9 / 98 3.7 / 114 3.2 | 76 4.8 / 96 3.8 / 130 2.8 | 81 4.5 / 104 3.5 / 135 2.7 | 79 4.6 / 111 3.3 / 135 2.7 | 83 4.5 / 101 3.6 / 135 2.7 | 83 4.4 / 101 3.6 / 135 2.7 | 79 4.6 / 104 3.5 / 130 2.8 | 81 4.5 / 104 3.5 / 135 2.7 |

# EXHIBIT I (continued)

| Ratio | Col 1 | Col 2 | Col 3 | Col 4 | Col 5 | Col 6 | Col 7 | Col 8 | Col 9 | Col 10 |
|---|---|---|---|---|---|---|---|---|---|---|
| Number of Statements | 10 / 27 / 38 | 18 / 32 / 43 | 18 / 36 / 51 | 22 / 35 / 41 | 17 / 32 / 43 | 17 / 29 / 45 | 19 / 38 / 44 | 20 / 31 / 45 | 20 / 31 / 45 | 17 / 32 / 43 |
| Cost of Sales/Payables | 36.6 / 13.4 / 9.6 | 20.8 / 11.5 / 8.5 | 19.8 / 10.5 / 7.2 | 16.8 / 10.3 / 8.9 | 21.0 / 11.5 / 8.4 | 21.5 / 12.7 / 8.2 | 19.7 / 12.0 / 8.3 | 18.4 / 11.9 / 8.2 | 18.6 / 11.6 / 8.2 | 21.0 / 11.5 / 8.4 |
| Sales/Working Capital | 3.9 / 5.7 / 10.8 | 3.6 / 5.1 / 9.0 | 4.4 / 6.4 / 8.9 | 5.9 / 8.1 / 11.9 | 4.3 / 6.0 / 9.8 | 4.0 / 5.6 / 9.0 | 3.8 / 5.9 / 8.9 | 4.1 / 5.4 / 8.6 | 4.0 / 5.8 / 9.6 | 4.3 / 6.0 / 9.8 |
| EBIT/Interest | (28) 6.0 / 2.8 / 1.0 | (57) 3.5 / 1.9 / 1.0 | (42) 7.1 / 3.9 / 2.0 | (18) 3.8 / 2.5 / 1.5 | (146) 5.0 / 2.4 / 1.4 | (154) 4.4 / 2.6 / 1.4 | (166) 4.2 / 2.3 / 1.2 | (174) 3.7 / 2.0 / 1.2 | (202) 4.7 / 2.0 / 1.1 | (145) 5.0 / 2.4 / 1.4 |
| Cash Flow/Cur. Mat. L/T/D | | (34) 5.5 / 2.4 / .9 | (39) 5.5 / 2.9 / 1.7 | (16) 4.9 / 2.0 / 1.1 | (98) 5.5 / 2.7 / 1.2 | (101) 6.7 / 2.4 / 1.2 | (123) 8.3 / 3.1 / 1.0 | (110) 8.3 / 2.5 / .9 | (130) 8.4 / 2.5 / .8 | (98) 5.5 / 2.7 / 1.2 |
| Fixed/Worth | .1 / .2 / .6 | .1 / .3 / .7 | .4 / .6 / .9 | .7 / .9 / 1.5 | .2 / .4 / .8 | .2 / .4 / .7 | .2 / .4 / .8 | .2 / .4 / .8 | .2 / .5 / .9 | .2 / .4 / .8 |
| Debt/Worth | .5 / 1.1 / 2.2 | .6 / 1.2 / 2.3 | .8 / 1.3 / 1.8 | 1.3 / 1.9 / 3.6 | .7 / 1.3 / 2.1 | .7 / 1.2 / 2.4 | .7 / 1.2 / 2.2 | .5 / 1.2 / 2.0 | .5 / 1.3 / 2.1 | .7 / 1.3 / 2.1 |
| % Profit Before Taxes/Tangible Net Worth | (30) 25.9 / 16.9 / 3.9 | (69) 19.4 / 6.9 / -1.1 | 29.8 / 15.3 / 7.4 | 28.3 / 20.6 / 7.6 | 24.2 / 11.9 / 4.4 | (175) 21.7 / 12.9 / 5.7 | (209) 20.6 / 10.9 / 2.1 | (228) 23.2 / 12.7 / 3.0 | (163) 23.6 / 11.9 / 2.0 | 24.2 / 11.9 / 4.4 |
| % Profit Before Taxes/Total Assets | 13.0 / 7.5 / .0 | 7.4 / 3.5 / -.5 | 13.0 / 7.1 / 3.3 | 10.2 / 8.4 / 1.8 | 9.9 / 5.0 / 1.2 | 9.8 / 5.1 / 1.9 | 9.4 / 4.3 / .8 | 11.9 / 5.2 / 1.1 | 11.3 / 5.0 / .7 | 9.9 / 5.0 / 1.2 |
| Sales/Net Fixed Assets | 71.1 / 30.4 / 9.4 | 49.7 / 15.4 / 8.0 | 15.0 / 10.9 / 6.5 | 12.1 / 6.2 / 5.4 | 30.3 / 12.3 / 7.0 | 29.1 / 14.1 / 7.3 | 28.4 / 11.9 / 6.6 | 33.2 / 13.5 / 7.2 | 23.2 / 11.7 / 6.4 | 30.3 / 12.3 / 7.0 |
| Sales/Total Assets | 3.2 / 2.6 / 1.9 | 2.7 / 2.2 / 1.8 | 2.7 / 2.2 / 1.7 | 2.9 / 2.3 / 1.6 | 2.8 / 2.2 / 1.8 | 2.8 / 2.2 / 1.9 | 2.8 / 2.1 / 1.7 | 2.8 / 2.1 / 1.7 | 2.7 / 2.1 / 1.7 | 2.8 / 2.2 / 1.8 |
| % Depr. Dep. Amort./Sales | (27) .5 / .9 / 1.8 | (62) .8 / 1.2 / 1.6 | 1.1 / 1.5 / 2.2 | 1.2 / 1.6 / 2.0 | .8 / 1.4 / 1.9 | (167) .7 / 1.1 / 1.6 | (194) .8 / 1.2 / 1.7 | (222) .8 / 1.3 / 1.9 | (149) .7 / 1.2 / 1.9 | .8 / 1.4 / 1.9 |
| % Lease & Rental Exp./Sales | (17) 1.7 / 2.4 / 5.5 | (42) 1.1 / 3.2 / 4.3 | 1.9 / 2.9 / 3.7 | (91) | 1.6 / 2.9 / 4.2 | (111) 1.5 / 3.1 / 4.2 | (112) 1.6 / 2.7 / 4.1 | (118) 1.7 / 3.3 / 4.3 | (81) 2.0 / 2.9 / 4.3 | 1.6 / 2.9 / 4.2 |
| % Officers' Comp/Sales | (12) 2.5 / 3.6 / 5.7 | (16) 1.8 / 2.4 / 3.6 | | (34) | 1.6 / 2.5 / 4.3 | (57) 1.1 / 2.0 / 4.0 | (51) 1.2 / 2.0 / 4.4 | (39) 1.3 / 3.6 / 5.6 | (34) 1.8 / 2.8 / 6.2 | 1.6 / 2.5 / 4.3 |
| Net Sales ($) | 42915M | 673199M | 2675825M | 3277794M | 6589733M | 3899515M | 7087455M | 7482025M | 7971118M | 6569733M |
| Total Assets ($) | 16833M | 246486M | 1076654M | 1418106M | 2758078M | 1853070M | 3083480M | 3236616M | 3406072M | 2758078M |

© Robert Morris Associates 1984

**M = $thousand    MM = $million**

See Pages 1 through 13 for Explanation of Ratios and Data

[1] RMA cautions that the Studies be regarded only as a general guideline and not as an absolute industry norm. This is due to limited samples within categories, the categorization of companies by their primary Standard Industrial Classification (SIC) number only, and different methods of operations by companies within the same industry. For these reasons, RMA recommends that the figures be used only as general guidelines in addition to other methods of financial analysis.

## EXHIBIT 2 Bostwick Stores, Inc.—Balance Sheets, January 31, 1984–88

| | | 1984 1/31 | 1985 1/31 | 1986 1/31 | 1987 1/31 | 1988 1/31 |
|---|---|---|---|---|---|---|
| | (000 OMITTED) | | | | | |
| 1 | CURRENT ASSETS | | | | | |
| 2 | CURRENT LIABILITIES | | | | | |
| 3 | WORKING CAPITAL | | | | | |
| 4 | TANGIBLE NET WORTH | | | | | |
| 5 | RATIO CURRENT ASSETS TO CURRENT LIAB. | | | | | |
| 6 | CASH. GOV. & REC. TO CURRENT LIAB. | | | | | |
| 7 | CURRENT DEBT TO NET WORTH | | | | | |
| 8 | TOTAL DEBT TO NET WORTH | | | | | |
| 9 | AV. RECEIVABLE COLLECTION PERIOD—DAYS | | | | | |
| 10 | AV. INVENTORY TURNOVER—TIMES | | | | | |
| 11 | DAYS INVENTORY ON HAND | | | | | |
| 12 | | | | | | |
| 13 | ASSETS: CASH | 153 | 46 | 50 | 83 | 128 |
| 14 | U.S. GOVERNMENT SECURITIES | | | | | |
| 15 | ACCOUNTS RECEIVABLE | 201 | 306 | 426 | 501 | 563 |
| 16 | NOTES RECEIVABLE | | | | | |
| 17 | RESERVE FOR BAD DEBTS | | | | | |
| 18 | INVENTORY | 310 | 368 | 383 | 345 | 405 |
| 19 | | | | | | |
| 20 | CURRENT ASSETS | 664 | 720 | 859 | 929 | 1.096 |
| 21 | LAND & BUILDINGS | | | | | |
| 22 | MACHINERY. EQUIPMENT & FIXTURES | | | | | |
| 23 | | | | | | |
| 24 | RESERVE FOR DEPRECIATION | | | | | |
| 25 | FIXED ASSETS | 77 | 94 | 88 | 73 | 75 |
| 26 | RECEIVABLES—MISCELLANEOUS | | | | | |
| 27 | CASH SURRENDER VALUE—LIFE INS. | | | | | |
| 28 | DUE FROM OFFICERS. EMP. OR AFFILIATES | | 4 | 19 | 23 | 11 |
| 29 | | | | | | |
| 30 | | | | | | |
| 31 | DEFERRED CHARGES & PREPAID EXPENSES | 13 | 7 | 6 | 5 | 4 |
| 32 | TOTAL ASSETS | 754 | 825 | 972 | 1030 | 1186 |
| 33 | LIABILITIES: NOTES PAYABLE—BANK | | | 94 | | 141 |
| 34 | NOTES PAYABLE—OTHER | | | | | |
| 35 | ACCOUNTS PAYABLE | 50 | 103 | 71 | 114 | 124 |
| 36 | RESERVE FOR FEDERAL INCOME TAXES | | | | | |
| 37 | ACCRUALS | 10 | 14 | 36 | 18 | 22 |
| 38 | CURRENT PORTION—DEFERRED DEBT | 23 | 24 | 24 | 32 | 32 |
| 39 | DUE TO OFFICERS. EMP. OR AFFILIATES | | | | | |
| 40 | | | | | | |
| 41 | | | | | | |
| 42 | | | | | | |
| 43 | CURRENT LIABILITIES | 83 | 141 | 225 | 164 | 319 |
| 44 | MORTGAGE DEBT: COUNTY NATL. | 34 | 11 | | | |
| 45 | FIRST NATIONAL BANK | | 107 | 94 | 83 | 73 |
| 46 | NORTH BANK | | | | 68 | 45 |
| 47 | TOTAL LIABILITIES | 117 | 259 | 319 | 315 | 437 |
| 48 | | | | | | |
| 49 | CAPITAL STOCK—PREFERRED | | | | | |
| 50 | CAPITAL STOCK—COMMON | | | | | |
| 51 | SURPLUS—CAPITAL OR PAID IN | | | | | |
| 52 | SURPLUS—EARNED | | | | | |
| 53 | NET WORTH | 637 | 566 | 653 | 715 | 749 |
| 54 | TOTAL LIAB. & NET WORTH | 754 | 825 | 972 | 1030 | 1186 |
| | CONTINGENT LIABILITY | | | | | |

## EXHIBIT 3    Bostwick Stores, Inc.—Income Statements, Years Ending January 31, 1984–88

| | (000 OMITTED) | 1984 year 1/31 | 1985 year 1/31 | 1986 year 1/31 | 1987 year 1/31 | 1988 year 1/31 |
|---|---|---|---|---|---|---|
| 1 | **SALES** | | | | | |
| 2 | | | | | | |
| 3 | LESS DISCOUNTS, RETURNS & ALLOWANCES | | | | | |
| 4 | **NET SALES** | 2.878 | 3.103 | 3.313 | 3.202 | 3.446 |
| 5 | COST OF GOODS—INVENTORY PERIOD BEGINNING | | | | | |
| 6 | PURCHASES | | | | | |
| 7 | LABOR | | | | | |
| 8 | MANUFACTURING EXPENSE | | | | | |
| 9 | | | | | | |
| 10 | TOTAL COST | | | | | |
| 11 | LESS INVENTORY PERIOD ENDED | | | | | |
| 12 | COST OF GOODS SOLD | 1.816 | 1.940 | 2.080 | 2.016 | 2.152 |
| 13 | | | | | | |
| 14 | **GROSS PROFIT** | 1.062 | 1.163 | 1.233 | 1.186 | 1.294 |
| 15 | OFFICERS' SALARIES | | | | | |
| 16 | OTHER SALARIES | | | | | |
| 17 | SELLING EXPENSE | 471 | 502 | 505 | 469 | 483 |
| 18 | GENERAL & ADMIN. EXP. | 386 | 445 | 486 | 488 | 545 |
| 19 | DEPRECIATION & AMORTIZATION | 34 | 15 | 28 | 26 | 30 |
| 20 | | | | | | |
| 21 | | | | | | |
| 22 | | | | | | |
| 23 | | | | | | |
| 24 | | | | | | |
| 25 | **TOTAL EXPENSES** | 891 | 962 | 1.019 | 983 | 1.058 |
| 26 | **OPERATING PROFIT** | 171 | 201 | 214 | 203 | 236 |
| 27 | OTHER INCOME—LEASED DEPARTMENTS | 13 | 13 | 15 | 13 | 15 |
| 28 | —SUNDRY | 4 | 8 | 19 | 39 | 43 |
| 29 | **OPERATING INCOME** | 188 | 222 | 248 | 255 | 294 |
| 30 | OTHER DEDUCTIONS: EMPLOYEE DISC. | 23 | 27 | 32 | 34 | 35 |
| 31 | | | | | | |
| 32 | **PROFIT BEFORE TAXES** | 165 | 195 | 216 | 221 | 259 |
| 33 | PROVISION FOR INCOME TAXES | | | | | |
| 34 | **NET PROFIT AFTER TAXES** | 165 | 195 | 216 | 221 | 259 |
| 35 | | | | | | |
| 36 | **SURPLUS PERIOD BEGINNING** | 654 | 637 | 566 | 653 | 715 |
| 37 | ADD | | | | | |
| 38 | PROFIT FOR PERIOD | 165 | 195 | 216 | 221 | 259 |
| 39 | ADJUSTMENT PRIOR YEARS' TAXES | | | | | |
| 40 | | | | | | |
| 41 | | | | | | |
| 42 | | | | | | |
| 43 | LESS: | | | | | |
| 44 | DIVIDENDS—PREFERRED STOCK | | | | | |
| 45 | DIVIDENDS—COMMON STOCK | | | | | |
| 46 | ADJUSTMENT PRIOR YEARS' TAXES | | | | | |
| 47 | WITHDRAWALS | 182 | 266 | 129 | 159 | 225 |
| 48 | | | | | | |
| 49 | | | | | | |
| 50 | **SURPLUS PERIOD ENDED** | 637 | 566 | 653 | 715 | 749 |
| 51 | RATIOS | | | | | |
| 52 | GROSS PROFIT MARGIN | | | | | |
| 53 | OPERATING PROFIT | | | | | |
| 54 | PROFIT AFTER TAXES | | | | | |

## EXHIBIT 4  Bostwick Stores, Inc.—Balance Sheet, May 31, 1988

|    | (000 OMITTED) | | 1988 5/31 | |
|----|---------------|--|-----------|--|
| 1  | **CURRENT ASSETS** | | | |
| 2  | **CURRENT LIABILITIES** | | | |
| 3  | **WORKING CAPITAL** | | | |
| 4  | **TANGIBLE NET WORTH** | | | |
| 5  | RATIO: | CURRENT ASSETS TO CURRENT LIAB. | | |
| 6  | | CASH. GOV. & REC. TO CURRENT LIAB. | | |
| 7  | | CURRENT DEBT TO NET WORTH | | |
| 8  | | TOTAL DEBT TO NET WORTH | | |
| 9  | AV RECEIVABLE COLLECTION PERIOD—DAYS | | | |
| 10 | AV. INVENTORY TURNOVER—TIMES | | | |
| 11 | DAYS INVENTORY ON HAND | | | |
| 12 | | | | |
| 13 | *ASSETS:* | CASH | | |
| 14 | | U.S. GOVERNMENT SECURITIES | 60 | |
| 15 | | ACCOUNTS RECEIVABLE | 538 | |
| 16 | | NOTES RECEIVABLE | | |
| 17 | | RESERVE FOR BAD DEBTS | | |
| 18 | | INVENTORY | 653 | |
| 19 | | | | |
| 20 | | **CURRENT ASSETS** | 1,251 | |
| 21 | | LAND & BUILDINGS | | |
| 22 | | MACHINERY. EQUIPMENT & FIXTURES | | |
| 23 | | | | |
| 24 | | RESERVE FOR DEPRECIATION | | |
| 25 | | **FIXED ASSETS** | 83 | |
| 26 | | RECEIVABLES—MISCELLANEOUS | | |
| 27 | | CASH SURRENDER VALUE—LIFE INS. | | |
| 28 | | DUE FROM OFFICERS, EMP. OR AFFILIATES | 2 | |
| 29 | | | | |
| 30 | | | | |
| 31 | | DEFERRED CHARGES & PREPAID EXPENSES | 11 | |
| 32 | | **TOTAL ASSETS** | 1,347 | |
| 33 | *LIABILITIES:* | NOTES PAYABLE—BANK | 203 | |
| 34 | | NOTES PAYABLE—OTHER | | |
| 35 | | ACCOUNTS PAYABLE | 255 | |
| 36 | | RESERVE FOR FEDERAL INCOME TAXES | | |
| 37 | | ACCRUALS | 32 | |
| 38 | | CURRENT PORTION—DEFERRED DEBT | 32 | |
| 39 | | DUE TO OFFICERS. EMP. OR AFFILIATES | | |
| 40 | | | | |
| 41 | | | | |
| 42 | | | | |
| 43 | | **CURRENT LIABILITIES** | 522 | |
| 44 | | MORTGAGE DEBT | | |
| 45 | | FIRST NATL. BANK | 62 | |
| 46 | | NORTH BANK | 29 | |
| 47 | | **TOTAL LIABILITIES** | 613 | |
| 48 | | | | |
| 49 | | CAPITAL STOCK—PREFERRED | | |
| 50 | | CAPITAL STOCK—COMMON | | |
| 51 | | SURPLUS—CAPITAL OR PAID IN | | |
| 52 | | SURPLUS—EARNED | | |
| 53 | | **NET WORTH** | 736 | |
| 54 | | TOTAL LIAB. & NET WORTH | 1,349 | |
| | CONTINGENT LIABILITY | | | |

## EXHIBIT 5 Bostwick Stores, Inc.—Income Statement, for Months Ending May 31, 1988

|  | (000 OMITTED) | 1988 4 mos 5/31 |
|---|---|---|
| 1 | **SALES** | 964 |
| 2 | | |
| 3 | LESS: DISCOUNTS, RETURNS & ALLOWANCES | |
| 4 | **NET SALES** | |
| 5 | COST OF GOODS—INVENTORY PERIOD BEGINNING | |
| 6 | PURCHASES | |
| 7 | LABOR | |
| 8 | MANUFACTURING EXPENSE | |
| 9 | | |
| 10 | TOTAL COST | |
| 11 | LESS: INVENTORY PERIOD ENDED | |
| 12 | COST OF GOODS SOLD | 598 |
| 13 | | |
| 14 | **GROSS PROFIT** | 366 |
| 15 | OFFICERS' SALARIES | |
| 16 | OTHER SALARIES | |
| 17 | SELLING EXPENSE | 153 |
| 18 | GENERAL & ADMIN. EXP. | 164 |
| 19 | DEPRECIATION & AMORTIZATION | 11 |
| 20 | | |
| 21 | | |
| 22 | | |
| 23 | | |
| 24 | | |
| 25 | TOTAL EXPENSES | 328 |
| 26 | **OPERATING PROFIT** | 38 |
| 27 | OTHER INCOME: LEASED DEPARTMENTS | 8 |
| 28 | SUNDRY | 15 |
| 29 | **OPERATING INCOME** | 61 |
| 30 | OTHER DEDUCTIONS: EMPLOYEE DISC. | 10 |
| 31 | | |
| 32 | **PROFIT BEFORE TAXES** | 51 |
| 33 | PROVISION FOR INCOME TAXES | |
| 34 | **NET PROFIT AFTER TAXES** | 51 |
| 35 | | |
| 36 | **SURPLUS PERIOD BEGINNING** | 749 |
| 37 | ADD: | |
| 38 | PROFIT FOR PERIOD | 51 |
| 39 | ADJUSTMENT PRIOR YEARS' TAXES | |
| 40 | | |
| 41 | | |
| 42 | | |
| 43 | LESS | |
| 44 | DIVIDENDS—PREFERRED STOCK | |
| 45 | DIVIDENDS—COMMON STOCK | |
| 46 | ADJUSTMENT PRIOR YEARS' TAXES | |
| 47 | WITHDRAWALS | 64 |
| 48 | | |
| 49 | | |
| 50 | **SURPLUS PERIOD ENDED** | 736 |
| 51 | RATIOS | |
| 52 | GROSS PROFIT MARGIN | |
| 53 | OPERATING PROFIT | |
| 54 | PROFIT AFTER TAXES | |

## EXHIBIT 6   Bostwick Stores, Inc.—Balance Sheets, September 30, 1983–87

| | | 1983 year 9/30 | 1984 year 9/30 | 1985 year 9/30 | 1986 year 9/30 | 1987 year 9/30 |
|---|---|---|---|---|---|---|
| | (000 OMITTED) | | | | | |
| 1 | **CURRENT ASSETS** | | | | | |
| 2 | **CURRENT LIABILITIES** | | | | | |
| 3 | **WORKING CAPITAL** | | | | | |
| 4 | **TANGIBLE NET WORTH** | | | | | |
| 5 | RATIO:   CURRENT ASSETS TO CURRENT LIAB. | | | | | |
| 6 |   CASH. GOV. & REC. TO CURRENT LIAB. | | | | | |
| 7 |   CURRENT DEBT TO NET WORTH | | | | | |
| 8 |   TOTAL DEBT TO NET WORTH | | | | | |
| 9 | AV. RECEIVABLE COLLECTION PERIOD—DAYS | | | | | |
| 10 | AV. INVENTORY TURNOVER—TIMES | | | | | |
| 11 | DAYS INVENTORY ON HAND | | | | | |
| 12 | | | | | | |
| 13 | ASSETS:   CASH | 11 | 36 | 2 | 1 | 3 |
| 14 |   U.S. GOVERNMENT SECURITIES | | | | | |
| 15 |   ACCOUNTS RECEIVABLE | | | | | |
| 16 |   NOTES RECEIVABLE | | | | | |
| 17 |   RESERVE FOR BAD DEBTS | | | | | |
| 18 |   INVENTORY | | | | | |
| 19 |   DUE FROM AFFILIATE | | | 49 | 27 | 48 |
| 20 |   **CURRENT ASSETS** | 11 | 36 | 51 | 28 | 51 |
| 21 |   LAND & BUILDINGS | | | | | |
| 22 |   MACHINERY, EQUIPMENT & FIXTURES | | | | | |
| 23 | | | | | | |
| 24 |   RESERVE FOR DEPRECIATION | | | | | |
| 25 |   **FIXED ASSETS** | 516 | 687 | 662 | 619 | 566 |
| 26 |   RECEIVABLES—MISCELLANEOUS | | | | | |
| 27 |   CASH SURRENDER VALUE—LIFE INS. | | | | | |
| 28 |   DUE FROM OFFICERS, EMP. OR AFFILIATES | | | | | |
| 29 | | | | | | |
| 30 | | | | | | |
| 31 |   DEFERRED CHARGES & PREPAID EXPENSES | | 1 | | | |
| 32 |   **TOTAL ASSETS** | 527 | 725 | 713 | 647 | 617 |
| 33 | LIABILITIES: NOTES PAYABLE—BANK | | | | | |
| 34 |   NOTES PAYABLE—OTHER | | | | | |
| 35 |   ACCOUNTS PAYABLE | | | | | |
| 36 |   RESERVE FOR FEDERAL INCOME TAXES | | | | | |
| 37 |   ACCRUALS | 1 | 3 | 5 | 4 | 1 |
| 38 |   CURRENT PORTION—DEFERRED DEBT MTGE. | 13 | 15 | 14 | 14 | 15 |
| 39 |   DUE TO OFFICERS. EMP. OR AFFILIATES | | | | | |
| 40 |   CPLTD—COUNTY NATL. | | 14 | 13 | 13 | 1 |
| 41 | | | | | | |
| 42 | | | | | | |
| 43 |   **CURRENT LIABILITIES** | 14 | 32 | 32 | 31 | 17 |
| 44 |   MORTGAGE DEBT | 355 | 342 | 327 | 313 | 298 |
| 45 |   COUNTY NATL. | | 28 | 14 | 1 | |
| 48 | | | | | | |
| 47 |   **TOTAL LIABILITIES** | 369 | 402 | 373 | 345 | 315 |
| 48 | | | | | | |
| 49 |   CAPITAL STOCK—PREFERRED | | | | | |
| 50 |   CAPITAL STOCK—COMMON | | | | | |
| 51 |   SURPLUS—CAPITAL OR PAID IN | | | | | |
| 52 |   SURPLUS—EARNED | | | | | |
| 53 |   **NET WORTH** | 158 | 323 | 340 | 302 | 302 |
| 54 |   TOTAL LIAB. & NET WORTH | 527 | 725 | 713 | 647 | 617 |
| | CONTINGENT LIABILITIES | | | | | |

**EXHIBIT 7 Bostwick Stores, Inc.—Income Statements, Years Ending September 30, 1983–87**

| | (000 OMITTED) | 1983 year 9/30 | 1984 year 9/30 | 1985 year 9/30 | 1986 year 9/30 | 1987 year 9/30 |
|---|---|---|---|---|---|---|
| 1 | **SALES** | | | | | |
| 2 | | | | | | |
| 3 | LESS: DISCOUNTS. RETURNS & ALLOWANCES | | | | | |
| 4 | **NET SALES** | 45 | 79 | 84 | 83 | 88 |
| 5 | COST OF GOODS—INVENTORY PERIOD BEGINNING | | | | | |
| 6 | PURCHASES | | | | | |
| 7 | LABOR | | | | | |
| 8 | MANUFACTURING EXPENSE | | | | | |
| 9 | | | | | | |
| 10 | TOTAL COST | | | | | |
| 11 | LESS: INVENTORY PERIOD ENDED | | | | | |
| 12 | LESS: COST OF GOODS SOLD | | | | | |
| 13 | | | | | | |
| 14 | **GROSS PROFIT** | | | | | |
| 15 | OFFICERS' SALARIES | | | | | |
| 16 | OTHER SALARIES | | | | | |
| 17 | SELLING EXPENSE | | | | | |
| 18 | GENERAL & ADMIN. EXP. | | | | | |
| 19 | DEPRECIATION & AMORTIZATION | 45 | 45 | 52 | 54 | 53 |
| 20 | INTEREST EXPENSE | 6 | 17 | 15 | 14 | 12 |
| 21 | | | | | | |
| 22 | | | | | | |
| 23 | | | | | | |
| 24 | | | | | | |
| 25 | TOTAL EXPENSES | 51 | 62 | 67 | 68 | 65 |
| 26 | **OPERATING PROFIT** | | | | | |
| 27 | OTHER INCOME | | | | | |
| 28 | | | | | | |
| 29 | **OPERATING INCOME** | | | | | |
| 30 | OTHER DEDUCTIONS | | | | | |
| 31 | | | | | | |
| 32 | **PROFIT BEFORE TAXES** | (6) | 17 | 17 | 15 | 23 |
| 33 | PROVISION FOR INCOME TAXES | | | | | |
| 34 | **NET PROFIT AFTER TAXES** | (6) | 17 | 17 | 15 | 23 |
| 35 | | | | | | |
| 36 | **SURPLUS PERIOD BEGINNING** | 164 | 158 | 323 | 340 | 302 |
| 37 | ADD: | | | | | |
| 38 | PROFIT FOR PERIOD | (6) | 17 | 17 | 15 | 23 |
| 39 | ADJUSTMENT PRIOR YEARS' TAXES | | | | | |
| 40 | OTHER ADDITIONS | | 148 | | | |
| 41 | | | | | | |
| 42 | | | | | | |
| 43 | LESS: | | | | | |
| 44 | DIVIDENDS—PREFERRED STOCK | | | | | |
| 45 | DIVIDENDS—COMMON STOCK | | | | | |
| 46 | ADJUSTMENT PRIOR YEARS' TAXES | | | | | |
| 47 | WITHDRAWALS | | | | 53 | 23 |
| 48 | | | | | | |
| 49 | | | | | | |
| 50 | **SURPLUS PERIOD ENDED** | 158 | 323 | 340 | 302 | 302 |
| 51 | RATIOS: | | | | | |
| 52 | GROSS PROFIT MARGIN | | | | | |
| 53 | OPERATING PROFIT | | | | | |
| 54 | PROFIT AFTER TAXES | | | | | |

CASE

15

# BERGNER CONSTRUCTION COMPANY*

In May 1988, Mr. Peter Davis, a newly appointed loan officer at Westside National Bank in Cleveland, Ohio, received a request from John Bergner, president of Bergner Construction Company, for an increase in his revolving credit line to $250,000. Bergner's borrowing relationships were presently established at FirstOhio Bank in Cleveland, where he had been a customer for the past five years. For various reasons, however, Bergner wanted to change banks and to increase his revolving line from $100,000 to $250,000, leaving his other credit needs unchanged. Mr. Bergner explained to Peter Davis that this additional credit was required to help finance a large construction project that his company had just been awarded by the Pepsi-Cola Bottling Company in Boulder, Colorado.

Bergner Construction Company, located in Cleveland, Ohio, was a mechanical contracting business, specializing in specialty construction projects in food and beverage manufacturing facilities. The company was a "custom-built" contractor, using primarily stainless steel to build the vessels and piping necessary for assembly lines in food and beverage processing. Like most specialty contractors, Bergner's installations were largely on a project-by-project basis, for which it provided engineering design and construction expertise to its clients. Companies of this kind required relatively little complex, specialized production equipment, and most inventory was associated with specific jobs in progress. Accordingly, Bergner Construction was thinly capitalized, like many firms in this kind of construction work.

The company's president, John Bergner, was 40 years of age. He held a degree in mechanical engineering from Ohio State University. Bergner began his career as a foreman for a large construction company that manufactured specialty food and beverage facilities. Having gathered several years of valuable on-the-job industry experience,

*This case was written by Sumon Mazumdar, Faculty of Management, McGill University, Montreal, Canada.

Mr. Bergner subsequently formed his own company, which was incorporated in 1982.

Mr. Bergner initially did business with the FirstOhio Bank of Cleveland, where his account was handled by Peter Davis. During the next five years, 1982–1987, a comfortable working relationship developed between the two men. Davis came to regard John Bergner as an honest and energetic entrepreneur. The banker found it easy to do business with his client, who was a pleasant, outgoing person clearly eager to expand his business.

In December 1987, Mr. Davis accepted a new position, with a higher salary and greater responsibility, at the Westside National Bank, also located in Cleveland. Accordingly, the construction company's account was transferred to another loan officer at FirstOhio in January 1988.

Bergner Construction Company had recorded a small net operating profit of $13,088 in 1987. During the first four months of 1988, however, the company's completed jobs slumped, leading to a loss of $53,556 for that period. Mr. Bergner explained to his new loan officer that this loss was due largely to problems encountered on one project, for which a former estimator had underestimated construction costs. These results did not truly reflect the firm's capabilities, in Mr. Bergner's opinion. He pointed out that his company had enjoyed a sales growth rate of 23 percent over the past two years, and projected sales by the end of 1988 were $1.3 million.

Bergner required a moderate increase in his credit line to cover these losses and to complete other projects that his firm had been awarded. He quickly learned, however, that the new loan officer at FirstOhio was quite reluctant to commit a larger line of credit for these purposes. Thus, in May 1988, John Bergner considered transferring his account to Westside National, where he hoped his business would continue to be handled by Mr. Davis, with whom he had enjoyed a satisfactory and understanding relationship.

After an initial meeting at Westside National

Bank, Mr. Davis recommended John Bergner's company at the bank's loan committee, stressing his honesty and positive business attitude. Davis strongly urged his bank to add Bergner's company as a new customer and to approve the credit request, which had, in effect, been declined by the FirstOhio Bank.

Peter Davis was a "character" lender. He felt most strongly that a crucial aspect in loan decisions was the integrity of the loan applicant. If he believed the applicant to be honest and knowledgeable about his business and if an adequate check of the applicant's credit history was satisfactory, Mr. Davis was often prepared to approve a loan, even if the client's financial statements might be considered somewhat weak.

In Bergner's case, the very nature of the contract construction business implied a low capital base, a factor that Davis argued should be considered in this case. Moreover, financial statements were often misleading, in Davis' opinion. He had concluded that the current somewhat weak financial state of Bergner's business did not imply an inability to manage his credit responsibilities properly. Indeed, Davis' faith in Bergner's integrity persuaded him that the proposed loan would be repaid, consistent with the company's past performance. It was important to Bergner that the present loan request be granted, since he was extremely anxious to proceed with the large Pepsi-Cola contract in Colorado, which would require additional financing before the project could be undertaken.

Peter Davis' polished presentation and eloquent appeal, however, left the committee undecided, and the decision was deferred, in part by limited time in committee, until the next meeting of the Loan Review Committee three days hence. The specific credit arrangements requested by Davis were as follows:

1. The sum of $100,000, which would be CD secured, the proceeds of which would be used to pay off Bergner's outstanding debt at FirstOhio Bank.

2. A $250,000 revolving line of credit, to be secured by accounts receivable and inventory (replacing an existing line of $100,000 at FirstOhio). The company's inventory consisted mainly of work in progress and raw materials.

3. A total of $128,000 in various equipment loans. These loans were secured by filings on various pieces of equipment, such as trucks, cars, forklifts, air compressors, and other tools. These loans were already approved and funded at FirstOhio. The loans and related security arrangements would also be moved, but this represented no increase in balances outstanding on this equipment. In most cases, the bank financed 100 percent of the original cost of equipment purchased.

Bergner Construction Company had limited its operations to the midwestern market, generally within a 500-mile radius of Cleveland. Mr. Bergner had always been anxious, however, to expand his business, and especially to search for contracts in other parts of the country to achieve greater geographical diversification. Accordingly, he had successfully bid for a renovation project at a Pepsi-Cola bottling plant in Boulder, Colorado, winning the bid in April 1988.

John Bergner felt that this new project offered an ideal opportunity to broaden his company's business contacts. This job would also represent the largest single construction project that his company had ever undertaken ($400,000), and he projected a 15 percent pretax profit as part of his winning bid. Its successful completion would, he hoped, improve prospects for future profitability.

For all these reasons, then, in May 1988 Mr. Bergner wanted to change his banking relationship by asking Peter Davis to move the Bergner account and to increase his revolving credit line to $250,000. Since Davis was a new loan officer at Westside and Bergner also represented a new customer, the Loan Review Committee realized they should carefully consider this credit request. Moreover, the amount involved would be substantial for Westside Bank.

The thinly capitalized structure of Bergner Construction Company was not, in Davis' mind, a significant handicap, since the contractual nature of the business did not require expensive long-term commitments to capital items such as plant and equipment. Questions were raised on this point, however, in the initial Loan Review Committee meeting.

Construction companies typically work on a project-to-project basis. If no single project is excessively dominant, then a loss on one does not imply that the firm's profit potential would be significantly affected.

Peter Davis was anxious to "sell" this new customer to the bank's Loan Review Committee, partly because of his confidence in Bergner and also to show to his new colleagues his approach to lending and loan decisions.

**EXHIBIT I    Balance Sheet—Bergner Construction Company (dollars)**

|  | 4/30/88 | | 12/31/87 | | 12/31/86 | |
|---|---|---|---|---|---|---|
| **Assets** | | | | | | |
| Current assets | | | | | | |
| Cash | 150,408 | | 5,699 | | 18,697 | |
| CD | 100,000 | | 102,200 | | 115,200 | |
| Accounts receivable | 419,628 | | 80,047 | | 55,346 | |
| Inventory | 135,044 | | 62,068 | | 11,137 | |
| Total current assets | | 805,080 | | 250,014 | | 200,380 |
| **Fixed assets** | | | | | | |
| Furniture and fixtures | 7,620 | | 6,430 | | 5,780 | |
| Leasehold improvements | 35,120 | | 30,000 | | 27,700 | |
| Automobiles and trucks | 73,079 | | 65,570 | | 49,052 | |
| Accumulated depreciation | (69,414) | | (40,011) | | (23,500) | |
| Total fixed assets | | 46,405 | | 61,989 | | 59,032 |
| **Other assets** | | | | | | |
| Deposits | 85,500 | | 44,161 | | 6,500 | |
| Total other assets | | 85,500 | | 44,161 | | 6,500 |
| Total assets | | $936,985 | | $356,164 | | $265,912 |
| **Liabilities** | | | | | | |
| Current liabilities | | | | | | |
| Accounts payable—taxes | 1,104 | | 1,071 | | 903 | |
| Accounts payable—trade | 37,102 | | 26,400 | | 11,000 | |
| Bank loans payable | 100,000 | | 61,000 | | 6,000 | |
| Accrued expenses | 13,894 | | 10,867 | | 3,394 | |
| Customer deposits | 596,430 | | 3,562 | | 5,982 | |
| Total current liabilities | | 748,530 | | 102,900 | | 27,279 |
| **Long-term liabilities** | | | | | | |
| Notes payable—equipment | 153,408 | | 169,147 | | 159,771 | |
| Total long-term liabilities | | 153,408 | | 169,147 | | 159,771 |
| Total liabilities | | 901,938 | | 272,047 | | 187,050 |
| **Equity** | | | | | | |
| Capital | 82,729 | | 67,615 | | 68,417 | |
| Current year profit (loss) | (47,682) | | 16,502 | | 10,445 | |
| Total net equity | | 35,047 | | 84,117 | | 78,862 |
| Total liabilities and equity | | $936,985 | | $356,164 | | $265,912 |

**EXHIBIT 2   Consolidated Income Statement—Bergner Construction Company**

| | 1/1/88–<br>4/30/88 | % | 1/1/87–<br>12/31/87 | % | 1/1/86–<br>12/30/86 | % |
|---|---|---|---|---|---|---|
| Income: | | | | | | |
| Contract sales | $571,173 | 97.0 | $ 970,411 | 95.0 | $707,607 | 90.0 |
| Noncontract sales | 17,665 | 3.0 | 51,074 | 5.0 | 78,623 | 10.0 |
| Total income | $588,838 | 100.0 | $1,021,485 | 100.0 | $786,230 | 100.0 |
| Cost of sales: | | | | | | |
| Noncontract cost | 13,543 | 2.3 | 30,682 | 3.0 | 39,311 | 5.0 |
| Noncontract cost—travel | 29,854 | 5.1 | 63,130 | 6.2 | 78,623 | 10.0 |
| Contract cost—material | 209,626 | 35.6 | 306,445 | 30.0 | 196,557 | 25.0 |
| Contract cost—labor | 141,321 | 24.0 | 296,230 | 29.0 | 235,869 | 30.0 |
| Lease cost | 23,555 | 4.0 | 71,503 | 7.0 | 51,450 | 6.6 |
| Contract cost—travel | 17,720 | 3.0 | 40,860 | 4.0 | 31,449 | 4.0 |
| Total cost of sales | 435,619 | 74.0 | 808,850 | 79.2 | 633,259 | 80.6 |
| Gross profit | $153,219 | 26.0 | $ 212,635 | 20.8 | $152,971 | 19.4 |
| Operating expenses: | | | | | | |
| Depreciation | 29,403 | 5.0 | 16,511 | 1.6 | 19,913 | 2.5 |
| Travel and entertainment | 34,788 | 5.9 | 59,820 | 5.9 | 29,719 | 3.8 |
| Interest | 24,617 | 4.1 | 11,700 | 1.1 | 15,789 | 2.0 |
| Professional fees | 5,422 | 0.9 | 5,822 | 0.6 | 13,027 | 1.7 |
| Salaries | 33,911 | 5.8 | 61,245 | 6.0 | 21,969 | 2.8 |
| Taxes (other than FIT) | 10,909 | 1.9 | 8,410 | 0.8 | 9,680 | 1.2 |
| Automobile expense | 8,312 | 1.4 | 5,321 | 0.5 | 7,502 | 0.9 |
| Rent | 20,172 | 3.4 | 6,940 | 0.7 | 6,953 | 0.9 |
| Telephone | 7,030 | 1.2 | 8,482 | 0.8 | 5,287 | 0.7 |
| Insurance | 19,420 | 3.3 | 7,484 | 0.7 | 3,895 | 0.5 |
| Other | 12,791 | 2.2 | 7,812 | 0.8 | 8,792 | 1.1 |
| Total operating expenses | 206,775 | 35.1 | 199,547 | 19.5 | 142,526 | 18.1 |
| Operating income | (53,556) | −9.1 | 13,088 | 1.3 | 10,445 | 1.3 |
| Other income | 5,874 | 1.0 | 3,414 | 0.3 | 0 | 0 |
| Net income | $ (47,682) | −8.1 | $ 16,502 | 1.6 | $ 10,445 | 1.3 |

**EXHIBIT 3  Financial Ratios—Bergner Construction Company**

|  | 4/30/88 | 12/31/87 | 12/31/86 |
|---|---|---|---|
| Liquidity |  |  |  |
| Current ratio | 1.07 | 2.42 | 7.34 |
| "Acid test" ratio | 0.89 | 1.82 | 6.93 |
| Leverage |  |  |  |
| Debt/total assets | 0.96 | 0.76 | 0.70 |
| Debt/equity | 25.73 | 3.23 | 2.37 |
| Activity |  |  |  |
| Inventory turnover[a] | 13.26× | 22.09× | 56.86× |
| Average collection period (days)[a] | 86.70 | 28.60 | 25.69 |
| Fixed asset turnover[a] | 32.59× | 16.88× | 13.31× |
| Profitability |  |  |  |
| Profit margin on sales | −8.1% | 1.6% | 1.3% |
| Return on total assets (ROA)[a] | −22.0% | 5.3% | 3.9% |
| Return on equity (ROE)[a] | −240.0% | 20.2% | 13.2% |

[a]Annualized.

# CASE 16  QUESTOR, INC.

Catherine Logan was president of Questor, Inc., a manufacturer of valves and pipe fittings. In April 1992, she visited Felix Fernandez, a loan officer for Golden West Bank, with a loan request. She gave Fernandez Questor's financial statements for the years 1990 and 1991 and for the most recent three-month period ending March 31, 1992. Logan indicated that she wanted Golden West Bank to provide Questor's banking requirements, including Questor's needs for loan funds.

She complained that her present bank had become careless in serving Questor's banking requirements and that the loan officers assigned to Questor's account were being changed frequently, causing her great inconvenience. She was frustrated with having to explain Questor's needs and business every time there was a change in loan officers. Recently, Questor's line of credit agreement with its present bank had expired, and the bank seemed to be delaying action on the firm's request for a much needed moderate increase in the line.

Logan informed Felix Fernandez that she would need as much as $1,000,000 during the next 12 months. She wanted part of the credit in 90-day notes and the rest on an intermediate-term basis. "Our sales volume continues to grow and our profits are good," she commented to Fernandez. "We have been in business for 15 years and we have been profitable every year. Our equipment is in good condition, and we will not have to expand our plant for at least three more years." Logan offered as references her current mortgage lender, Fairview Savings and Loan Association, and several of her major suppliers.

Later, Felix Fernandez made credit checks with these suppliers, who reported a pattern of generally prompt payment. They stated that Questor was usually prompt in meeting credit obligations. The highest credit reported by a single supplier was $150,000. However, Questor was not always able to take trade discounts, which all suppliers offered on a 2/10/net 30 basis.

Fairview Savings and Loan reported a balance of $275,000 owed on an original $500,000 loan. Payments of $25,000 per quarter were being made promptly. The loan from Fairview Savings was secured by land and buildings owned by Questor.

Felix Fernandez had not yet checked with Questor's present bank to discuss its experience with Questor. Golden West Bank was very anxious to establish a complete business relationship with Questor, but Fernandez was uncertain how to approach Questor's present bank and how to interpret what officers from that bank might tell him.

After Fernandez conducted his initial investigation, he called Catherine Logan to set up a meeting at the bank. At the meeting, Logan made a specific request for a $1,000,000 loan. In addition to the financial statements she provided earlier (Exhibits 1 through 3), she provided a personal financial statement (Exhibit 4). Fernandez had also received a ratio analysis on Questor from Golden West Bank's credit analysis department (Exhibit 5).

Logan indicated that Questor's inventory was composed of the following:

| | |
|---|---|
| Raw material | 40% |
| Work in process | 20% |
| Finished goods | 40% |

Fernandez was advised by another loan officer that the fractions of values that could be recovered on short notice for inventories such as Questor's were about 50, 0, and 50 percent, respectively, for raw, in-process, and finished inventories.

On Questor's accounts receivable, Fernandez wondered if those outstanding for more than 60 days actually could be collected. He was also worried because Questor continued currently to sell to customers with receivables older than 60 days, and he wondered if he should assign any value at all to the receivables of such customers. Finally, he decided to appraise accounts receivable that were on time at only the cost of production (cost of goods), about 70 percent of their book value.

## ASSIGNMENTS

1. *Amount of loan:* As a check against the $1,000,000 loan amount requested by Logan, determine how much Questor actually needs to borrow. (Estimate Questor's balance sheet for December 31, 1992, based on continued growth and industry average ratios for an average collection period and inventory turnover. Estimate December 1992 accounts payable based on taking a substantially higher amount of trade discounts than are presently taken.)

2. *Purpose:* Determine the purpose for the loan.

3. *Term for each type of borrowing:* Determine how much of the total amount loaned will be loaned short term and how much long term (or revolving).

4. *Collateral value and borrowing base:* Assuming that the bank secures the loan with Questor's accounts receivable and inventories, determine how much value can be recovered if Questor fails to pay. (Alternatively, determine how much Golden West Bank can safely lend against Questor's accounts receivable and inventories.)

5. *Repayment terms:* Establish a repayment schedule for each type of borrowing.

6. *Repayment source:* Identify the cash flow sources of repayment for each type of borrowing.

7. *Rate:* Establish the interest rate on each type of borrowing. (Specify in terms of points above the prime rate.)

8. *Guarantees, covenants, and other restrictions:* Specify the covenants to be placed on Questor. Describe the guarantees or other restrictions.

**EXHIBIT 1  Income and Expenses—Questor, Inc.**

|  | Three Months 1992 | 1991 | 1990 | 1989 |
|---|---|---|---|---|
| Sales revenue | $1,878,000 | $6,400,000 | $6,101,000 | $5,400,000 |
| Cost of goods sold | 1,333,380 | 4,480,000 | 4,209,000 | 3,780,000 |
| Gross profit | 544,620 | 1,920,000 | 1,892,000 | 1,620,000 |
| Operating expense | 423,845 | 1,362,000 | 1,359,000 | 1,127,000 |
| Net income before taxes and interest | 120,775 | 558,000 | 533,000 | 493,000 |
| Other expenses (includes interest) | 41,899 | 174,000 | 159,900 | 169,000 |
| Income taxes | 27,606 | 134,400 | 130,584 | 113,400 |
| Profit after taxes | $    51,270 | $   249,600 | $   242,516 | $   210,600 |

**EXHIBIT 2  Balance Sheet—Questor, Inc.**

|  | March 31 1992 | Dec. 31 1991 | Dec. 31 1990 | Dec. 31 1989 |
|---|---|---|---|---|
| Cash | $      67,800 | $    113,000 | $    139,320 | $    130,600 |
| Account receivable | 1,009,960 | 914,284 | 859,320 | 782,600 |
| Inventory | 1,780,000 | 1,357,600 | 1,315,200 | 1,111,800 |
| Current assets | 2,857,760 | 2,384,884 | 2,313,840 | 2,025,000 |
| Land | 100,000 | 100,000 | 100,000 | 100,000 |
| Plant and equipment | 614,000 | 610,000 | 602,700 | 598,000 |
| Depreciation | ($280,000) | ($270,000) | ($230,000) | ($190,000) |
| Net plant and equipment | 334,000 | 340,000 | 372,700 | 408,000 |
| Total assets | $3,291,760 | $2,824,884 | $2,786,540 | $2,533,000 |
| Notes payable (bank) | $    800,000 | $    800,000 | $    650,000 | $    650,000 |
| Accounts payable | 640,834 | 190,228 | 467,364 | 370,460 |
| Accrued expenses | 70,000 | 80,000 | 64,000 | 50,000 |
| Current liabilities | 1,510,834 | 1,070,228 | 1,181,364 | 1,070,460 |
| Long-term debt | 275,000 | 300,000 | 400,000 | 500,000 |
| Total liabilities | 1,785,834 | 1,370,228 | 1,581,364 | 1,570,460 |
| Capital | 100,000 | 100,000 | 100,000 | 100,000 |
| Retained earnings | 1,405,926 | 1,354,656 | 1,105,176 | 862,540 |
| Total stockholders' equity | 1,505,926 | 1,454,656 | 1,205,176 | 962,540 |
| Total liabilities and equity | $3,291,760 | $2,824,884 | $2,786,540 | $2,533,000 |

**EXHIBIT 3  Accounts Receivable Aging (March 31, 1992)—Questor, Inc.**

| Customer | Credit Extended Since Feb. 29, 1992 | Credit Extended During: | | | |
|---|---|---|---|---|---|
| | | Feb. 1992 | Jan. 1992 | Dec. 1991 | Before Dec. 1991 |
| Bunson, J. C. | $ 33,000 | $ 66,000 | | | |
| Carpenter Co. | 44,000 | | | | |
| Dalton Co. | | | $ 20,000 | | |
| Davidson Co. | 15,000 | | 15,000 | | |
| Fredrick Co. | | | | $ 6,000 | |
| Gaston, Inc. | 45,000 | | | | |
| Hardy Sons | | | | | $25,000 |
| Ivor | 6,000 | 5,000 | | 10,000 | |
| Logan, Inc. | 104,000 | | | | |
| Jefferson, Inc. | 52,000 | 3,600 | | | |
| Kessel Sons | 54,000 | 30,000 | 60,000 | 6,000 | 2,000 |
| Lamont Co. | 10,000 | | | | |
| Lawrence Sons | 35,600 | | | | |
| Massey, Inc. | | 15,000 | 30,000 | | 34,000 |
| Nestor | 12,000 | | | | |
| Olympia | 84,000 | | | | |
| Pinocle, Co. | | 4,000 | 10,000 | 10,000 | 10,000 |
| Trenton, Inc. | 45,000 | 8,000 | | | |
| Trilogy | 26,000 | 30,000 | | 5,000 | |
| Watson | (240) | | | | |
| Other | 40,000 | | | | |
| Total | $ 605,360 | $161,600 | $135,000 | $37,000 | $71,000 |
| Total of all receivables | $1,009,960 | | | | |

**EXHIBIT 4   Personal Financial Statement for Catherine and Cyril Logan (April 1, 1992)**

| Assets | | Liabilities and Equity | |
|---|---|---|---|
| Cash | $ 24,000 | Notes payable—banks | $ 150,000 |
| Marketable securities | 108,000 | Notes payable—Questor, Inc. | 65,000 |
| Loan receivables from Logan, Inc. | 80,000 | Mortgage on home | 335,000 |
| Residence | 550,000 | Total liabilities | 550,000 |
| Automobiles | 44,000 | Equity | 1,821,926 |
| Personal property | 60,000 | | |
| Stock of Questor, Inc. (book value) | 1,505,926 | | |
| Total assets | $2,371,926 | Total liabilities and equity | $2,371,926 |

| | |
|---|---|
| Salary (1991) | $150,000 |
| Bonus (estimated) | 30,000 |
| Other | 2,000 |
| Total Income | $182,000 |

## EXHIBIT 5  Financial Ratios—Questor, Inc.

|  | 1992[a] | 1991 | 1990 | 1989 | Industry Avg., 1991 |
|---|---|---|---|---|---|
| **Liquidity Ratios** | | | | | |
| Current ratio $= \dfrac{\text{current assets}}{\text{current liabilities}}$ | 1.892 | 2.228 | 1.959 | 1.892 | 2.100 |
| Quick ratios $= \dfrac{\text{current assets} - \text{inventory}}{\text{current liabilities}}$ | 0.713 | 0.960 | 0.845 | 0.853 | 1.000 |
| **Activity Ratios** | | | | | |
| Average collection period $= \dfrac{\text{accounts receivable}}{\text{annual sales rev./365 days}}$ (days) | 49.07 | 52.14 | 51.41 | 52.90 | 49.00 |
| Inventory turnover $= \dfrac{\text{costs of goods sold}}{\text{avg. inventory}}$ (times) | 3.400 | 3.352 | 3.468 | — | 3.600 |
| **Financial Leverage Ratios** | | | | | |
| Debt to equity $= \dfrac{\text{total liabilities}}{\text{tot. stockholders' equity}}$ | 1.186 | 0.942 | 1.312 | 1.632 | 1.500 |
| Coverage of interest expenses $= \dfrac{\text{net income before taxes and interest}}{\text{interest expenses}^b}$ | 8.99 | 10.15 | 10.15 | 8.57 | 3.50 |
| **Profitability Ratios** | | | | | |
| Gross profit margin $= \dfrac{\text{sales revenue} - \text{cost of goods sold}}{\text{sales revenue}}$ | 29.00% | 30.00% | 31.01% | 30.00% | 30.70% |
| Net profit margin $= \dfrac{\text{profit after taxes}}{\text{sales revenue}}$ | 2.73% | 3.90% | 3.98% | 3.90% | 3.60% |
| Return on total assets $= \dfrac{\text{profit after taxes}}{\text{total assets}}$ | 6.23% | 8.84% | 8.70% | 8.31% | 5.07% |
| Return on equity $= \dfrac{\text{profit after taxes}}{\text{tot. stockholders' equity}}$ | 13.62% | 17.16% | 20.12% | 21.88% | 17.00% |

[a] 1992 quarterly figures are annualized.
[b] Interest expenses = interest-bearing liabilities × assumed 10% interest rate.

**CASE**

# 17

# FIRST INTERSTATE NATIONAL BANK

## GEOGRAPHIC LOCATION AND HISTORY

The First Interstate National Bank (FINB), with total deposits of $65 million, was located in what was, until three years ago, an agricultural community 10 miles distant from a large city in Iowa. Since its establishment in the late 1940s, the bank had experienced slow but healthy growth, catering to the banking needs of townspeople and farmers, most of whom were personally well known to all the bank staff.

## ECONOMIC CHANGES

In 1984, a major oil company decided to relocate a large section of its executive and administrative staff to new offices just outside the town's boundaries. In the same year, construction began on a large residential development aimed at middle-class homeowners. Since that time, FINB had realized exceptional growth in both deposits and loans, especially consumer lending, which by 1987 totaled $8.5 million outstanding. All evidence pointed to continued demand for still higher consumer credit.

## STAFFING

With the exception of the president and executive vice-president (who was also the senior credit officer), the bank's lending staff consisted of five officers. Two of these officers serviced primarily commercial, real estate, and agricultural loans. The remaining three officers handled all consumer-related requests.

The two commercial loan officers had been trained by the senior credit officer. One of the consumer loan officers had been with the bank since it opened, and training of the two other consumer lenders had been more or less left up to her. The consumer loan officers received excellent support from both loan operations and the credit section, thus relieving them of nearly all clerical functions.

## PORTFOLIO CONDITION

Two months ago, a profitability study submitted to the president and board of directors indicated that, although growth was continuing in the consumer loan portfolio, profitability had declined due to delinquency losses and low rates. It was recognized that the demographic profile of the bank's customer base had changed dramatically. Accordingly, a knowledgeable and experienced consumer loan manager was employed to reverse the declining profitability trend.

After performing an audit of the portfolio and an evaluation of the staff, the consumer loan manager identified the following problem areas:

1. Little or no written documentation could be found on consumer borrowers, other than some incomplete applications accompanied only by credit bureau reports.

2. In cases in which borrower information was obtained, no basis for loan decisions was evident either for approvals or for rejections.

3. Average losses on auto repossessions had been greater than national or state averages.

4. Five percent of the losses over the past year on automobiles were directly attributable to physical damage losses of the collateral, and no insurance coverage was evident at the time of repossession.

5. Thirty-day and other delinquent accounts were being contacted by either mail-out notices or letters sent out by the individual loan officers at month end.

6. Many single-maturity loans had been renewed without reduction, and files contained no liquidation agreements.

7. Extensions on installment payments appeared excessive.

8. Many errors on forms and incorrect collateral documents were noted.

9. There appeared to be no consistency to consumer loan rates and terms.

10. Loan officers were unaware of any lending or overdraft limitations.

11. Several "balloon" contracts had been noted, together with other unattractive loans.

12. There was evidently confusion between loan officers, loan operations, and the credit section relating to loan officers' responsibilities.

13. Loan officers appeared to base loan decisions primarily on intuitive reasons rather than on an analysis of facts, sound credit principles, acquisition costs, and potential exposure.

### RECOMMENDATIONS

The consumer loan manager recommended that an extensive staff training program be implemented and a written credit policy adopted.

Both recommendations were approved. After a consumer credit policy was submitted, however, the senior credit officer indicated reluctance to approve some facets of it. His reluctance was based on feelings that the policy might be overrestrictive and demoralizing to personnel, create additional expense and paperwork, and act as a deterrent to the acquisition of loans.

Accordingly a meeting was scheduled by the senior credit officer to discuss the proposed policy with all concerned. A copy of the draft policy is included as Exhibit 1.

---

**EXHIBIT 1    First Interstate National Bank Consumer Credit Policies—A Draft Proposal, June 2, 1988**

## GENERAL STATEMENT AND PURPOSE

It is the intent of the consumer lending section, in accordance with total bank objectives, to increase growth and earnings while contributing to the development of the community through the employment of funds invested in a profitable and liquid consumer loan portfolio.

To achieve these objectives certain standards, authorizations, responsibilities, and guidelines must be set forth in order to provide affected personnel with direction, development, and control.

It is recognized that all conditions, as well as objectives and goals, are subject to change. As a result, this policy will be reviewed quarterly or at any time deemed necessary by the senior credit officer or the consumer loan manager.

## ORGANIZATION CHART

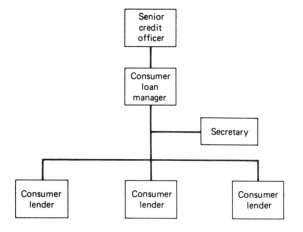

**EXHIBIT I**    *(continued)*

I. Lending Guidelines
  A. *Service Area*
     The service area of First Interstate National Bank shall be considered within a 15-mile radius of the bank's location.
  B. *Loan Eligibility*
     Loan requests will be entertained only for bank depositors. However, the opening of a new deposit account at the time of application may constitute eligibility.
  C. *Minimum Loans*
     Single maturity—$1,000.00.
     Installment—$500.00.

     Single maturity—Minimum 12 percent simple; term maximum 12 months, with reduction each 90 days.
     Secured new auto—Minimum 7.5 percent add-on; term maximum 42 months.
     New auto—Minimum 7 percent add-on; term maximum 36 months.
     Used auto (one year old)—Minimum 7.5 percent add-on; term maximum 30 months.
     Used auto (two years old)—Minimum 8 percent add-on; term maximum 24 months.
     Used auto (three years old)—Minimum 8.5 percent add-on; term maximum 18 months.

     Any financing on autos older than three years pledged as collateral should be considered as a personal loan not to exceed a term of 12 months at the maximum rate of 9 percent add-on.

     New cars primarily used for business purposes will be limited to a maximum term of 30 months and a 7.5 percent add-on rate.

     Home improvement loans (insured program):
     Maximum $25,000—Maturity 120 months; rate 7.5 percent add-on.
     Less than $2,500—Maximum maturity 60 months; rate 7.0 percent add-on.

     All home improvement loans exceeding a $5,000 net advance or 60-month term must have the manager's joint approval with the loan officer.

     Secured Savings:
     Minimum installment rates for time or saving deposits pledged as collateral—6.5 percent, not to exceed 36 months' maturity.
     Minimum single maturity—1½ percent over prime on loans exceeding $1,000, with a floor of 1½ percent of deposit interest; maximum 10 percent simple interest on a 365-day base computation.

     Boat Loans:
     New boats—7.5 percent minimum; maturity 36 months.
     Used boats (one-year model)—8 percent minimum; maturity 30 months.
     All others—9 percent, not to exceed 24 months.

     Appliances, Furniture, etc.:
     All such requests fall into the personal loan category. Except for special considerations, these applications should be treated as unsecured credits, not to exceed 12 months at a minimum rate of 9 percent add-on.

---

**EXHIBIT I** *(continued)*

---

D. *Down Payments*

All new-car requests for 42-month financing will require a minimum down payment of 20 percent of the selling price. All other new-car loan requests should have a minimum of 12 to 15 percent of the selling price. Used-car financing should not exceed NADA loan value.

Boat loans—required minimum down payment is 15 percent of the selling price. Home improvement loans—subject to mortgage equity and borrower creditworthiness.

E. *Unattractive Credits*

1. Single-maturity auto loans—As a matter of policy, no auto loans will be approved without the written authorization of the manager or the senior credit officer.
2. "Balloon" notes—Requests of this type should be discouraged and will not be approved without the written authorization of the manager or the senior credit officer.
3. Consolidation loans—Unless 100 percent collateralized, this type of loan will not be approved without the written authorization of the manager or the senior credit officer.
4. Speculative ventures—Loans to finance commodity issues, "get-rich-quick" real estate, and so on will not be approved.
5. Commercial requests—All commercial requests will be referred to the commercial loan officers.

F. *Special Requests*

Consumer-related loan requests such as mobile home, recreational vehicle, and cosigner or guarantor loans should be referred to the manager.

G. *Applicant Requirements and Qualifications*

1. Effective with this policy, all new borrowers will have a file established consisting of an application, a credit investigation, and any other information allowable by law pertaining to the borrower. New applicants will be required to complete a written application form. Loan requests on existing or former borrowers having an in-file credit investigation older than one year must be revised through the credit bureau and third-party sources if necessary. Credit applications older than two years will require new applications.
2. Stability—Applicant must have six-month occupational stability in present employment unless previous employment was in a similar or related field. Applicant must show previous concurrent employment and residence of three years.
3. Minimum income—No limitations are placed on income; however, lenders will be requested to compute total monthly net income and monthly expenditures.
4. Creditworthiness—Since this is a subjective decision, it must be left to the loan officer's discretion.

H. *Installment Extensions*

No more than one extension per 12 months of contract will be granted without the manager's written joint agreement with the loan officer.

I. *Overdrafts*

No overdrafts will be approved for borrowers having delinquent payments without the written authorization of the manager.

**EXHIBIT I**    *(continued)*

J. *Single-Maturity Repayment Agreements*
Lenders will require repayment agreements satisfactory to the bank and the borrower. Such agreements will be documented and retained in the borrower's file. Deviations from such agreements should be discouraged.

K. *Financial Statements*
All applications for unsecured loans of $2,500 or more must be accompanied by a financial statement in the applicant's credit file.

II. Authorizations

A. *Lending*
Loan Manager:
Secured—$25,000.
Unsecured—$12,500.
No restrictions of terms.

Loan Officers:
Secured installment—$12,500; maximum term 42 months.
Unsecured installment—$4,500; maximum term 24 months.
Single-maturity secured—$12,500; maximum term 12 months.
Single-maturity unsecured—$4,500; maximum term 12 months.
Home improvement—$9,000; maximum term 60 months.

These authorizations pertain to the net aggregate advanced for each individual borrower.

The loan manager may join a loan officer to the sum of both loan limits.

B. *Overdraft Limits*
All authorized loan officers will have overdraft limits up to the same amount as unsecured, single-maturity lending limits.

C. *Repossessions*
Only the loan manager or the senior credit officer may authorize repossessions.

D. *Charge-offs*
Only the loan manager will determine the uncollectibility of a loan and make charge-off recommendations to the senior credit officer.

III. Loan Officer Responsibilities

A. *Applicant Information*
Loan officers will be responsible for ensuring that factual information is obtained through applicant interview, credit bureau reports, and third-party reporting sources relating to a loan request and that applicants and updates conform to this policy.

B. *Analysis*
Loan officers will be responsible for confirming collateral insurance through an agent prior to making a loan decision where such coverage is required on pledged collateral. Additionally, the approving loan officer will be responsible for follow-up efforts in the event of cancellations, expirations, or terminations of such insurance.

C. *Repossessions*
Only the loan manager or the senior credit officer may authorize repossessions.

---

**EXHIBIT I**    *(continued)*

---

    D. *Documentation*

        Special emphasis is placed on each loan officer's responsibility for documenting all information and retaining such information on file pertaining to the borrower.

    E. *Loan Closing*

        Although clerical personnel will complete all legal documents, loan officers are responsible for proper forms, accuracy, and legality prior to closing. Loan officers will ensure during the closing that the borrower is aware of the contractual agreements and that legal disclosure is made.

    F. *Collections*

        Loan officers will be responsible for collection follow-up, skip-tracing, and so on. Letter contact will be discouraged and personal phone contact will be required. Delinquent nonseasoned accounts (less than six months) will be contacted on the 15th day from the due date.

    G. *Regulatory Compliance*

        Although a separate consumer regulation compliance policy will be implemented, all loan officers will be charged with the responsibility for obtaining a working knowledge of and complying fully with all federal and state regulations governing the lending function.

IV. Delinquency and Loan Loss Measures

    Loan officers will be required to maintain a delinquency 30-days-and-over percentage, not to exceed 1.5 percent of their total monthly outstanding loans. Losses should not exceed 0.25 percent of individual outstanding loans at year end.

V. Loan Review

    A. *Loans and Pending Applications*

        All new loans and pending applications will be reviewed on a daily basis by the loan manager and loan officers during the morning loan meetings from 7:45 to 8:30.

    B. *Delinquency and Collateral Insurance*

        Delinquency and collateral insurance follow-up will be reviewed by the loan manager with each loan officer on a weekly basis.

    C. *Charge-offs*

        Potential charge-offs will be reviewed by the loan manager and the individual loan officer on the third week of each month for month-end charge-off recommendations. Additionally, charge-off loan applications will be used for training purposes.

    D. *Rejected Applications*

        Rejected applications will be reviewed weekly for regulatory compliance, documentation, and loan judgment quality. Exceptions will be utilized for training purposes.

    E. *Installment Extensions*

        The loan manager will review daily all the loan extensions granted.

VI. Training

    In-bank training will consist of the following:

        1. Morning loan meeting.

        2. Weekly training meeting.

**EXHIBIT I** *(continued)*

American Institute of Banking courses will be encouraged, and loan officers meeting the necessary requirements will be scheduled for formal outside schooling at the bank's expense.

VII. Evaluation

All lenders will be evaluated on an annual basis and counseling will be conducted during a quarterly review. Primary considerations in the evaluation of the performance will consist of the following:

1. Loan volume.
2. Delinquency.
3. Losses.
4. Credit life insurance penetration.

5. Average portfolio effective rate.
6. Credit policy and regulatory compliance.
7. Justified customer complaints.
8. New business.

## CONCLUSION

The purpose of this policy is to provide direction and development for lending personnel while exercising control to attain bank objectives. It should not, however, be utilized by loan officers as a crutch to lay blame, discourage profitable loan acquisition, deter customer service, or detract from the bank's image. Moreover, the quoting of policy to customers may detract from the credibility and authority of the loan officer.

It is recommended that no policy can encompass all the situations and conditions related to every loan request. Flexibility must be exercised for a policy to work effectively. As a result, individual judgment and discretion is encouraged within reasonable and justifiable limits.

---

## CASE 18 — CALBANK LEASING CORPORATION*

In mid-1984, Sam Farrell was trying to complete the structuring of a leveraged lease financing package for negotiation with a prospective client. He reflected with satisfaction on the final commitment he had received that morning from an equity investor who was willing to put equity funds into the project. Farrell knew it was not going to be a cut-and-dried negotiation. The client, California Investment Partnership, had taken some unusual initiatives before approaching Far-

rell, and, as a result, he was uncertain about the position he would take.

Sam Farrell was vice-president of marketing for CalBank Leasing Corporation (CLC) and was responsible for developing leasing packages for possible funding through his organization. CLC was a subsidiary of CalBank, N.A., located in Los Angeles, California, and the sixth largest commercial bank on the West Coast. Farrell had met with the management team of California Investment Partnership (CIP) several weeks earlier to discuss the financing of capital equipment to be installed near an oil reservoir near Bakersfield, California.

CLC and its parent, CalBank, held lease financing outstanding of nearly $300 million. The

*This case was prepared by C. Dana Bickford, First City National Bank in Houston, Texas, and Donald G. Simonson, University of New Mexico.

leasing portfolio was an important profit center that contributed 8 percent of the parent's bottom-line earnings in 1983. Most of the leases in the portfolio were outright leases funded through CalBank resources. However, the larger leases increasingly were handled through leveraged lease packages involving long-term debt financing by a third party. By policy, the bank favored leasing capital equipment, such as major pieces of production or construction equipment. Special-purpose structures to house production equipment and processes often were included. However, CLC avoided lease financing of other types of real property such as commercial buildings, real estate development, and other improvements to land.

### THE PROPOSAL

CIP was in the process of assembling a project to install a "cogeneration" plant in one of the heavy oil fields near Bakersfield. The plant would produce both thermal (steam) and electrical energy from the burning of raw crude oil. The capital investment required to complete the plant totalled $8 million, of which CIP was able to provide only $500,000. CIP's management team knew that their modest investment potential was insufficient to qualify for a project-type debt financing; they knew that most lenders would require the investment firm to put in 25 to 40 percent, or roughly $2 to $3 million.

As an alternative, Farrell explained the possibility of a leveraged lease package to be managed by CLC. Under this plan, CLC would attempt to structure and place a leveraged lease in which its parent, CalBank, N.A., would provide interim construction financing and CLC would find an equity investor who would be willing to commit $1.6 million, or 20 percent, to the project. It was this crucial part of the package that Farrell had secured that morning by getting a commitment from an equity investor.

The long-term debt component of the funding of the plant to be leased would be provided by a long-term lender such as a bank, insurance firm, or pension fund. According to Chester Leopold, chief operating officer for CIP, a long-term lender had already committed verbally to the permanent debt component of the financing, and a formal commitment letter would be available in a matter of days.

### DESCRIPTION OF THE COGENERATION PROCESS

The term *cogeneration* applies to the joint production of thermal and electrical energy from a single plant. Cogeneration plants typically use a hydrocarbon fuel (such as gasoline, natural gas, or fuel oil) to produce electricity and thermal energy (steam) simultaneously. In the project being undertaken by CIP, the electricity produced would be sold to Pacific Gas and Electric, a large California public utility. Fuel for the process would be heavy crude oil produced just off the plant site and sold to CIP by the oil producer. The waste heat resulting from the generation of electricity would be captured and used to produce steam, which would be sold, in turn, to the oil producer. The steam would be used by the producer to enhance production of heavy crude in a nearby oil reservoir. Cogeneration facilities typically obtain 35 to 40 percent greater fuel efficiency than power plants that do not utilize the waste heat resulting from generating electricity.

CIP had negotiated a nine-year contract with the oil company to supply steam under a take-or-pay contract. That is, if for some reason the oil company was unable to take deliveries of steam as agreed, the company would have to pay for the steam as if it had actually taken delivery. Conversely, if CIP was unable to provide the steam for some period of time during the life of the contract, the oil company would be obligated to continue payments set by a predetermined schedule. CIP would be obliged to provide the steam, once its production capability returned, either at the end of the contract or in the form of increased amounts during the remaining contract life, at the oil company's option.

CIP's contract with the oil company also provided for a fuel supply for the cogeneration plant. The oil company would provide CIP with raw crude oil to be used as the fuel source for the cogeneration plant's combustors. A unique aspect of the plant was that it would utilize a modified gas turbine that would burn the heavy crude oil produced from the oil field. The advantages of burning this type of fuel were its low cost compared to refined fuels and its availability on site from the reservoir under production.

## CONTRACT FOR COGENERATION PLANT AND EQUIPMENT

Farrell was somewhat surprised to learn that CIP had already signed a turnkey installation contract with a European manufacturer, Industrias Popular Español (IPE), for the plant and equipment needed to complete the project. IPE warranted the performance of the installation in terms of power and steam output, as well as fuel consumption in conformance with CIP's specifications. Farrell considered it unusual that a commitment of this sort was so far advanced before the permanent financing of the project was finalized.

Chester Leopold further advised Farrell that IPE had already filled orders for most of the major pieces of the equipment. Both the equipment and the liability for the equipment appear on CIP's latest interim financial statement provided for Farrell's review. IPE provided the data in Exhibit 1 as its estimate of the value and degree of completion.

All of the units were assembled at IPE's local warehouse. IPE had transferred title to the equipment to CIP so that CIP could offer the units as collateral in any financing. IPE held a second lien on the equipment pending payment in full for the plant.

In the event of a default under any bank or lease agreement, IPE agreed to make a best efforts attempt to sell the equipment as a package elsewhere. If this attempt were not successful, IPE would do its best to assist the bank in disposing of the equipment by other means.

At their meeting with Farrell several weeks ago, the CIP team indicated that they had already contracted with Pacific Gas and Electric to deliver power produced by the plant for a period of seven years from the date operations began. The contract appeared to be quite favorable to both parties.

An eight-year pro forma operations statement was provided by Leopold, as shown in Exhibit 2. Also, a detailed monthly operations forecast for 1985 is given in Exhibit 3. An analysis of the expected performance of the lease, shown in Exhibit 4, had been prepared by Sam Farrell for his successful presentation to the equity investor.

## CIP MANAGEMENT

Chester Leopold had assumed the responsibility of coordinating the financing for CIP. Leopold was 50 years old and previously had worked for three different West Coast banks after several years as a stockbroker for Merrill Lynch. He also served as a director of CIP.

Warren Blume, age 42, was in charge of the cogeneration activities for CIP. Blume had attended three universities and since 1976 had been active in research, evaluation, and development of cogeneration technology and its application to enhanced oil recovery operations.

Jacques LeBoux, age 42, was the president and founder of CIP. He was a foreign national but was educated in the United States. LeBoux had worked in project engineering jobs with various public and private companies both in the United States and abroad. From 1973 to 1979, he was the chairman of the board for his own land development, home building, and construction company in his native country. Since 1979, he had been exclusively involved with the diversification and growth of CIP. LeBoux was the only one of the partners who had accumulated a significant personal net worth. His financial statement is summarized as follows:

### Jacques LeBoux, January 1984

| Assets | | Liabilities and Net Worth | |
|---|---|---|---|
| Cash | $    200,000 | Short-term notes | $    500,000 |
| Real estate | 10,300,000 | Mortgage | 800,000 |
| CIP investment | 9,000,000 | Long-term notes[a] | 5,000,000 |
| Home | 1,000,000 | Total liabilities | $ 6,100,000 |
| Notes receivable | 1,500,000 | Equity | 15,900,000 |
| Total assets | $22,000,000 | Total liabilities and equity | $22,000,000 |

[a]Long-term notes are secured by income-producing properties and without recourse to Mr. LeBoux.

CIP's financial statement was summarized by Leopold as follows:

### California Investment Partnership, January 30, 1984

| Assets | | Liabilities and Net Worth | |
|---|---|---|---|
| Cash | $    50,000 | Accounts payable | $ 1,000,000 |
| Accounts receivable | 500,000 | Supplier financing | 3,600,000 |
| Plant 1 | 9,000,000 | Long-term debt | 5,000,000 |
| Plant 2 (work in progress) | 5,800,000 | Total liabilities | $ 9,600,000 |
| Notes receivable partners | 4,000,000 | Partners' equity | 9,750,000 |
| Total assets | $19,350,000 | Total liabilities plus equity | $19,350,000 |

### THE LEASE PACKAGE

Farrell had obtained a commitment on the morning in question from an equity investor who agreed to participate in the leveraged lease outlined below. The relationships in the lease are diagrammed in Exhibits 5 and 6.

#### Equipment Cost
There is an $8 million all-in cost. A minimum of $7,750,000 would qualify as Section 38 property, which qualifies for a 10 percent investment tax credit and five years ACRS (Accelerated Cost Recovery System).

#### Lease Expiration Alternatives
1. The equipment may be returned to CLC.
2. CIP may purchase the equipment at its then fair market value.
3. The lease may be renewed at the then fair market renewal rent.

#### Other Provisions
1. The proposal is contingent on CIP's ability to secure senior financing in the amount of at least 80 percent of the final, all-in equipment cost, to include installation capitalized interest. The lease payment would be adjusted to reflect the interest rate obtained. At a fixed interest rate of 15.5 percent, the quarterly lease payment will equal 5.1563 percent of the total equipment cost.

2. As an additional incentive to enter into this transaction, CIP would pay CLC a minimum of 12 percent of its pretax profit each year during the lease term. If CIP failed to achieve pretax profits in any particular year, there would be no liability for that year.

3. The commitment is contingent upon CLC's review and approval of the financial statements of all parties involved, the contracts between the parties, and mutually satisfactory documentation.

4. CLC will receive an up-front, nonrefundable fee of 1 percent of the lease amount, or $80,000.

### BANK FINANCING

CIP asked CalBank to provide an interim construction loan of approximately $3 million to move the equipment to the Bakersfield area and bring the plant to operational status. It was anticipated that the loan would be outstanding for a period of 120 to 150 days while construction was under way. Repayment would come from funding of the lease by CLC and the long-term lender.

Farrell was not sure what to make of the unconventional sequence of events in which CIP had already arranged for fabrication of the cogeneration equipment and even held legal title to it prior to arranging for financing. Normally, the details of a lease agreement would all be documented carefully before such action took place. The funding then would occur when the lessee signed a letter of acceptance of the completed plant.

CIP had specifically requested that the construction loan be without recourse to any of the CIP partners. CIP requested funding under the interim construction loan within two weeks. Farrell and Leopold had an appointment with a senior loan officer at CalBank to discuss the interim financing. They knew they must press for an early decision because contracts in the lease commitment called for the plant to be on stream in five months. The construction period would take nearly four months.

In summary, the sources and applications of funds would be as follows:

**Sources**

| | |
|---|---|
| Lease | $1,600,000 |
| Long-term debt | 6,400,000 |
| CIP miscellaneous contributions | 300,000 |
| Total | $8,300,000 |

**Uses**

| | |
|---|---|
| Payment to IPE | $3,600,000 |
| Construction, moving start-up costs | 1,550,000 |
| Repayment of interim construction loans | 3,150,000 |
| Total | $8,300,000 |

---

**EXHIBIT 1    Estimate of Value**

| Equipment | Estimated Fair Market Value | Percentage Complete | Available Collateral |
|---|---|---|---|
| Turbines and generators | $3,700,000 | 100 | $3,700,000 |
| Recuperators | 300,000 | 100 | 300,000 |
| Boilers and scrubbers | 1,300,000 | 30 | 396,000 |
| Total | $5,300,000 | | $4,396,000 |

**EXHIBIT 2** California Investment Partnership—Operations Forecast, 1985–1992 (dollars in thousands)

| | 1985 | 1986 | 1987 | 1988 | 1989 | 1990 | 1991 | 1992 |
|---|---|---|---|---|---|---|---|---|
| Total revenue | $7,023 | $10,535 | $11,167 | $11,837 | $12,547 | $13,300 | $14,098 | $14,943 |
| Operating expenses | 4,022 | 6,033 | 6,395 | 6,779 | 7,185 | 7,617 | 8,074 | 8,558 |
| G&A expense | 1,500 | 2,250 | 2,385 | 2,528 | 2,680 | 2,841 | 3,011 | 3,192 |
| Lease costs | 1,650 | 1,650 | 1,650 | 1,650 | 1,650 | 1,650 | 1,650 | 1,650 |
| Pretax profit/(loss) | ($149) | $602 | $737 | $880 | $1,032 | $1,192 | $1,363 | $1,543 |

**EXHIBIT 3** California Investment Partnership—Monthly Operations Forecast, 1985 (dollars in thousands)

| Income Statement—Financial | Jan. | Feb. | Mar. | Apr. | May | June | Jul. | Aug. | Sept. | Oct. | Nov. | Dec. | Total | Percent |
|---|---|---|---|---|---|---|---|---|---|---|---|---|---|---|
| Revenue | 371 | 315 | 578 | 559 | 747 | 657 | 679 | 679 | 723 | 578 | 559 | 578 | 7023 | 100.00% |
| Operating expenses | | | | | | | | | | | | | | |
| Fuel costs | 186 | 174 | 186 | 180 | 186 | 180 | 186 | 186 | 180 | 186 | 180 | 186 | 2199 | 31.31% |
| Direct payroll and benefits | 39 | 39 | 39 | 39 | 39 | 39 | 39 | 39 | 39 | 39 | 39 | 39 | 469 | 6.68 |
| Plant operating costs | 101 | 101 | 101 | 101 | 101 | 101 | 101 | 101 | 101 | 101 | 101 | 101 | 1212 | 17.26 |
| Power discount | 8 | 7 | 13 | 13 | 13 | 12 | 12 | 12 | 13 | 13 | 13 | 13 | 142 | 2.02 |
| Total operating expenses | 335 | 321 | 339 | 333 | 339 | 332 | 338 | 338 | 333 | 339 | 333 | 339 | 4022 | 57.27% |
| Operating income | 36 | −7 | 238 | 226 | 408 | 325 | 341 | 341 | 390 | 238 | 226 | 238 | 3001 | 42.73% |
| Site overhead | 0 | 0 | 0 | 0 | 0 | 0 | 0 | 0 | 0 | 0 | 0 | 0 | 0 | 0.00 |
| Reserve-engine rebuild | 0 | 0 | 0 | 0 | 0 | 0 | 0 | 0 | 0 | 0 | 0 | 0 | 0 | 0.00 |
| Depreciation—20 years | 40 | 40 | 40 | 40 | 40 | 40 | 40 | 40 | 40 | 40 | 40 | 40 | 480 | 6.83 |
| General and administrative | 35 | 35 | 35 | 35 | 35 | 35 | 35 | 35 | 35 | 35 | 35 | 35 | 420 | 5.98 |
| Interest | 76 | 76 | 76 | 76 | 76 | 76 | 76 | 75 | 74 | 73 | 73 | 72 | 898 | 12.79 |
| Plant lease costs | 105 | 105 | 105 | 105 | 105 | 105 | 105 | 105 | 105 | 105 | 105 | 105 | 1254 | 17.86 |
| Income before CNC fees and tax | −220 | −262 | −17 | −29 | 152 | 70 | 86 | 86 | 136 | −14 | −26 | −13 | −51 | −0.73% |
| CNC fee | 0 | 0 | 0 | 0 | 0 | 0 | 0 | 0 | 0 | 0 | 0 | 0 | 0 | 0.00 |
| Profit before tax | −220 | −262 | −17 | −29 | 152 | 70 | 86 | 86 | 136 | −14 | −26 | −13 | −51 | −0.73% |
| Taxes on income | 0 | 0 | 0 | 0 | 0 | 0 | 0 | 0 | 0 | 0 | 0 | 0 | 0 | 0.00 |
| Profits after tax | −220 | −262 | −17 | −29 | 152 | 70 | 86 | 86 | 136 | −14 | −26 | −13 | −51 | −0.73% |
| Cash flow | −180 | −222 | 23 | 11 | 192 | 110 | 126 | 126 | 176 | 26 | 14 | 27 | 429 | 6.11% |

**EXHIBIT 4  Leverage Lease Analysis for Equity Investors, Not Including 12 Percent Pretax Profit Kicker**

| End of Year | (1) Initial Equity Participation Less ITC[a] (Net) | (2) Lease Payment Receipt[b] | (3) Depreciation[c] | (4) Loan Interest Payment[d] | (5) Pretax Profit (2) − (3) − (4) | (6) Taxes (40 Percent)[e] | (7) Total Loan Payment[f] | (8) Cash Flows[g] |
|---|---|---|---|---|---|---|---|---|
| 0 | ($800,000) | | | | | | | ($ 800,000) |
| 1 | | $1,650,000 | $1,368,000 | $1,240,000 | ($ 958,000) | ($383,200) | $914,286 | (121,086) |
| 2 | | 1,650,000 | 2,508,000 | 1,062,857 | (1,920,857) | (768,342) | 914,286 | 441,199 |
| 3 | | 1,650,000 | 1,900,000 | 885,714 | (1,135,714) | (454,286) | 914,286 | 304,286 |
| 4 | | 1,650,000 | 1,216,000 | 708,571 | (274,571) | (109,828) | 914,286 | 136,971 |
| 5 | | 1,650,000 | 608,000 | 531,429 | 510,571 | 204,228 | 914,286 | 57 |
| 6 | | 1,650,000 | — | 354,286 | 1,295,714 | 518,286 | 914,286 | (136,858) |
| 7 | | 3,250,000 | — | 177,143 | 3,072,857 | 909,143[h] | 914,286 | 1,249,428 |

[a] $1,600,000 − (0.1)(8,000,000) = $800,000.

[b] 5.1563% × $8,000,000 × 4. In year 7, add $1,600,000 for the assumed 20% residual value, which is taxed at the 20% capital gains rate.

[c] Per 1985 federal tax guide; Section 38 property with five-year ACRS and 10% ITC.

[d] Year 1: $8,000,000 × 0.155 = $1,240,000
Year 2: $6,757,143 × 0.155 = 1,062,857
Year 3: $5,714,286 × 0.155 = 885,714
Year 4: $4,571,429 × 0.155 = 708,571
Year 5: $3,428,571 × 0.155 = 531,429
Year 6: $2,285,714 × 0.155 = 354,286
Year 7: $1,142,857 × 0.155 = 177,143

[e] Parentheses indicate a tax credit.

[f] $6,400,000 ÷ 7 = $914,286 per year.

[g] (1) + (2) − (4) − (6) − (7)
Assumes that the tax benefits flow through to the investors.

[h] $1,650,000 − 177,143 = 1,472,857 × 0.4 = $589,143
Salvage value    1,600,000 × 0.2 = 320,000
                 $909,143

569

## EXHIBIT 5    Ownership and Initial Funding Diagram

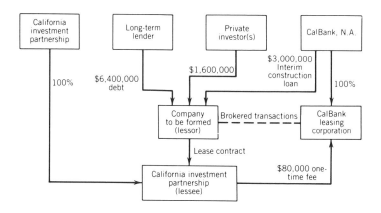

### Lease and Debt Payments

## EXHIBIT 6    Contractual Relationships

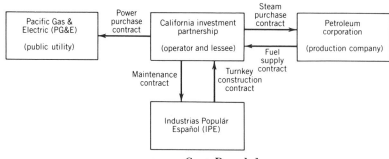

### Cost Breakdown

| | |
|---|---:|
| Turnkey equipment installation | $6,500,000 |
| Foundation and site preparation | 250,000 |
| California sales tax | 250,000 |
| Interest during construction | 400,000 |
| Start-up and working capital | 350,000 |
| Finance costs, fees, and contingency | 250,000 |
| | $8,000,000 |

**CASE**

# 18

## APPENDIX: NOTES ON LEVERAGED LEASING

Leasing is often viewed by financial management as an alternative means of medium- to long-term financing. Tax, accounting, and shareholder considerations are all significant in the evaluation of leasing as a financing alternative.

Once the lessee makes decisions regarding its equipment needs, that is, the manufacture, special features, terms of warranties, guarantees, delivery, installation, and services, the lessee then approaches a potential lessor to negotiate the term of the lease, rental rates, costs that will be capitalized into the lease, options at the end of the lease agreement, and other details. The financial attractiveness of a lease depends a great deal upon the tax benefits to the lessee and lessor. In a financial lease (as opposed to an operating lease), the lessor claims depreciation deductions and the lessee deducts the full lease payment as an expense. An investment tax credit (ITC) may be claimed by the lessor or, by agreement, by the lessee. The lessor owns the leased equipment at the end of the lease term.

A leveraged lease involves at least three parties: a lessee, a lessor, and a long-term lender. The lessor in a leveraged lease becomes the owner of the equipment by providing a percentage (20–40 percent) of the necessary capital. The remainder of the capital is provided by a long-term lender on a nonrecourse basis to the lessor. The loan is typically secured by a first lien on the equipment, an assignment of the lease, and an assignment of the lease rental payments. The cost of the loan is a function of the credit standing of the lessee. The lease rate varies with the debt rate and with the overall risk of the transaction. The lessor can claim all tax benefits incidental to ownership of the leased asset even though the lessor provides only 20–40 percent of the necessary capital.

The lessee also gains significant benefits. Among other things, the lessee has no up-front capital outlay, can closely match its revenue streams with the costs associated with its use of the asset, and can indirectly gain the benefit of the tax advantages of the lessor's ownership, since some of these advantages are passed on to the lessee in the form of a lower implied rate of interest on the lease. Of course, leasing is a preferred method of financing only to the extent that the total-cost rate of leasing is below the cost rate of financing an outright purchase.

# INTEGRATIVE
# BANK FINANCIAL
# DECISIONS

# CHAPTER 15

# Interest Margin and Sensitivity Management

Preceding chapters have discussed policies and management techniques for most of the key assets and liabilities areas. Attracting deposits, borrowed funds, and capital have been discussed in detail. Policies and techniques for managing securities have been introduced and evaluated. The theme in these areas of bank management has been consistent with the framework of maximizing returns consistent with a reasonable level of risk to maximize the shareholders' investment in the bank. The remaining link is to integrate these areas into a system of asset–liability management. This chapter emphasizes managing interest margin, interest sensitivity, duration, and hedging in an overall asset–liability management system.

## PRIMARY OBJECTIVES OF INTEREST MARGIN AND SENSITIVITY MANAGEMENT

As previously discussed, the overall objective of a bank should be to balance its return and risks in a way that maximizes the bank's market value to its owners. Relating this objective to interest sensitivity management, a bank should try to earn the highest margin it can in a manner consistent with reasonable stability in the interest margin. Although these concepts have been primary banking objectives for many years, interest sensitivity began receiving prime attention only in the late 1970s and early 1980s. By the late 1980s and early 1990s, banks had broadened interest sensitivity to include the changes in asset and liability values as well as interest flows. Attention to interest sensitivity has been intensified by strongly increased competition that has narrowed interest margins, and by external economic conditions, particularly fluctuating interest rates, which may cause bank earnings to become relatively more volatile. Also, in the current environment, in which confidence is such an important ingredient of successful bank management, there is a greater need for reasonable stability in bank interest margins and earnings. It seems likely that these conditions will continue to affect interest sensitivity management in the future.

## Measures of Interest Margin

The interest margin for a bank is the difference between all interest revenues on bank assets and all interest expenses on bank funds. One area bankers are not settled on is what to do with the provision for loan losses. Some bankers include the provision as part of interest expenses; others think it belongs with other expenses. Separate interest margins on specific types of assets or liabilities may also be calculated, but they are often determined by subjective allocations of revenues or expenses. The major emphasis in this chapter is on the overall interest margin. The three most common measures of a bank's overall interest margin are *dollar net interest margin*, *percent net interest margin*, and *spread*. All these terms appear in literature on bank management. They are often used interchangeably; however, the distinctions may be important and should be understood by serious students of banking. Table 15-1 contains a simplified version of the balance sheet and income statement of Community National Bank to illustrate these measures.

The *dollar net interest margin* is the difference between all interest revenues (adjusted to a tax-equivalent basis) and all interest expenses. This dollar figure is helpful in ascertaining how well the bank can cover its other expenses. In Table 15-1 the dollar net interest margin before and after the provision for loan losses is calculated. The *net interest margin in percentage terms* is the dollar net interest cost (in this table, after the loan loss provision) divided by the bank's earning assets. Since this is a relative term, it is more helpful in measuring the changes and trends in interest margin and in comparing interest margins among banks. *Spread*, a relative measure, is the difference between interest returns (interest revenues divided by earning assets) and interest costs (interest expenses excluding the loan loss provision divided by interest-bearing funds). Advocates of spread as a measure of interest sensitivity believe that spread measures trends, swings, and relative margins, as well as percentage net interest margin, and that spread is a superior measure when a bank wants to investigate reasons for good or bad margin performances.

*Interest sensitivity* refers to the sensitivity of or fluctuations in interest margin because of endogenous and exogenous factors. Endogenous factors include the composition of a bank's assets and liability, the quality and maturity of loans, and the maturity of attracted funds. Exogenous factors include general economic conditions and the level of interest rates. A bank can attempt to manage the endogenous factors, but it can only try to anticipate the exogenous factors.

**TABLE 15-1    Measures of Interest Margin—Community National Bank Average Balances, 1992 (dollars in thousands)**

| | | | |
|---|---|---|---|
| Cash and due from banks | $ 13,205 | Demand deposits | $ 21,632 |
| Short-term instruments | 1,504 | NOW and Super NOW | 19,107 |
| Securities | 42,101 | Savings and time deposits | 89,935 |
| Loans (net) | 82,676 | Borrowing and other liabilities | 4,650 |
| Other assets | 6,672 | Equity capital | 10,834 |
| | $146,158 | | $146,158 |

*Income Statement, 1992*

| | | |
|---|---|---|
| Interest income (taxable equivalent) | $12,768 | |
| Other revenues | 1,547 | $14,315 |
| Less: Interest expense | $ 7,363 | |
| Provision for loan losses | 517 | |
| Other expenses | 4,658 | $12,538 |
| Operating income (taxable equivalent) | | $ 1,777 |
| Taxes (taxable equivalent) | | 575 |
| Net income | | $ 1,202 |

Interest margin measures:

Dollar net interest margin
(before loan loss provision):

Interest revenues − Interest expense
$12,768 − 7,363 = $5,405

Dollar net interest margin
(after loan loss provision):

Interest revenues − (Interest exp. + Loan loss provision)
$12,768 − (7,363 + 517) = $4,888

Percent net interest margin
(after loan loss provision):

$$\frac{\text{Interest revs.} - (\text{Int. exp.} + \text{Loan loss prov.})}{\text{Earning assets}}$$

$$\frac{\$12,768 - (7,363 + 517)}{\$126,281} = 3.87\%$$

Interest spread:

$$\frac{\text{Interest revenues}}{\text{Earning assets}} - \frac{\text{Interest expenses}}{\text{Int.-bearing funds}}$$

$$\frac{\$12,768}{\$126,281} - \frac{\$7,363}{\$103,692}$$

$$10.11\% - 7.11\% = 3.00\%$$

# OBTAINING AN ADEQUATE INTEREST MARGIN

Obtaining an interest margin adequate to cover a bank's burden (the net of other expenses less other income) and to earn a satisfactory return on the owners' investment in the bank is as important as, if not more important than, reasonable stability in the interest margin. A stable interest margin at a low level is not consistent with the banking objective of maximizing the value of the owners' investment in the bank. Management should seek to obtain the highest interest margin possible within credit risk, liquidity risk, and capital risk constraints, as well as the interest rate risk (sensitivity) considerations discussed in the following section.

Competitive markets for both sources of funds and uses of funds constrain the bank's ability to earn a higher interest margin. For example, assume that a bank has a target "spread" of 4 percent, but its average return on earning assets is 10 percent and its average cost of funds is 7 percent. The bank can obtain its target spread by increasing its average return on assets or decreasing its cost of funds, or some combination thereof, by 1 percent. This may be difficult if competitive returns on acceptable composition and risk asset alternatives are 10 percent and competitive costs of acceptable composition and liability alternatives are 7 percent. Either the bank has to increase the risk associated with its assets or liabilities or it has to accept the spread at least partially dictated by the competitive markets.

## An Example Illustrating Yields Necessary for an Adequate Margin

Community National Bank, which was used as an example in Chapters 2, 3, and 4, serves again here as an example of a model, starting with the return on equity, recognizing the interest sensitivity of assets and liabilities, and showing the yield necessary on loans that will be repriced in the coming year. Table 15-2 presents the necessary information for estimating the required yields on sensitive assets for the Community National Bank. Data on the past performance of this bank appear in Tables 2-1 through 2-3 but are not essential.

---

**TABLE 15-2   Information for Estimating Required Yields on Sensitive Assets for Community National Bank (dollars in millions)**

---

1. The bank's holdings of vault cash, deposits with the Federal Reserve and other banks, and other cash items in 1992 are expected to be:
   22% of non-interest-bearing demand deposits
   18% of interest-bearing demand deposits
   3% of all time and savings deposits
2. The bank's investment in premises and equipment and other nonearning assets is expected to be 4% in 1993.
3. During 1993, the bank expects its net resources to average $160 million. The average amount and the investable amount of the various fund sources are projected as follows (amounts in millions of dollars):

**TABLE 15-6**    *(continued)*

|  | Average Amount | Percentage Usable | Amount Investable |
|---|---|---|---|
| Demand deposits, non-interest-bearing | $ 32 | 74% | $ 23.68 |
| Demand deposits, interest-bearing | 12 | 78 | 9.36 |
| Passbook savings | 6 | 98 | 5.58 |
| Money market accounts | 25 | 93 | 23.25 |
| Savings certificates | 20 | 93 | 18.60 |
| CDs $100,000 and over | 34 | 93 | 31.62 |
| Public and other time deposits | 12 | 93 | 11.16 |
| Short-term borrowing | 6 | 96 | 5.76 |
| Other liabilities | 1 | 96 | .96 |
| Stockholders' equity | 12 | 96 | 11.52 |
| Total sources of funds | $160 | | $141.49 |

4. The bank's target rate of return on equity is 16 percent after taxes. Its marginal income tax rate is 34%; therefore, the pretax return is $16/(1 - .34)$, or 24.2%.
5. Costs of each type of funding (percentage):

|  | Interest Cost, 1992 | Est. Int. Cost, 1993 | Net Processing Cost, 1993 |
|---|---|---|---|
| Demand deposits, non-interest-bearing | .0% | .0% | 4.6% |
| Demand deposits, interest-bearing | 3.1 | 3.0 | 2.5 |
| Passbook savings | 4.3 | 4.5 | 1.0 |
| Money market certificates | 5.8 | 5.5 | 0.6 |
| Savings certificates | 7.7 | 7.0 | 0.2 |
| CDs $100,000 and over | 8.1 | 7.5 | 0.1 |
| Public and other time deposits | 8.0 | 7.5 | 0.2 |
| Short-term borrowing | 5.6 | 6.0 | 0.1 |
| Other liabilities | 7.8 | 7.0 | 0.1 |
| Stockholders' equity | | 24.2 | 0.0 |

6. Expenses other than interest for 1993 are estimated to be $2.2 million in net processing costs and $1.8 million in net other costs (other expenses of $3.8 million less other income of $2.0 million), for total net noninterest expenses of $4.0 million.
7. Forecast average assets for 1993 (in millions of dollars):

|  | Interest Sensitive | Nonsensitive | Total |
|---|---|---|---|
| Cash and due from banks | | $12.1 | $ 12.1 |
| Short-term securities and interest | $ 8.5 | | 8.5 |
| Long-term securities | | 26.0 | 26.0 |
| Loans | 70.0 | 37.0 | 107.0 |
| Bank premise and equipment | | 3.9 | 3.9 |
| Other assets (nonearning) | | 2.5 | 2.5 |
| Total | | | $160.0 |

8. Projected return on short-term securities purchased in 1993 is 5.0%, and projected return on loans is 11%.

The typical starting point of such an analysis is to estimate the required overall returns based on the projected cost-of-funds figures in Table 15-2. The estimated interest cost figures should recognize the sensitivity or nonsensitivity to interest rates in these cost figures. For example, in 1992, when rates tended to rise, average rates on the few nonsensitive sources, such as demand deposits, did not change, but average rates on such sensitive sources as money market certificates or larger CDs rose considerably. The rise in such average rates would depend on the old rate, the maturity of liabilities (sources) outstanding at the end of 1992, and the new rates when the liabilities matured.

Table 15-3 illustrates the calculation of the required overall returns on earning assets based on the projected average cost of funds for 1993. The overall cost of acquiring funds can be estimated by dividing the summation of the total dollar acquisition cost, $12.276 million (Column 3) in this example, by the amount investable, $141.5 million (Column 4) in this example. The percentage return required to cover interest costs on separate sources of funds (Column 5) is calculated by dividing the dollar cost of each source (Column 3) by the amount investable from each source (Column 4). The relative weighting in Column 6 was obtained by dividing the amount for each source (Column 4) by the amount investable, $141.5 million. Finally, each segment's contribution to the weighted return required on investable assets (Column 7) was calculated by multiplying the return required on each source (Column 5) by its relative weighting (Column 6). The total of the contributions to weighted required returns is, of course, equal to the returns required on earning assets, which was previously calculated from the totals.

The stated objective is to obtain an interest margin adequate to cover other costs and to earn an adequate return on the owners' investment; however, costs other than those required to attract funds and income other than interest income have been ignored in the calculations. These cost and income figures can be incorporated by adding in all costs other than the acquisition costs already incorporated, net of all noninterest income items ($3.8 million less $2.0 million) divided by earning assets ($141.5 million) to the previously calculated required return (8.68 percent).

This resulting required return to cover total net costs of 9.95 percent includes an after-tax return to equity holders of 16 percent. This return, adjusted to a before-tax rate by dividing by 1 minus the marginal bank income tax rate, was treated as a cost of funds similar to other sources. If the forecasted interest rates were approximately correct and the bank earned above 9.95 percent on its assets, the residual after-tax return on equity would be above 16 percent and vice versa. The concern is how to employ earning assets, which are a mixture of sensitive and nonsensitive assets, so that they will yield an average of 9.95 percent or above.

### Effects of Rate Sensitivity of Assets

Community National Bank is used in Table 15-4 to demonstrate a simplified worksheet that can be used to calculate the yields required on newly priced,

**TABLE 15-3  Required Overall Returns Based on Projected Cost of Funds (dollars in millions)**

| Types of Funds | (1) Average Amount | (2) Interest and Net Acquisition Costs | (3) Total $ Costs (1) × (2) | (4) Amount Investable | (5) Cost on Amount Investable | (6) Relative Weight | (7) Contribution to Weighted Cost |
|---|---|---|---|---|---|---|---|
| Demand deposits, non-interest-bearing | $ 32 | 4.6% | $ 1.472 | $ 23.68 | 6.22% | 16.74% | 1.04% |
| Demand deposits, interest-bearing | 12 | 5.5 | 0.660 | 9.36 | 7.05 | 6.62 | 0.47 |
| Passbook savings | 6 | 5.5 | 0.330 | 5.58 | 5.91 | 3.94 | 0.23 |
| Money market accounts | 25 | 6.1 | 1.525 | 23.25 | 6.56 | 16.43 | 1.08 |
| Savings certificates | 20 | 7.2 | 1.440 | 18.60 | 7.74 | 13.15 | 1.02 |
| CDs $100,000 and over | 34 | 7.6 | 2.584 | 31.62 | 8.17 | 22.35 | 1.83 |
| Public and other time deposits | 12 | 7.7 | 0.924 | 11.16 | 8.28 | 7.89 | 0.65 |
| Short-term borrowing | 6 | 6.1 | 0.366 | 5.76 | 6.35 | 4.07 | 0.26 |
| Other liabilities | 1 | 7.1 | 0.071 | 0.96 | 7.40 | 0.68 | 0.05 |
| Stockholders' equity | 12 | 24.2 | 2.904 | 11.52 | 25.21 | 8.14 | 2.05 |
| Total | $160 | | $12.276 | $141.49 | | 100.00% | 8.68% |

Return required on earning assets to cover cost of acquiring funds: $12.276/$141.49 = 8.68%.
Return required on earning assets to cover total net cost of funds: 8.68% + 1.8/141.49 = 9.95%.

**TABLE 15-4** **Worksheet for Calculation of the Yield Required on Newly Priced, Interest-Sensitive Loans (dollars in thousands)**

| Asset Category | Forecasted Average for 1993 | Yield on Nonsensitive Assets | Yield on Sensitive Assets (Old) | Yield on Sensitive Assets (New) | Average Yield | Returns |
|---|---|---|---|---|---|---|
| Short-term securities | $  8,500 | | 4.0% | 5.0% | 4.5% | $    383 |
| Long-term securities | 26,000 | 9.0% | | | 9.0 | 2,340 |
| Loans (nonsensitive) | 37,000 | 10.0 | | | 10.0 | 3,700 |
| Loans (sensitive) | 70,000 | | 10.0 | (3)[a] | (2)[a] | (1)[a] |
| Total earning assets | $141,500 | | | | 9.95% | $14,076 |
| Nonearning assets | 18,500 | | | | 0 | 0 |
| Total assets | $160,000 | | | | 8.80% | $14,076 |

[a]Number in parentheses indicates calculation of the answer in Table 15-5.

interest-sensitive assets. The key characteristic of the worksheet is that to obtain the targeted return on equity, the bank must earn 9.95 percent on its earning asset of $141.5 million, or $14,076 million. The yields on nonsensitive loans and long-term securities are known, and the dollar returns of $3.70 million and $2.34 million, respectively, should be reasonable estimates. Estimated dollar returns on rate-sensitive loans and short-term securities are more complex. In the case of short-term securities, Community National felt its securities, which were yielding 4 percent at the start of the year, would mature about evenly during the year and that the average yield on newly purchased securities

**TABLE 15-5** **Calculation of the Yield Reported on Newly Priced, Interest-Sensitive Loans (dollars in thousands)**

| | | | |
|---|---|---|---|
| 1. Total dollar return on all assets | | $14,076 | |
| Dollar returns on: | | | |
| Short-term securities | $    383 | | |
| Long-term securities | 2,340 | | |
| Nonsensitive loans | 3,700 | | |
| Cash, premises, etc. | 0 | 6,423 | |
| Required dollar return on sensitive loans | | $ 7,653 | (1)[a] |

2. Required average yield on all sensitive loans: 7,653/70,000 = 10.93%     (2)
3. Required yield on newly priced sensitive loans:

$$\frac{7,653 - 3,500}{70,000 - 35,000} = \frac{4,153}{35,000} = 11.87\% \qquad (3)$$

[a]Numbers in parentheses represent answers in Table 15-4.

would be 5 percent. The average yield on the $8.5 million of short-term securities would then be 4.5 percent, or $383,000.

A calculation similar to that performed on short-term securities could be performed for rate-sensitive loans if the rates on currently outstanding loans are known; if there are reasonable estimates of the repricing, renewal, and maturity profiles of these loans; and if the average rate on newly priced loans can be forecast. A slightly different approach is taken. The current rate and repricing profile are estimated, and the required yield on newly priced, interest-sensitive loans to earn 16 percent on equity is calculated. Table 15-5 shows that the calculations can be made by first finding the required dollar yield on sensitive loans by subtracting the returns on short-term and long-term securities and nonsensitive loans from the total return required on all assets. The required average yield on sensitive loans can then be calculated by dividing the required dollar yields on sensitive loans by the average amount of sensitive loans. Finally, if sensitive loans will be repriced about evenly during the year, the required yield on newly priced, sensitive loans can be calculated by subtracting the dollar yield at the old sensitive rate and the average amount at the old rate from the numerator and denominator, respectively. The resulting dollar amount divided by the average amount repriced during the year is the average required percentage yield on newly priced, sensitive loans (11.87 percent for Community National).

Two final comments about using this type of model seem appropriate. First, the real world is more complex than this simplified model. For example, the growth rates of different types of loans vary, and loan prepayments and extensions occur. This model, however, may be made considerably more complex than this simplified example. The authors have worked with banks that have considerably more complex models (generally on microcomputers), which are based on the same basic ideas. Second, even the simplified model presented in this section can be flexibly used. For example, a bank can forecast all rates for the coming year and project the resulting rate of return on equity. Or a bank can leave the new rate on sensitive short-term securities as an unknown to see if the rate calculated by dividing the dollar return on sensitive securities by the forecasted amount of sensitive securities is reasonable in the expected environment. The required yield on newly priced, sensitive loans can then be calculated by dividing the dollar return on all sensitive loans less the dollar yield on sensitive loans at the previous yield by the average newly priced, sensitive loans.

The required yield on newly priced, sensitive loans can then be compared with the bank's estimates of competitive market rates for the coming year. If market rates are expected to be lower than the required yield, as was the case for the Community National example, the bank will probably earn less than the targeted 16 percent on equity, unless the asset–liability structure is changed or more risk is taken to increase returns. The bank is likely to earn above 16 percent on equity if expected market rates exceed the required yield on newly priced, sensitive loans.

## MANAGING INTEREST SENSITIVITY

As stated earlier, the causes of fluctuations in interest margins are classified broadly into endogenous (or internal) factors and exogenous (or external) factors. The exogenous factors are examined first. Banks have little control over cyclical movement in savings or credit demands, fiscal and monetary policy, and the resulting fluctuations in interest rates. Although the resulting economic fluctuations never follow exactly the same pattern, market analysts have conceived a useful, if highly simplified, scenario of the typical economic cycle. Business borrowing is said to be weak at the beginning of an economic upturn and strong in the final stages. Household borrowing spurts ahead at the beginning of the cycle but peaks well before business borrowing. Monetary policy and tightness mostly influence household borrowing behavior. As the availability of funds decreases, borrowing terms tighten and interest rates rise, producing a decline in household borrowing. Business, on the other hand, finds it profitable to borrow at progressively higher rates because of perceived market opportunities that persist late into the economic expansion. With a downturn in the business cycle, demand for business output and, thus, business borrowing eventually decline. Federal deficit financing increases in this stage in order to sustain or increase planned government expenditures in the face of shortfalls in tax revenues.

### Volume, Mix, and Rate

From a banking perspective, this scenario holds profound implications. The acceleration in household and, especially, business borrowing during economic expansion, coupled with rising interest rates, ought to have an abnormal effect on banks' interest margin. The sources of such an effect can be summarized in terms of rate, volume, and mix.

Volume effects occur simply because intense credit demands during periods of rapid economic growth typically force a higher rate of credit production and, therefore, higher levels of bank assets and liabilities. Mix effects usually stem from the shift in most bank portfolios toward high-yield assets (e.g., loans) and away from low-yield assets (e.g., U.S. Treasury securities), whereas the mix of most bank resources shifts toward relatively more purchased funds in the form of either large CDs or short-term borrowed funds. Rate effects in economic expansions tend to benefit the net interest margins as asset yields rise, but this benefit is reduced by negative rate effects as the marginal cost of funds rises.

### Endogenous Factors and Varying Performance

Endogenous factors include the composition of a bank's assets and liabilities, the quality and maturity of loans, and the cost and maturity of attracted funds. The wide disparity in interest sensitivity performance among individual banks, and predictions that interest rates may have relatively large and rapid fluctuations in coming years, indicate that most banks should develop a system to manage their interest sensitivity. The most widely used system in the 1980s and early 1990s was the so-called funds gap management. This system is a management tool that has been designed for the purpose of maintaining a high and relatively stable interest margin throughout the entire rate cycle.

## FUNDS GAP MANAGEMENT

In the traditional funds gap management system, management is asked to separate all items on each side of the bank's balance sheet into groups of items whose cash flows are either sensitive or insensitive to changes in short-term interest rates. Thus, an asset or liability is identified as sensitive if cash flows from the asset or liability change in the same direction and general magnitude as the change in short-term rates. The cash flows of insensitive (or nonsensitive) assets or liabilities do not change within the relevant time period. Some of these insensitive assets or liabilities do not have interest payments or costs at all.

### Funds Gap as a Method of Managing Interest Sensitivity

Figure 15-1 illustrates this system and gives examples of sensitive and nonsensitive assets and liabilities. It is important to remember that interest sensitivity is the distinction, not maturity. A 10-year note where the rate changes with the prime would be interest sensitive. Figure 15-1 illustrates three basic financing relationships: $S_B$ represents sensitive assets financed by sensitive liabilities, $G_B$ represents sensitive assets financed by nonsensitive liabilities, and $N_B$ represents nonsensitive assets financed by nonsensitive liabilities and common equity. Typically, assets, liabilities, and equity are valued in book value terms, and the interest sensitivity of cash flows is used to classify assets and liabilities. Common equity is usually treated as a nonsensitive liability.

Several measures obtainable from Figure 15-1 can be useful to bank management. The most common measure is the *funds gap* or *gap*, which refers to the dollar amount by which sensitive assets exceed sensitive liabilities. The gap is negative if sensitive liabilities exceed sensitive assets. The ratio of sensitive assets divided by sensitive liabilities is also widely used. A ratio above 1.0 indicates that sensitive assets exceed sensitive liabilities. The reverse is true for a ratio below 1.0. A balanced interest sensitivity position would be a zero dollar gap or a sensitivity ratio of 1.0. The final measure is a comparison of sensitive assets as a percentage of total assets to sensitive liabilities as a percentage of total liabilities and net worth.

Figure 15-1 illustrates a bank with a positive funds gap ($G_B$), as one whose sensitive assets exceed its sensitive liabilities. Under rising short-term rates, this positive gap would increase the interest margin (the difference between interest income and interest expense). Declining short-term rates, with a positive gap, would exert downward pressure on the interest margin. On the other

**FIGURE 15-1 Illustration of Traditional Gap Management (Assets and Liabilities at Book Values)**

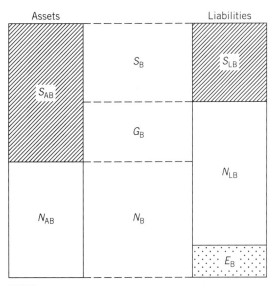

Assets | Liabilities

$S_{AB}$ | $S_B$ | $S_{LB}$
$N_{AB}$ | $G_B$ | $N_{LB}$
 | $N_B$ | $E_B$

▨ Assets and liabilities receiving cash flows sensitive to short-term rates.

☐ Assets and liabilities receiving cash flows nonsensitive to short-term rates.

⊡ Book value of equity capital.

Sensitive assets include Federal funds sold, short-term securities, and variable-rate loans.
Sensitive liabilities include short-maturity CDs and Federal funds purchased.
Nonsensitive assets include fixed-rate loans, long-term securities, and bank premises.
Nonsensitive liabilities include long-term CDs and debt capital. Equity capital included common stock, surplus, undivided profits, and equity reserves.

hand, if sensitive assets were less than sensitive liabilities, there would be a negative funds gap. With a negative gap, the interest margin would decline if short-term rates rose and increase if short-term rates fell.

**Managing the Gap**

The implications for bank management seem straightforward. If management expects interest rates to rise, it should widen the funds gap. On the other hand, if management expects interest rates to decline, it should narrow the bank's funds gap. If used effectively, such gap management decisions should lead to higher returns for a given interest rate risk level or reduced interest rate risk for a given return level.

## Concerns about Traditional Funds Gap Management

There are five categories of concerns relating to whether gap management can achieve such lofty goals:

1. What time period is appropriate to use in determining whether assets and liabilities are rate sensitive?
2. Can bank management predict the direction, magnitude, and timing of interest rate movements?
3. Can bank management flexibly adjust assets and liabilities to obtain the desired gap?
4. Do interest rates on different securities change by the same magnitude?
5. Is gap management myopic, because it focuses only on the interest sensitivity resulting from current flows and ignores reinvestment risk and potentially significant changes in the values of bank assets and liabilities usually deemed to be insensitive from a cash flow standpoint?

Each of these concerns and possible ways of overcoming them will be discussed in the following paragraphs.

## "Maturity Buckets" Gap Model

The concern about the relevant period in which assets and liabilities are sensitive to rate changes is important. A bank that uses six-month money market certificates extensively may have a large positive gap if the time period is one month and may have a negative gap if the time period is six months. A bank that reprices loans annually and has significant amounts of sensitive liabilities may have a balanced sensitivity position for a year but substantial changes in its interest margin during years in which rates change substantially.

Table 15-6 illustrates an interest sensitivity worksheet, which many banks have begun using to overcome the deficiency of selecting just one time period. Such worksheets present an interest sensitivity profile for the bank at a given time for several so-called maturity buckets. In Table 15-6 Community National Bank was very liability sensitive at each of the maturity periods as of December 31, 1992. An increase in rates would hurt this bank's interest margin in a short period of time, whereas a decrease in rates would improve its interest margin. While Community National is liability sensitive at all maturity periods, it is not unusual to find a bank that is asset sensitive for some periods and liability sensitive for others, or vice versa. Some banks have a policy of maintaining balanced long-term interest sensitivity—say, for six months or a year—but purposely mismatch in short-run maturity periods. The idea is to control interest rate risk while taking advantage of predicted short-run movements in interest rates. Balanced long-term interest sensitivity means that earnings will be hurt for only a quarter or two if the bank is wrong in anticipating rate move-

**TABLE 15-6   Interest Sensitivity Worksheet—Community National Bank as of 12/31/92 (dollars in thousands)**

| | w/i 1 Month | Cumulative w/i 3 Months | Cumulative w/i 6 Months | Cumulative w/i 1 Year | Nonsensitive | Total |
|---|---|---|---|---|---|---|
| **Assets** | | | | | | |
| Cash and due from banks | 0 | 0 | 0 | 0 | 13,205 | 13,205 |
| Short-term instruments | 1,504 | 1,504 | 1,504 | 1,504 | 0 | 1,504 |
| Investment securities | 300 | 3,120 | 4,081 | 5,731 | 26,370 | 32,101 |
| Commercial loans | 27,281 | 29,930 | 35,421 | 38,153 | 664 | 38,817 |
| Consumer loans | 2,307 | 5,783 | 11,680 | 20,731 | 11,410 | 32,141 |
| R.E. and other loans (net) | 298 | 879 | 1,703 | 3,673 | 18,045 | 21,718 |
| Other assets | 0 | 0 | 0 | 560 | 6,112 | 6,672 |
| Total assets | 31,698 | 41,216 | 54,389 | 70,352 | 75,806 | 146,158 |
| | | | | | | |
| **Liabilities and Capital** | | | | | | |
| Demand deposits | 0 | 0 | 0 | 0 | 31,632 | 31,632 |
| NOW and Super NOW | 9,107 | 9,107 | 9,107 | 9,107 | 0 | 9,107 |
| Passbook savings | 0 | 0 | 0 | 0 | 6,843 | 6,843 |
| Money market accounts | 20,012 | 20,012 | 20,012 | 20,012 | 0 | 20,012 |
| Savings certificates | 1,341 | 3,426 | 6,204 | 10,493 | 8,845 | 19,338 |
| CDs $100,000 and over | 2,794 | 11,412 | 19,897 | 30,630 | 1,448 | 32,078 |
| Public and other deposits | 380 | 1,607 | 3,014 | 7,781 | 3,883 | 11,664 |
| Short-term borrowing | 3,379 | 3,559 | 3,559 | 3,559 | 0 | 3,559 |
| Other liabilities | 0 | 0 | 32 | 167 | 924 | 1,091 |
| Shareholders' equity | 0 | 0 | 0 | 0 | 10,834 | 10,834 |
| Total liabilities and capital | 37,013 | 49,123 | 61,825 | 81,749 | 64,409 | 146,158 |

*Measures of Interest Sensitivity*

**In One Month**

Interest sensitivity ratio $= \dfrac{\text{Sensitive assets}}{\text{Sensitive liabs.}} = \dfrac{31,698}{37,013} = 0.86 \times$

Dollar int. sens. GAP = Sens. assets − sens. liabs. = 31,698 − 37,013 = −5,315

**In Three Months**

Interest sensitivity ratio $= \dfrac{\text{Sensitive assets}}{\text{Sensitive liabs.}} = \dfrac{41,216}{49,123} = 0.84 \times$

Dollar int. sens. GAP = Sens. assets − sens. liabs. = 41,216 − 49,123 = −7,907

**In Six Months**

Interest sensitivity ratio $= \dfrac{\text{Sensitive assets}}{\text{Sensitive liabs.}} = \dfrac{54,389}{61,825} = 0.88 \times$

Dollar int. sens. GAP = Sens. assets − sens. liabs. = 54,389 − 61,825 = −7,436

**TABLE 15-2**   (continued)

| | w/i 1 Month | Cumulative w/i 3 Months | w/i 6 Months | w/i 1 Year | Nonsensitive | Total |
|---|---|---|---|---|---|---|

**In One Year**

Interest sensitivity ratio $= \dfrac{\text{Sensitive assets}}{\text{Sensitive liabs.}} = \dfrac{70,352}{81,749} = 0.86\times$

Dollar int. sens. GAP = Sens. assets − sens. liabs. = 70,352 − 81,749 = −11,397

**Nonsensitive (Over one Year)**

Nonsensitive ratio $= \dfrac{\text{Nonsens. assets}}{\text{Nonsens. liabs.}} = \dfrac{75,806}{64,409} = 1.18\times$

Dollar nonsensitive GAP = Nonsens. assets − nonsens. liabs. = 75,806 − 64,409 = +11,397

ments. One possible difficulty in using such a strategy is that the interest sensitivity profile can change rapidly if maturing securities are invested in assets with different sensitivities or if maturing deposits are funded from sources with different sensitivities. Thus, a new worksheet should be prepared at least monthly and more often if substantial amounts of assets or liabilities mature during the month.

### "Dynamic" Gap Analysis

More recently, attention has focused on the so-called dynamic interest sensitivity gaps. These gaps require forecasting of interest rates and the expected changes in the balance sheet for several periods in the future. Given these forecasts, the dynamic gap report portrays the way the gaps are expected to be structured at certain future periods.

Dynamic gap reports are a feature of many microcomputer software models. These reports have been criticized as producing information overload. A recurrent problem of such information overload is that the basic purpose gets overlooked. Users of dynamic gap reports tend to get hung up on interest rate forecasts and balance sheet considerations. The gap concept is useful only if it gives some indication of the expected behavior of the net interest margin and, by extension, earnings. Simulating financial performance by emphasizing earnings with gap management as a by-product under various future interest rate scenarios and future business mixes would seem to provide more useful information for management decisions.

### Predicting Interest Rates and Flexibility in Gap Management

The concern about the ability of bankers, or anyone else for that matter, to predict interest rates is real. In effect, advocates of regular or dynamic gap management argue that bank managers can outpredict the market on the future course of interest rates. This assertion seems questionable. However, a cause for equal, if not greater, concern is the corollary assertion that, particularly for banks that do not believe they can outpredict the market on interest rates, interest rate risk is minimized when interest-sensitive assets equal interest-sensitive liabilities. The fallacy of this assumption is discussed in the paragraphs covering the third and fourth concerns about traditional gap management.

A bank's flexibility in adjusting its assets and liabilities to achieve its desired gap position can also be questioned. For example, can a community bank located in a particular market rapidly change the mix of either its assets or liabilities to achieve a desired position? There is also the question of the effects on a bank's customers. Successful gap management by a bank may mean that the bank's customers have positioned themselves improperly for interest rate movements.

### Similar Magnitude of Rate Changes among Securities

Even if a bank has positioned itself flexibly for predicted interest rate movements, funds gap management may not lead to the targeted results. One of the primary reasons for this problem is that a basic assumption of traditional funds gap management is that interest rates on all securities change in the same direction and in similar magnitude. This assumption means that there are parallel shifts in the yield curve, that is, if the rate of 90-day Treasury bills rises 1 percent, the rate on 30-year Treasury bonds or bank passbook savings accounts will rise the same 1 percent. The risk that the interest rates on different financial assets and liabilities may change in different magnitudes is called *basis risk*. While no one can say for sure, basis risk appears to be the rule rather than the exception in past years. Table 15-7 illustrates basis risk and shows how some banks have attempted to standardize funds gap analysis for basis risk.

In this table, it is assumed that an example bank, ABC Bank, has only two repricing assets and two repricing liabilities. Since repricing liabilities exceed repricing assets by $10 million, we say that ABC Bank has a negative gap of $10 million. Under traditional gap analysis, if interest rates decline, the bank would expect its interest margin to improve. The interest margin may not improve, however, if rates change by different magnitudes on the different assets and liabilities. Using the rate sensitivities in Table 15-7, we find that ABC Bank's interest margin was hurt when rates declined. In effect the traditional gap ensured that rates on all assets and liabilities change by the same magnitude. One method to overcome this weakness in part is to attempt to standardize the funds gap measure so that it is measured relative to the change in one key interest rate. This is done in Table 15-7. Such standardization is not an exact science. Rates on different securities may change differently when rates rise than when rates fall. Nevertheless, one or several estimations

**TABLE 15-7    ABC Bank—Basis Risk and Standardized Gaps**

1. Short-term traditional gap (dollars in millions)

| *Repricing Assets* | | *Repricing Liabilities* | |
|---|---|---|---|
| Federal funds sold | 50 | Passbook savings | 50 |
| Adj.-rate loans | 40 | Savings certificates | 50 |
| | 90 | | 100 |

Negative traditional funds gap of $10 million.

2. Rates fall 1%, which traditional gap management (assuming that rates on all assets and liabilities change 1%) indicates should improve the bank's interest margin by $.1 million.

3. Instead of falling by the same magnitude, assume that when the rate on Federal funds falls 1%, the rate on the loans falls .7%, the rate on passbook savings falls .5%, and the rate on savings certificates falls .4%. The bank's interest margin deteriorates rather than improves. Proof:

$$\$50 \text{ mn.} \times 1\% = \$.50 \text{ mn.} \qquad \text{interest revenue decrease}$$
$$\$40 \text{ mn.} \times .7\% = \$.28 \text{ mn.} \qquad \text{interest revenue decrease}$$
$$\$50 \text{ mn.} \times .5\% = \$.25 \text{ mn.} \qquad \text{interest revenue increase}$$
$$\$50 \text{ mn.} \times .4\% = \underline{\$.20 \text{ mn.}} \qquad \text{interest revenue increase}$$

$$\text{Total } \$.33 \text{ mn.} \qquad \text{interest margin } \underline{\text{decline}}$$

4. If ABC Bank believes that the magnitudes in (3) will be more representative of the future than equal changes in all rates, then it should standardize the gap by multiplying the dollar amounts by how much they will change for a given percentage change in one rate (the Federal funds rate is used in this example). The standardized gap for ABC Bank (in $ millions) is:

| Federal funds | $50 | Passbook savings | $25 |
|---|---|---|---|
| Adj.-rate loans | 28 | Savings certificates | 20 |
| | 78 | | 45 |

Positive standardized gap of $23 million.

5. If rates on different securities change closer to the magnitudes in (3) rather than changing at the same magnitude, the standardized gap will be a better measure of change in the bank's interest margin.

---

of standardized gaps seems more consistent with the real world than the traditional gap.

## Ignoring Changes in Values

The fifth concern about traditional funds gap management is that it focuses solely on the effects on the current interest margin. Changes in the value of assets, liabilities, and the resulting residual equity caused by changes in interest rates are ignored. In our opinion, both the gap and changes in the nonsensitive portion of a bank's assets and liabilities can affect a bank's value. Even if there is no funds gap, the bank still may be subject to substantial interest rate risk. Furthermore, it may be possible to offset a mismatch in sensitive assets and liabilities by a carefully designed position in nonsensitive assets and liabilities. Economic values rather than book values and current cash flows should be emphasized in interest sensitivity analysis.[1] The first part of Chapter 16 focuses on how a bank can estimate the effect of changes in interest rates on the values of assets, liabilities, and equity.

## POSSIBLE STRATEGIES FOR MANAGING INTEREST SENSITIVITY

Although these concerns are real, gap management still appears to be a helpful tool. This is particularly true if a frequently updated interest sensitivity profile is used, if management is aware of practical problems in predicting rates and managing the interest positions of borrowers and depositors, and if management standardizes for basis risk and keeps track of changes in values. Given these conditions, funds gap measures are good indicators of the direction and possibly the size of interest margins for a given increase or decrease in interest rates. With this in mind, management should explore four potential strategies that utilize gap management: (1) accepting margin fluctuations, (2) managing the gap over rate cycles, (3) achieving gap targets with typical assets or liabilities, and (4) achieving gap targets using artificial hedges. These strategies are not mutually exclusive; some banks may use two or more strategies.

### Accept Margin Fluctuations

The first strategy is to accept fluctuation in interest margins as one of the risks of banking and go on about a bank's business of filling depositors' and borrowers' needs. Such a strategy implies that a bank's market should control the destiny of the bank's interest sensitivity. A bank in a suburban community might have a large negative gap because nonsensitive mortgages dominate assets and short-term CDs dominate liabilities. A wholesale bank might have a large positive gap if nearly all of its assets are priced to vary with the LIBOR, yet many of its deposits are demand deposits and long-term CDs. The loan and deposit markets of these two banks practically force them to hope that rates will fall or rise, respectively. Movements in the opposite direction to that anticipated would be the bank's interest rate risk. This strategy was used successfully by many banks during the 1950s and 1960s because rate fluctuations were moderate. However, the increased volatility of interest rates in the late 1970s and early 1980s and the expectation for continued volatility make this a questionable strategy. Most banks cannot afford the sizable rate risk

---

[1]Donald Simonson and George H. Hempel, "Improving Gap Management as a Technique for Controlling Interest Rate Risk," *Journal of Bank Research* (Summer 1982), pp. 36–42.

often inherent in the practice of letting the market determine the bank's interest sensitivity position.

## Manage the Gap over the Rate Cycle

The second strategy emphasizes managing the funds gap over the rate cycle. Such a strategy would indicate positive movement in the gap—more sensitive assets or less sensitive liabilities or both—when rates are expected to increase. When rate declines are anticipated, the funds gap should narrow or become more negative—less sensitive assets or more sensitive liabilities or both. Problems with implementing this strategy include the questionable ability to outguess the market on interest rate movement and the desirability of managing borrowers and depositors in order to achieve the bank's objectives at the borrowers' or depositors' expense. In general, this strategy is used by some larger banks that have big staffs responsible for economic and rate predictions and that have entry into a large variety of impersonal financial markets. Some of these banks have publicly stated that they must use gap management based on their expectations for interest rates because they are unable to earn a high enough margin on many of their loans to large multinational companies. One way in which some of these banks try to control the risks of gap strategies is to maintain gaps for short periods and then close the gaps quickly if the interest rate scenario does not work out as anticipated. Another way is to limit cyclical gap management to shorter maturities while balancing the gap for longer-term periods. (Banks choosing such a strategy should probably use the duration and immunization concepts discussed in the next chapter to make sure they are limiting rate risk.)

## Achieve Gap Targets with Bank Assets and Liabilities

The third strategy is to achieve the targeted gap level by managing typical bank assets and liabilities. This strategy could be used in conjunction with gap targets from the preceding strategy or to achieve a balanced gap position. For example, a medium-sized bank with limited staff and limited access to financial markets may decide not to take an interest rate risk by seeking a balanced gap position. If, in order to remain competitive, such a bank is forced to use six-month savings certificates extensively, it may jeopardize its balanced gap position. Using this strategy, the bank should adjust its asset structure to match the interest sensitivity of its liabilities. Such action may be difficult for a bank with limited access to other markets.

## Achieve Gap Targets with Artificial Hedges

The final strategy is to use artificial hedges—financial futures, options, or interest rate swaps—to achieve the funds gap target. (This strategy is detailed in Chapter 16.)

## SUMMARY

Although no single-risk management program can be applied to all institutions, there appear to be several universal asset–liability truths. First, interest rate risk and spread management for banks will become increasingly important, because spreads will continue to be squeezed by competition and open-market pressures. Moreover, taking positions based on interest rate expectations will be necessary because it is unlikely that fee income can be boosted enough to offset declines being experienced in banks' net interest margins. Second, renewed interest rate volatility remains an ever-present threat. Institutions that must expose themselves to gain a few extra basis points of spread also must be carefully positioned to survive large, unexpected changes in interest rates.

Recent vast changes in the financial markets promise to continue and will demand much greater sophistication of asset–liability managers than ever before. And the rate of innovation in markets will probably accelerate.

With that in mind, banks must do their best to fortify themselves for the dynamic environment of the future. Primarily, they must continue to develop the most professional asset–liability function possible. In addition, this function should be led by professionals who can use advanced technology and who constantly upgrade their knowledge of financial markets and instruments. Chapter 16 explores some of the advanced alternatives for measuring and managing interest rate risk.

## Discussion Questions

1. Explain the differences between dollar net interest margin, percent net interest margin, and spread. How would you treat the provisions for loan losses in these calculations?
2. What should be the objectives of a bank in managing its interest margin?
3. What types of cost must a bank cover in order to earn its target return on equity? How do non-rate-sensitive assets affect the required return on rate-sensitive assets?
4. Explain the differences between rate, volume, and mix effects on a bank's net interest margin.
5. Describe the traditional funds gap management system. How should a bank manage its funds gap?
6. Discuss potential concerns about the effectiveness of traditional funds gap management. Do these concerns negate the effectiveness of gap management?
7. Evaluate the advantages and disadvantages of four potential gap management strategies:
   a. Accept margin fluctuations.
   b. Manage the gap over rate cycles.
   c. Achieve gap targets with bank assets and liabilities.
   d. Achieve gap targets with artificial hedges.

# CHAPTER 16

# Advanced Alternatives for Measuring and Managing Interest Rate Risk

The goal of most bankers is not to eliminate risk or even to minimize it. Their goal is to assume risk and control it while making an acceptable profit. Nowhere is this insight more relevant than in banks' asset–liability management efforts. In general, bankers must manage and not necessarily eliminate interest rate risk. In the process, they must generate returns that are at least commensurate with the interest rate risk or funding risk that they take. The effect of interest rate risk on banks' security portfolio values, especially trading account values, has always been a matter of concern; however, only in the last decade or so have bankers focused attention on the interest rate risk for the total balance sheet.

## CRITIQUE OF GAP MANAGEMENT

As with any tool of bank management, the first function of asset–liability tools is dependable measurement. A major premise is that interest rate exposure—the quintessential asset–liability focus—is manageable only if it is measurable. The most common tool for asset–liability management and control systems is the interest-sensitivity gap report presented in Chapter 15.

The gap report requires the preparer to classify assets and liabilities according to time periods called *buckets* in which the assets and liabilities are expected to be repriced. Asset and liability items are repriced at an extant market rate of interest when (1) they mature, (2) they contractually repay a portion of their principal, (3) their interest rate is contractually reset according to a market-rate index, or (4) they are paid or withdrawn by the customer in

**TABLE 16-1 Simplified Gap Report and Estimate of Earnings Sensitivity (dollars in millions)**

| | Time Bucket | | Change in Annual Earnings |
|---|---|---|---|
| | 0–3 Months | 3–12 Months | |
| Interest-sensitive assets | $ 30 | $ 30 | |
| Interest-sensitive liabilities | $ 70 | $ 10 | |
| Gap | − 40 | + 20 | |
| Earnings impact with 1% rise in interest rates | − .350 | + .125 | − .225 |

advance of maturity. The differences (gaps) between expected asset repricings and liability repricings for each time bucket are indicators of an institution's earnings exposure to the general movement of interest rates.

Thus, if an institution's interest-sensitive assets exceed its interest-sensitive liabilities (a positive gap) for a certain time bucket, the institution allegedly will have a net exposure to reinvestment risk during that time frame. Alternatively, when interest-sensitive liabilities exceed interest-sensitive assets (a negative gap), the institution will have a net exposure to refinancing risk. *Net reinvestment risk* causes the net interest margin to depend on the extant interest rates at which assets are repriced. *Net refinancing risk* (i.e., negative reinvestment risk), on the other hand, causes the net interest margin to depend more upon liability repricing rates.

These simple gap management techniques are not a sufficient basis for an effective asset–liability program. Most bankers now believe that the gap report alone does not provide meaningful answers. At best, they find that it is valuable for raising a host of issues surrounding the management of earnings volatility. Gap reports do not directly report anything about earnings volatility. At best, they are simply a proxy for earnings volatility.

An appealing but somewhat misleading use of the gap report is to impute the interest sensitivity of annual earnings. Table 16-1 shows ABC Bank's extremely simplified gap report with just a 0- to 3-month bucket and a 3- to 12-month bucket. If interest rates increase immediately by a uniform 1 percent for all interest-sensitive assets and liabilities, ABC will realize an estimated $225,000 decline in annual earnings. The estimate is based on repricings occurring at a uniform rate within the buckets or, on average, at the midpoint of the time range represented by each bucket. For example, the estimated annual earnings impact in the zero- to three-month bucket is − $40 million (gap) times 1 percent (rise in rates) times 10.5/12 (the average remaining fraction of the year during which the zero- to three-month repricings will be effective), which equals − $350,000.

The gap concept is easy to communicate and easy to understand. While simplicity is one of its strengths, however, gap reporting also understates the complexity of asset–liability processes and the rigor needed to understand them.

In general, changes in spreads between asset yields and liability rates are difficult to track. Assets and liabilities are not all identically sensitive to interest rate movements. At a minimum, asset–liability managers should factor in the usual behavior of the yield curve, in which greater rate fluctuations are associated with short-term items rather than with long-term items. Also, spreads can change in a direction that is opposite to the direction that gap intuition indicates. For example, spreads for a liability-sensitive institution might decline even in a falling-rate environment. This can occur when expiring low-rate term deposits roll over at higher rates than those at which they were previously booked.

Figure 16-1 illustrates this point. Originally, at an earlier stage of the interest rate cycle, the liability was priced at 6 percent. At a later stage of the cycle, when interest rates are falling, the liability is repriced at 8 percent. Thus, despite declining market interest rates, the liability becomes repriced at a higher rate than it carried previously.

The meaning of these and other defects is that gap management is not adequate for an effective asset–liability program. Even a position in which interest-sensitive assets are set equal to interest-sensitive liabilities—called a *gap-matched* position—does not insulate a bank from interest rate fluctuations. For example, it is possible that as interest rates decline, asset yields might reprice 300 basis points lower, while liability rates reprice only 100 basis points lower. Thus, it is not sufficient just to be matched. It is vital to understand what may happen in different interest rate environments.

**FIGURE 16-1    Liability Pricing Timing over an Interest Rate Cycle**

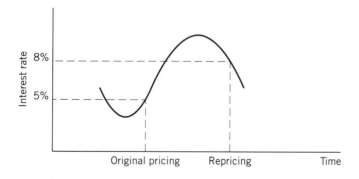

**TABLE 16-2  Earnings Simulation Results**

|  | Change in Earnings | |
|---|---|---|
|  | Upward<br>Shift in Yield Curve | Downward<br>Shift in Yield Curve |
| Variable-rate funding | − $ 6.0 million | + $10.5 million |
| Fixed-rate funding | + $13.0 million | − $20.8 million |

## SIMULATION SYSTEMS

Advances in personal computer technology and the development and refinement of asset–liability software have made earnings simulation models an increasingly practical tool for asset–liability management and control. Skillful simulation modeling can overcome the lack of insight and misleading information that are characteristic of simple gap management. Simulation software must be capable of manipulating the voluminous forward data required by the simulation technique. *Forward data* consist of the bank's estimates of new business activity, including the premature termination of certain existing and future loan and deposit contracts, under alternative interest rate and other environmental scenarios. *Simulation* is an iterative process in which the simulation model produces complete earnings results for each specific set of values for the relevant environmental factors. The process lets the banker observe a pattern of earnings implied in the present and planned balance sheet under, most commonly, alternative forecasts of future yield curves.

Table 16-2 shows a simplified set of earnings results. XYZ Bank has tested alternative funding strategies that emphasize a short-term, variable-rate funding program, on the one hand, and a long-term, fixed-rate funding program, on the other. Each funding program is mapped against interest rate forecasts of upward- and downward-shifting yield curves.

The results call attention to the high degree of earnings exposure associated with the long-term funding program. While the earnings improvement of $13 million in a rising-rate scenario is superior to any outcome for the short-funding alternative, XYZ's downside risk of − $20.8 million under the long-term program is probably unacceptable.

With well-developed software, earnings simulation can be increased to any degree of sophistication desired. At a minimum, the software should readily handle basis (spread) risk and correlated interest rate risk (rate sensitivity of prepayments of assets or early withdrawals of liabilities).

In actuality, early attempts at simulation were simply attempts to animate or articulate the basic static gap report. This resulted in the so-called dynamic gap, or forward gap, which simulated the static gap that would occur in the future. To arrive at this forward gap, much of the same forward data used in a complete simulation had to be input. Unlike the forward earnings emphasis of simulation, however, the emphasis tended to be on gap for gap's sake. That is, instead of focusing on earnings, it focused on the amount of the repricing mismatch at each time bucket.

Simulation does not offer the appeal of conceptual simplicity that is associated with gap analysis. It relies on many detailed data that are usually manageable only with rapid-processing computers. The process requires asset–liability managers to specify unique relationships between balance-sheet volume, mix, and spreads for each interest rate scenario. To be correct, it is necessary to specify these relationships definitively and not to assume, given numerous possible interest rate scenarios, that everything else remains constant. In other words, one cannot just apply a new set of yields and rates to a set of asset and liability volumes and proportions that are constant for all rate scenarios. In the real world, bank balance sheets change dramatically with the radically different business conditions implied with different interest rate environments. Falling interest rates, for example, might imply declining loan demand, prepayment of loans, rising securities volume, declining purchased funds, and so forth. Most smaller banks do not have the time or expertise to specify their simulation exercises so finitely. Large banks are more likely to derive valuable insights from simulation, but only if they are willing to provide the expertise needed to specify volume, mix, and spread dynamics knowledgeably.

## THE DURATION CONCEPT

Interest rate risk can be defined as the effect of changes in interest rates on the value of a single asset, the value of a portfolio of assets, or the difference in the values of a portfolio of assets and a portfolio of the liabilities that fund the assets. The last difference is, of course, the net worth of the asset owner's balance sheet.

### Single-Payment Assets

For the change in the value of an asset consisting of a single cash payment, given a change in interest rates, let $V_1$ be the value of a financial asset with a single payment of $C$ dollars to be received in $n$ years. Assume for simplicity that interest rates $(R)$ are the same for all maturities. Then differential calculus is applied to this simple equation to solve for the change in $V_1$ due to a change in $R$:

$$V_1 = \frac{C}{(1 + R)^n} \tag{16-1}$$

$$dV_1 = \frac{-nC}{(1 + R)^{n+1}} \, dR \tag{16-2}$$

When both sides of Equation 16-2 are divided by $V_1$ (Equation 16-1), we find the percentage change in $V_1$.

$$\frac{dV_1}{V_1} = -n\frac{dR}{1+R} \tag{16-3}$$

Because we are using calculus, Equation 16-3 applies to only infinitesimal changes, $d$, in $R$; however, it can be restated to give a reasonable approximation when changes, $\Delta$, in $R$ are finite, but still small.

$$\frac{\Delta V_1}{V_1} = -n\frac{\Delta R}{1+R} \tag{16-4}$$

Equations 16-3 and 16-4 show that there is an approximately linear relationship between the percentage change in $V_1$ ($dV_1/V_1$ or $\Delta V_1/V_1$) and $R$. Suppose that $R$ initially was 10 percent and $\Delta R$ was an increase of 1 percent. Further assume two single-payment assets, one of which has a maturity of one year and the other a maturity of five years. Substituting in Equation 16-4:

$$\frac{\Delta V_1}{V_1} = -1\left(\frac{.01}{1.10}\right) = -0.91\% \text{ for the one-year asset}$$

and

$$\frac{\Delta V_1}{V_1} = -5\left(\frac{.01}{1.10}\right) = -4.55\% \text{ for the five-year asset}$$

The significance of these results is simply that the five-year asset's price is five times more volatile than that of the one-year asset ($-4.55\%$ is five times $-0.91\%$). In reality, $n$ is an index of their respective interest rate risks.

**Multipayment Assets**

The index $n$ is also the duration of the single-payment asset. However, maturity and duration are equal only for single-payment assets. Duration can be derived as an index of interest rate risk for multipayment assets as well; however, maturity does not provide such an index for multipayment assets.

Let $V_2$ be the value of an $n$-maturity asset that generates a series of $m$ cash flows, $C_t$.

$$V_m = \frac{C_1}{1+R} + \frac{C_2}{(1+R)^2} + \frac{C_3}{(1+R)^3} + \cdots + \frac{C_n}{(1+R)^n} = \sum_{t=1}^{n}\frac{C_t}{(1+R)^t} \tag{16-5}$$

The differential of Equation 16-5 for infinitesimal changes in $V_m$ is

$$dV_m = -\left[\frac{(1)C_1}{(1+R)^2} + \frac{(2)C_2}{(1+R)^3} + \cdots + \frac{(n)C_n}{(1+R)^{n+1}}\right]dR \qquad (16\text{-}6)$$

Now we divide Equation 16-6 by $V_m$ (Equation 16-5) to obtain

$$\frac{dV_m}{V_m} = -\left[\frac{(1)C_1}{1+R} + \frac{(2)C_2}{(1+R)^2} + \cdots + \frac{(n)C_n}{(1+R)^n}\right]\frac{dR}{1+R}\bigg/V_m \qquad (16\text{-}7)$$

which can be written

$$\frac{dV_m}{V_m} = -\left[\frac{\sum_{t=1}^{n} C_t(t)/(1+R)^t}{\sum_{t=1}^{n} C_t/(1+R)^t}\right]\frac{dR}{1+R} \qquad (16\text{-}8)$$

In Equation 16-8 the term in brackets is duration $(D)$; therefore, Equation 16-8 can be written

$$\frac{dV_m}{V_m} = -D\frac{dR}{1+R} \qquad (16\text{-}9)$$

An approximation for finite, but small, changes in $R$ is

$$\frac{\Delta V_m}{V_m} = -D\frac{\Delta R}{1+R} \qquad (16\text{-}10)$$

Notice that Equation 16-10 is identical in form to Equation 16-4, which dealt with single-payment securities. Thus, duration is simply an index of interest rate risk that captures the cash-flow pattern of complex (multipayment) assets. The $t$ value in the numerator of Equation 16-8 signifies that duration is a time-weighted average of the present value of the series of cash flows. In its role as an index of interest rate risk, the duration of a multipayment asset $(D)$ is analogous to the maturity of a single-payment asset $(n)$.

Table 16-3 presents a sample calculation of the duration of a seven-year bond that makes a $120 coupon payment each year and returns the entire $1,000 principal in year 7. The bond is discounted at a market interest rate of 12 percent. Note that the bond's duration of 5.11 years is, as expected, less than its maturity. If the market rate shifts from 12 percent to 13 percent, the change in the bond's value will be

$$\frac{\Delta V_m}{V_m} = -5.11\left(\frac{.01}{1.12}\right) = -4.56\%$$

**TABLE 16-3   Duration of a 12% Coupon, Seven-Year Bond Priced at Par**

| (1) Year | (2) Cash Flow | (3) Present Value of $1 at 12% | (4) Present Value of Cash Flow | (5) Weighted Flows (1) × (4) |
|---|---|---|---|---|
| 1 | $  120 | 0.8929 | $107.15 | $107.1 |
| 2 | 120 | 0.7972 | 95.66 | 191.3 |
| 3 | 120 | 0.7118 | 85.42 | 256.3 |
| 4 | 120 | 0.6355 | 76.26 | 305.0 |
| 5 | 120 | 0.5674 | 68.09 | 340.5 |
| 6 | 120 | 0.5066 | 60.79 | 364.7 |
| 7 | 1,120 | 0.4523 | 506.58 | 3,546.1 |
| | | | $999.95[a] | $5,107.0 |

Duration = (5)/Price = 5,107.0/1,000 = 5.11 years

[a]This figure does not equal $1,000 due to rounding factors.

For this interest rate shift, $\Delta V_m$ will be $-\$45.63$, and the bond's price will fall from $1,000 to $954.37. If changes in interest rates are large, one must be concerned with convexity which is addressed later in this chapter.

## MARKET VALUE ACCOUNTING

In the context of asset–liability management, duration is applied in order to measure the exposure of the bank's value to changes in interest rates. Managers of financial institutions instinctively understand that the value of the bank, as indicated by the accounting book values of assets and liabilities, does not reflect true economic value. Most items on a bank's balance sheets are nominal contracts that define future cash inflow streams (assets) and cash outflow streams (liabilities). Unlike book values, the present values of these contractual streams change when market rates of interest change, or debtors' repayment prospects deteriorate, or when option features are likely to be exercised, thereby truncating cash-flow schedules. In short, a system of market value accounting that considers shifting patterns of discounted cash flow has advantages over book-value accounting both in the measurement of economic performance and as a basis for decision making. In effect, market values of assets and liabilities summarize meaningful information about institutions' future interest-related benefits and costs that are not evident in their book values.

In reality, the term *market value accounting* may be misleading when applied to firms' net worth. The market value of net worth connotes firms' valuation by the stock market, which incorporates the values of attributes that include, but also go well beyond, the bank's currently held assets and liabilities. These additional attributes include the market's valuation of earnings from future operations (operating value) and of future business that may be attracted because of accumulated goodwill (franchise value).

Many analysts use the term *current or fair value accounting* to designate the market value of assets on the books less the market value of liabilities on the books. We use the term *portfolio net worth*, coined by Toevs and Haney,[1] to express the economic value of a bank.

## THE DURATION GAP

The duration of an entire portfolio of assets or of liabilities can be derived from information on the portfolio's future cash flows and market discount rates. Ideally, by approximately matching the duration of its portfolio of assets with that of its portfolio of liabilities, a bank can control all of the interest rate exposure of its portfolio net worth. When asset and liability durations are matched, general interest rate movements should have roughly the same effect on the values of the firm's assets and liabilities, thereby protecting portfolio net worth.

*Duration gap* is a measure of the mismatch of asset and liability durations and, theoretically at least, provides an index of the interest rate exposure of portfolio net worth. The expression for duration gap ($DG$) is

$$DG = D_A - \left(\frac{L}{A}\right)D_L \qquad (16\text{-}11)$$

where   $A$ = market value of assets
         $L$ = market value of liabilities
         $D_A$ = duration of assets
         $D_L$ = duration of liabilities

In Equation 16-11 the duration of liabilities is weighted by the ratio of the market values of liabilities to assets in order to recognize that the difference in these two magnitudes affects the amount by which each will change with a change in interest rates.

The expression for the impact of interest rate changes on portfolio net worth as a percentage of assets is

$$\frac{\Delta PNW}{A} = -DG\frac{\Delta R}{1 + R} \qquad (16\text{-}12)$$

The example in Table 16-4 demonstrates the change in portfolio net worth with changes in interest rates. Notice that the simplified balance sheet is

[1]Alden L. Toevs and William C. Haney, *Measuring and Managing Interest Rate Risk: A Guide to Asset/Liability Models Used in Banks and Thrifts* (New York: Morgan Stanley), October 1984.

**TABLE 16-4    Interest Rate Exposure of Balance Sheet (dollars in millions)**

| | Present Economic Value | Years Duration | Economic Value after Rate Increase of 2% |
|---|---|---|---|
| **Assets** | | | |
| Securities | | | |
| Liquid | $ 150 | 0.5 | $148.6 |
| Investment | 100 | 3.5 | 93.6 |
| Loans | | | |
| Floating | 400 | 0 | 400.0 |
| Fixed-rate | 350 | 2.0 | 337.3 |
| Total assets | $1,000 | 1.125 | $979.5 |
| **Liabilities & Net Worth** | | | |
| Transaction deposits | $ 400 | 0 | $400.0 |
| CDs and other time deposits | | | |
| Short-term | 350 | 0.4 | 347.5 |
| Long-term | 150 | 2.5 | 143.7 |
| Net worth | 100 | 5.0[a] | 88.3[b] |
| Total liabilities & net worth | $1,000 | 1.015 | $979.5 |

DL (without net worth) = 0.572

[a] Approximately $(1 - r)/r$, where (arbitrarily) $r$ = return on equity = 25% before taxes. Net worth absorbs the residual adjustment.

[b] Decreased 11.7%.

presented in terms of economic values before and after a 2 percent shift in interest rates. The bank in the example has calculated the duration in years for each of several portfolios of assets and liabilities; for instance, the bank's $150 million short-term (liquid) securities portfolio is deemed to have a duration of 0.5 year. The duration estimate of 5.0 years for portfolio net worth is shown for the sake of completeness, but it does not enter into the calculation of the change in portfolio net worth. As indicated, for a 2 percent uniform increase in all interest rates, portfolio net worth falls by $11.7 million, from $100 million to $88.3 million.

From Equation 16-11 and using the dollar-weighted durations of assets and liabilities, the duration gap for the bank in Table 16-4 is

$$DG = D_A - \frac{L}{A} \times D_L$$

$$= 1.125 - \left(\frac{900}{1,000}\right) \times .572 = .610$$

(16-13)

According to Equation 16-12, the percentage change in the ratio of portfolio net worth to assets can be approximated by

$$\frac{\Delta PNW}{A} = -DG \times \frac{\Delta R}{1 - R}$$

Assuming an initial discount rate of 10 percent,

$$\frac{\Delta PNW}{\$1,000,000,000} = -.610 \times \frac{.02}{1.10} = -11.10\% \tag{16-14}$$

$$\Delta PNW = \$1,000,000,000 \times (-11.10\%) = -\$11.1 \text{ million} \tag{16-15}$$

Notice that the approximate change in portfolio net worth of $11.1 million given in Equation 16-15 is somewhat less than the $11.7 million calculated directly in Table 16-4. Recall that technically the linearity of changes in value with changes in interest rates applies only to infinitesimal changes in interest rates. The finite 2 percent change assumed in Table 16-4 produces a slightly nonlinear result.

## CONVEXITY AND HIGHER-ORDER DURATION

The nonlinearity of changes in portfolio net worth values with changes in interest rates is described as *convexity*. This property can be seen graphically in Figure 16-1, which traces the value path of portfolio net worth with different levels of interest rates. The convex shape of the value path comes about because mathematically interest rate declines cause larger positive changes in value than the negative changes in value caused by interest rate increases. Convexity differs from bank to bank because of differences in the cash inflows and outflows implied in different banks' assets and liabilities. The amount of convexity affects the size of the error in the simple linear duration equation for the interest rate volatility of value given earlier in Equation 16-10.

In Figure 16-2, simple linear duration is represented as the slope of a straight line tangent to the value path. As an index of the changes in value associated with changes in interest rates, its usefulness deteriorates as the change in rates becomes larger. A further definition of convexity is the amount of the change that is not picked up by the linearity result of simple duration. It has been demonstrated that the second and third derivatives of value (recall that simple duration is based on the first derivative) provide measures that account for convexity. In addition, these higher-order derivatives, in conjunction with simple duration, appear to anticipate changes in value associated with erratic, nonparallel shifts in the term structure of interest rates. In other words, these additional duration measures more accurately track value changes brought on by complicated—and not unusual—changes in the level, slope, and curvature of the term structure.

---

**FIGURE 16-2  Convexity of Bank Portfolio Net Worth**

---

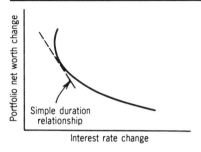

---

The expression for the second order duration as applied to a multipayment asset can be reduced to the following rather simple form:

$$D_2 = \left[ \frac{\sum\limits_{t=1}^{n} \dfrac{C_t(t^2 + t)}{(1 + R)^t}}{\sum\limits_{t=1}^{n} \dfrac{C_t}{(1 + R)^t}} \right] \frac{\Delta R}{(1 + R)^2} \qquad (16\text{-}16)$$

where $D_2$ = second derivative of value with respect to $R$

Note that the second derivative expression closely resembles Equation 16-10 (for simple duration), except that the present values in the numerator are multiplied by time squared plus time to receipt of each cash flow. This duration measure must be used in addition to simple duration, which still explains most of the value volatility. It also adds materially to the complexity of the duration concept.

## RETROSPECTIVE: DURATION, GAP MANAGEMENT, AND SIMULATION

In contrast to duration matching, gap management addresses matching of the near-term repricing volumes of assets and liabilities; it tends to ignore the interest elasticity of long-term assets and liabilities. Inherently, gap matching attempts to stabilize earnings, while, as noted, duration matching attempts to stabilize the portfolio net worth value.

Bankers adhere to gap matching rather than to duration matching because they are oriented to short-term earnings objectives, not portfolio net worth values. This bias toward earnings would not hold up, of course, if banks and thrifts adhered to mark-to-market accounting (market value accounting) principles. If they did so, the impact of interest rate movements on the values of loans, securities, and various funding sources would immediately be clear. Duration undoubtedly would be more apparent in a world of mark-to-market accounting than it is now. At present, duration is not well understood; perhaps its greatest drawback is that it is difficult to explain to nonfinancial managers.

In any event, the practical value of duration appears to be limited. Critics point out that duration values are unstable with the passage of time. Contractual cash flows change, defaults occur, reinvestment opportunities vary, and assumptions about future business fail to hold. As a result, the critics argue, to be correctly matched, the asset and liability durations must be continually rebalanced and readjusted.

In fairness, these criticisms also apply to dynamic gap measures, as well as to simulation. Proponents of simulation seem to argue, however, that the iterative nature of simulation overcomes uncertainties related to changing cash flows, defaults, future business assumptions, and so forth. Their point is that the multiple runs required in simulation permit the user to alter these variables from run to run. Thus, the uncertainties are reflected in the range of the simulation results and can be properly evaluated. One must be cautious about such reassurances, however, because the relationships *between* the variables surely change from one interest rate scenario to the next.

Despite the critics, duration appears to be getting more attention from practical asset–liability managers. Not surprisingly, given the greater length of their assets, S&Ls are more likely to apply duration techniques to monitor their asset–liability duration gaps than are commercial banks.

## RESTRUCTURING THE BALANCE SHEET

There are many means by which banks can restructure their balance sheets to alter undesired fluctuations of earnings or portfolio net worth. The most transparent means involve making direct changes in the repricing or cash-flow characteristics of conventional (cash) asset and liability instruments. For example, an institution can replace its daily rollover program of Federal funds sales with sales placed directly for terms of days or weeks; fixed-rate loan programs can be converted to floating-rate loans; term deposit rates can be bid up to replace short-term deposits with long-term deposits; and long-term securities can be effectively shortened by using them in repurchase agreements.

There are occasions, however, when traditional cash instruments cannot be used feasibly to alter the risk characteristics of balance-sheet portfolios.

Fortunately, there are nontraditional alternatives for changing (hedging) these characteristics by using so-called derivative securities, such as futures, options, securitized assets, and interest rate swaps.

These market innovations are permanently changing the tools and methods of asset–liability management. Futures or options programs enable banks to offset the effects of undesired deposit repricings. Interest rate swaps permit banks to fix their "long books" by exchanging floating-rate payments for fixed-rate payments. This leads to a lock-in of liability rates without the need for developing a client market for costly long-term liabilities. Securitizing loan assets permits banks or thrifts to create salable capital market instruments from their relatively homogeneous portfolios of auto loans, credit card loans, mortgages, or commercial loans. By positioning such assets for possible sale on short notice, banks or thrifts can quickly adjust their asset–liability matching or can create immediate cash to cover liquidity needs. (Loan securitization was discussed in depth in Chapter 17.)

## Interest Rate Futures

*Interest rate futures* contracts allow banks to shift interest rate risk to the market for financial futures. Interest rate futures are analogous to futures contracts on commodities, such as corn or soybeans, and on precious metals, such as gold or platinum. Commodities futures in the United States have existed since the nineteenth century to reduce price risk in agriculture, in mining, and in industries that depend on supplies of commodities or metals. They are contracts to make or take delivery of the subject commodity at some future date. For example, suppose that in March at the start of the growing season, a farmer is concerned about the price he might receive for his corn crop in September. He can sell his corn in the September futures market for $1.50 per bushel. September's price is thus secured in March for a crop that does not even exist. In September, whether the spot market price stands at $1.30 or $1.80, the farmer must make delivery at $1.50 (representing, respectively, an opportunity gain of 20 cents per bushel or an opportunity loss of 30 cents per bushel).

Financial futures have been in existence only since 1975, but they operate the same way. One can commit to a price to sell or buy a security at some future date. For example, in March a trader may acquire a futures contract to sell a nominal $1 million Treasury bill in September at an index value of 93.55. (The index value represents the annualized discounted percentage of the nominal maturity value of 100.) As with commodity futures, the trader locks in September's price in March on a security—the September Treasury bill—that will not exist until September. When September arrives, the trader must make delivery of the Treasury bill whether the spot price at the time is 92.75 (an opportunity loss) or 94.40 (an opportunity gain). In reality, in the financial futures market, only a few futures contracts are settled by actually making or taking delivery of the underlying security. Most futures contracts are settled or closed when holders execute an offsetting futures contract well in advance of the delivery date. For example, a holder of a contract to take future delivery of a given 90-day Treasury bill (a buy or *long* contract) usually closes his or her position later by selling (or going *short*) a contract on the identical Treasury bill. The two transactions are fully offsetting.

Interest rate futures contracts are written against the following instruments: U.S. Treasury bonds, U.S. Treasury notes, U.S. Treasury bills, GNMA collateralized depository receipts, domestic CDs, and three-month Eurodollar time deposits. The most active of these contracts are the Eurodollar and the Treasury bond contracts.

For banks, there are two kinds of balance-sheet hedges—asset hedges and liability hedges—that can be implemented using futures. An *asset hedge* is designed to transform the effective interest rate maturity of an asset. To extend the maturity of an asset, futures contracts (Treasury securities, GNMAs) are bought; to reduce the maturity of an asset, futures contracts are sold. A *liability hedge* is designed to transform the effective interest maturity of a liability. To extend the effective maturity of a liability, futures contracts (CDs, Eurodollars, Treasury bills) are sold; to reduce the effective maturity of a liability, futures contracts are bought. Basically, hedges using financial futures are designed either to maintain the market value of the asset or liability or to reduce net interest income risk.

The profitability of the combined transactions depends on the price movement of the original futures contract while the holder's position is open. Futures pricing is linked to current prices on cash instruments by the *cost-of-carry* concept, defined as the interest cost of carrying deliverable securities until the futures contract expires. This linkage exists because of cash and futures market arbitrage—after accounting for interest carrying costs—in which the two markets present alternative means for acquiring and selling the same securities. The holder of a buy (long) contract profits from declining current interest rates and the associated rise in the contract price because of the opportunity to take delivery of the underlying security at a contract price below the current market price. That is, the holder closes his or her position by buying at the earlier low contract price and selling at the present high price.

The workings of the market for financial futures make futures a useful hedging tool for banks. Because the price of the futures contract moves with current and expected interest rate movements, a bank can buy or sell a futures contract to offset some of the impact a change in interest rates would have because of the bank's funds gap position.

Table 16-5 gives an example of a so-called anticipatory hedge for a liability-sensitive bank. The bank wishes to hedge against a rise in the cost of $10 million worth of its six-month CDs, a large volume of which will roll over three months from now. The bank sells 20 June 90-day Eurodollar futures contracts with a nominal value of $1 million each to hedge against a rise in the cost of CDs. Twenty such contracts are used against the $10 million worth of CDs because the dollar interest cost on a six-month CD changes approximately

**TABLE 16-5  A Bank's Anticipatory Hedge of Six-Month CDs**

|  | Cash Transactions | Futures Transactions |
|---|---|---|
| January 1, 1991 | Bank expects a sharp rise in CD rates by April<br>Current CD rate = 7% | Bank sells 20 June 91 90-day Eurodollar CD futures contracts at a price of 92.70 (7.30%) |
| April 1, 1991 | Bank rolls over $10 million of six-month CDs<br>Spot CD rate = 9% | Bank offsets its hedge by buying 20 June 91 Eurodollar CD futures contracts at 90.90 (9.10%) |
| Summary | Interest cost due to rate rise in CD market (2%)<br><br>Increased cost<br>1/2 year × 2% × $10,000,000 = $100,000 | Yield gain on futures position due to decline (rise) in futures price (rate) − 1.80 (1.80%)<br>Gain<br>20 contracts × 1/4 year × 1.80% × $1,000,000 = $90,000 |

| | |
|---|---|
| Cost | $100,000 |
| Gain | $90,000 |
| Net loss | $10,000 |

twice as much as the interest yield on a single 90-day Eurodollar futures contract; this is due to the difference in their term in maturity (one is six months, the other three months).

The results show that CD rates did in fact rise by 2 percent, from 7 to 9 percent, between January and April. The futures hedge, however, largely protected the bank against the resulting $100,000 increase in the cost of funding the loan. (The hedge was not perfect because of *basis risk*; the price, or yield, on the Eurodollar CD futures did not change by exactly the same magnitude as the change in the CD rate.)

In addition to offsetting liability sensitivity—a negative gap—banks can view such a hedge as a vehicle for offering fixed-rate loans. In addition, banks can advise borrowers on booking futures positions for their own accounts to hedge against rate increases on floating-rate loans. To date, only a small number of banks are active users of the futures markets. It is likely that an increasing number of banks will become informed on futures-hedging techniques as the competition for business loans continues to intensify.

### Options

The second instrument for hedging interest rate risk is *options*. An option represents the right (rather than an obligation, as is the case with futures) to buy or sell a specified quantity and quality of an underlying asset at a given price on or before a stipulated date. A *call* is an option to buy the specified asset at a strike price, and a *put* is an option to sell the specified asset at a strike price on or before the specified date. Both calls and puts can be bought or sold.

Although gains or losses from futures positions are limited only by the price of the underlying asset, options allow purchasers or sellers (writers) to separate their upside and downside risk. For example, the purchaser of a call (put) retains upside (downside) profit opportunities. The net profit on a purchased call (put) equals the underlying asset's increase above (decrease below) the option's exercise price minus the option premium. Since the option is exercised only at the purchaser's discretion, however, a purchased option can be considered a limited-risk instrument. The maximum loss—the premium paid to purchase the option—is set when the position is established. On the other hand, there is no comparable limitation on risk in writing (selling) an option. While the option writer's maximum profit is the premium received from the option buyer, his or her potential loss equals the adverse movement of the underlying asset's price from the option's exercise price, minus the option premium. In effect, the option writer is guaranteed a gross receipt equal to the option premium, but his or her return may be considerably less, since he or she may suffer a virtually unlimited net loss.

Put and call contracts are now available on numerous financial instruments and indices—individual stocks, Treasury bills, Treasury bonds, mortgage instruments, stock indices, and options on futures contracts on Treasury securities. Although a single futures position can neutralize rate exposure on an underlying asset or liability a similar hedge with options would require either simultaneous put and call transactions, both at a premium, or so-called delta hedging, which entails continuous adjustments (hence, significant transaction costs).

The most straightforward use of options by banks is to hedge an asset–liability gap position with options on interest rate futures. Figure 16-3 illustrates the payoff from such an application. A put option on an interest rate futures contract bought to hedge a liability-sensitive position is shown in Figure 16-3A; a similar call option bought to hedge an asset-sensitive position is shown in Figure 16-3B. The dashed lines show the value of the option contract as interest rates fall, moving from left to right. The thin solid line shows the change either in the portfolio's net worth value or in net interest income for the bank. For liability-sensitive banks this line rises with falling interest rates, and for asset-sensitive banks it falls as rates fall. The composite outcome is shown by the heavy solid line and demonstrates that the bank is hedged against unfavorable rate movements while retaining a positive payoff (net of the cost of the options) in the case of favorable rate movements. (A more detailed exposition of the use of option concepts in pricing bank products and services is presented in Chapter 17.)

### FIGURE 16-3 Insuring against Interest Rate Sensitivity with Options

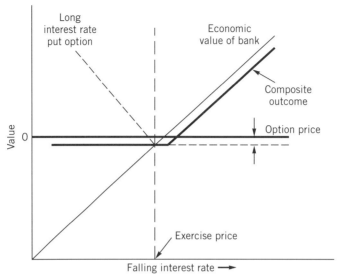

Part A.  Liability-sensitive bank (using purchased put option)

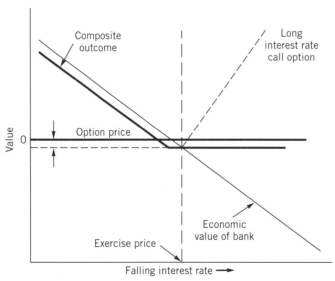

Part B.  Asset-sensitive bank (using purchased call option)

**Interest Rate Swaps**

A third method of hedging an asset–liability interest-sensitivity or duration position artificially is through *interest rate swaps*. An interest rate swap is a transaction in which two parties exchange a series of cash flows representing interest payments on an agreed-upon amount of underlying principal. Although this notional amount is usually linked to underlying liabilities or assets of the two parties, there is no exchange of principal. Generally, one party pays a floating rate of interest and the other party pays a fixed rate of interest; however, in some swaps, both parties pay a floating rate of interest based on different indices. Maturities of swaps run from 2 to 12 years, with most transactions running from 3 to 7 years. The net difference in interest payments is settled quarterly, semiannually, or annually (with semiannual settlement being the most common) by remittance of the difference in interest payments by the owning party. Swaps can involve interest received on assets or interest paid on liabilities.

There are two major economic rationale underlying a fixed-rate, floating-rate swap. First, a party that has one form of mismatched interest sensitivity or duration position (such as a party with primarily fixed-rate assets financed primarily with floating-rate liabilities) may undertake a swap with a party mismatched in the other direction (such as floating-rate assets financed primarily with fixed-rate liabilities). Second, a swap may match two parties that possess different *relative* financing advantages in long-term, fixed-rate markets and short-term, floating-rate markets. One party will have a cost (or yield) advantage over the other when it comes to acquiring long-term, fixed-rate funds (or assets), but it will have a smaller comparative advantage in the shorter-term credit markets. By leveraging on the ability of this stronger party (more creditworthy, more liquid, or whatever) to access longer-term markets, a swap allows the other party indirectly to obtain fixed financing rates, which would otherwise be unavailable to that party. (In a manner similar to the theory of comparative advantage in trade, the relative advantage, not the absolute advantage, is the essential ingredient for such swaps.) Either or both parties in both situations may be a bank or banks.

Table 16-6 presents an example of an interest rate swap. Party 1 might be a bank desiring more floating-rate assets (it needs more interest-sensitive assets to achieve its desired position), while party 2 is a bank that wants more assets with rates fixed for three years to achieve its desired interest-sensitivity or duration position. These two parties swap the difference in interest flows for three years on a notional amount of $10 million ($5 million to $100 million is the usual range of notional amounts). Party 1's interest payment is the three-year Treasury note rate of 12.10 percent less 0.10 percent, or 12 percent; party 2's interest payment is the annual average yield on 91-day Treasury bills. If Treasury bills averaged 10 percent in year 1, party 1 would pay party 2 $200,000 in an annual settlement. If the bills averaged 12 percent in year 2, no payment would be exchanged. If the bills averaged 14 percent in year 3, party 2 would pay party 1 $200,000 in an annual settlement. Note that both

---

### TABLE 16-6  Example of an Interest Rate Swap

---

*Elements of an Interest Rate Swap*

| | |
|---|---|
| Notational principal | $10,000,000 |
| Term | 3 years |
| Settlement | Annual |

**Fixed Rate**
3-year Treasury note yield
minus 10 basis points = 12.00%

```
┌─────────┐         Fixed          ┌─────────┐
│  Party  │        ══════⟹         │  Party  │
│    1    │        Floating        │    2    │
│         │        ⟸──────         │         │
└─────────┘                        └─────────┘
```

**Floating Rate**
91-day Treasury bill yield = 10.00%

*Interest Payment Exchange*

Year 1:   Fixed rate − 12.00%
          Floating rate − 10.00%
   Party 1 pays party 2 $200,000
Year 2:        Rates rise 2.00%
          Fixed rate − 12.00%
       Floating rate − 12.00%
          No payments made
Year 3:        Rates rise 2.00%
          Fixed rate − 12.00%
       Floating rate − 14.00%
   Party 2 pays party 1 $200,000

---

parties have achieved their objective; party 1 has achieved a yield similar to those on 91-day Treasury bills on the $10 million, and party 2 has obtained a three-year fixed yield on the notional amount. Swaps are also made on liabilities to parties that want to change the rate sensitivity of their liabilities.

Because no principal is involved, the only payment at risk is the difference in interest yields (or costs), meaning that credit risk is limited. Even this limited risk can be reduced further by L/Cs, collateral, or other protective devices. This limited credit risk means that stronger banks or other parties are reasonably comfortable with swaps with weaker or smaller banks or other parties. For example, a smaller or weaker bank can utilize swaps to create potentially significant amounts of long-term, fixed-cost financing that would otherwise be available only at prohibitive costs. These banks can potentially offer fixed-rate financing to both commercial and retail customers in virtually all market environments. On the other hand, a stronger bank can often utilize swaps with weaker banks to create variable-rate funding with gains, such as advantageous rates and reduced costs, which outweigh minimally higher credit risk. Both banks (or parties) can adjust their interest-sensitivity or duration positions without altering their underlying asset or liability positions. Swaps are also used to change a floating rate of interest from one index to another and to obtain income without the use of assets by taking market positions. The many advantages of swaps account for their growth as a hedging instrument. In 1981, under $1 billion in swap transactions occurred. By 1992 the notional amount of interest rate swaps had passed $1 trillion.

Interest rate swaps do have several potential disadvantages that should be weighed carefully against their advantages. One disadvantage results from the fact that, unlike a futures or options position, the swap transaction is irreversible. A second disadvantage is that there are legal expenses associated with establishing the swap, and there are relatively high transaction costs if a broker is involved. These costs may eliminate the relative rate advantage associated with swaps. Moreover, swaps must usually be transacted in larger amounts to spread legal and transactions costs; therefore, some smaller banks that would gain from swaps cannot participate. Third, at times, yield curve differences may be so large that one of the swapping parties may be unable to earn an adequate interest margin. Finally, the swap is not an entirely riskless transaction from a credit standpoint. Care should be taken to ensure that interest rate risk is not replaced with more significant credit risk.

## THE FUTURE OF RISK MANAGEMENT

While no single risk management program can be applied to all institutions, there appear to be several universal asset–liability truths. First, interest rate risk and spread management for banks will become increasingly important because spreads will continue to be squeezed by competition and open-market pressures. Moreover, taking positions based on interest rate expectations will be necessary because it is unlikely that fee income can be boosted enough to offset declines being experienced in banks' net interest margins. Second, renewed interest rate volatility remains an ever-present threat. Institutions that must expose themselves to gain a few extra basis points of spread also must be carefully positioned to survive large, unexpected changes in interest rates.

Recent vast changes in the financial markets promise to continue and will demand much greater sophistication of asset–liability managers than ever before. And the rate of innovation in markets will probably accelerate.

With that in mind, banks must do their best to fortify themselves for the dynamic environment of the future. Primarily, they must continue to develop the most professional asset–liability function possible. And the function should be led by professionals who can use advanced technology and who constantly upgrade their knowledge of financial markets and instruments.

## Discussion Questions

1. What is duration? How is duration measured? What is the relationship between duration and maturity? How does duration relate to market price?
2. Do you believe that immunization is the key to managing a bank's interest-sensitivity position? Explain your reasons.
3. Describe how a bank might use financial futures to manage its interest-sensitivity position.
4. What are the advantages and disadvantages of using options in managing a bank's interest-sensitivity position?
5. What are interest rate swaps? How can a bank effectively use swaps to manage its interest-sensitivity position?

# CHAPTER 17

# Innovations in Products and Pricing

Historically, banks relied upon U.S. government securities and tax-exempt municipal bonds to provide liquidity for future loan demands and, in the interim, to supplement income. Banks whose markets at times fail to provide abundant loan volumes may find themselves depending on securities income as an enduring principal component of their total income, along with loans, for significant periods of time. These banks face a dilemma because the traditional forms of bank investments do not produce yields sufficient to replace the revenues banks usually expect to earn on loans. For example, U.S. Treasury securities are unlikely to offer yields that exceed banks' cost of funds unless banks acquire longer-term securities with typically higher yields and accept the interest rate risk involved. Moreover, following enactment of the Tax Reform Act of 1986, most new municipal bonds no longer gave banks the benefits of tax-exempt income and did not provide tax-equivalent spreads over the cost of bank funds of the magnitude provided in the past.

Now, however, newer and higher-yielding forms of investment are available to banks. These investments usually entail greater credit risk and other types of risk than the more traditional bank investments covered in Chapter 7. Among the many banks with the need for higher investment income, it has become crucial to know whether and how to use these new investment media.

In addition to these new instruments, a substantial and increasing part of banks' business is off the balance sheet and is not reflected in conventional on–balance sheet assets or liabilities. This is especially true for money center and large regional banks whose access to previously large, profitable loans has shrunk because of lower-cost competition from open financial markets. As part of the effort to offset such lost income, these banks have increased their supplies of so-called contingent credit products such as standby letters of credit (L/Cs) and credit lines, as well as financial derivatives like interest rate swaps.

Contingent products are also embedded in more conventional bank assets and liabilities. Banks add value to many services extended to customers by offering contingent claims or options. For example, fixed-rate mortgage or business borrowers are given the option to pay off their loans if market interest rates decline, enticing borrowers to refinance their debt at lower borrowing rates. Other customers get other options. Term depositors can withdraw their funds before maturity, usually for a fee, if they find more attractive interest rates during a rise in market interest rates.

The contingent nature of off–balance sheet products is similar to the options offered on conventional, on–balance sheet products. When customers receive loan commitments, for example, they gain the privilege of drawing upon bank credit if and when funds are needed. These funds can be taken at the customer's option.

From banks' viewpoints, the flexibility of their products is limited only by bankers' imagination and the desire to please and serve their customers. However, each option granted to customers sets up contingent liabilities for the bank. In every case, the bank must do something—extinguish borrowers' debts, redeem deposits, extend credit—at the customer's request. Each such obligation potentially causes the bank to incur costs or relinquish an opportunity for profit.

We start this chapter by examining several nontraditional instruments available to and used by banks. After evaluating these instruments, we turn to pricing concepts for contingent claims, such as loan commitments and L/Cs. Contingent claims or options pricing is also applied to certain loan price-setting techniques involving interest rate floors, caps, collars, and other option features frequently associated with lending.

Finally, we review another kind of off–balance sheet activity: the sale and securitization of loans. Although such loans are temporarily warehoused on the balance sheet, their sale qualifies them as an off–balance sheet activity that appears to reduce the cost of loans and to intensify the utilization of available bank credit.

## CAPITAL MARKET ALTERNATIVE INVESTMENTS

For loan-deficient banks to achieve the higher yields on investments required to make up for a significant part of unavailable loan revenues, they must consider longer-term, capital market investment alternatives. With nontraditional capital market investment, banks must accept not only credit or marketability risk but also interest rate (or price) risk. Furthermore, with the fastest-growing segment of bank investments—mortgage derivative securities—banks are faced with the additional risk of mortgagors' prepayment behavior.

Table 17-1 lists several kinds of nontraditional investment instruments available to bank portfolio managers.

## TABLE 17-1    Alternative Investments Used by Banks

Mortgage derivatives
   Fixed-rate mortgage-backed securities, 15 years
   Fixed-rate mortgage-backed securities, 30 years
   Adjustable-rate mortgage-backed securitiess
   Collateralized mortgage obligations (CMO)
      ▪ sequential class
      ▪ planned amortization class
      ▪ targeted amortization class
   Interest only–principal only securities (IO-PO)
   Real estate mortgage investment conduits (REMIC)
Small Business Administration–guaranteed loan pools
Mutual funds
Government investment certificates
Corporate debt securities

## Mortgage Derivatives

A secondary mortgage market was first conceived by the federal government with the creation of the Federal National Mortgage Association (FNMA or Fannie Mae) in 1938. This government-sponsored corporation was chartered to purchase mortgages from lenders and resell them to investors. Its purpose was to provide home buyers with capital to overcome regional shortages of funds. In due course, FNMA and two subsequently founded government agencies—the Government National Mortgage Association (GNMA or Ginnie Mae) and the Federal Home Loan Mortgage Corporation (FHLMC or Freddie Mac)—began buying home loans from lenders, packaging them into securities, and providing explicit (in the case of GNMA) or implicit (in the cases of FNMA and FHLMC) guarantees on the packages. The securitization and guarantee of home mortgages through vehicles such as participation certificates offered by the agencies greatly enhanced the flow of loans for housing finance. Table 17-2 displays the growth in the amount of funds raised through securitized sources for one- to four-family housing. As of the end of the first quarter of 1992, the FHLMC estimated that 43 percent of all mortgages are securitized. Mortgage securitization has increased dramatically as the variety of instruments has grown.

Mortgages and mortgage-backed securities (MBS) constitute callable investments because mortgagors are granted the option to pay off their mortgages before maturity. Confronted with an indeterminate term on mortgage securities, investors demand a yield premium above the yield available on noncallable securities of similar credit and price risk. MBS are analogous to a sinking fund bond with an unknown retirement formula.

The factors that determine mortgage prepayment rates are well known, but unfortunately, they are subject to variation. Demographic factors are rela-

**TABLE 17-2    Securitization of One- to Four-Family Home Mortgages (dollars in millions)**

|      | Total 1- to 4-Family Originations | GNMA | FHLMC | FNMA | Percent Securitized |
|------|----------------------------------|---------|---------|---------|---------------------|
| 1976 | $112,785 | $12,315 | $1,073 |          | 11.87% |
| 1977 | 161,963 | 14,324 | 3,939 |          | 11.28 |
| 1978 | 185,036 | 9,451 | 5,282 |          | 7.96 |
| 1979 | 187,091 | 22,054 | 3,288 |          | 13.55 |
| 1980 | 133,762 | 17,473 | 1,772 |          | 14.39 |
| 1981 | 97,278 | 11,916 | 2,999 | $    717 | 15.97 |
| 1982 | 96,956 | 13,150 | 23,111 | 13,733 | 51.56 |
| 1983 | 201,863 | 40,910 | 14,931 | 10,671 | 36.61 |
| 1984 | 203,705 | 20,131 | 12,980 | 10,884 | 27.84 |
| 1985 | 289,800 | 32,164 | 29,565 | 18,772 | 9.49 |
| 1986 | 499,400 | 48,724 | 70,985 | 42,187 | 48.81 |
| 1987 | 507,200 | 54,858 | 41,262 | 42,786 |  |
| 1988 | 446,300 | 22,972 | 13,772 | 38,290 |  |
| 1989 | 452,900 | 27,840 | 46,464 | 49,982 |  |
| 1990 | 458,400 | 35,246 | 43,489 | 71,601 |  |

SOURCES: *Federal Reserve Bulletin*, various issues; *Statistical Abstract of the United States.*

tively more predictable than interest rate factors. Demographic data, such as the geographic region of the mortgaged houses and the occupation and age of the mortgagors, determine mortgagors' mobility and, therefore, a fairly constant basic rate of prepayment. In addition, mortgagors are inclined to prepay and refinance their homes when market interest rates on new mortgages fall sufficiently below the coupon rates on their existing mortgages. For securitized pools of mortgages, the constant prepayment rate (CPR) varies markedly for different combinations of the pools' coupon rates and the current market interest rate on new mortgages.

### Prepayment Effects on Yields

Most of the $1 trillion international market for MBS includes mortgages that grant mortgagors nearly unlimited prepayment privileges. Figure 17-1 illustrates the effects of changes in mortgage interest rates on the CPRs and cash flows of a 30-year, fixed-rate FHLMC mortgage bearing a coupon of 10 percent. As Figure 17-1A indicates, the interest rate on fixed-rate, 30-year mortgages fell over 100 basis points during 1992. As the market rates fell, many holders of 10 percent and higher-rate mortgages found that they could profitably pay the loan fees and other transaction costs to refinance their mortgages at market rates. Typically, mortgage holders refinance when the market rate falls approximately 2 percent below the rate on their mortgages. Figure 17-1B depicts the resulting rapid rise in the CPR over a six-month holding period. These rates actually continued to rise after October 1992 as market rates fell to levels close

**FIGURE 17-1A and B    Mortgage Rates and MBS Prepayments**

A  Mortgage rates

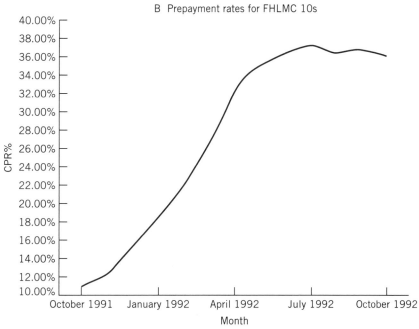

B  Prepayment rates for FHLMC 10s

**FIGURE 17-1C   Principal and Interest Payments**

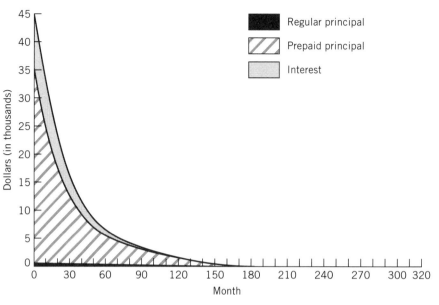

to 7 percent. An extremely rapid rate of prepayments produced a radical change in the cash flow pattern of MBS, which resulted in a large amount of prepaid principal being received prematurely by investors, as shown in Figure 17-1C. Bank and thrift institution holders of these securities incurred significant reinvestment penalties because they had to reinvest these cash flows at a time when reinvestment rates were low.

In summary, the interaction of market rates, CPR, and prices on MBS is a known and rather predictable phenomenon. The CPR increases when the current market rate falls below a security's coupon rate by about 2 percent or more. The pattern of prepayments can be forecast with reasonable accuracy for different interest rate environments. Once prepayment rates are forecast, the prices on MBS can be calculated in a straightforward manner. With higher CPRs, cash flows accelerate, shortening the duration; on premium-priced securities, yields are reduced. The accelerated cash flows we examined for the FHLMC 10s in Figure 17-1B shortened their duration to 1.90 years and reduced their yield. The dramatically shortened duration of these securities qualified them as short-term investments despite the roughly 320 months remaining to final maturity. Therefore, when investors compared this FHLMC security in October 1992 with competitive investment opportunities, they should have looked to investment alternatives on the short-term end of the yield curve.

### Premium MBS Investment Analysis

To assess the potential benefit of purchasing a government agency–backed premium MBS, investors compare its performance with that of U.S. Treasury securities of comparable maturities. The MBS must provide an adequate yield spread over Treasury yields to compensate investors for the risk of prepayment. To be comparable, the Treasury security should have the same duration as the MBS. Normally, duration serves as a measure of the price sensitivity of securities. However, prepayment risk on a premium MBS subjects it to changes in yield and duration as market rates change, rendering duration unsatisfactory as a measure of price sensitivity. (One investment banker has called the duration measure a "rubber ruler" when applied to MBS.)

Given the uncertainty of MBS durations, we can estimate some realistic outcomes on premium MBSs and several possible alternative investments in U.S. Treasury securities. Figure 17-2 shows six-month holding period rates of return on a premium GNMA 11.5 percent security, assuming various CPRs and initial prices. Parts A, B, and C of the figure show rates of return under constant, falling, and rising market rates for the GNMA (priced initially at 107.5) and on one-, two-, and three-year Treasury securities. We assume an initial money market rate of 5.5 percent. In Figure 17-2A, rates remain constant and prices remain flat over the six-month holding period. Under these conditions, the GNMA yields 8.0 percent, somewhat more than the yields on each of the Treasury securities. The GNMA yield is based on an assumption of a rather fast 3 percent monthly CPR.

If market rates decline 100 basis points, as in Figure 17-2B, the rates of return on the one-, two-, and three-year Treasuries increase substantially because of price appreciation. For the GNMA, assuming an increase in CPR to 3.5 percent and a price rise to 108.5, the rate of return rises moderately to 9.02 percent. If market rates rise 100 basis points instead, as in Figure 17-2C, the rates of return on all three Treasuries issues fall well below money market rates. If the GNMA 11.5s' price falls to, say, 106.5 and its monthly CPR declines to 2.0 percent, the GNMA will produce an annualized yield of 7.2 percent, or considerably more than the Treasury notes. Typically, the GNMA security provides the best defensive position in a bearish (rising-rate) market. It also outperforms comparable Treasury securities in a constant-rate environment. As a caution, however, the outcomes described for the GNMA 11.5s resulted from assumptions we made about how the speed of prepayments was affected by various market rates of interest. As market conditions change, shifts in prepayment rates change the nature of MBS. The key to successful investment choices requires an understanding and careful analysis of projected prepayments.

### Adjustable-Rate MBS

In addition to the large volume of securitized, fixed-rate mortgages, there is a smaller but growing volume of securitized adjustable-rate mortgages (ARMs).

**FIGURE 17-2**    **A. Premium MBS Rates of Return[a] Compared to Various Treasury Securities Return on 11.5% GNMAs for a Six-Month Holding Period**

| Monthly Constant Prepayment Rate | Price at Sale | | | | | | | | |
|---|---|---|---|---|---|---|---|---|---|
| | 105.5 | 106.0 | 106.5 | 107.0 | 107.5 | 108.0 | 108.5 | 109.0 | 109.5 |
| 0.5% | 6.66% | 7.56% | 8.46% | 9.36% | 10.26% | 11.16% | 12.06% | 12.96% | 13.86% |
| 1.0% | 6.28 | 7.15 | 8.03 | 8.90 | 9.77 | 10.65 | 11.52 | 12.39 | 13.27 |
| 1.5% | 5.91 | 6.76 | 7.61 | 8.46 | 9.30 | 10.15 | 11.00 | 11.84 | 12.69 |
| 2.0% | 5.56 | 6.38 | 7.20 | 8.02 | 8.84 | 9.66 | 10.49 | 11.31 | 12.13 |
| 2.5% | 5.20 | 6.00 | 6.80 | 7.60 | 8.38 | 9.19 | 9.99 | 10.78 | 11.58 |
| 3.0% | 4.86 | 5.63 | 6.41 | 7.18 | 7.95 | 8.73 | 9.50 | 10.27 | 11.04 |
| 3.5% | 4.53 | 5.28 | 6.03 | 6.78 | 7.52 | 8.27 | 9.02 | 9.77 | 10.52 |
| 4.0% | 4.20 | 4.93 | 5.65 | 6.38 | 7.10 | 7.83 | 8.56 | 9.28 | 10.01 |
| 4.5% | 3.88 | 4.59 | 5.29 | 5.99 | 6.88 | 7.40 | 8.10 | 8.81 | 9.51 |
| 5.0% | 3.57 | 4.25 | 4.93 | 5.62 | 6.30 | 6.98 | 7.66 | 8.34 | 9.03 |

[a]Rate of return is defined as the sum of the capital gain (loss), the cash flow (principal and interest), and the reinvestment earnings all divided by the value of the original investment.

Source: U.S. League Investment Services.

The volume of new ARMs is highly cyclical and tends to increase most when mortgage rates are falling.

The pricing of ARM securities is considerably more volatile than the pricing of comparable Treasury securities with maturities equal to the ARM rate reset intervals. Like fixed-rate mortgages, ARMs may carry not only the risks of default (conventional MBS), interest rate risk, and liquidity risk, but also prepayment risk. In addition, however, because ARMs rates can only be reset up to a contractual cap set on their adjustability, they possess *basis risk*—defined for these purposes as the risk that rate adjustment caps may prevent ARM securities from being adjusted with increases (decreases) in the underlying index (in this case, the Treasury bill rate plus 150 basis points and an annual adjustment cap of 1 percent). Now suppose that the one-year Treasury bill rate rises from 7.5 to 9.5 percent. The ARM security, with an initial rate of 9.0 percent, is limited this year to an adjustment to 10.0 percent. Barring further changes in the Treasury bill rate, it will take another full year before the ARM rate can be set at 11.0 percent, its expected spread over the Treasury bill.

The rate-resetting characteristic of the ARMs issued by FHLMC, FNMA, and GNMA are described in Table 17-3.

Repayment risk presents a threat to the value of ARM securities purchased at a premium. In early 1987, the FNMA's rate, based on the Eleventh Federal Home Loan Bank's cost of funds, was well above rates on fixed-rate mortgages. This rate disparity prompted widespread prepayment of ARMs and refinancing at fixed rates. Subsequently, the ARMs rate fell quickly as the

**FIGURE 17-2** *(continued)*    **B. Premium MBS Rates of Return Compared to Those of Various Treasury Securities**

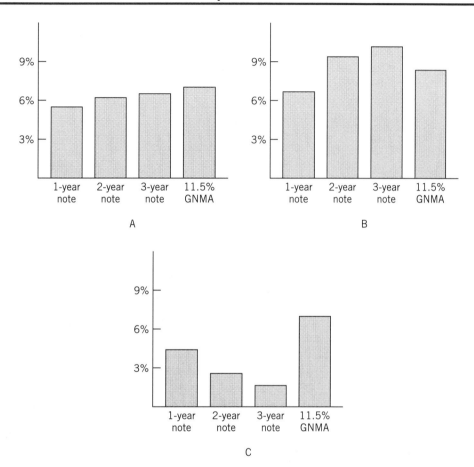

**TABLE 17-3    Rate Reset Characteristics**

|  | **FHLMC** | **FNMA** | **GNMA** |
|---|---|---|---|
| Index | 1-year Treasury bill | 11th FHLB District cost of funds | 1-year Treasury bill |
| Spread over index | 200 basis points (b.p.) | 200 b.p. | 150 b.p. |
| Rate cap, annual | 2% | 2% | 1% |
| Lifetime cap over initial rate | 6% | 6% | 5% |
| Reset frequency | Annually | Annually | Annually |

cost-of-funds index declined and, along with the earlier rapid prepayments, caused FNMA ARM prices to fall precipitously.

An irony of the reduction in interest rates on the premium FNMA ARMs in the spring of 1987 was that these securities' prices were falling at the same time that market interest rates were falling. The Eleventh District cost-of-funds index used to set FNMA mortgage rates in any current month actually is derived from the cost of funds three months earlier. Changes in the cost-of-funds index, in other words, lag behind changes in money market rates. As a result, they tend to remain above falling money market rates and to fall below rising money market rates.

Table 17-4 presents the relationship between ARM securities yields and various projected constant prepayment rates.

## Multiclass Securities

Securitization of pools of single-family home mortgages has forced investors and analysts to understand and quantify the insidious problem of prepayment risk. In the 1980s, new generations of securitized mortgages were introduced to address prepayment risk by redistributing it among various classes. These derivative securities—collateralized mortgage obligations (CMOs) and stripped mortgaged-backed securities (SMBSs)—created securities with unique risk–return characteristics.

CMOs separate mortgage pools into short-, medium-, and long-term classes called *tranches*. These tranches clarify for investors the repayment rate to be expected on mortgage-backed investments. Investors who seek a rapid return on their funds can buy a short-term tranche, say, a three-year CMO. Long-term investors can acquire a portion of a 20-year tranche. Each class is assigned a fixed, floating, or zero interest rate; a fixed principal amount; and a set of payment conditions. Short-term CMO investors sustain relatively little prepayment risk and receive a corresponding return; long-term investors bear relatively greater prepayment risk and, consequently, are paid a premium rate. Generally, CMOs are packaged in "vanilla" or sequential-pay tranches

## TABLE 17-4    FNMA Adjustable-Rate MBS

| Gross Coupon[a] | Price | CPR% Projected Yields | | | | | |
|---|---|---|---|---|---|---|---|
| | | 0% | 5% | 10% | 15% | 20% | 30% |
| 8.0 | 102½ | 7.82 | 7.68 | 7.54 | 7.38 | 7.21 | 6.83 |
| 9.0 | 102½ | 8.82 | 8.69 | 8.53 | 8.37 | 8.19 | 7.81 |
| 10.0 | 102½ | 9.83 | 9.69 | 9.53 | 9.36 | 9.18 | 8.79 |
| 11.0 | 102½ | 10.85 | 10.70 | 10.53 | 10.36 | 10.17 | 9.77 |

[a]Eleventh FHLB District cost of funds + 125 basis points.

that pay out the underlying principal only after previous classes have been retired. Therefore, short-term tranche investors receive all of their principal before medium-term investors do, and, as a result, are subject to a lower price sensitivity risk. Figures 17-3A and 17-3B illustrate the basic structure and the allocation of cash flows and the outstanding principal balances of a typical CMO or real estate mortgage investment conduit.

REMICs present still another variation of the problem of prepayment risk and its effect on the investment properties of the affected securities. REMICs are an extension of the basic CMO type of contract. They were created on January 1, 1987, by the Tax Reform Act of 1986, which removed various Internal Revenue Service regulations that imposed burdensome costs on CMO issuers and investors. REMIC legislation removed barriers to entry for certain multiclass MBS issuers and expanded the demand for multiclass securities by financial institutions. Today virtually all multiclass securities are issued in REMIC form. Their acceptance is growing; FNMA and FHLMC alone issued $98 billion worth of REMIC securities in 1990.

The cash flows associated with CMOs and REMICs are distributed according to the securities' tranche structure, as noted earlier. The cash flows occur as follows:

1. Interest payments are made simultaneously to all bond classes. (The actual interest cash flow to any zero accrual bonds is applied to repayment of principal.)

## FIGURE 17-3A   Building Blocks for REMICs

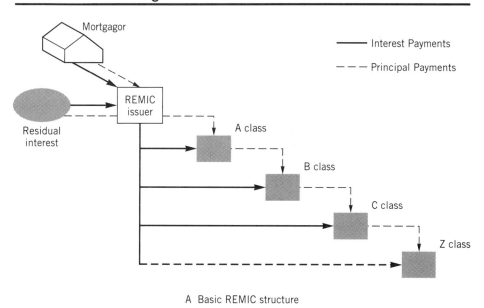

A  Basic REMIC structure

## FIGURE 17-3B

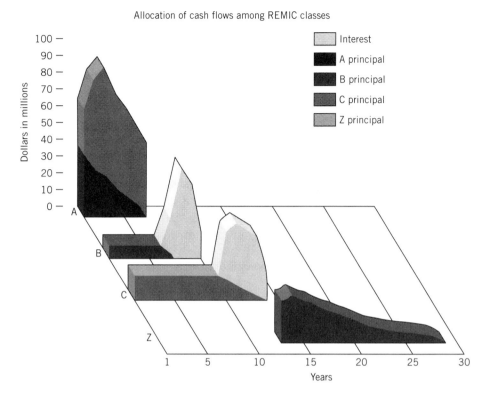

Allocation of cash flows among REMIC classes

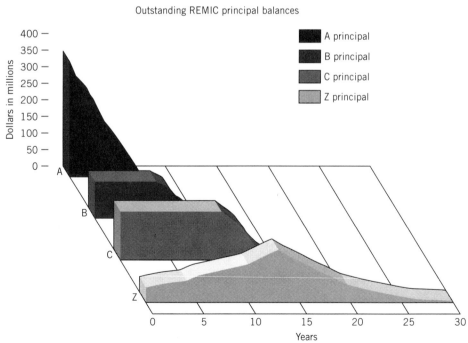

Outstanding REMIC principal balances

**FIGURE 17-3C**

Building a PAC–principal cash flows

| ■ A PAC | ▨ C PAC | ▥ D PAC | □ H PAC | ■ Companion tranches |

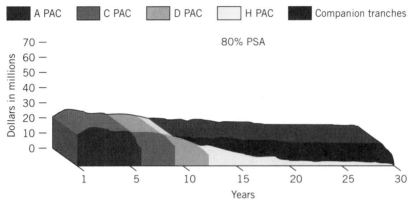

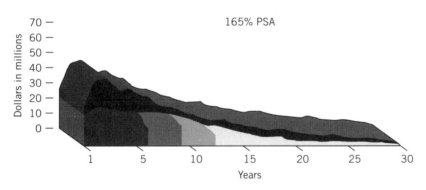

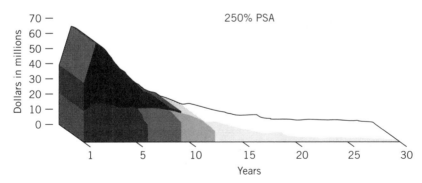

**FIGURE 17-3D**

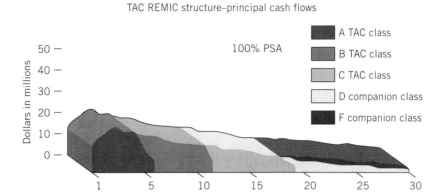

TAC REMIC structure–principal cash flows

100% PSA

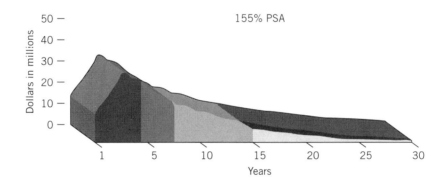

155% PSA

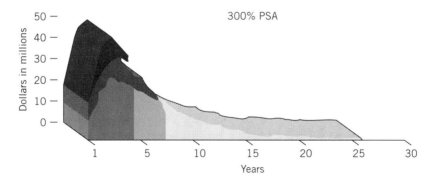

300% PSA

2. Principal repayments are used to retire the bond tranches sequentially. All principal payments on the collateral are directed first to retiring the shortest-maturity (designated *A-class*) bonds.
3. After these bonds are completely retired, principal payments on the collateral are directed to retirement of the next-shortest (*B-class*) bond. This process continues until all the bonds are retired.
4. Payments to owners of residual equity are made periodically. After the required interest and principal payments have been made to bondholders, any excess cash flow can be paid on a pro-rata basis to owners of equity interests.

The primary source of residual cash flow is the positive spread between the bond coupons and the coupons on the underlying collateral. Other sources include income from investing monthly cash flows pending distribution to bondholders and excess prepayments.

Table 17-5 shows the changes in the average life of each tranche, the zero coupon (terminal years' principal) bond, and residual equity as prepayment rates vary. The prepayment measure used for CMOs and REMICs is based on the Public Securities Association estimates for prepayment speed ("PSA speed") and average life of the class affected. The average life declines most rapidly for longer-term tranches and for the zero coupon bond as prepayment rates accelerate. Yield declines associated with changing lives are smaller for shorter-term tranches.

CMOs may also be packaged with PACs (planned amortization classes) and TACs (targeted amortization classes), which are similar to sinking fund bonds. A PAC, instead of producing interest cash flows until the principal is paid back for a given tranche, pays out principal on specific payment schedules. The CPR on the collateral underlying the PAC is held constant as long as the PSA speeds remain within a given protected range known as the *PAC band*. The PACs are issued within the REMIC structure with companion or support tranches. The support tranches absorb excess cash flows and make up for shortfalls. Because the support tranches bear most of the prepayment risk of the pool, their lives vary greatly. PACs are also purchased with different average lives, but they offer reduced volatility and provide the greatest certainty of cash flows of all MBS. TACs are similar to PACs except that protection is provided only against increasing prepayments and early retirement. In other words, if CPRs speed up, companion tranches will absorb cash flows to prevent retirement of the TAC; but if CPRs slow, the average life of the TAC increases. Usually TACs are not issued as isolated securities but are incorporated as support classes within PAC structures. Figures 17-3C and 17-3D show the principal cash flows of a PAC and a TAC at various prepayment speeds.

SMBSs, sometimes referred to as *interest only–principal only (IO–PO)*, separate MBS into principal payments and interest payments. IO segments perform better in sustained rising-rate environments because their cash flow patterns are heavily loaded toward the early years and the cash flows become available for reinvestment at higher and higher rates. PO segments perform

**TABLE 17-5  Multiclass Securities—Average Life and Prepayment Rates**

| Prepayment Speed[a] | A Tranche | | B Tranche | | C Tranche | | Z Tranche (0 Coupon) | | Residual Equity | |
|---|---|---|---|---|---|---|---|---|---|---|
| | Projected Maturity[b] | Average Life[c] | Projected Maturity[b] | Average Life[c] | Projected Maturity[b] | Average Life[c] | Projected Maturity[b] | Average Life[c] | Projected Maturity[b] | Average Life[c] |
| 100% | 4.5 | 2.45 | 6.5 | 5.45 | 10 | 8.33 | 29 | 15.78 | None | 3 |
| 200% | 3 | 1.59 | 4 | 3.45 | 7.5 | 5.59 | 29 | 13.98 | None | 2.5 |
| 300% | 2 | 1.25 | 3 | 2.56 | 5.5 | 4.24 | 29 | 9.44 | None | 2 |

[a]Prepayment speeds represent percentages of the Public Securities Association standard prepayment model.

[b]Number of years by which the bonds should be completely retired.

[c]Average life is the average time to the receipt of principal weighted by the size of each principal payment.

SOURCE: U.S. League Investment Service, Inc.

well in falling-rate environments. This property of IOs, whereby IO prices are positively related to interest rates, has increased investors' interest in them as a natural hedge against the decline in prices on normal securities when interest rates rise.

To appreciate the hedging capability of IOs, we analyze interest and principal cash flows on a $100 million pool of mortgages, given alternative CPRs. Figure 17-4A shows the cumulative cash flows that will result if no changes in CPRs occur. By the time the mortgage matures, the borrower has paid in almost twice as much interest as the principal originally borrowed. Because there is no prepayment of principal, interest payments accumulate rapidly, to become the dominant component of cash flows.

Figures 17-4B and 17-4C show the cumulative cash flows generated by this mortgage pool with, respectively, a 12 percent and a 24 percent CPR. Prepayments of principal cause a lesser accumulation of interest payments. With principal payments, on the other hand, differences in prepayment rates change the timing of the receipt of payments but do not change the total payment; obviously, $100 million must be paid. However, with respect to the IO, neither the timing of receipt nor the total amount of the cash flow is guaranteed. Thus, the purchaser of the IO who assumes a CPR of 12 percent can experience wide variance in total returns with swings in the prepayment rate.

The volatility in the timing and size of the IO is reflected in Figure 17-5A. This figure shows that the price volatility of either the IO or the PO component will exceed the price volatility of the whole mortgage. The relatively greater price sensitivity of the IO, combined with its positive price–interest rate relationship, makes it useful for hedging. For example, assume that a 9 percent mortgage pool is priced at par (the points of intersection in Figures 17-5B and 17-5C) and has a 6 percent CPR. Now if interest rates rise 2 percent, causing a decline in CPR to 4 percent, the price of the pool decreases to approximately 88.3 percent of par. If, alternatively, interest rates fall 2 percent (accompanied by an increase in the assumed CPR to 21 percent), the pool's price increases to 106.2 percent of par. In contrast, the IO portion of the mortgage undergoes a much wider swing in price. If, for example, the IO strip is priced at 54.5, given a 6 percent CPR assumption, it may increase in price to 60.1, or by 10.7 percent with a 2 percent rise in rates. If rates decline 2 percent, on the other hand, the IO's price will decrease to 28.8, or by 47 percent. Note that the price of the mortgage is the sum of the prices of its IO and PO components.

The performance of the IO strip as a hedge vehicle improves with the price volatility of the instrument. For instance, Figure 17-5B contrasts the price volatility of an IO strip from a pool of 11 percent mortgages with the volatility of an IO strip from a 9 percent pool.

As interest rates increase, the prepayment speeds of the 11 percent mortgages will decrease more rapidly from much higher levels. This results in greater price appreciation on the 11 percent IO strip. Conversely, as interest rates fall, the prepayment speed on the 11 percent collateral will pick up much faster, thereby depressing the IO's price very quickly.

**FIGURE 17-4  Cumulative Cash Flows for $100,000 Mortgage**

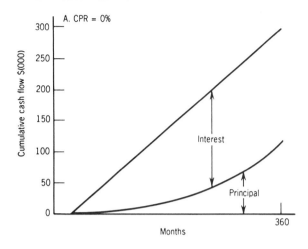

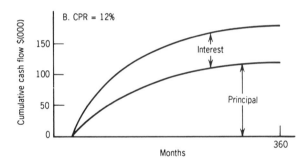

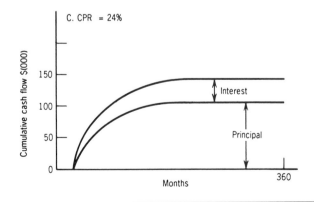

## FIGURE 17-5    Price Volatility of Pools, IOs, and POs

A. Pool of 9% mortgages

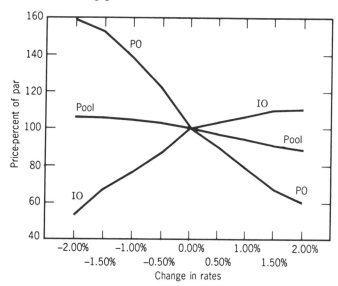

B. 9% IO versus 11% IO

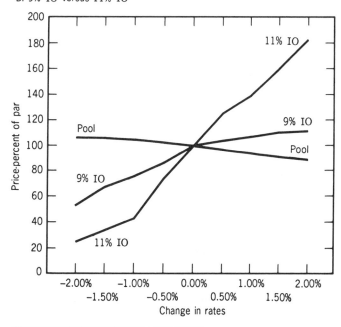

**TABLE 17-6   Typical SBA Loan Pool Offerings**

| Quarterly Adjustable | Price | CPR (%) | Yield | Average Life (years) | Maturity (years) |
|---|---|---|---|---|---|
| Prime + .875 | 106.75 | 6% | 8.34% | 9.2 | 20 |
| Prime + .875 | 104.75 | 6 | 8.01 | 5.3 | 10 |
| Prime + .875 | 103.50 | 6 | 7.96 | 2.9 | 5 |
| Prime − .125 | 103.00 | 6 | 7.95 | 9.8 | 22 |
| Prime − .125 | 102.75 | 6 | 7.87 | 6.1 | 15 |

IO and PO strips clearly have the potential for price depreciation and negative holding period returns. Investors must analyze the effect of prepayment risk by simulating the impact of varying prepayment assumptions on the mortgage collateral supporting the payments of interest or principal.

The hedging character of IO strips may not be as attractive as investors might assume. If interest rates decline even for a short period of time, prepayments will occur and will permanently deplete the basis of future interest payments. Even if interest rates rise later, reducing prepayment rates, earlier high rates of principal reduction will reduce future interest payments.

### Small Business Administration Loan Pools

In addition to MBS, bank portfolio managers have access to securities backed by Small Business Administration (SBA) guaranteed loan pools. These pools are backed by the full faith and credit of the U.S. government. They vary in stated maturity from 5 to 25 years. Prepayments on the pools are subject to significant change. Rates on pools are adjusted to a published prime rate at a spread ranging from −100 to +200 basis points. Table 17-6 lists some typical SBA-pool-backed security offerings.

### Debt Securities Mutual Funds

Another, less commonly used investment vehicle for banks' investment portfolios is debt securities mutual funds. These funds are typically open-end mutual funds that purchase and manage a portfolio of debt securities funded by a continual sale of shares to investors. In addition, such mutual funds offer immediate redemption of shares on demand. A mutual fund serves as a conduit. It pays no taxes on the interest and capital gains flowing through to its investors. Investors benefit from mutual fund holdings because of the funds' diversification and professional management of a portfolio of debt securities. Mutual fund shares simply reflect the risk and return characteristics of the securities they hold in their portfolios. Mutual funds comprising intermediate-term debt securities, for example, typically produce yields and exposure to interest rate risk commensurate with an intermediate position on the yield curve.

Mutual funds that invest in longer-term debt instruments, such as MBS, similarly exhibit the risks of a portfolio of such securities. When managed successfully, mutual funds have the potential to deliver a more consistent flow of income with less variance of principal than can be achieved by direct investment. On the other hand, some debt securities mutual funds may target high returns, and may adopt strategies to lengthen maturities and purchase premium-priced securities that may increase the volatility of their share values. Finally, the size of the fund allows fine tuning and some economies of scale that are not available to the smaller portfolios of individual institutions.

## PRICING CONCEPTS FOR CONTINGENT CLAIMS

### Option Pricing

From bank customers' viewpoints, the options previously described have value for which the customers are prepared to pay. Additionally, banks traditionally have exacted a price for many of these options. In the past several years, however, a more systematic means of approaching pricing has developed. More generally, there is a systematic way of conceptualizing countless banking services that involve bank contingent liabilities.

The common thread running through contingent claims services is that they all contain options features. They are part of a broad class of services that fit into a pricing methodology stemming from research on contingent claims (options) in the contemporary theory of finance. Contrary to popular belief, the option pricing methodology can be greatly simplified to make it practical and implementable. In this regard, theoretical mathematical option pricing formulas have been modified and adapted for the pricing of bank services that entail contingent liabilities.

Options pricing theory sharpens bankers' intuition about fee-based products or services. Bankers who recognize the options pricing analogy to the setting of fee income will also be quick to recognize the crucial potential for product innovation and greater fee income.

An *option* is a right, but not an obligation, to buy or sell something (a security, service, product, etc.) at a price guaranteed over a specified period of time; if the option is not exercised by its maturity date, it expires. Options are called *contingent claims* because their value is contingent upon the value of an underlying security, service, or product.

An option is analogous to an insurance policy, and the option price is analogous to an insurance premium. For example, a loan commitment (a loan put option) provides the prospective borrower with the right to "put" its debt to the bank. The commitment provides credit availability insurance to cover the possibility that funds will be needed in the future. The commitment fee (option price) represents an insurance premium. The feature that distinguishes

---

**FIGURE 17-6  Bank's Payoff Profile for a Fixed-Rate Loan Commitment (Selling a Put)**

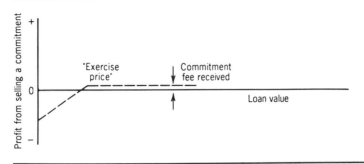

---

an option is that risk is not shared between the parties to an option agreement. Instead, risk is transferred from the buyer to the seller.

### Pricing Loan Commitments

With fixed-rate loan commitments, the bank (seller) acquires the risk of finding the funds agreed upon if the commitment option is exercised and bears the price risk of an increase in market borrowing rates. The commitment insures the potential borrower (buyer of the option) against liquidity risk in the event that funds are needed. The prospective borrower is not obligated to exercise the option to borrow and probably will not do so if market borrowing rates decline.

The bank's payoff profile for a fixed-rate loan commitment is illustrated in Figure 17-6. The vertical axis shows the profit outcome for selling the loan commitment upon maturity. The horizontal axis reflects the value of the amount to be committed upon demand. If market borrowing interest rates rise, the prospective loan value to the bank tends to fall because the bank is obliged to commit funds at below-market rates. With the rise in rates, of course, the customer is inclined to borrow at the now bargain rate fixed earlier. Falling loan values are associated with movement to the left in Figure 17-6. In this instance, the profitability of the commitment, illustrated by the dashed line, quickly becomes negative.

On the other hand, if market borrowing rates fall, the value of a loan rises (movement to the right in the figure). Now the borrower is either disinclined to borrow or else will attempt to borrow from cheaper alternative sources. Thus, the bank's upside profit potential on the commitment is effectively capped at the level of the commitment fee (the flat portion of the dashed line).

The outcome for the buyer of the put option commitment is an upside-down version of the diagram representing the bank's outcome (Figure 17-7). If interest rates rise, the loan value falls (movement to the left), enabling the

**FIGURE 17-7    Loan Customer's Payoff Profile for Receiving a Loan Commitment (Buying a Put)**

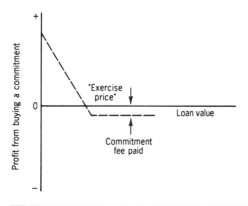

customer to profit because the customer is able to "put" underpriced debt to the bank. As market borrowing rates fall (movement to the right), the customer probably will reject the offer of fixed-rate credit from the bank. In that case, the customer's downside outcome is simply the cost of the commitment fee. Together, Figures 17-6 and 17-7 clearly illustrate the asymmetry of the risk involved in fixed-rate loan commitments. The seller of the loan put option (the bank) may bear considerable downside risk if borrowing rates rise, whereas the buyer of the put (customer) suffers no downside risk. The buyer of the put, however, is guaranteed a modest and known loss if rates decline.

Several ingredients need to be known to price a loan commitment option. An obvious ingredient is value in the underlying loan market. Also included is the *exercise price*, which is the loan value at which the customer can clearly borrow and achieve a positive payoff; in options terminology, a positive payoff signifies that the option is *in the money*. Other elements are the borrowing rate, the time to maturity of the option, and, crucially important, the volatility of the value of loans in the underlying loan market.

### Simplified Option Pricing

The challenge in option pricing is to model the volatility factor of the contingent or underlying entity. The more elegant option pricing models, beginning with the Black-Scholes model published in 1973, relate to complex common stock return distributions and are not easily applied to practical banking applications. More practical debt-type models have been developed, however, and are based on modeling the randomness of interest rate changes. Interest rate changes are then related to corresponding prices of the underlying debt instrument.

The most appealing debt-type model is one that models interest rate changes as a simple *binomial* process. Although researchers developed the background for the binomial model in the 1970s, it has only recently received attention in banking circles. The binomial model captures the volatility of the underlying debt by assuming that the relevant interest rate either increases or decreases by a specified amount from one period to the next. Thus, for example, the borrowing rate on loans that underlie a fixed-rate commitment maturing one period into the future can either increase or decrease from its starting value.

Consider a one-year commitment to lend $100 for a year at the market rate of 10 percent. Such a loan would have a repayment obligation of $110 at the end of the year. Assume that the market borrowing interest rate may either rise or fall by 20 percent of its starting level by the end of the year. If the rate rises, the present value of the underlying loan will fall below $100 because the $110 ending value is now discounted at the higher rate.

If the market rate rises by 20 percent, from a borrowing rate of 10 percent to 12 percent, the loan value becomes $110/1.12 = $98.21 one year hence. If the rate falls to 8 percent, the loan value becomes $110/1.08 = $101.85. Would-be borrowers would not be motivated to borrow at an above-market rate and would simply allow the commitment to expire unexercised. In the first instance, the commitment value is $100 − 98.21 = $1.79. In the second instance, the commitment value is zero because the customer can find alternative sources of credit at lower prices and will not call the commitment. If the 20 percent up-and-down rate movements each had a probability of 0.5, an appropriate minimum price for the commitment would be 0.5 ($1.79) + 0.5(0) = $0.895.

## Deriving Future Interest Rates

Admittedly, the pricing problem is more complicated than this simple example implies. Interest rate changes occur frequently, and they set up a more complex array of loan values. The binomial methodology permits the banker to model a more sophisticated interest rate change process that is consistent with the banker's estimate of the expected mean and volatility of future interest rates. Given these estimates, the method is used to generate the many paths that interest rates might take over the supposed life of the loan commitment. Then the lender calculates the commitment's values for each path and takes the average.

The interest rate paths evolve from the simple assumption, discussed earlier, that the change in the interest rate is either up or down by a like amount each period, say every month. When this up-or-down process is followed sequentially, a whole latticework of future possible interest rates is produced. Figure 17-8 shows the branching out of numerous rate paths over several periods, starting with a single initial rate of 10 percent. The amount of up-and-down movement (2 percent in Figure 17-8) can be adjusted to produce an interest rate distribution with volatility and other parameters that are

---

**FIGURE 17-8   Option Pricing Interest Rate Paths, Four-Period Loan**

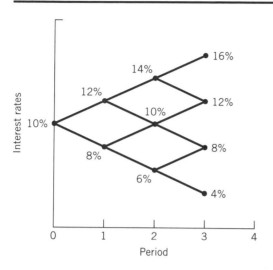

---

consistent with past or expected parameters. To be sure, the lattice becomes very complex when it is generated for, say, 360 months, but this complexity can be readily handled with sufficient computer power.

The lender next assigns values to the loan commitment, using a back-wardation approach. The computer first prices the commitment for each possible interest rate at the last period, assigning an equal 50-50 probability to each increase and decrease from prior periods' interest rate outcomes. Then the pricing step is backed up to the next-earlier period, the later-period prices are discounted, and expected present values are taken as of the earlier period. The new present values then become the basis for discounting back to the next earlier period. A value of zero is assigned to the commitment for interest rates in the lattice below the contracted loan commitment rate because, at those interest rates, the commitment option is valueless to the borrower and will not be exercised.

The end result is that when this pricing model is calculated sequentially back to the present, the expected value at the present is obtained. The value is a function of all possible future interest rate paths. In short, the value of the commitment option is obtained by the model as the expected present value.

## Interest Rate Cap Agreements

The option pricing procedures for loan commitments are conceptually the same as interest rate caps and are easily applied to interest rate caps on loans. An *interest rate cap* guarantees a variable-rate borrower that the loan rate will not exceed a maximum interest rate. The interest rate on a variable-rate loan is periodically "reset" or "repriced" according to a reference market rate of interest, such as LIBOR, during the life of the loan. If the reference rate has penetrated the guaranteed level on one of the reset dates, the borrower's rate is capped at the guarantee.

Alternatively, the borrower may purchase an interest rate cap guarantee agreement separately from the loan agreement itself. Under a stand-alone agreement such as this, the seller of the agreement makes a cash payment to the borrower when the borrowing rate exceeds the guaranteed level. The cash payment is equal to the difference between the actual borrowing rate and the guaranteed rate times the notional amount, typically the loan amount, of the guarantee agreement. Thus, the purchaser of the agreement (the borrower) is protected against rising interest rates and may still benefit from falling interest rates.

The following example illustrates the cash flows involved in a cap agreement. Suppose that on October 1, 1989 a manufacturer obtains a variable-rate $10 million loan for 18 months, with the rate set at the beginning of each quarter at a spread over the three-month LIBOR rate. The first rate is set at the start of the loan, and the last rate is set 15 months from the starting date. The firm acquires a rate cap guarantee of 10.0 percent, which establishes the maximum cost of the loan at 10.0 percent plus the cost of the guarantee agreement. The example demonstrates that when the borrowing or actual rate is above the cap, a cash payment is made.

| Reset Date | Cap Rate | Actual Rate | Difference | Days Applied | Savings at Days/360 | Eff. Rate |
|---|---|---|---|---|---|---|
| Jan. 1, 1990 | 10.0% | 9.50% | −.5% | 91 | 0 | 9.50% |
| Apr. 1, 1990 | 10.0% | 10.85% | .85% | 91 | $21,486 | 10.00% |
| Jul. 1, 1990 | 10.0% | 11.10% | 1.10% | 91 | $27,806 | 10.00% |
| Oct. 1, 1990 | 10.0% | 9.80% | −.2% | 91 | 0 | 9.80% |
| Jan. 1, 1991 | 10.0% | 11.00% | 1.00% | 91 | $25,278 | 10.00% |
| | | | | Total = | $74,570 | 9.86% |

The price at which a cap rate guarantee should be sold is subject to the option pricing techniques, including the modeling of the interest rate change process, presented earlier in this chapter. If a cap rate guarantee is made part of the original bank loan agreement, the bank should incorporate the price as part of the loan fee. If the guarantee is sold as a stand-alone agreement, the selling institution should simply charge a direct fee.

In either case, the seller can hedge the obvious risk in cap agreements by purchasing put options on Eurodollars. Actually, because cap agreements expose the seller to the resetting of rates at future dates, the seller must deal in options on Eurodollar futures. The Eurodollar futures market offers contracts out to 18 months; longer agreements would require the additional risk of rolling the 18-month limitation forward as time progresses.

Prices on cap agreements are sensitive to the length of the agreement and to the level of the cap guarantee required. Both longer-term agreements and lower caps (*striking prices*) increase the likelihood that the borrowing or market rate will exceed the cap rate. Prices, as a result, are higher for longer terms and lower caps. Current banking practice appears to favor a maximum term of about two years.

### Floors and Collars

An interest rate floor guarantee is the opposite of the cap guarantee arrangement. Just as a cap protects against a rise in the borrowing rate above a guaranteed level, the floor protects against a decrease in the borrowing rate below a guaranteed level. However, the flow of benefits is reversed. When a floor agreement is incorporated in a variable-rate loan contract, the lender becomes the beneficiary when the market rate falls below the guaranteed level. The borrower gives up the benefits of downside interest rate movements beyond the guarantee. The pricing of a floor agreement, therefore, entails reduced loan fees, lower borrowing rates, or other concessions to the borrower.

Collars simply incorporate both a cap and a floor agreement. Collars contain a borrower's variable interest rate within a band between the floor and cap rates over the life of the agreement. The pricing of collars is determined by the levels for the two guarantees relative to current and expected interest rates.

Figure 17-9 illustrates the differences in effective cost rates to the borrower for a cap, collar, and floor.

---

**FIGURE 17-9    Effective Cost Rates for a Cap, Collar, and Floor**

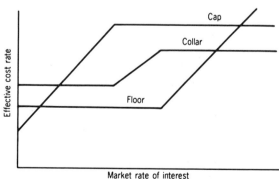

**FIGURE 17-10   The Standby Letter of Credit Relational Triangle**

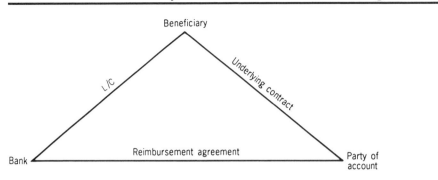

## Pricing Standby L/Cs

Like loan commitments, L/Cs are put options. The issuing bank accepts a liability to pay off the indebtedness of part of the account, contingent on the nonperformance of that party in honoring the claim of a beneficiary. The issuing bank receives a fee—the price—for bearing the liquidity and credit exposures that the beneficiary would otherwise bear.

Legally, the L/C is but one contract in a larger transaction that involves contingent consideration and liability between three parties. Figure 17-10 shows that three contracts actually link the parties.

First in importance (from the bank's viewpoint) is the contract between the bank and the beneficiary (the L/C) that constitutes a performance guarantee in which the bank will back up the debtor and pay off the beneficiary if the debtor defaults. Second is the reimbursement agreement between the bank and the party of account, which obligates the party of account to "make good" to the bank if it fails to perform on its obligation to the beneficiary, triggering the bank's backup payoff. Third, the underlying contract establishes the party of account's payment obligation to the beneficiary.

The bank's objective is to compute the minimum fee it must charge the account party for the bank's commitment to pay off the beneficiary. The account party (debtor) buys the right to "put to the bank" its payment obligation (due the beneficiary) in the event that it cannot perform on that obligation. At issue is how the value of the account party's reimbursement obligation (IOU) to the bank compares with the amount of its payment obligation to the beneficiary.

Clearly, if the account party's IOU is valued at less than the party's payment obligation, the bank will experience a net payout. If the value of the account party's IOU exceeds its payment obligation to the beneficiary, the bank will not experience a payout. Using analysis and intuition, the bank should generate estimates of the probabilities that the account party will totally fail to perform, partially perform, and fully perform.

Suppose that the party of account had borrowings of $10 million from an insurance company lender due in one year. The debtor's bank issues an L/C for the lender's benefit and determines that the debtor's repayment capacity (value of the IOU) in one year will be $10 million or more with a probability of .97, $8 million with a probability of .02, and $0 with a probability of .01. Assume that the current one-year riskless rate of interest is 6 percent.

The underlying analogy to option pricing is straightforward: The $10 million payment due the lender (beneficiary) is analogous to the option's exercise price. The alternative values of the debtor's IOU are three states of nature that describe the volatility of the valuation of the security underlying the option.

Under each state of nature, the value of the bank's commitment is equal to the difference between the exercise price of the value of the underlying security discounted to the present. Following this approach, the calculated minimum price (P) that should attach to the bank's commitment is

$$P - [.97 \times (\$10,000,000 - \$10,000,000) + .02 (\$10,000,000 - \$8,000,000)$$
$$+ .01 (\$10,000,000 - \$0)] \div 1.06 = \$132,075$$

The divisor of 1.06 is the annual discount rate applied to the L/C's expected value one year hence. The dollar value of $132,075 represents 1.32 percent of the exercise price.

The calculation does not, however, incorporate the cost of equity support that is likely to be introduced by regulations pertaining to bank capital. Suppose that regulators insist on literal 6 percent capital support and bank stockholders require a 16 percent return after taxes. A quick calculation, including grossing up the 16 percent to a pretax basis, indicates that the bank might conclude that it should charge another $145,000 to cover its capital costs. That would raise the fee to 2.78 percent.

In actuality, it is probably not legitimate to load in the bank's cost of capital at full value. The minimum price P is the value (cost) of the party of account's expected payment for nonperformance and already reflects the risk therein. Thus, it may be redundant to build in the full-risk premium implied in a 16 percent shareholder rate of return.

As a caveat, the options pricing analogy in this example again greatly simplifies more complete formulations developed in finance research. As discussed earlier, valuation of the underlying firm can be made quite rigorous. For example, the firm's value might be modeled as a function of the distribution of commodity prices or prices on debt instruments to which the firm's value might respond.

## Loan Portfolio Insurance

Options technology also is appropriate in providing protection for banks' loan portfolios against movements in commodity prices that might impair borrowers' ability to repay. Bankers have become highly aware of the need to hedge

---

**FIGURE 17-11   Loan Payoffs**

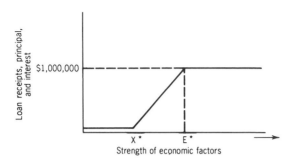

---

against credit risk because of heavy losses experienced by many banks with concentrations of loans in the agricultural, energy, and mortgage sectors.

A method by which a bank might self-insure against systematic credit risks involves a tightly controlled investment program in assets that produce increased payoffs as the bank's loan portfolio falters. It requires constructing a position with a payoff profile that mimics put options. The pseudo-options would be created so that their returns run counter to the deterioration of the underlying economic factors that affect the bank.

The payoff profile of a bank's loan portfolio is depicted as the solid line shown in Figure 17-11. The vertical axis is the payoff in terms of loan receipts of principal and interest. The horizontal axis is the strength of underlying economic factors that affect debtors' ability to repay their loans. Moving left of $E^*$, economic factors deteriorate such that borrowers cannot fully service their loans from the bank. A good case in point might be the crude oil market, in which falling oil prices and a chaotic world market progressively impair debt serviceability by borrowers in a community dependent upon oil production.

Alternatively, the falling price of corn or wheat might produce economic factors that impair debt service by a whole array of borrowers in an agricultural community. In any case, loan payoffs to the bank fall with deterioration in income and in the value of borrowers' collateral (oil rigs, farmland, homes). The bottom occurs when economic factors deteriorate to $X^*$ in Figure 17-11, where nothing can be recovered on the loan. The problem tends to be a systematic one, because the deterioration of common economic factors affects alike business income and assets, real estate values, and incomes of consumer debtors.

A positive shift in economic factors, moving to the right of $E^*$ on the horizontal axis of Figure 17-11, produces only limited benefits to bank loan portfolios. With good economic factors, the loan payoff profile reaches a maximum of $1 million, but then it flattens out, since beyond point $E^*$ banks do not participate in borrowers' rising profits. New profits earned under a stronger economy permit borrowers to repay loans, loan terms might cap the flow of

**FIGURE 17-12   Loan Payoffs with Synthetic Option Positions**

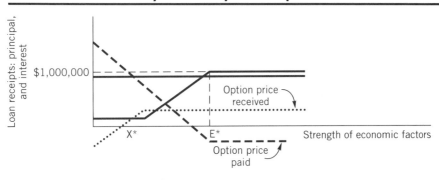

fees and interest revenues, and floating-rate loans are often refinanced with fixed-rate loans.

Now suppose that in financial markets, banks purchase put options on the economic factors that underlie the performance of their loan portfolios. Assume, in options terminology, that one put option is purchased carrying an exercise price of $E^*$ and a second put option is sold carrying an exercise price of $X^*$. In Figure 17-12 the payoff profile for the purchased option is the dashed line, and the profile for the written or sold option is the dotted line. The vertical distance of the flat portion of the dashed profile line below the horizontal axis is the option price paid for the purchased put, and the distance of the flat portion of the dotted line above the axis is the selling price received for the sold option.

Akin to a vertical-spread trading strategy used by options traders, the joint payoff of the two put option positions combined with the loan portfolio payoff is shown by the heavy solid line in Figure 17-12. This line is the result of simply adding up the vertical distances of the dashed, dotted, and original solid lines. The heavy line falls slightly below the maximum $1 million payoff because of the net cost of the options transactions. This slight vertical distance is, in fact, the cost of loan portfolio insurance.

Although highly simplified in this example, the underlying logic can be applied to a wide range of problems. Systematic credit exposure problems are usually multidimensional, calling for a pair of options on each identified economic factor. For example, corn farmers are best modeled with at least two key factors—corn prices and fuel costs. This would require transactions involving corn options and crude oil options.

For the scheme to work, options must be replicated or synthesized where there are no organized markets for certain kinds of options. The technology for replicating options is not difficult; various commodities contracts exist, including futures, that might serve as synthesizing vehicles. As with any innovation, the test for implementing option-based insurance on bank loan portfolios will be banks' skill in developing personnel and control systems to make effective use of options technology.

## LOAN SALES AND SECURITIZATION

Banks engage in another type of off–balance sheet activity when they sell loans. Loans are sold either outright, to pension funds and other banks, or via securitized pools of mortgages, consumer loans, or commercial loans for sale to secondary market investors. Bank pooling of mortgage loans for sale as mortgage-backed securities (MBS) actually began about 1970. The sale of consumer and commercial loans, however, is a recent and revolutionary phenomenon in which banks are liquidating what were historically considered nonmarketable assets.

The volume of both types of sales—MBS and conventional loan sales—began to boom in the mid-1980s. Annual sales volumes in the early 1990s indicated that as much as $4 trillion worth of MBS was sold by all sellers, with loan sales by commercial banks accounting for about one-quarter of the total.

### Mortgage-Backed Securities

The market for MBS is dominated by issues bearing government guarantees. The largest issuer is the GNMA, which authorizes pass-through securities that are serviced by the cash flows from a pool of mortgages originated by GNMA-approved lenders. GNMA guarantees these mortgages against default but accepts only Federal Housing Authority (FHA), Veterans Administration (VA), or Farm Home Administration (FmHA) mortgages.

FNMA and FHLMC purchase mostly conventional mortgages from banks and issue MBS. FHLMC's securities are guaranteed pass-throughs called *participation certificates (PCs)*. In 1980, FHLMC began to offer its PCs for mortgages held on lending institutions' balance sheets. This move permitted many institutions to mobilize heretofore inert assets and to refresh their liquidity. The volume of PCs also boomed as a result of this action.

The private-sector MBS market evolved more gradually than the government-guaranteed market. Private activity began to boom in the early to mid-1980s, when a new type of intermediary called the *private mortgage conduit* appeared. Conduits act as an intermediary between mortgage originators and investors and serve to pool the mortgages of many small lenders. The conduits issue pass-through securities to the originating lenders, proving them with greater liquidity and diversification. Private MBS issuers suffer a disadvantage, however, compared with public agency issues because, unlike the latter, they do not offer a guarantee. Private issuers have responded by offering their own guarantees, including sinking fund set-asides, and have made private MBS issues nearly as attractive as government-backed issues.

### Consumer Loan Sales

Beginning in the mid-1980s, commercial banks began to apply the principles of the secondary mortgage market to create securities pools backed by their loans to consumers. The banks' reasoning was the same as for securitized mortgage loans: to transform risky, illiquid loans such as credit card receivables into much less risky and more liquid securities. These types of asset-backed securities were originally offered in 1985. The market for such securities has grown dramatically from $9 billion in 1987 to over $50 billion in 1992.

Such securities allow the banks to make consumer loans and then quickly move them off the balance sheet to reduce their capital requirements. The two most common forms of consumer-loan pools have become popularly known as CARs (certificates of automobile receivables) and CARDs (certificates for amortizing revolving debt). Similar loan pools have been formed with backing by boat loans, truck leases, and others, but CARs and CARDs have been the most widely accepted because of investors' preferences, because of the homogeneous nature of the underlying loans, and because historical data on default and prepayment rates are more available and reliable.

CARs are generally backed by a pool of four- to five-year automobile installment loans. These securities have an average life of about two years. CARs have been highly successful, in part, because banks have considerable experience with such loans, making it easier to identify the securities' risk. However, from the banks' perspective, the short-term nature of the loans backing the securities means that origination and securitization costs must be recovered over a relatively short period of time. As a result, the securitization process puts pressure on the loans' profitability.

CARDs, on the other hand, are backed by the revolving debt from credit card receivables and generally have a longer life than CARs, averaging two to seven years. CARDs may offer investors better protection than CARs because they are supported by highly liquid, *revolving* loans. Bank issuers can tailor the securities' maturities and offer speedy liquidation. An example of a CARD is Citibank's Citi Credit Card Trust, which securitized $2.2 billion of the bank's $13.4 billion in credit card receivables from 1988 to 1990.

Securities sold for investment into pools such as Citibank's are created by forming a portfolio of good-quality performing loans. A backup pool of loans is earmarked to replace loans that are paid down. As shown in Figure 17-13, a trust is then formed to receive the loans' principal and interest payments. PCs are then sold to investors (usually at $1,000 par value) based on the cash flows from the loans, although some capital may be placed up front by the bank in a spread account. The PCs are sold to the investors at a yield below the assets' (loans') yield, usually at a spread over the Treasury rate of about 100 basis points. This large earnings spread tends to reduce the bank's required capital contribution and increases liquidity. As shown in Figure 17-13, the excess flows are available for reinvestment in the bank's loan portfolio.

Table 17-7 shows the hypothetical earnings on a credit card securitization program. The bank generates a net flow of 3.395 percent on its loans, and

---

**FIGURE 17-13   Cash Flows for Credit Card Securitization**

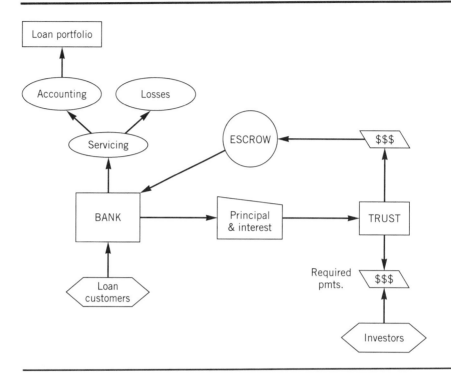

---

**TABLE 17-7   Yield on a Credit Card Securitization Program**

| | |
|---|---|
| **Bank Income** | |
| Loan yield | 17.66% |
| Less: charge-offs | 3.25% |
| Net yield | 14.41% |
| **Expenses** | |
| Servicing | 1.25% |
| L/C fee | 0.25% |
| Trust fee | 0.50% |
| Interest on PCs | 9.00% |
| Total expenses | 11.00% |
| **Excess** | 3.41% |
| To escrow (spread acct.) | 0.015% |
| Net flow | 3.395% |

investors receive attractive returns on a low-risk investment. The example is based on a $100 million CARD pool with a three-year maturity that yields 8.5 percent. In 1992, revolving card debt backing such pools averaged a yield of 17.66 percent.

Because such loan pools are not backed by federal agency guarantees, as most mortgage-backed instruments are, CARs and CARDs are set up with credit and collateral enhancements that exceed the par value of the security by 10 to 15 percent. This ensures that principal payments are not lost in cases of delinquency and default. Some trusts automatically repay principal once a level of default is reached. Additional principal insurance for these securities may be obtained through L/Cs.

## Commercial Loan Sales

In the strictest sense, the sale of commercial loans by banks is an old practice. For a long time, banks have sold participations in loans they originate to peer or correspondent banks. A recent call report verified the popularity of this practice and indicated that over 8,000 banks out of a sample of 11,461 sold loans sometime during 1992.

A new dimension to commercial loan sales has emerged, however, through the sales of outstanding single loans to a wide variety of bank and nonbank investors. Volume estimates for this type of activity in 1985 reached as high as $50 billion at one point during the 1980s. Commercial loan sales differ from MBS, CARs, and CARDs. Typically they involve single loans rather than pools. As a rule, they are sold without recourse. Loan sales activity is most prominent among money center banks, with the nine largest U.S. bank participants accounting for about 40 percent of the volume. Most loans sold are of short maturity, with about one-third of the volume in overnight loans. Another one-third of the volume is in loans with maturities of up to 30 days. Most commercial loans sold are credits produced more or less routinely from loan commitments to major, high-quality corporations.

Many of the banks selling loans, including virtually all money center banks, use a technique known as *stripping*, in which only the short-term obligations of longer-term loans are sold to loan buyers. This approach enhances the quality (reduces the risk) of the sale because the buyer avoids the loan's longer-term exposure to default and the possibility of a refinancing crisis at the loan's maturity.

Medium- to long-term loan sales have been slower to develop because of the customized nature and greater credit risk of longer-term loans. In addition, the special customer relationships that exist in the longer run, including the portfolio of bank services the customer uses, make longer-term credits difficult to detach for sales to more impersonal markets.

Originating banks almost always retain the servicing of loans sold, and frequently they play a role—at the buyer's request—in resolving disputes or claims due to defaults. The clear documentation of loans is crucial to their salability. Short-term loans are easier to structure according to standardized documentation. Longer-term loans are more difficult to standardize because the uniqueness of loan terms increases in proportion to the loans' maturities.

## Benefits of Loan Sales and Securitization

Recent research has sought to explain the perceived advantages to banks that sell loans outright or securitize them for sale through investment bankers. One prominent theme is that loan sales permit avoidance of regulatory "taxes." According to this reasoning, loans that are warehoused on banks' balance sheets are subject to regulatory taxes that invariably occur when banks finance assets. Loans that are sold, of course, are relieved of financing requirements and therefore do not create such taxes. Regulatory taxes include reserve requirements and deposit insurance premiums on the issue of deposits and capital requirements that periodically force the issue of equity. In addition, because equity is not tax deductible, the returns the bank must earn for equity holders are subject to corporate income taxes. All these taxes, reserve requirements, deposit insurance premiums, capital requirements, and corporate income taxes provide an incentive for banks to focus on selling loans they originate instead of holding them on their balance sheets.

George Pennacchi, of the University of Pennsylvania, has presented an example of the costs imposed by regulatory taxes on warehoused loans.[1] The financing cost can be expressed as follows:

$$\text{Cost of deposits and equity to finance loans} = \frac{ck_e}{(1-t)} + (1-c)(k_d + IP)$$

where $c$ is the bank's required capital ratio, $k_e$ is the after-tax cost of equity (the return required by equity holders), $t$ is the corporate income tax rate, $k_d$ is the interest cost of deposits, and $IP$ is the deposit insurance premium.

In addition, deposits are subject to a reserve requirement $(RR)$ that must be set aside in nonearning reserves. For every dollar raised to finance loans, therefore, only $c + (1 - c)(1 - RR)$ can be used. The reserve requirement raises the cost of loan financing as indicated by the following equation:

$$\text{Financing cost for warehoused loans} = \frac{ck_e}{(1-t)} + \frac{(1-c)(k_d + IP)}{[c + (1-c)(1-RR)]}$$

Suppose that a bank that warehouses loans must compete for funds by paying 5 percent to depositors and returning 15 percent after tax to equity holders. If the required capital ratio $(c)$ is .10 percent, the tax rate $(t)$ is 34 percent, the deposit insurance premium $(IP)$ is 0.250 percent, and the reserve requirement $(RR)$ is 3 percent, then

---

[1] George G. Pennacchi, "Advantages and Optimal Structuring of Banks Loan Sales," working paper, University of Pennsylvania (August 1987).

$$\frac{.10(.15)}{(1 - .34)} + \frac{(1 - 0.1)(.05 + 0.0025)}{[.1 + (1 - .1)(1 - .03)]} = .0713$$

Now assume that investors expect only a 5 percent return on the purchase of loans, that is, an amount equal to the return on deposits. In this example, banks would be unable to compete by warehousing rather than selling loans because they would require an additional 213 basis points—the unfavorable excess over money market financing rates.

Christine Pavel and David Phillis of the Federal Reserve Bank of Chicago have shown that other reasons probably also explain why banks are willing to sell loans.[2] Loan sales may permit banks to diversify their loan portfolios. Banks may specialize in originating certain loan types or their portfolios may be too concentrated geographically. Loan sales permit them to offload certain loans and to acquire other types of assets.

A compelling motive for loan sales is to improve bank liquidity management. A leading example of this motive is the system developed by Bankers Trust Company. This banking firm views loan sales as a continuous part of its asset and liability management process.

In the view of Bankers Trust's management, the *absence* of loan liquification techniques mismatches efforts at balance sheet management.[3] Balance sheet management, as practiced in most regional and money center banks, typically combines operation of a loan warehousing facility with aggressive pursuit of liabilities. Funds are moved forcefully against an immobile loan portfolio to control costs, market risk, and interest rate risk. In these banks, liability management is active and asset management is passive. The tactics of the asset and liability management committee are tuned to the bank's liabilities. Even the development of interest rate risk management tools, such as swaps, options, and loan price caps, is an attempt to solve problems resulting from aggressive liability management.

In contrast, Bankers Trust urges a more balanced approach. The firm believes that asset and liability management should be balanced by addressing investor markets through loan sales and deposit sales, respectively. Both types of sales are conducted continuously to maximize the risk-adjusted yield on the total loan portfolio: Liquidity is demanded of the asset side as well as the liability side of the balance sheet.

Bankers Trust's style of active asset management centers on the efforts of loan product managers. These officers focus intensely on loan documentation standards to ensure loan liquidity and salability. For further portfolio flexibility, the product managers are also responsible for reconfiguring existing assets to make them salable.

---

[2] Christine Pavel and David Phillis, "Why Commercial Banks Sell Loans: An Empirical Analysis," *Economic Perspectives*, Federal Research Bank of Chicago, Vol. 11 (September-October 1987), pp. 3–14.

[3] See Donald G. Simonson, "Loan Sales: So the Music Doesn't Stop," *United States Banker* (April 1986), pp. 56–57.

Loan liquification is seen as an inseparable part of the bank's global strategy, with links to investors in Hong Kong, London, and New York. The Bankers Trust concept puts investor markets (buyers of the loan product) in the same loop as the loan product managers. Loans are structured as products to be participated out to the world markets. The firm benefits from greater funds flexibility and responsiveness to borrowers, and it gains greater market efficiency by matching users of capital with pools of capital.

Through loan sales, according to Bankers Trust, bank capital is used more intensely and bank liquidity is enhanced. Moreover, the bank increases its underwriting income to offset the pricing pressures on conventional loan business that all large banks are experiencing. Loan salability also enhances diversification by giving the bank access to borrowers who otherwise may not be acceptable to its portfolio by reason of concentration limits or exposure policies.

### Regulatory Issues

Important regulatory problems surrounding bank loan sales remain to be solved. Can loan sales be structured, through creative origination and selling techniques, to avoid significant recourse to the bank? If not, loan sales will certainly cause a call on bank capital. Also, recourse might mean that the proceeds from loan sales will be treated as deposits and as reservable, adding to the cost of selling loans for the purpose of regenerating funds. On the other hand, should not sales with recourse be viewed as superior to collateralized borrowing (which in most instances need not be reservable)? Answers to these questions are being formulated by the Financial Accounting Standards Board, by the Comptroller of the Currency, and in the marketplace as each gains experience with loan sales. Clearly, the most troublesome regulatory questions have to do with the implications for the capital adequacy of selling institutions. At present, it appears that the supervisory examining apparatus is not equipped to deal with this kind of off–balance sheet activity.

New capital requirements on loan sales with recourse appear to restore the regulatory tax that banks hope to escape when they sell loans. Nevertheless, other incentives appear sufficient to ensure the continuation and growth of loan sales activity. For some large banks, it seems clear that loan sales reduce liquidity risk. This type of banking risk exists simply because no bank has complete match funding; in aggregate, liabilities mature at times that are different from those of assets. Conventionally, liquidity risk becomes a crisis when investors stop accepting a bank's liabilities. But banks that master the knowledge and techniques for liquidating loans enjoy an extra liquidity reserve.

### MBS and Options Pricing

In addition to being the most significant market for loan sales, the MBS market has become vitally important as a supply of high-yielding investments for banks. This was especially true for thousands of small banks in loan-deficient markets in the eastern and western United States in the early 1990s. The price behavior of MBS, however, appears to be irrational because of the difficulty of understanding prepayment patterns on these securities. An inopportune choice, however, can result in considerable loss, because interest rate movements can produce a rapid drop in certain MBS prices.

In particular, when the price on the MBS pool rises slightly above par, a precipitous fall in price may ensue. Prices at and above par value reflect the convergence of market interest rates on the coupon rate of the subject MBS pool. This coupon–market rate convergence increases the chances of a pending rush by mortgagors to refinance. It is a hallmark of the mortgage contract that borrowers can simply pay down their old mortgages at any time without penalty. For the banks with MBS in their investment portfolios, exposure to interest rate movements is increased by this "free" prepayment provision.

The potential for prepayments makes the MBS investment choice complex. The choice cannot be based on comparing observable yield spreads—for example, the reported difference between the yield on an MBS and the yield on a Treasury security of like duration. In reality, the primary reason MBS trade at positive yields over Treasuries is because of the prepayment effect, which must be incorporated to gauge the true yield. The prepayment privilege amounts to a call option sold to the borrower by the investors. Thus, the standard fixed-rate mortgage is best understood as a hybrid security composed of a conventional fixed-income security issued by the borrower plus a call option purchased by the borrower. As with any call option, the prepayment privilege grants the borrower the right to call in the debt at a favorable price but does not obligate the borrower to do so at an unfavorable price. This right gives the option a separable positive value, which causes the borrower to accede to a higher coupon (take a lower value for issuing the debt) than he or she would if there was no possibility of prepayment.

The value of the option changes as market interest rates change. For low-coupon mortgages in high interest rate environments, the option has little value (i.e., it is far out of the money). As the market rate converges on the mortgage's coupon, the option takes on increasing value and is in the money. The value of the prepayment option differs for different MBS pools because of different features in the pools, especially their coupons.

Thus, the root of the dilemma in choosing among MBS is that there are differences in the value of the call options embedded in the value of each MBS. This is why, in short, investors cannot use raw spreads between MBS pools or between MBS and comparable Treasuries to determine which MBS is favorably priced. Should yields decline, one MBS is likely to prepay more rapidly than another, and these prepayments occur just when the investor least wants them. The prepayments suppress the price increases that would be produced on a noncallable, fixed-income security when interest rates decline. This phenomenon—called *price compression*—causes the yield on an in-the-money MBS to exceed the yield on an out-of-the-money MBS.

Figure 17-14 shows how the price of an MBS compares with the price of a security with no call option (such as a noncallable bond) at various interest

**FIGURE 17-14   Price Compression on Mortgage Backed Securities**

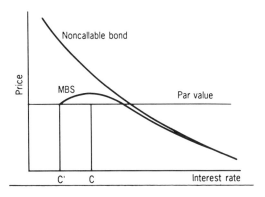

rates. $C$ on the interest rate axis is the MBS coupon rate, and $C'$ is the coupon level to which market coupon rates must fall to make it worthwhile for the borrower to prepay and refinance. Of course, borrowers incur front-end costs when they take out a new mortgage and, to justify refinancing, they must obtain a new coupon sufficiently below the old coupon to overcome these costs. The typically downward-sloping price curve for the noncallable bond is not a straight line but is somewhat convex. This *convexity* comes about because, mathematically, interest rate declines cause larger positive changes in price than the negative changes in price caused by interest rate increases. Convexity is a desirable property for a security to have. It represents the extent to which price changes are more favorable than if prices and interest rates were linearly related. Convexity differs from one security to another mainly because of differences in securities' coupon rates.

Unlike noncallable instruments' price curves, the MBS price curve has a perverse shape and becomes concave as market interest rates decline toward $C$. The perversity—called *negative convexity*—stems from the prepayment option coming into the money and causing falling prices in a bizarre combination with falling interest rates. More precisely, then, the primary reason MBS trade at positive yield spreads over Treasuries is this negative convexity characteristic.

In choosing the most favorably priced MBS for an investment portfolio, the investor needs to estimate the value of each MBS' prepayment option. The sophisticated approach taken by Wall Street investment bankers is to compute the value of MBS' options under myriad future interest rate scenarios, in the manner of the binomial interest rate lattice presented earlier in this chapter. The value of the prepayment option is the difference between the expected present value derived from the binomial model and the value of a noncallable bond.

With this value—or, more precisely, the yield implied—called the *option-adjusted yield*, the investor can draw apt yield comparisons with Treasury securities of like duration. The comparisons can be used to indicate the most underpriced MBS.

There is somewhat more to the issue of modeling MBS price and yield spreads, including the difficult issue of modeling prepayment behavior by unpredictable mortgagors. But it is important for bankers to understand the essence of the approach outlined earlier when investing in MBS. The intuitions derived from the approach should at least sharpen bankers' ability to evaluate buy recommendations from MBS brokers.

## SUMMARY

The dominant characteristic of most bank off–balance sheet activity is the contingent nature of these activities. For example, modern banks conduct a large volume of business by selling the right to obtain credit under circumstances that are often unfavorable to the bank. Loan commitments, such as line-of-credit and revolving-credit agreements and L/Cs, including standby and commercial L/Cs, are primary examples of contingent liability activities.

In addition, banks carry assets on their balance sheets whose values are contingent upon market interest rates and other prices set in the economy. Fixed and cap rate loans and loans with prepayment options are some leading examples of assets whose values are market sensitive.

Option pricing techniques offer a method of pricing all of these contingent-claim bank products. Perhaps equally important, option pricing provides insights into the value of such products. These insights can be gained from simplified and intuitively appealing approaches to option pricing.

Bank loan sales and securitization represent another kind of off–balance sheet activity. Loan selling appears to offer a lower-cost means of creating credit, and it enhances the management of liquidity, interest sensitivity, and capital.

## Discussion Questions

1. Review the costs and benefits of the creation of a secondary mortgage market supported by government sponsored agencies such as FNMA, GNMA, and FHLMC. Discuss how the liquidity and risk of financial institution providers of mortgage funds change with the introduction of a secondary market. Who bears the risk of default? How is the cost of mortgage funds affected?

2. What are the difficulties of comparing the returns on mortgage-backed securities with standard Treasury securities "of comparable maturities"? Critique investors' practice of judging MBS on the basis of "spread over Treasury".

3. How would you expect the interest rate banks set on adjustable-rate mortgages to be affected by an increase in the annual rate cap, the lifetime cap and interest rate expectations? Defend your answer with a numerical example

(e.g. assume annual caps rise from 1½% to 2%, lifetime caps rise from 5% to 6%, interest rates are expected to rise).

4. Explain the structure of cash flows to the various tranches of a CMO. Give a rationale for the risks and prices borne by the various tranch investors. Review the cashflow structure for Planned Amortization Class (PAC) securities and give the reasoning behind such a structure.

5. Criticize the following statement: "Interest-only strips are negatively affected by rising rates because, as prepayments decrease (with rising rates), interest payments are frozen at the original rates on the underlying mortgage."

6. A bank offers a deposit account in which the depositor is allowed to make later additions to the account at the original interest rate (even though markets rates may have fallen). Explain the appropriate pricing (interest rate) on this account, using the concepts of options-pricing theory.

7. Suppose your company obtains a $1 million six-month commitment from its bank to lend at 8 percent. Assume that there is agreement universally that interest rates on such loans will either rise to 9 percent or fall to 7 percent with equal probabilities of 0.5 and that your company will surely borrow the $1 million, but only if market rates rise to 9%. Calculate an appropriate commitment fee for this deal.

8. In terms of options-pricing methodology, describe how a bank should develop the pricing on a loan cap to be sold to a corporate borrower.

9. In the securitization of consumer loans such as automobile loans and credit card loans (CARs, CARDs), the ultimate investor is willing to accept a return on the securities much less than the return the bank receives on the underlying loans. Explain.

10. What is the estimated 1993 cost of financing warehoused loans, considering that risk-based capital ratios increased to 10 percent for "well-capitalized" banks, deposit insurance premium costs are 0.25 percent, equity holders require 16 percent returns after taxes of 34 percent? Assume reserve requirements are 3 percent.

11. Congress has discussed setting up a secondary market for loans to small business to enable banks to securitize their loans such entities. Discuss the difficulties of such a market compared to markets for other securitized loans (home mortgages, consumer loans, large commercial loans).

# CHAPTER 18

# Bank Mergers and Acquisitions

Consolidation in the number of banks in the United States during the 1980s and early 1990s was an epochal and ongoing event. During this period, more mergers occurred in the banking industry than in any other industry. Much of the merger activity was driven by new kinds of economic pressures and by the lifting of restrictive regulations that previously had isolated banks from competition. Continuing economic and deregulatory pressures probably will prompt many more mergers during the mid-1990s. Some observers believe that the number of commercial banks will shrink, from more than 14,000 in the late 1980s to 10,000 and possibly fewer by the mid-1990s.

Evidence of consolidations comes from the records of new banks, bank mergers and acquisitions, and bank failures. Figure 18-1 shows the structural changes among insured commercial banks over the last decade. Table 18-1 presents the record on overall bank consolidations and mergers for most of the post–World War II era. Table 18-2 lists the annual number of bank failures. (Failed banks almost always are added to the numbers of consolidations because they are usually absorbed into another existing bank.)

## PRESSURE ON BANK PROFITS

Changes in legislation, regulation, and competition in banking, as well as trends in the economy, have influenced the profitability and, therefore, viability of many banks, leading them to fail or to combine with financially stronger and better-managed institutions. The following phenomena are affecting banks' longer-term profitability outlook:

**FIGURE 18-1** **Structural Changes among FDIC-Insured Commercial Banks, 1980–1992**

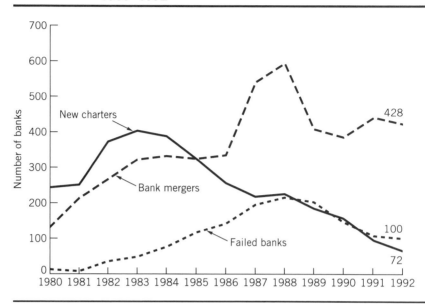

SOURCE: *Quarterly Banking Profile* (Washington, D.C.: 1992, FDIC).

1. *New competition for banks has developed from both financial and non-financial firms.* Thrift institutions now compete for bank transactions accounts and for traditional bank lending markets. In addition, various types of nondeposit firms offer banklike financial services. Many of these firms are less heavily regulated than banks and are able to exploit the synergies of offering banklike services in conjunction with activities forbidden to banks, such as securities underwriting and selling insurance.

2. *Banks and thrift institutions have lost the legal protection of the cost of their funds and their monopoly on offering consumer savings accounts.* Congress was forced to deregulate interest rates on consumer time and savings accounts and to authorize interest-bearing checking accounts to enable banks to compete with unregulated and booming money market funds and other investment media. These steps, as principal parts of the major banking legislation passed in 1980 and 1982, coupled with the growing consumer demand for nonbank investment media, denied banks and thrifts their accustomed protection from interest rate competition and, most likely, hurt their profitability.

3. *Banks' position as credit-granting intermediaries has been eroded by alternative lower-cost forms of credit extension.* The financial markets, in particular, the commercial paper market and the bond market, more and more directly supply credit to borrowers. The transactions cost of direct credit inter-

**TABLE 18-1  Combinations Due to Absorption, Considerations, and Mergers**[a]

| Year | | Year | |
|------|-----|------|-----|
| 1949 | 80 | 1971 | 103 |
| 1950 | 93 | 1972 | 126 |
| 1951 | 81 | 1973 | 102 |
| 1952 | 101 | 1974 | 126 |
| 1953 | 116 | 1975 | 99 |
| 1954 | 209 | 1976 | 144 |
| 1955 | 232 | 1977 | 161 |
| 1956 | 189 | 1978 | 182 |
| 1957 | 161 | 1979 | 235 |
| 1958 | 153 | 1980 | 136 |
| 1959 | 169 | 1981 | 232 |
| 1960 | 132 | 1982 | 310 |
| 1961 | 138 | 1983 | 457 |
| 1962 | 183 | 1984 | 418 |
| 1963 | 154 | 1985 | 504 |
| 1964 | 138 | 1986 | 327 |
| 1965 | 149 | 1987 | 531 |
| 1966 | 133 | 1988 | 594 |
| 1967 | 137 | 1989 | 409 |
| 1968 | 134 | 1990 | 398 |
| 1969 | 153 | 1991 | 448 |
| 1970 | 155 | 1992 | 428 |

[a]Combinations include commercial banks, stock savings banks, nondeposit trust companies, and mutual savings banks.

SOURCE: *Annual Reports of the FDIC* and *Quarterly Banking Profile* (Washington, D.C.: FDIC), various years.

mediation is only a small fraction of the cost of the traditional arrangement of bank deposit-loan intermediation. One consequence has been the reduction in banks' share of the market for large, short-term borrowings by nonfinancial corporations (from 85 percent in the mid-1960s to just under 40 percent in the early 1990s). This direct market competition applies further pressure to bank profit margins.

## FEDERAL AGENCIES' ROLE IN MERGERS

The analysis and approval of bank mergers is put in the hands of the three federal banking regulatory agencies, as well as the Department of Justice. There are two major pieces of legislation that control bank mergers: the Bank Merger Act of 1966 and the Bank Holding Company Act of 1956 (along with its amendments of 1966 and 1970). Under the Bank Merger Act, either the

**TABLE 18-2** **Number of Banks Closed because of Financial Difficulties, 1934–1992**

| Year | Total | Year | Total |
|------|-------|------|-------|
| 1934 | 61 | 1964 | 8 |
| 1935 | 32 | 1965 | 9 |
| 1936 | 72 | 1966 | 8 |
| 1937 | 84 | 1967 | 4 |
| 1938 | 81 | 1968 | 3 |
| 1939 | 72 | 1969 | 9 |
| 1940 | 48 | 1970 | 8 |
| 1941 | 17 | 1971 | 6 |
| 1942 | 23 | 1972 | 3 |
| 1943 | 5 | 1973 | 6 |
| 1944 | 2 | 1974 | 4 |
| 1945 | 1 | 1975 | 14 |
| 1946 | 2 | 1976 | 17 |
| 1947 | 6 | 1977 | 6 |
| 1948 | 3 | 1978 | 7 |
| 1949 | 9 | 1979 | 10 |
| 1950 | 5 | 1980 | 10 |
| 1951 | 5 | 1981 | 10 |
| 1952 | 4 | 1982 | 42 |
| 1953 | 5 | 1983 | 48 |
| 1954 | 4 | 1984 | 78 |
| 1955 | 5 | 1985 | 118 |
| 1956 | 3 | 1986 | 144 |
| 1957 | 3 | 1987 | 201 |
| 1958 | 9 | 1988 | 221 |
| 1959 | 3 | 1989 | 201 |
| 1960 | 2 | 1990 | 144 |
| 1961 | 9 | 1991 | 118 |
| 1962 | 3 | 1992 | 100 |
| 1963 | 2 | | |

SOURCE: *Annual Reports of the FDIC* and *Quarterly Banking Profile* (Washington, D.C.: FDIC), various years.

Office of the Comptroller of the Currency (OCC), the FDIC, or the Board of Governors of the Federal Reserve System (FRB) must conduct its own competitive analysis before approving a bank merger. The OCC, FDIC, or FRB has jurisdiction where the surviving bank is, respectively, a national bank, a federally insured state-chartered bank that is not a member of the Federal Reserve, or a state-chartered member of the Federal Reserve. The agency with jurisdiction is required to apply the competitive standard in the Bank Merger Act, which states that a merger shall not be approved if it will significantly lessen competition or create a monopoly. This standard basically restates the procompetitive and antitrust criteria set forth in the Clayton Act and the Sherman Act.

Under the Bank Holding Company Act, the FRB must rule on the acceptability of acquisitions of banks or bank holding companies by a bank holding company. In all merger and acquisition cases, application must be made to the Justice Department not less than 30 days before consummation. The Justice Department then has 30 days to review the transaction on the basis of anticompetitive factors. If the reviewing banking agency subsequently approves the transaction in spite of a negative finding by the Justice Department, the latter has 30 days more to decide whether to sue. In the case of bank holding company acquisitions of nonbanks, the FRB must make a determination as to whether the transaction is "so closely related to banking . . . as to be a proper incident thereto."

In recent practice, the antitrust division of the Department of Justice has not offered significant resistance to mergers and acquisitions of financial institutions. During a two and one-half year period in the late 1980s, the Department reviewed over 4,000 applications and issued only a half dozen or so adverse findings. Only two mergers or acquisitions were actually denied on competitive effect grounds during the same period.

As a practical matter, the multiple possible jurisdictions involving one of the three banking agencies presents choices to a bank holding company that is in an acquisition mode. In practice, each of the three banking regulatory agencies applies somewhat different criteria in its competitive analyses. The individual holding company, in effect, may have some latitude in choosing its reviewing agency. If the company seeks to avoid an FRB ruling, for example, it can merge the target bank with an affiliate bank instead of acquiring it directly. The acquisition ruling would then be made by the agency with jurisdiction over either the target bank or the preexisting affiliate, whichever is designated as the surviving bank.

It is also possible to avoid an FRB ruling and still arrange for the target bank and all affiliate banks to survive. The holding company can obtain a charter for a new bank and treat it as a shell or "phantom" bank. Then the acquired bank can be merged into the shell bank, which would bestow its charter on the surviving institution, thereby assuring a ruling by the desired regulatory agency.

## The Agencies' Approaches to Merger Standards

The regulatory agencies analyze the anticompetitive effects of bank mergers and acquisitions on the banking product market and the geographic market as defined for purposes of regulation. The analyses must first define these markets as they pertain to the institutions that are parties to a proposed merger or acquisition.

**Product Market**   The concept of a banking product market is dynamic and has been modified over the years. The first standard for defining such a market was established in *United States* v. *Philadelphia National Bank,* a landmark case decided by the U.S. Supreme Court in 1963. This case first denoted commercial banking as a distinct line of commerce in the sense of the Clayton Act. This act forbids acquisitions within a line of commerce in which the effect "may be substantially to lessen competition, or to tend to create a monopoly." In the *Philadelphia National Bank* case, the court viewed the product market for banks as a cluster of financial services rather than as just one service. Institutions that offered some but not a complete package of banking services (e.g., thrift institutions) were not considered in competitive analyses and were precluded as competitors that potentially offset banks' market power. As a result, in computing the concentration of banking power, only commercial banks, and not other financial institutions, were considered as competitors for bank customers. The Court adjusted this view somewhat in its *United States* v. *Connecticut National Bank* decision in 1974, when it recognized that the mix of services emerging in nonbank financial institutions might make them significant competitors for commercial banking customers.

Subsequent to the *Connecticut National Bank* decision, of course, thrift institutions have been granted authority to offer consumer loans and transactions accounts and to hold up to 10 percent of their assets in commercial loans. In addition, credit unions have created increasingly strong competition for consumer loans and transactions accounts. More subtle differences between banks and other sources of financial services (e.g., the widespread issuance and use of credit cards) have been eroded as well. As a result, the regulatory view of commercial banking as a line of commerce that is insulated from competition has changed to acknowledge the influence of other, banklike providers of financial services.

The regulatory agencies are now receptive, therefore, to evidence of broader competition within product markets in determining the competitive effect of an acquisition. In general, the agencies focus on total deposits as a surrogate for the product market. In this context, the FRB has recently used the total deposits of commercial banks plus one-half of thrift institution deposits. The OCC, on the other hand, takes into account the totals of bank, thrift, and other nonbank deposits. The FDIC has still another approach and has recently used a broader array of services offered by all providers to determine the effect of acquisitions on consumers and small businesses whose alternatives for financial services are limited to a local market.

**Geographic Markets** The regulatory agencies also define the geographic market that is relevant to the competitive effects of a merger or acquisition. The method is to identify the area in which an acquiring bank might be capable of exercising monopoly power—that is, the area where it can profit by controlling prices and the volume or quality of services without driving away too much business. To do this, the agencies must consider where, physically, the subject bank derives its business, its office locations, and the area from which it tries to attract business.

The *Philadelphia National Bank* case decision recognized that each banking service might have a different geographic market. In the Court's view, banks' large customers can usually conduct their banking business outside of their community. Small customers, on the other hand, tend to be constrained "to bank offices in their immediate neighborhood."

The Justice Department starts with standard metropolitan areas as defined by Rand-McNally for urban settings. In the case of rural settings, it starts with countywide markets. It tries to determine customers' practical alternatives for banking services other than the offices of the acquired bank. To decide on the practical alternatives available, it considers such data as distances to banking offices, the economic profile of the community served, zip code demographics, commuting and traffic patterns, and the coverage of advertising media.

The banking agencies each apply variations of this type of geographic market test. The OCC examines markets that are already shared by the two merging banks and uses a proximity measure based on distances between population concentrations and alternative banking offices. The FDIC, and to some extent the FRB, introduces economic measures, advertising markets, and the distribution of community public services to define relevant geographic markets.

In combination, the defined product and geographic markets permit an assessment of the competitive effects of a merger or acquisition. A summary concentration measure is used that gives an indication of the distribution of market power among firms in the market. Historically, the Herfindahl index, computed by summing the squares of the market shares of all firms, has been used. If the consolidation of the proposed acquiring and target institutions produces too large an index number for the market in question, excessive concentration is indicated. Such a result ordinarily would be grounds for disapproving the proposed acquisition or merger.

There are, however, mitigating factors to a finding of anticompetitive effects inferred by excessive structural concentration. The Justice Department gives consideration to such factors because they may tend to introduce *pro*competitive influences that outweigh the possibly *anti*competitive effects of concentration. For example, the Justice Department recognizes that intensified price and service competition might result despite an increase in concentration. Also, the consolidation of small banks may improve their economies of scales and result in cost savings that make them more formidable competitors with large institutions. In addition, the Department recognizes that the ease of potential entry by other strong financial institutions, given a shift toward monopolistic pricing in the market, serves to restrain the anticompetitive behavior of newly consolidated banks in that market.

The record indicates that the Justice Department has viewed these mitigating procompetitive factors quite favorably and generally has been reluctant to issue adverse findings or to deny bank mergers or acquisitions on grounds of excessive concentration. The logical conclusion is that the standard procedure of focusing on simplistic measures of market concentration lacks substance as a practical argument against consolidation.

# CONSOLIDATION OF FAILING BANKS

The overwhelming number of bank consolidations involve vibrant target institutions. The market for healthy banks is relatively open, except for geographical restrictions imposed by bank structure laws, and is subject to vigorous negotiation between buyers and sellers.

Consolidations involving failed or failing insured commercial banks, however, are different. In such cases, the owners of the distressed bank are removed from the process of selling the bank, and the FDIC assumes the role of receiver.

An analysis of Table 18-2 indicates that in the 40 years before 1980, failures were unusual and averaged only five per year. The surge in bank failures after 1981 was related to the staggering losses banks experienced in agricultural, energy, and commercial real estate lending.

In dealing with bank failures, the FDIC has several options to protect depositors and the insurance fund (see Table 18-3 for a summary). In particular, the agency is required by public policy to utilize the option that minimizes the loss to the insurance fund. The most common option, and the most frequent loss-minimizing option, appears to be the *purchase and assumption (P&A)*. In the P&A option, the FDIC seeks to have a strong financial institution take over the failed bank.

Over the past two decades, the FDIC has used the P&A method about 75 percent of the time. In a P&A, the FDIC conducts an auction, usually within 24 hours of its closing of the bank. The FDIC takes sealed bids on a uniform package containing the failing bank's good earning assets, bank premises, and the operating franchise. In addition, the FDIC furnishes cash to make the acquired assets (less the premium paid) equal to the assumed liabilities. (Table 18-4 gives an example of the packaged assets in a P&A auction and the new bank balance sheet after the FDIC input of cash.) The successful bidder assumes the liabilities of the failed bank and the good assets but is given a put on the loans that, upon more careful analysis, it does not wish to keep. The FDIC's policy is to accept the put of up to 100 percent of acquired assets for a period of about 50 days following the award to the successful bidder. The agency invites only bidders that exhibit strong operating results and a strong capital position. Because it does not want to publicize the pending closing of a failing bank, the auction is conducted with a good deal of secrecy and dispatch. Often the result has been a highly charged flurry of potential buyers who are forced to analyze the failing bank in a cloistered environment under considerable time pressure.

The FDIC's second most common means of failed bank resolution is the *deposit payoff*. In this method, insured depositors receive direct payments from the FDIC. The failed bank's residual asset values are then used to pay off uninsured depositors. In practice, this method has usually been extended to cover the claims of uninsured depositors as well as those of insured depositors. In the early 1990s, however, the FDIC used a *modified payoff* in which uninsured depositors recovered only 85 percent of their funds above the $100,000 insured amount.

**TABLE 18-3     Types of FDIC Transactions Options for Dealing with Bank Failures**

1. Purchase and Assumption (P&A)
   - A sealed-bid auction is held on a uniform package consisting of the failing bank's good loans, premises, securities, and the rights to operate the bank.
   - The winning bank bidder assumes the liabilities of the failed bank.
   - The winning bidder takes the good loans and gets a put-back of loans it does not want up to 100 percent for about 50 days.
   - The FDIC liquidates unwanted assets.
2. Deposit Payoff or Modified Payoff
   - The failing bank is liquidated.
   - Only insured depositors can be sure of getting paid off fully.
   - Uninsured depositors are partially paid off (modified payoff) from residual asset values.
3. Insured Deposit Transfer
   - Deposits and services are transferred to a healthy bank (instead of paying off depositors up to the insurance limit).
   - The FDIC gives the receiver certificates for uninsured deposits.
4. Open Bank Assistance
   - The acquiring bank is assisted in acquiring a failing bank by infusing cash. The FDIC takes notes or preferred stock of the acquirer.
   - The failing bank is not closed.
5. Whole Bank or Total Asset P&A
   - The acquirer submits a bid (usually negative) for all assets of the failing bank; put-back is not permitted.
   - The acquirer files a management plan, capital plan, collection program, and other intentions for the bank with the FDIC.
   - Bids are usually required within 48 hours.
6. Bridge Bank
   - The FDIC operates the failing bank for the time period necessary to identify a qualified buyer.

Another method for dealing with failed banks is the *insured deposit transfer*. Under this method, insured deposits are simply transferred to a healthy institution in the community without disruption of service to the depositors. The FDIC then gives uninsured depositors receiver certificates in support of these depositors' claims. The deposit transfer approach is used when the failed bank has a significant amount of potential and contingent claims.

Infrequently, the FDIC provides *open bank assistance*. This option merges a bank that is in danger of failing with a sound institution, thus avoiding closure of the distressed bank and a possible liquidation. In this case, the FDIC injects capital by purchasing nonvoting securities of the acquiring bank on terms favorable to the acquiring bank. The FDIC intends, in this instance, to recover its capital assistance through future earnings of the bank. (This assistance may also include, however, a no-strings supplementary payment of

**TABLE 18-4    P&A Transaction Details (dollars in thousands)**

| Failed Bank Package | | | | |
|---|---|---|---|---|
| **Assets** | | | **Liabilities** | |
| Cash and due from banks | $ 4,000 | | Demand deposits | $14,000 |
| Federal funds sold | 5,000 | | Time and savings deposits | 42,000 |
| Securities | 5,000 | | Accrued interest on | |
| Net loans | 15,000 | | deposits | 400 |
| Total | $29,000 | | | $56,400 |

| Post-P&A Bank | | | | |
|---|---|---|---|---|
| **Assets** | | | **Liabilities** | |
| Cash and due from banks | $35,000[a] | | Demand deposits | $14,000 |
| Federal funds sold | 5,000 | | Time and savings deposits | 42,000 |
| Securities | 5,000 | | Accrued interest on | |
| Net loans | 15,000 | | deposits | 400 |
| | $60,000 | | Stockholders' equity | 3,600[b] |
| | | | | $60,000 |

[a] Includes cash furnished by FDIC.

[b] Assumes a required capital ratio of 6%.

cash.) Open bank assistance has not been used often; however, a noteworthy instance of its use was the $4 billion rescue package the FDIC provided to Continental Illinois National Bank in 1984.

Recently, the FDIC has used new and innovative approaches to encourage healthy institutions to bid on failing banks. In 1987 it introduced the *whole bank purchase plan*, or the *total asset takeover*. In this approach, bidders submit any bid, including a possibly negative bid, that specifies the amount the FDIC must pay the bidder to take all of the assets of a failed bank. Unlike the P&A, this approach has the advantage of placing the task of liquidating the failed bank's bad assets with the acquiring institution. It has been argued persuasively that private institutions, and not the FDIC, have the knowledge and capacity to ensure a more orderly liquidation of troubled assets. Under this approach, of course, asset put-backs are ruled out.

Another innovation that addresses the problem of orderly liquidation is the *bridge bank*, which was adopted by Congress in June 1987. This approach permits the FDIC to take over a failed bank and to keep it in business for whatever time it takes to find a buyer. This approach avoids the usually pressurized P&A process in which bidders must analyze and bid within 24 hours. Such pressure has undoubtedly discouraged potential bidders and increased the FDIC's costs of failure resolution.

Congress also agreed to permit out-of-state institutions to acquire large problem banks rather than to close them for lack of in-state buyers. In this view, the Competitive Equality Banking Act of 1987 renewed the emergency acquisition provisions of the Garn–St. Germain Depository Institutions Act of 1982.

## FDIC Performance in P&A Auctions

There have been several recent attempts to measure the effects of the FDIC's P&A policies. This is an important issue, given the public policy directive requiring the FDIC to minimize losses to the insurance fund. P&A auction performance probably eventually affects bank customers because the prices they pay for bank services at least partly reflect bank costs, including the cost of FDIC insurance premiums. Also, P&A performance probably affects all taxpayers because, ultimately, they stand behind the implied "full faith and credit" guarantee of deposit insurance.[1] The core of the P&A issue is whether the FDIC adequately shares in the going-concern value of the failed bank. If it does not, then it can be concluded that the FDIC uneconomically transfers part of the value of the deposit insurance fund to the acquiring bank.

Several researchers have employed an innovative test to determine whether the FDIC gives value away. Their methodology analyzes the behavior of an acquiring bank's share prices at around the time that the stock market became aware of the potential and actual mergers. Using this approach, the researchers observed the rates of return on the stock of acquiring banks to determine whether the daily return was abnormal, relative to the expected risk-adjusted return, during the period before and after the merger. If returns to acquiring banks' shareholders were greater than normal, it would indicate that the FDIC received too little (disbursed too much) in P&A auctions.

In one of the earliest reviews, Richard H. Pettway and Jack W. Thrifts studied 11 banks' and bank holding companies' share prices for the 60 trading days prior to a merger the firms undertook and for the 50 trading days just after the merger. The mergers occurred between 1973 and 1980. The sample of merger cases was a disappointingly small proportion of the 64 P&A mergers that occurred between 1972 and 1981. The sample, however, was composed of the only acquiring banks that had active and continuously traded shares during the trading period analyzed.[2]

Pettway and Trifts found that the abnormal returns on the stock of acquiring banks declined by significant amounts. They concluded, therefore, that the winning bids submitted by acquiring banks were viewed as excessive by the market compared to the expected gains from the mergers. The tentative conclusion suggested that the FDIC did not give away value.[3]

---

[1] In this sense, the FDIC implicitly offers more than insurance as it is traditionally understood; it offers, in essence, a financial guarantee backed by the taxation powers of the federal government.

[2] Richard H. Pettway and Jack W. Thrifts, "Do Banks Overbid When Acquiring Failed Banks," *Financial Management* (Fall 1985), pp. 5–15.

[3] Ibid.

A more recent study draws the opposite conclusion. In this study, the two researchers, Christopher James and Peggy Weir, concluded that shareholders of the acquiring bank realized abnormal returns that readily exceeded the banks' costs of preparing and submitting bids. The James and Weir sample consisted of 19 P&As that occurred from 1973 to 1983. They conducted more extensive tests and concluded that winning bidders in P&A auctions pay less than the going-concern value of failed banks, which means that the P&As transferred wealth from the FDIC insurance fund to the winning bidders. The researchers blamed this transfer of wealth on the FDIC's restrictions on bidder lists and the unrealistic time pressure involved in the process.[4]

The latter result, if true, serves as an indictment of the FDIC's P&A procedures. The result seems to be supported by other evidence that demonstrates the superior postauction performance of banks acquired in P&As. Unencumbered by poor-quality assets, acquired banks appear to have more freedom than peer banks in their market to exploit business opportunities, and the FDIC is not adequately compensated for conferring this advantage to successful bidders.

## DEREGULATION OF INTERSTATE BANKING

A central factor in the accelerating consolidation of banks is the liberalization of laws and regulations governing bank expansion. The primary legal limitations on commercial bank expansion are set forth in the McFadden Act of 1927 and the Douglas Amendment to the Bank Holding Company Act of 1956. In combination, these two acts historically blocked bank expansion across state lines. The McFadden Act restricts national banks to the branching laws of the state in which they are chartered, effectively preventing banks from operating branches outside of their home state. The Douglas Amendment prohibits bank holding companies from acquiring banks in other states unless permitted by the acquiree's home state.

Over the years, several states have opened their intrastate markets by liberalizing branching on a local or statewide basis and by approving the formation of intrastate multibank holding companies. While these intrastate developments gave rise to new branches and to within-state mergers, the legislative developments of the 1980s and early 1990s reduced barriers to *interstate* mergers and acquisitions.

Congress provided for the possibility of interstate acquisitions of troubled financial institutions in the Garn–St. Germain Depository Institutions Act of 1982. Under the emergency provisions of the act, out-of-state organizations were permitted to acquire troubled banks if the loss of the bank would threaten the stability of the financial system or if the acquisition would substantially reduce the FDIC's potential loss. Several major acquisitions were effected

[4]Christopher James and Peggy Weir, "An Analysis of FDIC Failed Bank Auctions," *Journal of Monetary Economics* (Spring 1989), pp. 141–153.

under this provision, including the 1983 acquisition of SeaFirst Corporation in the state of Washington by Bank of America of California and the 1986 acquisition of the First National Bank of Oklahoma City, Oklahoma, by the First Interstate Corporation of California.

Interstate banking was considered in arguments over the two most recent banking laws passed by Congress—the Financial Institution Reform, Recovery, and Enforcement Act (FIRREA) in 1989 and the Federal Deposit Insurance Corporation Improvement Act (FDICIA) in 1991. Congress, however, chose to avoid the often emotional issue of interstate banking, so this issue remained unresolved.

### Erosion via the Douglas Amendment

Although the Garn–St. Germain Depository Institutions Act signaled congressional recognition of the appropriateness of interstate bank acquisitions, the more significant development for interstate acquisitions has been the erosion of the restrictive power of the Douglas Amendment. This development began in earnest in 1982 when New York State passed rather unrestricted interstate banking legislation. This legislation had the effect of putting other states on notice regarding several New York banks' aspirations for geographic expansion. Indeed, upper New York State banks moved aggressively to buy the largest banks in Maine, which had passed permissive interstate banking legislation in the mid-1970s. Two other New England states, Massachusetts and Connecticut, reacted to New York's move by quickly passing interstate banking legislation that restricted out-of-state entry to only one another's banks, as well as to banks in Maine and New Hampshire.

The Massachusetts and Connecticut laws were acknowledged as an effort to ensure in-state control, increase the mass of the institutions within their respective states to a less vulnerable size, and offset the perceived territorial ambitions of the huge New York banks. Similar regionally restricted interstate developments ensued in other parts of the United States, including a particularly successful pact among southeastern states. The exclusionary concept inherent in regionally restricted pacts was viewed by some as a violation of three principal clauses of the U.S. Constitution—the commerce clause, the compact clause, and the equal protection clause.

In 1985, a landmark decision by the Supreme Court in *Northeast Bancorp, Inc.* v. *Board of Governors of the Federal Reserve System* resolved these objections in favor of regional reciprocal statutes. This case arose when Citicorp, a New York bank holding company, and two Connecticut banking institutions opposed the FRB's approval of two interstate acquisitions between Massachusetts and Connecticut banking firms. The acquisitions were based on the Massachusetts and Connecticut regional reciprocal statutes.

The Supreme Court's decision removed the uncertainties surrounding regionally restricted banking statutes and triggered a wave of regional activity. Following closely upon New England's lead, a southeastern banking region had already begun to gel in 1984, when the key states of Florida, Georgia,

# FIGURE 18-2 Interstate Banking as of January 1, 1989

New Hampshire
CT, ME, MA, RI, VT

New Hampshire
CT, ME, MA, RI, VT

Rhode Island*
CT, ME, NH, RI, VI

Connecticut
MA, ME, NH, RI, VI

New Jersey +
DE, PA

Delaware *
MD, NJ, OH, PA, DC

Maryland
AL, DE, FL, GA, KY, LA
NC, PA, SC, VA, WV, DC

District of Columbia*

Maine*

Vermont ▲
CT, NH, ME,
MA, RI

New York +

Pennsylvania +
DE, KY, MD,
OH, WV, DC

Virginia +
AL, FL, GA, KY,
LA, MD, NC, SC,
TN, WV, DC

North Carolina
AL, FL, GA, KY, LA, MD,
SC, TN, VA, WV, DC

West Virginia +
AL, GA, IL,
IN, LA, MD,
MO, NC, PA,
SC, TN, VA,
WI

South Carolina
AL, FL, GA, KY,
LA, MD, NC,
SC, TN, VA,
DC

Florida
AL, GA,
LA, MD,
NC, SC,
TN, VA,
WV, DC

Michigan +
IL, IN, WI

Ohio +
IN, PA, WI,
DE

Kentucky +
AL, GA, IL, IN,
LA, MD, MO, PA,
SC, VA, WV

Georgia
AL, FL, GA, KY,
LA, MD, NC,
SC, TN, VA,
DC

Indiana ▲
IL, KY, MI,
OH, WI,
WV

Tennessee
AL, FL, GA, KY, LA, MD,
MO, MS, NC, SC, VA, WV

Alabama
TL, GA, KY,
LA, MD, MS,
NC, SC, TN,
VA, WV, DC

Wisconsin
IL, IN, KY,
MI, MN,
OH

Illinois ▲
IL, KY, MI,
MO, WI

Missouri
IL, KY,
OK, TN

Mississippi
AL, LA, TN

Minnesota
WI

Iowa

Arkansas

Louisiana +
AL, FL, GA,
MO, MS,
NC, SC,
TN, VA

North Dakota

South Dakota

Nebraska

Kansas

Oklahoma*

Texas*

Montana

Wyoming*

Colorado

New Mexico

Washington*
CA, OR

Oregon ▲
AK, AZ, CA, HI,
ID, NV, UT, WA

Idaho*

Utah*

Arizona*

Nevada*

California ▲
AK, AZ, NV,
ID, OR, TX,
UT, WA

Hawaii

Alaska*

* LEGEND

+ Unrestricted, National Interstate Banking

Reciprocal National Interstate Banking

The following additional states may enter under this legislation: Alaska, Arizona, Idaho, Kentucky, Louisiana, Maine, Michigan, Nevada, New Jersey, New York, Oklahoma, Ohio, Rhode Island, Texas, Utah, Washington, West Virginia, Wyoming, and District of Columbia

▲ National Trigger to be effective after January 1, 1989

SOURCE: Unpublished listing from Board of Governors of the Federal Reserve System.

and North Carolina passed regional reciprocal statutes. These states' statutes generally framed a region of about 13 southeastern states plus the District of Columbia and established a model for ensuing legislation in the other affected states. By 1985, other significant regional interstate legislation and acquisitions had occurred rapidly in Illinois, Indiana, Michigan, and Ohio.

The regional pacts stimulated a flurry of interstate mergers that created a number of superregional bank holding companies, including Bank One (Ohio), Bank of New England (Massachusetts), First Union Corp. (North Carolina), NCNB Corp. (North Carolina), and SunTrust Banks Inc. (Georgia). Such institutions appeared to fulfill one of the intended results of regional consolidations—that is, to create institutions with the capacity to compete with New York and California banks in preparation for the arrival of full interstate banking. Indeed, by 1987, the strength of several of the superregionals was such that their market valuations exceeded those of many New York money center banking institutions. Figure 18-2 summarizes the scope of interstate banking permitted by each state as of January 1, 1989.

More changes occurred in the early 1990s as regional restrictions became nullified by "national triggers" in many states' interstate statutes. In 1992, national interstate banking was permitted by law in Michigan, New Jersey, Ohio, Pennsylvania, Texas, Florida, Illinois, Indiana, and Massachusetts. In addition, the money center state of California joined New York with interstate legislation, leaving both of them free to venture into previously restricted markets. However, with the exception of Citicorp, Morgan Guaranty, and Bankers Trust, New York money center banks appear to have little advantage, in market capitalization terms, over several of the emerging superregionals. Moreover, Morgan Guaranty and Bankers Trust are fundamentally positioned as wholesale banking companies with little interest in acquiring traditional banks.

The interstate banking phenomena that marked the decade of the 1980s produced some important trends that should continue through the mid-1990s.

1. Small banks have not played a major role in interstate activity. Consolidation among small banks will continue in viable intrastate markets.
2. Several superregional banking organizations are emerging in both the Northeast (Pennsylvania through New England and exclusive of New York City firms) and the Southeast. Several of these firms boasted assets of more than $50 billion in early 1993.
3. Atlanta increasingly will be recognized as the seat of the powerful southeastern regional pact. It will join New York, Los Angeles, and Chicago as a major financial center.
4. Even with interstate banking, many large banking organizations probably will not venture far out of their regions.
5. High bank stock prices in 1992 and 1993 encouraged acquisitions.

## PREMIUMS PAID IN BANK MERGERS

In bank merger and acquisition transactions, a buyer evaluates the target bank (the bank to be acquired) and determines the returns expected from such factors as the target balance sheet, service delivery and revenue capacity, personnel, market position, and vitality of the market served. Then, summing together the values implied in all of these factors, the buyer sets the price or premium it is willing to pay for the target bank. The seller is not passive in this process. The rational behavior for the seller is to try to position the target bank most attractively. The net result of the give-and-take between buyers and sellers has been merger prices that recently have exceeded two times book value—a value that implies assumptions by the buyer of truly heroic future earnings and growth rates.

Instinctively, and mathematically for that matter, such premiums appear to be excessive. One possibility is that sellers bargain more purposefully than buyers. Selling banks are almost always smaller, and probably more of them are closely held by owners who participate in the negotiations. If so, their greater self-interest in the outcome might motivate tougher bargaining positions on their part.

## Determining the Value of a Potential Merger

With such large premiums being paid, it is important to understand how to determine the value of a target bank. Two steps should precede the valuation itself. First, the acquiring bank should determine its acquisition goals and priorities. The goals, to be ranked in order of importance, might include maximizing shareholder wealth, maximizing profits, minimizing risk, increasing management prestige, achieving growth rate targets, entering new markets, and achieving economies of scale. The ranked goals should be consistent with the bank's overall corporate objectives. Second, the acquiring bank or bank holding company should carefully evaluate its own performance. This self-assessment enhances the ability of the acquiring bank to set objectives and permits flexibility in terms of what the management considers to be important aspects of the preacquisition posture.

There are several methods that might be used in the valuation of the prospective bank. Conceptually, the market values of the acquiring and target banks should be used to establish an exchange ratio. There might be a 15 to 25 percent premium over the relative market values in recognition of the extra value of acquiring control, possible synergies, entry into a new market, and so forth. While this method seems conceptually appropriate, it is very unusual to find a merger in which both stocks are widely traded.

Other methods commonly used to develop a range of values and exchange ratios that compare an acquiring bank, without the proposed acquisition, and a target bank include book value comparisons, price–earnings comparisons, and earnings comparisons (past and predicted). These methods are, however, conceptually weak.

Two methods seem to be the most appropriate valuation techniques. The first method is to revalue the assets and liabilities of the target bank. On the asset side, securities are valued at their current market prices and loans are revalued at an estimated market price reflecting both credit risk and interest rate risk. Other assets are also revalued at estimated market values. On the liability side, longer-term CDs and capital notes are valued at estimated market prices. The resulting revalued liabilities are subtracted from the revalued assets to give an adjusted equity value that should approximate a realistic market value for the target bank. The acquiring bank may have to go through the same evaluation process for itself if its stock is not actively traded. The acquisition should be completed based on the relative adjusted equity values of the two parties, with a small premium usually accruing to the seller because the acquiring bank is gaining intangibles (entry into a new market, control, etc.). The difficulty of this method is in estimating values for many of the target bank's assets and liabilities.

The second method is to consider the acquisition of a bank as an investment decision. This method assumes that pricing a bank is no different from pricing any other investment. The expected return on the present value of the cash flows from the investment is compared with the desired return of the acquiring bank. The acquiring bank must determine whether the expected return justifies the risk of the investment.

There are three key variables to consider when using this investment approach: (1) the cash flows expected from the acquisition, (2) the terminal value of the acquisition (usually at the time cash flows become too hard to estimate), and (3) the acceptable rate of return. Measuring these three variables is difficult, and the acquiring and target banks often have different estimates. The size and timing of future income and dividend streams are difficult to measure. (The trick is to project the acquired bank's contribution to the consolidated bank's future cash flows.) Although the target bank's past earnings are a guide to what the future may bring, more efficient use of the target bank's resources could generate even larger cash flows. The terminal value is usually a very rough estimate based on book value at the future time or expected earnings times some average price–earnings multiple. The rate of return used as the discount rate is estimated by what the acquiring bank must pay to attract more capital.

By discounting the expected future cash flows and terminal value to their present values, using the required rate of return, the acquiring and target banks can determine a price that can be justified in economic terms. Prospective sellers can estimate the value of the bank, assuming no change in ownership, and prospective buyers can estimate the value based on the cash flow they expect as the new owners. Since most buyers believe they can do more with an acquisition than the current owners, there is generally a gap between the two values. Ideally, the gap should serve as the negotiating range.

In practice, unfortunately, a seller frequently focuses on the merger market value, which is often much higher than the amount that can be justified in economic terms. At this point, either the deal falls through (even though the offer exceeds the current value of the bank to its shareholders) or the acquiring bank pays the price necessary to complete the transaction and then earns a lower rate of return than required in view of the risk.

In an example from Robert Bullington and Arnold Jensen (see Table 18-5),

## TABLE 18-5  Investment Valuation of a Bank

| Year | Beginning Book Value | Net Income at 18% | Earnings Retained at 10% | Cash Flow Available | Present Value at 15% |
|------|---------------------|-------------------|--------------------------|---------------------|----------------------|
| 1 | $100.00 | $18.00 | $10.00 | $ 8.00 | $6.96 |
| 2 | 110.00 | 19.80 | 11.00 | 8.80 | 6.65 |
| 3 | 121.00 | 21.80 | 12.10 | 9.70 | 6.38 |
| 4 | 133.10 | 24.00 | 13.30 | 10.70 | 6.12 |
| 5 | 146.40 | 26.40 | 14.60 | 11.80 | 5.86 |
| 6 | 161.00 | 29.00 | 16.10 | 12.90 | 5.57 |
| 7 | 177.10 | 31.90 | 17.70 | 14.20 | 5.33 |
| 8 | 194.80 | 35.10 | 19.50 | 15.60 | 5.10 |
| 9 | 214.20 | 38.60 | 21.40 | 17.20 | 4.88 |
| 10 | 235.70 | 42.40 | 23.60 | 18.80 | 4.64 |
| 11 | 259.30 | | | | |
| | | | | | $57.59 |

Add the present value of the bank's book value at the end of year 10:
$259.30 × 0.247 (present value factor)                     +64.05

$121.64

SOURCE: Robert A. Bullington and Arnold E. Jensen, "Pricing a Bank," *Bankers Magazine* (May/June 1981), pp. 94–98.

the target bank is expected to earn 18 percent on its book equity for 10 years, which is 3 percent above the acquiring bank's required rate of return. After 10 years, the return will decline to the rate required. Further, assets are expected to grow at a rate of 10 percent per year. Given these assumptions, the bank is worth approximately 122 percent of book value. Bullington and Jensen calculated that if the same bank can earn 20 percent on equity for 10 years, the justifiable premium would increase to 37 percent of book value. (Even if the bank earns 20 percent for 10 years and grows at 20 percent per year instead of 10 percent, the premium increases to only 57 percent of today's book value.)[5]

Using this method, past premiums, which averaged over twice the book value, often seem hard to justify. One reason could be that a number of non-quantifiable factors influence prices significantly and positively. A second reason could be that the acquiring bank assumes that the target bank will earn exceptional returns and will benefit from exceptional growth over a long period of time. A third reason could be that the market has valued the acquiring bank's stock too high, and the acquiring bank is really not paying as high a premium as it seems. Finally, strong demand for a limited supply of acquirable banks may inflate the premiums beyond economic justification.

[5]Robert A. Bullington and Arnold E. Jensen, "Pricing a Bank," *Bankers Magazine* (May/June, 1981), pp. 94–98.

Each of these reasons has some validity in explaining the high premiums in some merger situations. Nevertheless, many mergers and acquisitions have taken place at values that cannot be economically justified. Even if exceptional returns, growth, and synergies should materialize, the acquiring bank has often given all of the anticipated benefits to the seller while taking all of the risk that results will match the acquirer's high expectations. Banks should be able to justify acquisitions economically (recognizing nonquantifiable factors realistically); if they cannot, then they should examine other options.

## What Buyers Pay For

In bank merger and acquisition transactions, buyers view a target bank as they would any other investment: Targets are a set of present-value-generating activities.[6] Buyers gather information that enables them to form expectations regarding the size and timing of future cash flows as well as appropriate discount rates. Usually a buyer believes that the economic value of a target bank is being only partly achieved under existing management. The buyer expects to gain by exploiting management expertise, untapped revenue enhancements, operating synergies, and strategic value.

Typically, a buyer has more human resources and can use them to manage the combined entity more efficiently. Actually, there is a managerial expertise premium because large acquiring banks can transfer their more highly developed skills to smaller acquirees.

Revenue enhancements arise from blending the product menus of acquiring and target banks to generate new sales. With the best of the available products, the flow of increased sales volume through a bigger delivery system is expected to produce larger cash flows.

Operating synergies occur because of economies of scale and/or economies of scope that result from a merger. *Economies of scale* are invoked when nonoperational expenses are reduced by eliminating some senior managers, excess data processing capacity, and redundant marketing. Moreover, there is recent evidence of economies of "superscale" that arise from the greater ability of large banks to invest in technology. Technological change, it seems, has a positive economies-of-scale bias that provides large banks with a competitive edge. *Economies of scope*, defined as the complementary production of multiple products using a common resource base, also produce certain benefits, such as graphic diversification, convenience, and image enhancement.

Any buyer's view of value is a distinctly private one. It is based on buyer-specific resources and skills in building earnings within its own stratagem. Sellers, on the other hand, adopt their own view. Their frame of reference for value is some market-comparable price based on many merger and acquisition transactions in a broader market. The bidder in a merger negotiation must

---

[6]This discussion is based on Donald G. Simonson, "Do Bank Sellers Play Better Poker?" *United States Banker* (January 1988), pp. 11–12.

**TABLE 18-6   The Attributes Buyers Pay for in Merger and Acquisition Transactions**

| | Direction of Relationship | |
|---|---|---|
| Attribute | Expected | Test Result |
| 1. Return on equity, 4-year average | + | − |
| 2. Capital–asset ratio[a] | − | − |
| 3. Loans–earning assets ratio[a] | + | + |
| 4. Investments over 5 years to total assets[a] | + | + |
| 5. Loan charge-offs to earning assets | + | + |
| 6. Assets of acquirer to assets of acquired[a] | + | + |
| 7. Market concentration index | + | − |
| 8. Market share of core deposits | + | + |
| 9. Banking capacity in market per capita | − | − |
| 10. Cash portion of sales price | − | − |
| 11. Interstate deal? (Yes or no)[a] | + | + |

[a]Results for this attribute were statistically significant, that is, acquiring banks are most likely to pay for these attributes.

SOURCE: Adapted from Robert Rogowski and Donald Simonson, "Bank Merger Pricing Premiums and Interstate Bidding," in *Bank Mergers: Current Issues and Perspectives* (Chicago: Kleiver Press, 1989), p. 137.

ascertain whether the target bank is worth the market-comparable valuation chosen by the seller.

Robert Rogowski and Donald Simonson studied a group of 137 completed acquisitions in order to determine the role played by different attributes of selling banks in setting merger premiums. The attributes they investigated included the targets' historical operating results (including the contemporary balance sheet), market factors, the mix of securities and cash exchanged in the sale, and the influence of interstate bidding. Table 18-6 lists the attributes that were tested, the direction of the expected relationship between each attribute and the price–book ratio, and the direction of the relationship that was actually indicated in the statistical results.[7]

Recent earnings, in terms of the last four years' return on equity, was a positive factor in merger premiums, although, surprisingly, the relationship was not very significant in a statistical sense. In the cases studied, buyers apparently did not always pay for past earnings. Where capital is concerned, on the other hand, a statistically significant negative premium associated with higher levels of capital for the target bank seemed logical. Buyers saw no reason to pay for marginal book capital. A caution is due here, though, because there is an arithmetic connection that automatically links capital to price–book values; obviously higher capital is reflected directly in the denominator of the price–book ratio and must reduce the latter. Still, the results probably concur with the likelihood that buyers will not pay for extra book capital.

[7]Robert Rogowski and Donald Simonson, "Bank Merger Pricing Premiums and Interstate Bidding," in *Bank Mergers: Current Issues and Perspectives* (Chicago: Kleiver Press, 1989).

Loans on a target bank's balance sheet add significant value. Banks with large amounts of loans appear to attract buyers who are motivated by access to a fresh loan source. Another significant attribute over the last decade studied was the amount of long-maturity bonds held. Because the period was one of falling interest rates, most long-term bonds carried premiums that were not reflected in book capital. Any aggregate premium of this sort should be at least equal to the gains possible from liquidating the bonds.

A target's current loan charge-offs also tend to increase the merger premium. One explanation is that charge-offs indicate a properly conservative accounting policy and, moreover, might suggest that the target bank has purged itself of bad loans. Another crucial variable, the ratio of acquirer bank assets to acquired bank assets, also explained a significant merger premium. This result suggests that size differential is a good proxy for the buyer's perceived ability to upgrade the target bank's technology and to provide a more diverse product menu.

Market factors for this example appear to be rather weak. Concentration in a target bank's market (the widely used Herfindahl index), in theory, should permit monopolistic pricing and make entry by a buyer more attractive. Tests of the market-oriented attributes of market share and of the banking capacity in place confirmed expectations of a positive and negative pricing relationship, respectively. The statistical properties, however, showed these two relationships to be extremely weak if they do exist.

The method of purchase seemingly also affects the acquisition prices paid. The larger the stock portion of an offer to buy (a stock-for-stock deal), the higher the price. A buyer's offer of stock appears to indicate that the acquiring bank does not believe, at the very least, that its stock is undervalued and quite likely believes that it is overvalued. Apparently sellers hold out for a more favorable stock exchange ratio and a "higher" price (in stock price terms). Consistent with this assumption, when more cash (less stock) is in the offer, the price tends to be lower.

The role of interstate bidding provided additional important information. When an interstate transaction was consummated—that is, when the acquiring bank and the target bank were from different states—a significant premium was paid. It was estimated that, on average, an interstate acquisition produced a premium of about one-quarter of book value more than an intrastate acquisition.

## Discussion Questions

1. Has the number of newly chartered banks been greater than the number of banks that have been closed? Why or why not?
2. Why has the number of bank mergers and acquisitions been growing in recent years? What are the implications of this trend for the banking industry?
3. Discuss what the regulatory agencies evaluate before approving a merger or acquisition. Has regulatory approval been a hindrance to recent mergers?

4. Do acquiring banks tend to pay substantial premiums for acquired banks? Explain why or why not.

5. Discuss the advantages and disadvantages of the following two bank valuation techniques:

   a. Revaluation of assets and liabilities.

   b. Present value of expected cash flows.

6. Evaluate the various options which may be used for dealing with the acquisition of failed banks.

7. Do you believe Congress will approve interstate banking by 1996? Give your reasons why or why not.

# CHAPTER 19

# International Banking*

Up to this point, this book has covered the many facets of management of commercial banks within the U.S. economy and financial system. The reasons for confining our analysis to the problems of domestic bank financial management are simple. Most U.S. banks have little involvement with international banking and international financial management. Moreover, the import–export sector represents a modest share of the U.S. economy compared with its share in most other economies of the world.

But the view that bankers in the United States are insulated from international financial markets is shortsighted. The international perspective of U.S. money center banks is radically different from the insulated view; these banks depend significantly on the international dimension of their operations. Eurodollar funds have had a profound influence on the liquidity of the entire U.S. banking system for many years. Even small banks have investment opportunities in foreign financial instruments, including Eurodollar deposits and loan participations.

This chapter covers most other aspects of international bank management: (1) a profile of the organizational forms used to conduct international banking; (2) the foreign exchange market; (3) the Eurocurrency markets, especially the Eurodollar market; (4) the financial management of a bank or bank affiliate in a foreign setting; and (5) a review of international lending activities of U.S. banks. The chapter ends with a brief discussion of U.S. use of foreign financing and of foreign banks in the United States.

*The sections on Lending to Developing Countries, Impact of Increasing U.S. Dependency on Foreign Financing, and Foreign Banks in the U.S. were written by Sumon Mazumdar, Faculty of Management, McGill University, Montreal, Canada.

## PROFILE OF ORGANIZATIONAL FORMS

International banking, for our purposes, refers to banking transactions that involve one or more parties located outside of the United States. Competition in international banking includes commercial banks that are active international lenders from their headquarters country, or via branches, from foreign locations. Some banks operate investment banking subsidiaries overseas that underwrite foreign bonds and other foreign securities. International banking has changed from a highly segmented industry in which individual geographic markets were controlled by just a few banks to a highly integrated capital market in which potential competition for major financing includes hundreds of banks.

There are probably several motives for banks to expand internationally. The most straightforward motive is for banks to follow their customers when they conduct operations abroad. As American corporations aggressively extended their operations overseas during the 1960s and 1970s, their U.S. banks followed. Similarly, Japanese and European banks followed their domestic corporate customers to foreign markets in the 1970s. Partly, this motivation is a defensive one, because banks want to maintain and consolidate relationships with domestic corporate customers that develop needs for international banking services. Also, banks feel they know more about their customers' particular needs and can serve them more efficiently than local banks, even in a foreign setting.

Banks also expand internationally to diversify their bases. They invest in loan products whose characteristics differ from those of domestic loans, and the pattern of demand for foreign loans may offset fluctuations in domestic loan demand and thus help to stabilize overall bank earnings.

## TYPES OF ORGANIZATION

Banks can adopt several legal forms of organization in entering the international banking arena. The most important of these are listed in the following paragraphs, with comments describing the scope of their activities.[1]

### Edge Act and Agreement Corporations

Edge Act and Agreement corporations permit banks to conduct international banking business in the United States from offices in financial centers outside their home states. For example, a Dallas bank might open Edge subsidiaries in cities that are important to international trade, such as New York, Miami, and Los Angeles. Edge corporations are chartered under Section 25(a) of the Federal Reserve Act and are not subject to state banking laws. The state-chartered and supervised counterparts to Edge corporations are called *Agree-*

---

[1]Parts of this section are adapted from Richard K. Abrams, "Regional Banks and International Banking," *Economic Review*, Federal Reserve Bank of Kansas City (November 1980), pp. 3–14.

*ment corporations* because they must agree to the same restrictions that apply to Edge Act subsidiaries. Edges, but not Agreements, must be capitalized to at least $2 million. Edge corporations conduct international operations abroad through their domestic offices. This permits local corporations to conduct their international financial activities through local banks.

### Shell Branches and Representative Offices

Shell branches are overseas offices established to participate in the Eurocurrency markets for booking Eurodollar liabilities for the bank or for issuing foreign loans. They are located in financially obscure places, such as the Bahamas, where they operate virtually free of local taxes; they are not interested in conducting local business. Representative offices are the foreign counterpart to domestic loan production offices. They are minimally staffed, do not take deposits, and essentially do the groundwork on loans made to local borrowers from the U.S. headquarters.

### Full-Service Foreign Branches

The full-service foreign branch is an extension of the headquarters bank. As such, it can conduct all the same banking activities as the home bank. Some foreign branches, particularly those in London, manage books (balance sheets) that run into many billions of dollars. Branches conduct a wholesale banking business based to a large extent on deposits purchased from the network of international banks known as the *interbank market*. They normally are unable to develop a local base of core deposits. Foreign branches are prohibited in some countries, including Canada and Mexico. In some other countries, branches are not established because they are not safe due to the risk of expropriation.

### Merchant Banks

Foreign branches of U.S. banks have a far narrower range of activities than the banks of most other nations, particularly Great Britain, as a result of Glass-Steagall prohibitions on investment banking. Several U.S. money center banks have established investment banking subsidiaries to compete with the merchant banking activities of British banks. British merchant banks are permitted to specialize in investment banking activities such as underwriting stock and bond issues, tailoring mergers and acquisitions, advising customers on portfolio management, and a host of nonlending financial activities. Although they desire this kind of business within the branch proper, U.S. banks are content to segregate it in a separate, nonbanking subsidiary because they feel that merchant banking requires substantially different types of personnel, described as *deal makers*, from commercial banking, where personnel are somewhat more procedure oriented. The investment banking subsidiary may also manage loan syndications, although this activity typically is centered in a department within the branch.[2]

### Consortium Banks

Some U.S. banks have joined with banks from other nations to form consortium banks. These banks conduct many of the activities of investment banking subsidiaries. Consortia of large banks can provide a huge capacity for managing and funding syndicated loans. Consortia of smaller banks give the participating banks opportunities to participate in middle-sized Eurofinancings that otherwise would far exceed their individual capacities.

### International Banking Facilities

An important new organizational form is the international banking facility (IBF). IBFs were authorized in December 1981 by the Federal Reserve to permit banks and other depository institutions to conduct international banking activities from within the United States on a basis similar to that enjoyed by foreign branches and subsidiaries of U.S. banks. In permitting IBFs, the Fed's basic intent was to return such activity to the United States.

IBFs provide banks with a relatively unregulated environment similar to the environment their foreign branches and subsidiaries find overseas. Deposits from foreigners have no reserve requirements and no interest rate limitations. Also, IBFs are exempt from deposit insurance coverage and the assessments associated with insurance. These exemptions permit IBFs to compete more effectively for foreign deposits and to offer competitive loan rates to foreigners. Deposits must be at least $100,000, and loans can be made only to foreigners.

Most of an IBF's assets consist of loans to foreign-based businesses and foreign governments and central banks for use outside the United States. Their funds come from placements by institutions in the international interbank network and from foreign governments and official institutions.

## FOREIGN EXCHANGE MARKET

*Foreign exchange* refers to the use of one currency to purchase another—for example, the use of U.S. dollars ($) to purchase British pounds (£). Foreign exchange is conducted in a worldwide chain of markets, the largest of which are probably London, Frankfurt, Zurich, and New York, in that order. There are many important but somewhat smaller centers for foreign exchange, such as Hong Kong, Paris, Singapore, and Tokyo. There are no physical marketplaces for foreign exchange as there are for stocks, such as the New York Stock Exchange, or financial futures, such as the Chicago Board of Trade. As

---

[2]Loan syndications are discussed in Chapter 14.

a result, it is difficult to know what volume of foreign exchange occurs in each of the markets.

The markets are linked together into one global market by a highly sophisticated communications network. The major participants in the market have telephone and telequote lines open to the major trading center 24 hours each day. Price movements occur simultaneously in the major centers as economic and financial news breaks. Thus, the markets are quite efficient, absorbing and transmitting information immediately as it is generated.

## Spot Market and Forward Market

In reality, there are two types of foreign exchange markets, which are distinguished by the dimension of time. The first type, the *spot market*, deals in currencies bought and sold for essentially immediate settlement on delivery. Actually, spot market transactions are cleared (payment is made) on the so-called *value date*, normally two days after the buyer and seller agree on the transaction. The other type of foreign exchange market is the *forward market*. In the forward market, currencies are bought and sold for future delivery at an agreed-upon exchange rate. Again, the value date is the date of delivery. Contracts or agreements in the forward market can have maturities that range from several days to months and even years.

The structure of foreign exchange markets is illustrated in Figure 19-1. The ultimate (nonbank) buyers and sellers of currencies typically conduct their transactions through their local bank or primary bank of account. The customer's bank interacts with upstream correspondent banks or directly with money center banks. These banks, in turn, clear their foreign transactions through the network of international banks (the interbank market) or through foreign exchange brokers.

Several special exchanges offer institutionalized access to the forward market. As shown in Figure 19-1, these include the International Money Market in Chicago and the London International Financial Futures Exchange. The two exchanges deal in rigidly standardized versions of forward contracts called *futures contracts*. In the early 1980s, the Philadelphia Stock Exchange introduced another means of trading in foreign exchange in the form of *currency options*. Participants in this market can purchase contingent claims on foreign currencies that need be exercised only if movements in exchange rates make it profitable to do so. Banks are the largest factor in the currency futures and options exchanges. However, individuals can access these markets, mostly for hedging purposes, with or without a bank's assistance.

## Foreign Exchange Quotations

Exchange rates can be stated either in units of foreign currency to the home currency, the *direct rate*, or in units of the home currency to the foreign currency, the *indirect rate*. The direct rate in U.S. dollars for, say, German

---

**FIGURE 19-1    Structure of Foreign Exchange Markets**

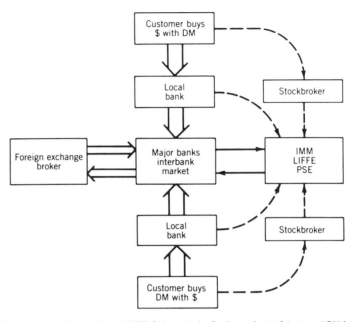

NOTE: The International Money Market (IMM) Chicago trades foreign exchange futures and DM futures options.
The London International Financial Futures Exchange (LIFFE) trades foreign exchange futures.
The Philadelphia Stock Exchange (PSE) trades foreign currency options.

---

deutsche marks (DM) is expressed as

$$\frac{DM1.70}{\$}$$

The numerator (DM) is known as the *unit of account*, and the denominator ($) is the unit of the currency being priced.

One can use the concept of a *cross rate* to derive the exchange rate between two currencies based on the prices of each currency in terms of a third currency. For example, to get the price of deutsche marks in terms of British pounds (£):

Given:      DM1.70/$
            £0.67/$

Simply solve:   $\dfrac{1.70/\$}{0.67/\$}$ = DM2.54/£

Forward exchange rates are expressed in terms of *swap rates* or forward *discount* or *premium*. Swap rates are stated in terms of the points of discount or premium from the spot rate. For example, if the three-month forward rate for deutsche marks was DM1.65/$ and the spot rate was DM1.70/$, then the dollar discount would be DM0.05, or five points. A forward discount or premium is expressed in terms of percent per annum when the forward price is lower or higher, respectively, than the spot price. The forward dollar discount from the foregoing example can be calculated as follows:

$$\text{Forward discount (or premium)} = \frac{\text{Forward} - \text{Spot}}{\text{Spot}}$$

$$\times \frac{12}{\text{Number of months forward}}$$

$$= \frac{1.65 - 1.70}{1.70} \times \frac{12}{3}$$

$$= -0.1176, \text{ or } 11.76\% \text{ per annum discount}$$

Several needs motivate the exchange of currencies. One obvious need is that of individuals and corporations who have overseas activities. For example, individuals purchase the indigenous currency to buy goods and services when visiting a foreign land; domestic corporations buy foreign currencies to acquire foreign products. Corporations hedge their commitments to future transactions by taking positions in the forward market. For example, suppose that a U.S. importer is obligated to pay pounds sterling for British goods six months in the future and the spot rate is £0.67/$. The risk is that pounds will appreciate relative to dollars, thereby increasing the importer's dollar cost. The importer can hedge against this risk by buying pounds in the forward market at, say, £0.65/$ for delivery in six months. The importer locks in the cost of pounds, which, although more expensive than the current spot rate (£0.65/$ instead of £0.67/$), insures against a precipitous movement in the exchange rate to, say, £0.55/$. The exchanges for overseas activities and hedge transactions by individuals and corporations are called *outright exchanges*. Contrary to common impressions, outright exchanges make up only a minuscule share of the foreign exchange market.

In truth, the dominant foreign exchange activity is spot trading and swaps between banks. Interbank trading entails major banks taking speculative positions and hedges in various currencies. In this activity, banks churn huge volumes of currencies for the purpose of adjusting their currency exposures or in the hope of making profits from short-term ripples in exchange rates. Although a large share of interbank transactions is in the spot market, a substantial volume also occurs as *swaps*. A swap is the forward-to-spot sale (purchase) of a currency coupled with a reversing forward purchase (sale) for a different value date. The size of the sale and purchase positions are the same, and both transactions take place between the same two banks; only the value dates differ. Suppose that a U.S. bank sold dollars for British pounds in the spot market in a swap against a three-month forward purchase of dollars for pounds. The net intended effect would be simply to increase the bank's exposure to the pound for a three-month period. Other financial institutions, such as investment banks and brokerage houses, are also active in swaps or forward trading.

### Interest Arbitrage

Differences in interest rates between two countries sometimes give rise to arbitrage opportunities in foreign exchange markets. *Arbitrage* refers to the riskless opportunities for profit that become available when an asset, such as currency holdings, carries different prices in two markets. For example, if the rate on three-month CDs was higher than the rate on three-month Eurodollar deposits (after adjustments for reserve requirements, FDIC insurance assessments, and other costs), arbitrageurs could profit by selling Eurodollar deposits and investing in CDs.

Interest rate arbitrage opportunities involve the concept of interest rate parity. In a perfect world, interest rates should be the same everywhere. They are not the same, of course, because of differences in inflationary expectations from currency to currency, differences in intrinsic economic growth, and non-economic effects, such as government regulations that impede the flow of capital. The tenets of interest rate parity do not hold that interest rates must be the same everywhere; rather, they imply that the differences between interest rates in a country and the rest of the world should be reflected in the relationship between spot and forward exchange rates. For example, if the one-year interest rate is 10 percent in the United States and 8 percent in the United Kingdom, the one-year forward rate for pounds sterling should be at a 2 percent premium. That is because, in effect, the opportunity cost of holding pounds is 2 percent less than that for holding dollars. In general:

| *The currency with:* | *Ought to have:* |
|---|---|
| higher interest rate | discount in forward markets |
| lower interest rate | premium in forward markets |

assuming that no other influences are expected to affect exchange rates. If interest rate differentials and the forward discount or premium are not equal (again, assuming no other effects), then interest rate arbitrage will occur. In the example given, if one-year forward pounds were at a 4 percent premium instead of the 2 percent premium signaled by the U.S.–U.K. interest rate differential, interest rate arbitrageurs would sell forward pounds against dollars.

## INTEREST RATE SWAPS

Speculators, including international banks, may conclude that interest rate differentials existing between two countries are not justified by economic conditions and that they will soon adjust. They can do swaps through the forward markets to attempt to profit from the expected adjustment in the rate differential. Suppose that one-year forward pounds reflect the present 2 percent interest rate difference between U.S. and U.K. one-year rates. Assume that the spot rate is £0.67/$ at present. Suppose, further, that a speculator believes U.S. rates will rise to 12 percent, producing a 4 percent differential. With one-year forward rates with the spot rate = 0.67/$, we have the following scenario:

| | Forward Rate | 12-Month Point Premium | Point Premium/Month |
|---|---|---|---|
| 2% premium on £ | 0.6566 | 0.0134 | 0.00112 |
| 4% premium on £ | 0.6432 | 0.0268 | 0.00223 |

If the forward market has not adjusted to the 4 percent rate differential expected by the speculator, the one-year forward rate will still be £0.6566/$, or a 2 percent premium on the spot rate. However, the speculator expects the forward market to adjust to a 4 percent differential in one-year rates, which infers a one-year forward exchange rate of £0.6432. The speculator can execute a swap by doing the following:

1. Selling forward pounds for delivery in one year.
2. Buying forward pounds to be received in one month.

Assuming that the forward markets adjust one month from now to recognize a newly expected 4 percent interest rate differential, the speculator will have a profit on the original sale of one-year (now 11-month) pounds. The value of this contract will go from £0.6566/$ to £0.6454/$, yielding a profit of £0.6566/$ − £0.6454/$ = £0.0112/$.[3]

Note that, consistent with the definition of a swap, the interest rate speculator held equal positions on the short (sell) and long (buy) sides of the market; only the value dates were different. This protects against the risk of holding a net exchange position in which, for example, the spot rate might shift for other reasons. Upon the maturity of the one-month contract, the speculator can close the original 12-month (now 11-month) position and take the profit.

## THE EUROCURRENCY MARKETS

The Eurocurrency markets involve banking units that lend and/or borrow funds denominated in a currency that is not native to the country in which the banking unit is located. The markets are comparatively unrestricted and unregu-

---

[3]The new 11-month forward rate is spot rate − point premium per month × 11 months × £0.67/$ − £0.00223/$ × 11 = £0.645/$.

lated by individual governments; therefore, they freely transcend international boundaries. The volume of Eurocurrencies in the world market is extremely large. In 1992 it consisted of over $3 trillion, measured as the gross foreign currency deposits in banks outside of the United States.[4] The markets have grown dramatically from a base of $100 billion in 1970 to their present size. The Eurodollar accounts for 75 to 80 percent of the market's total size. Belying their name, Euromarket deposits are not restricted to Eurodollars and European-based derivatives, such as Europounds, Eurofrancs, and Euromarks. Also included are non-European currency derivatives such as Japanese yen and Singapore dollars.

The Eurocurrency markets are important to U.S. banking, as evidenced by the fact that over one-half of the transactions of U.S. money center banks are conducted in the Euromarket. Operating through foreign branches and subsidiaries or through IBFs, U.S. banks accept deposits and make loans in relation to foreign entities and foreign-based U.S. customers. Eurodollar deposits can be taken free of reserve requirements and interest rate limitations. And even though money center banks and many regional banks dominate U.S. activity in the Eurodollar market, an increasing number of small banks participate in the market by investing in Eurodollar deposits. Finally, the investment banking subsidiaries of the U.S. banks (merchant banking subsidiaries) participate by underwriting Eurocurrency securities from their foreign locations, principally London.

*Eurodollars* are defined as dollar liabilities of banks (or U.S. bank foreign affiliates) located outside of the United States or of IBFs. Typically, Eurodollars are initially created when a customer of a U.S. bank shifts (i.e., wires) dollars from a U.S. bank to a foreign bank or a U.S. bank foreign affiliate. The customer, in effect, gives up a dollar deposit and gains a Eurodollar deposit.

The growth of the Eurodollar market can be traced to its universal acceptance in the financing of international trade. In this role, it replaced the British pound, which had been the world trade standard, when it was obvious that the pound had become chronically weak during the 1950s. British banks actually led the transition to dollars in the 1950s, recognizing that the financing of trade required a plentiful and strong currency. A more recent stimulus to the growth of and dominance by the Eurodollar in Eurocurrency markets originated with the rise in oil prices in the 1970s and early 1980s. With this price increase, the Organization of Petroleum Exporting Countries (OPEC) nations earned huge amounts of dollars from their oil exports. The OPEC nations deposited these funds in the Eurodollar market, where the banks of deposit loaned the funds to oil-importing nations to enable the latter to finance massive balance-of-payments deficits. The rate of growth from OPEC nations has slowed as world oil prices have stabilized; however, the Japanese invested part of their large trade overflows in the Eurodollar market in the past 10 years.

---

[4] *World Financial Markets* (New York: Morgan Guaranty Trust Co.), 1993.

# BANK FINANCIAL MANAGEMENT IN A FOREIGN ENVIRONMENT

Banks' foreign operations are conducted in two possible currency regimes. One is the Eurocurrency regime, in which the bank takes deposits and makes loans in currencies other than that of the host country. For example, a U.S. bank that manages dollars in its London branch or pounds sterling in its Brussels branch is operating in Eurocurrency markets in terms of, respectively, Eurodollars and Europounds. Alternatively, a U.S. bank might manage sterling-denominated assets and liabilities in its London branch. In this case, the bank is competing in a domestic or local-currency market.

Our discussion will focus mainly on operations in the Eurocurrency regime, where the vast majority of U.S. bank foreign operations are conducted; we will not devote much discussion to local-currency markets. Operations in Eurocurrencies are distinctly different from operations in the local currency. The Euromarket is essentially unregulated and is a true international capital market. Local currency operations, on the other hand, are controlled by the regulatory authorities of the host country.

The position of U.S. bank operations abroad is unique among large international banks because the Euromarket is dominated by the dollar or, more accurately, the Eurodollar. Thus, foreign subsidiaries of U.S. banks conduct much of their operations in their native currency, the dollar, but they do so in foreign lands. In managing their foreign banking operations in, say, Eurodollars, banks must deal with assets and liabilities whose characteristics are different from those on their domestic balance sheet. In market terminology, a bank's portfolio of Eurodollar assets and liabilities is referred to as its Eurodollar *book*.

## Eurodollar Liabilities

Bank funds in a bank's Eurodollar book are almost all fixed-rate deposits with specific maturities. The deposits usually fall in a maturity range of one week to six months, although some maturities may be as short as one day and some as long as five years. Eurodollar time deposits are mostly interbank liabilities; that is, they are placed on deposit by other banks in a network called the *interbank placement market*. Participating banks usually negotiate directly with one another in arranging for placements, although some interbank placements are arranged by brokers. Eurobankers refer to interbank placements as *redeposits*. The market for redeposits, or interbank placements, permits the participating banks to work out differences in their needs for liquidity and for matching liability maturities with asset maturities.

Eurodollar time deposits can be disadvantageous to depositors because their fixed maturities make them illiquid. As a solution to the illiquidity problem, large international banks, as well as some mid-size banks, offer negotiable Eurodollar CDs. Investors can sell their Eurodollar CDs before maturity in an active secondary market. Because of this liquidity factor, issuing banks are able to offer Eurodollar CDs at rates below LIBOR.[5] The CD market is thin, however, and Eurobanks cannot issue large volumes of CDs without putting upward pressure on the interest rate. This concern and the easy availability of time deposits from the interbank market make CDs less important than they are in U.S. domestic markets.

In addition to time deposits and CDs, Eurobanks receive funds, known as *call money*, that can be withdrawn on overnight notice. Depositors are willing to take lower rates on call money because they value its high degree of liquidity. Nevertheless, some call money is held on deposit for a while, making some portion of it an effectively long-term and cheap funding source. Foreign banks in local markets, such as U.S. bank branches in London or Paris, do not receive large amounts of call money, as much of it is in local currency deposited in locally headquartered banks.

A final category of deposit is *current accounts*, the foreign equivalent of demand deposits. Current account money is not available to nondomestic banks overseas, as this money is in native currency deposited by local firms and individuals in local institutions.

Eurodollar time deposits often carry slightly higher interest rates than comparable U.S. domestic bank deposits, despite the fact that the latter are subject to reserve requirements and insurance premiums. One reason is the fear in some cases that authorities in the country where Eurodollars are deposited might block the movement of the funds back to a foreign depositor. Also, the soundness of some foreign banks that take Eurodollar deposits is less certain than is the case for large U.S. banks. In part, this is because the disclosure of financial information on foreign banks is far less complete and regulatory examinations may be less rigorous.

### Eurodollar Assets

Just as Eurodollar deposits differ from U.S. domestic deposits, Eurodollar lending differs from U.S. bank domestic lending. Virtually all Eurodollar loans are priced at some spread over LIBOR, and the spread is typically small. Most of the loans are large wholesale credits; essentially none are retail size. Borrowers include U.S. firms that need to finance foreign activities, foreign firms that need to finance activity across their national borders, and foreign governments. Loans may be directly from one foreign banking entity to a borrower, or, as discussed elsewhere, they may be syndicated.

Eurobank loans are almost never made as fixed-rate loans. Occasionally, loans are made for terms as long as 10 years to finance capital projects, but the loan rate is reset at a regular interval, usually every 3 or 6 months. Most Eurobank loans are short term, however, and are similarly repriced on so-called rollover dates. The loan agreement is up for renewal on rollover dates, but there is no commitment to a longer term.

---

[5]LIBOR is the rate set on term Eurodollar deposits.

Other earning assets that a Eurobank usually holds include interbank placements and foreign currency bonds. The latter potentially give the bank a longer-maturity asset that might be useful for tailoring a certain interest rate exposure, depending on the bank's outlook for interest rates. Also, holding a portfolio asset denominated in a foreign currency permits the bank to manage its exposure in that currency, including taking a speculative position on exchange rates if it desires.

Most Eurobank assets and liabilities are renewed and repriced at fixed short-term intervals, unlike U.S. domestic balance sheets, for which many deposit and loan maturities and repricings are uncertain. As a result, Eurobankers have better opportunities than U.S. domestic bankers to control the matching (or mismatching) of asset–liability maturities. Eurobankers can attempt to improve upon the narrow spread available on matched funding by carefully managing a mismatch. For example, funding six-month loans with three-month deposits in lieu of six-month deposits might prove more profitable, given a positively sloped yield curve where long-term rates are greater than short-term rates. Such a borrow-short, lend-long mismatch is called a *short book* in Euromarket terminology, and it clearly incurs interest rate risk. The risk of a short book is that short-term rates might rise by the time the three-month deposit is rolled over. Bankers who mismatch Eurodollar asset and liability maturities or repricing dates clearly must try to "read" the U.S. interest rate outlook with great skill and care, because Eurodollar rates move with U.S. domestic rates. Compared with U.S. domestic banks, Eurobanks have developed a greater propensity for such mismatches, and they seem to have fine-tuned their skills at running a mismatched book.

## INTERNATIONAL LENDING BY U.S. BANKS

Foreign lending by the domestic and foreign offices of U.S. banks grew very rapidly throughout the 1970s until 1982. In August 1982, economic problems in Mexico led its government to request a suspension of payments on its loans from international banks. Soon thereafter several other governments followed suit. At that time, U.S. banks accounted for about half of all international bank loans outstanding worldwide. The extraordinary penetration of foreign loan markets was, of course, stimulated by profit opportunities, and the impact on the earnings of the largest money center banks was extremely important. International earnings frequently accounted for over half of the total annual earnings of the largest money center banks. For Citicorp in New York City, international earnings provided over 80 percent of the bank's earnings over a period of several years.

Foreign lending by banks takes place through both their domestic offices and their foreign branches. Before 1960, most foreign credits were extended by U.S. banks to foreigners and to U.S. companies that were investing in their own foreign operations; in many ways, U.S. banks were a unique source of capital in a capital-short world.

**TABLE 19-1 Latin Nations' Debt Profiles**

| Country | Total External Debt (billions) | Debt Service Ratio (%) | Population (millions) |
|---|---|---|---|
| Argentina | $ 54 | 52 | 28 |
| Brazil | 113 | 32 | 141 |
| Colombia | 13 | 19 | 27 |
| Mexico | 103 | 40 | 80 |
| Panama | 3.8 | NA | 2.3 |
| Peru | 14 | 10 | 18.7 |
| Uruguay | 5 | 24 | 2.9 |
| Venezuela | 33 | 33 | 17 |

SOURCE: Reuters Electronic Financial Reports, June 1988.

## Lending to Developing Countries

During the 1970s, U.S. banks rapidly expanded their lending to the developing countries of the world. They were especially active in recycling dollars that flowed to oil-exporting nations after the extremely high increases in world oil prices that occurred in 1973–1974 and 1979–1980. With these increases, the OPEC nations rapidly built up their deposits with U.S. banks. Conversely, the developing countries of Africa, Asia, and Latin America borrowed huge sums from U.S. banks to cover their balance-of-payments pressures resulting from the increased cost of oil and rising imports.

U.S. bank loans to developing countries other than those in OPEC grew at rates of 15 to 30 percent per year from 1976 to 1981.[6] This growth rate declined to about 5 percent in 1983 following the payments crisis that led to a restructuring of loans to Mexico, Argentina, Brazil, Chile, Nigeria, and several other developing nations during 1982 and 1983. U.S. banks and their regulatory authorities became alarmed over economic deterioration in developing countries, and the banks moved to reduce sharply their lending to these countries. Much of the new lending during 1983–1988 was to enable countries to reschedule their debts to international banks.[7] Table 19-1 summarizes eight of the latter nations' debt profiles.

The debt restructuring had a significant impact on debtors and creditors alike. Developing countries, in an attempt to pay off their foreign debt, implemented austerity programs and tried to generate forced savings by reducing

[6]Harry S. Terrell, "Bank Lending to Developing Countries: Recent Developments and Some Considerations for the Future," *Federal Reserve Bulletin* (October 1984), pp. 755–763.

[7]Jay H. Newman, "LDC Debt: The Secondary Market, the Banks, and New Investments in the Developing Countries," *Columbia Journal of World Business* (Fall 1986), pp. 112–114.

imports. These steps had the adverse effect of reducing in-country investment from 24.3 percent of GNP in 1977–1982 to 18.5 percent of GNP in 1983–1985, hampering economic growth. Moreover, expansionary monetary policies aimed at ameliorating the debt burden aggravated the inflationary tendencies in the developing countries' economies.

To deal with the deteriorating quality of their Third World loans, commercial lenders were forced to increase their reserve provisions. In addition, new lending to Third World nations was curtailed. U.S. banks' loans to these countries fell sharply, from $107 billion in 1983 to $90.5 billion by February 1985.[8] The ratio of Third World loans to bank capital at the largest U.S. money center banks declined significantly, from 230 percent in 1982 to 160 percent in February 1987.

Reform measures were implemented to rectify banks' Third World debt exposure. These measures consist broadly of relief and market reforms. Relief measures, on a case-by-case basis, were undertaken to forgive or reschedule existing developing-country debt obligations. The International Monetary Fund (IMF) initiated such an approach in 1982 to assist Mexico by lending it about $3.9 billion to stimulate its economy. Commercial banks lent Mexico an additional $5 billion and rescheduled its existing debt obligations. In return, the Mexican government agreed to pursue more austere monetary and fiscal policies. Similar schemes were undertaken for other debtor countries in the late 1980s and early 1990s. Several countries, for example Mexico, Chile, and Argentina, have had some success in improving their economies and ability to service debt in the early 1990s.

Market reforms include debt–equity swaps (the exchange of banks' creditor positions in certain developing countries for an equity stake in physical assets of those countries), privatization of government enterprise, improvement in government efficiency, and direct investment. Some of these measures attempt to promote voluntary lending and to help the debtor countries achieve sustained economic growth. One proposal aimed at promoting growth was the 1985 program suggested by the U.S. Secretary of the Treasury, James Baker. The Baker Plan took a long-run perspective on the debt crisis and suggested structural changes in the domestic economies of the debtor nations. Such changes included trade liberalization, elimination of subsidies, tax reform, development of domestic capital markets, and other deregulatory measures to stimulate growth.

In this context, it is interesting to note the evolution of the secondary market in developing-country debt and the increasing support of debt–equity swaps and other financial innovations. At the initial stages of the debt crisis, commercial banks began trading loans to hedge against the country-risk exposure of their international loan portfolios. As debt capitalization schemes gained momentum, a cash market in developing-country loans began to grow, which by 1985 was about $2 to $3 billion in size. In 1985, Chile began a formal

---

[8]Patricia Vertmin and Villian Cooper, *The Latin American Debt Crisis and U.S. Trade* (Washington, D.C.: Congressional Research Service, Library of Congress), January 14, 1987.

scheme to convert its outstanding foreign debt into Chilean equity holdings. Ecuador, Mexico, and the Philippines instituted similar programs in 1986, followed by Argentina, Brazil, Venezuela, Uruguay, and others in 1987. Such schemes accelerated the growth of the secondary loan market, which was $5 to $6 billion in 1986 and was estimated to be nearly $10 to $12 billion in 1987. The most optimistic projections hold that by the mid-1990s, as much as 25 percent of the outstanding debt of developing countries may be retired by swapping the debt for private or public enterprises in these countries. But a large fraction of these holdings would be in the hands of foreigners, and it remains to be seen if developing-country governments are prepared to pave the path of economic growth at the cost of nationalist interests. Thus, the debt problem is not merely a financial one but a political issue as well.[9]

Country risk will continue to plague large banks that were active in extending loans to poor, non-oil-exporting countries, as those nations continue to run deficits in their current accounts. How have U.S. banks and the international financial system coped with the problem of developing-country external debt?

Several developments have reduced U.S. bank exposure. For one thing, the new external financing needs of developing countries have been held to levels that are well below those of 1976–1982 as these countries' growths hold at more modest rates and as industrialized economies grow and increase imports from developing economies. Second, banks have further reduced their loans to developing countries and such official bodies as the IMF and the Bank for International Settlements will increase their participation. Finally, banks with large developing-country exposure have written down these loans.

## Impact of Increasing U.S. Dependency on Foreign Financing

Although not a specific problem for banks, the increasing dependency of the United States on foreign financing will have a large impact on international banking. This impact is best understood in terms of two related developments: the growth of U.S. debt to foreigners and foreign-owned banks' presence in the United States.

From the beginning of this century until the 1970s, Americans consistently invested their savings abroad to reap the rewards of higher returns. But in the 1980s there was a dramatic reversal in the direction of capital flows. U.S. borrowing began to escalate at a pace so rapid that in less than a decade, by the late 1980s, U.S. debt had far exceeded the peak creditor position that America had enjoyed in the past. This sudden swing in the capital account was due not merely to increased purchases of U.S. assets by foreigners, but also to a marked decline in U.S. investment abroad. Other industrial nations, including several major U.S. creditors, had capital surpluses over the same

[9]Rudiger Dornbusch, "Our LDC Debt," *NBER Summary Report: The United States in the World Economy*, ed. by Martin Feldstein (New Haven, Conn.: National Bureau of Economic Research, 1987), pp. 23–27.

period. It is interesting to note that the aggregate balance-of-payments deficit for the developing countries over the same period appears to be rather trivial in scale compared with the U.S. deficits.

Several reasons have been suggested to explain this phenomenon. Imperfections in global capital markets, such as large transactions costs and capital controls by foreign governments, have been reduced over the years, making foreign borrowing easier for Americans. Further, the relatively low probability of default risk in the United States compared with such risk in politically unstable regions such as Latin America may have prompted the flight of capital from those parts of the world to the United States. The significant differential between Eurodollar and U.S. interest rates during 1979–1982 suggests that foreigners perceived investment in the United States to be less risky and, in consequence, were willing to accept lower returns for their U.S. asset holdings. Following August 1982, however, the differential reduced rapidly, contradicting the view of the United States as a safe haven for investments.

Perhaps the most important cause of capital flowing into the United States in recent years may be the large relative increase in U.S. interest rates after 1980 compared with foreign interest rates. U.S. rates rose above foreign rates in the early 1980s and reached a differential of about 3 percent by 1987. These higher U.S. rates undoubtedly provided an incentive for much of the marked increase in capital inflows into this country.

The rise in U.S. interest rates probably occurred for several reasons. First, a huge increase in the federal budget deficit probably drove up interest rates. Throughout the 1970s the deficit averaged less than 2 percent of GNP. Following the 1981–1983 federal tax cuts, however, the deficit grew to about 5 percent of GNP. Second, total net saving—the net private saving left over after funding the government deficit—also fell by 3 percent of GNP as of 1985, compounding the deficit problem. Finally, dollar outflows accelerated as the U.S. trade deficit widened dramatically during most of the 1980s. U.S. consumer spending boomed during the period, and American tastes switched noticeably to foreign durable goods.

The resulting shortage in the domestic supply of U.S. funds was overcome by higher U.S. interest rates, which attracted foreign financial investment. At the same time, Japan, Germany, and the United Kingdom reduced their budget deficits, enabling them to lend more to the United States.[10]

The sharp depreciation of the dollar in the late 1980s and early 1990s reduced the trade deficit to about $80 billion. Nevertheless the U.S. net debt position was expected to reach about $900 billion by the end of 1992. Significantly, the obligations of interest and principal payments on this debt will have to be met in the 1990s and beyond. Clearly, then, considering this debt service burden, the trade balance deficit must improve by considerably more than $80 billion in order to reduce the current account deficit to zero and to avoid further increases in the U.S. external debt.

---

[10] Jeffrey A. Frankel, "International Capital Flows and Domestic Economic Policies," *NBER Summary Report: The United States in the World Economy*, pp. 33–38.

The U.S. external debt alarms many observers, because it may subject the American economy to terms that might be dictated by its foreign creditors. If foreign confidence in the dollar continues to fall, there could be a renewed flight of capital from the United States, driving up interest rates, crowding out domestic investment, and decreasing economic growth.

### Foreign Banks in the United States

International banking activities have surged as a result of the globalization of world capital markets, ongoing financial innovations, and the growth of multinational corporations. Banks have expanded their business abroad in an effort to meet the needs of their existing domestic corporate customers as these customers have expanded their domain of operations abroad. This is true for U.S. banks as well as for the banking community throughout the industrial world.

Foreign banking activity in the United States has escalated rapidly in recent years. There were 1,014 foreign bank offices in the United States in 1987 (435 of them located in New York) compared with 975 in 1986. These banks have aggressively expanded their business loan portfolios, buying substantial loans from American banks. Thus, business loans at the U.S. branch offices of foreign banks grew five times faster than at U.S.-owned banks in 1987, with 77 percent of such growth being appropriated by the Japanese banks in this country. The four largest foreign banks in the United States in 1987, with assets totaling $107.6 billion in their U.S. offices, were Japanese. In terms of business loan portfolio size alone, however, the Hongkong and Shanghai Banking Corporation was the largest, with $7.5 billion in outstanding loans in 1987. The United Kingdom is the second largest foreign banking entity in the United States after the Japanese. Twelve British banks had 47 offices in the United States in 1987, with $13.9 billion in outstanding loans, or 10 percent of all business loans held by foreign banks in the United States.[11] Japan's dominance of foreign banking in the United States may be attributed to several factors. The Japanese Economic Institute of America has listed some of the key factors:

1. Liberalization of the Japanese capital market.
2. The growth of the Japanese economy and the Japanese balance-of-payments surplus.
3. The increased number of Japanese corporations in the United States.
4. The additional opportunities, such as trust banking, that the U.S. banking system offers Japanese banks that are not available to them at home.

It is well known that many foreign banks in the United States operate with regulatory capital requirements of as little as one-half of the requirements for

---

[11] L. Michael Cacace, "Foreign Banks in U.S. Boost Loan Purchases," *American Banker* (February 23, 1988), pp. 7–8.

U.S. banks. These banks can afford to earn less on loans and other earning assets and still provide a competitive return to their shareholders. Therefore, the increasing presence of foreign banks in the United States can be expected to lower profitability in U.S. banking and induce U.S. banks to take greater risks.

## SUMMARY

Our survey of international banking covered topics and issues that form the background for managing banks with foreign activities. Banks must choose from a variety of organizational forms when they undertake international banking business. International banking can involve a formal organizational presence overseas; on the other hand, it might involve only a special organization within the United States. An overseas organization can be complex, including full wholesale service branches, or simple, such as a shell or representative office, as business activity requires. Alternatively international banking business can be conducted with only a domestic presence through organizational forms that exempt the bank from certain U.S. domestic banking restraints.

International banking requires that participants deal in multiple currencies whose value relationships are constantly changing. These value relationships are settled continuously in the foreign exchange market. Banks use hedging and swap techniques to manage exposure to their currency positions. They also assist customers in reducing the foreign exchange risk associated with international trade.

The context of most international banking activity is the Eurocurrency markets. International banks conduct most of their foreign operations in nonnative currencies. The market is essentially unregulated and represents a huge, efficient resource in international finance. Eurodollars are the dominant unit of account of most bank assets and liabilities held in nonnative currencies.

The assets and liabilities of a Eurodollar book have different characteristics from those of a U.S. domestic banking operation. Most Eurodollar assets and liabilities are repriced at regular and short intervals. The concept of core funds has little meaning to Eurobanks, most of whose funds are comprised of time money of specific duration, much of which is placed by other banks. An interbank placement market allows banks to resolve their problems of maturity matching of liabilities against assets.

International lending by U.S. banks went through two important phases in the 1970s and 1980s. Until 1982, lending to the developing countries was increasing rapidly. These nations were under pressure to finance large deficits in their balance of payments. These deficits stemmed from soaring costs of energy and excessive imports used to fuel a high rate of economic growth. Beginning in 1982, a series of defaults by developing nations imperiled the large international loan portfolios of most U.S. money center banks. The outlook for these loans remains uncertain in the early 1990s as steps are taken to impose more economic discipline on the large debtor nations.

The dramatic net capital inflows into the United States in the last several years have meant that the rest of the world owns more U.S. financial and real assets than the United States owns of their financial and real assets. Foreign banks have followed this capital inflow and have dramatically increased their presence in the U.S. banking market.

## Discussion Questions

1. Distinguish between the motives U.S. banks have for establishing
   a. Edge corporations.
   b. Shell branches.
   c. Full-service foreign branches.
   d. Merchant banking subsidiaries.
   What primary types of business are conducted by each of these institutions?
2. Edge corporations and IBFs are both formed within the borders of the United States. What are the primary differences between these two entities?
3. Foreign exchange can be traded in spot, forward, futures, or option contracts. Define each type of contract and state how it differs from the others.
4. From the following, compute the dollar price of deutsche marks:
   $1.25/£
   DM3.00/£
   What is the *direct rate* for dollars in terms of pounds?
5. Three-month forward pounds are selling at a 5 percent per annum discount to spot dollars. The spot rate is £0.8/$. Compute the forward rate.
6. Critique the following statement: "Traders can use the forward market to guard against deterioration in the spot exchange rate."
7. Define and cite the motivation for interbank currency swaps.
8. Suppose that six-month interest rates in Germany and the United States are 6 percent and 7 percent, respectively. The spot exchange rate is DM3.50/$. If interest rate parity holds, what should be the six-month forward rate?
9. Define Eurocurrency markets. Why are Eurocurrency markets dominated by Eurodollars?
10. Most U.S. banks operating overseas conduct most of their activities in Eurocurrencies rather than in the local currency. Discuss some difficulties a foreign branch of a U.S. bank might have operating in a local currency.
11. Discuss differences in management of the interest rate exposure of the balance sheet in Eurobanks versus domestic banks.
12. Discuss the impact of increasing U.S. dependency on foreign financing in the later 1980s. Is that dependency changing in the 1990s?

# CHAPTER 20

# Long-Range Planning
# for Future Performance

In the past, bank managers tended to spend most of their time dealing with short-term and often nonintegrated problems, such as attracting loans, measuring seasonal deposit movements, and estimating the liquidity of the securities portfolio. Since the banking environment was relatively static, most banks did not have much incentive to look beyond the annual budget or profit plan. This static environment no longer exists, however. Continuing rapid changes in economic, technological, regulatory, and competitive factors have made and seem likely to continue to make banks subject to ongoing dynamic change. It can now be concluded that successful bank managers cannot sit back and let the future happen to them; they must implement longer-term plans that will help them to succeed in a dynamic future environment while incorporating short-run operating decisions into their long-run plans.

## MANAGING RETURN–RISK TRADE-OFFS
## TO MAXIMIZE OWNERS' POSITION

Once a bank has decided what markets it wants to serve—that is, what the bank wants to be—it must make policy-level decisions about its return targets and the risks it is willing to take to achieve these targets. These return–risk trade-offs should be made so as to maximize the value of the bank to its owners.

### Measuring Returns and Risks

The primary measures of returns and risks were introduced in Chapter 3, and more sophisticated measures were discussed in subsequent chapters. The purpose here is to summarize the beginning measures a bank may use. Readers interested in greater detail on measures should review the relevant chapters.

The return-on-equity model provides the primary return measures. The first return measure is the interest margin in percentage terms, which is interest income minus interest expense divided by earning assets. Interest income less both interest expense and other expenses (net of other income) divided by revenues is labeled the *net margin*. This net margin times asset utilization (revenues divided by assets) equals the return on assets. When the return on assets is multiplied by the leverage multiplier (assets divided by equity), the result is the return on equity. The return on equity (net income divided by equity capital) is the most important measure of banking returns because it is influenced by how well the bank has performed on all other return categories and because it indicates whether a bank can compete for private sources of capital in the U.S. economy. (More detail on these and other return measures can be found in Chapters 2, 3, 4, and 9).

The risk measures are related to the return measures because in order to earn adequate returns, a bank must take risks. A beginning measure of the liquidity risk of a bank is approximated by comparing a proxy for the bank's liquidity needs, its deposits, with a proxy for the bank's liquidity sources, its short-term securities. Although both variables are only rough approximations—funding loans may be a major liquidity need and purchasing liabilities may be an important source of liquidity—the relationship is an indicator of many banks' liquidity risk. (More sophisticated measures of liquidity risk—for example, liquidity needs based on predicted fluctuations of loans and deposits compared with sources of liquidity or a liquidity profile of all assets and liabilities compared with the projected growth of loans and deposits—appear in Chapter 5.)

The ratio of interest-sensitive assets to interest-sensitive liabilities can be used as a first approximation of a bank's interest rate risk. Particularly in periods of wide interest rate movements, this ratio reflects the risk of lower returns. If a bank has a ratio above 1.0, the bank's returns will usually be lower if interest rates decline. A bank's returns will also be lower if the bank has a ratio below 1.0 and interest rates increase. Given the difficulty of predicting interest rates, at least some banks have concluded that the way to minimize interest rate risk is to have an interest-sensitivity ratio close to 1.0. Such a ratio may be hard for some banks to achieve and often may be reached only at the cost of lower returns on assets such as short-term securities or variable-rate loans. (More sophisticated measures of interest rate risk, such as a multiperiod interest-sensitivity profile, duration measures, and simulation, were discussed in detail in Chapter 16.)

The credit risk of a bank is often estimated by examining the relationship between the loans and either the provision of loan losses for the loan loss reserve. The credit risk in the loan portfolio may also be estimated by looking at loans classified as below average by the bank's examiners or management. Credit risk in the security portfolio may be estimated by an examination of bond ratings. (More sophisticated measures of credit risk appear in Chapters 11, 12, and 13.)

The capital risk of a bank can be measured by examining what percentage of the bank's capital risk assets are covered by its capital. The capital risk is inversely related to the leverage multiplier and, therefore, to the return on equity. When a bank chooses (assuming that this is allowed by its regulators) to take more capital risk, its leverage multiplier and return on equity, all else being equal, are higher. If the bank chooses (or is forced to choose) lower capital risk, its leverage multiplier and return on equity are lower. (More sophisticated measures of a bank's capital risk are described in Chapters 8 and 9.)

## Interrelationships between Returns and Risks

Commercial banks must take some risks in order to earn acceptable returns for their stockholders. Banks' primary final product, usable funds, must be in a form or provide utility that direct or indirect borrowers could not obtain directly from savers. For example, a bank might buy substantial amounts of short-term funds that it would lend for a longer term at a higher rate. The bank would be taking liquidity risk (the inability to meet short-term fund demands) and interest rate risk (the threat of large earning fluctuations because interest costs would change more rapidly than interest returns) in order to earn acceptable returns. The bank might take more credit risk (an increase in the probability that the borrower will be unable to pay as promised) to increase returns. Or a bank might take more capital risk (a decline in the capital cushion by which assets exceed liabilities) to leverage earnings so that the return to common stockholders is higher.

Table 20-1 summarizes the impact of increasing each of the primary risk categories on the typical earnings categories. Although it is difficult to estimate the exact path and magnitude of increasing these categories of risks, there is little doubt that the return on equity will usually be higher, other things being equal, by increasing the risk taken in any of the categories. One exception would be that the bank would take so many risks that it would have declining

---

**TABLE 20-1    The Impact of Increasing Risks on Returns**

| Return Measures | *Effect of Increasing Risks in Primary Categories* | | | |
|---|---|---|---|---|
| | **Interest Rate Risk** | **Credit Risk** | **Liquidity Risk** | **Capital Risk** |
| Interest margin | + | 0 | + | |
| Net margin | + | 0 | + | |
| Asset utilization | | + | + | |
| Return on assets | + | + | + | |
| Leverage multiplier | | | | + |
| Return on equity | + | + | + | + |

+ High probability that increased risk will increase return category.

0 Medium probability that increased risk will increase return category.

returns and possibly fail. The reverse will also usually be true; that is, if a bank decreases the risk taken in one of the risk categories, return on equity will be lower. It is essential to review the environment expected in the mid-1990s, its effects on return–risk trade-offs, and the bank's current position before deciding which categories of risk a bank should increase or decrease.

### Setting Objectives for Returns and Risks

What degree of total risks should a bank take in order to increase returns? How much of which types of risks should a bank take? The answers to these questions are difficult and not exact. For assistance, a bank can look at its own past performance and ask if it is satisfied with the returns obtained and the risks taken. Return and risk measures for similar individual banks or peer groups of banks can be compared with similar measures for the bank; however, exact answers are hard to come by. Constraints, such as the nature of a bank's market, the level of competition it faces, the areas in which it has special management expertise, and the stance of its regulators, mean that each bank has individual characteristics that affect its desired return–risk trade-offs.

The first step for bank managers is to examine how other similar individual banks and groups of banks have made their return–risk decisions. Any bank can obtain such information on other individual banks or peer groups from the FDIC, the Federal Reserve, the Comptroller of the Currency, or numerous private bank service companies. Many banks' regulatory reports include a comparison with peer-group banks. The second step is to compare a bank's performance (return and risk) measures with those of selected similar banks. Significant variances between a bank's performance measures and those of similar banks should be justified. There are many justifiable reasons for differences (different markets, different management philosophies, etc.); however, many banks may find one or several areas for improvement. The final step is to set reasonable (challenging, but attainable) objectives, given a bank's past performance, the performance of its peers, and its environment.

### Illustrating Potential Changes in Return–Risk Trade-offs

Figure 20-1 presents the changes in conceptual return–risk trade-offs that are likely to occur in coming years. The return on equity is used as the return measure on the vertical axis. The risk measure on the horizontal axis remains the same, even if the actual risk may change as the environment changes. In Figure 20-1A, under current conditions, the return on equity rises slowly then at an increasing rate, until the risk of substantial credit failures causes the return to fall. In the predicted future environment, however, returns are likely to be lower for each credit-risk level, and the point at which returns decline, even though credit risk increases, will probably occur at a lower credit risk. The primary reason for these predictions is an economic environment with moderate real growth. In certain regions, some basic industries (energy, agriculture, and real estate) are having economic problems. In addition, there is

**FIGURE 20-1    Shape of Changing Return–Risk Trade-offs. A For Credit Risk. B For Liquidity Risk. C For Interest Rate Risk. D For Capital Risk. E For the Four Risk Categories Combined.**

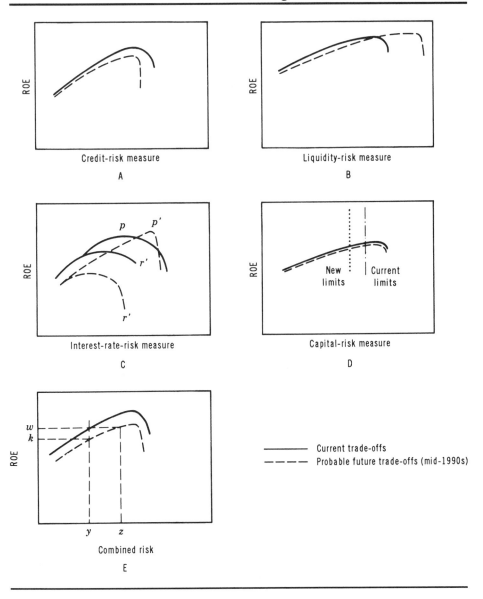

great competition among banks (nationwide banking) and between banks and nonfinancial companies. To keep returns at their current level, a bank may have to increase its credit risk.

The return–liquidity risk trade-offs appear in Figure 20-1B. Currently, the return on equity increases until the bank begins facing a serious liquidity problem. Under deregulation, when pricing will probably be more of a funds management problem than quantity, returns tend to be about the same or slightly higher for a given risk level, and the liquidity risk (measured in a consistent manner) will be higher before the bank faces a serious liquidity problem. On the other hand, questions about the safety of the banking system may lead to quality liquidity concerns. Nevertheless, this may be an area in which the risk measure and return may increase, but the bank will not be taking additional risk because of the predicted environment.

The return–interest rate risk trade-offs are traced in Figure 20-1C. In the current environment, banks are often able to increase their return on equity by taking greater interest rate risk. The increase in returns also depends on the ability of the bank to predict interest rates. As a bank increases its interest rate risk, its success or failure in increasing returns will be more and more dependent on its ability to outguess the general market on rate movements. As illustrated by line $P$ in the figure, a bank that actively manages its interest rate risk and successfully predicts interest rates may increase its return over a broader risk range. The cost of incorrect rate predictions becomes greater as interest rate risk is increased, and a bank with only average rate-prediction abilities (depicted by $r$) will find its returns declining considerably earlier. If interest rate fluctuations intensify and a narrowing interest margin occurs, as predicted for the future, management of interest rate risk becomes even more complex. The most likely scenario is that if a bank decides to take more interest rate risk to try to maintain returns, it will face a higher probability of declining returns. In other words, the cost of not predicting interest rates correctly (so that the bank stays on line $p$) may be greater (line $r$) because of the changed environment.

There will probably not be substantial changes in the return–capital risk trade-offs depicted in Figure 20-1D. By increasing capital risk, a bank will increase its leverage multiplier and resulting return on equity, for a given return on assets, about as much in the future as at present. The typical management goal seems to be to take about as much capital risk as regulators will allow (possibly allowing some flexibility for future growth). The risk weighting of assets and off–balance sheet items and leverage ratios for determining capital needs adopted by regulators will tend to restrict some banks from taking as much capital risk. The vertical lines in Figure 20-1D reflect these potential regulatory limits.

Finally, Figure 20-1E illustrates the effects on returns of the four risk measures in combination. Over most of the potential risk range, returns increase as combined risks increase. At some point, the risk of wide fluctuations in earnings, and possible failure, becomes great enough that returns may actually decline. Generally, bank management does not approach the point where the return on equity is highest because the bank needs flexibility and the return–risk line is really the mean of a probability distribution that widens as risks become higher. In the next few years, the predicted environment may cause the return–risk trade-off curve to shift downward and to the left. Returns will be lower for a given level of risk, and returns will begin declining at a lower risk level. For example, a bank taking $y$ risks to obtain $w$ return on equity would see its return on equity fall to $x$. The only way to maintain the bank's return on equity at $w$ would be for it to increase the risks it takes to $z$.

Assuming that $w$ is at or close to the minimum acceptable return level of a bank, the bank faces some difficult management decisions in the coming environment. For most banks, the same level of credit risk and interest rate risk will cause returns to fall. Some banks may be able to reverse some of this decline by increasing liquidity risk; however, because of regulatory pressures, the leverage multiplier resulting from capital risk is likely to fall slightly or, at best, remain the same. In order to keep returns at or close to their current levels, banks may have to seek higher returns by taking greater credit or interest rate risk. The actions to be taken depend heavily on the current position and the areas of management expertise of the individual bank.

## Key Steps in Making Future Return–Risk Decisions

Successful integrative bank management in the 1990s will require at least four substantive steps. The first step is to measure the return–risk trade-offs for each of the four risk categories. This step includes accurate measurement of each of the four risk categories and reasonable estimates of how increasing or reducing that risk category would affect returns. A bank cannot make rational management decisions without this information.

The second step is to evaluate honestly and accurately the bank's management and market strengths and weaknesses. For example, a bank may recognize that it has a strong commercial lending department but a weak location for consumer lending. Another bank may find that because of its location, its major market and management strength is in consumer lending. A large bank located in a financial center may have the ability and staff to predict interest rates, to conduct interest arbitrages, and so on, while a smaller rural bank's activity in these areas should probably be limited. A bank should take relatively more risks in those areas in which it has the greatest management and market strengths.

The third step is for the bank, after considering its current return–risk positions and its areas of management and market strengths, to determine its target mix of risk objectives for the environment expected in the next few years. The basic constraint on this mix is that the combined risk should produce an acceptable return on equity. For example, determinants of future credit risk include the bank's current credit risk, the effect of the future environment on its market location, and its management expertise in credit analysis. Future liquidity risk should probably depend on its current liquidity position, its ability to borrow liquidity, and possible declining liquidity needs as the bank is able to increase its control over attracting funds.

Future interest rate risk is difficult to control because a bank can be substantially constrained by its current net interest-sensitivity and duration position, and because wide future fluctuations in rates may make a given net interest-sensitivity and duration position even more risky. Nevertheless, a bank should have a target that is affected by its current interest rate risk, its managerial expertise in predicting rates, and its predictions about future rate fluctuations. If its target differs significantly from its current position, the bank can do one of three things: (1) accept that its target position is unattainable in the near future and try to live with its current position; (2) try to move rapidly toward its target by making substantial changes, such as selling most of the mortgage portfolio or making new installment loans only at variable rates; or (3) use interest rate swaps, financial futures, or options to move the bank to its targeted interest-rate-risk position.

The determinants of future capital risk include management's desire for a larger equity multiplier, the bank's current capital-risk position, and the new regulatory capital requirements. Although this is a potential area for improving bank returns, it seems likely that narrower profit margins and regulatory toughness will limit meaningful return improvement for most banks in the next few years.

The fourth and final step is to have a good risk management system. A bank should have an estimate of what will happen to its earnings, and to the value of its assets and liabilities, if interest rates rise or fall and if credit quality declines due to regional or nationwide recessions of varying severity. The estimated effects of several forms of liquidity pressures should also be simulated. In addition, for a bank with substantial international business, the estimated earnings and value effects of changing exchange rates and country risk should be simulated. With such a risk management system, a bank can make decisions regarding interest rate hedging, currency swaps, credit enhancements, and so forth if the risks of earnings or value changes are too great.

### Case Situations Illustrating Return–Risk Choices

The following situations are a few examples of how different individual banks must take different types of risks in order to obtain acceptable returns in the 1990s.

Bank A has approximately $55 billion in assets and is located in a money center city. The majority of its loans are to good-quality national corporations at very competitive rates, and its leverage multiplier exceeds 17. The new risk-based capital rules will limit this bank because of its high level of off–balance sheet items. It has a large portfolio management group that spends considerable time examining rate trends and special security opportunities. Bank A may have to extend its liquidity risk and credit risk within limits set by management and the bank's regulators. The bank's access to many markets makes liability management (funding) the bank's major source of liquidity. Some middle-market loan customers may have to be courted. If returns are still below an acceptable level, Bank A may also be justified in taking some additional interest rate risks by actively managing its interest-sensitivity position and duration gap. In spite of increasing rate fluctuations, the probability of higher returns in this area of management strength may be greater than in the competitive national loan market.

Bank B has slightly over $90 million in assets and is a community bank that emphasizes small business, agricultural, and individual loans in its community. Bank B has a larger margin and return on assets than Bank A; however, Bank B's leverage multiplier is 14, so its return on equity is only slightly above Bank A's. Bank B has slightly lower liquidity risk and capital risk than Bank A. Management believes that the effects of reregulation will include an even lower profit margin and greater interest rate risk for Bank B because more of its liabilities will be interest sensitive. Suggestions for Bank B would include (1) taking somewhat greater liquidity risk, (2) reducing interest rate risk by increasing rate sensitivity on assets or using interest rate swaps or financial futures, and (3) increasing credit risk in those areas in which the bank has a competitive advantage. Bank B probably has no business hoping to take advantage of rate movements, and it should maintain the ratio of interest-sensitive assets to interest-sensitive liabilities as close to 1.0 as possible. It should learn to measure the duration of its assets and liabilities to control value fluctuations. If the bank must take additional risks to earn an acceptable return, these risks should be taken in the areas of the bank's greatest management and market strengths.

Bank C is a regional bank that has approximately $15 billion in total assets. Its interest margin, return on assets, and return on equity have suffered in the last few years because the bank has experienced a significant decline in their loan portfolio. Bank C's management wonders what to do, particularly because the bank seems to be taking as much interest rate risk as it wants and will have substantial earnings fluctuations if its assets become less rate-sensitive and if interest rates fluctuate more in the coming environment. Advice is easy; action is difficult. For example, it is easy to say that the bank should make more variable rate commercial and consumer loans; however, there is little demand for such loans in Bank C's market. Suggestions would include an investigation of the possibilities of (1) increasing the bank's loan portfolio and credit risk by improving the bank's sales culture; (2) emphasizing liability management to meet liquidity needs; (3) making estimates of the duration of the bank's assets and liabilities; and (4) using interest rate swaps, options, or financial futures to attain the bank's desired interest sensitivity and duration position.

There are probably as many different case situations as there are banks. The primary task of a bank's managers is to measure accurately the risks the bank is currently taking to obtain returns. The managers can then make rational decisions, in light of their prediction for the future environment and their assessment of the bank's strengths and weaknesses, about which risks must be taken in order to earn acceptable returns.

## THE STRATEGIC PLANNING PROCESS

*Strategic planning* is the portion of long-range planning in which management determines what the bank will be like in the future. Strategic planning involves developing a set of objectives the bank wants to attain and the means with which to achieve these results. Although forecasting may be part of strategic planning, it is not the same as strategic planning. *Forecasting* attempts to measure the most probable course of future events, or, more typically, probability ranges of future events, based on assumptions and judgment as well as objective methods. Forecasting measures where the bank is most likely to be, not where it wants to be.

There are two other misconceptions often associated with strategic planning that managers must understand. First, strategic planning does *not* deal with future bank decisions; it deals with futurity of present decisions. The primary question facing the bank planner is not what the bank should do tomorrow, but rather what the bank should do today to achieve its objectives in an uncertain tomorrow. Second, strategic planning is *not* an attempt to eliminate or even minimize risk. Instead, strategic planning should enable the bank to choose rationally among risk-taking courses of action.

Strategic planning can probably be best achieved by answering four basic questions:

1. Where is the bank now?
2. What are the bank's objectives in the future?
3. What does management want the bank to be like in about five years?
4. How will management get to this desired position?

Although such questions at first seem trite, if they are broadly applied, they form the bases for strategic planning.

### Analysis of Past Performance

A system for analyzing past performance was introduced in Chapter 3. Many of the subsequent chapters also discussed more sophisticated measures of performance for specific areas of bank management. In addition to the formal financial measures discussed in these chapters, the bank needs to ask more general questions. What is the scope of its business? What markets is it in? Has it identified those markets on which it hopes to focus? How is it perceived by its community, by its competitors, and by its customers? What areas of strength and weakness can be identified in its organization? What provisions have been made for management succession? Answers to such questions, as well as a thorough analysis of financial performance, are the first steps in strategic planning. A bank must know where it has been and where it is before it can decide where it wants to be.

## Setting Objectives

The next step in strategic planning is to formulate a statement of the objectives the bank wants to achieve in roughly the next five years. The formulation of objectives can involve either top management alone or top management in conjunction with other bank personnel. The more involved the personnel are, the more likely the plan is to gain greater commitment by the entire bank. To be effective, the strategic plan must have a detailed implementation procedure. All management levels must be wholeheartedly committed to the plan for its implementation to be successful.

Objectives should be as definitive as possible. Objectives such as increased growth, a gain in market share, and improved efficiency are inappropriate. Objectives should be stated in terms that are quantifiable and measurable; this way, performance can be monitored. Planning may become too broad in scope, dealing with what may happen in the future rather than being specific about what management goals are and how to achieve them. Certain areas and key issues must be identified, and plans must be able to respond to these areas. Objectives should be selective and should pertain to those areas that are most relevant to management considerations. The key objective of managing risk and return so as to maximize the value of the bank to its shareholders was discussed in the preceding section. Other important areas in which to set objectives are discussed in the following sections.

**Corporate Objectives**    Corporate objectives comprise the broadest area to consider. What kind of bank do we want to be? What should our community image be? Why are we in business? Although these questions are broad in nature, they can be answered in specific terms.

**Management Development Objectives**    Areas that are weak in leadership abilities must be determined, and steps must be taken to develop expertise in these areas. If promotion and training can be accomplished from within, this should be done; if not, outside training or new experts should be investigated.

**Organizational Structure Objectives**    The number of organizational units should be in proportion to asset size and earnings capabilities. Having too few departments results in a volume too large to handle; having too many departments results in loss of efficiency due to excessive paperwork and high costs of excess personnel.

**Operational Objectives**    Increased operational efficiency can be viewed from personnel and equipment standpoints. Teller, proof, bookkeeping, new accounts, and other heavily personnel-oriented departments would benefit from review. Workload and staffing requirements must be consistent with customer service, scheduling, and output needs. Data processing and proof-transit operations should be consistent with the workload and the amount of data flow. Examples of possible problems in this area include revision of computer and data processing equipment, personnel turnover, and communications between staff and management.

**Marketing Objectives**   Marketing programs have become increasingly important in bank planning. Analysis of competition and market share can develop facts that are relevant to creating marketing objectives. Customer analysis is crucial in deciding what kinds of services can and should be offered. The marketing mix must be defined, and higher or lower levels of concentration in each area must be determined.

**Financial Objectives**   Traditional objectives of planning have centered on financial objectives. Evaluation of deposit growth, revenue growth, loan volume, and earnings growth are the key factors to consider. Responsibility may be assigned to profit areas, and measurement of results must be accurate. Economic factors and conditions will be guides to how much to expect realistically from profit areas such as the lending function.

**Capital Objectives**   The need for bank capital should be anticipated in light of the projected growth in resources and the ability of the bank to generate funds internally. The bank should spend considerable time assessing how the proposed risk-based capital system will affect the bank's asset allocation and use of off–balance sheet items as well as the impact on its future capital position.

## The Bank in the Future

After establishing its future objectives, the bank needs to determine what the bank will be like in the future if these objectives are achieved. A key concern must be the implications of the bank's future customer base. This customer base consists of businesses, governmental units, and individuals to whom the bank lends and from whom it borrows. A bank's customer base goes a long way in determining what the bank will be like.

One approach to determining what the bank will be like in the future is to start with a forecast that assumes that the bank will keep its current customer base and, given the anticipated environment, then project what the bank will be like in five years. Using assumptions about policies on the bank's return–risk trade-offs, bank management then should construct a rough pro forma balance sheet. Based on the proposed balance sheet and rate forecasts, projected income statements could also be prepared. Usually the items on the pro forma balance sheet constructed in this manner will not balance, bank returns will not be high enough, and the bank's top management will not be pleased with the results. Therefore, additional efforts must be made to restructure the bank to meet the anticipated future environment and to do better than the do-nothing forecast.

The response to this original forecast should be to ask what the bank can do or what it needs to do to get its performance to the desired level. For example, can the bank change its relative prices within its existing customer base to alter the magnitude of the funding it receives or of the loans it makes? Alternatively, the bank may seek to change its customer base. In a growth situation, the bank may want to increase the number of markets within which it operates. On the other hand, if loan demand is predicted not to grow sufficiently to justify the quantity of funds the bank forecasts it will attract, the bank may have to get out of some liability markets. Changes such as these must be run through the forecasting process to ensure that the new results come closer to the balance sheet and profit figures desired by the bank. Several repetitions of this process may be necessary before management feels comfortable with the plan and the customer base implied by the plan.

Another approach is nearly the reverse of the first. In this second approach, top management first declares where they would like the bank to be at the end of five years. Because management has chosen the plan, the bank's customer base should be as desired, the resulting balance sheet should be in balance, and the anticipated income statement should be consistent with the bank's return objectives. The second step is to determine whether this final position and the desired return figures are attainable—that is, whether the bank's current position and the expected future environment will allow such results. This step is usually achieved by putting together a forecast that assumes that the bank will change nothing but will just respond passively to the expected environment.

The focus of this approach should be to discern how much the forecasted results differ from the desired plan. If, as is likely, the proposed plan is different from the forecast, then management must go back to the drawing board to determine what changes must be made to achieve the desired position. The effort, therefore, must be one of gradually approaching the position desired by the bank. The first approach, on the other hand, involves a restructuring to arrive at the bank's desired position.

## Achieving the Desired Position

The final step in strategic planning is to convert the chosen objectives and strategies into specific assignments and responsibilities. A desirable way to accomplish this may be through a group of activities designated as action programs. *Action programs* are communicated in the bank through specific assignments that identify specific projects, assign responsibilities, identify resources required, establish steps to be taken, and set completion dates. These action programs should answer the following question: What is the bank going to do today that will enable it to meet its objectives for the future? The action programs are developed through the joint efforts of the planning committee, top management, and other managers. The board and top management review and approve the finalized action programs. As a result, commitments are made at all levels of responsibility within the organization.

One characteristic of these action plans is that they should be flexible enough to allow bank managers to consider alternative methods and courses of action to achieve the desired results. This does not mean that managers should discard proven practices and give in to change in an indiscriminate fashion; however, as the banking industry moves further into the 1990s, it must plan change and do so in a manner that will preserve the position of the banks as providers of financial services.

In addition to management direction, the establishment of action programs provides specific numbers for activities undertaken that can be used to monitor performance. The measurement of variance from plans provides the basis for a periodic review of progress toward established objectives. The essence of control for strategies is the ability to establish reasonable standards of performance expected from each department or division of the bank. Standards are derived from the sequential steps stated as part of the action programs and from targets in budgets and strategies. Performance can be measured against the standards established, and corrective action can be undertaken.

Tracking performance is difficult because the assumed environment underlying the action programs may have changed and the bank manager may have made adjustments to match the current expectations for the future environment. Sometimes organizational changes can cause difficulty, with the new manager being assigned the problems of or reaping the benefits of preceding administrators. To track performance accurately, a sophisticated, flexible accounting system is needed to keep up with all of the changes in plans. A tracking system is also needed to provide the base for a periodic review of progress. The control phase that is part of the review is based on setting standards for the sequence of steps in action programs, measuring performance against those standards, and taking corrective action to regain the planned position.

## The Weak Planning Track Record of Banks

One study indicates that in most banks the concept of long-range planning may be given a great deal of lip service but relatively little actual implementation. Richard Sapp[1] received 302 responses from a random sample selected from all insured commercial banks with assets of more than $10 million. The responses showed a strong emphasis on forward planning on a one-year basis; three-fourths of the respondents said that they prepared operating budgets covering one year or less. The other one-fourth admitted that they never planned ahead one year. When the time frame was extended to two years, the

[1]Richard W. Sapp, "Banks Look Ahead: A Survey of Bank Planning," *The Magazine of Bank Administration* (July 1980), pp. 87–88.

percentage of the banks preparing plans fell to approximately three-fifths of the respondents. However, if long-range planning is construed to mean the setting of targets on a basis beyond two years, slightly over two-thirds admitted that they did not include long-range planning in their management functions. Roughly two-fifths of the largest banks in this study—those with assets in excess of $500 million—stated that their planning process did not extend beyond a two-year time frame.

There is a strong element of irony in such figures on bank planning. Any credit officer of one of those major banks, when approached with a loan request by a commercial customer, would insist on pro forma balance sheets and income or cash flows showing the business' plans for future growth and profitability and reflecting known and projected industry conditions and trends. Yet in two out of five cases, that officer represents a major bank that does not plan beyond two years. Is it logical for banks to demand more from their customers than they expect of themselves?

## IMPROVING BANK PERFORMANCE IN A CHALLENGING PERIOD

There has been considerable discussion about the relatively poor performance of commercial banks in recent years. Only a limited number of banks have had earnings and price performance even close to those of other types of business. In spite of massive federal assistance and favorable interest rates, there were 995 bank failures in the last six years (1987–1992), and there were still 787 problem banks at the end of 1992.[2] The names of problem or failed banks, such as Penn Square Bank, SeaFirst, M Corp, Bank of New England, First National Bank of Midland, Continental Illinois Bank, First City, and First RepublicBank are better known to the public than the names of the high-performing banks.

Directors and managers of commercial banks are quick to respond that these are trying times for banks. Other financial intermediaries and even some nonfinancial firms have been allowed to sell financial products and services heretofore reserved exclusively for commercial banks. Many of these competitors are not subject to the strict regulatory requirements imposed on banks (reserves, liquidity, and capital). Competition among banks has also intensified because some aggressive banks (usually through their bank holding companies) have found ways around legally created geographic barriers and have begun competing in out-of-state markets. The product and geographic protections that banks used to enjoy are gone.

Other environmental and regulatory conditions beyond the control of bank directors and managers are equally difficult. Banks now must price their financial products and services. Most banks have also been forced into a more expensive mixture of sources of funds. If that is not enough, the Federal Re-

---

[2]*Quarterly Banking Profile* (Washington, D.C.: FDIC, 1993).

serve may be forced to allow interest rates to fluctuate fairly widely in the 1990s. Attempts to overcome fluctuating interest margins by pricing loans at floating rates have come back to haunt some banks in the form of problem loans. Technological changes that will be beneficial to banking in the long run are also proving costly to implement. And this list of challenges goes on.

While it is true that the current environment is more challenging for commercial banks, an equally important cause of the relatively poor performance of many banks has been weak management (and direction). Recognition that weak management has occurred is the first step in improving bank performance. The primary causes of the relatively poor performance of many commercial banks in recent years include large credit losses, rising costs of sources of funds, inadequate liquidity, declining business loan demand, and mismatched interest-sensitivity and duration position.

The only one of these causes we can blame partially on the banking environment is the rising cost of funds. The external factors that led to the rising costs of sources of funds came gradually—beginning in the early 1970s with the lifting of Regulation Q on time deposits of $100,000 and over—and probably should have been overcome with good planning and pricing. Well-managed banks generally had adequate lead time to price their products and services so that their interest margins were not hurt.

The other primary causes of weak bank performance were related to management performance. Bank lending practices that nearly ignored credit risk were widespread. Additional questionable practices included rapid loan growth without adequate trained personnel and documentation; concentration in one or a few industries; no verification of collateral; self-serving loans; ignoring country risk; selecting and paying loan officers strictly on the basis of their success in booking loans; and ignoring what interest rate risk would do to many of the bank's loan customers. Most of these unacceptable lending practices were approved implicitly by the bank's board and top management, who chose to pay little attention to their bank's lending practices.

Bank management's record on liquidity and interest sensitivity seems nearly as bad. How can any director or manager ignore the fact that his or her bank has practically no liquid assets and that often over one-half of the bank's funds are purchased from completely impersonal sources, such as brokerage firms (which furnish large amounts of funds from many sources for the highest-rate-paying banks), foreign banks, large companies, and foreign businesses? One or more of the following scenarios seems likely: (1) these impersonal sources of funds will demand high rates, hurting the bank's interest margin; (2) in an effort to maintain interest margins, a bank will take greater risks; and (3) as these risks become evident to these impersonal sources, such sources will withdraw their funds. If the third scenario occurs, the bank lacking any source of liquidity either fails or must be subsidized by the government.

Banks that had more rate-sensitive liabilities than rate-sensitive assets faced severely declining profits when rates rose rapidly in 1981 and 1982. Managers of most such mismatched banks swore they would never again allow their banks to be vulnerable to rate changes in either direction. Unfortunately, memories are short, and some banks again sought higher profits in the steep yield curve environment of the early 1990s by buying short-term funds and employing these funds in longer-term, higher-yielding assets. Other banks made variable-rate loans that were financed primarily by longer-term CDs. An interest rate sensitivity mismatch of significant magnitude either toward an asset- or a liability-sensitive position would seem to make the unlikely assumption that banks can outguess the market on interest rate movements. Furthermore, bankers ignored the use of duration measures, which approximate changes in the values of assets or liabilities, rather than the earnings flow changes estimated by interest-sensitivity measures.

## Essential Bank Financial Management Actions

While the environment has been and likely will continue to be tough, many well-managed banks will be more than just survivors—they will be good performers. Good management in the future will require special emphasis in five specific areas: (1) good management information systems, (2) selection of appropriate markets and products, (3) appropriate compensation of bank management for performance, (4) knowledge of modern financial instruments and techniques, and (5) appropriate financial management strategies to achieve goals.

**Good Management Information Systems**   While good information systems do not ensure good management, the lack of them ensures uninformed bank management decisions. Although success or severe problems may depend on regional economies and luck, one of the best predictors of bank performance is the adequacy of the bank's information system.

**Selection of Appropriate Markets and Products**   Most banks' strategic plans should probably start with the assumption that within a few years, only a small number of financial institutions will sell a full line of financial products and services throughout the world. These financial supermarkets will be huge and will face their own set of problems (such as intensive competition and diseconomies of scale). Most of the remaining banks need to select carefully their geographic markets and the financial products and services they want to sell in those markets. If they do this carefully in areas in which they have a competitive advantage, there is no question that they can easily outperform the financial supermarkets in selected areas.

While the selection of products and markets will depend on the bank's size, location, regional economy, and so forth, three general comments may kindle some new ideas in this area. First, most of the over 11,000 commercial banks in the United States have selected middle-sized businesses (which lack access to money and capital markets) and upper-middle-income households as their target markets. While this makes sense for each bank individually, selection by most banks means that there will be limited profitability for most banks due to the limited customer base and the increased competition. For some banks, markets ignored by other banks may prove to be a more profitable choice.

Second, in addition to any geographic or regional selection, commercial banks can choose from among a large number of relatively new financial products and services. These examples include origination and servicing of mortgages (which are then sold to other institutions); personal financial planning services; equipment leasing; brokerage of interest rate swaps for customers; data processing services; agricultural financial planning; underwriting of acceptable revenue bonds and other securities; credit union, finance company, and pension fund management consultants; sharing profits with insurance, travel, mortgage, or real estate agencies in the bank and its branches; and loan production offices. In general, financial products and services that are based on sharing revenues or profits should be emphasized whenever possible.

Third, the bank holding company offers a considerably broader spectrum of product and service choices. While holding companies need Federal Reserve approval, activities in areas such as finance companies, mortgage companies, travel agencies, leasing companies, discount brokerage firms (although these are proving not to be very profitable for most banks), and financial planning companies are generally acceptable. It is too early to generalize on other holding company–proposed alternatives, such as security underwriting firms, savings and loan associations, credit unions, life insurance companies, pension funds, and a host of other potential choices. Also, holding company activities have been used to partially overcome geographic restrictions on banks. Clearly, banks and bank holding companies have a number of alternatives from which to make product selections. The key for most banks is the appropriate selection of a few choices. Relative advantages in location and management skills are two selection criteria that banks should use.

**Appropriate Compensation**   Most bankers realize that banks can no longer get away with being the lowest-paying business in town. (Indeed, the banks that have continued to use this philosophy, which was popularized in the 1960s and 1970s, are most likely to be the banks that disappear in the 1990s.) Banks remain way behind many other financial and nonfinancial businesses in providing compensation plans that emphasize (1) keeping key managers and (2) encouraging the type of performance that owners desire. Many banks still try to emphasize position rather than pay and an orderly salary schedule by position within the bank. This is a pattern that can lead to failure.

Keeping key managers and encouraging desired performance should be the primary objectives of a bank's compensation plan. To keep key performers, a bank must pay as much as or more than other financial or nonfinancial firms. For example, should a bank wonder why its data processing system is weak if it pays its data processing manager $50,000 a year, when positions with similar responsibilities pay $80,000? Under these circumstances, most good data processing managers will not stay with the bank. Should a bank wonder why it continually loses municipal bond salespersons who are paid a $50,000 annual salary when they can earn an average of over $100,000 annually in commissions doing the same job for a brokerage firm? Banks must compensate competitively for the task performed.

The second objective, compensation to encourage the type of performance desired by bank owners, is often more difficult to achieve. For some banking positions (such as a bond salesperson) there is little, if any, conflict between the owners' desires and the level of activity or volume. Compensation plans for such positions can be based on volume or activity. For the majority of banking positions, however, there is the age-old conflict between the level (and often profitability) of the activity versus the risks taken. Owners generally believe that their return–risk objectives are achieved by maximizing the market price of the bank's common stock, but it is difficult to operationalize this objective into a compensation plan.

There are four key elements in good compensation plans for banks. First, compensation should be organized so that the bank is paying competitively for the task performed. Second, the compensation plan should be flexible enough so that managers in lower-ranked positions can get higher overall compensation than higher-ranked managers. Third, all key officers should have some of their compensation linked to the performance of the bank's stock price (stock options are the most common form used for such compensation). Finally, some managers should also have some form of performance-specific compensation that considers the level (and profitability) of the activity for which the manager is responsible and recognizes any change in risk due to this person's activities. Interestingly enough, banks that pay productive managers well need fewer managers and have lower salary and benefit expenses relative to assets, revenues, and profits. Nonperforming managers do not stay with such banks.[3]

### Knowledge of Modern Financial Instruments and Techniques
Banks should understand the potential return and risk effects of new financial instruments, such as mortgage-backed or pass-through securities (or tranches thereof), bonds with put options, zero-coupon securities, floating-rate preferred stock, and bond mutual funds. The effects of the globalization of financial markets should be understood, and the potential benefits and costs of derivative securities (such as interest rate swaps, currency swaps, options, and financial futures) should be carefully studied. New secondary markets for selling bank assets and the process of securitization of bank assets should also be understood by bank management. It is essential that these and similar financial instruments and techniques be understood if a bank is to be successful in a challenging environment.

### Appropriate Financial Management Strategies    It is not enough to
select appropriate markets and products and to pay good managers based on performance. The end result must be a bank whose financial performance

---

[3]For more specifics on incentive compensation, see James T. Brinks and A. W. Smith, Jr., "Incentive Compensation for Bank Management," *The Bankers Magazine* (March/April 1982), pp. 74–80.

(usually evaluated by market price) reflects these good financial markets and products managed appropriately by good people. A bank's market price usually reflects two basic elements—the bank's earnings multiplied by the price–earnings multiple, which tends to reflect the risks the bank has taken and its future prospects. The basic factors affecting these two elements need to be understood in order to improve bank performance.

If a bank's performance is not what the bank's owners, directors, and top management desire, what can be done? Usually the appropriate action is to increase earnings without commensurate increases in risks (although in high-risk banks, risks should be reduced without commensurate declines in earnings). Looking at earnings, however, we find that of the three controllable earnings inputs—net margin, asset utilization, and leverage—only the net margin can be strongly affected by bank management. Asset utilization and the leverage multiplier are generally already close to regulatory limits.

There are five primary areas of potential margin improvement:

1.  Interest revenue
2.  − Interest expense
3.  − <u>Provision for loan losses</u>
    = Interest margin (after provision)
4.  + Noninterest income
5.  − <u>Noninterest expense</u>
    = Net margin

Improvement in any of these key margin areas must be approached with a keen eye to the risk implications of any earnings improvement. For example, interest revenues may be improved by taking on more credit risk, interest rate risk, or liquidity risk. The essential element is to have the gain of increased earnings clearly outweigh the impact of increased risks.

There are five potential strategies that banks may want to consider to increase net margin without a commensurate increase in risks:

1. Increase interest income by taking more interest rate risk, but hedge this risk with (less costly) financial futures or interest rate swaps.
2. Systematically control interest expenses by using a pricing model to determine how much the bank can afford to pay on deposits and borrowed funds.
3. Improve control over loan losses through better risk assessment and collection policies and practices. In addition, banks with relatively large amounts of problem loans may wish to consider the sale of their weak loans (and equity in the borrower) to venture capital firms that are able to take higher risks in hopes of achieving considerably higher returns.
4. Increase noninterest income by selling more financial products and services on a fee or partial fee basis. The evaluation of new products and services should consider management expertise in the potential area, as well as the additional risk the bank would undertake.
5. Most banks need to achieve better control over noninterest expense. Lower

overall relative salary and benefits expenses can be achieved by proper compensation plans, and overhead expenses must be controlled.

Prudent financial management also means that banks should refrain from certain practices, including (1) taking higher credit risk to compensate for rising expenses; (2) taking security gains to make net income higher (at the cost of lower future earnings); (3) lengthening the loan or security portfolio, or both, without balancing interest-sensitivity changes; (4) ignoring the increasing interest sensitivity of primary sources of new funding; (5) getting into financial product and service areas in which the bank has no management expertise; and (6) thinking that larger size necessarily will lead to higher earnings.

## SUMMARY

Probably the most important decision most banks have to make in the challenging environment of the mid-1990s is how much and what types of risks the bank must take to earn a satisfactory return. Successful bank management in this period will require at least three substantive steps. First, management must measure the bank's current return–risk trade-offs for each of the four risk categories. Second, strengths and weaknesses in management talents and market position must be honestly and accurately evaluated. Third, the bank's board and top management must determine the bank's target level and mix of risks for the environment expected in the next few years. The basic constraint is that the combined risk should produce acceptable returns and the highest value for the owners' investment in the bank.

Strategic planning is necessary for achieving the desired return–risk position by providing a means to deal with change. The change in economic conditions, growth and diversification, and increased competition must be projected and dealt with effectively. If change is allowed to sneak up on management, the bank has little chance to utilize the change to any extent and will probably be overwhelmed. One warning concerning strategic planning is that it must be reassessed with some degree of regularity. Plans must be flexible enough to adapt to external or internal conditions that had not been anticipated. Knowing that change is a given element, the bank can exercise some degree of control if management is forced to think about change and its implications for the future.

Improving bank performance will be difficult in the challenging next few years. The external environment—competition, geographic and product deregulation, and so on—will continue to make good performance difficult. The biggest danger in improving bank performance, however, has been and will probably continue to be weak management. Nevertheless, well-managed commercial banks will generally have improved performance in the coming challenging period. Good management in the future will require emphasis on five specific areas: (1) good management information systems, (2) selection of appropriate markets and products, (3) appropriate compensation of bank management for performance, (4) knowledge of modern financial instruments and techniques, and (5) appropriate financial management to achieve the bank's goals.

## Discussion Questions

1. Give two concrete examples of the interrelationships between returns and risks in a commercial bank.
2. What do you think the banking environment will be like in the next year or so? How will your predictions affect future return–risk trade-offs?
3. What are the three key steps a bank should take in managing its future return–risk decision? Explain possible future return–risk choices for a bank you know (or one of the case banks).
4. Discuss each of the four basic questions that should be answered in the strategic planning process.
5. According to the authors, what were the four primary causes of banking problems in the late 1980s? Do you agree or disagree?
6. Select the market services and products you believe a bank you know (or one of the case banks) can profitably sell in the mid-1990s.
7. Develop a plan for compensating loan officers in a $500 million commercial bank. Cite problems faced in developing the compensation plan.
8. Evaluate each of the five potential financial management strategies that banks may want to consider to increase net margin without a commensurate increase in risks.

# FIRST NATIONAL BANK

Warren Hastings, president of First National Bank (FNB), was reviewing an economic forecast he had just received from the bank's New York correspondent for the year 1988. The report commented briefly on national trends in business and finance, and it contained a projection for 1988–1989 of various important series, including interest rates. Since Mr. Hastings would soon be convening the weekly meeting of his bank's Asset and Liability Committee (ALCO), he read with particular attention the opinions about future directions for market rates and economic activity. Hastings hoped the commentary would give him a somewhat clearer sense of direction and help him chair the ALCO discussion the following day. He always found the ALCO meetings difficult because so many different and often conflicting opinions and suggestions were voiced during a typical session. He assumed that this week's meeting would produce the same widely varied and sometimes confusing commentary.

## BACKGROUND

FNB was a moderate-sized regional bank in the western Mountain states, with assets totaling a little over $2 billion at year-end 1987. The bank was broadly diversified, with its loan volume about evenly divided among commercial, real estate, and consumer lending. FNB had only a modest involvement with international business, and it had made no foreign loans. The bank's financial statements appear in Exhibits 1–5.

Loan growth had been generally flat the past two years, and the bank had experienced increasing difficulties with problem credits. These were serious enough that the bank had received greater than normal scrutiny from bank examiners from the Comptroller of the Currency. Mr. Hastings was also concerned over the possibility that one of the bank credit agencies might lower its quality ratings on the bank's CDs, almost surely raising funding costs should the downrating occur.

In part because of heavy competition, particularly from local S&Ls, core deposits at FNB had not grown at the same rate as loans. Accordingly, the bank had turned to the national market for funding by placing some large CDs through brokers and other direct sources. The bank also purchased Federal funds on a regular basis from smaller banks in the region, as well as occasionally using national brokers for the same purpose.

After a long history as a locally supported and funded bank, removed from the volatility of national money markets, FNB now found itself increasingly confronted with problems of liquidity, interest sensitivity, marginal costing, transfer pricing, and other issues that in past years had been mostly the concern of larger banks. As a result, Hastings began relying more and more on discussions in the ALCO to shape his thinking on operating decisions, which had a pronounced effect on profitability.

Asset and liability management had become increasingly central to FNB's operations. In recent years, interest rates were much more volatile and hence less predictable. At the same time, bank deregulation had led directly to a greater volume of interest-bearing liabilities (the end of free deposits) and consequently to pressure on net interest margins.

The combination of greater interest rate volatility and higher cost of deposits obliged banks to manage more carefully the maturity and composition of both assets and liabilities to protect net interest margin. This increased awareness of the need to match the maturities of assets and liabilities led to a growing management view that there should normally be no gap, that is, assets and liabilities maturing in a particular time frame (say 0–90 days) should be approximately equal. On a policy exception basis, then, senior bank management could decide whether it was desirable to position the bank deliberately in a positive-gap (more interest-sensitive assets than liabilities) or a negative-gap posture (the reverse), depending on management's view of probable interest rate movements.

Many bankers, however, chose not "to bet the bank" by positioning it to either a positive or negative gap and thereby exposing themselves to losses that could be serious if interest rates moved opposite to their expectations. Effectively, then, the goal for Mr. Hastings in asset–liability management was to protect earnings by managing net interest margins, with care to maintain adequate liquidity while not taking much risk with either a large positive or negative gap in matching asset and liability maturities. To accomplish that goal, the ALCO paid particular attention to the following factors:

1. Economic conditions.
2. Interest rate projections.
3. Sources of funding.
4. Liquidity needs.
5. Volume variances (loans and deposits).
6. Interest rate sensitivity.
7. Maturity distributions of assets and liabilities.
8. Net interest margins.

It was particularly important to coordinate the ALCO decisions with other bank operating goals, especially with regard to profitability.

## MEMBERS OF THE ALCO

The weekly meeting of the ALCO brought together a cross section of the bank's operating personnel, some of whom had responsibilities that could be conflicting (e.g., the officer responsible for managing liquidity and the chief loan officer). The ALCO had specific responsibility for setting policy and procedures to coordinate maturities of assets and liabilities so that there would be no gap (or relatively little gap), positively or negatively, between the times these assets and liabilities would mature and hence be repriced.

The only time there should be a positive or negative gap in asset and liability maturities would be when the ALCO recommended to Hastings, as a matter of policy, that the bank should be placed deliberately in such a position.

The regular members of the ALCO committee were as follows:

1. President of FNB.
2. Chief commercial loan officer.
3. Chief consumer loan officer (also in charge of all branch offices).
4. Chief financial officer (accounting and control).
5. Funds management officer (responsible for monitoring and maintaining the maturity pattern of bank assets and liabilities and for monitoring the implementation of the ALCO directives).
6. Investment officer (manager of the securities portfolio).
7. Recording secretary.

As part of FNB's officer development program, Mr. Hastings also invited a few younger officers to attend each ALCO meeting. They were encouraged to participate in the discussions, even though their experience in banking and economics was limited.

Mr. Hastings chaired the ALCO meetings and consequently was responsible for their final decisions. He well understood that there was no single correct answer to the questions reviewed by the committee. Hastings found it helpful to encourage complete, frank, and occasionally heated debate on the agenda topics. There often was strong disagreement, but all participants realized that there was nothing personal in the financial and economic issues discussed.

The agenda for the next weekly ALCO meeting is summarized here:

| Topic | Discussant |
| --- | --- |
| 1. Economic and interest rate outlook | President |
| 2. Interest-sensitivity report and gap position | Chief financial officer |
| 3. Investment portfolio strategies | Investment officer |
| 4. Liquidity | Consumer banking officer |
| 5. Funding strategies | Funds management officer |
| 6. Funding cost for fixed-rate loans | Chief commercial lending officer |

## THE MEETING

The meeting began with Mr. Hastings summarizing the near-term economic outlook based on his reading of various reports and commentaries by national and regional bank economists. (See Exhibit 6 for the outlook that Mr. Hastings generally agreed with, supplied by FNB's principal correspondent bank.)

The chief financial officer then presented his interest-sensitivity report, commenting that FNB had a moderate liability-sensitive position (negative gap). He argued that in the economic environment discussed earlier, this moderate negative gap was "just right for us." He noted that if rates declined, the bank's net interest margin and profitability would increase. If interest rates should rise, however, he concluded that loan demand would probably be strong; hence, lending rates would strengthen and the bank could offset higher deposit costs with greater loan interest income. In his mind, therefore, the present negative-gap position was both justified and appropriate for FNB. His opinion, however, sparked considerable discussion and some strong disagreement.

For example, one officer argued that FNB was probably far more liability sensitive than the report suggested. If interest rates started to rise, she observed, the prime rate on loans would inevitably lag behind higher deposit rates because of competition and perhaps from the political pressures that operate to slow rising interest rates, especially during a presidential election year. If this occurred, the bank's cost of funds would rise rapidly and net interest margins would suffer.

Another more subtle argument was raised: Most commercial demand deposits are, in effect, interest sensitive (even though no actual interest is paid on them) because they are maintained to compensate for bank services provided, the "payment" based on an earnings credit rate. The argument was made that when interest rates rise, lower deposit balances are needed to pay for the same services; hence, excess commercial demand deposit balances would run out of the bank, requiring replacement with other deposits, such as Federal funds or CDs. Another officer immediately commented that describing non-interest-bearing demand deposits as interest sensitive was a "crazy idea." There then ensued a very spirited

discussion about whether FNB should have *any* negative gap for any reason, even if some economists were forecasting a pattern of declining interest rates through the first two quarters of 1988.

The investment officer also pointed out that there were some large blocks of U.S. Treasury securities maturing in the current and following months. These securities had been purchased five years earlier, when interest rates were much higher. To protect the bank's income, he strongly favored a decision to reinvest the proceeds from these securities in like issues of at least equal maturity, if not longer. The chief financial officer strongly objected, in part because of his concern about FNB's negative gap. He was seconded in his opposition to reestablishing the position in five-year (or longer) U.S. Treasury securities by the funds management officer, who was concerned about FNB's actual and potential liquidity requirements.

The chief commercial loan officer was frequently critical of decisions to invest bank assets in longer-term securities. He was convinced that the money could be placed in prime rate loans that return a higher effective yield—100 to 200 basis points better, he believed. There then developed considerable disagreement on the probable direction and magnitude of interest rate changes during the balance of 1988. The investment officer firmly believed that interest rates would continue to decline throughout the year. This would make bonds particularly attractive as investments, since a higher interest rate would be locked in by committing now, plus the opportunity for higher bond prices if interest rates did indeed decline. The chief loan officer argued forcefully that "banks are in the lending business" and that the real key to bank profitability was good-quality loans, not bonds. "A bank should make most of its money on its loan portfolio, not in its bond portfolio," he argued.

For the past several months, the funds management officer had been expressing growing concern about FNB's liquidity position. Loans had been growing a little faster than core deposits. To meet its funding needs, the bank had accepted an increasing volume of funds in the national market by using large-denomination CDs placed through brokers, primarily in the 30–60-day cate-

gory. There was concern about the ability to renew these CDs continually at attractive market
rates, especially if there was any change in FNB's
credit rating by independent credit agencies, such
as Keefe, Bruyette, and Woods. Mr. Hastings was
particularly concerned about a lowered credit
rating, since he believed FNB's recent financial
performance was somewhat marginal for its present rating.

The funds manager suggested a switch from
the shorter (and hence more vulnerable) CDs to
maturities ranging from six months to two years.
Proceeds could then be invested in Federal funds
sold and Eurodollar deposits to offset the cost of
these funds. He particularly emphasized the fact
that FNB's liquid asset ratios were below those
of its peer group; hence, this strategy would improve apparent liquidity and help reestablish balance sheet strength. The criticism was immediately raised that such actions would produce a
"negative yield," that is, the proposed CD purchases would carry an interest rate higher than
the one that would be earned from the sale of
Federal funds and Eurodollar deposits. Given already existing profit pressures, several persons
were openly scornful of such action, prompting
the funds manager to comment, "I'm sorry, but
liquidity does have a price!"

A bold alternative strategy was proposed. The
consumer banking officer suggested that FNB
pay higher rates on individual money market accounts. She noted that S&Ls in the area were
paying 50 to 100 basis points more than FNB,
which was resulting, in her opinion, in loss of deposit market share. Her rather pungent comment
was, "Why acquire more hot money to protect
yourself against hot money, and do it at a loss,
only to gross up the balance sheet for ostensible
liquidity purposes?" Moreover, both the commercial and consumer loan officers, who were evaluated in large part by their ability to book loans,
were concerned that FNB might have to reduce
loan growth because of funding pressures. They
argued, therefore, that liquidity concerns were
overstated in any case and that there was extra
liquidity in the loan portfolio because of steady
loan runoff from maturing credits plus the ability
to sell participations in loans to other institutions.
The loan officers also commented that some of
the peer group banks did not have as much loan

demand and hence would clearly appear more
liquid, but with presumably less profit potential
for shareholders.

Toward the end of the meeting, Mr. Hastings
asked the funds manager to outline his strategy
for the month ahead, which would still be subject
to adjustment based on the ALCO's final conclusions. The funds manager then summarized his
estimates of cash flow based on projected net
loan growth, investment runoff, and likely normal
deposit changes. He then reported on deposit
liabilities that would be needed to balance funds
needs.

Mr. Hastings decided not to prolong the
ALCO discussions further, saying that he would
make the final decisions after studying the issues
raised in the meeting.

Before the group adjourned, however, there
was one final policy issue on the agenda. The commercial loan officer stated that he was losing
fixed-rate loan business to competitors who
were undercutting him on interest rate quotations. His department was being charged an apparently high rate for fixed-cost money because
the internal rate set by the funds manager was
the full marginal cost of these funds. The bank
used a matched-maturity marginal cost of funds.
For example, for a five-year, fixed-rate loan, the
commercial loan officer would be charged the
then current rate for five-year U.S. government
securities plus 80 basis points, which is the premium the bank pays over the U.S. government's
cost of funds in that particular category.

The concern, rather vigorously expressed by
the chief loan officer, was that he was being
charged the full marginal cost of funds but that
in actual fact the funds management officer was
"short-funding" the loan with lower-cost, short-
maturity funds. To prove his point, he looked
at the interest-sensitivity report, which clearly
showed that the bank was short-funded or liability sensitive. He said, "If someone benefits from
these lower-cost funds, why shouldn't it be the
loan officer, whose work generates the majority
of bank profits?" The chief financial officer, who
had designed and implemented the matched-
maturity funding system, argued: "You can't have
everyone going around designing his or her gap
program for bank assets and liabilities. It may look
okay when interest rates are low, but we could

get ourselves into a real earnings squeeze if interest rates rose." In a somewhat testy response, the commercial loan officer asked why the funds manager could "gap" the bank, but he could not—and the loan officers earned most of the bank's profit! A very spirited discussion ensued.

Mr. Hastings concluded that it was time to adjourn the meeting, promising to consider the issues raised and report his conclusions at the regular executive committee scheduled for the following afternoon.

## QUESTIONS TO BE ANSWERED

After the secretary had typed up her notes of the meeting, Hastings reviewed them, noting the following questions that required an opinion or decision:

1. Should FNB be negatively gapped now, given the economic forecast information at hand?

2. What practical events might materially change the forecast?

3. What should the investment officer do about the $40 million in securities maturing in the next 60 days?

4. Should the bank make a conscious effort to increase its liquidity now, even if that might negatively impact profits?

5. Should a new, more competitive strategy be introduced to pay higher interest rates for money market accounts?

6. Should the bank adopt a more conservative strategy in purchasing deposits in terms of mix, source, and maturity?

7. Specifically, did the matched-maturity cost of funds approach in pricing loans really make sense, especially if, as he believed, it was causing FNB to lose some lending business?

---

## EXHIBIT I   First National Bank—Balance Sheets (dollars in thousands)

|  | December 31, 1987 | December 31, 1986 |
|---|---|---|
| **Assets** | | |
| Cash and due from banks | $ 462,827 | $ 605,712 |
| Interest-bearing deposits with banks | 177,005 | 82,000 |
| Investment securities: | | |
| U.S. Treasury | 245,437 | 105,238 |
| U.S. government agencies | 1,384 | 46,955 |
| States and political subdivisions | 202,410 | 269,870 |
| Other investment securities | 6,288 | 6,207 |
| Total investment securities | 455,519 | 428,270 |
| Trading account securities | 30,472 | 57,795 |
| Federal funds sold and securities purchased under agreements to resell | 227,484 | 161,340 |
| Loans | 1,347,234 | 1,397,482 |
| Lease financing | 34,849 | 42,111 |
| Less: allowance for possible losses | 28,328 | 19,919 |
| Net loans and lease financing | 1,353,755 | 1,419,674 |
| Foreclosed real estate | 5,710 | 6,503 |
| Premises and equipment | 76,907 | 60,116 |
| Customers' liability on acceptances outstanding | 1,834 | 768 |
| Other assets | 66,298 | 96,528 |
| Total assets | $2,857,811 | $2,918,706 |

**EXHIBIT I** (continued)

| | December 31, 1987 | December 31, 1986 |
|---|---|---|
| **Liabilities and Shareholders' Equity** | | |
| Deposits: | | |
| Demand, without interest | $ 780,167 | $ 884,205 |
| Checking with interest | 113,224 | 65,962 |
| Regular savings | 39,566 | 35,400 |
| Money market | 339,362 | 307,658 |
| CDs over $100,000 | 500,938 | 601,778 |
| Other time deposits | 106,184 | 105,568 |
| Foreign time deposits | 92,741 | 61,372 |
| Total deposits | 1,972,182 | 2,081,943 |
| Federal funds purchased and securities sold under repurchase agreements | 577,322 | 519,179 |
| Liabilities for borrowed money | 83,822 | 59,567 |
| Mortgage indebtedness | –0– | –0– |
| Accrued income taxes payable | 19,123 | 19,110 |
| Acceptances outstanding | 1,834 | 768 |
| Other liabilities | 32,232 | 79,027 |
| Total liabilities | 2,686,515 | 2,759,594 |
| Subordinated notes | 7,000 | 7,000 |
| Shareholders' equity: | | |
| Common stock, $10 par value: 1,325,000 shares | | |
| Authorized & 1,156,000 shares outstanding at Dec. 31 | 11,560 | 11,560 |
| Surplus | 34,468 | 34,468 |
| Undivided profits | 118,268 | 106,084 |
| Total shareholders' equity | 164,296 | 152,112 |
| Total liabilities and shareholders' equity | $2,857,811 | $2,918,706 |

**EXHIBIT 2    First National Bank—Income Statements for Years Ending December 31 (dollars in thousands)**

| | 1987 | 1986 |
|---|---|---|
| **Interest Income** | | |
| Interest on deposits with banks | $ 7,326 | $ 5,030 |
| Interest and fees on loans | 139,243 | 167,665 |
| Interest on investment securities | | |
| U.S. Treasury | 13,048 | 12,225 |
| U.S. government agencies | 2,969 | 4,846 |
| States and political subdivisions | 17,775 | 13,366 |
| Other investment securities | 317 | (755) |
| Interest on trading account securities | 2,055 | 1,154 |
| Interest on Federal funds sold and securities purchased under agreements to resell | 11,891 | 9,507 |
| Interest on lease financing | 1,943 | 2,446 |
| Total interest income | 196,567 | 215,484 |
| **Interest Expense** | | |
| Interest on deposits | 80,890 | 90,812 |
| Interest on Federal funds purchased and securities sold under repurchase agreements | 30,001 | 35,548 |
| Interest on borrowed money | 5,366 | 4,752 |
| Less: capitalized interest | 2,889 | 1,626 |
| Total interest expense | 113,368 | 129,486 |
| **Net Interest Margin** | 83,199 | 85,998 |
| Provision for losses | 29,600 | 13,850 |
| Net interest margin after provision for losses | 53,599 | 72,148 |
| **Noninterest Income** | | |
| Trust income | 18,337 | 16,453 |
| Service charges on deposits | 14,596 | 12,543 |
| Other service charges, commissions, and fees | 15,898 | 16,326 |
| Securities gains (losses) | 4,346 | 3,341 |
| Other income | 18,798 | 16,532 |
| Total noninterest income | 71,975 | 65,195 |
| **Noninterest Expense** | | |
| Salaries | 36,894 | 38,609 |
| Pension and employee benefits | 4,851 | 5,641 |
| Net occupancy expense | 7,918 | 5,555 |
| Furniture and equipment expense | 6,873 | 6,485 |
| Marketing and community relations | 2,784 | 2,799 |
| Data processing services purchased | 20,781 | 22,577 |
| Other expense | 22,601 | 26,737 |
| Total noninterest expense | 102,702 | 108,403 |
| Income before income taxes | 22,872 | 25,940 |
| Applicable income taxes | (516) | (4,089) |
| Net income | $ 22,356 | $ 21,851 |

## EXHIBIT 3 First National Bank—Summary Financial Ratios Compared to Peer Group Data

| | 12/31/87 | | | 12/31/86 | | | 12/31/85 | | | 12/31/84 | | 12/31/83 | |
| --- | --- | --- | --- | --- | --- | --- | --- | --- | --- | --- | --- | --- | --- |
| | Bank | Peer 3 | Pct | Bank | Peer 3 | Pct | Bank | Peer 3 | Pct | Bank | Peer 3 | Bank | Peer 3 |
| **Earnings and Profitability** | | | | | | | | | | | | | |
| Percent of average assets: | | | | | | | | | | | | | |
| Net interest income (TE) | 3.68 | 4.42 | 21 | 3.86 | 4.40 | 24 | 3.73 | 4.31 | 23 | 3.82 | 4.19 | 4.29 | 4.34 |
| + Noninterest income | 2.56 | 1.31 | 89 | 2.38 | 1.23 | 92 | 1.63 | 1.27 | 79 | 1.30 | 1.11 | 1.13 | 1.09 |
| − Overhead expense | 3.77 | 3.56 | 63 | 4.17 | 3.61 | 70 | 3.77 | 3.61 | 56 | 3.53 | 3.59 | 3.54 | 3.56 |
| − Provision for loan losses | 1.12 | 0.53 | 83 | 0.54 | 0.41 | 73 | 0.31 | 0.40 | 42 | 0.56 | 0.37 | 0.71 | 0.36 |
| = Pretax operating income (TE) | 1.33 | 1.60 | 32 | 1.52 | 1.65 | 41 | 1.27 | 1.58 | 31 | 1.04 | 1.28 | 1.17 | 1.52 |
| + Securities gains (losses) | 0.16 | 0.09 | 77 | 0.13 | 0.04 | 87 | 0.00 | 0.00 | 67 | −0.05 | 0.00 | −0.10 | −0.07 |
| = Pretax net oper. inc. (TE) | 1.49 | 1.72 | 33 | 1.65 | 1.70 | 45 | 1.26 | 1.54 | 31 | 0.99 | 1.28 | 1.07 | 1.42 |
| Net operating income | 0.84 | 0.94 | 38 | 0.97 | 0.93 | 50 | 0.75 | 0.88 | 34 | 0.60 | 0.74 | 0.60 | 0.83 |
| Adj. net oper. income | 1.16 | 1.09 | 54 | 1.02 | 1.06 | 46 | 0.81 | 0.95 | 32 | 0.50 | 0.81 | 0.98 | 0.89 |
| Adj. net income | 0.95 | 0.96 | 45 | 0.90 | 0.93 | 44 | 0.69 | 0.83 | 33 | 0.49 | 0.69 | 0.79 | 0.78 |
| Net income | 0.84 | 0.95 | 35 | 0.97 | 0.95 | 49 | 0.75 | 0.87 | 33 | 0.60 | 0.75 | 0.60 | 0.83 |
| Percent of avg. earning assets: | | | | | | | | | | | | | |
| Interest income (TE) | 10.15 | 10.40 | 34 | 11.50 | 11.37 | 54 | 12.86 | 12.45 | 73 | 12.32 | 11.74 | 15.03 | 13.63 |
| Interest expense | 5.54 | 5.54 | 50 | 6.56 | 6.46 | 54 | 8.11 | 7.61 | 74 | 7.39 | 6.95 | 9.43 | 8.61 |
| Net int. income (TE) | 4.62 | 4.92 | 36 | 4.94 | 4.94 | 49 | 4.75 | 4.87 | 47 | 4.92 | 4.76 | 5.60 | 5.05 |
| **Loans and Lease Losses, Reserves, and Noncurrent Loans and Leases** | | | | | | | | | | | | | |
| Net loss to avg. tot. ln. and lease | 1.55 | 0.61 | 85 | 0.86 | 0.48 | 82 | 0.43 | 0.48 | 54 | 1.12 | 0.59 | 0.54 | 0.56 |
| Earn coverage of net loss (×) | 2.27 | 7.12 | 22 | 3.15 | 8.36 | 23 | 4.74 | 7.83 | 36 | 1.78 | 6.54 | 4.17 | 6.49 |
| Loss reserve to net losses (×) | 1.34 | 3.73 | 18 | 1.59 | 4.20 | 18 | 3.07 | 4.03 | 48 | 1.18 | 3.36 | 2.76 | 3.09 |
| Loss resv. to tot. loans and leases | 2.05 | 1.33 | 89 | 1.38 | 1.22 | 70 | 1.24 | 1.22 | 59 | 1.33 | 1.25 | 1.42 | 1.26 |
| Percent of noncurrent loans and leases | 5.02 | 1.62 | 94 | 2.52 | 1.71 | 77 | 1.53 | 1.97 | 64 | 3.31 | 2.40 | N/A | 2.62 |
| **Liquidity and Rate Sensitivity** | | | | | | | | | | | | | |
| Volatile liability dependence | 42.62 | 16.17 | 87 | 47.97 | 16.54 | 89 | 52.64 | 17.04 | 89 | 50.52 | 16.91 | 61.51 | 21.88 |
| Net loans and leases to assets | 47.37 | 60.84 | 10 | 48.64 | 59.20 | 15 | 56.31 | 58.57 | 38 | 53.79 | 53.43 | 58.83 | 51.22 |
| Net assets repriceable in 1 year or less to assets | −8.49 | −4.70 | 36 | −5.94 | −1.92 | 28 | 3.36 | −1.61 | 72 | 8.16 | −1.92 | N/A | N/A |
| **Capitalization** | | | | | | | | | | | | | |
| Primary capital to avg. assets | 7.41 | 7.35 | 60 | 6.47 | 7.13 | 23 | 6.53 | 6.93 | 35 | 6.33 | 6.59 | 5.73 | 6.68 |
| Cash dividends to net income | 45.50 | 35.44 | 68 | 35.17 | 38.27 | 44 | 43.97 | 38.67 | 64 | 57.00 | 42.95 | 51.43 | 45.48 |
| Ret. earns to avg. total equity | 7.69 | 8.84 | 40 | 11.26 | 8.84 | 67 | 7.63 | 8.44 | 44 | 4.73 | 6.77 | 5.73 | 7.01 |
| **Growth Rates** | | | | | | | | | | | | | |
| Assets | −2.09 | 12.71 | 10 | 10.90 | 12.77 | 41 | 7.67 | 12.27 | 30 | 4.60 | 10.79 | 2.25 | 10.32 |
| Primary capital | 16.04 | 13.92 | 61 | 6.47 | 13.07 | 17 | 7.56 | 14.45 | 27 | 15.96 | 8.17 | 12.45 | 9.20 |
| Net loans and leases | −4.64 | 14.56 | 10 | −4.20 | 13.83 | 05 | 12.71 | 25.24 | 26 | −4.36 | 14.46 | 11.40 | 9.15 |
| Volatile liabilities | 1.04 | 6.98 | 42 | 3.80 | 17.34 | 31 | 3.38 | 14.15 | 35 | −0.14 | −3.12 | 12.05 | 11.05 |

**EXHIBIT 4  First National Bank—Analysis of Repricing Opportunities as of December 31, 1987**

| | 1 Day | 3 Months | 3–6 Mos | 6–12 Mos | 1–5 Years | 5 Years | All Other | Total | % Assets |
|---|---|---|---|---|---|---|---|---|---|
| **Repricing opportunities for:** | | | | | | | | | |
| Total loans and leases | 764,228 | 112,228 | 47,962 | 22,720 | 250,630 | 126,032 | | 1,323,800 | 46.32 |
| Debt securities | 4,503 | 3,000 | 10,026 | 67,561 | 207,640 | 162,789 | | 455,519 | 15.94 |
| Trading account assets | | 30,472 | | | | | | 30,472 | 1.07 |
| Other interest-bearing assets | 236,984 | 159,000 | 0 | 0 | 8,505 | 0 | | 404,489 | 14.15 |
| Total interest-bearing assets | 1,005,715 | 304,700 | 57,988 | 90,281 | 466,775 | 288,821 | | 2,214,280 | 77.48 |
| Loan and lease loss reserve | | | | | | | -28,328 | -28,328 | -0.99 |
| Nonaccrual loans | | | | | | | 59,378 | 59,378 | 2.08 |
| All other assets | | | | | | | 612,481 | 612,481 | 21.43 |
| Total assets | 1,005,715 | 304,700 | 57,988 | 90,281 | 466,775 | 288,821 | 643,531 | 2,857,811 | |
| Deposits in foreign offices | 92,741 | 0 | 0 | 0 | 0 | 0 | | 92,741 | 3.25 |
| CDs over $100,000 | 0 | 183,133 | 44,366 | 21,293 | 62,023 | 4,207 | | 315,022 | 11.02 |
| Other time deposits | 185,916 | 25,859 | 19,051 | 15,250 | 41,820 | 4,204 | | 292,100 | 10.22 |
| MMDA savings & unregulated NOW | | 452,586 | | | | | | 452,586 | 15.84 |
| Other savings & regulated NOW | | | | | | | 39,382 | 39,382 | 1.38 |
| Treasury notes | | 44,188 | | | | | | 44,188 | 1.55 |
| Mortgages & capitalized leases | | | | | | | 0 | 0 | 0.00 |
| Other nondeposit int.-bear. liabs. | 616,980 | 0 | 0 | 0 | 0 | 7,000 | 0 | 623,980 | 21.83 |
| Total int.-bearing liabilities | 895,637 | 705,766 | 63,417 | 36,543 | 103,843 | 15,411 | 39,382 | 1,859,999 | 65.08 |
| Demand deposits | | | | | | | 780,352 | 780,352 | 27.31 |
| All other liabilities | | | | | | | 53,164 | 53,164 | 1.86 |
| Total liabilities | 895,637 | 705,766 | 63,417 | 36,543 | 103,843 | 15,411 | 872,898 | 2,693,515 | 94.25 |
| Total equity (excluding limited-life pref. stock) | | | | | | | 164,296 | 164,296 | 5.75 |
| Total liabilities and capital | 895,637 | 705,766 | 63,417 | 36,543 | 103,843 | 15,411 | 1,037,194 | 2,857,811 | |
| Net positions—total assets less liabilities and capital | 110,078 | -401,066 | -5,429 | 53,738 | 362,932 | 273,410 | -393,663 | 0 | |
| **Cumulative positions:** | | | | | | | | | |
| Total assets | 1,005,715 | 1,310,415 | 1,368,403 | 1,458,684 | 1,925,459 | 2,214,280 | | 2,857,811 | |
| Total liabilities & capital | 895,637 | 1,601,403 | 1,664,820 | 1,701,363 | 1,805,206 | 1,820,617 | | 2,857,811 | |
| Total asset less liab. & cap. | 110,078 | -290,988 | -296,417 | -242,679 | 120,253 | 393,663 | | 0 | |
| **Estimated distribution for banks electing option 2 on Schedule J:** | | | | | | | | | |
| Residential RE loans (est.)[a] | 1,330 | 1,330 | 1,330 | 2,660 | 21,280 | 75,598 | | 99,198 | 3.47 |
| Consumer installment Ins. (est.)[a] | 1,234 | 1,234 | 1,234 | 2,468 | 3,639 | 0 | | 8,575 | 0.30 |

[a]Based on estimated payments for the latest quarter.

731

**EXHIBIT 5  First National Bank—Analysis of Repricing Opportunities (Summary): Cumulative Gap Comparisons for Interest-Bearing Assets and Liabilities**

| Percent of Assets Repriced Within | 12/31/87 | | | | | | | | | Bank Cumulative Net History | | | |
| --- | --- | --- | --- | --- | --- | --- | --- | --- | --- | --- | --- | --- | --- |
| | Assets | | | Liabilities | | | Net Position | | | | | | |
| | Bank | Peer 3 | Pct | Bank | Peer 3 | Pct | Bank | Peer 3 | Pct | 12/31/86 | 12/31/85 | 12/31/84 | 12/31/83 |
| 1 day | 35.19 | 29.66 | 67 | 31.34 | 8.44 | 98 | 3.85 | 21.19 | 08 | 20.45 | 23.39 | 28.75 | N/A |
| 3 months | 45.85 | 44.03 | 60 | 56.04 | 49.90 | 78 | −10.18 | −6.00 | 32 | −6.14 | −0.93 | 9.07 | N/A |
| 6 months | 47.88 | 47.88 | 53 | 58.26 | 55.15 | 67 | −10.37 | −6.93 | 34 | −6.97 | −3.63 | 8.30 | N/A |
| 12 months | 51.04 | 53.83 | 44 | 59.53 | 58.66 | 57 | −8.49 | −4.70 | 36 | −5.94 | 3.36 | 8.16 | N/A |
| 5 years | 67.38 | 76.51 | 10 | 63.17 | 64.12 | 43 | 4.21 | 12.53 | 20 | 6.31 | 8.09 | 14.19 | N/A |

**EXHIBIT 6    First National Bank—Economic Outlook, February 29, 1988**

| | Major Economic Indicators | | | | | | | | |
| --- | --- | --- | --- | --- | --- | --- | --- | --- | --- |
| | Forecast | | | | | | Annual Levels | | |
| | 1988.1 | 1988.2 | 1988.3 | 1988.4 | 1989.1 | 1989.2 | 1987 | 1988 | 1989 |
| | | | | | | | *Year-Over-Year % Change* | | |
| GNP percent change in annual rate | 0.8 | 1.7 | 3.2 | 3.0 | 0.8 | 0.0 | 2.9 | 2.6 | 1.4 |
| Composition of real GNP growth, | | | | | | | | | |
| Final sales | 3.9 | 1.5 | 3.1 | 3.2 | −0.5 | 0.7 | 2.0 | 2.9 | 1.2 |
| Change in inventories | −3.0 | 0.2 | 0.0 | −0.3 | 1.3 | −0.8 | 1.9 | −0.8 | −0.4 |
| **Indicators or Real Activity** | | | | | | | *Annual Levels* | | |
| Housing starts (pvt.) | 1,488.0 | 1,558.9 | 1,558.0 | 1,573.9 | 1,415.4 | 1,346.5 | 1,634.3 | 1,554.7 | 1,367.6 |
| Sales of domestic autos | 7.5 | 6.8 | 7.4 | 6.7 | 7.0 | 6.6 | 7.1 | 7.1 | 6.6 |
| Industrial production (mfg.) | 133.2 | 133.4 | 134.6 | 136.0 | 136.1 | 135.6 | 129.8 | 134.3 | 135.8 |
| Capacity util. (mfg.) | 82.4 | 82.5 | 82.8 | 83.0 | 82.4 | 81.4 | 81.0 | 82.7 | 81.3 |
| Unemployment rate (civ.) | 5.8 | 6.0 | 6.0 | 5.9 | 5.9 | 6.2 | 6.2 | 5.9 | 6.2 |
| **Prices, Productivity, and Costs** | | | | | | | *Yr./yr. % Chg.* | | |
| GNP deflator % chg. | 3.1 | 3.2 | 2.9 | 2.7 | 4.2 | 3.8 | 3.0 | 3.0 | 3.4 |
| CPI (all urban) % chg. | 3.6 | 4.3 | 4.3 | 4.4 | 4.0 | 2.7 | 3.7 | 4.0 | 3.3 |
| PPI (finished) % chg. | 1.9 | 3.9 | 3.4 | 5.5 | 4.9 | 3.1 | 2.1 | 2.6 | 4.0 |
| Comp. per man-hour % chg. | 5.6 | 4.2 | 4.2 | 4.4 | 6.8 | 4.5 | 2.8 | 4.3 | 5.0 |
| Output per hour % chg. | −1.3 | 0.6 | 1.8 | 1.3 | −0.2 | −0.1 | 0.8 | 0.6 | 0.6 |
| Unit labor cost & chg. | 6.9 | 3.6 | 2.4 | 3.1 | 7.0 | 4.6 | 2.0 | 3.6 | 4.3 |
| **Money and Interest Rates** | | | | | | | *Yr./yr. % Chg. or Levels* | | |
| Nonborrowed reserves | 6.2 | 9.3 | 5.4 | 4.1 | −3.7 | 2.3 | 14.2 | 5.0 | 2.4 |
| Money supply (MI) % chg. | 5.0 | 6.7 | 5.7 | 5.4 | 2.9 | 2.5 | 10.5 | 4.8 | 4.0 |
| MI velocity % chg. | −1.1 | −1.6 | 0.4 | 0.3 | 2.1 | 1.2 | −4.3 | 0.8 | 0.9 |
| Prime rate | 8.5 | 8.0 | 8.2 | 8.5 | 9.3 | 9.5 | 8.2 | 8.3 | 9.5 |
| Treasury bill rate (3 mo.) | 5.6 | 5.2 | 5.4 | 5.6 | 6.2 | 6.4 | 5.8 | 5.4 | 6.4 |
| Yield on 3-year govt. secs. | 8.5 | 8.2 | 8.5 | 8.8 | 9.8 | 10.0 | 8.6 | 8.5 | 10.0 |
| Federal funds rate | 6.6 | 6.1 | 6.3 | 6.6 | 7.3 | 7.5 | 6.7 | 6.4 | 7.4 |
| **Incomes and Related Measures** | | | | | | | *Yr./yr. % Chg. or Levels* | | |
| Net exports | −109.4 | −107.1 | −107.3 | −95.1 | −85.9 | −76.0 | −135.7 | −104.7 | −70.3 |
| Real pers. disp. inc. % chg. | 3.3 | 0.7 | 2.4 | 1.3 | 3.0 | 1.4 | 1.2 | 2.7 | 1.9 |
| Personal saving rate % | 4.9 | 4.8 | 4.7 | 4.8 | 5.6 | 5.8 | 3.8 | 4.8 | 5.9 |
| Federal deficit (FY) | −166.3 | −159.5 | −164.1 | −166.8 | −165.0 | −172.7 | −158.6 | −162.8 | −171.3 |
| Exchange rate (index) | 90.2 | 88.5 | 86.3 | 83.8 | 82.9 | 82.1 | 96.9 | 87.2 | 81.5 |
| Price of imported oil s/b | 17.2 | 17.0 | 17.4 | 17.8 | 17.8 | 17.8 | 18.1 | 17.4 | 17.9 |

**EXHIBIT 6** (Continued)

734

*Major Economic Indicators*

| | Forecast | | | | | | Yr./yr. % Chg. or Levels | | |
| | 1988.1 | 1988.2 | 1988.3 | 1988.4 | 1989.1 | 1989.2 | 1987 | 1988 | 1989 |
|---|---|---|---|---|---|---|---|---|---|
| Foreign GNP % chg. | 2.1 | 2.2 | 2.9 | 4.1 | 1.7 | 1.7 | 2.4 | 2.5 | 2.3 |
| Gross national product | 3,885.9 | 3,902.7 | 3,933.2 | 3,961.9 | 3,970.2 | 3,970.0 | 2.9 | 2.6 | 1.4 |
| % chg. annual rate | 0.8 | 1.7 | 3.2 | 3.0 | 0.8 | 0.0 | 2.9 | 2.6 | 1.4 |
| Pers. consumption exp. | 2,521.0 | 2,528.0 | 2,546.6 | 2,552.0 | 2,549.4 | 2,552.2 | 1.9 | 1.6 | 0.7 |
| % chg. annual rate | 3.3 | 1.1 | 3.0 | 0.8 | -0.4 | 0.4 | 1.9 | 1.6 | 0.7 |
| Durable goods | 396.6 | 393.9 | 399.8 | 399.1 | 391.5 | 387.9 | 1.2 | 2.4 | -2.3 |
| Nondurable goods | 870.8 | 870.9 | 876.1 | 878.6 | 880.6 | 883.3 | 0.0 | -0.3 | 1.2 |
| Services | 1,253.6 | 1,263.2 | 1,270.7 | 1,274.3 | 1,277.3 | 1,281.1 | 3.5 | 2.8 | 1.4 |
| Gross pvt. DCH investment | 689.1 | 697.6 | 704.4 | 707.2 | 717.1 | 702.0 | 4.9 | 2.0 | -0.7 |
| Fixed investment | 661.9 | 668.2 | 674.5 | 679.9 | 677.0 | 669.4 | 0.6 | 4.2 | -0.4 |
| Nonresidential | 468.2 | 473.9 | 479.2 | 484.5 | 485.8 | 484.9 | 0.9 | 6.4 | 1.5 |
| % chg. annual rate | 4.4 | 5.0 | 4.6 | 4.5 | 1.1 | -0.8 | 0.9 | 6.4 | 1.5 |
| Structures | 129.6 | 130.1 | 131.0 | 131.3 | 130.9 | 130.0 | -4.6 | 5.1 | -0.7 |
| Equipment | 338.6 | 343.8 | 348.2 | 353.2 | 354.9 | 354.8 | 3.2 | 6.9 | 2.4 |
| Residential | 193.7 | 194.3 | 195.3 | 195.4 | 191.2 | 184.5 | 0.0 | -0.9 | -5.2 |
| % chg. annual rate | -7.0 | 1.2 | 2.1 | 0.1 | -8.3 | -13.2 | 0.0 | -0.9 | -5.2 |
| Change in inventories | 27.2 | 29.4 | 29.9 | 27.3 | 40.1 | 32.6 | 42.0 | 28.5 | 26.5 |
| Net exports | -109.4 | -107.1 | -107.3 | -95.1 | -85.9 | -76.0 | -135.7 | -104.7 | -70.3 |
| Exports | 474.1 | 487.8 | 500.9 | 515.1 | 525.2 | 534.7 | 12.8 | 16.2 | 9.0 |
| % chg. annual rate | 20.3 | 12.1 | 11.2 | 11.8 | 8.1 | 7.5 | 12.8 | 16.2 | 9.0 |
| Nonag. merchandise | 286.6 | 297.4 | 307.7 | 318.1 | 326.3 | 333.8 | 14.8 | 22.9 | 11.4 |
| AG merchandise | 37.1 | 38.4 | 39.8 | 41.5 | 42.1 | 43.2 | 17.1 | 10.6 | 11.3 |
| Services | 150.5 | 152.1 | 153.4 | 155.5 | 156.8 | 157.8 | 8.5 | 6.1 | 3.7 |
| Imports | 583.5 | 594.9 | 608.2 | 610.2 | 611.1 | 610.8 | 7.3 | 6.8 | 1.7 |
| % chg. annual rate | -3.7 | 8.0 | 9.3 | 1.3 | 0.6 | -0.2 | 7.3 | 6.8 | 1.7 |
| Nonpetro. merchandise | 378.2 | 384.2 | 389.3 | 392.5 | 392.3 | 387.3 | 6.1 | 5.3 | -0.4 |
| Petro. & products | 75.8 | 78.1 | 83.6 | 79.3 | 77.5 | 79.6 | 4.0 | 2.5 | 1.5 |
| Service | 129.5 | 132.6 | 135.4 | 138.4 | 141.2 | 143.9 | 13.7 | 14.3 | 7.9 |
| Government purchases of | | | | | | | | | |
| Goods and services | 785.2 | 784.2 | 789.5 | 797.9 | 789.6 | 791.9 | 2.5 | 2.0 | 1.0 |
| % chg. annual rate | -5.5 | -0.5 | 2.7 | 4.3 | -4.1 | 1.2 | 2.5 | 2.0 | 1.0 |
| Federal | 341.5 | 337.3 | 339.4 | 345.7 | 336.0 | 336.3 | 1.6 | 0.9 | -0.2 |
| Defense | 263.8 | 259.3 | 258.4 | 258.0 | 258.8 | 259.4 | 5.4 | -1.6 | 0.0 |
| Nondefense | 77.6 | 78.0 | 81.0 | 87.8 | 77.1 | 77.0 | -9.9 | 10.0 | -0.9 |
| State and local | 443.7 | 446.9 | 450.1 | 452.2 | 453.6 | 455.5 | 3.2 | 2.9 | 1.9 |

SOURCE: First Republic Bank, Dallas, Texas, Economics Department.

## CASE 20    GRANTLAND NATIONAL BANK

### INTRODUCTION

Early in 1991, Mr. Gregory Mc-Clure, the recently named president and chief executive officer of Grantland National Bank (GNB), was reviewing his strategic business plan for the years 1991 and 1992 that he had presented to the bank's parent holding company, Grantland Financial Corporation, in the fall of 1990. The plan approved by the holding company's top management projected earnings just over the break-even level in 1991 and a return on assets (ROA) of 1 percent in the next year that would match the 1990 performance of the average bank in GNB's peer group.

The year just ended, 1990, had been particularly disappointing for GNB because of its sharply deteriorating earnings performance. As shown in the following table, over the last three years, GNB's ROA and return on equity (ROE) measures had declined, while the same profitability measures for the average bank in GNB's peer group had improved.

There were several reasons for the substantial increase in the loss provision and loss reserve in 1990. First, the reserve for loan and lease losses had probably been too low in 1989. GNB had believed that its conservative lending policies, high collateral requirements, and credit review functions would keep the quality of its loans, nearly all of which were made in the local communities within its market area, well above that of most of its peers. Few of the bank's loans were related to agriculture, Third World borrowers, energy, highly leveraged transactions, or commercial real estate, which had led to the severe credit problems of many banks. Many of GNB's loans classified as "other real estate loans" were credits to small business firms based primarily on cash flows or current asset values, with the real estate collateral as a secondary source of repayment. Thus, while many banks in the country were beset with substantial loan delinquencies, renegotiations, and charge-offs, GNB's management was confident that it was correctly re-

|  | 1988 | | 1989 | | 1990 | |
|---|---|---|---|---|---|---|
|  | **ROA** | **ROE** | **ROA** | **ROE** | **ROA** | **ROE** |
| GNB | 1.34% | 17.10% | 1.09% | 14.60% | (0.32%) | (5.00%) |
| Peer group | 0.64 | 8.72 | 0.81 | 10.77 | 1.05 | 13.96 |

### CAUSES OF THE EARNINGS DECLINE

Clearly, the major cause of the earnings plunge was the increase in the loan loss provision, which rose from $2,123,000 in 1989 to $6,647,000 in 1990, as shown in Exhibit 6. After adjustments for loans and leases written off as losses and recoveries, the reserve for loan and lease losses rose from $1,955,000 in 1989 to $3,649,000 in 1990. Despite the increase, the loss reserve fell from about 57 percent of 90-days-and-over past-due and noncurrent loans and leases in 1989 to 26 percent in 1990.

porting only a relatively small volume of credit problems. Mr. McClure, who became GNB's chief executive officer in the summer of 1990, had concluded that GNB's credit underwriting had avoided the adverse effects from the slower economic activity in the bank's market area.

A second reason for the large loss provision in 1990 was the increased scrutiny and critical evaluation of the loan portfolio by the bank's examiners. Because of many banks' severe lending problems throughout the country, Mr. McClure believed that the recent examination of the loan portfolio was far harsher than previous examinations. He also thought that GNB would benefit in future years from the examiners' and the bank's own tougher evaluation of loan credit quality with more loss recoveries. But, Mr. McClure wondered, who would provide the financing for the business turnaround needed to get GNB's market area growing again?

The third reason for the increased loan loss provision was a decision made by GNB's parent, Grantland Financial Corporation. When the examiners increased the volume of adversely classified loans and leases, which required the bank to raise the loan loss provision and make the loan loss reserve larger, Grantland Financial's senior management decided to "bite as much of the bullet" as they could in 1990 rather than spread the loan problems over several years.

## THE BANK

GNB was the smallest of the 11 bank affiliates of Grantland Financial Corporation, a multibank holding company whose banks operated in four midwestern states. At the end of 1990, GNB had total resources of $417 million and served its two-county market area with 17 offices and a staff of 235 full-time equivalent officers and employees (see Exhibit 1).

GNB's business strategy was summarized in its published mission statement: "Grantland National Bank is a community-oriented bank whose skilled and friendly professional people are dedicated to serving the financial needs of its customers today and in the future."

One of GNB's officers observed that the bank's key distinction was how it treated its customers, not how it charged them. By developing a strong interest in community affairs through active participation in many civic organizations and clubs, and by taking a leadership role in programs benefiting youth, GNB paid serious attention to improving its communities.

The attitude of treating customers as friends and of involving the bank deeply in community affairs was embraced by the entire staff. This philosophy was in sharp contrast to the transaction-oriented, highly automated, and more impersonal institutional style of some more aggressive banks. The key questions in developing account relationships were: Does the potential customer have a

strong reason to want to bank at GNB? Can the bank develop a long-term relationship with the customer? Customer service, not pricing, was viewed as the key to maintaining long-term banking customer relationships. As a consequence, potential customers who were overly sensitive to pricing were usually not pursued by GNB.

The bank's loan committee was convened weekly, and even more frequently if necessary, to accommodate customers and to consider loans in excess of individual officers' loan limits. Lending authorities were based on each officer's experience and seniority, and ranged from $150,000 on a secured basis and $50,000 unsecured for senior loan officers to $25,000 secured and $5,000 unsecured for junior officers. For loans that were presented to the loan committee, a unanimous vote was required to approve the credit.

GNB's commercial business was primarily small, family-owned and -operated firms, a market niche ignored by many competitors. The bank's officer calling program was directed at small industrial companies operating within its market area with annual sales between $5 and $15 million. Selected businesses with sales below $5 million were also targeted. The bank provided financing primarily for working capital purposes. Potential losses seemed reasonably reserved for, but new loans of acceptable quality were proving increasingly hard to find.

Although GNB showed a concentration of real estate loans, problems had been avoided until 1990 by the absence of larger development and commercial real estate loans. As already noted, most of the bank's "other real estate loans" were related to credits to small operating companies, with the real estate collateral serving as a secondary source of repayment.

## MANAGEMENT ISSUES

Mr. McClure realized that one of the issues central to a successful turnaround of GNB in 1991 would be the attitude of the bank's officers and employees in dealing with an operating loss for the first time in the bank's recent history. Facing a difficult economic situation both locally and nationally presented an additional challenge. The bank's low staff turnover rate and the continuity of senior management were essential ingredients for achieving forecasted goals. To replace and retrain personnel was a time-consuming but relatively easy task; however, to find employees with the abilities and personalities to embrace GNB's philosophy of dedication to customers and communities served was much more difficult.

As he looked at 1991 and beyond, Mr. McClure hoped for improvements in the bank's net interest margin, which, as a percentage of average total assets, had declined from 4.57 percent in 1989 to 3.84 percent in 1990. He pondered how to achieve this improvement. He knew that loan quality must be kept high so that the provision for loan losses would not require an increase. He was also concerned that the bank not take excessive interest rate or liquidity risks. Mr. McClure also wondered how GNB could increase noninterest or fee-based income while controlling noninterest expense.

Many courses of action were limited by existing requirements. For example, Mr. McClure estimated that the provision for loan and lease losses would probably have to be close to $4 million in 1991 to keep the examiners happy. Growth was also constrained by a relatively low capital position at the beginning of 1991. Furthermore, GNB would have to pay its holding company $900,000 in cash dividends so that Grantland Financial Corporation could meet its debt repayments. Mr. McClure had studied the risk-based capital rules coming in 1992 so that GNB would also meet these guidelines.

As he looked out of his third-floor window on a gray winter's day early in 1991, Mr. McClure wondered if GNB could achieve its performance targets of a slight profit in 1991 and an ROA of about 1 percent in 1992 within these constraints without taking excessive risks.

To assist Mr. McClure in his evaluation of GNB's recent performance and profit goals for the next two years, Ms. Helen Rajak, senior vice-president and chief financial officer, had prepared Exhibits 1 through 7. These statements contain balance sheet and income statement data for the bank and its peer group of banks with total assets of $300 to $500 million and three or more banking offices.

## QUESTIONS

1. Ignore the year 1990 just ended. Consider the two-year period 1988–1989, when the earnings performance of GNB was significantly better than that of the average peer group bank, as shown by the ROA and ROE measures.
   a. Explain how GNB achieved its superior earnings performance.
   b. Compare GNB's risk exposure with that of the average peer group bank. Evaluate the bank's relative credit risk, interest rate risk, liquidity risk, and capital-risk exposures.
   c. Summarize GNB's relative strengths and weaknesses as of the end of 1989.
2. Consider the year 1990.
   a. How do you explain the loss suffered by GNB?
   b. Evaluate the risk exposure of GNB at the end of the year compared with the risk position of the average peer group bank.
   c. What were the strengths and weaknesses of GNB at the end of 1990?
3. Under the risk-based capital guidelines, as of the end of 1990, GNB's risk-adjusted assets (in millions of dollars) were as follows:

| Risk Category | Risk Weight | Total Assets | Risk-Adjusted Assets |
|---|---|---|---|
| Category 1 | 0% | $102.9 | $ 0.0 |
| Category 2 | 20 | 78.4 | 15.7 |
| Category 3 | 50 | 38.2 | 19.1 |
| Category 4 | 100 | 200.9 | 200.9 |
| Off–balance sheet | Varies | 0.0 | 6.1 |
| Totals | | $420.4 | $241.8 |

Under the risk-based capital rules, half of total required capital (known as *Tier I capital*) must be composed of common stockholders' equity and non-cumulative perpetual preferred stock less goodwill. The other half (known as *Tier II capital*) may include subordinated debt, limited-life preferred stock, and loan loss reserves (up to 1.50 percent of risk-adjusted assets at the end of 1990 and 1.25 percent at the end of 1992). Total Tier II capital cannot exceed total Tier I capital.

As of year-end 1990, banks were required to comply with a minimum ratio of capital to risk-adjusted assets of 7.25 percent (3.625 percent of which had to be Tier I). When the capital rules became fully effective at the end of 1992, the minimum required capital ratio would be 8 percent (4 percent for Tier I capital).

Evaluate GNB's position against the risk-based capital guidelines.

4. GNB's profit targets are to operate just over the break-even level in 1991 and to earn an ROA of about 1 percent in 1992. Are these goals attainable? Make specific recommendations for steps that the bank should take to restore its profitability.

## EXHIBIT 1    Grantland National Bank—Balance Sheet as of December 31 (dollars in thousands)

|  | 1990 | 1989 | 1988 |
|---|---|---|---|
| Noninterest cash and due from banks | $ 22,022 | $ 14,282 | $ 14,796 |
| Money market investments: |  |  |  |
| Interest-bearing bank balances | 31,400 | 32,800 | 40,600 |
| Federal funds sold | 16,800 | 14,820 | 11,000 |
| Total money market investments | 48,200 | 47,620 | 51,600 |
| Investment securities: |  |  |  |
| U.S. Treasury and agency securities | 86,912 | 54,482 | 44,516 |
| State and local government securities | 33,496 | 34,498 | 33,026 |
| All other securities | 1,228 | 1,600 | 1,472 |
| Total investment securities | 121,636 | 90,580 | 79,014 |
| Loans and leases: |  |  |  |
| Commercial and industrial | 78,848 | 99,638 | 58,390 |
| Real estate loans | 96,958 | 91,864 | 94,432 |
| Consumer loans | 28,042 | 20,220 | 20,456 |
| All other loans and leases | 3,479 | 3,084 | 2,741 |
| Total loans and leases | 207,327 | 214,806 | 176,019 |
| Less reserve for loan and lease losses | 3,649 | 1,955 | 1,514 |
| Net loans and leases | 203,678 | 212,851 | 174,505 |
| Bank premises and equipment, net | 13,370 | 12,610 | 11,228 |
| Other assets | 7,904 | 6,836 | 6,122 |
| Total assets | 416,810 | 384,779 | 337,265 |
| Total earning assets | $377,163 | $353,006 | $306,633 |
| Non-interest-bearing demand deposits | $ 65,536 | $ 53,604 | $ 51,498 |
| Interest-bearing deposits: |  |  |  |
| Transactions accounts | 36,544 | 33,352 | 29,748 |
| Money market deposit accounts | 31,950 | 38,100 | 32,588 |
| Regular savings | 34,344 | 32,548 | 30,232 |

**EXHIBIT I**   *(continued)*

|  | 1990 | 1989 | 1988 |
|---|---|---|---|
| Time deposits under $100,000 | 144,856 | 122,976 | 105,106 |
| Time deposits $100,000 and over | 70,740 | 70,038 | 53,336 |
| Total interest-bearing deposits | 318,434 | 297,014 | 251,010 |
| Total deposit liabilities | 383,970 | 350,618 | 302,508 |
| Short-term borrowings | 3,118 | 3,345 | 5,200 |
| Other liabilities | 4,288 | 3,112 | 3,104 |
| Total liabilities | 391,376 | 357,075 | 310,812 |
| Shareholders' equity | 25,434 | 27,704 | 26,453 |
| Total liabilities and shareholders' equity | $416,810 | $384,779 | $337,265 |

**EXHIBIT 2   Grantland National Bank—Year-end Loan and Investment Portfolios**

|  | *1990* | | *1989* | | *1988* | |
|---|---|---|---|---|---|---|
|  | **GNB** | **Peers** | **GNB** | **Peers** | **GNB** | **Peers** |
| *Loan Mix as a Percent of Total Loans* | | | | | | |
| Commercial and industrial | 39.05 | 27.28 | 34.36 | 29.39 | 28.34 | 30.41 |
| Real estate: | | | | | | |
|   Construction and development | 5.44 | 4.84 | 6.52 | 4.15 | 7.32 | 5.65 |
|   1–4-family residential | 13.35 | 25.45 | 17.40 | 24.04 | 19.98 | 22.03 |
|   Home equity | 4.14 | 5.03 | 3.10 | 3.49 | 1.26 | 2.21 |
|   Other real estate | 22.93 | 15.84 | 24.36 | 17.66 | 27.88 | 17.61 |
|   Total real estate | 45.86 | 51.16 | 51.38 | 49.34 | 56.44 | 47.56 |
| Loans to individuals | 13.24 | 19.25 | 12.63 | 18.61 | 13.46 | 19.51 |
| All other loans and leases | 1.85 | 2.31 | 1.63 | 2.66 | 1.76 | 2.52 |
|   Total loans and leases | 100.00 | 100.00 | 100.00 | 100.00 | 100.00 | 100.00 |
| *Investment Mix as a Percent of Total Investments* | | | | | | |
| U.S. Treasuries and federal agencies | 70.34 | 69.38 | 59.73 | 68.88 | 56.54 | 63.09 |
| State and local government securities | 27.55 | 21.68 | 38.11 | 22.58 | 41.07 | 29.46 |
| Other securities | 2.11 | 8.94 | 2.16 | 8.54 | 2.39 | 7.45 |
|   Total investment securities | 100.00 | 100.00 | 100.00 | 100.00 | 100.00 | 100.00 |
| *Investment Maturities as a Percent of Total Investments* | | | | | | |
| Under one year | 31.27 | 34.87 | 33.75 | 33.78 | 37.49 | 28.42 |
| One to five years | 41.47 | 39.42 | 28.93 | 43.51 | 31.93 | 42.25 |
| Over five years | 27.26 | 25.71 | 37.32 | 22.71 | 30.58 | 29.33 |
|   Total investment securities | 100.00 | 100.00 | 100.00 | 100.00 | 100.00 | 100.00 |

**EXHIBIT 3    Grantland National Bank—Average Balance Sheet (dollars in thousands)**

|  | 1990 | 1989 | 1988 |
|---|---|---|---|
| Noninterest cash and due from banks | $ 18,188 | $ 12,879 | $ 12,508 |
| Money market investments: |  |  |  |
| Interest-bearing bank balances | 29,239 | 34,531 | 51,289 |
| Federal funds sold | 14,354 | 14,010 | 11,766 |
| Total money market investments | 43,593 | 48,541 | 63,055 |
| Investment securities: |  |  |  |
| U.S. Treasury and agency securities | 78,827 | 49,744 | 36,653 |
| State and local government securities | 30,870 | 31,736 | 26,627 |
| All other securities | 2,365 | 1,804 | 1,547 |
| Total investment securities | 112,062 | 83,284 | 64,827 |
| Loans and leases: |  |  |  |
| Commercial and industrial | 84,292 | 66,229 | 47,322 |
| Real estate loans | 99,012 | 99,035 | 94,228 |
| Consumer loans | 28,586 | 24,344 | 22,469 |
| All other loans and leases | 3,996 | 3,142 | 2,934 |
| Total loans and leases | 215,886 | 192,750 | 166,953 |
| Less reserve for loan and lease losses | 2,977 | 1,804 | 1,547 |
| Net loans and leases | 212,909 | 190,946 | 165,406 |
| Bank premises and equipment, net | 13,457 | 11,817 | 10,864 |
| Other assets | 7,585 | 6,333 | 5,706 |
| Total assets | $407,794 | $353,800 | $322,366 |
| Total earning assets | $371,541 | $324,575 | $294,835 |
| Non-interest-bearing demand deposits | $ 60,598 | $ 49,885 | $ 46,808 |
| Interest-bearing deposits: |  |  |  |
| Transactions accounts | 34,581 | 30,356 | 28,658 |
| Money market deposit accounts | 33,521 | 34,496 | 37,298 |
| Regular savings | 34,459 | 32,019 | 29,077 |
| Time deposits under $100,000 | 138,691 | 113,994 | 98,677 |
| Time deposits $100,000 and over | 72,260 | 60,394 | 50,450 |
| Total interest-bearing deposits | 313,512 | 271,259 | 244,160 |
| Total deposit liabilities | 374,110 | 321,144 | 290,968 |
| Short-term borrowings | 3,181 | 2,830 | 2,934 |
| Other liabilities | 4,119 | 3,397 | 3,191 |
| Total liabilities | 381,410 | 327,371 | 297,093 |
| Shareholders' equity | 26,384 | 26,429 | 25,273 |
| Total liabilities and shareholders' equity | $407,794 | $353,800 | $322,366 |

**EXHIBIT 4  Grantland National Bank—Asset and Liability Distribution as a Percentage of Average Total Assets**

| | 1990 | | 1989 | | 1988 | |
|---|---|---|---|---|---|---|
| | Grantland | Peers | Grantland | Peers | Grantland | Peers |
| Noninterest cash and due from banks | 4.46 | 5.47 | 3.64 | 5.37 | 3.88 | 5.65 |
| Money market investments: | | | | | | |
| Interest-bearing bank balances | 7.17 | 3.01 | 9.76 | 2.76 | 15.91 | 3.87 |
| Federal funds sold | 3.52 | 4.49 | 3.96 | 6.29 | 3.65 | 8.16 |
| Total money market investments | 10.69 | 7.50 | 13.72 | 9.05 | 19.56 | 12.03 |
| Investment securities: | | | | | | |
| U.S. Treasury and agency securities | 19.33 | 16.45 | 14.06 | 17.11 | 11.37 | 14.22 |
| State and local government securities | 7.57 | 5.14 | 8.97 | 5.61 | 8.26 | 6.64 |
| All other securities | 0.58 | 2.12 | 0.51 | 2.12 | 0.48 | 1.68 |
| Total investment securities | 27.48 | 23.71 | 23.54 | 24.84 | 20.11 | 22.54 |
| Loans and leases: | | | | | | |
| Commercial and industrial | 20.67 | 16.39 | 18.72 | 16.91 | 14.68 | 17.16 |
| Real estate loans: | | | | | | |
| Construction and development | 2.88 | 2.91 | 3.55 | 2.39 | 3.79 | 3.19 |
| One- to four-family residential | 7.07 | 15.29 | 9.48 | 13.83 | 10.35 | 12.43 |
| Home equity | 2.19 | 3.02 | 1.69 | 2.01 | 0.65 | 1.24 |
| Other real estate | 12.14 | 9.52 | 13.27 | 10.16 | 14.44 | 9.97 |
| Total real estate | 24.28 | 30.74 | 27.99 | 28.39 | 29.23 | 26.83 |
| Consumer loans | 7.01 | 11.57 | 6.88 | 10.71 | 6.97 | 11.01 |
| Other loans and leases | 0.98 | 1.39 | 0.89 | 1.53 | 0.91 | 1.42 |

**EXHIBIT 4** (continued)

| | 1990 | | 1989 | | 1988 | |
|---|---|---|---|---|---|---|
| | Grantland | Peers | Grantland | Peers | Grantland | Peers |
| Total loans and leases | 52.94 | 60.09 | 54.48 | 57.54 | 51.79 | 56.42 |
| Less loan & lease loss reserves | 0.73 | 0.81 | 0.51 | 0.82 | 0.48 | 0.76 |
| Net loans and leases | 52.21 | 59.28 | 53.97 | 56.72 | 51.31 | 55.66 |
| Bank premises and equipment, net | 3.29 | 2.01 | 3.34 | 1.88 | 3.37 | 1.87 |
| Other assets | 1.86 | 2.03 | 1.79 | 2.14 | 1.77 | 2.25 |
| Total assets | 100.00 | 100.00 | 100.00 | 100.00 | 100.00 | 100.00 |
| Total earning assets | 91.11 | 91.30 | 91.74 | 91.43 | 91.46 | 90.99 |
| Non-interest-bearing demand deposits | 14.86 | 15.27 | 14.10 | 15.47 | 14.52 | 15.70 |
| Interest-bearing deposits: | | | | | | |
| Transactions accounts | 8.48 | 9.62 | 8.58 | 8.96 | 8.89 | 8.38 |
| Money market deposit accounts | 8.22 | 13.38 | 9.75 | 14.99 | 11.57 | 15.84 |
| Regular savings | 8.45 | 9.46 | 9.05 | 8.79 | 9.02 | 8.10 |
| Time deposits under $100,000 | 34.01 | 29.41 | 32.22 | 24.74 | 30.61 | 24.68 |
| Time deposits $100,000 and over | 17.72 | 12.48 | 17.07 | 16.94 | 15.65 | 17.96 |
| Total interest-bearing deposits | 76.88 | 74.35 | 76.67 | 74.42 | 75.74 | 74.96 |
| Total deposit liabilities | 91.74 | 89.62 | 90.77 | 89.89 | 90.26 | 90.66 |
| Short-term borrowings | 0.78 | 1.76 | 0.80 | 1.57 | 0.91 | 1.55 |
| Other liabilities | 1.01 | 1.10 | 0.96 | 1.02 | 0.99 | 1.05 |
| Total liabilities | 93.53 | 92.48 | 92.53 | 92.48 | 92.16 | 92.66 |
| Shareholders' equity | 6.47 | 7.52 | 7.47 | 7.52 | 7.84 | 7.34 |
| Total liabilities & equity capital | 100.00 | 100.00 | 100.00 | 100.00 | 100.00 | 100.00 |
| Average total assets ($ in thousands) | 407,794 | | 353,800 | | 322,366 | |

**EXHIBIT 5  Grantland National Bank—Income Statement, Taxable-Equivalent Basis, Percentage of Average Total Assets (dollars in thousands)**

| | 1990 Grantland $ | 1990 Grantland % | 1990 Peers % | 1989 Grantland $ | 1989 Grantland % | 1989 Peers % | 1988 Grantland $ | 1988 Grantland % | 1988 Peers % |
|---|---|---|---|---|---|---|---|---|---|
| Interest income: | | | | | | | | | |
| Loans and leases | 24,913 | 6.11 | 7.12 | 22,956 | 6.49 | 6.10 | 19,330 | 6.00 | 5.81 |
| Investment securities | 10,736 | 2.64 | 2.34 | 7,936 | 2.24 | 2.28 | 6,793 | 2.11 | 2.20 |
| Interest-bearing bank balances | 2,254 | 0.55 | 0.25 | 2,569 | 0.73 | 0.21 | 3,606 | 1.12 | 0.28 |
| Federal funds sold | 1,062 | 0.26 | 0.35 | 1,020 | 0.29 | 0.47 | 824 | 0.25 | 0.58 |
| Total interest income | 38,965 | 9.56 | 10.06 | 34,481 | 9.75 | 9.06 | 30,553 | 9.48 | 8.87 |
| Interest expense: | | | | | | | | | |
| Interest on deposits | 23,043 | 5.65 | 5.25 | 18,091 | 5.12 | 4.77 | 15,591 | 4.84 | 4.70 |
| Interest on short-term borrowings | 264 | 0.07 | 0.14 | 211 | 0.06 | 0.11 | 192 | 0.06 | 0.10 |
| Total interest expense | 23,307 | 5.72 | 5.39 | 18,302 | 5.18 | 4.88 | 15,783 | 4.90 | 4.80 |
| Net interest margin | 15,658 | 3.84 | 4.67 | 16,179 | 4.57 | 4.18 | 14,770 | 4.58 | 4.07 |
| Provision for loan & lease losses | 6,647 | 1.63 | 0.37 | 2,123 | 0.60 | 0.53 | 967 | 0.30 | 0.70 |
| Adjusted net interest margin | 9,011 | 2.21 | 4.30 | 14,056 | 3.97 | 3.65 | 13,803 | 4.28 | 3.37 |
| Noninterest income | 3,874 | 0.95 | 0.87 | 3,290 | 0.93 | 0.85 | 2,901 | 0.90 | 0.82 |
| Noninterest expense: | | | | | | | | | |
| Personnel | 6,729 | 1.65 | 1.69 | 5,661 | 1.60 | 1.51 | 4,997 | 1.55 | 1.47 |
| Occupancy and equipment | 1,427 | 0.35 | 0.57 | 920 | 0.26 | 0.46 | 774 | 0.24 | 0.45 |
| Other noninterest expense | 6,729 | 1.65 | 1.32 | 4,918 | 1.39 | 1.30 | 4,384 | 1.36 | 1.30 |
| Total noninterest expense | 14,885 | 3.65 | 3.58 | 11,499 | 3.25 | 3.27 | 10,155 | 3.15 | 3.22 |
| Net overhead burden | 11,011 | 2.70 | 2.71 | 8,209 | 2.32 | 2.42 | 7,254 | 2.25 | 2.40 |
| Income before income taxes | (2,000) | (0.49) | 1.59 | 5,847 | 1.65 | 1.23 | 6,549 | 2.03 | 0.97 |
| Applicable income taxes | (680) | (0.17) | 0.54 | 1,988 | 0.56 | 0.42 | 2,227 | 0.69 | 0.33 |
| Net income | (1,320) | (0.32) | 1.05 | 3,859 | 1.09 | 0.81 | 4,322 | 1.34 | 0.64 |
| Cash dividends | 950 | | | 2,608 | | | 3,240 | | |

**EXHIBIT 6 Grantland National Bank—Analysis of Loan and Lease Loss Reserve and Problem Loans (dollars in thousands)**

|  | 1990 | 1989 | 1988 | 1987 | 1986 |
|---|---|---|---|---|---|
| Balance, beginning of the year | 1,955 | 1,514 | 1,617 | 1,385 | 1,716 |
| Gross loan and lease losses | 5,409 | 2,013 | 1,224 | 974 | 1,741 |
| Recoveries | 456 | 331 | 154 | 347 | 453 |
| Net loan and lease losses | 4,953 | 1,682 | 1,070 | 627 | 1,288 |
| Provision for loan and lease losses | 6,647 | 2,123 | 967 | 859 | 957 |
| Balance, end of the year | 3,649 | 1,955 | 1,514 | 1,617 | 1,385 |
| Problem loans: |  |  |  |  |  |
| Past due loans 30–89 days | 7,548 | 11,665 | 4,127 | 4,050 | 3,196 |
| Past due loans 90 days and over | 439 | 690 | 1,005 | 708 | 710 |
| Nonaccrual loans and leases | 13,493 | 2,758 | 289 | 168 | 1,224 |
| Renegotiated | 1,431 | 1,230 | 0 | 0 | 0 |

**EXHIBIT 7  Grantland National Bank—Interest Rate Sensitivity Report Maturity and Repricing Distribution of Earning Assets and Interest-Paying Liabilities Cumulative Amount and as a Percent of Assets, December 31, 1990 (dollars in thousands)**

| | Repriced within 3 Months | | | Repriced within 12 Months | | |
| | Grantland National | | Peers | Grantland National | | Peers |
| | $ | % | % | $ | % | % |
|---|---|---|---|---|---|---|
| Earning assets: | | | | | | |
| Money market investments | 26,220 | 6.29 | 6.16 | 48,200 | 11.56 | 8.18 |
| Investment securities | 11,264 | 2.70 | 2.48 | 38,036 | 9.13 | 8.27 |
| Loans and leases | 78,841 | 18.92 | 27.61 | 101,730 | 24.41 | 36.04 |
| Total earning assets | 116,325 | 27.91 | 36.25 | 187,966 | 45.10 | 52.49 |
| Interest-paying liabilities: | | | | | | |
| Transactions accounts | 36,544 | 8.77 | 9.62 | 36,544 | 8.77 | 9.62 |
| Money market deposit accounts | 31,950 | 7.67 | 13.38 | 31,950 | 7.67 | 13.38 |
| Regular savings | | | .15 | 3,435 | .82 | .95 |
| Time deposits under $100,000 | 50,700 | 12.16 | 10.29 | 108,642 | 26.07 | 22.06 |
| Time deposits $100,000 and over | 45,981 | 11.03 | 7.49 | 63,666 | 15.27 | 10.61 |
| Short-term borrowings | 3,118 | .75 | 1.80 | 3,118 | .75 | 1.80 |
| Total interest-paying liabilities | 168,293 | 40.38 | 42.73 | 247,355 | 59.35 | 58.42 |
| Gap (earning assets − interest-paying liabilities) | (51,968) | (12.47) | (6.48) | (59,389) | (14.25) | (5.93) |

| CASE | CENTRAN NATIONAL BANK |
|---|---|
| **21** | |

Centran National Bank (CNB) was the largest independent bank in the state. At the end of 1987 the bank had total resources of $2.6 billion, and its staff of about 1,900 officers and employees operated 80 offices, primarily located in the state's metropolitan areas.

The senior management of CNB had recently decided that there was an increasing need for more long-range planning, given the many significant changes in the competition, structure, and regulatory environment of all financial institutions, especially banks. Accordingly, Mr. Wilson Harwood was appointed to the newly created position of director, strategic planning. In past years there had been very little longer-range planning beyond the annual budget and profit planning cycle. It had been concluded, however, that CNB's size and expected future growth required more attention to shifting competitive trends and the bank's need to adapt to change.

Harwood, age 38, had been employed at CNB for 7 years and recently had been promoted to senior vice-president. His prior experience with the bank had involved primarily the accounting and controllership areas. Harwood had no prior experience with long-range planning concepts and procedures; however, he was regarded as "a good numbers man."

Shortly after assuming his new duties, Harwood concluded that a useful initial step in the forward planning process would be a thorough performance review clarifying where CNB stood now relative to its peer-group competitors, as well as an assessment of the bank's principal strengths and weaknesses. He reasoned that a close analysis of the financial and operating data should provide a clear picture of relative profitability. Harwood intended such a review to focus on the risks related to liquidity, credit, interest rate exposure, and capital.

With a comprehensive review at hand, Harwood believed he could then begin to formulate ideas and alternative possibilities for the bank's future growth.

CNB's banking offices were located in highly competitive markets. There were 337 banks in the state, operating over 2,600 full-service branches. CNB's offices also competed with thrifts, finance companies, and other financial institutions. Additionally, out-of-state bank and nonbank providers of financial services were becoming more important competitors in CNB's major metropolitan markets.

CNB's branches were grouped into three geographic regions, each headed by an executive vice-president. The bank's organizational philosophy was to afford each region strong local autonomy for operations in its respective communities, coupled with rigorous centralized financial controls.

Over the past five years, CNB's total resources had grown from $1.1 to $2.6 billion, an annual growth rate of about 19 percent. Much of this growth had been achieved through the purchase of smaller banks. Most of these acquisitions involved the exchange of common stock. It was CNB's policy to use its common stock for acquisitions so that equity was increased in proportion to the assets acquired.

In 1987, CNB's net income was $30 million, a gain of more than 13 percent over the $26.5 million earned in 1986. Earnings were $2.22 per share compared with $1.96 in 1986, and cash dividends were increased from $0.625 to $0.75 per share. The bank's return on average total assets was maintained at 1.23 percent, and return on average shareholders' equity was 16.4 percent.

CNB's earning performance in 1987 was driven by significant increases in the loan portfolio—notably consumer installment, credit card, and commercial loans—and in tax-exempt securities. This growth in earning assets was funded primarily by core deposits that moderated the bank's reliance on large deposit liabilities and resulted in a slight increase in net interest margin.

Following are selected excerpts from management's discussion and analysis of CNB's operations in the bank's 1987 annual report:

Because loan and deposit portfolios are independently dynamic, maturities are often mismatched. These mismatches, if left unmanaged, could subject the bank's earnings stream to random change in market interest rates. The bank's Asset and Liability Management Committee sets guidelines within which maturity and repricing mismatches are managed. By actively restructuring the securities portfolio, in both size and content, as market opportunities become available, the bank is able to offset undesirable asset and liability mismatches as they occur. The bank can also foster the objective of maximizing the "total rate of return" performance of the securities portfolio as measured by interest income, realized gains and losses, and the change in portfolio market value from period to period. The bank has maintained that the impact of changes in interest rates can be minimized by properly matching maturing and repricing opportunities of assets and liabilities. Changes in interest rates become less significant under this operating philosophy, which concentrates on managing the net interest margin instead of guessing at the direction of future interest rates. The narrow range of the bank's net interest margins of 5.01 to 5.68 percent over the past five years, which included periods of highly volatile interest rates, confirms the value of this strategy.

Four areas—credit card balances, student loans, small and middle-market commercial credits and equipment leasing, and automobile leasing—account for over one-fifth of the bank's loan portfolio and collectively generate yields approximating twice the prime rate. The bank's commercial and lease portfolios are diversified, as no single industry concentration exceeds 10 percent of total loans and leases. The bank's exposure in the troubled areas of oil and gas, agriculture, and foreign loans remains very small.

The ability to maintain, or have access to, sufficient funds for potential customer demands is the focus of liquidity management. The bank's net short-term assets are the first and most reliable source of incremental funds. The next liquidity source is our network of banking offices, providing access to a growing market of retail deposits. The third layer of the liquidity management system is the ability to access large liabilities in our local markets. The final source for incremental liquidity is the ability to access large liabilities, including Federal funds, jumbo certificates, and brokered deposits, in the national marketplace. By bank policy, total dependence on large local and national market liabilities is maintained at less than 25 percent of earning assets net of money market investments. Large liability dependence was 21.35 percent at year-end 1987 compared with 18.14 percent at year-end 1986.

The bank historically has sought to maintain superior levels of capital compared with peer organizations. At year-end 1987, the primary capital ratio was 8.44 percent, well in excess of the regulators' minimum requirement of 5.5 percent. For the year, average common equity represented 7.48 percent of average total assets. Capital ratios are maintained through matching dividend increases to earnings gains. Dividends paid as a percentage of net income have averaged between 32 and 35 percent.

Exhibits 1 through 6 contain the 1985–1987 financial data for CNB, as well as selected peer-group data for all U.S. commercial banks with total assets of $1 to $3 billion.

**EXHIBIT I    Centran National Bank—Average Balance Sheet (dollars in millions)**

|  | 1987 | | 1986 | | 1985 | |
|---|---|---|---|---|---|---|
|  | $ | % | $ | % | $ | % |
| Cash and due from banks | 176 | 7.20 | 165 | 7.65 | 147 | 7.76 |
| Investment securities: | | | | | | |
|   Taxable securities | 241 | 9.86 | 211 | 9.78 | 180 | 9.51 |
|   Tax-exempt securities | 235 | 9.61 | 170 | 7.88 | 126 | 6.65 |
|     Total investment securities | 476 | 19.47 | 381 | 17.66 | 306 | 16.16 |
| Interest-bearing deposits with banks | 76 | 3.11 | 102 | 4.73 | 156 | 8.24 |
| Federal funds sold and resales | 42 | 1.72 | 59 | 2.73 | 43 | 2.27 |
| Loans and lease financing: | | | | | | |
|   Commercial, financial, agricultural | 741 | 30.31 | 604 | 27.99 | 524 | 27.67 |
|   Real estate—construction | 60 | 2.45 | 62 | 2.87 | 59 | 3.12 |
|   Real estate—mortgage | 216 | 8.83 | 215 | 9.96 | 214 | 11.30 |
|   Consumer and credit card | 537 | 21.96 | 456 | 21.13 | 341 | 18.00 |
|   Lease financing | 44 | 1.80 | 33 | 1.53 | 27 | 1.42 |
|     Total loans and leases | 1,598 | 65.35 | 1,370 | 63.48 | 1,165 | 61.51 |
|     Lease reserve for losses | 21 | .86 | 17 | .79 | 14 | .74 |
|     Net loans and leases | 1,577 | 64.49 | 1,353 | 62.69 | 1,151 | 60.77 |
| Bank premises and equipment, net | 43 | 1.76 | 42 | 1.95 | 40 | 2.11 |
| Acceptances and other assets | 55 | 2.25 | 56 | 2.59 | 51 | 2.69 |
|   Total assets | 2,445 | 100.00 | 2,158 | 100.00 | 1,894 | 100.00 |
|     Total earning assets | 2,192 | 89.65 | 1,912 | 88.60 | 1,670 | 88.17 |
| Demand deposits—non-interest-bearing | 340 | 13.91 | 312 | 14.46 | 282 | 14.89 |
| Interest-bearing deposits: | | | | | | |
|   Demand deposits—interest-bearing | 189 | 7.73 | 151 | 7.00 | 130 | 6.86 |
|   Regular and money market savings | 500 | 20.45 | 405 | 18.77 | 352 | 18.59 |
|   Time accounts under $100M | 509 | 20.82 | 486 | 22.52 | 419 | 22.12 |
|   Time accounts $100M and over | 365 | 14.93 | 350 | 16.22 | 311 | 16.42 |
|     Total interest-bearing deposits | 1,563 | 63.93 | 1,392 | 64.51 | 1,212 | 63.99 |
|     Total deposits | 1,903 | 77.84 | 1,704 | 78.97 | 1,494 | 78.88 |
| Short-term borrowings | 302 | 12.35 | 234 | 10.84 | 209 | 11.03 |
| Acceptances and other liabilities | 57 | 2.33 | 59 | 2.73 | 56 | 2.96 |
|   Total liabilities | 2,262 | 92.52 | 1,997 | 92.54 | 1,759 | 92.87 |
| Shareholders' equity | 183 | 7.48 | 161 | 7.46 | 135 | 7.13 |
|   Total liabilities and equity capital | 2,445 | 100.00 | 2,158 | 100.00 | 1,894 | 100.00 |
| Average shares of common stock outstanding (in millions) | 13.3 | | 13.1 | | 12.8 | |
| Book value per share | $13.76 | | $12.29 | | $10.55 | |

**EXHIBIT 2   Centran National Bank—Income Statement, Years Ended December 31, Tax-Equivalent Basis (dollars in millions)**

|  | 1987 | | 1986 | | 1985 | |
|---|---|---|---|---|---|---|
|  | $ | % | $ | % | $ | % |
| Interest income: | | | | | | |
| Loans and leases | 195.4 | 65.40 | 182.5 | 65.46 | 162.3 | 64.79 |
| Investment securities: | | | | | | |
| Taxable | 21.2 | 7.10 | 21.9 | 7.86 | 19.5 | 7.78 |
| Tax-exempt | 32.4 | 10.84 | 25.3 | 9.07 | 18.3 | 7.30 |
| Interest-bearing deposits | 5.5 | 1.84 | 8.9 | 3.19 | 16.8 | 6.71 |
| Federal funds sold | 2.9 | .97 | 4.8 | 1.72 | 4.7 | 1.87 |
| Total interest income | 257.4 | 86.15 | 243.4 | 87.30 | 221.6 | 88.46 |
| Noninterest income: | | | | | | |
| Service charges, deposit accounts | 8.7 | 2.91 | 7.9 | 2.83 | 7.0 | 2.79 |
| Trust fees | 6.3 | 2.11 | 5.4 | 1.94 | 5.2 | 2.08 |
| Securities gains (losses) | 3.8 | 1.27 | .2 | .07 | .1 | .04 |
| Other noninterest income | 22.6 | 7.56 | 21.9 | 7.86 | 16.6 | 6.63 |
| Total noninterest income | 41.4 | 13.85 | 35.4 | 12.70 | 28.9 | 11.54 |
| Total operating income | 298.8 | 100.0 | 278.8 | 100.00 | 250.5 | 100.0 |
| Interest expense: | | | | | | |
| Interest on deposits | 112.2 | 37.55 | 116.1 | 41.64 | 109.1 | 43.55 |
| Interest on short-term borrowings | 20.7 | 6.93 | 19.3 | 6.92 | 21.3 | 8.50 |
| Total interest expense | 132.9 | 44.48 | 135.4 | 48.56 | 130.4 | 52.05 |
| Provision for loan losses | 19.5 | 6.53 | 16.8 | 6.03 | 12.4 | 4.95 |
| Noninterest expense: | | | | | | |
| Personnel | 42.1 | 14.09 | 37.1 | 13.31 | 33.2 | 13.26 |
| Occupancy and equipment | 11.3 | 3.78 | 9.5 | 3.41 | 8.7 | 3.47 |
| Other noninterest expense | 37.9 | 12.68 | 31.7 | 11.37 | 26.0 | 10.38 |
| Total noninterest expense | 91.3 | 30.55 | 78.3 | 28.09 | 67.9 | 27.11 |
| Total operating expense | 243.7 | 81.56 | 230.5 | 82.68 | 210.7 | 84.11 |
| Income before income taxes | 55.1 | 18.44 | 48.3 | 17.32 | 39.8 | 15.89 |
| Applicable income tax | 25.1 | 8.40 | 21.8 | 7.82 | 18.3 | 7.31 |
| Net income | 30.0 | 10.04 | 26.5 | 9.50 | 21.5 | 8.58 |

**EXHIBIT 3   Centran National Bank—Income Statement, Tax-Equivalent Basis, Percentage of Average Total Assets**

|  | 1987 | 1986 | 1985 |
|---|---|---|---|
| Interest income: | | | |
| Loans and leases | 7.99% | 8.46% | 8.57% |
| Investment securities | 2.19 | 2.19 | 1.99 |
| Interest-bearing deposits | .23 | .41 | .89 |
| Federal funds sold | .12 | .22 | .25 |
| Total interest income | 10.53 | 11.28 | 11.70 |
| Interest expense: | | | |
| Interest on deposits | 4.59 | 5.38 | 5.76 |
| Interest on short-term borrowings | .85 | .89 | 1.13 |
| Total interest expense | 5.44 | 6.27 | 6.89 |
| Net interest margin | 5.09 | 5.01 | 4.81 |
| Provision for loan losses | .80 | .78 | .65 |
| Adjusted net interest margin | 4.29 | 4.23 | 4.16 |
| Noninterest income: | | | |
| Service charges on deposit accounts | .36 | .37 | .37 |
| Trust fees | .26 | .25 | .27 |
| Securities gains (losses) | .16 | .01 | — |
| Other noninterest income | .92 | 1.01 | .88 |
| Total noninterest income | 1.70 | 1.64 | 1.52 |
| Noninterest expense: | | | |
| Personnel | 1.72 | 1.72 | 1.75 |
| Occupancy and equipment | .46 | .44 | .46 |
| Other noninterest expense | 1.55 | 1.47 | 1.37 |
| Total noninterest expense | 3.73 | 3.63 | 3.58 |
| Net overhead burden | 2.03 | 1.99 | 2.06 |
| Income before income taxes | 2.26 | 2.24 | 2.10 |
| Applicable income taxes | 1.03 | 1.01 | .97 |
| Net income | 1.23 | 1.23 | 1.13 |
| As a percentage of average earning assets: | | | |
| Total interest income | 11.74% | 12.73% | 13.27% |
| Total interest expense | 6.06 | 7.08 | 7.81 |
| Net interest margin | 5.68% | 5.65% | 5.46% |

**EXHIBIT 4** **Centran National Bank—Asset and Liability Maturity Repricing Schedule, December 31, 1987 (dollars in millions)**

| | Within 3 Months | 4 to 6 Months | 7 to 12 Months | 1 to 5 Years | Years | Total |
|---|---|---|---|---|---|---|
| Earning assets: | | | | | | |
|   Interest-bearing deposits | $86 | $4 | $5 | | | $95 |
|   Securities | 31 | 47 | 35 | $172 | $194 | 479 |
|   Loans and leases: | | | | | | |
|     Variable-rate: | | | | | | |
|       Commercial | 632 | 5 | | | | 637 |
|       Real estate, mortgage | 41 | 11 | 3 | 8 | | 63 |
|       Other | 138 | | | | | 138 |
|     Fixed-rate: | | | | | | |
|       Commercial | 24 | 11 | 11 | 56 | 63 | 165 |
|       Real estate, mortgage | 11 | 5 | 10 | 52 | 67 | 145 |
|       Other | 69 | 36 | 66 | 246 | 167 | 584 |
|   Total loans and leases | 915 | 68 | 90 | 362 | 297 | 1,732 |
|   Total earning assets | $1,032 | $119 | $130 | $534 | $491 | $2,306 |
| Interest-bearing liabilities: | | | | | | |
|   Demand—interest-bearing | $141 | $6 | $12 | $72 | | $231 |
|   Regular and money market savings | 235 | 19 | 36 | 199 | $72 | 561 |
|   Time deposits less than $100M | 197 | 115 | 83 | 160 | 16 | 571 |
|   Time deposits $100M and over | 114 | 25 | 14 | 67 | | 220 |
|   Purchased funds | 347 | | | | | 347 |
| Total interest-bearing liabilities | $1,034 | $165 | $145 | $498 | $88 | $1,930 |
| GAP | (2) | (46) | (15) | 36 | 403 | 376 |
| Cumulative GAP | (2) | (48) | (63) | (27) | 376 | 376 |
| Cumulative GAP as a percent of earning assets | (0.9)% | (2.08)% | (2.73)% | (1.17%) | 16.31% | 16.31% |

**752**

### EXHIBIT 5 Centran National Bank—Peer Group Data (All Insured Coml. Banks with Assets of $1 to $3 Billion)

| | Centran | | | Peers | | |
|---|---|---|---|---|---|---|
| | 1987 | 1986 | 1985 | 1987 | 1986 | 1985 |
| **1. Year-end maturities of investment securities:** | | | | | | |
| Under 1 year | 21.92% | 16.01% | 5.12% | 29.67% | 33.60% | 32.76% |
| 1 to 5 years | 45.77 | 41.50 | 46.13 | 42.87 | 38.72 | 39.02 |
| 5 to 10 years | 16.27 | 20.52 | 22.56 | 13.85 | 15.02 | 13.40 |
| Over 10 years | 16.04 | 21.97 | 26.19 | 13.61 | 12.66 | 14.72 |
| **2. Year-end market to book value:** | | | | | | |
| Taxable securities | 102.05% | 102.73% | 98.96% | 101.60% | 101.49% | 99.48% |
| Tax-exempt securities | 106.84 | 100.97 | 94.92 | 103.05 | 96.79 | 90.30 |
| **3. Yield on average investment securities:** | | | | | | |
| Taxable securities | 8.80% | 10.38% | 10.83% | 8.95% | 10.29% | 10.77% |
| Tax-exempt securities—tax equivalent | 13.79 | 14.88 | 14.52 | 12.59 | 12.42 | 12.24 |
| Total securities—tax equivalent | 11.26% | 12.39% | 12.35% | 10.17% | 11.29% | 11.54% |
| **4. Provision for loan losses:** | | | | | | |
| Provision/average total assets | 0.80% | 0.78% | 0.65% | 0.61% | 0.49% | 0.41% |
| Provision/average total loans and leases | 1.22 | 1.23 | 1.06 | 0.97 | 0.79 | 0.69 |
| **5. Loan and lease losses:** | | | | | | |
| Gross losses/average total loans and leases | 1.36% | 1.31% | 1.05% | 0.80% | 0.65% | 0.64% |
| Recoveries/average total loans and leases | 0.35 | 0.29 | 0.29 | 0.15 | 0.16 | 0.17 |
| Net losses/average total loans and leases | 1.01% | 1.02% | 0.76% | 0.65% | 0.49% | 0.47% |
| **6. Loan loss reserve:** | | | | | | |
| Ending reserve/total loans and leases | 1.39% | 1.28% | 1.22% | 1.33% | 1.22% | 1.18% |
| Ending reserve/net loan losses | 1.50× | 1.39× | 1.65× | 3.73× | 4.20× | 4.02× |
| **7. Earnings coverage of net loan and lease losses** | 3.31× | 3.29× | 4.28× | 7.12× | 8.36× | 7.83× |
| **8. Nonperforming assets/year-end loans and leases** | 2.12% | 2.06% | 2.43% | 1.62% | 1.85% | 2.12% |
| **9. Yield on loans and leases** | 12.23% | 13.32% | 13.93% | 11.03% | 12.00% | 12.60% |
| **10. Yield on deposits with banks** | 7.24% | 8.73% | 10.77% | 7.76% | 9.11% | 10.95% |
| **11. Yield on Federal funds sold** | 6.90% | 8.14% | 10.93% | 6.86% | 8.19% | 10.41% |
| **12. Profitability ratios:** | | | | | | |
| Net profit margin—tax equivalent | 10.04% | 9.51% | 8.58% | 8.39% | 7.88% | 6.89% |
| Asset yield or utilization—tax equivalent | 12.22 | 12.92 | 13.23 | 10.85 | 11.55 | 12.34 |

| | | | | | | |
|---|---|---|---|---|---|---|
| Return on average total assets | 1.23 | 1.23 | 1.13 | .91 | .91 | .85 |
| Leverage multiplier | 13.36× | 13.40× | 14.03× | 15.95× | 16.26× | 16.81× |
| Return on average equity capital | 16.39% | 16.46% | 15.93% | 14.51% | 14.79% | 14.23% |
| 13. Noninterest income/average total assets | 1.70% | 1.64% | 1.52% | 1.40% | 1.27% | 1.23% |
| 14. Personnel expense: | | | | | | |
| Number of FTE employees | 1,898 | 1,854 | 1,773 | | | |
| Personnel expense per FTE employee | $22,181 | $20,011 | $18,725 | $25,470 | $24,510 | $23,710 |
| FTE employees per $1 million average assets | 0.78 | 0.86 | 0.94 | 0.64 | 0.70 | 0.74 |
| 15. Fund costs: | | | | | | |
| All interest-paying funds | 7.13% | 8.33% | 9.18% | 6.68% | 7.82% | 9.26% |
| All interest-paying deposits | 7.18 | 8.34 | 9.00 | 6.70 | 7.81 | 9.09 |
| Federal funds purchased | 6.85 | 8.25 | 10.19 | 6.46 | 7.84 | 9.95 |
| 16. Interest rate sensitivity (percent of assets) | | | | | | |
| Three months | 39.62% | 33.31% | 33.52% | 44.03% | 44.21% | 44.12% |
| Six months | 44.18 | 38.23 | 39.02 | 47.88 | 48.59 | 49.40 |
| One year | 49.13 | 46.63 | 44.10 | 53.83 | 54.42 | 55.52 |
| Liabilities repriced within: | | | | | | |
| Three months | 39.69% | 34.74% | 31.87% | 49.90% | 46.93% | 46.12% |
| Six months | 46.03 | 41.20 | 39.27 | 55.15 | 52.78 | 52.91 |
| One year | 51.59 | 47.69 | 43.88 | 58.66 | 56.57 | 56.46 |
| Cumulative gap: | | | | | | |
| Three months | (.07%) | (1.43%) | 1.65% | (5.87%) | (2.72%) | (2.00%) |
| Six months | (1.85) | (2.97) | (.25) | (7.27) | (4.19) | (3.51) |
| One year | (2.42) | (1.06) | .22 | (4.83) | (2.15) | (.94) |
| 17. Liquidity measures | | | | | | |
| Temporary investments/total assets | 9.08% | 10.29% | 11.35% | 12.68% | 14.26% | 16.00% |
| Core deposits/total assets | 62.90 | 62.74 | 62.46 | 65.56 | 64.68 | 61.81 |
| Volatile liabilities/total assets | 27.28 | 27.07 | 27.46 | 25.88 | 26.69 | 29.65 |
| Volatile liability dependence | 22.83 | 21.64 | 21.17 | 17.65 | 16.03 | 19.21 |
| Short-term borrowings/equity capital | 1.65× | 1.45× | 1.55× | 1.69× | 1.69× | 1.97× |
| 18. Capital measures: | | | | | | |
| Primary capital/total assets | 8.34% | 8.25% | 7.87% | 7.10% | 6.90% | 6.65% |
| Total capital/total assets | 8.34 | 8.25 | 7.87 | 7.35 | 7.25 | 7.00 |
| Primary capital/total loans and leases | 12.77 | 12.99 | 12.79 | 11.23 | 11.16 | 11.22 |
| Total capital/total loans and leases | 12.77 | 12.99 | 12.79 | 11.63 | 11.73 | 11.81 |
| 19. End-of-period growth rates: | | | | | | |
| Total assets | 5.45% | 17.44% | 17.09% | 12.71% | 12.77% | 12.27% |
| Total loans and leases | 14.78 | 15.25 | 28.37 | 15.24 | 17.60 | 15.24 |
| Equity capital | 12.29 | 22.18 | 18.09 | 14.91 | 16.47 | 13.40 |
| Total capital | 13.25 | 22.05 | 19.38 | 14.26 | 16.71 | 13.27 |
| 20. Cash dividends declared/net income | 33.80% | 31.90% | 32.50% | 38.51% | 38.60% | 39.28% |
| 21. Internal capital generation rate | 10.85% | 11.21% | 10.75% | 8.92% | 9.08% | 8.64% |

**EXHIBIT 6** **Centran National Bank—Comparative Financial Analysis**

| | 1987 | 1986 | 1985 |
|---|---|---|---|
| **Composition of Assets and Liabilities** | | | |
| 1. Distribution of average total assets | | | |
|   a. Cash and due from banks | | | |
|     Centran | 7.20% | 7.65% | 7.76% |
|     Peer group | 8.04 | 8.12 | 8.28 |
|     Difference | (0.84%) | (0.47%) | (0.52%) |
|   b. Investment securities | | | |
|     Centran | 19.47% | 17.66% | 16.16% |
|     Peer group | 17.66 | 17.98 | 18.53 |
|     Difference | (1.81%) | (1.32%) | (2.37%) |
|   c. Taxable securities | | | |
|     Centran | 9.86% | 9.78% | 9.51% |
|     Peer group | 11.40 | 10.81 | 12.01 |
|     Difference | (1.54%) | (1.03%) | (2.50%) |
|   d. Tax-exempt securities | | | |
|     Centran | 9.61% | 7.88% | 6.65% |
|     Peer group | 6.26 | 7.17 | 6.52 |
|     Difference | 3.35% | 0.71% | 0.13% |
|   e. Net loans and leases | | | |
|     Centran | 64.49% | 62.69% | 60.77% |
|     Peer group | 62.38 | 61.07 | 58.58 |
|     Difference | 2.11% | 1.62% | 2.19% |
|   f. Earning assets | | | |
|     Centran | 89.65% | 88.60% | 88.17% |
|     Peer group | 88.31 | 88.02 | 87.73 |
|     Difference | 1.34% | 0.58% | 0.44% |
| 2. Distribution of total loans and leases | | | |
|   a. Commercial, financial, agricultural | | | |
|     Centran | 46.37% | 44.09% | 44.98% |
|     Peer group | 43.57 | 44.13 | 45.62 |
|     Difference | 2.80% | (0.04%) | (0.64%) |
|   b. Real estate—construction | | | |
|     Centran | 3.76% | 4.53% | 5.06% |
|     Peer group | 6.52 | 5.97 | 5.96 |
|     Difference | (2.76%) | (1.44%) | (0.90%) |
|   c. Real estate—mortgage | | | |
|     Centran | 13.52% | 15.69% | 18.37% |
|     Peer group | 23.13 | 23.53 | 23.85 |
|     Difference | (9.61%) | (7.84%) | (5.48%) |
|   d. Consumer installment and credit card | | | |
|     Centran | 33.69% | 33.28% | 29.27% |
|     Peer group | 25.17 | 24.58 | 22.66 |
|     Difference | 8.43% | 8.70% | 6.61% |

**EXHIBIT 6** *(continued)*

| | 1987 | 1986 | 1985 |
|---|---|---|---|
| **3. Year-end maturities of investment securities** | | | |
| **a. Under one year** | | | |
| Centran | 21.92% | 16.01% | 5.12% |
| Peer group | 29.67 | 33.60 | 32.76 |
| Difference | (7.75%) | (17.59%) | (27.64%) |
| **b. One to five years** | | | |
| Centran | 45.77% | 41.50% | 46.13% |
| Peer group | 42.87 | 38.72 | 39.12 |
| Difference | 2.90% | 2.78% | 7.01% |
| **c. Five to 10 years** | | | |
| Centran | 16.27% | 20.52% | 22.56% |
| Peer group | 13.85 | 15.02 | 13.40 |
| Difference | 2.42% | 5.50% | 9.16% |
| **d. Over 10 years** | | | |
| Centran | 16.04% | 21.97% | 26.19% |
| Peer group | 13.61 | 12.66 | 14.72 |
| Difference | 2.43% | 9.31% | 11.47% |
| **4. Distribution of liabilities and equity capital** | | | |
| **a. Demand deposits—non-interest-bearing** | | | |
| Centran | 13.91% | 14.46% | 14.89% |
| Peer group | 18.73 | 19.17 | 19.78 |
| Difference | (4.83%) | (4.71%) | (4.89%) |
| **b. Non-interest-bearing demand, regular and money market savings** | | | |
| Centran | 28.18% | 25.77% | 25.45% |
| Peer group | 29.37 | 26.79 | 23.72 |
| Difference | (1.19%) | (1.02%) | 1.73% |
| **c. Time accounts under $100,000** | | | |
| Centran | 20.82% | 22.52% | 22.12% |
| Peer group | 17.46 | 18.72 | 18.31 |
| Difference | 3.36% | 3.80% | 3.81% |
| **d. Time accounts $100,000 and over** | | | |
| Centran | 14.93% | 16.22% | 16.42% |
| Peer group | 12.96 | 13.90 | 14.70 |
| Difference | 1.97% | 2.32% | 1.72% |
| **e. Equity capital** | | | |
| Centran | 7.48% | 7.46% | 7.13% |
| Peer group | 6.27 | 6.15 | 5.95 |
| Difference | 1.21% | 1.31% | 1.18% |

**EXHIBIT 6**  (continued)

|  | 1987 | 1986 | 1985 |
|---|---|---|---|
| **Profitability Measures** | | | |
| 5. Return on average total assets | | | |
|     Centran | 1.23% | 1.23% | 1.13% |
|     Peer group | 0.91 | 0.91 | 0.85 |
|       Difference | 0.32% | 0.32% | 0.28% |
| 6. Return on average equity capital | | | |
|     Centran | 16.39% | 16.46% | 15.93% |
|     Peer group | 14.51 | 14.79 | 14.23 |
|       Difference | 1.88% | 1.67% | 1.70% |
| **Components of Profitability** | | | |
| 7. Net profit margin—taxable equivalent | | | |
|     Centran | 10.04% | 9.51% | 8.58% |
|     Peer group | 8.39 | 7.88 | 6.89 |
|       Difference | 1.65% | 1.63% | 1.69% |
| 8. Asset yield or asset utilization—taxable equivalent | | | |
|     Centran | 12.22% | 12.92% | 13.23% |
|     Peer group | 10.85 | 11.55 | 12.34 |
|       Difference | 1.37% | 1.37% | .89% |
| 9. Leverage multiplier or equity multiplier | | | |
|     Centran | 13.36× | 13.40× | 14.03× |
|     Peer group | 15.95 | 16.26 | 16.81 |
|       Difference | (2.59×) | (2.86×) | (2.78×) |
| **Analysis of Net Profit Margin** | | | |
| 10. Expense control measures | | | |
|   a. Total expenses/average total assets | | | |
|       Centran | 9.97% | 10.68% | 11.12% |
|       Peer group | 9.16 | 9.87 | 10.77 |
|         Difference | 0.81% | 0.81% | 0.35% |
|     (i) Interest expense | | | |
|       Centran | 5.44% | 6.27% | 6.89% |
|       Peer group | 4.99 | 5.77 | 6.77 |
|         Difference | 0.45% | 0.50% | 0.12% |
|     (ii) Provision for loan losses | | | |
|       Centran | 0.80% | 0.78% | 0.65% |
|       Peer group | 0.61 | 0.49 | 0.41 |
|         Difference | 0.19% | 0.29% | 0.24% |
|     (iii) Personnel expense | | | |
|       Centran | 1.72% | 1.72% | 1.75% |
|       Peer group | 1.63 | 1.71 | 1.78 |
|         Difference | 0.09% | 0.01% | (0.03%) |

**EXHIBIT 6**    (continued)

| | 1987 | 1986 | 1985 |
|---|---|---|---|
| b. Personnel expense/FTE employees | | | |
| Centran | $22,181 | $20,011 | $18,725 |
| Peer group | 25,470 | 24,510 | 23,710 |
| Difference | ($3,289) | ($4,499) | ($4,985) |
| c. FTE employees/$1MM of average assets | | | |
| Centran | 0.78 | 0.86 | 0.94 |
| Peer group | 0.64 | 0.70 | 0.74 |
| Difference | 0.14 | 0.16 | 0.20 |
| d. Interest-paying funds/total assets | | | |
| Centran | 76.28% | 75.35% | 75.02% |
| Peer group | 72.96 | 72.55 | 72.03 |
| Difference | 3.32% | 2.80% | 2.99% |
| e. Interest on interest-paying funds | | | |
| Centran | 7.13% | 8.33% | 9.18% |
| Peer group | 6.68 | 7.82 | 9.26 |
| Difference | 0.45% | 0.51% | (0.08%) |
| 11. Spread management measures (as percent of average total assets) | | | |
| a. Total interest income—taxable equivalent | | | |
| Centran | 10.52% | 11.28% | 11.70% |
| Peer group | 9.45 | 10.28 | 11.11 |
| Difference | 1.07% | 1.00% | 0.59% |
| b. Less total interest expense | | | |
| Centran | 5.44% | 6.27% | 6.89% |
| Peer group | 4.99 | 5.77 | 6.77 |
| Difference | 0.45% | 0.50% | 0.12% |
| c. Equals net interest margin | | | |
| Centran | 5.09% | 5.01% | 4.81% |
| Peer group | 4.46 | 4.51 | 4.34 |
| Difference | 0.63% | 0.50% | 0.47% |
| d. Less provision for loan losses | | | |
| Centran | 0.80% | 0.78% | 0.65% |
| Peer group | 0.61 | 0.49 | 0.41 |
| Difference | 0.19% | 0.29% | 0.24% |
| e. Equals adjusted net interest margin | | | |
| Centran | 4.29% | 4.23% | 4.16% |
| Peer group | 3.85 | 4.02 | 3.93 |
| Difference | 0.44% | 0.21% | 0.23% |
| f. Noninterest income | | | |
| Centran | 1.70% | 1.64% | 1.52% |
| Peer group | 1.40 | 1.27 | 1.23 |
| Difference | 0.30% | 0.37% | 0.29% |

**EXHIBIT 6** *(continued)*

|  | 1987 | 1986 | 1985 |
|---|---|---|---|
| g.  Less noninterest expense | | | |
| Centran | 3.73% | 3.63% | 3.58% |
| Peer group | 3.56 | 3.61 | 3.59 |
| Difference | 0.17% | 0.02% | (0.01%) |
| h.  Equals net overhead burden | | | |
| Centran | (2.03%) | (1.99%) | (2.06%) |
| Peer group | (2.16) | (2.34) | (2.36) |
| Difference | (0.13%) | (0.35%) | (0.30%) |
| i.  Income before taxes—taxable equivalent | | | |
| Centran | 2.26% | 2.24% | 2.10% |
| Peer group | 1.69 | 1.68 | 1.57 |
| Difference | 0.57% | 0.56% | 0.53% |
| j.  Applicable income taxes—taxable equivalent | | | |
| Centran | 1.03% | 1.01% | 0.97% |
| Peer group | 0.78 | 0.77 | 0.72 |
| Difference | 0.25% | 0.24% | 0.25% |
| k.  Net income after taxes | | | |
| Centran | 1.23% | 1.23% | 1.13% |
| Peer group | 0.91 | 0.91 | 0.85 |
| Difference | 0.32% | 0.32% | 0.28% |
| | | | |
| **Analysis of Asset Yield** | | | |
| 12.  Yield on total loans and leases | | | |
| Centran | 12.23% | 13.32% | 13.93% |
| Peer group | 11.03 | 12.00 | 13.15 |
| Difference | 1.20% | 1.32% | 0.78% |
| 13.  Return on investment securities—taxable equivalent | | | |
| Centran | 11.26% | 12.39% | 12.35% |
| Peer group | 10.17 | 11.29 | 11.54 |
| Difference | 1.09% | 1.10% | 0.81% |
| 14.  Return on taxable securities | | | |
| Centran | 8.80% | 10.38% | 10.83% |
| Peer group | 8.95 | 10.29 | 10.77 |
| Difference | (0.15%) | 0.09% | 0.06% |
| 15.  Return on tax-exempt securities—taxable equivalent | | | |
| Centran | 13.79% | 14.88% | 14.52% |
| Peer group | 12.59 | 12.42 | 12.24 |
| Difference | 1.20% | 2.46% | 2.28% |

**EXHIBIT 6** *(continued)*

| | 1987 | 1986 | 1985 |
|---|---|---|---|
| 16. Yield on interest-bearing deposits | | | |
|     Centran | 7.24% | 8.73% | 10.77% |
|     Peer group | 7.76 | 9.11 | 10.95 |
|     Difference | (0.52%) | (0.38%) | (0.18%) |
| 17. Yield on Federal funds sold | | | |
|     Centran | 6.90% | 8.14% | 10.93% |
|     Peer group | 6.86 | 8.19 | 10.41 |
|     Difference | 0.04% | (0.05%) | 0.52% |
| 18. Noninterest income/average total assets | | | |
|     Centran | 1.70% | 1.64% | 1.52% |
|     Peer group | 1.40 | 1.27 | 1.23 |
|     Difference | 0.30% | 0.37% | 0.29% |
| **Interest Rate Sensitivity Analysis** | | | |
| 19. Cumulative gap as percent of assets | | | |
|     a. Three months | | | |
|       Centran | (0.07%) | (1.43%) | 1.65% |
|       Peer group | (5.87) | (2.72) | (2.00) |
|       Difference | 5.80% | 1.29% | 3.65% |
|     b. Six months | | | |
|       Centran | (1.85%) | (2.97%) | (0.25%) |
|       Peer group | (7.27) | (4.19) | (3.51) |
|       Difference | 5.42% | 1.22% | 3.26% |
|     c. One year | | | |
|       Centran | (2.42%) | (1.06%) | 0.22% |
|       Peer group | (4.83) | (2.15) | (0.94) |
|       Difference | 2.41% | 1.09% | 1.16% |
| **Analysis of Liquidity** | | | |
| 20. Core deposits/total assets | | | |
|     Centran | 62.90% | 62.74% | 62.46% |
|     Peer group | 65.56 | 64.68 | 61.81 |
|     Difference | (2.66%) | (1.94%) | 0.65% |
| 21. Volatile liabilities/total assets | | | |
|     Centran | 27.29% | 27.07% | 27.45% |
|     Peer group | 25.88 | 26.69 | 29.65 |
|     Difference | 1.41% | 0.38% | (2.20%) |
| **Analysis of Leverage and Capital Adequacy** | | | |
| 22. Primary capital/total assets | | | |
|     Centran | 8.34% | 8.25% | 7.87% |
|     Peer group | 7.10 | 6.90 | 6.65 |
|     Difference | 1.24% | 1.35% | 1.22% |

**EXHIBIT 6** *(continued)*

| | 1987 | 1986 | 1985 |
|---|---|---|---|
| 23. Ending loss reserve/total loans and leases | | | |
| Centran | 1.39% | 1.28% | 1.22% |
| Peer group | 1.33 | 1.22 | 1.18 |
| Difference | 0.06% | 0.06% | 0.04% |
| 24. Nonperforming assets/total loans and leases | | | |
| Centran | 2.12% | 2.06% | 2.43% |
| Peer group | 1.62 | 1.85 | 2.12 |
| Difference | 0.50% | 0.21% | 0.31% |
| 25. Ending loss reserve/net loan losses | | | |
| Centran | 1.50× | 1.39× | 1.65× |
| Peer group | 3.73 | 4.20 | 4.02 |
| Difference | (2.23×) | (2.81×) | (2.37×) |
| 26. Earnings coverage of net loan losses | | | |
| Centran | 3.31× | 3.29× | 4.28× |
| Peer group | 7.12 | 8.36 | 7.83 |
| Difference | (3.81×) | (5.07×) | (3.55×) |

**Analysis of Growth**

| | 1987 | 1986 | 1985 |
|---|---|---|---|
| 27. Growth rate of year-end total assets | | | |
| Centran | 5.45% | 17.44% | 17.09% |
| Peer group | 12.71 | 12.77 | 12.27 |
| Difference | (7.26%) | 4.67% | 4.82% |
| 28. Growth rate of year-end total loans | | | |
| Centran | 14.78% | 15.25% | 28.37% |
| Peer group | 15.24 | 17.60 | 15.24 |
| Difference | (0.46%) | (2.35%) | 13.13% |
| 29. Growth rate of year-end equity capital | | | |
| Centran | 12.29% | 22.18% | 18.09% |
| Peer group | 14.91 | 16.47 | 13.40 |
| Difference | (2.62%) | 5.71% | 4.69% |
| 30. Cash dividends declared/net income | | | |
| Centran | 33.80% | 31.90% | 32.50% |
| Peer group | 38.51 | 38.60 | 39.28 |
| Difference | (4.71%) | (6.70%) | (6.78%) |
| 31. Internal capital generation rate | | | |
| Centran | 10.85% | 11.21% | 10.75% |
| Peer group | 8.92 | 9.08 | 8.64 |
| Difference | 1.93% | 2.13% | 2.11% |

**Cost of Funds Analysis**

| | 1987 | 1986 | 1985 |
|---|---|---|---|
| 32. Interest on all interest-paying funds | | | |
| Centran | 7.13% | 8.33% | 9.18% |
| Peer group | 6.68 | 7.82 | 9.26 |
| Difference | 0.45% | 0.51% | (0.08%) |

## CASE 22    CITY FEDERAL SAVINGS AND LOAN ASSOCIATION*

In January 1984, John Lanning was reviewing the hedging program at City Federal Savings and Loan Association. The program involved the use of interest rate futures to hedge the institution's exposure to increases in interest rates. City Federal had been a particularly active user of futures since January 1982. However, up to the present, the firm had experienced losses amounting to $72 million on its futures positions.

Lanning recognized that there are two sides to every futures hedge—the cash side and the futures side. Generally, when one side loses, the other side gains. As a disciplined hedger, the firm must view the $72 million loss only as the inevitable losing side of the hedge. The gain side in this case was the appreciation in value of the cash position under the hedge. Lanning estimated this gain to be $89 million. The difference of $17 million between the cash side gain and the futures side loss resulted from basis risk and had nothing to do with interest rate risk, which was effectively eliminated by the hedge. He considered the fact that the difference was positive and favorable to be simply a matter of luck. He knew that, just as readily, it might have been negative and unfavorable.

### BACKGROUND

City Federal, located in Piscataway, New Jersey, was the 14th largest savings and loan association in the nation with total assets in excess of $6 billion (see Exhibits 1 and 2 for financial statements). It was the second most profitable publicly owned savings and loan association in the United States during both 1981 and 1982, and its return on assets placed it in the top 25 percent of S&Ls in 1983. The firm had grown rapidly during the past three years as a result of aggressive

*Parts of the case were adapted, with permission, from John Morris, "At City Federal, Hedging Turns $78.5 Million Loss into a $104 Million Gain," *American Banker*, September 14, 1983.

mortgage lending funded primarily by new retail deposits and, to a lesser extent, by wholesale funds in the form of "jumbo" CDs, wholesale repurchase agreements, and national distribution by brokerage houses of a limited amount of CDs. In addition, City Federal had embarked on an ambitious acquisition program in which it acquired two large savings and loan associations in Florida and two in New Jersey.

The firm also had been moving to diversify its product offerings. Management observed that "the savings and loan business, a two-product industry for so long, today has a wealth of potential product lines." Consumer lending had been recently introduced, and various service corporations within City Federal now offered trust, brokerage, mortgage banking, real estate appraisal, insurance, and other services.

### FINANCIAL POLICY

In 1980, John Lanning, Vice-President of Economics and Planning for City Federal, recognized the threat that rising interest rates posed to the firm's net income. In the savings and loan industry, this threat came from the funding of long-term, fixed-rate mortgages with short-term liabilities. Rising rates forced the cost of funds up, while the yield on mortgages remained constant. By late in 1980, the spread on many of City Federal's mortgages in relation to funding costs was negative and was rapidly deteriorating. With this in mind, Lanning successfully urged management to establish an Asset/Liability Management Committee (ALCO) to ensure that strict asset/liability management policies would be instituted and observed.

One of the first policies of the Committee was to see that new loans were funded at a good spread that was locked in by deposits or borrowings with interest rate sensitivity equivalent to the loans. That is, assets on the margin were to be matched with their funding in rate-sensitivity terms. Thus, the spread on all marginal activity was to be desensitized to interest rate changes.

This required lengthening the normal life of liabilities and shortening the life of assets.

The ALCO closely monitored the institution's short-term gap ratio. ALCO defined the gap ratio as rate-sensitive liabilities minus rate-sensitive assets divided by total assets. This measure gave a rough indication of the effect of rate changes on net income. For example, a gap ratio of 40 percent with $2.5 billion in total assets indicates that income before taxes will decrease roughly $10 million for every 1 percent increase in market interest rates (40 percent × $2.5 billion × 1 percent). Because of ALCO's efforts, as shown in Exhibit 3, the gap ratio had been steadily reduced through 1981–1983.

Some of this balance sheet restructuring had come about through the dramatic growth of sensitivity-matched assets and liabilities. The sheer weight of new assets and liabilities restructured the balance sheet by diluting the overall interest sensitivity associated with preexisting assets and liabilities. Thus, City Federal was managing to grow out of its large gap ratio.

In much the same way, City Federal's portfolio of fixed-rate mortgages, which were booked at low interest rates over the years, was being swamped by new loans carrying higher rates or rates that could be adjusted as rates changed in the market. One major source of the growth of new higher rate loans had been the association's acquisitions of other thrift institutions. Exhibit 4 shows a breakdown of the balance sheet in terms of the old, pre-1980 remaining portfolio, the merger portfolio, and the new portfolio remaining since 1980. This breakdown, and the associated yields and rates, demonstrated that City Federal could not rely on its old assets for profitability.

Acquired thrifts were folded into the balance sheet on a purchase accounting basis. Purchase accounting permitted City Federal to mark down or discount the value of loans from an acquired institution to a level that brought their yields up to current mortgage rates. The amount of this discount was then added to income during the roughly 12-year life of the loans.[1]

In general, Lanning believed much of the credit for controlling rate sensitivity was due to the association's system of allocating resources. Lanning's staff prepared a report called the *investment/funding matrix,* which set forth an analysis of all investment and funding opportunities available to the firm. The analysis arrayed and ranked each investment and source of funds by its rate sensitivity and maturity. This innovation pointed out attractive spread relationships along the yield curve. Exhibit 5 presents an example of the matrix and the associated yield/cost spreads on the yield curve.

It also alerted ALCO and management to the feasibility of new products, including consumer lending and the CAMP (City Affordable Mortgage Plan) loan by demonstrating the attractiveness of long-term deposits and borrowing. The CAMP program included many loans that carried attractive below-market interest rates in their early years resulting in increases in principal or negative amortization.

In addition, City Federal was a major player in secondary mortgage markets, originating and selling nearly $1 billion of loans in both 1982 and 1983.

## HEDGING PROGRAM

The asset–liability management program also gave rise to the use of the financial futures markets as a technique for redressing the gap. Beginning in August 1981, the Federal Home Loan Bank Board (FHLBB) permitted FSLIC-insured associations to use financial futures to manage interest rate risk. In general, associations were restricted to short positions, i.e., to sell futures contracts; they were prohibited from taking long positions, i.e., to buy contracts.[2]

With financial futures, City Federal was able to shorten the rate sensitivity of assets and to

---

[1] This addition to net income was offset somewhat by a charge against income consisting of amortized goodwill—any excess of the price over market value paid by City Federal. Goodwill

was amortized over a period of about 35 years. This increased reported profits artificially, as income was recognized faster than goodwill expense. Subsequent to most of City Federal's acquisitions, this accounting asymmetry was eliminated when regulatory authorities required acquiring firms to amortize goodwill over a time frame that was similar to the life of acquired loans.

[2] However, long positions were permitted in mortgage banking activities of thrift associations.

lengthen the rate sensitivity of liabilities. The use of futures made it practical to lock in new liability rates for longer periods to better match the rate sensitivity of new assets. Alternatively, futures were used to convert City's deep-discount, fixed-rate mortgages into variable-rate instruments.

Looking back over the nearly two years of using futures, Lanning believed that City Federal had conducted a successful hedging program. Exhibit 6 shows that net interest margin varied less than that of the industry as a whole. It had moved from 35 basis points in 1981 to 58 in 1982 to 136 in 1983. The rise in net interest margin stemmed from City Federal's diversification program and profitable spreads on its huge volume of new assets. But Lanning reasoned that the relative stability of its earnings could be partly attributed to the futures hedging program. Of course, this stability could be attributed more generally to the firm's investment/funding analysis that resulted in a huge volume of cash hedges by matching asset and liability maturities in addition to cash/futures hedging.

## TYPES OF HEDGES

City Federal embarked upon its hedging program in March 1982 when it was carrying a gap of $1 billion consisting of fixed-rate mortgages funded by six-month money market certificates and other short-term deposits. After watching rates on liabilities surge relentlessly during 1981, ALCO considered three solutions. First, it could absorb the violent swings in profits and do nothing. Second, it could hedge the entire gap against any further rate increases. However, this would ensure that an unacceptably high cost of funds would be locked in at the existing 14.9 percent rate on the firm's six-month money market CDs. Third, it could just hedge a part of the gap at different interest rates, locking in positive spreads whenever they could be identified. Then, if interest rates fell, additional hedges would be put on to hedge other portions of the gap. Of course, this staggered hedge would not work if interest rates rose further.

After carefully considering these three alternatives, ALCO chose the staggered hedge. ALCO estimated that if rates remained unchanged, the

Association would earn $12.7 million in 1982: It ultimately earned $13.2 million. If the entire gap had been hedged, profits would have been much lower at about $8.4 million. In a sense, then, the cost of eliminating the rate sensitivity (except basis risk)[3] with a whole gap hedge instead of a staggered hedge would have been the difference between the actual earnings and estimated earnings under the whole gap hedge—an amount equal to $4.8 million.

Eventually, City Federal's board approved nine types of hedges and set dollar limits on each. The specific hedges and limits in existence in June 1982 are listed in Exhibit 7. In any case, the board limited to $1.1 billion the aggregate cash positions that could be hedged.

## EFFECTIVENESS OF FUTURES HEDGING

Although futures were central to the financial policies of the past two years, it was difficult to assess their benefits because they were so intertwined with City Federal's overall risk management program. On the one hand, one could not ignore the fact of a $72 million loss on futures positions since March 1982. The futures position had actually fluctuated from a high of a positive $20 million to a low of a negative $100 million. Cynics could argue that the firm had bet on increases in interest rates and had lost the bet. Unavoidably, critics pointed to the fact that the losses on futures had been massive and that profits could have been much greater if the Association had simply avoided the futures markets. But Lanning reasoned that without its futures hedging program, the firm would have been a flagrant speculator and would have been exposed to a potential loss with no offsetting gain. His expectation had been that rates would fluctuate; he maintained that there had been no betting on rates moving in a specific direction.

City Federal used *hedge accounting,* in which gains or losses on futures were deferred and recognized over time according to a schedule that was consistent with the hedge purpose. Exhibit

---

[3]Basis risk is the potential that movements in futures prices will differ from the movement in prices of the cash position being hedged.

8 shows the adjustment to net interest margin through nine months of 1983 due to hedging activity. At that time (September 1983), a footnote to City Federal's quarterly report read:

As of September 30, 1983, the Association had deferred hedging losses of $71,779,000, which include $64,842,000 of losses on closed contracts and $6,937,000 of unrealized losses on 6,458 open contracts. Through the use of hedging, the Association has converted $456 million of fixed rate assets to variable rate assets and $137 million of short-term liabilities to fixed rate medium-term liabilities. The market appreciation on hedged assets and liabilities totaled approximately $89,438,000 which exceeded the deferred losses by $17,659,000.

As noted previously, futures hedging probably contributed significantly to the stability of City Federal's net interest margin.

The Association's board of directors was well versed in the costs and benefits of hedging. In fact, the board had indicated its enthusiastic support of Lanning's initiatives in futures hedging. Lanning was aware, however, of boards of directors of other firms that had not understood the nature of hedging with futures and were somewhat intolerant of losses on futures positions.

**EXHIBIT I    City Federal Savings and Loan Association and Subsidiaries—Statements of Consolidated Financial Condition (Unaudited) (dollars in thousands)**

|  | December 31, 1983 | December 31, 1982 | December 31, 1981 |
| --- | --- | --- | --- |
| **Assets** | | | |
| Cash | $    118,537 | $     97,110 | $     49,970 |
| Investment securities | 477,816 | 330,523 | 247,049 |
| First mortgage loans—net | 4,540,426 | 2,858,981 | 2,234,263 |
| Consumer loans—net | 888,749 | 748,006 | 545,073 |
| Accrued interest receivable on loans | 63,393 | 38,264 | 25,083 |
| Real estate owned or under development—net | 57,108 | 57,939 | 43,288 |
| Federal Home Loan Bank stock, at cost | 38,287 | 23,287 | 23,019 |
| Premises and equipment—net | 81,354 | 50,647 | 38,740 |
| Goodwill | 278,773 | 171,654 | 79,625 |
| Deferred hedging losses | 54,218 | 88,478 | — |
| Other assets | 133,261 | 89,460 | 60,914[a] |
| Total assets | $6,794,586 | $4,554,349 | $3,347,025 |

[a] Included deferred hedges losses not separately identified.

**EXHIBIT I**    *(continued)*

| | December 31, 1983 | December 31, 1982 | December 31, 1981 |
|---|---|---|---|
| **Liabilities and Stockholders' Equity** | | | |
| Retail funds | | | |
| Retail deposits | $4,220,716 | $2,630,675 | $2,151,590 |
| Retail repurchase agreements | 129,118 | 258,950 | 42,585 |
| Total retail funds | 4,349,834 | 2,889,625 | 2,194,175 |
| Wholesale funds | | | |
| Wholesale deposits, jumbo and broker CDs | 558,118 | 496,167 | 251,362 |
| Advances from Federal Home Loan Bank | 696,094 | 427,069 | 416,697 |
| Securities sold under agreements to repurchase | 460,543 | 283,542 | 181,716 |
| Other borrowings | 99,998 | 63,747 | 59,271 |
| Total wholesale funds | 1,814,753 | 1,270,525 | 909,046 |
| Loans in process | 211,915 | 156,516 | 105,035 |
| Advance payments by borrowers for taxes and insurance | 39,094 | 20,383 | 12,064 |
| Accounts payable and other liabilities | 122,983 | 59,595 | 29,480 |
| Total liabilities | 6,538,579 | 4,396,644 | 3,249,800 |
| Stockholders' equity | | | |
| Preferred stock, $2.20 cum. conv. $25 par value | $    50,000 | $    50,000 | — |
| $2.10 cum. conv., Series B, $25 par value | 63,500 | — | — |
| Common stock, $0.01 par value; issued and outstanding: 13,014,435 in 1983 and 6,394,164 in 1982 | 132 | 64 | $        30 |
| Additional paid-in capital | 27,869 | 28,812 | 28,759 |
| Retained earnings | 114,506 | 78,829 | 68,436 |
| Total stockholders' equity | $  256,007 | $  157,705 | $    97,225 |
| Total liabilities and stockholders' equity | $6,794,586 | $4,554,349 | $3,347,025 |

**EXHIBIT 2    City Federal Savings and Loan Association and Subsidiaries—Statements of Consolidated Income (dollars in thousands except per share data)**

| | Year Ended December 31, | | | |
| --- | --- | --- | --- | --- |
| | 1983 | 1982 | 1981 | 1980 |
| **Income** | | | | |
| Interest on mortgage loans | $ 417,647 | $ 305,545 | $ 179,511 | $ 149,434 |
| Interest on other loans | 116,407 | 100,340 | 52,821 | 20,476 |
| Interest and dividends on investments and deposits | 37,052 | 58,572 | 57,534 | 27,105 |
| Loan fees and service charges | 81,323 | 56,093 | 30,402 | 15,443 |
| Gain on sale of mortgage loans | 36,354 | 27,209 | 4,001 | 4,348 |
| Income (loss) from real estate operations | 1,063 | 2,901 | 2,330 | 2,554 |
| Other income | 8,470 | 5,322 | 2,066 | 453 |
| Total income | $ 698,316 | $ 555,982 | $ 328,665 | $ 219,813 |
| **Expenses** | | | | |
| Interest on retail funds | $ 343,898 | $ 292,774 | $ 189,372 | $ 133,444 |
| Interest on wholesale funds | 147,262 | 150,459 | 92,001 | 43,170 |
| Interest adjustment-hedging activity | 11,393 | 1,884 | — | — |
| General and administrative expenses | | | | |
| Compensation and employee benefits | 71,015 | 43,140 | 26,500 | 20,248 |
| Occupancy and office operations | 37,172 | 23,562 | 12,272 | 9,052 |
| Advertising | 6,070 | 6,248 | 5,743 | 4,568 |
| Other expenses | 24,911 | 16,604 | 9,498 | 6,519 |
| Provision for loan losses | 1,209 | 1,255 | 44 | 25 |
| Amortization of goodwill | 8,364 | 4,755 | — | — |
| Amortization of other intangible assets | 2,499 | 2,735 | — | — |
| Total expenses | $ 653,793 | $ 543,416 | $ 335,430 | $ 217,026 |
| Income (loss) before income taxes | 44,523 | 12,566 | (6,765) | 2,787 |
| Income taxes (benefit) | 601 | (623) | (5,400) | (562) |
| Net income (loss) | $ 42,554 | $ 13,189 | $ (1,365) | $ 3,349 |
| Earnings (loss) per share | | | | |
| Primary | $ 2.50 | $ 0.98 | $ (0.22) | $ 0.49[a] |
| Fully diluted | $ 2.11 | $ 0.95 | $ (0.22) | $ 0.49[a] |
| Average shares outstanding | | | | |
| Primary | 14,043,585 | 13,393,574 | 6,325,154 | 6,300,000 |
| Fully diluted | 20,187,374 | 13,943,628 | 6,325,154 | 6,300,000 |

[a]This amount represents earnings per share for the six months ended December 31, 1980, which is the period subsequent to conversion to a capital stock association.

**EXHIBIT 3    City Federal Savings and Loan Association—Interest Rate Sensitivity**

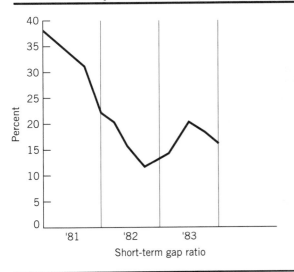

Short-term gap ratio

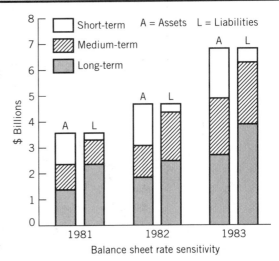

Balance sheet rate sensitivity

**EXHIBIT 4  City Federal Savings and Loan Association—Balance Sheet Composition: Old, New, and Merged Portfolios**

| | Old Portfolio Remaining (Pre-1980) | | Merger Portfolio | | New Portfolio | | Total 1983 | |
|---|---|---|---|---|---|---|---|---|
| | Thousands of Dollars | Percentage | Thousands of Dollars | Percentage | Thousands of Dollars | Percentage | Thousands of Dollars | Percentage |
| **Assets** | | | | | | | | |
| First mortgage loans | 956,000 | 8.61 | 569,871 | 16.93 | 2,119,834 | 13.44 | 3,645,705 | 12.72 |
| Consumer loans | 29,782 | 14.40 | 19,951 | 15.44 | 859,016 | 14.74 | 908,749 | 14.74 |
| Mortgage-backed securities | 98,135 | 8.33 | 120,693 | 13.10 | 506,642 | 8.98 | 725,470 | 9.58 |
| Investment securities | 22,284 | 6.90 | 32,121 | 9.49 | 516,283 | 10.30 | 570,688 | 10.12 |
| Total earning assets | 1,106,201 | 8.71 | 742,636 | 15.95 | 4,001,775 | 12.75 | 5,850,612 | 12.39 |
| Other assets | 56,691 | — | 304,572 | — | 370,796 | — | 732,059 | — |
| Total assets | 1,162,892 | | 1,047,208 | | 4,372,571 | | 6,582,671 | |
| **Liabilities** | | | | | | | | |
| Retail and wholesale funds | 1,094,186 | 10.02 | 1,047,208 | 10.02 | 4,007,671 | 10.02 | 6,149,065 | 10.02 |
| Total interest-bearing liabilities | 1,094,186 | 10.02 | 1,047,208 | 10.02 | 4,007,671 | 10.02 | 6,149,065 | 10.02 |
| Other liabilities | 68,706 | — | — | — | 364,900 | — | 433,606 | — |
| Total liabilities and equity | 1,162,892 | | 1,047,208 | | 4,372,571 | | 6,582,671 | |
| **Ratios** | | | | | | | | |
| Adjusted net interest yield spread | (1.21) | | 0.82 | | 2.56 | | 1.62 | |
| Net interest income | (13,385) | | 6,090 | | 102,275 | | 94,780 | |
| Percentage of earning asset portfolio | 18.91% | | 12.69% | | 68.40% | | 100% | |

**EXHIBIT 5   City Federal Savings and Loan Association—The Investment-Funding Matrix Sample Date: November 18, 1981**

*Ranking Investments*

| | Overnight | 30-Day | 60-Day | 90-Day | 180-Day | 360-Day | Medium-Term | Long-Term |
|---|---|---|---|---|---|---|---|---|
| 1st choice | 13.43 Fed funds | 12.86 Fed funds | 12.81 Fed funds | 12.94 Fed funds | 15.80 Alternate mortgage | 12.71 GNMA cash and carry | 19.77 Equity loan/GPM | 18.53 Conventional mortgage |
| 2nd choice | 10.42 FHLB-DDA | 12.68 Comm. paper | 12.67 Comm. paper | 12.60 Comm. paper | 14.71 Alternate mortgage/GPM | 12.24 FHLMC-360 | 19.08 Equity loan | 16.31 FHA/VA |
| 3rd choice | | 12.38 Bank. accept. | 12.35 Bank. accept. | 12.13 Bank. accept. | 12.63 Fed funds | 12.05 FNMA-360 | 18.99 Interest-only mortgage | 15.81 Corporate bond |

*Ranking Sources of Funds*

| | Overnight | 30-Day | 60-Day | 90-Day | 180-Day | 360-Day | Medium-Term | Long-Term |
|---|---|---|---|---|---|---|---|---|
| 1st choice | 12.60 Rev. repo | 12.37 Broker reverse | 12.37 Broker reverse | 11.82 Retail reverse | 12.44 Jumbo | 10.52 All Savers Cert. | 10.08 NOW | 15.92 Private sale |
| 2nd choice | 13.50 Fed funds | 12.69 Jumbo | 12.64 Jumbo | 12.37 Broker reverse | 12.50 Broker reverse | 14.38 FHLB advance | 12.73 Hedged MMC (6-month) | 17.42 FNMA/FHA auction |
| 3rd choice | 17.38 FHLB advance | 13.07 Comm. paper | 13.21 Comm. paper | 12.75 Jumbo | 12.83 Hedged jumbo (60-day) | | 14.89 FHLB advance | 17.53 FHLMC auction |

——— Maximum Investment Yield
- - - - Minimum Funds Cost

Percent axis: 20, 19, 18, 17, 16, 15, 14, 13, 12, 11, 10, 9

Horizontal axis: Overnight, 30 Day, 60 Day, 90 Day, 180 Day, 360 Day, Medium Term, Long Term

SOURCE: Reprinted from Proceedings of the Seventh Annual Conference, December 10–11, 1981, Federal Home Loan Bank of San Francisco, California.

---

**EXHIBIT 6** **City Federal Savings and Loan versus Industry: Net Interest Income to Average Assets, 1979–1983**

---

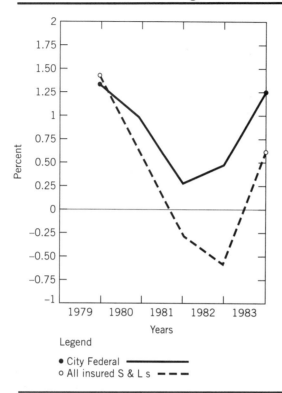

SOURCE: FHLBB Combined Financial Statements.

## EXHIBIT 7 City Federal Savings and Loan Association—Board of Directors Authorization for Types and Limits of Futures Hedges

The following types of hedges are specifically authorized:

1. Lock in the rate on six-month money market certificates for beyond the original six-months maturity and/or to shorten the effective life of assets. — Limit $200 million
2. Lock in the rate on jumbo CDs for 3 to 60 months. — Limit $150 million
3. Lock in the rate on 30-month money market certificates for beyond the original 30 months. — Limit $10 million
4. Lock in the rate on Federal funds for one month or longer. — Limit $5 million
5. Provide fixed-rate construction loans. — Limit $5 million
6. Hedge FHA/VA mortgage production. — Limit $5 million
7. Hedge the market value of fixed-payment mortgages, equity loans, and commercial loans. — Limit $650 million
8. Provide fixed-rate or capped-forward commitments for end-loan financing. — Limit $25 million
9. Lock in the rate on FHLB advances during the lag between commitment and takedown. — Limit $50 million

### Position Limits

| | |
|---|---|
| Treasury bill futures | $500 million |
| CD futures (or Treasury bill, if preferable) | $960 million |
| Treasury bond and note futures and GNMA futures and options | $710 million |

## EXHIBIT 8 City Federal Savings and Loan Association—Analysis of Net Interest Income, Including Adjustment Due to Hedging Activity (dollars in thousands)

| | Nine Months Ended September 30 | |
|---|---|---|
| | 1983 | 1982 |
| Interest income | | |
| Interest on loans | $374,127 | $294,355 |
| Interest on investments | 28,817 | 48,658 |
| Total interest income | 402,944 | 343,013 |
| Interest expense | | |
| Interest on retail funds | 240,086 | 215,241 |
| Interest on wholesale funds | 104,697 | 113,665 |
| Total interest expense | 344,783 | 328,906 |
| Net interest income | 58,161 | 14,107 |
| Interest adjustment hedging activity | (8,765) | (374) |
| Adjusted net interest income | $ 49,396 | $ 13,733 |
| Interest margin | 2.51% | 1.32% |
| Interest margin adjusted for the excess of interest-bearing liabilities over interest-earning assets and hedging activity | 1.41% | 0.49% |
| Income-earning assets as a percentage of interest-bearing liabilities at September 30 | 94.98% | 92.94% |

# GLOBAL MACHINERY AND METALS COMPANY, INC.

Mr. David Farmer, assistant vice-president at Motor City National Bank, Detroit, Michigan, was considering in early 1988 an expanded loan request from one of the bank's established customers—Global Machinery and Metals Company, Inc. (GMMC). David Farmer had only recently joined the Motor City Bank after two years of credit analysis and lending experience at a nearby competing institution. The GMMC account, which was established at the Motor City Bank about four years ago, had been brought to the bank by the officer whom Farmer had recently replaced; hence he had no prior contact or experience with the managers at GMMC, beyond his understanding that the account had been a satisfactory and profitable one for the bank since the relationship began in 1984.

David Farmer was approached by Wayne Newton, one of the principals of GMMC, with a request for a material expansion in the company's credit facilities. Newton was asking for an increased line of credit to $1 million and an increase in the letter of credit (L/C) line to $1 million.

The GMMC credits currently approved were as follows:

1. Line of credit: $500,000 at prime plus 2 percent.

2. L/C: $750,000 at prime plus 2 percent, with a fee of 1 percent per annum at issue plus 1 percent at funding.

The preceding authorized credit lines, which had been increased in 1985, were secured by all accounts receivable and inventory. Advances against those lines were based on 50 percent of eligible accounts receivable and 40 percent of inventory in amounts not to exceed the total credit approved.

The L/C line had been in constant use since its establishment in 1984 at or near the authorized limit. The line of credit was zeroed out in 1985 for about 60 days, for about 30 days in 1986, and was paid down to a low of $265,000 in 1987. Average usage in 1987 totaled $470,000. Mr. Newton told David Farmer that his current request for increased credit facilities resulted from

the continued rapid expansion of GMMC sales. Newton indicated that he would appreciate prompt consideration and approval by the bank of his request for increased credit. (See Exhibits 1 and 2).

GMMC was organized in 1965 as a sole proprietorship, owned and operated by Wayne Newton, who was 54 years of age. GMMC operated as a dealer for new and used machine tools. In 1980 Newton converted the firm to a corporation. At about the same time, he concluded that some diversification of product and activity would serve to reduce the firm's risk as well as increase its profitability. Accordingly, GMMC began importing finished steel products such as stainless steel rounds, angles, pipes, sheets, and plates, principally from Japan and, to a lesser extent, from Spain and Korea.

## METALS DIVISION

The metals division, whose sales had shown rapid growth in recent years, sold stainless steel products to about 450 customers in the South and Southwest. One client accounted for about 10 percent of total division sales; nearly all other buyers were significantly smaller, with no other customer accounting for as much as 3 percent of volume. Sales were managed through five salesmen, primarily to small and medium-sized distributors and fabricators. Mr. William Hardin, 46, directed the metals division and its sales staff. He operated in GMMC with a great deal of autonomy.

The GMMC metals division worked with three Japanese suppliers and one each in Spain and South Korea. The company could sell to its customers at prices approximately 20 percent less than competitors who offered equivalent U.S.-made products. This price advantage had allowed GMMC to expand its metals division sales volume quite rapidly.

Recently the company had begun building its inventory of stainless steel products in anticipation of voluntary industry import restrictions on supplies from Japan and Korea. Although GMMC enjoyed a significant price advantage on its imported stainless steel products, there were some important disadvantages to imported sources of supply. GMMC customers had to place their orders at least 60 days in advance of needed delivery. This put GMMC at some competitive disadvantage with domestic (U.S.) suppliers, who could respond to orders in four to six weeks. This situation led to apparent risks for GMMC related to any interruption of supply sources. For example, dock strikes, either in the country of origin or in the United States, could quickly affect supplies. Domestic sources of similar-quality stainless steel products would be available to replace imports, but at a substantially higher cost to GMMC. Almost all of the recent inventory growth had resulted from the growth of stainless steel sales plus recent purchases to hedge against possible import restrictions.

### MACHINE TOOL DIVISION

Mr. Wayne Newton closely supervised the activities of the machine tool division. Three salesmen serviced approximately 400 accounts, which were primarily machine shops and small manufacturers. GMMC frequently purchased surplus used machinery, and from time to time the company even bought entire small manufacturing plants, using in these cases various joint-venture partners. Sales by GMMC, when a large-scale purchase was made, would either be at auction or to existing customers within about 30 days.

When used machinery was purchased, it would be shipped to the company's facility for repair or refurbishing if that proved necessary. GMMC had maintained an excellent reputation for selling quality used machinery, and profit margins on this business were excellent.

### PRODUCT MIX

The product mixes for year-end 1985, 1986, and 1987 were as follows:

The company's records indicated that about 66% of the machine tool division's sales in 1986 resulted from used machinery, which accounted for 75 percent of the division's profitability.

### FACILITIES

The company owned office and warehouse space containing approximately 36,000 square feet. In addition, other warehouse and yard area was leased with annual payments of $25,000. The majority of GMMC's facilities had been constructed from materials acquired through purchase of closed manufacturing plants. Through use of company labor the cost of facilities had been held to a minimum without sacrificing function.

### STAFFING

The company employed a total of 18 people, none of whom were union members. Messrs. Newton and Hardin drew annual salaries of $50,000 each. They also participated in a bonus program based upon performance. Each of the two men earned a bonus of $50,000 in 1987. Common stock ownership was divided, with Mr. Newton owning 60 percent and Mr. Hardin holding 40 percent.

In his discussion at the bank, Mr. Newton summarized his credit requests to the bank officer, David Farmer, as follows:

GMMC wishes to increase its line of credit to $1,000,000 to strengthen our ability to buy closed manufacturing plants and/or surplus machinery on short notice and to enable the company to enter larger joint venture deals. We anticipate an average use for 1988 of $700,000, with a minimum of $300,000. We also want to use a portion of the credit line to finance increased stainless steel inventory from time to time in anticipation of supply interruptions. Finally, the increase we ask in the letter of credit line, to

| | 1987 | | 1986 | | 1985 | |
|---|---|---|---|---|---|---|
| | **Sales** | **Earnings** | **Sales** | **Earnings** | **Sales** | **Earnings** |
| Metals division | 79% | 73% | 73% | 66% | 45% | (14%) |
| Machine tool division | 21% | 27% | 27% | 34% | 55% | 114% |

$1,000,000 from the present $750,000, will help us finance additional stainless steel inventory to meet our steadily growing demand.

Mr. Farmer promised to review these requests and to respond to Mr. Newton within the next few days.

**EXHIBIT 1    Global Machinery and Metals, Inc.—Balance Sheets**

|  | 12/31/85 (Unaudited) | 12/31/86 (Unaudited) | 12/31/87 (Audited) |
|---|---|---|---|
| **Assets** | | | |
| Current assets: | | | |
| Cash | $ 54,500 | $ 76,420 | $ 62,370 |
| Receivables net of allowance for doubtful accounts (Note 1) | 457,676 | 787,442 | 972,154 |
| Inventories (Note 2) | 644,794 | 1,527,925 | 2,480,115 |
| Prepaid expenses | 6,608 | 7,677 | 10,802 |
| Total current assets | 1,163,578 | 2,399,464 | 3,525,441 |
| Property, plant, and equipment (at cost) | | | |
| Building | 54,800 | 54,800 | 54,800 |
| Equipment, furniture, and fixtures | 87,281 | 103,943 | 113,635 |
| Leasehold improvements | 18,760 | 23,434 | 23,434 |
| Land | 23,000 | 23,000 | 23,000 |
| Less: accumulated depreciation | (55,195) | (66,846) | (81,695) |
| Net property, plant, and equipment | 128,646 | 138,331 | 133,174 |
| Other assets | 632 | 704 | 423 |
| Total assets | $1,292,856 | $2,538,499 | $3,659,038 |
| **Liabilities** | | | |
| Current liabilities: | | | |
| Notes payable | $ 50,000 | $ 320,000 | $ 500,000 |
| Liability on L/Cs | 150,000 | 580,000 | 750,000 |
| Trade accounts payable | 388,730 | 746,572 | 1,093,557 |
| Accrued interest and taxes | 48,081 | 66,522 | 88,364 |
| Federal income taxes payable | 147,000 | 142,600 | 250,048 |
| Total current liabilities | 783,811 | 1,855,694 | 2,681,969 |
| **Equity** | | | |
| Common stock, 2,000 shares authorized and issued | 100,000 | 100,000 | 100,000 |
| Retained earnings | 409,045 | 582,805 | 877,069 |
| Total equity | 509,045 | 682,805 | 977,069 |
| Total liabilities and equity | $1,292,856 | $2,538,499 | $3,659,038 |

**EXHIBIT 2    Global Machinery and Metals, Inc.—Statement of Income**

|  | 1985 (Unaudited) | 1986 (Unaudited) | 1987 (Audited) |
|---|---|---|---|
| Net revenues | $2,654,526 | $4,330,934 | $5,229,695 |
| Costs and expenses |  |  |  |
|    Cost of goods sold | 1,688,268 | 3,111,927 | 3,759,491 |
|    Selling, general & administrative expenses | 582,804 | 849,151 | 873,670 |
| Total cost and expenses | 2,271,072 | 3,961,078 | 4,633,161 |
| Revenue after costs and expenses | 383,454 | 369,856 | 596,534 |
| Other income (expense) |  |  |  |
|    Miscellaneous income | 1,120 | (11,286) | 3,898 |
|    Interest income | (26,037) | (45,810) | (56,668) |
| Total other income | (24,917) | (57,096) | (52,770) |
| Income before federal taxes | 358,537 | 312,760 | 543,764 |
| Provision for federal income taxes | 160,500 | 139,000 | 249,500 |
| Net income | $   198,037 | $   173,760 | $   294,264 |

**Statement of Retained Income**

|  | 1985 (Unaudited) | 1986 (Unaudited) | 1987 (Audited) |
|---|---|---|---|
| Retained earnings—beginning of period | $   211,008 | $   409,045 | $   582,805 |
| Net income | 198,037 | 173,760 | 294,264 |
| Retained earnings—end of period | 409,045 | 582,805 | 877,069 |

*Note 1:* Bad debt expense:
  1987   $16,863
  1986     117
  1985   1,053
  The reserve for doubtful accounts totaled $12,114 as of 12/31/87.
*Note 2:* Inventories are stated at the lower of cost, first-in, first-out method, or market. Amounts of inventories used in computing cost of sales for periods covered by the financial statements are as follows:
  12/31/87   $2,480,115
  12/31/86   1,527,925
  12/31/85     671,402

---

**CASE**

**24**

# EDWARD EDWARDS COMPANY

## BACKGROUND

Edward Edwards was a manufacturer's representative acting on a commission basis only. He sold decorative accessories, pictures, lamps, and garden accessories, and he engaged in direct importing of similar items for his own account. His territory covered Texas, Oklahoma, New Mexico, Missouri, Arkansas, Mississippi, Tennessee, and Loui-

siana. Edwards' business was not seasonal, and he had two employees in addition to himself. His business was located in rented showroom space in a multistory building in Dallas' industrial section. The showrooms covered 2,000 square feet, and the premises were orderly.

The business had been started 22 years ago in Oklahoma City and was moved to Dallas in 1987. Edwards was 50 years old in 1992. He had worked for his father, who was also a manufacturer's representative, for about eight years prior to forming his own company.

## BANK RELATIONSHIP

Edwards had been a customer at Third Bank of Dallas for the past 10 years. Since that time he had steadily used the letter of credit (L/C) services in the bank's international department. Third Bank of Dallas had issued its first L/C to Edwards some eight years ago for $1,600 on a 100 percent cash secured basis. Additional L/Cs were issued that same year on the same collateral basis, none of which individually exceeded $2,500. No more than that amount was outstanding at any time during the year.

The following year, Third Bank continued to service Edwards' L/C requirements covering his foreign purchases but changed its collateral position to one of security solely by shipping documents, including full sets of clean-on-board ocean bills of lading drawn to shipper's order and bank endorsed. Under this arrangement, individual L/Cs up to $4,000 were issued, all payable against shipping documents and sight drafts. At no time did such outstanding credits exceed $6,000 in the aggregate.

Beginning in 1986, individual credits up to $5,000 were issued and aggregate outstandings reached $12,000, all on the same basis noted previously.

Due to projected sales increases for the period 1989–1991, Edwards requested a $20,000 line to cover L/Cs payable against sight drafts when accompanied by ocean shipping documents, including bills of lading as noted previously. Such bank credits would be secured by control of documents. This line would also cover financing of sight draft L/C payments for up to 120 days. The line of credit was granted, and the bank's experience with Edwards proved entirely satisfactory.

Edwards continued to operate under this line from 1989 to 1991. In 1992, he again asked that the bank increase the line from $20,000 to $40,000 and that drafts under L/Cs be drawn payable at 120 days after sight, thus giving rise to a banker's acceptance. Edwards' request for this change in the use of drafts arose because the Japanese banks through which his sight draft L/Cs had been utilized were offering more attractive financing charges covering Japanese exports than were available in the United States.

The discount rate in Japan on acceptances of up to 120 days, together with Third Bank's acceptance commission on 120-day drafts, would be less than Edwards' borrowing rate at Third Bank. These credits would be utilized to provide the funds to meet sight draft payments under L/Cs.

Edwards' unaudited financial statements for the past three years are summarized in Exhibits 1–3.

In discussions with Edwards, the bank indicated it would study his request, including the liabilities and responsibilities that would be included in the issuance of L/Cs and the bank's subsequent acceptance of drafts associated with those L/Cs. In making a decision, the lending officer knew she must be aware of the bank's role as the issuing bank, accepting and paying L/Cs for Edwards' account.

**EXHIBIT 1 Edward Edwards Company—Statement of Source and Application of Funds, Years Ended December 31, 1990, 1991, and 1992[a]**

| | 1990 | | 1991 | | 1992 | |
|---|---|---|---|---|---|---|
| Funds provided by: | | | | | | |
| Net earnings | | $17,932.37 | | $18,519.67 | | $20,006.54 |
| Adjust for depreciation charges not requiring funds | | 926.24 | | 934.99 | | 175.46 |
| Disposition of automobile | | 2,411.02 | | 0 | | 0 |
| Disposition of investments | | 0 | | 291.25 | | 0 |
| | | $21,269.63 | | $19,745.91 | | $20,182.00 |
| | | | | | | |
| Funds applied to: | | | | | | |
| Increase in working capital | | | | | | |
| Working capital, beginning of year | $23,978.94 | | $30,391.85 | | $38,083.37 | |
| Working capital, end of year | 15,333.75 | | 23,978.94 | | 30,391.85 | |
| | | 8,645.19 | | 6,412.91 | | 7,691.52 |
| Acquisition of automobile | | 3,173.42 | | 0 | | 0 |
| Acquisition of equipment | | 405.00 | | 350.00 | | 646.00 |
| Increase in other assets and investments | | 2,413.43 | | 0 | | 5,157.56 |
| Owner's net withdrawals and other | | 6,632.59 | | 12,983.00 | | 6,686.92 |
| | | $21,269.63 | | $19,745.91 | | $20,182.00 |

[a] All statements prepared from the books without audit.

**EXHIBIT 2  Edward Edwards Company—Balance Sheet, December 31, 1990, 1991, and 1992**

| | 1990 | | 1991 | | 1992 | |
|---|---|---|---|---|---|---|
| **Assets** | | | | | | |
| Current assets | | | | | | |
| Cash—business account | $ 3,967.53 | | $ 5,317.44 | | $16,712.10 | |
| Cash—personal account | 10,421.00 | $14,388.53 | 13,010.00 | $18,327.44 | 11,847.92 | $28,560.02 |
| Trade accounts receivable | | 5,628.37 | | 5,667.55 | | 6,056.24 |
| Merchandise inventory | | 15,500.42 | | 17,502.28 | | 22,309.56 |
| Prepaid expenses | | 60.00 | | 73.30 | | 0 |
| Total current assets | | $35,577.32 | | $41,570.57 | | $56,925.82 |
| Fixed assets | | | | | | |
| Automobile—business | 3,173.42 | | 3,173.42 | | 3,173.42 | |
| Automobile—personal | 2,751.00 | | 2,751.00 | | 2,751.00 | |
| Office and showroom equipment | 2,287.19 | | 2,637.19 | | 3,283.19 | |
| Total—at cost | 8,211.61 | | 8,561.61 | | 9,207.61 | |
| Less accumulated depreciation | 2,549.95 | 5,661.66 | 3,484.94 | 5,076.67 | 3,660.40 | 5,547.21 |
| Other assets and investments | | | | | | |
| Cash value of life insurance in force | 3,744.68 | | 3,744.68 | | 4,195.48 | |
| Contributions to retirement plan—General Motors | 1,400.00 | | 1,400.00 | | 1,400.00 | |
| Contributions to self-employed retirement plan | 500.00 | | 1,500.00 | | 3,871.07 | |

| | | | | | | |
|---|---:|---:|---:|---:|---:|---:|
| Corporation stocks and bonds | 11,780.00 | | 9,495.00 | | 13,300.00 | |
| Deposits | 35.00 | | 35.00 | | 35.00 | |
| U.S. savings bonds | 2,551.59 | | 1,745.34 | | 0 | |
| United Science Fund Plan | 0 | 20,011.27 | 1,800.00 | 19,720.02 | 2,076.03 | 24,877.58 |
| Total assets | | $61,250.25 | | $66,367.26 | | $87,350.61 |

## Liabilities and Owner's Equity

| | | | | | | |
|---|---:|---:|---:|---:|---:|---:|
| **Current liabilities** | | | | | | |
| Trade accounts payable | $ 1,383.50 | | $ 972.39 | | $18,005.80 | |
| Insurance loan payable | 376.53 | | 376.53 | | 275.59 | |
| Notes payable—bank | 6,192.69 | | 6,612.96 | | 0 | |
| Payroll taxes | 36.36 | | 217.82 | | 167.10 | |
| Income and self-employment taxes payable | 3,609.30 | | 2,999.02 | | 393.96 | |
| Total current liabilities | | 11,598.38 | | 11,178.72 | | 18,842.45 |
| **Owner's equity** | | | | | | |
| Balance, January 1 | $38,352.09 | | $49,651.87 | | $55,188.54 | |
| Net income | 17,932.37 | | 18,519.67 | | 20,006.54 | |
| Total | 56,284.46 | | 68,171.54 | | 75,195.08 | |
| Less owner's withdrawal and other | 6,632.59 | 49,651.87 | 12,983.00 | 55,188.54 | 6,686.92 | 68,508.16 |
| Total liabilities and owner's equity | | $61,250.25 | | $66,367.26 | | $87,350.61 |

**EXHIBIT 3  Edward Edwards Company[a]—Statement of Earnings, Years Ended 1990, 1991, and 1992**

| | 1990 | | 1991 | | 1992 | |
|---|---:|---:|---:|---:|---:|---:|
| Net sales | | $50,186.37 | | $81,420.00 | | $102,572.00 |
| Cost of sales | | | | | | |
| Inventory—beginning | $ 8,654.77 | | $15,500.42 | | $17,502.28 | |
| Purchases | 35,139.65 | | 49,828.67 | | 67,878.56 | |
| Merchandise available for sale | 43,794.42 | | 65,329.09 | | 85,380.84 | |
| Less inventory—ending | 15,500.42 | | 17,502.28 | | 22,309.56 | |
| Cost of sales | | 28,294.00 | | 47,826.81 | | 63,071.28 |
| Gross profit | | 21,892.37 | | 33,593.19 | | 39,501.62 |
| Commission income | | 19,363.72 | | 21,736.15 | | 22,976.39 |
| Rent subsidy | | 1,200.00 | | 1,200.00 | | 1,200.00 |
| Miscellaneous income | | 0 | | 114.18 | | 0 |
| Gross income | | $42,456.09 | | $56,643.52 | | $63,678.01 |
| Expenses | | | | | | |
| Accounting and legal | 600.00 | | 1,260.00 | | 825.00 | |
| Advertising | 320.58 | | 960.79 | | 1,209.64 | |
| Automobile expenses | 735.53 | | 692.19 | | 573.62 | |
| Bad debts charged off | 497.55 | | 1,171.44 | | 329.91 | |
| Customer contact | 197.86 | | 298.62 | | 219.71 | |
| Depreciation | 926.24 | | 934.99 | | 175.46 | |
| Dues and subscriptions | 91.36 | | 174.75 | | 0 | |
| Insurance | 294.09 | | 568.35 | | 533.88 | |
| Interest | 438.06 | | 709.90 | | 702.30 | |
| Office supplies | 570.58 | | 1,429.40 | | 1,009.86 | |
| Office and showroom rent | 8,238.03 | | 7,619.91 | | 8,793.72 | |
| Payroll taxes | 178.10 | | 155.61 | | 311.01 | |
| Repairs and maintenance | 0 | | 47.50 | | 139.72 | |
| Salaries | 4,289.96 | | 4,701.76 | | 7,635.59 | |
| Sales commissions | 6,877.41 | | 10,550.00 | | 14,716.26 | |
| Telephone | 664.47 | | 597.10 | | 656.19 | |
| Taxes—general | 65.10 | | 351.46 | | 320.79 | |
| Travel—lodging, meals, tips | 861.77 | | 891.53 | | 1,106.00 | |
| Travel—commercial fares | 343.87 | | 4,209.50 | | 3,266.39 | |
| Utilities | 588.15 | | 566.37 | | 567.49 | |
| Miscellaneous | 50.83 | | 233.04 | | 578.93 | |
| | | 26,829.54 | | 38,123.85 | | 43,671.47 |
| Net operating income | | 15,626.55 | | 18,159.67 | | 20,006.54 |
| Extraordinary income (expense) | | 2,305.82 | | 0 | | 0 |
| Net earnings | | $17,932.37 | | $18,159.67 | | $ 20,006.54 |

[a]Note: No provision has been made in this statement for income taxes accruing on the proprietor.

## CASE 25

# UNITED BANCSHARES, INC.

United Bancshares, Inc. (UBI) was planning to become a multibank holding company with the purchase outside its trading area of an independent bank named The Interchange National Bank. For the first time, recent legislation permitted holding companies in the state to own more than one affiliate bank.

Since 1973, UBI had been the parent holding company of United Bank and Trust, N.A., a $365 million bank in a midwestern unit banking state. In addition, UBI owned nonbanking subsidiaries that were active in venture capital and livestock credit. UBI's resources totaled $426 million, including a particularly strong capital position (see financial summaries in Exhibits 1 and 2). UBI's bank affiliate, United Bank and Trust, was the largest bank in Haneystown, a community of 45,000 located in the northern edge of the state. The bank held deposits totaling just over 50 percent of all deposits in the town's three banks and two S&Ls.

The United Bank and Trust's market area covered about a 30-mile radius around Haneystown, including several communities across the state line. In addition, United Bank maintained strong correspondent ties to many rural banks at distances as much as 250 miles from Haneystown.

### THE TARGET BANK

In late summer, 1984, UBI was attempting to complete negotiations for acquiring Interchange National Bank, which was located near a city of 700,000, 75 miles south of Haneystown. UBI's management believed this location would permit UBI to penetrate and compete effectively in the major city market.

Interchange Bank leased space in a new suburban high-rise building at an important expressway interchange. The expressway led to a distant western suburb of the major city and ran along a six-mile corridor consisting of middle- and upper-income homes and numerous light industrial firms. During the first half of 1984, building permits had been issued for over 3,000 residential units in the corridor. This represented over 60 percent of all such permits issued by the city during the period. Recognizing its strategic location, Dick Troxell, UBI's chief financial officer, proclaimed Interchange Bank's commercial potential to be "fantastic."

Interchange National's total assets were $55 million on June 30, 1984. The bank was controlled by R. B. Wolfe, an investor who held 60 percent of the common stock. The remaining 40 percent stock interest had been widely subscribed when the bank was incorporated in December 1981.

A stock purchase agreement had been drawn up by UBI calling for payment of $12,320,000 to the Interchange stockholders in return for 100 percent of the outstanding common stock.

Interchange Bank's board of directors had just approved the acquisition, and a special meeting of UBI's board had been called to act on the proposed agreement. Dick Troxell was preparing an analysis of the Interchange acquisition for the meeting. There were several aspects of this proposed merger, however, that continued to concern him.

### FINANCIAL STATUS OF INTERCHANGE NATIONAL

The financial statements on Interchange National appear in Exhibits 3 and 4. The bank's financial performance as of June 30, 1984, was unusually impressive as shown:

| | |
|---|---|
| Total assets | $55,245,000 |
| Total deposits | 45,860,000 |
| Net loans | 21,092,000 |
| Annualized earnings | 1,397,000[a] |

## Ratio Analysis

| | Interchange National Bank (Six Months, 1984) | All $25–50 Million Deposit Banks in the State (1983) |
|---|---|---|
| Return on assets | 2.53% | 1.18% |
| Return on equity | 16.23% | 13.37% |
| Loans/deposits | 46.00% | 52.00% |
| Capital/assets | 15.58% | 8.04% |

ª January–June 1984 income was $698,500.

Interchange National's financial reporting was on a cash basis for tax purposes, as was true for most small banks. Troxell hoped to incorporate Interchange's returns into UBI's financial reports in December 1984. Interchange had a federal income tax net operating loss carry-forward of about $375,000.

The bank's deposit base included $10 million in public funds and $5.1 million in large CDs held by Mr. Wolfe, the majority stockholder. In addition, Mr. Wolfe's demand deposit account fluctuated significantly, reaching a peak of $2 million on June 30, 1984.

### PROSPECTS FOR INTERCHANGE NATIONAL

In preparation for his final presentation of the acquisition proposal to UBI's board of directors, Dick Troxell projected financial statements on Interchange National for 1984–1993 (see Exhibits 6 and 7). These statements incorporated key assumptions about the growth potential for loans and deposits (Exhibit 5). In particular, the assumptions anticipated strong growth in commercial loans paralleled by significant increases in the demand deposits of commercial customers. The projections omitted, however, a major interest expense that would probably be associated with these commercial deposits in the future. It was assumed that U.S. banks would soon be permitted to pay explicit interest on commercial demand accounts by the Depository Institutions Deregulation Committee (DIDC), a federal government rule-making group comprising the heads of depository institutions' supervisory agencies in

Washington, D.C. Troxell realized that this additional interest expense was not reflected in Exhibit 7, but he reasoned that it might be offset by other factors such as increased spreads on loans and higher fee income.

An important financial characteristic of Interchange National was its extremely strong capital position. The bank's $8,400,000 equity was well in excess of the minimum 7 percent of total assets, the current guideline for capital adequacy established by the Comptroller of the Currency. Troxell wondered if the abundance of Interchange's capital was a positive or a negative factor in the acquisition. On the negative side, bank acquisition prices are usually determined as a multiple of equity book value. For Interchange National, the multiple was a reasonable 1.35. Because of Interchange's large equity in relation to assets, however, estimated to rise to $9.3 million by the closing of the sale, UBI would be paying $12.32 million for control of only about $60 million in assets.

As a positive aspect of Interchange's excessive capital, Troxell anticipated that UBI could "dividend" some of Interchange's $9.3 million capital "upstream." He knew that the Comptroller of the Currency generally limited upstream dividends to a maximum of a subsidiary's ongoing earnings, or the amount remaining after sufficient earnings were retained to maintain adequate capital in a growing subsidiary. He thought, however, that Interchange's strong capital position would permit the upstreaming of an amount in excess of $7 million, or about $2.3 million in capital, which then could be added back to UBI's capital after the purchase was closed. In a sense, then, the *net* purchase price would be about $10.02 million ($12.32 million less $2.3 million upstreamed) and not the stated price of $12.32 million.

Exhibits 6 and 7 did not take into account, however, the upstreaming of this excess equity capital. The financial projections assumed that Interchange's $9.3 million capital expected when the acquisition closed would remain in the bank. All earnings subsequent to closing would be upstreamed to UBI until assets grew to the point at which the capital–assets ratio fell to 8 percent. With growth beyond that point, enough earnings would be retained to maintain equity at a conservative 8 percent of assets.

## FINANCING THE ACQUISITION

The Federal Reserve's regulations limited UBI's methods of financing the acquisition. Holding company acquisitions were limited to a maximum debt financing equal to 75 percent for any subsidiary. Each acquisition was subject to the same financing limitations on a one-at-a-time evaluation; that is, no acquisition could be debt financed beyond the 75 percent limitation, regardless of how earlier subsidiaries were financed.

In UBI's case, even though its three existing subsidiaries were each fully financed by equity, future acquisitions would still require a minimum 25 percent equity down payment. Applications to the Federal Reserve with larger equity down payments were generally viewed more favorably. Troxell believed that a 100 percent cash equity deal for Interchange would create significant problems for UBI's overall acquisition program. For example, if UBI paid all cash for Interchange and then found that it could not gain the Comptroller of the Currency's approval to upstream additional dividends from its equity-rich United Bank and Trust subsidiary, UBI might not have enough cash for the required 25 percent down payment on future acquisitions.

With these factors in mind, Troxell believed UBI would be able to borrow $8.4 million, or about two-thirds of the $12.32 million acquisition price. This would require a cash equity payment of $3.92 million. He had been assured by a regional insurance firm that it would lend the necessary funds at a 12 percent interest rate. This loan would amortize over a nine-year period.

## CONSOLIDATED HOLDING COMPANY PERFORMANCE

Troxell believed that the ultimate test of the proposed acquisition would be its effect on UBI's performance. Exhibits 8 through 10 show projected changes in the earnings, cash flow, and performance of the holding company following the acquisition of Interchange National.

The sources of cash flowing to a holding company were controlled by law. The holding company incurred no tax liability on upstreamed dividends. Management fees collected from subsidiaries such as Interchange National were strictly limited. Holding company indebtedness was serviced from pretax earnings, including both interest and principal components.

Troxell knew that UBI's board of directors would focus closely on the merger's net income effect on the holding company. Exhibit 8 indicates a net income contribution up to $2.4 million by the year 1993. Although Exhibit 10 shows that the acquisition would slightly dilute the holding company's returns on assets and equity in the early years following the acquisition, the dilution effect would stem from UBI's unusually high returns before consolidation and not from subnormal returns on the new subsidiary.

In Troxell's view, the crucial economic test of the acquisition was its cash-flow effect. Exhibit 9 presents the annual cash-flow pattern from Interchange, and Exhibit 10 shows the net present value of the cash-flow pattern at various discount rates. He considered 16 percent to be an acceptable rate of return (i.e., discount rate).

Although the results indicated that the acquisition was amply profitable, Troxell knew the results were strongly influenced by some key assumptions. He wondered if it was conservative enough to assume a 1994 terminal value for Interchange Bank at the same 1.35 book multiple as the original acquisition. He also wondered about the outcome if a debt financing ratio well below the assumed two-thirds was used. Finally, he was concerned about presenting an overly optimistic picture of Interchange Bank's potential earnings.

**EXHIBIT I   United Bancshares, Inc., and Subsidiaries—Consolidated Balance Sheet (dollars in thousands)**

| | 1983 | 1982 |
|---|---|---|
| Cash and due from banks | $ 54,235 | $ 39,132 |
| Investment securities | | |
| U.S. government | 40,228 | 32,899 |
| Municipal and other tax-exempt | 69,942 | 74,229 |
| Other securities | 18,312 | 15,228 |
| Total investment securities | 128,482 | 122,356 |
| Loan discounts | | |
| Commercial | 141,580 | 135,040 |
| Real estate | 64,305 | 47,730 |
| Consumer | 20,828 | 21,922 |
| | 226,713 | 204,692 |
| Less: | | |
| Unearned discount | 2,106 | 2,538 |
| Allowance for possible loan losses | 2,022 | 2,729 |
| Net loans and discounts | 222,575 | 199,424 |
| Federal funds sold | – | 9,800 |
| Premises and equipment—net | 5,516 | 5,145 |
| Direct-lease financing | 4,986 | 5,168 |
| Other assets | 10,520 | 10,506 |
| Total assets | $426,314 | $391,531 |

| | 1983 | 1982 |
|---|---|---|
| **Deposits** | | |
| Total demand deposits | $113,049 | $164,688 |
| Savings | 23,686 | 12,644 |
| CDs | 143,265 | 88,570 |
| Total time deposits | 166,951 | 101,214 |
| Total deposits | 280,000 | 265,902 |
| Discounted loans | 29,557 | 31,076 |
| Federal funds purchased | 6,300 | 8,134 |
| Other borrowed funds | 38,587 | 19,234 |
| Accrued interest, tax, and expense | 12,040 | 11,811 |
| Total liabilities | 366,484 | 336,157 |
| **Shareholders' Equity** | | |
| Common stock, $2 par value per share, 14,735,000 shares outstanding | 2,947 | 2,947 |
| Capital surplus | 5,242 | 5,242 |
| Retained earnings | 51,641 | 47,185 |
| Total shareholders' equity | 59,830 | 55,374 |
| Total liabilities and equity | $426,314 | $391,531 |

**EXHIBIT 2   United Bancshares, Inc., and Subsidiaries—Consolidated Statements of Income (dollars in thousands)**

|  | 1983 | 1982 |
|---|---|---|
| Total interest revenue | $42,584 | $41,204 |
| Total interest expense | 23,264 | 23,195 |
| Net interest revenue | 19,320 | 18,009 |
| Provision for possible loan losses | 3,861 | 1,400 |
| Net interest revenue, less provision for possible loan losses | 15,459 | 16,609 |
| Total other revenue | 4,095 | 3,799 |
| Total other expenses | 12,228 | 10,499 |
| Income before income taxes and security transactions | 7,325 | 9,910 |
| Income taxes (credit) | (285) | 1,966 |
| Net income before securities transactions | 7,610 | 7,944 |
| Net securities gains after tax effect of $162,504 and $86,454 in 1983 and 1982 | 792 | 221 |
| Net income | $ 8,402 | $ 8,165 |

## EXHIBIT 3 United Bancshares, Inc.—Balance Sheet for Interchange National Bank, December 31, 1982, 1983, and June 30, 1984 (dollars in thousands)

| | June 30, 1984 | Dec. 31 1983 | Dec. 31 1982 |
|---|---|---|---|
| **Assets** | | | |
| Cash and due from banks | $ 7,459 | $ 2,411 | $11,152 |
| Interest-bearing deposits with bank | — | 1,456 | 5,152 |
| Investment securities | | | |
| U.S. Treasury securities | 18,931 | 10,893 | 12,660 |
| Obligations of state and political subdivisions | 1,916 | 2,255 | 2,747 |
| Other securities | 846 | 904 | 872 |
| Total investment securities | 21,693 | 14,022 | 16,279 |
| Federal funds sold | 3,466 | 3,010 | 1,400 |
| Loans | | | |
| Commercial | 16,192 | 12,516 | 4,014 |
| Real estate | 5,135 | 3,948 | 1,301 |
| Consumer | 351 | 316 | 395 |
| Less | | | |
| Unearned discount | 294 | 334 | 162 |
| Allowance for possible loan losses | 292 | 147 | 70 |
| Net loans | 21,092 | 16,297 | 5,478 |
| Premises and equipment, net | 655 | 583 | 581 |
| Accrued interest receivable | 855 | 888 | 821 |
| Other assets | 25 | 28 | — |
| Total assets | $55,245 | $38,695 | $40,863 |
| **Liabilities** | | | |
| Demand deposits | | | |
| Individuals, partnerships, and corporations | $22,023 | $12,307 | $16,009 |
| Public funds | 600 | 616 | 372 |
| Total demand deposits | 22,623 | 12,923 | 16,381 |
| **Time Deposits** | | | |
| Savings | 3,007 | 2,328 | 1,388 |
| CDs | 10,150 | 5,319 | 13,814 |
| Public funds—CDs | 10,080 | 9,867 | — |
| Total time deposits | 23,237 | 17,514 | 15,202 |
| Total deposits | 45,860 | 30,437 | 31,583 |
| Securities sold under agreement to repurchase | — | — | 1,400 |
| Other liabilities | 775 | 342 | 604 |
| Total liabilities | 46,635 | 30,779 | 33,587 |
| **Shareholders' Equity** | | | |
| Common stock | 3,500 | 3,500 | 3,500 |
| Surplus | 3,500 | 3,500 | 3,500 |
| Undivided profits | 911 | 916 | 276 |
| Current earnings | 699 | — | — |
| Total capital | 8,610 | 7,961 | 7,276 |
| Total liabilities and shareholders' equity | $55,245 | $38,695 | $40,863 |

**EXHIBIT 4  United Bancshares, Inc.—Income Statement for Interchange National Bank (dollars in thousands)**

| | Month of June, 1984 | Year Ending December 31, 1983 | Year Ending December 31, 1982 |
|---|---|---|---|
| **Interest Revenue** | | | |
| Loans | $165 | $2,080 | $304 |
| Investment securities | | | |
| U.S. Treasury securities | 164 | 1,838 | 926 |
| Obligations of state and political subdivisions | 40 | 314 | 13 |
| Other securities | 8 | 209 | 235 |
| Federal funds sold | 56 | 325 | 234 |
| Total interest revenue | 433 | 4,766 | 1,712 |
| **Interest Expense** | | | |
| Time deposits: | | | |
| Savings | 169 | 115 | 35 |
| CDs | — | 2,054 | 621 |
| NOW accounts | 41 | 29 | 3 |
| Other | 2 | 60 | 3 |
| Total interest expense | 212 | 2,258 | 662 |
| Net interest revenue | 221 | 2,507 | 1,050 |
| Provision for possible loan losses | 17 | 580 | 70 |
| Net interest revenue after provision for possible loan losses | 204 | 1,929 | 980 |
| **Other Operating Revenue** | | | |
| Bond trading revenue | — | — | 103 |
| Exchange and service-charge revenue | 40 | 183 | 23 |
| Other revenue | 1 | 8 | 4 |
| Total other operating revenue | 41 | 192 | 130 |
| **Other Operating Expense** | | | |
| Salaries and benefits | 61 | 613 | 273 |
| Occupancy expense | 30 | 365 | 153 |
| Other expense | 45 | 518 | 351 |
| Total other operating expense | 136 | 1,498 | 777 |
| Income before income taxes and security gains | 111 | 623 | 333 |
| Federal and state income taxes | 24 | 36 | 57 |
| Income before security gains | 87 | 587 | 276 |
| Security gains (losses) | — | 51 | — |
| Net income | $ 87 | $ 638 | $ 276 |

787

---

**EXHIBIT 5    United Bancshares, Inc.—Assumptions for Projection Model
for Interchange National Bank**

---

**Prime Rate and Pricing Assumptions**
Prime rate: assumed to be $11\frac{1}{2}\%$

**Asset Pricing**
Loans: priced at 2% above prime rate.
U.S. Treasury securities: priced at 2% below prime rate.
State and political obligations: priced at 1% above prime.
Other assets: priced at 3% (no relation to prime).
Federal funds: priced at $2\frac{1}{2}\%$ below prime.

**Liability Pricing**
Savings: priced at $5\frac{1}{4}\%$
CDs: priced at prime less 2%
NOW accounts: priced at $5\frac{1}{4}\%$
Other liabilities: priced at 10% (no relation to prime)

---

**EXHIBIT 6  United Bancshares, Inc.—Interchange National Bank Balance Sheet Projections (dollars in thousands)**

| | 1984 | 1985 | 1986 | 1987 | 1988 | 1989 | 1990 | 1991 | 1992 | 1993 |
|---|---|---|---|---|---|---|---|---|---|---|
| **Assets** | | | | | | | | | | |
| Cash and due | $ 592 | $ 622 | $ 652 | $ 686 | $ 699 | $ 713 | $ 728 | $ 742 | $ 757 | $ 771 |
| Deposit with banks | 7,053 | 7,406 | 7,776 | 8,165 | 8,574 | 9,002 | 9,451 | 9,925 | 10,420 | 10,942 |
| Income taxes refundable | 56 | 35 | 35 | 35 | 35 | 35 | 35 | 35 | 35 | 35 |
| **Securities** | | | | | | | | | | |
| U.S. Treasury securities | 21,298 | 26,622 | 33,278 | 41,598 | 45,758 | 50,334 | 55,367 | 60,904 | 66,294 | 73,693 |
| State and political obligations | 2,061 | 2,370 | 2,726 | 2,997 | 3,147 | 3,305 | 3,471 | 3,644 | 3,826 | 4,018 |
| Other securities | 636 | 636 | 636 | 636 | 636 | 636 | 636 | 636 | 636 | 636 |
| Total investment securities | 23,995 | 29,628 | 36,639 | 45,231 | 49,542 | 54,274 | 59,473 | 65,184 | 71,456 | 78,347 |
| Federal funds sold | 2,395 | 1,305 | — | — | | | | | | |
| **Loans** | | | | | | | | | | |
| Commercial loans | 18,250 | 22,813 | 28,517 | 35,645 | 39,210 | 43,131 | 47,445 | 52,188 | 57,407 | 63,148 |
| Real estate loans | 5,788 | 7,235 | 9,043 | 11,304 | 12,435 | 13,678 | 15,046 | 16,549 | 18,206 | 20,026 |
| Consumer loans | 396 | 496 | 619 | 774 | 851 | 937 | 1,030 | 1,133 | 1,246 | 1,371 |
| **Minus loan loss and unearned discounts** | | | | | | | | | | |
| Unearned discounts | 344 | 361 | 379 | 399 | 417 | 440 | 462 | 484 | 508 | 535 |
| Loan loss allowance | 245 | 305 | 382 | 477 | 525 | 577 | 636 | 699 | 769 | 846 |
| Net loans | 23,845 | 29,876 | 37,416 | 46,847 | 51,552 | 56,728 | 62,423 | 68,688 | 75,580 | 83,164 |
| Premises and equipment | 582 | 840 | 840 | 840 | 840 | 840 | 840 | 840 | 840 | 840 |
| Interest receivable | 952 | 1,095 | 1,259 | 1,448 | 1,593 | 1,751 | 1,928 | 2,120 | 1,632 | 2,565 |
| Other assets | 900 | 945 | 993 | 1,042 | 1,095 | 1,149 | 1,207 | 1,267 | 1,330 | 1,397 |
| Total assets | $60,371 | $71,751 | $85,611 | $104,294 | $113,928 | $124,494 | $136,083 | $148,799 | $162,751 | $178,062 |

# EXHIBIT 6 (continued)

|  | 1984 | 1985 | 1986 | 1987 | 1988 | 1989 | 1990 | 1991 | 1992 | 1993 |
|---|---|---|---|---|---|---|---|---|---|---|
| **Liabilities and Stockholders' Equity** | | | | | | | | | | |
| Deposits | | | | | | | | | | |
| Individual, partnerships and corporations | $24,175 | $30,219 | $34,752 | $39,965 | $43,961 | $48,357 | $53,193 | $58,512 | $64,364 | $70,799 |
| Public funds | 1,190 | 1,309 | 1,440 | 1,583 | 1,742 | 1,917 | 2,108 | 2,318 | 2,551 | 2,806 |
| Total demand deposits | 25,365 | 31,528 | 36,191 | 41,549 | 45,703 | 50,274 | 55,301 | 60,831 | 66,914 | 73,606 |
| Savings | 3,233 | 3,717 | 4,276 | 4,917 | 5,653 | 6,502 | 7,153 | 7,868 | 8,653 | 9,520 |
| CDs | 8,977 | 11,692 | 15,014 | 18,912 | 22,805 | 26,020 | 29,534 | 33,358 | 37,502 | 41,973 |
| Public funds—CDs | 12,473 | 13,720 | 15,092 | 16,601 | 18,262 | 20,087 | 22,096 | 24,305 | 26,736 | 29,410 |
| Total time deposits | 24,683 | 29,129 | 34,382 | 40,430 | 46,719 | 52,609 | 58,783 | 65,531 | 72,891 | 80,903 |
| Total deposits | 50,047 | 60,657 | 70,573 | 81,979 | 92,225 | 102,883 | 114,085 | 126,363 | 139,805 | 154,510 |
| Federal funds purchased | — | — | 3,864 | 11,054 | 10,345 | 9,498 | 8,842 | 8,134 | 7,385 | 6,607 |
| Repos | — | 700 | 700 | 700 | 700 | 700 | 700 | 700 | 700 | 700 |
| Interest payable | 218 | 251 | 288 | 332 | 382 | 440 | 505 | 581 | 668 | 769 |
| Other liabilities | 794 | 833 | 875 | 918 | 965 | 1,014 | 1,064 | 1,117 | 1,173 | 1,232 |
| Total liabilities | 51,059 | 62,440 | 76,300 | 94,983 | 104,617 | 114,534 | 125,196 | 136,895 | 149,731 | 163,817 |
| Stockholders' equity | | | | | | | | | | |
| Common stock | 3,500 | 3,500 | 3,500 | 3,500 | 3,500 | 3,500 | 3,500 | 3,500 | 3,500 | 3,500 |
| Surplus | 3,500 | 3,500 | 3,500 | 3,500 | 3,500 | 3,500 | 3,500 | 3,500 | 3,500 | 3,500 |
| Undivided profits | 2,311 | 2,311 | 2,311 | 2,311 | 2,311 | 2,960 | 3,886 | 4,904 | 6,020 | 7,245 |
| Total stockholders' equity | 9,311 | 9,311 | 9,311 | 9,311 | 9,311 | 9,960 | 10,886 | 11,904 | 13,020 | 14,245 |
| Total stockholders' equity and liability | $60,371 | $71,751 | $85,611 | $104,294 | $113,928 | $124,494 | $136,083 | $148,799 | $162,751 | $178,062 |

**EXHIBIT 7  United Bancshares, Inc.—Interchange National Bank Income Statement Projections** (dollars in thousands)

| | 1984 | 1985 | 1986 | 1987 | 1988 | 1989 | 1990 | 1991 | 1992 | 1993 |
|---|---|---|---|---|---|---|---|---|---|---|
| Interest income | | | | | | | | | | |
| Loans | $3,218 | $4,033 | $5,051 | $6,324 | $6,959 | $7,658 | $8,427 | $9,272 | $10,203 | $11,227 |
| U.S. Treasury | 2,023 | 2,529 | 3,175 | 3,952 | 4,347 | 4,781 | 5,260 | 5,786 | 6,364 | 7,001 |
| State and political | 258 | 297 | 340 | 375 | 393 | 413 | 434 | 455 | 479 | 503 |
| Other securities | 20 | 20 | 20 | 20 | 20 | 20 | 20 | 20 | 20 | 20 |
| Federal funds sold | 216 | 118 | — | — | — | — | — | — | — | — |
| Total interest revenue | 5,734 | 6,997 | 8,586 | 10,671 | 11,719 | 12,872 | 12,140 | 15,533 | 17,066 | 18,750 |
| Interest expense | | | | | | | | | | |
| Savings | 169 | 195 | 224 | 258 | 297 | 342 | 375 | 413 | 455 | 500 |
| CDs | 853 | 1,130 | 1,446 | 1,817 | 2,166 | 2,472 | 2,806 | 3,170 | 3,563 | 3,987 |
| NOW accounts | 655 | 720 | 792 | 872 | 959 | 1,054 | 1,161 | 1,275 | 1,404 | 1,544 |
| Other | 80 | 84 | 88 | 92 | 97 | 101 | 106 | 112 | 118 | 123 |
| Federal funds purchased | — | — | 367 | 1,050 | 983 | 902 | 840 | 773 | 701 | 627 |
| Total interest expense | 1,757 | 2,129 | 2,918 | 4,089 | 4,501 | 4,871 | 5,288 | 5,743 | 6,241 | 6,782 |
| Net interest revenue | 3,977 | 4,866 | 5,669 | 6,581 | 7,218 | 8,001 | 8,852 | 9,790 | 10,825 | 11,969 |
| Loan loss provision | 584 | 700 | 840 | 1,009 | 1,211 | 1,453 | 1,743 | 2,092 | 2,510 | 3,013 |
| Net internal revenue after loan loss | 3,394 | 4,166 | 4,829 | 5,572 | 6,007 | 6,548 | 7,109 | 7,699 | 8,315 | 8,956 |
| Other operating revenues | | | | | | | | | | |
| Bond trading revenue | — | 70 | 70 | 70 | 70 | 70 | 70 | 70 | 70 | 70 |
| Exchange and service charge | 187 | 195 | 206 | 216 | 226 | 238 | 249 | 262 | 276 | 288 |
| Other revenue | 8 | 10 | 10 | 11 | 13 | 14 | 15 | 17 | 18 | 20 |
| Total other operating revenues | 195 | 274 | 286 | 297 | 308 | 321 | 335 | 349 | 363 | 378 |
| Other operating expenses | | | | | | | | | | |
| Salaries and benefits | 906 | 1,077 | 1,228 | 1,406 | 1,567 | 1,741 | 1,929 | 2,135 | 2,358 | 2,603 |
| Occupancy expenses | 266 | 316 | 360 | 413 | 459 | 511 | 566 | 626 | 692 | 763 |
| Other expenses | 532 | 585 | 644 | 708 | 778 | 857 | 942 | 1,037 | 1,141 | 1,254 |
| Total other expenses | 1,704 | 1,977 | 2,232 | 2,526 | 2,804 | 3,109 | 3,438 | 3,798 | 4,190 | 4,620 |
| Income pretaxes and gain | 1,886 | 2,464 | 2,883 | 3,343 | 3,511 | 3,759 | 4,005 | 4,249 | 4,487 | 4,714 |
| Federal and state taxes | 906 | 1,183 | 1,384 | 1,604 | 1,686 | 1,805 | 1,922 | 2,040 | 2,153 | 2,262 |
| Income before securities transactions | 980 | 1,281 | 1,499 | 1,739 | 1,826 | 1,954 | 2,083 | 2,209 | 2,334 | 2,451 |
| Security gains (losses) | 56 | 56 | 56 | 56 | 56 | 56 | 56 | 56 | 56 | 56 |
| Net income | $1,036 | $1,337 | $1,555 | $1,795 | $1,882 | $2,010 | $2,139 | $2,265 | $2,390 | $2,507 |
| | | | *ROA and Asset Growth Analysis* | | | | | | | |
| Asset growth rate | — | 0.1885 | 0.1406 | 0.1452 | 0.1141 | 0.1122 | 0.1078 | 0.1062 | 0.1048 | 0.1034 |
| Return on assets | 0.0172 | 0.0186 | 0.0182 | 0.0172 | 0.0165 | 0.0161 | 0.0157 | 0.0152 | 0.0147 | 0.0141 |
| Initial outlay for entity | 12,320 | | | | | | | | | |

**EXHIBIT 8 United Bancshares, Inc.—Target Bank Effects on Holding Company (dollars in thousands)**

| | 1984 | 1985 | 1986 | 1987 | 1988 | 1989 | 1990 | 1991 | 1992 | 1993 |
|---|---|---|---|---|---|---|---|---|---|---|
| **Target-bank financial projections** | | | | | | | | | | |
| Assets | $60,371 | $71,151 | $86,611 | $104,294 | $113,928 | $124,494 | $136,083 | $148,799 | $162,751 | $178,062 |
| Management fees | 121 | 142 | 171 | 209 | 228 | 249 | 272 | 298 | 326 | 356 |
| Earnings | 1,036 | 1,337 | 1,555 | 1,795 | 1,882 | 2,010 | 2,139 | 2,265 | 2,390 | 2,507 |
| Ending minimum equity | 4,830 | 5,692 | 6,849 | 8,344 | 9,114 | 9,960 | 10,887 | 11,904 | 13,020 | 14,245 |
| Ending projected equity | 9,311 | 9,311 | 9,311 | 9,311 | 9,311 | 9,960 | 10,887 | 11,904 | 13,020 | 14,245 |
| Maximum dividends | 1,036 | 1,337 | 1,555 | 1,795 | 1,868 | 1,164 | 1,212 | 1,248 | 1,274 | 1,282 |
| **Parent loan information** | | | | | | | | | | |
| Parent loan payments | 1,487 | 1,487 | 1,487 | 1,487 | 1,487 | 1,487 | 1,487 | 1,487 | 1,487 | — |
| Parent loan balance, year end | 7,921 | 7,385 | 6,784 | 6,112 | 5,359 | 4,515 | 3,571 | 2,513 | 1,327 | — |
| **Holding company earnings** | | | | | | | | | | |
| Earnings from target bank | 1,036 | 1,337 | 1,555 | 1,795 | 1,882 | 2,010 | 2,139 | 2,265 | 2,390 | 2,507 |
| Add: Management fee | 121 | 142 | 171 | 209 | 228 | 249 | 272 | 298 | 326 | 356 |
| Less: Nondeductible goodwill | 198 | 198 | 198 | 198 | 198 | 198 | 198 | 198 | 198 | 198 |
| Less: Interest cost | 1,008 | 951 | 886 | 815 | 734 | 643 | 542 | 428 | 301 | 160 |
| Net before tax | (49) | 330 | 642 | 991 | 1,178 | 1,418 | 1,671 | 1,937 | 2,217 | 2,505 |
| Income tax | (408) | (372) | (329) | (279) | (233) | (181) | (124) | (60) | 12 | 90 |
| Net income effect on parent | 359 | 702 | 971 | 1,270 | 1,411 | 1,599 | 1,795 | 1,997 | 2,205 | 2,415 |
| Cumulative net effect | 359 | 1,061 | 2,032 | 3,302 | 4,713 | 6,312 | 8,107 | 10,104 | 12,309 | 14,724 |

**EXHIBIT 9  United Bancshares, Inc.—Consolidated Cash-Flow and Income Effects (dollars in thousands)**

| | 1984 | 1985 | 1986 | 1987 | 1988 | 1989 | 1990 | 1991 | 1992 | 1993 |
|---|---|---|---|---|---|---|---|---|---|---|
| **Holding company cash flows** | | | | | | | | | | |
| Upstream dividends | $ 1,036 | $1,337 | $1,555 | $1,795 | $1,868 | $1,164 | $1,212 | $1,248 | $1,274 | $ 1,282 |
| Management fees | 121 | 142 | 171 | 209 | 228 | 249 | 272 | 298 | 326 | 356 |
| Loan proceeds | 8,400 | — | — | — | — | — | — | — | — | — |
| Tax benefits | 408 | 372 | 329 | 279 | 233 | 181 | 124 | 60 | (12) | (90) |
| Total cash flows | 9,965 | 1,851 | 2,055 | 2,283 | 2,329 | 1,594 | 1,608 | 1,606 | 1,588 | 1,548 |
| Purchase of target bank | 12,320 | | | | | | | | | |
| Acquisition cost | 50 | | | | | | | | | |
| Debt payment | 1,487 | 1,487 | 1,487 | 1,487 | 1,487 | 1,487 | 1,487 | 1,487 | 1,487 | — |
| Total cash outflows | 13,857 | 1,487 | 1,487 | 1,487 | 1,487 | 1,487 | 1,487 | 1,487 | 1,487 | — |
| Net cash flow | (3,892) | 364 | 568 | 796 | 842 | 107 | 121 | 119 | 101 | 1,548 |
| Cumulative cash flow | (3,892) | (3,528) | (2,960) | (2,164) | (1,322) | (1,215) | (1,094) | (975) | (874) | 674 |
| | 1994 Ending Equity 1.35 Book Multiple That Target Was Purchased for | | | | | | | | | → 19,231 |
| **Consolidated net income effect** | | | | | | | | | | |
| Holding company net income | 359 | 702 | 971 | 1,270 | 1,411 | 1,599 | 1,795 | 1,997 | 2,205 | 2,415 |
| Opportunity cost—cum. cash position | (189) | (171) | (144) | (105) | (64) | (59) | (53) | (47) | (42) | 33 |
| Total consolidated net income effect | 170 | 531 | 827 | 1,165 | 1,347 | 1,540 | 1,742 | 1,950 | 2,163 | 2,448 |
| Cumulative consolidated net income effect | 170 | 701 | 1,528 | 2,693 | 4,040 | 5,580 | 7,322 | 9,272 | 11,435 | 13,883 |

793

# EXHIBIT 10 United Bancshares, Inc.—Acquisition Results Summary (dollars in thousands)

| | 1984 | 1985 | 1986 | 1987 | 1988 | 1989 | 1990 | 1991 | 1992 | 1993 |
|---|---|---|---|---|---|---|---|---|---|---|
| **Holding Company Totals** | | | | | | | | | | |
| Present holding company assets | $448,000 | $465,920 | $484,557 | $503,938 | $524,097 | $545,061 | $566,863 | $589,537 | $613,119 | $637,644 |
| Present holding company profits | 8,781 | 9,132 | 9,498 | 9,877 | 10,272 | 10,683 | 11,110 | 11,556 | 12,018 | 12,498 |
| Present holding company equity | 60,200 | 65,680 | 71,378 | 77,304 | 83,468 | 89,877 | 96,544 | 103,477 | 110,687 | 118,185 |
| New holding company assets | 508,371 | 537,071 | 570,168 | 608,232 | | 669,555 | 702,946 | 738,336 | 775,870 | 815,706 |
| New holding company profits | 8,951 | 9,663 | 10,325 | 11,042 | 11,619 | 12,223 | 12,852 | 13,506 | 14,181 | 14,946 |
| New holding company equity | 69,511 | 74,991 | 80,689 | 86,615 | 92,779 | 99,837 | 107,431 | 115,381 | 123,707 | 132,430 |
| Present ROA | 1.96% | 1.96% | 1.96% | 1.96% | 1.96% | 1.96% | 1.96% | 1.96% | 1.96% | 1.96% |
| Present ROE | 14.59% | 13.90% | 13.31% | 12.78% | 12.31% | 11.89% | 11.51% | 11.17% | 10.96% | 10.57% |
| New ROA | 1.76% | 1.80% | 1.81% | 1.82% | 1.82% | 1.83% | 1.83% | 1.83% | 1.83% | 1.83% |
| New ROE | 12.88% | 12.89% | 12.80% | 12.75% | 12.52% | 12.24% | 11.96% | 11.71% | 11.46% | 11.29% |
| **Valuation of Target Bank** | | | | | | | | | | |
| Times book value → | 1.1 | 1.3 | 1.5 | 1.7 | 1.9 | 2.0 | 2.25 | 2.5 | 2.75 | 3.0 |
| Times book value valuations | $10,010 | $11,830 | $13,650 | $15,470 | $17,290 | $18,200 | $20,475 | $22,750 | $25,025 | $27,300 |
| Times earning value → | 8 | 9 | 10 | 11 | 12 | 13 | 14 | | | |
| Times earnings valuations | $8,288 | $9,234 | $10,360 | $11,396 | $12,432 | $13,468 | $14,504 | | | |
| NPV discount rates | 8% | 10% | 12% | 14% | 16% | 18% | | | | |
| NPV valuation of 10 years' earnings | $12,035 | $10,879 | $9,876 | $9,003 | $8,240 | $7,570 | | | | |
| NPV valuation of 10 years' cash flows | $8,424 | $5,813 | $4,424 | $3,295 | $2,378 | $1,628 | | | | |

NOTE: Including ending equity at purchase times book value as a positive cash flow in 1994.

## CASE

# 26

## MADISON COUNTY NATIONAL BANK*

Charles Peterson was president and CEO of Madison County National Bank (MCNB), a community bank with total assets of over $52 million, located in Jackson, Tennessee. The city of Jackson served as the county seat of Madison County.

As with most other community bank CEOs, profitability was never far from Peterson's mind. Recently he had become increasingly interested in generating more fee (noninterest) income to improve the bank's earnings. Peterson was especially curious about new products and services that might generate greater fees and cross-selling opportunities.

Selling had really never received major attention within the bank, as evidenced by a lackluster officer call program. One of the new product opportunities of interest to Peterson was personal financial planning. Perhaps of equal concern was whether the bank was getting the most out of its existing products. How much time and attention should I devote to managing existing products better as opposed to studying new products and services? Peterson wondered.

### THE ECONOMY

Jackson, Tennessee's population totaled some 51,000 as of 1985, an increase from 49,000 in 1980. Jackson was located in west Tennessee on Interstate 40, some 126 miles west of Nashville and 80 miles east of Memphis. Jackson's recent labor force statistics indicated an unemployment rate of only 5.74 percent. The economy of Tennessee was generally strong, with Madison County sharing in this positive economic environment.

Agriculture represented an important part of the county's economic strength. Farmland comprised nearly 60 percent of the county's land area. Soybeans were the primary cash crop, followed by cotton, wheat, corn, and other grains (see Exhibits 1 and 2).

*Case adapted from a case by Philip White, University of Colorado, with his permission.

The commercial banks in Jackson all carried agricultural loans. The recent national decline in agriculture also existed in Madison County. Given prevailing land prices in the early 1980s, significant profits had been made in asset-based lending to agricultural customers. Now, however, local bankers were quite concerned that the cash flow required to repay these loans might not be sufficient, especially given lower prevailing land prices. At the start of 1987, with the exception of the agricultural sector, virtually every other economic indicator pointed to a continuing healthy economy in Madison County and in Jackson.

### COMPETITION

The historic strength of the local economy made it an attractive market for statewide bank holding companies, resulting in an increasingly competitive banking environment. The competitive situation in Jackson could only be described as one step short of open warfare. MCNB faced vigorous competition from three larger commercial banks. All were full-service banks that had been established much longer than MCNB. The overall financial condition of the competitor banks was sound. Each bank had sufficient resources to compete aggressively. Those banks that were part of statewide bank holding companies were in fact becoming much more skillful in marketing. Several S&Ls and credit unions were also becoming increasingly active and effective in the market. Comparative statistics on the four commercial banks are presented in Exhibits 3 and 4.

MCNB was one of two locally owned financial institutions, the other being Jackson National Bank (JNB). Both MCNB and JNB were somewhat more closely identified with the Jackson community than either First American National Bank (FANB) or Union Planters National Bank (UPNB), which were both members of statewide bank holding companies. JNB's growing correspondent activity, increasing emphasis on commercial customers, and formation of its own bank holding company had somewhat weakened its image as a community bank in recent years. MCNB had grown and prospered, positioning itself successfully as a quality community bank with a continuing commitment to the Madison County–Jackson market. Both JNB and MCNB believed they had attracted substantial new accounts based on their greater local ownership and identification.

## BACKGROUND

MCNB received its national bank charter in 1952. It had consistently focused on the retail market, although there had been some success in obtaining business from selected commercial customers.

As of January 1, 1987, MCNB operated attractively designed and maintained facilities at its main banking location, plus one full-service branch, two limited-service branches, and two 24-hour equipment locations (ATMs). The limited-service branches were designed to facilitate deposit and checking transactions and emphasized convenience. Peterson considered MCNB's facilities equal to or somewhat better than those of its primary competitors. The location of MCNB's branches and 24-hour ATMs provided basic market coverage. The competition's larger number of full-service branches did place MCNB at some disadvantage in terms of customer convenience. Given the higher cost of operating branches, however, Peterson was not sure that maintaining fewer branches was really a disadvantage. MCNB employed a staff of 32 full-time employees, 14 of whom were officers, and 15 part-time employees (see Exhibit 5).

MCNB's employees believed the bank had a strong board of directors that demonstrated good commitment and leadership. At a recent board meeting, the following resolution was passed:

*The Board of Directors of Madison County National Bank adopts the following strategic financial performance goals:*

| | |
|---|---|
| *Return on assets* | *1.20%* |
| *Annual growth in assets* | *10.00%* |
| *Minimum capital/assets ratio* | *7.50%* |

MCNB's common stock had limited distribution throughout the west Tennessee region. Three board members, however, controlled nearly 45 percent of the common stock. John Jacobson, chairman of the board, owned almost 20 percent of the shares outstanding. Mr. Jacobson had been in the automobile business for many years and owned Jackson's Oldsmobile–Cadillac dealership. The two other major shareholders were both from wealthy, well-established local families.

Charles Peterson was the only bank officer who was also a member of the board of directors. Over the past five years his common stock ownership had increased to slightly over 4 percent of the shares outstanding. Peterson was born in Tennessee and graduated in 1959 from the University of Tennessee in Knoxville with a degree in business administration. His banking education had included several American Bankers Association as well as Bank Administration Institute courses. In 1975 he graduated from the School of Banking of the South, sponsored by Louisiana State University in Baton Rouge. Charles Peterson was generally considered by both officers and staff members to be a "reasonably good human relations person," although everyone in the bank knew that numbers, not people, represented his primary banking skill.

## ISSUES TO BE ADDRESSED

The necessity of increasing MCNB's fee income had become increasingly clear during the past few years. As a result, one early decision was to offer discount brokerage, introduced in 1983, which thus far had experienced only limited success. Personal financial planning as a source of fee income had also been discussed from time to time at recent board meetings.

It has long been common for community bankers to answer questions and to counsel customers on personal financial matters, normally without any type of charge or fee. Answering questions and giving advice strengthens the relationship between customer and banker, and this type of activity frequently can lead to cross-selling opportunities for other bank products.

Pressure to increase fee income, coupled with the strong relationship between customers and bankers at MCNB, naturally led Peterson to consider a more formalized personal financial planning program for which a specified fee could be charged. Estimates of fee potential varied widely, from $100 to $3,500 or more from each customer using the service.

After considerable thought and some independent study, Peterson concluded that personal financial planning could cover a range of activities, from a basic personal financial analysis and summary report to a sophisticated and thorough analysis and comparably complete customer report.

Although Peterson believed that a number of topics could be covered in a personal financial planning report, he concluded that there should be little, if any, investment advice. More sophisticated, detailed analyses with specific investment suggestions would go beyond the basic plan and would be charged on an hourly basis.

One of the considerations in undertaking only a basic financial planning service involved the issue of bank–customer liability. By keeping the service basic, with advice limited to broad, general directions, Peterson believed that bank liability problems would be minimized. Peterson commented to one of the bank's directors: "I am unwilling to let the issue of liability move the focus of product review away from market potential and bottom-line profits." A more serious uncertainty, however, was whether customers would pay some $200 for a report that was general and did not give specific implementation recommendations.

Peterson concluded, however, that the bank could provide a "turnkey" product, using existing computer software programs, which comprised customer data collection, analysis, and reporting. He thought a tentative price for this basic service could be $200. Those customers who desired additional personal financial planning would be encouraged to commit to the extra services at an hourly rate, expected to range between $50 and $75. Peterson thought a bank officer (financial planner) would require about three hours of time to complete a basic customer plan.

Several crucial questions remained to be answered. First, who were the customers who might want this service, and how many of them were in the bank's market area? Second, how much would customers be willing to pay for this service?

Peterson had reached some preliminary market segmentation conclusions. He thought customers would include the following:

1. Savers and less aggressive investors, not traders or investors willing to take high risk.
2. Households with incomes greater than $35,000 with earners between ages 35 and 60.
3. Households with incomes greater than $40,000 with earners over age 60.
4. Professionals, managers, and self-employed individuals.

In addition to identifying the customer base and pricing the product, there were many questions about determining relevant costs and allocating overhead. Moreover, the timing of the future flow of income and expense was uncertain; hence, a question arose about the usefulness of using discounted present-value techniques to evaluate profitability.

An additional point that had substantial impact on Peterson's thinking was his belief that major segments of the banking industry had introduced very few new products in recent years that contributed to profitability. Peterson thought most new services had been designed as defensive measures to protect market share or to respond to deregulation. Relatively few new products had been offered specifically to attract new business and thus contribute new sources of profit.

The assumptions and framework Peterson decided to use for the projected personal financial planning services are presented in Appendixes A, B, and C. This approach, however, raised several important questions in Peterson's mind. First, should the performance criterion be net contribution dollars or net operating profit? The question focused on fixed-cost allocations and their impact on the proposed new product. Based on the argument that fixed costs would likely be only slightly affected by offering personal financial planning services, Peterson decided to proceed with net operating profit as the appropriate measure. The approach appeared consistent with efforts to leverage existing staff and overhead to increase fee income with, it was hoped, little impact on the bank's fixed costs.

Another issue, related to the data shown on line 12 of Appendixes B and C, entitled "Balance Adjustment and Supplementary Contribution," was whether, in offering this product, the bank's *overall* profits from all sources would increase. If profits were enhanced, then a portion of those incremental earnings should be associated with this product to reflect its true profit contribution. If the primary rationale for the new service was to defend the existing customer base, then some allocated earnings from other bank profit centers would be warranted to reflect the new service's true earnings (or so Peterson thought). Alternatively, if the new personal financial planning service was designed to be profitable on a fee-for-service basis, without considering profits from maintaining existing business or attracting new accounts, then any rationale for using the "Balance Adjustment" line was much less persuasive. More supplementary detail is included on operating aspects of the proposed new service, together with a forecast of anticipated results for the first three years.

With these data in mind, Charles Peterson was evaluating what decision he should make and what should be his recommendations to the board of directors about offering the personal financial planning service to MCNB's customers.

---

**APPENDIX A    Madison County National Bank—Supplementary Information: Personal Financial Planning Service**

1. Introduction date would be February 1, 1988.
2. All development and training would be completed in 1987.
3. The planning service would be tied to computer analysis of data provided by the client and checked by the interviewing officer.
4. For purposes of estimating sales volume by MCNB, it is necessary to estimate the total size of the target market segment. This is done by adding all households with incomes greater than $35,000. From Exhibit 2, this number was 2,115. Based on the fact that this represented 1980 data, this number was increased by 10 percent. Thus, the total number of households in this target market segment in Jackson, Tennessee, was estimated to be 2,327.
5. Of the total potential market of 2,327, it is estimated that 10 percent would be innovators and would be likely to consider buying this service in its first year in the marketplace.
6. MCNB would be able to achieve 20 percent penetration of the 233 innovators, for total first-year sales of 47 cases.
7. During the first year, MCNB would be the only bank in the Jackson market offering personal financial planning.
8. During the second year, the total number of households in the target market segment would be 2,280 (2,327 − 47). Further, it is assumed that the number of individuals who would consider personal financial services in the second year would be substantially greater. Thus, 25 percent of the 2,280, for a total of 570 households, are considered viable prospects for this service during the second year. Further, with the addition of another bank, it is reasonable to assume that total sales by the industry (two banks) would be somewhat greater than in year 1. Assuming total industry sales represented 30 percent penetration of the market, total sales would equal 171. Assuming that MCNB's market share was 40 percent, its total sales in year 2 would be 68 cases.
9. During year 2 there would be at least one other commercial bank competitor offering personal financial planning.
10. Using this same approach for year 3, the key estimates are as follows:
    a. Total potential households—2,109 (2,280 − 171).
    b. Total households interested in year 3—50 percent, or 1,055.
    c. Total industry penetration in year 3—35 percent, or 369 sales.
    d. MCNB's market share would be 30 percent, for total sales of 111 cases.

**APPENDIX A** *(continued)*

11. The price for this service will be $200.
12. The variable costs associated with providing this service are low. The primary variable costs are supplies, folders, forms, etc. Variable costs per sale are estimated to be $30.
13. Staff time would not be charged directly to the service. This is based on the concept of leveraging existing staff and overhead.
14. MCNB would purchase the hardware and software needed to provide the analysis of customer information consistent with the basic service being provided. Total hardware and software costs are estimated to be $7,000.
15. Staff training costs during the first year would total $3,000. This would include seminars, training courses, and materials for the officer providing the service.
16. Some additional development costs would be expected in year 1. It is anticipated that these costs would total $1,000 or less.
17. First-year marketing costs would total $7,654. This would include $1,000 for a lobby reception targeted at existing customers to kick off the new service. Finally, the reception would be a reward for the employees who have invested their time in training and would reinforce in their minds the importance of this new service. A total of $500 is budgeted for internal training. To reach individuals in the target market segment beyond those who are our present customers, direct mail would be the primary method of communication. Two mailings during year 1 are anticipated, with the cost per piece being $1.00, including postage. Assuming a total mailing of 2,327, the total costs of the direct mail program would be $4,654. Finally, the bank would host an educational seminar during the first year, featuring an outside speaker on some topic of interest to individuals in this target market segment. Total costs for the seminar would be budgeted at $1,500.
18. Year 2 marketing expenses are expected to total $7,840. This would include three direct mailings to approximately 2,280 prospects at a cost per mailing of $1.00. An additional $1,000 would be budgeted to cover other marketing actions implemented during the year.
19. MCNB would market this service aggressively to households in the target market segments. This would be done to increase sales of the service in the first and second years and would, it was hoped, lead to the transfer of some account relationships to MCNB from the other commercial banks.
20. No overhead costs would be charged to this service given that the overhead structure of the bank was already in place and would not be affected by this service.

**APPENDIX B  Madison County National Bank—Pro Forma Income Statement for Personal Financial Planning Services**

| Variable | Year 0 | Year 1 | Year 2 | Year 3 |
|---|---|---|---|---|
| 1. Market size—total units | | 2,327 | 2,280 | 2,109 |
|   a. Units actively considered (%) | | 10 | 25 | 50 |
|   b. Market potential (1 × 1a) | | 233 | 570 | 1,055 |
|   c. Number of competitors | | 1 | 2 | 2 |
|   d. Industry market penetration (%) | | 20 | 30 | 35 |
|   e. Total industry sales units (1b × 1d) | | 47 | 171 | 369 |
| 2. Market share (%) | | 100 | 40 | 30 |
| 3. Sales volume (units) | | 47 | 68 | 111 |
| 4. Price per unit ($) | | 200 | 200 | 200 |
| 5. Sales revenue ($) | | 9,400 | 13,600 | 22,200 |
| 6. Variable cost per unit ($) | | 30 | 30 | 30 |
| 7. Gross contribution margin per unit ($) (4 − 6) | | 170 | 170 | 170 |
| 8. Total variable costs ($) (3 × 6) | | 1,410 | 2,040 | 3,330 |
| 9. Gross contribution margin ($) (5 − 8) | | 7,990 | 11,560 | 18,870 |
| 10. Development and training costs ($) | (10,000) | 1,000 | 0 | 0 |
| 11. Marketing costs ($) | | 7,654 | 7,840 | 7,840 |
| 12. Balance adjustment and supplementary contribution ($) | | 0 | 0 | 0 |
| 13. Net contribution ($) (9 − [10 + 11] + 12) | (10,000) | (664) | 3,720 | 11,030 |
| 14. Allocated overhead ($) | | 0 | 0 | 0 |
| 15. Net operating profit ($) (13 − 14) | (10,000) | (664) | 3,720 | 11,030 |
| 16. Cumulative ($) | (10,000) | (10,664) | (6,944) | 4,086 |

**APPENDIX C  Madison County National Bank—Revised Pro Forma Income Statement for Personal Financial Planning Services**

| Variable | Year 0 | Year 1 | Year 2 | Year 3 |
|---|---|---|---|---|
| 1. Market size—total units | | 2,327 | 2,280 | 2,109 |
| a. Units actively considered (%) | | 10 | 25 | 50 |
| b. Market potential (1 × 1a) | | 233 | 570 | 1,055 |
| c. Number of competitors | | 1 | 2 | 2 |
| d. Industry market penetration (%) | | 20 | 30 | 35 |
| e. Total industry sales units (1b × 1d) | | 47 | 171 | 369 |
| 2. Market share (%) | | 100 | 40 | 30 |
| 3. Sales volume (units) (1c × 2) | | 47 | 68 | 111 |
| 4. Price per unit ($) | | 200 | 200 | 200 |
| 5. Sales revenue ($) | | 9,400 | 13,600 | 22,200 |
| 6. Variable cost per unit ($) | | 93 | 99 | 108 |
| 7. Gross contribution margin per unit (4) (4 − 6) | | 107 | 101 | 92 |
| 8. Total variable costs ($) (3 × 6) | | 4,371 | 6,732 | 11,988 |
| 9. Gross contribution margin ($) (5 − 8) | | 5,029 | 6,868 | 10,212 |
| 10. Development and training costs ($) | 10,000 | 1,300 | 1,384 | 2,260 |
| 11. Marketing costs ($) | | 12,383 | 14,833 | 15,826 |
| 12. Balance adjustment and supplementary contribution | | | | |
| a. New deposit balances (estimated income) ($) | | 5,875 | 8,500 | 13,875 |
| b. Fee income net (# × $30 ea.) | | 1,410 | 2,040 | 3,330 |
| c. New relationships not PFP (50 per year × $60) | | 3,000 | 3,000 | 3,000 |
| d. Additional service hours (# × 70 − hourly cost) | | 1,372 | 1,880 | 2,992 |
| e. Interest income from credit funding ($) | | 2,625 | 5,325 | 9,150 |
| f. Additional hours to previous customers (net) | | ____ | 550 | 1,100 |
| Total balance adjustment and supplementary contribution ($) | | 14,282 | 21,295 | 33,447 |
| 13. Net contribution ($) (9 − [10 + 11] + 12) | 10,000 | 5,628 | 11,946 | 25,573 |
| 14. Allocated overhead ($) | | 1,000 | 1,000 | 1,000 |
| 15. Net operating profit ($) (13 − 14) | 10,000 | 4,628 | 10,946 | 24,573 |
| 16. Discounted profit rate: 10% Factors: Yr 1 = .909; Yr 2 = .826; Yr 3 = .751 | | 4,207 | 9,041 | 18,454 |
| 17. Cumulative discounted cash flow ($) | 10,000 | 5,793 | 3,248 | 21,702 |

**EXHIBIT 1  Madison County, Tennessee—Information about Occupations of Employed Persons 16 Years of Age and Over**

| Occupation | Persons | Percent |
|---|---|---|
| Total employed persons 16 years of age and over | 35,735 | 100.0 |
| Managerial and professional specialty occupations: | | |
|   Executive, administrative, and managerial | 2,801 | 7.8 |
|   Professional and specialty occupations | 3,567 | 10.0 |
| Technical, sales, and administrative support occupations: | | |
|   Technicians and related support occupations | 923 | 2.6 |
|   Sales occupations | 4,044 | 11.3 |
|   Administrative support, including clerical | 4,653 | 13.0 |
| Service occupations: | | |
|   Private household occupations | 213 | 0.6 |
|   Protective services occupations | 463 | 1.3 |
|   Other service occupations | 3,861 | 10.8 |
| Farming, forestry, and fishing occupations | 635 | 1.8 |
| Precision production, craft, and repair occupations | 3,945 | 11.0 |
| Operators, fabricators, and laborers | | |
|   Machine operators, assemblers, and inspectors | 5,846 | 16.4 |
|   Transportation and material-moving occupations | 1,722 | 4.8 |
|   Handler, equipment cleaners, helpers, and laborers | 3,062 | 8.6 |

**EXHIBIT 2  Madison County, Tennessee—Income Statistics**

| | Number | Percent |
|---|---|---|
| Less than $2,500 | 1,928 | 7.2 |
| $2,500–$9,999 | 7,949 | 29.7 |
| $10,000–$17,499 | 6,231 | 23.4 |
| $17,500–$24,999 | 4,966 | 18.6 |
| $25,000–$34,999 | 3,525 | 13.2 |
| $35,000–$74,999 | 1,893 | 7.1 |
| $75,000 or more | 222 | 0.8 |
| Total | 26,714 | 100.0 |

SOURCE: Profile, University of Tennessee, 1980.

**EXHIBIT 3    Comparison of Financial Institutions—December 31, 1987 (dollars in thousands)**

|  | JNB* | FANB* | UPNB* | MCNB* |
|---|---|---|---|---|
| Investments | $ 57,196 | $ 36,302 | $ 28,844 | $14,989 |
| Net loans | 79,913 | 81,109 | 77,106 | 31,974 |
| Reserve for loan loss | 664 | 1,565 | 658 | 316 |
| Total assets | 162,103 | 148,561 | 130,257 | 52,137 |
| Demand deposits | 20,381 | 20,486 | 15,813 | 9,586 |
| Time and savings deposits | 111,640 | 103,766 | 98,891 | 37,061 |
| Total deposits | 132,021 | 124,252 | 114,704 | 46,647 |
| Interest income | 11,662 | 10,798 | 9,544 | 5,258 |
| Interest expense | 7,482 | 6,810 | 6,111 | 2,599 |
| Net interest income | 4,180 | 3,988 | 3,433 | 2,657 |
| Net after provision for loan loss | 3,383 | 3,763 | 3,208 | 2,447 |
| Noninterest income | 1,010 | 709 | 675 | 396 |
| Noninterest expense: |  |  |  |  |
|   Salary and benefits | 1,903 | 1,834 | 1,329 | 1,095 |
|   Occupancy | 340 | 217 | 205 | 229 |
|   Other operating expenses | 1,812 | 1,268 | 1,231 | 839 |
| Total noninterest expense | 4,055 | 3,319 | 2,765 | 2,163 |
| Taxes | (71) | 400 | 308 | 98 |
| Securities gains (losses) | 81 | (12) | 175 | 53 |
| Net income | 490 | 741 | 985 | 634 |
| Total capital | 12,673 | 9,198 | 8,809 | 3,715 |

*Abbreviations: JNB (Jackson National Bank), FANB (First American National Bank), UPNB (Union Planters National Bank), MCNB (Madison County National Bank).

**EXHIBIT 4    Additional Competitive Comparisons—December 31, 1987**

|  | JNB | FANB | UPNB | MCNB | Total |
|---|---|---|---|---|---|
| Demand deposits (000s) | $ 20,381 | $ 20,486 | $15,813 | $ 9,586 | $ 66,266 |
|   Market share (%) | 30.7 | 30.9 | 23.9 | 14.5 | 100 |
| Time and savings deposits (000s) | $111,640 | $103,766 | $98,891 | $37,061 | $351,358 |
|   Market share (%) | 31.8 | 29.5 | 28.1 | 10.6 | 100 |
| Loans (000s) | $ 79,913 | $ 81,109 | $77,106 | $31,974 | $270,102 |
|   Market share (%) | 29.6 | 30.0 | 28.5 | 11.9 | 100 |
| Trust assets (000s) | $ 9,299 | $ 30,690 | $ 9,185 | $ 5,428 | $ 54,602 |
|   Market share (%) | 17.1 | 56.2 | 9.9 | 9.9 | 100 |
| Full-service branches | 5 | 4 | 4 | 1 | 14 |
| Limited-service branches | 1 | 1 | 1 | 2 | 5 |
| 24-hour equipment locations | 5 | 3 | 3 | 2 | 13 |

**EXHIBIT 5   Madison County National Bank—Years Ending December 31, 1983–1987: Selected Indicators of Financial Performance (dollars in thousands)**

|  | 1987 | 1986 | 1985 | 1984 | 1983 |
|---|---|---|---|---|---|
| Investments | 14,989 | 13,751 | 9,366 | 7,365 | 10,029 |
| Net loans | 31,974 | 28,973 | 26,558 | 27,173 | 23,061 |
| Reserve for loan loss | 316 | 287 | 244 | 222 | 201 |
| Total assets | 52,137 | 47,392 | 41,824 | 40,004 | 37,908 |
| Demand deposits | 9,586 | 9,043 | 7,889 | 7,494 | 7,255 |
| Time and savings deposits | 37,061 | 33,352 | 26,524 | 24,210 | 22,851 |
| Total deposits | 46,647 | 42,395 | 34,413 | 31,704 | 30,106 |
| Interest income | 5,258 | 4,982 | 5,110 | 4,440 | 4,630 |
| Interest expense | 2,599 | 2,543 | 3,072 | 2,415 | 2,461 |
| Net interest income | 2,657 | 2,439 | 2,038 | 2,025 | 2,169 |
| Net after provision for loan loss | 2,447 | 2,238 | 1,903 | 1,915 | 2,021 |
| Noninterest income | 396 | 361 | 332 | 300 | 258 |
| Noninterest expense: |  |  |  |  |  |
|   Salary and benefits | 1,095 | 997 | 866 | 885 | 807 |
|   Occupancy | 229 | 197 | 154 | 138 | 122 |
|   Other operating expense | 839 | 763 | 840 | 725 | 701 |
|   Total noninterest expense | 2,163 | 1,957 | 1,860 | 1,748 | 1,630 |
| Taxes | 98 | 72 | (24) | 56 | 88 |
| Securities gains (losses) | 53 | 0 | 120 | 44 | (176) |
| Net income | 634 | 570 | 519 | 455 | 385 |
| Total capital | 3,715 | 3,383 | 3,081 | 2,770 | 2,477 |

## CASE 27

## TATE CITY BANK*

Brian Williams, vice-president of planning for the Tate City Bank, was reviewing a detailed marketing research study about his bank and its principal competitors. The bank's profitability had been up fairly sharply in the past few years; however, the bank's total size was essentially unchanged. By 1989, some members of the board of directors had become increasingly concerned about the bank's relative competitive position in

its market area, wondering whether the lack of asset growth was due to changes in the market environment or to management problems within Tate City Bank. Accordingly, the board of directors asked the bank's president to undertake a thorough review of the competitive situation and to report back to the board promptly. The study had been directed by Williams, who was now preparing to summarize its contents for discussion by the board of directors at their next monthly meeting.

Moreover, Williams hoped to use the market research study as a basis for identifying performance objectives that would become an integral

*This case is adapted from a case originally written by Dick Snelsire of Wachovia Corporation and is used with his permission.

part of a five-year strategic plan. The board of directors had also asked management to produce such a plan as a basis for measuring future operating results. Thus, the marketing research study would help identify how Tate City Bank was presently perceived by customers, as well as how the bank might adjust its operating and financial objectives in the next few years, all with the hope that financial results could be significantly improved.

## TRADE AREA ANALYSIS

Tate City, located in the Midwest, had a population of approximately 235,000 people in 1988. The bank's metropolitan area had a population of approximately 488,000. Employment totaled about 120,000. Over the past decade, the growth in Tate City's population and other key economic variables had been about average for the state. During the next 10 years, however, the population was expected to increase by 10 percent, with employment rising slightly faster, projected at 11 percent. Most employment was concentrated in small, diversified manufacturing and wholesale trade.

The headquarters of four banks were located in the city. Total deposits of the four banks in 1988 were $455 million, and loans totaled $309 million. The recent annual growth rates were 8.8 percent and 9.9 percent, respectively, for deposits and loans. There were no out-of-state or foreign banks with loan production offices within the county. State law allowed banks to branch within the county.

The population, composed of blue-collar workers and high-income professionals, had a pronounced ethnic background. In recent years, unemployment had averaged about 7 percent. Al-though loan interest rates were somewhat high, money was available. Non-price-competitive factors were, however, intense among the local banks.

Tate City Bank did not have a cash management department; however, several operations officers were skilled in cash management programs and had been adequately handling the needs of local middle-sized companies. The bank had an officer familiar with the handling of some traditional foreign trade transactions. A competitor, the American National Bank, offered cash management and international services. Two other local banks also provided these services through a Chicago correspondent. The Peoples Bank, the third largest in the city, was known as the "retail bank." In recent years, Peoples had been on the cutting edge of retail innovations, and the bank was rumored to be aggressively pursuing the commercial market within the county. Exhibit 1 includes selected questions from the employee attitude survey; Exhibits 2–4 include financial data for the banks and their peers.

## SUMMARY OF THE MARKETING RESEARCH STUDIES

The primary market research organized by Williams was conducted in three areas: small businesses, middle-market-sized companies, and consumers. A 30-minute telephone interview was the basis for each segment studied.

The following exhibits contain portions of the market research reports received. Exhibit 5 includes brief summary data on the four principal banks. Exhibit 6 presents a survey of the small business market; Exhibit 7 contains a review of middle market businesses. Exhibit 8 covers retail banking.

---

**EXHIBIT I   Tate City Bank—Selected Questions from Employee Attitude Survey**

This opinion survey was conducted to get employees' views of the Tate City Bank organization. The rating scale consists of three responses: agree, neutral, and disagree.

| | Agree | Neutral | Disagree |
|---|---|---|---|
| 1. The people I work with cooperate to get the job done. | 81% | 12% | 7% |
| 2. My job makes good use of my skills and abilities. | 69 | 24 | 7 |
| 3. I get appropriate recognition for my work. | 42 | 30 | 28 |
| 4. I like the kind of work I do. | 85 | 10 | 5 |
| 5. My superior never shows favoritism toward certain employees. | 21 | 23 | 56 |
| 6. I am proud to tell people I am a member of this bank. | 86 | 10 | 4 |
| 7. The bank is doing very well in meeting its social (public) responsibilities. | 72 | 22 | 6 |
| 8. The amount of pay I get for my job is very good. | 20 | 46 | 34 |
| 9. I have enough information to do my job well. | 78 | 20 | 2 |
| 10. Minorities' opportunities for advancement in the bank are the same as those of other employees. | 70 | 10 | 20 |
| 11. I am satisfied with the information received from top management on what's going on in the bank. | 52 | 38 | 10 |
| 12. I feel women's pay is the same as that of men for the same work. | 40 | 30 | 30 |
| 13. I believe that top management at the bank has a sincere interest in the satisfaction and well-being of its employees. | 67 | 20 | 13 |
| 14. The training that the bank has given me is adequate. | 52 | 13 | 35 |
| 15. We give customers the service we promise in our advertising. | 64 | 26 | 10 |
| 16. The morale of the bank staff is very good. | 71 | 20 | 9 |

**EXHIBIT 2   Tate City Bank—Statement of Condition (dollars in thousands)**

|  | 1985 | 1986 | 1987 | 1988 |
|---|---|---|---|---|
| **Assets** | | | | |
| Cash and due from banks | $ 32,034 | $ 15,611 | $ 21,978 | $ 20,124 |
| U.S. governments | 10,082 | 11,583 | 8,938 | 6,788 |
| U.S. agencies | 20,750 | 15,011 | 13,281 | 13,114 |
| Municipals | 19,075 | 17,447 | 16,599 | 18,153 |
| Other securities | 9,486 | 8,996 | 296 | 296 |
| Total securities | 59,403 | 53,037 | 39,114 | 38,351 |
| Loans | 85,149 | 85,543 | 85,553 | 90,447 |
| Gross loans | 85,149 | 85,543 | 85,553 | 90,447 |
| Less: unearned income | 3,681 | 3,552 | 3,397 | 3,326 |
| Less: reserve for losses | 522 | 716 | 795 | 867 |
| Net loans | 80,946 | 81,275 | 81,361 | 86,254 |
| Federal funds sold | 5,804 | 30,110 | 34,100 | 30,705 |
| Trading account securities | 290 | 261 | 671 | — |
| Premises and equipment | 4,808 | 4,985 | 4,902 | 5,037 |
| Other assets | 1,716 | 1,776 | 2,555 | 2,753 |
| Total assets | $185,001 | $187,055 | $184,681 | $183,224 |
| **Liabilities** | | | | |
| Demand deposits | $ 58,482 | $ 42,002 | $ 43,648 | $ 47,132 |
| Savings deposits | 72,060 | 73,468 | 77,115 | 79,164 |
| Total deposits | 130,542 | 115,470 | 120,763 | 126,296 |
| Federal funds purchased | 38,434 | 54,254 | 46,219 | 37,375 |
| Other liabilities | 4,839 | 5,322 | 4,792 | 5,502 |
| Total liabilities | 173,815 | 175,046 | 171,774 | 169,173 |
| Common stock | 2,000 | 2,000 | 2,000 | 2,000 |
| Surplus | 7,000 | 7,000 | 7,000 | 7,000 |
| Undivided profits | 2,186 | 3,009 | 3,906 | 5,051 |
| Total capital | 11,186 | 12,009 | 12,906 | 14,051 |
| Total liabilities and capital | $185,001 | $187,055 | $184,681 | $183,224 |

**EXHIBIT 3** Tate City Bank—Statement of Earnings (dollars in thousands)

| | 1985 | 1986 | 1987 | 1988 |
|---|---|---|---|---|
| **Interest Income** | | | | |
| Loans | $ 8,078 | $ 9,248 | $10,501 | $13,077 |
| Investment securities: | | | | |
|   U.S. governments | 731 | 829 | 975 | 954 |
|   U.S. agencies | 1,446 | 1,353 | 1,074 | 1,299 |
|   Municipals[a] | 1,099 | 864 | 1,012 | 1,053 |
|   Other securities | 72 | 98 | 17 | 19 |
|     Total securities | 3,348 | 3,144 | 3,078 | 3,325 |
| Federal funds sold | 1,132 | 3,854 | 6,276 | 6,665 |
| Interest-bearing bank balance | 245 | 778 | 398 | 307 |
| Trading account | — | — | 38 | 16 |
|   Interest income | 12,803 | 17,024 | 20,291 | 23,390 |
| **Interest Expense** | | | | |
| Interest paid on deposits | 4,400 | 4,722 | 5,894 | 7,961 |
| Federal funds purchased | 3,150 | 6,287 | 8,020 | 7,671 |
| Other interest expense | 167 | 39 | 68 | 59 |
|   Total interest expense | 7,717 | 11,048 | 13,982 | 15,691 |
| Net interest income | 5,086 | 5,976 | 6,309 | 7,699 |
| Provision for loan losses | 313 | 590 | 443 | 470 |
|   Net after provision | 4,773 | 5,386 | 5,866 | 7,229 |
| **Other Income** | | | | |
| Fees for trust services | — | — | 327 | 327 |
| Service charges | 601 | 774 | 207 | 252 |
| Miscellaneous income | — | — | 457 | 319 |
|   Total other income | 601 | 774 | 991 | 898 |
| **Other Expense** | | | | |
| Salaries | 2,113 | 2,341 | 2,366 | 2,418 |
| Employee benefits | — | — | 420 | 522 |
|   Total staff costs | 2,113 | 2,341 | 2,786 | 2,940 |
| Net occupancy | 396 | 367 | 300 | 390 |
| Equipment | 367 | 422 | — | — |
| Other expenses | 1,444 | 1,826 | 2,501 | 3,005 |
|   Total | 4,320 | 4,956 | 5,587 | 6,335 |
| Income before taxes | 1,054 | 1,204 | 1,270 | 1,792 |
| Taxes | 195 | 91 | 98 | 253 |
| Income before securities transactions | 859 | 1,113 | 1,172 | 1,539 |
| Securities gains (losses) | — | (49) | (16) | (105) |
|   Net income | $ 859 | $ 1,064 | $ 1,156 | $ 1,434 |

[a]Fully taxable equipment for 1985 = 2,035, for 1986 = 1,600, for 1987 = 1,874, and for 1988 = 1,950.

**EXHIBIT 4   Tate City Bank—Summary: Peer Group vs. Tate City Bank 1988 (Year-End Data)**

| Ratio | Tate City | Peer Group[a] |
|---|---|---|
| 1. Return on assets | 0.78% | 1.02% |
| 2. Return on equity | 10.20 | 13.68 |
| 3. Net interest margin | 5.43 | 5.28 |
| 4. Net charge-offs | 0.47 | 0.27 |
| 5. Recoveries to gross charge-offs | 36.93 | 22.30 |
| 6. Equity to total assets | 7.67 | 7.26 |

[a] For competitor banks in Tate City.

**EXHIBIT 5   General Market Information on Tate City Banks, Year Ending December 31, 1988**

| | American National | Tate City | Peoples Bank | Third Security |
|---|---|---|---|---|
| Total assets | $212MM | $183MM | $149MM | $114MM |
| Total deposits | $148MM | $126MM | $102MM | $79MM |
| Total loans | $100MM | $86MM | $74MM | $49MM |
| Number of branches | 10 | 7 | 6 | 4 |
| Number of ATMs | 6 | 3 | 6 | — |
| Return on assets | 0.94 | 0.84 | 1.01 | 0.75 |
| Loan–deposit ratio | 0.67 | 0.68 | 0.72 | 0.62 |

**EXHIBIT 6   Survey of the Small Business Market in Tate City (Businesses with Less Than $5 Million in Annual Sales)**

*Table 1*
*All Banks Presently Used*

| | Total |
|---|---|
| American National | 33% |
| Tate City Bank | 29 |
| Peoples Bank | 24 |
| Third Security Bank | 20 |
| First Federal Savings & Loan | 14 |

**EXHIBIT 6** *(continued)*

*Table 2*
*Person Responsible For*

| | Selecting Banks | Negotiating Loans | Signing Checks | Making Out Checks | Making Deposits |
|---|---|---|---|---|---|
| Owner/manager/president | 95% | 88% | 85% | 65% | 64% |
| Vice-pres./treasurer/assistant treasurer | 4 | 5 | 10 | 8 | 8 |
| Bookkeeper/clerk | 2 | 3 | 14 | 29 | 31 |

| | Making Up Payroll | Reconciling Statements |
|---|---|---|
| Owner/manager/president | 56% | 54% |
| Vice-pres./treasurer/assistant treasurer | 7 | 6 |
| Bookkeeper/clerk | 33 | 34 |

*Table 3*
*Relationship of Personal and Business Accounts*

**(Do you have a personal account at the same bank at which the company banks?)**

| | Total |
|---|---|
| Have business and personal accounts at same bank | 72% |
| Do not have | 24 |
| (No answer) | (4) |
| Which came first? | |
| Personal | 51 |
| Business | 24 |
| Same time | 7 |
| (No answer) | (18) |

*Table 4*
*Major Services Used at Primary Bank*

| | American National | Tate City | Peoples Bank | Third Security | 1st Federal S&L |
|---|---|---|---|---|---|
| Checking | 87% | 89% | 96% | 86% | 10% |
| Payroll | 15 | 10 | 17 | 12 | 20 |
| CD | 19 | 16 | 23 | 24 | 40 |
| Safe deposit | 21 | 24 | 35 | 24 | 15 |
| Short-term loans | 25 | 24 | 38 | 21 | 10 |
| Medium-term loans | 10 | 9 | 22 | 16 | 20 |
| Long-term loans | 9 | 9 | 7 | 10 | 67 |
| Other financing | 10 | 15 | 10 | 10 | 11 |

*Table 5*
*How I View My Bank*

| | Total |
|---|---|
| A place to borrow money | 13% |
| A place to deposit money | 55 |
| A way to pay bills | 18 |
| A source of information and advice | 7 |

**EXHIBIT 6**  (continued)

*Table 6*
*Deposit Activity*

|  | Total |
|---|---|
| **How Made** | |
| In person | 85% |
| Night depository | 6 |
| Mail | 1 |
| (No answer) | 8 |
| **Frequency** | |
| More than one per day | 8% |
| One per day | 32 |
| Three to four per week | 20 |
| One to two per week | 32 |
| Less than one per week | 5 |

*Table 7*
*Characteristics You Feel Describe the Bank*

| | Banks | | | | |
|---|---|---|---|---|---|
| | American National | Tate City | Peoples Bank | Third Security | 1st Federal S&L |
| Capable management | 74% | 74% | 70% | 73% | 72% |
| Reputable | 69 | 66 | 60 | 62 | 61 |
| Accurate bookkeeping | 63 | 46 | 58 | 57 | 53 |
| Accurate tellers | 58 | 41 | 50 | 51 | 51 |
| Friendly, personal | 53 | 45 | 61 | 52 | 54 |
| Fast teller service | 50 | 46 | 40 | 46 | 40 |
| Bank for big business | 55 | 45 | 32 | 30 | 6 |
| Eager for my business | 34 | 35 | 53 | 36 | 45 |
| Bank for small business | 40 | 34 | 46 | 34 | 12 |

*Table 8*
*Calling Officer Ratings—Percent Rated Good or Excellent (5 or 6)*
*(On Six-Point Scale on the Following Characteristics)*

| | American National | Tate City | Peoples Bank | Third Security | 1st Federal S&L |
|---|---|---|---|---|---|
| Friendly | 59% | 67% | 76% | 65% | 72% |
| Knows all banking services | 67 | 68 | 56 | 62 | 44 |
| Has specific bank service knowledge | 66 | 68 | 54 | 62 | 41 |
| Has general business knowledge | 64 | 66 | 64 | 60 | 67 |
| Can always reach him or her | 45 | 55 | 63 | 54 | 67 |
| Calls only at my request | 69 | 45 | 51 | 43 | 55 |
| Knows my business | 54 | 40 | 48 | 41 | 28 |
| Calls often | 19 | 27 | 35 | 18 | 4 |

**EXHIBIT 7  Survey of the Middle Market Businesses (Businesses with Annual Sales Greater Than $20 Million)**

Table 1
*Companies Located in Tate City with Sales Volume Greater Than $20 Million*

| $20–59MM | $60–599MM | $600MM+ | Total |
|---|---|---|---|
| 32 | 22 | 2 | 56 |

Table 2
*Companies Located in Tate City—Industry Classifications*

| Manufacturing | Wholesale Trade | Others | Total |
|---|---|---|---|
| 18 | 15 | 23 | 56 |

Table 3
*Market Share*

| | American National | Tate City Bank | Peoples Bank | Third Security Bank |
|---|---|---|---|---|
| Do business with | 71% | 61% | 43% | 36% |
| Solicit business | 4 | 11 | 21 | 11 |
| Total market coverage | 75 | 72 | 64 | 47 |

Table 4
*Increase in Importance over Last 12 Months (Base: Existing Customers)*

| | American National | Tate City Bank | Peoples Bank | Third Security Bank |
|---|---|---|---|---|
| Became more important | 10% | 17% | 41% | 10% |
| Became less important | 5 | 8 | 12 | — |
| Net increase | 5 | 9 | 29 | 10 |

Table 5
*Bank Image*

| | American National | Tate City Bank | Peoples Bank | Third Security Bank |
|---|---|---|---|---|
| Effective job for companies | 35% | 32% | 24% | 11% |
| Most innovative in new services | 25 | 11 | 14 | 7 |
| Lead bank for cash management | 26 | 11 | — | 4 |
| Lead bank for international services | 18 | 8 | — | 3 |

Table 6
*Evaluation of Calling Officers by Bank's Customers*

| | American National | Tate City Bank | Peoples Bank | Third Security Bank |
|---|---|---|---|---|
| Know bank's noncredit services | 40% | 53% | 50% | 30% |
| Meet company's credit needs | 60 | 59 | 42 | 20 |
| Know company's needs | 45 | 76 | 42 | 20 |
| Prompt follow-up | 60 | 76 | 50 | 50 |
| Try to earn more business | 40 | 59 | 42 | 50 |
| Easy to work with | 65 | 62 | 62 | 70 |
| Average six-factor score | 52 | 68 | 46 | 40 |

**EXHIBIT 7**   (continued)

### Table 7
### New Business Coverage

|  | American National | Tate City Bank | Peoples Bank | Third Security Bank |
|---|---|---|---|---|
| Call most frequently | 13% | 19% | 27% | 17% |
| Would add bank | 13 | 13 | 45 | — |

### Table 8
### Credit Services Used

|  | American National | Tate City Bank | Peoples Bank | Third Security Bank |
|---|---|---|---|---|
| Short-term credit | 59% | 68% | 67% | 53% |
| Revolving term credit | 49 | 39 | 67 | 45 |
| Real estate loan | 27 | 42 | 36 | 0 |
| Commercial financial | 29 | 45 | 0 | 0 |
| Equipment leasing | 29 | 32 | 33 | 17 |

### Table 9
### Noncredit Services Used

|  | American National | Tate City Bank | Peoples Bank | Third Security Bank |
|---|---|---|---|---|
| Cash management consulting | 49% | 25% | 17% | 14% |
| Financial planning | 10 | 19 | 17 | 0 |
| Pension and profit sharing | 37 | 42 | 37 | 36 |

### Table 10
### International Services Used

|  | American National | Tate City Bank | Peoples Bank | Third Security Bank |
|---|---|---|---|---|
| Letters of credit | 63% | 25% | 10% | 4% |
| Documentary collections | 27 | 11 | 9 | 4 |
| Foreign exchange | 32 | 13 | 10 | 6 |

### Table 11
### Bank's Borrowing Penetration: Borrowed in the Last 2 Years (Base: Each Bank's Customers)

|  | American National | Tate City Bank | Peoples Bank | Third Security Bank |
|---|---|---|---|---|
| From any bank | 65% | 76% | 87% | 70% |
| From this bank | 40 | 59 | 65 | 30 |
| Share of borrowers | 62 | 77 | 75 | 43 |

**EXHIBIT 8   Survey of Retail Banking Customers**

*Table 1*
*Probability of Changing Financial Institutions within the Coming Year*

| | | Main Financial Institution | | | | |
| | Total | American National | Tate City | Peoples Bank | Third Security | 1st Federal S&L |
|---|---|---|---|---|---|---|
| Definitely will change | 2% | 3% | 3% | 1% | 3% | 3% |
| Probably will change | 5 | 6 | 5 | 3 | 0 | 3 |
| Might change | 8 | 7 | 10 | 8 | 11 | 7 |
| Probably will not change | 36 | 38 | 39 | 43 | 38 | 41 |
| Definitely will not change | 38 | 36 | 34 | 33 | 38 | 38 |
| Hadn't thought about it | 11 | 11 | 10 | 12 | 11 | 7 |

*Table 2*
*Financial Institution Most Likely to Be Selected*

| | | Main Financial Institution | | | | |
| | Total | American National | Tate City | Peoples Bank | Third Security | 1st Federal S&L |
|---|---|---|---|---|---|---|
| American National | 14% | — | 25% | 16% | 16% | 21% |
| Tate City Bank | 11 | 19 | — | 17 | 11 | 14 |
| Peoples Bank | 4 | 6 | 6 | — | 5 | 7 |
| Third Security Bank | 3 | 5 | 1 | 3 | — | 3 |
| First Federal S&L | 3 | 2 | 4 | 5 | 3 | — |

*Table 3*
*Service Usage by Bank*

| | Main Financial Institution | | | | |
| | American National | Tate City | Peoples Bank | Third Security | 1st Federal S&L |
|---|---|---|---|---|---|
| Regular checking | 29% | 25% | 26% | 15% | 4% |
| Passbook savings | 22 | 20 | 21 | 14 | 23 |
| MasterCard | 33 | 19 | 32 | 15 | — |
| VISA | 7 | 50 | 23 | 13 | — |
| Mortgage loans | 7 | 8 | 11 | 6 | 33 |
| Statement savings | 21 | 24 | 25 | 15 | 13 |
| Banking machines | 26 | 20 | 18 | 10 | 1 |
| Overdraft protection | 22 | 26 | 24 | 6 | 1 |
| Auto loan | 17 | 15 | 19 | 15 | 3 |
| Int.-bearing checking | 22 | 26 | 24 | 13 | 3 |
| CD | 15 | 14 | 18 | 14 | 2 |
| 6-month money market cert. | 14 | 11 | 16 | 14 | 2 |
| Line of credit | 30 | 27 | 21 | 12 | 2 |
| IRA | 11 | 7 | 14 | 6 | 2 |
| Money market funds | 10 | 1 | 2 | 0 | 1 |
| Single-payment loan | 22 | 22 | 19 | 13 | 0 |
| Other installment loan | 8 | 20 | 12 | 12 | 3 |
| 30-month money market cert. | 17 | 15 | 13 | 12 | 15 |
| Trust service | 32 | 24 | 18 | 13 | 0 |

**EXHIBIT 8**   (continued)

*Table 4*
*Customer Data, 1988*

| | | Main Financial Institution | | | | |
|---|---|---|---|---|---|---|
| | **Total** | **American National** | **Tate City** | **Peoples Bank** | **Third Security** | **1st Federal S&L** |
| **Sex** | | | | | | |
| Male | 50% | 46% | 57% | 51% | 54% | 41% |
| Female | 50 | 54 | 43 | 49 | 46 | 59 |
| **Age** | | | | | | |
| Under 18 | — | — | — | — | — | — |
| 18–34 | 38 | 37 | 35 | 41 | 32 | 41 |
| 35–49 | 26 | 27 | 26 | 25 | 27 | 24 |
| 50–64 | 23 | 22 | 26 | 22 | 27 | 31 |
| 65 + | 12 | 13 | 11 | 10 | 14 | 3 |
| **Income** | | | | | | |
| Under $10M | 13 | 16 | 12 | 10 | 16 | 7 |
| $10M–$15M | 13 | 13 | 10 | 12 | 24 | 21 |
| $15M–$25M | 25 | 25 | 22 | 24 | 19 | 41 |
| $25M–$50M | 27 | 25 | 35 | 31 | 22 | 21 |
| $50M + | 6 | 6 | 8 | 9 | 3 | — |
| Refused | 16 | 15 | 13 | 14 | 16 | 10 |
| **Education** | | | | | | |
| HS or less | 47 | 50 | 45 | 37 | 65 | 45 |
| College | 43 | 40 | 43 | 43 | 27 | 45 |
| College + | 10 | 10 | 12 | 10 | 8 | 10 |
| **Occupation of Chief Wage Earner** | | | | | | |
| White collar | 46% | 42% | 50% | 51% | 32% | 62% |
| Blue collar | 34 | 34 | 33 | 30 | 43 | 28 |
| Other | 19 | 20 | 17 | 17 | 24 | 7 |
| **Primary Financial Decision Maker** | | | | | | |
| Male | 31% | 33% | 32% | 31% | 24% | 38% |
| Female | 22 | 24 | 19 | 22 | 16 | 14 |
| Mutual | 47 | 43 | 49 | 46 | 60 | 48 |

**EXHIBIT 8**  (continued)

*Table 5*
*Change in Distribution of Traditional Household Investments*

| Type Account/Investment | Year Ended | Previous Year | 2 Years Previous |
|---|---|---|---|
| Standard savings/passbook | 34% | 39% | 46% |
| 6-month MMC/30-month SSC | 30 | 21 | 0 |
| Other certificates | 21 | 29 | 45 |
| Money market mutual funds[a] | 5 | 2 | 0 |
| Treasury issues/savings bonds | 9 | 9 | 9 |
| Total | 100 | 100 | 100 |

[a]While included as investments, many have transaction account options available.

*Table 6*
*Reasons for Closing a Transaction Account by Bank*

| | | Banks | | | |
|---|---|---|---|---|---|
| | Total | American National | Tate City | Peoples Bank | Third Security |
| Moved residence | 25% | 17% | 20% | 12% | 9% |
| Service charges | 22 | 18 | — | 27 | 44 |
| Unfriendly/rude | 15 | 20 | 2 | 21 | 4 |
| Slow service | 11 | 15 | 36 | 5 | 10 |
| Inefficient personnel | 10 | 15 | 26 | 16 | 18 |
| Changed job location | 8 | 6 | 5 | 4 | 3 |
| Overdraft charges | 3 | — | 4 | 6 | 5 |
| Other | 3 | 8 | 4 | 5 | 3 |

*Table 7*
*Reasons for Opening a Transaction Account by Bank*

| | | Banks | | | |
|---|---|---|---|---|---|
| | Total | American National | Tate City | Peoples Bank | Third Security |
| Convenient to home | 36% | 40% | 30% | 38% | 42% |
| Convenient to work | 18 | 20 | 15 | 23 | 21 |
| Better service charges | 9 | 2 | 24 | 3 | 3 |
| Better quality service | 7 | 7 | 3 | 5 | 2 |
| Better or more services | 4 | 2 | 3 | 2 | 3 |
| Better hours | 3 | 12 | 1 | 4 | 2 |
| Previous dealings there | 8 | 9 | 4 | 10 | 15 |
| Best reputation | 6 | 6 | 5 | 8 | 5 |
| Other | 3 | 2 | 3 | 3 | 5 |

# Appendix: Bank President Simulation,[1] EE[2]

## INTRODUCTION

Bank President is a business management simulation game that puts you in charge of a large commercial bank. You must develop strategies and make decisions that determine the success or failure of your bank. Bank President is both educational and entertaining. It will teach you about managing a bank and introduce you to the concepts and terminology of banking, as well as give you an exciting and competitive game to play.

There can be from one to 10 banks in every Bank President game. Each player or team becomes the management of a different bank. The game is more realistic if there are two or more banks competing with each other, so the computer will act as president of one or more of the banks and play against you if you want it to.

Like the real world, Bank President is essentially a game of competition. There are fixed amounts of loans and deposits available in the economy at any time. These amounts are taken from actual historical data from the U.S. economy. All the banks in the game must compete with each other to get a share of these loans and deposits. For example, by raising its interest rates and increasing advertising, a bank can take deposits away from other banks in the game. Banks that do not respond to competitors' actions can find themselves with dwindling loan and deposit portfolios.

The game is played as a series of consecutive three-month intervals ("quarters"). Each quarter, Bank President gives the players comprehensive management reports showing the detailed financial performance of their own banks and summary reports on competitors, the economic environment, and the regulatory environment. These reports are available as a series of over 70 different charts and graphs that Bank President can

---

[1] Specifically prepared for this book by Lewis Lee Corporation. An order form to obtain the microcomputer diskette is available in the Instructor's Manual.

[2] *Educational Edition*, User's Manual for the IBM PC and Compatibles, Version 2.1. SYSTEM REQUIREMENTS: 640KB Memory DOS; 3.0 or higher.

display on both text and graphics monitors. The player can also obtain a hard copy summary report each quarter if there is a printer connected to the computer.

Players review these reports showing the results of last quarter, then make the decisions that determine what their banks will do in the coming quarter. Players can set interest rates for loans and deposits, raise or lower employee salaries, expand or contract premises, increase or decrease advertising budgets, buy and sell U.S. government securities, issue or redeem the bank's common stock and capital notes, declare a dividend to pay to stockholders, and make other important decisions every quarter.

Bank President contains a powerful and realistic financial model that it uses to calculate the effect of each bank's decisions. Bank President runs this model each quarter to simulate the operation of every bank in the game. The decisions made by each bank's management strongly influence how well the bank performs during the simulation. The model also considers competitors' actions and changes in the economic and regulatory environments in calculating the bank's results each quarter.

The model sets a market price for each bank's stock every quarter, in addition to providing detailed management and accounting reports.

The object of the game is to be a better bank manager than your opponents. Unless you and your opponents agree to use some other measure, stock price is the measure to use in rating the relative performance of the banks. The team whose bank has the highest stock price at the end of the game is the winner.

Your instructor will tell you whether you will play the game as individuals or teams. The following pages describe how an individual or team can play the Bank President Micro Simulation, either alone or versus other teams, using an IBM PC or Compatible.

These pages can be used as the players' manual for participants.

## INSTALLING BANK PRESIDENT ON HARD DISK

Bank President Educational Edition Version 2.1 performs best when played from hard disk. To install Bank President on hard disk, follow the procedure described below.

1. Make sure the computer is on, DOS has been loaded, and C is the default drive.
2. Create a subdirectory for Bank President by typing "md \bp" and pressing the enter key:

    C:\>md  \bp

3. Make "bp" the current directory by typing "cd \bp" and pressing the enter key:

    C:\>cd  \bp

4. Place the Bank President disk in drive A.
5. Type "copy a:*.*" and press the enter key:

    C:\BP>copy a:*.*

## STARTING BANK PRESIDENT

Although Bank President performs best when played from hard disk, it is also possible to play Bank President directly from diskette. The instructions below describe how to play Bank President from hard disk or from diskette.

### Playing Bank President from Hard Disk

1. If Bank President has not already been installed on your hard disk, install Bank President now using the instructions in the previous section.

2. Make sure the computer is on, DOS has been loaded, and C is the default drive.
3. Select the Bank President subdirectory by typing "cd\bp" and pressing the enter key:

C:\>cd \bp

4. Put the Bank President disk in drive A.
5. Type "bankpres" and press the enter key:

C:\BP>bankpres

## Playing Bank President from Diskette

1. Make sure the computer is on and DOS has been loaded. If the computer is off, remove all diskettes from the drives and turn on the computer. DOS should load from the hard disk.
2. Put the Bank President disk in drive A.
3. Make A the default drive by typing "a:" and pressing the enter key:

C:\>a:

4. Type "bankpres" and press the enter key:

A:\>bankpres

## THE MAIN MENU

The Main Menu is the primary point from which you select the task you want Bank President to perform. If you are playing from a student disk, the Main Menu contains these items:

| Menu Item |
| --- |
| Review Results and Make Decisions |
| Print a Summary of All Banks in this Game |
| Exit Bank President |
| List the Banks on this Disk |
| Identify the Current Game |

Cycle among the available menu choices by pressing the space bar one or more times. Press the enter key when the choice you want appears in the highlighted area.

Refer to later sections in this appendix for descriptions of each of these menu items.

## REVIEWING LAST QUARTER'S RESULTS

Before you make your decisions each quarter, you will want to analyze the results of the previous quarter. If you have a printer on your computer, you should begin your analysis of last quarter's results by looking at the summary printout available by selecting "Print a Summary of All Banks in this Game" at the Main Menu level.

Next, you should look at the 70 charts and graphs that show—in detail—your financial performance, competitor's results and actions, and the economic and regulatory environments. To view these charts and graphs, select "Review Results and Make Decisions" at the Main Menu level. Be sure the disk with your bank's data is in the drive when you give this command. You will have to enter your bank name and password (if your bank has one) before you will be allowed to see your bank's financial results.

Once your password has been validated, you will arrive at the Decisions/Results Menu. From here, you can select any of the charts, graphs, and tables showing last quarter's results, or you can select any of the decision input forms on which you make next quarter's decisions.

Some of the results charts and graphs are reached directly from the Decisions/Results Menu, but most are reached from submenus of the Decisions/Results Menu.

There are two ways to go through the results charts and graphs. One way is to select a specific chart or graph from the Decisions/Results Menu or one of its submenus. To do this, press the space bar until the highlighted area encloses the chart or graph you want, then press the enter key. The requested chart or graph will appear on the screen. Press F2 when you are ready to return to the menu from which you selected the chart or graph.

Another way to go through the charts and graphs is to use F5 and F6. When you get to the Decisions/Results Menu, just press F6. The first chart ("Common Stock Market Price") will appear on the screen. Press F6 again and the next chart or graph in sequence will appear on the screen. Continue using F6 until you have seen all 70 charts and graphs (or as many of them as you want to see). Use F5 whenever you want to back up and see the previous chart or graph again. You can see all 70 of the charts and graphs in only a few minutes by repeatedly using F6.

You can display the data used to create any chart or graph by pressing F7 while the chart or graph is displayed on your screen. Bank President will immediately replace the chart or graph with a data table. Press F7 again to restore the chart or graph to the screen.

It is very important that you learn to use the function keys available to you while you are looking at your results. If you will make a habit of looking at the bottom two lines of your monitor, Bank President will remind you which function keys are available to you at each point in the program. Function keys F1 through F7 are available to all Bank President users, and users with graphics monitors also have the use of F8.

Following is a brief description of each of the results charts and graphs.

**Decisions/Results Menu: Common Stock Market Price.** This chart shows the common stock market prices for all banks in the game, sorted from lowest stock price to highest stock price. Stock price is the best overall measure of your perfor-

mance and is usually used to determine the winner of the game.

**Balance Sheet Menu: Total Assets.** This chart summarizes the assets side of your balance sheet. Your major assets categories are cash, Fed funds sold, securities, loans, and premises. Cash consists of currency, funds on deposit with the Federal Reserve Bank, and float. Fed funds sold is money you have lent to other banks on a short-term basis. In Bank President, securities consist entirely of U.S. government T-bills and T-notes (money you have lent to the U.S. government). Loans represent money you have lent to businesses (commercial loans), individuals (consumer loans), and purchasers of real property (real estate loans). Premises are land and buildings used by the bank to conduct its business.

**Balance Sheet Menu: Change in Asset Balances.** This chart compares current asset balances with those of last quarter, so you can see what changes have occurred.

**Balance Sheet Menu: Detail for Cash Balances.** This chart breaks cash into its components: vault cash, reserves, and float. Vault cash (currency) is used to meet customer withdrawal demands. Reserves are funds kept on deposit with the Federal Reserve Bank and are held based on the level of deposits and the regulatory environment. Float is primarily checks in the process of being collected from other banks. All of these cash components are based on deposit levels and are not under the direct control of each player.

**Balance Sheet Menu: Securities Activity.** This chart summarizes the changes that took place in securities balances over the last quarter. Security purchases increase balances. Maturing securities and security sales decrease balances. Maturing securities are repaid automatically, while security purchases and sales are player decisions.

**Balance Sheet Menu: Loan Balances by Loan Type.** This chart separates loans into the categories of commercial loans, consumer loans, and real estate loans.

**Balance Sheet Menu: Commercial Loan Activity.** This chart shows the components of the net change in commercial loan balances during the last quarter. New loans increase balances. Loan payments and loan losses decrease balances. Each commercial loan is repaid in full with a single payment one year after the loan is made. Interest is paid quarterly.

**Balance Sheet Menu: Consumer Loan Activity.** This chart shows the components of the net change in consumer loan balances. New loans increase balances while loan payments and loan losses decrease balances. Consumer loans are repaid in equal quarterly payments over a three-year period. Each payment includes both principal and interest.

**Balance Sheet Menu: Real Estate Loan Activity.** This chart shows the components of the net change in total real estate loan balances (fixed-rate loans and variable-rate loans combined). New loans increase balances. Loan payments, loan losses, and loan sales decrease balances. See the discussion of the Loan Rates decision input form for details on how real estate loans are repaid.

**Balance Sheet Menu: Total Liabilities and Equity.** This chart summarizes the liabilities and equity side of your balance sheet. The major categories are deposits, Fed funds purchased, Federal Reserve Bank borrowing, capital notes, and equity. Deposits represent money your customers leave

with you in checking, savings, time deposit, and certificate of deposit accounts. Fed funds purchased is money you borrow from other banks on a short-term basis. Federal Reserve Bank borrowing is money you borrow from the Federal Reserve Bank on a short-term basis. Capital notes are issued when you borrow money from the general public. Equity consists of money received when you issue common stock, plus earnings retained by the bank. The bank's "capital," for purposes of calculating the capital adequacy ratio, is equity plus capital notes.

**Balance Sheet Menu: Change in Liability and Equity Balances.** This chart compares current liability and equity balances with those of last quarter, so you can see what changes have occurred.

**Balance Sheet Menu: Deposit Balances by Type.** This chart breaks down deposit balances into the various types of deposits: checking deposits, savings deposits, time deposits, and certificates of deposit. Checking deposits are checking accounts. Savings deposits are passbook savings accounts. Time deposits are amounts under $100,000 left on deposit for a specific period of time. Certificates of deposit (CDs) are amounts of $100,000 or more left on deposit for a specific period of time.

**Balance Sheet Menu: Time Deposit Activity.** This chart shows the components of the net change in time deposit balances. New time deposits increase balances. Maturing time deposits decrease balances. Time deposits are amounts under $100,000 left on deposit for a specific period of time (one year or five years in Bank President).

**Balance Sheet Menu: Certificate of Deposit Activity.** This chart shows the components of the net change in certificate of deposit balances. New certificates of deposit increase balances. Maturing certificates of deposit decrease balances. Certificates of deposit (CDs) are amounts of $100,000 or more left on deposit for a specific period of time (two quarters in Bank President). CDs are usually purchased by corporations or wealthy individuals.

**Balance Sheet Menu: Capital Notes Activity.** This chart shows the components of the net change in capital notes balances. New capital notes increase balances. Maturing capital notes and capital notes redeemed prior to maturity decrease balances.

**Balance Sheet Menu: Equity Accounts Activity.** This chart shows the components of the net change in equity. New stock issued increases equity. The dividend paid on common stock, and stock repurchased, decrease equity. If the bank is profitable, net income after taxes increases equity. If the bank loses money, net income (loss) after taxes decreases equity.

**Decisions/Results Menu: Average Asset Yield.** This chart shows the average rate of interest (yield) received by the bank for each category of assets, plus the weighted average yield of all assets that generate interest income. Cash and premises are excluded because they do not generate interest income.

**Decisions/Results Menu: Average Liability Yield.** This chart shows the average rate of interest paid by the bank for each liability category, plus the weighted average cost of all liabilities that incur interest expense. Equity is excluded because it does not directly incur interest expense.

**Income Statement Menu: Revenue and Expense Summary.** This is your income statement in chart form. Press F7 if you prefer to see your income statement in traditional table format. Interest revenue is the

amount of interest the bank receives from its loans and investments. Interest expense is the amount the bank pays for deposits and money it borrows from others. Fee income is derived from fees charged to customers on checking deposits, commercial loans, consumer loans, and real estate loans. Noninterest expense is the amount the bank spends on salaries, business development, and occupancy. Taxes are paid to federal, state, and local governments. Nonoperating income is the capital gain or loss (net of taxes) from the sale of securities or loans. Net income is the bank's profit or loss, after taxes.

**Income Statement Menu: Change in Revenues and Expenses.** This chart compares the current income statement with last quarter's income statement, item by item, so you can see what has changed. Interest margin is interest revenue minus interest expense.

**Income Statement Menu: Components of Interest Revenue.** This chart shows you the sources of your interest income. The amount of interest income obtained from each of the following is shown: Fed funds sold, securities, commercial loans, consumer loans, and real estate loans.

**Income Statement Menu: Components of Interest Expense.** This chart shows you the sources of your interest expense. Interest expense is broken down into these categories: Fed funds purchased, Federal Reserve Bank borrowing, checking deposits, savings deposits, time deposits, certificates of deposit, and capital notes.

**Income Statement Menu: Components of Noninterest Expense.** Noninterest expense is separated into its components: salaries, business development–deposits, business development–loans, and occupancy. The first three components are under the direct control of each bank. Occupancy is determined by the level of premises and the general price level (consumer price index).

**Funds Flow Menu: Sources of Funds Last Quarter.** Each quarter, funds become available for the bank to use. This chart shows the various sources that provided those funds last quarter. Funds are generated whenever asset balances decrease, or when liability balances increase. For example, funds are generated when a customer pays off a loan (a loan is an asset and a loan payment will reduce asset balances). Funds are also generated when a customer makes a deposit (a deposit is a liability and a new deposit will increase liability balances).

The possible sources of funds in a Bank President game are shown in the chart below.

**Funds Flow Menu: Uses of Funds Last Quarter.** This chart shows how the bank used the funds that were provided by the sources identified in the previous chart.

(Therefore, the total uses of funds shown in this chart will equal the total sources of funds shown in the previous chart.)

Increases in asset balances and decreases in liability and equity balances are uses of funds. For example, a bank can use funds to make a new loan (a loan is an asset and a new loan increases asset balances). Or, the bank can use funds to pay a depositor making a withdrawal from a deposit account (deposits are liabilities and withdrawing funds decreases liability balances).

The possible uses of funds in a Bank President game are shown in the chart on the following page.

**Asset/Liability Profile Menu: Assets Maturing Next Quarter.** This chart shows the amount of Fed funds sold and securities that will mature next quarter, and the amount of the principal repayment due on loans next quarter. These funds will be available to you next quarter.

**Asset/Liability Profile Menu: Liabilities Maturing Next Quarter.** This chart

| Sources of Funds | Explanation |
|---|---|
| **Decrease in Assets** | |
| Cash | Less cash was needed, so the excess was used for other purposes |
| Fed funds sold | Funds that were previously lent to another bank were repaid to this bank |
| Securities | The U.S. government repaid its debt to the bank on the due date, or the bank sold some securities before they matured |
| Loans | The total amount of loans outstanding decreased (loan payments plus loan sales exceeded new loans) |
| Premises | Funds previously invested in premises became available for other purposes |
| **Increase in Liabilities** | |
| Buy FF/FRB | The bank borrowed Fed funds from other banks, or borrowed from the Federal Reserve Bank |
| Deposits | Customers increased the balances in their accounts |
| Capital notes | The bank issued new capital notes in excess of those maturing or being redeemed |
| Equity | The bank's profit plus new issues of stock exceeded dividends and stock repurchases |

| Use of Funds | Explanation |
|---|---|
| **Increase in Assets** | |
| Cash | Funds were used to increase cash balances |
| Fed funds sold | Funds were lent to other banks |
| Securities | Funds were used to buy additional securities |
| Loans | Funds were used to make additional loans to customers |
| Premises | Funds were invested in additional land and buildings |
| **Decrease in Liabilities** | |
| Buy FF/FRB | Funds were used to repay Fed funds borrowed from other banks, or to repay amounts borrowed from the Federal Reserve Bank |
| Deposits | Customers decreased the balances in their accounts |
| Capital notes | Funds were used to repay capital notes at maturity, or redeem notes before maturity |
| Equity | The bank's dividend payments plus stock redeemed exceeded net income plus new stock issued |

shows the amount of Fed funds purchased and Federal Reserve Bank borrowing you will have to repay next quarter. It also shows the amount you will have to pay to depositors holding time deposits and certificates of deposit that mature next quarter, and the principal amount you must repay to holders of capital notes. You must come up with funds to cover all of these maturing liabilities.

**Asset/Liability Profile Menu: Asset/Liability Maturity Profile.** This chart divides assets and liabilities into groups based on the date of final maturity. The total asset balances and liability balances in each group are compared. This enables you to tell whether the maturity patterns of your assets and liabilities are well-matched. A mismatch in maturity pattern could indicate possible exposure to interest rate risk.

This chart excludes cash, premises, and equity because they do not mature in the ordinary sense.

**Asset/Liability Profile Menu: Asset/Liability Yield Profile.** This chart shows the interest rates being earned on the asset balances given in the Asset/Liability Maturity Profile chart, and the interest rates being paid on the liability balances. This lets you see the interest rate spread of assets and liabilities with matched maturity.

**Competitor Analysis Menu: Net Income.** This chart compares net income after tax for all banks in the game.

**Competitor Analysis Menu: Return on Equity.** This chart compares return on equity (ROE) for all banks in the game. The quarterly net income is annualized (multiplied by 4) in calculating ROE.

**Competitor Analysis Menu: Return on Assets.** This chart compares return on average assets (ROA) for all banks in the game. The quarterly net income is annualized (multiplied by 4) in calculating ROA.

**Competitor Analysis Menu: Earnings per Share.** This chart compares quarterly earnings per share (EPS) for all banks in the game.

**Competitor Analysis Menu: Dividend per Share.** This chart compares quarterly dividend per share for all banks in the game.

**Competitor Analysis Menu: Price/
Earnings Ratio.** This chart compares the
ratio of stock price to earnings for all banks
in the game. The quarterly earnings figure is
annualized (multiplied by 4) before it is divided into stock price.

**Competitor Analysis Menu: Capital
Adequacy Ratio.** This chart compares
the capital adequacy ratios of all banks in
the game. The capital adequacy ratio is defined as the actual amount of a bank's capital
divided by the required amount of capital.

Capital is defined as equity plus capital
notes for the purpose of calculating the capital adequacy ratio.

**Competitor Analysis Menu: Total Sala-
ries.** This chart compares total salary expense for all banks in the game.

**Competitor Analysis Menu: Total Busi-
ness Development Expense.** This chart
compares total business development expense for all banks in the game.

**Competitor Analysis Menu: Total
Assets.** This chart compares total asset
balances for all banks in the game.

**Competitor Analysis Menu: Total Secu-
rities plus Fed Funds Sold.** This chart
shows the total amount of securities plus Fed
funds sold for all banks in the game.

**Competitor Analysis Menu: Total
Loans.** This chart compares total loan balances for all banks in the game.

**Competitor Analysis Menu: Commer-
cial Loans.** This chart compares commercial loan balances for all banks in the game.

**Competitor Analysis Menu: Consumer
Loans.** This chart compares consumer
loan balances for all banks in the game.

**Competitor Analysis Menu: Real Estate
Loans.** This chart compares real estate
loan balances for all banks in the game.

**Competitor Analysis Menu: Net Prem-
ises.** This chart compares the level of net
premises for all banks in the game.

**Competitor Analysis Menu: Total De-
posits.** This chart compares total deposit
balances for all banks in the game.

**Competitor Analysis Menu: Checking
Deposits.** This chart compares checking
deposit balances for all banks in the game.

**Competitor Analysis Menu: Savings
Deposits.** This chart compares savings
deposit balances for all banks in the game.

**Competitor Analysis Menu: Time De-
posits.** This chart compares time deposit
balances for all banks in the game.

**Competitor Analysis Menu: Certificates
of Deposit.** This chart compares certificate of deposit (CD) balances for all banks
in the game.

**Competitor Analysis Menu: Fed Funds
Purchased.** This chart compares the
amount of Fed funds purchased by all banks
in the game.

**Competitor Analysis Menu: FRB Bor-
rowing.** This chart compares the amount
borrowed from the Federal Reserve Bank by
all banks in the game.

**Competitor Analysis Menu: Capital
Notes.** This chart compares capital notes
balances for all banks in the game.

**Competitor Analysis Menu: Total Eq-
uity.** This chart compares total equity for
all banks in the game.

**Loan/Deposit Rates Menu: Commercial Loans.** This chart compares the interest rates charged for commercial loans last quarter by all banks in the game.

**Loan/Deposit Rates Menu: Consumer Loans.** This chart compares the interest rates charged for consumer loans last quarter by all banks in the game.

**Loan/Deposit Rates Menu: Fixed Rate Real Estate Loans.** This chart compares the interest rates charged for fixed-rate real estate loans last quarter by all banks in the game.

**Loan/Deposit Rates Menu: Variable Rate Real Estate Loans.** This chart compares the interest rates charged for variable-rate real estate loans last quarter by all banks in the game.

**Loan/Deposit Rates Menu: Checking Deposits.** This chart compares the interest rates paid on checking deposit balances last quarter by all banks in the game.

**Loan/Deposit Rates Menu: Savings Deposits.** This chart compares the interest rates paid on savings deposit balances last quarter by all banks in the game.

**Loan/Deposit Rates Menu: One-Year Time Deposits.** This chart compares the interest rates paid on one-year time deposit balances last quarter by all banks in the game.

**Loan/Deposit Rates Menu: Five-Year Time Deposits.** This chart compares the interest rates paid on five-year time deposit balances last quarter by all banks in the game.

**Loan/Deposit Rates Menu: Six-Month Certificates of Deposit.** This chart compares the interest rates paid on six-month certificates of deposit last quarter by all banks in the game.

**Performance History Menu: Net Income.** This graph shows a 16-quarter history of net income after tax for your bank.

**Performance History Menu: Earnings/Share and Dividend/Share.** This graph shows a 16-quarter history of earnings per share and dividend per share for your bank.

**Performance History Menu: Total Assets.** This graph shows a 16-quarter history of total asset balances for your bank.

**Economic Environment Menu: Short Term Interest Rates.** This graph shows a 16-quarter history of the 3-month T-bill rate, the Fed funds rate, and the prime lending rate.

**Economic Environment Menu: T-Note Interest Rates.** This graph shows a 16-quarter history of interest rates for one-year, five-year, and 10-year T-notes.

**Economic Environment Menu: Consumer Price Index.** This graph shows a 16-quarter history of the consumer price index, scaled so that the value is 100 just before the game begins.

**Economic Environment Menu: GNP History and Forecast.** This graph shows a 12-quarter history and four-quarter forecast of Gross National Product (GNP).

## MAKING NEXT QUARTER'S DECISIONS

Each quarter, you should review the results of the previous quarter before making your decisions for the coming quarter. You can review last quarter's results by printing a summary report on the printer, or you can look at the 70 detailed charts and graphs available to you.

To make your decisions for the coming quarter, select "Review Results and Make Decisions" at the Main Menu level. You must enter your bank name and password (if your bank has one) before Bank President will allow you to make decisions for the bank. Also, the disk containing your bank's data must be in the drive.

After your password has been validated, you will get the Decisions/Results Menu on your screen. This menu has the 10 decision input forms listed in the following chart.

| Decision Input Forms | Decisions |
|---|---|
| Deposit interest rates | Checking deposit interest rate |
| | Savings deposit interest rate |
| | 1-year time deposit interest rate |
| | 5-year time deposit interest rate |
| | Certificate of deposit interest rate |
| Loan interest rates | Commercial loan interest rate |
| | Consumer loan interest rate |
| | Fixed-rate real estate loan rate |
| | Variable-rate real estate loan rate |
| Expenses and expansion | Salaries paid to employees |
| | Business development–deposits |
| | Business development–loans |
| | Premises |
| Divided declared | Dividend on the bank's common stock |
| Policy limits | Maximum new commercial loans |
| | Maximum new consumer loans |
| | Maximum new real estate loans |
| | Maximum new time deposits |
| | Maximum new certificates of deposit |
| | Maximum Fed funds purchased |
| | Maximum Federal Reserve Bank borrowing |
| Security purchases | 3-month T-bills |
| | 6-month T-bills |
| | 1-year T-notes |
| | 5-year T-notes |
| | 10-year T-notes |
| Security sales | 3–12-month maturity |
| | 1–2-year maturity |
| | 2–3-year maturity |
| | 4–5-year maturity |
| | 5–10-year maturity |
| Real estate loan sales | Fixed rate |
| | Variable rate |
| Capital notes | New 5-year notes |
| | New 10-year notes |
| | New 20-year notes |
| | Redeem old notes |
| Common stock | Amount of new issue |
| | Amount to repurchase |

There are two ways to go through the decision input forms. One way is to select a specific form from the Decisions/Results Menu. To do this, press the right arrow key (→) to tell Bank President that you want to select one of the items in the right column of the menu. Then, press the space bar until the highlighted area encloses the decision input form you want to use. When the form you want is highlighted, press the Enter key. The requested decision input form will appear on the screen. When you are finished with the form, press F2 and you will return to the Decisions/Results Menu.

Another way to go through the decision input forms is to use F3 and F4. When you get to the Decisions/Results Menu, just press F4. The first decision input form will appear on the screen. Press F4 again and the next decision input form in sequence will appear. Continue using F4 until you have seen all 10 decision input forms, at which point pressing F4 again will return you to the Decisions/Results Menu. Use F3 any time you want to back up and look at the previous decision input form again.

You will find Bank President much easier to play if you learn to use function keys F1 through F7 (and F8 if you have a graphics monitor). Bank President uses the bottom two lines of your screen to remind you of the function keys that are available at each point in the game. If you are ever in doubt about what to do, look to these two lines for help.

The 10 decision input forms contain a total of 40 decisions you can make each quarter. However, it is not necessary to make all 40 decisions each quarter to play Bank President well. Beginning players should concentrate on the 14 decisions in the first four forms, and use Forms 9 and 10 when they want to issue stock or capital notes. Intermediate players should concentrate on the same forms as beginners, and should add Forms 5 and 6 to the list. Advanced players will want to use all 10 forms.

When you are finished making decisions, return to the Decisions/Results Menu and press F2. Bank President will ask you whether or not your decisions are ready for next quarter. If you are finished making next quarter's decisions and are ready for the game to be advanced to the next quarter, select "This Bank's Decisions are Ready for Next Quarter." If you want to come back later and work on your decisions some more before the game advances to the next quarter, select "This Bank's Decisions are Not Yet Ready for Next Quarter." Be sure the disk with your bank's data is in the drive, because Bank President saves your decisions on the disk at this point.

For reference, the 10 decision input forms and 40 decisions are summarized here:

An explanation of the decisions you must make on each decision input form is given below.

## Deposit Interest Rates

On this decision input form, you set the interest rates you are going to pay depositors next quarter. You may set a different rate for each type of deposit.

If you set your deposit rates above those of other banks, you can take deposits away from others, since customers like to put their money where they receive the most interest. However, you will also have higher interest expenses because you will be paying out more interest to depositors. You can lose deposits to other banks if your deposit rates are too low.

In addition to being sensitive to interest rates, your deposit balances are also affected by the level of your premises, business development expenses and salaries, and the total amount of deposits available in the economy each quarter.

You should pay particular attention to the change in your deposit balances each quarter. If you are gaining or losing balances you should try to find out why this is happening by looking at what other banks are doing. You may discover that your rates are too high or too low, or that some other bank is deliberately trying to take business away from you by rapidly expanding premises and spending heavily on business development.

If you do not enter new deposit interest rates using this decision input form, Bank President will leave this quarter's rates in effect next quarter.

The regulatory environment sets a limit on the maximum interest rate you can pay for each type of deposit. If you specify rates higher than those currently allowed, Bank President will reduce your rates to the maximum permissible rates.

**Checking Deposits.** Checking deposits are checking accounts. You must decide what rate of interest (if any) you are going to pay on balances left in customers' accounts. You can take deposits away from other banks if your rates are higher than theirs. You can lose deposits if your rates are too low.

**Savings Deposits.** Savings deposits are passbook savings accounts. You must set the rate you are going to pay on balances left in customers' accounts. The higher the rate you pay, the more deposits you will attract. You can take deposits away from other banks if your rates are higher than theirs. You can lose deposits if your rates are too low.

**One-Year Time Deposits.** These are amounts under $100,000 left on deposit for one year. You must set the rate you will pay for the entire one-year term of new deposits received next quarter. To help you decide how much to pay for these deposits, the current one-year U.S. government Treasury note rate is shown directly opposite the area where you enter your rate for next quarter.

(Note that the one-year T-note rate could change before next quarter.)

**Five-Year Time Deposits.** These are amounts under $100,000 left on deposit for five years. You must set the rate you will pay for the entire five-year term of new deposits received next quarter. To help you decide how much to pay for these deposits, the current five-year U.S. government Treasury note rate is shown directly opposite the area where you enter your rate for next quarter. (Note that the five-year T-note rate could change before next quarter.)

**Certificates of Deposit.** CDs are amounts of $100,000 or more left on deposit for six months (two quarters). You must set the rate you will pay for the entire term of new CDs received next quarter. The current six-month U.S. government Treasury bill rate is shown opposite the area where you enter your CD rate for next quarter to help you set your rate. You will get few new CDs if your rate is below the six-month T-bill rate, because customers will buy Treasury bills instead of your CDs. (Note that the six-month T-bill rate could change before next quarter.)

## Loan Interest Rates

On this decision input form, you set the rates you are going to charge for loans next quarter. You may set a different rate for each type of loan.

If you set your loan rates lower than those of other banks, you can take loan business away from others, since customers prefer to borrow where interest rates are lower. However, you will then receive less interest income on each loan than you would if your rates were higher. You can lose loans to other banks if your rates are too high.

In addition to being sensitive to interest rates, your loan balances are also affected by the level of your premises, business development expenses and salaries, and the total amount of loan demand in the economy each quarter.

You should take note of the amount by which your loan balances change each quarter. If you are gaining or losing balances you should try to find out why this is happening by looking at what other banks are doing. You may discover that your rates are too high or too low, or that some other bank is making a deliberate effort to take business away from you by rapidly expanding premises and spending heavily on business development.

If you do not enter new loan interest rates using this decision input form, Bank President will leave this quarter's rates in effect next quarter.

The regulatory environment sets a limit on the maximum interest rate you can charge for each type of loan. If you specify rates higher than those currently allowed, Bank President will reduce your rates to the maximum permissible rates.

**Commercial Loans.** Commercial loans are loans to businesses. Principal is repaid in one payment at the end of one year (four quarters). Interest is paid quarterly. In Bank President, the interest rate is fixed for the life of the loan. You must set the rate you are going to charge for the one-year life of new commercial loans made next quarter.

To help you set your commercial loan rate, the "prime" lending rate prevailing in the economy this quarter is shown opposite the area where you enter your commercial loan rate. Note that prime may move up or down before next quarter so you may want to try to anticipate such movement. Also, you will want to consider what other banks in your game are charging for loans, since they may be charging rates considerably above or below the prevailing prime rate.

**Consumer Loans.** Consumer loans are made to individuals and are repaid in 12 equal quarterly payments that include both principal and interest. You must set the rate for new consumer loans made next quarter. The rate you set will be in effect for the life of the loan.

To help you set your consumer loan rate, the rate for consumer loans prevailing in the current economy is shown opposite the area where you enter your consumer loan rate. Note that the other banks in your game may be charging rates considerably above or below the rate prevailing in the economy. Also, the rate currently prevailing may change before next quarter.

**Fixed-Rate Real Estate Loans.** Fixed-rate real estate loans are secured with real property and are repaid in 80 equal quarterly payments that include both principal and interest. You must set the rate for new loans made next quarter. The rate you set will be in effect for the entire 20-year life of the loan.

To help you set your fixed-rate real estate loan rate, the rate currently prevailing in the economy is shown opposite the area where you enter your rate for next quarter. Note that the other banks in your game may be charging rates considerably higher or lower than this prevailing rate, and that the currently prevailing rate may change before next quarter.

**Variable-Rate Real Estate Loans.** Variable-rate real estate loans are secured by real property. They are repaid in 80 quarterly payments that include both principal and interest. The interest rate on these loans is revised once a year (every fourth quarter). The rate you set when you make your decisions is the rate that will be in effect during the first year. Bank President recalculates the interest rate every fourth quarter in the following way:

1. The one-year T-note rate at the time the loan was made is subtracted from the loan's original interest rate. The difference is called the "spread." For example, if the one-year T-note rate was 9 percent at the time a new 11 percent variable-rate loan was made, the spread would be 11 percent − 9 percent = 2 percent. The spread stays constant for the life of the loan.

2. Every fourth quarter, the interest rate of the loan is changed to the current one-year T-note rate plus the spread. For example, if the one-year T-note rate is 10 percent one year after a loan with a 2 percent spread is made, the new loan rate will be 10 percent + 2 percent = 12 percent. The new loan rate will be in effect for one year, after which time the loan rate will again be revised.

To help you set your variable-rate real estate loan rate, the rate currently prevailing in the economy is shown opposite the area where you enter your rate for next quarter. This rate may or may not be the same as that being charged by other banks in your game. Also, the prevailing rate may change before next quarter.

## Expenses and Expansion

This decision input form lets you set the salaries you pay employees, the amount you spend on new business development, and the amount you want to invest in premises.

If you do not enter new values for next quarter for any of these decisions, Bank President will keep the amount the same as it was this quarter.

**Salaries.** You must decide the total amount of your bank's payroll for next quarter. You cannot increase or decrease the total by more than 25 percent of the amount you paid last quarter. Salary increases that are less than or equal to the rise in the cost of living (CPI) are considered raises to existing employees. Increases above the rise in the cost of living are considered increases in the number of employees.

Salaries are one of your most important expenses. It is easy to pay too much or too little. Pay attention to your beginning salary levels, the cost of living, and the amounts being paid by other banks.

**Business Development—Deposits.** This is the amount you spend trying to get new deposits. It consists primarily of advertising and promotions. It is easy to spend too much or too little on business development. Watch what the other banks are doing, since the effect of your advertising depends largely on how much advertising your competitors are doing.

The amount you spend should depend on how badly you need deposits. If you have more deposits than you need, decrease business development—deposits. If you have too few deposits, increase business development—deposits.

**Business Development—Loans.** This is the amount you spend trying to get new loans. It consists primarily of advertising and promotions. The amount you spend should be influenced by how much other banks are spending and how badly you want more loans.

**Net Premises.** This is the amount of land and buildings used to conduct your bank's business. You specify the total amount you want each quarter. You cannot increase or decrease premises by more than 25 percent each quarter. Your premises may not exceed your bank's equity.

The number you enter is the number that will appear in the balance sheet category "Premises" next quarter.

## Dividend Declared

This decision input form lets you set the quarterly dividend you pay to holders of your common stock. The dividend is expressed as dollars per share. Bank President will automatically reduce the amount of your dividend if you attempt to pay out more than the amount of your retained earnings.

It is best to have a consistent dividend policy. For example, you could pay out a constant percentage (e.g., 40 percent) of quarterly earnings per share as a dividend each quarter: If quarterly EPS were $3.00, the quarterly dividend would be $1.20.

The common stock analysis that appears on the bottom of this form is intended to help you set your dividend each quarter. It shows (among other things) the amount of your EPS the previous quarter, to make it easy for you to set your dividend as a percentage of EPS.

If you do not set the amount of dividend you want to pay next quarter, Bank President will pay your shareholders the same dividend next quarter that you paid this quarter.

## Policy Limits

Policy limits let you set the maximum amount of new loans and deposits you will accept next quarter, and the maximum amount of Fed funds and Federal Reserve Bank borrowing you are willing to incur next quarter.

The best way to limit loan and deposit volume is through interest rates, not policy limits. For example, if you use high interest rates to limit loan volume, you get the benefit of the high interest rates on your loans as well as limiting loan volume. When you use low interest rates to hold down deposits, you pay out less interest to depositors as well as limiting deposit volume. Policy limits should be used only as a fail-safe mechanism in case you greatly misjudge the amount of loans and deposits you will get given your interest rates.

The Policy Limits decision input form shows you, in the column labeled "Refused," the amount of additional loans and deposits you turned down last quarter because of your policy limits. Increase your policy limits if you unintentionally refused loans or deposits last quarter.

Set your policy limits to 9999 if you do not want to have to worry about unintentionally limiting loans, deposits, or borrowing.

There are no policy limits available on checking and savings deposits, since there is no practical way to prevent customers from increasing balances in these accounts if they want to. Of course, if you really want to limit checking and savings accounts (few bankers do), simply pay low rates and your customers will move their accounts to banks paying higher rates.

If you do not change any of the policy limits, Bank President will leave the limits you set last quarter in effect for next quarter.

**Commercial Loan Limit.**  Specify (in millions of dollars) the maximum amount of new commercial loans you are willing to make next quarter.

**Consumer Loan Limit.**  Specify (in millions of dollars) the maximum amount of new consumer loans you are willing to make next quarter.

**Real Estate Loan Limit.**  Specify (in millions of dollars) the maximum amount of new real estate loans you are willing to make next quarter. The amount includes both fixed- and variable-rate loans.

**Time Deposit Limit.**  Specify (in millions of dollars) the maximum amount of new time deposits you are willing to accept from depositors next quarter. The amount includes both one-year and five-year time deposits.

**Certificates of Deposit Limit.** Specify (in millions of dollars) the maximum amount of new certificates of deposit you are willing to accept from depositors next quarter.

**Fed Funds Borrowing Limit.** Specify (in millions of dollars) the maximum amount you are willing to borrow from other banks on a short-term basis next quarter.

Bank President automatically borrows Fed funds for your bank any time it is short of funds. For example, if you make a large number of new loans, or buy a large number of securities, you must somehow come up with funds to complete these transactions. If you do not generate the funds through other sources (e.g., an increase in deposits), Bank President will get the required funds for your bank by arranging for your bank to borrow Fed funds from other banks in the economy. Your bank will be charged interest on these loans at the Fed funds rate. The loans must be repaid the following quarter (but you can borrow more Fed funds next quarter to repay the Fed funds you borrow this quarter).

The maximum amount of Fed funds a bank can borrow is equal to 25 percent of the bank's total assets. You can use the Fed funds Borrowing Limit to lower the maximum amount of Fed funds Bank President can borrow for your bank.

If your bank requires more Fed funds than the borrowing limit, or more than 25 percent of total assets, Bank President will first try to borrow from the Federal Reserve Bank. If you still do not have sufficient funds to meet your needs, Bank President will dispose of some of your bank's assets to lower funding requirements. In this event, Bank President will first cancel the purchase of new securities. Next, it will cancel new commercial loans. If such measures still do not generate sufficient funds to meet your needs, Bank President will go back to the Federal Reserve Bank and beg for funds to rescue your bank from the difficult financial position its

management has brought upon it. In this game, the Federal Reserve Bank always complies with such requests. You will be charged interest at the prevailing rate for funds borrowed from the Federal Reserve Bank.

**Federal Reserve Bank Borrowing Limit.** Specify (in millions of dollars) the maximum amount you are willing to borrow from the Federal Reserve Bank next quarter.

Federal Reserve Bank borrowing cannot exceed the amount specified in your regulatory environment. The limit is expressed as a percent of equity. See Regulatory Environment—Screen 1 for an explanation of how the regulatory environment limits Federal Reserve Bank borrowing. Since the Federal Reserve Bank requires you to pledge U.S. government securities equal to the amount of your borrowing, your Federal Reserve Bank borrowing also cannot exceed the amount of your securities. You can use the Federal Reserve Bank borrowing limit to further limit the amount of borrowing.

Bank President will automatically try to borrow from the Federal Reserve Bank if your bank needs the funds and has reached its limit on Fed funds borrowing. If your bank is in difficulty, the Federal Reserve Bank will act as a lender of last resort and rescue your bank even if doing so requires a loan larger than permitted by the above limits. Refer to the discussion in the Fed Funds Borrowing Limit section for details on how and why Bank President borrows Fed funds and from the Federal Reserve Bank on behalf of your bank.

You are charged interest at the prevailing Federal Reserve Bank discount rate for all funds you borrow from the Federal Reserve Bank. Loans must be repaid the following quarter (but you can borrow more funds next quarter to repay funds you borrow this quarter).

## Security Purchases

This decision input form lets you buy U.S. government securities next quarter. To help you decide how much to buy, the column "Securities Maturing" shows how much of your securities portfolio will mature next quarter. To increase your securities balances you must buy more than the amount maturing. To decrease your securities balances, buy less.

You can buy securities with maturities ranging from three months to 10 years. The current interest rate paid on each security is shown. Note that the interest rate could change before next quarter.

Bank President will not buy any securities for your next quarter unless you explicitly ask it to by filling in the amount on this decision input form. If you still have excess funds after buying the amount of securities you specify, Bank President will "sell" those funds in the Fed funds market rather than buy additional securities.

If you ask Bank President to buy more securities than the amount of funds your bank has available to invest, Bank President will attempt to get the funds you need from the Fed funds market and from the Federal Reserve Bank. If Bank President borrows up to your limit in the Fed funds market and reaches your borrowing limit at the Federal Reserve Bank without coming up with all the funds you need to buy the securities you asked for, Bank President will reduce the amount of securities it buys to the amount of funds it was able to get.

**Three-Month T-Bills.**  Specify (in millions of dollars) the amount of U.S. government Treasury bills with a three-month (one quarter) maturity you want to buy.

**Six-Month T-Bills.**  Specify (in millions of dollars) the amount of U.S. government Treasury bills with a six-month (two quarters) maturity you want to buy.

**One-Year T-Notes.**  Specify (in millions of dollars) the amount of U.S. government Treasury notes with a one-year (four quarters) maturity you want to buy.

**Five-Year T-Notes.**  Specify (in millions of dollars) the amount of U.S. government Treasury notes with a five-year (20 quarters) maturity you want to buy.

**10-Year T-Notes.**  Specify (in millions of dollars) the amount of U.S. government Treasury notes with a 10-year (40 quarters) maturity you want to buy.

## Security Sales

This decision input form lets you sell securities from your securities portfolio next quarter. Your portfolio is divided into "pools" based on the remaining maturity of the securities. When you sell securities, you must sell a uniform mix of securities from within a specific maturity pool. The first maturity pool is for securities with a remaining maturity of zero to three months. You may not sell from this pool next quarter because these securities are going to mature by the beginning of the quarter. You may sell from any or all of the other pools.

Three columns of information are given for each pool. The first column is "Par Value Held." This tells you the total amount you paid for the securities that are now in this pool. When you sell, you specify the amount of par value you want to sell. For example, to sell half of the securities in a given pool, you would enter one half of the par value shown as your decision input. The second column shows "Average Coupon Rate." This is the weighted average rate of interest you are receiving on the securities in the pool. The third column is "Current Market Value." This tells you how much you can get for your securities if you sell them. Note that the market value of securities in any pool is rarely equal to the par value. If interest rates are higher now than they were when you bought a particular security, its market value will be less than its par value. If rates have gone down since you bought a particular security, the market value will be higher than the par value. To ensure accuracy, Bank President calculates the market value of every individual security in each pool and sums these to get the amount shown for the pool.

Although you specify the amount you want to sell in terms of par value, the amount you receive is related to the market value rather than the par value. For example, if you want to sell 25 percent of the securities in a given pool, you would enter 25 percent of the par value of that pool as your decision. The amount you would receive when you sold these securities would be 25 percent of the market value. The difference between the par value sold and the market value received is your pretax gain or loss on the sale. If the par value is less than the market value you receive, the difference is a capital gain. Capital gains are taxed at one half of your regular income tax rate. If par value exceeds market value, you have a loss. Bank President gives you a tax credit at the regular income tax rate under the presumption that you will normally have sufficient income to be able to use the tax credit.

The maximum amount you may sell from each pool is the total par value of that pool. If you do not explicitly enter the amount of securities you want to sell next quarter, Bank President will not sell any of your securities for you. If your bank needs funds, Bank President will "purchase" funds in the Fed funds market rather than sell securities.

## Real Estate Loan Sales

This decision input form lets you sell loans from your real estate loan portfolio next quarter. When you sell loans, you must sell a uniform mix of either fixed-rate loans or variable-rate loans.

Three columns of information are given to help you decide how much to sell. "Total Loans Held" is the remaining principal balance due on the loans. When you sell loans, you specify the amount to sell in terms of remaining principal balance. For example, to sell half of your fixed-rate loans, you would enter an amount equal to one half of the "Total Loans Held" as your decision input. "Average Loan Rate" is the weighted average interest rate charged on the loans. "Current Market Value" is the amount you would get if you sold all the loans. Note that the market value of your loans is rarely equal to the remaining principal balance. If interest rates have gone up since you made a loan, the loan's market value will be less than the remaining principal balance. If interest rates have gone down, the market value will exceed the remaining principal balance. (For variable-rate loans, the market value is related to the size of the spread rather than the actual interest rate. Loans with a higher spread will have a higher market price. Variable-rate real estate loan spread is discussed in the "Loan Interest Rates" decision input section above.)

Although you specify the amount you want to sell in terms of "Total Loans Held," the amount you receive when you make the sale is related to the "Current Market Value." For example, if you want to sell 25 percent of your fixed-rate real estate loans, you would enter an amount equal to 25 percent of the "Total Loans Held." The amount you would receive from the sale would be 25 percent of the "Current Market Value." The difference between the amount sold and the amount received is your pretax gain or loss on the sale.

## Capital Notes

This decision input form lets you issue new capital notes, or redeem old notes, next quarter. Capital notes are issued when the bank borrows money from the general public. The regulatory environment sets an upper limit on the amount of capital notes you can issue, expressed as a percentage of your equity.

The regulatory environment also sets a minimum capital requirement, expressed as a percent of total assets. Both capital notes and equity are counted as capital for purposes of the minimum capital requirement. If your capital adequacy ratio (the ratio of your actual capital to required capital) falls below 1.0, you should issue new capital notes or common stock to raise the ratio above 1.0. If you do not do this, your bank will have less than the required amount of capital (which will hurt your stock price). Bank President will not automatically meet your minimum capital requirement for you—it is up to you to do so yourself.

An increase in your capital adequacy ratio will improve your stock price—all else being equal—but increases in the ratio above 1.4 will have little additional effect on your stock price. You may therefore want to repurchase capital notes or common stock if the ratio rises much above 1.4.

You can issue capital notes with an initial maturity of 5, 10, or 20 years. However, you must make sinking fund payments on these notes beginning in the quarter following their issue. The sinking fund payments are equal to the amount that would be required to retire the notes uniformly throughout the maturity period (repay the same amount of principal each quarter). For accounting purposes, the sinking fund payments are treated as reductions in the amount of capital notes outstanding.

Interest is paid quarterly on capital notes. Bank President automatically makes the sinking fund payments and the interest payments on existing capital notes each quarter.

An increase in your capital adequacy ratio will improve your stock price—all else being equal—but increases in the ratio above 1.4

will have little additional effect on your stock price. You may therefore want to repurchase common stock or capital notes if the ratio rises much above 1.4.

For accounting purposes, repurchased common stock is treated as a reduction in equity rather than as treasury stock.

Bank President will not issue or redeem common stock for you unless you explicitly ask it to do so using this decision input form.

**Amount to Issue.**   Specify (in millions of dollars) the amount of new common stock you want to issue next quarter. Bank President will reduce the amount you specify if necessary to ensure that you do not increase the total number of shares outstanding by more than 25 percent in any quarter.

Your net proceeds from each share sold is 95 percent of the "Market Price" shown at the bottom of the decision input form.

**Amount to Repurchase.**   Specify (in millions of dollars) the amount of the bank's outstanding common stock you want to repurchase next quarter. Bank President will reduce the amount you specify if necessary to ensure that you do not repurchase an amount exceeding 25 percent of your equity, or 50 percent of the total outstanding market value of your stock.

Your net cost for each share repurchased is 105 percent of the "Market Price" shown at the bottom of the decision input form.

## PRINTING A SUMMARY REPORT

Bank President can print a summary report of the game status if you have a printer connected to your computer. From the Main Menu, select "Print a Summary of All Banks in this Game."Be sure your printer is ready before you ask Bank President to print this report.

The summary report shows each bank's loan and deposit interest rates for the most recent quarter. It also shows a balance sheet, income statement, and performance summary for each bank, including stock prices and capital adequacy ratios.

The most detailed financial information about your bank, competitors, and the economic and regulatory environments can be obtained as a set of 70 different charts and graphs. Although this information comes out on your monitor screen, you can use the "Print Screen" capability to obtain hard copy if you have a printer. You may want to use F7 to convert each chart or graph to a table before you print it. Also, if you have a graphics monitor you may want to use F8 to convert graphics charts or graphs to text mode before you print them.

## EXITING BANK PRESIDENT

To make sure you do not lose any of your data, it is important to exit Bank President only from one of the several menus offering the choice: "Exit Bank President." If you exit this way, the current status of the game is automatically saved before you exit.

## STRATEGIES FOR SUCCESS

This section presents some simple techniques that beginning players can use to keep their banks in reasonable financial condition. These techniques are far less sophisticated than those used by bankers in the real world. In particular, these techniques call for the individual or team to manage the assets side of your balance sheet and the liabilities and equity side of your balance sheet independently. This is contrary to the essence of modern bank management, which calls for bankers to carefully match assets and liabilities. Nevertheless, a beginning player must start somewhere and following the rules presented in this chapter is still better than managing completely in the dark.

Players who are more advanced can use more sophisticated techniques such as maturity matching to run their banks in ways that should consistently lead to superior performance. Although teaching these advanced techniques is beyond the scope of this manual, the 70 charts and graphs Bank President displays every quarter give sufficient information for advanced players to use relatively sophisticated methods of bank management when they play the game.

The beginning player should set targets, in percentage terms, for each balance sheet and income statement item. Using a balance sheet similar to the initial balance sheet for Full Service Banks as an example, your balance sheet targets could be the following:

| Balance Sheet Item | Target |
|---|---|
| **Assets** | |
| Cash | 7.5% |
| Fed funds sold | 0% |
| Securities | 26.0% |
| Loans | 65.0% |
| Premises | 1.5% |
| Total assets | 100.0% |
| **Liabilities and Equity** | |
| Deposits | 89.5% |
| Fed funds purchased | 4.5% |
| FRB borrowing | 0% |
| Capital notes | 1.2% |
| Equity | 4.8% |
| Total liability and equity | 100.0% |

Note that these targets are examples only. The actual targets you set will depend on the regulatory environment in effect for your game. For example, the target for "Cash" above is 7.5 percent of total assets. If the reserve requirements on deposits were increased, the cash target would also have to be increased (remember that "Cash" includes reserves held at the Federal Reserve Bank). Also, the combined target of 6 percent for capital notes (1.2 percent) plus equity (4.8 percent) depends on the Minimum Capital Requirement of the regulatory environment. The point is that you should set targets for each balance sheet category, but you will have to give some thought to what the targets should be rather than just using the sample targets above.

Each quarter, you should compare your Bank President balance sheet for that quarter with your targets. If your current balance sheet is close to your targets, your decisions for the coming quarter can be similar to those for the previous quarter (adjusted for expected changes in interest rates). If your current balance sheet is moving away from your targets, you will need to act to bring the balance sheet closer to your targets. Some of the simple things you can do are the following:

In addition to balance sheet targets, you should also have income statement targets. These targets are expressed as a percentage of interest revenue. The following is an example of income statement targets:

| Income Statement Item | Target |
|---|---|
| Interest revenue + fee income | 100.0% |
| Interest expense | 60.0% |
| Noninterest expense | 20.0% |
| Taxes | 9.5% |
| Nonoperating income | 0% |
| Net income | 10.5% |

These targets are meant as examples only. The actual targets you set will have to take into consideration the economic and competitive environments of your game.

## Possible Actions to Take When Balance Sheet Items Are above or below Target Levels

| Balance Sheet Item | Action If above Target | Action If below Target |
|---|---|---|
| **Assets** | | |
| Cash | None | None |
| Fed funds sold | Buy securities or increase loans | Sell securities or decrease loans |
| Securities | Sell securities | Buy securities |
| Loans | Decrease loans (raise loan rates) | Increase loans (lower loan rates) |
| Premises | Decrease premises | Increase premises |
| **Liabilities and Equity** | | |
| Deposits | Decrease deposits (lower deposit rates) or issue capital notes or stock | Increase deposits (raise deposit rates) |
| Fed funds purchased | Sell securities, decrease loans (raise loan rates) or increase deposits (raise deposit rates) | Buy securities, increase loans (lower loan rates) or decrease CDs (lower CD rates) |
| FRB borrowing | Same as above | Same as above |
| Capital notes | Redeem old notes | Issue new notes |
| Equity | Repurchase stock | Issue new stock |

Each quarter, you should compare your Bank President income statement to your targets. If your income statement is close to target levels, you can continue into next quarter with current policies. If your income statement is moving away from your targets, you will want to act to correct the problem areas.

The table below gives some examples of actions you can take if your income statement is moving away from your targets.

Since Bank President is a competitive

## Possible Actions to Take When Income Statement Items Are above or below Target Levels

| Income Statement Item | Action If above Target | Action If below Target |
|---|---|---|
| Interest expense | Attempt to get more of your funds from low-cost sources such as checking and savings deposits and fewer of your funds from higher-cost sources such as CDs and Fed funds purchased. You may also be able to generate more interest revenue by shifting assets to higher yielding categories (e.g., making commercial loans instead of buying securities). Or your problem may be that you need to lower deposit rates and increase loan rates. | None—as long as you are satisfied with the level of deposits you are getting. Raise deposit interest rates if you want to attract more deposits. Lower loan rates if you are not getting enough loans. |
| Noninterest expense | Lower salaries or business development expense. | None—if you are satisfied with the amount of loans and deposits you are getting. Increase salaries, business development, or premises if you want more loans or deposits. |
| Taxes | None | None |
| Nonoperating income | None | Look for opportunities to sell securities and real estate loans at prices above book value. |
| Net income | None—if you are satisfied with the size of your bank. Invest for growth if you want to build a bigger bank. This could include increasing premises, salaries, and business development. | Increase interest revenue, decrease interest expense, or decrease noninterest expense. |

game, you may have to do things in response to competitive pressures that take you away from your income statement targets. For example, if a competitor raises interest rates on checking and savings deposits, you may also have to raise rates to avoid losing deposits. This could take you over target in the area of interest expense. Your task is to find ways to compete that allow you to remain profitable.

## APPENDIX A.
## STOCK PRICE CALCULATION

The factors that have the most influence on your stock price are: dividend/share, earnings/share, dividend growth rate, earnings growth rate, and capital adequacy. For all of these factors, Bank President uses a weighted average of values from several recent quarters rather than just the current values. Although both are considered, earnings from normal operations are more important than capital gains and losses in determining stock price.

The best way to achieve a high stock price is to consistently improve earnings/share and dividend/share, while maintaining a capital adequacy ratio greater than 1.0. (All else being equal, your stock price will go up if you increase your capital adequacy ratio, but by the time the ratio reaches 1.4 further increases have little effect.) One or two poor quarters will not decrease your stock price too much if you quickly return to normal earnings and dividend levels.

The size of your bank as measured by total assets has no effect at all on your stock price, except to the extent that size affects earnings and dividends.

## APPENDIX B. SUBMENU
## STRUCTURE FOR CHARTS
## AND GRAPHS

Bank President uses over 70 different charts, graphs, and tables to keep you in-

formed about the status of your bank, your competitors, and the economic and regulatory environments. These charts and graphs are reached from the Decisions/Results Menu, and the various submenus of the Decisions/Results Menu.

There are two ways you can go through the charts and graphs each quarter. One way is to select specific charts and graphs from the Decisions/Results Menu or one of its submenus. To do this, press the space bar until the item you want is in the highlighted area of the menu, then press the Enter key. The chart, graph, or submenu you selected will then appear on your monitor. Press F2 when you are ready to return to the previous menu.

Another way to go through the charts and graphs is to use the F5 and F6 keys. When you get to the Decisions/Results Menu, just press F6. The first chart in sequence ("Common Stock Market Price") will appear on your monitor. Press F6 again to see the next chart or graph in sequence. Continue using F6 to go through as many of the charts and graphs in sequence as you want. You can actually go through all 70 of the charts and graphs in just a few minutes using F6. Any time you want to back up and see the previously displayed chart or graph again, press F5.

Whenever you select a particular submenu from the Decisions/Results Menu, Bank President resets F6 such that pressing F6 will give you the first chart or graph in the submenu. For example, if you select "Income Statement" from the Decisions/Results Menu, Bank President will display the Income Statement Menu (a submenu of the Decisions/Results Menu). If you then press F6, Bank President will display the "Revenue and Expense Summary" chart—the first chart in the Income Statement Menu. Continued use of F6 will take you through the rest of the charts in the Income Statement Menu.

If you press F2 while a chart or graph is being displayed, Bank President will return you to the menu or submenu that contains the chart or graph. The following table shows which menu or submenu contains each of Bank President's charts and graphs.

You reach each chart or graph in the right column from the menu or submenu in the column to its left. The charts and graphs are shown in sequence (the same order they will appear in if you repeatedly press F6). Note: The regulatory environment tables cannot be reached using F6. You must select "Regulatory Environment" from the Decisions/Results Menu to see the two regulatory environment tables.

The following table covers the structure of the 70 charts and graphs.

## Structure for Charts and Graphs

| Menu or Submenu | Chart or Graph |
|---|---|
| Decisions/Results Menu | Common Stock Market Price |
| Balance Sheet Menu | Total Assets |
| | Change in Asset Balances |
| | Detail for Cash Balances |
| | Securities Activity |
| | Loan Balances by Loan Type |
| | Commercial Loan Activity |
| | Consumer Loan Activity |
| | Real Estate Loan Activity |
| | Total Liabilities and Equity |
| | Change in Liability and Equity Balances |
| | Deposit Balances by Type |
| | Time Deposit Activity |
| | Certificate of Deposit Activity |
| | Capital Notes Activity |
| | Equity Accounts Activity |
| Decisions/Results Menu | Average Asset Yield |
| | Average Liability Yield |
| Income Statement Menu | Revenue and Expense Summary |
| | Change in Revenues and Expenses |
| | Components of Interest Revenue |
| | Components of Interest Expense |
| | Components of Noninterest Expense |
| Funds Flow Menu | Sources of Funds Last Quarter |
| | Uses of Funds Last Quarter |
| Asset/Liability Profile Menu | Assets Maturing Next Quarter |
| | Liabilities Maturing Next Quarter |
| | Asset/Liability Maturity Profile |
| | Asset/Liability Yield Profile |

## Structure for Charts and Graphs    *(continued)*

| Menu or Submenu | Chart or Graph |
| --- | --- |
| Competitor Analysis Menu | Net Income |
| | Return on Equity |
| | Return on Assets |
| | Earnings per Share |
| | Dividend per Share |
| | Price/Earnings Ratio |
| | Capital Adequacy Ratio |
| | Total Salaries |
| | Total Business Development Expense |
| | Total Assets |
| | Total Securities plus Fed Funds Sold |
| | Total Loans |
| | Commercial Loans |
| | Consumer Loans |
| | Real Estate Loans |
| | Net Premises |
| | Total Deposits |
| | Checking Deposits |
| | Savings Deposits |
| | Time Deposits |
| | Certificates of Deposit |
| | Fed Funds Purchased |
| | FRB Borrowing |
| | Capital Notes |
| | Total Equity |
| Loan/Deposit Rates Menu | Commercial Loans |
| | Consumer Loans |
| | Fixed-Rate Real Estate Loans |
| | Variable-Rate Real Estate Loans |
| | Checking Deposits |
| | Savings Deposits |
| | One-Year Time Deposits |
| | Five-Year Time Deposits |
| | Six-Month Certificates of Deposit |
| Performance History Menu | Net Income |
| | Earnings/Share and Dividend/Share |
| | Total Assets |
| Economic Environment Menu | Short-Term Interest Rates |
| | T-Note Interest Rates |
| | Consumer Price Index |
| | GNP History and Forecast |
| Decisions/Results Menu | Regulatory Environment—Screen 1 |
| | Regulatory Environment—Screen 2 |

## APPENDIX C. FUNCTION KEY SUMMARY

Eight function keys are available in Bank President. If you learn to use these keys, you will find Bank President very easy to play. Descriptions of the keys follow.

**F1** Displays help information for the current screen. This key is available any time you see "F1—Help" at the bottom of your screen.

**F2** Back up or return to the previous menu. This key is available whenever it appears on the bottom of your screen.

**F3** Display the previous decision input form. This key is available whenever you select "Review Results and Make Decisions" from the Main Menu.

**F4** Display the next decision input form. Repeated use of F4 will display all decision input forms in sequence. F4 is available whenever you select "Review Results and Make Decisions" from the Main Menu.

**F5** Display the previous results chart or graph. This key is available whenever you select "Review Results and Make Decisions" from the Main Menu.

**F6** Display the next results chart or graph. Repeated use of F6 will display all charts and graphs in sequence. F6 is available whenever you select "Review Results and Make Decisions" from the Main Menu.

**F7** Display the data used to draw the current chart or graph, in table format. Pressing F7 again will restore the chart or graph. Use this key any time you see a chart or graph on the screen and want to see a data table instead of a chart or graph.

**F8** Convert graphics charts and graphs to text mode. Pressing F8 again will redraw the chart or graph in graphics mode. Charts and graphs do not look quite as nice in text mode, but they are easier to print using "Print Screen." This key is available on graphics monitors only, whenever a chart or graph is on the screen.

## CASE 4 (continued) United National Bank of Denver

Uniform Bank Performance Report

United National Bank of Denver: Summary Ratios

|  | 12/30/87 | | | 12/31/86 | | | 12/31/85 | | | 12/31/84 | | 12/31/83 | |
|---|---|---|---|---|---|---|---|---|---|---|---|---|---|
|  | Bank | Peer 3 | PCT | Bank | Peer 3 | PCT | Bank | Peer 3 | PCT | Bank | Peer 3 | Bank | Peer 3 |
| Average Assets ($000) | 2,593,676 | | | 2,646,582 | | | 2,560,312 | | | 2,370,681 | | 2,235,016 | |
| Net Income ($000) | 8,645 | | | 22,356 | | | 24,851 | | | 17,773 | | 13,373 | |
| No. banks in peer group | 205 | | | 204 | | | 192 | | | 171 | | 160 | |
| **Earnings and profitability** | | | | | | | | | | | | | |
| **Percent of average assets:** | | | | | | | | | | | | | |
| Net interest income (TE) | 3.27 | 4.16 | 14 | 3.66 | 4.42 | 21 | 3.86 | 4.40 | 24 | 3.73 | 4.31 | 3.82 | 4.19 |
| + Non-interest income | 2.37 | 1.28 | 87 | 2.56 | 1.31 | 89 | 2.38 | 1.23 | 92 | 1.63 | 1.27 | 1.30 | 1.11 |
| − Overhead expense | 4.21 | 3.48 | 77 | 3.77 | 3.56 | 63 | 4.17 | 3.61 | 70 | 3.77 | 3.61 | 3.53 | 3.59 |
| − Provision for loan losses | 1.04 | 0.49 | 83 | 1.12 | 0.54 | 83 | 0.54 | 0.41 | 73 | 0.31 | 0.40 | 0.56 | 0.37 |
| = Pretax operating income (TE) | 0.40 | 1.43 | 14 | 1.33 | 1.59 | 33 | 1.52 | 1.66 | 41 | 1.27 | 1.58 | 1.04 | 1.28 |
| + Securities gains (losses) | 0.06 | 0.03 | 79 | 0.16 | 0.09 | 77 | 0.13 | 0.04 | 87 | 0.00 | 0.00 | −0.05 | 0.00 |
| = Pretax net oper inc (TE) | 0.45 | 1.47 | 13 | 1.49 | 1.70 | 33 | 1.65 | 1.70 | 45 | 1.26 | 1.54 | 0.99 | 1.28 |
| Net operating income | 0.33 | 0.89 | 16 | 0.84 | 0.93 | 38 | 0.97 | 0.93 | 50 | 0.75 | 0.88 | 0.60 | 0.74 |
| Adj. net oper. income | 0.63 | 0.97 | 21 | 1.16 | 1.08 | 54 | 1.02 | 1.06 | 46 | 0.81 | 0.95 | 0.50 | 0.81 |
| Adj. net income | 0.44 | 0.87 | 19 | 0.96 | 0.96 | 47 | 0.90 | 0.93 | 44 | 0.69 | 0.83 | 0.49 | 0.69 |
| Net income | 0.33 | 0.90 | 16 | 0.84 | 0.94 | 36 | 0.97 | 0.95 | 49 | 0.75 | 0.87 | 0.60 | 0.75 |
| **Percent of avg earning assets:** | | | | | | | | | | | | | |
| Interest income (TE) | 9.34 | 9.67 | 26 | 10.15 | 10.38 | 34 | 11.50 | 11.37 | 54 | 12.86 | 12.45 | 12.32 | 11.74 |
| Interest expense | 5.30 | 5.13 | 62 | 5.54 | 5.53 | 50 | 6.56 | 6.46 | 54 | 8.11 | 7.61 | 7.39 | 6.95 |
| Net int income (TE) | 4.03 | 4.63 | 24 | 4.62 | 4.91 | 36 | 4.94 | 4.94 | 49 | 4.75 | 4.87 | 4.92 | 4.76 |

Uniform Bank Performance Report *(continued)*

United National Bank of Denver: Summary Ratios

| | Bank | Peer 3 | PCT | Bank | Peer 3 | PCT | Bank | Peer 3 | PCT | Bank | Peer 3 | Bank | Peer 3 |
|---|---|---|---|---|---|---|---|---|---|---|---|---|---|
| Loan and lease losses, reserves and | | | | | | | | | | | | | |
| Noncurrent loans and leases | | | | | | | | | | | | | |
| Net loss to avg. tot. loan and lease | 1.47 | 0.64 | 84 | 1.55 | 0.63 | 85 | 0.86 | 0.48 | 82 | 0.43 | 0.48 | 1.12 | 0.59 |
| Earn coverage of net loss (K) | 1.51 | 7.04 | 14 | 2.27 | 7.10 | 23 | 3.15 | 8.36 | 23 | 4.74 | 7.83 | 1.78 | 6.54 |
| Loss reserve to net losses (K) | 1.89 | 3.77 | 29 | 1.34 | 3.73 | 19 | 1.59 | 4.20 | 18 | 3.07 | 4.03 | 1.18 | 3.36 |
| Loss resv. to tot. loans and leases | 2.73 | 1.42 | 88 | 2.05 | 1.33 | 89 | 1.38 | 1.22 | 70 | 1.24 | 1.22 | 1.33 | 1.25 |
| % noncurrent loans and leases | 3.82 | 1.52 | 87 | 5.02 | 1.65 | 94 | 2.52 | 1.71 | 77 | 1.53 | 1.97 | 3.31 | 2.40 |
| Liquidity and rate sensitivity | | | | | | | | | | | | | |
| Volatile liability dependence | 42.00 | 20.36 | 87 | 42.62 | 15.70 | 87 | 47.97 | 16.54 | 89 | 52.64 | 17.04 | 50.52 | 16.91 |
| Net loans and leases to assets | 49.55 | 63.33 | 14 | 47.37 | 60.84 | 10 | 48.64 | 59.20 | 15 | 56.31 | 58.58 | 53.79 | 53.43 |
| Net assets repriceable in 1 yr or less to assets | -11.35 | -6.19 | 32 | -8.49 | -4.90 | 37 | -5.94 | -1.92 | 29 | 3.36 | -1.61 | 8.16 | -1.92 |
| Capitalization | | | | | | | | | | | | | |
| Prim capital to avg. assets | 8.05 | 7.54 | 70 | 7.41 | 7.35 | 60 | 6.47 | 7.13 | 23 | 6.53 | 6.93 | 6.33 | 6.59 |
| Cash dividends to net income | 117.47 | 39.68 | 96 | 45.50 | 35.87 | 67 | 35.17 | 38.13 | 44 | 43.97 | 38.73 | 57.00 | 42.95 |
| Net earns to avg. total equity | -0.93 | 7.02 | 15 | 7.69 | 8.71 | 41 | 11.26 | 8.88 | 67 | 7.63 | 8.43 | 4.73 | 6.77 |
| Growth rates | | | | | | | | | | | | | |
| Assets | -8.48 | 4.18 | 09 | -2.09 | 12.67 | 10 | 10.90 | 12.77 | 41 | 7.67 | 12.27 | 4.60 | 10.79 |
| Primary capital | 2.83 | 10.08 | 16 | 16.04 | 13.85 | 62 | 6.47 | 13.08 | 17 | 7.56 | 14.45 | 15.96 | 8.17 |
| Net loans and leases | -4.26 | 9.54 | 13 | -4.64 | 14.47 | 10 | -4.20 | 13.83 | 05 | 12.71 | 25.24 | -4.36 | 14.46 |
| Volatile liabilities | -7.89 | 24.40 | 18 | 1.04 | 6.41 | 42 | 3.80 | 17.46 | 31 | 3.38 | 14.15 | -0.14 | -3.12 |

845

United National Bank of Denver: Income Statement-Revenues and Expenses ($000)

| | 12/30/87 | 12/31/86 | 12/31/85 | 12/31/84 | 12/31/83 | Percent change 1 Year | Percent change 4 Years |
|---|---|---|---|---|---|---|---|
| Interest and fees on loans | 129,679 | 139,243 | 167,665 | 185,952 | 163,497 | -6.87 | -20.62 |
| Income from lease financing | 1,554 | 1,943 | 2,446 | 2,567 | 3,091 | -20.02 | -49.74 |
| Fully taxable | 130,276 | 139,393 | 167,675 | 186,977 | N/A | | |
| Tax exempt | 957 | 1,793 | 2,436 | 1,542 | N/A | | |
| Estimated tax benefit | 479 | 1,497 | 2,015 | 1,312 | N/A | | |
| Income on loans and leases (te) | 131,712 | 142,683 | 172,126 | 189,831 | 166,588 | | |
| U.S. Treas. and agency securities | 18,557 | 15,935 | 17,334 | 15,871 | 11,367 | 16.45 | 63.25 |
| Tax-exempt securities income | 15,148 | 17,775 | 13,366 | 8,751 | 11,493 | -14.78 | 31.80 |
| Estimated tax benefit | 7,497 | 15,136 | 11,417 | 7,437 | 9,769 | | |
| Other securities income | 541 | 383 | 0 | 0 | 78 | 41.25 | 593.59 |
| Investment int. income (te) | 41,743 | 49,229 | 42,117 | 32,059 | 32,707 | | |
| Interest on due from banks | 13,566 | 7,326 | 5,030 | 4,738 | 2,518 | 85.18 | 438.76 |
| Int on Fed Funds sold/resales | 8,581 | 11,891 | 9,507 | 11,714 | 11,121 | -27.84 | -22.84 |
| Trading account income | 961 | 2,055 | 1,154 | 741 | 547 | -53.24 | 75.69 |
| Total interest income (te) | 196,563 | 213,184 | 229,934 | 239,083 | 213,481 | | |
| Interest on CD's over $100M | 36,899 | 40,020 | 48,379 | 65,588 | 43,555 | -7.80 | -15.28 |
| Int. on deposits in foreign off | 4,808 | 5,016 | 5,553 | 5,666 | 4,201 | -4.15 | 14.45 |
| Interest on all other deposits | 34,188 | 35,854 | 36,880 | 29,544 | 39,642 | -4.65 | -13.76 |
| Int. on Fed Funds purch. and repos | 29,866 | 30,001 | 35,548 | 44,663 | 36,796 | -0.45 | -18.83 |
| Int. borrowed money (+note opt) | 5,331 | 4,771 | 4,062 | 4,449 | 3,241 | 11.74 | 64.49 |
| Int. on mortgages and leases | 0 | 0 | 96 | 203 | N/A | N/A | N/A |
| Int. on subord. notes and debs | 595 | 595 | 595 | 615 | 749 | 0.00 | -20.56 |
| Total interest expense | 111,687 | 116,257 | 131,113 | 150,728 | 128,184 | -3.93 | -12.87 |
| Net interest income (te) | 84,876 | 96,927 | 98,821 | 88,355 | 85,297 | | |
| Non-interest income | 61,355 | 67,645 | 60,836 | 38,536 | 29,095 | -9.30 | 110.88 |
| Adjusted operating income (te) | 146,231 | 164,572 | 159,657 | 126,891 | 114,392 | | |
| Overhead expense | 109,087 | 99,813 | 106,777 | 89,448 | 78,794 | 9.29 | 38.45 |
| Provision for loan losses | 26,892 | 29,600 | 13,850 | 7,450 | 12,435 | -9.15 | 116.26 |
| Prov.: allocated transfer risk | N/A | N/A | N/A | N/A | N/A | | |
| Pretax operating income (te) | 10,252 | 35,159 | 39,030 | 29,993 | 23,163 | | |
| Securities gains (losses) | 1,504 | 4,346 | 3,341 | -26 | -1,027 | -65.39 | -246.45 |
| Pretax net operating inc. (te) | 11,756 | 39,505 | 42,371 | 29,967 | 22,136 | | |
| Applicable income taxes | -4,865 | 516 | 4,088 | 3,445 | -1,006 | | |
| Current tax-equiv. adjustment | 3,780 | 16,633 | 13,432 | 8,749 | 9,769 | | |
| Other tax-equiv. adjustments | 4,196 | 0 | 0 | 0 | 0 | | |
| Applicable income taxes (te) | 3,111 | 17,149 | 17,520 | 12,194 | 8,763 | | |
| Net operating income | 8,645 | 22,356 | 24,851 | 17,773 | 13,373 | -61.33 | -35.35 |
| Net extraordinary items | 0 | 0 | 0 | 0 | 0 | | |
| Net income | 8,645 | 22,356 | 24,851 | 17,773 | 13,373 | -61.33 | -35.35 |
| Cash dividends declared | 10,155 | 10,172 | 8,740 | 7,815 | 7,623 | -0.17 | 33.22 |
| Retained earnings | -1,510 | 12,184 | 16,111 | 9,958 | 5,750 | -112.39 | -126.26 |
| Memo: net international income | 3,376 | 666 | -132 | -565 | 2,731 | 406.91 | 23.62 |

United National Bank of Denver

| Percent of average assets | 12/31/87 Bank | Peer 3 | PCT | 12/31/86 Bank | Peer 3 | PCT | 12/31/85 Bank | Peer 3 | PCT | 12/31/84 Bank | Peer 3 | 12/31/83 Bank | Peer 3 |
|---|---|---|---|---|---|---|---|---|---|---|---|---|---|
| Temporary investments | 18.52 | 11.02 | 83 | 18.20 | 13.33 | 76 | 13.90 | 15.07 | 49 | 11.70 | 16.26 | 14.65 | 18.46 |
| Core deposits | 47.30 | 63.44 | 14 | 48.24 | 65.02 | 13 | 48.61 | 65.01 | 15 | 46.59 | 62.45 | 44.34 | 60.27 |
| Volatile liabilities | 44.20 | 27.61 | 86 | 43.91 | 26.16 | 86 | 42.55 | 26.14 | 83 | 45.46 | 28.89 | 47.35 | 31.10 |
| **Liquidity ratios** | | | | | | | | | | | | | |
| Volatile liability dependence | 42.00 | 20.36 | 87 | 42.62 | 15.70 | 87 | 47.97 | 16.54 | 89 | 52.64 | 17.04 | 50.52 | 16.91 |
| Temp inv to volatile liab | 41.90 | 52.95 | 46 | 41.44 | 68.33 | 33 | 52.66 | 72.18 | 17 | 25.74 | 77.82 | 30.94 | 78.32 |
| Brokered deposits to deposits | 0.27 | 0.01 | 75 | 0.41 | 0.11 | 74 | 0.50 | 0.12 | 74 | 1.03 | 0.34 | 6.84 | 0.15 |
| Temp inv less vol liab to asset | -25.68 | -12.77 | 17 | -25.71 | -10.27 | 16 | -28.65 | -11.05 | 12 | -33.76 | -11.85 | -32.70 | -12.30 |
| Net loans and leases to deposits | 69.92 | 76.49 | 25 | 68.64 | 73.45 | 29 | 68.19 | 73.07 | 28 | 79.92 | 72.60 | 72.43 | 67.63 |
| Net loans and leases to core deposits | 104.77 | 92.03 | 73 | 98.20 | 87.17 | 73 | 100.06 | 89.67 | 73 | 120.87 | 92.12 | 121.32 | 87.23 |
| Net loans and leases to assets | 49.55 | 63.33 | 14 | 47.37 | 60.84 | 10 | 48.64 | 59.20 | 15 | 56.31 | 58.58 | 53.79 | 53.43 |
| Net loans, leases, and SBLC to asset | 55.38 | 65.42 | 18 | 53.01 | 63.33 | 19 | 55.40 | 62.04 | 25 | 62.60 | 61.25 | 57.79 | 55.94 |
| **Percent change in:** | | | | | | | | | | | | | |
| Temporary investments | -6.87 | -8.76 | 59 | 28.20 | 2.37 | 76 | 31.73 | 11.89 | 75 | -14.01 | 9.24 | 97.46 | 6.71 |
| Securities over 1 year | -18.25 | 8.48 | 15 | 14.50 | 16.86 | 51 | 56.95 | 20.89 | 81 | -22.83 | -10.56 | 24.51 | 4.73 |
| Net loans and leases | -4.26 | 9.54 | 13 | -4.64 | 14.47 | 10 | -4.20 | 13.83 | 05 | 12.71 | 25.24 | -4.36 | 14.46 |
| Core deposits | -10.26 | 0.79 | 12 | -2.84 | 15.37 | 04 | 15.72 | 11.22 | 70 | 13.13 | 12.85 | 9.42 | 18.50 |
| Volatile liabilities | -7.89 | 24.40 | 18 | 1.04 | 6.41 | 42 | 3.80 | 17.46 | 31 | 3.38 | 14.15 | -0.14 | -3.12 |
| Total assets | -8.48 | 4.18 | 09 | -2.09 | 12.67 | 10 | 10.90 | 12.77 | 41 | 7.67 | 12.27 | 4.60 | 10.79 |
| **Securities** | | | | | | | | | | | | | |
| **Percent of total securities:** | | | | | | | | | | | | | |
| U.S. treas. and agency | 58.76 | 59.79 | 40 | 53.88 | 56.90 | 41 | 36.63 | 54.76 | 21 | 52.14 | 57.62 | 52.26 | 51.62 |
| Municipals | 39.91 | 25.14 | 82 | 44.44 | 31.08 | 74 | 63.05 | 38.86 | 86 | 47.41 | 34.16 | 47.40 | 41.46 |
| Foreign securities | 0.00 | 0.05 | 54 | 0.00 | 0.07 | 47 | 0.00 | 0.08 | 47 | 0.00 | 0.10 | N/A | N/A |
| All other securities | 1.33 | 12.21 | 27 | 1.68 | 7.70 | 36 | 0.32 | 3.11 | 16 | 0.45 | 4.23 | 0.34 | 3.36 |
| Debt securities under 1 year | 34.69 | 28.07 | 65 | 18.68 | 29.28 | 32 | 24.42 | 33.51 | 34 | 35.39 | 32.67 | 16.05 | 32.31 |
| Debt securities 1 to 5 years | 38.36 | 42.40 | 43 | 45.58 | 42.47 | 58 | 33.30 | 38.63 | 40 | 33.14 | 39.03 | 48.62 | 38.05 |
| Debt securities 5 to 10 years | 16.81 | 12.13 | 70 | 20.85 | 13.37 | 77 | 22.08 | 14.94 | 76 | 23.71 | 13.31 | 23.05 | 15.52 |
| Debt securities over 10 years | 10.14 | 15.37 | 52 | 14.89 | 13.33 | 65 | 20.21 | 12.56 | 77 | 7.76 | 14.63 | 12.28 | 13.49 |

United National Bank of Denver: Relative Income Statement and Margin Analysis

| Percent of average assets | 12/30/87 | | | 12/31/86 | | | 12/31/85 | | | 12/31/84 | | 12/31/83 | |
|---|---|---|---|---|---|---|---|---|---|---|---|---|---|
| | Bank | Peer 3 | PCT | Bank | Peer 3 | PCT | Bank | Peer 3 | PCT | Bank | Peer 3 | Bank | Peer 3 |
| Interest income (te) | 7.58 | 8.71 | 10 | 8.03 | 9.36 | 11 | 8.98 | 10.20 | 08 | 10.08 | 11.06 | 9.55 | 10.32 |
| Less: interest expense | 4.31 | 4.66 | 31 | 4.39 | 5.00 | 15 | 5.12 | 5.77 | 17 | 6.36 | 6.77 | 5.74 | 6.11 |
| Equals: net int. income (te) | 3.27 | 4.16 | 14 | 3.66 | 4.42 | 21 | 3.86 | 4.40 | 24 | 3.73 | 4.31 | 3.82 | 4.19 |
| Plus: noninterest income | 2.37 | 1.28 | 87 | 2.56 | 1.31 | 89 | 2.38 | 1.23 | 92 | 1.63 | 1.27 | 1.30 | 1.11 |
| Equals: adj. oper. income (te) | 5.64 | 5.40 | 55 | 6.22 | 5.73 | 67 | 6.24 | 5.71 | 68 | 5.35 | 5.61 | 5.12 | 5.32 |
| Less: overhead expense | 4.21 | 3.48 | 77 | 3.77 | 3.56 | 63 | 4.17 | 3.61 | 70 | 3.77 | 3.61 | 3.53 | 3.59 |
| Less: provision for LN losses | 1.04 | 0.49 | 83 | 1.12 | 0.54 | 83 | 0.54 | 0.41 | 73 | 0.31 | 0.40 | 0.56 | 0.37 |
| Less: prov. allocated trans risk | N/A | N/A | | N/A | 0.08 | | N/A | 0.08 | | N/A | 0.01 | N/A | N/A |
| Plus: securities gains (losses) | 0.06 | 0.03 | 79 | 0.16 | 0.09 | 77 | 0.13 | 0.04 | 87 | 0.00 | 0.00 | −0.05 | 0.00 |
| Equals: pretax NOI (te) | 0.45 | 1.47 | 13 | 1.49 | 1.70 | 33 | 1.65 | 1.70 | 45 | 1.26 | 1.54 | 0.99 | 1.28 |
| Less: applicable inc. tax (te) | 0.12 | 0.65 | 10 | 0.65 | 0.80 | 32 | 0.68 | 0.76 | 39 | 0.51 | 0.71 | 0.39 | 0.57 |
| Equals: net operating income | 0.33 | 0.89 | 16 | 0.84 | 0.93 | 38 | 0.97 | 0.93 | 50 | 0.75 | 0.88 | 0.60 | 0.74 |
| Plus extraord. equals: net income | 0.33 | 0.90 | 16 | 0.84 | 0.94 | 36 | 0.97 | 0.95 | 49 | 0.75 | 0.87 | 0.60 | 0.75 |
| Margin analysis | | | | | | | | | | | | | |
| Avg. earning assets to avg. assets | 81.18 | 90.59 | 04 | 79.33 | 90.59 | 02 | 78.06 | 89.82 | 02 | 78.40 | 88.87 | 77.56 | 87.97 |
| Avg. int.-bearing funds to avg. assets | 67.11 | 75.69 | 12 | 65.06 | 74.80 | 10 | 63.95 | 74.11 | 06 | 66.29 | 73.24 | 66.36 | 72.16 |
| Int. inc. (te) to avg. earn. assets | 9.34 | 9.67 | 26 | 10.15 | 10.38 | 54 | 11.50 | 11.37 | 54 | 12.86 | 12.45 | 12.32 | 11.74 |
| Init. expense to avg. earn. assets | 5.30 | 5.13 | 62 | 5.54 | 5.53 | 50 | 6.56 | 6.46 | 54 | 8.11 | 7.61 | 7.39 | 6.95 |
| Net int. inc-te to avg. earn. assets | 4.03 | 4.63 | 24 | 4.62 | 4.91 | 36 | 4.94 | 4.94 | 49 | 4.75 | 4.87 | 4.92 | 4.76 |

United National Bank of Denver: Relative Income Statement and Margin Analysis *(continued)*

| Yield on or cost of: | 12/30/87 Bank | 12/30/87 Peer 3 | 12/30/87 PCT | 12/31/86 Bank | 12/31/86 Peer 3 | 12/31/86 PCT | 12/31/85 Bank | 12/31/85 Peer 3 | 12/31/85 PCT | 12/31/84 Bank | 12/31/84 Peer 3 | 12/31/83 Bank | 12/31/83 Peer 3 |
|---|---|---|---|---|---|---|---|---|---|---|---|---|---|
| Total loans and leases (te) | 10.06 | 10.20 | 37 | 10.45 | 10.80 | 29 | 11.89 | 11.88 | 50 | 13.52 | 13.04 | 12.43 | 12.23 |
| Loans in domestic offices | 10.17 | 10.01 | 60 | 10.50 | 10.49 | 52 | 11.90 | 11.55 | 70 | 13.60 | 12.75 | 12.57 | 12.29 |
| Real estate | 8.87 | 10.07 | 10 | 9.46 | 10.65 | 16 | 11.48 | 11.37 | 54 | 14.50 | 12.19 | 11.97 | 11.33 |
| Commercial and industrial | 8.86 | 9.18 | 35 | 8.57 | 9.49 | 19 | 10.01 | 10.94 | 18 | 12.43 | 12.60 | 11.16 | 11.78 |
| Individual | 16.39 | 11.98 | 91 | 16.82 | 12.74 | 92 | 39.72 | 13.81 | 99 | 18.66 | 14.58 | 16.57 | 13.99 |
| Agricultural | 9.01 | 9.32 | 36 | 9.53 | 8.77 | 60 | 11.14 | 10.13 | 54 | 13.36 | 12.50 | N/A | N/A |
| Loans in foreign offices | 8.45 | 6.94 | 75 | 8.80 | 8.21 | 60 | 14.35 | 10.15 | 95 | 6.65 | 11.37 | 16.78 | 10.72 |
| Total investmt securities (te) | 8.87 | 8.72 | 55 | 11.21 | 10.15 | 77 | 11.68 | 10.91 | 76 | 11.16 | 11.22 | 13.53 | 11.66 |
| U.S. Treas. and Agency | 6.86 | 7.88 | 17 | 7.67 | 8.93 | 14 | 9.56 | 10.19 | 23 | 9.90 | 10.77 | 9.85 | 10.66 |
| Municipals (book) | 7.99 | 7.11 | 77 | 7.78 | 6.88 | 81 | 7.59 | 6.71 | 77 | 7.06 | 6.65 | 7.20 | 7.03 |
| Municipals (te)* | 11.94 | 11.55 | 57 | 14.41 | 12.60 | 81 | 14.08 | 12.32 | 78 | 13.07 | 12.14 | 13.33 | 12.86 |
| Other securities | 5.50 | 5.99 | 34 | 12.88 | 7.30 | 96 | 0.00 | 8.18 | 01 | 0.00 | 8.94 | 1.20 | 5.66 |
| Interest-bearing bank balances | 7.40 | 7.36 | 62 | 2.93 | 7.77 | 66 | 8.46 | 9.11 | 24 | 10.58 | 10.95 | 10.31 | 9.79 |
| Federal Funds sold and resales | 6.74 | 6.73 | 56 | 6.85 | 6.86 | 50 | 8.27 | 8.18 | 66 | 10.50 | 10.41 | 9.24 | 9.35 |
| Total int.-bearing deposits | 6.26 | 6.11 | 71 | 6.72 | 6.70 | 54 | 7.98 | 7.81 | 62 | 9.31 | 9.09 | 8.49 | 8.43 |
| Transaction accounts | 4.45 | 4.76 | 23 | N/A | N/A | | N/A | N/A | | N/A | N/A | N/A | N/A |
| Money market deposit accounts | 5.32 | 5.32 | 60 | N/A | N/A | | N/A | N/A | | N/A | N/A | N/A | N/A |
| Other savings deposits | 5.65 | 5.08 | 89 | N/A | N/A | | N/A | N/A | | N/A | N/A | N/A | N/A |
| Large certs of deposit | 6.92 | 6.62 | 70 | 7.28 | 7.05 | 69 | 9.86 | 8.47 | 93 | 11.46 | 10.25 | 8.96 | 9.07 |
| All other time deposits | 6.58 | 7.19 | 24 | N/A | N/A | | N/A | N/A | | N/A | N/A | N/A | N/A |
| Foreign office deposits | 6.34 | 6.65 | 24 | 6.63 | 6.98 | 28 | 8.23 | 8.47 | 36 | 10.31 | 10.56 | 8.07 | 8.66 |
| Federal funds purch. & repos | 6.56 | 6.32 | 70 | 6.75 | 6.48 | 79 | 8.09 | 7.84 | 79 | 10.24 | 9.95 | 9.20 | 8.76 |
| Other borrowed money | 7.99 | 6.16 | 77 | 7.26 | 5.12 | 80 | 7.76 | 6.22 | 70 | 9.88 | 7.94 | 7.20 | 7.46 |
| Subordinated notes and debentures | 8.50 | 7.89 | 48 | 8.50 | 8.65 | 45 | 8.50 | 8.49 | 40 | 8.41 | 8.62 | 8.47 | 8.54 |
| All interest-bearing funds | 6.42 | 6.17 | 71 | 6.75 | 6.68 | 56 | 8.01 | 7.82 | 68 | 9.59 | 9.26 | 8.64 | 8.51 |

United National Bank of Denver: Balance Sheet-Assets Section ($000)

| | 12/30/87 | 12/31/86 | 12/31/85 | 12/31/84 | 12/31/83 | Percent change 1 Year | Percent change 4 Years |
|---|---|---|---|---|---|---|---|
| Real estate loans | 510,507 | 514,319 | 480,886 | 546,528 | 429,507 | −0.74 | 18.86 |
| Financial institutions loans | 24,397 | 1,232 | 8,338 | 6,102 | 135,301 | 1880.28 | −81.97 |
| Agricultural loans | 23,901 | 21,661 | 19,486 | 23,581 | 22,535 | 10.34 | 6.06 |
| Commercial and industrial loans | 335,710 | 305,590 | 363,573 | 411,689 | 411,687 | 9.86 | −18.46 |
| Loans to individuals | 270,223 | 288,463 | 276,648 | 258,148 | 263,262 | −6.32 | 2.64 |
| Municipal loans | 8,076 | 18,732 | 29,934 | 33,447 | N/A | −56.89 | N/A |
| Acceptances of other banks | 504 | 234 | 0 | 0 | N/A | 115.38 | N/A |
| Other loans in domestic offices | 115,446 | 188,380 | 219,182 | 182,637 | 34,824 | −38.72 | 231.51 |
| Foreign office loans and leases | 9,623 | 9,718 | 2,600 | 2,600 | 2,500 | −0.98 | 284.92 |
| Lease financing receivables | 34,477 | 34,849 | 42,111 | 38,892 | 36,438 | −1.07 | −5.38 |
| Gross loans and leases | 1,332,864 | 1,383,178 | 1,442,758 | 1,503,824 | 1,336,054 | −3.64 | −0.24 |
| Less: unearned income | 474 | 1,095 | 5,165 | 3,364 | 4,038 | | |
| Loss reserve | 36,372 | 28,328 | 19,919 | 18,585 | 17,189 | 28.40 | 111.60 |
| Transfer risk reserve | N/A | N/A | N/A | N/A | N/A | | |
| Net loans and leases | 1,296,018 | 1,353,755 | 1,419,674 | 1,481,877 | 1,314,827 | −4.26 | −1.43 |
| Securities over 1 year | 302,817 | 370,429 | 323,514 | 206,131 | 267,123 | −18.25 | 13.36 |
| Subtotal | 1,598,835 | 1,724,184 | 1,743,188 | 1,688,008 | 1,581,950 | | |
| Interest-bearing bank balances | 211,448 | 177,005 | 82,000 | 45,000 | 75,000 | 19.46 | 181.93 |
| Federal Funds sold and resales | 102,409 | 227,484 | 161,340 | 119,527 | 231,042 | | |
| Trading account assets | 9,612 | 30,472 | 57,795 | 31,306 | 1,204 | −68.46 | 698.34 |
| Debt securities 1 year and less | 160,834 | 85,090 | 104,524 | 112,109 | 50,856 | 89.02 | 216.25 |
| Temporary investments | 484,303 | 520,051 | 405,659 | 307,942 | 358,102 | −6.87 | 35.24 |
| Total earning assets | 2,083,138 | 2,244,235 | 2,148,847 | 1,995,950 | 1,940,052 | −7.18 | 7.38 |
| Nonint. cash and due from banks | 375,277 | 462,827 | 605,712 | 489,888 | 368,402 | −18.92 | 1.87 |
| Acceptances | 539 | 1,834 | 768 | 8,037 | 24,135 | | |
| Premises, fixed assets, cap. leases | 81,233 | 76,907 | 60,116 | 62,002 | 56,789 | 5.62 | 43.04 |
| Other real estate owned | 15,364 | 5,710 | 6,503 | 9,553 | 6,420 | 169.07 | 439.31 |
| Inv. in unconsolidated subsidiaries | 0 | 0 | 232 | 1,358 | 1,628 | | |
| Intangible assets | 0 | 0 | 0 | 0 | 0 | | |
| Other assets | 59,782 | 66,298 | 96,528 | 65,015 | 46,651 | | |
| Total assets | 2,615,333 | 2,857,811 | 2,918,706 | 2,631,803 | 2,444,277 | −8.48 | 7.00 |
| Average assets during quarter | 2,513,001 | 2,665,735 | 2,639,389 | 2,455,092 | 2,355,211 | −5.73 | 6.70 |

United National Bank of Denver: Balance Sheet-Liabilities nd Capital Section ($000)

| | 12/30/87 | 12/31/86 | 12/31/85 | 12/31/84 | 12/31/83 | Percent change 1 Year | 4 Years |
|---|---|---|---|---|---|---|---|
| Demand deposits | 665,087 | 780,352 | 884,205 | 741,082 | 700,982 | −14.77 | −5.12 |
| All NOW and ATS accounts | 122,931 | 120,163 | 61,037 | 59,466 | 57,021 | 2.30 | 62.81 |
| Super NOWs included in above | N/A | N/A | 28,110 | 22,383 | 18,487 | N/A | N/A |
| MMDA savings | 300,309 | 339,362 | 307,658 | 273,993 | 222,637 | −11.51 | 34.89 |
| Other savings deposits | 36,788 | 32,443 | 30,286 | 32,966 | 54,050 | 13.39 | −31.94 |
| Time deposits under $100M | 111,942 | 106,184 | 107,497 | 96,157 | 30,571 | 5.42 | 266.17 |
| Core deposits | 1,237,057 | 1,378,504 | 1,418,793 | 1,226,047 | 1,083,748 | −10.26 | 14.15 |
| Time deposits over $100M | 530,985 | 500,937 | 601,778 | 560,379 | 683,867 | 6.00 | −22.36 |
| Deposits held in foreign offices | 85,634 | 92,741 | 61,372 | 67,715 | 47,665 | −7.66 | 79.66 |
| Federal Funds purchased and resales | 486,063 | 577,346 | 519,179 | 514,210 | 391,017 | | |
| Other borrowings (+note opt) | 53,192 | 83,822 | 59,567 | 54,138 | 34,802 | −36.54 | 52.84 |
| Volatile liabilities | 1,155,874 | 1,254,846 | 1,241,896 | 1,196,442 | 1,157,351 | −7.89 | −0.13 |
| Acceptances | 539 | 1,834 | 768 | 8,037 | 24,135 | | |
| Other liabilities | 52,956 | 51,331 | 98,157 | 54,505 | 40,621 | | |
| Total liabilities | 2,446,426 | 2,683,515 | 2,759,594 | 2,485,031 | 2,305,855 | −8.91 | 5.83 |
| Mortgages and capitalized leases | 0 | 0 | 0 | 3,771 | 4,426 | N/A | −100.00 |
| Subordinated notes and debentures | 7,000 | 7,000 | 7,000 | 7,000 | 7,953 | 0.00 | −11.98 |
| Total liabilities and debt | 2,453,426 | 2,693,515 | 2,766,594 | 2,495,802 | 2,318,234 | −8.91 | 5.83 |
| Limited-life preferred stock | 0 | 0 | 0 | 0 | 0 | | |
| Common equity | 161,907 | 164,296 | 152,112 | 136,001 | 126,043 | −1.45 | 28.45 |
| Perpetual preferred stock | 0 | 0 | 0 | 0 | 0 | | |
| Total equity capital | 161,907 | 164,296 | 152,112 | 136,001 | 126,043 | −1.45 | 28.45 |
| Total liabilities and capital | 2,615,333 | 2,857,811 | 2,918,706 | 2,631,803 | 2,444,277 | −8.48 | 7.00 |

United National Bank of Denver: Balance Sheet-Percentage Composition of Assets and Liabilities

| Assets, percent of avg. assets | 12/30/87 | | | 12/31/86 | | | 12/31/85 | | | 12/31/84 | | 12/31/83 | |
|---|---|---|---|---|---|---|---|---|---|---|---|---|---|
| | Bank | Peer 3 | PCT | Bank | Peer 3 | PCT | Bank | Peer 3 | PCT | Bank | Peer 3 | Bank | Peer 3 |
| Total loans | 47.72 | 62.95 | 09 | 47.87 | 60.87 | 11 | 53.44 | 59.39 | 24 | 56.59 | 56.88 | 56.81 | 52.17 |
| Lease financing receivables | 1.22 | 0.58 | 79 | 1.35 | 0.55 | 80 | 1.46 | 0.61 | 80 | 1.44 | 0.56 | 1.63 | 0.53 |
| Less: loss reserves | 1.19 | 0.90 | 81 | 0.80 | 0.80 | 53 | 0.74 | 0.73 | 50 | 0.74 | 0.69 | 0.79 | 0.64 |
| Transfer risk reserve | N/A | N/A | | N/A | N/A | | N/A | 0.03 | | N/A | N/A | N/A | N/A |
| Net loans and leases | 47.75 | 62.77 | 10 | 48.42 | 60.90 | 12 | 54.17 | 59.56 | 25 | 57.29 | 57.30 | 57.65 | 52.52 |
| Securities over 1 year | 12.92 | 12.67 | 51 | 12.29 | 11.93 | 54 | 10.07 | 11.52 | 44 | 8.83 | 12.74 | 10.81 | 14.61 |
| Subtotal | 60.66 | 76.60 | 08 | 60.71 | 73.34 | 10 | 64.23 | 71.73 | 17 | 66.12 | 70.32 | 68.46 | 67.55 |
| Interest-bearing bank balances | 6.90 | 1.50 | 89 | 3.98 | 2.09 | 75 | 2.22 | 2.99 | 59 | 2.19 | 4.83 | 1.31 | 7.04 |
| Federal Funds sold and resales | 6.31 | 3.42 | 80 | 7.42 | 4.54 | 79 | 4.54 | 4.78 | 57 | 5.53 | 4.84 | 6.66 | 5.50 |
| Trading account assets | 0.57 | 0.03 | 92 | 1.25 | 0.10 | 93 | 1.07 | 0.11 | 93 | 0.62 | 0.12 | 0.24 | 0.20 |
| Debt securities 1 year and less | 4.06 | 4.95 | 50 | 3.17 | 5.42 | 31 | 3.93 | 6.06 | 34 | 3.45 | 5.85 | 1.25 | 5.70 |
| Temporary investments | 17.83 | 11.66 | 82 | 15.81 | 13.98 | 66 | 11.77 | 15.34 | 33 | 11.79 | 16.50 | 9.47 | 19.12 |
| Total earning assets | 78.50 | 88.36 | 03 | 76.52 | 87.92 | 02 | 76.00 | 87.56 | 02 | 77.92 | 86.97 | 77.93 | 86.80 |
| Nonint. cash and due from banks | 15.91 | 7.37 | 97 | 18.22 | 7.99 | 97 | 18.71 | 8.06 | 98 | 16.27 | 8.28 | 16.31 | 8.44 |
| Premises, fix assts, cap. leases | 2.90 | 1.47 | 94 | 2.39 | 1.48 | 88 | 2.33 | 1.63 | 86 | 2.45 | 1.73 | 2.33 | 1.71 |
| Other real estate owned | 0.44 | 0.14 | 83 | 0.22 | 0.18 | 67 | 0.31 | 0.21 | 72 | 0.35 | 0.21 | 0.29 | 0.23 |
| Acceptances and other assets | 2.24 | 2.19 | 63 | 2.65 | 2.12 | 77 | 2.65 | 2.37 | 71 | 3.02 | 2.68 | 3.14 | 2.75 |
| Subtotal | 21.50 | 11.64 | 96 | 23.48 | 12.08 | 97 | 24.00 | 12.44 | 97 | 22.08 | 13.03 | 22.07 | 13.20 |
| Total assets | 99.99 | 100.00 | | 100.00 | 100.00 | | 100.00 | 100.00 | | 99.99 | 100.00 | 100.00 | 100.00 |
| Standby letters of credit | 6.02 | 2.27 | 92 | 6.24 | 2.55 | 91 | 6.90 | 2.50 | 95 | 5.27 | 2.38 | 3.96 | 2.16 |

United National Bank of Denver: Balance Sheet-Percentage Composition of Assets and Liabilities *(continued)*

| Liabilities, percent of avg. assets | 12/30/87 Bank | Peer 3 | PCT | 12/31/86 Bank | Peer 3 | PCT | 12/31/85 Bank | Peer 3 | PCT | 12/31/84 Bank | Peer 3 | 12/31/83 Bank | Peer 3 |
|---|---|---|---|---|---|---|---|---|---|---|---|---|---|
| Demand deposits | 26.20 | 17.23 | 89 | 28.09 | 18.34 | 91 | 29.31 | 19.00 | 94 | 27.38 | 19.78 | 27.84 | 20.48 |
| All NOW and ATS accounts | 4.32 | 7.01 | 25 | 3.58 | 6.12 | 24 | 3.15 | 5.36 | 22 | 3.19 | 4.88 | 3.15 | 4.33 |
| Super NOWs included in above | N/A | N/A | | N/A | N/A | | 0.94 | 1.66 | 41 | 0.51 | 1.27 | 0.50 | 0.84 |
| MMDA savings | 12.61 | 15.30 | 33 | 11.98 | 16.04 | 28 | 10.83 | 14.77 | 27 | 10.24 | 12.11 | 7.26 | 9.26 |
| Other savings deposits | 1.28 | 7.20 | 10 | 1.06 | 6.16 | 09 | 1.16 | 6.26 | 10 | 1.75 | 6.70 | 3.04 | 8.09 |
| Time deposits under $100M | 3.93 | 16.74 | 09 | 3.83 | 17.03 | 10 | 3.74 | 18.32 | 08 | 2.92 | 17.89 | 3.25 | 17.05 |
| Core deposits | 48.33 | 64.27 | 13 | 48.54 | 64.03 | 16 | 48.18 | 63.86 | 16 | 45.49 | 61.57 | 44.54 | 59.29 |
| Time deposits over $100M | 19.08 | 12.28 | 79 | 19.74 | 12.39 | 79 | 21.72 | 13.40 | 79 | 24.45 | 14.40 | 25.62 | 15.87 |
| Deposits in foreign offices | 2.96 | 2.59 | 68 | 2.80 | 1.90 | 69 | 2.74 | 2.02 | 62 | 2.40 | 2.95 | 2.28 | 3.67 |
| Federal funds purch $ repos | 19.35 | 8.84 | 94 | 18.25 | 9.39 | 89 | 17.01 | 8.94 | 88 | 17.23 | 10.54 | 16.97 | 11.43 |
| Other borrowings (+note opt) | 2.37 | 1.17 | 82 | 2.30 | 1.21 | 81 | 2.05 | 1.23 | 76 | 1.79 | 1.16 | 1.91 | 1.39 |
| Volatile liabilities | 43.76 | 26.66 | 86 | 43.10 | 26.86 | 85 | 43.51 | 27.42 | 83 | 45.87 | 29.59 | 46.78 | 31.83 |
| Acceptances and other liabilities | 1.77 | 1.61 | 66 | 2.49 | 1.73 | 81 | 2.64 | 1.95 | 81 | 2.94 | 2.24 | 2.98 | 2.31 |
| Total liabilities (inc. mortg.) | 93.85 | 93.31 | 74 | 94.13 | 93.45 | 76 | 94.33 | 93.45 | 83 | 94.30 | 93.58 | 94.30 | 93.58 |
| Subordinated notes and debentures | 0.25 | 0.21 | 68 | 0.25 | 0.25 | 62 | 0.26 | 0.35 | 59 | 0.30 | 0.34 | 0.39 | 0.46 |
| All common and preferred capital | 5.89 | 6.49 | 30 | 5.62 | 6.28 | 27 | 5.41 | 6.15 | 21 | 5.40 | 5.95 | 5.31 | 5.93 |
| Total liabilities and capital | 100.00 | 100.00 | | 100.00 | 100.00 | | 100.00 | 100.00 | | 100.00 | 100.00 | 100.00 | 100.00 |
| Noninterest bearing deposits | 26.36 | 17.20 | 90 | 28.34 | 18.34 | 91 | 29.58 | 19.21 | 94 | 27.58 | 19.25 | 27.84 | 20.50 |
| Interest-bearing deposits | 44.00 | 62.10 | 09 | 42.74 | 60.73 | 08 | 43.06 | 61.23 | 05 | 44.26 | 58.96 | 44.60 | 57.48 |
| Total brokered deposits | 0.20 | 0.04 | 75 | 0.20 | 0.17 | 70 | 0.59 | 0.13 | 76 | 2.77 | 0.17 | 5.08 | 0.11 |

## United National Bank of Denver: Analysis of Allowance for Loan and Lease Losses and Loan Mix

### Change: loan and lease reserve ($000)

| | 12/30/87 | 12/31/86 | 12/31/85 | 12/31/84 | 12/31/83 |
|---|---|---|---|---|---|
| Beginning balance | 28,328 | 19,919 | 18,583 | 17,189 | 19,286 |
| Gross loan and lease losses | 21,030 | 22,322 | 14,605 | 7,710 | 15,784 |
| Recoveries | 1,740 | 1,131 | 2,091 | 1,654 | 1,252 |
| Net loan and lease losses | 19,290 | 21,191 | 12,514 | 6,056 | 14,532 |
| Provision for loan, lease loss | 26,892 | 29,600 | 13,850 | 7,450 | 12,435 |
| Other adjustments | 442 | 0 | 0 | 0 | 0 |
| Ending balance | 36,372 | 28,328 | 19,919 | 18,583 | 17,189 |
| Net atrr charge-offs | N/A | N/A | N/A | N/A | N/A |
| Other atrr changes (net) | N/A | N/A | N/A | N/A | N/A |
| Average total loans and leases | 1,309,380 | 1,365,560 | 1,447,506 | 1,403,859 | 1,339,743 |

### Analysis ratios

| | 12/30/87 | | | 12/31/86 | | | 12/31/85 | | | 12/31/84 | | 12/31/83 | |
|---|---|---|---|---|---|---|---|---|---|---|---|---|---|
| | Bank | Peer 3 | PCT | Bank | Peer 3 | PCT | Bank | Peer 3 | PCT | Bank | Peer 3 | Bank | Peer 3 |
| Loss provision to avg. assets | 1.04 | 0.49 | 83 | 1.12 | 0.54 | 83 | 0.54 | 0.41 | 73 | 0.31 | 0.40 | 0.56 | 0.37 |
| Loss prov to avg. tot. loans and leases | 2.05 | 0.76 | 85 | 2.17 | 0.89 | 88 | 0.96 | 0.65 | 80 | 0.53 | 0.63 | 0.95 | 0.69 |
| Net losses to avg. tot. loans and leases | 1.47 | 0.64 | 84 | 1.55 | 0.63 | 85 | 0.86 | 0.48 | 82 | 0.43 | 0.48 | 1.12 | 0.59 |
| Gross loss to avg. tot. loans and leases | 1.61 | 0.80 | 82 | 1.63 | 0.80 | 83 | 1.01 | 0.65 | 80 | 0.55 | 0.64 | 1.21 | 0.80 |
| Recoveries to avg. tot. loans and leases | 0.13 | 0.16 | 53 | 0.08 | 0.15 | 29 | 0.14 | 0.16 | 53 | 0.12 | 0.17 | 0.10 | 0.19 |
| Recoveries to prior period loss | 7.80 | 28.08 | 06 | 7.74 | 31.45 | 07 | 27.12 | 33.26 | 40 | 10.48 | 32.48 | 15.18 | 32.28 |
| Loss reserve to tot. loan and leases | 2.73 | 1.42 | 88 | 2.05 | 1.33 | 89 | 1.38 | 1.22 | 70 | 1.24 | 1.22 | 1.33 | 1.25 |
| Loss reserve to net losses (K) | 1.89 | 3.77 | 29 | 1.34 | 3.73 | 19 | 1.59 | 4.20 | 18 | 3.07 | 4.03 | 1.18 | 3.36 |
| Loss reserve to nonaccrual loans and leases | 0.99 | 2.05 | 14 | 0.48 | 2.01 | 23 | 0.78 | 1.52 | 23 | 1.11 | 1.27 | 0.43 | 1.14 |
| Earn coverage of net losses (K) | 1.51 | 7.04 | | 2.27 | 7.10 | | 3.15 | 8.36 | | 4.74 | 7.83 | 1.78 | 6.54 |

| | Bank | Peer 3 | PCT | Bank | Peer 3 | PCT | Bank | Peer 3 | PCT | Bank | Peer 3 | Bank | Peer 3 |
|---|---|---|---|---|---|---|---|---|---|---|---|---|---|
| **Loan mix, % of avg. gross loans and leases** | | | | | | | | | | | | | |
| Construction and development | 15.07 | 6.51 | 90 | 12.38 | 6.20 | 83 | 14.81 | 5.79 | 90 | 11.16 | 5.76 | 11.53 | 5.72 |
| 1-4-Family residential | 7.95 | 13.97 | 29 | 5.46 | 12.56 | 20 | 6.14 | 12.99 | 20 | 6.17 | 13.50 | 5.15 | 14.37 |
| Other real estate loans | 14.80 | 11.79 | 72 | 17.87 | 10.58 | 85 | 14.74 | 9.63 | 83 | 16.60 | 9.33 | 17.65 | 9.16 |
| Total real estate | 37.82 | 33.04 | 64 | 35.72 | 29.94 | 68 | 35.69 | 29.11 | 73 | 33.93 | 28.93 | 34.32 | 29.57 |
| Financial institutions | 1.43 | 1.11 | 70 | 0.41 | 1.30 | 46 | 0.43 | 2.09 | 37 | 6.21 | 3.22 | 8.57 | 4.94 |
| Agricultural loans | 1.83 | 0.30 | 88 | 1.61 | 0.36 | 88 | 1.57 | 0.47 | 82 | 2.02 | 0.66 | 1.83 | 0.65 |
| Commercial and industrial | 23.14 | 28.41 | 35 | 24.59 | 29.26 | 33 | 26.81 | 30.77 | 37 | 28.93 | 31.69 | 32.58 | 33.73 |
| Loans to individuals | 19.05 | 22.50 | 39 | 19.23 | 23.59 | 35 | 17.76 | 23.00 | 31 | 18.00 | 21.66 | 17.57 | 20.96 |
| Municipal loans | 0.91 | 4.18 | 29 | 1.82 | 5.19 | 32 | 2.24 | 5.35 | 31 | 1.93 | 4.06 | N/A | N/A |
| Acceptances of other banks | 0.11 | 0.00 | 84 | 0.03 | 0.00 | 81 | 0.00 | 0.02 | 66 | 0.00 | 0.04 | N/A | N/A |
| Loans, leases in foreign offices | 0.70 | 0.00 | 89 | 0.39 | 0.00 | 83 | 0.18 | 0.04 | 74 | 0.18 | 0.22 | 0.18 | 0.34 |
| All other loans | 12.54 | 3.04 | 95 | 13.46 | 3.39 | 94 | 12.66 | 3.44 | 93 | 6.33 | 3.84 | 2.17 | 3.56 |
| Lease financing receivables | 2.48 | 0.88 | 81 | 2.74 | 0.98 | 83 | 2.65 | 1.01 | 82 | 2.48 | 0.95 | 2.78 | 1.05 |
| **Memoranda (% of average total loans):** | | | | | | | | | | | | | |
| Commercial paper in loans | 0.00 | 0.00 | 90 | 0.00 | 0.00 | 89 | 0.00 | 0.00 | 90 | 0.00 | 0.00 | 0.00 | 0.00 |
| Officer, shareholder loans | 0.01 | 0.04 | 45 | 0.00 | 0.03 | 32 | 0.00 | 0.03 | 34 | 0.00 | 0.03 | 3.74 | 0.03 |
| Loan and lease commitments | 105.49 | 23.23 | 98 | 82.96 | 22.65 | 98 | 78.03 | 23.27 | 97 | 81.89 | 25.37 | 116.00 | 27.54 |
| Loans sold during the quarter | 7.24 | 0.73 | 91 | 18.26 | 1.19 | 98 | 5.20 | 1.45 | 87 | 4.29 | 1.50 | 0.50 | 1.43 |
| **Composition changes** | | | | | | | | | | | | | |
| Asset mix | 9.65 | 14.19 | 33 | 8.71 | 13.73 | 35 | 16.21 | 12.65 | 76 | 11.93 | 17.97 | 12.94 | 14.64 |
| Loan mix (including leases) | 11.81 | 12.97 | 50 | 11.83 | 12.81 | 51 | 10.96 | 11.69 | 57 | 29.72 | 17.07 | 14.45 | 13.84 |
| Liability mix | 9.25 | 17.53 | 14 | 19.84 | 23.10 | 33 | 7.64 | 15.47 | 12 | 21.05 | 52.23 | 24.88 | 53.21 |

## United National Bank of Denver: Analysis of Repricing Opportunities (continued)

### 12/30/87

| Percent of assets repriced within | Assets | | | Liabilities | | | Net position | | | Bank cumulative net history | | | |
|---|---|---|---|---|---|---|---|---|---|---|---|---|---|
| | Bank | Peer 3 | PCT | Bank | Peer 3 | PCT | Bank | Peer 3 | PCT | 09/30/87 | 06/30/87 | 03/31/87 | 12/31/86 |
| 1 Day | 32.15 | 28.90 | 59 | 22.33 | 7.63 | 96 | 9.82 | 21.26 | 18 | 8.07 | 7.05 | 1.99 | 3.85 |
| 3 Months | 40.76 | 41.98 | 44 | 56.02 | 49.37 | 80 | -15.27 | -6.66 | 23 | -10.87 | -10.62 | -7.29 | -10.18 |
| 6 months | 43.98 | 46.16 | 40 | 59.36 | 55.33 | 70 | -15.38 | -8.42 | 26 | -13.84 | -11.25 | -7.10 | -10.37 |
| 12 months | 50.37 | 52.62 | 42 | 61.72 | 59.73 | 59 | -11.35 | -6.19 | 32 | -12.31 | -11.47 | -7.53 | -8.49 |
| 5 Years | 69.67 | 76.99 | 18 | 64.16 | 65.80 | 40 | 5.51 | 11.02 | 27 | 2.33 | 1.83 | 5.16 | 4.21 |

## United National Bank of Denver: Capital Analysis

| | 12/30/87 | | | 09/30/87 | | | 06/30/87 | | | 03/31/87 | | 12/31/86 | |
|---|---|---|---|---|---|---|---|---|---|---|---|---|---|
| | Bank | Peer 3 | PCT | Bank | Peer 3 | PCT | Bank | Peer 3 | PCT | Bank | Peer 3 | Bank | Peer 3 |
| **Capital ratios:** | | | | | | | | | | | | | |
| **Percent of adj. average assets:** | | | | | | | | | | | | | |
| Primary capital | 8.05 | 7.54 | 70 | 7.41 | 7.35 | 60 | 6.47 | 7.13 | 23 | 6.53 | 6.93 | 6.33 | 6.59 |
| Primary and secondary capital | 8.05 | 7.72 | 66 | 7.41 | 7.57 | 51 | 6.73 | 7.43 | 23 | 6.53 | 7.30 | 6.37 | 7.03 |
| **Percent of risk assets:** | | | | | | | | | | | | | |
| Primary capital | 12.49 | 10.16 | 83 | 11.64 | 9.98 | 79 | 9.27 | 9.63 | 50 | 9.08 | 9.64 | 9.38 | 9.70 |
| Primary and secondary capital | 12.49 | 10.48 | 81 | 11.64 | 10.30 | 76 | 9.65 | 10.14 | 48 | 9.08 | 10.25 | 9.43 | 10.32 |
| **Percent of total equity:** | | | | | | | | | | | | | |
| Net loans and leases (K) | 8.00 | 9.88 | 23 | 8.24 | 9.98 | 24 | 9.33 | 9.98 | 36 | 10.90 | 9.96 | 10.43 | 9.47 |
| Subord notes and debentures | 4.32 | 3.06 | 70 | 4.26 | 4.15 | 65 | 4.60 | 6.03 | 60 | 5.15 | 5.46 | 6.31 | 7.82 |
| Long-term debt | 4.32 | 5.05 | 60 | 4.26 | 6.55 | 54 | 4.60 | 8.13 | 50 | 7.92 | 8.57 | 9.82 | 11.10 |
| **Percent of avg tot equity** | | | | | | | | | | | | | |
| Net income | 5.33 | 13.39 | 16 | 14.11 | 14.30 | 41 | 17.37 | 14.84 | 67 | 13.62 | 14.22 | 11.00 | 12.53 |
| Dividends | 6.26 | 5.90 | 53 | 6.42 | 5.54 | 59 | 6.11 | 5.71 | 54 | 5.99 | 5.59 | 6.27 | 5.41 |
| Retained earnings | -0.93 | 7.02 | 15 | 7.69 | 8.71 | 41 | 11.26 | 8.88 | 67 | 7.63 | 8.43 | 4.73 | 6.77 |
| **Other capital ratios:** | | | | | | | | | | | | | |
| Qualifying intang to prim cap | 0.00 | 0.15 | 61 | 0.00 | 0.21 | 61 | 0.00 | 0.18 | 64 | 0.00 | 0.57 | 0.00 | 0.10 |
| Equity capital to assets | 6.19 | 6.47 | 41 | 5.75 | 6.13 | 39 | 5.21 | 6.08 | 18 | 5.17 | 5.91 | 5.16 | 5.71 |
| Prim cap. to tot. loans and leases | 15.41 | 12.00 | 85 | 14.44 | 11.79 | 80 | 11.95 | 11.64 | 65 | 10.77 | 11.44 | 11.28 | 12.13 |
| **Growth rates:** | | | | | | | | | | | | | |
| Total equity capital | -1.45 | 9.05 | 11 | 8.01 | 11.89 | 33 | 11.85 | 12.31 | 55 | 7.90 | 13.41 | 14.31 | 7.93 |
| Primary capital | 2.83 | 10.08 | 16 | 16.04 | 13.85 | 62 | 6.47 | 13.08 | 17 | 7.56 | 14.45 | 15.96 | 8.17 |
| Equity growth less asst. growth | 7.03 | 3.96 | | 10.10 | -0.88 | | 0.95 | -0.34 | | 0.23 | 1.09 | 9.71 | -3.31 |

United National Bank of Denver: Summary Information for All Banks in State of Colorado

| | Average of All Banks in State | | | | | Banks with Assets- $Mill (12/30/87) | | |
|---|---|---|---|---|---|---|---|---|
| | 12/30/87 | 12/31/86 | 12/31/85 | 12/31/84 | 12/31/83 | 0-25 | 25-100 | 100+ |
| Total assets ($millions) | 25,018 | 26,001 | 25,593 | 24,248 | 22,249 | 3,339 | 8,155 | 13,524 |
| Net income ($millions) | 19 | 85 | 127 | 170 | 172 | -15 | 17 | 17 |
| Number of banks in tabulation | 460 | 471 | 469 | 447 | 401 | 258 | 164 | 38 |
| Earnings and profitability | | | | | | | | |
| Net int. inc. (te) to avg. assets | 4.99 | 5.19 | 5.64 | 5.88 | 5.91 | 5.13 | 4.89 | 4.45 |
| + Non-int. inc. to avg. assets | 1.32 | 1.21 | 1.26 | 1.23 | 1.16 | 1.34 | 1.25 | 1.45 |
| - Overhead exp. to avg. assets | 5.11 | 4.98 | 5.11 | 4.95 | 4.88 | 5.62 | 4.50 | 4.36 |
| - Prov. for LN loss to avg. asset. | 1.06 | 1.09 | 0.83 | 0.63 | 0.49 | 1.11 | 0.99 | 1.12 |
| = Pretax operating income (te) | 0.20 | 0.33 | 0.79 | 1.41 | 1.66 | -0.11 | 0.67 | 0.20 |
| + Securities gains (losses) | 0.02 | 0.12 | 0.02 | 0.00 | 0.01 | 0.02 | 0.02 | 0.03 |
| = Pretax net oper. inc. (te) | 0.25 | 0.49 | 0.86 | 1.41 | 1.67 | -0.07 | 0.74 | 0.26 |
| Net oper. inc. to avg. assets | 0.19 | 0.21 | 0.55 | 0.89 | 1.02 | 0.01 | 0.44 | 0.24 |
| Adj net oper. inc. to avg. assets | 0.36 | 0.39 | 0.65 | 1.06 | 1.12 | 0.22 | 0.56 | 0.35 |
| Net income to avg. assets | 0.20 | 0.22 | 0.56 | 0.90 | 1.03 | 0.02 | 0.45 | 0.25 |
| Int inc. (te) to avg. earn. assets | 10.51 | 11.43 | 12.76 | 13.97 | 13.21 | 10.74 | 10.31 | 9.89 |
| Int. expense to avg. earn. assets | 4.83 | 5.54 | 6.36 | 7.19 | 6.37 | 4.89 | 4.72 | 4.88 |
| Net int. inc.-te to avg. earn asst | 5.63 | 5.91 | 6.40 | 6.80 | 6.81 | 5.82 | 5.49 | 5.01 |
| Capitalization: | | | | | | | | |
| Member prin. capital to avg. assets | 9.35 | 9.28 | 9.94 | 9.95 | 9.79 | 9.62 | 9.02 | 9.02 |
| Nonmember prim. cap. to avg. assets | 9.30 | 9.26 | 9.91 | 9.95 | 9.79 | 9.56 | 9.01 | 8.96 |
| Cash dividends to net income | 49.72 | 48.02 | 46.97 | 42.39 | 47.28 | 41.29 | 57.12 | 63.50 |
| Ret. earn. to avg. total equity | -1.18 | -1.49 | 0.80 | 4.65 | 5.12 | -2.41 | 0.99 | -2.89 |
| Growth rates: | | | | | | | | |
| Assets | -1.94 | 5.87 | 7.94 | 12.87 | 14.42 | -1.64 | -1.73 | -4.87 |
| Primary capital | 0.24 | 0.55 | 3.50 | 5.52 | 6.63 | -1.31 | 3.14 | -3.18 |
| Core deposits | -1.69 | 10.87 | 10.05 | 10.81 | 21.15 | -0.46 | -2.31 | -6.71 |
| Volatile liabilities | 5.99 | -5.80 | 6.61 | 35.81 | 3.21 | 2.14 | 10.41 | 11.46 |

# Index

A number of informative Case Studies are listed in the index under the heading Case Studies. Page references followed by an italic "n" refer to material in a footnote.